CHILD 2e

Gabriela Martorell

Virginia Wesleyan University

CHILD, SECOND EDITION

Published by McGraw-Hill Education, 2 Penn Plaza, New York, NY 10121. Copyright ©2020 by McGraw-Hill Education. All rights reserved. Printed in the United States of America. Previous editions ©2013. No part of this publication may be reproduced or distributed in any form or by any means, or stored in a database or retrieval system, without the prior written consent of McGraw-Hill Education, including, but not limited to, in any network or other electronic storage or transmission, or broadcast for distance learning.

Some ancillaries, including electronic and print components, may not be available to customers outside the United States.

This book is printed on acid-free paper.

4 5 6 7 8 9 LWI 21 20

ISBN 978-1-260-50017-2 (bound edition)
MHID 1-260-50017-9 (bound edition)
ISBN 978-1-260-08201-2 (loose-leaf edition)
MHID 1-260-08201-6 (loose-leaf edition)

Portfolio Manager: *Ryan Treat*
Product Developer: *Kirstan Price*
Lead Product Developer: *Dawn Groundwater*
Marketing Managers: *AJ Laferrera; Olivia Kaiser*
Program Manager: *Kelly Heinrichs*
Content Project Managers: *Mary E. Powers (Core), Jodi Banowetz (Assessment)*
Buyer: *Laura Fuller*
Design: *Matt Diamond*
Content Licensing Specialist: *Ann Marie Jannette*
Cover Image: *©Brayden Howie/Shutterstock*
Compositor: *Aptara, Inc.*

All credits appearing on page or at the end of the book are considered to be an extension of the copyright page.

Cataloging-in-Publication Data is on file with the Library of Congress

The Internet addresses listed in the text were accurate at the time of publication. The inclusion of a website does not indicate an endorsement by the authors or McGraw-Hill Education, and McGraw-Hill Education does not guarantee the accuracy of the information presented at these sites.

mheducation.com/highered

BRIEF CONTENTS

Chapters

©Rubberball/PunchStock

ABOUT THE AUTHOR

Gabriela Martorell

Gabriela Martorell

Gabriela Alicia Martorell was born in Seattle, Washington, but moved as a toddler to Guatemala. At eight, she returned to the United States and lived in Northern California until leaving for her undergraduate training at the University of California, Davis. After obtaining her B.S. in Psychology, she earned her Ph.D. in Developmental and Evolutionary Psychology at the University of California, Santa Barbara. Since that time, she has taught at Portland State University, Norfolk State University, and her current full-time position as a Full Professor of Psychology at Virginia Wesleyan University.

Gabi has taught courses in Introductory Psychology, Research Methods, Lifespan Human Development, Infant Development, Child Development, Adolescent Development, Culture and Development, Evolutionary Psychology, Developmental Psychopathology, and capstone community-based learning courses in Early Childhood Education and Adulthood and Aging. She is committed to teaching, mentoring, and advising. She is currently a co-investigator for a National Science Foundation grant focused on student retention and success in science, technology, engineering, and math. She is also a volunteer trainer for Court Appointed Special Advocates and a group fitness instructor for the YMCA of South Hampton Roads.

CONTENTS

©Ariel Skelley/Blend Images/Getty Images

CHAPTER 2 CONCEPTION, HEREDITY, AND ENVIRONMENT 33

©Denis Kuvaev/Shutterstock

CHAPTER 3 PREGNANCY AND PRENATAL DEVELOPMENT 56

©Pixtal/age fotostock

CHAPTER

4 BIRTH AND THE NEWBORN 75

©Lisette Le Bon/Purestock/SuperStock

©lostinbids/Getty Images

©Roberto Westbrook/Getty Images

©Tetra Images/Getty Images

©Vicky Kasala/Getty Images

©Mint Images RF/Getty Images

©wavebreakmedia/Shutterstock

CHAPTER 12 COGNITIVE DEVELOPMENT IN MIDDLE CHILDHOOD 254

©FS Stock/Shutterstock

©wavebreakmedia/Shutterstock

CHAPTER **13** PSYCHOSOCIAL
DEVELOPMENT IN MIDDLE
CHILDHOOD 280

©Sergey Novikov/Shutterstock

CHAPTER **14** PHYSICAL DEVELOPMENT
AND HEALTH IN
ADOLESCENCE 304

©Caiaimage/Trevor Adeline/Getty Images

©Ian Lishman/Juice Images/Getty Images

CHAPTER 16 PSYCHOSOCIAL DEVELOPMENT IN ADOLESCENCE 344

©PeopleImages.com/Getty Images

Perspectives on Diversity

PREFACE

Child, second edition, is designed to be a brief but thorough account of human development from conception through adolescence, exposing students to culture and diversity and immersing them in practical application. *Child* combines a commitment to scholarly content, critical thinking, and real-life application of theory with a visually engaging and dynamic, interactive format. Written from a developmental framework and borrowing from multiple traditions and theoretical perspectives, *Child* also addresses the major periods of development and focuses on the important biological, psychological, and social forces driving change, highlighting theoretical distinctions, research findings, and new directions in the field. *Child* will engage your students and encourage the application of psychological concepts to everyday life.

Paired with McGraw-Hill Education **Connect**, a digital assignment and assessment platform that strengthens the link between faculty, students, and course work, instructors and students accomplish more in less time. Connect for Child Development includes assignable and assessable videos, quizzes, exercises, and interactivities, all associated with learning objectives. Interactive assignments and videos allow students to experience and apply their understanding of psychology to the world with fun and stimulating activities.

Diversity

In response to requests from faculty like you, substantial space has been devoted to addressing issues of diversity. When relevant, each chapter includes current U.S. statistics drawn from census data and national governmental databases, including not just major population trends but also demographic and statistical information on ethnic and racial minorities. In many cases, information on global statistics, trends, and cultural differences has been included as well.

Additionally, each chapter includes a *Perspectives on Diversity* feature. In this feature, a cross-cultural issue of interest is addressed from a global perspective. These features address a wide variety of topics, including, for example, cultural differences in beliefs about conception and fertility or attitudes toward corporal punishment or research-based features on topics such as prenatal care and infant mortality. A complete listing of *Perspectives on Diversity* can be found on page xvi.

Other forms of diversity have also been included. For example, the influence of socioeconomic status is highlighted

for topics such as low birth weight, school achievement, tested IQ, and family relationships. Information is also included on different family structures, including gay and lesbian parents, stepparents, divorced parents, and those families in which adults remain single by choice.

Current Research

Child, second edition, draws a current picture of the state of the field. In well-established areas of psychology, there is an emphasis on the inclusion of review articles and meta-analyses in order to capture the major trends found through decades of psychological research. In research areas with less information available, the emphasis is on the inclusion of the newest research available in that area.

The second edition of *Child* features expanded and updated coverage of many key areas, including brain development, gender differences and gender typing, aggression and bullying, and the influences of media on development. Topical areas that have arisen in the public consciousness in recent years have also been included. For example, new sections in the second edition examine topics such as opioid use during pregnancy, cultural influences on motor development, alcohol and nicotine use in adolescence, and transgender children.

Better Data, Smarter Revision, Improved Results

Students helped inform the revision of *Child*. Content revisions were informed by data collected anonymously through McGraw-Hill Education's SmartBook®:

Step 1. Data points showing concepts that caused students the most difficulty were anonymously collected from the SmartBook for the first edition of *Child*.

Step 2. The data were provided to the author in the form of a Heat Map, which graphically illustrates "hot spots" in the text that affect student learning (see image p. xviii).

Step 3. The author used the Heat Map data to refine the content and reinforce student comprehension in the new edition. Additional quiz questions and assignable activities were created for use in Connect to further support student success.

Because the Heat Map gave the author empirically based feedback at the paragraph and even sentence level, she was able to develop the new edition using precise student data that pinpointed concepts that gave students the most difficulty.

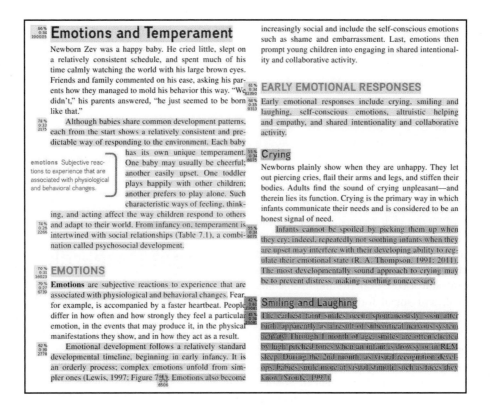

Support for Student Engagement

Child, second edition, offers a dynamic learning experience designed for today's students. The research-based content of *Child* is written around key learning objectives to support student mastery. *Did You Know?* features introduce relevant, interesting facts about concepts to further engage students. *Child* supports application of concepts and theories to the real world through the features *What Do You Do?* and *What Do You Think?* and with textual examples. The *Summary* and *Practice Quiz* at the end of each chapter provide students with opportunities to assess and confirm their learning.

Provide a Smarter Text and Better Value

SMARTBOOK®

New to this edition, **SmartBook** is now optimized for mobile and tablet and is accessible for students with disabilities. Content-wise, it has been enhanced with improved learning objectives that are measurable and observable to improve student outcomes. SmartBook personalizes learning to individual student needs, continually adapting to pinpoint knowledge gaps and focus learning on topics that need the most attention. Study time is more productive and, as a result, students are better prepared for class and coursework. For instructors, SmartBook tracks student progress and provides insights that can help guide teaching strategies.

Powerful Reporting

Whether a class is face-to-face, hybrid, or entirely online, Connect for Child Development provides tools and analytics to reduce the amount of time instructors need to administer their courses. Easy-to-use course management tools allow instructors to spend less time administering and more time teaching, while easy-to-use reporting features allow students to monitor their progress and optimize their study time.

- The **At-Risk Student Report** provides instructors with one-click access to a dashboard that identifies students who are at risk of dropping out of the course due to low engagement levels.

- The **Category Analysis Report** details student performance relative to specific learning objectives and goals, including APA outcomes and levels of Bloom's taxonomy.

- **Connect Insight** is a one-of-a-kind visual analytics dashboard—now available for both instructors and students—that provides at-a-glance information regarding student performance.

- The **LearnSmart Reports** allow instructors and students to easily monitor progress and pinpoint areas of weakness, giving each student a personalized study plan to achieve success.

Real People, Real World, Real Life

At the higher end of Bloom's taxonomy, the **McGraw-Hill Education Milestones video series** offers an observational tool that allows students to experience life as it unfolds, from infancy to late adulthood. This groundbreaking, longitudinal video series tracks the development of real children as they progress through the early stages of physical, social, and emotional development in their first few weeks, months, and years of life. Assignable and assessable within Connect, Milestones also includes interviews with adolescents and adults to reflect development throughout the entire life span.

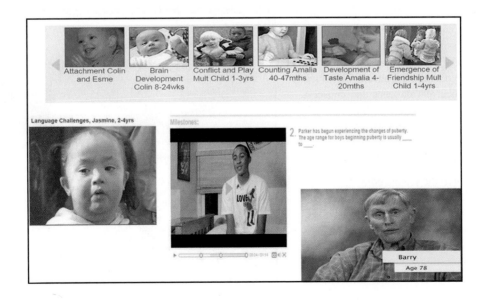

Preparing Students for Higher-Level Thinking

Also at the higher end of Bloom's, and new to the second edition, **Power of Process for Child Development** helps students improve critical-thinking skills and allows instructors to assess these skills efficiently and effectively in an online environment. Available through Connect, preloaded journal articles are available for instructors to assign. Using a scaffolded framework such as understanding, synthesizing, and analyzing, Power of Process moves students toward higher-level thinking and analysis.

Inform and Engage on Psychological Concepts

At the lower end of Bloom's taxonomy, students are introduced to **Concept Clips**—the dynamic, colorful graphics and stimulating animations that break down some of psychology's most difficult concepts in a step-by-step manner, engaging students and aiding in retention. They are assignable and assessable in Connect or can be used as a jumping-off point in class. Complete with audio narration, Concept Clips focus on topics such as object permanence and conservation, as well as theories and theorists like Bandura's social cognitive theory, Vygotsky's sociocultural theory, and Kuhl's language development theory.

Also for the lower levels of Bloom's Taxonomy:

- **NewsFlash:** New to the second edition, NewsFlash activities tie current news stories to key psychological principles and learning objectives. After interacting with a contemporary news story, students are assessed on their ability to make the connection between real life and research findings.

- **Interactivities:** Assignable through Connect, Interactivities engage students with content through experiential activities. New and updated activities include Neurons, Research Ethics, Prenatal Development, Kohlberg's Moral Reasoning, and Gardner's Theory of Multiple Intelligences.

Online Instructor Resources

The resources listed here accompany *Child*, second edition. Please contact your McGraw-Hill representative for details concerning the availability of these and other valuable materials that can help you design and enhance your course.

- **Instructor's Manual:** Broken down by chapter, this resource provides chapter outlines, suggested lecture topics, classroom activities and demonstrations, suggested student research projects, essay questions, and critical-thinking questions.

- **Test Bank and Computerized Test Bank:** This comprehensive Test Bank includes more than 1,500 multiple-choice, true-false, and short essay questions. Organized by chapter, the questions are designed to test factual, applied, and conceptual understanding. All test questions are available within TestGen™ software.

- **PowerPoint Slides:** The PowerPoint presentations, now with improved accessibility, highlight the key points of the chapter and include supporting visuals. All of the slides can be modified to meet individual needs.

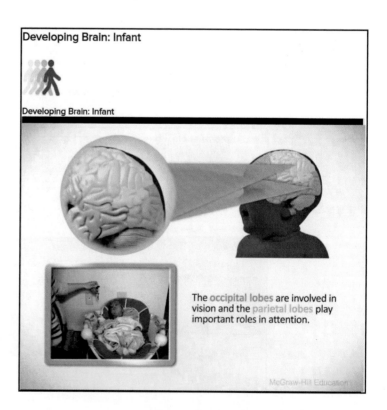

Developing Brain: Infant

The occipital lobes are involved in vision and the parietal lobes play important roles in attention.

McGraw-Hill Education

Chapter-by-Chapter List of Changes

Every chapter has been extensively revised and updated for the second edition, with new research findings, updated statistics, and expanded coverage of key topics.

Chapter 1 Introduction to Child Development

- New section on fields of study in child development.
- Expanded description of genetic and environmental influences on development.
- Updated statistics on U.S. household composition.
- Updated statistics on ethnic minority populations and trends in the United States.
- *Perspectives on Diversity* feature updated with demographic changes, effects of implementation of the Affordable Care Act, and potential changes to health insurance coverage under the new presidential administration.
- Added discussion of diversity within ethnic categories and ethnic gloss.
- Expanded discussion of active versus passive development and of continuous versus discontinuous development.
- Expanded discussion of Erikson's theory of psychosocial development.
- Added information about the history of learning theoretical approaches and why they gained prominence in the scientific community.
- Expanded description of Pavlov's research.
- Added specific examples of classical conditioning, positive and negative reinforcement and punishment, and the use of behavioral modification.
- Added critique of learning theories as an overarching framework of development.
- Expanded example of the processes of assimilation and accommodation.
- Added a specific example of scaffolding.
- New discussion of Vygotsky's experimental approach and expanded discussion of his impact on the field.
- New example of how quantitative data can be used to infer internal mental processes in information processing research.
- Added descriptions of each of Bronfenbrenner's systems, including the microsystem, mesosystem, exosystem, macrosystem, and chronosystem.
- Expanded descriptions of evolutionary theory and evolutionary psychology.
- New section on quantitative and qualitative research.
- Added information on qualitative research methods and goals.
- Expanded section on self-report measures.
- Added information on observer bias.
- Expanded information on pros and cons of case studies.
- New example of a spurious correlation.
- New material on operational definitions.
- New section on random assignment.
- Expanded description of field experiments.
- New material on the pros and cons of cross-sectional and longitudinal research designs.

Chapter 2 Conception, Heredity, and Environment

- Expanded discussion on causes of infertility.
- Updated statistics on infertility and the use of artificial reproductive technologies.
- Added coverage of the risks of multiple pregnancies and new guidelines for transfer of multiple embryos.
- Updated information and statistics on adoption.
- Revised discussion of recessive and dominant inheritance patterns.
- Expanded discussion of multifactorial transmission and epigenetic changes.
- Added material on racial and ethnic variations in prevalence of birth disorders.
- Revised discussion of heritability.
- Expanded discussion and examples of canalization and range of reaction.
- Expanded examples for nonshared environmental influences in the family.
- Expanded discussion of, and updated research on, the interaction of genes and environment on obesity, temperament, and schizophrenia.

Chapter 3 Pregnancy and Prenatal Development

- Expanded description of the placenta.
- Updated and expanded statistics on miscarriage.
- Expanded information on pain perception in fetuses.
- Updated research on auditory perception and auditory memory in fetuses.
- Updated information on weight gain and nutritional recommendations in pregnancy.
- Updated global statistics on malnutrition during pregnancy.
- Differentiation of malnutrition as a result of calorie deficit versus nutrient deficit.
- New information on the effects of Zika exposure during pregnancy.
- Updated information on rubella outbreaks in the United States.
- Revised section on maternal anxiety and stress.
- Updated statistics on maternal age.
- Expanded information on the influence of environmental hazards on pregnancy.

- New section on the influence of opioid exposure on pregnancy outcomes and neonatal abstinence syndrome.
- Expanded information on the transmission of alcohol and drugs through breast milk.
- Expanded information on the effects of tobacco smoke on pregnancy.
- Updated information on the risks associated with caffeine usage during pregnancy.
- Updated information on the effects of marijuana, cocaine, and methamphetamine use during pregnancy.
- Updated and expanded information on paternal factors in pregnancy.
- Added information on prenatal cell-free DNA scans.
- Updated *Perspectives on Diversity* feature on disparities in prenatal care around the world.

Chapter 4 Birth and the Newborn

- Updated statistics on childbirth, birth complications, and maternal mortality in the United States.
- New global statistics on childbirth, birth complications, and maternal mortality.
- Expanded information and updated research on outcomes associated with the use of doulas during childbirth.
- Expanded information on developmental changes and cultural variations in infant sleep patterns.
- Updated global and U.S. statistics on low-birth-weight babies.
- New information on the link between sleep organization and outcomes in preterm infants.
- Updated research on low-birth-weight babies, including long-term outcomes.
- Updated statistics on postmature infants.
- Updated statistics and research on stillbirth.
- Expanded information on neurological basis of parental bonding and on fathers' involvement in caregiving and play.

Chapter 5 Physical Development and Health, 0 to 3

- Expanded information on growth rates in the first 3 years of life.
- Added information on teething.
- Updated statistics on U.S. breast-feeding rates.
- Expanded information and new research on obesity in infancy.
- New section on malnutrition in infancy.
- New section on brain cells, including information on integration and differentiation of neurons.
- New section on myelination of neural pathways.
- Updated research on pain perception in newborns.

- Expanded information on the development of smell and taste and adaptive nature of taste preferences.
- Updated research on auditory discrimination in infancy.
- New information on infant preferences for and ability to discriminate facial stimuli.
- Updated research on visually directed reaching in infants and on haptic perception.
- New section on cultural influences on motor development.
- Updated statistics and information on global and U.S. infant mortality.
- Updated statistics on U.S. racial and ethnic disparities in infant mortality rates.
- Updated statistics and information on sudden infant death syndrome (SIDS), child injuries, and child maltreatment rates.
- Updated global and U.S. statistics and information on vaccination rates.
- Updated research on nonorganic failure to thrive in infancy and toddlerhood.
- Updated research on characteristics of abusive parents and household environments.
- New information on long-term outcomes of children placed in foster care.
- Expanded and updated information on long-term effects of maltreatment.

Chapter 6 Cognitive Development, 0 to 3

- Updated research example for the use of conditioning paradigms in infant research.
- Expanded discussion of Piaget's sensorimotor substages.
- Expanded discussion of the object concept, including new information on the a-not-b error.
- New section on imitation, including information on visible imitation, invisible imitation, deferred imitation, and preferences in imitation.
- New section on symbolic development, pictorial competence, and understanding of scale.
- New section on perceptual processing abilities.
- Expanded and updated information and research on information processing as a predictor of intelligence, on the development of categorization in infancy, and on the development of the understanding of causality.
- Expanded and updated discussion of violation-of-expectations research methodology.
- Expanded and updated information and research on the development of an understanding of number in infants.
- Expanded and updated information and research on the development of neural structures and their link to memory processes.

- Expanded discussion of the social constructionist approach and how it applies to early childhood education.
- Expanded discussion of the development of infant understanding of phonemic native language patterns.
- Updated research on the use of gestures in infants.
- Expanded information on language milestones in infancy and on syntactic development.
- New section on sign language development in deaf children.
- Expanded discussion of characteristics of early speech and language errors.
- Expanded discussion of and updated research on the role of social interaction in language development and on child-directed speech.

Chapter 7 Psychosocial Development, 0 to 3

- Expanded definition of emotion.
- Expanded discussion of and updated research on developmental changes in crying and in smiling and laughter in infancy.
- Expanded discussion of and updated research on the development of altruism and empathy, including new information on underlying brain neurology.
- Expanded information on the link between collaborative activities and the development of culture.
- Expanded discussion and updated research on stability of temperament, with particular attention on developmental changes in relative influence of genes and environment and cultural influences on stability.
- Expanded discussion of and updated research on behavioral inhibition.
- Expanded description of behaviors of resistantly attached infants.
- Expanded discussion on how attachment is established.
- Expanded discussion of and updated research on long-term effects of attachment.
- New information on physiological and neurological correlates of parental attachment history.
- Expanded discussion of mutual regulation, with the addition of new material on interactional synchrony and the role of oxytocin.
- Expanded discussion of and updated research on social referencing.
- Expanded description on the origins of the self-concept.
- Added information on cultural variations in the development of the self.
- Expanded discussion on the development of conscience, including new information on receptive cooperation.
- Expanded discussion and updated research on factors in the success of socialization.

- Expanded discussion and updated research on sex and gender differences in infants and toddlers.
- Expanded discussion on sibling influences.
- New information included on peer preferences.

Chapter 8 Physical Development and Health in Early Childhood

- Updated information on brain changes from 3 to 6 years of age.
- Expanded discussion and updated research on sleep disturbances.
- Expanded discussion and updated research and statistics on night terrors, sleepwalking, sleeptalking, and nightmares.
- Expanded discussion and updated research on the relationship between motor development, sports participation, and risk of overweight or obesity.
- Expanded discussion and updated research on the origins of handedness.
- Expanded discussion and updated research and statistics on obesity, including both global U.S. data on prevalence, causes, and recommended prevention strategies.
- Updated *Perspectives on Diversity* feature with current global data on prevalence and causes of mortality in the first 5 years of life.
- Updated discussion and research on undernutrition.
- Updated statistics for allergy prevalence in U.S. children.
- Expanded discussion and updated research and recommendations on the use of fluoride for the prevention of dental caries, including a critical analysis of research on fluoride toxicity.
- Updated global and U.S. statistics on accidental child injuries and deaths.
- Updated statistics and information on access to medical care for children living in poverty.
- Updated statistics on the influence of race and ethnicity on children's access to health care.
- Updated statistics on the prevalence and causes of homelessness in U.S. children.
- Updated statistics on the children's exposure to environmental contaminants.

Chapter 9 Cognitive Development in Early Childhood

- Expanded discussion and updated research on the understanding of causality in children.
- Expanded description of the development of the concept of identity in children.
- Expanded description of and updated research on animism.
- New information on long-term academic correlates of early number sense in children.

- Expanded description of irreversibility.
- New information on children's early understanding of mental states.
- Expanded description of and updated research on false beliefs, including links to other skills, neural correlates, and its relationship to lying.
- New section on distinguishing between appearance and reality.
- Added information on understanding fantastical elements in storybooks and the influence religious beliefs play.
- Updated information on the benefits of imaginative activities.
- Expanded discussion of and updated research on family influences, cultural influences, and neurological correlates of theory of mind development.
- New example of encoding.
- Expanded description of working memory, including information on the phonological loop, visuospatial sketchpad, and neurological correlation.
- Expanded discussion of and updated research on the development of executive control, its relationship to academic performance, and intervention programs for its improvement.
- New section on influences on memory retention.
- Updated research on the Flynn effect.
- Expanded discussion of and updated research on family influences on measured intelligence.
- New section on electronic media and cognitive processes.
- Expanded discussion of scaffolding and updated research illustrating its use in the classroom.
- Expanded discussion of fast mapping with the inclusion of updated research and an illustrative example.
- New section on private speech.
- Updated research on the development of literacy, including the impact of electronic devices.
- Updated research on the impact of compensatory preschool programs on child outcomes.
- Updated information on current funding status of universal preschool programs.
- Updated statistics on kindergarten attendance in the United States.
- Updated discussion of and research on kindergarten readiness and outcomes.

Chapter 10 Psychosocial Development in Early Childhood

- Updated research on cultural differences in self-definition.
- Expanded description of developmental changes in self-esteem from ages 5 to 7.
- Expanded discussion of and updated research on contingent self-esteem.

- New information on the differential influence of generic versus targeted praise on task perseverance.
- Coverage of understanding and regulating emotions separated into two distinct sections, expanded, and updated with current research.
- New information on cultural differences in the likelihood of feeling guilt, pride, and shame.
- Expanded discussion of and updated research on gender differences in children and on biological influences on gender development.
- New information on the development of transgender individuals.
- Expanded discussion of the consequences of differing reproductive strategies of men and women.
- Expanded discussion of the interaction between evolutionary and cultural processes in the determination of human behavior and psychology.
- Expanded discussion on Kohlberg's cognitive-developmental theory of gender and on gender schema theory.
- Updated research on family, peer, and cultural influences on gender socialization.
- Expanded discussion of and updated research on nonsocial play, with new information on reticent play.
- Expanded discussion of and updated research on the influence of gender on play styles.
- Expanded discussion of and updated research on cultural influences on play.
- New section on the adaptive functions of play.
- New information on negative outcomes associated with harsh parenting practices.
- Expanded discussion of and updated research on outcomes associated with the use of corporal punishment.
- New information on the use of and recommendations regarding corporal punishment in the U.S. educational system.
- Updated *Perspectives on Diversity* feature, with new information on U.S. and global prevalence in use of corporal punishment.
- Expanded cultural critique of Baumrind's parenting typology.
- Expanded discussion of and updated research on gender differences in aggression.
- New information on cultural influences on aggressive behavior.
- New section on fearfulness.

Chapter 11 Physical Development and Health in Middle Childhood

- Updated weight and height statistics for middle childhood in the United States, with new information on racial and ethnic variations.

- Updated and expanded statistics and discussion on the prevalence of and treatments for dental caries.
- Expanded discussion of and updated research on brain development in middle childhood.
- Expanded discussion of and updated research on nutritional needs and challenges in middle childhood, including new information on racial and ethnic differences in food consumption.
- Expanded discussion of and updated research on sleep statistics, needs, and problems in middle childhood.
- Updated statistics on activity levels in U.S. children.
- Expanded discussion of and updated research on the impact of recess.
- Updated statistics on participation in organized sports programs.
- Updated global and U.S. statistics for overweight and obesity in middle childhood.
- Updated research on the causes of obesity.
- Updated and expanded discussion on outcomes of childhood overweight and on the prevention and treatment of overweight.
- Expanded discussion of and updated research and statistics on childhood asthma, hypertension, and diabetes.
- Expanded discussion of and updated research on stuttering, including new information on neurological correlates.
- Updated statistics on accidental injuries.
- Updated research on childhood predictors of future antisocial behavior.
- Updated statistics on the prevalence of childhood depression.
- New information on the reasons for the rise of off-label drugs for the treatment of psychiatric conditions in children.

Chapter 12 Cognitive Development in Middle Childhood

- New section on developmental changes in the understanding of cause and effect.
- Expanded discussion of and updated research on seriation, transitive inferences, and class inclusion.
- Expanded discussion of and updated research on deductive reasoning.
- Expanded discussion of conservation.
- Expanded discussion on the development of an understanding of number and mathematics, including new information on number estimation and cultural context.
- New section on neurological development, culture, and schooling.
- Expanded discussion of and updated research on developmental influences on executive function.

- Expanded discussion of selective attention.
- Expanded discussion of and updated research on working memory and on metamemory.
- New section on mnemonics.
- New information on the Otis-Lennon School Ability Test (OLSAT8).
- Updated research critiquing the meaning of IQ tests.
- Expanded discussion and critique of Gardner's theory of multiple intelligences.
- Expanded description of Sternberg's Triarchic Abilities Test, including new information on tacit knowledge.
- New section on other directions in intelligence testing.
- Expanded discussion of and updated research on the relationship between genes and brain development.
- Updated research and discussion on the influence of race and ethnicity on IQ.
- New section on the influence of schooling in IQ.
- Expanded discussion of the development of literacy, including new information on the role of metacognitive processes and technology on emerging literacy.
- Updated research on gender differences in academic performance.
- Expanded discussion of and updated research on parental and peer influence on academic performance and on the influence of socioeconomic status on academic achievement.
- Updated information on educational reform efforts in the United States.
- Expanded discussion of and updated research on the impact of class size.
- Updated research on charter schools and homeschooling outcomes.
- Expanded discussion of and updated research on computer and Internet usage in schools.
- Updated statistics and information on second-language learning.
- Updated statistics on special education services and intellectual disabilities in school-age children in the United States.
- Updated statistics and information on attention deficit/hyperactivity disorder, including diagnosis rates by race/ethnicity.
- Expanded description of and updated statistics for giftedness.
- Updated research on the causes and correlated of giftedness and creativity.

Chapter 13 Psychosocial Development in Middle Childhood

- Expanded discussion of and updated research on emotional growth in middle childhood.

- Expanded discussion of and updated research on coregulation, including new information on cultural differences.
- Updated statistics and research on maternal employment, child care arrangements, and related outcomes.
- Updated statistics on U.S. child and family poverty rates.
- Updated research on outcomes related to child poverty.
- Updated statistics on family structure in the United States, with new information on the effect of father involvement on child outcomes.
- Updated statistics on U.S. divorce rates.
- Updated research on child outcomes associated with divorce and family conflict.
- Expanded discussion of and updated research on custody, visitation, and co-parenting.
- Updated research on long-term effects of divorce on children.
- Updated statistics and research on single-parent families, stepfamilies, and gay and lesbian families.
- Updated statistics, research, and discussion on cohabitating families.
- Expanded discussion of and updated research on adoption and outcomes of U.S. and foreign-born children.
- Expanded discussion of and updated research on sibling relationships, including new information on the influence of gender.
- New *Perspectives on Diversity* feature on bullying across the world.
- Expanded discussion of and updated research on peer relations, including new information on discrimination and the influence of group norms.
- Expanded discussion of and updated research on gender influences on peer groups.
- Expanded description of sociometric methodology.
- Expanded discussion of and updated research on correlates and outcomes of popularity, including new information on family and cultural influences.
- Expanded discussion of and updated research on friendship.
- Updated research on aggression and bullying.
- New section on aggression and social information processing.
- Expanded discussion of and updated research on the influence of media and electronics on aggression.
- Expanded discussion of and updated research on bullies and victims, including new information on cyberbullying.

Chapter 14 Physical Development and Health in Adolescence

- Updated and expanded statistics on timing of puberty by race/ethnicity.

- Expanded discussion and updated statistics on menarche.
- Expanded discussion of and updated research on influences on pubertal timing, with new information on the role of leptin and environmental toxins.
- Expanded discussion of and updated research on implications of early and late maturation.
- Expanded discussion of and updated research on brain development in adolescence and its consequences.
- New information on adolescent global health statistics.
- Updated statistics on physical activity in adolescence.
- Expanded discussion of and updated research on sleep needs and problems, with new information on racial and ethnic differences in sleep patterns and on negative outcomes associated with sleep deprivation.
- New section on prevalence of overweight and obesity, including both global and U.S. data.
- New section on causes and consequences of overweight and obesity.
- Expanded discussion of and updated research on body image and eating disorders, with new information on racial and ethnic differences in prevalence rates, global variations in prevalence rates, and peer influences.
- New information on binge eating disorder.
- Updated research on treatment outcomes for eating disorders.
- Updated statistics on adolescent trends in drug use and on drug and alcohol treatment rates.
- Updated and expanded statistics on global and U.S. trends in adolescent alcohol use.
- New information on the effect of alcohol on the developing brain.
- Updated statistics on marijuana usage, including new information about the effect of legalization on usage.
- Updated and expanded statistics on the use of tobacco products in adolescence.
- New section on the initiation of nicotine and alcohol use.
- Updated research on depression.
- New global statistics on death in adolescence and updated statistics for the United States.
- Updated statistics on deaths from motor accidents, with new information on the impact of distracted driving.
- Expanded discussion on and updated research for firearm-related deaths.
- Updated research and statistics on suicide.

Chapter 15 Cognitive Development in Adolescence

- New critique of Elkind's model of adolescent thought.
- Added information on the sequence in which various cognitive skills come on line.
- Revision of critique of Kohlberg's theory of moral development.

- Expanded discussion of and updated research on prosocial behavior and volunteer activity, with new information on cultural and peer influences.
- Expanded and updated statistics on U.S. students' academic achievement and graduation rates.
- Updated research on student motivation and self-efficacy.
- Updated research on adolescent brain differences between girls and boys.
- Updated statistics on doctoral degrees awarded by gender in the United States.
- Expanded discussion and updated research and statistics on the influence of technology on academic skills, including new information on the impact of multitasking on cognition.
- Updated research on the influence of parenting practices and peers on academics.
- Updated statistics on high school status dropout rate.
- Expanded discussion of and updated research on consequences of dropping out of high school.
- Updated research and discussion of the impact of gender on career goals.
- Added information on reasons some students select not to go to college.
- Expanded discussion of and updated research on the impact of working during high school on academics.

Chapter 16 Psychosocial Development in Adolescence

- Updated research on and expanded discussion and critique of Gilligan's theory of identity development in women.
- Expanded discussion of and updated research on ethnic factors in identity development, with new information on the impact of perceived discrimination and cultural socialization.
- New self-report data on same-sex experiences and sexual orientation in adolescence.
- Expanded discussion of and updated research on the origins of sexual orientation, including new material on the 2D:4D ratio.
- Expanded discussion of and updated research on homosexual and bisexual identity development, including new information on the process of coming out.
- Updated statistics on U.S. adolescent sexual behavior.
- Expanded discussion of and updated research on sexual risk taking, including new information on the influence of religiosity.
- Expanded discussion of and updated research on sexting.
- Updated statistics and research on the use of contraceptives.
- Expanded discussion of and updated research on sex education, including the addition of new information on the impact of media influences.

- Added information on global prevalence rates for sexually transmitted infections and updated statistics on U.S. rates.
- Expanded discussion of and updated research on human papilloma virus, including new information on vaccine effectiveness and fears of adverse side effects.
- Updated statistics for chlamydia, gonorrhea, and genital herpes, and updated statistics and expanded discussion for trichomoniasis.
- New information on hepatitis B.
- Updated statistics and research on human immunodeficiency virus (HIV).
- Added information on global adolescent pregnancy statistics, and updated research for the United States.
- New sections on outcomes of teen pregnancy and on preventing teen pregnancy.
- Expanded discussion of and updated research on individuation, with new information on cultural differences.
- Expanded discussion and critique of the influence of parenting styles.
- Expanded discussion of and updated research on parenting monitoring and self-disclosure, with new information on cultural variations.
- Expanded discussion of and updated research on the influence of family structure and atmosphere, with new information on gay and lesbian parents.
- Expanded discussion of and updated research on the impact of maternal employment.
- Expanded discussion of and updated research on adolescents and siblings.
- Updated research on the importance of friends.
- Updated statistics, discussion, and research on the social consequences of electronic communication.
- Updated research and discussion on romantic relationships, including new information on the impact of technology and electronic media.
- Updated research and statistics on dating violence.
- Expanded discussion of and updated research on biological influences on antisocial behaviors, including new information on physiological and neurological correlates.
- Updated research and discussion on family influences on antisocial behavior.
- Expanded discussion of and updated research on environmental influences on antisocial behavior.
- New section on long-term prospects for adolescents with antisocial behavior.
- Expanded discussion of and updated research on preventing and treating teen delinquency.
- Expanded discussion of cultural changes in the United States leading to the new developmental stage of emerging adulthood.

Acknowledgments

Many thanks to those faculty instructors whose insight and feedback contributed to the development of *Child*, second edition:

James Adams, *Skyline College*

Debra Ahola, *Schenectady County Community College*

Elmida Baghdaserians, *Los Angeles Valley College*

Steven Baron, *Montgomery County Community College*

Kathleen Bonnelle, *Lansing Community College*

Erik Cheries, *University of Massachusetts – Amherst*

Catherine Chou, *Southeast Missouri State University*

Shelby Clatterbuck, *Santiago Canyon College*

Shannon Coulter, *Moorpark College*

Dana Cox, *Cabrillo College*

Christie Cunningham, *Pellissippi State Community College*

Marcy Davidson, *Reedley College*

Katherine DeMuesy, *Kent State University – Stark*

Steven Dennis, *Brigham Young University – Idaho*

John Donnelly, *Indian River State College*

Patrick Dyer, *Indian River State College*

Wendy Eckenrod-Green, *Radford University*

Linda Fayard, *Mississippi Gulf Coast Community College*

Elaine Francisco, *Skyline College*

Jennifer Gadberry, *Southeast Missouri State University*

Ofelia Garcia, *Cabrillo College*

Wanda Gilbert, *Stanly Community College*

Pamela Guerra-Schmidt, *Columbia College*

Amanda Hill, *Palomar College*

Christie Honeycutt, *Stanly Community College*

Cathleen Hunt, *Pennsylvania State University*

Janice Jefferis, *El Camino College*

Janette Kopp, *Mississippi Gulf Coast Community College*

Dawn Ladiski, *Oklahoma City Community College*

Chantal Lamourelle, *Santa Ana College*

Regina Rei Lamourelle, *Santiago Canyon College*

Erika Lanning, *Chemeketa Community College*

Heidi Lyn, *University of Southern Mississippi*

Debra Maranto, *Mississippi Gulf Coast Community College*

Nancy Marsh, *Reedley College*

Janet Mason, *Diablo Valley College*

Krista McClain, *Skyline College*

Jessie Kosorok Mellor, *Palomar College*

Krisztina Micsinai, *Palomar College*

Amy Micu, *Reedley College*

Mary Beth Miller, *Fresno City College*

Kathleen Nikolai, *Harper College*

Laura Ochoa, *Bergen Community College*

Linda O'Connell-Knuth, *Waubonsee Community College*

Monique Paige, *Saddleback College*

Karin Pavelek, *Fullerton College*

Heather Pham, *Palomar College*

Lillian Pimentel-Stratton, *Bakersfield College*

Keith Radley, *University of Southern Mississippi*

Timothy Rarick, *Brigham Young University – Idaho*

Maidie Rosengarden, *Southwestern Oregon Community College*

Rita Rzezuski, *MassBay Community College*

Alex Schwartz, *Santa Monica College*

Lynn Shelley, *Westfield State University*

Jaime Shelton, *Stanly Community College*

Bethanne Shriner, *University of Wisconsin – Stout*

Jodi Sindlinger, *Slippery Rock University*

Marla Sturm-Gould, *Montgomery County Community College*

Laura Talcott, *Indiana University South Bend*

Donna Vaught, *University of North Carolina Wilmington*

Maris Wagener, *Yuba College*

Kristin Wesner, *Clarke University*

Brittany Wilson, *El Camino College*

Gina Wilson, *Palomar College*

Rebecca Wood, *Central Connecticut State University*

Christina Yousaf, *Eastern Illinois University*

Melissa Ysais, *Bakersfield College*

Elaine Zweig, *Collin College*

From Gabi Martorell: Thank you to my family, for encouraging and supporting me while picking up the slack that allowed me to fit in writing around our already crazy lives.

Chapter 1

Introduction to Child Development

©Ed-Imaging

What's to Come

> **The Study of Child Development**

> **Influences on Development**

> **Issues in Development**

> **Theories of Child Development**

> **Research Methods**

I n 1877, a young father sat gazing at his newborn son and, pen in hand, took careful notes on his child's behaviors. "During the first seven days various reflex actions, namely sneezing, hiccupping, yawning, stretching, and of course sucking and screaming, were well performed by my infant," the proud new father wrote. "On the seventh day, I touched the naked sole of his foot with a bit of paper, and he jerked it away, curling at the same time his toes, like a much older child when tickled. The perfection of these reflex movements shows that the extreme imperfection of the voluntary ones is not due to the state of the muscles or of the coordinating centres, but to that of the seat of the will."

The young Charles Darwin who theorized about his son's motor capacities was one of the first members of the field of child development. Although modern-day researchers are more likely to use electrodes to view the pattern of brain activation in a baby, show them computerized scenarios of imaginary events, or analyze microexpressions on a videotape, they share with Darwin an interest in the changes that emerge in childhood with extraordinary speed and organization. In this chapter, we outline the basics of the field of child development. We discuss how development is conceptualized, some major influences on development, and recurrent issues in the field. Last, we address the major theoretical perspectives and touch on how scientific data are collected.

• • • •

The Study of Child Development

Development begins at the moment of conception, and it does not cease until death. From the moment of conception, a single cell divides, and divides again, over and over, in an orchestrated, organized fashion. Although each child born of this process is a unique individual, development is nonetheless patterned and orderly and follows a blueprint laid out by our evolutionary history. Eventually, a living, breathing, squalling infant is born into our vast world and begins both to be influenced by and to influence the space around him or her. Babies grow, and become children, and then adolescents, and then adults. It is not until the heart ceases beating and the neurons of the brain stop firing that our stories end. This book is about the beginning chapters of that story.

child development The scientific study of processes of change and stability in human children.

social construction Concept about the nature of reality based on societally shared perceptions or assumptions.

The field of **child development** focuses on the scientific study of systematic processes of change and stability in human children. Developmental scientists look at ways in which children change from conception through adolescence and at characteristics that remain fairly stable. The study of child development is part of the broader study of human development, which covers the entire human life span from conception to death, and is organized around periods and domains of development.

THE FIELD OF CHILD DEVELOPMENT

While attempts to understand development have a long history, the scientific study of child development is a relatively new field. The first formal efforts to study the development of children involved "baby biographies," such as Charles Darwin's (1877) description of the difference between his infant son's voluntary and reflexive motor responses quoted at the beginning of this chapter. Although he is best known for evolutionary theory, Darwin kept careful records of his son's development, using them as a springboard for the development of his psychological theories. Other parent-scientists, such as philosopher Dietrich Tiedemann (1787) and developmental psychologist Jean Piaget (1954), kept similar diaries.

In the years following the development of baby diaries, scores of researchers followed in Darwin's footsteps, and more than 30 baby diaries were published in scientific journals (Dennis, 1936). While such efforts served a valuable purpose in that they allowed these scholars to develop ideas and introduced the scientific community to the concept of development as a field of inquiry, they had limited value outside of that. For instance, it is difficult to remain objective when describing one's own child, and what is true of one infant may not be true of all infants. Thus, as the field of child development matured, more scientifically rigorous approaches were used.

Contemporary researchers now use a wide variety of techniques to study children. Modern tools include sensitive instruments that measure eye movements, heart rate, blood pressure, muscle tension, and the like, illuminating previously hidden biological influences. Digital technology, including sensitive video recordings and computer-based analyses, allow researchers to scan babies' facial expressions in minute detail, or carefully analyze how caregivers and babies communicate with each other. Brain imaging techniques allow us to investigate the basis of our thought and behaviors at the neural level. All these advances are grounded in the scientific method, the organized body of methods developed by scientists to investigate the world. Much of this chapter will be focused on describing these techniques and how they are implemented in the study of development.

The scientific method, however, is not enough. Research must be grounded in theory. Theories are the lenses through which data are viewed and understood. They tell us what questions to ask, where to look for answers, and how to interpret what we find. Thus, this chapter will also outline the most important theoretical approaches that have shaped our understanding.

PERIODS OF DEVELOPMENT

Division of the life span into periods of development is a **social construction**: a concept or practice that is an invention of a particular culture or society. There is no objectively definable moment that an infant becomes a toddler, or a child becomes an adolescent, and indeed some age-related concepts may exist in some cultures, but be absent in others. For example, in many preindustrial societies, the concept of adolescence does not exist. What we consider to be adolescence is viewed as part of adult life.

In *Child*, we follow a sequence of five periods generally accepted in Western industrial societies. After examining the crucial changes that occur in the first period, before birth, we trace physical, cognitive, and psychosocial development through infancy, toddlerhood, early childhood, middle childhood, and adolescence (Table 1.1).

DOMAINS OF DEVELOPMENT

Developmental scientists study three broad domains, or areas, of the self—physical, cognitive, and psychosocial—in the different periods of development. **Physical development** includes growth of the body and brain, sensory capacities, motor skills, and health. **Cognitive development** includes learning, attention, memory, language, thinking, reasoning, and creativity. **Psychosocial development** includes emotions, personality, and social relationships. How and what behaviors are studied may reflect a researcher's stand on basic issues in the field.

For the sake of simplicity, *Child* is organized so each domain is addressed separately within the periods of child development defined earlier. However, child development is a complex and tangled spiderweb of multiple influences, and understanding these influences requires looking at them from multiple perspectives. Just as a fly caught on one thread of a web sends reverberations across the entire structure, development in one area sends ripples though all other areas. For example, a child with frequent ear infections may develop language more slowly than a child without this physical problem, and the failure to develop language may lead to feelings of frustration because of the difficulty in communicating with others. Thus, scholars of child development draw collaboratively from a wide range of disciplines, including psychology, psychiatry, sociology, anthropology, biology, genetics, education, history, and medicine.

WHAT DO YOU **DO**?

Early Childhood Education Teacher

Early childhood education teachers support children's early development in the classroom, focusing on infancy and toddlerhood. These teachers plan classrooms that encourage exploration and learning, lead developmentally appropriate activities, and guide their students. Early childhood education teachers may work in private or public schools. Often only an associate's degree is required to work in private settings, though lead teachers typically have at least a bachelor's degree. In public schools, early childhood education teachers must meet the licensure requirements to teach preschool through third grade of the particular state, which generally include a bachelor's degree, practicum or internship, and passage of state exams. To learn more about what an early childhood teacher does, visit www.naeyc.org.

©Glow Images

Child includes findings from research in all these fields. Throughout the text, links between the three major domains of development will be highlighted.

Influences on Development

"I feel sure, from what I have seen with my own infants, that the period of development of the several faculties will be found to differ considerably in different infants," wrote Darwin. He was referring to what are now known as **individual differences**—that is, differences among children in characteristics, influences, or developmental outcomes. Children differ in a range of areas, from gender to body build to energy level to personality. Heredity, environment, maturation, the contexts of their lives, and normative and nonnormative influences can impact how they develop. The timing of these variables is also a factor in development.

HEREDITY, ENVIRONMENT, AND MATURATION

Influences on development can be described in two primary ways. Some influences are internal and driven by heredity. Heredity can be conceptualized as the genetic roll of the dice. It consists of the inborn traits and characteristics provided by a child's biological parents. Other influences stem from outside the body, starting with the prenatal environment in the womb and continuing throughout life. The relative influence of nature (heredity and biological processes) and nurture (environmental influences) is fiercely debated, and theorists differ in the weight they assign to each.

Scientists have found ways to measure the contributions of nature and nurture to the development of specific traits within a population. For example, even though heredity strongly affects intelligence, environmental factors such as parental stimulation, education, and peer influences also affect it. Contemporary theorists and researchers are increasingly interested in explaining how nature and nurture work together rather than in arguing about which factor is more important.

Many typical changes of infancy and early childhood, such as the emergence of the abilities to walk and talk, are tied to **maturation** of the body and brain—the

physical development
Growth of body and brain, including biological and physiological patterns of change in sensory capacities, motor skills, and health.

cognitive development
Pattern of change in mental abilities, such as learning, attention, memory, language, thinking, reasoning, and creativity.

psychosocial development
Pattern of change in emotions, personality, and social relationships.

individual differences
Differences among children in characteristics, influences, or developmental outcomes.

maturation Unfolding of a universal natural sequence of physical and behavioral changes.

TABLE 1.1 Five Periods of Child Development

Age Period	Physical Developments	Cognitive Developments	Psychosocial Developments
Prenatal Period (conception to birth)	• Conception occurs by normal fertilization or other means. The genetic endowment interacts with environmental influences from the start. • Basic body structures and organs form; brain growth spurt begins. Physical growth is the most rapid in the life span. • Vulnerability to environmental influences is great.	• Abilities to learn and remember and to respond to sensory stimuli are developing.	• Fetus responds to mother's voice and develops a preference for it.
Infancy and Toddlerhood (birth to age 3)	• All senses and body systems operate at birth to varying degrees. The brain grows in complexity and influence. • Physical growth and development of motor skills are rapid.	• Ability to learn and ability to remember are present, even in the early weeks. • Use of symbols and ability to solve problems develop by end of 2nd year. • Comprehension and use of language develop rapidly.	• Attachment to parents and others forms. • Self-awareness develops. • Shift from dependence to autonomy begins. • Interest in other children increases.
Early Childhood (ages 3 to 6)	• Growth is steady; appearance becomes more slender and proportions more adultlike. • Appetite diminishes, and sleep problems are common. • Handedness appears; fine and gross motor skills and strength improve.	• Thinking is somewhat egocentric, but understanding of other people's perspectives grows. • Cognitive immaturity results in some illogical ideas about the world. • Memory and language improve. • Intelligence becomes more predictable. • Preschool experience is common, and kindergarten experience is more so.	• Gender identity develops. • Self-concept and understanding of emotions become more complex; self-esteem is global. • Independence, initiative, and self-control increase. • Play becomes more imaginative, more elaborate, and usually more social. • Altruism, aggression, and fearfulness are common. • Family is still the focus of social life, but other children become more important.
Middle Childhood (ages 6 to 11)	• Growth slows. • Strength and athletic skills improve. • Respiratory illnesses are common, but health is generally better than at any other time in life span.	• Egocentrism diminishes. Children begin to think logically but concretely. • Memory and language skills increase. • Cognitive gains permit children to benefit from formal schooling. Some children show special educational needs and strengths.	• Self-concept becomes more complex, affecting self-esteem. • Coregulation reflects gradual shift in control from parents to child. • Peers assume greater importance.
Adolescence (ages 11 to about 20)	• Physical growth and other changes are rapid and profound. • Reproductive maturity occurs. • Major health risks arise from behavioral issues, such as eating disorders and drug abuse.	• Ability to think abstractly and use scientific reasoning develops. • Immature thinking persists in some attitudes and behaviors. • Education focuses on preparation for college or vocation.	• Search for identity, including sexual identity, becomes central. • Relationships with parents are generally good. • Peer group may exert a positive or negative influence.

©Elke Van de Velde/Getty Images

©Rubberball Productions

©Nicole Hill/Rubberball/Getty Images

©Rubberball/Getty Images

unfolding of a universal, natural sequence of physical changes and behavior patterns. These maturational processes, which are seen most clearly in the early years, act in concert with the influences of heredity and environment. As children grow into adolescents and adults, individual differences in innate personal characteristics (heredity) and life experience (environment) play an increasing role as they adapt to the internal and external conditions.

CONTEXTS OF DEVELOPMENT

In Victorian England, fathers were generally remote figures and did not typically take part in child care activities. However, Charles Darwin was different. By all accounts he was a loving and involved father. His daughter described him as "the most delightful play-fellow, and the most perfect sympathizer." Modern-day fathers in the United States show a wider range of involvement; some fathers are completely absent from family life, some are closely involved with caregiving, and some even take on the role of a stay-at-home parent.

For a child, the immediate context normally is the family; the family in turn is subject to the wider and ever-changing influences of neighborhood, community, and society. How might the family experiences of Darwin's children have shaped them? And how would the wider societal norms interact with their immediate family environment?

For many children, the immediate context of development is the family. Since the 1980s, the number of people in the United States living in multigenerational households has steadily increased.

©realpeople/Shutterstock

Family

What type of family did you grow up in? If you lived with two parents, you were part of a nuclear family. The **nuclear family** is a household unit generally consisting of one or two parents and their children, whether biological, adopted, or stepchildren. Historically, the two-parent nuclear family has been the most common family unit in the United States and other Western societies. In 1960, 37 percent of households were composed of nuclear families. In 2014, only 16 percent of households could be described as such. The modern family structure is becoming increasingly diverse. We now see families of single or divorced parents, households that may include a stepparent and stepsiblings or a parent's live-in partner, and an increasing number of unmarried parents, gay and lesbian households with children, and mixed race households (Krogstad, 2014).

In Asia, Africa, and Latin America and among some U.S. families that trace their lineage to those countries, the **extended family**—a multigenerational kinship network of grandparents, aunts, uncles, cousins, and more distant relatives—is the traditional family form (Johnson et al., 2003). Today the extended-family household is becoming slightly less typical in some developing countries due to industrialization and migration to urban centers (Kinsella & Phillips, 2005). In the United States, however, economic pressures, housing shortages, and out-of-wedlock childbearing have helped to fuel a trend toward three- and even four-generational family households. In 2014, a record 19 percent of the U.S. population, or 60.6 million people, lived in multigenerational families. This number has been steadily increasing since the low reached in the early 1980s (Cohn & Passel, 2016).

> **nuclear family** Two-generational household unit consisting of one or two parents and their biological children, adopted children, or stepchildren.
>
> **extended family** Multigenerational kinship network of parents, children, and other relatives, sometimes living together in an extended-family household.
>
> **culture** A society's or group's total way of life, including customs, traditions, beliefs, values, language, and physical products—all learned behavior passed on from adults to children.
>
> **ethnic group** A group united by ancestry, race, religion, language, or national origin that contributes to a sense of shared identity.

Culture, Ethnicity, and Race

Culture, ethnicity, and race can influence child development. **Culture** refers to a society's or group's total way of life, including customs, traditions, laws, knowledge, beliefs, values, language, and physical products, from tools to artworks—all the behavior and attitudes that are learned, shared, and transmitted among members of a social group. Culture is constantly changing, often through contact with other cultures. Today, computers and telecommunications enhance cultural contact among adults and children alike; e-mail and social networking sites offer almost immediate communication across the globe.

An **ethnic group** consists of people united by a distinctive culture, ancestry, religion, language, or national origin, all of which contribute to a sense of shared identity and shared attitudes, beliefs, and values. Within large societies, ethnic groups

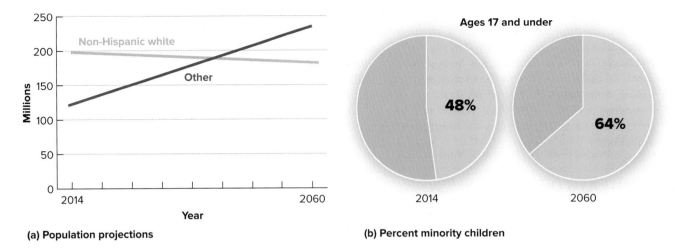

(a) Population projections

(b) Percent minority children

Ages 17 and under

FIGURE 1.1 **U.S. Ethnic Minority Population Projections: 2014–2060**

(a) According to Census Bureau projections, non-Hispanic whites are expected to remain the largest single racial and ethnic group in the United States, but beginning in about 2044, the group will make up less than 50% of the total U.S. population. In 2060, racial and ethnic minorities as a group are expected to make up 56% of the total population. (b) Also by 2060, "minority" children are expected to make up 64% of the total child population.

Source: S. L. Colby & J. M. Ortman, *Projections of the size and composition of the U.S. population: 2014 to 2060.* P25–1143. Washington, DC: U.S. Census Bureau, 2015.

may also be characterized by minority status. Ethnic minorities are those ethnic groups that have national or cultural traditions different from the majority of the population, and they are often affected by prejudice and discrimination. By 2044, due to rising immigration and high birthrates among immigrant families, ethnic minorities in the United States—roughly one-third of the population in 2008—are expected to become the majority (Colby & Ortman, 2015; Figure 1.1a and 1.1b). Geographic dispersion and adaptation to local conditions together with a steady rise in interracial marriages—in 2015, 1 in 6 new marriages in the United States was between people of different races (Bialik, 2017)—have produced a wide variety of physical and cultural characteristics within populations. According to a 2015 estimate, 2.6 percent of the U.S. population is of two or more races (United States Census Bureau, 2016).

Ethnic and cultural patterns affect child development by their influence on the composition of a household, its economic and social resources, the way its members act toward one another, the foods they eat, the games children play, the way they learn, how well they do in school, the occupations adults engage in, and the way family members think about and perceive the world. In time, however, immigrants tend to learn the language, customs, and attitudes needed to get along in the dominant culture, although many preserve some of their unique cultural practices and values (Johnson et al., 2003). *Perspectives on Diversity* explores characteristics of immigrant families in the United States.

It is worth considering what we mean when we speak of race. All humans belong to the same taxonomic classification—Homo sapiens. However, there are important differences in outward appearance of people from different geographical regions—note, for instance, the different skin color of people from northern European countries and from Africa.

socioeconomic status (SES) Combination of economic and social factors, that describe an individual or family, including income, education, and occupation.

These salient differences have led people to speak of individuals as being of different races. However, there is no clear scientific consensus on the definition of race, and it is impossible to measure reliably (Bonham, Warshauer-Baker, & Collins, 2005; Sternberg, Grigorenko, & Kidd, 2005). Human genetic variation occurs along a broad continuum, and 90 percent of such variation occurs *within* rather than *among* socially defined races (Ossorio & Duster, 2005). In other words, the differences between two people on the opposite ends of a distribution within one race are larger than the differences between two people of different races. Nevertheless, race as a social category clearly remains a factor in research because it makes a difference in "how individuals are treated, where they live, their employment opportunities, the quality of their health care, and whether [they] can fully participate" in their society (Smedley & Smedley, 2005, p. 23).

It is also worth noting that across broad ethnic and racial dimensions, there is still vast diversity within the categories themselves. For example, the term "Hispanics" encompasses a variety of different types of people: Cuban Americans; Central Americans, including Mexicans; South Americans; and those Hispanics who were born in the United States. Moreover, within these groupings, individuals may be white, black, Native American, or of mixed descent. When a term such as "Hispanics" is used to describe this diverse group as a single entity, this is known as ethnic gloss. Ethnic gloss is an overgeneralization that obscures or blurs variations within heterogenous groups.

Socioeconomic Status and Neighborhood

A family's **socioeconomic status (SES)** is based on family income, and the educational and occupational levels of the adults in the household. Throughout *Child,* we examine many studies that relate SES to developmental processes, such as mothers' verbal interactions with their children, and

Perspectives on Diversity

©Digital Vision/Getty Images

CHILDREN OF IMMIGRANT FAMILIES

The United States has always been a nation of immigrants and ethnic groups, but the primary ethnic origins of the immigrant population have shifted from Europe and Canada to Latin America, the Caribbean, Asia, and Africa. In 2009, about 80 percent of foreign-born families were from countries in Latin America and Asia (Greico & Trevalyan, 2010). Nearly one-fourth (24 percent) of U.S. children lived in immigrant families in 2007. The legal status of many immigrant families is uncertain. Approximately 5.1 million children under the age of 18 years—30 percent of children of immigrants and 7 percent of all children—have at least one parent who is unauthorized, although most (79 percent) of the children are themselves U.S. citizens (Capps, Fix & Zong, 2016). Faster growing than any other group of children in the country, children in immigrant families are the leading edge of the coming shift of racial and ethnic minorities to majority status. Whereas earlier waves of immigrants were almost entirely white and Christian, more than one-third (37 percent) of children in immigrant families have nonwhite parents. More immigrants come from Mexico (30 percent) than from any other country (www.census.gov). An estimated 5 million Mexican-born children or children of Mexican-born parents live in the United States.

Poverty is higher in children from immigrant families. Fifty-one percent of immigrant children live in poverty, as compared with 40 percent of all children in the United States. Having undocumented parents is an even greater risk; 75 percent of these children live in poverty (Capps et al., 2016). Access to health care is also an issue. While the implementation of the Affordable Care Act (ACA) led to significant gains in health care access for children in immigrant families, their health insurance coverage rates still lag behind those of children with nonimmigrant parents. Immigrant children with noncitizen parents show the lowest rates of all groups (Jarlenski, Baller, Borrero & Bennett, 2016). The future of the ACA is unclear in the Trump administration, as is the effect its repeal might have on children's health insurance coverage (Chaudry & Wimer, 2016).

As immigration fuels dramatic changes in the United States population, developmental issues affecting children in immigrant families will become increasingly important areas of research.

Sources: Unless otherwise cited, the source for this box is Hernandez, Denton, & Macartney (2008).

---

to developmental outcomes, such as health and cognitive performance. SES affects these processes and outcomes indirectly through the kinds of homes and neighborhoods people live in and the quality of nutrition, medical care, and schooling available to them.

Poverty is a problem worldwide. Although numbers have fallen by 1.1 billion since 1990, more than 757 million people lived on less than $1.90 a day in 2013. While countries such as China, Indonesia, and India have enjoyed some success in their efforts to eliminate poverty, sub-Saharan Africa lags behind and struggles greatly with this issue (World Bank, 2016). The decline in poverty is in large part due to the expanding global economy (United Nations, 2009). Still, too many children and families remain affected by poverty.

Poverty is also an issue in the United States (Figure 1.2). The number of children living in poor or low-income families increased during the recession of 2008 (Jiang, Ekono & Skinner, 2015). Currently, approximately

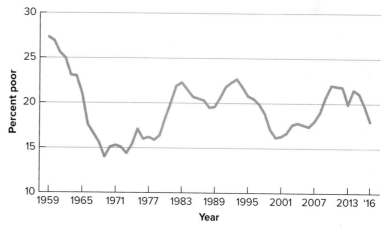

FIGURE 1.2 Child Poverty Rates—United States: 1959–2016

The child poverty rate dropped substantially in the 1960s, then rose significantly in the early 1980s. Great strides were made in decreasing child poverty in the late 1990s, owing in part to the strong economy. However, the child poverty rate began to rise again in 2007. Child poverty is closely tied to the overall health of the economy, rising in periods of recession.

Source: J. L. Semega, K. R. Fontenot, & M. A. Kollar, *U.S. Census Bureau, current population reports, P60–259, income and poverty in the United States: 2016.* Washington, DC: U.S. Government Printing Office, 2017.

risk factors Conditions that increase the likelihood of a negative developmental outcome.

normative Characteristic of an event that occurs in a similar way for most people in a group.

nonnormative Characteristic of an unusual event that happens to a particular person or a typical event that happens at an unusual time of life.

20 percent of children under the age of 18 live in poverty, and more than 40 percent of those children live in extreme poverty, defined as living on less than $2 per day per person (Children's Defense Fund, 2017). In total, about 18.5 million people in the United States live in poverty, and children comprise 6 million of those affected (Semega, Fontenot & Kollar, 2017). Although children from middle- and lower-income families are not as negatively affected as those below the poverty line, they nonetheless are at a disadvantage relative to wealthy peers with respect to employment insecurity and income inequality (Foundation for Child Development, 2015). In the United States, race or ethnicity are often associated with socioeconomic status. African American children, Asian and Pacific Islanders, and Hispanic children are more likely to live in poverty than their white counterparts (Kids Count Data Center, 2017).

Poverty is stressful and can damage children and families' physical, cognitive, and psychosocial well-being. Poor children are more likely than other children to go hungry,

to have frequent illnesses, to lack access to health care, to experience violence and family conflict, and to show emotional or behavioral problems (Coleman-Jensen, Nord, Andrews & Carlson, 2011; Schickedanz, Dreyer & Halfon, 2015; Eckenrode, Smith, McCarthy & Dineen, 2014; Yoshikawa, Aber & Beardsley, 2012). Their cognitive potential and school performance suffer as well (Wolf, Magnuson & Kimbro, 2017; Hair, Hanson, Wolfe & Pollak, 2015).

The harm poverty does is often indirect through its impact on parents' emotional state and parenting practices and on the home environment they create. Threats to well-being multiply if, as often happens, several **risk factors**, conditions that increase the likelihood of a negative outcome, are present. Moreover, the earlier poverty begins, the longer it lasts, and the higher the concentration of poverty in the community in which children live, the worse the outcomes for those children are (Chaudry & Wimer, 2016).

The composition of a neighborhood affects the way children develop. Living in a neighborhood with large numbers of poor people has been shown to impact physical health, well-being, and school readiness (Chaudry & Wimer, 2016; Cushon, Vu, Janzen & Muhajarine, 2011). Positive development can occur despite serious risk factors, however (Kim-Cohen, Moffitt, Caspi, & Taylor, 2004). For example, parents in poor families report being just as close to their children, they attend church with their families just as often, and they eat meals together as a family more often than wealthier families (Valladares & Moore, 2009). Strong family ties can also buffer children against the negative effects of poverty. Consider television star Oprah Winfrey, singer/songwriter Shania Twain, musician/producer Jay-Z, singer Justin Bieber, and former U.S. President Bill Clinton, all of whom grew up in poverty.

The Historical Context

At one time developmental scientists paid little attention to historical context—the time in which people live. Then, as the early longitudinal studies of childhood extended into the adult years, investigators began to focus on how certain experiences, tied to time and place, affect the course of people's lives. For example, because of the severe economic recession, record numbers of families moved in with relatives, leading to the largest increase in multigenerational families in modern history (Pew Research Center, 2010). This shift in family structure affects the influences to which children are exposed. Today, as we discuss in the next section, historical context is an important part of the study of child development.

NORMATIVE AND NONNORMATIVE INFLUENCES

To understand similarities and differences in development, we need to look at **normative** influences, biological or environmental events that affect many or most people in a society in similar ways, and at **nonnormative** influences,

One example of a normative age-graded influence might be the type of music that is popular during adolescence for a particular cohort.
©ZUMA Press, Inc./Alamy

events that touch only certain individuals (Baltes & Smith, 2004).

Normative age-graded influences are highly similar for people in a particular age group. The timing of biological events is fairly predictable within a normal range. For example, children do not experience puberty at age 3 or menopause at 12.

Normative history-graded influences are significant events (such as the Hurricane Katrina or the Japan tsunami) that shape the behavior and attitudes of a **historical generation**, a group of people who experience the event at a formative time in their lives. For example, the generations that came of age during the Depression and World War II tend to show a strong sense of social interdependence and trust that has declined among more recent generations (Rogler, 2002).

A historical generation is not the same as an age **cohort**, a group of people born at about the same time who experience similar influences. A historical generation may contain more than one cohort, but not all cohorts are part of historical generations unless they experience major, shaping historical events at a formative point in their lives (Rogler, 2002).

Nonnormative influences are unusual events that have a major impact on individual lives because they disturb the expected sequence of the life cycle. They are either typical events that happen at an atypical time of life, such as the death of a parent when a child is young, or atypical events, such as surviving a plane crash.

Taken together, the three types of influences—normative age-graded, normative history-graded, and nonnormative—contribute to the complexity of human development as well as to the challenges people experience in trying to build their lives.

TIMING OF INFLUENCES: CRITICAL OR SENSITIVE PERIODS

Konrad Lorenz (1957), an Austrian zoologist, got newborn ducklings to follow him as they would a mother duck. Lorenz showed that newly hatched ducklings will instinctively follow the first moving object they see. This phenomenon is called **imprinting**, and Lorenz believed it is automatic and irreversible. Usually, this instinctive bond is with the mother; but if the natural course of events is disturbed, other attachments, like the one to Lorenz—or none at all—can form. Imprinting, said Lorenz, is the result of a predisposition toward learning, the readiness of an organism's nervous system to acquire certain information during a brief critical period in early life.

A **critical period** is a specific time when a given event, or its absence, has a specific impact on development. If a necessary event does not occur during a critical period of maturation, normal development will not occur, and the resulting abnormal patterns are generally irreversible (Kuhl, Conboy, Padden, Nelson, & Pruitt, 2005).

Do human children experience critical periods as ducklings do? One example of a critical period occurs

during gestation. If a woman receives X-rays, takes certain drugs, or contracts certain diseases at certain times during pregnancy, the fetus may show specific ill effects, depending on the nature of the shock and on its timing. For example, exposure to rubella (measles) when the heart is forming will damage heart structure. However, this type of damage cannot occur after the heart has already been formed. Many environmental influences may affect development irreversibly after pregnancy as well. If a muscle problem interfering with the ability to focus both eyes on the same object is not corrected within a critical period early in childhood, depth perception probably will not develop normally (Bushnell & Boudreau, 1993).

The concept of critical periods in humans is controversial. Because many aspects of development, even in the biological/neurological domain, have been found to show **plasticity**, or modifiability of performance, it may be more useful to think about **sensitive periods**, when a developing person is especially responsive to certain kinds of experiences (Bruer, 2001).

historical generation A group of people strongly influenced by a major historical event during their formative period.

cohort A group of people born at about the same time.

imprinting Instinctive form of learning in which, during a critical period in early development, a young animal forms an attachment to the first moving object it sees, usually the mother.

critical period Specific time when a given event or its absence has a profound and specific impact on development.

plasticity Modifiability of performance.

sensitive periods Times in development when a given event or its absence usually has a strong effect on development.

Did you know?

The most critical time for a pregnancy is the first trimester when the major structures of the body are forming. Therefore, any adverse substances encountered during this time can profoundly affect the developing fetus. However, many women do not realize at first that they are pregnant. Luckily, nature has provided us with a safety net—the lack of a shared blood supply for approximately two weeks after conception diminishes the likelihood of exposure.

©PLAINVIEW/Getty Images

Issues in Development

Psychology is in many ways an outgrowth of philosophy, and just as philosophers ask basic questions about human nature, so do psychologists. Indeed, many of the ancient philosophical debates are echoed in the current controversies in psychology. What drives development? Is nature more important than nurture, or vice versa? Is development active or passive? Continuous or discontinuous? Different explanations, or models, of development have emerged out of debates over these issues.

IS DEVELOPMENT BASED MORE ON NATURE OR NURTURE?

Some influences on development originate primarily with **heredity** (nature), inborn traits or characteristics inherited from a child's biological parents. Other influences come largely from the inner and outer **environment** (nurture), the world outside the self, beginning in the womb, and the learning that comes from experience. Which of these factors—heredity or environment—has more impact on development?

Most researchers today agree that nature and nurture always work together. For example, while tall parents pass on "tall genes" to their children, and thus tend to have tall children, nutritional status in childhood also will affect eventual height.

heredity Inborn characteristics inherited from the biological parents.

environment Totality of nonhereditary, or experiential, influences on development.

quantitative change Change in number or amount, such as in height, weight, or size of vocabulary.

Did you know?

Calluses are the result of the environmental experience of repeated friction on skin—they offer protection against irritation. Yet they would never develop if not for genes that instruct the body to "develop a thick layer of skin when this happens." So—are calluses a product of nature or nurture? The answer is that they are both; they would not exist without both influences.

©Digital Vision

IS DEVELOPMENT ACTIVE OR PASSIVE?

Some models of development see it as passive. In this view, people are like machines that react to environmental input (Pepper, 1961). A machine is the sum of its parts. To understand it, we can break it down into its smallest components and then reassemble it. Fill a car with gas, turn the ignition key, press the accelerator, and the vehicle will move. In this view, human behavior is much the same: It results from the operation of biological parts in response to external or internal stimuli. If we know enough about how the human "machine" is put together and about the forces acting on it, we can predict what the person will do. Rather than being active and internally driven, development is reactive and externally driven. Psychologists who endorse this approach see the child as a hungry sponge, eagerly soaking up and responding to the world.

Other models see children as active, growing organisms that set their own development in motion. They do not just react; they initiate events. Thus, the driving force for change is internal. Environmental influences do not cause development, though they can speed or slow it. Because human behavior is viewed as an organic whole, it cannot be predicted by breaking it down into simple responses to environmental stimulation. In this view, children are not merely sponges soaking up experience, they also create experiences for themselves, actively searching for understanding and influencing those around them.

These two models are known as the mechanistic and organismic models of development, and both have a long history of philosophical debate as well as contemporary analogues in modern psychological theories.

The eighteenth century philosopher John Locke was an early proponent of mechanistic models. He believed that babies were born a *tabula rasa*—a blank slate upon which experience would write. Everything that they became and all aspects of their learning and development were shaped by environmental influences, both positive and negative. We see echoes of this approach in Freud's psychoanalytic theory and the behaviorist approaches, both discussed a little later in this chapter.

The French philosopher Jean Jacques Rousseau, by contrast, believed that children were born "noble savages" who would develop according to their own innate plan unless they became corrupted by society. In this view, children were active, growing organisms that were the architects of their own development. Similar beliefs about the active nature of development are also found in Erikson's psychosocial theory, Piaget's theory of cognitive development, and Brofenbrenner's ecological systems theory, also discussed later in this chapter.

IS DEVELOPMENT CONTINUOUS OR DISCONTINUOUS?

Mechanistic and organismic models also differ with respect to what they believe about how change occurs. Mechanistic theorists generally believe in continuous change, while organismic theories most commonly endorse discontinuous change.

Continuous change is gradual and incremental, like walking or crawling up a ramp. (Figure 1.3a). This is a **quantitative change**, a change in number or amount, such as in height, weight, size of vocabulary, or frequency of communication. A baby who can say 3 words at 12 months and then 20 words at 15 months experiences a quantitative change.

Did you know?

A good example of quantitative and qualitative change can be seen with pregnancy. Being 3 months versus 6 months pregnant is a quantitative change. It is not fundamentally different, just further along. But there is no such thing as being a little bit pregnant. You either are, or you are not—making this an example of qualitative change.

©Nancy Ney/Digital Vision/Getty Images

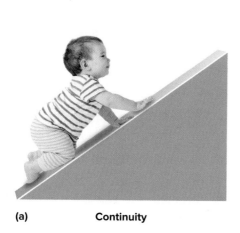

| (a) Continuity | (b) Stage theory (Discontinuity) |

FIGURE 1.3 The Nature of Change

A major difference among developmental theories is (**a**) whether it proceeds continuously, as learning theorists and information-processing theorists propose, or (**b**) whether development occurs in distinct stages, as Freud, Erikson, and Piaget maintained.

©Oksana Kuzmina/Shutterstock; ©Amos Morgan/Getty Images

Discontinuous or **qualitative change** is change in kind, structure, or organization. It is marked by the emergence of new phenomena that cannot be predicted easily on the basis of earlier functioning. The change from a nonverbal child to one who understands words and can communicate verbally is a qualitative change.

These theorists see development as occurring in a series of distinct stages, like stairsteps (Figure 1.3b). At each stage, children cope with different types of problems and develop different abilities. Each stage builds on the previous one and prepares the way for the next.

All stage theories imply qualitative change. Whenever you read or hear about a stage approach to development from Freud or Piaget or Kohlberg, one of the things they are arguing is that development at each stage is fundamentally different from development at other stages.

AN EMERGING CONSENSUS

There are many different viewpoints and controversies in the study of child development. However, as the field has matured, broad agreement has emerged on several fundamental points:

1. *All domains of development are interrelated.* Development in each of the different domains—physical, cognitive, and psychosocial—affects the others in a series of complex interactions. When a baby learns how to stand, this opens up a world of exploration, which then affects cognitive development. Walking triggers the development of attachment-related behaviors; just as soon as a baby is capable of getting away from Mommy, she is suddenly motivated to remain close. While we, of necessity, discuss the different domains

independently, in reality, they are constantly interacting with and affecting each other.

2. *Normal development includes a wide range of individual differences.* Each child, from the start, is unlike anyone else in the world. Some are fussy, some calm. Some smile widely at strangers, some hide behind a parent's legs. Some of the influences on individual development are inborn; others come from experience. Most often, these influences work together. These influences also include such factors as family size and composition, neighborhood, socioeconomic status, gender, race, ethnicity, and the presence or absence of physical, behavioral, or emotional disabilities.

> **qualitative change** Change in kind, structure, or organization, such as the change from nonverbal to verbal communication.

3. *Influences are bidirectional.* Children affect the environment around them as much as the environment shapes them. Outgoing babies smile at strangers, and so their environment includes the presence of friendly adults who interact readily with them. Shy babies shrink away from contact, so their environment may be characterized by the retreat of most adults.

4. *Historical and cultural contexts strongly influence development.* Each child develops within a specific environment bounded by time and place. Some babies are born in times of peace and prosperity, some during war. Some children live in technologically advanced urban environments, others in remote rural areas. These different experiences influence the paths of development.

5. *Early experience is important, but children can be remarkably resilient.* A traumatic incident or a severely deprived childhood may have grave emotional

consequences, but the effects of painful experience, such as growing up in poverty or the death of a parent, often can be overcome.

6. *Development in childhood affects development throughout the life span.* As long as people live, they have the potential to change in both positive and negative directions. Development is lifelong; from womb to tomb.

Now that you have had a brief introduction to the field of child development and its basic concepts, we can look more closely at the issues developmental scientists think about and how they do their work. In the following section, we expand upon these foundations and look more closely at influential theories of how development takes place and the methods investigators commonly use to study it.

Theories of Child Development

When Ahmed graduated from high school with honors in math and science, his father, an award-winning engineer, beamed. "The apple doesn't fall far from the tree," he said. Statements like this are informal, or intuitive, theories about why children develop as they do. Fundamentally, these are no different from the theories scientists develop. Like laypeople's informal theories, scientific theories are not dry, abstract, or esoteric. They deal with the substance of real life, and they are an attempt to explain the world around us.

theory Coherent set of logically related concepts that seeks to organize, explain, and predict data.

A scientific **theory** is a set of logically related concepts or statements that seek to describe and explain development and to predict what kinds of behavior might occur under certain conditions. Theories organize and explain data, the information gathered by research. Throughout *Child*, different aspects of development are explored through different theories. The major theories used in child development fall under five perspectives: psychoanalytic, learning, cognitive, contextual, and evolutionary/sociobiological (Table 1.2).

Did you know?

In scientific terminology, theories provide stronger evidence than laws. Laws are observations—we know that something happens, but we do not know why. Theories include causal explanations—we know that something happens, and we think we know why.

©McGraw-Hill Education/Charles D. Winters

PERSPECTIVE 1: PSYCHOANALYTIC

While most commonly associated with the work of Sigmund Freud, the term *psychoanalytic perspective* is actually a broader umbrella that incorporates an array of related perspectives, generally focused on the lasting effects of childhood experiences and unconscious drives and motivations. In the following section, we describe the two approaches most relevant to the study of child development—the psychosexual and psychosocial perspectives Sigmund Freud and Erik Erikson popularized.

TABLE 1.2 Five Perspectives on Human Development		
Perspective	**Important Theories**	**Basic Propositions**
Psychoanalytic	Freud's psychosexual theory Erikson's psychosocial theory	• Behavior is controlled by powerful unconscious urges. • Personality is influenced by society and develops through a series of crises.
Learning	Behaviorism, or traditional learning theory (Paviov, Skinner, Watson)	• People are responders; the environment controls behavior.
	Social learning (social cognitive) theory (Bandura)	• Children learn in a social context by observing and imitating models. • Children are active contributors to learning.
Cognitive	Piaget's cognitive-stage theory	• Qualitative changes in thought occur between infancy and adolescence. • Children are active initiators of development.
	Vygotsky's sociocultural theory Information-processing theory	• Social interaction is central to cognitive development. • Human beings are processors of symbols.
Contextual	Bronfenbrenner's bioecological theory	• Development occurs through interaction between a developing person and five surrounding, interlocking contextual systems of influences, from microsystem to chronosystem.
Evolutionary/ Sociobiological	Bowlby's attachment theory	• Human beings have the adaptive mechanisms to survive; critical or sensitive periods are stressed; evolutionary and biological bases for behavior and predisposition toward learning are important.

Developmental Psychologist

Developmental psychologists focus on life-span or developmental issues from conception through death, often specializing in a specific stage of the life span. A developmental psychologist might work in a hospital or private practice, or at a home for adolescents or a clinic for the elderly. Developmental psychologists might also research and teach at a university or work for the government or private corporations. For example, a developmental psychologist interested in infants might work for an early intervention program or at a toy company advising on the next developmentally appropriate "must have" toy. Alternatively, a developmental psychologist interested in emerging adulthood might work and teach at a university while also conducting research on college students' risky behaviors. Or a developmental psychologist might research ways to improve seniors' lives, such as increasing the time for a cross-walk signal to accommodate the elderly or implementing an exercise program for seniors. A master's degree or doctoral degree is required to become a developmental psychologist. To learn more about what a developmental psychologist does, visit www.apa.org.

©LWA/Larry Williams/ Blend Images

Sigmund Freud: Psychosexual Development

Sigmund Freud (1953, 1964a, 1964b), a Viennese physician, originated the **psychoanalytic perspective**. He believed that unconscious, universal biological drives shaped development. Freud also developed the now well-known concept of the unconscious, a vast psychic reserve unavailable to conscious experience. Here, warring aspects of the personality battled over how biological imperatives could be addressed in real life, with all the rules and social conventions found there.

Freud proposed that personality was composed of three parts: the id, the ego, and the superego. Newborns are governed by the id, which operates under the pleasure principle—the drive to seek immediate satisfaction of needs and desires. When gratification is delayed, as it is when infants have to wait to be fed, they begin to see themselves as separate from the outside world. The ego, which represents reason, develops gradually during the first year or so of life and operates under the reality principle. The ego's aim is to find realistic ways to gratify the id that are acceptable to the superego, which develops at about age 5 or 6. The superego includes the conscience and incorporates socially approved "shoulds" and "should nots" into the child's own value system. The superego is highly demanding; if its standards are not met, a child may feel guilty and anxious. The ego mediates between the impulses of the id and the demands of the superego.

psychoanalytic perspective View of human development as being shaped by unconscious forces.

> *"Anatomy is destiny."*
> *Sigmund Freud*

Technique Used	Stage-Oriented	Causal Emphasis	Active or Reactive Individual
Clinical observation	Yes	Innate factors modified by experience	Reactive
Clinical observation	Yes	Interaction of innate and experiential factors	Active
Rigorous scientific (experimental) procedures	No	Experience	Reactive
Rigorous scientific (experimental) procedures	No	Experience modified by innate factors	Active and reactive
Flexible interviews; meticulous observation	Yes	Interaction of innate and experiential factors	Active
Cross-cultural research; observation of child interacting with more competent person	No	Experience	Active
Laboratory research; technological monitoring of physiologic responses	No	Interaction of innate and experiential factors	Active
Naturalistic observation and analysis	No	Interaction of innate and experiential factors	Active
Naturalistic and laboratory observation	No	Interaction of innate and experiential factors	Active and reactive (theorists vary)

"Children love and want to be loved and they very much prefer the joy of accomplishment to the triumph of hateful failure." Erik Erikson

Freud proposed that development is shaped by an unvarying sequence of five stages of **psychosexual development** (Table 1.3) in which sensual pleasure shifts from one body zone to another. At each stage, the behavior that is the chief source of gratification (or frustration) changes.

According to Freud, if children receive too little or too much gratification in any of these stages, they are at risk of fixation—an arrest in development that can show up in adult personality. For example, babies whose needs are not met during the oral stage, when feeding is the main source of sensual pleasure, may grow up to become nail-biters or smokers. In the anal stage of development, occurring during the toddler years, if the mother did not handle toilet training appropriately a child might develop an anal fixation, and as an adult be obsessively clean and overly rigid, or, by contrast, excessively messy and undisciplined. The phallic stage of early childhood, when the zone of gratification presumably shifted to the genital region, is when Freud believed gender identity formed. He believed that children developed a sexual attraction to their opposite sex parent. He did not think this was abnormal or problematic; in fact, he believed it to be part of the typical developmental path children should take. He thought that children's attraction to their opposite sex parent also involved viewing the same-sex parents as a rival, aggressive impulses directed at the same-sex parent, and anxiety over these processes. In an attempt to allay their anxiety, children would identify with their same-sex parents. Freud termed this the Oedipus (for boys) and Electra (for girls) complex and believed it to be vital to the formation of an appropriate gender identity in adulthood. Following this, children would move into the relative calm of the latency stage of middle childhood, where social energies were redirected toward schoolwork, relationships, or hobbies. Finally, as children entered and moved through puberty, sexual urges would reemerge and could now be directed into socially approved channels. In the Victorian times in which Freud lived, this was defined as heterosexual relationships, or marriage, and children.

psychosexual development In Freudian theory, an unvarying sequence of stages of personality development during infancy, childhood, and adolescence in which gratification shifts from the mouth to the anus and then to the genitals.

psychosocial development In Erikson's eight-stage theory, the socially and culturally influenced process of development of the ego, or self.

Freud's theory made historic contributions and inspired a whole generation of followers, some of whom took psychoanalytic theory in new directions. Many of Freud's ideas, however, now are widely considered obsolete, cannot be scientifically tested, or have not been supported in research. Additionally, his ideas, shaped by the context of Victorian society and developed out of his interactions with his psychologically distressed clients, were culturally bound, relatively negative about human development, and often sexist. Yet several of his central themes have nonetheless stood the test of time. Freud made us aware of the importance of unconscious thoughts, feelings, and motivations; the role of childhood experiences in forming personality; the ambivalence of emotional responses, especially to parents; the role of mental representations of the self and others in establishing intimate relationships; and the path of normal development from an immature, dependent state to a mature, interdependent one. In all these ways, Freud left an indelible mark on psychoanalysis and developmental psychology (Westen, 1998).

Erik Erikson: Psychosocial Development

Erik Erikson (1902–1994) modified and extended Freudian theory by emphasizing the influence of society on the developing personality. He is notable in that he was one of the first theorists to emphasize the life-span perspective. Like Freud, and like all theorists who endorse stage theories of development, Erikson would argue for qualitative change. What happens at one stage, in theories such as these, is fundamentally different from what happens at other stages. However, unlike Freud, Erikson believed in active development and that people were motivated to resolve the issues that emerged during development.

Erikson's (1950) theory of **psychosocial development** covers eight stages across the life span (see Table 1.3). This was a notable departure from Freud's theories because of the emphasis on lifelong change. While Freud essentially stopped the developmental clock at adolescence, Erikson argued that the entire life span was marked by change and development. Each stage in his approach involved what Erikson originally called a "crisis" in personality—a major psychosocial theme that was particularly important at that time.

TABLE 1.3 Developmental Stages According to Freud, Erikson, and Piaget

Psychosexual Stages (Freud)	Psychosocial Stages (Erikson)	Cognitive Stages (Piaget)
Oral *(birth to 12–18 months)*. Baby's chief source of pleasure involves mouth-oriented activities (sucking and feeding).	**Basic trust versus mistrust** *(birth to 12–18 months)*. Baby develops sense of whether world is a good and safe place. Virtue: hope.	**Sensorimotor** *(birth to 2 years)*. Infant gradually becomes able to organize activities in relation to the environment through sensory and motor activity.
Anal *(12–18 months to 3 years)*. Child derives sensual gratification from withholding and expelling feces. Zone of gratification is anal region, and toilet training is important activity.	**Autonomy versus shame and doubt** *(12–18 months to 3 years)*. Child develops a balance of independence and self-sufficiency over shame and doubt. Virtue: will.	**Preoperational** *(2 to 7 years)*. Child develops a representational system and uses symbols to represent people, places, and events. Language and imaginative play are important manifestations of this stage. Thinking is still not logical.
Phallic *(3 to 6 years)*. Child becomes Child attached to parent of the other sex and later identifies with same-sex parent. Superego develops. Zone of gratification shifts to genital region.	**Initiative versus guilt** *(3 to 6 years)*. Child develops initiative when trying new activities and is not overwhelmed by guilt. Virtue: purpose.	
Latency *(6 years to puberty)*. Time of relative calm between more turbulent states.	**Industry versus inferiority** *(6 years to puberty)*. Child must learn skills of the culture or face feelings of incompetence. Virtue: skill.	**Concrete operations** *(7 to 11 years)*. Child can solve problems logically if focused on the here and now but cannot think abstractly.
Genital *(puberty through adulthood)*. Reemergence of sexual impulses of phallic stage, channeled into mature adult sexuality.	**Identity versus identity confusion** *(puberty to young adulthood)*. Adolescent must determine sense of self ("Who am I?") or experience confusion about roles. Virtue: fidelity.	**Formal operations** *(11 years through adulthood)*. Person can think abstractly, deal with hypothetical situations, and think about possibilities.
	Intimacy versus isolation *(young adulthood)*. Person seeks to make commitments to others; if unsuccessful, may suffer from isolation and self-absorption. Virtue: love.	
	Generativity versus stagnation *(middle adulthood)*. Mature adult is concerned with establishing and guiding the next generation or else feels personal impoverishment. Virtue: care.	
	Integrity versus despair *(late adulthood)*. Elderly person achieves acceptance of own life, allowing acceptance of death, or else despairs over inability to relive life. Virtue: wisdom.	

Note: All ages are approximate.

Each stage requires the balancing of a positive trait and a corresponding negative one. The critical theme of infancy, for example, is basic trust versus basic mistrust. People need to trust the world and the people in it, but they also need to learn some mistrust to protect themselves from danger. Successful resolution of one crisis puts the child in a particularly good position to address the next crisis, a process that occurs iteratively across the life span. So, to extend this example, in toddlerhood the critical theme is autonomy, or a sense of agency and independence. A child who successfully developed a sense of trust would be in a good position to develop this strength. After all, if you feel that others have your back, you are likely to try new things and thus develop new skills. By contrast, if you feel alone and uncertain, you can still develop autonomy, but it is more difficult. Ideally, each stage builds on the preceding one.

Erikson's theory is important for a number of reasons. First, while the crises that Erikson outlined were particular to one place and time—for example, across different cultures, not all children go to school, and not all people marry only in young adulthood—Erikson did make clear that social and cultural influences mattered. Erikson highlighted the social clock, the conventional, culturally preferred timing of important life events. Last, Erikson held a much more positive view of development than Freud. Freud focused more strongly on the ways in which development could go awry. Erikson, while acknowledging that crises could be resolved poorly, left room for improvement. At any point in the life span, development could shift in a positive direction, and a crisis might be successfully resolved and a new strength developed.

PERSPECTIVE 2: LEARNING

When psychology began to grow in prominence in the scientific community, its methods were not as advanced as they are now. This is true not just with respect to the tools we now employ—the video and computer equipment, the brain-scanning technology, and the measures that have been developed over the decades since then—but also in the means by which research is conducted. Psychology was critiqued, at that time rightly so, for its overly subjective approach to research. The learning perspective, or behaviorism, was in many ways a response to this.

Theorists within the **learning perspectives** argued that development was the result of learning, a relatively long-lasting change in development based on experience or adaptation to the environment. Learning theorists were not interested in the inner working of the mind, because those processes could not be directly observed. Because behavior is observable and countable and confers great objectivity, the focus was on behavior. Terms could be defined precisely, and theories could be tested scientifically in the laboratory, thus, in the opinion of proponents of this view, lending psychology greater legitimacy and respectability.

learning perspective View of human development that holds that changes in behavior result from experience.

classical conditioning Learning based on association of a stimulus that does not ordinarily elicit a particular response with another stimulus that does elicit the response.

Another aspect of learning approaches that was attractive to psychologists at the time was the view of the mind as a tabula rasa, a blank slate upon which experience could write. In this view, everything a person became depended upon experience. Thus, anyone, no matter what race, or whatever individual characteristics might be present, could be anything. This implied that the ills of the world could be fixed if psychologists could just figure the right way to raise children. While the child-rearing strategies proposed by behaviorists eventually fell out of favor, the idea that people were fundamentally the same held a powerful attraction.

Behaviorists also saw development as continuous, emphasizing incremental quantitative changes over time, and reactive, occurring in response to environmental input. The learning approach was the dominant ideology in the field of psychology in the 1950s. Two of the major subtheories were behaviorism and the social learning approach.

Learning Theory 1: Behaviorism

Behaviorism is a mechanistic approach in psychology centered around the observation of behaviors and the belief in the environment's strong influence. Behaviorists hold that human beings at all ages learn about the world by reacting to aspects of their environment that they find pleasing, painful, or threatening, and that these processes govern learning in all areas of development in the same way. In other words,

young children learn how to walk and how to talk via the same process—learned associations. Behavioral research focuses on associative learning in which a mental link is formed between two events. Two kinds of associative learning are classical conditioning and operant conditioning.

Classical Conditioning   Sometimes, discoveries are serendipitous. This is the case with one of the most influential theories developed in psychology. Ivan Pavlov (1849–1936) was a Russian physiologist studying the role of saliva in dogs' digestive processes. In order to collect saliva from the dogs, Pavlov would secure them with a harness to prevent them from lowering their head, and implant a saliva collection device on their throat. Because dogs salivate readily to meat, he would then place a bowl of meat underneath the dog. While conducting this research, Pavlov realized that the dogs, shortly after being introduced to the methodology, would salivate before the presentation of the meat. Once he realized this was occurring, he investigated this process, using a "bell" (in actuality a metronome that could be configured to release a certain number of clicks per minute) as a predictor for the arrival of the meat. This accidental breakthrough was the foundation for the discovery of **classical conditioning**, a type of learning in which a response (salivation) to a stimulus (a bell) is elicited after repeated association with a stimulus that normally elicits the response (food).

This research was extended by the American behaviorist John B. Watson (1878–1958) who applied stimulus-response theories to children, claiming he could mold any infant in any way he chose. In one of the earliest and most famous demonstrations of classical conditioning in human beings, he taught an 11-month-old baby known as "Little Albert" to fear a furry white rat (Watson & Rayner, 1920).

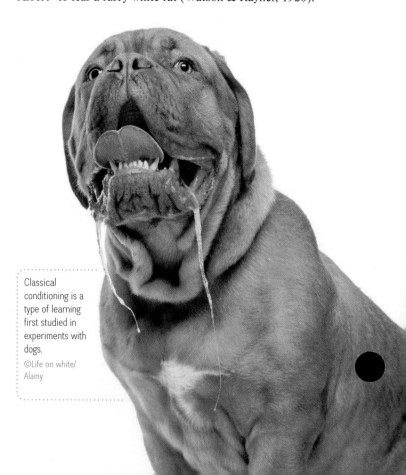

Classical conditioning is a type of learning first studied in experiments with dogs.
©Life on white/Alamy

> *"Give me a dozen healthy infants, well-formed, and my own specified world to bring them up in and I'll guarantee to take any one at random and train him to become any type of specialist I might select—doctor, lawyer, artist, merchant-chief and, yes, even beggar-man and thief, regardless of his talents, penchants, tendencies, abilities, vocations, and race of his ancestors." John Watson*

In this study, Albert was exposed to a loud noise when he started to stroke the rat. The noise frightened him, and he began to cry. After repeated pairings of the rat with the loud noise, Albert whimpered with fear when he saw the rat. Moreover, Albert also started showing fear responses to white rabbits and cats, and elderly men's beards. Although the study would be considered highly unethical today, it did demonstrate that a baby could be conditioned to fear something he or she had not been afraid of previously.

Classical conditioning occurs frequently in everyday life. In advertising, a common strategy is to associate a brand with a particular feeling by presenting a product repeatedly with an object that elicits positive feelings. For example, many fast-food restaurants run promotions in which toys are offered to children who eat there. Presumably, this will cause the children to form a positive association with visiting the restaurant, and hence result in loyalty to that brand. This can also work in a negative direction. For example, fear responses to objects such as a car or a dog may be the result of an accident or bad experience.

Operant Conditioning   Angel lies in his crib. When he starts to babble ("ma-ma-ma"), his mother smiles and repeats the syllables. Angel learns his behavior (babbling) can produce a desirable consequence (loving attention from a parent), so he learns to keep babbling to attract his mother's attention. An originally accidental behavior (babbling) has become a conditioned response.

This type of learning is called **operant conditioning**. The individual learns from the consequences of "operating" on the environment. Unlike classical conditioning, operant conditioning involves voluntary behavior, such as Angel's babbling, and the consequences rather than the predictors of behavior. If classical conditioning involves the "before" of actions, operant conditioning is about the "after."

The American psychologist B. F. Skinner (1904–1990), who formulated the principles of operant conditioning, found an organism will tend to repeat a response that has been reinforced by desirable consequences and will suppress a response that has been punished. Thus, **reinforcement** is the process by which a behavior is strengthened, increasing the likelihood the behavior will be repeated. In Angel's case, his mother's attention reinforces his babbling. **Punishment** is the process by which a behavior is weakened, decreasing the likelihood of repetition. If Angel's mother frowned when he babbled, he would be less likely to babble again.

Reinforcement and punishment can be positive, involving "adding" a stimulus to the environment, or "negative," involving the removal of a stimulus to the environment. For example, positive reinforcement is provided by Angel's mother's smiles and encouragement, and because this is reinforcing, it increases the likelihood that Angel will perform this action again. Negative reinforcement (commonly confused with punishment) should likewise result in a greater likelihood of a behavior occurring, but it should do so by removing a negative stimulus. A good example of this can be found in seatbelt alerts in cars. When the ignition key is turned and the seatbelt is not attached, an irritating sound is played. The sound shuts off immediately when the seatbelt is clicked close. The cessation of the sound (the removal of an unpleasant stimulus) is reinforcing (should result in a greater likelihood of the seatbelt being buckled the next time a person drives).

> **operant conditioning** Learning based on association of behavior with its consequences.
>
> **reinforcement** In operant conditioning, a process that increases the likelihood that a behavior will be repeated.
>
> **punishment** In operant conditioning, a process that decreases the likelihood that a behavior will be repeated.

The same process can be applied to punishment. An example of positive punishment is speaking sharply to a dog that got into the garbage. Presumably, the negative experience should result in a reduction of the likelihood of the dog misbehaving again. Punishment can also be negative. If two siblings are fighting over what to watch on television, and a parent decides to turn the television off, the children have experienced negative punishment. The removal of a positive stimulus (the television) should result in a reduced likelihood of fighting over the television again.

Reinforcement is most effective when it immediately follows a behavior. If a response is no longer reinforced, it will eventually be extinguished, that is, return to its original (baseline) level. If after a while, no one responds to Angel's babbling, he may babble less often.

Skinnerian psychology has been influential. For many years, the bulk of work in psychology occurred within this approach. Behavioral modification, a form of operant conditioning used to eliminate negative behaviors, has been widely used as a therapeutic approach for children with special needs. It has been extraordinarily effective in managing problem behaviors.

However, as an overarching theory of development, behaviorism falls short. While learning theorists advocated a tabula rasa approach, we know now that children come into the world with a host of individual differences that profoundly impact development. There is no room for such variability within the learning approach. Moreover, it has become clear that the "rules" for learning in different domains do not always follow behavioral predictions and can differ depending on what is being learned. For example, children learn language far more rapidly than learned associations can account for, and the way in which children learn to talk is fundamentally different from how they learn to walk. Last, psychologists have realized, over time, that while we cannot directly access what is going on in people's heads, we can use indirect measures (such as reaction time) to make objective scientific predictions and collect empirical data. Thus, the earlier reluctance to examine mental processes has abated as the field has progressed.

Learning Theory 2: Social Learning (Social Cognitive) Theory

As the psychological community began to realize that developmental theories that ignored all cognitive processes were incomplete, the original postulates of the behavioral approach were expanded by the American psychologist Albert Bandura (b. 1925). Bandura developed many of the principles of social learning theory in which behaviors are learned by observation. Whereas behaviorists saw the environment as the chief impetus for development, Bandura (1977, 1989) suggested that the impetus for development was bidirectional. He called this concept **reciprocal determinism**— the child acts on the world as the world acts on the child.

Classic social learning theory maintains that people learn appropriate social behavior chiefly by observing and imitating models—that is, by watching other people and learning both about what potential behaviors might be as well as the likely consequences of such behaviors. This process is called **observational learning**, or modeling. Observational learning can occur even if a person does not imitate the observed behavior. For example, Clara sees her older sister get disciplined for eating a cookie cooling on the counter, and thus restrains herself from doing the same thing.

reciprocal determinism Bandura's term for bidirectional forces that affect development.

observational learning Learning through watching the behavior of others.

self-efficacy Sense of one's capability to master challenges and achieve goals.

cognitive perspective Perspective that looks at the development of mental processes such as thinking.

organization Piaget's term for the creation of categories or systems of knowledge.

> "Coping with the demands of everyday life would be exceedingly trying if one could arrive at solutions to problems only by actually performing possible options and suffering the consequences."
> *Albert Bandura*

Bandura's (1989) updated version of social learning theory is social cognitive theory. The change of name reflects a greater emphasis on cognitive processes as central to development. Cognitive processes are at work as people observe models, learn "chunks" of behavior, and mentally put the chunks together into complex new behavior patterns. Rita, for example, imitates the toes-out walk of her dance teacher but models her dance steps after those of Carmen, a slightly more advanced student. Even so, Rita develops her own style of dancing by putting her observations together into a new pattern. As children experience success in areas of functioning, they also begin to develop a sense of **self-efficacy**, or confidence in their abilities.

PERSPECTIVE 3: COGNITIVE

Where behaviorists were reluctant to study the inner workings of the mind because they believed that events not directly observable could not be viewed through a scientific lens, cognitive psychologists argued this is exactly what research should illuminate. In the following section, we discuss three theoretical traditions within the **cognitive perspective**: Piaget's cognitive theory, Vygotsky's sociocultural theory, and the information-processing approach to cognition.

Jean Piaget's Cognitive-Stage Theory

The fields of both cognitive psychology and developmental psychology owe an enormous debt to the work of the Swiss theoretician Jean Piaget (1896–1980). Through his careful observations and thoughtful questions, Piaget developed a theory that reintroduced the concept of scientific inquiry into mental states. Because he developed a series of experimental paradigms that yielded hard observational data, he demonstrated that "real" science could indeed investigate hidden mental phenomena, as we will see throughout this text.

Piaget viewed development organismically, as the product of children's attempts to understand and act upon their world. He also believed in qualitative development, and thus his theory delineates a series of stages characterizing development at different ages. Piaget believed that children came equipped with a few basic capacities that allowed them to begin learning. Most importantly, development is initially based on motor activities such as reflexes. By rooting for a nipple, feeling a pebble, or exploring the boundaries of a room, young children first learn how to control and refine their movements, and then learn how to explore their world with their bodies. In this way, they develop a more accurate understanding of their surroundings and greater competence in dealing with them. This cognitive growth occurs through three interrelated processes: organization, adaptation, and equilibration.

Organization is the tendency to create categories, such as birds, by observing the characteristics that individual members of a category, such as sparrows and cardinals, have in common. According to Piaget, people create increasingly complex cognitive structures called **schemes**, or ways of organizing information about the world. These schemes can be either motor or mental in nature. Take sucking, for example. A newborn infant has a simple scheme for sucking but soon develops varied schemes for how to suck at the breast, a bottle, or a thumb. The infant may have to open her mouth wider, or turn her head to the side, or suck with varying strength.

Adaptation is Piaget's term for how children handle new information in light of what they already know. Adaptation occurs through two complementary processes: (1) **assimilation**, taking in new information and incorporating it into existing cognitive structures, and (2) **accommodation**, adjusting one's cognitive structures to fit the new information.

Equilibration—a constant striving for a stable balance—motivates the shift from assimilation to accommodation. For example, a child knows what birds are and sees a plane for the first time. The child labels the plane a "bird" (assimilation). Over time the child notes differences between planes and birds. For example, the child might notice that planes look different in picture books, even though both fly in the sky, and that birds have feathers, while planes are made of a hard, smooth surface. These observations bring about an uneasy motivational state known as disequilibrium. The child is then motivated to change her understanding to more closely reflect her observations—perhaps by learning the label for plane and realizing that planes and birds are not, after all, the same thing. In other words, accommodation has occurred and she is now at equilibrium. Throughout life, the quest for equilibrium is the driving force behind cognitive growth.

Piaget described cognitive development as occurring in four qualitative stages (listed in Table 1.3 and discussed in detail in later chapters). At each stage a child's mind develops a new way of operating. From infancy through adolescence, mental operations evolve from learning based on simple sensory and motor activity to logical, abstract thought. An implication of this view is that children's minds are not just miniature adult minds. They fundamentally think differently from adults.

While Piaget was profoundly influential in the field and provided a series of rough but useful benchmarks of development, he underestimated the abilities of infants and young children. Some contemporary psychologists question his distinct stages, pointing to evidence that cognitive development is more gradual and continuous (Courage & Howe, 2002). Others have pointed out that children's cognitive processes seem closely tied to specific content (what they are thinking about) as well as to the context of a problem and the kinds of information and thought a culture considers important (Case & Okamoto, 1996). We explore further critiques of Piaget's work in the chapters that follow.

> *"The principal goal of education in the schools should be creating men and women who are capable of doing new things, not simply repeating what other generations have done." Jean Piaget*

Lev Vygotsky's Sociocultural Theory

The Russian psychologist Lev Semyonovich Vygotsky (1896–1934) focused on the social and cultural processes that guide children's cognitive development. Whereas previous theorists viewed development as a primarily individual process, Vygotsky believed that learning was social and collaborative. Children, said Vygotsky, learn through social interaction and shared activities. Rather than believing in universal aspects of development, Vygostky believed there are as many ways to develop as there are different cultures and different experiences. While psychology as a field has increasingly incorporated issues of diversity into theory and research, Vygotsky's realization that culture matters was far ahead of his time and remains a fundamental and important contribution of his approach.

schemes Piaget's term for organized patterns of thought and behavior used in particular situations.

adaptation Piaget's term for adjustment to new information about the environment.

assimilation Piaget's term for incorporation of new information into an existing cognitive structure.

accommodation Piaget's term for changes in a cognitive structure to include new information.

equilibration Piaget's term for the tendency to seek a stable balance among cognitive elements; achieved through a balance between assimilation and accommodation.

According to Piaget, children's development is initially based on motor activities as they learn to explore the world with their bodies.

©lostinbids/Getty Images

> *"Through others, we become ourselves."*
> *Lev Vygotsky*

According to Vygotsky, adults or more advanced peers must help direct and organize a child's learning. This guidance is most effective in helping children cross the **zone of proximal development (ZPD)**, the imaginary psychological space between what children can do on their own and what they could achieve with another person's assistance. Over time, as a child's abilities increase, responsibility for directing and monitoring learning gradually shifts from the adult to the child—for example, when an adult teaches a child to float, the adult first supports the child in the water and then lets go gradually as the child's body relaxes into a horizontal position. This temporary support that parents, teachers, or others give a child is known as scaffolding.

For example, Noah receives a new puzzle for his birthday, but after emptying the pieces on the dining room table and trying to fit pieces together randomly, he makes little progress. His older sister sees him trying, sits next to him, and offers advice on how to begin. "Try putting all the pieces of the same color in piles," she says, "that makes it easier to see what goes together. You can look at the box for clues. And, if you do the edges first, then you have the outline already done." With his sister's coaching, Noah is able to start assembling the puzzle. His sister has provided him with scaffolding with her coaching and allowed Noah to move to the high end of his zone of proximal development and maximize his learning.

Vygotsky made significant contributions to the understanding of developmental processes. However, one aspect of his approach that initially made it difficult for psychologists to accept his work is that he did not use traditional quantitative experimental methodology. Rather than conducting a carefully controlled experiment, for example, Vygotsky was more likely to conduct experiments such as asking a toddler to draw a representation of an event, or putting two children who spoke different languages in a room and asking them to complete a task together. The data collected often consisted of detailed descriptions of what occurred, and contained little in the way of quantifiable information or statistics (Vygotsky, 1980). Vygotsky simply viewed experiments as different—rather than providing statistical tests of competing hypotheses, they were springboards for the development of understanding.

Despite the reluctance of the scientific community to embrace his experimental approach, Vygotsky's ideas have grown in stature and prominence as their implications for education and cognitive testing have become more apparent. For example, most intelligence tests assess what a child has already learned. By contrast, an intelligence test within the Vygotskian tradition might allow testers to offer hints to children who were having trouble answering a question, thereby focusing on that child's potential learning. Additionally, Vygotsky's ideas have had an enormous impact in early childhood education, and they show great promise for promoting the development of self-regulation, which later affects academic achievement (Barnett et al., 2008).

The Information-Processing Approach

The **information-processing approach** seeks to explain cognitive development by analyzing the processes involved in making sense of incoming information and performing tasks effectively. For example, theorists within this tradition focus on processes such as attention, memory, planning strategies, decision errors, decision making, and goal setting. The information-processing approach is not a single theory but a framework that undergirds a wide range of theories and research. Information-processing theorists view development as continuous. They note age-related increases in the speed, complexity, and efficiency of mental processing, and the variety of material that can be stored in memory. However, they do not consider those processes to be fundamentally different at different ages, just more sophisticated.

The most common model for this theory is that of a computer, which has certain inputs (such as sensory impressions) and certain outputs (such as behaviors). Information-processing theorists are interested in what happens in the middle. How does the brain use sensations and perceptions, say, of an unfamiliar word, to recognize that word again? Why does the same input sometimes result in different outputs? How do people gather, store, retrieve, and use information?

Note that many of the processes that these theorists investigate are internal. It is impossible to directly observe what paying attention to or remembering something looks like. However, it is possible to use indirect measures to infer what is happening inside a person's head. For example, one classic demonstration can be found in the Stroop Effect. When asked to indicate the color of font a word is written in, subjects are faster and more accurate doing so when the color term matches the font color the word is printed in. When they do not match, such as when the word "red" is printed in green font, subjects are slower to say what color the word is printed in. Presumably, the slowed time for the unmatched word and color are the result of interference. Why does this happen? According to Stroop (1935) an experienced reader cannot help but read the word. Because upon reading the word the concept (red) is activated, there is interference with the correct response (green). While this explanation is based on inference, and other scientists might argue about what it means, the result itself is an objective fact that can be tested scientifically.

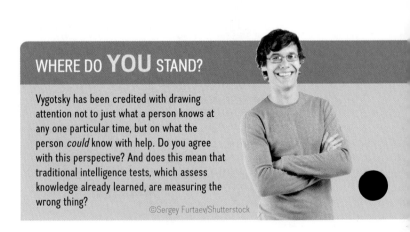

WHERE DO YOU STAND?

Vygotsky has been credited with drawing attention not to just what a person knows at any one particular time, but on what the person *could* know with help. Do you agree with this perspective? And does this mean that traditional intelligence tests, which assess knowledge already learned, are measuring the wrong thing?

©Sergey Furtaev/Shutterstock

The information-processing approach has taught us a great deal about the mechanics of how the mind works. It has also demonstrated that we *can* access cognitive processes, even though they are internal.

PERSPECTIVE 4: CONTEXTUAL

According to the **contextual perspective**, development can be understood only in its social context. Contextualists see the individual not as a separate entity interacting with the environment but as an inseparable part of it. Vygotsky's sociocultural theory, which we discussed as part of the cognitive perspective, also can be classified as contextual.

> *"Development, it turns out, occurs through this process of progressively more complex exchange between a child and somebody else—especially somebody who's crazy about that child."*
> *Urie Bronfenbrenner*

The American psychologist Urie Bronfenbrenner's (1917–2005) **bioecological theory** (1979, 1986, 1994; Bronfenbrenner & Morris, 1998) identifies five levels of environmental influence, ranging from very intimate to very broad: microsystem, mesosystem, exosystem, macrosystem, and chronosystem (Figure 1.4).

Bronfenbrenner's model is generally represented as a set of rings. In the middle of the rings is the developing child. Here, individual difference variables such as age, sex, health, abilities, or temperament are present. The child is not seen as just an outcome of development; this is an active viewpoint that views the child as an active shaper of development. But the child does not exist in isolation. To understand development, we must see the child within the context of the multiple environments surrounding her.

The *microsystem* consists of the everyday environment of home, work, school, or neighborhood. It includes face-to-face interactions with siblings, parents, friends, classmates, or later in life, spouses, work colleagues, or employers.

The *mesosystem* is the interlocking influence of microsystems. It may include linkages between home and school (such as a parent-teacher conference) or between the family and the peer group (such as the relationships that develop among families in a neighborhood peer group). Because of mesosystem interactions, environments in which a child does not directly participate may nonetheless influence her. For example, a parent's bad day at work may affect interactions with a child later that evening in a negative way. Despite never having actually gone to the workplace, a child is still affected by it.

The *exosystem* consists of interactions between a microsystem and an outside system or institution. Although the effects are indirect, they can still have a profound impact on a child. For example, countries differ with respect to policies on what type, if any, of maternal and paternal leave are available to new parents. Whether or not a parent has the option to stay home with a newborn is a substantial influence on development. Thus, government policies trickle down and can affect a child's day-to-day experiences.

The *macrosystem* consists of overarching cultural patterns, such as dominant beliefs, ideologies and economic and political systems. For example, individuals are affected by the type of political system they live in and might reasonably have different experiences if raised in an open democratic society versus an authoritarian regime with limited freedoms.

contextual perspective View of child development that sees the individual as inseparable from the social context.

bioecological theory Bronfenbrenner's approach to understanding processes and contexts of child development that identifies five levels of environmental influence.

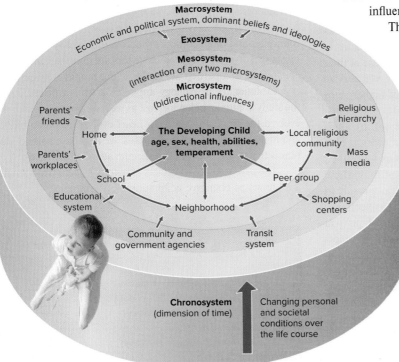

FIGURE 1.4 Bronfenbrenner's Bioecological Theory

Concentric circles show five levels of environmental influence on the individual, from the most intimate environment (the microsystem) to the broadest (the chronosystem)—all within the perpendicular dimension of time.

©Africa Studio/Shutterstock

Last, the *chronosystem* represents the dimension of time. Time marches on and changes occur. These can include changes in family composition (as when a new child is born or a divorce occurs), place of residence, or parents' employment, as well as larger events such as wars, ideological shifts, or economic cycles.

By looking at systems that affect individuals in and beyond the family, this bioecological approach helps us to see the variety of influences on development. The contextual perspective also reminds us that findings about child development in one culture or one group within a culture (such as white, middle-class Americans) may not apply equally to children in other societies or cultural groups.

PERSPECTIVE 5: EVOLUTIONARY/ SOCIOBIOLOGICAL

The **evolutionary/sociobiological perspective** originally proposed by E. O. Wilson (1975) focuses on evolutionary and biological bases of behavior. Influenced by Darwin's theory of evolution, it draws on findings of anthropology, ecology, genetics, ethology, and evolutionary psychology to explain the adaptive, or survival, value of behavior for an individual or species.

Darwin's theory of natural selection is one of the most important theoretical advances of modern science. It is elegant in its simplicity and profound in its implications. Although it was controversial when Darwin first proposed it, and remains controversial today, it is the cornerstone of the biological sciences and has many implications for human psychology.

Fundamentally, Darwin's theory can be broken down into a few major postulates. First, organisms vary. Second, there are never enough resources for all organisms to survive. Third, individual differences in organisms are heritable. The logical consequence of these simple statements is that some organisms, because of their particular characteristics, will survive and hence reproduce at higher rates than others. Their particular traits, then, will be passed on to their descendants in higher proportions, while characteristics of organisms that are not as well suited to the environment will not. Over vast spans of time, these small incremental changes in passed-down traits result in species change. This process is known as natural selection.

Natural selection is defined as the differential survival and reproduction of different variants of members of a species, and is the tool the natural world uses to shape evolutionary processes. While it is commonly described as "survival of the fittest" the key feature is in actuality reproductive success. Individuals with more adaptive traits pass on more of those traits to future generations. In this way, "fit" characteristics are selected to be passed on, and others die out.

Note that these traits can be physical (like a tiger's stripes, which allow it to blend into the background),

evolutionary/sociobiological perspective View of human development that focuses on evolutionary and biological bases of social behavior.

ethology Study of distinctive adaptive behaviors of species of animals that have evolved to increase survival of the species.

evolutionary psychology Application of Darwinian principles of natural selection and survival of the fittest to human psychology.

Did you know?

Charles Darwin was by all accounts a loving and involved father. He encouraged his children to participate in his research, collecting butterflies and plants in the countryside of his family home in Kent, England, and allowing them to draw and doodle on the backs of his scientific manuscripts. He also installed a wooden slide on the stairs and a rope swing on the second floor. At his home, now a museum, you can still see the same slide his children played on so long ago.

©Heritage Images/ Getty Images

behavioral (like the mating dances of many species of birds), or psychological (like a baby monkey's need to cling to and cuddle a warm soft body).

> *"In the distant future I see open fields for more important researches. Psychology will be based on a new foundation, that of the necessary acquirement of each mental power and capacity by gradation."* Charles Darwin

Ethology is the study of animal species' distinctive adaptive behaviors. Ethologists suggest that for each species certain innate behaviors, such as squirrels burying nuts in the fall and spiders spinning webs, have evolved to increase the odds of survival. By observing animals, usually in their natural surroundings and often comparing across different species, ethologists seek to identify which behaviors are universal and which are specific to a particular species or are modified by culture.

Evolutionary psychology applies Darwinian principles to the study of human behavior. Just as we have opposable thumbs evolved for manual dexterity, a heart evolved to pump blood, and lungs evolved to exchange gases, we also have parts of our brains that evolved to address specific adaptive problems.

The psychological products of natural selection in humans are known as cognitive adaptations. For example,

WHERE DO **YOU** STAND?

Evolutionary psychology is one of the most controversial perspectives in the field of psychology. Do you think evolution can explain animal behavior? Can it explain human psychology? Is there a qualitative difference between the two?
©Wayhome studio/Shutterstock

our brains have evolved to find certain faces and body types as attractive, to strive for dominance, and to perceive babies as cute, because these propensities addressed the adaptive problems of mate selection, access to resources, and survival of young.

Humans have a large number of cognitive adaptations. Most cognitive adaptations are tailored to a specific problem. For example, "morning sickness," the nausea experienced by many women early in their pregnancies, has been theorized to have evolved to protect the fetus from teratogens (harmful substances) during the first trimester of pregnancy when it is most vulnerable. In support of this, the types of foods women generally report aversions to are foods high in teratogens and morning sickness generally subsides after the first trimester (Flaxman & Sherman, 2008). Other adaptations, such as human intelligence, are viewed as having evolved to help people face a wide variety of problems flexibly (MacDonald, 1998). These types of cognitive adaptations, in our ancestral past, led to greater survival and reproduction.

Some cognitive adaptations may survive even if they no longer serve a useful purpose or are even harmful. This is because, relatively speaking, little time has passed since we first left the savannas and our hunter/gatherer lifestyle. Our cultural evolution has outpaced biological evolution. So, for example, our taste buds evolved in an environment where sugar and salt were rare treats and difficult to come by. When they were encountered, it was a good idea to consume as much as possible. Thus, humans evolved a taste preference for salty, fatty foods that in today's world, with its wealth of options, can result in unhealthy eating choices.

Evolutionary psychology, despite arguing that reproductive success is the key feature driving our adaptations, does not propose that people are consciously seeking to maximize their reproductive output. For example, people enjoy sexual activity even when it is not intended to lead to pregnancy. In the ancestral past where birth control was not available, sexual activity often led to pregnancy and hence greater reproductive success. Those people who had a greater desire for sex, and hence more sex, were likely to be more reproductively successful than those with less sexual desire. Thus, genes that code for sexual desire became more common. However, they are not necessarily related to a conscious desire for children. Rather, people tend to have sex because it feels good, just as natural selection designed it to feel.

Early critiques of evolutionary psychology argued that evolutionary approaches reduced human behavior to the dictates of genetic imperatives. However, despite arguing that ultimately the transmission of genes is what drives evolved behaviors, evolutionary psychology is not deterministic. Evolutionary psychologists place great weight on the environment to which humans adapt and the flexibility of the human mind.

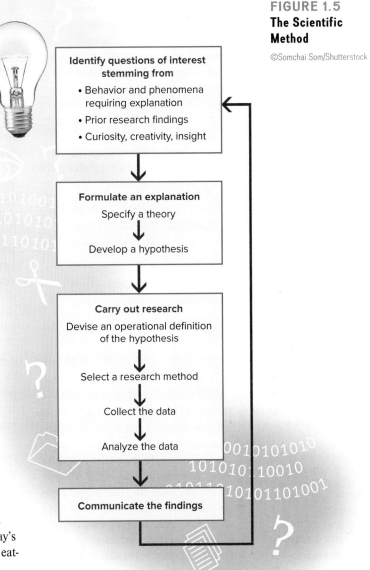

FIGURE 1.5
The Scientific Method

©Somchai Som/Shutterstock

Research Methods

Theories help frame our thinking—they tell us what is important, where to look for it, and how to study it. Theories generate **hypotheses**, or educated guesses, that further research can test. Sometimes research supports a hypothesis and the theory on which it was based. At other times, scientists must modify their theories to account for unexpected data. This process is known as the scientific method (Figure 1.5). In the following section, we review some of the major ways in which researchers collect such data and design their experiments.

QUANTITATIVE AND QUALITATIVE RESEARCH

Generally, when most people think of scientific research, they are thinking of what is called *quantitative research.*

hypotheses Possible explanations for phenomena, used to predict the outcome of research.

Quantitative research deals with objectively measurable, numerical data that can answer questions such as "how much?" or "how many?" and that is amenable to statistical analysis. For example, quantitative researchers might study the fear and anxiety children feel before surgery by asking them to answer questions, using a numerical scale, about how fearful or anxious they are. These data could then be compared to data for children not facing surgery to determine whether a statistically significant difference exists between the two groups.

Quantitative research on human development is based on the *scientific method*, which has traditionally characterized most scientific inquiry. Its usual steps are:

1. *Identification of a problem* to be studied, often on the basis of a theory or of previous research.

2. *Formulation of hypotheses* to be tested by research.

3. *Collection of data.*

4. *Statistical analysis of the data* to determine whether they support the hypothesis.

5. *Formation of tentative conclusions.*

6. *Dissemination of findings* so other observers can check, learn from, analyze, repeat, and build on the results.

naturalistic observation
Research method in which behavior is studied in natural settings without intervention or manipulation.

laboratory observation
Research method in which all participants are observed under the same controlled conditions.

Qualitative research, in contrast, focuses on the how and why of behavior. It more commonly involves nonnumerical (verbal or pictorial) descriptions of participants' subjective understanding, feelings, or beliefs about their experiences. Qualitative researchers might study the same subject areas as quantitative researchers, but their perspective informs both how they collect data and how they interpret it. For example, if qualitative researchers were to study children's emotional state prior to surgery, they might do so with unstructured interviews or by asking children to draw their perceptions of the upcoming event. Whereas the goal in quantitative research is to generate hypotheses from previous research and empirically test them, the goal in qualitative research is to understand the "story" of the event.

The selection of quantitative or qualitative methods may depend on the purpose of the study, how much is already known about the topic, and the researcher's theoretical orientation. Quantitative research often is done in controlled laboratory settings; qualitative research typically is conducted in everyday settings, such as the home or school.

FORMS OF DATA COLLECTION

The two forms of data collection development researchers most frequently use are self-reports (including diaries, visual techniques, interviews, and questionnaires) and naturalistic and laboratory observation.

Self-Reports

Self-report involves asking people for information. One form of self-report is a *diary* or log. Adolescents may be asked, for example, to record what they eat each day or the times when they feel depressed. In studying young children, *parental self-reports*—diaries, journals, interviews, or questionnaires—are commonly used, often together with other methods, such as videotaping or recording.

In a face-to-face or telephone *interview,* researchers ask questions about attitudes, opinions, or behavior. In a *structured interview*, each participant is asked the same set of questions. An *open-ended interview* is more flexible; the interviewer can vary the topics and order of questions and can ask follow-up questions based on the responses. To reach more people and to protect their privacy, researchers sometimes distribute a printed or online *questionnaire,* which participants fill out.

Self-report measures are meaningful and useful only if they are both valid (that is, the tests measure the abilities they claim to measure) and reliable (that is, the results are reasonably consistent from one time to another). In addition, any characteristics to be measured must be carefully operationalized—that is, defined solely in terms of the operations or procedures used to produce or measure a phenomenon.

By questioning a large number of people, investigators can get a broad picture—at least of what the respondents *say* they believe or do or did. However, people willing to participate in interviews or fill out questionnaires may not accurately represent the population as a whole. Furthermore, heavy reliance on self-reports may be unwise because people may not have thought about what they feel and think or honestly may not know. They may forget when and how events took place or may consciously or unconsciously distort their replies to fit what is considered socially desirable.

Naturalistic and Laboratory Observation

Observation can take two forms: naturalistic observation and laboratory observation. In **naturalistic observation**, researchers look at children in real-life settings. In **laboratory observation**, researchers observe and record behavior in a controlled situation. These are nonexperimental methods—researchers do not attempt to manipulate variables.

Both kinds of observation can provide valuable descriptions of behavior, but they have limitations. For one, they do not explain *why* people behave as they do, though the observers may suggest interpretations. They merely explain what people are doing. Additionally, an observer's presence can alter behavior. When people know they are being watched, they may act differently. Finally, there is a risk of *observer bias:* the researcher's tendency to interpret data to fit expectations or to emphasize some aspects and minimize others.

BASIC RESEARCH DESIGNS

Research designs most frequently used by development researchers include case studies, ethnographic studies, correlational studies, and experiments. Case studies and ethnographic studies are qualitative in nature, while correlational and experimental studies use quantitative methodology.

In naturalistic observation, a researcher might collect data by observing real-world events such as a teacher interacting with schoolchildren.
©Blend Images/John Lund/Marc Romanelli/Getty Images

Case Studies

A **case study** is a study of a single case or individual. Case studies may include careful observation and interpretation, or they may use behavioral or physiological measures and biographical, autobiographical, or documentary materials.

Case studies are particularly useful when studying something relatively rare, when it simply is not possible to find a large enough group of people with the characteristic in question to conduct a traditional laboratory study. Case studies can explore sources of behavior and can test treatments, and they suggest directions for further research. However, case studies do have shortcomings. While an intensive examination of a single individual can yield rich data, we cannot be sure that what is learned applies to all children. Thus, case studies have limited generalizability.

Ethnographic Studies

An **ethnographic study** is a case study of a culture. An ethnography seeks to describe the pattern of relationships, customs, beliefs, technology, arts, and traditions that make up a society's way of life. It uses a combination of methods, including informal, unstructured interviewing and participant observation. **Participant observation** is a form of naturalistic observation in which researchers live or participate in the societies or smaller groups they observe, as anthropologists often do for long periods of time. Because of ethnographers' close involvement with a culture, findings are especially open to observer bias. However, ethnographic studies can provide valuable information about cultural processes and help reduce cultural bias in theory and research.

Correlational Studies

A **correlational study** is an attempt to find a correlation, or statistical association, between two or more variables. Correlations are expressed in terms of direction (positive or negative) and magnitude (how strong they are). Two positively related variables increase or decrease together. For example, the more texting someone engages in while driving, the more likely the person is to get into a car crash. Two variables have a negative, or inverse, correlation if, as one increases, the other decreases. Studies show a negative correlation between the amount of time students spend on Facebook and the grades students receive. The more time students are on Facebook, the lower their grades are (Kirschner, 2010).

Correlations are reported as numbers ranging from +1.0 (a perfect positive relationship) to −1.0 (a perfect negative relationship). The closer a correlation comes to +1.0 or −1.0, the stronger the relationship, either positive or negative. A correlation of 0 means the variables have no relationship (Figure 1.6).

Although strong correlations suggest possible cause-and-effect relationships, these are merely hypotheses and need to be examined and tested critically. Correlation does not equal causation. It is possible that the causation goes the other way or that a third variable explains the relationship. For example, a strong positive correlation exists between the number of churches in a town and the number of liquor bottles found in the garbage cans of that town. One might theorize that heavy drinkers seek out religion, or alternatively, that religion drives people to drink. But a third variable, in this case population size, is the true causal influence. Larger towns have more churches, more garbage cans, and more liquor bottles in those cans. Churchgoing and drinking are associated with each other, but not in a causal way.

case study A study of a single subject, such as an individual or family.

ethnographic study In-depth study of a culture, which uses a variety of methods including participant observation.

participant observation Research method in which the observer lives with the people or participates in the activity being observed.

correlational study Research design intended to discover whether a statistical relationship between variables exists.

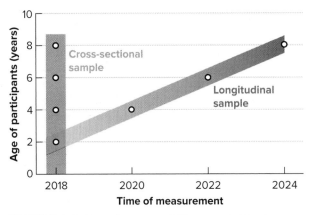

FIGURE 1.6 Developmental Research Designs

In the cross-sectional study, groups of 2-, 4-, 6-, and 8-year-olds were tested in 2018 to obtain data about age differences. In the longitudinal study, a group of children were first measured in 2018, when they were 2 years old; follow-up testing is done when the children are 4, 6, and 8 to measure age-related changes in performance.

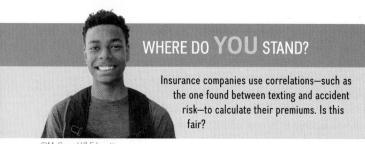
Experiments

While correlational studies are a valuable tool, their inability to establish causal relationships limits their use. Thus, psychologists often use experimental design. The only way to show with certainty that one variable causes another is through experimentation.

Groups and Variables An experiment is a controlled procedure that allows stronger causal statements to be made. A common way to conduct an experiment is to randomly divide the participants into two kinds of groups. An **experimental group** consists of people who are to be exposed to the experimental manipulation or treatment—the phenomenon the researcher wants to study. A **control group** consists of people who are similar to the experimental group but do not receive the treatment or may receive a different treatment. You can think of them as the "status quo"—what would happen if the variable of interest were not there.

For example, in one recent study, researchers were interested in whether or not bribing children to eat their vegetables is an effective strategy. In their study, roughly 400 4- to 6-year-olds were divided into two experimental and one control group. One group was bribed with a sticker to eat their least favorite vegetable, one group was bribed with verbal praise, and the remainder were given no reward for eating their vegetables. The results? After two weeks, the sticker group liked their vegetables as much (or little!) as the control group, however, they were more likely to eat more vegetables later even in the absence of bribery. The researchers concluded that bribery resulted in increased consumption of vegetables (Cooke et al., 2011).

In this experiment, the type of reward (sticker, verbal praise, or no reward) was the independent variable, and how many vegetables they ate at the conclusion of the study was the dependent variable. An **independent variable** is something the researcher directly manipulates to see if it has an effect on another variable. A **dependent variable** is the end measure that tells researchers whether their hypotheses were supported.

When conducting research, it is important to define exactly what is to be measured in a way that other researchers can replicate, or reproduce. For this purpose, researchers use an *operational definition*—a definition stated solely in terms of the operations used to measure a phenomenon. In the Cooke et al. (2011) study cited above, children's vegetable consumption was measured by weighing the vegetables before and after the children were given an opportunity to eat them. Had the researchers merely stated the children ate "more" vegetables, it would have been unclear exactly what this meant. Did the child need to consume the entire vegetable for it to count? Or was each bite counted? By specifying the variable precisely as grams of consumption, other researchers know exactly what was done, and can reproduce the study and comment on the results.

Random Assignment If an experiment finds a significant difference in the performance of the experimental and control groups, how do we know that the cause was the independent variable? For example, in the Cooke et al. (2011) study, what if the researchers had recruited one group of parents from a bulletin board posting at a fast-food restaurant and another group from a posting at a health food store? One might reasonably assume there might be preexisting differences between such groups. If all parents from the health food store were placed in the experimental group, the researchers might have found an effect, but it would be unclear why. We could not be sure that the incentives were the reason the children in those groups ate more vegetables; rather it might be because those children were already accustomed to eating vegetables and were more open to bribery. The best way to control for effects of such extraneous factors is *random assignment:* assigning the participants to groups in such a way that each person has an equal chance of being placed in any group.

If assignment is random and the sample is large enough, differences between groups should be evenly distributed so that the groups initially are as alike as possible in every respect except for the variable to be tested. Otherwise, unintended differences between the groups might *confound,* or contaminate, the results, and any conclusions drawn from the experiment would have to be viewed with suspicion.

Of course, with respect to some variables we might want to study, such as age, gender, and race/ethnicity, random assignment is not possible. We cannot assign Terry to be 5 years old and Brett to be 10, or one to be a boy and the other a girl. When studying such a variable, researchers can strengthen the validity of their conclusions by randomly selecting participants and by trying to make sure that they are statistically equivalent in other ways that might make a difference in the study.

Laboratory, Field, and Natural Experiments In a *laboratory experiment* the participants are brought to a laboratory, where they experience conditions the experimenter manipulates. This allows researchers to establish cause-and-effect relationships and permits replication. The tight control of a laboratory study allows researchers to be more certain that their independent variable caused change in their dependent variable. However, because of the artificiality of the laboratory experience, the results may not generalize to real life. People may not act as they typically would.

experimental group In an experiment, the group receiving the treatment under study.

control group In an experiment, a comparison group of people similar to those in the experimental group who do not receive the treatment under study.

independent variable In an experiment, the variable or condition the researcher directly manipulates to see if it has an effect on another variable.

dependent variable In an experiment, the condition that may or may not change as a result of changes in the independent variable.

People often have everyday hypotheses about how human psychology works but it is important to verify them through research. Experimental design has shown that bribery—at least with respect to eating your vegetables—works.

©karelnoppe/ Shutterstock

A *field experiment* is a controlled study conducted in an everyday setting, such as a home or school. Variables can still be manipulated, so causal claims can still be investigated. Because the experiments occur in the real world, there is more confidence that the behaviors seen are generalizable to natural behaviors. However, researchers have less control over events that may occur—the real world is often messy, and things do not always go as planned.

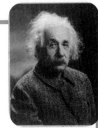

Did you know?

The process of science is based upon the assumption that you can never prove anything to be definitively true, you can only prove it to be false. Einstein summed up this concept nicely when he said, "No amount of experimentation can ever prove me right; a single experiment can prove me wrong."

Source: Library of Congress Prints and Photographs Division [LC-USZ62-60242]

When it is impossible for practical or ethical reasons to conduct a true experiment, a *natural experiment* may provide a way of studying certain events. A natural experiment, also called a quasi-experiment, compares people who have been accidentally "assigned" to separate groups by circumstances of life—for example, one group of children who were exposed to famine and another group who were not. A natural experiment, despite its name, is actually a correlational study because controlled manipulation of variables and random assignment to treatment groups are not possible.

DEVELOPMENTAL RESEARCH DESIGNS

Developmental researchers' primary task is to study change over time, but, just as there are different theoretical perspectives, there are also different ways of addressing the nuts and bolts of how this will be done. Cross-sectional and longitudinal studies (Figure 1.7) are the two most common research strategies used to study child development. Because each of these designs has drawbacks, researchers also have devised sequential designs.

In a **cross-sectional study**, children of different ages are assessed at one time. In one cross-sectional study, researchers presented 3- to 11-year-old children with scenarios depicting a story in which one character copied the ideas of another for a project in art class. At 3 to 4 years of age, children did not judge the copier negatively; however, by about 5 years of age, children judged copiers more negatively. These findings suggest a relatively sophisticated view about intellectual property—that ideas can be stolen (Olson & Shaw, 2010). However, we cannot draw such a conclusion with certainty. We don't know whether the 5-year-olds' awareness of mental activity when they were 3 years old was the same as that of the current 3-year-olds in the study. The only way to see whether change occurs with age is to conduct a longitudinal study of a particular person or group.

cross-sectional study Study designed to assess age-related differences, in which people of different ages are assessed on one occasion.

longitudinal study Study designed to assess changes in a sample over time.

In a **longitudinal study**, researchers study the same person or group of people more than once, sometimes years apart. For example, in one study, researchers were interested in whether or not Internet usage was associated with loneliness, and what the patterns were over time. The researchers found

FIGURE 1.7 Sequential Design

Two successive cross-sectional groups of 2, 4, 6, and 8 year olds are tested in 2018 and 2020. Also, a longitudinal study of a group of children first measured in 2018, when they were 2 years old, is followed by a similar longitudinal study of another group of children who are 2 years old in 2020.

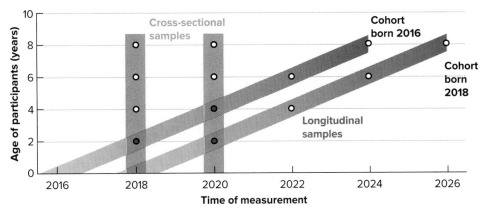

that people who were initially lonely and spent more and more time on the Web over the course of a year reported becoming more and more lonely and having lower life satisfaction at the conclusion of the study (Stepanikova, Nie & He, 2010).

sequential study Study design that combines cross-sectional and longitudinal designs.

Neither cross-sectional nor longitudinal design is superior. Rather, both designs have strengths and weaknesses (Table 1.4). For example, cross-sectional design is fast—we don't have to wait 30 years for results. This also makes it a more economical choice. Moreover, because participants are assessed only once, we don't have to consider attrition (people dropping out of the study) or repeated testing (which can produce practice effects). But cross-sectional design uses group averages, so individual differences and trajectories may be obscured. More important, the results can be affected by the differing experiences of people born at different times, as previously explained.

Longitudinal research shows a different and complementary set of strengths and weaknesses. Because the same people are studied over time, researchers can track individual patterns of continuity and change. This is more time-consuming and expensive than cross-sectional studies. In addition, repeated testing of participants can result in practice effects. For example, your performance on an intelligence test might get better over time from practice rather than from any increase in intelligence. Attrition (dropping out of the study) can be problematic in longitudinal research as well because it tends to be nonrandom, which can introduce a positive bias to the study. Practical issues, such as turnover in research personnel, loss of funding, or the development of new measures or methodologies, also can introduce potential problems with data collection.

The **sequential study** is a complex strategy designed to overcome the drawbacks of longitudinal and cross-sectional research. In this technique, researchers study people of different ages (like cross-sectional) over time (like longitudinal). A combination of cross-sectional and longitudinal sequences (as shown in Figure 1.7) can provide a more complete picture of development than would be possible with either alone.

ETHICS OF RESEARCH

Institutional review boards at colleges, universities, and other institutions that receive federal funding must review proposed research from an ethical standpoint. Guidelines of the American Psychological Association (2002) cover such issues as informed consent, avoidance of deception, protection of participants from harm and loss of dignity, guarantees of privacy and confidentiality, the right to decline or withdraw from an experiment at any time, and the investigators' responsibility for correcting any undesirable effects, such as anxiety or shame.

Right to Informed Consent

Informed consent exists when participants voluntarily agree to be in a study, are competent to give consent, are aware of the risks as well as the potential benefits, and are not being exploited. The National Commission for the Protection of Human Subjects of Biomedical and Behavioral Research (1978) recommends that children age 7 or over be asked to give their consent to take part in research and that any children's objections should be overruled only if the research promises direct benefit to the child.

Avoidance of Deception

Ethical guidelines call for withholding information only when it is essential to the study; and then investigators should avoid methods that could cause pain, anxiety, or harm. Participants should be debriefed afterward to let them know the true nature of the study and why deception was necessary and to make sure they have not suffered as a result.

Right to Privacy and Confidentiality

Research participants need to know that their information will be kept private and their responses are confidential. However, there are cases in which researchers are obligated to breach confidentiality—such as when an investigator discovers signs of abuse. Thus, researchers need to inform participants of their legal responsibility to report abuse or neglect or any other illegal activity of which they become aware, and confidentiality must be guarded otherwise.

TABLE 1.4 Cross-Sectional, Longitudinal, and Sequential Research

Type of Study	Procedure	Advantages	Disadvantages
Cross-sectional	Data are collected on people of different ages at the same time.	Can show similarities and differences among age groups; speedy, economical; presents no problem of attrition or repeated testing.	Cannot establish age effects; masks individual differences; be confounded by cohort effects.
Longitudinal	Data are collected on same person or persons over a period of time.	Can show age-related change or continuity; avoids confounding age with cohort effects.	Is time-consuming, expensive; presents problems of attrition, bias in sample, and effects of repeated testing; results may be valid only for cohort tested or sample studied.
Sequential	Data are collected on successive cross-sectional or longitudinal samples.	Can avoid drawbacks of both cross-sectional and longitudinal designs.	Requires large amount of time and effort and analysis of very complex data.

mastering the CHAPTER

©Ed-Imaging

Summary and Key Terms

The Study of Child Development

> Child development is the scientific study of the process of change and stability in human children.

> The concept of periods of development is a social construction.

> The three major domains of development are physical, cognitive, and psychosocial. Each affects the others.

KEY TERMS

Child development

Social construction

Physical development

Cognitive development

Psychosocial development

Influences on Development

> Influences on development come from both heredity and environment. Many typical changes during childhood are related to maturation. Individual differences tend to increase with age.

> In some societies, the nuclear family predominates; in others, the extended family.

> Important environmental influences stem from culture, ethnicity, race, and historical context. Race is a social construction.

> Socioeconomic status (SES) affects developmental processes and outcomes through the quality of home and neighborhood environments, nutrition, medical care, and schooling. Multiple risk factors increase the likelihood of poor outcomes.

> Influences may be normative (age-graded or history-graded) or nonnormative. There is evidence of critical or sensitive periods for certain kinds of early development.

KEY TERMS

Individual differences

Maturation

Nuclear family

Extended family

Culture

Ethnic group

Socioeconomic status (SES)

Risk factors

Normative

Nonnormative

Historical generation

Cohort

Imprinting

Critical period

Plasticity

Sensitive periods

Issues in Development

> Nature and nurture work together to influence development.

> Different models view development as active versus passive and as continuous versus discontinuous.

> Domains of development are interrelated and bidirectional. Normal development includes a wide range of individual differences, and children can be remarkably resilient.

> Historical and cultural contexts influence development, and childhood development affects development throughout the life span.

Theories of Child Development

> A theory is used to organize and explain data

> The psychoanalytic perspective sees development as motivated by unconscious drives or conflicts. Leading examples are Freud's and Erikson's theories.

> The learning perspective views development as a result of learning based on experience. Leading examples are Watson's and Skinner's behaviorism and Bandura's social learning (social cognitive) theory.

> The cognitive perspective is concerned with thought processes. Leading examples are Piaget's cognitive-stage theory, Vygotsky's sociocultural theory, and the information-processing approach.

> The contextual perspective focuses on the individual in a social context. A leading example is Bronfenbrenner's bioecological theory.

> The evolutionary/sociobiological perspective applies Darwinian principles of natural selection and survival of the fittest to human psychology.

Research Methods

> Research can be either quantitative or qualitative. Forms of data collection are self-reports and naturalistic and laboratory observation.

> A design is a plan for conducting research. Two qualitative designs used in developmental research are the case study and the ethnographic study. Cross-cultural research can help determine whether certain aspects of development are universal or culturally influenced.

> Two quantitative designs are the correlational study and the experiment. Only experiments can establish causal relationships.

> Experiments must be rigorously controlled to be valid. Random assignment of participants can help ensure validity. It is important to carefully define your variable with an operational definition. Ideally, experiments should be replicated.

> Laboratory experiments are easiest to control and replicate, but findings of field experiments may be more generalizable. Natural experiments may be useful in situations in which true experiments would be impractical or unethical.

> The two most common designs used to study age-related development are cross-sectional and longitudinal. Cross-sectional studies assess age differences; longitudinal studies describe continuity or change in the same participants.

> Ethical issues in research include the rights of participants to informed consent, avoidance of deception, and rights to privacy and confidentiality.

Practice Quiz

1. The study of child development involves both:
   a. children and adults.
   b. growth and emotions.
   c. humans and other species.
   d. change and stability.

2. Periods of child development could best be described as:
   a. invariant biological timelines.
   b. socially constructed agreements about important points in the life span.
   c. maturational processes shared by all humans.
   d. controversial concepts in the current literature and research.

3. If I am interested in how babies' memory capacity changes with age and how this might affect their ability to learn new words, I am primarily interested in the _____ domain of development.

4. Nine-month-old Sally is an active and smiley baby, while her playmate John is quiet and shy. The variations in their behavior are known as:
   a. emotional variants.
   b. social emotions.
   c. individual differences.
   d. maturation.

5. Which of these could best be described as a maturational process?
   a. learning to read.
   b. getting a tooth.
   c. understanding that another person is sad.
   d. knowing how to roller skate.

6. Important environmental influences include:
   a. ethnicity.
   b. home environment.
   c. neighborhood.
   d. culture.
   e. all of these.

7. An example of a normative influence is _____; an example of a nonnormative influence is

   _____.

8. While people generally learn to read in childhood, illiterate adults can learn to read later in life. However, most programs to promote literacy in adults have low success rates. Does this mean that childhood is a critical or sensitive period for learning how to read? Why or why not? _____

   _____

9. If you are a researcher interested in genetic influences on development, you are on the _____ side of the nature/nurture debate; if you are interested in how media impacts aggression, you are on the _____ side.

10. Which is the best example of passive development?
    a. Baby Joe loves interacting with other people and smiles widely at anybody whenever he catches the person's eye.
    b. Jessica is a highly aggressive girl who elicits negative behaviors from those around her.
    c. Ava learns not to interrupt her mother while she is talking to other adults because her mom always frowns at her when she does.
    d. Sophie pesters her mom until she finally signs her up for ballet lessons.

11. A puppy getting larger as it grows would be an example of _____ change, while a caterpillar turning into a butterfly would be an example of _____ change.

12. Which of the following is NOT a point of consensus about development?
    a. Development in different domains is interrrelated.
    b. The influences in child development flow from the environment to the child.
    c. History and culture influence development.
    d. Development occurs from conception to death.
    e. Early experiences are important, but children are resilient.

13. A theory is:
    a. an observation of something.
    b. a proven fact.
    c. a description or explanation of an observed phenomena.
    d. a statistical relationship between two variables.

14. If I believe that you are experiencing anxiety as an adult because your mother was rigid and stingy in her breast-feeding practices with you, I am probably a _____ theorist.

15. When my dog gets into the garbage can, I yell at him and tell him he is a bad dog. This is an example of _____ and is drawn from the _____ theoretical approach.
    a. adaptation; cognitive
    b. punishment; behaviorist
    c. gratification of an urge; psychoanalytic
    d. cross-species comparison; ethological

16. Three-year-old Ava has never seen a zebra. On a visit to the zoo, she points to a zebra and says, "horse!" Ava has just engaged in:
    a. the ZPD   c. equilibrium
    b. accommodation   d. assimilation

17. Bronfenbrenner would call the societal changes that were the result of the women's movement part of the:
    a. microsystem.
    b. mesosystem.
    c. exosystem.
    d. macrosystem.
    e. chronosystem.

18. An evolutionary psychologist would be most interested in studying which of the following?
    a. What is the relationship between television viewing and body image?
    b. How does your early relationship with your opposite sex parent impact later romantic relationships?
    c. How do physical attractiveness and amount of resources impact a man's versus a woman's likelihood of dating a person?
    d. How does neighborhood composition influence child development?

19. A study in which a researcher collects questionnaire data on exercise and health is probably a _____ study, while a study in which a researcher interviews people about why they do or do not exercise is probably a _____ study.

20. I believe that taking vitamins leads to increases in energy. So, I design a study in which my experimental group gets a vitamin, and my control group gets a placebo. Then, I assess both groups on how energetic they feel. What is my independent variable?
    a. the vitamin
    b. the placebo
    c. dose (i.e., vitamin or placebo)
    d. levels of energy

21. Susan takes a photo of her daughter every year on her birthday. Which developmental research design is this most similar to?
    a. cross-sectional
    b. longitudinal
    c. sequential
    d. correlational

22. If I am conducting research with a young child who becomes scared and screams, "no, no, no!" while I am trying to conduct data, and I back off and decide not to continue with the experiment, I am illustrating concern with the principle of _____.

Answers: 1–d; 2–b; 3–cognitive; 4–c; 5–b; 6–e; 7–Examples of normative influences might include biological events (such as puberty) and social events (such as entry into formal education). Examples of nonnormative events include unusual events that have a major impact on individual lives and may include either atypical timing (such as marriage in the early teens or the death of a parent when young) or atypical events (such as having a birth defect or being in an airplane crash); 8–That most literacy programs are not successful does not imply there is a critical or sensitive period for learning to read. Critical or sensitive periods usually result in permanent change. Older adults are capable of learning how to read, even if the programs are not generally successful; 9–Nature; nurture; 10–c; 11–quantitative; qualitative; 12–b; 13–c; 14–psychoanalytic; 15–b; 16–d; 17–e; 18–c; 19–quantitative; qualitative; 20–c; 21–b; 22–principle of respect

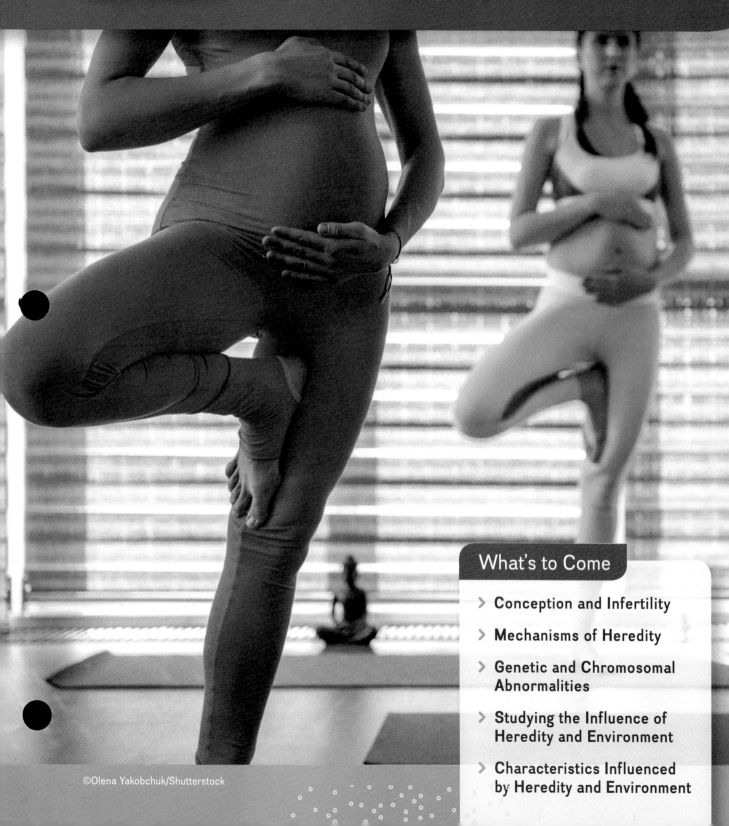

Chapter 2

Conception, Heredity, and Environment

©Olena Yakobchuk/Shutterstock

What's to Come

> **Conception and Infertility**

> **Mechanisms of Heredity**

> **Genetic and Chromosomal Abnormalities**

> **Studying the Influence of Heredity and Environment**

> **Characteristics Influenced by Heredity and Environment**

Before Tania and Paul were married, they talked about having children one day but agreed to wait until they were financially and emotionally secure as a couple before starting a family. After three years of marriage, they decided they were ready for parenthood. Tania carefully watched the calendar, counting the days after each menstrual period to take advantage of her "fertile window." When Tania had not yet become pregnant after two months, she wondered what might have gone wrong.

What Tania and Paul didn't realize is that although a woman is usually fertile between the 6th and 21st days of the menstrual cycle, the timing of the fertile window can be unpredictable (Wilcox, Dunson & Baird, 2000). This means that although conception is far more likely at certain times, she may be able to conceive any time during the month. Conversely, while conception is more likely during certain parts of the month, it may not always occur during that time. Indeed, the average woman takes about six months to conceive.

We begin this chapter by examining how a life is conceived. We consider the mechanisms and patterns of heredity—the inherited factors that affect development—and how genetic counseling can help couples decide whether to become parents. Finally, we look at how heredity and environment work together and their effects on development.

• • • •

Conception and Infertility

The arrival of a new family member effects an enormous change in the lives of caregivers. It involves sleepless nights and harried days, dirty diapers and stained onesies and, for most parents, an all-encompassing love for the squalling, squirming creature now in their care. In the following section, we address how this family addition is conceived. For some families, conception occurs easily; others need artificial reproductive technologies. For still other parents, the child arrives via adoption. For all families, however, this is the beginning of a new relationship filled with a multitude of both stressors and joys.

fertilization Union of sperm and ovum to produce a zygote; also called *conception*.

zygote One-celled organism resulting from fertilization.

FERTILIZATION

Fertilization, or conception, is the process by which sperm and ovum—the male and female gametes, or sex cells—combine to create a single cell called a **zygote**, which then duplicates itself again and again by cell division to produce all the cells that make up a baby. At birth, a female is believed to have about 2 million immature ova in her two ovaries, each ovum in its own small sac, or follicle. In a sexually mature woman, ovulation occurs about once every 28 days until menopause. After being expelled from the ovary, the ovum is swept along through one of the

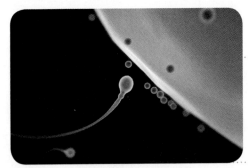

Conception occurs when a male's sperm cell penetrates a female's egg cell.
©MedicalRF.com

fallopian tubes by tiny hair cells, called cilia, toward the uterus, or womb.

Sperm are produced in the testicles (testes), or reproductive glands, of a mature male at a rate of several hundred million a day and are ejaculated in the semen at sexual climax. Deposited in the vagina, they try to swim through the cervix (the opening of the uterus) and into the fallopian tubes, but only a tiny fraction make it that far. As we will see, which sperm meets which ovum has tremendous implications for the person being conceived.

Fertilization typically occurs while the ovum is passing through the fallopian tube. If fertilization does not occur, the ovum and any sperm cells in the woman's body die. The sperm are absorbed by the woman's white blood cells, and the ovum passes through the uterus and exits through the vagina.

INFERTILITY

Tania and Paul tried to get pregnant for one long dispiriting year before seeing a fertility doctor. At the year mark, they joined the estimated 10 percent of U.S. couples ages 15 to 44 who experience infertility (Centers for Disease Control and Prevention [CDC], 2011). After a variety of tests, it was determined that Tania's eggs were low quality. While her chances of having a baby with her own eggs and her husband's sperm were still relatively good, pregnancy was not assured, even with the advances of modern medicine now available to prospective parents.

An estimated 6 percent of U.S. women aged 15 to 44 years old experience *infertility*: the inability to conceive a baby after 12 months of intercourse in the absence of birth control methods (CDC, 2017). Worldwide, about 1 in 4 couples have difficulty getting pregnant or maintaining a pregnancy to term (Mascarenhas, Flaxman, Boerma, Vanderpoel & Stevens, 2012).

Women's fertility begins to decline in their late twenties, with substantial decreases during their thirties. By their forties, many women are not able to become pregnant without the use of assisted reproductive technology, which is described in the next section. Men's fertility is less affected by age but begins to decline in the late thirties (Dunson, Colombo & Baird, 2002). Infertility can burden a relationship emotionally. Approximately 30 percent of couples are unable to become parents, and they show worse mental health outcomes than those couples who do succeed (Gameiro & Finnigan, 2017).

The most common cause of infertility in men is production of too few sperm. A sperm count lower than 60 million per ejaculation makes conception unlikely. In some instances an ejaculatory duct may be blocked, preventing the exit of sperm, or sperm may be unable to swim well enough to reach the cervix. Some cases of male infertility seem to have a genetic basis (O'Flynn, O'Brien, Varghese & Agarwal, 2010). For example, some men appear to have gene mutations that affect the quality and quantity of sperm they produce (Krausz, 2010).

In women, the common causes of infertility include the failure to produce ova or to produce normal ova; mucus in the cervix, which might prevent sperm from penetrating it; or a disease of the uterine lining, which might prevent implantation of the fertilized ovum. A major cause of declining fertility in women after age 30 is deterioration in the quality of ova (CDC, 2017). However, the most common cause is blockage of the fallopian tubes, preventing ova from reaching the uterus. In about half of these cases, the tubes are blocked by scar tissue from sexually transmitted infections (King, 1996). In addition, some women suffer from physical disorders affecting fertility, such as polycystic ovarian syndrome (Franks, 2009) or primary ovarian insufficiency (Welt, 2008).

In both men and women, modifiable environmental factors are related to infertility. For example, overweight men (Sallmen, Sandler, Hoppin, Blair & Day, 2006) and women (Maheshwari, 2010) are more likely to have issues with fertility. Smoking also appears to have a strong negative effect on fertility. Other factors, such as psychological stress, high levels of caffeine and alcohol consumption, and exposure to environmental pollutants, have been implicated, but the evidence for their negative effects is less strong (Hofman, Davies & Norman, 2007).

ASSISTED REPRODUCTIVE TECHNOLOGIES

Unless there is a known cause for failure to conceive, the chances of conception after trying for 18 months to 2 years are high (Dunson, 2002). For couples struggling with infertility, science offers several alternative ways to parenthood.

Assisted reproductive technology (ART), or conception through artificial means (International Committee for Monitoring Assisted Reproductive Technologies [ICMART], 2006) provides couples having difficulty conceiving naturally with a means to augment their fertility. Since it was first tested in 1978, estimates are that approximately 5 million children worldwide have been conceived through ART (Adamson, Tabangin, Macaluso & de Mouzon, 2013).

The simplest form of ART is *artificial insemination* in which sperm is injected into a woman's vagina, cervix, or uterus. This procedure can facilitate conception if a man has a low sperm count. If the man is infertile, a couple may choose artificial insemination by a donor. Artificial insemination is also used if there is no male partner (Brezina & Zhao, 2012).

In another common method, *in vitro fertilization* (IVF), a woman first receives fertility drugs to stimulate the production of multiple ova. Then the ova are surgically removed, fertilized in a laboratory dish, and implanted in the woman's uterus. These implanted ova are less likely to become established in the womb and thus more likely to result in miscarriage. In 2015, approximately 70 percent of IVF procedures using fresh, nondonor eggs did not result in a pregnancy (CDC, 2017). To increase the odds of success, it is common to transplant multiple ova; however, this procedure also increases the likelihood of multiple, usually premature births.

assisted reproductive technology (ART) Methods used to achieve conception through artificial means.

In 2006, nearly half (48 percent) of infants born through ART were twins or higher multiples (Saswati et al., 2009). In response to research demonstrating the increased risk for children of a multiples birth (Sazanova, Kallen, Thurin-Kjellbert, Wennerholm & Bergh, 2013; Qin et al., 2015), recommended guidelines now support single-embryo transfer coupled with later additional frozen embryo transfers for couples wanting multiple children. Some countries now also restrict the number of embryos that can legally be implanted (Brezina & Zhao, 2012). While fresh embryo transfers have greater success rates than frozen embryos, rates for frozen embryos have improved in recent years (Wong, Masternbroek & Repping, 2014). Because the transfer of multiple embryos has decreased, the percentage of twin or multiple births following ART has fallen to 26.5 percent in the United States (Kissin, Kulkami, et al., 2015) although this rate remains variable across different global regions (Maheshwari, Griffiths & Bhattacharya, 2010).

IVF also addresses severe male infertility. A single sperm can be injected into the ovum—a technique called *intracytoplasmic sperm injection* (ICSI). This procedure is now used in the majority of IVF cycles (Van Voorhis, 2007). Singleton infants conceived through IVF or ICSI are two to four times more likely than naturally conceived infants to have certain types of heart defects, cleft lip, and gastrointestinal defects, although the incidence of such defects is still small (Reefhuis et al., 2008).

WHAT DO YOU **DO**?

Fertility Specialist

Fertility specialists diagnose, counsel, and treat women who are having difficulty becoming pregnant and delivering a child. Based on the diagnosis, a fertility specialist might prescribe a fertility medication or conduct in vitro fertilization. Fertility specialists are medical doctors who work out of a hospital, a clinic, or private practice. As medical doctors, they must complete medical school, a residency, and pass board certification.

©Pixtal/AGE fotostock

©Digital Vision/Getty Images

Perspectives on Diversity

FOLK BELIEFS ABOUT CONCEPTION AND FERTILITY

Folk beliefs about the origin of new life have been common throughout history. The belief that children came from wells, springs, or rocks was common in northern and central Europe as recently as the early 1900s. Cosmic forces were believed to influence conception. A baby conceived under a new moon would be a boy; one conceived during the moon's last quarter, a girl (Gélis, 1991). Even today, beliefs about spiritual influences on conception persist in many traditional societies. Among the Warlpiri people of Australia, a baby conceived in a place associated with a particular spirit is believed to have been given life by that spirit (DeLoache & Gottlieb, 2000). Even in modern Western countries such as the United States, beliefs about how personality might be shaped by the time of year in which children are born persist—as the astrology sections in many newspapers and magazines attest.

Likewise, infertility is far from a new concern. To enhance fertility, ancient doctors advised men to eat fennel and women to drink lamb saliva and wear earthworm necklaces. It was recommended that, after intercourse, a woman lie flat with her legs crossed and avoid becoming angry (Fontanel & d'Harcourt, 1997, p. 10). By the Renaissance, the list of foods recommended to spur conception ranged from squabs and sparrows to cocks' combs and bulls' genitals. In the early seventeenth century, Loise Bourgeois, midwife to Queen Marie de Medicis of France, advocated bathing the vagina with chamomile, mallow, marjoram, and catmint boiled in white wine.

Women that bear only girls have been historically subject to sanctions, despite the irony that the father's sperm determines sex. In many villages in Nepal, it is common for a man whose wife has borne no sons to take a second wife. King Henry VIII's propensity to remove his wife's heads was in part due to their failure to produce a suitable male heir to the throne of England. Even now in the United States, folk beliefs still exist. To conceive a boy, mothers are advised to eat red meat or have sex standing up.

The prevalence of folk beliefs about all aspects of pregnancy speaks to the great wonder of how we become who we are. Even now—despite our ability to see the baby in the womb with ultrasound technology and to test for disorders in fetuses via prenatal genetic testing—the specifics of how the unique mix of genes a baby receives results in a completely new individual remains a delightful mystery.

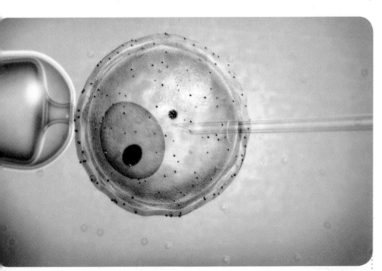
In vitro fertilization (IVF) is a technique in which egg cells are fertilized in a laboratory dish before being implanted in the uterus. In the commonly used fertilization procedure intracytoplasmic sperm injection (ICSI), a single sperm is injected directly into the egg.
©MedicalRF.com

Sarah Jessica Parker and Matthew Broderick's twin daughters were born via a surrogate.
©Robin Layton/Handout/Getty Images

A woman who is producing poor-quality ova or who has had her ovaries removed may try ovum transfer. In this procedure, a donor egg from a fertile younger woman is fertilized in the laboratory and implanted in the prospective mother's uterus. IVF using donor eggs tends to be successful (Van Voorhis, 2007). Alternatively, the ovum can be fertilized in the donor's body by artificial insemination. The embryo is retrieved from the donor and inserted into the recipient's uterus. This is a promising technique for women undergoing cancer treatments, which may damage eggs, and for women with polycystic ovarian syndrome, which interferes with sex hormone regulation and ovulation (Chian, Uzelac & Nargund, 2013).

Although success rates have improved, only 30 percent of any single trial of ART resulted in a successful pregnancy in 2015 (CDC, 2017c). The likelihood of success with IVF using a mother's own ova drops precipitously as a woman gets older (Van Voorhis, 2007).

ART can result in a tangled web of legal, ethical, and psychological dilemmas (ISLAT Working Group, 1998; Schwartz, 2003). Should the children know about their parentage? Should genetic tests be performed on prospective donors and surrogates? When IVF results in multiple fertilized ova, should some be discarded to improve the chances of health for the survivors? Science has outpaced our legal system, and there are serious questions about ethics and legal oversight that have not yet been addressed.

The issues multiply when a *surrogate mother* is involved (Schwartz, 2003). The surrogate, a fertile woman, is impregnated by the prospective father, usually by artificial insemination. She agrees to carry the baby to term and give it to the father and his partner. But who is the real parent—the surrogate or the woman whose baby she bears? What if a surrogate wants to keep the baby, as has happened in a few highly publicized cases? What if the intended parents refuse to go through with the contract? Will the use of surrogates result in a breeder class of disadvantaged women who carry the babies of the well-to-do?

Surrogacy rates in the United States have increased from 1.0 percent of assisted reproductive technology cycles in 1999 to 2.4 percent in 2014 (Perkins, Boulet, Jamieson & Kissin, 2016; Perkins, Boulet, Levine, Jamieson & Kissin, 2018). Courts in most states view surrogacy contracts as unenforceable, and some states have either banned the practice or placed strict conditions on it. The American Academy of Pediatrics (AAP) Committee on Bioethics (1992) recommends that surrogacy be considered a tentative, preconception adoption agreement. The committee also recommends a prebirth agreement on the period of time in which the surrogate may assert parental rights. Some countries, such as France and Italy, have banned commercial surrogacy. In the United States, it is illegal in some states and legal in others, and regulations differ from state to state (Perkins et al., 2018).

ADOPTION

While a desire to adopt children is not contingent upon not being able to bear biological children, it is certainly an option for those faced with infertility. If a woman cannot conceive on her own, and she is either unwilling or unable to conceive with the ART, adoption is an alternative. In 2010, an estimated 2 percent of children under the age of 18 lived with adoptive parents, or approximately 1.3 million to 1.5 million children (Kreider & Lofquist, 2014). Adopted children are more likely to be African American, Asian, American Indian, or Alaska Native than the general population, although less likely to be Hispanic. About 14 percent of adopted boys and 19 percent of adopted girls are foreign born. The higher international adoption rate for girls appears

WHAT DO YOU **DO**?

Social Worker

Social workers help people in many different ways. Depending on the area of practice, a social worker might work with a couple to adopt a child from outside the United States, coordinate services for a child with a developmental disorder, provide support and guidance for homeless families, or help pregnant teenagers plan for their changing lives. A bachelor's degree in social work (B.S.W) is required for an entry-level social work position. However, many social workers earn master's degrees in social work (M.S.W.) in order to advance. Social workers work within agencies, schools, hospitals, and institutions. To learn more about what social workers do, visit www.socialworkers.org.

©Purestock/SuperStock

More than a million U.S. children live with adoptive parents. While adopted children are more likely to have special health care needs, most score well on measures of social and emotional well-being.
©Photodisc/Getty Images

to be driven by a larger number of girls adopted from Asian countries. Adopted children are also more likely to have a disability or special health care needs (Kreider & Lofquist, 2014). However, most adopted children are healthy and fare well on most indices of social and emotional well-being (Vandivere, Malm & Radel, 2009).

In 2008, most adoptions occurred through publicly funded adoption agencies (46 percent) or through intercountry adoption (13 percent) (Child Welfare Information Gateway, 2011). Since the mid-1970s, the percentage of never-married women who adopt out their children has declined from about 9 percent to less than 1 percent of live births (Jones, 2008), due in part to society's increasing acceptance of unwed mothers.

In general, single adults and married couples may adopt. Additionally, stepparents can adopt the child of a spouse if the spouse has legal custody of the child. Many states do not specify a minimum age for adopting parents, while other states allow adults aged 18 years or older to adopt children and several states call for a minimum age of 21 (Colorado, Delaware, and Oklahoma) or 25 years (Georgia and Idaho). Six states also require that adopting parents are at least 10 years older than the child, a number that rises to 14 years in Puerto Rico and 15 years in Idaho (Child Welfare Information Gateway, 2016). While state laws on same-sex adoption varied widely, in June 2017, the U.S. Supreme Court ruled that same-sex couples were to be treated as equal under the law, and same-sex adoption is now legal in all 50 states.

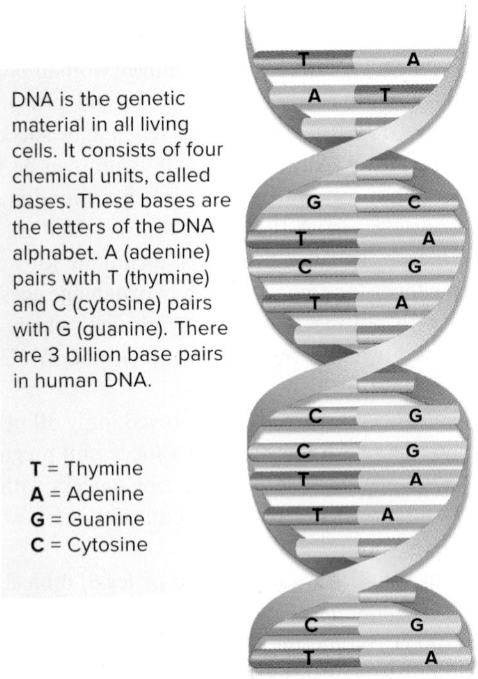

Mechanisms of Heredity

The science of genetics is the study of heredity—the inborn factors from the biological parents that affect development. When the ovum and sperm unite, they endow the baby-to-be with a genetic makeup that influences a wide range of characteristics, from color of hair to health, intellect, and personality.

THE GENETIC CODE

The fundamental unit of heredity is a chemical called **deoxyribonucleic acid (DNA)**. The double-helix structure of DNA resembles a long, spiraling ladder whose steps are made of pairs of chemical units called *bases* (Figure 2.1). The bases—adenine, thymine, cytosine and guanine—are the "letters" of the genetic code, which cellular machinery "reads."

Chromosomes are coils of DNA that consist of smaller segments called **genes** and are found in every cell in the human body. Each gene has a specific location on its

DNA is the genetic material in all living cells. It consists of four chemical units, called bases. These bases are the letters of the DNA alphabet. A (adenine) pairs with T (thymine) and C (cytosine) pairs with G (guanine). There are 3 billion base pairs in human DNA.

T = Thymine
A = Adenine
G = Guanine
C = Cytosine

FIGURE 2.1 DNA: The Genetic Code

Source: Adapted from Ritter, J. "Scientists close in on DNA code." *Chicago Sun-Times*, November 23, 1999, p. 7.

chromosome and contains thousands of bases. The sequence of bases in a gene tells the cell how to make the proteins that enable it to carry out its specific functions. The complete sequence of genes in the human body constitutes the **human genome**. Of course, every human has a unique genome. The human genome is not meant to be a recipe for making a particular human. Rather, the human genome is a reference point, or representative genome, that shows the location of all human genes.

Every cell in the normal human body except the sex cells (sperm and ova) has 23 pairs of chromosomes—46 chromosomes in all. Through a type of cell division called *meiosis*, each sex cell ends up with only 23 chromosomes. Thus, when sperm and ovum fuse at conception, they produce a zygote with 46 chromosomes: 23 from the father and 23 from the mother (Figure 2.2).

At the moment of conception, the single-celled zygote receives all the biological information needed to guide its development into a unique individual. Through *mitosis*, a process by which the nonsex cells divide in half over and over again, the DNA replicates itself so each newly formed cell is a genetic copy with the same hereditary information. As the cells divide, they differentiate, specializing in a variety of complex bodily functions that enable the child to grow and develop.

Genes spring into action when they are turned on or off, either by external environmental factors such as nutrition or stress, or by internal factors such as hormone levels in the mother or fetus. Thus, from the start, heredity and environment are intertwined.

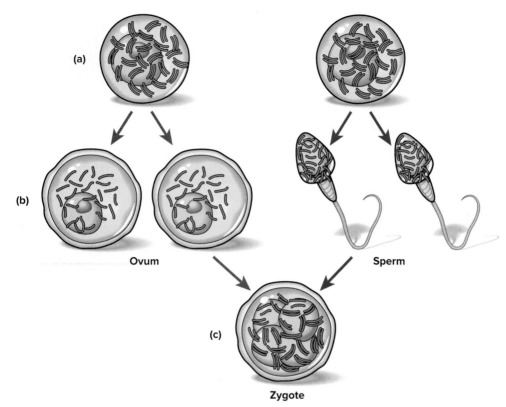

FIGURE 2.2 Hereditary Composition of the Zygote

(**a**) Body cells of women and men contain 23 pairs of chromosomes, which carry the genes, the basic units of inheritance. (**b**) Each sex cell (ovum and sperm) has only 23 single chromosomes because of meiosis, a special kind of cell division in which the total number of chromosomes is halved. (**c**) At fertilization, the 23 chromosomes from the sperm join the 23 from the ovum so that the zygote receives 46 chromosomes, or 23 pairs.

SEX DETERMINATION

Twenty-two of our 23 pairs of chromosomes are **autosomes**, chromosomes that aren't related to sexual expression. The 23rd pair are **sex chromosomes**—one from the father and one from the mother—that govern the baby's sex. Females have two X chromosomes (XX), and males have one of each type (XY). Each sperm cell has an equal chance of carrying an X or a Y, and thus it is the father who determines sex.

Did you know?

The Greek philosopher Aristotle believed that baby girls result from disturbances in "normal" male development? This is particularly notable because embryos are female by default.

©karapas/123RF

Sexual differentiation is a more complex process than simple gene determination. Early in development, the embryo's rudimentary reproductive system appears almost identical in males and in females. Surprisingly, sexual differentiation

is not automatic. However, on the Y chromosome is a gene called the *SRY* gene. Research with mice has found that once hormones signal the *SRY* gene to turn on, cell differentiation and formation of the testes is triggered. At 6 to 8 weeks after conception, the testes start to produce the male hormone testosterone. Exposure of a genetically male embryo to steady, high levels of testosterone ordinarily results in the development of a male body with male sexual organs (Kashimada & Koopman, 2010; Hughes, 2004). Without this hormonal influence, a genetically male mouse will develop genitals that appear female rather than male. Thus, male development for a genetically male fetus is not automatic. It is likely that a similar mechanism occurs in human males.

The development of the female reproductive system is equally complex and depends on a number of genetic variants. These variants promote ovarian development and inhibit testicular development (Ono & Harley, 2013). This includes the HOX genes (Taylor, 2000) and a signaling molecule called *Wnt-4*, a variant form of which can masculinize a genetically female fetus (Biason-Lauber, Konrad, Navratil & Shoenle, 2004).

PATTERNS OF GENETIC TRANSMISSION

During the 1860s, Gregor Mendel, an Austrian monk, laid the foundation for our understanding of patterns of inheritance. By crossbreeding strains of peas, he discovered two fundamental principles of genetics. First, traits could be either dominant or recessive. *Dominant traits* are always expressed, while *recessive traits* are expressed only if both copies of the gene are recessive. Second, traits are passed down independently of each other. For example, the color of your hair and your height are both heritable traits that are not linked.

While Mendel's groundbreaking insights were the beginning of the study of genetics, we now know that the genetic picture in humans is far more complex than he ever imagined. Moreover, who we are is not just a product of our genetic code, but also depends on that code's interaction with the environment. In the following section, we discuss dominant and recessive transmission as well as the transmission of multifactorial traits. Last, we discuss how epigenetic processes can

autosomes In humans, the 22 pairs of chromosomes not related to sexual expression.

sex chromosomes Pair of chromosomes that determines sex; XY in the normal human male, XX in the normal human female.

alleles Two or more alternative forms of a gene that can occupy the same position on paired chromosomes and affect the same trait.

homozygous Possessing two identical alleles for a trait.

heterozygous Possessing differing alleles for a trait.

dominant inheritance Pattern of inheritance in which, when a child receives different alleles, only the dominant one is expressed.

recessive inheritance Pattern of inheritance in which a child receives identical recessive alleles, resulting in expression of a nondominant trait.

mutations Permanent alterations in genes or chromosomes that usually produce harmful characteristics but provide the raw material of evolution.

multifactorial transmission Combination of genetic and environmental factors to produce certain complex traits.

alter the expression of the underlying genetic code.

Dominant and Recessive Inheritance

Genes that can produce alternative expressions of a characteristic, such as the presence or absence of dimples, are called **alleles**. Alleles are the different version of a particular gene. Every person receives one maternal and one paternal allele for any given trait. When both alleles are the same, the person is **homozygous** for the characteristic; when they are different, the person is **heterozygous**. In **dominant inheritance**, when an offspring receives at least one dominant allele for a trait, it will be expressed. **Recessive inheritance**, or the expression of a recessive trait, occurs only when a person receives two recessive alleles, one from each parent.

Let's take red hair as an example. Because red hair is a recessive trait, you must receive two recessive copies (r) of the gene—one from each parent—in order to express red hair. Having hair that is not red (R; brown in this example) is a dominant trait, so you will have brown hair if you receive at least one copy (R) from either parent (Rr or RR) (Figure 2.3). If you receive one copy of the red hair allele (r) and one copy of an allele for brown hair (R), you are heterozygous (Rr); if you

Dimples are an example of dominant inheritance: If you inherit one allele for the trait from either parent, you will have dimples.
©Jajmo/Shutterstock

have two copies of the allele for brown hair, you are homozygous dominant (RR). In both of these cases, you will have brown hair. If you inherited one allele for red hair from each parent, you are homozygous recessive for this trait (rr) and will have red hair. Thus the only situation in which you would have red hair is if you received two recessive copies (r), one from each parent.

Traits may also be affected by **mutations**, permanent alterations in genetic material. Mutations, such as the spontaneous dominant mutation known as achondroplasia which results in dwarfism, are generally due to copying errors and are usually harmful.

Multifactorial Transmission

Environmental experience modifies the expression of the genotype for most traits—a phenomenon called **multifactorial transmission**. Multifactorial transmission illustrates the action of nature and nurture and how they mutually and

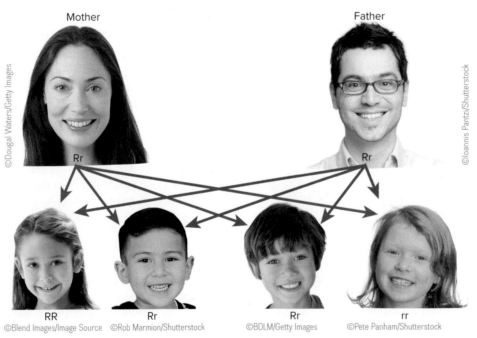

Mother — Rr
©Dougal Waters/Getty Images

Father — Rr
©Ioannis Pantzi/Shutterstock

RR
©Blend Images/Image Source

Rr
©Rob Marmion/Shutterstock

Rr
©BDLM/Getty Images

rr
©Pete Panham/Shutterstock

FIGURE 2.3 Dominant and Recessive Inheritance
Because of dominant inheritance, the same observable phenotype (in this case, brown hair) can result from two different genotypes (RR and Rr). A phenotype expressing a recessive characteristic (such as red hair) must have a homozygous recessive genotype (rr).

reciprocally affect outcomes. Imagine that Rio has inherited athletic talent and comes from a family of avid athletes. If his family nurtures his talent and he practices regularly, he may become, for example, a skilled soccer player. However, if he is not encouraged and not motivated to engage in athletics, his genotype for athletic ability may not be expressed (or may be expressed to a lesser extent) in his phenotype. Some physical characteristics (including height and weight) and most psychological characteristics (such as intelligence and musical ability) are products of multifactorial transmission.

Many disorders arise when an inherited predisposition (an abnormal variant of a normal gene) interacts with an environmental factor, either before or after birth. Attention-deficit/hyperactivity disorder (ADHD) is one of several behavioral disorders thought to be transmitted multifactorially (Yang et al., 2013).

Did you know?

Eye color is often used as an example of dominant-recessive genetic transmission, and generally, it does follow a recessive/dominant pattern with brown eyes dominant over blue or green eyes. However, as it turns out, eye color is more complex than this and is influenced by at least three different genes.

©RapidEye/
Getty Images

EPIGENESIS: ENVIRONMENTAL INFLUENCE ON GENE EXPRESSION

Who you are is a product of your genes as well as the environmental influences you are exposed to. Your **genotype** is what is coded in your genes—the recipe for making you. It may be expressed in varying ways. What is expressed—who you actually are—is your **phenotype**. For example, if you have dimples, that trait is part of your phenotype, the observable characteristics through which your genotype, or underlying genetic makeup, is expressed. Except for monozygotic twins, identical twins who started out as a single fertilized ovum, no two people have the same genotype. The phenotype is the genotype in action. The difference between genotype and phenotype helps explain why a clone, a genetic copy of an individual, or even an identical twin can never be an exact duplicate of another person. The environment has an effect; thus, phenotypic differences emerge even between genetically identical twins.

Mounting evidence suggests that gene expression is controlled by reversible chemical reactions that turn genes on or off as they are needed but that do not change the underlying genetic code. This phenomenon is called **epigenesis**. Epigenesis works via chemical molecules, or "tags," attached to a gene that affect the way a cell "reads" the gene's DNA. Because every cell in the body inherits the same DNA sequence, the function of the chemical tags is to differentiate various types of body cells, such as brain cells, skin cells,

and liver cells—somewhat like placing sticky notes in your textbook to tell you where to look for information. These tags work by "switching" particular genes on or off during embryonic formation. Having mapped the human genome, scientists are joining forces internationally to decode the epigenome (Mayo Foundation for Medical Education and Research, 2009).

Environmental factors, such as nutrition, smoking, sleep habits, stress, and physical activity can cause epigenetic changes (Wong et al., 2014). In turn, these epigenetic changes can contribute to such common ailments as cancer, diabetes, and heart disease (Dawson & Kouzarides, 2012; Slomko, Heo & Einstein, 2012; Webster, Yan & Marsden, 2013). It may explain why one monozygotic twin is susceptible to a disease such as schizophrenia whereas the other twin is not, and why some twins get the same disease but at different ages (Fraga et al., 2005; Wong, Gottesman & Petronis, 2005). Environmental influences can also be social in nature. For example, social isolation can lead to a variety of health vulnerabilities including cardiovascular disease, decreased immune responses, and an increased risk of inflammation-related diseases (Cole, 2009).

genotype Genetic makeup of a person, containing both expressed and unexpressed characteristics.

phenotype Observable characteristics of a person.

epigenesis Mechanism that turns genes on or off and determines functions of body cells.

Epigenetic changes are more likely to occur in response to environmental triggers during critical or sensitive periods of development such as puberty and pregnancy (Mayo Foundation for Medical Education and Research, 2009; Rakyan & Beck, 2006). Epigenetic modifications, especially those that occur early in life, may be heritable. Studies of human sperm cells found age-related epigenetic variations capable of being passed on to future generations (Rakyan & Beck, 2006).

Despite having identical genes, the epigenome of twins diverges over time because of different environmental influences, leading to different expression of those genes.
©Mark Hunt/Huntstock/Corbis

Genetic and Chromosomal Abnormalities

After two failed IVF attempts, Tania and Paul were finally pregnant. Early ultrasound tests indicated that, luckily, only one embryo had implanted and Tania was pregnant with a singleton. In her first trimester, Tania had undergone initial screenings. Everything had gone well, and there was no indication of a genetic or developmental disorder. At 20 weeks pregnant, Tania went to her obstetrician for a midpregnancy anatomy scan. Now she would find out the sex of her baby and be screened for soft markers of disorders. Soft markers are physical abnormalities that can be seen on an ultrasound; they indicate an increased risk of having a baby with a genetic disorder. By looking for various soft markers—shorter legs, a thicker nuchal fold (skin on the back of the neck) and heart abnormalities—Tania's doctor could give her an idea of whether or not her baby was likely to have certain developmental disorders.

Most birth disorders are fairly rare, affecting only about 3 percent of live births (Centers for Disease Control and Prevention, 2018). Nevertheless, they are the leading cause of infant death in the United States, accounting for approximately 20 percent of infant deaths (Mathews, MacDorman & Thoma, 2015). Rates of disorders vary with race and ethnicity. For example, Hispanic infants have a higher occurrence of neural tube and ear defects than do non-Hispanic white infants but lower rates of hypospadias (when the opening of the penis is on the underside rather than the tip). African American infants are more likely to have one type of a neural tube defect known as an encephalocele (in which the skull does not close correctly and part of the brain protrudes outside the head) and trisomy 18 (where an extra chromosome results in a condition called Edwards syndrome and severe developmental delays) and less likely to have cleft lip or palate, or gastrointestinal abnormalities. Asian American infants are not at higher risk for any birth defects, but are at lower risk for a wide range of disorders (Canfield et al., 2014). Survival rates also differ by ethnicity. In particular, African American and Hispanic infants are at higher risk than non-Hispanic white infants (Wang et al., 2015).

The most prevalent defects are cleft lip and cleft palate, followed by Down syndrome, a chromosomal disorder we will discuss later in the chapter. Other serious malformations involve the eye; the face; the mouth; or the circulatory, digestive, or musculoskeletal systems (Parker et al., 2010).

Not all genetic or chromosomal abnormalities are apparent at birth. Table 2.1 lists some of the disorders caused by genetic and chromosomal abnormalities. Tay-Sachs, a fatal degenerative disease of the central nervous system most common in Jews of eastern European ancestry, and sickle-cell anemia, a blood disorder more common among African Americans, do not generally appear until at least 6 months of age. Likewise, cystic fibrosis, a condition most common in people of northern European descent in which excess mucus accumulates in the lungs and digestive tract, may not appear until age 4. Some diseases show an even later onset, such as glaucoma, a disease in which fluid pressure builds up in the eyes, and Huntington's disease, a progressive degeneration of the nervous system, which do not typically appear before middle age.

It is in genetic defects and diseases that we see most clearly the operation of dominant and recessive transmission, and also of a variation, sex-linked inheritance, discussed in a subsequent section.

DOMINANT OR RECESSIVE INHERITANCE OF DEFECTS

Most of the time, typical genes are dominant over those carrying abnormal traits, but sometimes the gene for an abnormal trait is dominant. When this is the case, even one copy of the "bad" gene will result in a child expressing the disorder. Among the 1,800 disorders known to be transmitted by dominant inheritance are achondroplasia (a type of dwarfism) and Huntington's disease. Although they can be serious, defects transmitted by dominant inheritance are less likely to be lethal at an early age than those transmitted by recessive inheritance. This is because if a dominant gene is lethal at an early age, then affected children would be likely to die before reproducing. Therefore, that gene would soon disappear from the population.

Recessive defects are expressed only if the child is homozygous for that gene; in other words, a child must inherit a copy of the recessive gene from each parent to be affected. Because recessive genes are not expressed if the parent is heterozygous for that trait, both parents may be carriers without realizing it. In this case any child they had would have a 25 percent chance of getting both of the recessive copies, and thus expressing the trait. Defects transmitted by recessive genes tend to be lethal at an earlier age, in contrast to those transmitted by dominant genes as they can be passed down to the next generation by carriers. Tay-Sachs disease, for example, occurs only if both parents are carriers of the defective gene; children with this degenerative condition typically die by age 4 or 5.

TABLE 2.1 Some Birth Defects

Problem	Characteristics of Condition	Who Is at Risk	What Can Be Done
Alpha-1 antitrypsin deficiency	Enzyme deficiency that can lead to cirrhosis of the liver in early infancy and emphysema and degenerative lung disease in middle age.	1 in 1,000 white births	No treatment.
Alpha thalassemia	Severe anemia that reduces ability of the blood to carry oxygen; nearly all affected infants are stillborn or die soon after birth.	Primarily families of Malaysian, African, and Southeast Asian descent	Frequent blood transfusions.
Beta thalassemia (Cooley's anemia)	Severe anemia resulting in weakness, fatigue, and frequent illness; usually fatal in adolescence or young adulthood.	Primarily families of Mediterranean descent	Frequent blood transfusions.
Cystic fibrosis	Overproduction of mucus, which collects in the lungs and digestive tract; children do not grow normally and usually do not live beyond age 30; the most common inherited *lethal* defect among white people.	1 in 2,000 white births	Daily physical therapy to loosen mucus; antibiotics for lung infections; enzymes to improve digestion; gene therapy (in experimental stage).
Duchenne muscular dystrophy	Fatal disease usually found in males, marked by muscle weakness; minor intellectual disability is common; respiratory failure and death usually occur in young adulthood.	1 in 3,000 to 5,000 male births	No treatment.
Hemophilia	Excessive bleeding, usually found in males; in its most severe form, can lead to crippling arthritis in adulthood.	1 in 10,000 families with a history of hemophilia	Frequent transfusions of blood with clotting factors.
Neural-tube defects Anencephaly	Absence of brain tissues; infants are stillborn or die soon after birth.	1 in 1,000	No treatment.
Spina bifida	Incompletely closed spinal canal, resulting in muscle weakness or paralysis and loss of bladder and bowel control; often accompanied by hydrocephalus, an accumulation of spinal fluid in the brain, which can lead to intellectual disability.	1 in 1,000	Surgery to close spinal canal prevents further injury; shunt placed in brain drains excess fluid and prevents intellectual disability.
Phenylketonuria (PKU)	Metabolic disorder resulting in intellectual disability.	1 in 15,000	Special diet begun in first few weeks of life can prevent intellectual disability.
Polycystic kidney disease	*Infantile form:* enlarged kidneys, leading to respiratory problems and congestive heart failure. *Adult form:* kidney pain, kidney stones, and hypertension resulting in chronic kidney failure.	1 in 1,000	Kidney transplants.
Sickle-cell anemia	Deformed, fragile red blood cells that can clog the blood vessels, depriving the body of oxygen; symptoms include severe pain, stunted growth, frequent infections, leg ulcers, gallstones, susceptibility to pneumonia, and stroke.	1 in 500 African Americans	Painkillers, transfusions for anemia and to prevent stroke, antibiotics for infections.
Tay-Sachs disease	Degenerative disease of the brain and nerve cells, resulting in death before age 5.	Historically found mainly in eastern European Jews	No treatment.

Source: Adapted from AAP Committee on Genetics, 1996; NIH Consensus Development Panel, 2001; Tisdale, 1988, pp. 68–69.

Some traits are only partly dominant or partly recessive. In **incomplete dominance**, a trait is not fully expressed. For example, people with one sickle-cell allele and one normal allele do not have sickle-cell anemia, but they do show some manifestations of the condition, such as shortness of breath at high altitudes.

SEX-LINKED INHERITANCE OF DEFECTS

Certain recessive disorders are transmitted by **sex-linked inheritance**. They are linked to genes on the sex chromosomes and affect male and female children differently (Figure 2.4). In humans, the Y chromosome is smaller and carries fewer genes than the X chromosome. Remember that males are XY, and females are XX. One consequence of this is that females receive two copies of any gene carried on the X chromosome, whereas males receive only one. Therefore, males are more likely to be affected by any trait carried on

incomplete dominance Pattern of inheritance in which a child receives two different alleles, resulting in partial expression of a trait.

sex-linked inheritance Pattern of inheritance in which certain characteristics carried on the X chromosome inherited from the mother are transmitted differently to her male and female offspring.

the X chromosome because they only have one chance to get it right.

When a mother is a carrier of a sex-linked disorder—in other words, when she is heterozygous for an allele carried on the sex chromosomes—she has a 50 percent chance of passing that gene on to her children. A male child has a 50 percent chance of getting the faulty gene and having the disorder because there is no back-up copy. A female child, even if she gets a copy of the faulty gene from her mother, will receive another allele from her father. Red-green color blindness is one of these sex-linked conditions. Another is hemophilia, a disorder in which blood does not clot when it should.

Occasionally, a female inherits a sex-linked condition. For example, if her father has hemophilia and her mother also happens to be a carrier for the disorder, the daughter has a 50 percent chance of receiving the abnormal X chromosome from each parent and having the disease.

CHROMOSOMAL ABNORMALITIES

Chromosomal abnormalities typically occur because of errors in cell division. For example, Klinefelter syndrome, found only in males, is caused by an extra female sex chromosome (shown by the pattern XXY). While some boys born with Klinefelter may not show any symptoms, others may have impaired fertility; problems with language or reading; and they are often tall, with long legs and a short trunk. Klinefelter occurs in approximately 1 out of 500 males (NICHD, 2007). Turner syndrome results from a missing sex chromosome (XO) and is found only in females. Girls with Turner syndrome tend to have a webbed neck, low-set ears, and short stature; they are usually infertile (NICHD, 2007). Estimates are that Turner syndrome occurs in 1 out of every 2,000 live births (Donaldson, Gault, Tan & Dunger, 2006). In yet another variation, Triple X syndrome results from an extra X chromosome. Also known as trisomy X, it is associated with delayed language and motor development and affects approximately 1 in 1,000 females (National Library

FIGURE 2.4 **Sex-Linked Recessive Inheritance**

In the most common form, the female sex chromosome of an unaffected mother carries one recessive abnormal gene and one dominant normal one (X). The father has one normal male X and Y chromosome complement.

©Jack Hollingsworth/Getty Images; ©Image Source/Getty Images; ©Gelpi/Shutterstock; ©Jiang Jin/Purestock/SuperStock

Carrier mother   **Normal father**

X X   X Y

The odds for each *male* child are 50/50:
1. 50% risk of inheriting the abnormal X and the disorder
2. 50% chance of inheriting normal X and Y chromosomes

The odds for each *female* child are 50/50:
1. 50% chance of inheriting one abnormal X, to be a carrier like mother
2. 50% chance of inheriting no abnormal genes

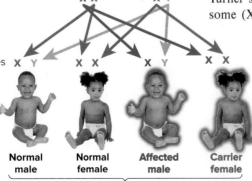

X Y   X X   X Y   X X

Normal male   **Normal female**   **Affected male**   **Carrier female**

Possible hereditary results

Early intervention for children with Down syndrome provides cognitive, social, and emotional benefits and can help them achieve important skills.
©Denis Kuvaev/Shutterstock

Did you know?

Rather than having the three familiar branching lines on their palm, children with Down syndrome are more likely to have one horizontal line across their palms, a characteristic known as the single transverse palmar crease. This trait sometimes occurs in the general population, but it is more likely in children with Down syndrome.

©Michal and Yossi Rotem/Shutterstock

of Medicine, n.d.). The likelihood of genetic errors may increase in offspring of women age 35 or older (University of Virginia Health System, 2004).

The most common genetic disorder in children is **Down syndrome** (Parker et al., 2010). It is responsible for about 40 percent of cases of moderate-to-severe intellectual disability (Pennington, Moon, Edgin, Stedron & Nadel, 2003) as defined by performance on an intelligence test. The condition is also called *trisomy-21* because it is characterized in more than 90 percent of cases by an extra 21st chromosome. The most obvious physical characteristic associated with Down syndrome is a downward-sloping skin fold at the inner corners of the eyes. Children with Down syndrome also tend to have slowed growth; poor muscle tone; congenital heart defects; thick hands; ear infections and early hearing loss; and impaired communication, language, memory, and motor skills (Davis, 2008).

Slightly under 14 of every 10,000 live births is a child with Down syndrome (Parker et al., 2010). Although the risk of having a child with Down syndrome rises with age of the mother (Society for Neuroscience, 2008), because of the higher birthrates of younger women, there are actually more young mothers with children with Down

syndrome (National Institute of Child Health and Human Development, 2008). In 95 percent of cases, the extra chromosome seems to come from the mother's ovum; in the other 5 percent, from the father's sperm (Antonarakis & Down Syndrome Collaborative Group, 1991).

With early intervention the prognosis for children with Down syndrome is brighter than once thought. Children with Down syndrome, like other children with disabilities, tend to benefit cognitively, socially, and emotionally when placed in regular classrooms rather than in special schools (Davis, 2008) and when given regular, intensive therapies to help them achieve important skills. As adults, many live in small group homes and support themselves; they tend to do well in structured job situations. More than 70 percent of people with Down syndrome live into their sixties, but they are at elevated risk of early death from various causes, including leukemia, cancer, Alzheimer's disease, and cardiovascular disease (Hill et al., 2003; Bittles, Bower, Hussain & Glasson, 2006).

Down syndrome Chromosomal disorder characterized by moderate-to-severe intellectual disability and by such physical signs as a downward-sloping skin fold at the inner corners of the eyes.

genetic counseling Clinical service that advises prospective parents of their probable risk of having children with hereditary defects.

GENETIC COUNSELING AND TESTING

Tania's anatomy scan showed two soft markers for Down syndrome, and she was told that her risk for having an affected child was thus 1 in 23. Tania and Paul had a decision to make. They could opt to live with those risks and proceed with the pregnancy with no further intervention, or they could schedule an *amniocentesis*–a genetic test that would definitely tell whether or not the child would be affected but would also put Tania at a small risk of miscarriage. Tania and Paul weren't sure what to do.

Genetic counseling can help prospective parents like Paul and Tania assess their risk of bearing children with genetic or

WHAT DO YOU **DO**?

Genetic Counselor

Geneticists are experts in the area of genes and heredity. For example, genetic counselors work with prospective or soon-to-be parents to consult on genetically based disorders that might occur in their child. They often work with patients to create a genetic family tree, determine if testing is needed, help interpret results from testing, and counsel patients as they make decisions related to findings. For example, a couple who are both of eastern European descent might consult a genetic counselor regarding risk of Tay-Sachs disease. Or a couple with one child with a particular disorder that research has shown to have a genetic basis might consult a genetic counselor before trying to become pregnant again. A master's degree is required to become a genetic counselor. Graduate programs are very competitive. Visit www.nsgc.org for more information about genetic counselors.

©Purestock/SuperStock

heritability Statistical estimate of contribution of heredity to individual differences in a specific trait within a given population at a particular time.

chromosomal defects. People who have already had a child with a genetic defect, who have a family history of hereditary illness, who suffer from conditions known or suspected to be inherited, or who come from ethnic groups at higher-than-average risk of passing on genes for certain diseases can get information about their likelihood of producing affected children. A genetic counselor tries to help clients understand the mathematical risk of a particular condition, explains its implications, and presents information about alternate courses of action. Screening for disorders can either happen before pregnancy, when parents can be screened for the presence of recessive genetic disorders, or after conception via genetic assessments such as chorionic villi sampling (CVS) and amniocentesis. These will be discussed in greater detail in Chapter 3.

Geneticists have made great contributions to the prevention of birth defects. For example, since so many Jewish couples have been tested for genes that carry Tay-Sachs, a fatal disease involving degeneration of mental and physical abilities, far fewer Jewish babies have been born with the disease (Kolata, 2003). Similarly, screening and counseling women of childbearing age from Mediterranean countries, where beta thalassemia (severe anemia that is generally fatal in adolescence or young adulthood) is common, have resulted in a decline in births of affected babies and greater knowledge of the risks of being a carrier (Cao, Rosatelli, Monni & Galanello, 2002).

Studying the Influence of Heredity and Environment

How much of who we are is due to heredity and how much is due to environment? Although certain rare physical disorders are virtually 100 percent inherited, phenotypes for more complex normal traits, such as those having to do with health, intelligence, and personality, are subject to a complex array of hereditary and environmental forces. Here we explore how scientists study the influences of heredity and environment and how these two forces work together.

MEASURING HERITABILITY

Heritability is a statistical estimate of how much heredity contributes to variations in a specific trait at a certain time within a given population. Heritability does not refer to the relative influence of heredity and environment in a particular individual. It merely indicates the statistical extent to which genes contribute to a trait among a group of people.

Heritability is expressed as a percentage ranging from 0.0 to 1.0; the higher the number, the greater the heritability of a trait. A heritability estimate of 1.0 indicates that genes are 100 percent responsible for variances in the trait within the population. For example, the heritability of eye color approaches 1.0—whether or not your eyes are blue or brown is not driven by environment.

Heritability cannot be measured directly. Thus, researchers in behavioral genetics have developed indirect methods for assessing the relationship between the expression of traits and the genetic and environmental factors influencing them. Although there are variations in the details, the underlying logic of the approaches in these types of studies is the same.

Our phenotype results from the joint action of genetic and environmental influences. Fortunately, we can estimate the shared genetic influences between two people relatively easily. If two people are unrelated, we know they are not likely to share any genes. If two people are identical twins, we know they share all their genes. If two people are fraternal twins, siblings, or parents, they share roughly 50 percent of their genes with each other. If we know, on average, how many genes people share, then we can measure how similar they are on traits (that is, their concordance rate) and work backward to determine the relative environmental influences. Therefore, if heredity has a large influence on a particular trait, identical twins should be more alike on that trait that fraternal twins, and adopted children should be more like their biological parents than their adoptive parents. Note that this can be carried out to more distant genetic relatives as well. For traits with strong genetic influences, for example, siblings should be more similar than cousins on that trait.

A genetic counselor can help a family determine the mathematical risk that their children will be born with a genetic condition.

©Jupiterimages/Getty Images

Much of heritability research compares identical twins, who share 100 percent of their genes, with fraternal twins, who share roughly 50 percent of their genes, on traits thought to be influenced by genes.

©Image Source/Getty Images

Twin studies compare pairs of monozygotic, or identical, twins with same-sex dizygotic, or fraternal, twins. Monozygotic twins are twice as genetically similar, on average, as dizygotic twins. When monozygotic twins are more alike, or more *concordant*, on a trait than dizygotic twins, we see the likely effects of heredity. As an extension of this, twins raised in either their biological family or an adoptive family can be studied.

HOW HEREDITY AND ENVIRONMENT WORK TOGETHER

In actuality, as noted above, the effects of genetic influences, especially on behavioral traits, are rarely inevitable. Even in a trait strongly influenced by heredity, the environment can have substantial impact (Rutter, 2002). In fact, environmental interventions sometimes can overcome genetically determined conditions. For example, phenylketonuria (PKU) is a recessive genetic disorder—if children are born with the faulty genes coding for PKU then they are unable to metabolize phenylalanine, an amino acid found in animal proteins such as milk, cheese, and meat, and in artificial sweeteners such as aspartame. If people with PKU eat these foods, they are unable to break down phenylalanine. Infants born with this condition, if untreated, appear typical for a few months. However, as the phenylalanine builds up in their brains, it reaches toxic levels that eventually result in irreversible and severe brain damage. Fortunately, a strict diet begun soon after birth can prevent intellectual disability and allow these children to experience normal health and life span (Widaman, 2009). Thus, despite this disorder being strongly influenced by genetics, the environment nonetheless impacts the effect it has on the developing human.

From conception on, a combination of constitutional (biological and psychological), social, economic, and cultural factors help shape development. The more advantageous these circumstances, the greater the likelihood of optimum development. Here we consider several ways in which inheritance and experience work together.

We can also use the environment to estimate influences. If the environment exerts a large influence on a trait, people who live together should be more similar than those that live apart, and shared genes should matter less. For example, in this situation, we might compare adopted children to their biological and adoptive parents. If adopted children are more similar to their adoptive parents than their biological parents on a trait, then that trait is likely influenced strongly by the environment.

Essentially, this approach boils down to comparisons of shared genes, the same or different environments, and concordance rates. Using these three variables allows researchers to make an estimate of the relative influence of genes and environment on a trait. Three types of studies are most commonly used in investigations such as these: family, adoption, and twin studies.

In *family studies*, researchers measure the degree to which biological relatives share certain traits and determine whether or not the closeness of the familial relationship is associated with the degree of similarity. In other words, the more closely two people are related, the more likely they will be similar on a trait if that trait is indeed genetically influenced. Therefore, researchers use concordance rates on traits to infer genetic influences. For example, one would expect full siblings to be more similar on a trait than half-siblings, who share only one parent.

Adoption studies look at similarities between adopted children and their adoptive families and also between adopted children and their biological families. When adopted children are more like their biological parents and siblings in a particular trait (say, obesity), we see the influence of heredity. When they resemble their adoptive families more, we see the influence of environment.

Reaction Range and Canalization

Many characteristics vary, within limits, under differing hereditary or environmental conditions. The concepts of reaction range and canalization can help us visualize how this happens.

Reaction range is the conventional term for a range of potential expressions of a hereditary trait. Body size, for example, depends largely on biological processes, which are genetically regulated. Tall people have tall children, and short people have short children. Even so, a range of sizes is possible. In societies in which nutrition has dramatically improved, an entire generation has grown up to tower over the generation before (Cole, 2003). The better fed children

reaction range Potential variability, depending on environmental conditions, in the expression of a hereditary trait.

share their parents' genes, but have responded to a healthier world. Ultimately, height has genetic limits. We don't see typically developing people who are only 1 foot tall, or who are 10 feet tall.

Heredity can influence whether a reaction range is wide or narrow. In other words, the genotype places limits on the range of possible phenotypes. For example, a child born with a defect producing mild cognitive limitations is better able to respond to a favorable environment than a child born with more severe limitations. The child with a mild impairment has a wider range of reaction.

Some traits have an extremely narrow range of reaction. The metaphor of **canalization** illustrates how heredity restricts the range of development for some traits. After a heavy storm, the rainwater that has fallen on a pavement has to go somewhere. If the street has potholes, the water will fill them. If deep canals have been dug along the edges of the street, the water will flow into the canals. Highly canalized traits, such as eye color, are analogous to the deep canals. They are strongly programmed by genes, and there is little opportunity for variance in their expression. Because of the deep, genetically dug channel, it would take an extreme change in environment to alter their course. The canal is too deep for the water to easily slosh over.

In the ancestral past, an inability to walk or talk would have had profound adaptive consequences. Because they are so important, natural selection has designed them to develop in a predictable and reliable way within a variety of environments and a multitude of influences. They are too important to be left to chance. Thus, traits such as these tend to be highly canalized. With respect to motor development, typical babies follow a predictable sequence: crawling, walking, and running, in that order, at certain approximate ages. This sequence is said to be canalized, in that children will follow this same blueprint irrespective of many variations in the environment. A similar process occurs for language. Despite differences in linguistic environments, babies the world over reach language milestones at approximately the same time and in the same order. Cognition and personality, however, are not highly canalized. They are more subject to variations in experience: the kinds of families children grow up in, the schools they attend,

Even if well fed in childhood, two different people may reach different heights, reflecting the influence of their genes.
©RunPhoto/Getty Images

and the people they encounter. Consider reading. The environment plays a large part in reading skills development. Parents who play letter and word games and who read to their children are likely to have children who learn to read earlier than if these skills are not encouraged or reinforced. And children who are not taught to read do not learn to do so spontaneously.

Genotype–Environment Interaction

Genotype-environment interaction usually refers to the effects of similar environmental conditions on genetically different individuals. A discussion of these interactions is a way to conceptualize and talk about the different ways nature and nurture interact. To take a familiar example, many children are exposed to pollen and dust, but those with a genetic predisposition are more likely to develop allergic reactions (Sordillo et al., 2015). Interactions can work the other way as well: Genetically similar children often develop differently depending on their home environments (Collins, Maccoby, Steinberg, Hetherington & Bornstein, 2000). A child born with a difficult temperament may develop adjustment problems in one family and thrive in another, depending largely on how parents respond to the child. Thus it is the interaction of hereditary and environmental factors, not just one or the other, that produces certain outcomes. In reality, there are multiple ways in which individual differences—driven by genetics—and the environment interact to produce outcomes.

Genotype–Environment Correlation

The environment often reflects or reinforces genetic differences. This tendency is called **genotype-environment correlation**,

canalization Limitation on variance of expression of certain inherited characteristics.

genotype–environment interaction Effect of the interaction between genes and the environment on phenotypic variation.

genotype–environment correlation Tendency of certain genetic and environmental influences to reinforce each other; may be passive, reactive (evocative), or active.

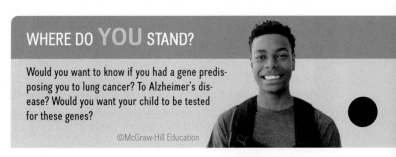

WHERE DO YOU STAND?

Would you want to know if you had a gene predisposing you to lung cancer? To Alzheimer's disease? Would you want your child to be tested for these genes?

©McGraw-Hill Education

and it works in three ways to strengthen the phenotypic expression of a genotypic tendency (Bergeman & Plomin, 1989; Scarr, 1992; Scarr & McCartney, 1983):

- *Active correlations*: Children actively select experiences that are consistent with their genetic tendencies. A shy child is more likely than an outgoing child to spend time in solitary pursuits. An adolescent with a talent for music probably will seek out musical friends, take music classes, and go to concerts if such opportunities are available. This tendency to seek out environments compatible with one's genotype is called *niche-picking*; it helps explain why identical twins reared apart tend to be quite similar. Children are always involved in creating the environment they inhabit, but their ability to find niches for themselves increases with age and independence.

- *Passive correlations*: You not only inherit genes from your parents, you also inherit environments. For example, a musical parent is likely to create a home environment in which music is heard regularly, to give a child music lessons, and to take the child to musical events. If the child inherited the parent's musical talent, the child's musicality will reflect a combination of genetic and environmental influences. This type of correlation is called passive because the child does not control it. Passive correlations are most applicable to young children, whose parents have a great deal of control over their early experiences. In addition, passive correlations function only when a child is living with a biologically related parent.

- *Reactive, or evocative, correlations*: Children with differing genetic makeup evoke different responses from adults. If a child shows interest and ability in music, parents who are not musically inclined may react by making a special effort to provide that child with musical experiences. This response, in turn, strengthens the child's genetic inclination toward music.

What Makes Siblings So Different?

You might assume that siblings, as they share approximately 50 percent of their genes, might be very similar to each other. However, siblings can differ greatly in intellect and especially in personality, and this difference increases with age (Plomin & Daniels, 2011). One reason may be genetic differences, which lead children to need different kinds of stimulation or to respond differently to a similar home environment, and thus develop along increasingly divergent paths. For example, twin studies have identified that genetic differences between siblings in part drive how family conflict is experienced (Horwitz et al., 2010).

An example of a passive genotype-environment correlation is a child whose parents both pass along genes for musical talent and provide a musically rich environment (lessons, musical events). The child isn't actively controlling his environment; he inherits both genes and the environment from his parents.
©Rubberball/Punchstock

In addition, there are also **nonshared environmental effects** that result from the unique environment in which each child in a family grows up. Children in a family have a shared environment—the home they live in, the people in it, and the activities a family jointly engages in—but even if they are twins, they also have experiences that their brothers and sisters do not share. Parents and siblings may treat each child differently; a firstborn gets undivided attention, but later-borns must compete for it. Certain events, such as illnesses and accidents, and experiences outside the home affect one child and not another. Indeed, some researchers have concluded that although heredity accounts for most of the similarities between siblings, the nonshared environment accounts for most of the differences (Hetherington, Reiss & Plomin, 2013). We can also extend the conversation about genotype-environment correlations to explain some of the effects of the nonshared environment on siblings' experiences. Children's genetic differences may lead parents to react to them differently and treat them differently. One child may be shy and elicit more gentle behavior from parents, another may be bold and be given greater freedom and encouragement to explore. Children also mold their environments by the choices they make—what they do and with whom—and their genetic makeup influences these choices. A child who loves to read may spend hours in solitude, while an athletic and sociable child may prefer to be outside playing with others. Thus, not only will the child's talents (such as reading or athleticism) develop differently, but their social lives will be different as well. These differences tend to be accentuated as children grow older and have more experiences outside the family (Plomin, 1996; Scarr, 1992).

> **nonshared environmental effects** The unique environment in which each child grows up, consisting of distinctive influences or influences that affect one child differently than another.

Did you know?

Every person has unique fingerprints—even identical twins. While the basic whorls, loops, and ridges of the fingertips of identical twins are similar in their broad patterns, they are not exact copies.

©Digital Vision/ Getty Images

Characteristics Influenced by Heredity and Environment

A full four years after their first try to become pregnant, Tania and Paul finally had a baby girl. Even from the first day at the hospital, their daughter behaved and acted differently from the other children in the nursery with distinct likes, dislikes, and patterns of behaviors. Although it would take years for her abilities and tendencies to emerge fully, many of the tiny baby's characteristics were already in place. While developmentalists have studied heredity–environment interactions in great detail, it is unlikely that the true complexity of this dynamic relationship will ever be known. Nonetheless, some general truths have emerged in the areas of physical and physiological traits, intelligence, personality, and psychopathology.

obesity Extreme overweight in relation to age, sex, height, and body type.

PHYSICAL AND PHYSIOLOGICAL TRAITS

Not only do monozygotic twins generally look alike, but they also are more concordant than dizygotic twins in their risk for medical disorders such as high blood pressure, heart disease, stroke, rheumatoid arthritis, peptic ulcers, and epilepsy (Bevan et al., 2012; Brass, Isaacsohn, Merikangas & Robinette, 1992; Plomin, Owen & McGuffin, 1994). Life span, too, seems to be influenced by genes (Hjelmborg et al., 2006).

Obesity is measured by body mass index, or BMI (comparison of weight to height). Children between the 85th and 95th percentiles are classified as overweight, and those above the 95th percentile as obese (Ogden, Carroll, Curtin, Lamb & Flegal, 2010). The risk of obesity is 2 to 3 times higher for a child with a family history of obesity, especially severe obesity (Nirmala et al., 2008). Therefore, we might reasonably conclude that obesity involves genetic contributions.

Research shows that obesity is indeed affected by genetics. There is a not "a" gene for obesity, rather it is a multifactorial condition. Twin studies, adoption studies, and other research suggest that 40 to 70 percent of the risk is genetic (Willyard, 2014). More than 430 genes or chromosome regions are associated with obesity (Nirmala, Reddy & Reddy, 2008; Snyder et al., 2004). There are also small subsets of obese people who have a genetic profile making them particularly prone to obesity; for instance, one such subset includes obese adults suffering from a deletion of approximately 30 genes (Bochukova et al., 2009).

However, this increased risk is not solely genetic. Environmental experiences also contribute to obesity (Willyard, 2014). The kind and amount of food eaten in a particular home and the amount of exercise that is encouraged can increase or decrease the likelihood that a child will become obese. Moreover, the wider social context is at play as well. Obesity rates rise in countries with rapid socioeconomic growth and increases in gross domestic product (Min, Chiu & Wang, 2013). In Western countries, obesity likely stems from the interaction of a genetic predisposition with overeating, supersized portions, and inadequate exercise (Arner, 2000).

INTELLIGENCE

Heredity exerts a strong influence on general intelligence, as measured by intelligence tests, and a moderate effect on specific abilities such as memory, verbal ability, and spatial ability (Plomin & Spinath, 2004). While specific genes might contribute to intelligence (Posthuma & de Geus, 2006), intelligence is influenced by the effects of large numbers of genes working together.

Indirect evidence of the role of heredity in intelligence comes from adoption and twin studies. Adopted children's scores on standardized intelligence tests are consistently closer to the scores of their biological mothers than to those of their adoptive parents and siblings; monozygotic twins are more alike in intelligence than dizygotic twins (Petrill et al., 2004; Plomin & DeFries, 1999).

Intelligence also depends in part on brain size and structure, which are under strong genetic control

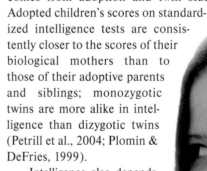

The nonshared environment accounts for many of the differences between siblings.
©Image Source

(Toga & Thompson, 2005). Experience counts, too; an enriched or impoverished environment can substantially affect the development and expression of innate ability (Ceci & Gilstrap, 2000). Environmental influence is greater, and heritability lower, among poor families than among more economically privileged families (Nisbett et al., 2012).

TEMPERAMENT AND PERSONALITY

When babies are exposed to a new experience, say riding on a train or playing with a new noisy toy, some infants respond with interest and excitement, and others with apprehension and withdrawal. Some babies are active, others less so. Some babies sleep and eat at the same time every day, others have difficulty settling into a consistent schedule. Right from the beginning, infants are utterly unique. Psychologists call these unique and characteristic ways of approaching and reacting to environmental stimuli **temperament**. Temperament is largely inborn and is relatively consistent over the years, although it may respond to special experiences or parental handling (Thomas & Chess, 1984; Thomas, Chess & Birch, 1968). In support of the role of genes, siblings—both twins and nontwins—tend to be similar in temperament on such traits as positive affect, activity level (Saudino & Micalizzi, 2015), and behavioral regulation (Gagne & Saudino, 2010).

Temperament is believed to underlie adult personality. Given the genetic contributions found for temperament, then, one would assume personality research should also illustrate hereditary influences. This is indeed the case. Scientists have identified genes directly linked with specific aspects of personality such as neuroticism and extraversion (Vinkhuyzen et al., 2012). Overall, the heritability of personality traits appears to be around 40 percent (Vukasovic & Bratko, 2015), and there is little evidence of shared environmental influence (Plomin, 2011). As with intelligence, genetic influences on personality appear to become more important with age (Briley & Tucker-Drob, 2014) and are shaped in part by active niche-picking (Kandler & Zapko-Willmes, 2017).

PSYCHOPATHOLOGY

There is evidence for a hereditary influence on such mental disorders as schizophrenia, autism, alcoholism, and depression. All tend to run in families and to show greater concordance between monozygotic twins than between dizygotic twins. However, heredity alone does not produce such disorders; an inherited tendency can be triggered by environmental factors.

Schizophrenia is an example of the interaction of heredity and genetics. *Schizophrenia* is a neurological disorder that affects about 1 percent of the U.S. population each year (Society for Neuroscience, 2008). It is characterized by loss of contact with reality; hallucinations and delusions; loss of

Because temperament is genetically influenced, it is not unusual for siblings to have similar temperaments.
©Fancy Collection/SuperStock

coherent, logical thought; and inappropriate emotionality. Estimates of heritability range from 60 to 80 percent (Schwab & Wildenauer, 2013). A wide array of rare gene mutations, some of which involve missing or duplicated segments of DNA, may increase susceptibility to schizophrenia (Chen et al., 2009; Vrijenhoek et al., 2008; Walsh et al., 2008). However, monozygotic twins are not always concordant for schizophrenia, perhaps due to epigenetic processes (Bonsch et al., 2012).

Researchers also have looked at possible nongenetic influences, such as a series of neurological insults in fetal life (Debnath, Venkatasubramanian & Berk, 2015), exposure to influenza or rubella (Brown, 2012), or the mother's loss of a close relative in the first trimester of pregnancy (Khashan et al., 2008). Infants born in urban areas or those whose mothers experienced obstetric complications or who were poor or severely deprived as a result of war or famine are at higher risk (Rapoport, Giedd & Gogtay, 2012) as are infants born during the winter months (Martinez-Ortega et al., 2011). Advanced paternal age is also a risk factor for schizophrenia (Byrne, Agerbo, Ewald, Eaton & Mortensen, 2003), and there are indications that, at least for boys, very young fathers may put children at elevated risk as well (Miller et al., 2010).

temperament Characteristic disposition, or style of approaching and reacting to situations.

mastering the CHAPTER

Summary and Key Terms

Conception and Infertility

> Fertilization, the union of an ovum and a sperm, results in the formation of a one-celled zygote, which then duplicates itself by cell division.

> The most common cause of infertility in men is low sperm count; the most common cause in women is blockage of the fallopian tubes.

> Assisted reproductive technology can help overcome infertility but may involve ethnical and practical issues. Adoption is also an option for those faced with infertility, but people adopt children for other reasons as well.

KEY TERMS

Fertilization	Zygote	Assisted reproductive technology (ART)

Mechanisms of Heredity

> The basic functional units of heredity are the genes, which are made of deoxyribonucleic acid (DNA). DNA carries the genetic code. Each gene is located by function in a definite position on a particular chromosome. The complete sequence of genes in the human body is called the human genome.

> At conception, each normal human being receives 23 chromosomes from the mother and 23 from the father. These form 23 pairs of chromosomes—22 pairs of autosomes and 1 pair of sex chromosomes. A child who receives an X chromosome from each parent is genetically female. A child who receives a Y chromosome from the father is genetically male.

> The simplest patterns of genetic transmission are dominant and recessive inheritance. When a pair of alleles are the same, a person is homozygous for the trait; when they are different, the person is heterozygous.

> Most normal human characteristics are the result of polygenic or multifactorial transmission. Dominant inheritance and multifactorial transmission explain why a person's phenotype does not always express the underlying genotype.

> The epigenetic framework controls the functions of particular genes; it can be affected by environmental factors.

KEY TERMS

Deoxyribonucleic acid (DNA)	Alleles	Multifactorial transmission
Chromosomes	Homozygous	Genotype
Genes	Heterozygous	Phenotype
Human genome	Dominant inheritance	Epigenesis
Autosomes	Recessive inheritance	
Sex chromosomes	Mutations	

Genetic and Chromosomal Abnormalities

> Birth defects and diseases may result from dominant, recessive, or sex-linked inheritance; or from chromosomal abnormalities.

> Through genetic counseling, prospective parents can receive information about the mathematical odds of bearing children with certain defects. Genetic testing involves risks as well as benefits.

KEY TERMS

Incomplete dominance	Down syndrome
Sex-linked inheritance	Genetic counseling

Studying the Influence of Heredity and Environment

> Research in behavioral genetics is based on the assumption that the relative influences of heredity and environment within a population can be measured statistically. If heredity is an important influence on a trait, genetically closer persons will be more similar in that trait.

> Family studies, adoption studies, and studies of twins enable researchers to measure the heritability of specific traits.

> The concepts of reaction range, canalization, genotype-environment interaction, genotype-environment correlation, and niche-picking describe ways in which heredity and environment work together.

> Siblings tend to be more different than alike in intelligence and personality. According to some behavioral geneticists, heredity accounts for most of the similarity, and nonshared environmental effects account for most of the difference.

KEY TERMS

Heritability	Canalization	Genotype environment correlation
Reaction range	Genotype-environment interaction	Nonshared environmental effects

Characteristics Influenced by Heredity and Environment

> Obesity, longevity, intelligence, temperament, and other aspects of personality are influenced by both heredity and environment.

> Schizophrenia is a highly heritable neurological disorder that also is environmentally influenced.

KEY TERMS

Obesity	Temperament

Practice Quiz

1. In conception, the moment when genes are combined and a new individual is formed is:
   a. when the fertilized egg implants in the uterus.
   b. when the sperm breaks through the egg and fuses with it.
   c. during meiosis when the pairs of chromosomes are halved and gametes are produced.
   d. when the one-celled zygote starts replicating itself.

2. The most common cause of infertility in men is _____, and the most common cause of infertility in women is _____.

3. In vitro fertilization involves:
   a. injecting sperm directly into a woman's vagina, cervix, or uterus.
   b. injecting a woman with a variety of hormones to stimulate egg production.
   c. the removal and fertilization of a woman's eggs, and the subsequent implantation back into the woman's uterus.
   d. b and c
   e. a, b, and c

4. What is the major trend in adoption in the United States?_____

   _____

5. Which is the best analogy for what genes do?
   a. a set of on/off buttons on a switchboard
   b. a large balloon that fills and deflates on a cycle
   c. a set of instructions for making a person
   d. a chalkboard upon which experiences are written

6. Humans have _____ pairs of chromosomes. Of those, _____ are autosomes and _____ is/are sex chromosomes. Males are _____ and females are ____.

7. Under what condition would a recessive trait be displayed?
   a. when both genes in a pair are dominant
   b. when the first gene in a pair is recessive and the second is dominant
   c. when the first gene in a pair is dominant and the second is recessive
   d. when both genes in a pair are recessive

8. Skin cells and stomach cells are expressed differently from each other because:
   a. they code for different genes
   b. epigenetic tags instruct some genes to turn on and some to turn off
   c. they differentiate over time as they adapt to their local environment
   d. This is untrue: They are expressed in an identical way regardless of location.

9. Consider a trait coded for by a recessive gene. Which of the following people will express the trait?
   a. a woman who is heterozygous for the recessive trait
   b. a man who is heterozygous for the recessive trait
   c. a woman who is a homozygous for the dominant trait
   d. a man who is homozygous for the recessive trait

10. Sex-linked traits:
    a. are usually passed from father to son.
    b. are never manifested in females.
    c. can be carried by females who do not display them.
    d. are carried by dominant genes.

11. A chromosomal disorder characterized by moderate-to-severe intellectual disability and a downward sloping skin fold at the inner corners of the eyes is called:
    a. cystic fibrosis.   c. Down syndrome.
    b. Tay-Sachs disease.   d. sickle-cell anemia.

12. Which of the following is the best description of what is done in an amniocentesis or chorionic villi test?
    a. Parents are assessed to see if they carry any recessive genes that might lead to a disorder prior to becoming pregnant.
    b. Parents are asked to meet with a genetic counselor and are told about different genetic disorders.
    c. Pregnant mothers are given blood tests to determine hormone levels in their blood.
    d. Fetal cells are extracted from the pregnant mother and tested in a lab.

13. If we find that identical twins are more concordant on a trait than fraternal twins, we can deduce that the trait is strongly influenced by _____.

14. Jiro is born to very athletic parents, who provide him with genes for athleticism. They also provide him with an environment rich in opportunity to engage in athletic activities. Because of his genes, he is uniquely well suited to take advantage of the environment his parents provide. Which of the following best describes the interaction of heredity and environment?
    a. active genotype–environment correlations
    b. passive genotype–environment correlations
    c. evocative genotype–environment correlations
    d. niche-picking

15. Although Roberto's adoptive parents are short in stature, he is growing tall like his biological mother. What might we conclude about Roberto's height?
    a. It is influenced primarily by environment.
    b. It is influenced primarily by heredity.
    c. Nutrition did not influence his height.
    d. It is primarily a result of independent segregation.

16. Which of the following statements supports the assertion that genes influence intelligence?
   a. Siblings are rarely similar in intelligence.
   b. Monozygotic twins are more similar in intelligence than dizygotic twins.
   c. Genetic influences on intelligence seem to decrease with age.
   d. Adoptive children are more similar in intelligence to their adoptive parents than their biological parents.

17. What are two temperamental traits in which genetic influences have been identified?

_____

_____

18. Which of the following statements is evidence that schizophrenia is not entirely due to genetics?
   a. Infants born in urban areas are at greater risk.
   b. Advanced paternal age is a risk factor.
   c. Siblings who have a close family member with schizophrenia are at higher risk.
   d. Not all monozygotic twins are concordant for schizophrenia.

Answers: 1–b; 2–The most common cause of infertility in men is production of too few sperm, and the most common cause of infertility in women is blockage of the fallopian tubes; 3–d; 4–The major trend in U.S. adoption is a decline in the number of never-married women who adopt out their babies.; 5–c; 6–Humans have 23 pairs of chromosomes. Of those, 22 are autosomes and 1 is/are sex chromosomes. Males are XY and females are XX; 7–d; 8–b; 9–d; 10–c; 11–c; 12–d; 13–genes; 14–b; 15–b; 16–b; 17–Temperament traits shown to be impacted by genetics include behavioral regulation, activity, sociability, emotionality, and neuroticism; 18–d

What's to Come

©Pixtal/AGE fotostock

n 1971 writer Michael Dorris adopted a 3-year-old Sioux boy whose mother drank heavily during her pregnancy. The boy, Abel, was small for his age, was not toilet trained, and could speak only about 20 words. Dorris was convinced that with a positive environment, the young child could catch up. Unfortunately, the damage was too great. At 4, Abel was still in diapers and weighed only 27 pounds. He could not remember his playmates' names; he was hyperactive; and he had severe, inexplicable seizures. As he entered primary school, he had difficulty learning tasks such as counting or identifying primary colors, and he tested as having an IQ in the 60s. Although he eventually learned to read and write, he was never able to add, subtract, count money, or complete other essential life tasks.

By the time Abel Dorris became a teen, the medical community had identified the origin of his difficulties: *fetal alcohol syndrome (FAS)*. High levels of prenatal alcohol exposure cause brain damage and harm other body organs. There is no cure. Abel's story is a devastating reminder of prospective biological parents' responsibility for the crucial development that goes on before birth. The womb is the developing child's first environment. In this chapter, we look at prenatal development, tracing how the fertilized ovum becomes an embryo and then a fetus, environmental factors that can affect the child-to-be, and techniques for determining whether development is proceeding normally.

• • • •

Stages of Prenatal Development

Ethan and Sophia had decided to try to become pregnant. One Tuesday morning, Sophia woke up feeling no different than she had on any other day. However, deep inside her body within her fallopian tubes, a tiny sperm had broken through her egg's defenses and conception had occurred. While Sophia did not know it at the time, the tiny fertilized egg had begun a 9-month gestation journey after which, if all went well, a newborn child would be delivered into her arms.

PRINCIPLES OF GROWTH

The prenatal period of development, between conception and birth, is called **gestation**. The normal range of gestation is 37 to 41 weeks (Martin et al., 2009). Prenatal development takes place in three stages: germinal, embryonic, and fetal. During these stages, the fertilized ovum, or *zygote*, grows into an embryo and then a fetus. (Table 3.1 summarizes the stages of prenatal development.)

Both before and after birth, development proceeds according to two fundamental principles: growth and motor development occur from the top down and from the center of the body outward. The **cephalocaudal principle**, from

Latin, meaning "head to tail," dictates that development proceeds from the head to the lower part of the trunk. An embryo's head, brain, and eyes develop earliest and are disproportionately large until the other parts catch up. At 2 months of gestation, the embryo's head is half the length of the body. By the time of birth, the head is only one-fourth the length of the body but is still disproportionately large. According to the **proximodistal principle**, from Latin, meaning "near to far," development proceeds from parts near the center of the body to outer ones. The embryo's head and trunk develop before the limbs, and the arms and legs before the fingers and toes.

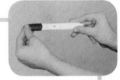
THE GERMINAL STAGE

The **germinal stage** includes the first two weeks of development after fertilization. During this time, the zygote divides, becomes more complex, and is implanted in the wall of the uterus (Figure 3.1).

Within 36 hours after fertilization, the zygote enters a period of rapid cell division and duplication, or *mitosis*. Some 72 hours after fertilization, it has divided into 16 to 32 cells; 24 hours later it has 64 cells.

While the fertilized ovum is dividing, it is also making its way down the fallopian tube to the uterus, a journey of 3 or 4 days. Its form changes into a *blastocyst*, a fluid-filled sphere that floats freely in the uterus until the 6th day after fertilization, when it begins to implant itself in the uterine wall. Where the egg implants will determine the placement of the placenta.

gestation The prenatal period of development, between conception and birth.

cephalocaudal principle Principle that development proceeds in a head-to-tail direction; that is, that upper parts of the body develop before lower parts of the trunk.

proximodistal principle Principle that development proceeds from within to without; that is, that parts of the body near the center develop before the extremities.

germinal stage First 2 weeks of prenatal development, characterized by rapid cell division, increasing complexity and differentiation, and implantation in the wall of the uterus.

TABLE 3.1 Milestones in Prenatal Development

Age	Accomplishments
3 weeks	Nervous system begins to form
4 weeks	Heart begins to beat
5 weeks	Head continues rapid growth
8 weeks	Almost all body parts are differentiated
12 weeks	Growth of head slows Formation of red blood cells by liver slows
14 weeks	Begins to coordinate limb movement
16 weeks	Possible to visually determine baby's sex Ultrasound shows clearly defined bone structure
20 weeks	Possible to hear heartbeat with stethoscope Baby covered by fine downy hair called lanugo Fetal movements called quickening are felt by mother
21 weeks	Rapid eye movements commence Substantial weight gain
24 weeks	Fingernails can be seen
28 weeks	Eyes open and close Lungs capable of breathing
32 weeks	Skin pink and smooth Chubby appearance
38 weeks	Nervous system can carry out some integrative functions Reacts to light Usually assumes upside-down position as birth approaches

1 month
©Biophoto Associates/Science Source

3 months
©Science Pictures Ltd/Science Photo Library/Getty Images

5 months
©James Stevenson/Science Source

Source: G. Leifer, *Introduction to maternity and pediatric nursing.* St. Louis: Saunders, 2003; K. Moore & T. Persaud, *Before we are born: Essentials for embryology and birth defects.* Philadelphia: Saunders, 2003; and D. Olds, M. London & P. Ladewig, *Maternal-newborn nursing.* Reading, MA: Addison-Wesley, 1996.

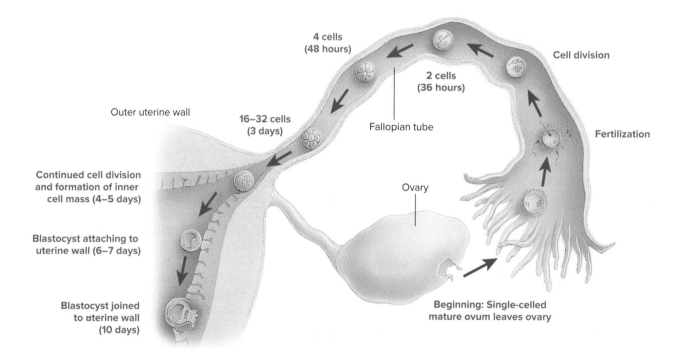

FIGURE 3.1 Early Development of a Human Embryo

This simplified diagram shows the progress of the ovum as it leaves the ovary, is fertilized in the fallopian tube, and then divides while traveling to the lining of the uterus. Now a blastocyst, it is implanted in the uterus, where it will grow larger and more complex until it is ready to be born.

FIGURE 3.2 The Developing Embryo

Throughout its development, the embryo (here approximately 6 weeks gestational age) is enclosed and cushioned by the expandable, fluid-filled amniotic cavity. The umbilical cord develops to contain the embryonic blood vessels that carry blood to and from the placenta. Diffusion across the chorionic villi removes wastes from the embryonic blood and adds nutrients and oxygen without commingling of maternal and embryonic blood.

©Brand X Pictures/PunchStock

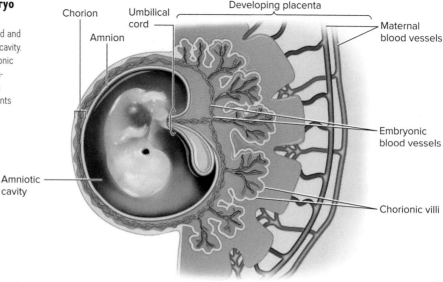

Chorion
Umbilical cord
Amnion
Developing placenta
Maternal blood vessels
Embryonic blood vessels
Chorionic villi
Amniotic cavity

Only about 10 to 20 percent of fertilized ova complete the task of implantation and continue to develop.

Before implantation, as cell differentiation begins, some cells around the edge of the blastocyst cluster on one side to form the *embryonic disk*, a thickened cell mass from which the embryo begins to develop. This mass is already differentiating into two layers. The upper layer, the *ectoderm*, will become the outer layer of skin, the nails, hair, teeth, sensory organs, and the nervous system, including the brain and spinal cord. The lower layer, the *endoderm*, will become the digestive system, liver, pancreas, salivary glands, and respiratory system. Later, a middle layer, the *mesoderm*, will develop and differentiate into the inner layer of skin, muscles, skeleton, and the excretory and circulatory systems.

Other parts of the blastocyst begin to develop into organs that will nurture and protect the embryo (Figure 3.2). The *amniotic sac* is a fluid-filled membrane that encases the developing embryo, giving it room to move. The *placenta*, which contains both maternal and embryonic tissue, develops in the uterus to allow oxygen, nourishment, and wastes to pass between mother and embryo. It is connected to the embryo by the *umbilical cord*. Nutrients from the mother pass from her blood to the embryonic blood vessels and are then carried, via the umbilical cord, to the embryo. In turn, embryonic blood vessels in the umbilical cord carry embryonic wastes to the placenta, where they can be eliminated by maternal blood vessels. The mother and embryo's circulatory systems are not directly linked, instead this exchange occurs by diffusion across the blood vessel walls. The placenta also helps to combat internal infection and gives the unborn child immunity to various diseases. It produces the hormones that support pregnancy, prepare the mother's breasts for lactation, and eventually stimulate the uterine contractions that will expel the baby from the mother's body.

THE EMBRYONIC STAGE

Sophia woke up one morning with sore breasts. Oddly, her much-loved morning coffee did not smell good; in fact, the smell of it made her feel slightly nauseated. Some hours later she realized these might be early signs of pregnancy—and a pregnancy test later that day indicated that a conception had indeed occurred. Sophia had entered the embroyonic stage, when most women first realize they are pregnant.

During the **embryonic stage**, from about 2 to 8 weeks, the organs and major body systems—respiratory, digestive, and nervous—develop rapidly. Because the major organ systems and overall body structure are in the process of forming (organogenesis), the embryo is most vulnerable during this time (Figure 3.3). Defects that occur at this point in the pregnancy are likely to be more serious than those that occur later.

embryonic stage Second stage of prenatal development (2 to 8 weeks), characterized by rapid growth and development of major body systems and organs.

spontaneous abortion Natural expulsion from the uterus of an embryo that cannot survive outside the womb; also called *miscarriage.*

The most severely defective embryos usually do not survive beyond the first *trimester*, or 3-month period, of pregnancy. A **spontaneous abortion,** commonly called a *miscarriage,* is the expulsion from the uterus of an embryo or fetus that is unable to survive outside the womb. A miscarriage that occurs after 20 weeks of gestation is generally characterized as a stillbirth. Because many spontaneous abortions occur before a woman realizes she is pregnant, it is difficult to estimate rates. But, as many as 1 in 4 recognized pregnancies end in miscarriage. Estimates are that this results in approximately 1 million fetal deaths each year in the United States alone (MacDorman & Gregory, 2015). Most miscarriages occur during the first trimester (American College of Obstetricians and Gynecologists, 2015) and 50 to 70 percent involve chromosomal abnormalities (Hogge, 2003). Smoking, drinking alcohol, and drug use

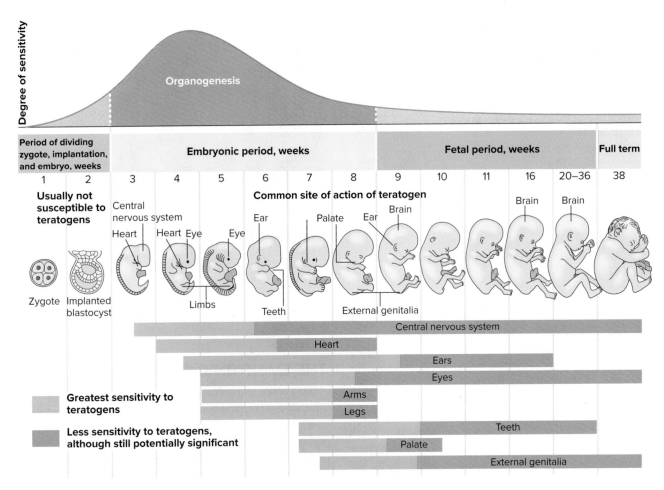

FIGURE 3.3 **Sensitive Periods in Prenatal Development**

fetal stage Final stage of prenatal development (from 8 weeks to birth), characterized by increased differentiation of body parts and greatly enlarged body size.

increase the risks of miscarriage, especially later in the pregnancy. Miscarriages are more common in African American women and American Indian or Alaska Native women and in both young and older (greater than 35 years of age) mothers; they are also more likely to occur in pregnancies involving twins or higher order multiples (MacDorman & Gregory, 2015).

Males are more likely than females to be spontaneously aborted or to be *stillborn* (dead at or after the 20th week of gestation). Thus, although about 125 males are conceived for every 100 females—a fact that has been attributed to the greater mobility of sperm carrying the smaller Y chromosome—only about 105 boys are born for every 100 girls (Martin, Hamilton, Osterman, Driscoll & Drake, 2018). Males' greater vulnerability continues after birth: More die early in life, and at every age they are more susceptible to many disorders. As a result, there are only about 97 males for every 100 females in the United States (U.S. Census Bureau, 2018).

Did you know?

Most miscarriages occur early in the pregnancy—before a heartbeat can be heard. Women often agonize over their choices and the things they did or did not do when they lose a pregnancy. However, most early miscarriages—by some estimates as much as 70 percent—are due to chromosomal abnormalities; these pregnancies were never viable. Miscarriage later in pregnancy, however, are more likely to be the result of smoking, drinking alcohol, or drug use.

©Adam Gault/agefotostock

THE FETAL STAGE

Sophia and Ethan had visited their obstetrician at seven weeks gestation, and they heard for the first time the tiny, rapid heartbeat of their developing baby. Once that milestone has been passed, the chances of miscarriage drop dramatically. Sophia and Ethan now knew their chances of having a healthy baby born in approximately seven months were high. They had entered the fetal period of development.

The appearance of the first bone cells at about 8 weeks signals the beginning of the **fetal stage**, the final stage of gestation. During this period, the fetus grows rapidly to

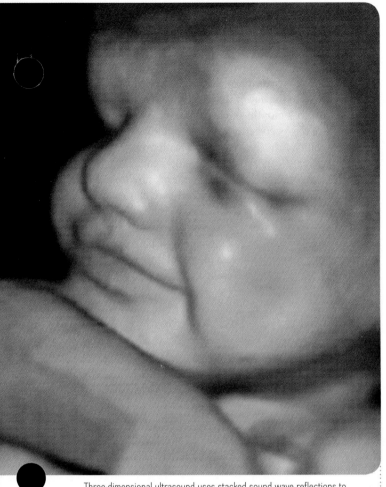

Three-dimensional ultrasound uses stacked sound wave reflections to produce a computer-aided image of the developing fetus.

©LookatSciences/Medical Images

facial events) at 36 weeks of gestation (Reissland, Francis & Mason, 2013).

Scientists can observe fetal movement through **ultrasound**, high-frequency sound waves that allow them to detect the outline of the fetus. Other instruments can monitor heart rate, changes in activity level, states of sleep and wakefulness, and cardiac reactivity.

ultrasound Prenatal medical procedure using high-frequency sound waves to detect the outline of a fetus and its movements; used to determine whether a pregnancy is progressing normally.

neurons Nerve cells.

The movements and activity level of fetuses show marked individual differences, and their heart rates vary in regularity and speed. There also are differences between males and females. Male fetuses, regardless of size, are more active and tend to move more vigorously than female fetuses throughout gestation (Almli, Ball & Wheeler, 2001). Thus infant boys' tendency to be more active than girls may be at least partly inborn (DiPietro et al., 2002).

Beginning during the 8th week of gestation, an estimated 250,000 immature **neurons**—nerve cells—are produced every minute. The number of neurons increases most rapidly between the 25th week of gestation and the first few months after birth. Originally the neurons are simply cell bodies with a nucleus, or center, composed of deoxyribonucleic acid (DNA), which contains the cell's genetic programming. As the brain grows, these rudimentary cells migrate to various parts of the brain (Bystron, Rakic, Molnar & Blakemore, 2006). Most of the neurons in the higher areas of the brain are in place by 20 weeks of gestation, and the structure becomes fairly well defined during the next 12 weeks.

From about the 12th week of gestation, the fetus swallows and inhales some of the amniotic fluid in which it floats. Mature taste cells appear at about 14 weeks of gestation. The olfactory system, which controls the sense of smell, also is well developed before birth (Savage, Fisher & Birch, 2007). The amniotic fluid contains substances that cross the placenta from the mother's bloodstream and enter the fetus's bloodstream.

Fetuses respond to the mother's voice and heartbeat and the vibrations of her body, suggesting that they can hear and feel. Responses to sound and vibration seem to begin at 26 weeks of gestation, increase, and then reach a plateau at about 32 weeks (Kisilevsky & Haines, 2010; Kisilevsky, Muir & Low, 1992). Voices, especially women's voices, and particularly those of the mother, seem to be particularly relevant for fetuses. For example, heart rate data indicate that fetuses prefer their mother's voice to those of other women

about 20 times its previous length, organs and body systems become more complex, and the fetus puts on a layer of fat in preparation for birth. Right up to that moment, "finishing touches" such as fingernails, toenails, and eyelashes continue to develop.

Fetuses are not passive passengers in their mothers' wombs. They breathe, kick, turn, flex their bodies, do somersaults, squint, swallow, make fists, hiccup, and suck their thumbs. The flexible membranes of the uterine walls and amniotic sac, which surround the protective buffer of amniotic fluid, permit and stimulate limited movement, and after approximately 16 to 25 weeks of gestation, the movements are strong enough for expectant mothers to detect them. Fetal movement is positively related to later well-being and developmental outcomes (Mesbah et al., 2011). Fetuses also can feel pain, but it is unlikely they do so before the third trimester. This is because many of the relevant structures, most notably the cortex (where consciousness is believed to reside), are immature at this point (Bellieni & Buonocore, 2012). For example, the thalamocortical pathways responsible for pain perception do not appear to be functional until the 29th to 30th week (Kostovic & Judas, 2010). Moreover, facial expressions of pain are almost absent at 24 weeks (5 percent of facial events), but appear more frequently (21.2 percent of

Did you know?

There are indications that early exposure to different flavors in the amniotic fluid may influence later taste preferences (Beauchamp & Mennella, 2009).

©lynx/iconotec.com/Glow Images

A fetus near full term responds to music and voices. A neonate prefers female voices to male voices and shows a preference for her or his own mother's voice.

©Jim Arbogast/Purestock/SuperStock

Influences on Prenatal Development

Generally, we think of environmental influences as those that occur once we are born. However, it is important to remember that on the day of their birth, infants have already been exposed to 9 months of environmental influences, and this exposure has occurred during a period of rapid growth and vulnerability. A healthy pregnancy with proper nutrition and prenatal care can promote development and put the newborn on an optimal path. However, exposure to harmful substances or suboptimal nutrition and care can result in a baby being born vulnerable and at risk. Here, we consider the primary source of early environmental influences—the mother. We also consider the influences of paternal factors in a pregnancy, which, while less pivotal in development, can nonetheless impact the developing child.

MATERNAL FACTORS

In traditional societies, pregnancy is recognized as a dangerous time for both a woman and her unborn baby. Among the Beng of West Africa's Ivory Coast, for example, a woman who has "taken a belly" is warned to stay away from corpses, lest her baby be born diseased; not to offend someone who might curse her pregnancy; and not to eat certain foods, such as pureed yams, lest her labor be difficult (Gottlieb, 2000). Some of these folk beliefs may have a basis in fact. The prenatal environment is the mother's body, and virtually everything that affects her well-being, from her diet to her moods, may alter her unborn child's environment and influence its growth and health.

Alcohol, bacteria from spoiled food, and even the hormones produced by a highly stressed pregnant mother's body can all have negative effects on a developing fetus. They are examples of **teratogens**, environmental agents, such as a virus, a drug, or radiation, which can interfere with normal prenatal development. Teratogens have their most damaging effects on systems that are developing during the time that the exposure occurs (refer back to Figure 3.3). In other words, there are sensitive periods of development during which exposure to teratogens will cause maximal harm.

Not all environmental hazards are equally risky for all fetuses. Sometimes vulnerability may depend on a gene either in the fetus or in the mother. For example, fetuses with a particular variant of a growth gene, called *transforming growth factor alpha*, have greater risk than other fetuses of developing a cleft palate if the mother smokes while pregnant (Zeiger Beaty & Liang, 2005). The timing of exposure (refer back to Figure 3.3), the dose, duration, and interaction with other teratogenic factors also may make a difference.

Nutrition and Maternal Weight

Pregnant women typically need 300 to 500 additional calories a day, including extra protein. Women of normal weight and body build who gain 16 to 40 pounds are less likely to

(Jardri et al., 2012). In addition, fetuses nearing full term recognize the voice of their mother (Voegtline, Costigan, Pater & DiPietro, 2013) prefer it to that of their father (Lee & Kisilevsky, 2014). While fetuses, starting at approximately 33 weeks of gestation, orient toward and attend to music (Kisilevsky, Hains, Jacquet, Granier-Deferre & Lecanuet, 2004), speech is a stronger draw. Near-term fetuses exposed to either music or speech show heart rate changes consistent with more focused attention toward and increased processing for music over speech (Granier-Deferre, Ribiero, Jacquet & Bassareau, 2011). Once born, neonates prefer female voices to male voices and their mother's native language to other languages (Pino, 2016) as illustrated by their willingness to suck longer on a modified pacifier rigged to play a tape as long they suck on it. Hungry infants, no matter on which side they are held, turn toward the breast in the direction from which they hear the mother's voice (Noirot & Algeria, 1983). A preference for the mother's voice may have an evolutionary survival function: to help newborns locate the source of food.

Fetuses learn and remember as they near the end of the pregnancy. Heart rate data indicate that fetuses have some ability to remember auditory material for short periods of time (Pino, 2016). Current estimates suggest that fetal memory begins to function at approximately 30 weeks, when fetuses are able to hold information in memory for 10 minutes. By 34 weeks, they are able to remember information for a period of 1 month (Dirix, Nijhuis, Jongsma & Hornstra, 2009). Moreover, fetuses not only remember and recognize voices, but they also have some limited ability to reproduce them. In one study, newborn infants used distinctly different intonation patterns in their cries that mirrored aspects of their mothers' native language (Mampe, Friederici, Christophe & Wermke, 2009).

teratogen Environmental agent, such as a virus, a drug, or radiation, that can interfere with normal prenatal development and cause developmental abnormalities.

have birth complications or to bear babies whose weight at birth is dangerously low or overly high. Yet about 1 in 3 mothers gain more or less than the recommended amounts (Martin et al., 2009). If a woman does not gain enough, her baby is likely to suffer growth retardation in the womb, to be born prematurely, to experience distress during labor and delivery, or to die at or near birth. Interestingly, some research indicates that not eating enough calories during pregnancy might put children at risk for later obesity, perhaps by setting their metabolism to burn fewer calories (Caballero, 2006). A woman who gains too much weight risks having a large baby that needs to be delivered by induced labor or surgically by cesarean section (Martin et al., 2009). In addition, very large babies are more likely to become overweight or obese later in life (Hillier et al., 2008).

Desirable weight gain depends on body mass index (BMI) before pregnancy. Women who are overweight or obese before becoming pregnant or in the early months of pregnancy tend to have longer deliveries, need more health care services (Chu et al., 2008), and are more likely to bear infants with birth defects (Gilboa et al., 2009; Stothard, Tennant, Bell & Rankin, 2009). Obesity also increases the risk of other complications of pregnancy, including miscarriage, difficulty inducing labor, and a greater likelihood of cesarean delivery (Brousseau, 2006; Chu et al., 2008). Current recommendations are that women who are underweight should gain 28 to 40 pounds, normal weight women should gain 25 to 35 pounds, overweight women should gain 15 to 25 pounds, and obese women should gain only 11 to 20 pounds (American College of Obstetrics and Gynecology, 2013).

While appropriate weight gain is an important factor in the health of a pregnancy, it is not the only factor. What an expectant mother eats is also important. For example, an omega-E fatty acid, docosahexaenoic acid (DHA) found in certain fish, such as Atlantic salmon and tuna, has been found to impact a variety of outcomes. DHA is found in the central nervous system and the retina of the eye, and it is believed to be important to the development of these areas (Bradbury, 2011). One mechanism of action may be its direct influence. For example, newborns whose mothers consumed DHA showed more mature sleep patterns, a sign of advanced development, than infants whose mothers' blood had lower levels of DHA (Cheruku, Montgomery-Downs, Farkas, Thoman & Lammie-Keefe, 2002), and also were more attentive at 12 and 18 months (Colombo et al., 2004). There are also effects on the health of the pregnancy. Mothers who consume higher levels of DHA are more likely to have heavier babies (a sign of good health) and longer gestational periods, and are at decreased risk of preterm birth (Carlson et al., 2013; Salvig & Lamont, 2011).

Folic acid, or folate (a B vitamin), found in leafy vegetables and in fortified cereals, is critical in a pregnant woman's diet. Inadequate levels of folic acid can leave babies at risk of developing a neurological defect such as anencephaly, a condition in which the brain is formed incompletely or improperly, or spina bifida, a condition in which the baby's spinal cord is not fully enclosed. Addition of folic acid to enriched grain products has been mandatory in the United States since 1998, reducing the incidence of these defects by approximately 1,300 children a year (Williams et al., 2015). Milder folic acid deficiencies in pregnant mothers can result in less severe, but still troubling problems. For example, low folate levels during pregnancy have been associated with later attention-deficit/hyperactivity in 7- to 9-year-old children (Schlotz et al., 2009).

Women of childbearing age are urged to eat plentiful fresh fruits or vegetables or take a folate supplement even before getting pregnant as damage can occur during the early weeks of gestation (American Academy of Pediatrics [AAP] Committee on Genetics, 1999). It is estimated that if all women took 5 milligrams of folic acid each day before pregnancy and during the first trimester an estimated 85 percent of neural-tube defects could be prevented (Wald, 2004).

Malnutrition

Malnutrition is a global problem that affects millions of people a year. Worldwide, approximately 800 million people suffer from calorie deficiency, and 2 billion suffer from micronutrient deficiency (International Food Policy Research Institute,

Did you know?

For many years it was a mystery why China had the highest incidence of anencephaly and spina bifida. The reason? Traditionally, Chinese couples marry in January or February and try to conceive as soon as possible. Thus their pregnancies often begin in the winter, when rural women have little access to fresh fruits and vegetables, important sources of folic acid. Programs to give folic acid supplements to pregnant mothers have drastically reduced the incidence of these birth defects in China (Berry et al., 1999).

©Getty Images

2016). Micronutrients are vitamins or minerals that are needed in small quantities, but have a profound negative effect if absent. Either form of malnutrition during pregnancy is an urgent issue as it can not only hurt the expectant mother and her child, but also exert effects across generations (Martorell & Zongrone, 2012). For example, children who are malnourished in early childhood can be stunted, and this stunting, in women, is associated with a higher risk of birth complications (Black et al., 2008) and the birth of smaller babies (Victora et al., 2008).

Some expectant mothers suffer from a calorie deficit. This can result in fetal growth restriction and low birth weight. Additionally, babies born to mothers who do not consume sufficient calories have a higher risk of death and surviving babies may be stunted (Black et al., 2013). Expectant mothers can also suffer from micronutrient deficiencies in vitamins or minerals. For example, vitamin A and zinc deficiencies result in a higher risk of death for both child and mother (Black et al., 2013) and babies born to mothers with a vitamin D deficiency may suffer from weak or soft bones (Anastasiou, Karras, Bais, Grant, Kotsa & Goulis, 2017).

It is important to identify malnutrition early in pregnancy so that it can be treated. Malnourished women who take caloric dietary supplements while pregnant tend to have bigger, healthier, more active, and more visually alert infants (Brown, 1987; Vuori et al., 1979; Imdad & Bhutta, 2011). Similarly, micronutrient supplementation for malnourished expectant mothers results in larger babies and fewer stillbirths (Haider & Bhutta, 2012).

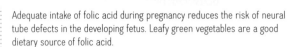

Adequate intake of folic acid during pregnancy reduces the risk of neural tube defects in the developing fetus. Leafy green vegetables are a good dietary source of folic acid.
©rubberball/Getty Images

Physical Activity and Strenuous Work

Among the Ifaluk of the Western Caroline Islands, women are advised not to harvest crops during the first 7 months of pregnancy, when the developing fetus is thought to be weak, but resume manual labor during the last 2 months to encourage a speedy delivery (Le, 2000). Actually, moderate exercise any time during pregnancy does not seem to endanger the fetuses of healthy women. Regular exercise prevents constipation and improves respiration, circulation, muscle tone, and skin elasticity, all of which contribute to a more comfortable pregnancy and an easier, safer delivery (Committee on Obstetric Practice, 2002). However, strenuous working conditions, occupational fatigue, and long working hours may be associated with a greater risk of premature birth (Bell, Zimmerman & Diehr, 2008).

acquired immune deficiency syndrome (AIDS) Viral disease that undermines effective functioning of the immune system.

The American College of Obstetricians and Gynecologists (2016) recommends that women in low-risk pregnancies should be guided by their own abilities and stamina. The safest course seems to be for pregnant women to exercise moderately, not pushing themselves and not raising their heart rate above 150, and, as with any exercise, to taper off at the end of each session rather than stop abruptly.

Maternal Illnesses

Both prospective parents should try to avoid all infections, including common colds and flu. A mother who does contract an infection should have it treated promptly. Among the diseases that can cause serious problems for her offspring are AIDS, rubella, toxoplasmosis, Zika, and diabetes.

Acquired immune deficiency syndrome (AIDS) is a disease caused by the human immunodeficiency virus (HIV), which undermines functioning of the immune system. An infected mother can pass the virus to the fetus's bloodstream through the placenta during pregnancy, labor, or delivery, or after birth through breast milk. The biggest risk factor for HIV transmission is a mother who is unaware she has it. In the United States, new pediatric AIDS cases have declined steadily since 1992 due to routine testing and treatment of pregnant women and newborn babies and to advances in the prevention, detection, and treatment of HIV infection in infants. The risk of transmission also can be reduced by choosing cesarean delivery, especially when an infected woman has not been treated for HIV, and by promotion of alternatives to breast-feeding among high-risk women (CDC, 2006a).

Rubella (German measles), if contracted by a woman before her 11th week of pregnancy, is almost certain to cause deafness and heart defects in her baby. Chances of catching rubella during pregnancy have been greatly reduced in Europe and the United States since the late 1960s, when a vaccine was developed that is now routinely administered to infants and children. Recent efforts in less developed countries to provide rubella vaccinations have resulted in a decrease of more than 80 percent of reported rubella from 2000 to 2009 (Reef, Strebel, Dabbagh, Gacic-Dobo & Cochi, 2011). However, the United States has seen a recent recurrence of rubella. These outbreaks most likely stem from the importation of the disease from international travel. Most of the people who were infected were not vaccinated (Clemmons et al., 2015).

An infection called *toxoplasmosis*, caused by a parasite harbored in the bodies of cattle, sheep, and pigs, and in the intestinal tracts of cats, typically produces either no symptoms or symptoms like those of the common cold. In an expectant woman, however, especially in the 2nd and 3rd trimesters of

Toxoplasmosis is an infection that is dangerous to a developing fetus. It can be carried in the intestinal tract of cats, so pregnant women should avoid emptying or cleaning a litter box.

©Andrey_Kuzmin/Shutterstock

pregnancy, it can cause fetal brain damage, severely impaired eyesight or blindness, seizures, miscarriage, stillbirth, or death of the baby. If the baby survives, there may be later problems, including eye infections, hearing loss, and learning disabilities. Treatment with antiparasitic drugs during the first year of life

Moderate, regular exercise is beneficial for pregnant women and does not seem to endanger the fetus.

©Tanya Constantine/Blend Images

can reduce brain and eye damage (McLeod et al., 2006). To avoid infection, expectant mothers should not eat raw or rare meat, should peel or thoroughly wash raw fruits and vegetables, and should not dig in a garden where cat feces may be buried. Women who have a cat can have it checked for the disease and should have someone else empty the litter box (March of Dimes Foundation, 2012).

In early 2015, an epidemic of a mosquito-borne illness called Zika originated in Brazil, and from there it spread rapidly to other countries in South America, Central America, the Caribbean, and North America. In adults, the Zika virus results in relatively mild symptoms, including a fever, rash, headache, joint pain, red eyes, and muscle pain. The symptoms generally abate quickly, and most adults recover easily (Centers for Disease Control, 2017). However, pregnant women who become infected with the virus are more likely to give birth to a baby with microcephaly, an abnormally small head, as well as other structural abnormalities. Additionally, many of these babies suffer from seizures, developmental delays, motor abnormalities, feeding problems, and hearing and vision problems (Centers for Disease Control, 2017). Estimates are that approximately 6 percent of mothers infected during pregnancy will give birth to an affected baby, a number that rises to 11 percent if the infection occurs during the first trimester (Honein et al., 2017). While Zika infection can result from travel to tropical locations, it has been found within the continental United States as well (Shapiro-Mendoza et al., 2017). There is currently no treatment for Zika, thus recommendations focus on prevention, especially with respect to the prevention of mosquito bites. Pregnant women are advised against traveling to countries where Zika is prevalent, and, when in areas with mosquitos, encouraged to use repellent and wear long-sleeved shirts and pants.

Offspring of mothers with diabetes are 3 to 4 times more likely than offspring of other women to develop a wide range of birth defects (Correa et al., 2008). Research on mice suggests why: High blood glucose levels, typical in diabetics, deprive an embryo of oxygen, with resulting cell damage, during the first 8 weeks of pregnancy when its organs are forming. Women with diabetes need to be sure their blood glucose levels are in the normal range before becoming pregnant (Li, Chase, Jung, Smith, & Loeken, 2005). Use of multivitamin supplements during the first 3 months of pregnancy can help reduce the risk of diabetes-associated birth defects (Correa, Botto, Liu, Mulinare & Erickson, 2003).

Maternal Anxiety and Stress

Some tension and worry during pregnancy are normal and do not necessarily increase risks of birth complications (Littleton, Breitkopf & Berenson, 2006). Moderate maternal anxiety may even spur organization of the developing brain. In one study, newborns whose mothers experienced moderate levels of both positive and negative stress showed signs of accelerated neurological development (DiPietro et al., 2010). In a series of studies, 2-year-olds whose mothers had shown moderate anxiety midway through pregnancy scored higher on measures of motor and mental development than did age-mates whose mothers had not shown anxiety during pregnancy (DiPietro, 2004; DiPietro, Novak, Costigan, Atella & Reusing, 2006).

However, unusual or extreme maternal stress during pregnancy may have harmful effects on the unborn child (Dingfelder, 2004; Huizink, Mulder & Buitelaar, 2004). For example, a mother's self-reported stress and anxiety during pregnancy has been associated with more active and irritable temperament in newborns (DiPietro et al., 2010), inattentiveness during a developmental assessment in 8-month-olds (Huizink, Robles de Medina, Mulder, Visser & Buitelaar, 2002), and negative emotionality or behavioral disorders in early childhood (Martin, Noyes, Wisenbaker & Huttunen, 2000; O'Connor, Heron, Golding, Beveridge & Glover, 2002). Additionally, chronic stress can result in preterm delivery, perhaps through the action of elevated levels of stress hormones (which are implicated in the onset of labor) or the resulting dampened immune functioning, which makes women more vulnerable to inflammatory diseases and infection that can also trigger labor (Schetter, 2009).

Depression may have also have negative effects on development. Children of mothers who were depressed during pregnancy were more likely to be born premature (Grogoriadis et al., 2013), be developmentally delayed as toddlers (Deave, Heron, Evants & Emond, 2008) and show elevated levels of violent and antisocial behaviors in adolescence (Hay, Pawlby, Waters, Perra & Sharp, 2010).

Maternal Age

Birthrates of U.S. women in their thirties and forties are at their highest levels since the 1960s, in part due to fertility treatments—an example of a history-graded influence (Martin et al., 2010). From 2000 to 2014, there was a 23 percent increase in first births for women over the age of 35 years, for all ethnic and racial groups, and in all states (Mathews & Hamilton, 2016).

Tina Fey, a successful comedian and writer, had her two daughters at ages 35 and 41.
©Lawrence Schwartzwald/Splash New/Newscom

The chance of miscarriage or stillbirth rises with maternal age and reaches 90 percent for women age 45 or older. Women 30 to 35 are more likely to suffer complications due to diabetes, high blood pressure, or severe bleeding. There is also higher risk of premature delivery, retarded fetal growth, birth defects, and chromosomal abnormalities, such as Down syndrome. However, due to widespread screening among older expectant mothers, fewer babies with malformations are born today (Heffner, 2004).

Adolescent mothers tend to have premature or underweight babies—perhaps because a young girl's still-growing body consumes vital nutrients the fetus needs (Martin et al., 2007) or, more likely, because of inadequate or missing prenatal care (Malabarey, Balayla,

Klam, Shrim & Abenhaim, 2012). These newborns are at heightened risk of death in the first month, disabilities, or health problems. While rates of teen pregnancy in the United States have been in a steady, long-term decline, they are still among the highest of industrialized nations (Hamilton & Ventura, 2012).

Outside Environmental Hazards

Prenatal development can also be affected by air pollution, chemicals, radiation, extremes of heat and humidity, and other environmental factors. Pregnant women who regularly breathe air that contains high levels of fine combustion-related particles such as gas fumes and smoke are more likely to bear infants who are premature or undersized (Parker, Woodruff, Basu & Shoendorf, 2005; Pedersen et al., 2013) or have chromosomal abnormalities (Bocskay et al., 2005). Exposure to high concentrations of disinfection by-products is associated with low birth weight and congenital abnormalities (Nieuwenhuijsen, Dadvand, Grellier, Martinez & Vrijheid, 2013). Two insecticides, chlorpyrifos and diazinon, are associated with stunted prenatal growth (Whyatt et al., 2004).

Fetal exposure to low levels of environmental toxins, such as lead, mercury, and dioxin, as well as nicotine and ethanol, may help explain the sharp rise in asthma, allergies, and autoimmune disorders such as lupus (Dietert, 2005). Both maternal exposure to the hydrocarbons and the children's asthma symptoms were associated with epigenetic changes in the gene ACSL3, which affects the lungs (Perera et al., 2009). Childhood cancers, including leukemia, have been linked to pregnant mothers' drinking chemically contaminated groundwater (Boyles, 2002) and use of home pesticides (Menegaux et al., 2006). Infants exposed prenatally even to low levels of lead are born smaller and shorter than unexposed babies (Xie et al., 2013) and tend to show IQ deficits during childhood (Schnaas et al., 2006).

Women who have routine dental X-rays during pregnancy triple their risk of having full-term, low-birth-weight babies (Hujoel, Bollen, Noonan & del Aguila, 2004). In utero exposure to radiation has been linked to miscarriage, intellectual disabilities, small head size, increased cancer risk, and lowered IQ (Groen, Bay & Lim, 2012). The risk of problems from the single use of medical diagnostic procedures is low. However, in nuclear disasters, such as the Chernobyl or Fukishima Daiichi nuclear plant accidents in 1996 and 2011, where radiation exposure is high, pregnant women are likely to be at extremely elevated risk for adverse pregnancy outcomes (Groen, Bae & Lim, 2012).

Drug Intake

Almost everything an expectant mother takes in makes its way to the uterus. Drugs may cross the placenta, just as oxygen, carbon dioxide, and water do. Vulnerability is greatest in the first few months of gestation, when development is most rapid.

What are the effects of the use of specific drugs during pregnancy? Let's look at the influence of prescription drugs, then at alcohol, nicotine, and caffeine, and finally at the influence of marijuana, cocaine, and methamphetamine.

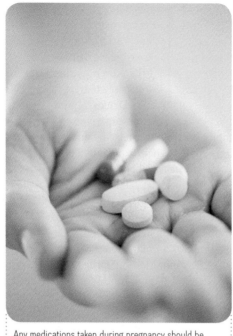

Any medications taken during pregnancy should be cleared with an obstetrician.
©JGI/Jamie Grill/Blend Images

Medical Drugs   Louisa was thrilled to have become pregnant, especially so soon after starting to try to conceive. However, she soon became incapacitated by severe morning sickness, throwing up multiple times over the course of the day. After meeting with her doctor about her nausea, he prescribed thalidomide, then a new drug. Louisa was relieved when her nausea and vomiting stopped. However, when her new baby was born with malformed arms and missing legs, it became clear that the drug did not come without a cost. Louisa's baby joined the roughly 12,000 babies born in the late 1950s with severe birth defects as a result of maternal ingestion of thalidomide during sensitive periods of development. The thalidomide disaster sensitized medical professionals and the public to the potential dangers of taking drugs while pregnant; since then, doctors and pregnant women alike have exercised great care in using medication during pregnancy.

Among the prescription drugs that may be harmful when taken during pregnancy are the antibiotic tetracycline; certain barbiturates, opiates, and other central nervous system depressants; several hormones, including diethylstilbestrol (DES)

Did you know?

While animal research has its place in medical testing, it also has limitations. Thalidomide was tested on animals before being prescribed for pregnant woman and indicated no ill effects. However, in humans, it quickly became clear that thalidomide was closely linked to major birth defects.
©sidsnapper/Getty Images

and androgens; certain anticancer drugs, such as methotrexate; Accutane, a drug often prescribed for severe acne (Briggs, Freeman & Yaffe, 2012; Koren, Pastuszak & Ito, 1998); drugs used to treat epilepsy (U.S Food and Drug Administration, 2011). Angiotensin-converting enzyme (ACE) inhibitors and nonsteroidal anti-inflammatory drugs (NSAIDs), such as naproxen and ibuprofen, have been linked to birth defects when taken any time from the first trimester on (Cooper et al., 2006; Ofori, Oraichi, Blais, Rey, & Berard, 2006). In addition, certain antipsychotic drugs used to manage severe psychiatric disorders may have potential effects on the fetus, including withdrawal symptoms at birth (Hudak & Tan, 2012; Einarson & Boskovic, 2009).

The AAP Committee on Drugs (2001) recommends that no medication be prescribed for a pregnant or breast-feeding woman unless it is essential for her health or her child's. When practical and consistent with controlling her symptoms, a woman should be withdrawn from psychiatric medication prior to conception. Infants whose mothers took antidepressants, such as Prozac, during pregnancy tend to show signs of disrupted neurobehavioral activity such as a tendency to startle easily and a decreased tendency to form a regular sleep cycle (Zeskind & Stephens, 2004), and are at increased risk of severe respiratory failure (Chambers et al., 2006). Certain drugs such as lithium that are used to manage severe psychiatric disorders may have serious potential effects on the fetus, including withdrawal symptoms at birth (AAP Committee on Drugs, 2000). If medication is necessary, the most effective drug with the fewest side effects should be selected. Pregnant women should not take over-the-counter drugs without consulting a doctor.

Research has shown that most psychiatric drugs administered to a lactating woman can be found in her breast milk. The concentration tends to be low, and therefore, there is little likelihood of an effect on the infant. Thus there appears to be no concrete evidence at the present time for recommending that a woman taking psychiatric medication avoid breast-feeding. However, it must be emphasized that a mother who chooses to breast-feed while on medication should observe the baby for signs of drug effects (AAP Committee on Drugs, 2001).

Opioids

In recent years, the number of pregnant women abusing legal and illegal opioids has risen (Martin, Longinaker & Terplan, 2015; Kocherlakota, 2014). While opioid use has not been implicated in birth defects, it is associated with small babies, fetal death, preterm labor, and aspiration of meconium (Center for Substance Abuse Treatment, 2008). Moreover, babies born to drug-addicted mothers are often addicted themselves and go through withdrawal once they are born and no longer receiving the drug. This results in neonate abstinence syndrome, a condition in which newborns may show sleep disturbances, tremors, difficulty regulating their bodies, irritability and crying, diarrhea, fever,

and feeding difficulties (Jansson & Velez, 2012). Long-term effects include deficiencies in growth as well as attentional, memory, and perceptual problems. However, studies on cognitive outcomes are conflicting, and results may be due to other variables (such as socioeconomic status or other drug use) that are correlated with opiate use (Behnke, Smith & Committee on Substance Abuse, 2013). Punitive measures such as jailing pregnant women who use these drugs have been shown to be ineffective. This has led to calls to address the opioid crisis in pregnant women as a public health problem rather than a law enforcement issue (Patrick & Schiff, 2017).

Alcohol Like Abel Dorris, whose story opened this chapter, as many as 5 in 1,000 infants born in the United States suffer from **fetal alcohol syndrome (FAS)**, a combination of retarded growth, facial and bodily malformations, and disorders of the central nervous system. Prenatal alcohol exposure is the most common cause of intellectual disability and the leading preventable cause of birth defects in the United States (Sacks, Gonzalez, Bouchery, Tomedi & Brewer, 2015).

The more the mother drinks, the greater the effects. Moderate or heavy drinking during pregnancy seems to disturb an infant's neurological and behavioral functioning; this may affect early social interaction with the mother, which is vital to emotional development (Hannigan & Armant, 2000). Heavy drinkers who continue to drink after becoming pregnant are likely to have babies with smaller skulls and brains than babies of nondrinking women or expectant mothers who stop drinking (Handmaker et al., 2006).

FAS problems can include, in infancy, reduced responsiveness to stimuli, slow reaction time, and reduced visual acuity (sharpness of vision) (Carter et al., 2005). FAS problems throughout childhood include short attention span, distractibility, restlessness, hyperactivity, learning disabilities, memory deficits, and mood disorders (Sokol et al., 2003), as well as aggressiveness and problem behavior (Sood et al., 2001). Some FAS problems recede after birth; but others, such as intellectual disability, behavioral and learning problems, and hyperactivity, tend to persist. Enriching these children's education or general environment does not always seem to enhance their cognitive development (Kerns, Don, Mateer & Streissguth, 1997), but recent interventions targeted at cognitive skills in children with FAS are showing promise (Paley & O'Connor, 2011). Children with FAS may be less likely to develop behavioral and mental health problems if they are diagnosed early and are reared in stable, nurturing environments (Streissguth et al., 2004).

Nicotine Maternal smoking has been identified as the single most important factor in low birth weight in developed countries (DiFranza, Aligne & Weitzman, 2004). Women who smoke during pregnancy are more than 1½ times as likely as nonsmokers to bear babies of low birth weight who are less than 5½ pounds at birth. While even light smoking (fewer than five cigarettes a day) is associated with a greater risk of low birth weight (Martin et al., 2007) the effect is dose dependent. Thus, those mothers who

The Centers for Disease Control estimates that approximately 8.4% of women smoke during pregnancy (Curtin & Mathews, 2016). Rates are highest among pregnant women with less than a high school education and those who do not receive early prenatal care.
©Monkey Business Images Ltd/Getty Images

smoke more than 20 cigarettes a day have the smallest babies (Ko et al., 2014).

Tobacco use during pregnancy also brings increased risks of miscarriage, growth retardation, stillbirth, small head circumference, sudden infant death, colic (uncontrollable, extended crying for no apparent reason) in early infancy, hyperkinetic disorder (excessive movement), and long-term respiratory, neurological, cognitive, attentional, and behavioral problems (AAP Committee on Substance Abuse, 2001; DiFranza, Aligne & Weitzman, 2004; Froehlich et al., 2009; Linnet et al., 2005; Shah, Sullivan & Carter, 2006; Smith et al., 2006). The effects of prenatal exposure to secondhand smoke on development tend to be worse when children also experience socioeconomic hardship during the first 2 years of life (Rauh et al., 2004) when they are exposed to additional teratogens such as lead (Froehlich et al., 2009), or deprived of necessary nutrients such as folic acid (Mook-Kanamori et al., 2010) at the same time. However, not all fetuses respond in the same way. Some are more robust than others by virtue of their genotype and seem to be less affected by moderate maternal smoking (Price, Grosser,

Plomin & Jaffee, 2010). Secondhand smoke has similar effects and has been linked with low birth weight, infant respiratory infections, sudden infant death, and cancer in childhood and adulthood (Kharrazi et al., 2004).

Caffeine   Can the caffeine a pregnant woman consumes in coffee, tea, cola, or chocolate cause trouble for her fetus? Research results have been mixed. It does seem clear that caffeine is *not* a teratogen for human babies (Christian & Brent, 2001). However, studies have found a slightly increased risk of miscarriage, stillbirth, and low birth weight in mothers who consume caffeine while pregnant (Greenwood et al., 2014) and there are suggestions that risk may increase with dosage (Chen et al., 2014). Thus, while results are unclear, current recommendations on limiting caffeine to 200 milligrams or less (about one cup of coffee) are still in place.

Marijuana, Cocaine, and Methamphetamine   Marijuana is the most commonly used illegal drug during pregnancy, and rates of women who report using marijuana while pregnant have risen sharply in the last 10 years (Martin, Longinaker, Mark, Chisholm & Terplan, 2015), perhaps as a result of more liberal usage laws in many states. Research on marijuana is difficult. For example, many pregnant women who smoke marijuana also smoke cigarettes or consume alcohol, and socioeconomic factors also seem to be important (Metz & Stickrath, 2015). However, research does show that while marijuana exposure is not associated with low birth weight, preterm delivery (Mark, Desai & Terplan, 2016), or decreases in general intelligence (Behnke, Smith & Committee on Substance Abuse, 2013), it has been implicated in subtle deficits in problem-solving skills (Fried, 2002), and learning and memory problems (Richardson, Ryan, Willford, Day & Goldschmidt, 2002). This may explain why marijuana exposure during the prenatal period is also associated with decreases in academic achievement (Goldschmidt, Richardson, Cornelius & Day, 2004).

Cocaine use during pregnancy has been associated with spontaneous abortion, delayed growth, premature labor, low birth weight, small head size, birth defects, and impaired neurological development (Chiriboga, Brust, Bateman & Hauser, 1999; March of Dimes Birth Defects Foundation, 2004a; Shankaran et al., 2004). In some studies, cocaine-exposed newborns show acute withdrawal symptoms and sleep disturbances (O'Brien & Jeffery, 2002). It appears that cocaine may preferentially affect areas of the brain involved in attention and executive functioning (Behnke et al., 2013). Other studies, however, have found no specific connection between prenatal cocaine exposure and physical, motor, cognitive, emotional, or behavioral deficits that could not also be attributed to other risk factors, such as low birth weight; exposure to tobacco, alcohol, or marijuana; or a poor home environment (Frank, Augustyn, Knight, Pell & Zuckerman, 2001; Messinger et al., 2004; Singer et al., 2004).

Prenatal methamphetamine exposure is associated with fetal growth restriction (Smith et al., 2006). Additionally, prenatal exposure to methamphetamines has been implicated in fetal brain damage to areas of the brain involved in learning, memory, and control (Roussotte et al., 2011). Methamphetamine-exposed children also have less white matter in their brains, a finding that has implications for the developmental delays commonly found in such children (Cloak, Ernst, Hedemark & Chang, 2009).

Early treatment for alcohol, nicotine, and other substance abuse can greatly improve health outcomes. Among 2,073 women enrolled in an early prenatal care program, risks of stillbirth, preterm delivery, low birth weight, and placental separation from the uterus were no higher than for a control group of 46,553 women with no evidence of substance abuse, whereas risks for 156 untreated substance abusers were dramatically higher (Goler, Armstrong, Taillac, & Osejo, 2008).

Drugs and Breast-feeding

There has been a great deal of research into the effects of drugs on prenatal development; however, far less data exist on the effects of the consumption of these substances during breast-feeding. A recent review indicates that approximately half of women in Western countries consume alcohol while breast-feeding. While alcohol does pass into breast milk, the amounts are equivalent to the mother's blood alcohol level. Thus, even in a case of theoretical binge drinking, infants would not be exposed to clinically relevant amounts of alcohol, even despite their slower rate of alcohol metabolism. Research has shown, however, that breast milk yield declines temporarily while drinking alcohol (Haastrup, Pottegard & Damkier, 2014). Of course, this discussion does not include the effects of alcohol consumption on the mother's behavior, which may be compromised if intake is excessive.

Other drugs may also be transmitted into breast milk. For example, antidepressants and anti-anxiety drugs have been detected at low levels in human breast milk (Fortinguerra, Clavenna & Bonati, 2009). Generally, recommendations for the use of medically prescribed drugs are that women are provided with information about the risks and benefits associated with each drug, and they can come to a decision in consultation with a health care provider. A number of variables should be assessed, such as whether the infant was born premature or has underlying medical conditions, the half-life of the drug (how long it takes the drug to leave the body), or whether data exist for that particular drug. For most drugs, the benefits of breast-feeding outweigh the risks of taking the drug (Sachs, 2013). For example, while anti-epileptic drug (AED) exposure in utero has been shown to be associated with cognitive impairment at 3 years of age (Meador et al., 2009), infants who breast-feed from mothers who take AEDs show no adverse effects on their cognitive processes. Additionally, when compared to infants who do not breast-feed, they show a cognitive advantage at 6 years of age (Meador et al., 2014).

PATERNAL FACTORS

Sophia was careful during her pregnancy to eat healthfully, and she diligently avoided alcohol and her favorite sushi restaurant. Did Ethan need to do the same thing? What is the father's role in early environmental influences?

While the woman's exposure to teratogens has a larger effect on a pregnancy, a man's exposure to deleterious substances can still exert an effect on it. A man's exposure to lead, marijuana, or tobacco smoke, large amounts of alcohol or radiation, DES, pesticides, or high ozone levels may result in abnormal or poor quality sperm (Sokol et al., 2006). Offspring of men working at a nuclear processing plant were at elevated risk of stillbirth (Parker, Pearce, Dickinson, Aitkin & Craft, 1999) and those born to men stationed on military vessels were at elevated risk of infant mortality and their mothers were at risk for dangerously high blood pressure during pregnancy (Baste et al., 2012). Babies whose fathers had diagnostic X-rays within the year before conception or had high lead exposure at work tended to have low birth weight and slowed fetal growth (Chen & Wang, 2006; Lin, Hwang, Marshall & Marion, 1998; Shea, Little & the ALSPAC Study Team, 1997).

Men who smoke have an increased likelihood of transmitting genetic abnormalities (AAP Committee on Substance Abuse, 2001) and heart defects (Deng et al., 2013). A pregnant woman's exposure to the father's secondhand smoke has been linked with asthma (Simond, To, Moneiddin, Stieb & Dell, 2014), attentional problems (Langley, Heron,

Did you know?

When drinking, many breast-feeding mothers will "pump and dump"—extract their breast milk using a pump and then discard the milk. However, while women may want to pump to avoid engorgement or maintain supply, if they do not, the alcohol will be filtered out of their breast milk, just as it is in the blood.

©Burke/Triolo Productions/ Getty Images

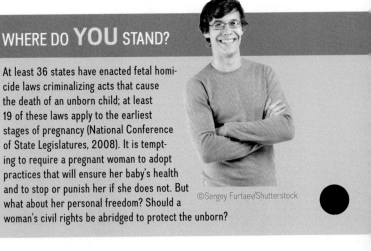

WHERE DO YOU STAND?

At least 36 states have enacted fetal homicide laws criminalizing acts that cause the death of an unborn child; at least 19 of these laws apply to the earliest stages of pregnancy (National Conference of State Legislatures, 2008). It is tempting to require a pregnant woman to adopt practices that will ensure her baby's health and to stop or punish her if she does not. But what about her personal freedom? Should a woman's civil rights be abridged to protect the unborn?

©Sergey Furtaev/Shutterstock

Smith & Thapar, 2012), low birth weight (Rubin, Krasilnikoff, Leventhal, Weile & Berget, 1986), and cancer in childhood and adulthood (Ji et al., 1997). In a study of 214 nonsmoking mothers in New York City, exposure to *both* paternal smoking and urban air pollution resulted in a 7 percent reduction in birth weight and a 3 percent reduction in head circumference (Perera et al., 2004).

Older fathers may be a significant source of birth defects due to damaged or deteriorated sperm. Birthrates for fathers ages 30 to 49 have risen significantly since 1980 (Martin et al., 2009). Advancing paternal age is associated with increases in the risk of several rare conditions, including dwarfism (Wyrobek et al., 2006). Advanced age of the father also may be a factor in a disproportionate number of cases of schizophrenia (Byrne, Agerbo, Ewald, Eaton & Mortensen, 2003; Malaspina et al., 2001), bipolar disorder (Frans et al., 2008), and autism and related disorders (Reichenberg et al., 2006; Tsuchiya et al., 2008).

Monitoring Prenatal Development

Sophia's pregnancy was proceeding in a textbook fashion from the outside. But because of the development of modern prenatal assessment tools now available to expectant parents, Sophia and Ethan could opt to do any number of tests to assess their baby's health. Because Sophia was under 35 and had no obvious risk factors, their doctor suggested they use ultrasound and blood tests to get a risk assessment of their baby's health. Happily, the baby appeared to be healthy and thriving, and so the young parents opted against further genetic testing.

Not long ago, almost the only decision parents had to make about their babies before birth was the decision to conceive. Most of what happened in the intervening months was beyond their control. Now scientists have developed an array of tools to assess an unborn baby's progress and well-being.

Progress is being made in noninvasive procedures, such as ultrasound and blood tests, to detect chromosomal abnormalities. Screening is most effective when begun during the first trimester (Simpson, 2005). In one study, a combination of three noninvasive tests conducted at 11 weeks of gestation

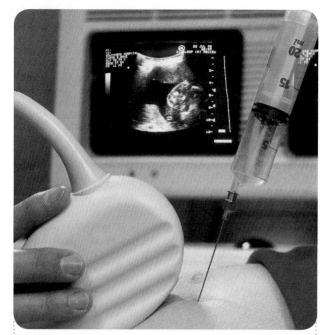

In both chorionic villus sampling and amniocentesis, an ultrasound machine can be used to guide the procedure.
©Saturn Stills/Science Source

predicted the presence of Down syndrome with 87 percent accuracy. When the 11-week tests were followed by further noninvasive testing early in the second trimester, accuracy reached 96 percent (Malone et al., 2005).

Other assessment techniques include *prenatal cell-free DNA scans*, in which fetal DNA is extracted from the mother's blood and tested. These tests have been shown to be useful for early detection of genetic problems (Sparks, Struble, Wang, Song & Oliphant, 2012; Mazloom et al., 2013), although they are not always definitive (American College of Obstetricians and Gynocologists, 2015).

Other, more invasive assessment techniques are also available. *Amniocentesis* is a procedure in which a sample of amniotic fluid is withdrawn for analysis. In *chorionic villus sampling*, tissue from the membrane surrounding the fetus is removed and analyzed. Both procedures provide definitive evidence of a genetic issue. Contrary to previous findings, amniocentesis and chorionic villus sampling, which can be used earlier in pregnancy, carry only a slightly higher miscarriage risk than these noninvasive procedures (Caughey, Hopkins & Norton, 2006; Eddleman et al., 2006). *Embryoscopy*, the insertion of a tiny viewing scope into the mother's uterus through the abdominal wall for a direct look at the embryo, can help diagnose nonchromosomal disorders, and *umbilical cord sampling* allows direct access to fetal DNA in the blood vessels of the umbilical cord for diagnosis.

Screening for defects and diseases is only one reason for the importance of early prenatal care. Early, high-quality prenatal care, which includes educational, social, and

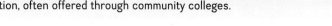

WHAT DO YOU **DO?**

Ultrasound Technician or Sonographer

Ultrasound technicians operate ultrasound machines that take diagnostic images. An ultrasound technician may take images of a fetus to monitor proper development, as well as images to help diagnose medical conditions, such as cancer. A radiologist evaluates the images ultrasound technicians take. To become an ultrasound technician, one needs to complete an ultrasound technician or sonographer course and receive certification, often offered through community colleges.

©Monkey Business Images/Shutterstock

©Digital Vision/Getty Images

Perspectives on Diversity

DISPARITIES IN PRENATAL CARE

In developing countries, 1 in 4 pregnant women do not receive prenatal care (United Nations Children's Fund [UNICEF], 2007), and about 2 out of 10 give birth without a skilled attendant (World Health Organization, 2017a). These facts may help explain why 46 percent of deaths of children under age 5 occur during the first 4 weeks of life from complications of birth (World Health Organization, 2017b).

In the United States prenatal care is widespread, but not universal as in many European countries, and it lacks uniform national standards and guaranteed financial coverage. Use of early prenatal care (during the first 3 months of pregnancy) rose modestly between 1990 and 2003 but then plateaued and declined slightly in 2006, possibly due to changes in welfare and Medicaid policies (Martin et al., 2010). In 2016, 6 percent of expectant mothers received late or no prenatal care during their pregnancies; another 17 percent did not begin prenatal care until the second trimester (Martin et al, 2018).

Historically, rates of low birth weight and premature birth continue to rise. Why? One answer is the increasing number of multiple births, which often are early births, with heightened risk of death within the first year. However, new data suggest that this increase may have finally peaked, as rates of premature delivery have decreased, particularly for triplets and higher order multiples (Martin, Hamilton, Osterman, Driscoll & Mathews, 2017).

A second answer is that the benefits of prenatal care are not evenly distributed. Although usage of prenatal care has grown, especially among ethnic groups that have tended not to receive early care, the women most at risk of bearing low-birth-weight babies—teenage and unmarried women, those with little education, and some minority women—are still least likely to receive it (Partridge, Balayla, Holcroft & Abenhaim, 2012; Martin et al., 2006).

A related concern is an ethnic disparity in fetal and postbirth mortality. After adjusting for such risk factors as SES, overweight, smoking, hypertension, and diabetes, the chances of perinatal death (death between 20 weeks of gestation and 1 week after birth) remain 3.4 times higher for non-Hispanic blacks, 1.5 times higher for Hispanics, and 1.9 times higher for other minorities than for non-Hispanic whites (Healy et al., 2006).

Good prenatal care can give every child the best possible chance for entering the world in good condition to meet the challenges of life outside the womb—challenges we discuss in the next chapter.

---

nutritional services, can help prevent maternal or infant death and other birth complications. It can provide first-time mothers with information about pregnancy, childbirth, and infant care. Poor women who get prenatal care benefit by being put in touch with other needed services, and they are more likely to get medical care for their infants after birth (Shiono & Behrman, 1995). The amount of prenatal care received by a woman is linearly related to positive outcomes (Partridge, Balayla, Holcroft & Abenhaim, 2012).

mastering the CHAPTER

©Pixtal/AGE fotostock

Summary and Key Terms

Stages of Prenatal Development

> Prenatal development occurs in three stages of gestation: the germinal, embryonic, and fetal stages.

> Growth and development both before and after birth follow the cephalocaudal principle (head to tail) and the proximodistal principle (center outward).

> As many as 1 in 4 recognized pregnancies end in miscarriage, usually in the first trimester of pregnancy.

> As fetuses grow, they move less, but more vigorously. Swallowing amniotic fluid, which contains substances from the mother's body, stimulates taste and smell. Fetuses seem able to hear, respond to music and speech, recognize their mothers' voices, learn, and remember.

KEY TERMS

Gestation	Embryonic stage	Ultrasound
Cephalocaudal principle	Spontaneous abortion	Neurons
Proximodistal principle	Fetal stage	Teratogen
Germinal stage		

Influences on Prenatal Development

> The developing organism can be greatly affected by its prenatal environment. The likelihood of a birth defect may depend on the timing and intensity of an environmental event and its interaction with genetic factors.

> Important environmental influences involving the mother include nutrition, physical activity, transmission of maternal illnesses or infections, maternal stress, maternal age, external environmental hazards, and intake of alcohol or other drugs, including nicotine. External influences also may affect the father's sperm.

KEY TERMS

Acquired immune deficiency syndrome (AIDS)	Fetal alcohol syndrome (FAS)

Monitoring Prenatal Development

> Ultrasound, prenatal cell-free DNA scans, amniocentesis, chorionic villus sampling, umbilical cord sampling, and maternal blood tests can be used to determine whether an unborn baby is developing normally.

> Early, high-quality prenatal care is essential for healthy development. It can lead to detection of defects and disorders and may help reduce maternal and infant death, low birth weight, and other birth complications.

> Racial/ethnic disparities in prenatal care may be a factor in disparities in low birth weight and perinatal death.

Practice Quiz

1. Because of the proximodistal principle, we would expect that an embryo's:
   a. head would develop before the arms.
   b. arms would develop before the legs.
   c. arms would develop before the fingers.
   d. feet would develop before the heart.

2. The zygote implants in the uterine wall during:
   a. the germinal stage of development.
   b. the embryonic stage of development.
   c. the fetal stage of development.
   d. the germinal or embryonic stage; it varies for each zygote.

3. The developing child is most sensitive to teratogens during the embryonic stage of development because:
   a. it has not yet implanted and thus does not have an umbilical cord.
   b. the fetus becomes more active during this time and thus metabolizes substances more quickly.
   c. the major organ systems and body structures are forming during this time.
   d. this is not true; the developing child is most sensitive to teratogens during the fetal stage of development.

4. During the fetal stage of development, the developing child:
   a. is unable to perceive any sensory stimulation.
   b. can perceive some limited sensory information and appears to be able to use it to learn from it.
   c. can perceive sensory information at nearly adult levels.
   d. this information is not known because it is impossible to test for it.

5. List three maternal factors that can negatively impact a pregnancy.
   a. _____
   b. _____
   c. _____

6. One's age during a pregnancy is a risk factor:
   a. only for mothers.
   b. only for fathers.
   c. for neither parent.
   d. for both parents, although for mothers to a greater degree.
   e. for both parents, although for fathers to a greater degree.

7. Inadequate maternal intake of which of the following is linked to increased risk of spina bifida?
   a. vitamin D
   b. docosahexanoic acid
   c. folic acid
   d. zinc

8. Which of the following maternal infections is linked to microcephaly, seizures, and developmental delays in an infant?
   a. influenza
   b. Zika
   c. acquired immune deficiency syndrome
   d. rubella

9. Pregnant women should avoid emptying cat litter boxes due to risk of _____, a parasitic infection.

10. Which of the following tests assess the genetic risk for the child?
    a. maternal blood tests
    b. chorionic villi sampling
    c. embryoscopy
    d. amniocentesis
    e. b and d

Answers: 1–c; 2–a; 3–c; 4–b.; 5–Among the maternal factors that can impact a pregnancy are exposure to teratogens, nutrition and weight, physical activity and strenuous work, drug intake, illness, stress, age, and environmental hazards; 6–d; 7–c; 8–b; 9–toxoplasmosis; 10–e

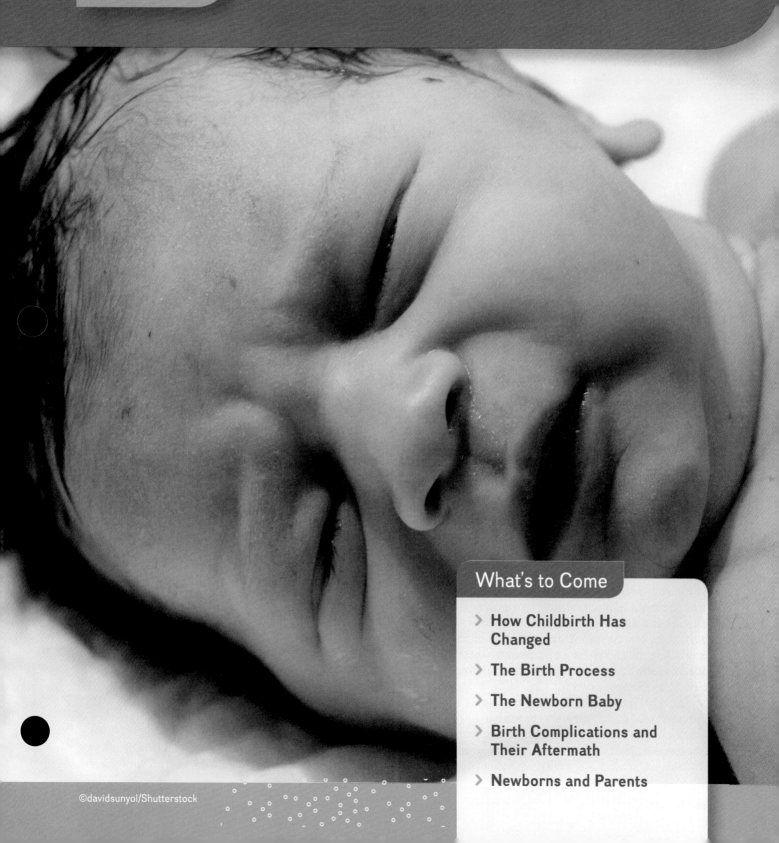

4 Birth and the Newborn

©davidsunyol/Shutterstock

Emily rocked back and forth slowly as she paged through her newest purchase—a book describing the birthing process and the early months of life of a newborn child. She bit her lip thoughtfully, taking careful notes in the margins and underlining passages she found important. Eight months ago when she had realized she was pregnant with her first child, she had looked forward to its arrival with unbridled anticipation. Nine months had seemed an eternity away. But now, as the end of her pregnancy approached, she felt a mix of excitement and apprehension. After her long pregnancy, she was tired of swollen feet, heartburn, and feeling out of breath. She was looking forward to meeting her son. But what would labor be like? Would it hurt a lot? What would it be like to have a newborn? Would she know what to do? Emily rested her hand on her swollen belly, rubbing it in small circles, and sighed.

In this chapter, we describe the first steps in the journey of life outside the womb. We describe how babies come into the world, what they look like, and how their body systems work. We discuss techniques that assess newborn health and the different ways birth complications affect development. We also consider how the birth of a baby affects the people most vital to the infant's well-being: the parents.

● ● ● ●

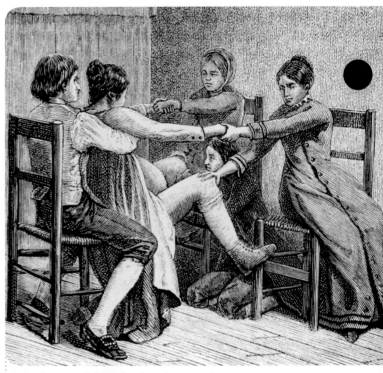

In this illustration of childbirth in the early nineteenth century, a woman gives birth at home with the assistance of family members and a midwife with no formal training.
©Everett Collection Inc/Alamy

How Childbirth Has Changed

Customs surrounding childbirth reflect a culture's beliefs, values, and resources. A Mayan woman in Yucatan gives birth in the hammock she sleeps in every night; both the father-to-be and a midwife are expected to be present. To evade evil spirits, mother and child remain at home for a week (Jordan, 1993). By contrast, among the Ngoni in East Africa, men are excluded from the birth experience. And in rural Thailand, a new mother generally resumes normal activity within a few hours of giving birth (Gardiner & Kozmitzki, 2005). While cultural differences regarding childbirth abound, differences can also be seen across time within many countries as childbirth and labor became increasingly medicalized and moved from the home to hospital settings.

Childbirth in earlier times was "a struggle with death" (Fontanel & d'Harcourt, 1997) for both mother and baby. In seventeenth- and eighteenth-century France, a woman had a 1 in 10 chance of dying while or shortly after giving birth. Thousands of babies were stillborn, and 1 out of 4 born alive died during the 1st year. At the end of the nineteenth century in England and Wales, an expectant mother was almost 50 times more likely to die in childbirth than a woman giving birth today (Saunders, 1997).

At this time, childbirth in Europe and in the United States followed similar patterns. The woman, surrounded by female relatives and neighbors, sat up in her bed or perhaps in the stable, modestly draped in a sheet; she might stand, walk around, or squat over a birth stool. Chinks in the walls, doors, and windows were stuffed with cloth to keep out chills and evil spirits. Neither the prospective father nor doctors were present, although midwives without formal training often were. Salves made of viper fat, eel gall, powdered donkey hoof, chameleon tongue, snake skin, or hare skin might be rubbed on the prospective mother's abdomen to ease her pain or hasten her labor. The midwives' ministrations sometimes did more harm than good. A sixteenth-century textbook instructed midwives to stretch and dilate the membranes of the genital parts and cut or break them with their fingernails, to urge the patient to go up and down stairs screaming at the top of her lungs, to help her bear down by pressing on her belly, and to pull out the placenta immediately after the birth (Fontanel & d'Harcourt, 1997).

At the start of the twentieth century, childbirth began to be professionalized in the United States, at least in urban settings. The growing use of maternity hospitals led to safer, more antiseptic conditions for childbirth, which reduced mortality for women. In 1900, only 5 percent of U.S. deliveries occurred in hospitals; by 1920, in some cities 65 percent did (Scholten, 1985). A similar trend took place in Europe. Most recently, in the United States 98.7 percent of babies are born in hospitals, and 86.1 percent of births are attended by physicians (Martin, Hamilton, Ventura, Osterman & Mathews, 2013).

The dramatic reductions in risks surrounding pregnancy and childbirth in industrialized countries are largely due to the availability of antibiotics, blood transfusions, safe anesthesia, improved hygiene, and drugs for inducing labor. In addition, improvements in prenatal assessment and care make it far more likely that a baby will be born healthy.

Hospitals may offer birthing rooms that provide a less medicalized childbirth experience.

©Science Photo Library/Alamy

Mortality rates for both mothers and children have decreased dramatically. For example, in 1940 there were 47.0 infant deaths per 1,000 live births; by 2015, this rate had decreased to 5.82 infant deaths per 1,000 live births. Postnatal survival rates have also increased. In 1940 the postnatal death rate was 18.3 infant deaths per 1,000 live births, a number that fell to 1.88 deaths in 2014 (Kochanek, Murphy, Xu & Tejada-Vera, 2016).

Still, childbirth is not risk-free for women or babies. Among the nearly 4 million U.S. women who gave birth in 2014, approximately 14.4 women out of every 1,000 experienced complications, including blood transfusions, hysterectomy, the use of a ventilator, or other complications. This number has risen steadily in the last 15 years. The increase—almost 200 percent from 1993 to 2014—is likely due to a variety of factors, including increases in maternal age, prepregnancy obesity, preexisting medical conditions, and cesarean delivery (Centers for Disease Control and Prevention, 2015). Black women, obese women, those with difficult medical histories, those who had previous cesarean deliveries, and those who had several children are at elevated risk of hemorrhage and other dangerous complications (Bernstein, 2003).

Childbirth is still a dangerous endeavor in some developing countries in sub-Saharan Africa and South Asia. There, 60 million women deliver at home each year without the benefit of skilled care, and until recently more than 500,000 women and 4 million newborns died in or shortly after childbirth (Sines, Syed, Wall & Worley, 2007). There are promising trends in maternal mortality though. Estimates suggest that maternal mortality dropped to approximately 289,000 in 2013, representing a 45 percent decline from 1990 (World Health Organization & UNICEF, 2014).

While childbirth is undoubtedly safer with the advances of modern medicine, the medicalization of childbirth has nonetheless had social and emotional costs that some women are rejecting. Today a small but growing percentage of women in developed countries are going back to the intimate, personal experience of home birth (MacDorman, Menacker & Declercq, 2010). Home births are usually attended by a trained nurse-midwife, ideally with the resources of medical science close at hand. Arrangements may be made with a physician and a nearby hospital in case an emergency arises. Some studies suggest that planned home births with speedy transfer to a hospital available in case of need can be as safe as hospital births for low-risk deliveries attended by skilled, certified midwives or nurse-midwives (American College of Nurse-Midwives, 2016). However, the American College of Obstetricians and Gynecologists (2017) and the American Medical Association (AMA House of Delegates, 2008) point out that complications can arise suddenly, even in low-risk pregnancies, and hospitals or accredited birthing centers are best equipped to respond to such emergencies.

Today hospitals are finding ways to humanize childbirth. Labor and delivery may take place in a comfortable birthing room, under soft lights, with the father or partner present as a coach and older siblings invited to visit after the birth. Rooming-in policies allow a baby to stay in the mother's room much or all of the time. These changes allow hospitals to allay concerns about an overly medicalized experience while still providing a safe environment in the event of complications.

The Birth Process

Emily woke up with some strange sensations in her belly. She had felt the baby, her first, moving all through her second and third trimesters, but this felt different. Her due date was still 2 weeks off. Could she be feeling the birth contractions she had heard and read so much about? Was she in labor?

Labor is an apt term for the process of giving birth. Birth is hard work for both mother and baby, chiefly because of the size of the fetal head. However, from an evolutionary perspective, the advantage of an enlarged head that can contain a brain capable of advanced thought outweighs the difficulty of passing through the birth canal (Bjorklund & Pellegrini, 2000).

Labor is brought on by a series of uterine, cervical, and other changes that begin about 2 weeks before delivery. While the definitive trigger for the advent of labor is unclear, it is at least partially due to hormones released by the placenta and fetus (Mendelson, 2009). The uterine contractions that expel the fetus begin—typically about 266 days after conception—as tightenings of the uterus. A woman may have felt false contractions, known as Braxton-Hicks contractions, at times during the final months of pregnancy. These contractions may help tone the uterine muscles and promote the flow of blood to the placenta, but they are mild, irregular, and do not result in any of the cervical changes required for birth to take place. In comparison, real labor contractions are more frequent, rhythmic, and painful, and they increase in frequency and intensity.

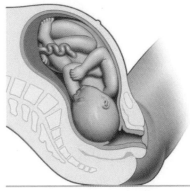
STAGES OF CHILDBIRTH

Labor takes place in three overlapping stages (Figure 4.1). The first stage, dilation of the cervix, is the longest; it typically lasts 12 to 14 hours for a woman having her first child. In subsequent births the first stage tends to be shorter. During this stage, regular and increasingly frequent uterine contractions—15 to 20 minutes apart at first—cause the cervix to shorten and dilate, or widen, in preparation for delivery. Toward the end of the first stage, contractions occur every 2 to 5 minutes. This stage lasts until the cervix is fully open (10 centimeters, or about 4 inches) so the baby can descend into the birth canal.

The second stage, descent and emergence of the baby, typically lasts up to 1 or 2 hours. It begins when the baby's head starts to move through the cervix into the vaginal canal, and it ends when the baby emerges completely from the mother's body. Mothers often feel a strong urge to push at this time. If this stage lasts longer than 2 hours, signaling that the baby may need help, a doctor may use vacuum extraction with a suction cup to pull the baby out of the mother's body. The use of forceps—an instrument shaped like a large pair of salad tongs—is increasingly rare, occurring at less than 1 percent of births (Martin, Hamilton, Osterman, Driscoll & Drake, 2018). At the end of this stage, the baby is born but is still attached to the placenta in the mother's body by the umbilical cord, which must be cut and clamped.

WHAT DO YOU **DO**?

Labor and Delivery Nurse

©Pixtal/AGE Fotostock

Labor and delivery nurses, also called perinatal nurses, typically take care of the medical and emotional needs of mother and baby during labor and delivery. They are often responsible for caring for pregnant mothers admitted into the hospital prior to delivery for monitoring of potentially problematic conditions. In addition, they assist pregnant women who come to the hospital to deliver, and help them determine if they are indeed in labor and ready for admission. During the labor process, they are responsible for managing the mother's overall care, monitoring changes in her cervix, watching the baby's heart rate, supporting the mother in pain management, and ultimately assisting the physician in the baby's delivery. After the birth, the labor and delivery nurse will examine the baby and sometimes help the mother begin to breast-feed. Labor and delivery nurses are typically registered nurses (RNs). To become a registered nurse, one must pass the NCLEX-RN exam. Individuals taking this exam typically have completed a four-year nursing degree program or an associate's degree in nursing program. In addition to the proper educational credentials, labor and delivery nurses need to have unique personal qualifications such as being emotionally respondent to mom and dad during and after labor and delivery. To learn more about becoming a nurse, go to: www.nursingworld.org.

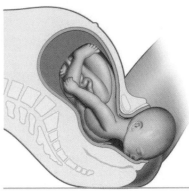

Stage one: Baby positions itself

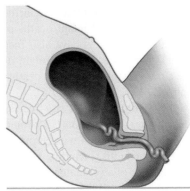

Stage two: Baby begins to emerge

Stage three: Placenta is expelled

FIGURE 4.1 The Stages of Birth

The third stage, expulsion of the placenta, lasts between 10 and 60 minutes. During this stage the placenta and the remainder of the umbilical cord are expelled from the mother.

LABOR AND DELIVERY OPTIONS

With the development of varied methods to manage difficult labor and deliveries have come a wealth of medical and nonmedical options for women to take advantage of during the birthing process. In the following section, we discuss the use of fetal monitors as well as birthing options for expectant women.

Electronic Fetal Monitoring

Electronic fetal monitoring can track the fetus's heartbeat during labor and can help detect serious problems. In 2004, the procedure was used in 89 percent of live births in the United States (Chen, Chauhan, Ananth, Vintzileos & Abuhamad, 2013). While electronic fetal monitoring can provide valuable information in high-risk deliveries, it can have major drawbacks if used routinely in low-risk pregnancies. It is costly; it restricts the mother's movements during labor; and most important, it has an extremely high false-positive rate, suggesting that fetuses are in trouble when they are not. Such warnings may prompt doctors to deliver by the riskier cesarean method rather than the vaginal one (Banta & Thacker, 2001).

Vaginal versus Cesarean Delivery

The usual method of childbirth is vaginal delivery. Alternatively, **cesarean delivery** can surgically remove the baby from the uterus through an incision in the mother's abdomen. Use of this procedure increased in European countries during the 1990s; (Gibbons et al., 2010). In the United States, cesarean birthrates peaked in 2009 at 32.9 percent. Although still high, the rate in 2016 was 31.9 percent, a decline for the fourth year in a row (Martin et al., 2018).

The operation is commonly performed when labor progresses too slowly, when the fetus seems to be in trouble, or when the mother is bleeding vaginally. A cesarean is often needed when the fetus is in the breech position (feet or buttocks first) or in the transverse position (lying crosswise in the uterus), or when the head is too big to pass through the mother's pelvis. In addition, a cesarean delivery is more likely to occur when labor is induced, as is common in women whose pregnancy progresses past 40 weeks (Wilson, Effken, & Butler, 2010).

The increase in cesarean rates can be attributed to many factors. One is a rising proportion of older first-time mothers, who are more likely to have multiple births, and of very premature infants (Martin, Hamilton et al., 2010). Physicians' fear of malpractice suits and women's preferences also may play a part in the choice of cesarean deliveries (Ecker & Frigoletto, 2007; Martin et al., 2009), as may the increased revenue hospitals generate with cesarean rather than vaginal births.

Cesarean deliveries carry risks of serious complications for the mother, such as bleeding, infection, damage to pelvic organs, postoperative pain, and heightened risks of problems in future pregnancies (Ecker & Frigoletto, 2007). They also deprive the baby of important benefits of normal birth, including the surge of hormones that clears the lungs of excess fluid, the mobilization of stored fuel to nourish cells, and the movement of blood to the heart and brain. In making the baby more alert and ready to interact with another person, these hormones may also promote bonding with the mother (Lagercrantz & Slotkin, 1986). Vaginal delivery also stimulates the release of oxytocin, a hormone involved in uterine contractions that stimulates maternal behavior in animals. There are indications that oxytocin may have similar effects in humans (Swain et al., 2008). Further, breast-feeding can be negatively impacted in mothers who undergo cesarean deliveries, which may impede bonding (Zanardo et al., 2010).

Once a woman has had one cesarean delivery, many physicians warn that she should only attempt a vaginal birth after cesarean (VBAC) with caution. VBACs have been associated with greater, though still low, risks of uterine rupture and brain damage (Landon et al., 2004) as well as infant death (Smith, Pell, Cameron, & Dobbie, 2002). However, other research shows risks associated with repeat cesarean deliveries, including postpartum endometriosis (a painful condition in which uterine cells are found outside of the uterus), complications related to the use of anesthesia, or hysterectomy (Fong et al., 2016). Today, if a woman has had a cesarean delivery and attempts a vaginal birth, chances of a successful VBAC are about 12 percent (National Center for Health Statistics, 2015).

electronic fetal monitoring Mechanical monitoring of fetal heartbeat during labor and delivery.

cesarean delivery Delivery of a baby by surgical removal from the uterus.

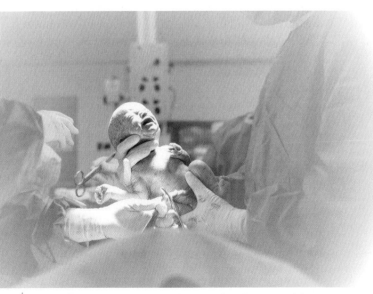

In a cesarean delivery, a baby is surgically removed from the uterus. A little over 30 percent of babies in the United States are born by cesarean delivery.
©Martin Valigursky/Alamy

Medicated versus Nonmedicated Delivery

Emily and her husband had attended a childbirth preparation class at her hospital. The class offered the prospective parents various options for childbirth, and Emily puzzled over what she wanted to experience for her own labor and delivery. Should she focus on learning pain management techniques and attempt a medication-free birth? Should she request an epidural? How might these different choices impact both her and her new baby?

For centuries, pain was considered an unavoidable part of giving birth. Then, in the mid-nineteenth century, sedation with ether or chloroform became common practice as more births took place in hospitals (Fontanel & d'Harcourt, 1997).

Because of growing concerns that the use of drugs might pose risks for babies, and a desire for both parents to participate fully in a natural, empowering experience, several alternative methods of **natural**, or **prepared**, **childbirth** were developed during the twentieth century. The most common model of natural childbirth is the *Lamaze method*, introduced by the French obstetrician Fernand Lamaze in the late 1950s. The woman is trained to pant or breathe rapidly in sync with the increasing intensity of her contractions and to concentrate on other sensations to ease the perception of pain. She learns to relax her muscles as a conditioned response to the voice of her coach (usually the prospective father, a friend, or a midwife), who attends classes with her, takes part in the delivery, and helps with the exercises.

natural, or prepared, childbirth Method of childbirth that seeks to reduce or eliminate the use of drugs, enable both parents to participate fully, and control perceptions of pain.

Today, improvements in medicated delivery have led many mothers to choose pain relief. General anesthesia, which renders the woman completely unconscious and greatly increases the risks to mother and baby, is rarely used, even in cesarean births (Eltzschig, Lieberman, & Camann, 2003). Approximately 60 percent of women use a regional anesthesia known as an *epidural block* (Eltzschig et al., 2003). During an epidural, an anesthetic is injected into the spinal cord between the vertebrae in the lumbar (lower) region; this blocks the nerve pathways that would carry the sensation of pain to the brain. Epidurals given early can shorten labor with no added risk of needing cesarean delivery (Wong, Gottesman, & Petronis, 2005) and allow the woman to participate in the birth process. However, these drugs do pass through the placenta to the fetal blood supply and tissues; thus there are some relatively minor risks associated with their use.

In many traditional cultures, and increasingly in developed countries, childbearing women are attended by a *doula*, an experienced mentor, coach, and helper who can give emotional support and information about what is happening and can stay at a

Katie Holmes reportedly used a Scientology "quiet birth" method for her delivery of daughter Suri.
©Toby Canham/Getty Images

woman's bedside throughout labor. A doula does not actively participate in the delivery but supports the mother throughout the process. There is growing evidence that offering women support during pregnancy and the birthing process is associated with better outcomes. For example, in one study, expectant mothers who participated in prenatal education classes with a doula were less likely to give birth to a low-birth-weight baby or have birth complications and more likely to successfully initiate breast-feeding than expectant mothers who participated in the same classes, but without the support of a doula (Gruber, Cupito & Dobson, 2013). Other studies have found that women who give birth with the assistance of a doula are almost 41 percent less likely to have a cesarean delivery than women who give birth without such support (Kozhimannil, Hardeman, Attanasio, Blauer-Peterson & O'Brien, 2013). Doulas also provide an economic benefit. Infants born before 37 weeks of gestation—currently 1 in 9 in the United States—incur medical costs that average approximately 10 times what the costs are for a full-term infant. Additionally, cesarean deliveries are double the cost of vaginal births. Thus, the use of doulas is a cost-effective strategy and, if funded by insurance, would

©nycshooter/Getty Images

WHAT DO YOU **DO**?

Anesthesiologist

An anesthesiologist is a medical doctor who administers anesthetic medication. During labor, an anesthesiologist performs the epidural, if requested. The anesthesiologist also provides pain medication for women undergoing a cesarean delivery. An anesthesiologist must earn a medical degree, complete a residency, and pass a comprehensive exam in order to practice. To learn more about becoming an anesthesiologist, go to: www.asahq.org.

A doula, or experienced helper, stays at a woman's bedside throughout labor and provides emotional support. Research has found that women attended by doulas tend to have shorter labor and easier deliveries.

©Brand X Pictures

result in significant overall savings (Kozhimannil, Hardeman, Alarid-Escudero, Vogelsang, Blauer-Peterson & Howell, 2016). Unfortunately, doulas are often not covered by insurance, and cost is the largest barrier most women face in securing the support of a doula (Strauss, Giessler & McAllister, 2015). Ethnic minorities, including African Americans, Hispanics, American Indians, and others, have higher rates of cesarean delivery, preterm birth, neonatal and maternal mortality, and congenital abnormalities than white mothers (Bryant, Worjoloh, Caughey & Washington, 2010). Given the strong relationship in the United States between race and socioeconomic status, the implication of this is that those expectant mothers who would most benefit from the support of a doula are often the least likely to be able to do so.

Some expectant mothers also work with *midwives*. Although certification processes vary, midwives are generally trained to provide care during pregnancy, labor, and the postpartum period; many also offer assistance in breast-feeding and other primary care services to women.

The Newborn Baby

Emily and her husband cuddled her newborn—after 11 hours of labor she had given birth to a healthy 7-pound baby boy. While he seemed so helpless in many ways—kicking his legs and tightly curled fists and peering around with his murky gray eyes—in other ways he seemed to know exactly what to do. He nursed vigorously, cried when he was hungry or needed changing, and calmed when held by an adult. Emily was exhausted from caring for her new baby, but she was overjoyed at her new role in life and falling more in love with her new son every day.

The **neonatal period**, the first 4 weeks of life, is a time of transition from the uterus, where a fetus is supported entirely by the mother, to an independent existence. What are the physical characteristics of newborn babies, and how are they equipped for this crucial transition?

SIZE AND APPEARANCE

In the United Stated, an average newborn, or **neonate**, is about 20 inches long and weighs about 7½ pounds. At birth, the vast majority of full-term babies weigh between 5½ and 10 pounds and are between 18 and 22 inches long. Boys tend to be slightly longer and heavier than girls, and a firstborn child is likely to weigh less at birth than laterborns. When the baby is born, the mother produces a special high-protein type of milk called *colostrum*. This provides babies with important immunological substances and has laxative effects that help babies begin to eliminate toxins. However, colostrum contains less fat and calories than breast milk. Thus, in their first few days, neonates lose as much as 10 percent of their body weight. Babies begin to gain weight by about the 5th day when the mother's milk comes in and are generally back to birth weight by the 10th to the 14th day.

New babies have distinctive features, including a large head, red skin, various temporary skin conditions or blotches, permanent birthmarks, and a receding chin, which makes it easier to nurse. In addition, there are *fontanels*—soft spots on the head covered with a tough membrane—where an infant's

neonatal period First 4 weeks of life, a time of transition from intrauterine dependency to independent existence.

neonate Newborn baby, up to 4 weeks old.

WHAT DO YOU **DO?**

©Sam Edwards/ AGE fotostock

Doula

A certified doula supports women emotionally during labor and childbirth. A doula helps the mother create a birth plan and supports the mother and her partner during labor and delivery. After the baby's birth, a postpartum doula helps the family adjust to the new baby, does light housekeeping and cooking, and supports the mother during her recovery. Becoming a doula requires certification that varies from attending workshops to childbirth education series. To learn more about being a doula, go to: www.dona.org.

skull bones are not yet fused. This allows for flexibility in shape, which eases the passage of the neonate through the birth canal. In the first 18 months of life, the plates of the skull gradually fuse together.

Many newborns have a pinkish cast; their skin is so thin it barely covers the capillaries through which blood flows. However, a baby's skin color can vary greatly, depending on its age, racial/ethnic origin, health status, temperature, the environment, and whether the baby is crying. During the first few days, some neonates are very hairy because some of the *lanugo*, a fuzzy prenatal hair on the shoulders, back, forehead, and cheeks, has not yet fallen off. Almost all new babies are covered with *vernix caseosa* ("cheesy varnish"), a white, oily, cheeselike substance that is formed in the womb by secretions from the fetal oil glands and protects against infection. This coating is absorbed into the skin after birth.

©Julia Raketic/Shutterstock

REFLEXES

Infants are born with a set of newborn reflexes. Some, like the rooting reflex, where a baby turns its head toward a soft touch on the cheek and begins to search for a nipple, and the sucking reflex are clearly related to

survival needs. Others are holdovers from our adaptive past, as when babies grasp whatever is placed in their palm much as baby monkeys cling to their mother's fur. Still other reflexes do not appear to have a clear function. For example, when a baby's head is turned to one side, one arm extends and one bends back, as if the baby were getting ready to fire an arrow. The origins of this tonic neck reflex are unclear.

The proper appearance and disappearance of reflexes are related to neurological organization and are a marker of good health. Many diminish over time; their continued persistence after they should have disappeared can be evidence of neurological problems. Chapter 5 covers reflexes in greater detail.

BODY SYSTEMS

Before birth, blood circulation, respiration, nourishment, elimination of waste, and temperature regulation are accomplished through the mother's body. After birth, all of the baby's systems and functions

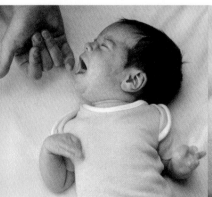

The rooting reflex.
©Elizabeth Crews/The Image Works

The sucking reflex.
©Alik Mulikov/Shutterstock

The grasping reflex.
©DAJ/Getty Images

The Moro reflex.
©Elizabeth Crews/The Image Works

TABLE 4.1 A Comparison of Prenatal and Postnatal Life

Characteristic	Prenatal Life	Postnatal Life
Environment	Amniotic fluid	Air
Temperature	Relatively constant	Fluctuates with atmosphere
Stimulation	Minimal	All senses stimulated by various stimuli
Nutrition	Dependent on mother's blood	Dependent on external food and functioning of digestive system
Oxygen supply	Passed from maternal bloodstream via placenta	Passed from neonate's lungs to pulmonary blood vessels
Metabolic elimination	Passed into maternal bloodstream via placenta	Discharged by skin, kidneys, lungs, and gastrointestinal tract

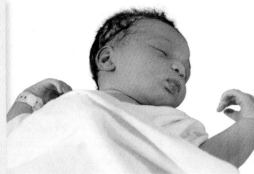

©Photodisc Collection/Getty Images

must operate on their own (Table 4.1). Most of this transition occurs during the first 4 to 6 hours after delivery (Ferber & Makhoul, 2004).

The fetus and mother have separate circulatory systems and separate heartbeats; the fetus's blood is cleansed through the umbilical cord, which carries used blood to the placenta and returns a fresh supply. A neonate's heartbeat is fast and irregular at first, and blood pressure does not stabilize until about the 10th day of life.

The fetus gets oxygen and carries away carbon dioxide through the umbilical cord. Once birth occurs, a newborn must start breathing for itself. Most babies start to breathe as soon as they are exposed to air. A baby who has not begun within about 5 minutes may suffer permanent brain injury from **anoxia**, lack of oxygen, or hypoxia, a reduced oxygen supply. Anoxia or hypoxia may occur during delivery as a result of repeated compression of the placenta and umbilical cord with each contraction, or after the birth occurs if the baby has difficulty taking in sufficient amounts of air. Babies have only one-tenth the lung capacity of adults and are susceptible to respiratory problems that can cause permanent brain damage and lead to mental retardation, behavior problems, or even death.

Many babies are born alert and ready to begin feeding. Full-term babies have a strong sucking reflex to take in milk and their own gastrointestinal secretions to digest it. Babies must also eliminate toxins from their bodies independently. During the first few days, infants secrete *meconium*, a stringy, greenish-black waste matter formed in the fetal intestinal tract. In addition, babies begin to urinate regularly; the volume of urine is proportionate to food intake.

The layers of fat that develop during the last 2 months of fetal life enable healthy full-term infants to keep their body temperature constant after birth despite changes in air temperature. Newborn babies also maintain body temperature by increasing their activity when air temperature drops. These early fat deposits also give babies a reserve of energy until their mother's milk comes in.

Three or 4 days after birth, about half of all babies, and a larger proportion of babies born prematurely, develop **neonatal jaundice**: their skin and eyeballs look yellow. The immaturity of the liver and failure to filter out bilirubin, a by-product resulting from the breakdown of red blood cells, cause this kind of jaundice. Usually neonatal jaundice is not serious, does not need treatment, and has no long-term effects. However, severe jaundice that is not monitored and treated promptly can result in brain damage.

anoxia Lack of oxygen, which may cause brain damage.

neonatal jaundice Condition in many newborn babies caused by immaturity of the liver and evidenced by a yellowish appearance; can cause brain damage if not treated promptly.

Apgar scale Standard measurement of a newborn's condition; it assesses appearance, pulse, grimace, activity, and respiration.

MEDICAL AND BEHAVIORAL ASSESSMENT

Although the great majority of births result in normal, healthy babies, some do not. The first few minutes, days, and weeks after birth are crucial for development. It is important to know as soon as possible whether a baby has any problem that needs special care.

The Apgar Scale

One minute after delivery and 5 minutes after birth, most babies are assessed using the **Apgar scale** (Figure 4.2). Its name helps

Did you know?

The fontanels on an infant's head allow the head to be molded so it can fit through the mother's birth canal. Because of this, babies born vaginally often have misshapen heads for about a week after birth, while babies born via cesarean have rounded heads.

©Steven Lam/Photodisc/Getty Images

us remember its five subtests: (1) *a*ppearance (color), (2) *p*ulse (heart rate), (3) *g*rimace (reflex irritability), (4) *a*ctivity (muscle tone), and (5) *r*espiration (breathing). The newborn is rated 0, 1, or 2 on each measure, for a maximum score of 10. A 5-minute score of 7 to 10—achieved by 98.4 percent of babies born in the United States in 2006—indicates the baby is in good to excellent condition (Martin et al., 2009). A score of 5 to 7 at 1 minute may mean the baby needs help to establish breathing, and the test should be repeated every 5 minutes up to 20 minutes (AAP Committee on Fetus and Newborn & American College of Obstetricians and Gynecologists [ACOG] Committee on Obstetric Practice, 2006).

A score below 5 is rare and may reflect a variety of problems. For example, the heart or respiratory system may not be working at peak levels. In this event, a mask may be placed over the newborn's face to pump oxygen directly into the lungs or, if breathing still does not start, a tube can be placed in the windpipe. In addition, medications and fluids may be administered through the blood vessels in the umbilical cord to strengthen the heartbeat. If resuscitation is successful, bringing the baby's score to 5 or more, long-term damage is unlikely. Scores of 0 to 3 at 10, 15, and 20 minutes after birth are increasingly associated with cerebral palsy (muscular impairment due to brain damage prenatally or during birth) or other neurological problems (American College of Obstetricians and Gynecologists, 2015). Prematurity, low birth weight, trauma, infection, birth defects, medication given to the mother, and other conditions may affect the scores (AAP Committee on Fetus and Newborn & ACOG Committee on Obstetric Practice, 2006).

Brazelton Neonatal Behavioral Assessment Scale (NBAS) Neurological and behavioral test to measure a neonate's responses to the environment.

The Brazelton Scale

The **Brazelton Neonatal Behavioral Assessment Scale (NBAS)** is used to assess neonates' responsiveness to their environment, to identify strengths and vulnerabilities in neurological functioning, and to predict future development. The test is suitable for infants up to 2 months old; it assesses (1) motor organization as shown by such behaviors as activity level and the ability to bring a hand to the mouth; (2) reflexes; (3) changes in state, such as irritability, excitability, and ability to quiet down after being upset; (4) attention and interactive capacities, as shown by general alertness and response to visual and auditory stimuli; and (5) indications of central nervous system instability, such as tremors and changes in skin color (Brazelton, 1973, 1984; Brazelton & Nugent, 1995, 2001). The NBAS takes about 30 minutes, and scores are based on a baby's best performance. It is most commonly used in research applications, although it is useful as an educational tool for parents and in interventions.

Neonatal Screening for Medical Conditions

As mentioned in Chapter 2, children who inherit the enzyme disorder phenylketonuria, or PKU, will develop permanent intellectual disability unless fed a special diet beginning in the first 3 to 6 weeks of life (National Institute of Child Health and Human Development, 2017). Screening tests administered soon after birth often can discover this and other correctable defects; in the case of PKU, environmental intervention can prevent the manifestation of the disease. Generally, blood is collected via a heelstick from newborn babies at the hospital and used to screen for this and other conditions.

Routine screening of all newborn babies for such rare conditions as PKU (1 in 15,000 births), congenital hypothyroidism (1 in 3,600 to 5,000), galactosemia (1 in 60,000 to 80,000), and other, even rarer, disorders is expensive. Yet the cost of testing thousands of newborns to detect one case of a rare disease may be less than the cost of caring for one person with significant disability for a lifetime. The Recommended Uniform Screening Panel, developed by the U.S. government in conjunction with professionals in the field, includes 34 core

FIGURE 4.2

The Apgar Scale

Score	0	1	2
Heart rate	Absent	Slow—less than 100 beats per minute	Fast—100–140 beats per minute
Respiratory rate	No breathing for more than one minute	Irregular and slow	Good breathing with normal crying
Muscle tone	Limp and flaccid	Weak, inactive, but some flexion of extremities	Strong, active motion
Body color	Blue and pale	Body pink, but extremities blue	Entire body pink
Reflex irritability	No response	Grimace	Coughing, sneezing, and crying

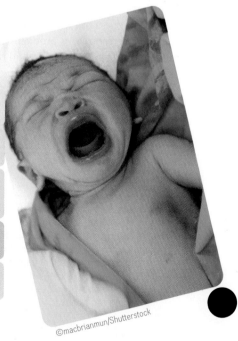
©macbrianmun/Shutterstock

conditions and 26 secondary conditions for which it recommends screening all newborns. However, states vary with respect to which conditions they include (United States Department of Health and Human Services, 2017).

STATES OF AROUSAL AND ACTIVITY LEVELS

Are you an early bird or a night owl? Do you work most effectively in the morning or in the afternoon? When do you get hungry? We all have internal biological clocks that regulate our states of arousal and activity over the course of a day. Babies also have an internal clock that regulates their daily cycles of eating, sleeping, elimination, and even their moods. These periodic cycles of wakefulness, sleep, and activity, which govern an infant's **state of arousal,** or degree of alertness (Table 4.2), seem to be inborn and highly individual. Changes in state are coordinated by multiple areas of the brain (Tokariev, Videman, Palva & Vanhatalo, 2016) and are accompanied by changes in the functioning of virtually all body systems (Ingersoll & Thoman, 1999; Scher, Epstein & Tirosh, 2004). The establishment of "stable and distinct" states of arousal is associated with newborn health and positive outcomes because they are a marker of neurological organization. For example, preterm infants who show more organized sleep patterns early in life have better outcomes at 5 years of age (Weisman, Magori-Cohen, Louzoun, Eidelman & Feldman, 2011).

Youngest babies sleep the most and wake up the most frequently. Parents report that from 0 to 2 months of age, infants sleep about 14.5 hours a day and wake 1.7 times per night (Galland, Taylor, Elder & Herbison, 2012). In the daytime, infants from 0 to 5 months will generally nap about 3 hours a day. Newborns' sleep alternates between quiet (regular) and active (irregular) sleep. Active sleep is the equivalent of rapid eye movement (REM) sleep, which in adults is associated with dreaming. Active sleep appears rhythmically in cycles of about 1 hour and accounts for up to 50 percent of a newborn's total sleep time (Hoban, 2004).

At 2 months of age, the average baby's longest nightly sleep period will be 5.7 hours long, a number that rises to 8.3 hours a night at 6 to 24 months of age. By a year, most babies will sleep 12.6 hours a night total with 0.7 wakings each evening. With respect to daytime napping, a similar developmental trend emerges. By 1 to 2 years of age, most children are napping only about an hour a day (Galland et al., 2012).

state of arousal Infant's physiological and behavioral status at a given moment in the periodic daily cycle of wakefulness, sleep, and activity.

TABLE 4.2 States of Arousal in Infancy

State	Eyes	Breathing	Movements	Responsiveness
Regular sleep	Closed; no eye movements	Regular and slow	None, except for sudden, generalized startles	Cannot be aroused by mild stimuli.
Irregular sleep	Closed; occasional rapid eye movements	Irregular	Muscles twitch, but no major movements	Sounds or light bring smiles or grimaces in sleep.
Drowsiness	Open or closed	Irregular	Somewhat active	May smile, startle, suck, or have erections in response to stimuli.
Alert inactivity	Open	Even	Quiet; may move head, or limbs, and trunk while looking around	An interesting environment (with people, things to watch); may initiate or maintain this state.
Waking activity	Open	Irregular	Much activity	External stimuli (such as hunger, cold, pain, being restrained, or being laid down) bring about more activity, perhaps starting with soft whimpering and gentle movements and turning into a rhythmic crescendo of crying or kicking, or perhaps beginning and enduring as uncoordinated thrashing and spasmodic screeching.

Source: Adapted from H. F. R. Prechtl & D. J. Beintema, "The neurological examination of the full-term newborn infant." *Clinics in Developmental Medicine, 12* (1964), and P. H. Woff, "The natural history of crying and other vocalizations in early infancy." In B. M. Foss (Ed.), *Determinants of infant behavior* (Vol. 4, pp 81–109). London: Methuen, 1969.
©Image Source/Veer

A 2-year-old typically sleeps about 13 hours a day, including naps. The amount of REM sleep also decreases. By age 3, REM sleep declines to less than 30 percent of daily sleep time, and this number continues to decrease steadily throughout life (Hoban, 2004).

Babies' sleep schedules vary across cultures. Among the Micronesian Truk, babies and children have no regular sleep schedules; they fall asleep whenever they feel tired (Broude, 1995). When there is a bedtime it may differ widely by country; the average bedtime in Australia and New Zealand is 7:43 p.m., while in India, the average bedtime is 10:26 p.m. (Mindell, Sadeh, Kwon & Goh, 2013). Mothers in rural Kenya allow their babies to nurse as they please, and their 4-month-olds continue to sleep only 4 hours at a stretch (Broude, 1995). In many predominantly Asian countries, bedtimes are later and total sleep time is shorter than in predominately Caucasian countries (Mindell, Sadeh, Wiegand, How & Goh, 2010; Galland, Taylor, Elder & Herbison, 2010). In the United States, many parents spend a great deal of energy trying, often unsuccessfully, to change babies' states, mostly by soothing a fussy infant to sleep. This is common; across different cultures, parents are likely to report sleeping problems

on the part of their children. However, despite different sleep patterns, over the course of a 24-hour day, young children get roughly equivalent amounts of sleep, often making up lost nighttime sleep with daytime naps (Mindell, Sadeh, Kwon & Goh, 2013). Still, sleep problems are an important issue to address; low-quality infant sleep has been associated with later attention and behavioral problems (Sadeh et al., 2015).

Birth Complications and Their Aftermath

Emily and her husband were fortunate: She had good prenatal care, a healthy pregnancy, and her newborn son was born without complications. As in Emily's case, the great majority of births result in normal, healthy babies; some, sadly, do not. Some infants are born prematurely or very small, some remain in the womb too long, and some are born dead or die soon after birth. Let's look at these potential complications of birth and how they can be avoided or treated to maximize the chances of favorable outcomes.

LOW BIRTH WEIGHT

Low-birth-weight babies weigh less than 5½ pounds (2,500 grams) at birth; they may be either preterm (born early) or small-for-date (born small by comparison to other babies of the same age), or both (Figure 4.3). More than 43 percent of **preterm (premature) infants**, born before completing the 37th week of pregnancy, are of low birth weight (Martin et al., 2009). **Small-for-date (small-for-gestational-age) infants**, who may or may not be preterm, weigh less than 90 percent of babies born at the same age. Their small size is generally a result of inadequate prenatal nutrition, which slows fetal growth.

Factors increasing the likelihood a woman will have an underweight baby include:

- *Demographic and socioeconomic factors,* such as being African American, under age 17 or over 40, poor, unmarried, or undereducated, and being born in certain regions, such as the southern and plains states (Martin, Hamilton, Osterman, Driscoll & Mathews, 2017; Thompson, Goodman, Chang, & Stukel, 2005)

- *Medical factors predating the pregnancy,* such as having no children or more than four, being short or thin, having had previous low-birth-weight infants or multiple miscarriages, having particular genetic variants associated with higher risk (National Institutes of Health, 2010a), having been low

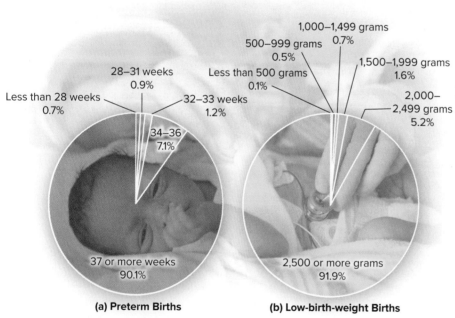

FIGURE 4.3 Birth Complications

Percentages of live births were: (a) preterm (less than 37 weeks gestation); or (b) low birth weight (less than 2,500 grams). Low-birth-weight babies can be preterm or small-for-date, or both.

Source: J. A. Martin, B. E. Hamilton, M. J. K. Osterman, A. K. Driscoll, and P. Drake, "Births: Final data for 2016." *National Vital Statistics Reports, 67*(1), Hyattsville, MD: National Center for Health Statistics, 2018.

©ERproductions Ltd/Blend Images

birth weight oneself, or having genital or urinary abnormalities or chronic hypertension

- *Prenatal behavioral and environmental factors*, such as poor nutrition; inadequate prenatal care; smoking; use of alcohol or other drugs; or exposure to stress, high altitude, or toxic substances
- *Medical conditions*, such as vaginal bleeding, infections, high or low blood pressure, anemia, too little weight gain, and having last given birth less than 12 months or more than 5 years ago (Arias, MacDorman, Strobino, & Guyer, 2003; O'Leary, Nassar, Kurinczuk, & Bower, 2009; Zhu, Rolfs, Nangle, & Horan, 1999; DeFranco, Stamilio, Boslaugh, Gross, & Muglia, 2007)

An estimated 15 percent of all infants worldwide are born with low birth weight, and the percentages are far greater in less economically developed countries. The true extent of low birth weight may be much higher because nearly half of the newborns in the developing world are not weighed at birth (UNICEF, 2013). Low birth weight in developing regions stems primarily from the mother's poor health and nutrition. In the industrialized world, smoking during pregnancy is the leading factor in low birth weight (UNICEF & WHO, 2004).

In the United States, 8.2 percent of infants born in 2016 were low-birth-weight babies—a number that has increased slightly since 2012. In the same year, 9.9 percent of U.S. infants were preterm. Much of the incidence of low-birth-weight and preterm births is due to delayed childbearing, multiple births, use of fertility drugs, and induced and cesarean deliveries. The risk of both preterm delivery and low birth weight increases rapidly with the number of babies being carried, approaching 100 percent for quadruplets (Martin et al., 2018).

In 2015 and 2016, the late preterm birthrate rose slightly, up to 7.1 percent, after declining each year from 2007 to 2014 (Martin et al., 2018). Late preterm infants, delivered between 34 and 36 weeks of gestation, tend to weigh more and to fare better than those born earlier in gestation, but in comparison with full-term babies, they too are at greater risk of early death or adverse effects such as respiratory distress, hospitalization, and brain injuries (Martin, Hamilton et al., 2009).

Birth weight and length of gestation are the two most important predictors of an infant's survival and health (Mathews & MacDorman, 2008). Together they constitute the second leading cause of death in infancy in the United States after birth defects (Kochanek, Murphy, Xu & Tejada-Vera, 2016). Preterm birth is involved in nearly half of neurological birth defects, such as cerebral palsy, and more than one-third of infant death. Altogether, low-birth-weight infants account for more than two-thirds of infant deaths. Internationally, low birth weight is an underlying factor in 60 to 80 percent of neonatal deaths worldwide (UNICEF, 2008a).

The United States has been more successful than any other country in saving low-birth-weight babies, but the rate of such births to U.S. women remains higher than in some European and Asian nations (MacDorman & Mathews, 2009). Preventing preterm births would greatly increase the number of babies who survive the first year of life. In the last decade, some countries have halved deaths attributed to preterm delivery, most notably with training and the provision of equipment and supplies. For example, even low-tech changes such as ensuring appropriate warmth, support for breast-feeding, and training in basic care for infections and breathing problems can reduce mortality rates.

Immediate Treatment and Outcomes

The most pressing fear regarding very small babies is that they will die in infancy. Because their immune systems are not fully developed, they are especially vulnerable to infection, which has been linked to slowed growth and developmental delays (Stoll et al., 2004). Moreover, they sometimes require a variety of aggressive interventions such as intramuscular injections or intubation, the insertion of a chest or feeding tube. Such invasive procedures increase the chances of infection. Also, these infants' nervous systems may be too immature for them to perform basic survival functions, such as sucking, so they may need to be fed intravenously (through the veins). Because they do not have enough fat to insulate them and to generate heat, it is hard for them to stay warm.

A low-birth-weight or at-risk preterm baby is placed in an isolette, an antiseptic, temperature-controlled crib, and fed through tubes. To counteract the sensory impoverishment of life in an isolette, hospital workers and parents are encouraged to give these small babies special handling. Preterm babies are especially at risk for slowed growth and developmental delays (Scharf, Stroustrup, Conaway & DeBoer, 2016), although

TABLE 4.3 Percentage of Low-Birth-Weight Infants by Selected United Nations Regions, 2008–2012

	% Low-Birth-Weight Infants
WORLD	15
LEAST DEVELOPED COUNTRIES	13
SUB-SAHARAN AFRICA	13
Eastern and Southern Africa	11
West and Central Africa	14
SOUTH ASIA	28
EAST ASIA AND PACIFIC	6
LATIN AMERICA AND CARIBBEAN	9

*Data refer to the most recent year available during 2008–2012.

Source: UNICEF, *The State of the World's Children: 2014 in Numbers. Every Child Counts. Revealing Disparities, Advancing Children's Rights.* www.unicef.org/sowc2014/numbers/

girls tend to be hardier than boys (Glass, Costarino, Stayer, Brett, Cladis & Davis, 2015).

Babies who are born prematurely may not have fully developed biological clocks (Levitt, 2003), which may disrupt sleep processes. Compared with full-term infants, premature infants are more alert and wakeful and have longer stretches of quiet sleep and more REMs in active sleep. Their sleep is more fragmented, with more transitions between sleeping and waking (Ingersoll & Thoman, 1999; Holditch-Davis, Scher, Schwartz & Hudson-Barr, 2004). The more disorganized their sleep is, the worse their later outcomes seem to be. For example, preterm infants who primarily cycled between quiet sleep and wakefulness at 37 weeks of gestational age showed better outcomes when compared to preterm infants who primarily cycled between states of high arousal such as active sleep and cry, or shorter episodes of active and quiet sleep. The measured outcomes included better neonatal neuromaturation at discharge from the hospital; better emotion regulation at 3 and 6 months; more advanced cognitive development at 6, 12, and 24 months; and higher verbal IQ, executive function, and symbolic competence at 5 years of age (Weisman, Magori-Cohen, Louzoun, Eidelman & Feldman, 2011).

Gentle massage seems to foster growth, weight gain, motor activity, cognitive development, behavioral and neurological organization, and can shorten the hospital stay (Field, Diego & Hernandez-Reif, 2007; Procianoy, Mendes & Silveira, 2010; Guzzetta et al., 2011). Kangaroo care, a method of skin-to-skin contact in which a newborn is laid face down between the mother's breasts for an hour or so at a time after birth, seems to reduce stress on the central nervous system and helps with self-regulation of sleep and activity (Ferber & Makhoul, 2004). It has been associated with reductions in preterm infant mortality (Lawn, Mwansa-Kambafwile, Horta, Barros & Cousens, 2010).

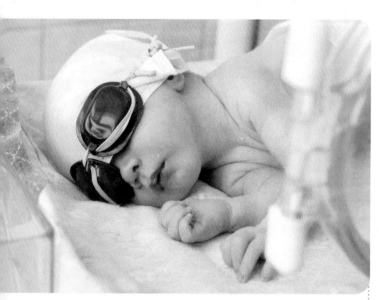

Preterm infants face many immediate health challenges, but special handling can help improve outcomes.
©Li_Al/Shutterstock

Respiratory distress syndrome, also called hyaline membrane disease, is common in preterm babies who lack an adequate amount of *surfactant*, an essential lung-coating substance that keeps air sacs from collapsing. These babies may breathe irregularly or stop breathing altogether. Since the late 1990s, administering surfactant to high-risk preterm newborns has dramatically increased survival rates (Glass et al., 2015) as well as their neurological and developmental status at 18 to 22 months (Vohr, Wright, Poole, & McDonald for the NICHD Neonatal Research Network Follow-up Study, 2005). In one study, the percentage of extremely low-birth-weight infants who survived unimpaired increased from 32 percent to approximately 50 percent (Wilson-Costello et al., 2007).

Long-Term Outcomes

Even if low-birth-weight babies survive the dangerous early days, their trials may not be over. While most survivors of prematurity, even when born very young and small, live productive and happy lives, they are at greater risk for a host of adverse health outcomes when compared to adults who were born full term (Doyle & Anderson, 2010). For example, preterm infants are at higher risk of high blood pressure (Parkinson, Hyde, Gale, Santhakumaran & Modi, 2013), both preterm and small-for-date infants are at increased risk of adult-onset diabetes, and small-for-date infants appear to be at increased risk of cardiovascular disease (Hofman et al., 2004; Sperling, 2004). In addition, preterm birth is associated with a heightened risk of death throughout childhood, diminished reproductive rates in adulthood, and, for women, increased risk of bearing preterm infants themselves (Swamy, Ostbye & Skjaerven, 2008). Generally, the shorter the period of gestation, the greater the likelihood of cerebral palsy, intellectual disability, autistic disorders, and low educational and job-related income levels (Moster Lie, & Markestad, 2008).

In longitudinal studies of extremely low-birth-weight infants (about 1 to 2 pounds at birth) and infants born before 26 weeks of gestation, the survivors tend to be smaller than full-term children and are more likely to have neurological, sensory, cognitive, educational, and behavioral problems (Hutchinson et al., 2013; Samara, Marlow & Wolke for the EPICure Study Group, 2008). Cognitive deficits, especially in memory and information-processing speed, have been noted among very low-birth-weight babies (those weighing less than 1,500 grams or 3½ pounds at birth) by age 5 or 6

Did you know?

Think of the lungs as a balloon: Surfactant is the substance that keeps the balloon inflated.
©C Squared Studios/Getty Images

Low-birth-weight infants are at higher risk for a variety of physical, cognitive, and behavioral issues, but positive environmental factors can make a difference. Most small and premature infants go on to live healthy and productive lives.
©Ron Nickel/Design Pics

months, continuing throughout childhood (Rose & Feldman, 2000; Rose, Feldman & Jankowski, 2002), adolescence (Litt et al., 2012), and persisting into adulthood (Fearon et al., 2004; Greene, 2002; Hack et al., 2002; Hardy, Kuh, Langenberg, & Wadsworth, 2003). Very-low-birthweight children and adolescents also tend to have more behavioral and mental health problems than those born at normal weight (Hack et al., 2004) as well as impaired motor development both in the first year of life and throughout childhood and adolescence (de Kieviet, Piek, Aarnoudse-Moens & Oosterlaan, 2009).

However, environmental factors can make a difference. Factors such as maternal education, two-parent family structure, and higher SES are associated with positive developmental outcomes for preterm infants (Voss, Jungmann, Wachtendorf & Neubaur, 2012; Saigal et al., 2006). Parenting matters as well; when parents are low in anger and criticism, their preterm babies have better outcomes (Poehlmann-Tynan et al., 2015); and when preterm babies have mothers who are low in anxiety they are more likely to be high in cognitive development and low in internalizing behavioral problems as toddlers (Zelkowitz, Na, Wang, Bardin & Papageorgiou, 2011). Babies are highly resilient, and a high-quality postnatal environment can do much to moderate the potential effects of being born small.

POSTMATURITY

When people think about birth complications, they generally think about babies being born too early or too small. However, babies can also be affected by staying too long in the womb. In fact, approximately 7 percent of pregnant women in the United States have not given birth after 42 or more weeks of gestation (Galal, Symonds, Murray, Petraglia & Smith, 2012). At that point, a baby is considered **postmature**.

Postmature babies tend to be long and thin as they continue to grow in the womb, but the placenta becomes less efficient as the pregnancy progresses, resulting in decreased levels of nutrients and oxygen available to the baby. The baby's greater size also complicates labor; the mother has to deliver a baby the size of a normal 1-month-old.

postmature A fetus not yet born as of 42 weeks' gestation.

stillbirth Death of a fetus at or after the 20th week of gestation.

Because postmature fetuses are at risk of brain damage or even death, doctors sometimes induce labor or perform cesarean deliveries. The increasing use of both of these techniques probably explains a decline in postterm births in recent years (Martin et al., 2006).

STILLBIRTH

Stillbirth, the sudden death of a fetus at or after the 20th week of gestation, is a tragic union of opposites—birth and death. Sometimes fetal death is diagnosed prenatally; in other cases, the baby's death is discovered during labor or delivery. Worldwide, about 3.2 million fetuses are stillborn annually (Lawn et al., 2010). In the United States, the incidence of stillbirth has fallen steadily since 1990. The reduction in stillbirths may be due to electronic fetal monitoring, ultrasound, measures to identify fetuses at risk for restricted growth, and even corrective prenatal surgery in the womb (Goldenberg, Kirby & Culhane, 2004). Still, in 2013, there were almost 24,000 stillbirths in the United States, a number representing 5.96 fetal deaths for every 1,000 live births. Boys are more likely to be stillborn than girls, non-Hispanic black fetuses are more likely to be stillborn than fetuses of other racial/ethnic groups, and twins and higher multiples are more likely to be stillborn than singletons (MacDorman & Gregory, 2015).

Although the cause of stillbirth is often not clear, many stillborn fetuses are small for gestational age, indicating malnourishment in the womb (MacDorman & Gregory, 2015). Fetuses believed to have problems can have prenatal surgery in the womb to correct congenital problems or be delivered prematurely (Goldenberg, Kirby & Culhane, 2004). Interventions such as these could prevent a large proportion of stillbirths (Bhutta et al., 2011).

Newborns and Parents

Emily and her husband were thrilled with their new baby, but unanticipated challenges came with that joy. Their baby, as is typical for newborns, woke every few hours wanting to feed; he needed constant care and seemed to spend every early evening crying without any identifiable reason the frantic parents could find for distress. Emily and her husband found themselves irritable, overtired, and stressed by both their new baby and the unending stream of advice given to the new parents.

Childbirth is a major transition, not only for the baby, but also for the parents. Suddenly almost all their time and energy, it seems, is focused on this newcomer in their lives.

©Digital Vision/Getty Images

INFANT CARE: A CROSS-CULTURAL VIEW

Infant care practices vary greatly around the world. In Bali, infants are believed to be ancestors brought to life and thus must be treated with utmost dignity and respect. The Beng of West Africa think young babies can understand all languages, whereas people in the Micronesian atoll of Ifaluk believe babies cannot understand language at all, and therefore adults do not speak to them (DeLoache & Gottlieb, 2000).

In some societies infants have multiple caregivers. Among the Efe of central Africa, for example, infants typically receive care from five or more people per hour and are routinely breast-fed by other women besides the mother (Tronick, Morelli & Ivey, 1992). Among the Gusii in western Kenya, where

infant mortality is high, parents keep their infants close to them, respond quickly when they cry, and feed them on demand (LeVine, 1994). The same is true of Aka foragers in central Africa who live in small groups marked by sharing, cooperation, and concern about danger. However, Ngandu farmers in the same region, who tend to live farther apart and to stay in one place for long periods of time, are more likely to leave their infants alone (Hewlett, Lamb, Shannon, Leyendecker, & Schölmerich, 1998).

We need to remember that patterns of interaction we take for granted may be culture-based. Moreover, from the very first day, the ways in which babies' needs and desires are managed begins the lifelong process of socialization.

Parents, and perhaps siblings, are getting acquainted with the baby and developing emotional bonds. Especially with a first birth, a newborn brings insistent demands that challenge the parents' ability to cope—and may affect their marital relationship.

CHILDBIRTH AND BONDING

How and when does the mother-infant bond—the close, caring connection between mother and newborn—develop? Some researchers studying this topic have followed the ethological approach (introduced in Chapter 1), which considers behavior in human beings, as in animals, to be biologically influenced and emphasizes critical or sensitive periods for development of certain behaviors.

John Bowlby (1960) suggested that we are prewired by natural selection to want to care for infants. We find them cute, not because there is anything objectively cute about them but because our minds see them that way. We find their cries unpleasant and rush to help them because those parents who took good care of their newborns passed their genes on to us. In other words, we are biologically prepared by evolution to engage in the parenting relationship. From an evolutionary perspective, parental bonding is a mechanism that ensures the parents invest the tremendous energy and resources needed to enable a helpless infant to survive and reproduce.

There is a neurological basis for parental bonding. For example, research has shown that we are not only wired to see babies as cute, but also to find their sounds and smells endearing, and that these stimuli capture our attention rapidly and trigger caregiving behaviors (Kringelbach, Stark,

Alexander, Bornstein & Steing, 2016). Additionally, adults' brains, in an area of the frontal cortex involved in processing feelings of reward and pleasure, show an almost immediate surge of activity in response to unfamiliar infants' faces but not to the equally attractive faces of unfamiliar adults (Kringelbach et al., 2008). Similarly, our brains respond more quickly to infant cries than to those of adults (Young et al., 2015). In short, our brains show evidence of specific parental circuitry designed by natural selection to help us bond with and care for children.

Fathers, like mothers, form close bonds with their babies. This may even be influenced at a biological level;

Fathers can form close bonds with their infants.
©Lisette Le Bon/Purestock/SuperStock

When given the choice, infant rhesus monkeys spend more time clinging to a warm, soft terry-cloth mother even if the alternative, a wire surrogate mother, provides the food.
©Martin Rogers/Getty Images

there are indications that involved fathers show decreases in testosterone levels over the course of a pregnancy, suggesting their physiology is helping them prepare for engagement in parenting behaviors (Gray, Yang & Pope Jr., 2006; Gettler, McDade, Feranil & Kuzawa, 2011). Fathers who are present at the birth of a child often see the event as a "peak emotional experience" (May & Perrin, 1985) or as the best thing that has happened to them (Longworth & Kingdon, 2010). But a man can become emotionally committed to his newborn whether or not he attended the birth (Palkovitz, 1985), although this relationship is often impacted by the quality of the relationship between the mother and father (Fagan, Palkovitz, Roy & Farrie, 2009).

THE MOTHER-INFANT BOND

For many years, psychology theorists thought babies bonded to their parents because parents provided food, which babies naturally enjoyed. Over time, babies would start to associate their parents with the provision of food and would then become attached to them. A series of pioneering experiments with monkeys by Harry Harlow and his colleagues (Harlow & Zimmerman, 1959) established that more than feeding is involved in the mother-infant bond. In these experiments, rhesus monkeys were separated from their mothers

and raised in a laboratory. The infant monkeys were put into cages with two kinds of surrogate "mothers": a plain cylindrical wire-mesh form with an attached bottle for nursing or a form covered with terry cloth that provided no food. The essential question was "to which mother would the baby monkeys become attached?" If earlier theorists were right, the babies should have become attached to the wire "mother" because she provided food. However, the monkeys actually became attached to the soft terry-cloth "mother." When the monkeys were allowed to spend time with either kind of "mother," they all spent more time—indeed the majority of their time—clinging to and cuddling with the cloth surrogates.

It is hardly surprising that a dummy mother would not provide the same kinds of stimulation and opportunities for positive development as a live mother. These studies show that feeding is not the most important thing babies get from their mothers. Mothering includes the comfort of close bodily contact and, at least in monkeys, the satisfaction of an innate need to cling.

THE FATHER'S ROLE

The fathering role has different meanings in different cultures. It may be taken or shared by someone other than the biological father: the mother's brother, as in Botswana, where young mothers remain with their childhood family until their partners are in their forties, or a grandfather, as in Vietnam (Engle & Breaux, 1998; Richardson, 1995; Townsend, 1997). In some societies, fathers are more involved in their young children's lives—economically, emotionally, and in time spent—than in other cultures, and this may change over historical time periods as well (Engle & Breaux, 1998).

In China, fathers tend to be stern and aloof, and their children respect and fear them. Men rarely hold infants. Fathers interact more with toddlers but perform child care duties only if the mother is absent. However, urbanization and maternal employment are changing these attitudes. Fathers—especially college-educated fathers—now seek more intimate relationships with children, especially sons (Engle & Breaux, 1998). Alternately, among the Aka of central Africa, fathers are as nurturant and emotionally supportive as mothers. In fact, "Aka fathers provide more direct infant care than fathers in any other known society" (Hewlett, 1992, p. 169).

In the United States and some other countries, fathers' involvement in caregiving and play has greatly increased since 1970 as more mothers have begun to work outside the home and concepts of fathering have changed (Cabrera, Tamis-LaMonda, Bradley, Hofferth & Lamb, 2000; Wood & Repetti, 2004). For example, married fathers spent more than twice as much time with child care (6.5 hours) and housework (9.7 hours) in 2000 than they did in 1965 (Bianchi, Robinson & Milkie, 2006). On weekends, as their children get older, the time fathers spend with their children is more equal to that of mothers (Yeung et al., 2001). Work affects this as well. Fathers with long working hours report wanting more time to spend with their children but being unable to do so (Milkie, Mattingly, Nomaguchi, Bianchi & Robinson, 2004). A father's frequent and positive involvement with his child, from infancy on, is directly related to the child's well-being and physical, cognitive, and social development (Cabrera et al., 2000; Shannon, Tamis-LeMonda, London & Cabrera, 2002).

HOW PARENTHOOD AFFECTS MARITAL SATISFACTION

How does parenthood affect the relationship between marriage partners? Results are mixed. Some studies show that marital satisfaction typically declines during the child-raising years—and the more children, the greater the decline. Moreover, mothers of young infants tend to feel the effects most strongly. For example, only 38 percent of new mothers report high marital satisfaction compared with 62 percent of childless wives (Twenge, Campbell & Foster, 2003).

Why do these declines occur? New parents are likely to experience stressors that can affect their health and state of mind. Taking care of newborn babies is difficult and often comes with sleep deprivation, uncertainty, and isolation. Nighttime crying, for example, is associated with a decrease in marital satisfaction in the 1st year of the child's life (Meijer & van den Wittenboer, 2007). If the woman was working outside the home and is now staying home, the burden of housework and child care may fall mostly on her. Indeed, the division of household tasks is a common issue among new parents (Schulz, Cowan & Cowan, 2006). Many couples find their relationship becoming more "traditional" following the birth of a child, with the woman often engaging in the bulk of caregiving and housekeeping (Cox & Paley, 2003). The perceptions of unfairness and inequity that result from this process can damage the marital relationship (Dew & Wilcox, 2011).

However, the picture is not all bad. Other studies tell a different story, and it may be that additional variables are needed to truly understand the effect of a new baby. For example, whether or not the couple was happy prior to the pregnancy, whether or not the pregnancy was planned, and the age of parents affects marital satisfaction after the birth of a child (Lawrence, Rothman, Cobb, Rothman & Bradbury, 2008; Nelson, Kushlev, English, Dunn & Lyubomirsky, 2013). Other studies have found no differences in marital satisfaction

in the first year of marriage for couples that do and do not have children (McHale & Huston, 1985), and some data indicate that parents have greater happiness, positive emotions, and meaning in life than non-parents (Nelson et al., 2013).

A recent attempt to make sense of these contrasting findings suggests that when studies are examined in concert, a small but significant decrease in marital satisfaction is common 1 to 2 years after the birth of a child. However, this decline is also found in married couples without a child. Thus it may be a general relational process rather than one specific to the parenting transition (Mitnick, Heyman & Slep, 2009).

There are indications, too, that declines in satisfaction are not inevitable. Parents who participate in professionally led couples discussion groups about parenting issues and relationships, beginning in the last trimester of pregnancy, report significantly smaller declines in satisfaction (Schulz et al., 2006). Additionally, the marital relationships of parents who have secure attachments weather the birth of a child more effectively than those who are anxious or avoidant in their relationships (Kohn et al., 2012). Factors outside the home matter as well. A good work-life balance, and the consequent reduction in stress, is also associated with less of a decline in marital satisfaction following the birth of a child (van Steenbergen, Kluwer & Karney, 2011). It may be that the adjustment is easier when parents have more accurate perceptions of the impact a new child is likely to have on the marriage and the necessary resources to handle the increased responsibility and stress a newborn brings (Kalmuss, Davidson & Cushman, 1992).

The birth of a baby, as momentous an achievement as it is, marks the start of a challenging but rewarding journey. In Chapter 5, we start to examine the rapidly growing understanding of the physical developments of infancy and toddlerhood, mindful of the fact that physical, cognitive, and psychosocial development are always intertwined.

Planning, open discussion, and a good work-life balance can all help a couple handle the challenging transition to parenthood.
©Ned Frisk Photography/Brand X Pictures/Jupiterimages

WHAT DO YOU THINK?

The general finding about parenthood is that parents report less marital satisfaction than nonparents. But are the right groups being compared? Some people don't have children because they don't want them. Some people don't have children because they can't. How might these differences impact the statistics about parenting and happiness?

©McGraw-Hill Education

mastering the CHAPTER

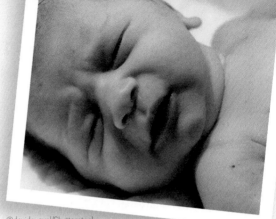

©davidsunyol/Shutterstock

Summary and Key Terms

How Childbirth Has Changed

> In Europe and the United States, childbirth before the twentieth century was risky for both mothers and infants. Birth was a female ritual that occurred at home and was attended by a midwife. Pain relief was minimal.

> Childbirth began to be professionalized in the twentieth century. Births took place in hospitals and

were attended by physicians. Medical advances dramatically improved safety.

> Today, delivery at home or in birth centers attended by midwives can be a relatively safe alternative to physician-attended hospital delivery for women with low-risk pregnancies.

The Birth Process

> The birth process consists of three stages: (1) dilation of the cervix, (2) descent and emergence of the baby, and (3) expulsion of the umbilical cord and the placenta.

> Electronic fetal monitoring is widely used and can detect signs of fetal distress.

> About 32 percent of births in the United States are by cesarean delivery.

> Alternative methods of prepared childbirth can minimize the need for painkilling drugs and maximize parents' active involvement. Modern epidurals can give effective pain relief with smaller doses of medication than in the past.

> The presence of a doula can provide physical benefits as well as emotional support.

> KEY TERMS

Electronic fetal monitoring	Cesarean delivery	Natural, or prepared, childbirth

The Newborn Baby

> The neonatal period is a time of transition from the uterus to independent existence. During the first few days, the neonate loses weight and then regains it; the lanugo (prenatal hair) falls off, and the protective coating of vernix caseosa is absorbed into the skin. The fontanels (soft spots) in the skull close within the first 18 months.

> Infants are born with multiple reflexes, including the sucking reflex and the rooting reflex.

> At birth, the circulatory, respiratory, digestive, elimination, and temperature regulation systems become independent of the mother's. If a newborn cannot start breathing within about five minutes, brain injury may

occur. Within three to four days after birth, many babies develop neonatal jaundice due to immaturity of the liver.

> At 1 minute and 5 minutes after birth, a neonate's Apgar score can indicate how well he or she is adjusting to extrauterine life. The Brazelton Neonatal Behavioral Assessment Scale can predict future development. Neonatal screening is done for certain rare medical conditions, such as PKU and congenital hypothyroidism.

> A newborn's state of arousal is governed by periodic cycles of wakefulness, sleep, and activity. Sleep takes up the major, but a diminishing, amount of a neonate's time. Cultural customs affect sleep patterns.

> KEY TERMS

Neonatal period	Neonatal jaundice	Brazelton Neonatal Behavioral Assessment Scale (NBAS)
Neonate	Apgar scale	State of arousal
Anoxia		

Birth Complications and Their Aftermath

> Complications of childbirth include low birth weight, pre- or postmature birth, and stillbirth.

> Low-birth-weight babies may be either preterm (premature) or small for gestational age. Low birth weight is a major factor in infant mortality and can cause long-term physical and cognitive problems.

> A supportive postnatal environment and other protective factors often can improve the outcome for babies suffering from birth complications.

KEY TERMS

Low-birth-weight babies
Preterm (premature) infants

Small-for-date (small-for-gestational-age) infants

Postmature
Stillbirth

Newborns and Parents

> Researchers following the ethological approach suggest that there is a sensitive period for the formation of the mother-infant bond. Human brains show evidence of specific responses designed to help bond with and care for children. Fathers can bond with their babies whether or not they are present at birth.

> Infants have strong needs for maternal closeness and warmth as well as for food.

> Fathering roles and child-raising practices vary across cultures.

> Research findings on the impact of parenthood on the relationship between marriage partners have been mixed; becoming a parent is stressful, but other factors such as a couple's relationship prior to pregnancy are also important.

Practice Quiz

1. Women in the industrialized world who give birth today have benefited from a dramatic reduction in risks surrounding pregnancy and childbirth, due to:
   a. use of antibiotics
   b. use of anesthesia
   c. implementation of prenatal care
   d. all of the above

2. What are the three stages of the birth process?
   a. _____
   b. _____
   c. _____

3. List two options for pain management during delivery:
   a. _____
   b. _____

4. Describe what a newborn baby looks like.
   _____
   _____
   _____
   _____
   _____
   _____
   _____

5. Reflexes are a good way to assess a newborn's health because:
   a. they should develop rapidly following birth
   b. they are a marker of neurological organization
   c. they don't require any learning
   d. this is incorrect; reflexes have little to do with newborn health

6. A few days after birth, a baby develops a yellowish tinge to the skin and the eyeballs. These symptoms indicate _____, which is due to immaturity of the _____.
   a. anoxia; liver
   b. anoxia; kidneys
   c. neonatal jaundice; liver
   d. neonatal jaundice; kidneys

7. What screening tests assesses a baby's health at 1 and 5 minutes after birth has occurred?
   a. Brazelton Neonatal Assessment
   b. heelstick and blood draw
   c. Apgar scale
   d. amniocentesis

8. What are states of arousal?
   a. how excited or angry a baby becomes in response to environmental stimulation
   b. the sleep cycles of a newborn
   c. times where the baby is awake or drowsy
   d. periodic cycles of wakefulness, sleep, and activity

9. A baby born at or near her due date, but smaller than other babies born at the same age, would be called a:
   a. preterm baby
   b. postmature birth
   c. small-for-date baby
   d. stillbirth

10. Postmature babies are at risk for
   a. high volume of amniotic fluid, which puts pressure on the brain
   b. brain damage
   c. hyaline membrane disease
   d. respiratory distress syndrome

11. Which of the following would be the least likely feature of a stillborn baby?
   a. African American
   b. a twin
   c. a girl
   d. small-for-date

12. According to ethologists parents love their babies because:
   a. they are prewired to engage in attachment relationships by natural selection
   b. they are worried that people would respond negatively if it appeared they did not love their baby
   c. they learned from their culture that this is what parents are supposed to do
   d. they imprint on their babies

13. According to research with young primates, what is the most important thing mothers provide?
   a. protection against aggressive others
   b. physical contact and warmth
   c. food
   d. water

14. From infancy on, a father's frequent and positive involvement with his child is directly related to:
   a. level of educational achievement
   b. the child's social, cognitive, and physical development
   c. marital satisfaction
   d. the child's ability to self-regulate

15. Marital satisfaction typically _____ during the child-raising years.
   a. increases
   b. decreases
   c. increases, then decreases
   d. decreases, then increases

Answers: 1. d; 2. First Stage: Dilation of the Cervix; Second Stage: Descent and Emergence of the Infant; Third Stage: Expulsion of the Placenta; 3. lamaze method; epidural block; 4. Healthy full-term infants are on average 20 inches long and weigh 7½ pounds. They have a large head, various skin conditions, a receding chin, and may have a misshapen head. They are covered with lanugo (soft downy hair) and vernix caseosa (a cheesy substance). They may also have swollen breast tissue and genitals; 5. b; 6. c; 7. c; 8. b; 9. c; 10. b; 11. c; 12. a; 13. b; 14. b; 15. b

hen William was born, he was 19½ inches long and weighed 7½ pounds. He slept in short bursts most of the day and night and cried when he needed to be fed, changed, or soothed. Over the next 12 months, William grew nearly 10 inches and gained 20 pounds. Although he was not walking by himself when he turned 1, he could stand or cruise around the room while holding on to something or, when motivated, crawl with astonishing speed. Using gestures, such as outstretched arms when he wanted to be picked up, and a small vocabulary of one-word utterances, William could make his needs and desires clear. To his parents' relief he now slept through the night and took two short naps during the day. William was a typically developing infant, who at 12 months was on the verge of toddlerhood.

Infancy begins at birth and ends when a child begins walking and stringing words together—usually between 12 and 18 months. Toddlerhood lasts from about 18 to 36 months, a period when children become more verbal, independent, and able to move about. Although we focus on infants' and toddlers' physical development in this chapter, on their cognitive development in Chapter 6, and on their psychosocial development in Chapter 7, we will see many examples of how these aspects of development intertwine. All areas of development are interrelated, and development proceeds in a complex, reciprocal fashion.

In this chapter, we examine typical growth patterns of body and brain, and we see how a nourishing environment can stimulate both. We explore how sensory perception goes hand in hand with motor skills and shapes the astoundingly rapid development of the brain. And we discuss threats to infants' life and health, including abuse and neglect, and ways to prevent them.

● ● ● ●

Early Growth and Physical Development

The first three years are a time of explosive growth and development. Never again will a person grow so quickly or change so rapidly. Despite its rapid growth, however, the developing body grows in an orderly and patterned way. For growth to be optimal, good nutrition and healthy eating habits are important. We discuss these processes in the following sections.

PRINCIPLES OF EARLY GROWTH AND PHYSICAL DEVELOPMENT

An infant's head is gigantic compared to the rest of its body. If you had the same body proportions as an infant, your head would approach the size of a watermelon. This highlights the cephalocaudal principle of early growth and physical development. According to the *cephalocaudal principle*, growth occurs from top down. Thus, a newborn baby's head is disproportionately large. At 1 year, the brain is 70 percent of its adult weight, but the rest of the body is only 10 to 20 percent of adult weight. The head becomes proportionately smaller as the child grows in height and the lower parts of the body develop (Figure 5.1). Sensory and motor development follow the same principle; infants see objects before they can control their torso, and they learn to use the upper parts of the body before the lower parts.

According to the *proximodistal principle*, growth and motor development proceed from the center of the body outward. For example, babies first develop the ability to use their upper arms and upper legs, then the forearms and forelegs, then hands and feet, and finally fingers and toes.

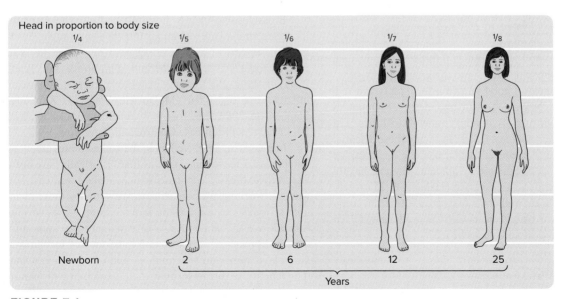

FIGURE 5.1

Changes in Proportions of the Human Body

PHYSICAL GROWTH

Growth is faster in the first few months of life than it ever will be again. By 5 months, the average U.S. baby boy's birth weight has doubled to nearly 16 pounds and has more than tripled to exceed 25 pounds by 1 year. This rapid growth rate tapers off during the 2nd and 3rd years. A boy typically gains about 5½ pounds by his second birthday and 3 more pounds by his third, when he tips the scales at almost 34 pounds. A boy's height typically increases by 10 inches during the 1st year (making the average 1-year-old boy about 30 inches tall), by 5 inches during the 2nd year (the average 2-year-old boy is about 3 feet tall), and by 2½ inches during the 3rd year (to approach 39 inches). Girls follow a similar pattern but are slightly smaller at most ages (Kuczmarski et al., 2000; McDowell et al., 2008). As a baby grows into a toddler, body shape and proportions change too; a 3-year-old typically is slender compared with a chubby, potbellied 1-year-old.

The genes an infant inherits strongly influence whether the child will be tall or short, thin or stocky, or somewhere in between. This genetic influence interacts with environmental influences, such as nutrition and living conditions, to determine characteristics. Today, children in many developed countries are growing taller and maturing at an earlier age than children did a century ago, probably because of better nutrition, improved sanitation and medical care, and decreases in child labor. Teething usually begins around 3 or 4 months, when infants begin grabbing almost everything in sight to put into their mouths, but the first tooth may not actually arrive until sometime between 5 and 9 months, or even later. By the first birthday, babies generally have six to eight teeth; by age 2½, they have a mouthful of 20.

Actress Maggie Gyllenhaal breast feeds her daughter Ramona.
©Hector Vallenilla, Pacificcoastn/Newscom

NUTRITION

Like most babies, William was an avid eater from birth. Whether breast-feeding or taking a bottle from his dad, he seemed happiest while eating. Cereals and other solid foods were gradually introduced before his first birthday, and William happily adjusted to this new experience. As he matured into toddlerhood, he became pickier—gobbling down his favorite foods with gusto and throwing others, such as broccoli and green peppers, onto the ground in disgust.

The importance of good nutrition for infants and toddlers is critical. Normal growth and brain development require the proper mix of vitamins, minerals, calories, and high-quality protein sources. Failure to secure these essential substances can have effects lasting far past the early years in areas as diverse as cognitive development, physical health, work capacity, and earning power (Habicht & Martorell, 2010). Babies who eat well in the first year are smarter, stronger, healthier, and better suited to life's challenges. Given this, how and what should babies be fed?

Breast-feeding

Through most of human history, all babies were breast-fed. With the advent of dependable refrigeration, pasteurization, and sterilization in the first decade of the twentieth century, manufacturers began to develop formulas to modify and enrich cow's milk for infant consumption. During the next half-century, formula feeding became the norm in the United States and some other industrialized countries. By 1971, only 25 percent of U.S. mothers even tried to nurse (Ryan, 1997).

Breast-feeding in U.S. hospitals and elsewhere greatly increased after a United Nations initiative encouraging institutional support of breast-feeding went into effect in 1991 (Merewood, Mehta, Chamberlain, Philipp, & Bauchner, 2005). By 1992–1993, approximately 60 percent of American infants were breast-fed (McDowell, Wang, & Kennedy-Stephenson, 2008), and rose to 82.5 percent of newborns in 2014 (Centers for Disease Control and Prevention, 2017).

Increases in breast-feeding in the United States are most notable in socioeconomic groups that historically have been less likely to breast-feed: black women, teenage women, poor women, working women, and those with no more than high school education. Postpartum maternity leave, flexible scheduling, the ability to take relatively frequent and extended breaks at work to pump milk, privacy for nursing mothers at work and at school, as well as education about the benefits of breast-feeding, and availability of breast pumping facilities might increase its prevalence in these groups (Guendelman et al., 2009; Ryan, Wenjun & Acosta, 2002; Taveras et al., 2003).

With regard to nutrition, breast-feeding is almost always best for infants (Table 5.1). It should begin immediately after birth and continue for at least 1 year, longer if the mother and baby wish (Eidelman et al., 2012). The American Academy of Pediatrics [AAP] Section on Breastfeeding (2005) recommends that babies be exclusively breast-fed for 6 months. Breast-feeding has economic as well as health benefits. If 90 percent of the U.S. mothers in the study complied with the AAP's recommendation to breast-feed for 6 months, potentially 911 infant deaths could be prevented and the United States could save $13 billion annually (Bartick & Reinhold, 2010).

A variety of social factors can make it difficult for women to follow this initiative. Such factors as a short or absent postpartum maternity leave, lack of flexible scheduling, an inability to take relatively frequent and extended breaks at work to pump milk, and a lack of privacy make it difficult to sustain breast-feeding (Guendelman et al., 2009). Thus, many women, even if they desire to breast feed, are unable to do so and must use formula. The only acceptable alternative to breast milk is an iron-fortified formula that is based on either cow's milk or soy protein and contains supplemental vitamins and minerals. Infants weaned during the 1st year should receive iron-fortified formula. At 1 year, babies can switch to cow's milk.

Breast-feeding is inadvisable if a mother is infected with the acquired immune deficiency syndrome (AIDS) virus or any other infectious illness, if she has untreated active tuberculosis, if she has been exposed to radiation, or if she is taking any drug that would not be safe for the baby (AAP Section on Breastfeeding, 2005). The risk of transmitting human immunodeficiency virus (HIV) infection to an infant continues as long as an infected mother breast-feeds (Breast-feeding and HIV International Transmission Study Group, 2004), although this risk can be reduced via the use of zidovudine and/or nevirapine during the first 14 weeks of life (Kumwenda et al., 2008).

Overweight in Infancy

Obesity, defined in infants as having a weight for height in the 95th percentile, has increased in infancy as it has in all age groups in the United States. In 2011–2012, the prevalence of obesity in children birth to age 2 was 8.1 percent (Ogden, Carrol, Kit & Flegal, 2014), with the highest rates found in American Indians or Alaska Natives (20.7 percent) and Latinos (17.9 percent) (Polhamus, Dalenius, Mackintosh, Smith, & Grummer-Strawn, 2011).

TABLE 5.1 Benefits of Breast-feeding

Breast-fed babies . . .

- Are less likely to contract infectious illnesses such as diarrhea; respiratory infections; otitis media (an infection of the middle ear); and staphylococcal, bacterial, and urinary tract infections.
- Have a lower risk of SIDS and of postneonatal death.
- Have less risk of inflammatory bowel disease.
- Have better visual acuity, neurological development, and long-term cardiovascular health, including cholesterol levels.
- Are less likely to develop obesity, asthma, eczema, diabetes, lymphoma, childhood leukemia, and Hodgkin's disease.
- Are less likely to show language and motor delays.
- Score slightly higher on cognitive tests at school age and into young adulthood, but cognitive benefits have been questioned.
- Have fewer cavities and are less likely to need braces.

Breast-feeding mothers . . .

- Enjoy quicker recovery from childbirth with less risk of postpartum bleeding.
- Are more likely to return to their prepregnancy weight and less likely to develop long-term obesity.
- Have reduced risk of anemia and decreased risk of repeat pregnancy while breast-feeding.
- Report feeling more confident and less anxious.
- Are less likely to develop osteoporosis or ovarian and premenopausal breast cancer.

Sources: American Academy of Pediatrics, "Benefits of breastfeeding" (2018 fact sheet), retrieved from www.aap.org/en-us/avocacy-and-policy/aap/health-initiatives/Breastfeeding/Pages/Benefits-of-Breastfeeding.aspx; R. E. Black, S. S. Morris & J. Bryce, "Where and why are 10 million children dying every year?" *The Lancet, 361,* no. 9376 (2003), 2226–2234; A. Chen & W. J. Rogan, "Breastfeeding and the risk of postneonatal death in the United States," *Pediatrics, 113,* no. 5 (2004), e435–e439; D. L. Dee, R. Li, L. C. Lee & L. M. Grummer-Strawn, "Associations between breastfeeding practices and young children's language and motor skill development," *Pediatrics, 119,* Supplement 1 (2007), S92–S98; M. S. Kramer, F. Aboud, E. Mironova, I. Vanilovich, R. W. Platt, L. Matush ... & J. P. Collet, "Breastfeeding and child cognitive development: New evidence from a large randomized trial," *Archives of General Psychiatry, 65,* no. 5 (2008), 578–584; C. I. Lanting, M. Huisman, E. R. Boersma, B. C. L. Touwen & V. Fidler, "Neurological differences between 9-year-old children fed breast-milk or formula-milk as babies," *The Lancet, 344,* no. 8933 (1994), 1319–1322; E. L. Mortensen, K. F. Michaelson, S. A. Sanders & J. M. Reinisch, "The association between duration of breastfeeding and adult intelligence," *Journal of the American Medical Association, 287* (2002), 2365–2371; I. U. Ogbuanu, W. Karmaus, S. H. Arshad, R. J. Kurukulaaratchy & S. Ewart, "Effect of breastfeeding duration on lung function at age 10 years: A prospective birth cohort study," *Thorax, 64,* no. 1 (2009), 62–66; C. G. Owen, P. H. Whincup, K. Odoki, J. A. Gilg & D. G. Cook, "Infant feeding and blood cholesterol: A study in adolescents and a systematic review," *Pediatrics, 110,* no. 3 (2002), 597–608; A. Singhal, T. J. Cole, M. Fewtrell & A. Lucas, "Breastmilk feeding and lipoprotein profile in adolescents born preterm: Follow-up of a prospective randomised study," *The Lancet, 363,* no. 9421 (2004), 1571–1578.

A recent review including data from 282 studies identified a variety of risk factors found in infants and toddlers from 0 to 2 years of age that are associated with later risk of obesity in children. Children born to mothers who had a higher prepregnancy body mass index (BMI) or who gained a great deal of weight during the pregnancy were at higher risk, as were infants who weighed a great deal at birth or gained weight quickly as infants. Additionally, prenatal tobacco exposure was also implicated. Other factors were associated, but not as strongly. These included a maternal diagnosis of gestational diabetes, enrollment in child care, inappropriate bottle use, being introduced to solid food before the age of 4 months, and the use of antibiotics for the infant. These data suggest that efforts to prevent obesity in children should begin with modifiable factors in the infant and toddler period (Baidal et al., 2016).

What should babies be fed? Pediatric experts recommend that iron-enriched solid foods—usually beginning with cereal—should be introduced gradually between ages 6 and 12 months (AAP Section on Breastfeeding, 2005). Unfortunately, many parents do not follow these guidelines. According to random telephone interviews with parents and caregivers of more than 3,000 U.S. infants and toddlers, 29 percent of infants are given solid food before 4 months, 17 percent drink juice before 6 months, and 20 percent drink cow's milk before 12 months. By 7 to 24 months, the median food intake is 20 to 30 percent above normal daily requirements (Fox, Pac, Devaney, & Jankowski, 2004). Thirty percent of 19- to 24-month-old children eat no fruit, and French fries are the most commonly consumed vegetable in this age group. Sixty percent eat baked desserts, 20 percent candy, and 44 percent sweetened beverages on a daily basis (American Heart Association [AHA] et al., 2006).

Malnutrition

While infants and toddlers in the United States may eat too much, in many low-income communities around the world, malnutrition in early life is widespread—and often fatal. Malnutrition is implicated in more than half of deaths of children globally, and many children are irreversibly damaged by age 2 (UNICEF, 2015c). Undernourished children are at high risk for stunted growth and poor health and functioning throughout life (Martorell, 2010), although intervention programs that provide nutrition supplements, nutrition education, health care, and financial assistance for the family can result in better growth and lower rates of anemia for enrolled infants (Rivera et al., 2004).

Chronic malnutrition is caused by factors such as poverty, low-quality foods, poor dietary patterns, contaminated water, unsanitary conditions, insufficient hygiene, inadequate health care, and diarrheal diseases and other infections. Approximately 3.1 million children around the world die each year from chronic malnutrition, accounting for 45 percent of all deaths of children under 5 (UNICEF, 2017, May). Worldwide, 25 percent of children under 5 are malnourished; most of these children live in West/Central Africa, Southeast Asia, Latin America, and the Caribbean (Lake, 2015). Malnutrition is not confined to developing countries. In North America, 13.1 million children in the United States, 1.1 million in Canada, and 2.5 million in Mexico are undernourished (Patterson, 2017).

The Brain and Reflex Behavior

Holding a newborn has been compared to "holding a three-pound bag of corn" (Wingert & Underwood, 1997). But underneath the flailing limbs, fuzzy eyesight, and wailing cries of newborn infants, the brain is already starting to change and grow with amazing speed as it takes in environmental information and starts to make sense of the new world. How does this happen? How does a baby move from uncontrolled movements and reflexes to deliberate actions? Are these emerging skills reflected in the structure of the brain?

BUILDING THE BRAIN

The brain's growth occurs in fits and starts called brain growth spurts. Beginning about 3 weeks after conception, the brain gradually develops from a long hollow tube into a spherical mass of cells (Figure 5.2). By birth, the spinal cord

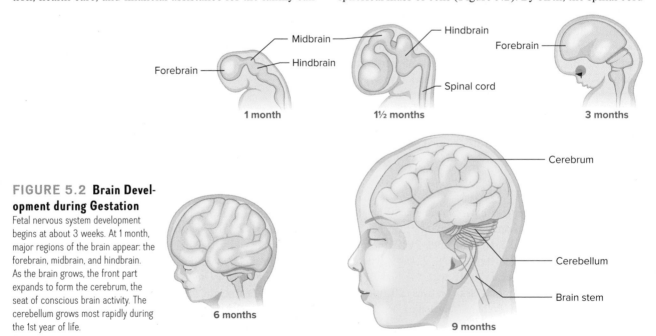

FIGURE 5.2 Brain Development during Gestation
Fetal nervous system development begins at about 3 weeks. At 1 month, major regions of the brain appear: the forebrain, midbrain, and hindbrain. As the brain grows, the front part expands to form the cerebrum, the seat of conscious brain activity. The cerebellum grows most rapidly during the 1st year of life.

and brain stem, the part of the brain responsible for basic bodily functions such as breathing, heart rate, body temperature, and the sleep-wake cycle, are nearly complete. The brain at birth is only about one-fourth to one-third of its eventual adult volume (Toga, Thompson, & Sowell, 2006). The cerebellum, the part of the brain that maintains balance and motor coordination, grows fastest during the 1st year of life (Knickmeyer, et al., 2008). By age 3 the typical child's brain will weigh 3½ pounds, nearly 90 percent of its eventual adult weight (Gabbard, 1996).

The cerebrum, which resembles a giant wrinkled walnut, is the largest part of the brain; it is divided into right and left halves, or hemispheres, each with specialized functions. This specialization of the hemispheres is called lateralization. The left hemisphere is the center of language and logical thinking. The right hemisphere processes visual and spatial information, enabling us to read maps or draw. Joining the two hemispheres is a tough band of tissue called the corpus callosum. If you were looking at a side view of one-half of the human brain, the corpus callosum would resemble the cross-section of a mushroom cap. The corpus callosum is like a giant switchboard of fibers connecting the hemispheres and allowing them to share information and coordinate commands. It grows dramatically during childhood, reaching adult size by about age 10.

Each cerebral hemisphere has four lobes, or sections: the occipital, parietal, temporal, and frontal lobes, which control different functions (Figure 5.3) and develop at different rates. The regions of the cerebral cortex that govern vision, hearing, and other sensory information grow rapidly in the first few months after birth and are mature by 6 months, but the areas of the frontal cortex responsible for abstract thought, mental associations, remembering, and deliberate motor responses grow little during this period and

remain immature through adolescence (Gilmore et al., 2007). The growth of the brain is a lifelong process fundamental to physical, cognitive, and emotional development.

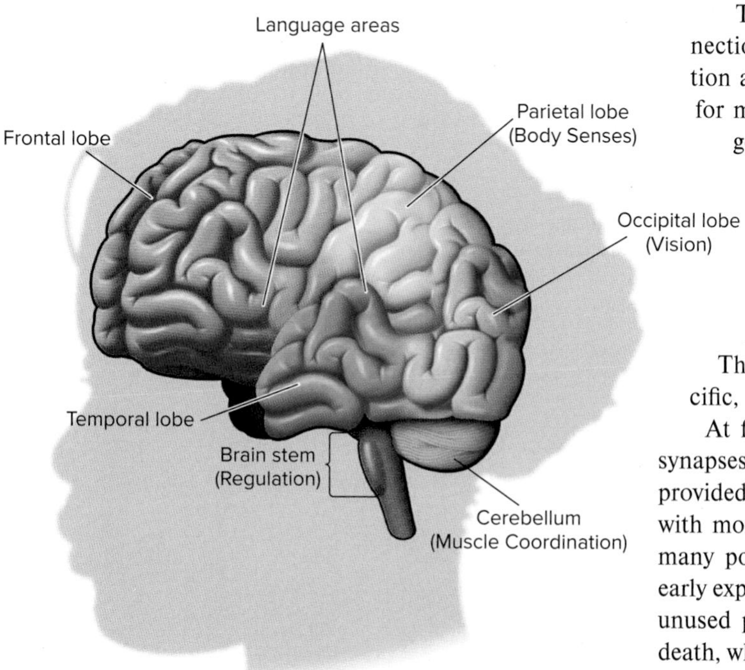

Brain Cells

The brain is composed of neurons and glial cells. **Neurons**, or nerve cells, send and receive information. Glia, or glial cells, nourish and protect the neurons. They are the support system for our neurons.

Beginning in the 2nd month of gestation, an estimated 250,000 immature neurons are produced every minute through cell division (mitosis). At birth, most of the more than 100 billion neurons in a mature brain are already formed but are not yet fully developed. The number of neurons increases most rapidly between the 25th week of gestation and the first few months after birth. This cell proliferation is accompanied by a dramatic growth in cell size.

Originally the neurons are simply cell bodies with a nucleus, or center, composed of deoxyribonucleic acid (DNA), which contains the cell's genetic programming. As the brain grows, these rudimentary cells migrate to various parts of the brain (Bystron, Rakic, Molnar & Blakemore, 2006). Most of the neurons in the cortex are in place by 20 weeks of gestation, and its structure becomes fairly well defined during the next 12 weeks.

Once in place, the neurons sprout axons and dendrites—narrow, branching, fiberlike extensions. Axons send signals to other neurons, and dendrites receive incoming messages from them, through synapses, tiny gaps, which are bridged with the help of chemicals called neurotransmitters that are released by the neurons. Eventually, a particular neuron may have anywhere from 5,000 to 100,000 synaptic connections.

The multiplication of dendrites and synaptic connections, especially during the last 2½ months of gestation and the first 6 months to 2 years of life, accounts for much of the brain's growth and permits the emergence of new perceptual, cognitive, and motor abilities. As the neurons multiply, migrate to their assigned locations, and develop connections, they undergo the complementary processes of integration and differentiation. Through **integration**, the neurons that control various groups of muscles coordinate their activities. Through **differentiation**, each neuron takes on a specific, specialized structure and function.

At first the brain produces many more neurons and synapses than it needs. The large number of excess neurons provided by this early proliferation give the brain flexibility—with more connections available than will ever be needed, many potential paths are open for the growing brain. As early experience shapes the brain, the paths are selected, and unused paths are pruned away. This process involves cell death, which may sound negative but is a way to calibrate the developing brain to the local environment. This process begins during the prenatal period and continues after birth.

> **Neurons** Nerve cells.
>
> **Integration** Process by which neurons coordinate the activities of muscle groups.
>
> **Differentiation** Process by which cells acquire specialized structures and functions.

Language areas
Frontal lobe
Parietal lobe (Body Senses)
Occipital lobe (Vision)
Temporal lobe
Brain stem (Regulation)
Cerebellum (Muscle Coordination)

FIGURE 5.3 **The Human Brain**

Only about half the neurons originally produced survive and function in adulthood (Society for Neuroscience, 2008). Yet, even as unneeded neurons die, others may continue to form during adult life (Deng, Aimone & Gage, 2010; Gould, Reeves, Graziano & Gross, 1999). Meanwhile, connections among cortical cells continue to strengthen and to become more reliable and precise, enabling more flexible and more advanced motor and cognitive functioning (Society for Neuroscience, 2008).

Myelination

Much of the credit for efficiency of neural communication goes to the glia that coat the neural pathways with a fatty substance called myelin. This process of **myelination** enables signals to travel faster and more smoothly. Myelination begins about halfway through gestation, peaks during the first year of life, continues into adolescence (Dubois et al., 2014) and persists through the third decade of life (Bartzokis et al., 2010).

In the fetus, myelin development progresses from the center out. Sensory pathways, including the somatosensory, visual, and auditory pathways, are generally myelinized before motor pathways, and the occipital pole (the posterior end of the occipital lobe) is myelinized before the temporal and frontal poles. Last, projection fibers (nerve tracts that connect the cortex with lower parts of the brain and spinal cord) are myelinized prior to association fibers (nerve tracts that connect cortical areas within the cerebral hemisphere) (Qiu, Mori & Miller, 2015). It has been argued that this sequence exists because before higher cortical areas can use information, they must be able to access stable inputs. Therefore, the primary cortical areas are myelinated first (Guillery, 2005).

Myelination continues to occur rapidly throughout infancy, accelerating at 12 to 16 months, and then slowing again from 2 to 5 years of age (Deoni, Dean III, O'muircheartaigh, Dirks & Jerskey, 2012). At 5 years of age, the myelinated white matter volume in the brain is approximately 80 percent of that found in adults (Deoni et al., 2011).

EARLY REFLEXES

If you were to release an infant in a swimming pool, the baby will hold his or her breath, divert any ingested water into the stomach, and show movements of the arms and legs that are coordinated and strong enough for propulsion through a few feet through the water. This is known as the diving reflex; while it is one of the more puzzling behaviors babies come equipped with, it occurs in all neurologically normal babies.

Reflex behaviors are automatic, innate responses to stimulation. (See Table 5.2.) Human babies have an estimated 27 major reflexes, which are present at birth or soon after (Noble & Boyd, 2012). They are controlled by the lower brain centers that govern other involuntary processes, such

Myelination Process of coating neural pathways with a fatty substance called myelin, which enables faster communication between cells.

reflex behaviors Automatic, involuntary, innate responses to stimulation.

TABLE 5.2 Early Human Reflexes

Reflex	Stimulation	Baby's Behavior	Typical Age of Appearance	Typical Age of Disappearance
Moro	Baby is dropped or hears loud noise.	Extends legs, arms, and fingers; arches back, draws back head.	7th month of gestation	3 months
Darwinian (grasping)	Palm of baby's hand is stroked.	Makes strong fist, can be raised to standing position if both fists are closed around a stick.	7th month of gestation	4 months
Tonic neck	Baby is laid down on back.	Turns head to one side, assumes "fencer" position, extends arms and legs on preferred side, flexes opposite limbs.	7th month of gestation	5 months
Babkin	Both of baby's palms are stroked at once.	Mouth opens, eyes close, neck flexes, head tilts forward.	Birth	3 months
Babinski	Sole of baby's foot is stroked.	Toes fan out, foot twists in.	Birth	4 months
Rooting	Baby's cheek or lower lip is stroked with finger or nipple.	Head turns, mouth opens, sucking movements begin.	Birth	9 months
Walking	Baby is held under arms, with bare feet touching flat surface.	Makes steplike motions that look like well-coordinated walking.	1 month	4 months
Swimming	Baby is put into water face down.	Makes well-coordinated swimming movements.	1 month	4 months

as breathing and heart rate. Both the presence of reflexes and the disappearance of unneeded reflexes on schedule are signs of neurological development. Primitive reflexes, such as sucking, rooting for the nipple, and the Moro reflex (a response to being startled or beginning to fall), are related to instinctive needs for survival and protection. Some primitive reflexes may be part of humankind's evolutionary legacy. One example is the grasping reflex in which infants tightly grasp any object placed in their palm; presumably this is a holdover from our ancestral past when we held on to our primate mothers' fur as they scrambled among the trees.

As the higher brain centers become active during the first 2 to 4 months, babies begin to show postural reflexes—reactions to changes in position or balance. For example, infants who are tilted downward extend their arms in the parachute reflex, an instinctive attempt to break a fall. Locomotor reflexes, such as the walking reflex, resemble voluntary movements and may impede the development of voluntary movements unless they disappear.

Most of the early reflexes disappear during the first 6 months to 1 year. Reflexes that continue to serve protective functions, such as blinking, yawning, coughing, gagging, sneezing, and shivering remain.

BRAIN PLASTICITY

Although the brain's early development is in large part genetically directed, its structure is continually modified by environmental experiences; this modifiability is called **plasticity**. Because of plasticity, early experiences can have lasting effects on the capacity of the brain to learn and store information (Society for Neuroscience, 2008). Plasticity may be an evolutionary mechanism to enable adaptation to environmental change (Gomez-Robles, Hopkins & Sherwood, 2013; Toga, Thompson & Sowell, 2006).

The brain is like a car—it needs gas, brake fuel, oil, coolant, and other substances to perform at peak efficiency. When a brain is malnourished, it cannot form new connections or add appropriate amounts of myelin to the axons of nerve cells because it lacks the required substances to do so. In addition, exposure to hazardous drugs, environmental toxins, or maternal stress can threaten the developing brain. For example, early abuse or sensory impoverishment can delay neural development or negatively affect brain structure (Glaser, 2000). The lack of enriching experiences may inhibit the normal process of **cell death** and the streamlining of neural connections, resulting in smaller head size and reduced brain activity (C. A. Nelson, 2008).

If certain neural connections are not made early in life, these brain circuits may shut down forever (Society for Neuroscience, 2008). For example, children with a "lazy eye" who are not treated when young will forever lose the ability to process visual input through the affected eye, even if their muscle control is later corrected.

But just as negative experiences can affect the brain adversely, positive experiences or an enriched environment can spur brain development and even make up for past deprivation (Black, 1998; Society for Neuroscience, 2008).

Animals raised in toy-filled cages sprout more axons, dendrites, and synapses than animals raised in bare cages (Society for Neuroscience, 2008). Such findings have sparked successful efforts to stimulate the brain development of premature infants (Als et al., 2004) and children with Down syndrome, and to help victims of brain damage recover function.

Ethical constraints prevent controlled experiments on the effects of profound environmental deprivation on human infants and young children. However, the thousands of orphaned or abandoned children who had spent virtually their entire lives in overcrowded Romanian orphanages offered a natural experiment (Beckett et al., 2006). The Bucharest Early Intervention Project (BEIP) has studied these children—one group abandoned at birth and placed in institutions; a second

> **plasticity** Modifiability of the brain through experience.
>
> **cell death** In brain development, normal elimination of excess cells to achieve more efficient functioning.

While children are generally less accepting of bitter or sour foods, those offered a wider range of flavors in early childhood often have less restricted preferences later in life.

©stockphoto for you/Shutterstock

group abandoned at birth and placed in institutions but then randomly assigned to foster care; and a comparison group living with their biological parents. Findings so far suggest that long-term institutional care in severely deprived settings has a profound negative effect on many areas of development, including physical growth, cognitive development, and social-emotional functioning, but that foster care can help prevent problems in many of these areas. Age of adoption, length of previous institutionalization, and the specific features of the institutional experience were key factors in the children's prospects for improvement (C. A. Nelson, 2008). This suggests that high-quality foster care may moderate the adverse effects of early institutionalization (Moulson, Fox, Zeanah, & Nelson, 2009). Similarly, a high-quality adoptive home, especially if an adoption occurs earlier than 4 months of age, can mitigate early institutionalization (Audet & Le Mare, 2011).

Early Sensory Capacities

The regions of the developing brain that control sensory information grow rapidly during the first few months of life, enabling newborn infants to make fairly good sense of what they touch, see, smell, taste, and hear (Gilmore et al., 2007). It does not take long, for example, for newborns to recognize the smell of their mother's breast milk on a piece of cloth or to learn the sound of her voice.

TOUCH AND PAIN

Anytime you have comforted a crying baby by cuddling her or tickled a drowsy child to wake him up, you have made use of perhaps the most important sense in infancy: touch. Touch is the first sense to develop; for the first several months it is the most mature sensory system. By 32 weeks of gestation, all body parts are sensitive to touch, and this sensitivity increases during the first 5 days of life (Haith, 1986; Field, 2010). When a newborn's cheek is stroked near the mouth, the baby responds by trying to find a nipple, a reflex that is probably an evolved survival mechanism (Rakison, 2005).

In the past, physicians performing surgery on newborn babies, such as circumcision, often used no anesthesia in the mistaken belief that neonates could not feel pain, felt it only briefly, or did not have the memory capacity to remember and thus be affected by it. However, there is evidence that, as discussed in Chapter 3, the capacity for pain perception emerges sometimes in the third trimester of pregnancy (Bellieni &

Buonocore, 2012; Kostovic & Judas, 2010; Reissland, Francis & Mason, 2013). Newborns can and do feel pain, and they become more sensitive to it during their first few days. Anesthesia is dangerous for young infants, however; so when possible, alternative methods of pain management are used for minor procedures such as circumcision, a heelstick, or vaccines. For example, infants show a decreased pain response when they are held or cuddled, especially with skin-to-skin contact, and either breast-fed or given a sweet solution to suck on (Johnston et al., 2014; Campbell-Yeo, Fernandes, & Johnston, 2011).

SMELL AND TASTE

The senses of smell and taste begin to develop in the womb. Flavors from food the mother has consumed are found in amniotic fluid (Cooke & Fildes, 2011), thus a preference for certain tastes and smells can be developed in utero. Moreover, flavor from the foods that the mother eats are also transmitted via breast milk (Ventura & Worobey, 2013). Therefore, exposure to the flavors of healthy foods through breast-feeding may improve acceptance of healthy foods after weaning and later in life (Mennella, 2014). The taste preferences developed in infancy may last into early childhood; children offered different flavors in early infancy later have less restricted food preferences (Trabulsi & Mennella, 2012).

Certain taste preferences seem to be largely innate and appear to reflect an adaptive preference for signals for high-calorie, high-protein foods and an aversion toward signals that a food may be poisonous or toxic (Ventura & Worobey, 2013). These preferences exist most strongly for sweet and bitter flavors (Mennella & Bobowski, 2015). Newborns much prefer sweet tastes to sour, bitter, or salty taste (Menella, 2014). This inborn sweet tooth may help a baby adapt to life outside the womb, as breast milk is quite sweet (Ventura & Menella, 2011). Newborns also strongly dislike bitter flavors, likely a survival mechanism given the toxic nature of many bitter substances (Beauchamp & Mennella, 2011).

HEARING

Auditory discrimination develops rapidly after birth. Even in the womb, fetuses can tell new speech sounds from those they have heard before (Partanen, Kujala, Naatanen, Liitola, Sambeth & Huotilainen, 2013). In addition, infants as young as 2 days old were able to recognize a word they heard up to a day earlier (Swain, Zelazo & Clitfon, 1993). At 1 month, babies can distinguish sounds as close as *ba* and *pa* (Eimas, Siqueland, Jusczyk & Vigorito, 1971). By 11 to 17 weeks, infants are able to both recognize and remember entire sentences after a brief delay (Dehaene-Lambertz et al., 2006). By 4 months, infants' brains are showing lateralization for language, as occurs in adults. By this age, the left side of infants' brain responds preferentially to speech, especially that of their native language, over other sounds (Minagawa-Kawai et al., 2010). There are even indications that infants can recognize music that is typical of their culture from a young age (Virtala, Huotilainen, Partanen, Fellman & Tervaniemi, 2013) and by 4 months of age prefer music typical of their cultural experiences (Soley & Hannon, 2010).

Did you know?

It is developmentally typical for children to become picky eaters in the toddler years; up to 78 percent of the variance in pickiness is genetic. The other 22 percent is the part you can affect by exposing children to varied flavors (Cook, Haworth, & Wardle, 2007).

©Ingram Publishing/ SuperStock

Because hearing is a key to language development and hearing impairments are the most common cause of speech delays, hearing impairments should be identified as early as possible. Hearing loss occurs in 1 to 3 of 1,000 infants (Gaffney, Gamble, Costa, Holstrum & Boyle, 2003).

SIGHT

What does a baby see when in his or her parents' arms? Vision is the least developed sense at birth. From an evolutionary developmental perspective, the other senses are more directly related to a newborn's survival. Visual perception and the ability to use visual information—identifying caregivers, finding food, and avoiding dangers—become more important as infants become more alert and active (Rakison, 2005).

Newborns' eyes are smaller than adults' eyes, the retinal structures are incomplete, and the optic nerve is underdeveloped. A neonate's eyes focus best from about 1 foot away—just about the typical distance from the face of a person holding a newborn. This is probably not an accident; this focusing distance may have evolved to promote mother-infant bonding.

Newborns blink at bright lights. Their peripheral vision is very narrow; it more than doubles between 2 and 10 weeks of age (Tronick, 1972). The ability to follow a moving target also develops rapidly in the first months, as does color perception (Haith, 1986). The development of these abilities is tied closely to cortical maturation (Braddick & Atkinson, 2011).

Visual acuity at birth is approximately 20/400 but improves rapidly, reaching the 20/20 level by about 8 months (Kellman & Arterberry, 1998). Binocular vision—the use of both eyes to focus, enabling depth and distance perception—usually does not develop until 4 or 5 months (Bushnell & Boudreau, 1993).

Infants show a special affinity for faces. From the very beginning, infants prefer to look at human faces more than almost any other stimuli (Pascalis & Kelly, 2009). Even though their vision is not operating at peak levels, infants are nonetheless able to discriminate between individual faces within hours after birth (Sugden & Marquis, 2017). Infants prefer to look at their own mother's face, and the faces of attractive strangers more than unattractive strangers (Pascalis & Kelly, 2009). Within a few months after birth,

WHAT DO YOU DO?

Audiologist

Audiologists test hearing and diagnose hearing impairments. Audiologists work with individuals that may have hearing, balance, and other related ear problems. For example, an audiologist might help determine if the cause of a toddler's speech delay could be a hearing problem. All states require different licensures for audiologists, a master's degree is required, and a doctoral degree is becoming increasingly necessary. To learn more about becoming an audiologist, visit www.audiology.com and www.asha.org.

infants begin to pay close attention to human eyes over other features (Dupierrix et al., 2014). Between about 4 and 8 months of age, when learning language, infants pay particular attention to the mouth. Then, at approximately a year of age, as they begin to master some of the basics of language, their attention shifts back to the eyes (Lewkowicz & Hansen-Tift, 2012). Infants also show some ability to categorize racial groups on the basis of facial data. At 3 months, infants look longer at own-race faces. By 9 months, they look longer at other race faces, and they seem to process own-race faces more efficiently (Liu et al., 2015), paying more attention to their eyes (Xiao, Xiao, Quinn, Anzures & Lee, 2013). Generally, infants seem to show privileged attention to faces, a tendency that is likely the result of a dedicated neural system for the processing of facial stimuli.

Early screening is essential to detect problems that interfere with vision. Infants should be examined by 6 months for visual fixation preference, ocular alignment, and signs of eye disease. Formal vision screening should begin by age 3 (American Optometric Association, 2018). Doctors' offices have modified eye charts for toddlers specifically for this purpose; in place of letters are shapes easily recognized by most toddlers such as stars, hearts, and circles.

Motor Development

While William flailed and thrashed around in his crib when first born and was floppy and uncoordinated when held, his parents noticed a continual and rapid increase in his ability to control his body's movements. By about 4 months he was rolling over and could no longer be left unattended on his changing table without risking a fall. By 6 months he was sitting up by himself, although he had a tendency to topple over when reaching for a toy and needed help to reach a sitting position. And just after his 1st birthday, William took his first, halting, unaided steps. He was a typically developing baby, showing the same patterned timeline of development as humans worldwide.

MILESTONES

Motor development is marked by a series of milestones that develop systematically (Figure 5.4). Babies are driven to

Did you know?

Infants show an innate preference for faces, which is presumably in the service of mother-infant bonding. Even before they understand what faces are, newborns will gaze at them for extended periods of time.

©Ingram Publishing

WHAT DO YOU **DO**?

Occupational Therapist

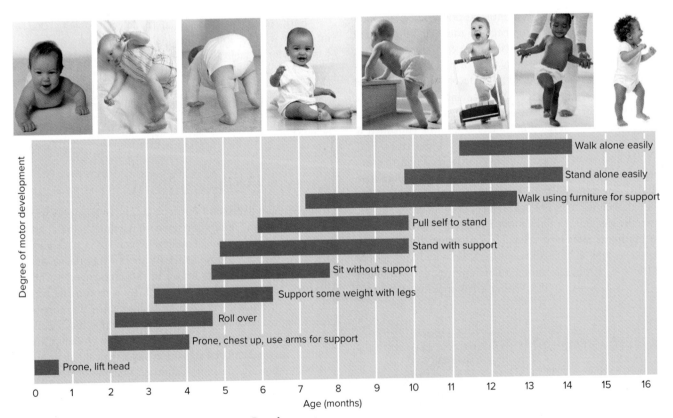

©Corbis/SuperStock

Occupational therapists help individuals with mental, physical, or developmental disabilities improve their ability to perform everyday tasks at home and in working environments. Such activities may consist of computer usage, dressing, eating, or cooking. For example, an occupational therapist might help a toddler with a developmental disorder use utensils or manipulate toys. They work in a range of settings, including hospitals, rehabilitation clinics, private practices, schools, and mental health facilities. A master's degree or higher is required in most states. To learn more about becoming an occupational therapist, visit www.aota.org.

which thumb and index finger meet at the tips to form a circle, making it possible to pick up tiny objects.

The **Denver Developmental Screening Test** (Frankenburg, Dodds, Fandal, Kazuk, & Cohrs, 1975) charts normal progress between 1 month and 6 years. The test measures **gross motor skills** involving the use of large muscle groups, such as rolling over and catching a ball, and **fine motor skills** requiring precise coordination of small muscles, such as grasping a rattle and copying a circle. Generally, gross motor development occurs before fine motor development, and the Denver test provides a guideline of the approximate timeline different skills should come on board. It also assesses language development, personality, and social development. When we talk about what the "average" baby can do, we refer to the 50 percent Denver norms. However, it is important to remember that normality covers a wide range.

The pace of motor development responds to certain cultural factors. In Uganda, for example, babies generally walk at 10 months as compared with 12 months in the United States and 15 months in France (Gardiner & Kozmitzki, 2005). Asian babies tend to develop these skills more slowly. Such differences may be related in part to ethnic differences in temperament or may reflect a culture's child-rearing practices (Gardiner & Kozmitzki, 2005). Normal development

Denver Developmental Screening Test Screening test given to children age 1 month to 6 years to determine whether they are developing normally.

gross motor skills Physical skills that involve the large muscles.

fine motor skills Physical skills that involve the small muscles and eye-hand coordination.

develop these skills and need nothing more than room to move and freedom to see what they can do. Babies first learn simple skills and then combine them into increasingly complex systems of action, which permit a wider or more precise range of movement and more effective control of the environment. In developing the precision grip, for example, an infant first tries to rake things up with the whole hand, fingers closing against the palm. Later the baby masters the pincer grasp, in

FIGURE 5.4 **Milestones in Gross Motor Development**

Source: Frankenburg, W. K., & Dodds, J. B. "The Denver Development Screening Test." *Journal of Pediatrics*, vol. 71, August 1967, 181–191.

©Barbara Penoyar/Getty Images; ©Digital Vision/Getty Images; ©Image Source/Alamy; ©Victoria Blackie/Getty Images; ©Digital Vision; ©OJO Images Ltd/Alamy; ©Corbis/PictureQuest; ©lostinbids/Getty Images

need not follow the same timetable to reach the same destination, and there are many paths leading to proficiency in motor movements. Key milestones in the first three years of life relate to head control, hand control, and locomotion.

Head Control

At birth, most infants can turn their heads from side to side while lying on their backs. While lying chest down, many can lift their heads enough to turn them. Within the first 2 to 3 months, they lift their heads higher and higher—sometimes to a point at which they lose their balance and roll over on their backs. By 4 months, almost all infants can keep their heads erect while being held or supported in a sitting position.

Hand Control

Babies are born with a grasping reflex. If the palm of an infant's hand is stroked, the hand closes tightly. At about 3 months, most infants can grasp an object of moderate size, such as a rattle, but have trouble holding a small object. Next, they begin to grasp objects with one hand and transfer them to the other, and then to hold, but not pick up, small objects. Between 7 and 11 months, their hands become coordinated enough to pick up a tiny object, such as a pea, using the pincer grasp. By 15 months, the average baby can build a tower of two cubes. A few months after the third birthday, the average toddler can copy a circle fairly well.

Locomotion

After 3 months, the average baby begins to roll over deliberately—first from front to back and then from back to front. The average baby can sit without support by 6 months and can assume a sitting position without help by about 8 months.

Between 6 and 10 months, most babies begin to get around by creeping or crawling. This achievement of self-locomotion has striking cognitive and psychosocial benefits (Karasik, Tamis-LeMonda, & Adolph, 2011). Crawling infants become more sensitive to where objects are, how big

At 4 to 5 months, infants start reaching for objects. They can grasp objects of moderate size, but the ability to pick up and hold small objects develops later.
©Tetra Images/Corbis

they are, whether they can be moved, and how they look. Crawling helps babies learn to better judge distances and perceive depth. They learn to look to caregivers for clues as to whether a situation is secure or frightening—a skill known as social referencing (Campos, Sorce, Emde & Svejda, 2013). Crawling is not technically a motor milestone. Some babies move directly from sitting to walking, sometimes scooting on their bottoms in place of crawling.

By holding on to a helping hand or a piece of furniture, the average baby can stand at a little past 7 months. The average baby can let go and stand well alone at about 11 months. At this point, the baby is ready to learn how to walk. Babies often practice standing and walking more than 6 hours a day, on and off, and may take enough steps to cover the length of 29 football fields! Within a few weeks the baby is walking fairly well and thus achieves the status of toddler.

During the 2nd year, children begin to climb stairs one at a time, putting one foot after another on each step; later, they will alternate feet. Walking down stairs comes later. In their 2nd year, toddlers also begin to run and jump. By age 3, most children can balance briefly on one foot and begin to hop.

MOTOR DEVELOPMENT AND PERCEPTION

Motor experience sharpens and modifies infants' perceptual understanding of what is likely to happen if they move in a certain way. This two-way connection between perception

WHAT DO YOU DO?

Physical Therapist

©Pixtal/agefotostock

Physical therapists work with individuals who have physical disabilities or limitations resulting from an injury or developmental delay. They diagnose and then create and implement treatment plans to improve patient movement and overall functionality. For example, a toddler who broke his leg might need physical therapy as part of the recovery process. Physical therapists need to have strong interpersonal skills due to the extensive interaction required with patients, family members, doctors, and other medical professionals. Physical therapists work in a variety of settings, including hospitals, clinics, private practices, and schools. A physical therapist needs a bachelor's or master's degree in physical therapy, and also needs to meet state-specific licensure requirements. To learn more about becoming a physical therapist, go to www.apta.org.

and action, mediated by the developing brain, gives infants useful information about themselves and their world (Adolph & Eppler, 2002) and appears to be fairly well coordinated from birth (von Hofsten, 2004).

Infants begin reaching for objects at about 4 to 5 months, but initially, they are not very good at it. Their reaching trajectory is halting and generally contains multiple corrections and changes in direction before they are able to successfully grasp an object. For many years, researchers believed that this process was primarily under the control of vision (White, Castle & Held, 1964; McDonnell, 1975; Bushnell, 1985). However, as researchers investigated further, they began to doubt this assertion. For example, they realized that young infants could locate unseen objects by sound, and they could locate objects in the dark and by using their memory of the object's location, even if the object were moving (McCall & Clifton, 1999; McCarty, Clifton, Ashmead, Lee & Goubet, 2001; Robin, Berthier & Clifton, 1996). Indeed, at 6 months of age, infants could successfully reach for objects in the dark faster than they could in the light, although by 12 months, this process reversed (Berthier & Carrico, 2010).

More recently, researchers have realized that in younger infants, early corrective movements are more likely to be illustrating immature cerebellar development. The immature cerebellum is only able to provide a rough guideline of movements used in reaching, which must be then corrected in order to be successful (Berthier, 2011).

Younger infants are more likely to correct their reaching movements using proprioceptive feedback from their muscles and joints and haptic (relating to touch) information rather than vision (Berthier & Carrico, 2010; Corbetta, Thurman, Weiner, Guan & Williams, 2014). While they look at objects they reach for, this information is not the primary source of information for their corrective actions. Rather, they reach first, and then the eyes follow (Corbetta et al., 2014).

Depth perception, the ability to perceive objects and surfaces in three dimensions, depends on cues that affect the image of an object on the retina of the eye where the sensory receptors cells are located. These cues involve both binocular coordination and motor control (Bushnell & Boudreau, 1993). Kinetic cues are produced by movement of the object or the observer, or both. To find out whether an object is moving, a baby might hold his or her head still for a moment, an ability well established by about 3 months.

Haptic perception involves the ability to acquire information by handling objects rather than just looking at them. This includes putting objects in the mouth—a common means of exploration in infancy. The tongue's multiple receptors are capable of fine-grained discrimination and can provide a wealth of information.

depth perception Ability to perceive objects and surfaces in three dimensions.

haptic perception Ability to acquire information about properties of objects, such as size, weight, and texture, by handling them.

visual cliff Apparatus designed to give an illusion of depth and used to assess depth perception in infants.

ecological theory of perception Theory developed by Eleanor and James Gibson that describes developing motor and perceptual abilities as interdependent parts of a functional system that guides behavior in varying contexts.

Infants appear capable of using haptic information even prenatally. Babies who were born as early as 28 weeks of gestation were able to recognize and remember features of objects that were placed in their hands (Marcus, Lejeune, Berne-Audeoud, Gentaz & Debillon, 2012). However, infants are limited by their motor development. It is only after babies develop enough hand-eye coordination to reach for objects and grasp them, generally at about 5 to 7 months, that they can use their sense of touch to explore the objects within their reach (Bushnell & Bondreau, 1993).

THEORIES OF MOTOR DEVELOPMENT

Developmental psychologists are interested not just in documenting the sequence and timing of events, but also in understanding the underlying processes. Given the complexity of motor development, it is not surprising that a variety of theoretical perspectives have been proposed as explanatory frameworks. Here, we focus on two of the most important approaches: the ecological theory of perception and the dynamic systems theory.

Ecological Theory of Perception

In a classic experiment by Richard Walk and Eleanor Gibson (1961), 6-month-old babies were placed on a clear acrylic tabletop laid over a checkerboard pattern that created the illusion of a vertical drop—a **visual cliff**—in the center of the table. Would the infants perceive this illusion of depth? The babies did see a difference between the "ledge" and the "drop." They crawled freely on the "ledge" but avoided the "drop," even when they saw their mothers beckoning from the far side of the table.

According to Eleanor Gibson's and James J. Gibson's **ecological theory of perception** (E. J. Gibson, 1969; J. J. Gibson, 1979; Gibson & Pick, 2000), babies continually gauge their abilities and their surroundings and adapt their

The visual cliff.
©Mark Richards/PhotoEdit

movements accordingly, devising new strategies as needed. This process of "learning to learn" (Adolph, 2008, p. 214) involves visual and manual exploration, testing alternatives, and flexible problem solving. In visual cliff experiments, infants who have been crawling for some time are more likely than new crawlers to avoid the cliff. Likewise, when faced with a downward slope, infants who have just begun to crawl or walk seem unaware of the limits of their abilities and plunge recklessly down. In time, however, their judgment becomes more accurate and their explorations more discerning as they practice their new skills and learn from experience how far they can push their limits without losing their balance (Adolph, 2008).

According to Gibson's theory, locomotion does not develop in functionally related stages. Instead, "each problem space has its own . . . learning curve" (Adolph, 2008, p. 214). Babies who learn how far they can reach for a toy across a gap while in a sitting position must acquire this knowledge anew when they begin to crawl. Likewise, when crawling babies who have mastered slopes begin to walk, they have to learn to cope with slopes all over again (Adolph & Eppler, 2002).

Dynamic Systems Theory

The typical sequence of motor development was traditionally thought to be genetically programmed—a largely automatic, preordained series of steps directed by the maturing brain. Today, many developmental scientists consider this view too simple. Instead, according to Esther Thelen (1995; Smith & Thelen, 2003), motor development is a continuous process of interaction between baby and environment.

Thelen pointed to the walking reflex—stepping movements a neonate makes when held upright with the feet touching a surface. This behavior usually disappears by the 4th month. These movements do not appear again until late in the 1st year. The usual explanation for the reemerging movement is that the original reflex is replaced by a new—and deliberate—skill now controlled by the developing brain. But, as Thelen observed, a newborn's stepping involves the same movements the neonate makes while lying down and kicking. Why would stepping stop, whereas kicking continues? She proposed the answer might be that babies' legs become thicker and heavier during the early months, but the muscles are not yet strong enough to carry the increased weight (Thelen, 1995) and so walking attempts disappear. In fact, when infants who had stopped stepping were held in warm water, which helps support their legs, stepping reappeared.

Thelen argued there is no single, simple cause—such as maturation—that sufficiently explains motor development. Infant and environment form an interconnected, continually changing system, which includes such variables as the infant's motivation and muscular strength and the environmental affordances that are available. Environmental affordances are the qualities of the environment, or objects in it, that allow an individual to perform an action. For example, a safe environment affords exploration, and balls afford throwing. Ultimately, as babies act upon their environments,

they try various combinations of movements and select those that are most efficient. Their solutions must be flexible, or subject to modification in changing circumstances, because the environment and the baby's body are constantly changing. The maturing brain is only one part of it.

According to Thelen's **dynamic systems theory (DST)**, typical babies develop the same skills in the same order because they are built approximately the same way and have similar physical challenges and needs. Thus they eventually discover that walking is more efficient than crawling in most situations. However, this discovery arises from each particular baby's physical characteristics and experience in a particular context, which explains why some babies learn to walk earlier than others.

> **dynamic systems theory (DST)** Thelen's theory that holds that motor development is a dynamic process of active coordination of multiple systems within the infant in relation to the environment.

Cultural Influences on Motor Development

Although motor development follows a virtually universal sequence, its *pace* does respond to cultural factors. For example, according to some research, African babies tend to be more advanced. For example, in Ghana, 9-month-old infants are better at reaching and grasping, and they are more likely to be able to sit, stand, or walk than infants from China or the United States (Angulo-Barroso et al., 2011). In Uganda, babies typically walk at 10 months, as compared with 12 months in the United States and 15 months in France. Similarly, Brazilian children, who are encouraged to play physically active and expressive games, outperform British children in running and walking (Victora, Victora & Barros, 1990). Such differences may, in part, be related to ethnic differences in temperament (Kaplan & Dove, 1987) or may reflect a culture's child-rearing practices (Venetsanou & Kambas, 2010).

Some cultures actively encourage early development of motor skills. In many African and West Indian cultures in which infants show advanced motor development, adults use special handling routines, such as bouncing and stepping exercises, to strengthen babies' muscles. In one study, Jamaican infants, whose mothers used such handling routines daily, sat, crawled, and walked earlier than English infants, whose mothers gave them no such special handling (Hopkins & Westra, 1988; 1990). In Western countries, motor intervention programs that encourage locomotor skills in young children have been shown to accelerate some forms of motor development, such as horizontal jumping or skipping (Deli, Bakle & Zachopoulou, 2006).

On the other hand, some cultures discourage early motor development. Children of the Ache in eastern Paraguay do not begin to walk until age 18 to 20 months. Ache mothers pull their babies back to their laps when the infants begin to crawl away. Yet, as 8- to 10-year-olds, Ache children climb tall trees, chop branches, and play in ways that enhance their motor skills (Kaplan & Dove, 1987). Normal development, then, need not follow the same timetable to reach the same destination.

Health

William was born to parents with the resources to provide him with good nutrition, enriching experiences, and quality health care. Perhaps most important, his parents were also loving, kind, and able to help him establish trust in others and confidence in his own fledgling abilities. William lived in a sunny world filled with toys and affection. He was lucky—many babies do not grow up in these circumstances, and they face numerous physical and emotional risks in early childhood. What are the risks such children face?

INFANT MORTALITY

Great strides have been made in protecting the lives of new babies, but these advances are not evenly distributed. In 2015, there were 5.9 million worldwide deaths of children 5 years of age and younger (World Health Organization, 2015). Of those deaths, 2.7 million were infants 28 days or younger (UNICEF, 2015a). The vast majority of these early deaths are in developing countries, especially in South Asia and West and Central Africa (World Health Organization, 2013; Figure 5.5).

The chief causes of neonatal death worldwide are preterm birth complications (35 percent), childbirth complications (24 percent), and sepsis (15 percent). Many of these deaths are preventable, resulting from a combination of poverty, poor maternal health and nutrition, infection, and inadequate medical care (UNICEF, 2015a). Although maternal mortality declined 44 percent from 1990 to 2015, the number of women and girls who die in childbirth is still about 303,000 a year. Most of these

infant mortality rate Proportion of babies born alive who die within the 1st year.

deaths (27 percent) are due to hemorrhage, with preexisting medical conditions, eclampsia, embolisms, and complications of unsafe abortions also playing a role (UNICEF, 2015b). About two-thirds of maternal deaths occur during the immediate postnatal period, and infants whose mothers have died are more likely to die than infants whose mothers remain alive (Sines, Syed, Wall & Worley, 2007). As with neonatal deaths, many of these deaths are preventable.

In the United States, **the infant mortality rate**—the proportion of babies who die within the 1st year—has fallen almost continuously since the beginning of the twentieth century, when 100 infants died for every 1,000 born alive. By 2015, the rate had fallen to 5.9 infant deaths per 1,000 live births (Murphy, Xu, Kochanek, Curtin & Arias, 2017). More than half of U.S. infant deaths take place in the first week of life, and about two-thirds occur during the neonatal period (Heron et al., 2009).

Birth defects and genetic abnormalities are the leading cause of infant deaths in the United States, followed by disorders related to prematurity or low birth weight, sudden infant death syndrome (SIDS), maternal complications of pregnancy, accidents, and complications of the placenta, umbilical cord, and membranes (Murphy et al., 2017). In 2005, more than two-thirds of all deaths in infancy were of preterm babies, and more than half were of very preterm infants (Mathews & MacDorman, 2008).

The overall improvement in U.S. infant mortality rates since 1990 is attributable largely to prevention of SIDS (discussed in the next section) as well as to effective treatment for respiratory distress and medical advances in keeping very small babies alive (Arias et al., 2003). Still, mainly because of the prevalence of preterm births and low birth weight, U.S. babies have less chance of reaching their 1st

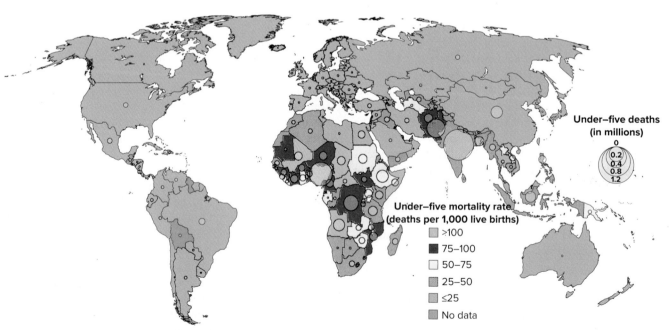

Figure 5.5 Under-5 Mortality Rate, 2015

Most neonatal deaths occur in sub-Saharan Africa and Asia.

Source: UNICEF, *Committing to Child Survival: A Promised Renewed, Progress Report 2015.* New York: UNICEF, 2016.

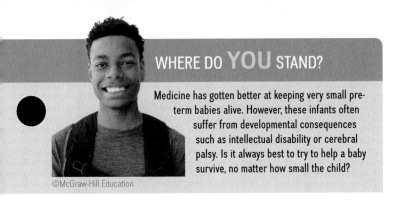

birthday than do babies in many other developed countries (MacDorman & Mathews, 2009). The U.S. infant mortality rate in 2008 was higher than in 44 countries worldwide (Kaiser Family Foundation, 2017).

Racial/Ethnic Disparities in Infant Mortality

Infant mortality in the United States has declined from 6.86 deaths per 1,000 live births in 2005 to 5.90 in 2015 (Murphy et al., 2017). While this decline exists for all races and ethnic groups, large disparities remain. The infant mortality rate of black babies (11.73 deaths per 1,000 live births) is over twice as large as that of non-Hispanic white (4.82) and Hispanic (5.20) babies (Murphy et al.,). This disparity has been attributed to the greater prevalence of low birth weight and SIDS among African Americans. Similarly, infant mortality among Native Americans and Alaska Natives is about 1½

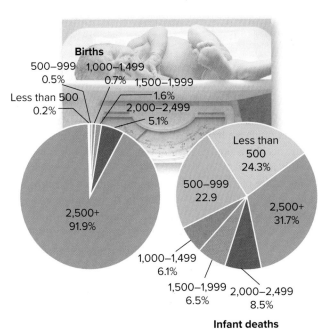

FIGURE 5.6 Infant Birth and Mortality Statistics by Weight

Percentage of live births and infant deaths by birth weight in grams: United States, 2005. Low-birth-weight babies constitute less than 10 percent of live births but nearly 70 percent of infant deaths.

Source: T. J. Mathews, M. F. MacDorman, & M. E. Thoma, "Infant mortality statistics from the 2013 period linked birth/infant death data set," *National Vital Statistics Reports, 64*, no. 9 (2015); Hyattsville, MD: National Center for Health Statistics.

©Luke Schmidt/Shutterstock

times that among white babies, in this case due to SIDS and fetal alcohol syndrome (American Public Health Association, 2004; Mathews & MacDorman, 2008).

Racial or ethnic disparities in access to and quality of health care for minority children (National Center for Health Statistics, 2016) clearly help account for differences in mortality, but behavioral factors also may play a part. Obesity, smoking, and alcohol consumption contribute to poor outcomes of pregnancy. African Americans have the highest obesity rates, and Native Americans and Alaska Natives tend to be heavy smokers and drinkers. Rates of prenatal care vary from about 89 percent of non-Hispanic white expectant mothers down to about 76 percent of Native Americans and Alaska Natives (National Center for Health Statistics [NCHS], 2006). Because risk factors for infant mortality vary among ethnic groups, efforts to further reduce infant deaths need to focus on factors specific to each group (Hesso & Fuentes, 2005).

Sudden Infant Death Syndrome

Sudden infant death syndrome (SIDS), sometimes called crib death, is the sudden death of an infant under age 1 in which the cause of death remains unexplained after a thorough investigation that includes an autopsy. SIDS accounts for 7 percent of infant mortality rates (Mathews, MacDorman & Thoma, 2015). It peaks between 2 and 3 months and is most common among African American and American Indian/Alaska Native babies, boy babies, those born preterm, and those whose mothers are young and received late or no prenatal care (AAP Task Force on Sudden Infant Death Syndrome, 2005).

SIDS most likely results from a combination of factors. An underlying biological defect may make some infants vulnerable during a critical period to certain contributing or triggering experiences, such as prenatal exposure to smoke—one of the major identified risk factors. There may be genetic mutations affecting the heart that predispose children to SIDS as well (Arnestad et al., 2007; Wang et al., 2007). In the absence of any risk factors, SIDS is rare. Babies who die from SIDS frequently have multiple risk factors (Ostfeld, Esposity, Perl & Hegyl, 2010).

An important clue has emerged from the discovery of defects in the brain stem, which regulates breathing, heartbeat, body temperature, and arousal (Machaalani & Waters, 2014). These defects may prevent SIDS babies who are sleeping face down or on their sides from waking or turning their heads when they breathe stale air containing carbon dioxide trapped under their blankets (Panigraphy et al., 2000). Similarly, babies who have low levels of serotonin may not awaken under conditions of oxygen deprivation and carbon dioxide buildup and are thus at greater risk as well (Duncan et al., 2010).

Research strongly supports a relationship between SIDS and sleeping on the stomach. SIDS rates declined in the United States by 53 percent between 1992 and 2001 (AAP Task Force on Sudden Infant Death Syndrome, 2005) and in some other countries by as much as 70 percent following recommendations that healthy babies be laid down to sleep

sudden infant death syndrome (SIDS) Sudden and unexplained death of an apparently healthy infant.

Perspectives on Diversity

©Digital Vision/Getty Images

SLEEP CUSTOMS

In many cultures, co-sleeping with young infants is expected. For example, Gusii infants in Kenya fall asleep in someone's arms or on a caregiver's back. In many societies, infants sleep in the same room with their mothers for the first few years of life and frequently in the same bed, making it easier to nurse at night (Broude, 1995). Mayan mothers sleep with children until the birth of a new baby, and even express shock at the idea that anyone would let a baby sleep in a room all alone (Morelli, Rogoff, Oppenheim & Goldsmith, 1992).

Although parents in the United States are likely to have their child sleep in the same room but not in the same bed, co-sleeping has become more popular in recent years. The percentage of babies in the United States that sleep with their parents has more than doubled between 1993 and 2000 (Brenner et al., 2003); at 2 weeks of age, approximately 42 percent of American infants sleep with a parent (Hauck, Signore, Fein & Raju, 2008).

Some researchers have argued that co-sleeping is a safe and desirable choice (Goldberg & Keller, 2007). The physical closeness of mother and baby facilitates breast-feeding, touching, and maternal responsiveness (Ball, 2009).

However, under certain conditions, bed sharing can increase the risk of sudden infant death syndrome or suffocation. The risk seems to be particularly high when the infant is under 11 weeks, when more than one person co-sleeps with the baby, or when a bed sharer has been smoking, drinking alcohol, or is overtired (AAP Task Force on Sudden Infant Death Syndrome, 2005).

Sources: F. R. Hauck, C. Signore, S. B. Fein & T. N. Raju, "Infant sleeping arrangements and practices during the first year of life," *Pediatrics, 122*, Supplement 2 (2008), S113–S120; W. A. Goldberg & M. A. Keller, "Co-sleeping during infancy and early childhood: Key findings and future directions," *Infant and Child Development, 16*, no. 4 (2007), 457–469; H. L. Ball, "Bed-sharing and co-sleeping: research overview," *New Digest, 48* (2009), 22–27.

---

on their backs (Dwyer, Ponsonby, Blizzard, Newman & Cochrane, 1995; Hunt, 1996; Skadberg, Morild & Markestad, 1998; Willinger, Hoffman & Hartford, 1994).

The American Academy of Pediatrics (Moon & Fu, 2012) also recommends that infants *not* sleep on soft surfaces, such as pillows, quilts, or sheepskin, or under loose covers, which, especially when the infant is face down, may increase the risk of overheating or rebreathing (breathing the infant's own exhaled carbon dioxide). Current recommendations for risk reduction also include sleeping in the parent's room, but on a separate surface, avoiding tobacco smoke, the use of a pacifier, and avoiding the use of breathing monitors as a strategy to reduce the risk of SIDS. Additionally, some research has supported the use of a fan with a further reduction in SIDS risk (Coleman-Phox, Odouli & Li, 2008).

Injuries

Unintentional injuries are the fifth leading cause of death in infancy in the United States (Murphy et al., 2017). Infants have the second highest death rate from unintentional injuries among children and adolescents, exceeded only by 15- to 19-year-olds. About 90 percent of all injury deaths in infancy are due to one of four causes: suffocation, motor vehicle traffic, drowning,

and residential burns or fires (Pressley, Barlow, Kendig & Paneth-Pollak, 2007). About two-thirds of injury deaths in the 1st year of life are by suffocation. Among children ages 1 to 4, traffic accidents are the leading cause of unintentional injury deaths, followed by drowning and burns. Falls are by far the major cause of nonfatal injuries in both infancy (52 percent) and toddlerhood (43 percent). Boys of all ages are more likely to be injured and to die from their injuries than girls (Borse et al., 2008). African American infants are 2½ times as likely to die of injuries as white infants and more than 3 times as likely to be victims of homicide (Tomashek, Hsia & Iyasu, 2003). These statistics speak to the importance of baby-proofing the environment because many accidents are avoidable.

IMMUNIZATIONS

Such once-familiar and sometimes fatal childhood illnesses as measles, pertussis (whooping cough), and polio are now largely preventable, thanks to the development of vaccines that mobilize the body's natural defenses. Unfortunately, many children still are not adequately protected.

Worldwide, more than 86 percent of children received routine vaccinations during their 1st year in 2016 (UNICEF, 2017).

Did you know?

The original paper linking autism and vaccines was formally retracted by the *Lancet* in February 2010 amid allegations that the primary researcher, Andrew Wakefield, had committed deliberate scientific fraud and had financial conflicts of interest that colored his findings.

©Science Photo Library/Alamy

Another parental worry is that infants receive too many vaccines for their immune system to handle safely. Actually, the opposite is true. Multiple vaccines fortify the immune system against a variety of bacteria and viruses and reduce related infections (Offit et al., 2002). One day at a typical children's museum exposes children to a far greater immune system load than a regular course of vaccines.

The Global Immunization Vision Strategy for 2006–2015 seeks to extend routine vaccinations to every eligible person (Department of Immunization, Vaccines and Biologicals, WHO; United National Children's Fund; Global Immunization Division, National Center for Immunization and Respiratory Diseases & McMorrow, 2006).

In the United States, thanks to a nationwide immunization initiative, over 90 percent of 19- to 35-month-olds had completed a recommended series of childhood vaccinations, including measles, mumps, rubella, hepatitis B, and chicken pox. Still, many children, especially poor or African American children, lack one or more of the required shots and there are regional differences in coverage (Centers for Disease Control and Prevention, 2014).

Some parents hesitate to immunize their children because of speculation that certain vaccines—particularly the diphtheria-pertussis-tetanus (DPT) and measles-mumps-rubella (MMR) vaccines—may cause autism or other neurodevelopmental disorders. However, there is no empirical evidence that this link exists. A recent meta-analysis representing data from more than 1.26 million children showed no link between autism, autism-spectrum disorders, intellectual disability, and vaccines (Taylor, Swerdfeger & Eslick, 2014). Despite this data, however, many parents elect not to vaccinate their children, or vaccinate them incompletely or on a delayed schedule. This, as well as imported disease from international travel, has resulted in a resurgence of some diseases (Ventola, 2016). For example, with over 8 percent of children who are eligible for vaccination left unprotected against measles, outbreaks of the disease have occurred in vulnerable communities (National Center for Health Statistics, 2017). Currently, exemptions for religious or philosophical reasons are allowed in many states, and in some areas, the exemption rate is as high as 20 percent (Ventola, 2016).

Charlize Theron, an Oscar winning actor, is the survivor of a traumatic childhood. At age 15, her mother shot and killed her father after he came home drunk and began shooting at and verbally abusing them.

©Jaguar PS/Shutterstock

CHILD MALTREATMENT

Although most parents are loving and nurturing, some cannot or will not take proper care of their children and some deliberately harm them. Maltreatment can take several specific forms and the same child can be a victim of more than one kind (U.S. Department of Health and Human Services [USDHHS], Administration on Children, Youth and Families, 2008):

- Physical abuse: injury to the body through punching, beating, kicking, or burning.

- Neglect: failure to meet a child's basic needs, such as food, clothing, medical care, protection, and supervision.

- Sexual abuse: any sexual activity involving a child and an older person.

- Emotional maltreatment: includes rejection; terrorization; isolation; exploitation; degradation; ridicule; or failure to provide emotional support, love, and affection.

State and local child protective service agencies received an estimated 3.4 million referrals for alleged maltreatment of 6.2 million children in 2015, a 9 percent increase from 2011. About 75 percent of children identified as maltreated were neglected, 17.2 percent were physically abused, and 8.4 percent were sexually abused. Emotional maltreatment was not included in this analysis, however, as it often co-occurs with the other forms of abuse. In 2015, an estimated 1,670 children, or about five a day, died of maltreatment, and the actual number may well have been considerably higher (USDHHS, Administration on Children, Youth and Families, 2017; Child Welfare

Information Gateway, 2017). Of those children, 72.9 percent of them died as a result of neglect either alone or in combination with other maltreatment types, and 43.9 percent of them died as a result of physical abuse either alone or in combination with other maltreatment types (Child Welfare Information Gateway, 2017).

Maltreatment in Infancy and Toddlerhood

Children are abused and neglected at all ages, but the highest rates of victimization and of death from maltreatment are for infants and toddlers age 3 and younger. Babies younger than a year of age account for 49.4 percent of child maltreatment fatalities, and children from 1 to 3 years of age account for another 31.5 percent. A number of factors increase the vulnerability of young children, including their small size, dependency, and inability to defend themselves (Children's Welfare Information Gateway, 2017).

nonorganic failure to thrive In infancy, lack of appropriate growth for no known medical cause, accompanied by poor developmental and emotional functioning.

shaken baby syndrome Form of maltreatment in which shaking an infant or toddler can cause brain damage, paralysis, or death.

Babies who do not receive nurturance and affection or who are neglected sometimes suffer from **nonorganic failure to thrive** (FTT), slowed or arrested physical growth with no known medical cause, accompanied by poor developmental and emotional functioning. Symptoms may include lack of appropriate weight gain, irritability, excessive sleepiness and fatigue, avoidance of eye contact, lack of smiling or vocalizing, and delayed motor development. In short, they neither grow nor develop normally despite a lack of underlying physical or medical causes.

FTT can result from a combination of inadequate nutrition, difficulties in breast-feeding, improper formula preparation or feeding techniques, and disturbed interactions with parents. Infants whose mother or primary caregiver is depressed, abuses alcohol or other substances, is under severe stress, or does not show warmth or affection toward the baby are also at heightened risk (Block, Krebs, the Committee on Child Abuse and Neglect & the Committee on Nutrition, 2005; Lucile Packard Children's Hospital at Stanford, 2009).

Some researchers have questioned the role of maltreatment in FTT. They point out that while it can be the case that maltreatment, maternal mental health, or maternal addiction have been associated with FTT, FTT also regularly occurs in situations in which these variables do not seem to be present. Thus, they argue, FTT is not always the result of disruptions in the parent-child relationship. Rather, FTT may be a growth pattern that reflects insufficient caloric intake (Shields, Wacogne & Wright, 2012). The reasons for undernutrition are multifaceted and may result from such factors as feeding or eating difficulties, problems with food absorption, food insecurity, developmental delays, gastroesophageal reflux, conditioned food aversions, excessive juice intake, or chronic disease (Jaffe, 2011).

Head trauma is the leading cause of death in child abuse cases in the United States (Dowshen, Crowley & Palusci,

2004) and can result from a baby being shaken, dropped, or thrown. **Shaken baby syndrome** is found mainly in children under 2, most often in infants. The baby's weak neck muscles and heavy head result in the brain bouncing back and forth inside the skull during a shaking episode, with damage even more likely if the baby is thrown into bed or against a wall. This can cause bruising, bleeding, and swelling, and can lead to permanent and severe brain damage, paralysis, and even death (AAP, 2000; National Institute of Neurological Disorders and Stroke [NINDS], 2006).

Contributing Factors

Often, abusive adults appear to be just like everyone else; no identifying behavior or characteristic determines who will or will not abuse a child. Parents—either acting alone or in concert with another parent—are responsible for 77.7 percent of the child fatalities that result from child maltreatment (Child Welfare Information Gateway, 2017). Slightly over 6 percent of perpetrators are other relatives, and almost 4 percent are unmarried partners of parents. Slightly more than half (54.1 percent) are women, and the race of the perpetrator is generally the same as the race of the victim (USDHHS, 2017).

Characteristics of the household environment are related to the likelihood a child will be physically abused (Jaffee et al., 2004). A disproportionate number of abused and neglected children are in large, poor, or single-parent families, which tend to be under stress and to have trouble meeting children's needs (USDHHS, 2017; Dubowitz et al., 2011). Parents who abuse children tend to use harsh or controlling parenting practices (Bugental et al., (2010). Moreover, they often have issues with intimate partner violence (Guedes & Mikton, 2013; Hamby, Finkelhor, Turner & Ormrod, 2010). Substance abuse is a factor in approximately a quarter of cases of maltreatment (USDHHS, 2017). Sexual abuse often occurs along with other family disturbances such as physical abuse, emotional maltreatment, substance abuse, and family violence (Kellogg & the Committee on Child Abuse and Neglect, 2005).

Abuse may begin when a parent who is already anxious, depressed, or hostile tries to control a child physically but loses self-control and ends up shaking or beating the child. Yet what pushes one parent over the edge, another may take in stride. Although many neglect cases occur in very poor families, most low-income parents do not neglect or abuse their children.

Abuse and neglect reflect the interplay of multiple layers of contributing factors; in addition to family characteristics there are cultural factors that increase the likelihood of maltreatment. Two cultural factors associated with child abuse are societal violence and physical punishment of children. For example, more frequent use of corporal punishment is related to higher rates of violence in societies (Lansford & Dodge, 2008). In the United States, homicide, domestic violence, and rape are common, and many states still permit corporal punishment in schools. Overall, the use of corporal punishment has been trending down in the

United States in recent decades. However, slightly more than 8 out of 10 parents of preschoolers and about half of parents of school-age children still report using physical punishment at home (Zolotor, Theodore, Runyan, Chang & Laskey, 2011; Straus, 2010).

Helping Families in Trouble

Preventing maltreatment before it occurs is an effective, fiscally sound policy. Some prevention activities, such as public service announcements, aim to raise awareness among the general population. Others, such as parenting classes for single teen mothers, are targeted to high-risk families or to families where abuse or neglect has already occurred (Child Welfare Information Gateway, 2008b).

If maltreatment is suspected, Child Protective Services agencies investigate claims and determine what steps, if any, need to be taken. Agency staff may try to help the family resolve their problems or arrange for alternative care for children who cannot safely remain at home (USDHHS, Administration on Children, Youth and Families, 2017). Services for abused children and their parents include shelters, education in parenting skills, and therapy. However, availability of these services is often limited (Burns et al., 2004).

When authorities remove children from their homes, the usual alternative is to put the children in foster care. Foster care removes a child from immediate danger, but it is often unstable, further alienates the child from the family, and may turn out to be another abusive situation. Often a child's basic health and educational needs are not met in foster care (David and Lucile Packard Foundation, 2004; National Research Council [NRC], 1993b). In part because of a scarcity of traditional foster homes and an increasing caseload, a growing proportion of placements are in kinship foster care, under the care of grandparents or other family members (Berrick, 1998; Geen, 2004). Although most foster children who leave the system are reunited with their families, about 28 percent reenter foster care within the next 10 years (Wulczyn, 2004). Children who have been in foster care are more likely than other children to become homeless, to commit crimes, and to become teenage mothers (David and Lucile Packard Foundation, 2004), as well as to suffer mental or physical health problems in adulthood (Zlotnick, Tam & Soman, 2012).

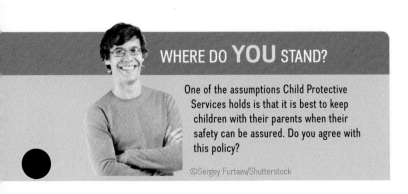

WHERE DO YOU STAND?

One of the assumptions Child Protective Services holds is that it is best to keep children with their parents when their safety can be assured. Do you agree with this policy?

©Sergey Furtaev/Shutterstock

Did you know?

Prison inmates, both male and female, are more likely to have been abused as children than nonincarcerated adults (Carlson & Shafer, 2010).

©Ingram Publishing/SuperStock

Long-Term Effects of Maltreatment

Without help, maltreated children may grow up with problems and continue the cycle of maltreatment when they have children of their own. Abuse and neglect in childhood results in an elevated risk that the victims will, when grown, become abusers as well (Child Welfare Information Gateway, 2013). An estimated one-third of adults who were abused and neglected in childhood victimize their own children (National Clearinghouse on Child Abuse and Neglect Information [NCCANI], 2004).

Consequences of maltreatment in childhood may include poor physical, mental, and emotional health and impaired brain development (Glaser, 2000; Twardosz, 2010). Children who are maltreated may be less effective at regulating their emotions, and their peer relationships may suffer (Kim & Cicchetti, 2010). Additionally, there may be cognitive, language, attentional, and academic difficulties; as well as problems with attachment and social relationships (National Clearinghouse on Child Abuse and Neglect Information [NCCANI], 2004; Child Welfare Information Gateway, 2013; Twardosz, 2010). In adolescence there is a heightened risk of poor academic achievement, delinquency, teenage pregnancy, risky sexual behaviors, mental illness, alcohol and drug use, and suicide (Norman et al., 2012; NCCANI, 2004). There are also long-term influences on physical health. Adults who were abused tend to suffer from poor health and to develop fatal illnesses, such as stroke, cancer, and heart disease (Leeb, Lewis & Zolotar, 2011). Lastly, adults who were abused as children have lower levels of education, are less likely to be employed, earn less money, and have fewer assets than adults who were not abused as children, an effect that is stronger for women (Currie & Spatz Widom, 2010).

Sexual abuse is particularly harmful. Sexually abused children often become sexually active at an earlier age and tend to have higher numbers of sexual partners than children who were not sexually abused. Sexually abused children are more likely to mistrust people and to engage in violence in their relationships (Fergusson, Boden & Horwood, 2008; Friesen, Woodward, Horwood & Fergusson, 2009). As adults, children who were sexually abused tend to be more anxious, depressed, or suicidal, and are more likely to be diagnosed with post-traumatic stress disorder. They are also more likely to abuse drugs and alcohol (Fergusson, McLeon & Horwood, 2013; Fergusson, Boden & Horwood, 2008).

Moreover, sexual abuse may also compromise physical health: Sexual abuse survivors are more likely to be obese or suffer from stress-related or autoimmune disorders (D. R. Wilson, 2010).

Why do some abused children grow up to become antisocial or abusive, while others do not? One possible difference is genetic; some genotypes may be more resistant to trauma than others (Caspi et al., 2002; Jaffee et al., 2005). Many maltreated children show remarkable resilience.

Optimism, self-esteem, intelligence, creativity, humor, and independence are also protective factors, as is the social support of a caring adult (NCCANI, 2004). In Chapter 14 we further discuss factors that affect resilience.

Fortunately, most babies survive and grow up healthy and well cared for. Their physical development forms the underpinning for the cognitive and psychosocial developments that enable infants and toddlers to become more at home in their world, as we will see in Chapters 7 and 8.

Maltreated children are at higher risk for a variety of physical, emotional, and social problems. However, many show remarkable resistance.
©279photo Studio/Shutterstock

mastering the CHAPTER

©Nimazi/Shutterstock

Summary and Key Terms

Early Growth and Physical Development

> Normal physical growth and sensory and motor development proceed according to the cephalocaudal and proximodistal principles.

> A child's body grows most dramatically during the 1st year of life; growth proceeds at a rapid but diminishing rate throughout the first 3 years.

> Breast-feeding offers many health advantages and sensory and cognitive benefits. Social factors can make it difficult for women to breast-feed.

> Babies are at risk of becoming obese adults if they have obese parents or grow very quickly in the first year.

The Brain and Reflex Behavior

> The brain grows most rapidly during the months before and immediately after birth as neurons migrate to their assigned locations, form synaptic connections, and undergo integration and differentiation. Cell death and myelination improve the efficiency of the nervous system.

> Reflex behaviors—primitive, locomotor, and postural— are indications of neurological status. Most early

reflexes drop out during the 1st year as voluntary, cortical control develops.

> Especially during the early period of rapid growth, environmental experiences can influence brain development positively or negatively.

> **KEY TERMS**

Neurons	**Myelination**	**Plasticity**
Integration	**Reflex behaviors**	**Cell death**
Differentiation		

Early Sensory Capacities

> Sensory capacities, present from birth and even in the womb, develop rapidly in the first months of life. Very young infants show pronounced abilities to discriminate between stimuli.

> Touch is the first sense to develop and mature. The senses of smell, taste, and hearing begin to develop in the womb. Newborns are sensitive to pain.

> Vision is the least well-developed sense at birth.

Motor Development

> Motor skills develop in a certain sequence, which may depend on maturation, context, experience, and motivation. Simple skills combine into increasingly complex systems. Cultural practices may influence the pace of early motor development.

> Self-locomotion brings about changes in all domains of development.

> Perception is intimately related to motor development. Depth perception and haptic perception develop in the first half of the 1st year.

> According to Gibson's ecological theory, sensory perception and motor activity are coordinated from birth, helping infants figure out how to navigate in their environment.

> Thelen's dynamic systems theory holds that infants develop motor skills, not by maturation alone but by active coordination of multiple systems of action within a changing environment.

Health

> The vast majority of infant deaths occur in developing countries. Postnatal care can reduce infant mortality.

> Although infant mortality has diminished in the United States, it is still disturbingly high, especially among African American babies. Birth defects are the leading cause of death in infancy.

> Sudden infant death syndrome (SIDS) is a leading cause of postneonatal death in the United States. SIDS rates have declined markedly following recommendations to lay babies on their backs to sleep.

> Vaccine-preventable diseases have declined as immunization rates have improved, but many preschoolers are not fully protected.

> Forms of maltreatment are physical abuse, neglect, sexual abuse, and emotional maltreatment. Maltreatment can interfere with physical, cognitive, emotional, and social development, and its effect can continue into adulthood. Still, many maltreated children show remarkable resilience.

Practice Quiz

1. The reason babies learn how to use their arms before using their legs has to do with the _____, while the reason babies learn how to use their arms before grasping objects has to do with the _____.

2. What are the recommended foods for babies according to the ages listed below?
   a. 6 months of age and younger _____
   b. 6–12 months of age _____

3. In general, the areas of the brain responsible for sensation and perception _____, while areas of the brain specialized for higher cognitive functions _____.
   a. develop slowly over a number of years; are absent at birth
   b. develop rapidly in the first few months after birth; remain immature through adolescence
   c. develop prenatally; develop rapidly in the first few months after birth
   d. develop slowly over a number of years; develop prenatally

4. Neurological health can be gauged by:
   a. the presence of reflexes when they are supposed to be there
   b. the absence of reflexes by the age of 6 months
   c. the disappearance of reflexes on schedule
   d. a and c

5. Rooting is an example of a _____ reflex and the walking reflex is an example of a _____ reflex.

6. What kind of environmental experiences are likely to have a negative effect on early brain development?

   _____
   _____

7. At birth, the most mature sensory system is _____.

8. Babies whose mothers consume garlic while pregnant seem to like the smell of garlic more than those babies whose mothers did not consume garlic while pregnant. This suggests that:
   a. liking garlic is an innate preference
   b. babies learn to like certain flavors or smells prenatally
   c. babies learn to like certain flavors or smells postnatally
   d. babies must be taught to like garlic

9. It is important to identify hearing impairments early in life because:
   a. if they are not identified by six months of age the neural pathways for auditory information will disappear
   b. being able to respond to parents is heavily dependent upon hearing

   c. hearing is key to language development
   d. hearing impairments can lead to failure to thrive

10. What are three differences between an infant's and an adult's eyes?

    _____
    _____
    _____

11. What motor skills are developing at the following ages:

    0–3 months _____

    3–6 months _____

    6–12 months _____

    12–24 months _____

    24–36 months _____

12. The best way to describe the way perception and motor development are related to each other is:
    a. perception leads to advances in motor development
    b. motor development leads to changes in perceptual abilities
    c. perception and motor development do not influence each other
    d. perception and motor development mutually influence each other

13. Which would be the best analogy of a developing child's development according to the ecological theory of perception?
    a. a person carefully following instructions in a manual
    b. a magician waving a wand to cast a spell
    c. a scientist exploring the world
    d. a gambler rolling dice multiple times

14. What are two reasons infant mortality rates in African American babies might be higher than those for white babies?

    _____
    _____
    _____

15. Evidence suggests the link between autism and vaccines:
    a. does not exist
    b. is very strong
    c. exists, but only for the measles vaccine
    d. exists, but only for boys

16. Name three contributing factors to child maltreatment.

    _____
    _____
    _____

Answers: 1–cephalocaudal; proximodistal; 2–(a) Breast milk; (b) iron-enriched solid foods; 3–b; 4–d; 5–primitive; locomotor; 6–exposure to hazardous drugs, environmental toxins, maternal stress, malnutrition, early abuse, and sensory impoverishment; 7–touch; 8–b; 9–c; 10–Newborn eyes are smaller than adults', their retinal structure is incomplete, and the optic nerve is underdeveloped; 11–See Table 5.3; 12–d; 13–c; 14–The prevalence of low birth weight and SIDS is higher in African American populations; 15–a; 16–Contributing factors to maltreatment include family variables (large, poor, single-parent, high stress, disorganized, critical, uncommunicative), community characteristics (rampant crime, lack of community services and facilities, lack of social support networks, weak political leadership), and cultural values (high levels of societal violence, physical punishment of children seen as appropriate).

What's to Come

©JGI/Jamie Grill/Getty Images

When Ava was born, the most obvious sign of her development over time was her rapid increase in size and her motor skill development. However, even bigger changes were occurring in her mind. As an infant, she focused her wide eyes thoughtfully on objects she found interesting, or clumsily pulled toys toward her mouth to explore them. As she began to crawl and then walk, her world grew with her. She used her hands, eyes, and ears to learn more about the world around her, shaking and throwing toys, pointing at objects that interested her, saying her first word, and tracing her fingers over magazines as if they were iPad touchscreens. In three years, she went from a helpless infant to a busy toddler, full of questions and comments about the expanding world around her. In this chapter, we will be studying cognitive development—the series of achievements that supported Ava's newfound abilities.

As in any area, looking at multiple perspectives helps us in our quest for understanding. First, we'll explore six fundamental approaches in the study of cognition to see how each provides a more complete understanding of development. Then, we will move on to language—a fundamental achievement of the first three years made possible by increases in cognition—and discuss some of the influences on language development, its typical progression, and how to prepare children for later literacy.

• • • •

Behaviorist Approach: Basic Mechanics of Learning

The **behaviorist approach** to cognitive development is concerned with how we learn—that is, how behavior changes in response to experience. Babies are born with the ability to learn from what they see, hear, smell, taste, and touch. This ability then develops as part of the child's cognitive development. Classical conditioning and operant conditions are two important processes behaviorists study to understand how we learn.

CLASSICAL CONDITIONING

Eager to capture Ava's memorable moments in photos, her father took pictures of the infant smiling, crawling, and showing off her other achievements. Whenever the flash went off, Ava blinked. One evening when Ava was 11 months old, she saw her father hold the camera up to his eye—and she blinked before the flash. She had learned to associate the camera with the bright light, so the sight of the camera alone activated her blinking reflex.

Ava's blinking is an example of **classical conditioning** in which a person learns to make a reflex or involuntary response (in this case, blinking) to a stimulus (the camera) that originally did not provoke the response. Classical conditioning enables infants to anticipate an event before it

happens by forming associations between stimuli (such as the camera and the flash) that regularly occur together. Classically conditioned learning becomes extinct, or fades, if it is not reinforced by repeated association. Thus, if Ava frequently saw the camera without the flash, she would eventually stop blinking.

OPERANT CONDITIONING

In contrast, in **operant conditioning** the learner operates, or acts, on the environment. The infant learns to make a certain response to an environmental stimulus (e.g., babbling at the sight of parents) to produce a particular effect (e.g., smiles). Operant conditioning can either involve reinforcements, which increase behaviors, or punishments, which decrease behaviors. Conditioning can also be positive (adding a stimulus to the environment) or negative (removing a stimulus from the environment). For example, praising a child for sharing is an example of positive reinforcement because the addition of a positive stimulus (praise) should lead to the repetition of the behavior (sharing).

By contrast, the seat belt buzzer's sudden cessation as soon as the seat belt is fastened is negative reinforcement because the removal of the irritating stimulus (the buzzer) leads to a greater likelihood of the target behavior (buckling the seat belt).

Infants cannot talk, they have limited motor control, and researchers must be creative if they are to determine what babies know and understand. Fortunately, conditioning paradigms in research allow investigators to ask questions of babies in

behaviorist approach Approach to the study of cognitive development that is concerned with the basic mechanics of learning.

classical conditioning Learning based on associating a stimulus that does not ordinarily elicit a particular response with another stimulus that does elicit the response.

operant conditioning Learning based on reinforcement and punishment.

Babies 2 to 6 months old who learn that kicking activates a mobile remember this skill even if the mobile is removed for up to 2 weeks. When the mobile is returned, the baby starts kicking as soon as he sees it.
©Alivepix/Shutterstock

ways they can answer. For example, in one experiment, researchers operantly conditioned 3-month-old infants to kick to activate a mobile attached to one ankle by a ribbon. Babies were trained at this task in the presence of either a coconut or cherry scent, thus classically conditioning the presence of the scent and the ability to control the mobile with their body movements. Previous research had shown that babies this young forget what they learn one week later. However, when the infants were cued with the scent and mobile a day before being tested again, they were able to remember the relationship between their kicking and the mobile's movements. Thus, the babies' responses showed that babies were able to use contextual cues (i.e., the scent) to retrieve memories (Suss, Gaylord & Fagen, 2012).

Psychometric Approach: Developmental and Intelligence Testing

psychometric approach Approach that seeks to quantitatively measure the different factors that make up intelligence and predict future performance.

intelligent behavior Behavior that is goal oriented and adaptive to circumstances and conditions of life.

IQ (intelligence quotient) tests Psychometric tests that seek to measure intelligence by comparing a test-taker's performance with standardized norms.

Bayley Scales of Infant and Toddler Development Standardized test of infants' and toddlers' mental and motor development.

Home Observation for Measurement of the Environment (HOME) Instrument designed to measure the influence of the home environment on children's cognitive growth.

The **psychometric approach** to child development measures quantitative differences in abilities that make up intelligences by using tests that indicate or predict these abilities. Although there is no clear scientific consensus on a definition of intelligence, most professionals agree that **intelligent behavior** is goal oriented and adaptive. Intelligence enables people to acquire, remember, and use knowledge; to understand concepts and relationships; and to solve everyday problems.

The most well-known approach to intelligence is psychometric. The goals of psychometric testing are to measure the factors thought to make up intelligence, such as comprehension and reasoning, and to then predict future performance, such as school achievement. **IQ (intelligence quotient) tests** consist of questions or tasks that are supposed to show how much of the measured abilities a person has, by comparing that person's performance with standardized norms. Using the psychometric approach, three areas of interest related to cognitive development during ages 0 to 3 are intelligence testing, assessing the impact of the home environment, and early intervention.

TESTING INFANTS AND TODDLERS

It is difficult to measure infants' intelligence. Babies cannot tell us what they know and how they think, so the most obvious way to gauge their intelligence is to assess what they can do. But if they do not grasp a rattle, it is hard to tell whether they do not know how, do not feel like doing it, do not realize what is expected of them, or have simply lost interest. However, it is possible to test their developmental functioning. Developmental tests compare a baby's performance on tasks with established age-graded norms.

The **Bayley Scales of Infant and Toddler Development** is a widely used developmental test designed to assess children from 1 month to 3½ years. Scores on the Bayley-III (Bayley, 2005) indicate a child's strengths and weaknesses in five developmental areas: cognitive, language, motor, social-emotional, and adaptive behavior. Separate scores, called developmental quotients (DQs), are calculated for each scale. DQs are most useful for early detection of emotional disturbances and sensory, neurological, and environmental deficits, and in helping parents and professionals plan for a child's needs.

ASSESSING THE IMPACT OF THE HOME ENVIRONMENT

We know inheritance and experience both influence intelligence. Given this, what characteristics of the early home environment might influence intelligence and cognitive development?

Using the **Home Observation for Measurement of the Environment (HOME)** (Bradley, 1989), trained observers interview the primary caregiver and rate on a yes-or-no checklist the intellectual stimulation and support observed in a child's home. The version for infants and toddlers (Table 6.1) lasts about 1 hour. HOME scores are significantly correlated with measures of cognitive development (Totsika & Sylva, 2004).

Factors identified as important include parental responsiveness, the number of books in the home, the presence of playthings that encourage the development of concepts, and parents' involvement in children's play. These factors have been consistently associated with kindergarten achievement scores, language competence, and motor and social development (Bradley, Corwyn, Burchinal, McAdoo & Coll, 2001). Keep in mind that HOME items are correlations and not necessarily causal. Therefore, all we can say is that these factors are associated with high intelligence and achievement. Intelligent, well-educated parents may be more likely to provide a positive, stimulating home environment.

TABLE 6.1 The Infant-Toddler HOME Inventory (ages 0 to 3)

Name of Subscale	Description	Example Item
Emotional and verbal responsivity of the primary caregiver (items 1–11)	The communicative and affective interactions between the caregiver and the child	Mother spontaneously vocalizes to the child at least twice during visit Mother caresses or kisses child at least once during visit
Avoidance of restriction and punishment (items 12–19)	How the adult disciplines the child	Primary caregiver (PC) does not shout at child during visit PC does not express overt annoyance with or hostility toward the child
Organization of the physical and temporal environment (items 20–25)	How the child's time is organized outside the family house. What the child's personal space looks like	When PC is away, care is provided by one of three regular substitutes The child's play environment appears safe and free of hazards
Provision of appropriate play materials (items 26–34)	Presence of several types of toys available to the child and appropriate for his/her age	Child has one or more large muscle activity toys or pieces of equipment Provides equipment appropriate to age, such as infant seat, infant rocker, playpen
Parental involvement with the child (items 35–40)	How the adult interacts physically with the child	PC tends to keep child within visual range and look at him/her often PC talks to child while doing her work
Opportunities for variety in daily stimulation (items 41–45)	The way the child's daily routine is designed to incorporate social meetings with people other than the mother	Father provides some caregiving every day. Family visits or receives visits from relatives approximately once a month

Source: Totsika, V., & Sylva, K. "The Home Observation for Measurement of the Environment revisited." *Child and Adolescent Mental Health*, vol. 9, 2004, 25–35.

EARLY INTERVENTION

Early intervention is a systematic process of planning and providing therapeutic and educational services for families that need help in meeting infants', toddlers', and preschool children's developmental needs.

The best support for the effectiveness of early intervention programs is from data from Project CARE (Wasik, Ramey, Bryant & Sparling, 1990) and the Abecedarian (ABC) Project (Ramey & Campbell, 1991; Campbell, Ramey, Pungello, Sparling & Miller-Johnson (2002). In each project, an experimental group from 6 weeks through age 5 was enrolled in Partners for Learning, a full-day, year-round early childhood education program at a university child development center. Control groups received pediatric and social work services, formula, and home visits, as the experimental groups did, but they were not enrolled in Partners for Learning (Ramey & Ramey, 2003).

> **early intervention** Systematic process of providing services to help families meet young children's developmental needs.

In both projects, the children who received the early intervention showed a widening advantage over the control groups in developmental test scores between 12 and 18 months. By age 3, the average IQ of the Abecedarian experimental group was 101 and that of the CARE experimental group 105, as compared with only 84 and 93 for the control groups (Ramey & Ramey, 1998).

These findings and others like them (Camilli, Vargas, Ryan & Barnett, 2010) show that early educational intervention can help offset environmental risks and provide significant benefits. The most effective early

WHAT DO YOU **DO**?

Early Intervention Specialist

Early intervention specialists work with young children who have sensory, physical, or cognitive disabilities; emotional challenges; or a developmental delay. They collaborate with families, doctors, and other specialists to provide the child with support. Early intervention specialists may work with young children in their homes, visit them at their child care center, or meet with children brought to them in a professional setting. Requirements for becoming an early intervention specialist vary by state, but the typical requirement is a bachelor's degree with an endorsement or certification in early intervention. To learn more about becoming an early intervention specialist, visit www.naset.org.

©Teresa De Paul/ Blend Images

interventions are those that (1) start early and continue throughout the preschool years; (2) are time-intensive; (3) are based in a child development center and not just in parental training; (4) take a comprehensive approach; and (5) are tailored to individual needs. As occurred in Project CARE and the ABC Project, initial gains tend to diminish without sufficient ongoing environmental support (Brooks-Gunn, 2003).

Piagetian Approach: The Sensorimotor Stage

The **Piagetian approach** to cognitive development looks at changes, or stages, in the quality of cognitive functioning. It is concerned with how the mind structures its activities and adapts to the environment. The first of Piaget's four stages of cognitive development is the sensorimotor stage. During this stage, from birth to approximately age 2, infants learn about themselves and their world through their developing sensory and motor activity as they change from creatures who respond primarily through reflexes and random behavior into goal-oriented toddlers.

Piagetian approach Approach to the study of cognitive development that describes qualitative stages in cognitive functioning.

Circular reactions Piaget's term for behaviors performed by an infant that stimulate their own repetition.

SENSORIMOTOR SUBSTAGES

The sensorimotor stage consists of six substages (Table 6.2). During the first five substages, babies learn to coordinate input from their senses and organize their activities in relation to their environment. During the sixth substage, they progress from trial-and-error learning to the use of symbols and concepts to solve problems.

Much of this early cognitive growth comes about through **circular reactions** in which an infant learns to reproduce events originally discovered by chance. Initially, an activity

Children progress in cognitive development as they explore their world and try new activities.
©Comstock Images/Getty Images

such as sucking produces an enjoyable feeling that the baby wants to repeat. The repetition produces pleasure, which motivates the baby to do it yet again. The originally chance behavior has been consolidated into a new scheme. These are called circular reactions because they stimulate their own repetition. They can be broken down into six substages of increasing complexity and engagement with the environment.

In the first substage (birth to about 1 month), neonates practice their reflexes. For example, newborns suck reflexively when their lips are touched. But they soon learn to find the nipple even when they are not touched, and they suck at times when they are not hungry. Infants thus modify and extend the scheme for sucking.

In the second substage (about 1 to 4 months), babies learn to purposely repeat a pleasurable bodily sensation first achieved by chance (Figure 6.1). Piaget called this a primary circular reaction. Also, they begin to turn toward sounds, showing the ability to coordinate different kinds of sensory information (vision and hearing).

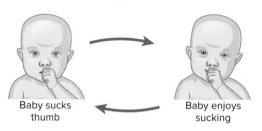

Baby sucks thumb   Baby enjoys sucking

(a) Primary circular reaction: Action and response both involve infant's own body (1 to 4 months).

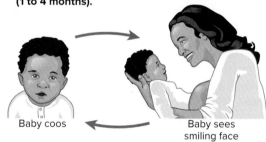

Baby coos   Baby sees smiling face

(b) Secondary circular reaction: Action gets a response from another person or object, leading to baby's repeating original action (4 to 8 months).

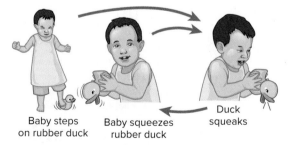

Baby steps on rubber duck   Baby squeezes rubber duck   Duck squeaks

(c) Tertiary circular reaction: Action gets one pleasing result, leading baby to perform similar actions to get similar results (12 to 18 months).

FIGURE 6.1 Primary, Secondary and Tertiary Circular Reactions

TABLE 6.2 Six Substages of Piaget's Sensorimotor Stage of Cognitive Development*

Substages	Ages	Description	Behavior
1. Use of reflexes	Birth to 1 month	Infants exercise their inborn reflexes and gain some control over them. They do not coordinate information from their senses. They do not grasp an object they are looking at.	Dorri begins sucking when her mother's breast is in her mouth.
2. Primary circular reactions	1 to 4 months	Infants repeat pleasurable behaviors that first occur by chance (such as thumbsucking). Activities focus on the infant's body rather than the effects of the behavior on the environment. Infants make first acquired adaptations; that is, they suck different objects differently. They begin to coordinate sensory information and grasp objects.	When given a bottle, Dylan, who is usually breast-fed, is able to adjust his sucking to the rubber nipple.
3. Secondary circular reactions	4 to 8 months	Infants become more interested in the environment; they repeat actions that bring interesting results (such as shaking a rattle) and prolong interesting experiences. Actions are intentional but not initially goal directed.	Alejandro pushes pieces of dry cereal over the edge of his high-chair tray one at a time and watches each piece as it falls to the floor.
4. Coordination of secondary schemes	8 to 12 months	Behavior is more deliberate and purposeful (intentional) as infants coordinate previously learned schemes (such as looking at and grasping a rattle) and use previously learned behaviors to attain their goals (such as crawling across the room to get a desired toy). They can anticipate events.	Anica pushes the button on her musical nursery rhyme book, and "Twinkle, Twinkle, Little Star" plays. She pushes this button over and over again, choosing it instead of the buttons for the other songs.
5. Tertiary circular reactions	12 to 18 months	Toddlers show curiosity and experimentation; they purposefully vary their actions to see results (for example, by shaking different rattles to hear their sounds). They actively explore their world to determine what is novel about an object, event, or situation. They try new activities and use trial and error in solving problems.	When Bjorn's big sister holds his favorite board book up to his crib bars, he reaches for it. His first efforts to bring the book into his crib fail because the book is too wide. Soon, Bjorn turns the book sideways and hugs it, delighted with his success.
6. Mental combinations	18 to 24 months	Because toddlers can mentally represent events, they are no longer confined to trial and error to solve problems. Symbolic thought enables toddlers to begin to think about events and anticipate their consequences without always resorting to action. Toddlers begin to demonstrate insight. They can use symbols, such as gestures and words, and can pretend.	Jenny plays with her shape box, searching carefully for the right hole for each shape before trying—and succeeding.

*Infants show enormous cognitive growth during Piaget's sensorimotor stage, as they learn about the world through their senses and their motor activities. Note their progress in problem solving and the coordination of sensory information. All ages are approximate.

The third substage (about 4 to 8 months) coincides with a new interest in manipulating objects and learning about their properties. Babies also intentionally repeat an action not merely for its own sake, as in the second substage, but to get results beyond the infant's own body. For example, a baby this age might repeatedly shake a rattle to hear the noise or coo when a friendly face appears so that it stays longer.

By the time infants reach the fourth substage, coordination of secondary schemes, they have built upon the few schemes they were born with. They have learned to generalize from past experiences to solve new problems. They will crawl to get something they want, grab it, or push away a barrier to it. They try out, modify, and coordinate previous schemes to find one that works. This substage marks the development of complex, goal-directed behavior.

In the fifth substage (about 12 to 18 months), babies begin to experiment to see what will happen. They now vary a behavior to see what might happen. For example, a toddler may squeeze a rubber duck, then step on it, then throw it, in order to see if all three actions result in squeaks. By trial and error, toddlers try behaviors until they find the best way to attain a goal.

The sixth substage (about 18 months to 2 years) is a transition to the preoperational stage of early childhood. Representational ability—the ability to mentally represent objects and actions in memory, largely through symbols such as words, numbers, and mental pictures—frees toddlers from immediate experience. They can pretend, and their representational ability affects the sophistication of their pretending. They can think about actions before taking them and try solutions in their mind. They no longer have to go through laborious trial and error in the real world to picture the difference between what might happen when food is thrown or dropped from different heights off the side of their high chair.

During these six substages, infants develop the ability to think and remember, and develop knowledge about the physical world. Researchers have found that some of these developments conform fairly closely to Piaget's observations, but others may occur earlier than Piaget claimed.

OBJECT CONCEPT

In his close observations of children, Piaget noted that infants under the age of about 8 months act as if an object no longer exists once it is out of their line of sight. This led to his theorizing about the object concept—the understanding that objects have independent existence, characteristics, and locations in space.

One aspect of the object concept is object permanence, the realization that something continues to exist when out of sight. At first, infants appear to have no such concept. If you hide an interesting toy, babies will not show any obvious sign they understand it still exists. However, by 18 to 24 months, almost all babies understand that objects have independent existences and will reliably search for hidden objects. According to Piaget, object permanence develops gradually during the sensorimotor stage as children develop the ability to symbolically represent objects.

Visible imitation Imitation with parts of one's body that one can see.

Invisible imitation Imitation with parts of one's body that one cannot see.

Deferred imitation Piaget's term for reproduction of an observed behavior after the passage of time by calling up a stored symbol of it.

Some research suggests that babies may fail to physically search for hidden objects because they cannot yet carry out a two-step sequence of actions, such as lifting the cover of a box and then grasping the object. Methods based only on infants' looking behavior eliminate the need for coordination with motor activity and thus can be used at very early ages. With this technique, we can get a better assessment of what babies really know.

Over the next few months, this ability continues to develop. For example, infants will continue to look for an object in the place where they first found it after seeing it hidden, even if they were later shown the object being moved to a new location (the A-not-B error). Somewhere between 5 and 8 months they start *looking* at the correct location where the object was moved, but do not reach for it. At about 9 to 10 months, infants will start looking and reaching for the object in the correct location (Cuevas & Bell, 2010). At 12

to 18 months, most infants will reliably search for an object in the last place they saw it hidden. However, they will not search for it in a place where they did *not* see it hidden. At 18 to 24 months, object permanence is fully achieved; toddlers will look for an object even if they did not see it hidden.

IMITATION

One-year-old Clara watches as her older sister brushes her hair. When her sister puts the brush down, Clara picks it up and tries to brush her own hair.

Imitation becomes increasingly valuable late in the first year of life as babies try new skills (Nelson, 2005). Piaget noted this behavior in his own observations and maintained that **visible imitation**—imitation that uses body parts such as hands or feet that babies can see—develops first and is then followed by **invisible imitation**—imitation that involves parts of the body that babies cannot see—at 9 months.

Whether or not newborns can imitate is a controversial subject. Initially, studies seemed to indicate that newborns could imitate adults by opening their mouths and sticking out their tongues (Meltzoff & Moore, 1989). Some researchers argued that this early imitative behavior was the basis for later social cognition (Meltzoff, 2007). Others argued that infants have an innate predisposition to imitate human faces that may serve the evolutionary purpose of communication with a caregiver (Rakison, 2005). Finally, some researchers argued that the tongue thrust was not imitation at all, and might simply be exploratory behavior triggered by the sight of a narrow, pointed object approaching an infant's mouth (Kagan, 2008). More recent longitudinal research concluded that under more carefully controlled testing conditions, the apparent imitation disappeared (Oostenbroek et al., 2016). Thus, this finding remains in dispute (Meltzoff et al., 2017).

Piaget believed that children under 18 months could not engage in **deferred imitation**, a more complex ability requiring long-term memory. Deferred imitation is the reproduction of an observed behavior after the passage of time. As the behavior is no longer happening, deferred imitation requires that a stored representation of the action be recalled. Piaget argued that young children could not engage in deferred imitation because they lacked the ability to retain mental representations. However, deferred imitation of novel or complex events seems to begin earlier than Piaget thought, by about 6 to 9 months (Bauer, 2002). For example, in one study 6-month-old German and Cameroonian infants were able to imitate how an adult interacted with a doll after a 10-minute delay (Goertz et al., 2011). The ability to hold material in memory over a longer time span increases with age. For example, by 9 months, more than 40 percent of infants can reproduce two steps, such as dropping a toy car down a vertical chute and then pushing a car with a rod to make it roll to the end of a ramp and turn on a light. Moreover, they can do this after a delay of 1 month (Bauer 2002; Bauer, Wiebe, Carver, Waters & Nelson, 2003).

By 14 months of age, toddlers show preferences about whom they imitate from. For example, they are more likely to imitate from people who speak the same language they do (Buttelmann, Zmyj, Daum & Carpenter, 2013). At 15 months,

Did you know?

Another sign—indeed the most important and obvious one—of a toddler's emerging symbolic capacities is language. Words are symbols—the word "key" for example, is a verbal symbol for the class of things that unlock doors.

©Spike Mafford/Getty Images

they show a bias toward imitating a peer; however, this switches to a bias toward imitating an adult at 24 months (Seehagen & Herbert, 2011). At 4 years of age, they are more likely to imitate from those who are the same gender they are (Grace, David & Ryan, 2008). In explaining results such as these, some theorists have argued that children's imitation varies depending on their goals. When children are trying to communicate similarity or forge social bonds, they are more likely to imitate from others who are like them, such as other children. When children are trying to learn new things, they are likely to imitate from those whom they think they can learn the most from, such as adults (Zmyj & Seehagen, 2013).

SYMBOLIC DEVELOPMENT, PICTORIAL COMPETENCE, AND UNDERSTANDING OF SCALE

Much of the knowledge people acquire about their world is gained through symbols, intentional representations of reality. Learning to interpret symbols is an essential task of childhood. One aspect of symbolic development is the growth of pictorial competence, the ability to understand the nature of pictures (DeLoache, Pierroutsakos & Uttal, 2003). For example, consider how suns are represented in children's books. Generally they are drawn as yellow circles with radiating spires. A child who understands that this graphic stands in for the ball of light in the sky has attained some degree of pictorial competence.

Until about 15 months, infants use their hands to explore pictures as if they were objects—rubbing, patting, or attempting to lift a depicted object off the page. By about 19 months children are able to point at a picture of an object while saying its name, demonstrating an understanding that a picture is a symbol of something else (DeLoache et al., 2003). By age 2, children understand that a picture is *both* an object and a symbol (Preissler & Bloom, 2007).

Picture books support children's acquisition of information about the world. However, research suggests that the ability to learn from books is influenced by cultural experiences. Twenty-month-old Tanzanian children who had previously not had experience with books were able to recognize familiar objects in books presented to them by a researcher, but were not able to learn a label for a novel object (a gold s-shaped hook) first presented to them in a book, and then in real life. By approximately 27 months they were able to learn the word for the novel object from a picture book and apply it to the real object correctly, and by 34 months they were able to apply what they learned to a different exemplar of that novel object (a silver s-shaped hook) (Walker, Walker & Ganea, 2013). What can be learned from pictures is also affected by the medium in which the information is presented. In one study, children under the age of 2 years did not learn the word for a novel object presented via an e-book, although they easily learned the word presented in a traditional print book. It was not until after 2 years of age that children were able to use e-books in this fashion (Strouse & Ganea, 2017).

What about television? Although toddlers may spend a good deal of time watching television, at first they seem unaware that what they are seeing is a representation of reality (Troseth, Saylor & Archer, 2006). This makes it difficult for them to use the information presented on television effectively (Barr, 2010). For example, 12- to 18-month-old children were better able to imitate an adult's actions (helping a puppet ring a bell) when they saw an adult performing the action in front of them than when they saw a video of the same thing (Barr, Muentener & Garcia, 2007). In one series of experiments, 2½-year-olds were able to locate an object hidden in an adjoining room after watching a video of an adult hiding it, but 2-year-olds could not. Yet the younger children were able to find the object if they watched through a window as it was hidden (Troseth & DeLoache, 1998). Apparently, what the 2-year-olds lacked was representational understanding of screen images.

Have you ever seen toddlers try to put on a hat that is too small for their head, or sit in a chair much too tiny to hold them? This is known as a scale error—a momentary misperception of the relative sizes of objects (DeLoache, LoBue, Vanderborght & Chiong, 2013). In one study, 18- to 36-month-olds were first allowed to interact with play objects that fit their body size, such as a toy car to ride in or a plastic slide to slide down. Then the life-size objects were replaced with miniature replicas. The children tried to slide down the tiny slides and squeeze their bodies into the miniature cars. Why would they still treat the objects as if they were full size?

The researchers suggested that these actions might in part be based on a lack of impulse control—the children wanted to play with the objects so badly that they ignored perceptual information about size. However, toddlers might also be exhibiting faulty communication between immature brain systems. One brain system enables the child to recognize and categorize an object ("That's a chair") and to plan what to do with it ("I'm going to sit in it"). A separate system may be involved in perceiving the size of the object and using visual information to control actions pertaining to it ("It's big enough to sit in"). When communication between these areas breaks down, children momentarily, and amusingly, treat the objects as if they were full size (DeLoache, Uttal & Rosengren, 2004).

Infants use their hands to explore pictures as if they were objects until they are about 15 months of age. As they develop symbolic understanding, usually by age 2, they come to realize that a picture is both a symbol and an object.
©Roberto Westbrook/Getty Images

The **dual representation hypothesis** offers yet another proposed explanation for scale errors. An object such as a toy chair has two potential representations. The chair is both an object in its own right, as well as a symbol for a class of things ("chairs"). According to this hypothesis, it is difficult for toddlers to simultaneously mentally represent both the actual object and the symbolic nature of what it stands for. In other words, they can either focus on the particular chair they are faced with ("This is a miniature chair") or the symbol and what it represents ("Chairs are for sitting in"), and so they may confuse the two (DeLoache, 2011).

EVALUATING PIAGET'S SENSORIMOTOR STAGE

According to Piaget, the journey from reflex behavior to the beginnings of thought is a long, slow one; children do not make the breakthrough to conceptual thought until the last half of the 2nd year. More recent research using simplified tasks and modern tools suggests that certain limitations Piaget saw in infants' early cognitive abilities, such as object permanence, may instead have reflected immature linguistic and motor skills. The answers Piaget received were as much a function of the ways in which he asked the questions as they were a reflection of young children's actual abilities.

In terms of describing what children do under certain circumstances, and the basic progression of skills, Piaget was correct. However, in some ways infants and toddlers are more cognitively competent than Piaget imagined. It is true, as Piaget observed, that immature forms of cognition precede more mature forms. However, he may have been mistaken in emphasizing motor experience as the primary engine of cognitive growth. Infants' perceptions are far ahead of their motor abilities, and today's methods enable researchers to make observations and inferences about those perceptions. The relationship between perception and cognition is a major area of investigation; we discuss it in the next section.

Dual representation hypothesis Proposal that children under age 3 have difficulty grasping spatial relationships because of the need to keep more than one mental representation in mind at the same time.

information-processing approach Approach to the study of cognitive development by observing and analyzing processes involved in perceiving and handling information.

habituation Type of learning in which familiarity with a stimulus reduces, slows, or stops a response.

dishabituation Increase in responsiveness after presentation of a new stimulus.

Information-Processing Approach: Perceptions and Representations

The **information-processing approach** focuses on perception, learning, memory, and problem solving. It aims to discover how children process information from the time they encounter it until they use it. Information-processing researchers analyze the separate parts of a complex task to figure out what abilities are necessary for each part of the task and at what age these abilities develop, often by using children's attentional processes to infer what the children know. Key aspects of information processing related to the 0 to 3 age range include habituation, visual-processing abilities, information processing as a predictor of intelligence, and the relationship to the development of Piagetian abilities.

HABITUATION

At about 6 weeks, Stefan lies peacefully in his crib near a window, sucking a pacifier. It is a cloudy day, but suddenly the sun breaks through, and an angular shaft of light appears on the end of the crib. Stefan stops sucking for a few moments, staring intently at the pattern of light and shade. Then he looks away and starts sucking again. A vast body of research in infant development underlies the analysis of this simple behavior.

When doing research with infants, researchers need to figure out how to ask questions in ways that babies can answer. **Habituation** is a type of learning in which continued exposure to a stimulus (such as a shaft of light) reduces attention to that stimulus (such as looking away). In other words, familiarity breeds boredom. Researchers study habituation in newborns by repeatedly presenting a stimulus, usually a sound or visual pattern, and then monitoring such responses as heart rate, sucking, eye movements, and brain activity. A baby who has been sucking typically stops or sucks less vigorously when the stimulus is first presented and pays attention to the new stimulus—somewhat like an adult who might stop talking for an instant when he or she notices something interesting going on. However, after a while, the stimuli loses its novelty and no longer causes the baby to suck less. Resumption of vigorous sucking shows the infant has habituated to the stimulus. A new sight or sound, however, will capture the baby's attention, and the baby will again stop or reduce sucking. This response to a new stimulus is called **dishabituation**.

Researchers gauge the efficiency of infants' information processing by measuring how quickly babies habituate, how quickly they reorient to new stimuli, and how much time they spend looking at the new and the old. Liking to look at new things and quickly habituating to them correlates with

Did you know?

Habituation is a general property of our nervous systems. Have you ever worn uncomfortable shoes? You may have noticed your feet hurt more when you stand after sitting for a while than they do while walking around. That's because when you walk around, you habituate to the pain. When you sit down, and then stand again, you feel the pain in its full intensity anew because you have become dishabituated.

©denisfilm/123RF

later signs of cognitive development. In fact, as we will see, speed of habituation and other information-processing abilities show promise as predictors of intelligence (Rose, Feldman, Jankowski & Van Rossem, 2012; Fagan, Holland & Wheeler, 2007).

VISUAL PROCESSING ABILITIES

Researchers assume the more time a baby spends looking at something, the more the baby must like it—an assumption that has been used to develop the **visual preference** paradigm. Researchers merely present two stimuli and observe which one babies look at more. As a result, they have determined that babies less than 2 days old prefer curved lines to straight lines, complex patterns to simple patterns, three-dimensional objects to two-dimensional objects, and moving objects to stationary objects. Newborns also prefer pictures of faces or facelike configurations to pictures of other things. Last, infants tend to prefer new sights to familiar ones (Rakison, 2005; Turati, Simion, Milani & Umilta, 2002), which is known as novelty preference.

We can examine **visual recognition memory** using a similar method. Babies like to look at new things. If we show a baby two stimuli side by side and the baby looks longer at a novel stimuli than a familiar one, we can assume he or she recognized the familiar stimulus. In other words, because the novel stimulus is new, it is more interesting and thus warrants a better look.

Did you know?

Pointing helps regulate joint attention and does not need to be taught to neurotypical babies.

©anetta/Shutterstock

PERCEPTUAL PROCESSING ABILITIES

Contrary to Piaget's view, such studies suggest that a rudimentary representational ability exists at birth or very soon after and quickly becomes more efficient. Individual differences in efficiency of information processing reflect the speed with which infants form and refer to such mental images. When shown two sights at the same time, infants who quickly shift attention from one to another tend to have better recognition memory and stronger novelty preference than infants who take longer looks at a single sight (Jankowsky, Rose & Feldman, 2001).

Speed of processing increases rapidly during infants' 1st year. It continues to increase during the 2nd and 3rd years, as toddlers become better able to distinguish new information from information they have already processed (Rose, Jankowski & Feldman, 2002; Zelazo, Kearsley & Stack, 1995).

Auditory discrimination studies are also usually based on attentional preference. This ability may emerge prenatally. In one study, fetuses were played recordings of various adults reading a story in either their parents' native language or a novel language. Heart rate data indicated that the fetuses paid increased attention to both their mother's voice and stories read in a novel language (Kisilevsky et al., 2009). At birth, infants also have the ability to remember some sounds. Infants who heard a certain speech sound one day after birth remembered that sound 24 hours later, as shown by a reduced tendency to turn their heads toward the sound (Swain, Zelazo & Clifton, 1993). However, these memory traces, at least initially, are brief and subject to interference and forgetting (Benavides-Varela et al., 2011).

Piaget held that the senses are unconnected at birth and are only gradually integrated through experience. However, this integration begins almost immediately. The fact that neonates will look at a source of sound shows that at the very least they associate hearing and sight. A more sophisticated ability is cross-modal transfer, the ability to use information gained from one sense to guide another—as when a person negotiates a dark room by feeling for the location of familiar objects. In one study, 1-month-olds showed that they could transfer information gained from sucking (touch) to vision. When the infants saw a rigid object (a hard plastic cylinder) and a flexible one (a wet sponge) being manipulated by a pair of hands, the infants looked longer at the object they had just sucked (Gibson & Walker, 1984).

Researchers also study how attention itself develops. From birth to about 2 months, the amount of time infants typically gaze at a new sight increases (Colombo, 2002). Between about 4 to 8 months, looking time shortens, with the fastest decline seen at 4 to 6 months (Colombo et al., 2010). Presumably, this is because infants learn to scan objects more efficiently and thus shift attention more rapidly. Indeed, those infants who look for less time at novel stimuli show better memory for it later (Reynolds, Guy & Zhang, 2011) and have better executive control in early childhood (Cuevas & Bell, 2010). Later in the 1st year and into the 2nd, when sustaining attention becomes more voluntary and task-oriented, looking time plateaus or increases, especially for more complex stimuli (Colombo et al., 2004).

The capacity for **joint attention**—which is of fundamental importance to social interaction, language acquisition, and the understanding of others' intentions and mental states—develops between 10 and 12 months, when babies follow an adults' gaze by looking or pointing in the same direction (Behne, Liszkowski, Carpenter & Tomasello, 2012). Young children who follow an adults' gaze at 10 to 11 months have a larger vocabulary at 18 months, 2 years, and 2½ years than those who do not (Brooks & Meltzoff, 2005; 2008; 2015). The use of pointing by children to capture the attention of adults around them has strong positive effects on children's language

visual preference Tendency of infants to spend more time looking at one sight than another.

visual recognition memory Ability to distinguish a familiar visual stimulus from an unfamiliar stimulus when shown both at the same time.

joint attention Involves understanding that you and I have a shared focus of attention.

comprehension and production (Colonnesi, Stams, Koster & Noom, 2010).

Watching television may impede attentional development, although the data are unclear. One widely cited study found that the more hours children spent viewing television at ages 1 and 3, the more likely they were to have attentional problems by age 7 (Christakis, Zimmerman, DiGiuseppe & McCarty, 2004). However, follow-up work in this area suggested the association between television viewing and attentional problems was only true for those children who watched more than seven hours of television a day, and even that association disappeared when maternal achievement and family income were included in analyses (Foster & Watkins, 2010).

INFORMATION PROCESSING AS A PREDICTOR OF INTELLIGENCE

Because of a weak correlation between infants' scores on developmental tests such as the Bayley Scales and their later IQ (Bjorklund & Causey, 2017), many psychologists assumed that the cognitive functioning of infants had little in common with that of older children and adults. However, when cognitive functioning is examined more closely, some aspects of mental development do seem to be fairly continuous from birth (Courage & Howe, 2002).

Four core cognitive domains appear to be associated with later IQ: attention, processing speed, memory, and representational competence (as indexed by cross-modal transfer and the ability to anticipate future events). In one study, performance on these tasks in infancy (7 and 12 months) was related to performance on the same tasks in toddlerhood (24 and 36 months) as well as to performance on IQ tests at 11 years of age (Rose, Feldman, Jankowski & Van Rossem, 2012). Similar relationships to school performance have been found for the ability to shift attention rapidly (Hitzert, Van Braeckel, Bos, Hunnius & Geuze, 2014) and the ability to inhibit attention toward irrelevant stimuli (Markant & Amso, 2014). This provides evidence for the continuity of cognitive processes. Essentially, children who, from the start, are efficient at attending to, taking in, and interpreting sensory information score well on later intelligence tests (Colombo, Kapa & Curtindale, 2010). However, other items, such as performance on motor skills, do not relate well to later IQ.

INFORMATION PROCESSING AND THE DEVELOPMENT OF PIAGETIAN ABILITIES

As we discussed earlier, several of the cognitive abilities Piaget identified as developing toward the end of the sensorimotor stage seem to arise much earlier. Research on infants' visual processing has given developmental scientists a window into the timing of such cognitive developments as categorization, causality, object permanence, and number—all of which depend on formation of mental representations.

Categorization

Adults can understand that plants and animals are both living things but a television is not. Furthermore, they can understand that some animals are pets, that among those pets are cats and dogs, and that a mastiff is a type of dog. These nested relationships are known as *categories.* Dividing the world into meaningful categories is vital to thinking about objects or concepts and their relationships. It is the foundation of language, reasoning, problem solving, and memory.

According to Piaget, the ability to group things into categories does not appear until around 18 months. Yet, by looking longer at items in a new category, even 3-month-olds seem to know, for example, that a dog is not a cat (French, Mareschal, Mermillod & Quinn, 2004). Indeed, brain imaging has found that basic components of the neural structures needed to support categorization are functional within the first 6 months of life (Quinn, Westerlund & Nelson, 2006). Experience matters too. After being presented with a variety of photographs of pets, 4-month-old infants with pets at home were better at recognizing individual cats and forming categories representing cats than infants without pets at home (Kovack-Lesh, Horst & Oakes, 2008).

Infants at first seem to categorize on the basis of *perceptual* features, such as shape, color, and pattern, but by 12 to 14 months their categories become *conceptual,* based on real-world knowledge, particularly of function (Mandler, 1998; 2007). In one series of experiments, 10- and 11-month-olds recognized that chairs with zebra-striped upholstery belong in the category of furniture, not animals (Pauen, 2002). As time goes on, these concepts become more specific. For example, 2-year-olds understand that categories such as "car" and "airplane" are nested within the overall category of "vehicles" (Mandler, 2007).

Categorization is not limited to visual stimuli. There is evidence that 3-month-old babies categorize words differently than tones (Ferry, Hespos & Waxman, 2010) and can even categorize musical chords into dissonant versus consonant and major versus minor dimensions (Virtala, Huotilainen, Partanen, Fellman & Tervaniemi, 2013). Furthermore, in the 2nd year, language becomes a factor in the ability to categorize. In one study, 14-month-olds who understood more words were more flexible in their categorizing than those with smaller understood vocabularies (Ellis & Oakes, 2006).

Did you know?

Of all primates, humans have the largest amount of sclera—the white part of the eye. Theorists have speculated this helps us more easily engage in joint attention activities. The large sclera allows us to more easily see where others around us are looking.

©Image Source/Getty Images

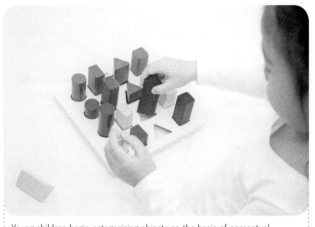
Young children begin categorizing objects on the basis of perceptual features like shape and color.
©paulaphoto/Shutterstock

Causality

Eight-month-old Aviva accidentally squeezes her toy duck and it quacks. Startled, she drops it, and then, staring at it intently, she squeezes it again. Aviva is beginning to understand causality—the principle that one event (squeezing) causes another (quacking). Piaget believed that at about 4 to 6 months, as infants become able to grasp objects, they begin to recognize that they can act on their environment. However, he believed that they did not yet know that causes must come before effects, and that forces outside of themselves can make things happen. He maintained that this understanding develops slowly during infants' 1st year.

However, information-processing studies suggest that an understanding of causality emerges earlier. In one study, infants as young as 4½ months were able to understand simple causality (a ball knocking another ball out of position). However, only those infants who had practiced playing with a Velcro-covered ball and Velcro mittens—allowing them to easily manipulate the ball despite their immature motor control, and therefore practice performing causal actions—were able to do so (Rakison & Krogh, 2012). By 6 months of age, this ability is more robust and does not require training (Leslie, 1995). Moreover, by 8 months of age, infants make causal attributions for simple events even when they cannot see the actual moment of contact between the two objects (Muentener & Carey, 2010). And by 10 to 12 months old, the types of inferences made by infants become even more sophisticated. For example, 10- to 12-month-olds looked longer when a hand emerged from the opposite side of a stage onto which a beanbag had been thrown than when the hand emerged from the same side as the beanbag, suggesting the infants understood that the hand had probably thrown the beanbag. The infants did not have the same reaction when a toy train rather than a hand appeared or when the thrown object was a self-propelled puppet (Saxe, Tenenbaum & Carey, 2005).

It may be that, with age, infants accumulate more information about how objects behave, thus they are better able to see causality as a general principle operating in a variety of situations (Cohen & Amsel, 1998; Cohen, Chaput & Cashon, 2002). Increasing experience with the environment may also be a factor. For example, 7-month-olds who had begun to crawl recognized self-propulsion of objects, but non-crawling 7-month-olds did not. This finding suggests that infants' ability to identify self-propelled motion is linked to the development of self-locomotion, which gives them new ways of understanding objects in their world (Cicchino & Rakison, 2008). Self-locomotion has also been linked to infants' ability to predict the goal of other people's intentional failed actions (like trying, but failing, to reach an object) (Brandone, 2015).

Violation of Expectations Research

When Piaget investigated object permanence, he used infants' motor responses to gauge whether or not infants understood that a hidden object still existed. Their failure to reach for the hidden object was interpreted to mean they did not. However, it was possible that infants understood object permanence but could not demonstrate this knowledge with motor activity. At that time, infant development research methodologies were more limited. Researchers needed to ask babies the question in a way they could answer.

If in the course of your everyday life, you encountered something outside of your expectations, you would probably stop to look at it to try to figure out why it was occurring. Babies are no different. When they encounter something that is puzzling or surprising, they scrutinize it until they have analyzed it to their satisfaction and it is no longer interesting. Because they are capable of controlling their visual behavior to some degree, this gives researchers a way to ask them what they know.

Violation of expectations begins with a familiarization phase in which infants see an event happen normally. After the infant becomes bored and has habituated to this procedure (most commonly as indexed by looking away), the event is changed in a way that conflicts with—or violates—normal expectations. If the baby looks longer at this changed event, researchers assume the additional interest shown by the baby implies that the baby is surprised.

For example, in one experiment, infants as young as 3½ months were first shown an animation of a carrot moving back and forth behind a screen (Hespos & Baillargeon, 2008). The center of the screen was notched, and a tall carrot should have shown momentarily as it moved in front of the notch. In the "possible" event, the carrot could be seen as it passed in front of the notch. In the "impossible" event, the carrot would appear at one side, never show in the middle, and then emerge out the opposite side. Infants showed surprise by looking longer at the "impossible" event, indicating that the "impossible" event violated their expectations (Figure 6.2).

This type of research has been important for the study of object permanence because for the babies to be surprised by the carrot's failure to

violation-of-expectations research Research method in which dishabituation to a stimulus that conflicts with experience is taken as evidence that an infant recognizes the new stimulus as surprising.

FIGURE 6.2 Violation-of-Expectations Research

How early do infants show object permanence? In this violation-of-expectations experiment, 3½-month-olds watched a short carrot and then a tall carrot slide along a track, disappear behind a screen, and then reappear. After they became accustomed to seeing these events, the opaque screen was replaced by a screen with a large notch at the top. The short carrot did not appear in the notch when passing behind the screen; the tall carrot, which should have appeared in the notch, also did not. The babies looked longer at the tall, than at the short, carrot event, suggesting that they were surprised that the tall carrot did not reappear in the notch.

Source: Baillargeon, R., & DeVos, J. "Object permanence in young infants: Further evidence." *Child Development*, vol. 62, 1991, 1227–1246.

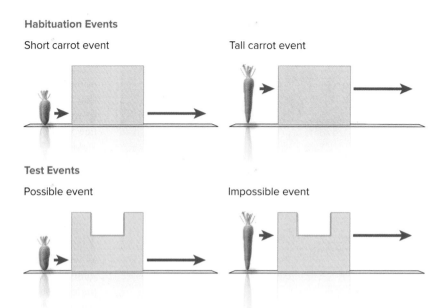

show, they needed to be able to remember that the carrot continued to exist. Thus, it provided evidence for the development of the ability at much younger ages than Piaget thought possible. Moreover, this methodology has allowed researchers to investigate a wider series of questions about what infants do and do not expect about the world and allowed us to ask these questions at much earlier ages than would otherwise be possible. For example, we now know that infants have object permanence, expect that objects should not appear and disappear randomly, and realize that you should not be able to hide tall objects inside of short objects (Baillargeon, 2004). More generally, it appears infants have a skeletal understanding of physical concepts such as gravity, inertia, and physical continuity. Some researchers have argued that, at some level, infants have innate, naïve expectations about the physical principles of the world around them (Baillargeon & Carey, 2012).

Number

The violation-of-expectations paradigm can also be used to ask babies questions about their understanding of numbers. In one study, infants watched as Mickey Mouse dolls were placed behind a screen, and a doll was either added or taken away. The screen then was lifted to reveal either the number of dolls that should have been there or a different number of dolls. Babies looked longer at surprising "wrong" answers than at expected "right" ones, suggesting that they had mentally computed the right answers (Wynn, 1992). Subsequent to this classic study, multiple programs of research supported infants' ability to discriminate between small sets of numbers (Baillargeon & Carey, 2012). Theorists argued that this data suggested babies have an innate rudimentary ability to add and subtract.

Critics argued the infants might simply have been responding perceptually to the puzzling presence or the

absence of the doll behind the screen (Cohen & Marks, 2002; Haith, 1998). In other words, they may have merely noticed differences in the overall contours, area, or collective mass of sets of objects rather than compared the number of objects in the sets (Mix, Huttenlocher & Levine, 2002).

In response to such criticisms, McCrink and Wynn (2004) designed an experiment that used numbers too large for mere perceptual discrimination. Nine-month-old infants saw five abstract objects go behind an opaque square. Five more objects then appeared and went behind the square. The infants looked longer when the screen dropped to reveal five objects than when it revealed 10. This supported an early numerical system rather than a perceptual process. Other research has supported similar conclusions. For example, newborns are able to relate a visual array of 4 or 12 triangles or circles with the auditory presentation of 4 or 12 sounds (such as "tu-tu-tu-tu" or "ra-ra-ra-ra"). This suggests that even at this early age, number is an abstract concept that can be represented across different sensory modalities (Izard, Sann, Spelke & Streri, 2009). In preschool, the ability to estimate approximate numbers is related to later mathematical achievement, suggesting continuity in this process (Bonny & Lourenco, 2013).

Some theorists have suggested that there are two core systems for the representation of number. One system is designed for keeping track of small numbers of individual objects. A second system is designed for representing large numbers of approximate magnitude (Feigenson, Dehaene & Spelke, 2004). In support of this assertion, brain imaging research conducted on 6- to 7-month-olds showed that when infants viewed visual arrays of one to three items, areas in the occipital and temporal areas of the brain were more active, while arrays of 8 to 32 objects led to more activity in parietal sites (Hyde & Spelke, 2011).

Violation-of-expectations studies and other recent information-processing research with infants raises the possibility that at least rudimentary forms of categorization, causal reasoning, naïve physics, and number sense may be present in the early months of life. One proposal is that infants are born with reasoning abilities—*innate learning mechanisms* that help them make sense of the information they encounter—or that they acquire these abilities very early (Baillargeon, Gertner & Wu, 2011). Some investigators go further, suggesting that infants at birth may already have intuitive *core knowledge* of basic physical principles in the form of specialized brain modules that help infants organize their perceptions and experience (Spelke, 2017; Baillargeon & Carey, 2012).

Cognitive Neuroscience Approach: The Brain's Cognitive Structures

The **cognitive neuroscience approach** examines the hardware of the central nervous system to identify what brain structures are involved in specific areas of cognition. Current brain research bears out Piaget's assumption that neurological maturation is a major factor in cognitive development. Brain growth spurts (periods of rapid growth and development) do indeed coincide with changes in cognitive behavior (Fischer, 2008).

Some researchers have used brain scans to determine which brain structures are tied to cognitive functions and to chart developmental changes. These brain scans provide physical evidence of the location of two separate long-term memory systems—implicit and explicit—that acquire and store different kinds of information and mature at different rates (Bauer, DeBoer & Lukowski, 2007). **Implicit memory** refers to remembering that occurs without effort or even conscious awareness; for example, knowing how to tie your shoe or throw a ball. It most commonly pertains to habits and skills. Implicit memory seems to develop early and is demonstrated by such actions as an infant's kicking on seeing a familiar mobile (Nelson, 2005). **Explicit memory**, also called declarative memory, is conscious or intentional recollection, usually of facts, names, events, or other things that can be stated or declared. Delayed imitation of complex behaviors is evidence that declarative memory has developed. This is because delayed imitation requires a representation of a behavior to be stored in memory. While infants cannot yet speak, and thus the memory cannot technically be "declared," this is nonetheless a demonstration of symbolic representation (Bauer et al., 2007).

In early infancy, when the structures responsible for memory storage are not fully formed, memories are relatively fleeting. The rapid growth of the *hippocampus,* a structure deep in the temporal lobes, along with the development of cortical structures coordinated by the hippocampal formation make longer-lasting memories possible (Lavenex & Lavenex, 2013; Uematsu et al., 2012; Bauer et al., 2003).

The *prefrontal cortex* (the large portion of the frontal lobe directly behind the forehead) is believed to control many aspects of cognition. This part of the brain develops more slowly than any other (Teffer & Semendeferi, 2012;

Diamond, 2002) making it more sensitive to environmental disruption (Kolb et al., 2012). During the second half of the 1st year, the prefrontal cortex and associated circuitry develop the capacity for working memory (Pelphrey et al., 2004). Working memory is short-term storage of information the brain is actively processing, or working on. For example, when you try to estimate how much an item on sale will cost, you are using working memory to make the calculations. Working memory can be overwhelmed, as when someone speaks to you while you try to calculate the sale price.

Working memory appears relatively late in development and may be responsible for the slow development of object permanence, which seems to be seated in a rearward area of the prefrontal cortex (Bell, 2012; Nelson, 1995). By 12 months, this region may be developed enough to permit an infant to avoid the A-not-B error by controlling the impulse to search in a place where the object previously was found (Bell & Fox, 1992; Diamond, 1991).

Although memory systems continue to develop beyond infancy, the early emergence of the brain's memory structures underlines the importance of environmental stimulation from the first months of life. Social-contextual theorists and researchers pay particular attention to the impact of environmental influences.

Social-Contextual Approach: Learning from Caregivers

The **social-contextual approach** examines the environment's effect on the learning process. Researchers influenced by Vygotsky's sociocultural theory study how cultural context affects early social interactions that may promote cognitive competence. **Guided participation** refers to mutual interactions with adults that help structure children's activities and bridge the gap between a child's understanding and an adult's. This concept was inspired by Vygotsky's view of learning as a collaborative process. Guided participation often occurs in shared play and in ordinary, everyday activities in which children informally learn the skills, knowledge, and values important in their culture, much as an apprentice would.

In a series of cross-cultural studies (Goncu, Mistry & Mosier, 2000; Rogoff, Mistry, Goncu & Mosier, 1993), researchers visited the homes of 1- to 2-year-old children in four culturally different places: a Mayan town in Guatemala, a tribal village in India, and middle-class urban neighborhoods in Salt Lake City and Turkey.

cognitive neuroscience approach Approach to the study of cognitive development that links brain processes with cognitive ones.

implicit memory Unconscious recall, generally of habits and skills; sometimes called *procedural memory.*

explicit memory Intentional and conscious memory, generally of facts, names, and events; sometimes called *declarative memory.*

social-contextual approach Approach to the study of cognitive development that focuses on environmental influences, particularly parents and other caregivers.

guided participation Participation of an adult in a child's activity in a manner that helps to structure the activity and to bring the child's understanding of it closer to that of the adult.

As adults share everyday activities, this guided participation helps a child informally learn skills, knowledge, and values.
©Image Source Trading Ltd/Shutterstock, ©Hero/Corbis/Glow Images

The investigators interviewed caregivers about their child-rearing practices and watched them help the toddlers learn to dress themselves and to play with unfamiliar toys.

Cultural differences affected the types of guided participation the researchers observed. In the Guatemalan town and the Indian village, the children customarily played while the mother worked nearby. When children needed to be shown how to do something, such as tie their shoes, the mothers tended to provide an initial demonstration and instruction, and then allow the children to take over while they remained available to help if needed. The instruction was primarily nonverbal. The U.S. toddlers, who had full-time caregivers, interacted with adults in the context of child's play rather than work or social worlds. Caregivers managed and motivated children's learning with praise and excitement. Their instruction was highly verbal in nature, often consisting of "lessons." Turkish families, who were in transition from a rural to an urban way of life, showed a pattern somewhere in between.

The cultural context influences the way caregivers contribute to cognitive development. Direct adult involvement in children's play and learning may be better adapted to a middle-class urban community, in which parents or caregivers have more time, greater verbal skills, and possibly more interest in children's play and learning, than to a rural community in a developing country, in which children frequently observe and participate in adults' work activities (Rogoff et al., 1993). However, despite the different means by which caregivers teach their children valuable life skills, all children learn the things they need to be effective members of society.

The social constructionist approach has been influential in early childhood education. Research has shown that preschool programs that are highly focused on academic skills are not necessarily ideal for young children (Bodrova, 2008; Hirsch-Pasek, 1991). Indeed, such programs may even result in lower academic achievement later in school (Marcon, 2002). However, programs based on Vygotsky's philosophies have been shown to be an effective route for the transmission of academic concepts within the context of classroom routines and play. For example, a geometry lesson in which 4- to 5-year-old children donned detective hats and were guided through solving a "mystery of the shapes" sorting task where they were asked to discover the secret distinguishing "real" shapes from "fake" ones was more effective in teaching shape knowledge than either didactic teaching or free play (Fisher, Hirsh-Pasek, Newcombe & Golinkoff, 2013).

Additionally, social constructionist approaches to early childhood education may have positive effects on other variables important for later academic achievement. For example, when compared to children enrolled in a child-centered preschool and kindergarten, children in a highly academic program did significantly worse on a number of motivational measures. The children in the academically oriented programs rated their own abilities as lower, expected less success in academics, were more dependent on adults, were less proud of their accomplishments, and found school more worrisome (Stipek, Feiler, Daniels & Milburn, 1995).

Language Development

When Ava was a small baby, far before she ever spoke her first word, she was already communicating a great deal to her parents. Through smiles, crying, laughing, facial expressions, and sounds of pleasure and pain, she let her parents know exactly how she was feeling. However, when she said her first word—"ba"—uttered in response to the birds outside her window, she had crossed a threshold of profound importance.

Language is a communication system based on words and grammar, and it is inextricably intertwined with cognition. A certain level of cognitive development is necessary for language; once language develops, it promotes cognitive development. Once children know words, they can use them to represent objects and actions. They can reflect on people, places, and things, and they can communicate their needs, feelings, and ideas to exert control over their lives.

Is linguistic ability learned or inborn? In the 1950s, a debate raged between two schools of thought: one led by B. F. Skinner, the foremost proponent of learning theory, and the other by the linguist Noam Chomsky.

TABLE 6.3 Language Milestones from Birth to 3 Years

Age in Months	Development
Birth	Can perceive speech, cry, make some response to sound.
1½ to 3	Coos and laughs.
3	Plays with speech sounds.
5 to 6	Recognizes frequently heard sound patterns.
6 to 7	Recognizes all phonemes of native language.
6 to 10	Babbles in strings of consonants and vowels.
9	Uses gestures to communicate and plays gesture games.
9 to 10	Intentionally imitates sounds.
9 to 12	Uses a few social gestures.
10 to 12	No longer can discriminate sounds not in own language.
10 to 14	Says first word (usually a label for something).
10 to 18	Says single words.
12 to 13	Understands symbolic function of naming; passive vocabulary grows.
13	Uses more elaborate gestures.
14	Uses symbolic gesturing.
16 to 24	Learns many new words, expanding expressive vocabulary rapidly, going from about 50 words to as many as 400; uses verbs and adjectives.
18 to 24	Says first sentence (2 words).
20	Uses fewer gestures; names more things.
20 to 22	Has comprehension spurt.
24	Uses many two-word phrases; no longer babbles; wants to talk.
30	Learns new words almost every day; speaks in combinations of three or more words; understands very well; makes grammatical mistakes.
36	Says up to 1,000 words, 80 percent intelligible; makes some mistakes in syntax.

Sources: E. Bates, B. O'Connell, C. Shore & J. D. Osofsky, "Language and communication in infancy," in J. D. Osofsky (Ed.), *Handbook of infant development* (2nd ed.) New York: Wiley, 1987; A. J. Capute, B. K. Shapiro, & F. B. Palmer, "Marking the milestones of language development," *Contemporary Pediatrics, 4* (1987), 24; P. K. Kuhl, "Early language acquisition: Cracking the speech code," *Nature Reviews Neuroscience, 5*, no. 11 (2004), 831; C. E. Lalonde & J. F. Werker, "Cognitive influences on cross-language speech perception in infancy," *Infant Behavior and Development, 18*, no. 4 (1995), 459–475; E. H. Lenneberg, "On explaining language," *Science, 164*, no. 3880 (1969), 635–643.

Skinner (1957) maintained that language learning, like all learning, is based on experience. According to Skinner, there is nothing innate about language; rather, children learn language the same way they learn all things—through environmental influences. According to learning theory, children learn language through operant conditioning. At first, babies utter sounds at random. By chance, some of these sounds may approximate speech (e.g., "da"), and parents generally reinforce these vocalizations with smiles, attention, and praise. Gradually, by selectively reinforcing closer and closer approximations to adult speech (e.g., "dada"), parents shape their children's emerging language abilities. In addition, as children develop, they begin to imitate words as well, which their parents also reinforce. Over time, these processes result in the emergence of speech. Although the child can participate actively via imitation, this is predominantly a passive view of language development.

Chomsky's view is called **nativism**. It emphasizes the active role of the learner. Chomsky (1957, 1972, 1995) proposed that the human brain has an innate capacity for acquiring language; babies learn to talk as naturally as they learn to walk. It is part of our species heritage. He suggested that an inborn language acquisition device (LAD) programs children's brains to analyze the language they hear and figure out its rules. Nativists point out that almost all children master their native language in the same age-related sequence. For example, most babies learn to speak in active voice prior to passive voice. The fact that there is so much consistency, and that babies learn it so easily and without formal teaching, suggests that our brains are specialized for language (Gannon, Holloway, Broadfield & Braun, 1998). In addition, newborns appear to have "perceptual mechanisms that are tuned to the properties of speech" (Eimas, 1985, p. 49), making it more likely they will pay attention to language, thus supporting learning. Last, nativists point to the sensitive periods for language acquisition in support of their position.

Most developmental scientists today believe that language acquisition, like most other aspects of development, depends on an intertwining of nature and nurture. Children have an inborn capacity to acquire language, which may be activated or constrained by experience.

nativism Theory that human beings have an inborn capacity for language acquisition.

Now let's look first at the typical sequence of language development (Table 6.3). Next we will note special characteristics of early speech and then examine competing explanations of how infants acquire language.

Did you know?

Infants have distinct cries for hunger and pain. The higher the need for assistance, the higher the frequency of the cry (Dessureau, Kurowski, & Thompson, 1998).

©Stockbyte/Getty Images

SEQUENCE OF EARLY LANGUAGE DEVELOPMENT

Before babies can use words, they make their needs and feelings known through sounds that progress from crying to cooing and babbling, then to accidental imitation, and finally to deliberate imitation. These sounds are known as **prelinguistic speech**. They go hand in hand with calibration of babies' perceptual system with their native language. Babies are then ready to engage in language, an ability expressed both with their gestures as well as their first words and sentences.

Early Vocalization

Crying is a newborn's first means of communication and has great adaptive value. Different pitches, patterns, and intensities signal hunger, sleepiness, or anger (Lester & Boukydis, 1985). Adults find crying aversive for a reason—it motivates them to find the source of the problem and fix it. Thus, crying has great adaptive value.

prelinguistic speech Forerunner of linguistic speech; utterance of sounds that are not words. Includes crying, cooing, babbling, and accidental and deliberate imitation of sounds without understanding their meaning.

Between 6 weeks and 3 months, babies start cooing when they are happy—squealing, gurgling, and making vowel sounds like "ahhh." At about 3 to 6 months, babies begin to play with speech sounds, matching the sounds they hear from people around them.

Babbling—repeating consonant-vowel strings, such as "ma-ma-ma-ma"—occurs between 6 and 10 months. Babbling is not real language because it does not hold meaning for the baby, but it becomes more wordlike over time.

Imitation is a key to early language development. First, infants accidentally imitate language sounds. Generally, they are reinforced by their parent's positive responses, and thus encouraged to produce such sounds more and more over time. Then, at about 9 to 10 months, infants deliberately imitate sounds without understanding them. Once they have a repertoire of sounds, they string them together in patterns that sound like language but seem to have no meaning. Once infants become familiar with the sounds of words and phrases, they begin to attach meanings to them (Fernald, Perfors, & Marchman, 2006).

Perceiving Language Sounds and Structure

Imitation of language sounds requires the ability to perceive subtle differences between sounds. Infants' brains seem to be preset to distinguish basic linguistic units and patterns, and categorize them as similar or different (Kuhl, 2010).

Phonemes are the smallest units of sound in speech. For example, the word *dog* has three phonemes: the *d,* the *o,* and the *g* sound. Every language has its own unique phonology, or system of sounds, that are used in the production of speech. At first, infants can discriminate the sounds of any language. In time, however, exposure to a native language commits the brain's neural networks to further learning of the patterns of the infant's native language and constrains future learning of nonnative language patterns (Kuhl & Rivera-Gaxiola, 2008). This exposure can either occur prenatally or postnatally. If a mother speaks two languages regularly during pregnancy, her newborn baby will recognize both languages and be more interested in listening to speakers in the languages he or she was previously exposed to. Even more important, the baby will show differential responses to both languages, suggesting that even newborns have some understanding that two language systems are involved, and that they are sensitive not just to the overall sounds but to the patterns and rhythms that distinguish the two languages (Byers-Heinlein, Burns & Werker, 2010).

By 6 to 7 months, hearing babies have learned to recognize the phonemes used in their native language (Kuhl, Williams, Lacerda, Stevens & Lindblom, 1992), and by 8 months they begin to lose sensitivity to phonemes that are not used in their native language (Gervain & Mehler, 2010). By the end of the 1st year, babies lose their sensitivity to sounds that are not part of the language or languages they usually hear spoken. This process begins earlier for vowels and later for consonants (Kuhl & Rivera-Gaxiola, 2008). The ability to discriminate native-language sounds at this age predicts individual differences in language abilities during the 2nd year (Tsao, Liu & Kuhl, 2004), whereas nonnative sound discrimination does not (Kuhl, Conboy, Padden, Nelson & Pruitt, 2005). The increased sensitivity to native sounds helps the child more efficiently acquire language. Interestingly, analogous processes occur in deaf children with gestures (Kuhl & Rivera-Gaxiola, 2008).

How does this change occur? One hypothesis is that infants mentally compute the relative frequency of particular phonetic sequences in their language and learn to ignore sequences they infrequently hear (Werker, Yeung & Yoshida, 2012; Kuhl, 2004). Another hypothesis is that early language experience modifies neural structures, facilitating detection of word patterns in the native language while suppressing attention to nonnative patterns that would slow native language learning. In support of this, toddlers who at 7½ months had shown better neural discrimination of native phonemes were more advanced in word production and sentence complexity at 24 months and at 30 months than toddlers who, at 7½ months, had been better able to discriminate phonetic contrasts in nonnative languages (Kuhl & Rivera-Gaxiola, 2008).

In addition to learning what the phonemes in their language are, babies also learn the rules for how they fit together. For example, in English, the sound combination in "kib" is acceptable, although "kib" is not a word. However, the nonsense word "bnik" breaks the phonological rules in English as a "b" and an "n" are not typically found next to each other within the same word. Between 6 and 12 months, babies begin to become aware of the phonological rules of their language. Research with infants supports this and suggests that they may have a mechanism for discerning abstract rules of sentence structure (Saffran, Pollak, Seibel & Shkolnik, 2007).

Kristin Bell, like many parents, used sign language with her young children before they were fully verbal.

©WENN Ltd/Alamy

Babies also begin to recognize sound patterns they hear frequently, such as their name. Five-month-old infants listen longer to their name than to other names (Newman, 2005). Infants at 8 months discern perceptual cues such as syllables that usually occur together (such as *ba* and *by*) and store these possible word forms in memory. They also notice pronunciation, stress placed on syllables, and changes in pitch. This early auditory learning lays the foundation for later vocabulary growth (Swingley, 2008).

Gestures

Before babies can speak, they point (Liszkowski, Carpenter & Tomasello, 2008). At 11 months, Maika pointed to her cup to show she wanted it. By 12 months, Maika learned some conventional social gestures: waving bye-bye and nodding her head to mean yes. By about 13 months, she used more elaborate representational gestures; for example, she would hold an empty cup to her mouth to show she wanted a drink or hold up her arms to show that she wanted to be picked up.

Symbolic gestures, such as blowing to mean hot or sniffing to mean flower, often emerge around the same time as babies say their first words, and they function much like words. By using them, babies show they understand that symbols can refer to specific objects, events, desires, and conditions. Gestures usually appear before children have a vocabulary of 25 words, and they drop out when children learn and can say the word for the idea they were gesturing (Lock, Young, Service & Chandler, 1990). Girls show a developmental advantage and use gestures at a slightly earlier age than do boys (Ozcaliskan & Goldin-Meadow, 2010). Both hearing and deaf children use gestures in much the same ways (Goldin-Meadow, 2007).

The use of gestures seems to help babies learn to talk. Pointing, for example, is positively correlated with later language development (Colonnesi, Stams, Koster & Noom, 2010) and early gestures in general are a good predictor of later vocabulary size (Goldin-Meadow, 2007). In one study, parents' use of gestures predicted their child's use of gestures at 14 months, which in turn predicted the size of the child's vocabulary at 42 months (Rowe, Özçaliskan & Goldin-Meadow, 2008). These data, however, refer to the spontaneous use of gestures and may not apply to the deliberate training of gestures to infants. Teaching preverbal children to use sign language has not been shown to accelerate their language development, but it also does not appear to be harmful (Kirk, Howlett, Pine & Fletcher, 2013; Fitzpatrick, Thibert, Grandpierre & Johnson, 2014).

First Words

The average baby says a first word between 10 and 14 months, initiating **linguistic speech**—verbal expression that conveys meaning. At first an infant's total verbal repertoire is likely to be "mama" or "dada." Or it may be a simple syllable that has more than one meaning depending on the context in which the child utters it. "Da" may mean "I want that," "I want to go out," or "Where's Daddy?" A word like this, which expresses a complete thought, is called a **holophrase**.

linguistic speech Verbal expression designed to convey meaning.

holophrase Single word that conveys a complete thought.

Babies understand many words before they can use them. Six-month-olds look longer at a video of their mothers when they hear the word "mommy" and of their fathers when they hear "daddy" (Tincoff & Jusczyk, 1999). By 13 months, most children understand that a word stands for a specific thing or event, and they can quickly learn the meaning of a new word (Woodward, Markman & Fitzsimmons, 1994; Gurteen, Horne & Erjavec, 2011).

Between 10 months and 2 years, there is a shift from simple associations to following social cues. At 10 months, infants tend to assume a new word they hear refers to whatever object they find most interesting, whether or not the name is correct for that object. At 12 months, they begin to pay attention to cues from adults, such as looking or pointing at an object while saying its name. However, they still learn words only for interesting objects and ignore uninteresting ones. By 18 to 24 months, children follow social cues in learning words, regardless of the intrinsic interest of the objects (Golinkoff & Hirsh-Pasek, 2006; Pruden, Hirsh-Pasek, Golinkoff & Hennon, 2006). At 24 months, children quickly recognize the names of familiar objects in the absence of visual cues (Swingley & Fernald, 2002). Additionally, if presented with a familiar object and novel object, 24-month-old children will assume a novel term refers to the novel object, and quickly learn and remember that term (Spiegel & Halberda, 2011).

Receptive vocabulary—what infants understand—continues to grow as verbal comprehension gradually becomes faster and more accurate and efficient (Fernald,

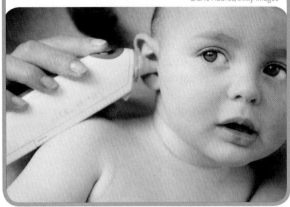

the 2nd year (Fernald et al., 2006) as well as an understanding that things belong in categories (Courage & Howe, 2002).

Nouns seem to be the easiest type of word to learn (Waxman et al., 2013), perhaps because it is easier to form a mental image of nouns (McDonough, Song, Hirsh-Pasek, Golinkoff & Lannon, 2011) and "imageability" is associated with learning and memory (O'Neill, 2005). In a cross-cultural study, Spanish, Dutch, French, Hebrew, Italian, Korean, and U.S. parents all reported that their 20-month-old children knew more nouns than any other class of words (Bornstein et al., 2004). A similar advantage has emerged for nouns in laboratory studies where children have been taught novel nouns and verbs (Imai et al., 2008).

First Sentences

The next linguistic breakthrough comes when a toddler puts two words together to express one idea ("Dolly fall"). Generally, children do this between 18 and 24 months, but this age range varies greatly. Although prelinguistic speech is closely tied to chronological age, linguistic speech is not. Most children who begin talking fairly late catch up eventually.

A child's first sentences typically deal with everyday events, things, people, or activities (Rice, 1989). Children often use **telegraphic speech**, consisting of only a few essential words. So when Rita says, "Damma deep," she means "Grandma is sweeping the floor." Children's use of telegraphic speech and the form it takes vary, depending on the language being learned (Slobin, 1983). Word order of first sentences generally conforms to what a child hears; Rita, for example, does not say, "Deep Damma," when she sees her grandmother pushing a broom. Children show their implicit understanding of the fundamental rules for putting sentences together—or syntax—with the word order they use. Syntax is why a sentence like "man bites dog" differs from "dog bites man," and it allows us to understand and produce an infinite number of utterances.

Between 20 and 30 months, children show increasing competence in syntax. At this age, children also become more comfortable with articles (*a, the*), prepositions (*in, on*), conjunctions (*and, but*), plurals, verb forms, and forms of the verb *to be* (*am, are, is*). They also become increasingly aware of the communicative purpose of speech and of whether their words are being understood (Dunham, Dunham & O'Keefe, 2000; Shwe & Markman, 1997)—a sign of growing sensitivity to the mental lives of others. By age 3, speech is fluent, longer, and more complex. In the third year of life, the average child's sentence will be approximately three or four words long (Rice et al., 2010).

> **telegraphic speech** Early form of sentence use consisting of only a few essential words.

Perfors & Marchman, 2006). Generally, infants have a far greater receptive vocabulary than an expressive—or spoken—vocabulary. By 18 months, 3 out of 4 children can understand 150 words and can say 50 of them (Kuhl, 2004). Children with larger vocabularies and quicker reaction times can recognize spoken words from just the first part of the word. For example, when they hear "daw" or "ki," they will point to a picture of a dog or kitten (Fernald, Swingley & Pinto, 2001). This early language learning is closely related to later cognitive development. In a longitudinal study, children's speed of recognition of spoken words and vocabulary size at 25 months predicted linguistic and cognitive skills at 8 years (Marchman & Fernald, 2008).

Addition of new words to the *expressive* (spoken) *vocabulary* is slow at first. Then, sometime between 16 and 24 months, a "naming explosion" may occur (Ganger & Brent, 2004). Within a few months, many toddlers go from saying about 50 words to saying several hundred (Courage & Howe, 2002). Rapid gains in spoken vocabulary reflect increases in speed and accuracy of word recognition during

Language Development in Deaf Children

Deaf babies seem to learn sign language in much the same fashion and in the same sequence as hearing infants learn speech,

Perspectives on Diversity

©Digital Vision/Getty Images

INVENTING SIGN LANGUAGE

There are hundreds of different languages across the world. But this diversity reflects a deep universal commonality—we are made for language. It is part of our species heritage.

Even when we have only the bits and pieces of language, we are adept at developing it. Consider the following example. In Nicaragua prior to the fall of the Sandinista government, deaf children were raised by their hearing parents who generally could not speak sign language. As a result, these children were raised in linguistic isolation and never truly learned language. Although they would use a variety of signs with their families, there was no syntax or grammatical complexity—they spoke in a pidgin of sorts. In the 1980s, after the fall of the Sandinista government, the first schools for the deaf were established. At this point deaf Nicaraguan schoolchildren spontaneously developed a true sign language, which, as adapted by successive cohorts of deaf Nicaraguan children, has evolved from simple gestures into words and sentences that follow linguistic rules (Senghas, Kita & Ozyürek, 2004). Without assistance from adults, without rewards or encouragement, without anything but their own desire to communicate and their own innate understanding, the children created a brand new language out of their shared experience.

All sign languages, including American Sign Language, probably came into existence through a similar process. Thus the development of new sign languages offers a unique opportunity to glimpse language in its infant stages and watch it grow. The development of new languages such as this suggests a recipe for human language: All you need are rudimentary communication symbols and a group of interacting children, and nature will do the rest.

---

providing they are raised in a language-rich environment (Lederberg, Schick & Spencer, 2013). Just as hearing babies of hearing parents imitate vocal utterances, deaf babies of deaf parents seem to imitate the sign language they see their parents using, first stringing together meaningless motions and then repeating them over and over in what has been called hand-babbling. As parents reinforce these gestures, the babies attach meaning to them (Petitto & Marentette, 1991; Petitto, Holowka, Sergio & Ostry, 2001).

Deaf babies begin hand-babbling between ages 7 and 10 months, about the age when hearing infants begin voice-babbling (Petitto et al., 2001). Deaf babies also begin to use sentences in sign language at about the same time that hearing babies begin to speak in sentences (Meier, 1991). These observations suggest that an inborn language capacity may underlie the acquisition of both spoken and signed language and that advances in both kinds of language are tied to brain maturation (Kuhl, 2010).

Did you know?

Just like hearing babies, deaf babies of deaf parents imitate the sign language they see their parents using, and they even "hand-babble"!

©JGI/Jamie Grill/Getty Images

CHARACTERISTICS OF EARLY SPEECH

Early speech has a character all its own—no matter what language a child is speaking (Slobin, 1970; 1990). As we have seen, children simplify. They use telegraphic speech to say just enough to get their meaning across ("No drink milk!").

Young children understand grammatical relationships they cannot yet express. For example, Nina understands that a dog is chasing a cat but does not yet produce multiple-word sentences easily, so her sentence comes out as "Puppy chase" rather than "The puppy is chasing the kitty." The order of the words shows she understand the underlying syntactic rules: She does not say "Kitty chase."

Children also make mistakes with respect to what category a word describes by either underextending or overextending word meaning. When they underextend word meanings, they use words in too narrow of a category. For example, Lisa knows their family pet is a "doggy." However, she shakes her head no when her mother points out other dogs outside their home. To her, her dog, and only her dog, is a "doggy." Lisa is underextending the word doggy by restricting it to only her pet.

Alternatively, children also overextend word meanings by using words in too broad of a category. At 14 months, Amir jumped in excitement at the sight of a gray-haired man on the television screen and shouted, "Gampa!" Amir was overgeneralizing, or overextending, a word. He thought that because his grandfather had gray hair, all gray-haired men could be called "Grandpa."

Young children also overregularize rules. Overregularization is a language error, but it nonetheless illustrates children's growing knowledge of syntax. It occurs when children inappropriately apply a syntactical rule. For instance, when children say sentences such as "Daddy goed to the store" or "I drawed that," they are applying the English language rule "add -ed to a verb to make it past tense." It takes a while for children to learn the rule as well as the exceptions to it. For example, children commonly use the exceptions to the rule first. They generally learn these by rote for phrases they commonly hear ("Daddy went to the store"). Then they learn the rule and use that to fill in the blanks when they can't recall the exception ("Daddy goed to the store"). By early school age, as they become more proficient in language, they memorize the exceptions and begin to apply them, once again saying the phrase correctly ("Daddy went to the store").

INFLUENCES ON LANGUAGE DEVELOPMENT

What determines how quickly and how well children learn to understand and use language? Research has focused on influences both inside and outside the child.

Brain Development

Our brains have structures that have been shown to be directly implicated in language use (Friederici, 2011). Thus, it is not surprising the tremendous brain growth during the early months and years is closely linked with language development. The brain stems and pons, the most primitive parts of the brain and the earliest to develop, control a newborn's cries. Repetitive babbling may emerge with the maturation of parts of the motor cortex, which control movements of the face and larynx. A link exists between the brain's phonetic perception and motor systems as early as 6 months—a connection that strengthens by 6 to 12 months (Imada et al., 2006). The development of language actively affects brain networks, committing them to the recognition of native language sounds only (Kuhl et al., 2005). In other words, language exposure helps shape the developing brain, and then the developing brain helps the infant learn language.

Brain scans confirm the sequence of vocabulary development outlined earlier in this chapter. In about 98 percent of people, the left hemisphere is dominant for language (Knecht et al., 2000). Brain activation tends to focus on the left temporal and parietal lobes in toddlers with large vocabularies, whereas in toddlers with smaller vocabularies, brain activation is more scattered (Kuhl & Rivera-Gaxiola, 2008). Cortical regions associated with language continue to develop until at least the late preschool years or beyond—some, even until adulthood.

Social Interaction: The Role of Parents and Caregivers

Language is a social act. It requires interaction. Language takes not only the necessary biological machinery and cognitive capacity but also interaction with a live communicative partner. Children who grow up without normal social contact do not develop language normally (Fromkin, Krashen, Curtiss, Rigler & Rigler, 1974). Neither do children who are exposed to language only through television. For example, in one experiment, 9-month-old English-speaking infants learned and retained Mandarin when they played and interacted with adults speaking Mandarin, but not when they merely watched television in Mandarin (Kuhl & Rivera-Gaxiola, 2008). A series of experiments on baby vocabulary videos showed that infants and toddlers did not learn new words from videos (DeLoache et al., 2010; Richert, Robb, Fender & Wartella, 2010), even when researchers made sure the infants were paying attention to the content of the video (Krcmar, 2011).

Babies learn language from other people. As Bronfenbrenner's bioecological model would predict, the age of caregivers, the way they interact with an infant, child care experience, and, later, schooling and peers all affect the course of language acquisition. The milestones of language development described in this chapter are typical of Western, middle-class children who are spoken to directly. They are not necessarily typical in all cultures, nor at all socioeconomic levels (Hoff, 2006).

At the babbling stage, adults help an infant advance toward true speech by repeating the sounds the baby makes and rewarding her efforts. Most babies find this engaging and repeat the sounds back. Parents' imitation of babies' sounds affects the amount of

Did you know?

When children are first learning language, they use the correct grammatical form—Daddy went to the store, I drew the picture, the plane flew. The later overregularization of these phrases—Daddy goed to the store, I drawed the picture, the plane flied—looks like backsliding, but actually illustrates progress in language learning. Children have internalized the rule; rather than merely parroting back the correct form they heard previously, they are now changing verb forms on the fly according to the rules of grammar. Because English is full of irregular verbs such as *go* and *drew*, however, toddlers get the verbs that "break the rule" wrong.

©Life on white/Alamy

infant vocalization (Goldstein, King & West, 2003) and the pace of language learning (Schmitt, Simpson & Friend, 2011). It also helps babies experience the social aspect of speech (Kuhl, 2004). When babies begin to talk, parents or caregivers can boost vocabulary development by repeating their first words and pronouncing them correctly.

Socially contingent interactions help children learn new words (Roseberry, Hirsh-Pasek & Golinkoff, 2014), as does joint attention (Hoff, 2006). In one longitudinal study, mothers' responsiveness to 9-month-olds' and, even more so, to 13-month-olds' vocalization and play predicted the timing of language milestones (Tamis-LeMonda, Bornstein & Baumwell, 2001). This is not surprising; a shared understanding and focus on an event or object coupled with maternal labeling is an extremely supportive framework for language acquisition.

A strong relationship exists between the frequency of specific words in mothers' speech and the order in which children learn these words (Brent & Siskind, 2001) as well as between mothers' talkativeness and the size of toddlers' vocabularies (Schmitt et al., 2011). Mothers with higher socioeconomic status tend to use richer vocabularies and longer utterances, and their 2-year-olds have larger spoken

vocabularies (Hoff, 2003; Ramey & Ramey, 2003; Rowe, 2012). By age 3, vocabularies of low-income children vary greatly, depending in large part on the diversity of word types they have heard their mothers use (Pan, Rowe, Singer & Snow, 2005). Parental sensitivity and responsiveness can act as a buffer, however. Specifically, low-income parents' sensitivity, positive regard for the child, and cognitive stimulation provided during play predicted their child's receptive vocabulary and cognitive development at ages 2 and 3 (Tamis-LeMonda, Shannon, Cabrera & Lamb, 2004).

In households where more than one language is spoken, babies achieve similar milestones in each language on the same schedule as children who hear only one language (Petitto & Kovelman, 2003). However, children learning two languages tend to have smaller vocabularies in each language than children learning only one language (Hoff, 2006). Bilingual children often use elements of both languages, sometimes in the same utterance—a phenomenon called code mixing (Petitto & Kovelman, 2003). In Montreal, children as young as 2 in dual-language households differentiate between the two languages, using French with a French-speaking parent and English with an English-speaking parent (Genesee, Nicoladis & Paradis, 1995). This ability to shift from one language to another is called code switching.

child-directed speech (CDS) Form of speech often used in talking to babies or toddlers; includes slow, simplified speech, a high-pitched tone, exaggerated vowel sounds, short words and sentences, and much repetition; also called *parentese*.

Use of Child-Directed Speech

When you talk to an infant or toddler, if you speak slowly in a sing-song, high-pitched voice with exaggerated ups and downs, simplify your speech, exaggerate vowel sounds, and use short words and sentences and repetition, you are engaging in **child-directed speech (CDS)**, sometimes called

Language requires interaction, and while parents play an important role, so do experiences outside the home such as interactions with other children.

©Panorama Productions Inc./Alamy

By reading aloud to and asking questions about the pictures in the book, this father helps his child build language skills and learn how letters look and sound.

©Hero/Corbis/Glow Images

parentese, motherese, or baby talk. Most adults and even children do it naturally, and other babyish stimuli, such as puppies or kittens, also can elicit it.

Some investigators challenge the value of CDS, contending that babies speak sooner and better if they are exposed to more complex adult speech (Oshima-Takane, Goodz & Derevensky, 1996). However, "baby talk" has been documented in many cultures, including the United States, Russia, Sweden, Australia, Thailand, Spain, Syria, England, Italy, France, Germany, and others (Kuhl et al., 1997; Kitamura, Thanavishuth, Burnham & Luksaneeyanawin, 2001; Cooper & Aslin, 1990; Ferguson, 1964). The ubiquity of this language form across cultures suggests it is universal in nature and serves a function.

Many researchers believe that CDS helps infants learn their native language or at least pick it up faster by exaggerating and directing attention to the distinguishing features of speech sounds (Kuhl et al., 2005). Moreover, infants are "captured" attentionally by the sound and find it highly engaging, resulting in more rapid learning (Golinkoff, Can, Sodernstrom & Hirsh-Pasek, 2015; Spinelli, Fasolo & Mesman, 2017). There are data that support this view. For example, infants, even before a month of age, clearly prefer to hear CDS (Dunst, Gorman & Hanby, 2012; Cooper & Aslin, 1990). In one study, infants who experienced more CDS had larger expressive vocabularies at 2 years of age and seemed to be more adept at processing language (Weisleder & Fernald, 2013). Laboratory data also highlight the support that CDS provides. For example, 21-month-old children were only able to learn new words when CDS speech was used. However, 27-month-old children, who were more sophisticated in their language abilities, were able to use adult-directed speech to learn new words (Ma, Golinkoff, Houson & Hirsh-Pasek, 2011).

PREPARING FOR LITERACY

Most babies love to be read to. The frequency with which caregivers read to them can influence how well children speak and eventually how well and how soon they develop literacy—the ability to read and write. In a study of 2,581 low-income families, about half of the mothers reported reading daily to their preschool children between 14 months and 3 years. Children who had been read to daily had better cognitive and language skills at age 3 (Raikes et al., 2006) and better reading comprehension at age 7 than did their peers (Crain-Thoreson & Dale, 1992; Sénéchal & LeFevre, 2002). Data such as these suggest that intervention programs targeting home variables such as reading to children could be highly effective (Forget-Dubois et al., 2009).

The way parents or caregivers read to children makes a difference. Adults tend to have one of three styles of reading to children: the describer, comprehender, and performance-oriented style. A describer focuses on describing what is going on in the pictures and invites the child to do so as well ("What are the Mom and Dad having for breakfast?"). A comprehender encourages the child to look more deeply at the meaning of a story and make inferences and predictions ("What do you think the lion will do now?"). A performance-oriented reader reads the story straight through, introducing the main themes beforehand and asking questions afterward. An adult's read-aloud style is best tailored to the child's needs and skills. In one study, the describer style resulted in the greatest overall benefits for vocabulary and print skills, but the performance-oriented style was more beneficial for children who started out with large vocabularies (Reese & Cox, 1999).

mastering the CHAPTER

©JGI/Jamie Grill/Getty Images

Summary and Key Terms

Behaviorist Approach: Basic Mechanics of Learning

> Two simple types of learning that behaviorists study are classical conditioning and operant conditioning.

KEY TERMS

| Behaviorist approach | Classical conditioning | Operant conditioning |

Psychometric Approach: Developmental and Intelligence Testing

> Psychometric tests measure factors presumed to make up intelligence.

> Developmental tests, such as the Bayley Scales of Infant and Toddler Development, can indicate current functioning and help parents and professionals plan for a child's needs.

> The home environment may affect measured intelligence. If the home environment does not meet a child's developmental needs, early intervention may be needed.

KEY TERMS

Psychometric approach
Intelligent behavior
IQ (intelligence quotient)

Bailey Scales of Infant and Toddler Development

Home Observation for Measurement of the Environment (HOME)
Early intervention

Piagetian Approach: The Sensorimotor Stage

> During Piaget's sensorimotor stage, infants' schemes become more elaborate. They progress from primary to secondary to tertiary circular reactions and finally to the development of representational ability, which makes possible deferred imitation, pretending, and problem solving.

> Object permanence develops gradually, according to Piaget. Research suggests that a number of abilities, including imitation and object permanence, develop earlier than Piaget described.

> Children also develop pictorial competence and a better understanding of scale.

KEY TERMS

Piagetian approach
Circular reactions

Visible imitation
Invisible imitation

Deferred imitation
Dual representation hypothesis

Information-Processing Approach: Perceptions and Representations

> Information-processing researchers observe and analyze processes involved in handling information.

In infants, they look at habituation and other signs of visual and perceptual abilities.

> Indicators of the efficiency of infants' information processing, such as speed of habituation, tend to predict later intelligence.

> Information-processing research techniques such as habituation, novelty preference, and the violation-of-expectations method have yielded evidence that infants as young as 3 to 6 months may have a rudimentary grasp of such Piagetian abilities as categorization, causality, object permanence, a sense of number, and an ability to reason about characteristics of the physical world.

> **KEY TERMS**
>
> | | | |
> |---|---|---|
> | Information-processing approach | Visual preference | Violation-of-expectations research |
> | Habituation | Visual recognition memory | |
> | Dishabituation | Joint attention | |

Cognitive Neuroscience Approach: The Brain's Cognitive Structures

> Explicit memory and implicit memory are located in different brain structures.

> Working memory emerges by 12 months of age.

> Neurological developments help explain the emergence of Piagetian skills and memory abilities

> **KEY TERMS**
>
> | | | |
> |---|---|---|
> | Cognitive neuroscience approach | Implicit memory | Explicit memory |

Social-Contextual Approach: Learning from Caregivers

> Social interactions with adults contribute to cognitive competence through shared activities that help children learn skills, knowledge, and values important in their culture.

> Cultural context affects the way caregivers contribute to cognitive development.

> **KEY TERMS**
>
> | | |
> |---|---|
> | Social-contextual approach | Guided participation |

Language Development

> The acquisition of language is an important aspect of cognitive development. Humans appear to have an inborn capacity for acquiring language, which is affected by experience.

> Prelinguistic speech includes crying, cooing, babbling, and imitating language sounds. By 6 to 7 months, babies have learned the basic sounds of their language. Perception of categories of sounds in the native language may commit the neural circuitry to further learning in that language only. Children who hear two languages at home generally learn both at the same rate as children who hear only one language.

> Before they say their first word, babies use gestures. The first word typically comes sometime between 10 and 14 months. For many toddlers, a naming explosion occurs between 16 and 24 months. The first brief sentences generally come between 18 and 24 months. By age 3, syntax and communicative abilities are fairly well developed.

> Early speech is characterized by oversimplification, underextending and overextending word meanings, and overregularizing rules.

> Influences on language development include neural maturation and social interaction. Family characteristics such as socioeconomic status, adult language use, and maternal responsiveness affect a child's vocabulary development.

> Child-directed speech (CDS) seems to have cognitive, emotional, and social benefits, and infants show a preference for it.

> Reading aloud to a child from an early age helps pave the way for literacy.

> **KEY TERMS**
>
> | | | |
> |---|---|---|
> | Nativism | Linguistic speech | Telegraphic speech |
> | Prelinguistic speech | Holophrase | Child-directed speech (CDS) |

Practice Quiz

1. Which of the following is an example of classical conditioning?
   a. Clara smiles more after her mother gives her attention for doing so.
   b. John is less likely to hit his brother after being punished by his parents for hitting.
   c. Maria does not like how cucumbers taste.
   d. Michael learns the sound of the front door being opened means his mother is getting home from work.

2. In operant conditioning, a _____ results in a greater chance of a behavior being performed, while a _____ results in a decrease in the chance a behavior will be performed.

3. What are the five developmental areas assessed by the Bayley scales of infant development?

   _____
   _____
   _____

4. List four factors in the home that have been identified as being important for intelligence.

   _____
   _____
   _____

5. What is the best way to characterize the findings of studies on intervention programs?
   a. Intervention programs result in few, if any, gains in intelligence.
   b. Intervention programs show no immediate effects, although they often show later benefits.
   c. Intervention programs show strong initial gains that fade without ongoing environmental support.
   d. Intervention programs result in strong and long-lasting gains in intelligence.

6. Baby Gus kicks his legs over and over again, and seems to enjoy repeating the action. Piaget would say this is an example of a:
   a. primary circular reaction.
   b. secondary circular reaction.
   c. tertiary circular reaction.
   d. object permanence.

7. Infants under the age of 6 months do not generally cry in response to separations from their mothers; however, by 1 year, they strongly protest maternal separation and are not easily calmed by strangers. How might this be related to object permanence?

   _____
   _____
   _____

8. In general, many abilities Piaget researched develop earlier than he thought they did. Why did he underestimate infants' abilities?
   a. He did not use brain imaging techniques.
   b. He relied on immature linguistic and motor skills to assess cognitive development.
   c. He did not use careful research methodology and design.
   d. He did not conduct longitudinal work.

9. Habituation is most like which of the following states?
   a. interest
   b. fear
   c. affection
   d. boredom

10. If a baby looks longer at a picture of a face than a square, what do researchers take this as evidence of?
    a. Babies don't like squares.
    b. Babies cannot tell the difference between faces and squares.
    c. Babies like faces better than squares.
    d. Babies like squares better than faces.

11. Speed of habituation seems to be related to later intelligence. Why might this be?
    a. Easily bored babies are always eager to learn new things.
    b. Rapid habituation indicates a child who can quickly process information.
    c. Speed of habituation is related to learning words more quickly, and verbal abilities are then related to intelligence.
    d. This is untrue; rapid habituation actually indicates rushed and shallow processing, which then leads to less learning over time.

12. In general, research conducted using babies' visual responses to stimuli suggests they develop an understanding of concepts such as categorization, causality, object permanence, and a primitive understanding of number _____ than Piaget thought they did.
    a. earlier
    b. later
    c. at about the same time
    d. the research has not shown a consistent pattern across different areas of knowledge

13. Knowing how to tie a shoelace is an example of _____ memory, while knowing what the word "dog" means is an example of _____ memory.

14. Which is the best way to characterize what social contextual theorists believe?
    a. The best way for children to learn is in formal educational settings.
    b. While different cultures use different techniques, all children learn the things they need to learn to be effective members of their culture.
    c. The most important contextual variable is the extended family system.
    d. Despite cultural differences, most human traits can be characterized as universals that do not vary across cultures.

15. Which of the following is the correct order of acquisition?
    a. babble, coo, cry, telegraphic speech
    b. telegraphic speech, babble, coo, cry
    c. cry, coo, babble, telegraphic speech
    d. cry, babble, coo, telegraphic speech

16. Why is it significant that Cora says "want juice" instead of "juice want"?
    a. It shows Cora understands pragmatics.
    b. It illustrates Cora's knowledge of syntactic rules.
    c. It shows semantic knowledge.
    d. It is telegraphic speech.

17. What are two ways in which parents often promote language development?

    _____
    _____
    _____

18. Provide a sentence that might be said by each of the three types of readers while reading a story to a young child.

    Describer: _____
    Comprehender: _____
    Performer: _____

What's to Come

> Emotions and Temperament

> Attachment

> The Developing Self

> Relationships with Other Children

Z ev was a difficult baby from the start. He cried vigorously at diaper changes, if he was cold or hungry, and, when he was older, strongly protested being held by anyone but his mother. But his parents' gentle handling built his confidence over time. And although at 18 months he would still check in visually with his parents before picking up a new toy or taking a potential risk, Zev would happily toddle around a new playground as long as they stayed nearby. At age 3, although he was frightened the first day he was dropped off at preschool, the trust he felt in his parents led him to expect other people to be good to him too, and he was able to haltingly establish new relationships with other children. All of these related developments occurring during the fundamental first 3 years of life exist under the umbrella of psychosocial development, the topic of this chapter.

In this chapter, we examine the role of attachment in development. We discuss early emotional development, individual differences, and early experiences that impact the formation of this foundational system. We then examine how peer relationships, including relationships with siblings, impact development.

• • • •

Emotions and Temperament

Newborn Alex was a happy baby. He cried little, slept on a relatively consistent schedule, and spent much of his time calmly watching the world with his large brown eyes. Friends and family commented on his ease, asking his parents how they managed to mold his behavior this way. "We didn't," his parents answered, "he just seemed to be born like that."

Although babies share common development patterns, each from the start shows a relatively consistent and predictable way of responding to the environment known as temperament. Each baby has its own unique temperament. One baby may usually be cheerful; another easily upset. One toddler plays happily with other children; another prefers to play alone. Such characteristic ways of feeling, thinking, and acting affect the way children respond to others and adapt to their world. Eventually, temperament becomes what we think of as personality, the relatively consistent blend of emotions, thought, and behavior that makes each person unique. From infancy on, temperament and personality development are intertwined with social relationships (Table 7.1), a combination called psychosocial development.

EMOTIONS

Emotions, such as fear, anger, or joy, are subjective reactions to experience that are associated with physiological and behavioral changes. For example, the subjective feeling of fear is associated with changes in and increase in heart rate, more rapid breathing, and an exaggerated startle response. A person's characteristic pattern of emotional reactions begins to develop during infancy and is a basic element of temperament and, later, personality. People differ in how often and how strongly they feel a particular emotion, in the kinds of events that may produce it, in the physical manifestations they show, and in how they act as a result. Culture also influences the way people feel about a situation and the way they show their emotions. Newborns clearly feel emotions, and they emerge over development in a predictable sequence.

Emotional development follows a relatively standard developmental timeline, beginning in early infancy. It is an orderly process; complex emotions unfold from simpler ones (Lewis, 1997; Figure 7.1). Emotions also become increasingly social and include the self-conscious emotions such as

emotions Subjective reactions to experience that are associated with physiological and behavioral changes.

TABLE 7.1 Highlights of Infants' and Toddlers' Psychosocial Development, Birth to 36 Months	
Approximate Age, Months	**Characteristics**
0–3	Infants are open to stimulation. They begin to show interest and curiosity, and they smile readily at people.
3–6	Infants can anticipate what is about to happen and experience disappointment when it does not. They show this by becoming angry or acting warily. They smile, coo, and laugh often. This is a time of social awakening and early reciprocal exchanges between the baby and the caregiver.
6–9	Infants play "social games" and try to get responses from people. They "talk" to, touch, and cajole other babies to get them to respond. They express more differentiated emotions, showing joy, fear, anger, and surprise.
9–12	Infants are intensely preoccupied with their principal caregiver, may become afraid of strangers, and act subdued in new situations. By 1 year, they communicate emotions more clearly, showing moods, ambivalence, and gradations of feeling.
12–18	Toddlers explore their environment, using the people they are most attached to as a secure base. As they master the environment, they become more confident and more eager to assert themselves.
18–36	Toddlers sometimes become anxious because they now realize how much they are separating from their caregiver. They work out their awareness of their limitations in fantasy and in play and by identifying with adults.

Source: Adapted from L. A. Sroufe, "The coherence of individual development: Early care, attachment, and subsequent developmental issues," *American Psychologist, 34,* no. 10 (1979), 834.

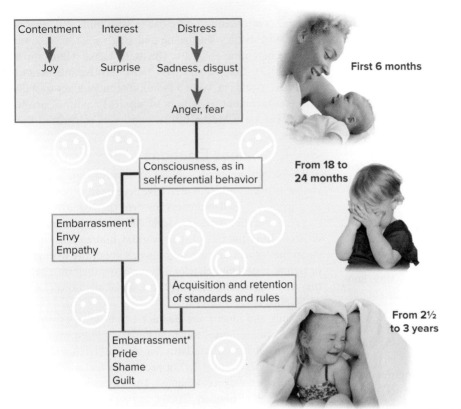

FIGURE 7.1 Differentiation of Emotions

The primary, or basic, emotions emerge during the first 6 months or so; the self-conscious emotions develop around 18 to 24 months, as a result of the emergence of self-awareness (consciousness of self) together with accumulation of knowledge about societal standards and rules.

There are two kinds of embarrassment. The earlier kind does not involve evaluation of behavior and may simply be a response to being singled out as the object of attention. The second kind, evaluative embarrassment, which emerges during the 3rd year, is a mild form of shame.

Source: Adapted from M. Lewis, M., "The self in self-conscious emotions." In S. G. Snodgrass & R. L. Thompson (Eds.), *The self across psychology: Self-recognition, self-awareness, and the self-concept* (Vol. 818). New York: Annals of the New York Academy of Sciences, 1997. Fig 1, p. 120.

©Blend Images/SuperStock; ©Lensation photos/Shutterstock; ©Kristy-Anne Glubish/Design Pics

shame and embarrassment. Last, emotions then prompt young children into engaging in shared intentionality and collaborative activity.

EARLY EMOTIONAL RESPONSES

Early emotional responses include crying, smiling and laughing, self-conscious emotions, altruistic helping and empathy, and shared intentionality and collaborative activity.

Crying

Newborns plainly show when they are unhappy. They let out piercing cries, flail their arms and legs, and stiffen their bodies. Adults find the sound of crying unpleasant—and therein lies its function. Crying is the primary way in which infants communicate their needs and is considered to be an honest signal of need. Human brains, particularly those of parents, are wired to respond to such sounds with caregiving behaviors (Swain, Lorberbaum, Kose & Strathearn, 2007; Kim, Strathearn & Swain, 2016), although their high pitch can sometimes put children at risk for harsh parenting (Out, Pieper, Bakermans-Kranenburg, Zeskind & van IJzendoorn, 2010).

Crying is the earliest and most powerful way infants can communicate their needs. There are four patterns of crying (Wolff, 1969): the basic hunger cry (a rhythmic cry, which is not always associated with hunger); the angry cry (a variation of the rhythmic cry, in which excess air is forced through the vocal cords); the pain cry (a sudden onset of loud crying without preliminary moaning, sometimes followed by holding the breath); and the frustration cry (two or three drawn-out cries, with no prolonged breath-holding) (Wood &

Gustafson, 2001). Features of infants' cries are related to their physiological state. A higher pitch and a more monotonic vocalization is associated with autonomic system activity during stressful procedures in infants (Stewart et al., 2013) and is more characteristic of the cries of preterm infants, who generally have higher needs, than full-term infants of the equivalent age (Shinya, Kawai, Niwa, Myowa-Yamakoshi, 2016).

As children age, they begin to realize that crying serves a communicative function. By 5 months of age, babies have learned to monitor their caregivers' expressions, and if ignored will first cry harder in an attempt to get attention, and then stop crying if their attempt is unsuccessful (Goldstein, Schwade & Bornstein, 2009). Boys and girls, as infants, show similar patterns of sadness and anger; however, by the toddler years, boys express more anger than girls (Chaplin & Aldao, 2013).

Some parents worry that picking up a crying baby will spoil the infant. However, this is not the case, especially when levels of distress are high. For example, if parents wait it may become more difficult to soothe the baby; and such a pattern, if experienced repeatedly, may interfere with an infant's developing ability to regulate his or her own emotional state (R. A. Thompson, 2011). Indeed, mothers' rapid and sensitive response to crying is associated with later social competence and positive adjustment, regardless of whether or not babies cry frequently or rarely (Leerkes, Blankson & O'Brien, 2009). The most developmentally sound approach to crying may be to prevent distress when possible, making soothing unnecessary.

Smiling and Laughing

The earliest faint smiles occur spontaneously soon after birth, apparently as a result of subcortical nervous system activity. Through 1 month of age, smiles are often elicited by high-pitched tones when an infant is drowsy or in REM sleep. During the 2nd month, as visual recognition develops, babies smile more at visual stimuli, such as faces they know (Sroufe, 1997).

Social smiling, when newborn infants gaze and smile at their parents, develops in the second month of life. Babies generally start using a social smile at the same time and in the same way regardless of culture. However, by 12 weeks of age, infants smile at others more or less frequently depending on the responses of adults around them (Wormann, Holodynski, Kartner & Keller, 2012). Laughter is a smile-linked vocalization that becomes more common between 4 and 12 months when it may signify the most intense positive emotion (Salkind, 2005).

Parents often try to elicit smiles and laughs from their young children by clowning. Clowning includes silly, non-verbal behaviors such as odd facial expressions or sounds, or actions like revealing a usually hidden body part (such as a belly button), or imitating another's odd actions. Clowning is generally paired with affective cues such as smiles, laughs, and eye contact. Babies try to join in the humor, most commonly starting at 3 months of age, by shrieking or making faces (Mireault, Poutre et al., 2012). Babies' humor gradually becomes more complex with age. A 6-month-old may giggle in response to the mother making unusual sounds or appearing with a towel over her face; a 10-month-old may laughingly try to put the towel back on her face when it falls off. This change reflects cognitive development: By laughing at the unexpected, babies show that they know what to expect; by turning the tables, they show awareness that they can make things happen (Sroufe, 1997).

By 12 to 15 months, infants are intentionally communicating to others about objects. **Anticipatory smiling**—in which infants smile at an object and then gaze at an adult while continuing to smile—rises sharply between 8 and 10 months and seems to be among the first types of communication in which the infant refers to an object or experience.

Positive affective processes are reciprocal. Mothers low in stress and high in positive emotionality and effortful control tend to have babies who smile and laugh a lot. In turn, babies who smile and laugh a lot elicit fewer negative parenting behaviors (Bridgett, Laake, Gartstein & Dorn, 2013). Infants who have more positive interactions with their parents at 3 and 6 months are more likely to show secure attachment at a year of age (Mireault, Sparrow, Poutre, Perdue & Macke, 2012).

Self-Conscious Emotions

Self-conscious emotions, such as embarrassment, envy, and shame arise only after children have developed self-awareness at about age 3. **Self-awareness** involves the cognitive understanding that they have a recognizable identity, separate and different from the rest of their world. Children must understand that others might have opinions about the wrongness or rightness of their behavior different from their own before they can understand and feel these social emotions (Lewis, 1998; 2007).

Guilt and shame are distinct emotions, even though both may be responses to wrongdoing. Children who fail to live up to behavioral standards may feel guilty, that is, regret their behavior, but they do not necessarily feel a lack of self-worth as when they feel ashamed. Their focus is on a bad act, not a bad self (Eisenberg, 2000).

Altruistic Helping and Empathy

A guest of 18-month-old Zev's father—a person Zev had never seen—dropped his pen on the floor; it rolled under a cabinet, where the guest couldn't reach it. Zev was small enough to crawl under the cabinet, retrieve the pen, and give it to the guest. By acting out of concern for a stranger with no expectation of reward, Zev showed **altruistic behavior** (Warneken & Tomasello, 2006).

The roots of altruism can be seen in early empathic reactions in infancy. For example, 2- to 3-month-old infants react to others' emotional expressions (Tomasello, 2007), and infants at 1, 3, 6, and 9 months of age respond to the cries of other infants with cries of their own and facial expressions of distress (Geangu, Benga, Stahl & Striano, 2010). Infants also form "opinions" about others on the basis of their social behaviors. In one series of experiments (Hamlin & Wynn, 2011), infants watched as a puppet tried to open a box. In one condition, a second "Opener" puppet helped the first puppet open the box, and in another condition a "Closer" puppet interfered by jumping on the box to slam it shut. When later given the choice, 3-month-old infants preferred to look at and 5-month-old infants preferred to reach for the Opener puppet.

Infants like helpers, and altruistic behavior also seems to come naturally to them. In one study, infants at 12 months of age spontaneously helped an adult reach or find a toy that had fallen out of reach. By 15 months of age, infants also seemed to have expectations about fairness, as illustrated by their tendency to stare longer at an unfair distribution of goods than at an equal distribution. Those infants who looked the longest at the unequal sharing were also more likely to themselves share toys later (Sommerville, Schmidt,

---

anticipatory smiling Infant smiles at an object and then gazes at an adult while still smiling.

self-conscious emotions Emotions, such as embarrassment, shame, and pride, that depend on self-awareness.

self-awareness Realization that one's existence and functioning are separate from those of other people and things.

altruistic behavior Activity intended to help another person with no expectation of reward.

Did you know?

Because early smiles are often the result of internal changes, and one internal change commonly experienced by newborns is gas, such smiles used to be known as "windy grins."

©Katrina Elena/Shutterstock

Young children exhibit altruism and begin to collaborate with caregivers in joint activities.

©Ariel Skelley/Blend Images/AP Images

person is not helped (Hepach, Vaish & Tomasello, 2012).

Some theorists doubt the conclusions that have been reached about mirror neurons. They point out, for example, that people sometimes feel empathy for others even without the action of mirror neurons. They argue this theory, while intriguing, lacks direct empirical support (Lamm & Majdandzic, 2015).

empathy Ability to put oneself in another person's place and feel what the other person feels.

mirror neurons Neurons that fire when a person does something or observes someone else doing the same thing.

temperament Characteristic disposition or style of approaching and reacting to situations.

Shared Intentionality and Collaborative Activity

The motivation to help and share along with the ability to understand others' intentions together contribute to an important development between 9 and 12 months of age—collaboration with caregivers in joint activities, such as a child passing a pair of socks to her mother in order to help while getting dressed.

Collaborative activities increase during the 2nd year of life as toddlers become more adept at communication. At 12 months, Zev points at a ball to show that he wants to play a game of rolling it back and forth with his father. When the ball rolls under a chair, he points to let his father know where it is. The vocabulary explosion that frequently occurs during the 2nd year enables more complex and flexible collaborative communication with others (Tomasello, 2007).

These types of interactions are quintessentially human. Although many of our closest relatives, such as chimpanzees, are able to communicate and learn from each other in impressive and sophisticated ways, they do not share with us our ability and motivation to engage in socially coordinated actions with shared goals. Some researchers have argued that this ability, more than others, accounts for our impressive creation of cultural artifacts and institutions. In this view, our biologically shaped transmission of collaborative learning has led to our unique success as a species in this area (Tomasello & Moll, 2010).

TEMPERAMENT

Temperament is a person's characteristic, biologically based way of approaching and reacting to people and situations (Thomas & Chess, 1977). One toddler may happily run toward a large dog, eager to pet it; another may shrink back in fear. Temperament may affect not only the way children approach and react to the outside world, but also the way they regulate their mental, emotional, and behavioral functioning (Rothbart, Ahadi & Evans, 2000; Rueda & Rothbart, 2009). Individual differences in temperament form the core of the developing personality.

Temperament Patterns

To better appreciate how temperament affects behavior, let's look at three children. Sarita was a cheerful, calm baby who ate, slept, and eliminated at regular times. She greeted each day

Yun & Burns, 2013). Other research has also documented that well before the 2nd birthday, children are likely to help others, share belongings and food, and offer comfort at the distress of others (Dunfield, Kuhlmeier, O'Connell & Kelley, 2011; Warneken & Tomasello, 2009). Interestingly, the tendency to share, to help, and to comfort seem to be unrelated to each other, presumably reflecting separate developmental trajectories. In other words, a baby who shares may not necessarily tend to comfort or help (Dunfield & Kuhlmeier, 2013). Nonetheless, Zahn-Waxler and colleagues (1992) have concluded that such behavior may collectively reflect **empathy**, the ability to imagine how another person might feel in a particular situation.

Research in neurobiology has identified special brain cells called **mirror neurons**, which may underlie empathy and altruism. Mirror neurons fire when a person does something but also when he or she observes someone else doing the same thing. By "mirroring" the activities and motivations of others, they may help a person to see the world from someone else's point of view (Iacoboni, 2008; Iacoboni & Mazziotta, 2007; Oberman & Ramachandran, 2007). Interestingly, infants also show similar sympathetic nervous system arousal when they help someone directly *and* when they see a third party doing the helping. They do not show the same pattern of arousal if the

How do you think Sarita, Caroline, and Ariana would respond to this dog?
©Photodisc/Getty Images

easy children Children with a generally happy temperament, regular biological rhythms, and a readiness to accept new experiences.

difficult children Children with irritable temperament, irregular biological rhythms, and intense emotional responses.

slow-to-warm-up children Children whose temperament is generally mild but who are hesitant about accepting new experiences.

and most people with a smile; the only sign she was awake during the night was the tinkle of the musical toy in her crib. When Caroline, the second child, woke up, she would open her mouth to cry before she even opened her eyes. She slept little; she laughed and cried loudly; and she had to be convinced that new people and new experiences were not threatening before she would have anything to do with them. The last child, Ariana, was mild in her responses. She did not like most new situations, but if allowed to proceed at her own slow pace, she would eventually become interested and involved.

Sarita, Caroline, and Ariana illustrate the three main types of temperament found by the New York Longitudinal Study (NYLS). In this pioneering study, researchers followed 133 infants into adulthood. The researchers asked their parents how active the children were; how regular their hunger, sleep, and bowel habits were; how readily they accepted new people and situations; how they adapted to changes in routine; how sensitive they were to sensory stimuli; whether their mood tended to be joyful or unhappy; and whether they

persisted at tasks. The researchers used these data to place children into one of three categories (Table 7.2).

- Forty percent were **easy children** like Sarita: They were generally happy, rhythmic in biological functioning, and accepting of new experiences.
- Ten percent were what the researchers called **difficult children** like Caroline: They were more irritable and harder to please, irregular in biological rhythms, and more intense in expressing emotion.
- Fifteen percent were **slow-to-warm-up children** like Ariana: They were mild but slow to adapt to new people and situations (Thomas & Chess, 1977, 1984).

While Thomas and Chess's research captured broad temperament trends, many children (including 35 percent of the NYLS sample) do not fit neatly into any of these three categories. For example, a baby may eat and sleep regularly but be afraid of strangers. Another child may warm up slowly to new foods but adapt quickly to new babysitters (Thomas & Chess, 1984). A child may laugh intensely but not show intense frustration, and a child with rhythmic toilet habits may have irregular sleeping patterns (Rothbart, Ahadi & Evans, 2000). All these variations are normal.

Stability of Temperament

From the beginning, babies show different patterns of sleeping, fussing, and activity. For example, despite how babies' abilities change vastly in almost all areas over the first year of life, stability in temperament from 2 to 13 months of age is quite high (Bornstein et al., 2015). Studies using the Infant Behavior Questionnaire (IBQ), a parental report instrument, have found strong links between infant temperament and childhood personality at age 7 (Rothbart, Ahadi, Hershey & Fisher, 2001). Similarly, researchers investigating positive emotionality, negative emotionality, and constraint (a dimension reflecting the tendency to behave in a controlled fashion) have found stability in these traits from toddlerhood to early childhood, and then from early childhood to middle childhood (Neppl et al., 2010). Other research, using temperament types similar to those of the NYLS, found that temperament at age 3 closely predicts aspects of personality at ages 18 and 21 (Caspi, 2000). Thus, a wealth of research suggests temperament is a relatively stable individual difference, perhaps because it is largely inborn and strongly influenced by genetics (Braungart, Plomin, DeFries & Fulker, 1992; Schmitz, Saudino, Plomin, Fulker & DeFries, 1996).

Current conceptions of temperament view genetic influences as being strongest early in life, with greater influence wielded by the environment over time (Shiner et al., 2012). Temperament develops as various emotions and self-regulatory capacities appear (Rothbart et al., 2000) and can change in response to parental treatment and other life experiences (Kagan & Snidman, 2004). For example, culturally influenced child-rearing practices may influence temperament. Research has shown that infants from the United States are rated by their parents as higher in activity level, vocalization, frustration, and pleasure than babies from both Italy and

TABLE 7.2 Categories of Temperment

Easy Child	Difficult Child	Slow-to-Warm-Up Child
Has moods of mild to moderate intensity, usually positive.	Displays intense and frequently negative moods; cries often and loudly; also laughs loudly.	Has mildly intense reactions, both positive and negative.
Responds well to novelty and change. Quickly develops regular sleep and feeding schedules.	Responds poorly to novelty and change. Sleeps and eats irregularly.	Responds slowly to novelty and change. Sleeps and eats more regularly than the difficult child, less regularly than the easy child.
Takes to new foods easily.	Accepts new foods slowly.	
Smiles at strangers.	Is suspicious of strangers.	
Adapts easily to new situations.	Adapts slowly to new situations.	Shows mildly negative initial response to new stimuli (a first encounter with a new person, place, or situation).
Accepts most frustrations with little fuss.	Reacts to frustration with tantrums.	
Adapts quickly to new routines and rules of new games.	Adjusts slowly to new routines.	Gradually develops liking for new stimuli after repeated, unpressured exposures.

Adapted from Thomas, A. and Chess, S. "Genesis and evolution of behavioral disorders: From infancy to adult life." Reprinted with permission from the American Journal of Psychiatry, 141, 1984, pp. 1–9. Copyright 1984 by the American Psychiatric Association. Reproduced with permission.

Norway, who are rated as more cuddly and easy to soothe (Montirosso, Cozzi, Putnam, Gartstein, & Borgatti, 2010; Cozzi et al., 2013; Sung, Beijers, Gartstein, de Weerth & Putnam, 2015). Researchers suggest this may be because mothers in the United States foster greater individuality and assertiveness. In another study, Japanese and Russian infants tended to show higher levels of fear, while babies from Poland and the United States showed higher positive affectivity and vocal reactivity (Gartstein, Slobodskaya, Olaf Zylicz, Gosztyla & Nakagawa, 2010). In this case, one proposed influence was the cultural dimension of collectivism and individualism.

Goodness of Fit

Children differ, and their ideal environments differ as well. According to the NYLS, the key to healthy adjustment is **goodness of fit**, the match between a child's temperament and the environmental demands. A shy child will do better with gentle handling, a bold one with more stimulation. Goodness of fit is a descriptor of the child-caregiver relationship but can also be used to describe the fit between the child and the wider social context.

For example, children also differ in their susceptibility to environmental influences. For example, infants with difficult temperaments may be more susceptible to the quality of parenting than infants with easy or slow-to-warm-up temperaments and may need more emotional support and respect for their autonomy (Stright, Gallagher, & Kelley, 2008).

Behavioral Inhibition

In longitudinal research with about 500 children starting in infancy, Jerome Kagan and his colleagues studied an aspect of temperament called *behavioral inhibition*. Behavioral inhibition has to do with how boldly or cautiously a child

approaches unfamiliar objects and situations (Kagan, Reznick, Clarke, Snidman & Garcia-Coll, 1984).

Behavioral inhibition is most clearly seen when babies are presented with novel stimuli. When babies high in behavioral inhibition are presented with a new stimulus, they became physiologically aroused, pumping their arms and legs vigorously and sometimes arching their backs. This feeling of being overaroused is unpleasant for them, and most start to fuss and cry. Approximately 20 percent of babies respond in this way. Babies low in behavioral inhibition, however,

goodness of fit Appropriateness of environmental demands and constraints to a child's temperament.

Behaviorally inhibited children are cautious or fearful in unfamiliar situations, a pattern that often continues. However, experiences can affect these early tendencies, and children may develop their own strategies for reducing anxiety.

©Image Source/Getty Images

respond quite differently. When presented with a new stimulus, these babies are relaxed. They show little distress or motor activity, and often calmly stare at new stimuli, sometimes smiling at it. About 40 percent of babies respond in this manner. These differences between babies are theorized to be the result of an underlying difference in physiology. Inhibited children may be born with an unusually excitable amygdala. The amygdala detects and reacts to unfamiliar events, and, in the case of behaviorally inhibited children, responds vigorously and easily to most novel events (Kagan & Snidman, 2004; Kagan, 2012). Moreover, children who are highly behaviorally inhibited tend to show greater right frontal EEG (electroencephalographic) asymmetry (Fox, Henderson, Rubin, Calkins & Schmidt, 2001; Smith & Bell, 2010), a pattern that has been associated more broadly with a tendency toward retreat and withdrawal (Coan & Allen, 2004).

If behavioral inhibition is indeed due to an underlying physiological arousal pattern, then we should expect some consistency in patterns of behavior over time. This is the case. Infants who are identified as inhibited or uninhibited seemed to maintain these patterns over time (Kagan, 1997; Kagan & Snidman, 2004). Many highly inhibited infants remain so through the first two years of age (Fox, Henderson, Rubin, Calkins & Schmidt, 2001). Inhibited toddlers are likely to turn into shy 7-year-olds (Kagan, Reznick, Snidman, Gibbons & Johnson, 1988) and behaviorally inhibited 8- to 12-year-old children are less likely as young adults to have a positive, active social life and more likely to live close to their family of origin in adulthood (Gest, 1997). Behavioral inhibition has also been associated with a heightened risk of developing a social anxiety disorder later in life (Clauss & Blackford, 2012).

However, experience can moderate or accentuate early tendencies. Behaviorally inhibited children were more likely to outgrow their inhibition if parents did not completely shield them from new situations and instead supported them during anxiety-provoking situations (Park, Belsky, Putnam & Crnic, 1997), and they were no more likely to suffer from anxiety disorders if

basic trust versus basic mistrust Erikson's first stage in psychosocial development, in which infants develop a sense of the reliability of people and objects.

their mothers encouraged independence and were not overly controlling (Lewis-Morrarty et al., 2012). In other research, when mothers responded neutrally to infants who were behaviorally inhibited, the inhibition tended to remain stable or increase (Fox, Hane & Pine, 2007). Children may themselves develop buffering strategies. For example, while behaviorally inhibited toddlers with an attentional bias toward threat have been shown to be at risk for social withdrawal in childhood and adolescence (Perez-Edgar et al., 2011; Perez-Edgar et al., 2010), other research has shown that those toddlers who are better at shifting their attention are protected against later anxiety symptoms, perhaps because they are able to utilize their cognitive processes to regulate their negative reactivity (White, McDermott, Degnan, Henderson & Fox, 2013). In other words, when you can pull your attention away from scary things, perhaps they are less scary. Other environmental influences, such as birth order, race/ethnicity, culture, relationships with teachers and peers, and unpredictable events also can reinforce or soften a child's original temperament bias (Kagan & Snidman, 2004).

Attachment

How does a dependent newborn, who has a limited emotional repertoire and pressing physical needs, become a child with complex feelings and the abilities to understand and control them? Much of this development revolves around issues regarding relationships with caregivers, especially in the development of trust, attachments, and mutual regulation.

DEVELOPING TRUST

Human babies depend on others for food, protection, and their very lives for a far longer period than the young of most other mammals. For example, baby rats are with their mothers for only about a month; many baby mammals stay with their mothers only for breeding season. How do human infants—with their need for extended maternal care—come to trust their needs will be met? According to Erikson (1950), early experiences are the key.

The first of Erikson's eight stages in psychosocial development (refer to Table 1.3) is **basic trust versus basic mistrust**. This stage begins in infancy and continues until about 18 months. In these early months, babies need to develop a balance between trust, which lets them form intimate relationships, and mistrust, which enables them to protect themselves. If trust predominates, as it should, children develop hope: the belief they can fulfill their needs and obtain their desires (Erikson, 1982). If mistrust predominates, children will view the world as unfriendly and unpredictable and will have trouble forming quality relationships.

The critical element in developing trust is sensitive, responsive, consistent caregiving. Erikson saw the feeding situation as the setting for establishing the right mix of trust and mistrust. Can the baby count on being fed when hungry, and can the baby therefore trust the mother as a representative of the world? (Erikson, 1950, p. 247).

Did you know?

Infants identified at 4 months as highly behaviorally inhibited are generally noisy and active in response to a new stimulus, but at 2 years of age they tend to be shy and withdrawn. The difference in response can be attributed to children's increasing ability to regulate themselves behaviorally. A child scared by an unfamiliar stimulus at 4 months can do nothing but squirm in its presence. A child of 2 years faced with the same event can retreat to safety.

©DreamPictures/Vanessa Gavalya/Blend Images/AP Images

DEVELOPING ATTACHMENTS

A young colt follows his mother, trotting quickly to catch up when he falls too far behind. A kitten purrs with pleasure, kneading her mother's stomach as she nurses. A baby rhesus monkey clings to his mother's soft fur with tiny hands. And, in a dark room late at night, a newborn infant snuggles close to her mother and is soothed by her calm voice and warm body. All of these processes illustrate one of the oldest mammalian characteristics—the attachment bond.

Attachment is a reciprocal, enduring emotional tie between an infant and a caregiver, each of whom contributes to the quality of the relationship. From an evolutionary point of view, attachments have profound adaptive value for babies, ensuring that their psychosocial and physical needs will be met.

Attachment Patterns

The study of attachment owes much to the ethologist John Bowlby (1951), a pioneer in the study of bonding. From his knowledge of animal studies and from observations of disturbed children in a London psychoanalytic clinic, Bowlby became convinced of the importance of the mother-baby bond. Mary Ainsworth (1967), a student of Bowlby's in the early 1950s, went on to study attachment in African babies in Uganda through naturalistic observation in their homes. Ainsworth later developed the **Strange Situation**, a now classic laboratory-based technique designed to assess attachment patterns between a 10- to 24-month-old infant and an adult.

The Strange Situation consists of a sequence of eight short episodes of gradually increasing stress designed to trigger the emergence of attachment-related behaviors. During that time, the mother twice leaves the baby in an unfamiliar room. Upon her return, the mother gives comfort if the baby seems to need it (Ainsworth, Blehar, Waters & Wall, 1978). Of particular concern is the baby's response each time the mother returns.

When Ainsworth and her colleagues observed 1-year-olds in the Strange Situation and at home, they found three main patterns of attachment. There is **secure attachment**—the most common category into which about 60 to 75 percent of low-risk North American babies fall. And there are two forms of insecure attachment: **avoidant** (15 to 25 percent) and ambivalent, or **resistant** (10 to 15 percent) (Vondra & Barnett, 1999). Security of attachment to father and mother is usually quite similar (Fox, Kimmerly & Schafer, 1991; Brown, Schoppe-Sullivan, Mangelsdorf & Neff, 2010).

attachment Reciprocal, enduring tie between two people—especially between infant and caregiver—each of whom contributes to the quality of the relationship.

Strange Situation Laboratory technique used to study infant attachment.

secure attachment Pattern in which an infant is quickly and effectively able to find comfort from a caregiver when faced with a stressful situation.

avoidant attachment Pattern in which an infant rarely cries when separated from the primary caregiver and avoids contact on his or her return.

resistant (ambivalent) attachment Pattern in which an infant becomes anxious before the primary caregiver leaves, is extremely upset during his or her absence, and both seeks and resists contact on his or her return.

Did you know?

In the Strange Situation, what the baby does when the mother is gone—and thus not available—is not diagnostic of attachment classification. The crucial behaviors emerge upon the mother's return. This makes sense because in order to assess attachment, we need to see how the baby uses the mother for comfort when under stress, something that is impossible if the mother is not there.

©Ale Ventura/AP Images

Babies with secure attachment might cry or protest when a caregiver leaves but they obtain the comfort they need quickly and effectively upon her return, and they calm easily upon contact. If they do not become upset at separations, they nonetheless illustrate their preference for the mother over strangers when she reenters the room, often greeting her with smiles and vocalizations. Babies with avoidant attachment are outwardly unaffected by a caregiver leaving or returning. They show little positive or negative emotion to the mother's return, and often deliberately ignore a mother's attempts to get their attention when she comes back. Babies with resistant (ambivalent) attachment become anxious even before a caregiver leaves and become increasingly upset when he or she departs. Upon the caregiver's return, resistant babies seek contact while at the same time resisting it. They tend to remain upset for long periods—kicking, squirming, screaming, refusing to be distracted with toys, sometimes arching back and away from contact. They show a mix of proximity seeking and angry behaviors and are very difficult to comfort. These three attachment patterns are universal in all cultures in which they have been studied—cultures as different as those in Africa, China, and Israel—though the percentage of infants in each category varies (van IJzendoorn & Sagi-Schwartz, 2008).

Note that in all of these cases what the baby does during the caregiver's *absence* is not diagnostic of attachment categorization. What is diagnostic is what the babies do when the caregiver *returns*. The important component of the attachment relationship is how the babies use a caregiver to obtain comfort while in his or her presence.

disorganized-disoriented attachment Pattern in which an infant, after separation from the primary caregiver, shows contradictory behaviors on his or her return.

Other research (Main & Solomon, 1986) identified a fourth pattern, **disorganized-disoriented attachment**. Babies with the disorganized pattern seem to lack a cohesive strategy for dealing with Strange Situation stress. Instead, they show contradictory, repetitive, or misdirected movements and emotions. They may greet the mother brightly when she returns but then turn away or approach her without looking at her, freeze during moments of stress, or show repetitive, self-stimulatory movements called stereotypies. They often seem confused and afraid (Carlson, 1998).

Disorganized attachment is thought to occur in at least 10 percent of low-risk infants but in much higher proportions in certain at-risk populations, such as babies with mothers who are insensitive, intrusive, or abusive; who are fearful; or who have suffered unresolved loss or have unresolved feelings about their childhood attachment to their own parents. Disorganized attachment is a reliable predictor of later behavioral and adjustment problems (Bernier & Meins, 2008; Carlson, 1998).

How Attachment Is Established

According to Bowlby, attachment styles are the result of repeated interactions with a caregiver. For example, if every time a baby cries the mother responds quickly and sensitively to that bid for comfort, over time the baby comes to expect it. By contrast, if a mother responds inconsistently to crying, babies form a very different set of expectations regarding the likely responses of the mother to their cries.

Bowlby called these sets of expectations working models and theorized that these early working models became the blueprint for the dynamics of that relationship. As long as the mother continues to act the same way, the model holds up. If her behavior changes—not just once or twice but repeatedly—the baby may revise the model, and security of attachment may change. Because the working model emerges as a result of interactions between both partners in the relationship, babies can have different working models (and attachment styles) with different people.

A baby's working model of attachment is related to Erikson's concept of basic trust. Secure attachment reflects trust; insecure attachment, mistrust. Securely attached babies have learned to trust not only their caregivers but also their own ability to get what they need. Not surprisingly, mothers of securely attached infants and toddlers tend to be sensitive and responsive (Ainsworth, Blehar, Waters & Wall, 1978; Braungart-Rieker, Garwood, Powers & Wang, 2001). A secure base allows children to explore their environment more effectively because they know they can rely on their caregivers to quickly come to the rescue if needed. Equally important are mutual interaction, stimulation, a positive attitude, warmth and acceptance, and emotional support (De Wolff & van IJzendoorn, 1997; Lundy, 2003).

A child who exhibits a strong preference for his caregivers and distress when they leave is experiencing stranger anxiety and separation anxiety.
©Hill Street Studios/Blend Images/AP Images

The Role of Temperament in Attachment

How much influence does temperament exert on attachment and in what ways? Neurological or physiological conditions may underlie temperament differences in attachment. For example, variability in heart rate is associated with irritability, and heart rate seems to vary more in insecurely attached infants (Izard, Porges, Simons, Haynes & Cohen, 1991).

However, attachment is a relational process—that is, child temperament and parenting interact. For example, in one series of studies 15-day-old infants classified as irritable were much more likely than nonirritable infants to be avoidantly attached at 1 year unless their mothers had been instructed on how to soothe their babies (Van den Boom, 1994). Thus an infant's irritability may work against the development of secure attachment, but not if the mother has the skills to cope with the baby's temperament (Rothbart et al., 2000). Thus, goodness of fit between parent and child may well be a key to understanding security of attachment. By the same token, however, a poor fit may put a child at elevated risk. For example, another study found infants who were highly behaviorally inhibited were at particularly high risk for resistant attachment when their mothers also reported having high anxiety themselves (Stevenson-Hinde, Shouldice & Chicot, 2011).

Stranger and Separation Anxiety

Alex was always a friendly baby, smiling at strangers and going to them, continuing to coo happily as long as someone— anyone—was around. Now, at 8 months, he prefers to stay in his mother's arms when a new person approaches and clings to his parents when they try to leave him with a babysitter. Alex is experiencing two types of typical infant anxiety— **stranger anxiety**, wariness of a person he does not know, and **separation anxiety**, distress when a familiar caregiver leaves him.

Babies rarely react negatively to strangers before age 6 months, commonly do so by 8 or 9 months, and do so more and more throughout the rest of the 1st year (Sroufe, 1997).

This change may reflect cognitive development. Alex's stranger anxiety involves memory for faces, the ability to compare the stranger's appearance with his mother's, and perhaps the recollection of situations in which he has been left with a stranger (Lewis, 1997; Sroufe, 1997).

Long-Term Effects of Attachment

As attachment theory proposes, security of attachment seems to affect emotional, social, and cognitive competence, presumably through the action of internal working models (Sroufe, Coffino & Carlson, 2010). Most notably, the more secure a child's attachment to a nurturing adult, the more likely that the child will develop good relationships with others. A recent meta-analysis including over 80 studies and 4,000 children concluded that attachment security in infancy is associated with peer competence across childhood and early adolescence, while insecurity, regardless of subtype, is associated with lower peer competence (Groh et al., 2014).

Securely attached toddlers tend to have larger, more varied vocabularies than those who are insecurely attached (Meins, 1998), and in preschool these children use more words reflecting mental states (McQuaid, Bigelow, McLaughlin & MacLean, 2008). They show less stress in adapting to child care (Ahnert, Gunnar, Lamb & Barthel, 2004), have more positive interactions with peers, and their friendly overtures are more likely to be accepted (Fagot, 1997). Insecurely attached toddlers tend to show more negative emotions (fear, distress, and anger), whereas securely attached children are more joyful (Kochanska, 2001).

Between ages 3 and 5, securely attached children are likely to be more curious, competent, empathic, resilient, and self-confident; to get along better with other children; and to form closer friendships than children who were insecurely attached as infants (Elicker, Englund & Sroufe, 1992; Jacobson & Wille, 1986; Youngblade & Belsky, 1992). They interact more positively with parents, preschool teachers, and peers; are better able to resolve conflicts; and tend to have a more positive self-image (Elicker et al., 1992; Verschueren, Marcoen & Schoefs, 1996; Sroufe, Egeland, Carlson & Collins, 2005). In middle childhood and adolescence, securely attached children tend to have the closest, most stable friendships (Schneider, Atkinson & Tardif, 2001; Sroufe, Carlson & Shulman, 1993) and to be socially well adjusted (Jaffari-Bimmel, Juffer, van IJzendoorn, Bakersmans-Kranenburg & Mooijaart, 2006). Secure attachment in infancy also influences the quality of attachment to a romantic partner in young adulthood (Simpson, Collins, Tran & Haydon, 2007).

Insecurely attached children, in contrast, often are more likely to have inhibitions and negative emotions in toddlerhood, hostility toward other children at age 5, and dependency during the school years (Calkins & Fox, 1992; Fearon, Bakersman-Kranenburg, van IJzendoorn, Lapsley & Roisman, 2010; Kochanska, 2001; Lyons-Ruth,

> **stranger anxiety** Wariness of strange people and places, shown by some infants from age 6 to 12 months.
>
> **separation anxiety** Distress shown by someone, typically an infant, when a familiar caregiver leaves.

Alpern & Repacholi, 1993; Sroufe, Carlson & Shulman, 1993). They also are more likely to show evidence of externalizing behaviors such as aggression and conduct problems. This appears to be more true for boys, for clinically referred children, and when the attachment assessments are based on observational data (Fearon et al., 2010). Those with disorganized attachment are more likely to have behavior problems at all levels of schooling and psychiatric disorders at age 17 (Carlson, 1998).

Transmission of Attachment Patterns

The *Adult Attachment Interview* (AAI) (George, Kaplan, & Main, 1985; Main, 1995) asks adults to recall and interpret feelings and experiences related to their childhood attachments. Studies using the AAI have found that the way adults recall early experiences with parents or caregivers is related to their emotional well-being and may influence the way they respond to their own children (Dykas & Cassidy, 2011; Adam, Gunnar & Tanaka, 2004). A mother who recalls being securely attached to her mother or who has effectively dealt with memories of insecure attachment is better at recognizing her baby's attachment behaviors, responding encouragingly, and helping the baby form a secure attachment to her (Bretherton, 1990). Mothers who are preoccupied with their past attachment relationships tend to show anger and intrusiveness in interactions with their children. Depressed mothers who dismiss memories of their past attachments tend to be cold and unresponsive to their children (Adam et al., 2004).

> **mutual regulation** Process by which infant and caregiver communicate emotional states to each other and respond appropriately.
>
> **interactional synchrony** The synchronized coordination of behavior and affect between a caregiver and infant.

Parents' attachment history also influences their perceptions of their baby's temperament, and those perceptions may affect the parent-child relationship (Pesonen et al., 2003). Some of these processes may occur outside of awareness at a physiological level. For example, when viewing their own infant's smiling face, mothers who reported a secure attachment style on the AAI showed greater activation in areas of the brain (hypothalamus/pituitary and ventral striatum) associated with reward, as well as release of oxytocin (a neurohormone involved in social processes), while mothers with insecure or dismissing styles did not. The differences while viewing their own infants' sad faces were even more striking. Here, mothers with a secure AAI style continued to show activation in reward areas, while mothers with insecure/dismissing styles showed activation in areas (ventral striatum) more closely associated with feelings of pain or disgust (Strathearn, Fonagy, Amico & Montague, 2009). Additional research has found that adults with insecure attachment representations also show greater amygdala activation and respond with greater irritation than do securely attached adults to infant cries (Riem, Bakersmans-Kranenburg, van IJzendoorn, Out & Rombouts, 2012).

Fortunately, the cycle of insecure attachment can be broken. Interventions that focus on maternal sensitivity—teaching mothers to more accurately "read" their babies' emotional signals—are effective in influencing infants' security (Klein-Velderman, Bakermans-Kranenburg, Juffer & van IJzendoorn, 2006).

MUTUAL REGULATION

At 1 month, Zev gazed attentively at his mother's face. At 2 months, when his mother smiled at him and rubbed his tummy, he smiled back. By the 3rd month, Zev smiled first, inviting his mother to play (Lavelli & Fogel, 2005).

Infants have a strong drive to communicate with others—they want and need to do so. The ability of both infant and caregiver to respond appropriately and sensitively to each other's mental and emotional states is known as **mutual regulation**. Ideally, caregivers and infants have high **interactional synchrony**—where both unconsciously coordinate their behavior and affect in a rhythmic back-and-forth manner, responding appropriately and effectively to each other's signals in an interactive dance. Infants take an active part in this by sending behavioral signals, like smiling, that influence the way caregivers behave toward them.

Some of this interactional synchrony may be expressed at a biological level. For example, when mothers and infants are interacting face-to-face in a synchronous fashion, their heart rates become synchronized with lags of less than one second. This process does not occur during asynchronous periods of interaction (Feldman, Magori-Cohen, Galili, Singer & Louzoun, 2011). Additionally, the release of oxytocin, a hormone related in bonding processes in mammals, has been found to be related to parenting behaviors in humans. In fathers, oxytocin levels are related to playful behaviors. In mothers, oxytocin levels are related to positive affect, affectionate touch, and "baby talk"—all markers of sensitive parenting (Gordon, Zagoory-Sharon, Leckman & Feldman, 2010).

Typically, interaction shifts between well-regulated states and poorly regulated states. When an interaction is highly synchronous, the baby tends to be joyful, or at least interested (Tronick, 1989; Lowe at al., 2012). However, when a mother or caregiver is not synchronous in her interaction with the baby—for example, if an invitation to play is ignored or an adult is overly intrusive—the baby can become stressed or physiologically aroused (Haley & Stansbury, 2003). From this process, babies learn how to send signals and what to do when their signals are not effective. Even young infants can perceive emotions others express and can adjust their own behavior accordingly (Legerstee & Varghese, 2001; Montague & Walker-Andrews, 2001).

Not surprisingly, there are links to later social behaviors. Children whose mothers were high in interactional synchrony when young are more likely later to be better at regulating their behavior, to comply with parental requests, to have higher IQ, to use more words referencing mental states (such as "think"), and to have fewer behavioral problems (Feldman, 2007). It may be that mutual regulation processes help them learn to read others' behavior and to respond appropriately.

Measuring Mutual Regulation

Mutual regulation in 2- to 9-month-old infants is measured using the **still-face paradigm** (Tronick, Als, Adamson, Wise & Brazelton, 1978). First, the mother interacts in a normal fashion in order to establish a baseline of behaviors. Then, in the still-face episode, the mother suddenly becomes stony-faced, silent, and unresponsive, avoiding eye contact. During the still-face episode, infants tend to stop smiling and look-ing at the mother. They may make faces, sounds, or gestures, often in an attempt to draw the mother's attention, and they express more negative affect. They may touch themselves, their clothing, or a chair, apparently to comfort themselves or to relieve the emotional stress the mother's unexpected behavior created. In essence, they become dysregulated (Weinberg & Tronick, 1996; Mesman, Van IJzendoorn & Bakersmans-Kranenburg, 2009).

How do infants react after the still-face procedure? Most babies continue to show sad or angry facial expressions, "pick-me-up" gestures, distancing, and indications of stress, and they have an increased tendency to fuss and cry. Their behavior, compared to that of the baseline episode, is more negative, suggesting they are still recovering and the negative feelings stirred by a breakdown in mutual regulation were not readily eased (Weinberg & Tronick, 1996; Mesman et al., 2009).

Social Referencing

Zev and his mother are visiting a new playground for the first time. Zev's mother places him on the ground; he looks around, taking in the toys, laughing children, and bright col-ors. Still unsure, he turns back toward his mother, makes eye contact, and notes her warm smile. Comforted by this, he begins to explore his environment.

When babies look at their caregivers upon encountering an ambiguous, confusing, or unfamiliar situation, they are engaging in **social referencing**, seeking out emotional infor-mation to guide behavior (Hertenstein & Campos, 2004). For example, when exposed to jiggling or vibrating toys, both 12- and 18-month-olds moved closer to or farther from the toys depending on the experimenters' expressed emotional reactions ("Yecch!" or "Nice!") (Moses, Baldwin, Rosicky & Tidball, 2001). In another experiment (Hertenstein & Campos, 2004), whether 14-month-olds touched plastic creatures that dropped within their reach was related to the positive or negative emotions they had seen an adult express about the same objects an hour before. As children age, social referencing becomes more complex. For example, it becomes less dependent on facial expression and more dependent on language. Additionally, while younger infants tend to check in with adults regardless of what type of stimu-lus they encounter, older infants tend to check in only when a stimulus or situation is ambiguous (Kim & Kwak, 2011). Children also become pickier about whom they seek infor-mation. Between the ages of 4 and 5 years, they are more likely to trust information that comes from their mother than from a stranger (Corriveau et al., 2009).

Social referencing may play a role in such key develop-ments of toddlerhood as the rise of self-conscious emotions (embarrassment and pride), the development of a sense of self, and the processes of socialization and internalization.

The Developing Self

About halfway between their first and second birthdays, babies become tod-dlers. This transformation can be seen in such physical and cognitive skills as walking and talking, and also in the ways children express their personali-ties and interact with others. A toddler becomes a more active, intentional partner in interactions and sometimes ini-tiates them. This helps a toddler gain communicative skills and social competence and motivate compliance with a par-ent's wishes (Harrist & Waugh, 2002).

Three key areas of psychosocial development for tod-dles are the emerging sense of self; the growth of autonomy, or self-determination; and socialization, or internalization of behavioral standards.

THE EMERGING SENSE OF SELF

The **self-concept** is our image of ourselves—our total picture of our abilities and traits. It describes what we know and feel about ourselves and guides our actions (Harter, 1998). When and how does the self-concept develop? From a jumble of seemingly isolated experiences (say, from one breast-feeding session to another), infants begin to extract consistent pat-terns that form rudimentary concepts of self and other. Depending on what kind of care the infant receives and how she or he responds, pleasant or unpleasant emotions become

> **still-face paradigm** Research procedure used to measure mutual regulation in infants 2 to 9 months old.
>
> **social referencing** Under-standing an ambiguous situa-tion by seeking out another person's perception of it.
>
> **self-concept** Sense of self; descriptive and evaluative mental picture of one's abili-ties and traits.

By 18 to 24 months, children have developed self-awareness and recognize themselves in a mirror.
©InkkStudios/Getty Images

connected with experiences that play an important part in the growing concept of the self (Harter, 1998).

When does the self-concept develop? By at least 3 months infants pay attention to their mirror image (Courage & Howe, 2002). Four- to 9-month-olds show more interest in images of others than of themselves (Rochat & Striano, 2002). This early perceptual discrimination may be the foundation of the conceptual self-concept that develops in the middle of the 2nd year.

Between 4 and 10 months, when infants learn to reach, grasp, and make things happen, they experience a sense of personal agency, the realization that they can control external events. At about this time infants develop self-coherence, the sense of being a physical whole with boundaries separate from the rest of their world (Harter, 1998). These developments occur in interaction with caregivers in games such as peeka-boo in which the infant becomes increasingly aware of the difference between self and other ("I see you!").

Did you know?

Chimpanzees and dolphins also pass the self-recognition task (Reiss & Marino, 2000); they will twist and turn to view a stripe of paint on their body in a mirror. ©Life on white/Alamy

autonomy versus shame and doubt Erikson's second stage in psychosocial development, in which children achieve a balance between self-determination and control by others.

The emergence of self-recognition ("the idea of me")—a conscious knowledge of the self as a distinct, identifiable being (Lewis, 2003)—builds on this dawning perceptual discrimination between self and others. Self-recognition can be tested by studying whether infants recognize themselves in a mirror (Lewis & Carmody, 2008). In a classic line of research, investigators dabbed rouge on the noses of 6- to 24-month-olds and sat them in front of a mirror. Three-fourths of 18-month-olds and all 24-month-olds touched their red noses more often than before, whereas babies younger than 15 months never did. This behavior suggests the 18- and 24-month-olds had self-awareness. They knew they did not normally have red noses and recognized the image in the mirror as their own (Lewis & Brooks, 1974).

Pretend play, which typically begins during the last half of the 2nd year, is an early indication of the ability to understand others' mental states as well as the child's own (Lewis & Carmody, 2008). A third measure or sign of self-recognition is the use of first-person pronouns, such as me and mine, usually at 20 to 24 months (Lewis & Carmody, 2008). A positive correlation between the usage of pronouns and mirror self-recognition has been found cross-culturally (Kartner, Keller, Chaudhary & Yovsi, 2012). Between 19 and 30 months, children's rapid language development also enables them to think and talk about the self and to incorporate

parents' verbal descriptions ("You're so smart!" "What a big boy!") into their emerging self-image (Stipek, Gralinski & Kopp, 1990). Similarly, toddlers of this age demonstrate self-understanding through acknowledging objects that belong to them and those that belong to others (Fasig, 2000). Interestingly, those children with older siblings show greater self-awareness and social understanding than those without older siblings (Taumoepeau & Reese, 2014). Culture matters too; children from autonomy-supporting cultural contexts, such as German and Indian urban samples, recognize themselves in a mirror earlier than do children from cultures stressing relatedness and interactional goals, such as Indian and Nso rural samples (Kartner et al., 2012).

Brain maturation underlies the development of self-representation. Magnetic resonance imaging (MRI) scans of 15- to 30-month-olds showed that signal intensities in a specific brain region, the left temporo-parietal junction, were strongest in children, regardless of age, who recognized their image in a mirror, engaged in pretend play with others, and used personal pronouns (Lewis & Carmody, 2008).

DEVELOPING AUTONOMY

As children mature they are driven to seek independence from the very adults to whom they are attached. "I do it!" is the common phrase as toddlers use their developing muscles and minds to try to do everything on their own—not only to walk, but to feed and dress themselves and to explore their world.

Erikson (1950) identified the period from about 18 months to 3 years as the second stage in psychosocial development, **autonomy versus shame and doubt**. Having come through infancy with a sense of basic trust in the world and an awakening self-awareness, toddlers begin to substitute their own judgment for their caregivers'. The strength that emerges during this stage is will. As children are better able

This toddler is showing autonomy—the drive to exert her own power and try to do things on her own.
©Image Source

Perspectives on Diversity

©Digital Vision/Getty Images

STRUGGLES WITH TODDLERS

Are the terrible twos a normal phase in child development? Although many Western parents and psychologists think so, this transition does not appear to be universal.

One arena in which issues of autonomy and control appear in Western cultures is in sibling conflicts over toys. To explore these issues, a cross-cultural study compared 16 San Pedro Guatemalan families with 16 middle-class European American families in Salt Lake City (Mosier & Rogoff, 2003). All of the families had toddlers and older siblings. The researchers handed the mother a series of attractive objects and, in the presence of the older sibling, asked the mother to help the toddler operate them.

The older siblings in Salt Lake City often tried to take and play with the objects. However, the older San Pedro children would offer to help their younger siblings work the objects, or the two children would play with them together. When there was a conflict over possession of the objects, San Pedro mothers favored the toddlers and gave them the toy. In more than one-third of the interactions in Salt Lake City,

however, the mothers tried to treat both children equally, negotiating with them or suggesting they take turns or share.

What explains these cultural contrasts? A clue emerged when the mothers were asked at what age children can be held responsible for their actions. Most of the Salt Lake City mothers maintained their toddlers already understood the consequences of touching prohibited objects. Yet all but one of the San Pedro mothers placed the age of understanding social consequences of actions much later—between 2 and 3 years. The Salt Lake City mothers regarded their toddlers as capable of intentional misbehavior and punished their toddlers for it; most San Pedro mothers did not.

The researchers suggest the terrible twos may be a phase specific to societies such as the United States that place individual freedom before the needs of the group. Research such as this suggests that in societies that place higher value on group needs, freedom of choice does still exist, but it goes hand in hand with interdependence, responsibility, and expectations of cooperation.

---

to make their wishes understood, they become more powerful and independent. Since unlimited freedom is neither safe nor healthy, said Erikson, shame and doubt have a necessary place. Toddlers need adults to set appropriate limits, and shame and doubt help them recognize the need for those limits.

In the United States, the "terrible twos" are a normal sign of the drive for autonomy. This drive typically shows itself in the form of negativism, that is, the tendency to shout "No!" just for the sake of resisting authority. Almost all U.S. children show negativism to some degree; it usually begins before age 2, tends to peak at about 3½ to 4, and declines by age 6. Caregivers who view children's expressions of self-will as a normal, healthy striving for independence and not as stubbornness, can help them learn self-control, contribute to their sense of competence, and avoid excessive conflict.

Many U.S. parents might be surprised to hear that the terrible twos are not universal. In some developing countries, the transition from infancy to early childhood is relatively smooth and harmonious, as we discuss in *Perspectives on Diversity*.

SOCIALIZATION

Moral development—the process by which children grow to understand what is right or wrong—is a complex ongoing process that encompasses cognitive, emotional, and environmental influences. Moral development is based on the internalization of parental beliefs, a process known as socialization.

Socialization is the process by which children develop habits, skills, values, and motives that make them responsible, productive members of society. Compliance with parental expectations is a first step toward compliance with societal standards; however, the ultimate goal is **internalization** of these standards. Children who are successfully socialized no longer merely obey rules or commands to get rewards or avoid punishment; they have made society's standards their own (Kochanska, Tjebkes, & Forman, 1998; Kochanska, 2002). Areas of

> **socialization** Development of habits, skills, values, and motives shared by responsible, productive members of a society.
>
> **internalization** During socialization, process by which children accept societal standards of conduct as their own.

socialization that are developing during the toddler years include self-regulation and conscience. Both internal and external factors impact successful socialization.

Developing Self-Regulation

Zev, age 2, is about to poke his finger into an electric outlet. In his child-proofed apartment, the sockets are covered, but they aren't covered here in his grandmother's home. When Zev hears his father shout "No!" the toddler pulls his arm back. The next time he goes near an outlet, he starts to point his finger, hesitates, and then says "No." He has stopped himself from doing something he remembers he is not supposed to do. He is beginning to show **self-regulation**: control of his behavior to conform to a caregiver's demands or expectations, even when the caregiver is not present.

Before they can control their behavior, children may need to be able to regulate their attentional processes and to modulate negative emotions (Eisenberg, 2000). Attentional regulation enables children to develop willpower and cope with frustration (Sethi, Mischel, Aber, Shoda & Rodriguez, 2000). For example, control of attentional processes might allow a child to distract herself enough that she manages not to steal the cookies temptingly cooling on the counter.

The growth of self-regulation parallels the development of the self-conscious and evaluative emotions, such as empathy, shame, and guilt (Lewis, 1998). It requires the ability to wait for gratification. It is correlated with measures of conscience development, such as resisting temptation and making amends for wrongdoing (Eisenberg, 2000). In most children, the full development of self-regulation takes at least 3 years (Kopp, 1982).

Developing Conscience

While young children often cooperate with parental dictates because they know they are supposed to, the goal of parenting is development of a **conscience**. A conscience includes both emotional discomfort about doing something wrong and the ability to refrain from doing it. Conscience depends on the willingness to do the right thing because a child believes it is right, not, as in self-regulation, just because someone else said so.

Kochanska and her colleagues (1993, 1995, 1997a, 1997b) have looked for the origins of conscience. Researchers videotaped 103 children aged 26 to 41 months with their mothers playing together with toys. After a free-play period of about an hour, a mother would give her child 15 minutes to put away the toys. The laboratory where the research occurred had a special shelf with other, unusually attractive toys, such as a bubble gum machine, a walkie-talkie, and a music box. The child was told not to touch anything on that shelf. The experimenter asked the mother to go into an adjoining room, leaving the child alone for the cleanup. A few minutes later, a woman entered, played with several of the forbidden toys, and then left the child alone again for 8 minutes.

Some children could put the toys away as long as their parents were there to remind them. These children showed what is called **situational compliance**. They needed the extra assistance provided by their parents' presence and prompts to complete the task. However, other children seemed to have internalized their parents' requests more fully. These children showed **committed compliance**—that is, they were committed to following requests and could do so without their parents' direct intervention. They were able to clean up and not touch the toys without reminders or lapses. (Kochanska, Coy & Murray, 2001).

The roots of committed compliance go back to infancy. Committed compliers, most typically girls, tend to be those who, at 8 to 10 months, could refrain from touching when told, "No!" (Kochanska, Tjebkes & Forman, 1998). Mothers of committed compliers, as contrasted with mothers of situational compliers, were more sensitive and responsive with their children as infants (Kochanska et al., 2010) and, once the children were toddlers, tended to rely on gentle guidance rather than force, threats, or other forms of negative control (Eisenberg, 2000; Kochanska, Friesenborg, Lange & Martel, 2004). Committed compliance tends to increase with age, whereas situational compliance decreases.

Receptive cooperation goes beyond committed compliance. It is a child's eager willingness to cooperate with a parent, not only in disciplinary situations, but also in a variety of daily interactions, including routines, chores, hygiene, and play. In a longitudinal study of 101 children, those who were prone to anger, who received unresponsive parenting, or who were insecurely attached at 15 months also tended to be low in receptive cooperation in toddlerhood. Children who were securely attached and whose mothers had been responsive to the child during infancy tended to be high in receptive cooperation (Kochasnka, Aksan & Carlson, 2005).

Factors in the Success of Socialization

Not all children respond in the same way to parental efforts to socialize them. For example, a temperamentally fearful toddler may respond better to gentle reminders than to strong admonitions, whereas a more bold toddler may require more assertive parenting (Kochanska, Aksan & Joy, 2007). The opposite is also true; children of similar temperament respond differently to different parenting strategies. For instance, temperamentally bold toddlers whose mothers responded to their approach behaviors in a constructive way (for example, by teaching coping skills) tended to later be reported by their teachers as socially competent and well-behaved, whereas bold toddlers whose mothers responded to their approach behaviors in an nonsupportive fashion (for example, with criticism or punishment) tended to later be described as disruptive in a classroom setting (Root & Stifter, 2010).

Secure attachment and a warm, mutually responsive, parent-child relationship seem to foster committed compliance and conscience development (Kochanska et al., 2010). Emotional socialization seems to be important too. Parents who talk to their 18- to 30-month-old children about emotions tend to have toddlers who are quicker to help others (Brownell, Svetlova, Anderson, Nichols & Drummond, 2013). By reading their parents' emotional responses to their behavior, children continually absorb information about what conduct their parents approve of. The quality of their relationship with their parents affects this emerging skill. Maternal sensitivity, parents' tendency to use mental terms when talking to the child, and support of the child's autonomous behavior are all important influences (Bernier, Carlson & Whipple, 2010). In one study, researchers observed mothers and children in lengthy, naturalistic interactions: caregiving routines, preparing and eating meals, playing, relaxing, and doing household chores. Children who had mutually responsive relationships with their mothers at the age of 2 tended in early school age to show *moral emotions* such as guilt and empathy; *moral conduct* in the face of strong temptation to break rules; and *moral cognition,* as judged by their response to hypothetical, age-appropriate moral dilemmas (Kochanska, 2002).

Constructive conflict that involves negotiation, reasoning, and resolution can help children develop moral understanding by enabling them to see another point of view. In one observational study, 2½-year-olds whose mothers gave clear explanations for their requests, compromised, discussed emotions, or bargained with the child were better able to resist temptation at age 3 than children whose mothers had threatened, teased, insisted, or given in (Laible & Thompson, 2002).

GENDER

Being male or female affects how people look, move their bodies, work, play, and dress. It influences what they think about themselves and what others think of them. All these characteristics—and more—are included in the word *gender*: what it means to be male or female.

Did you know?

The term *sex* refers to biological differences between males and females, for example, that females have two X chromosomes while males have one X and one Y. *Gender* refers to the social construction of what that biological difference means.

©OJO Images/AP Images

The following discussion focuses primarily on gender differences, a controversial area in the field of psychology. Most of the differences are small—indeed the controversy would not exist if the differences were large and obvious. However, it is important to note prior to this discussion that while there are small differences, overall males and females are more alike than different (Hyde, 2005).

Sex and Gender Differences in Infants and Toddlers

Measurable differences between baby boys and baby girls are few, at least in U.S. samples. Boys are a bit longer and heavier and may be slightly stronger and more active, but they are physically more vulnerable from conception on. Girls are less reactive to stress and more likely to survive infancy (Fryar, Gu, Ogden & Flegal, 2016; Bale & Epperson, 2015; Davis & Emory, 1995; Keenan & Shaw, 1997; Stevenson et. al., 2000). Boys' brains at birth are about 10 percent larger than girls' brains, a difference that continues into adulthood (Gilmore et al., 2007; Ruigrok et al., 2014). Despite these differences, they achieve the motor milestones of infancy at about the same times.

There is some evidence for differences in social behavior between boys and girls. For instance, girls are rated as more cuddly (Benenson, Philippoussis & Leeb, 1999), are more interested in faces and better at discriminating facial expressions (Connellan, Baron-Cohen, Wheelwright, Batki & Aluwalia, 2000; McClure, 2000), show fewer externalizing emotions (Chaplin & Aldao, 2013); and are better than boys at regulating their distress during and quicker to recover from still-face procedures than boys (Weinberg, Tronick, Cohn & Olson, 1999). Still, such differences are relatively small and have not always been found consistently (Alexander & Wilcox, 2012).

However, there are some consistently identified and robust early behavioral differences between boys and girls, including a preference for toys, play activities, and playmates of the same sex. A preference for sex-typed toys, such as trucks for boys and dolls for girls, appears as young as 3 months of age (Alexander, Wilcox & Woods, 2009). While children at 12, 18, and 24 months of age show little preference for sex-typed colors (indeed, both seem to prefer reds over blues), they do continue to show sex-typed toy preferences (Jadva, Hines & Golombok, 2010). By the age of 2½ years, girls start to prefer the color pink, and boys start to actively avoid it (LoBue & DeLoache, 2011). By 3 years of age, girls, but not boys, will show more interest in novel toys labeled as being for their sex and decorated in the appropriate masculine or feminine color (Weisgram, Fulchur & Dinella, 2014).

Are sex-typed toy preferences innate or the product of socialization processes? There are several lines of evidence germane to this question. First, toy preferences emerge early in development, at 3 months of age, and before infants could have formed an understanding of masculine or feminine conceptual categories. Second, similar sex-typed toy preferences have been found in non-human primates

There are some indications that sex-typed toy preferences may be affected by innate factors.
©Tetra Images/Getty Images

Musician John Legend walks hand in hand with daughter Luna.
©Robert Kamau/GC Images/Getty Images

(Hassett, Siebert & Wallen, 2008). For example, in one study female vervets played longer with dolls and pots, while male vervets spent more time playing with cars and balls (Alexander & Hines, 2002). Third, testosterone levels in infancy predict later sex-typed toy preferences (Lamminmaki et al., 2012). These findings suggest that basic sex-typed toy preferences are to some extent innate and do not result from gender socialization processes. Other factors that emerge later, such as color or shape preferences, may be more subject to social influences.

Toddlers, and to a lesser extent babies, prefer to play with others of the same sex (Campbell, Shirley, Heywood & Crook, 2000). This may perhaps be because boys as young as 17 months tend to play more actively and aggressively than girls (Baillargeon et al., 2007). For example, in one study, 57 3-year-old children were observed during free play. Most children, and especially the girls, preferred to play with same-sex peers. The children's gender role awareness and toy preferences did not impact their propensity to play with same-sex peers. However, their play styles did. Very active and aggressive boys and very sensitive girls were the least likely to play with opposite sex peers (Moller & Serbin, 1996). Some theorists have argued that the segregation seen in boys' and girls' play is a result of these differences in play styles. Girls play with girls and boys play with boys, not because they necessarily want to play with someone who is the same sex, but because most children enjoy playing with someone who plays like they do (Maccoby, 1990).

Play style is likely to be influenced by prenatal androgen exposure. One clue can be found by looking at girls with congenital adrenal hyperplasia (CAH), a genetic condition involving the overproduction of androgens (such as testosterone) in utero. These girls generally have play styles that are more typical of boys. Additionally, despite identifying as

gender-typing Socialization process by which children, at an early age, learn appropriate gender roles.

girls, they have a greater preference for male playmates than unaffected girls (Pasterski et al., 2011).

How Parents Shape Gender Differences

U.S. parents begin to influence boys' and girls' personalities very early. Fathers, especially, promote **gender-typing**, the process by which children learn behavior their culture considers appropriate for each sex (Bronstein, 1988; Lytton & Romney, 1991). Fathers treat boys and girls more differently than mothers do, even during the 1st year (Snow, Jacklin & Maccoby, 1983). During the 2nd year, fathers talk more and spend more time with sons than with daughters (Lamb, 1981). Mothers talk more, and more supportively, to daughters than to sons (Leaper, Anderson & Sanders, 1998), and girls at this age tend to be more talkative than boys (Leaper & Smith, 2004). Fathers, overall, play with their children more than mothers do (Lewis & Lamb, 2003) and play more roughly with sons and show more sensitivity to daughters (Kelley, Smith, Green, Berndt & Rogers, 1998; Lindsey, Cremeens & Caldera, 2010).

However, a highly physical style of play, characteristic of many fathers in the United States, is not typical of fathers in all cultures. Swedish and German fathers usually do not play with their babies this way (Lamb, Frodi, Frodi & Hwang, 1982). African Aka fathers (Hewlett, 1987) and those in New Delhi, India, also tend to play gently with small children (Roopnarine, Hooper, Ahmeduzzaman & Pollack, 1993). Such cross-cultural variations suggest that rough play may be a biologically based gender difference but is strongly culturally influenced.

Relationships with Other Children

Although parents exert a major influence on children's lives, relationships with other children—both in the home and out of it—are important too. These relationships shape and mold us over time, and they become increasingly important with age.

SIBLINGS

If you have brothers or sisters, your relationships with them are likely to be the longest lasting you will ever have. They share your roots: They knew you when you were young, they accepted or rejected the same parental values, and they probably deal with you more candidly than almost anyone else you know.

Sibling relationships begin with the birth of a new baby and continue to develop positively and negatively throughout childhood.

Affection and cooperation are common in sibling relationships.
©LWA/Sharie Kennedy/Blend Images/AP Images

WHAT DO YOU DO?

Child Psychologist

Child psychologists support mental well-being through assessments and therapies. Child psychologists working with young children are often involved because of a trauma or suspected disability. For example, a child psychologist may work with a preschooler who experienced the loss of a parent or with a toddler who parents and the pediatrician suspect may be on the autism spectrum. Child psychologists may work in hospitals, clinics, or in private practices. Becoming a child psychologist typically requires a doctoral degree, which includes an internship. To learn more about what a child psychologist does, visit www.apa.org.

The earliest, most frequent, and most intense disputes among siblings are over property rights or access to the mother. Although exasperated adults may not always see it that way, sibling disputes and their settlement are socialization opportunities, in which children learn to stand up for principles and negotiate disagreements, in part because the involuntary nature of the relationship ensures that interactions will continue (Howe, Rinaldi, Jennings & Petrakos, 2002). Lessons and skills learned from interactions with siblings—such as conflict and cooperation—carry over to relationships outside the home (Brody, 1998; Kim, McHale, Crouter & Osgood, 2007). Another arena for socialization is joint dramatic play. Siblings who frequently play "let's pretend" develop a history of shared understandings that enable them to more easily resolve issues and build on each other's ideas (Howe, Petrakos, Rinaldi & LeFebvre, 2005).

As babies begin to move around and become more assertive, they inevitably have conflict with siblings—at least in U.S. culture. Sibling conflict increases dramatically after the younger child reaches 18 months (Vandell & Bailey, 1992). During the next few months, younger siblings begin to participate more fully in family interactions. As they do, they become more aware of others' intentions and feelings. They begin to recognize what kind of behavior will upset or annoy an older brother or sister and what behavior is considered naughty or good (Dunn & Munn, 1985; Recchia & Howe, 2009).

Despite the frequency of conflict, sibling rivalry is *not* the main pattern between brothers and sisters early in life. Affection, interest, companionship, and influence are also prevalent in sibling relationships. Indeed, prosocial and play-oriented behaviors are more common than rivalry, hostility, and competition. Older siblings initiate more behavior, both friendly and unfriendly; while younger siblings tend to imitate the older ones. As the children age, they tend to become less physical and more verbal in showing both aggression and care and affection (Abramovitch, Corter, Pepler & Stanhope, 1986). Because older siblings tend to dominate younger ones, the quality of the relationship is more affected by the emotional and social adjustment of the older child than the younger one (Pike, Coldwell & Dunn, 2005). Generally, same-sex siblings, particularly girls, are closer and play together more peaceably than boy-girl pairs (Kier & Lewis, 1998).

The quality of sibling relationships tends to carry over to relationships with other children. A child who is aggressive with siblings is likely to be aggressive with friends as well (Abramovitch et al., 1986). For example, children who victimize their siblings are more likely to be bullied or to bully others, and children who are victimized by their siblings are more likely to be bullied (Tippett & Wolke, 2015). By the same token, siblings who frequently play amicably together tend to develop prosocial behaviors (Pike et al., 2005).

Likewise, friendships can influence sibling relationships. Older siblings who have experienced a good relationship with a friend before the birth of a sibling are likely to treat their younger siblings better and are less likely to develop antisocial behavior in adolescence (Kramer & Kowal, 2005). For a young child at risk for behavioral problems, a positive relationship with *either* a sibling or a friend can buffer the effects of a negative relationship with the other (McElwain & Volling, 2005).

PEERS

Infants and, even more so, toddlers show interest in people outside the home, particularly people their own size. During the first few months, they look, smile, and coo at other babies. From about 6 to 12 months, they increasingly smile at, touch, and babble to them (Hay, Pedersen & Nash, 1982). From about 1½ to almost 3, children show growing interest in and increased understanding of what other children do (Eckerman, Davis & Didow, 1989). Preschoolers usually like to play with children of the same age, sex, and gender. They also prefer prosocial playmates who can provide them with positive experiences (Hartup & Stevens, 1999; Hart, DeWolf, Wozniak & Burts, 1992; Fishbein & Imai, 1993) and who are advanced in theory of mind (Slaughter, Imuta, Peterson & Henry, 2015). Preschoolers reject disruptive, demanding, intrusive, or aggressive children (Ramsey & Lasquade, 1996; Roopnarine & Honig, 1985; Sebanc, 2003). As children become older, their preferences become more sophisticated and start focusing less on physical traits and more on characteristics such as doing things together, liking and caring for each other, and sharing and helping one another (Furman & Bierman, 1983).

Games such as follow-the-leader help toddlers connect with other children and pave the way for more complex games during the preschool years (Eckerman et al., 1989). Imitation of each other's actions leads to more frequent verbal communication ("You go in playhouse" or "Look at me"), which helps peers coordinate joint activity (Eckerman & Didow, 1996). Cooperative activity develops during the 2nd and 3rd years as social understanding grows (Brownell, Ramani & Zerwas, 2006). Beginning at about 4 years, children will start to conform to peer pressure and sometimes go along with the group even when they disagree with an action (Haun & Tomasello, 2011). Conflict can also have a purpose; it helps children learn how to negotiate and resolve disputes (Caplan, Vespo, Pedersen & Hay, 1991).

Preschool-age children usually prefer to play with others of the same age and sex, and they favor playmates who provide positive experiences.
©Glow Images

mastering the CHAPTER

©PeopleImages/Getty Images

Summary and Key Terms

Emotions and Temperament

> Emotional development is orderly; complex emotions seem to develop from earlier, simpler ones. Crying, smiling, and laughing are early signs of emotion.

> Brain development is closely linked with emotional development. Self-conscious and self-evaluative emotions arise after the development of self-awareness.

> Altruistic behavior and empathy typically emerge during the second year of life and may result from the activity of mirror neurons. The roots of empathy can be seen in early infancy.

> Between 9 and 12 months, infants begin to collaborate with caregivers on joint activities.

> Many children seem to fall into one of three categories of temperament: "easy," "difficult," and "slow-to-warm-up." Temperamental patterns appear to have a biological basis. They are generally stable but can be modified by experience.

> Goodness of fit between a child's temperament and environmental demands aids adjustment.

> Cross-cultural differences in temperament may reflect child-raising practices.

KEY TERMS

Emotions	Altruistic behavior	Easy children
Anticipatory smiling	Empathy	Difficult children
Self-conscious emotions	Mirror Neurons	Slow-to-warm-up children
Self-awareness	Temperament	Goodness of fit

Attachment

> According to Erikson, infants in the first 18 months are in the first stage of personality development, basic sense of trust versus mistrust. Sensitive, responsive, consistent caregiving is the key to successful resolution of this conflict.

> Research based on the Strange Situation has found four patterns of attachment: secure, avoidant, ambivalent (resistant), and disorganized-disoriented.

> Attachment patterns may depend on a baby's temperament as well as on the quality of parenting and may have long-term implications for development.

> Stranger anxiety and separation anxiety may arise during the second half of the 1st year.

> A parent's memories of childhood attachment can influence his or her own child's attachment.

> Mutual regulation enables babies to play an active part in regulating their emotional states.

> Social referencing has been observed by 12 months.

KEY TERMS

Basic trust versus basic mistrust	Resistant (ambivalent) attachment	Separation anxiety
Attachment	Disorganized-disoriented attachment	Mutual regulation
Strange Situation		Interactional synchrony
Secure attachment	Stranger anxiety	Still-face paradigm
Avoidant attachment		Social referencing

The Developing Self

> The sense of self arises between 4 and 10 months, as infants begin to perceive a difference between self and others.

> The self-concept builds on the perceptual sense of self and develops between 15 and 24 months with the emergence of self-awareness and self-recognition.

> Erikson's second stage concerns autonomy versus shame and doubt. In U.S. culture, negativism is a normal manifestation of the shift from external control to self-control.

> Socialization, which rests on internalization of societally approved standards, begins with the development of self-regulation.

> A precursor of conscience is committed compliance to a caregiver's demands. Children who show receptive cooperation can be active partners in their socialization.

> Parenting practices, a child's temperament, the quality of the parent-child relationship, and cultural and socioeconomic factors may affect the ease and success of socialization.

> Although significant gender differences typically do not appear until after infancy, U.S. fathers, especially, promote early gender-typing.

KEY TERMS

Self-concept

Autonomy versus shame and doubt

Socialization

Internalization

Self-regulation

Conscience

Situational compliance

Committed compliance

Receptive cooperation

Gender-typing

Relationships with Other Children

> Sibling relationships play a distinct role in socialization and influence relationships outside the home.

> Between ages 1½ and 3 years, children tend to show more interest in and understanding of other children.

Practice Quiz

1. The earliest form of communication babies use is:
   a. smiles, to show they are happy
   b. eye gaze, to get a parent's attention
   c. cries, to show they are unhappy
   d. none of the above; babies cannot easily communicate in infancy

2. The self-conscious emotions (e.g., embarrassment, shame, and pride) require self-awareness. Self-awareness is required because _____
   _____
   _____

3. When guests show up at her parent's dinner party, Esme hides behind her father's legs and avoids contact with the guests. However, a half-hour later, she sits on a guest's lap and chatters happily away. With respect to temperament, Esme is likely to be:
   a. easy
   b. difficult
   c. slow to warm up
   d. high in behavioral inhibition

4. Erikson argued that the first stage of psychosocial development involved developing a sense of trust. The following parental characteristics most important for this are:
   a. being biological (as opposed to adoptive) parents
   b. being a mother (as opposed to a father)
   c. being of higher socioeconomic status
   d. being sensitive, responsive, and consistent in caregiving

5. The Strange Situation is used to assess attachment in the laboratory. Describe two events in the real world in which babies would be expected to show attachment behaviors.
   _____
   _____
   _____
   _____

6. April cries loudly when her mother leaves the room during the Strange Situation, but she quiets immediately upon her return, snuggling in close to her mother. John cries loudly when his mother leaves the room, but upon her return, continues to cry in an angry fashion for some time. April is likely to have a _____ attachment style, while John is likely to have a _____ attachment style.
   a. secure; resistant
   b. resistant; secure

   c. resistant; avoidant
   d. avoidant; secure
   e. avoidant; resistant

7. What are two variables that influence the development of attachment in infants?
   _____
   _____

8. Eight-month-old Gus cries loudly when carried by people he does not know well. Gus is showing:
   a. separation anxiety
   b. stranger anxiety
   c. temperament
   d. social referencing

9. Generally, babies respond to the still-face paradigm with:
   a. flat emotional affect
   b. emotional distress
   c. increased physical activity
   d. increased vocalizations

10. Two-year-old Billy reaches up to touch his new haircut after looking at himself in the mirror. Billy is exhibiting:
    a. self-coherence
    b. self-regulation
    c. internalization
    d. self-awareness

11. Committed compliance involves _____, while situational compliance involves _____.

12. Shy babies can become overwhelmed with harsh parenting techniques, while very bold babies may need a firmer hand. The match between child temperament and parenting techniques can be considered as an issue of:
    a. receptive cooperation
    b. mutual synchrony
    c. goodness-of-fit
    d. gender

13. What are two factors that impact successful socialization?
    _____
    _____

14. What is one of the earliest behavioral differences between boys and girls? _____
    _____

15. Gender-typing can be defined as:
   a. a genetic test to determine sex
   b. highly characteristic play styles
   c. a culture's adult sex roles
   d. the process by which children learn the appropriate behaviors for their sex

16. What are three factors that impact how children respond to the birth of a new sibling? _____
_____
_____

17. Conflict within peer relationships:
   a. is always bad
   b. can be useful for learning skills such as the resolution of disputes
   c. drops sharply once children attain language
   d. increases sharply once children attain language
   e. is rare in preschool children

Answers: 1–c; 2–Self-awareness involves the cognitive understanding one has a recognizable identity, separate and different from the rest of their world. This is required for the self-conscious emotions because children must understand others might have opinions about the wrongness or rightness of their behavior different from their own before they can understand and feel these social emotions; 3–c; 4–d; 5–Any situation in which an infant is separated and then reunited with parents would be expected to elicit attachment-related behaviors. For example, you might expect similar processes at day care drop-offs and pick-ups, or when parents leave a child with an alterative caregiver such as a babysitter or nanny. 6–secure; resistant; 7–Among the variables that influence attachment are parenting practices (such as how sensitive or responsive the parent is) and infant temperament; 8–b; 9–b; 10–d; 11–Committed compliance involves willingly following the order given by parents without reminders or lapses, while situation compliance involves following orders given by parents with prompting; 12–c; 13–Factors that impact successful socialization include how parents socialize a child, child temperament, the quality of the parent-child relationship, security of attachment, observational learning from parents' behavior, and the mutual responsiveness of parent and child; 14–One of the earliest behavioral differences between boys and girls is a preference for toys, play activities, and playmates of the same sex; 15–d; 16–Among the factors that impact how a child responds to the birth of a new sibling are the older child's age, the quality of his or her relationship with the mother, and the family atmosphere; 17–b

Physical Development and Health in Early Childhood

What's to Come

> Physical Growth

> Sleep

> Motor Development

> Health and Safety

©Vicky Kasala/Getty Images

t was Eva's first day of kindergarten. As her father drove her to school, he reflected on how much she had changed in just a few short years. At age 2, Eva had been a chunky baby with round cheeks and brown curls, enthusiastically toddling around her rapidly expanding world. Now, at 5, Eva had lost her baby belly and her limbs had lengthened. She could hop on either foot, walk backward, and easily use utensils. She chattered away and asked questions about everything around her, and she had strong preferences about foods, clothes, and toys.

In this chapter, we will discuss physical development during the years from 3 to 6. In early childhood, children's body proportions change and they get taller and slimmer. They need less sleep and are more likely to develop sleep problems. They improve in running, hopping, skipping, jumping, and throwing balls. They also become better at tying shoelaces (in bows instead of knots), drawing with crayons (on paper rather than on walls), and pouring cereal (into the bowl, not onto the floor), and they also begin to show a preference for using either the right or left hand. As a group, they also encounter a range of health and safety risks, from obesity to allergies to those with environmental bases.

• • • •

Physical Growth

While children's growth is most rapid in infancy and toddlerhood, early childhood is a time of great changes and advances in physical growth and development. This change is clearly apparent in the physical dimensions of the body. Less outwardly apparent but still profoundly important are the changes that occur within the brain. In the following section, we detail some of these important advancements.

HEIGHT AND WEIGHT

Children grow rapidly between ages 3 and 6 but less quickly than in infancy and toddlerhood. At about age 3, they begin to take on the slender, athletic appearance of childhood. As abdominal muscles develop, the toddler potbelly tightens. The trunk, arms, and legs grow longer. The head is still relatively large, but the other parts of the body continue to catch up as proportions steadily become more adultlike. Both boys and girls typically grow 2 to 3 inches a year during early childhood and gain about 4 to 6 pounds annually (Table 8.1). Boys' slight edge in height and weight continues until the growth spurt of puberty that generally starts a few years earlier in girls; thus for a short while, boys have a growth advantage.

Muscular and skeletal growth progresses, making children stronger. Cartilage turns to bone at a faster rate than before, and bones become harder, giving the child a firmer shape and protecting the internal organs. The increased capacities of the respiratory and circulatory systems build physical stamina and, along with the developing immune system, keep children healthier.

TABLE 8.1 Physical Growth, Ages 3 to 6 (50th percentile*)

Age	Height (inches)		Weight (pounds)	
	Boys	Girls	Boys	Girls
3	39	36.6	35.3	34.5
4	42	41.7	40.8	40.3
5	44.8	44.2	46.6	45.0
6	47.2	46.7	52.8	52.4

*Fifty percent of children in each category are above this height or weight level, and 50 percent are below it.

Source: C.D. Fryar, Q. Gu & K.M. Flegal, "Anthropometric reference data for children and adults: United States, 2011–2014." National Center for Health Statistics, Vital Health Statistics 3(39), 2016.

THE BRAIN

By age 3, the brain is approximately 90 percent of adult weight (Gabbard, 1996). From ages 3 to 6, the most rapid brain growth occurs in the frontal areas that regulate planning and goal setting, and the density of synapses in the prefrontal cortex peaks at age 4 (Lenroot & Giedd, 2006). This "exuberant connectivity" will gradually be pruned back over time as a result of experience, a process that underlies the great plasticity of the human brain (Innocenti & Price, 2005). In addition, myelin (a fatty substance that coats the axons of nerve fibers and accelerates neural conduction) continues to form (Giedd & Rapoport, 2010). By age 6, the brain has attained about 90 percent of its peak volume (Stiles & Jernigan, 2010). From ages 6 to 11, rapid brain growth occurs in areas that support associative thinking, language, and spatial relations (Thompson et al., 2000).

The *corpus callosum* is a thick band of nerve fibers that connects both hemispheres of the brain and allows them to communicate more rapidly and effectively with each other (Toga, Thompson & Sowell, 2006), allowing improved coordination of the senses, attention and arousal, and speech and hearing (Lenroot & Giedd, 2006). The corpus callosum continues to be myelinized throughout childhood and adolescence, with peak volume occurring later in boys than in girls (Luders, Thompson & Toga, 2010).

Sleep

"Just one more drink of water," begged Eva, and 20 minutes later, "I need to go potty." Finally, Eva fell asleep at 10:00 PM, occasionally mumbling in her sleep. Late at night, her parents woke to screaming. Her father ran into the bedroom to find Eva sitting up, bleary-eyed and confused. After a pat on the back, she settled back down, and the next morning, did not remember waking. Eva's sleep patterns are typical of young school-aged children, as we will see in the following section.

An object such as a favorite toy or blanket can serve as a bedtime companion and help young children transition to falling asleep on their own.
©Purestock/SuperStock

Sleep patterns change throughout the growing-up years (Iglowstein, Jenni, Molinari & Largo, 2003; Figure 8.1), and early childhood has its own distinct rhythms. By age 5, most U.S. children average about 11 hours of sleep at night and give up daytime naps (Hoban, 2004).

Bedtime may bring on a form of separation anxiety, and the child may do all she or he can to avoid it. More than half of U.S. parents or caregivers report their preschool child stalls at bedtime and that it takes 15 minutes or more for the child to fall asleep. About one-third of preschoolers actively resist going to bed, and more than one-third wake up at least once each night (National Sleep Foundation, 2004). Regular, consistent sleep routines can help minimize these problems. Children are likely to want a light left on and to sleep with a favorite toy or blanket. Such transitional objects, used repeatedly as bedtime companions, help a child shift from the dependence of infancy to the independence of later

childhood. Young children who have become accustomed to going to sleep while feeding or rocking, however, may find it hard to fall asleep on their own (Hoban, 2004). Moreover, some children, even once they do get to sleep, show sleep disturbances that make it difficult for them to stay asleep.

SLEEP DISTURBANCES

About a third of parents or caregivers of children aged 1 to 5 years say their child has a sleep problem (Bruni & Novelli, 2010). Sleep disturbances may be caused by accidental activation of the brain's motor control system (Hobson & Silvestri, 1999), by incomplete arousal from a deep sleep (Hoban, 2004), or by disordered breathing or restless leg movements (Guilleminault, Palombini, Pelayo, & Chervin, 2003). These disturbances tend to run in families (Caylak, 2009) and are often associated with separation anxiety (Petit, Touchette, Tremblay, Boivin, & Montplaisir, 2007), nasal abnormalities, and overweight (Bixler et al., 2009). The problems are particularly prevalent in children with physical or learning disabilities. Sleep problems are reported in 86 percent of such children aged up to 6 years (Bruni & Novelli, 2010).

In most cases, sleep problems are occasional and are usually outgrown (Mason & Pack, 2007). Many sleep issues are the result of ineffective parenting practices that exacerbate rather than ease the problem (Sadeh, Tikotzky & Scher, 2010). For instance, allowing young children to nap in the daytime to catch up on sleep can result in difficulty getting to sleep later that evening. Persistent sleep problems may indicate an emotional, physiological, or neurological condition that needs to be examined. For example, colic, difficult temperament, premature birth, and altered circadian rhythm have been proposed as mechanisms responsible for the onset of disordered sleep (Bruni & Novelli, 2010). Possible sleep disturbances that include night terrors, walking and talking while asleep, and nightmares.

> **night terrors** Abrupt awakening from a deep sleep in a state of agitation.

Night Terrors

A child who experiences a **night terror** appears to awaken abruptly from a deep sleep early in the night in a state of

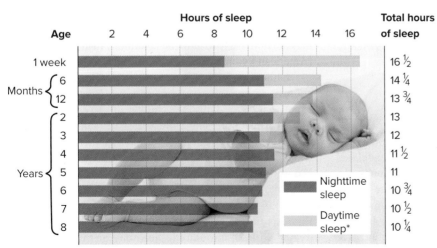

	Hours of sleep									Total hours of sleep
Age	2	4	6	8	10	12	14	16		
1 week										16 ½
Months 6										14 ¼
Months 12										13 ¾
Years 2										13
3										12
4										11 ½
5										11
6										10 ¾
7										10 ½
8										10 ¼

■ Nighttime sleep
□ Daytime sleep*

*Divided into typical number of naps per day. Length of naps may be quite variable.

FIGURE 8.1 Sleep Requirements in Childhood

Unlike infants, who sleep about as long day and night, preschoolers get all or almost all their sleep in one long nighttime period. The number of hours of sleep steadily decreases throughout childhood, but individual children may need more or fewer hours than shown here.

Source: M. McDowell, C. Fryar, C. Ogden & K. Flegal, "Anthropometeric Reference Data for Children and Adults: United States, 2003–2006," *National Health Statistics Report*, No. 10, October 22, 2008.
©JGI/Blend Images

agitation. The child may scream and sit up in bed, breathing rapidly and staring or thrashing about. Yet he is not really awake. He quiets down quickly and remembers nothing about the episode the next morning. Night terrors generally peak at about 1½ years of age (Petit et al., 2015), are common between 2.5 to 4 years of age, and decline thereafter (Petit et al., 2007). Prevalence estimates of night terrors vary widely, but current data suggest that about 56 percent of children will experience an episode at least once (Petit et al., 2015). Some researchers have proposed night terrors are related to anxiety (Petit et al., 2007), and other studies have provided evidence for the strong role genetic influences play in their occurrence (Nguyen et al., 2008; Barclay & Gregory, 2013).

Sleepwalking and Sleeptalking

Walking and talking during sleep are fairly common in early and middle childhood. It is estimated that approximately 5 percent of children sleepwalk (Stallman & Kohler, 2016), and approximately 37 percent sleeptalk (Laberge et al., 2000).

sleepwalking Walking around and sometimes performing other functions while asleep.

sleeptalking Talking while asleep.

nightmares A bad dream, sometimes brought on by staying up too late, eating a heavy meal close to bedtime, or overexcitement.

enuresis Repeated urination in clothing or in bed.

Sleepwalking, sleeptalking, and night terrors share many characteristics. They all occur during slow wave sleep and are more common when children are sleep deprived, have a fever or are on medications, or when conditions are noisy. Moreover, during their occurrence, children are generally unresponsive to external stimulation and are confused. Some researchers have suggested that these events represent different manifestations of the same underlying disorder. There are several lines of evidence for this assertion. Sleepwalkers and people with sleep terrors tend to have family members who sleepwalk, have sleep terrors, or both. Parents who have a history of sleepwalking or sleeptalking tend to have children who have night terrors, and young children who have night terrors tend to later sleepwalk (Petit et al., 2015).

Sleepwalking and sleeptalking are generally harmless, and their frequency declines as children age. It is best not to interrupt sleepwalking or night terrors because interruptions may confuse and further frighten the child (Hoban, 2004). Rather, the child can be quietly guided back to the bedroom and tucked in to sleep.

Nightmares

Nightmares are common during early childhood (Petit et al., 2007). The occurrence of nightmares has been related to difficult child temperament, high overall childhood anxiety, and bedtime parenting practices that promote dependency (Moore, 2012). They usually occur toward morning and are often brought on by staying up too late, eating a heavy meal close to bedtime, or overexcitement (Vgontzas & Kales, 1999). Sometimes watching an action-packed

Did you know?

Sleeping less than 12 hours a day as an infant is associated with an increased risk of being overweight in preschool and childhood (Taveras, Rifas-Shiman, Oken, Gunderson, & Gillman, 2008).

©AP Images

television program, seeing a terrifying movie, or hearing a frightening bedtime story have been implicated, although results on this are inconsistent (Schredl, Anders, Hellreigel & Rehn, 2008).

An occasional bad dream is no cause for alarm, but frequent or persistent nightmares, especially those that make a child fearful or anxious during waking hours, may signal excessive stress (Kovachy et al., 2013; Hoban, 2004) and are correlated with emotional, attentional, and conduct problems (Schredl, Fricke-Oerkermann, Mitschke, Wiater & Lehmkuhl, 2009; Li et al., 2011).

BED-WETTING

Most children stay dry, day and night, by age 3 to 5, but **enuresis**, repeated, involuntary urination at night by children old enough to be expected to have bladder control, is not unusual. About 10 to 15 percent of 5-year-olds, more commonly boys, wet the bed regularly, often while sleeping deeply. More than half outgrow bed-wetting by age 8 without special help (Community Paediatrics Committee, 2005).

Preschool children normally recognize the feeling of a full bladder while asleep and awaken to empty it. Children who wet the bed do not yet have this awareness. Enuresis runs in families, suggesting that genetics may play a role. The discovery of the approximate site of a gene linked to enuresis (Eiberg, 1995; von Gontard, Heron, & Joinson, 2011) points to heredity as a major factor, possibly in combination with slow motor maturation (von Gontard, Schmelzer, Seifen, & Pukrop, 2001), sleep apnea (Umlauf & Chasens, 2003), allergies, or poor behavioral control (Goleman, 1995). About 75 percent of bed-wetters have a close relative who also wets the bed, and identical twins are more concordant (meaning, they are both likely to have the condition) than fraternal twins (American Psychiatric Association, 1994).

Children and their parents need to be reassured that enuresis is common and not serious. Treatment is most effective if delayed until the child is able to understand and follow instruction. The child is not to blame and should not be punished. Generally parents need not seek professional help unless children themselves are distressed by bed-wetting. Enuresis that persists beyond age 8 to 10 may be related to poor self-concept or other psychological problems (Community Paediatrics Committee, 2005). Enuresis that is particularly persistent is most commonly treated with an antidiuretic hormone or nighttime alarm (Walle et al., 2012).

TABLE 8.2 Gross Motor Skills in Early Childhood		
3 Year Olds	**4 Year Olds**	**5 Year Olds**
• Cannot turn or stop suddenly or quickly	• Have more effective control of stopping, starting, and turning	• Can start, turn, and stop effectively in games
• Can jump a distance of 15 to 24 inches	• Can jump a distance of 24 to 33 inches	• Can make a running jump of 28 to 36 inches
• Can ascend a stairway alternating feet, unaided	• Can descend a long stairway alternating feet, if supported	• Can descend a long stairway alternating feet, unaided
• Can hop, using largely an irregular series of jumps with some variations added	• Can hop four to six steps on one foot	• Can easily hop a distance of 16 feet

Source: Corbin, 1973.

Motor Development

Children ages 3 to 6 make great advances in motor skill developments—both **gross motor skills** such as running and jumping, which involve the large muscles (Table 8.2), and **fine motor skills**, which are manipulative skills such as buttoning and drawing that involve eye-hand and small-muscle coordination. They also begin to show a preference for using either the right or left hand.

GROSS MOTOR SKILLS AND FINE MOTOR SKILLS

At 3, Eva could walk a straight line and jump a short distance. At 4, she could hop a few steps on one foot. At 5, she could jump nearly 3 feet and hop for 16 feet, and she was learning to roller-skate.

Motor skills do not develop in isolation. The skills that emerge in early childhood build on the achievements of infancy and toddlerhood. Development of the sensory and motor areas of the cerebral cortex permits better coordination between what children want to do and what they can do. Their bones and muscles are stronger, and their lung capacity is greater, making it possible to run, jump, and climb farther, faster, and better.

gross motor skills Physical skills that involve the large muscles.

fine motor skills Physical skills that involve the small muscles and eye-hand coordination.

At about 2½, children begin to jump with both feet, a skill they have not been able to master before this time. Hopping is hard to master until about 4. Going upstairs is easier than going down; by 3½, most children comfortably alternate feet going up, but they don't easily descend that way until about age 5. Skipping is challenging; although some 4-year-olds can skip, most children cannot do it until age 6 (Corbin, 1973). Of course, children vary in adeptness, depending on their genetics and their opportunities to learn and practice motor skills.

Motor coordination in childhood tends to be a relatively stable trait over time (Vandorpe et al., 2012). The gross motor skills developed during early childhood are the basis for sports, dancing, and other activities that often begin in middle childhood. Thus, it is perhaps not surprising that motor coordination also predicts participation in sports (Vandorpe et al., 2012). Motor coordination has also been associated with both childhood and adolescent levels of physical activity (Lopes, Rodrigues, Maia & Malina, 2011; Barnett, Van Beurden, Morgan, Brooks & Beard, 2009). Moreover, poor motor coordination has been associated with an

Physical changes such as stronger muscles and bones facilitate development of new motor skills during early childhood. By age 2½, most children have mastered jumping with both feet.
©Ariel Skelley/Blend Images/Getty Images

increased risk of obesity or overweight in children in what is likely to be a reciprocal relationship (D'Hondt et al., 2013; D'Hondt et al., 2014). Interventions designed to increase motor coordination in young children have at times been shown to be an effective means of improving their motor abilities (Riethmuller, Jones & Okely, 2009). However, children under 6 are rarely ready to take part in any organized sport. If the demands of the sport exceed the child's physical and motor capabilities, this can leave the child frustrated (AAP Committee on Sports Medicine and Fitness & Committee on School Health, 2001).

Young children develop best physically when they can be active at an appropriate maturational level in unstructured free-play. Parents and teachers can help by offering young children the opportunity to climb and jump on safe, properly sized equipment, by providing balls and other toys small enough to be grasped easily and soft enough to be safe, and by offering gentle coaching when a child seems to need help.

Gains in fine motor skills, such as tying shoelaces and cutting with scissors, allow young children to take more responsibility for their personal care. At 3, Eva can pour milk into her cereal bowl, eat with silverware, and use the toilet alone. She can also draw a circle and a rudimentary person that doesn't have arms. At 4, she can dress herself with help. She can cut along a line, draw a fairly complete person, make designs and crude letters, and fold paper into a double triangle. At 5, Eva can dress herself without much help, copy a square or triangle, and draw a more elaborate person than before.

HANDEDNESS

Handedness, the preference for using one hand over the other, is usually evident by about age 3. Because the left hemisphere of the brain, which controls the right side of the body, is usually dominant, 90 percent of people favor their right side (Coren, 2012). Handedness is not always clear-cut; not everybody prefers one hand for every task. Boys are more likely to be left-handed than are girls. For every 100 left-handed girls there are 123 left-handed boys (Papadatou-Pastou, Martin, Munafo, & Jones, 2008).

handedness Preference for using a particular hand.

Is handedness genetic or environmental? The answer to this question is controversial. Some researchers argue for genetic explanations citing, for example, that left-handedness runs in families and the high heritability estimates between twins (Medland et al., 2009; Lien, Chen, Hsiao & Tsuang, 2015). Identifying the genetic mechanism has been elusive; while inheritance patterns appear to suggest single gene inheritance, the genes themselves have not been easy to find, and some evidence suggests handedness may actually be the result of many genes working together (McManus, Davison & Armour, 2013; Armour, Davison & McManus, 2014).

Other researchers have argued that the environment must be more important since a variety of factors seem to be related to increased likelihood of left-handedness. For

Improvements in fine motor skills allow children to take more responsibility for such tasks as dressing themselves, tying their shoelaces, and pouring food into a bowl.
©Image Source/AP Images

example, children who were low birth weight or who had a difficult delivery are more likely to be left-handed (Alibeik & Angaji, 2010; Domellof, Johansson & Ronnqvist, 2011). Moreover, female twins from opposite-sex twin pairs are less likely to be left-handed than female twins from same-sex twin pairs, perhaps because of the influence of the testosterone provided by an opposite-sex male twin (Vuoksimaa, Eriksson, Pulkkinen, Rose & Kaprio, 2010). As further evidence of environmental effects, children who attend schools are more likely to be right-handed than children who do not receive a formal education (Geuze et al., 2012). Both viewpoints—nature and nurture—may hold some truth.

Did you know?

If you are right-handed but break your right hand as a child, you are likely to learn how to use your left hand well and may even stay left-handed after your break heals.

©Poznyakov/Shutterstock

Health and Safety

A few weeks before starting kindergarten, Eva's mother took her to the doctor for her annual healthy child check-up and required vaccinations for starting school. While some parents in the United States worry about potential negative effects of vaccines, Eva's mother knew the benefits outweigh the low risk of complications. As the doctor immunized Eva against the major diseases of childhood, Eva's mother remembered her grandfather's shriveled leg—the result of a bout with polio

Perspectives on Diversity

©Digital Vision/Getty Images

SURVIVING THE FIRST 5 YEARS OF LIFE

In the United States, we have grown accustomed to assuming our children will have good health. A child's death is a rare event in most families. But this is not true across the world. In many countries, surviving childhood is not guaranteed, and the death of a young child is shockingly common. Still, things have improved. The chances of a child living to his or her 5th birthday have nearly tripled during the past 50 years. Worldwide, more than 17 million children under the age of 5 died in 1970. In 2015, this number dropped to 5.9 million deaths (UNICEF, 2016). Globally the under-5 mortality rate decreased 53 percent from 1990 to 2015 (WHO, 2015).

International efforts to improve child health focus on the first 5 years of life because nearly 90 percent of deaths in children under age 15 occur during those years. Worldwide, 70 percent of deaths in children under the age of 5 are attributed to seven issues: pneumonia, preterm birth complications, intrapartum complications, diarrhea, congenital abnormalities, neonatal sepsis, and malaria. Excluding birth complications, nearly 50 percent of all children's deaths were caused by communicable diseases such as pneumonia, meningitis, tetanus, diarrhea, malaria, measles, sepsis, and AIDS (UNICEF, 2016). Almost all of child deaths (98 percent) occur in the poorest regions of developing countries, where nutrition is inadequate, water is unsafe, and sanitary facilities are lacking (UNICEF, 2015).

Significant progress was made between 1990 and 2015. East Asia, the Pacific, Latin America, and the Caribbean showed a 66 percent reduction in the under-5 mortality rates. Out of the 196 countries in the world, 62 countries have reduced their under-5 mortality rate by 65 percent or more, and 74 more countries cut their under-5 mortality rate by at least 50 percent. Globally, 70 percent of the countries with available data had at least a 50 percent reduction in under-5 mortality rate (UNICEF, 2016).

The risk of a child dying by age 5 is still the highest in the sub-Saharan Africa and Southern Asian regions, which accounted for 81 percent of deaths in 2015 (WHO, 2015). Though significant progress has been made, six of the seven countries with under-5 mortality rates over 100 deaths per 1,000 births are African countries. In 2015, Angola had the highest rate of under 5 deaths worldwide at 157 deaths per 1,000 births and Somalia was the second highest with 137 deaths per 1,000 births (UNICEF, 2016).

In children under 5, boys have a significantly higher mortality rate than girls. Boys are more vulnerable to infections, respiratory distress, prematurity, and other birth complications. In China and India, where families traditionally prefer boys, this trend is reversed. Young girls have a higher risk of dying through abandonment, neglect, or infanticide (WHO, 2015). India has a 4 percent higher mortality rate for girls and China has a 33 percent higher rate.

A global effort is being made to reduce child mortality rates. With the increase of health care and home care for children around the world, great strides are being made. The biggest focus is on improved family care, nutrition supplementation, and breast-feeding practices. These approaches are accompanied by interventions for maternal health, including skilled care during pregnancy and childbirth. Other successful programs focus on vaccinations, antibiotics, and insecticide-treated bed nets (UNICEF, 2015).

---

in childhood. Because of widespread immunization, Eva would probably not have to worry about preventable diseases such polio, rubella, and mumps. In the developing world, however, many preventable diseases still take a large toll.

In the United States, advances in public health have made many of the previously common childhood illnesses, accidents, and deaths rare. However, children nonetheless continue to face risks to optimal development. Some children eat too much food and may become overweight or obese, while others suffer from malnourishment. Some children need to be careful not to consume foods they are allergic to. Oral health is also an issue; not all children practice good habits or have access to dentists. While deaths in childhood are relatively few compared with deaths in adulthood, and most childhood deaths are caused by injury rather than illness (Heron et al., 2009), some children live in risky environments that increase the chances of accidents.

OBESITY

Worldwide, an estimated 41 million children under age 5 were obese in 2015. If current trends continue, 70 million children under age 5 will be overweight or obese by 2025 (World Health Organization, 2017). Rates are rising more quickly in developing countries with less income (World Health Organization, 2017).

Obesity is a serious problem among U.S. preschoolers. In 2015–2016, almost 14 percent of 2- to 5-year-olds had a body mass index (BMI) at or above the 95th percentile for their age; this number was slightly higher in boys than girls. This number was highest in Hispanic children (25.8 percent), followed by African American (22 percent) and white children (14.1 percent), with the lowest obesity rates found in Asian American children (11 percent) (Hales, Carroll, Fryar & Ogden, 2017). Overweight was also an issue; approximately 23 percent of children aged 2 to 5 years old have a body mass index at or above the 85th percentile for their age, with findings for gender and ethnicity mirroring those for obesity (Ogden, Carroll, Kit & Flegal, 2014). Children who come from families lower on the socioeconomic ladder are more likely to be obese (Ogden, Lamb, Carroll & Flegal, 2010; Skelton, Cook, Auinger, Klein & Barlow, 2009). While prevalence rates had for a time leveled off in the United States (Ogden, Carroll, Fryar & Flegal, 2015), they once again rose last year (Hales et al., 2017).

A tendency toward obesity can be hereditary, but the main factors driving the obesity epidemic are environmental (AAP, 2004). Excessive weight gain hinges on increases in caloric intake, changes in diet composition, declining levels of physical activity and changes in the gut microbiome (Sahoo et al., 2015; Ng et al., 2014). One particularly important factor may be the availability of highly processed, energy-dense, nutrient-poor foods (Crino, Sacks, Vandevijvere, Swinburn & Neal, 2015).

Prevention of obesity in the early years, when excessive weight gain usually begins, is critical; the long-term success of treatment, especially when it is delayed, is limited (AAP Committee on Nutrition, 2003; Quattrin, Liu, Shaw, Shine & Chiang, 2005). Overweight children, especially those who have overweight parents, tend to become obese adults (Singh, Mulder, Twisk, Van Mechelen & Chinapaw, 2008) and excess body mass is a threat to health (Biro & Wien, 2010; Franks et al., 2010). Thus, early childhood is a good time to treat obesity, when a child's diet is still subject to parental influence or control (Quattrin et al., 2005). Trends toward childhood obesity can be identified as early as 6 months of age, and the earlier interventions start for at-risk children, the more likely they are to be effective (De Onis, Blossner & Borghi, 2010).

As growth slows, preschoolers need fewer calories in proportion to their weight than they did when younger. A key to preventing obesity may be to make sure older preschoolers are served appropriate portions (Rolls, Engell & Birch, 2000; Table 8.3). Children 1 or 2 years old who are at risk of being overweight or of obesity may be given reduced-fat milk

TABLE 8.3 Encouraging Healthy Eating Habits

- Parents, not children, should choose mealtimes.
- If the child is not overweight, allow him or her to decide how much to eat. Don't pressure the child to clean the plate.
- Serve portions appropriate to the child's size and age.
- Serve simple, easily identifiable foods. Preschoolers often balk at mixed dishes such as casseroles.
- Serve finger foods as often as possible.
- Introduce only one new food at a time, along with familiar food the child likes. Offer small servings of new or disliked foods; give second helpings if wanted.
- After a reasonable time, remove the food and do not serve more until the next meal. A healthy child will not suffer from missing a meal, and children need to learn that certain times are appropriate for eating.
- Give the child a choice of foods containing similar nutrients: rye or whole wheat bread, a peach or an apple, yogurt or milk.
- Serve nonfat or lowfat dairy products as sources of calcium and protein.
- Encourage a child to help prepare food; a child can help make sandwiches or mix and spoon out cookie dough.
- Limit snacking while watching television. Discourage nutrient-poor foods such as salty snacks, fried foods, ice cream, cookies, and sweetened beverages, and instead suggest nutritious snack foods, such as fruits and raw vegetables.
- Turn childish delights to advantage. Serve food in appealing dishes; dress it up with garnishes or little toys; make a party out of a meal.
- Don't fight rituals in which a child eats foods one at a time, in a certain order.
- Have regular family meals. Make mealtimes pleasant with conversation on interesting topics, keeping talk about eating itself to a minimum.

Sources: American Heart Association, S.S. Gidding, B. A. Dennison, L. L. Birch, S. R. Daniels, M. W. Gillman, E. L. Van Horn, "Dietary recommendations for children and adolescents: A guide for practitioners," *Pediatrics,* 118, no. 3 (2006), 544–559; B. J. Rolls, D. Engell & L. L. Birch, "Serving portion size influences 5-year-old but not 3-year-old children's food intake," *Journal of the American Dietetic Association,* 100 (2000), 232–234; and E. R. Williams & M. A. Caliendo, *Nutrition: Principles, Issues, and Applications.* New York: McGraw-Hill, 1984.

instead of whole milk; after age 2 they can drink fat-free milk (Daniels, Greer & the Committee on Nutrition, 2008). Too little physical activity is an important factor in obesity as well. In a longitudinal study of 8,158 U.S. children, each additional hour of watching TV more than 2 hours per day increased the likelihood of obesity at age 30 by 7 percent, presumably because each additional hour of television replaces an hour of physical activity (Viner & Cole, 2005).

Data suggest that three factors are important in the prevention of obesity: (1) regularly eating an evening meal as a family, (2) getting adequate sleep, and (3) watching less than 2 hours of television a day (Anderson & Whitaker, 2010).

What children eat is as important as how much they eat. To avoid obesity and prevent cardiac problems, young children should get only about 30 percent of their total calories from fat, and no more than one-third of fat calories should come from saturated fat. Although well-planned vegetarian diets are healthy, most children should eat lean meat and dairy foods that provide protein, iron, and calcium. Milk and other dairy products should be skim or low fat (AAP Committee on Nutrition, 2006).

UNDERNUTRITION

In 2011, approximately 101 million children were underweight and another 165 million were stunted from lack of adequate nutrients and calories. Undernutrition is an underlying cause in about a third of worldwide deaths for children under 5 (WHO, 2013). South Asia has the highest level of undernutrition; 33 percent of children under age 5 in South Asia are moderately or severely underweight as compared to 22 percent in West and Central Africa, 3 percent in Latin America and the Caribbean, and 15 percent of young children worldwide (UNICEF, 2015). Even in the United States, 18 percent of children under age 18 lived in food-insecure households in 2015 (Federal Interagency Forum on Child and Family Statistics, 2017).

Because undernourished children usually live in extremely deprived circumstances, the specific effects of poor nutrition are hard to determine. However, taken together, these deprivations may negatively affect not only growth and physical well-being but cognitive and psychosocial development as well (Martorell, Melgar, Maluccio, Stein & Rivera, 2010), and the effects may be long lasting (Liu, Raine, Venables, Dalais & Mednick, 2003). For example, in one series of longitudinal studies in Guatemala, children who were supplemented early in childhood performed better than control children in adolescence on a variety of cognitive tasks (Pollitt, Gorman, Engle, Rivera & Martorell, 1995) and in tests of physical work capacity (Martorell, 1995).

Studies suggest effects of undernutrition on growth can be lessened with improved diet (Engle et al., 2007), but the most effective treatments go beyond physical care. For example, a longitudinal study of severely undernourished Jamaican children found that an intervention in which mothers were shown how to make toys and stimulate their children's intellect resulted in significant IQ gains relative to a control group that received only medical care (Grantham-McGregor,

Powell, Walker, Chang & Fletcher, 1994). Similarly, in another study in Mauritia, 3- to 5-year-olds received nutritional supplements and medical examinations and were placed in special preschools with small classes. At age 17, these children had lower rates of antisocial behavior and mental health problems than a control group (Raine, Mellingen, Lui, Venables & Mednick, 2003).

FOOD ALLERGIES

A food allergy is an abnormal immune system response to a specific food. Reactions can range from tingling in the mouth and hives to more serious, life-threatening reactions like shortness of breath and even death. Ninety percent of food allergies can be attributed to eight foods: milk, eggs, peanuts, tree nuts, fish, soy, wheat, and shellfish (Boyce et al., 2010). Food allergies are more prevalent in children than adults, and most children will outgrow their allergies (Branum & Lukacs, 2008). In 2012, about 6 out of every 100 children suffered from some type of food allergy (Bloom, Jones & Freeman, 2013). Children who suffer from food allergies are, on average, smaller and shorter than children without food allergies (Sova et al., 2013; Flammarion et al., 2011). Additionally, while morbidity and mortality as a result of allergic reactions are generally low given most families' vigilance in monitoring food intake, there are negative psychosocial consequences to having food allergies. These include an increased risk of anxiety and depression, constraints on the types of activities that can be participated in by a family, and negative influences on school attendance and participation (Cummings, Knibb, King & Lucas, 2010).

Research on children under age 18 has demonstrated an increase in the prevalence of skin and food allergies over the past 10 years (Figure 8.2). There is no clear pattern to this increase, and it exists equally for boys and girls and across different races and ethnicities (Branum & Lukacs, 2008; Jackson, Howie & Akinbami, 2013). Children with food allergies are more likely to come from families of higher socioeconomic status (Jackson et al., 2013).

Changes in diet, how foods are processed, and decreased vitamin D based upon less exposure to the sun have all been suggested as contributors to the increase in allergy rates. A theory that society is too clean and that children's immune systems are less mature because they are not exposed to enough dirt and germs has also been explored. The link between eczema and food allergies has also led some researchers to theorize that sensitization to allergens develops through skin exposure (Lack, 2008). Additionally, better awareness by doctors and parents might factor into the reported increases. Although possible explanations abound, not enough evidence exists to pinpoint a cause.

ORAL HEALTH

Poor oral health and untreated disease can impact quality of life. Oral health is an important component of overall health. It starts in childhood with two common areas of oral health of concern to parents: thumbsucking and tooth decay.

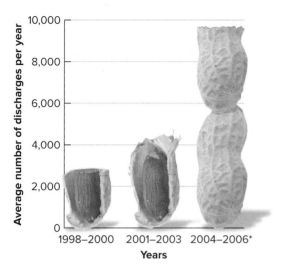

FIGURE 8.2 Food Allergy Hospitalization Trends

Average number of hospital discharges per year among children under age 18 years with any diagnosis related to food allergy: United States, 1998–2006. Recent data show diagnoses related to food allergies have increased among children birth to 17 years old.

*Statistically significant trend.

Source: Centers for Disease Control and Prevention, *National health interview survey*, Hyattsville, MD: U.S. Department of Health and Human Services, 2008.

©Keigh Leighton/Alamy

Suri Cruise with a pacifier at 4 years of age. Prolonged usage may lead to dental problems.

©PacificCoastNews/Newscom

By age 3, all the primary (baby) teeth are in place, and the permanent teeth, which will begin to appear at about age 6, are developing. Thus parents usually can safely ignore the common habit of thumbsucking in children under age 4. If children stop sucking thumbs or fingers by that age, their permanent teeth are not likely to be affected (American Dental Assocation [ADA], 2007).

Fluoride is a mineral essential for the maintenance and solidification of bones (Giri, 2016). At low levels, flouride has been shown to reduce the incidence of **dental caries,** or cavities (dos Santos, Nadanovsky & de Oliveira, 2013). Fluoride can be administered topically, via toothpaste, mouthwashes or gels; or systemically, via supplements or

dental caries Tooth decay, a cavity.

the water supply (Buzalaf & Levy, 2011). Given the low risk and high effectiveness of fluoridated toothpaste, topical administration is now generally recommended (Tubert-Jeannin et al., 2011).

Some parents avoid fluoride out of concerns about its toxicity. It is true that high levels of fluoride have been associated in some studies with lower IQ. For example, one meta-analysis of 27 epidemiological studies conducted over 22 years indicated that there was a link between high fluoride exposure and lower IQ in young children (Choi, Sun, Zhang & Grandjean, 2012). However, such studies are difficult to interpret. For instance, the data analyzed in the Choi et al. (2012) study was drawn from studies in China and Iran, and the high fluoride exposure groups had levels of fluoride far higher than is legal in any U.S. water supply.

WHAT DO YOU **DO?**

Dentist

©Karin Dreyer/ Blend Images

Dentists care for teeth and the mouth. The American Academy of Pediatric Dentistry recommends children start visiting the dentist when the first teeth appear. With young children, dentists will check to ensure teeth are coming in as expected and there are no cavities or problems. One reason for early visits to the dentist is to get children comfortable with the experience. Most dental students complete a nonspecific undergraduate degree that focuses on biology, science, and anatomy before pursuing a four-year dental program. Dentists work in shared or private practices. To learn more about dentistry, visit www.aapd.org.

Moreover, the fluoride in the samples was generally naturally occurring and was more typical of rural than urban areas. Urban areas tend to have water treatment plants that *reduce* fluoride levels in water supplies (along with other potentially harmful substances as well). Given the general finding that children from urban areas score higher on IQ tests than children from rural areas, this provides an alternative explanation for such a finding. Thus, this and other similar findings may be a result of methodological confounds. Moreover, other research on fluoride has shown that low levels of fluoride do not result in IQ declines (Broadbent et al., 2015).

Tooth decay in early childhood often stems from overconsumption of sweetened milk and juices in infancy together with a lack of regular dental care. Some of the worst effects have been found in children who take bottles to bed with them and bathe their teeth in sugar over the course of an afternoon or evening (AAP, 2009. Though decay in primary teeth has declined overall from the early 1970s, there has been a slight reverse in this trend since the mid-1990s (Centers for Disease Control and Prevention [CDC], 2007b). Disadvantaged children still have more untreated cavities than other children (Bloom, Cohen, Vickerie & Wondimu, 2003).

ACCIDENTAL INJURIES AND DEATHS

While Eva was generally a compliant child, one day when her mother was in the other room, she danced and jumped on the couch and fell to the floor. The impact of the fall broke a bone in her upper arm.

Young children are naturally venturesome and often are unaware of danger. Although most cuts, bumps, and scrapes are "kissed away" and quickly forgotten, some accidental injuries result in lasting damage or death. Worldwide, estimates are that approximately 5.9 million children under the age of 5 died in 2015 (You, Hug, Ejdemyr & Beise, 2015), a 53 percent decrease from 1990 (World Health Organization, 2015). Most child deaths are the result of infectious disease or neonatal complications; however, more than 830,000 children die each year from burns, drowning, car crashes, falls, poisonings, and other accidents (World Health Organization, 2008). Almost all of child deaths (98 percent) occur in the poorest regions of developing countries, where nutrition is inadequate, water is unsafe, and sanitary facilities are lacking (UNICEF, 2015).

In the United States, deaths in childhood are relatively few compared with deaths in adulthood, and accidents are the leading cause of death in the United States for children from the ages of 5 to 12 years of age (Kochanek, Murphy, Xu & Tejada-Vera, 2016). All 50 states and the District of Columbia require young children to ride in specially designed car seats or wear seat belts. Recommendations are that 4-year-olds should use forward-facing car seats with a harness until they reach the top weight or height limit for their seat. After that, belt-positioning booster seats should be used until children are big enough to fit a seat belt properly, with the lap belt across their thighs and

Car seats can significantly reduce the risk of injury in a car accident.
©moodboard/Corbis

the shoulder belt snug against the shoulder and chest. Airbags are designed to protect adults, not children. They have been shown to increase the risk of fatal injury to children under age 13 who are riding in the front seat. Campaigns to keep children in the back seats of cars have reduced the number of child deaths in motor vehicle crashes by 200 a year from 1996 to 2003 (Glassbrenner, Carra & Nichols, 2005). However, car accidents continue to be the leading cause of death for children 4 years of age and older (Durbin, 2011).

Most deaths from injuries, especially among preschoolers, occur in the home—from fires, drowning in bathtubs, suffocation, poisoning, or falls (Nagaraja et al., 2005). Everyday medications, such as aspirin, acetaminophen, cold

Did you know?

Hollywood is wrong—drowning children don't call for help, noisily splashing and kicking in the water. Rather, they are silent and glassy eyed, and anytime their mouth comes up above the surface of the water, they are busy breathing, not calling for help.

©Moment Open/Getty Images

and cough preparations, and even vitamins can be dangerous to inquisitive young children. From 2001 to 2003, more than 50,000 children age 4 and under were treated each year in U.S. hospital emergency departments for unintentional exposure to prescription and over-the-counter medicines (Burt, Annest, Ballesteros & Budnitz, 2006).

U.S. laws requiring childproof caps on medicine bottles and other dangerous household products, regulation of product safety, car seats for young children, mandatory helmets for bicycle riders, and safe storage of firearms and of medicines have improved child safety. Table 8.4 summarizes suggestions for reducing accident risks in various settings.

ENVIRONMENTAL INFLUENCES ON HEALTH

Why do some children have more illnesses or injuries than others? Genetic heritage contributes: Some children seem predisposed toward some medical conditions. However, environmental factors, including socioeconomic status, race and ethnicity, homelessness, and exposure to pollutants, play major roles.

Socioeconomic Status

The lower a family's socioeconomic status, the greater a child's risks of illness, injury, and death (Braveman, Cubbin, Egerter, Williams & Pamuk, 2010; Olson, Diekema, Elliott & Renier, 2010). Poor children are more likely than other children to have chronic conditions and activity limitations, to lack health insurance, and to have unmet medical and dental needs. Children living in poverty—21 percent of children under the age of 6 and disproportionately minority children—are more likely than other children to have chronic conditions and activity limitations, to lack health insurance, and to have unmet medical and dental needs (Federal Interagency Forum on Child and Family Statistics, 2017).

Medicaid, a government program that provides medical assistance to eligible low-income persons and families,

TABLE 8.4 Reducing Accident Risks for Children

Activity	Precautions
Bicycling	Helmets reduce risk of head injury by 85 percent and brain injury by 88 percent.
Skateboarding and rollerblading	Children should wear helmets and protective padding on knees, elbows, and wrists.
Using fireworks	Families should not purchase fireworks for home use.
Lawn mowing	Children under 12 should not operate walk-behind mowers; those under 14 should not operate ride-on mowers; small children should not be close to a moving mower.
Swimming	Swimming pools should not be installed in backyards of homes with children under 5; pools already in place need a high fence all around, with gates having high, out-of-reach, self-closing latches. Adults need to watch children very closely near pools, lakes, and other bodies of water.
Playing on a playground	A safe surface under swings, slides, and other equipment can be 10-inch-deep sand, 12-inch-deep wood chips, or rubber outdoor mats; separate areas should be maintained for active play and quiet play, for older and younger children.
Using firearms	Guns should be kept unloaded and locked up, with bullets locked in a separate place; children should not have access to keys; adults should talk with children about the risks of gun injury.
Eating	To prevent choking, young children should not eat hard candies, nuts, grapes, and hot dogs (unless sliced lengthwise, then across); food should be cut into small pieces; children should not eat while talking, running, jumping, or lying down.
Ingesting toxic substances	Only drugs and toxic household products with safety caps should be used; toxic products should be stored out of children's reach. Suspected poisoning should be reported immediately to the nearest poison control center.
Riding in motor vehicles	Young children should sit in approved car seats, in the back seat. Adults should observe traffic laws and avoid aggressive drivers.

Source: Adapted in part from American Academy of Pediatrics, *Injury violence and poison prevention* (2018), retrieved from https://www.aap.org/en-us/advocacy-and-policy/aap-health-initiatives/Injury-Violence-Poison-Prevention/Pages/default.aspx; F. Rivera, "Pediatric injury control in 1999. Where do we go from here?" *Pediatrics*, 103, no. 4 (1999), 883–888; and M. Shannon, "Ingestion of toxic substances by children," *New England Journal of Medicine*, 342 (2000), 186-191.

©Michael N. Paras/agefotostock

has been a safety net for many poor children since 1965. However, it had not reached millions of children whose families earned too much to qualify but too little to afford private insurance. In 1993, 14 percent of children did not have health insurance (Federal Interagency Forum on Child and Family Statistics, 2017). In 1997 the federal government created the State Children's Health Insurance Program (SCHIP) to help states extend health care coverage to uninsured children in poor and near-poor families. Legislation passed in 2009 expanded the program and extended the coverage from 7 million to 11 million children (Centers for Medicare and Medicaid Services, 2009). Even with that expansion, there were about 9 million uninsured children in the United States (Devoe, Ray, Krois & Carlson, 2010). The passage of the Affordable Care Act of 2010 reduced this number. Among the provisions were the expansion of benefits to many previously ineligible poor families, elimination of pre-existing condition coverage exclusions, oral and vision coverage for children, and initiatives to prevent and address childhood obesity. In 2015, the number of uninsured children dropped to 4.5 percent, a historic low (Federal Interagency Forum on Child and Family Statistics, 2017). In December of 2017, the passage of President Trump's Tax Cuts and Jobs Act of 2017 repealed the individual mandate—the requirement that all Americans carry a minimum level of health insurance or face a fee. The repeal of the individual mandate took effect in 2018. While the effects of the repeal remain to be seen, the non-partisan Congressional Budget Office (2017) estimates that this will result in 4 million more uninsured people by 2019, and 13 million more uninsured people by 2027.

Race/Ethnicity

Access to quality health care is a particular problem among black and Latino children, especially those who are poor (Flores, 2010). According to the Children's Legal Defense Fund (2014), 1 in 7 Latino children and 1 in 11 black children are uninsured compared with a rate of 1 in 15 for white children. Language and cultural barriers and the need for more Latino care providers may help explain some of these disparities (Betancourt, Green, Carrillo & Ananeh-Firempong, 2016). Even Asian American children, who tend to be in better health than non-Hispanic white children, are less likely to access and use health care, perhaps because of similar barriers (National Center for Health Statistics, 2017; NCHS, 2005; Yu, Huang & Singh, 2004).

Homelessness

Homelessness results from circumstances that force people to choose between food, shelter, and other basic needs. Since the 1980s, as affordable rental housing has become scarce and poverty has spread, homelessness has increased dramatically in the United States. Factors that contribute to homelessness include lack of employment opportunities, declines in public assistance funds, lack of affordable health care, domestic violence, mental illness, and addiction (National

Years	Number of homeless children
2013	2,484,000
2010	1,610,000
2006	1,555,000

Number of homeless children

FIGURE 8.3 Number of Homeless Children. 2006–2013

The number of U.S. homeless children has increased significantly in recent years, from about 1 in 50 children in 2006 to 1 in 30 children in 2013.

Source: Data from E. L. Bassuk, C. Murphy, N. T. Coupe, R. R. Kenney & C. A. Beach, America's youngest outcasts 2010: State report card on child homelessness. *The National Center on Family Homelessness.* 2011. Retrieved from www.homelesschildrenamerica.org/media/NCFH_AmericaOutcast2010_web.pdf

©Africa Studio/Shutterstock

Coalition for the Homeless, 2017). In 2011, there were an estimated 1.6 million homeless children in the United States (Bassuk, Murphy, Coupe, Kenney & Beach, 2011). This number increased to 2.5 million by 2014 (America's Youngest Outcasts, 2014).

Families now make up roughly 31 percent of the homeless population on any given night, and the proportion is higher in rural areas (Henry, Cortes & Morris, 2013). While the overall economy of the United States has improved, the benefits have not reached the very poor, and the number of homeless children has increased to about 1 in every 30 children (Figure 8.3 America's Youngest Outcasts, 2014). Many homeless families are headed by single mothers in their twenties (Park, Metraux & Culhane, 2010). Often these families are fleeing domestic violence (National Coalition for the Homeless, 2018).

Many homeless children spend their crucial early years in unstable, insecure, and often unsanitary environments. They and their parents may be cut off from a supportive community, family and institutional resources, and from ready access to medical care and schooling. These children suffer more physical health problems than poor children who have homes, and they are more likely to have a low birth weight or need neonatal care in infancy. Homeless children also tend to suffer from depression and anxiety and to have academic and behavior problems (Hwang et al., 2010; Bassuk, Richard & Tsertvadze, 2015; Herbers et al., 2012; Richards, Merrill & Baksh, 2011). More research is needed on evidence-based interventions to tackle the multitude of risk factors that homeless children are exposed to (Zlotnick, Tam & Zerger, 2012).

Exposure to Smoking, Air Pollution, Pesticides, and Lead

Smoking is bad for everyone; however, children, with their still-developing lungs and faster rate of respiration, are particularly sensitive to the damaging effects of exposure (Constant et al., 2011). Parental smoking is a preventable cause

Exposure to parental smoke harms a child's still-developing lungs and increases risk for a variety of respiratory problems.

©Frédéric Cirou/AP Images

of childhood illness and death. The potential damage caused by exposure to tobacco smoke is greatest during the early years of life (DiFranza, Aligne & Weitzman, 2004). Children exposed to parental smoke are at increased risk of respiratory infections such as bronchitis and pneumonia, ear problems, worsened asthma, and slowed lung growth. From 1988 to 1994, about 85 percent of children between the ages of 4 and 11 showed evidence of exposure to second-hand smoke. From 2011 to 2012, this number dropped to 40 percent (Federal Interagency Forum on Child and Family Statistics, 2017).

Air pollution is associated with increased risks of death and of chronic respiratory disease. Environmental contaminants also may play a role in certain childhood cancers, neurological disorders, attention-deficit/hyperactivity disorder, and mental retardation (Woodruff et al., 2004). In 2015, 59 percent of U.S. children lived in counties that failed to meet one or more national air quality standards (Federal Interagency Forum on Child and Family Statistics, 2017).

Children are more vulnerable than adults to chronic pesticide damage (Federal Interagency Forum on Child and Family Statistics, 2017). There is some, evidence that low-dose pesticide exposure may affect the developing brain (Jurewicz & Hanke, 2008). Pesticide exposure is greater in children in agricultural and inner-city families (Dilworth-Bart & Moore, 2006). More than half of all reported pesticide poisonings—almost 50,000 per year—occur in children younger than age 6 (Weiss et al., 2004).

Children can get elevated concentrations of lead from lead-contaminated food or water, from airborne industrial wastes, from putting contaminated fingers in their mouths, or from inhaling dust or playing with paint chips in homes or schools where there is lead-based paint. Lead poisoning can seriously interfere with cognitive development and can lead to neurological and behavioral problems (AAP Committee on Environmental Health, 2005; Federal Interagency Forum on Child and Family Statistics, 2017). Very high levels of blood lead concentration may cause headaches, abdominal pain, loss of appetite, agitation, or lethargy, and eventually vomiting, stupor, and convulsions (AAP Committee on Environmental Health, 2005).

Children's median blood lead levels dropped by 89 percent in the United States from 1976 to 2002 due to laws mandating removal of lead from gasoline and paints and reducing smokestack emissions (Federal Interagency Forum on Child and Family Statistics, 2005). The number of children with elevated levels of lead in their blood has declined, from about 25 percent in 1994 to 1.2 percent in 2014; still, many children are at risk due to lead in dust, paint chips, and other sources, and rates of elevated lead levels are highest among non-Hispanic blacks and children living in poverty (Federal Interagency Forum for Child and Family Statistics, 2017).

mastering the CHAPTER

©Vicky Kasala/Getty Images

Summary and Key Terms

Physical Growth

> Physical growth continues during the years from 3 to 6, but more slowly than before. Boys are slightly taller, heavier, and more muscular than girls. Internal body systems are maturing.

> By age 6, the brain has attained about 90 percent of its peak volume. A gradual change in the corpus

callosum permits more rapid transmission of information and better integration between brain hemispheres.

> From ages 3 to 6, the most rapid brain growth occurs in the frontal areas that regulate the planning and goal setting.

Sleep

> Sleep patterns change during early childhood. It is normal for preschool children to develop bedtime rituals that delay going to sleep.

> Occasional sleepwalking, sleeptalking, nightmares, and night terrors are common, but prolonged bedtime

struggles or persistent sleep problems may indicate excessive stress.

> Bed-wetting is common and is usually outgrown without special help.

KEY TERMS

Night terrors	Sleeptalking	Enuresis
Sleepwalking	Nightmares	

Motor Development

> Children progress rapidly in gross and fine motor skills, developing more complex systems of action.

> Handedness is usually evident by age 3, reflecting dominance by one hemisphere of the brain.

KEY TERMS

Gross motor skills	Fine motor skills	Handedness

Health and Safety

> Although major contagious illnesses are rare today in industrialized countries, preventable disease continues to be a major problem in the developing world.

> Preschool children generally eat less, and need less, in proportion to their weight than they did when younger. The prevalence of obesity has increased among preschoolers; the tendency toward obesity can be hereditary, but environmental factors drive the obesity epidemic. Factors important in obesity

prevention include eating an evening meal as a family, getting adequate sleep, and limiting television viewing.

> Undernutrition can affect all aspects of development. Although undernutrition is more common in developing countries, many U.S. children live in food-insecure households.

> Food and skin allergies are becoming increasingly common among children, but most children will outgrow their allergies.

- Tooth decay has decreased since the 1970s but remains a problem among disadvantaged children. Overconsumption of sweet beverages and lack of regular dental care are risk factors.

- Thumbsucking can safely be ignored unless it continues beyond age 4, when permanent teeth begin to develop.

- Accidents, most commonly motor vehicle injuries, are the leading cause of death in childhood in the United States.

- Environmental factors such as living in poverty, lack of access to quality health care, homelessness, parental smoking, air pollution, and pesticides increase the risks of illness or injury. Lead poisoning can have serious physical, cognitive, and behavioral effects.

KEY TERMS

Dental caries

Practice Quiz

1. Between the ages of 3 to 6 years, children's growth:
   a. speeds up relative to growth in infancy and toddlerhood
   b. continues, but slows relative to growth in infancy and toddlerhood
   c. slows down dramatically until puberty
   d. may slow down or speed up, depending on the individual child

2. What are three bodily changes that occur in early childhood?
   _____
   _____
   _____

3. The most rapid brain growth from ages 3 to 6 is in:
   a. the corpus callosum
   b. the brain stem
   c. motor areas of the brain
   d. the frontal lobes

4. Which of the following is abnormal in young children and cause for medical or behavioral intervention?
   a. attempts to delay bedtime
   b. enuresis (wetting the bed)
   c. night terrors
   d. nightmares
   e. all of the above are normal

5. Enuresis runs in families, and identical twins are more likely to be concordant for this behavior than fraternal twins. This suggests that:
   a. parents are probably responsible for it because of poor parenting practices
   b. punishment is an appropriate means by which to address bed-wetting
   c. there are likely to be genetic factors that contribute to enuresis
   d. bed alarms are likely to be ineffective

6. An example of a gross motor skill is _____, and an example of a fine motor skill is _____.

7. Being left-handed is more common in:
   a. boys
   b. girls
   c. neither

8. List two variables related to risk of overweight or obesity in children.
   _____
   _____

9. Children who are undernourished are likely to:
   a. do poorly on arithmetic tests
   b. repeat a grade
   c. be very shy
   d. have difficulty getting along with other children

10. Which of the following is theorized to be a contributing variable to food allergies?
    a. age
    b. changes in the modern diet
    c. "too clean" environments
    d. all of the above

11. Which of the following is likely to have the worst oral health?
    a. a 3 year old who sucks her thumb frequently
    b. a 2 year old who takes a bottle of juice to bed nightly
    c. a 5 year old who brushes daily but does not floss
    d. a 4 year old who receives fluoride through his water supply

12. When riding in a car, young children:
    a. need to use a seat belt, but no other precautions are necessary
    b. should use a car or booster seat
    c. should not sit in the front seat
    d. b and c

13. What are three reasons children of lower socioeconomic status might have worse health than those of higher socioeconomic status?
    _____
    _____
    _____

14. Homeless families are more likely to be from _____ areas and to be headed by _____.
    a. rural; two-parent families
    b. rural; single mothers
    c. urban; two-parent families
    d. urban; single mothers

15. Damage from tobacco exposure is _____ during the early years of life.
    a. worse
    b. unlikely to result in long-lasting damage
    c. rare
    d. illegal

©Mint Images Limited/Alamy

A young researcher sat across from 6-year-old Schi. "What is memory?" he asked him, pen in hand ready to take notes on the child's response. Schi glanced up at the scientist, "When you remember something," he stated simply. "But how do you remember?" the researcher pressed. "Well," the little boy answered, "It suddenly comes into the mind. When you've been told something, it comes into your mind, then it goes out and then it comes back . . . into the sky."

While most people would smile at such flights of fancy and move on, the young researcher interviewing Schi was none other than Jean Piaget. Piaget would use Schi's interviews, as well as those of other children of varying ages, to help him develop his theories of cognitive development. Through Piaget's brilliant musings and careful analysis of children's behavior, the seeds of both the cognitive revolution and developmental psychology as a field were planted.

Piaget was one among a number of researchers who have advanced our knowledge of children's cognition. While he focused on children's logical errors, others have focused on their information-processing capacities, how to measure their intelligence, what social factors help them learn, their use of language, and how all these factors can be used to design and implement quality early childhood education.

In this chapter, we examine Piaget's theoretical approach of cognitive development in early childhood. We will see how children's thinking advances after toddlerhood and in what ways it remains immature. We also consider Vygotsky, a contemporary of Piaget's, as well as the modern extensions of their early work. We examine the beginnings of autobiographical memory, and we compare psychometric intelligence tests with assessments based on Vygotsky's theories. We look at children's increasing fluency with language and how this impacts other domains of development. Finally, we look at the widening world of preschool and kindergarten.

• • • •

Piagetian Approach: The Preoperational Child

Jean Piaget called early childhood the **preoperational stage** of cognitive development because children of this age are not ready to engage in logical mental operations. This period is characterized by a great expansion in the use of symbolic thought, or representational ability, which first emerges near the end of the sensorimotor stage, and is most notably illustrated by the growth of language abilities. In this section we look at advances and immature aspects of preoperational thought as well as the development of theory of mind.

ADVANCES OF PREOPERATIONAL THOUGHT

As children's cognitive development proceeds, they begin to think in fundamentally different ways. Young children are grounded in the concrete here-and-now, according to Piaget, and the fundamental achievements in cognitive ability stem from advances in symbolic thought. These advances are accompanied by a growing understanding that was previously impossible of objects in space, causality, identities and categorization, and number.

The Symbolic Function

"I want ice cream!" announces Lila, age 4, trudging indoors from the hot, dusty backyard. She has not seen anything that triggered this desire—no open freezer door, no television commercial. She no longer needs a sensory cue to think about something—she can remember ice cream and she purposefully seeks it out. This is an illustration of the **symbolic function**, the ability to use symbols, or mental representations. For example, language is a symbolic representational system. The word *key* is a symbol for the object that we use to open doors. Without symbols, people could not communicate verbally, make change, read maps, or treasure photos of distant loved ones.

Preschool children show the symbolic function through deferred imitation, pretend play, and language. Deferred imitation, which becomes more common after 18 months, is based on having kept a mental representation of an observed action—as when 3-year-old Bart scolds his little sister, using the same words he heard his father say to the delivery boy who was late bringing the pizza. In **pretend play**, also called fantasy play, dramatic play, or imaginary play, children may make an object, such as a doll, represent, or symbolize, something else, such as a person. For example, a child may hold up a remote control to her ear while pretending to talk on a cell phone. Language is also symbolic; words stand for objects and concepts in our world. When we see the emergence of language in young children, we have a wide and clear window into their increasing use of symbolic function.

Objects Space

Another ability related to the development of symbolic function is representations of the world. Most children do not reliably grasp the relationships between pictures, maps, or scale models and the larger or smaller objects or spaces they represent until at least age 3. Older preschoolers can use simple maps, and they can transfer the spatial understanding gained from working with models to maps and vice versa. So, for example, older preschoolers can view a scale model

preoperational stage In Piaget's theory, the second major stage of cognitive development in which children become more sophisticated in their use of symbolic thought but are not yet able to use logic.

symbolic function Piaget's term for ability to use mental representations (words, numbers, or images) to which a child has attached meaning.

pretend play Play involving imaginary people or situations; also called fantasy play, dramatic play, or imaginary play.

of a room, be shown on that model where a toy is hidden, and then find the toy in the actual room (DeLoache, 2011).

Causality

Piaget maintained that preoperational children cannot yet reason logically about cause and effect. Instead, he said, they reason by **transduction**. They mentally link two events close in time, whether or not there is logically a causal relationship. For example, Luis may think that his "bad" thoughts or behavior caused his own or his sister's illness or his parents' divorce.

Piaget was incorrect in believing that young children could not understand causality. When tested in situations that are appropriate to their overall level of cognitive development, young children do grasp cause and effect. For example, naturalistic observations of 2½- to 5-year-olds' everyday language showed flexible causal reasoning. Children listed both physical ("The scissors have to be clean so I can cut better") and social-conventional ("I have to stop now because you said to") causes for their actions (Hickling & Wellman, 2001). Research has also supported their ability to engage in causal reasoning. In one study, children were shown two small lights and one large light. Pressing on one of the small lights, which was attached to the large light by a wire, caused the large light to illuminate. Four-year-old children were able to understand that a relevant change (switching the wire connection to the other small light) would alter the causal sequence, but an irrelevant change (moving a block near the light) would not (Buchanan & Sobel, 2011). By the age of 4, most children are able to understand that observed events have a cause, and may in fact have more than one cause. They are also able to revise their opinion about a cause if new evidence emerges that suggests they might be wrong, and understand that even if a cause is not immediately apparent or present, it still may be a good explanation for an event (Fernbach, Macris & Sobel, 2012).

transduction In Piaget's terminology, preoperational child's tendency to mentally link particular experiences, whether or not there is logically a causal relationship.

animism Tendency to attribute life to objects that are not alive.

Identities and Categorization

Preschool children also develop a better understanding of *identities:* the concept that people and many things are fundamentally the same even if they change in outward form, size, or appearance. For example, putting on a wig does not make a person a different person; rather, it is just a surface change in appearance. This understanding underlies the emerging self-concept, and many of the processes involved in understanding the identity of others are mirrored in the understanding of one's own identity.

Categorization, or classification, requires a child to identify similarities and differences between classes of objects. By age 4, many children can classify by two criteria, such as color and shape. Children use this ability to order many aspects of their lives, categorizing people as "good" or "bad," "nice" or "mean," and so forth.

One type of categorization is the ability to distinguish living from nonliving things. When Piaget asked young children whether the wind and the clouds were alive, their answers led him to think they were confused. The tendency to attribute life to objects that are not alive is called **animism**. However, when later researchers questioned 3- and 4-year-olds about something more familiar to them—differences between a rock, a person, and a doll—the children showed they understood that people are alive and rocks and dolls are not (Gelman, Spelke & Meck, 1983; Jipson & Gelman, 2007). In general, it appears that children attribute animism to items that share characteristics with living things: things that move, make sounds, or have lifelike features such as eyes (Opfer & Gelman, 2011). For example, after watching a robot stack a pile of blocks, children were likely to attribute cognitive, behavioral, and especially affective characteristics to a robot (Beran, Ramirez-Serrano, Kuzyk, Fior & Nugent, 2011).

Number

Multiple lines of research have shown that infants have a rudimentary sense of number. Research suggests that infants as young as 4½ months indicate, with longer looking times and increased staring, that if one doll is added to another doll, there should be two dolls, not just one. By 6 months of age they can "count" higher and know that 8 dots are different from 16 dots (Libertus & Brannon, 2010). Other research has found that ordinality—the concept of comparing quantities (more or less, bigger or smaller)—seems to begin around 9 to 11 months (Suanda, Tompson & Brannon, 2008).

The cardinality principle, where children understand that the number of items in a set is the same regardless of how they are arranged, and that the last number counted is the total number of items in the set regardless of how they are counted, starts to develop at about 2½ years of age. However, this ability is based in practical situations, such as checking to see which one of two plates has more cookies in it (Gelman, 2006). When asked to count six items, children younger than 3½ tend to recite the number-names (one through six) but not to say how many total items there are (six). Most children do not consistently apply the cardinality principle in counting until age 3½ or older (Sarnecka & Carey, 2007).

By age 4, most children can say one tree is bigger than another or one cup holds more juice than another. If they have one cookie and then get another, they know they have more cookies than they had before. By age 5, most children can count to 20 or more and know the relative sizes of the numbers 1 through 10 (Siegler, 1998). By the time they enter elementary school, most children have developed basic "number sense" (Jordan, Kaplan, Oláh, & Locunia, 2006). This basic level of number skills (Table 9.1) includes counting, number knowledge (ordinality), number transformations (simple addition and subtraction), estimation ("Is this group of dots more or less than 5?"), and recognition of number patterns (2 plus 2 equals 4, and so does 3 plus 1).

Socioeconomic status (SES) and preschool experience affect how rapidly children advance in math. By age 4,

TABLE 9.1 Key Elements of Number Sense in Young Children

Area	Components
Counting	• Grasping one-to-one correspondence • Knowing stable order and cardinality principles • Knowing the count sequence
Number knowledge	• Discriminating and coordinating quantities • Making numerical magnitude comparisons
Number transformation	• Simple addition and subtraction • Calculating in story problems and nonverbal contexts • Calculating "in the head"
Estimation	• Approximating or estimating set sizes • Using reference points
Number patterns	• Copying number patterns • Extending number patterns • Discerning numerical relationships

Source: Adapted from N. C. Jordan, D. Kaplan, L. N. Olah & M. N. Locunia, "Number sense growth in kindergarten: A longitudinal investigation of children at risk for mathematics difficulties," *Child Development*, 77 (2006), 153–175.

©BananaStock/PunchStock

children from middle-income families have markedly better number skills than children from lower-income families, and their initial advantage tends to continue. Children whose preschool teachers do a lot of "math talk," such as asking children to help count days on a calendar, tend to make greater gains than children whose teachers do not use this technique (Klibanoff, Levine, Huttenlocher, Vasilyeva, & Hedges, 2006). Finally, playing number board games with children enhances their numerical knowledge, especially if they are from low SES backgrounds (Siegler, 2009). Numerical competence is important; how well children understand numbers in kindergarten predicts their academic performance in math through third grade (Jordan, Glutting & Ramineni, 2010) and deficient number sense has been associated with mathematical learning disabilities (Mazzocco, Feigenson & Halberda, 2011).

PREOPERATIONAL THOUGHT

According to Piaget, one of the main characteristics of pre-operational thought is **centration**, the tendency to focus on one aspect of a situation and neglect others—for example, noting the height of a glass of juice but not the width. This is an immature area of preoperational thought for children age 3 to 5. Piaget argued that preschoolers come to illogical conclusions because they cannot **decenter**—that is, focus on more than one aspect of a situation at one time. Two forms of centration are egocentrism and conservation.

Egocentrism

Egocentrism is the inability to consider another person's point of view. According to Piaget, young children center so much on their own point of view they cannot take in another's. Egocentrism may help explain why young children

sometimes have trouble separating reality from what goes on inside their heads and why they may show confusion about what causes what. When Emily believes her "bad thoughts" have made her brother sick or that she caused her parents' marital troubles, she is thinking egocentrically.

To study egocentrism, Piaget designed the three-mountain task (Figure 9.1). A child sits facing a table that holds three large mounds. A doll is placed on a chair at the opposite side of the table. The investigator asks the child how the mountains would look from the doll's vantage point. Piaget found that young children usually described the mountains from their own perspective and could not take a point of view different from their own (Piaget & Inhelder, 1967).

However, when children are asked to describe others' view in a more simple and familiar way, their performance improves. In one study, a child was instructed to select one object from a set of objects by an experimenter who could only see some of the objects. The researchers found that children as young as 3 were able to take the experimenter's perspective. For example, two of the objects were rubber ducks—one small and one large. In one condition, the experimenter could only see one of the rubber ducks. When the child heard the instructions to retrieve the rubber duck, the child more often selected the rubber duck that the experimenter could see, even though the child could see both rubber ducks (Nilsen & Graham, 2009).

centration In Piaget's theory, tendency of preoperational children to focus on one aspect of a situation and neglect others.

decenter In Piaget's terminology, to think simultaneously about several aspects of a situation.

egocentrism Piaget's term for an inability to consider another person's point of view; a characteristic of young children's thought.

FIGURE 9.1 Piaget's Three Mountains Task

A preoperational child is unable to describe the mountains from the doll's point of view—an indication of egocentrism, according to Piaget.

Why were these children able to take another person's point of view when those doing the mountain task were not? Most children do not look at mountains and do not think about what other people might see when looking at one, but most preschoolers know something about hiding. Thus young children may show egocentrism primarily in situations beyond their immediate experience.

Conservation

A classic example of centration is the failure to understand **conservation**, the fact that two equal things remain so if their appearance is altered, so long as nothing is added or taken away. In Piaget's classic conservation of liquid task, a child is shown two identical clear glasses, each short and wide and each holding the same amount of water. The child is then asked, "Is the amount of water in the two glasses the same?" When the child agrees, the researcher pours the water in one glass into a tall, thin third glass. Then, the child is asked, "Do both glasses contain the same amount of water? Or does one contain more? Why?" In early childhood—even after watching the water being poured out of one of the short, fat glasses into a tall, thin glass or even after pouring it himself—children will say either the taller glass or the wider one contains more water. When asked why, they tend to say the glass is taller or wider, taking into account only one of the relevant dimensions. Why do children make this error? Their responses are influenced by two immature aspects of thought: centration and **irreversibility**. Centration involves focusing on one dimension while ignoring the other. Preoperational children cannot consider height and width at the same time because they cannot decenter, or consider multiple attributes of an object or situation. In addition, children are limited by irreversibility: failure to mentally reverse an action.

conservation Piaget's term for awareness that two objects that are equal according to a certain measure remain equal in the face of perceptual alteration so long as nothing has been added to or taken away from either object.

irreversibility Piaget's term for a preoperational child's failure to understand that an operation can go in two or more directions.

theory of mind Awareness and understanding of mental processes of others.

Because their thinking is concrete, preoperational children cannot realize that the original state of the water can be restored by pouring it back into the other glass, and thus it must be the same. Preoperational children commonly think as if they were watching a slide show with a series of static frames: They focus on successive states, said Piaget, and do not recognize the transformation from one state to another.

THEORY OF MIND

Amalia, age 4, hates brussels sprouts, but when her father asks for them to be passed at the dinner table, she places the bowl in her father's hands. She now understands her father might like brussels sprouts, even though she herself finds them highly suspect. In understanding this, Amalia is illustrating her emerging understanding of others' mental states.

Piaget (1929) was interested in this growing ability, and to investigate it he asked children such questions as "Where do dreams come from?" and "What do you think with?" On the basis of the answers, he concluded that children younger than 6 cannot distinguish between thoughts or dreams and real physical entities. However, more recent research indicates that between ages 2 and 5, children's knowledge about mental processes and their ability to distinguish between mental states and reality grows dramatically. For example, at 2 years of age children readily engage in pretend play. At 3 years of age they can use deception in simple games and predict others' actions on the basis of their desires. And at 4 to 5 years of age they understand that a person can believe something that they themselves know is not true (Frye, 2014). Let's take a closer look at the development of theory of mind.

Theory of mind is the understanding that others have their own thoughts, beliefs, desires, and intentions. Having a theory of mind allows us to understand and predict others' behavior and makes the social world understandable. Different people may have different theories of mind depending upon social experiences. Theory of mind includes knowledge of thinking about mental states, false beliefs, and distinguishing between fantasy and reality.

Knowledge about Thinking and Mental States

Between ages 3 and 5, children come to understand that thinking goes on inside the mind; that it can deal with either

Conservation of liquid.
©Marmaduke St. John/Alamy

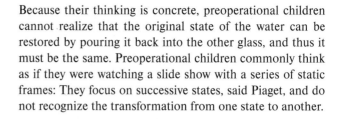

Did you know?

We can best see the complexity and importance of theory of mind by looking at what happens when it does not work well. One fundamental deficit in children with autism is the failure to develop an adequate theory of mind. Without it, children with autism are adrift in a sea of social confusion.

©Jirus Malawong/Shutterstock

real or imaginary things, and that thinking is different from seeing, talking, touching, and knowing (Flavell, 2000). They understand that thinking about the past or the future might make someone feel sad or happy (Lagatutta, 2014). They start to expect people to act in accordance with their beliefs, and when asked to explain people's behavior they use words like *want* or *think*. They also know that people's expressions might not necessarily match their internal state (Wellman, 2014) and realize that you can manipulate others' mental states to deceive or tease them (Miller, 2009). By 5 years of age, they understand that if they are sad about something, they can try to think about something else or decide they don't want something anymore to feel better (Davis, Levine, Lench & Quas, 2010).

However, preschoolers generally believe that mental activity starts and stops. Preschoolers also have little or no awareness that they or other people think in words, or "talk to themselves in their heads" (Flavell, Green, Flavell & Grossman, 1997). It is not until a few years later that they understand that they can be wrong about what someone else thinks (Miller, 2009) and that the mind is continuously active (Flavell, 2000).

The recognition that others have mental states accompanies the decline of egocentrism and the development of empathy (Povinelli & Giambrone, 2001). In the following sections, we will look more closely at some of the abilities related to the understanding of mental states.

Did you know?

Children do not fully realize they cannot control their dreams until about age 11 (Woolley & Boerger, 2002).

©BananaStock/PunchStock

False Beliefs

A researcher shows 3-year-old Madeline a cookie box and asks what is in it. "Cookies," she says. But when Madeline opens the box, she finds crayons, not cookies. "What will a child who hasn't opened the box think is in it?" the researcher asks. "Crayons," says Madeline, not understanding that another child would be fooled by the box just as she was (Flavell, 2000).

The understanding that people can hold false beliefs flows from the realization that people can hold incorrect mental representations of reality. For example, if you see your mother searching for an umbrella, but you know it's not raining outside, you can understand that she *thinks* it's raining, even if it is not. This ability is generally tested with what is called a false belief task. Although infants as young as 13 months can illustrate some understanding of the mental states of others if asked in an appropriate (nonverbal) manner (Scott & Baillargeon, 2009), it is not until about 4 years of age that children consistently pass false belief tasks (Baillargeon, Scott & He, 2010). It is not until 5 to 6 years of

age that children understand second-order false beliefs—that they may have an incorrect belief about what someone else believes (Miller, 2009).

Three-year-olds' failure to recognize false beliefs may stem from a variety of different processes. Piagetian researchers have suggested it stems from egocentric thinking (Lillard & Curenton, 1999). Other researchers have pointed to general processing mechanisms and predictive abilities (Berthiaume, Shultz & Onishi, 2013). Still other researchers have argued that reasoning about false beliefs is likely to be a highly specialized skill with separate processing capabilities (Leslie, Friedman & German, 2004).

There are links between the ability to pass false belief tasks and language (Low, 2010; Rubio-Fernandez & Geurtz, 2013) and attentional and inhibitory processes (Leslie et al., 2004). Culturally diverse research has revealed a consistent association between executive functioning ability and theory of mind (Devine & Hughes, 2014). Research on the brain has shown that somewhat different areas of the brain are active during different types of false belief tasks (Shurz, Aichhorn, Martin & Perner, 2013). Moreover, even after they have mastered false belief tasks, children's brain waveforms are different from those of adults, suggesting continued change over time (Meinhardt, Sodian, Thoermer, Dohnel & Sommer, 2011). Thus, it may be that a variety of different processes underlie children's developing abilities in this area.

Deception is an effort to plant a false belief in someone else's mind. Not surprisingly, performance on the false belief task has been repeatedly shown to predict the ability to lie (Lee, 2013; Talwar & Lee, 2008; Bigelow & Dugas, 2009). Thus, while most people do not view the ability to lie as a positive trait, it is nonetheless a developmental milestone illustrative of advances.

Generally children become capable of telling simple lies, such as claiming they received a winning card in a game (Ahern, Lyon & Quas, 2011) or denying looking at a hidden toy they were instructed to avoid (Evans & Lee, 2013), at about 3 years of age. However, when asked follow-up questions to their lie that if answered would reveal their deception, such as what kind of toy it was, young children fail to hide their knowledge (Evans & Lee, 2013). It is not until almost 8 years of age that children become better able to think about what they should and should not know, and thus conceal their transgressions more effectively (Talwar & Lee, 2008). Furthermore, as children age and become more aware of social conventions as well as others' feelings, they become more likely to lie out of politeness or a desire to avoid hurting others' feelings. For example, they are more likely to tell an experimenter that they liked an unattractive gift when in reality they did not (Xu, Bau, Fu, Talwar & Lee, 2010).

Distinguishing between Appearance and Reality

According to Piaget, not until about age 5 or 6 do children begin to understand the distinction between what *seems* to be and what *is*. Initial research seemed to support this view; however, more recent studies have found this ability emerging between 3 and 4 years of age.

In one classic series of experiments (Flavell, Green & Flavell, 1986), 3-year-olds seemed to confuse appearance and reality in a variety of tests. For example, when the children put on special sunglasses that made milk look green, they said the milk *was* green. Similarly, 3-year-olds thought that a sponge that looked like a rock was a rock, even after being shown the sponge in use (Flavell, Flavell & Green, 1983).

Later research showed that 3-year-old children could answer questions about reality and appearance correctly under certain circumstances. For example, when children were asked questions about how to use a sponge that looked like a rock, they answered incorrectly. However, when the experimenter indicated a sponge was needed to clean up some spilled water, the children were able to hand over the correct item (Sapp, Lee & Muir, 2000). Later research showed that if children were presented with two objects, such as an eraser that looked like a chocolate bar and a real chocolate bar, and asked to hand an experimenter "the real one" they were able to select the correct item (Moll & Tomasello, 2012). Similarly, 3-year-old children were able to understand that an adult looking through a yellow screen at a blue object saw it as green, as evidenced by correctly selecting the blue toy after being asked "can you put the green one in the bag for me?" (Moll & Meltzoff, 2011). It may be that children do understand the difference between appearance and reality, but have difficulty displaying their knowledge in traditional tasks that require verbal responses. When you ask them to display their knowledge via their actions, they are better able to do so.

Distinguishing between Fantasy and Reality

Sometime between 18 months and 3 years, children learn to distinguish between real and imagined events. Three-year-olds know the difference between a real dog and a dog in a dream, and between something invisible, such as air, and something imaginary. They can pretend and can tell when someone else is pretending (Flavell, 2000). By age 3, and, in some cases, by age 2, they know that pretense is intentional; they can

tell the difference between trying to do something and pretending to do the same thing (Rakoczy, Tomasello, & Striano, 2004).

While more inclined to believe in storybook characters than older children, 3-year-olds are still skeptical about whether or not characters in books are real or pretend, especially if those books contain fantastical elements (Woolley & Cox, 2007). By the age of 4, most children, if given the choice, complete stories with real-world causal laws rather than magical or fantastical elements (Weisberg, Sobel, Goodstein & Bloom, 2013). Religion can influence this process. Children raised in religious households are more likely to believe the protagonists in stories with fantastical elements are real if they think the stories are religious in nature than are children raised in secular households (Corriveau, Chen & Harris, 2015). If told a particular story is a bible story, 5-year-olds are more likely to assert magical events in the story are possible in real life (Woolley & Cox, 2007).

Children often engage in magical thinking as a way to explain events that do not seem to have obvious realistic explanation or simply to indulge in the pleasures of pretending—as with the belief in imaginary companions. Magical thinking in children age 3 and older does not seem to stem from

Imaginative activities have been shown to have developmental benefits.
©Terry Vine/Blend Images

confusion between fantasy and reality, and it tends to decline near the end of the preschool period (Woolley, Phelps, Davis, & Mandell, 1999). Moreover, there are indications that imaginative activities may offer developmental benefits. In one study, children who had imaginary companions used richer and more elaborate narrative structure than children without imaginary companions when asked to recount a personal story (Trionfi & Reese, 2009). Other research has shown that children who watched a movie with magical themes later scored higher on creativity tests and drew more imaginative impossible objects, even though their beliefs about magic were unaffected (Subbotsky, Hysted & Jones, 2010).

All in all, then, the research on various theory-of-mind topics suggests that young children may have a clearer picture of reality than Piaget believed.

Individual Differences in Theory-of-Mind Development

Some children develop theory-of-mind abilities earlier than others. In part, this development reflects brain maturation and general improvements in cognition. What other influences explain individual differences?

Infant social attention has been closely linked to theory-of-mind development (Wellman & Liu, 2004). Several lines of research show that infants who are better at paying attention to others as infants show more facility with theory-of-mind tasks at 4 years of age (Wellman, Lopez-Duran, LaBounty & Hamilton, 2008; Aschersleben, Hofer & Jovanovic, 2008). Social competence also matters and contributes to an understanding of thoughts and emotions. Children whose teachers and peers rate them high on social skills are better able to recognize false beliefs, to distinguish between real and pretend emotion, and to take another person's point of view (Cassidy, Werner, Rourke, Zubernis & Balaraman, 2003). Findings such as these suggest continuity in social cognition and that skills build on each other over time.

The kind of talk a young child hears at home may also affect the child's understanding of mental states. A mother's

©Paul Burns/Blend Images

reference to others' thoughts and knowledge is a consistent predictor of a child's later mental state language (Dunn, 2006). Being bilingual may also help. Bilingual children do somewhat better on certain theory-of-mind tasks (Kovacs, 2009). Bilingual children know that an object or idea can be represented linguistically in more than one way, and this may help them see that different people may have different perspectives. Bilingual children also recognize the need to match their language to that of their partner, making them more aware of others' mental states (Bialystok & Senman, 2004; Goetz, 2003).

Families that encourage pretend play stimulate the development of theory-of-mind skills. As children play roles, they assume others' perspectives. Talking with children about how the characters in a story feel helps them develop social understanding (Lillard & Curenton, 1999). Theory of mind has been positively related to reading storybooks, perhaps because parents and children often discuss characters and their desires, beliefs or emotions (Mar, Tackett & Moore, 2010). Having siblings is also associated positively with theory of mind development (McAlister & Peterson, 2013).

While cross-cultural studies have shown few differences in basic abilities (Callaghan et al., 2005), culture can lead to variations in patterns of development. For example, in one study, 5- to 6-year-old British children were found to be advanced in theory-of-mind development relative to Japanese and Italian children, an effect the researchers suggested was likely the result of formal schooling (Hughes et al., 2014). In another study, while Iranian and Australian children from 3 to 9 years of age had overall equivalent theory-of-mind scores, Iranian children were able to understand sarcasm earlier, and Australian children were able to understand that others might have different beliefs than them earlier (Shahaeian, Nielsen, Peterson & Slaughter, 2014).

Brain development is also necessary for theory of mind. In particular, neural activity in the prefrontal cortex has been identified as important (Mitchell, Banaji & MacRae, 2005). For example, in one study, children who were able to correctly reason about the mental states of characters in animated scenarios showed brain wave activation in their left frontal cortex, much as the adults in the study did. However, those children who were not able to correctly pass the task did not (Liu, Sabbagh, Gehring & Wellman, 2009).

Did you know?

Note that conservation requires children to hold two aspects in mind at once—for example, height and width. Likewise, understanding false beliefs also requires children to hold two things in mind at once: what the person thinks and what is actually true.

©McGraw-Hill Education/Tara McDermott, photographer

Some researchers have urged caution in interpreting the results of brain imaging research, and pointed out that related subjects such as empathy and "mind-reading" need to be clearly delineated (Singer, 2006). Given its complexity, it is likely multiple areas are involved in processing theory of mind. For example, in one model, two processing loops that underlie theory-of-mind processing have been proposed. The cognitive network, composed of the dorsomedial prefrontal cortex, the dorsal anterior cingulate cortex, and the dorsal striatum, makes inferences about knowledge and beliefs. The affective network, composed of the ventromedial and orbito-frontal cortices, the ventral anterior cingulate cortex, the amygdala, and the ventral striatum, makes inferences about emotions (Abu-Akel & Shamay-Tsoory, 2011).

An incomplete or ineffective theory of mind may be a sign of a cognitive or developmental impairment. Individuals with this type of impairment have difficulty determining the intentions of others, lack understanding of how their behavior affects others, and have a difficult time with social reciprocity. Research suggests that children with autism are deficient in theory of mind, and that this is a core feature of autism (Baron-Cohen, Leslie & Frith, 1985).

Information-Processing Approach: Memory Development

When recalling events, young children tend to focus on exact details, while simultaneously failing to notice important aspects of a situation, such as when and where an event occurred. However, as they improve in attention and in the speed and efficiency of information processing, their memories also improve, and they begin to form long-lasting memories more focused on the "gist" of what happened. In the following sections, we summarize key changes that occur from ages 3 to 6 in these processes.

BASIC PROCESSES AND CAPACITIES

Information-processing theorists think of memory as a filing system that has three steps: encoding, storage, and retrieval (Figure 9.2). **Encoding,** processes by which information is prepared for long-term storage and later retrieval, is like putting information in a folder to be filed in memory; it attaches a "code" or "label" to the information so it will be easier to find when needed. For example, if you were asked to list "things that are red" you might list apple, stop sign, and heart. Presumably, all these items were tagged in memory with the concept "red" when they were originally encoded. Events are encoded along with information about the context in which they are encountered. **Storage,**

encoding Process by which information is prepared for long-term storage and later retrieval.

storage Retention of information in memory for future use.

retrieval Process by which information is accessed or recalled from memory storage.

sensory memory Initial, brief, temporary storage of sensory information.

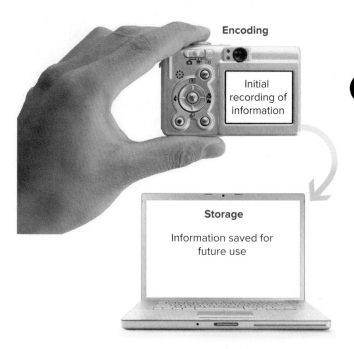

Encoding

Initial recording of information

Storage

Information saved for future use

Retrieval

Recovery of stored information

FIGURE 9.2
Memory Systems
Memory is like a filing system with three steps: encoding, storage and retrieval.
©Garret Bautista/Getty Images; ©D. Hurst/Alamy; ©McGraw-Hill Education/Gary He

the retention of information for future use, is putting the folder away in the filing cabinet. **Retrieval,** the processes by which information is accessed from memory storage, occurs when the information is needed; the child then searches for the file and takes it out. Difficulties in any of these processes can impact memory.

The way the brain stores information is believed to be universal, though the efficiency of the system varies from one person to another (Siegler, 1998). Information-processing models depict the brain as containing three storehouses: sensory memory, working memory, and long-term memory.

Sensory memory is a temporary storehouse for incoming sensory information that decays rapidly. Sensory memory

Did you know?

Have you ever had the experience of talking to someone, not hearing them, asking, "What?" and then actually hearing them by the time the question leaves your mouth? That's your sensory memory at play.

©Blend Images/AP Images

shows little change from infancy on (Siegler, 1998). However, without processing (encoding), sensory memories fade quickly.

Information being encoded or retrieved is kept in **working memory**, a short-term storehouse for information a person is actively working on, trying to understand, remember, or think about. According to a widely used model, a **central executive** controls processing operations in working memory (Baddeley, 1998, 2001). The central executive orders information encoded for transfer to **long-term memory**, a storehouse of virtually unlimited capacity that holds information for long periods. The central executive also retrieves information from long-term memory for further processing. It is assisted by two subsystems, the phonological loop, which aids in the processing of verbal information, and the visuospatial sketchpad, which maintains and manipulates visual information.

Brain imaging studies have found that working memory is located partly in the prefrontal cortex (Nelson et al., 2000). Functions controlled by the central executive are found in a variety of regions in the frontal lobes and in some posterior, primarily parietal, areas. Functions controlled by the phonological loop are found in the left hemisphere in the inferior parietal areas and anterior temporal frontal areas, including Broca's area, the premotor cortex, and the sensory motor association cortex. Functions controlled by the visuospatial sketchpad are found in the right hemisphere in the occipital and inferior frontal areas (Gathercole, Pickering, Ambridge & Wearing, 2004).

The efficiency of working memory is limited by its capacity. Researchers can assess the capacity of working memory by asking children to recall a series of scrambled digits (for example, 2-8-3-7-5-1 if they heard 1-5-7-3-8-2). The capacity of working memory—in this case the number of digits a child can recall backward—increases rapidly. At age 4, children typically remember only two digits; at 12 they typically remember six (Zelazo, Muller, Frye & Marcovitch, 2003). All basic components of working memory are in place by 6 years of age, and increase linearly with age until approximately 14 to 15 years (Gathercole et al., 2004).

The growth of working memory permits the development of **executive function**, the conscious control of thoughts, emotions, and actions to accomplish goals or to solve problems (McCabe, Roediger, McDaniel, Balota & Hambrick, 2010). Executive function enables children to plan and carry out goal-directed mental activity (Zelazo & Carlson, 2012), and it is often useful when children need to focus their attention on something or override an inappropriate response. For example, despite being eager for a turn, a child might wait in line for a slide, knowing that to cut the line would result in disciplinary action from the teacher. Executive function probably emerges around the end of an infant's 1st year and develops in spurts with age. Changes in executive function between ages 2 and 5 enable children to make up and use complex rules for solving problems (Zelazo et al., 2003).

Executive function may explain why working memory is positively associated with academic performance, in fact, to a greater degree than is IQ (Alloway & Alloway, 2010). These findings have held for both literacy and numeracy skills, and for children from low-income families, ethnic minority children; children born preterm, and children with attentional problems (Welsh, Nix, Blair, Bierman & Nelson, 2010; Mulder, Pitchford & Marlow, 2010; Alloway, Gathercole, & Elliott, 2010). Because of this association, attempts have been made to increase working memory capacity via training and intervention programs. Generally, such attempts have been successful in improving working memory (Melby-Lervag & Hulme, 2013; Diamond & Lee, 2011) and are in fact associated with changes in brain activity and dopamine receptor density (Klingberg, 2010). Some programs, especially those focused on literacy, have shown success (Dahlin, 2011; Titz & Karbach, 2014; Holmes & Gathercole, 2014). Other programs have had difficulty with the generalizability of training to other areas and have not resulted in academic gains (Rapport, Orban, Kofler & Friedman, 2013; Dunning, Holmes & Gathercole, 2013), and some have even shown declines in academic performance as a result of training (Roberts et al., 2016).

Placing material in memory is not enough, it must also be retrieved to be used. Recognition and recall are types of retrieval. **Recognition** is the ability to identify something encountered before—for example, picking out a missing mitten from a lost-and-found box. **Recall** is the ability to reproduce knowledge from memory—for example, describing the mitten to someone.

Preschool children, like those in all age groups, do better on recognition than on recall, but both abilities improve with age. The more familiar children are with an item, the better they can recall it. However, young children often fail to use strategies for remembering—even strategies they already know—unless reminded, and they sometimes choose inefficient memory strategies (Schwenck, Bjorklund, & Schneider, 2009; Whitebread et al., 2009). This tendency

working memory Short-term storage of information being actively processed.

central executive In Baddeley's model, element of working memory that controls the processing of information.

long-term memory Storage of virtually unlimited capacity that holds information for long periods.

executive function Conscious control of thoughts, emotions, and actions to accomplish goals or solve problems.

recognition Ability to identify a previously encountered stimulus.

recall Ability to reproduce material from memory.

As children get older, they develop more efficient memory strategies to improve recognition and recall.

©Lia_Skyfox/Shutterstock

Autobiographical memory, a type of episodic memory, refers to memories of distinctive experiences that form a person's life history. Not everything in episodic memory becomes part of autobiographical memory—only those memories that have a special, personal meaning to the child (Fivush, 2011). Autobiographical memory generally emerges between ages 3 and 4 (Nelson, 2005).

A suggested explanation for the relatively slow arrival of autobiographical memory is that children cannot store in memory events pertaining to their own lives until they develop a self-concept (Nelson & Fivush, 2004). Also critical is the emergence of language, which enables children to share memories and organize them into personal narratives (Nelson, 2005). Parents who spend more time reminiscing about and discussing past events have children who form more coherent autobiographical memories (Fivush, Habermas, Waters & Zaman, 2011).

INFLUENCES ON MEMORY RETENTION

Why do some memories last longer than others? One important factor is the uniqueness of the event. When events are rare or unusual, children seem to remember them better (Peterson, 2011). Children, as they get older, are also more likely to remember unique details of an event for which they have a generic script (Brubacher, Glisic, Powers & Powell, 2011). Moreover, events with emotional impact seem to be remembered better (Buchanan, 2007), although some evidence suggests attention is focused on central aspects of the situation rather than on peripheral details (Levine & Edelstein, 2009). So, for example, if you were frightened by a scary film, you might show enhanced memory for events in the film but forget if you bought candy or who you went with. Still another factor is children's active participation. Preschoolers tend to remember things they did better than things they merely saw (Murachver, Pipe, Gordon, Owens & Fivush, 1996).

Finally, the way adults talk with a child about experiences strongly affects autobiographical memory (Fivush et al., 2011; Fivush & Haden, 2006). Why might this be the case? The **social interaction model,** based on Vygotsky's sociocultural approach, provides a rationale. Theorists argue that children collaboratively construct autobiographical memories with parents or other adults as they talk about events, such as might occur when a mother and child leaf through a photo album and talk about past events.

Parents differ with respect to how they talk about past events (Fivush & Haden, 2006). When a child gets stuck, adults with a *low elaborative style* repeat their own previous statements or questions. Such a parent might ask, "Do you remember how we traveled to Florida?" and then, receiving no answer, ask, "How did we get there? We went in the _____." A parent with a *high elaborative style* would ask a question that elicits more information: "Did we go by car or by plane?" The use of more elaboration on the part of parents results in richer memories for their children (Reese & Newcombe, 2007).

The relationship between elaborative, parent-guided reminiscing and children's autobiographical memory has

not to generate efficient strategies may reflect lack of awareness about how a strategy would be useful (Sophian, Wood & Vong, 1995). Older children, particularly once they begin formal schooling, tend to become more efficient in the spontaneous use of memory strategies (Schneider, 2008).

CHILDHOOD MEMORY

Three types of childhood memory that serve different functions have been identified: generic, episodic, and autobiographical (Nelson, 1993; Bauer, 2006).

generic memory Memory that produces scripts of familiar routines to guide behavior.

script General remembered outline of a familiar, repeated event, used to guide behavior.

episodic memory Long-term memory of specific experiences or events, linked to time and place.

autobiographical memory A type of episodic memory of distinctive experiences that form a person's life history.

social interaction model Model, based on Vygotsky's sociocultural theory, that proposes children construct autobiographical memories through conversation with adults about shared events.

Generic memory, which begins at about age 2, produces a **script**, a general outline of a familiar, repeated event, such as riding the bus to preschool or having lunch at Grandma's house. It helps a child know what to expect and how to act.

Episodic memory refers to awareness of having experienced a particular event that occurred at a specific time and place, like a particularly fun time at the park on a sunny day. Given a young child's limited memory capacity, episodic memories are temporary. Unless they recur several times, in which case they are transferred to generic memory, they last for a few weeks or months and then fade. For example, getting vaccinated at the pediatrician's office might originally be an episodic memory. Over time and repeated visits, a child might form a generic memory of the doctor's office being a place where shots are administered. Talking about events with parents often helps children remember them on a long-term basis, presumably by providing verbal labels for aspects of an event and giving it an orderly, comprehensible structure (Nelson & Fivush, 2004).

been replicated widely across cultures. However, mothers in middle-class Western cultures tend toward more elaboration than mothers in non-Western cultures (Fivush & Haden, 2006). In reminiscing with 3-year-olds, U.S. mothers might say, "Do you remember when you went swimming at Nana's? What did you do that was really neat?" Chinese mothers tend to ask leading questions, leaving little for the child to add new information ("What did you play at the place of skiing? Sat on the ice ship, right?") (Nelson & Fivush, 2004).

Psychometric and Vygotskian Approaches: Intelligence

Intelligence is one factor that may affect the strength of early cognitive skills such as memory capacity and language. Intelligence is traditionally measured through psychometric tests, however environmental factors may influence their accuracy. Tests of cognitive potential, developed based on Vygotsky's theories allow additional information about intelligence.

TRADITIONAL PSYCHOMETRIC MEASURES

Three- to 5-year-old children are more proficient with language than younger children, so intelligence tests for this age group can include more verbal items. These tests, beginning at age 5, tend to be fairly reliable in predicting measured intelligence and school success later in childhood. The two most commonly used individual intelligence tests for preschoolers are the Stanford-Binet Intelligence Scale and the Wechsler Preschool and Primary Scale of Intelligence.

The **Stanford-Binet Intelligence Scale** is used for children ages 2 and up and takes 45 to 60 minutes to complete. The child is asked to define words, string beads, build with blocks, identify the missing parts of a picture, trace mazes, and show an understanding of numbers. The child's score is supposed to measure fluid reasoning (the ability to solve abstract or novel problems), knowledge, quantitative reasoning, visual-spatial processing, and working memory. The 5th edition includes nonverbal methods of testing all five of these dimensions of cognition and permits comparisons of verbal and nonverbal performance. In addition to providing a full-scale intelligence quotient (IQ), the Stanford-Binet yields separate measures of verbal and nonverbal IQ plus composite scores spanning the five cognitive dimensions.

The **Wechsler Preschool and Primary Scale of Intelligence, Revised (WPPSI-III)** is an individual test that takes 30 to 60 minutes. It has separate levels for ages 2½ to 4 and 4 to 7, and it yields separate verbal and performance scores as well as a combined score. The most current version includes subtests designed to measure both verbal and nonverbal fluid reasoning, receptive versus expressive vocabulary, and processing speed. The WPPSI-III has been validated for special populations, such as children with intellectual disabilities, developmental delays, language disorders, and autistic disorders.

INFLUENCES ON MEASURED INTELLIGENCE

A common misconception is that IQ scores represent a fixed quantity of inborn intelligence. In reality, an IQ score is simply a measure of how well a child can do certain tasks at a certain time in comparison with others of the same age. This can be used to identify both gifted children, as well as children who need extra assistance. Thus, children who might benefit from special attention can be provided with appropriate programming. In addition, most tests have been in use for some time, and as such they are standardized, normed, and reliable. Moreover, they do indeed help predict academic achievement. However, there are also negatives to IQ testing. Most notably, they may track children inappropriately, and while many people interpret them to be an indicator of innate ability, in reality IQ tests more reflect experiences. Indeed, test scores of children in many industrialized countries have risen steadily since testing began, forcing test developers to raise standardized norms (Flynn, 1984, 1987). This trend was thought to reflect better nutrition in early childhood, exposure to educational television and preschools, better-educated parents, smaller families in which each child receives more attention, and a wide variety of mentally demanding games, as well as changes in the tests themselves.

Some researchers believed that the trend slowed and even reversed in the 1970s and 1980s, at least in industrialized countries, perhaps because such influences had reached a saturation point (Sundet, Barlaug & Torjussen, 2004; Teasdale & Owen, 2008). However, recent meta-analyses suggest that average IQ continues to rise at a rate of 2.3 points per decade (Trahan, Stuebing, Fletcher & Hiscock, 2014).

The degree to which family environment influences a child's intelligence is difficult to specify. Some of parents' influence on intelligence comes from their genetic contribution, and some results from the fact that they provide a child's earliest environment for learning. Twin and adoption studies suggest that family life has its strongest influence on IQ

Stanford-Binet Intelligence Scale Individual intelligence test for ages 2 and up, used to measure knowledge, quantitative reasoning, visual-spatial processing, and working memory.

Wechsler Preschool and Primary Scale of Intelligence, Revised (WPPSI-III) Individual intelligence test for children ages 2½ to 7 that yields verbal and performance scores as well as a combined score.

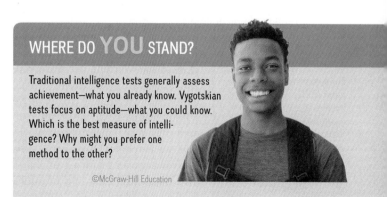

WHERE DO YOU STAND?

Traditional intelligence tests generally assess achievement—what you already know. Vygotskian tests focus on aptitude—what you could know. Which is the best measure of intelligence? Why might you prefer one method to the other?

©McGraw-Hill Education

in early childhood, and this influence diminishes greatly by adolescence (Bouchard, 2013; Haworth et al., 2010).

The correlation between socioeconomic status and IQ is well documented (Strenze, 2007). Family income is associated with cognitive development and achievement in the preschool years and beyond. Family economic circumstances can exert a powerful influence, not so much in themselves as in the way they affect other factors such as health, stress, parenting practices, and the atmosphere in the home (Jenkins, Woolley, Hooper & De Bellis, 2014; NICHD Early Child Care Research Network, 2005a).

The relationship between IQ and socioeconomic status interacts with other variables. For example, children in deprived families tend to have lower IQs. However, poor children with an outgoing temperament, warm mothering, and stimulating activities in the home (which may be influenced by parental IQ) tend to do better than other economically deprived children (Kim-Cohen, Moffitt, Caspi & Taylor, 2004). Environmental differences also seem to matter more for some children than others. Children at risk may be more influenced by negative environments. For example, research has shown that children with low IQ show greater negative effects as a result of low socioeconomic status than do those with high IQ (Hanscombe et al., 2012). Also, the IQ of children from homes of higher economic status is more strongly affected by genetic influences, while the IQ of children from homes of the lowest socioeconomic status is driven more by environmental deprivation (Turkheimer, Haley, Waldron, D'Onofrio & Gottesman, 2003).

ELECTRONIC MEDIA AND COGNITIVE PROCESSES

Preschool-age children comprehend the symbolic nature of television and can readily imitate behaviors they see. Exposure to television during the first few years of life has been negatively associated with academic outcomes (Pagani, Fitzpatrick, Barnett & Dubow, 2010) and cognitive development, especially when the television is left on for long periods or when young children are exposed to high levels of adult programming (Barr, Lauricella, Zack & Calvert, 2010). Some researchers have also found that the fast-paced programming common now in many children's shows negatively impacts executive functioning and the ability to sustain attention in preschool children (Lillard & Peterson, 2011).

While certain kinds of programming do appear to be harmful to young children's cognitive development, the type of television watched is also important, and high-quality children's programming can result in cognitive enhancements (Kirkorian, Wartella & Anderson, 2008). For example, *Sesame Street,* developed specifically to improve school readiness in inner-city children, has been repeatedly shown to improve outcomes. Viewing *Sesame Street* is associated with a host of positive outcomes, including cognitive proficiency, literacy, and numeracy

zone of proximal development (ZPD) Vygotsky's term for the difference between what a child can do alone and what the child can do with help.

scaffolding Temporary support to help a child master a task.

(Mares & Pan, 2013). Similar findings have emerged for other educational programming such as *Blue's Clues* and *Dora the Explorer* (Kirkorian et al., 2008). It is clear that program content is an important mediator. Additionally, parents who limit screen time, select well-designed, age-appropriate programs, and view the programs with their children can maximize the benefits of media.

While for many years television was the most frequently used media source, the use of home computers, tablets, cellular phones, and other such devices has grown rapidly in recent years. Because of the now ubiquitous nature of these devices, the American Academy of Pediatrics (2016) issued new guidelines to encompass usage of all electronics. The recommendations state that children from 2 to 5 years of age should spend no more than an hour a day on *any* screen media, and that parents should watch programming with their children and discuss it. For children 6 and older, there should be consistent limits and designated media-free times. As with television, the most important variable is content. Children can learn from educational media, but pure entertainment and violent content are negatively associated with cognitive competence and academic achievement (Kirkorian et al., 2008).

MEASUREMENT AND TEACHING BASED ON VYGOTSKY'S THEORY

According to Vygotsky, children learn by internalizing the results of interactions with adults. This interactive learning is most effective in helping children cross the **zone of proximal development (ZPD)**, the imaginary psychological space between what they are already able to do by themselves and what they could do with help. The ZPD can be assessed by dynamic tests that provide a better measure of children's intellectual potential than do traditional psychometric tests. Examiners help the child when necessary by asking questions, giving examples or demonstrations, and offering feedback, making the test itself a learning situation.

The ZPD, in combination with the related concept of **scaffolding**, also can help parents and teachers efficiently guide children's cognitive progress. Scaffolding is the supportive assistance that a more sophisticated interaction partner provides, and ideally it should be aimed at the ZPD. For

Did you know?

Vygotsky argued that pretend play was an ideal situation for learning. The "rules" of pretend play require children to stretch their abilities and to work at the higher end of their ZPD. For example, if two children are playing an emergency rescue game, then one must lie still until rescued, which requires self-regulation and inhibition of impulses. The rules of the game provide the scaffolding that help the child achieve this.

©SteveDF/Getty Images

Perspectives on Diversity

©Digital Vision/Getty Images

PATHS TO LEARNING

In the United States and other Western nations, the primary way in which children learn the skills they need to have to be productive adult members of society is via formal education. In other words, they attend school. However, Vygotsky's theory of sociocultural development, which implies there are as many paths to effective development as there are potential interactions between "teachers" and "learners," suggests there might be alternative ways that children could learn about their world.

Barbara Rogoff (2003), who has conducted extensive cross-cultural research focused on the different ways in which cultural communities affect the development of children, has studied this idea. In her work, she has found that nonindustrialized cultures, rather than send children away to learn in a classroom, are more likely to involve children in everyday activities and experiences, which then transmit valuable cultural information and practical skills. For example, a young Mayan child might accompany her mother to the market, and while playing at her mother's feet, hear her mother negotiate a price for an item she is selling, thereby learning about currency conversions and mathematics. The child may be viewed as an apprentice, who acquires vital cultural knowledge through daily life practices and routine activities.

Rogoff's research demonstrates that while formal educational practices in Western countries may be ideal for the transmission of information, it does not have to be this way. Other cultures have varying, and equally valid, ways of teaching their children what they need to know.

example, consider what happens when you are trying to learn a new skill, such as playing pool. When you play with someone who is worse than you, you are not likely to improve. Likewise, when you play with someone who is a master, their skills are so above yours that they overwhelm you. However, playing with someone who is just a bit better than you is likely to challenge you, illustrate strategies you might be successful at, and result in the greatest amount of learning.

Ideally, scaffolding is lessened as children gain in skills. The less able a child is to do a task, the more scaffolding, or support, an adult must give. As the child can do more and more, the adult helps less and less. When the child can do the job alone, the adult takes away the scaffold that is no longer needed.

Scaffolding helps children learn. For example, when the mothers of 2-year-old children helped maintain their child's interests by scaffolding their attention—by asking questions, making comments, or offering choices—their children tended to show more independence and cognitive sophistication at 3½ to 4½ years of age (Landry, Smith, Swank & Miller-Loncar, 2000). Teachers can also influence children's growing abilities. Prekindergarten children who receive scaffolding are better able to regulate their own learning when they get to kindergarten (Neitzel & Stright, 2003). First graders struggling with reading showed greater gains in their abilities when their teachers prompted them to use sources of information they were ignoring to decode difficult words when they got stuck (Rodgers, D'Agostino, Harmey, Kelly & Brownfield, 2016). Teachers who scaffolded the group discussions of their fourth grade classrooms had students who later modeled their behavior on that of the teachers', for example, by remembering to use evidence to support their statements (Jadallah et al., 2011).

Language Development

Preschoolers are full of questions: "How many sleeps until tomorrow?" "Who filled the river with water?" "Do babies have muscles?" "Do smells come from inside my nose?" Young children's growing facility with language helps them express their unique view of the world. Between ages 3 and 6, children make rapid advances in vocabulary, grammar and syntax, and pragmatics and social speech. The child who, at age 3, describes how Daddy "hatches" wood (chops with a hatchet) or asks Mommy to "piece" her food (cut it into little pieces) may, by age 5, tell her mother, "Don't be ridiculous!" or proudly point to her toys and say, "See how I organized everything?" In this section, we will discuss major changes in language development. We will also address delayed language, as well as the contribution language makes to preliteracy.

AREAS OF LANGUAGE DEVELOPMENT

During the early childhood years, key language development occurs in the areas of vocabulary, grammar and syntax, and pragmatics and social speech.

Vocabulary

At age 3 the average child knows and can use 900 to 1,000 words. By age 6, a child typically has an expressive (speaking) vocabulary of 2,600 words and understands more than 20,000. With the help of formal schooling, a child's passive, or receptive, vocabulary—words she or he can understand—will quadruple to 80,000 words by the time the child enters high school (Owens, 1996).

fast mapping Process by which a child absorbs the meaning of a new word after hearing it once or twice in conversation.

This rapid expansion of vocabulary may occur through **fast mapping**, which allows a child to pick up the approximate meaning of a new word after hearing it only once or twice in conversation (Spiegel & Halberda, 2011). Using the context, children seem to form a quick hypothesis about the meaning of the word. For example, suppose a child is at the zoo and encounters an emu for the first time. The mother might point to the emu and say, "Look at the emu over there." The child might use what she knows about the rules for forming words, about the context, and about the subject to form a hypothesis about the meaning of the word *emu*. Names of objects (nouns) seem to be easier to fast map than names of actions (verbs), even across different languages (Imai et al., 2008).

Grammar and Syntax

The ways children combine syllables into words, and words into sentences, grow increasingly sophisticated during early childhood. In this context, grammar does not refer to the lessons learned in seventh grade English class; rather, it refers to the deep underlying structure of a language that enables us to both produce and understand utterances.

This preschool girl can use her growing vocabulary and knowledge of grammar and syntax to communicate more effectively. She has learned how to ask for things, carry on a conversation, and tell a joke or story.

©Blend Images/AP Images

Syntax is a related concept and involves the rules for putting together sentences in a particular language.

At age 3, children typically begin to use plurals, possessives, and past tense, and they know the difference between I, you, and we. They can ask—and answer—what and where questions. However, their sentences are generally short, simple, and declarative ("Kitty wants milk").

Between ages 4 and 5, sentences average four to five words and may be declarative ("I'm a girl"), negative ("I'm not hungry"), interrogative ("Why can't I go outside?"), or imperative ("Catch the ball!"). Four-year-olds use complex, multiclause sentences ("I'm eating because I'm hungry") more frequently if their parents often use such sentences (Huttenlocher, Vasilyeva, Cymerman, & Levine, 2002). Children this age tend to string sentences together in long run-on stories (". . . And then . . . And then . . .").

Children are also affected by their peers. When children interact with peers who have strong language skills, this results in a small but significant positive effect on their own language (Mashburn, Justice, Downer & Pianta, 2009). In some respects, comprehension may be immature. For example, 4-year-old Noah can carry out a command that includes more than one step ("Pick up your toys and put them in the cupboard"). However, if his mother tells him, "You may watch TV after you pick up your toys," he may process the words in the order in which he hears them and think he can first watch television and then pick up his toys.

By ages 5 to 7, children's speech has become quite adult-like. They speak in longer and more complicated sentences. They use more conjunctions, prepositions, and articles. They use compound and complex sentences and can handle all parts of speech.

Still, although preschool-age children speak fluently, comprehensibly, and fairly grammatically, they have yet to master many fine points of language. They rarely use the passive voice ("I was dressed by Grandpa"), conditional sentences ("If I were big, I could drive the bus"), or the auxiliary verb *have* ("I have seen that lady before") (C. S. Chomsky, 1969). They often make errors because they have not yet learned exceptions to rules. Saying "holded" instead of "held" or "eated" instead of "ate" is a normal sign of linguistic progress. When young children discover a rule, such as adding *-ed* to a verb for past tense, they tend to overgeneralize—to use it even with words that do not conform to the rule. Eventually, they notice that *-ed* is not always used to form the past tense of a verb.

Pragmatics and Social Speech

When Clara was 3, she would ask for a cookie by demanding, "Cookie now!" However, as she got older, she realized that

Did you know?

Pragmatics is related to theory of mind. To understand how to use language socially, you have to be able to put yourself in other people's shoes.

©JGI/Jamie Grill/ Getty Images

asking, "Momma, can I have a cookie please?" was far more effective.

As children learn vocabulary, grammar, and syntax, they become more competent in **pragmatics**, the social context of language. This includes knowing how to ask for things, how to tell a story or joke, how to begin and continue a conversation, and how to adjust comments to the listener's perspective (Rice, 1982).

With improved pronunciation and grammar, it becomes easier for others to understand what children say. Most 3-year-olds are talkative, and they pay attention to the effect of their speech on others. If people cannot understand them, they try to explain themselves more clearly.

Most 5-year-olds can adapt what they say to what the listener knows. They can use words to resolve disputes, and they use more polite language and fewer direct commands in talking to adults than to other children. Almost half of 5-year-olds can stick to a conversational topic for about a dozen turns—if they are comfortable with their partner and if the topic is one they know and care about (Owens, 1996).

PRIVATE SPEECH

Jenna, age 4, was alone in her room painting. When she finished, she was overheard saying aloud, "Now I have to put the pictures somewhere to dry. I'll put them by the window. They need to get dry now."

Private speech—talking aloud to oneself with no intent to communicate with others—is normal and common in childhood. Theorists have disagreed on the precise nature of private speech. Piaget (1962) saw private speech as a sign of cognitive immaturity, and he believed that children were simply vocalizing whatever was on their minds. Vygotsky (1962) viewed private speech as a special form of communication: conversation with the self. He believed private speech was part of the learning process.

Research generally supports Vygotsky. There is evidence for the role of private speech in self-regulation (Day & Smith, 2013; Lidstone, Meins & Fernyhough, 2011). Private speech tends to increase when children are trying to solve problems or perform difficult tasks, especially without adult supervision (Berk, 1992). The use of private speech in young children also predicts their autobiographical memory (AL-Nahlah, Meins & Fernyhough, 2012), creativity (Daugherty & White, 2008), and spelling proficiency (Aram, Abili & Elad, 2014). Findings such as these support Vygotsky's view that private speech was part and parcel of learning rather than Piaget's view that it was merely reflecting ongoing mental activity.

Vygotsky proposed that private speech increases during the preschool years and then fades away during the early part of middle childhood as children become more able to guide and master their actions.

DELAYED LANGUAGE DEVELOPMENT

The fact that Albert Einstein did not start to speak until he was between 2 and 3 years old (Isaacson, 2007) may encourage parents of other children whose speech develops later than usual. The prevalence of speech delays in children from 2 to 7 years of age has been reported to be from 2.3 to 19 percent (McLaughlin, 2011).

Hearing problems, head and facial abnormalities, premature birth, family history, socioeconomic factors, and some developmental delays are all associated with speech and language delays (Dale et al., 1998; U.S. Preventive Services Task Force, 2006). Heredity seems to play a major role (Newbury & Monaco, 2010; Spinath, Price, Dale & Plomin, 2004), and boys are more likely than girls to be late talkers (U.S. Preventive Services Task Force, 2006).

Many children who speak late, especially those whose comprehension is normal, eventually catch up. One of the largest studies to date on language emergence determined that 80 percent of children with language delays at age 2 catch up with their peers by age 7 (Rice, Taylor & Zubrick, 2008). However, some 40 to 60 percent of children with early language delays, if left untreated, may experience far-reaching cognitive, social, and emotional consequences (McLaughlin, 2011; U.S. Preventive Services Task Force, 2006).

PREPARATION FOR LITERACY

What is the link between language and literacy? While for all normally developing children, language is as natural as learning how to grasp a rattle or walk, we are not designed by natural selection for literacy. Rather, reading borrows from a variety of systems—vision, audition, memory, language, motor skills, and more. It is a testament to our flexibility and intelligence as a species that most children readily learn to read; however, it is not an easy or natural task, and by the time a child learns to read his or her first word, he or she has already mastered many skills. **Emergent literacy** refers to the development of these skills. Language is necessary for literacy, but it is by no means enough.

Prereading skills can be divided into two types: (1) oral language skills,

> **pragmatics** Practical knowledge needed to use language for communicative purposes.
>
> **private speech** Talking aloud to oneself with no intent to communicate with others.
>
> **emergent literacy** Preschoolers' development of skills, knowledge, and attitudes that underlie reading and writing.

Reading involves skills from multiple systems, including vision, motor skills, memory, and language.
©Blend Images/Getty Images

such as vocabulary, syntax, narrative structure, and the understanding that language is used to communicate; and (2) specific phonological skills (linking letters with sounds) that help in decoding the printed word. Each of these types of skills seems to have its own independent effect (NICHD Early Child Care Research Network, 2005b).

Social interaction promotes emergent literacy. Children are more likely to become good readers and writers if, during the preschool years, parents provide appropriate conversational challenges—if they use a rich vocabulary and read and talk about books, and if they center dinner-table talk on the day's activities, on mutually remembered past events, or on questions about why people do things and how things work (Reese, 1995; Reese, Sparks & Leyva, 2010). Similar positive effects are found for preschool teachers. Children whose preschool teachers used sophisticated vocabulary during free play had larger vocabularies and better reading comprehension in fourth grade providing they had good receptive vocabulary in kindergarten (Dickinson & Porche, 2011).

As children learn the skills they will need to translate the written word into speech, they also learn that writing can express ideas, thoughts, and feelings. Preschool children in the United States pretend to write by scribbling, lining up their marks from left to right (Levin & Bus, 2003; Brenneman, Massey, Machado & Gelman, 1996). Later they begin using letters, numbers, and letterlike shapes to represent words, syllables, or phonemes. Often their spelling is so inventive that they cannot read it themselves (Whitehurst & Lonigan, 1998; 2001).

Reading to children is one of the most effective paths to literacy (Evans & Shaw, 2008). Fifty-five percent of U.S. children ages 3 to 5 and not in kindergarten are read to daily by a family member (Federal Interagency Forum on Child and Family Statistics, 2011). Children who are read to from an early age learn that reading and writing in English move from left to right and from top to bottom and that words are separated by spaces. They also are motivated to learn to read (Whitehurst & Lonigan, 2001; Baker, 2013). There are suggestions that these processes may be altered (Korat & Or, 2010) or interrupted (Parish-Morris, Mahajan, Hirsh-Pasek, Golinkoff & Collins, 2013) when reading is conducted on electronic devices.

Early Childhood Education

Going to preschool around age 3 is an important step that widens a child's physical, cognitive, and social environment. The transition to kindergarten, the beginning of "real school," at age 5 is another momentous step. Preschool enrollments have increased dramatically over the last 20 years, and approximately 57 percent of preschool children are enrolled in some form of center-based child care setting (National Center for Education Statistics, 2012).

WHAT DO YOU **DO?**

Preschool Teacher

Preschool teachers support the learning of young children, typically between the ages of 3 and 6. There are a variety of preschool approaches, but all emphasize the importance of developmentally appropriate strategies with which to engage their students. Preschool teachers work in both public and private school settings. Lead preschool teachers typically require at least a bachelor's degree and licensure. Assistant teachers may only require an associate's degree. If you plan to teach in a preschool that takes a particular approach, for example, Montessori, you may need to receive training in that particular approach. To learn more about becoming a preschool teacher, visit www.naeyc.org.

©Don Hammond/ Design Pics

TYPES OF PRESCHOOLS

Preschools vary greatly in their goals and curriculums. In some countries, such as China, preschools provide academic preparation for schooling. In contrast, many preschools in the United States have followed progressive, child-centered philosophies stressing social and emotional growth in line with young children's developmental needs. Two of the most influential programs, Montessori and Reggio Emilia, were founded on similar philosophical premises.

Montessori and Reggio Emilia Methods

The Montessori method, introduced by Maria Montessori in 1907, is based on the belief that children's natural intelligence involves rational, spiritual, and empirical aspects (Edwards, 2003). Montessori stresses the importance of children learning independently at their own pace in multiage classrooms as they work with developmentally appropriate materials and self-chosen tasks. Teachers serve as guides, and older children help younger ones (Montessori, 1995). An evaluation of Montessori education in Milwaukee found that 5-year-old Montessori students were better prepared for elementary school in reading and math than children who attended other types of preschools (Lillard & Else-Quest, 2006).

Children enrolled in high-quality compensatory preschool programs such as Head Start make gains in vocabulary and early reading scores.
©Mint Images RF/Getty Images

The Reggio Emilia approach, named for the town in Italy in which the movement first started in the 1940s, is a less formal model than Montessori. Children are highly valued, considered capable, and given the opportunity to explore what they desire. Teachers follow children's interests and support them in exploring and investigating ideas and feelings through words, movement, dramatic play, and music. Learning is purposeful but less defined than with the Montessori curriculum. Teachers ask questions that draw out children's ideas and then create flexible plans to explore these ideas with the children. Classrooms are carefully constructed to offer complexity, beauty, organization, and a sense of well-being (Edwards, 2002).

Compensatory Preschool Programs

Compensatory preschool programs are designed to aid children who would otherwise enter school poorly prepared to learn. Since the 1960s, large-scale programs have been developed to help such children compensate for what they have missed and to prepare them for school.

Generally, research has shown that children who are enrolled in compensatory preschool programs show academic and cognitive gains (Camilli, Vargas, Ryan & Barnett, 2010), and these effects are stronger for children who are low in cognitive potential, have parents with a low educational level, or attend programs for more hours per week (Lee, Zhai, Brooks-Gunn, Han & Waldfogel, 2014; Bitler, Hoynes & Domina, 2014). However, teachers and researchers in early childhood education generally work within a model of the whole child, seeking not just to enhance cognitive skills but also to improve physical health and to foster self-confidence and social skills. The best known of the early intervention programs in the United States is Project Head Start, a federally funded program launched in 1965. Head Start provides medical, dental, and mental health care; social services; and at least one hot meal a day. About 1 out of 3 Head Start children are from non-English-speaking homes (predominantly Hispanic) and a majority live in single-mother homes (Administration for Children and Families, 2006).

Has Head Start lived up to its name? Children enrolled in Head Start show academic and social gains in multiple, but not all, target areas immediately following their participation (Camilla et al., 2010). Head Start children make gains in vocabulary, letter recognition, early writing, early mathematics, and social skills. The gap between their vocabulary and early reading scores and national norms narrows significantly. Furthermore, their skills continue to progress in kindergarten. Gains are closely related to parental involvement (Administration for Children and Families, 2006).

Some reports suggest that these gains are not maintained over time. These reports have been controversial, in part due to the complexity of comparing outcomes of diverse children in varying programs. About half the number of children who apply for but do not get into Head Start find alternative child care arrangements. Thus the control group—those children who did not participate in Head Start—experience a variety of different child care situations rather than the lack of *any* enriching child care experiences. Some researchers

argue that this might help explain why many children who do not participate in Head Start seemed to "catch up" to program participants by first grade (National Forum on Early Childhood Policy and Programs, 2010).

An analysis of long-term effects of Head Start suggests that even though benefits lessen with time (Ludwig & Phillips, 2007) the benefits outweigh the costs (Puma et al., 2012). Children from Head Start and other compensatory programs were less likely to be placed in special education or to repeat a grade and were more likely to finish high school than low-income children who did not attend such programs (Deming, 2009). "Graduates" of similar programs were much less likely to become juvenile delinquents or to become pregnant in their teens (Schweinhart, 2007). There were also differences in long-term outcomes for males and females. At ages 27 and 40, men were less likely to have been involved in criminal activity and more likely to be employed and have a higher income than controls. For women, there were positive effects on both education and employment at age 19 and 27, and negative effects on criminal activity at age 40 (Heckman, Moon, Pinto, Savelyev & Yavitz, 2010; Reynolds, Temple, Ou, Arteaga & White, 2011). Outcomes are best with earlier and longer-lasting intervention through high-quality, center-based programs (Brooks-Gunn, 2003; Zigler & Styfco, 2001).

What happens after children leave preschool affects their likelihood of retaining the benefits of early intervention programs. A growing consensus among early childhood educators is that the most effective way to ensure that gains achieved in early intervention and compensatory education programs are maintained is through a systematic program extending from prekindergarten through third grade (Bogard & Takanishi, 2005). For example, children who participated in early intervention programs and then attended high-performing schools retained many of their academic and behavioral outcomes, whereas those children who then attended low-performing schools lost much of that advantage (Zhai, Raver & Jones, 2012).

Universal Preschool

The correlation between quality early childhood education and future academic success has been closely investigated. Studies have indicated that the gaps in academic achievement between low-SES and middle-class students in the United States can be documented before children enter school (Sawhill, 2006). These findings have prompted interest in—and debate over—the development of universal preschool, a national system for early care and education using the public schools. The goal of programs such as this is to improve school readiness and educational success by (1) providing access to high-quality child care and developmentally appropriate preschool, especially for low- or middle-income children, (2) building parent involvement, and (3) providing support services for parents that enhance family functioning. Preliminary findings from one such program have indicated enhanced academic skills through second grade by children who have attended preschool (Henrich, Ginicola, Finn-Stevenson & Zigler, 2006). Critics argue the cost is too high and protest tax increases to fund them.

In recent years, the overall trend has been toward increased commitment to universal preschool.
©IT Stock Free/Alamy

In the United States, 43 states as well as the District of Columbia and Guam provide some form of publicly funded preschool, serving about 1.5 million 3- to 4-year-olds. In 2016, roughly 5 percent of 3-year-olds and 32 percent of 4-year-olds were enrolled. Quality and access vary widely. For example, six states have programs that meet all 10 benchmarks for quality standards, while seven states offer no programs (National Institute for Early Education Research, 2017). Despite these disparities in funding and access across states, the overall trend in recent years has been toward increased commitment for universal preschool. However, continued funding for such programs is not certain.

KINDERGARTEN

Originally a year of transition between the relative freedom of home or preschool and the structure of grade school, kindergarten in the United States has become more like first grade. Children spend less time on self-chosen activities and more time on worksheets and preparing to read. A successful transition to kindergarten lays the foundation for future academic achievement (Schulting, Malone, & Dodge, 2005).

Although some states do not require kindergarten programs or kindergarten attendance, most 5-year-olds attend kindergarten. Since the late 1970s, an increasing number of kindergarteners spend a full day in school, rather than the traditional half day (Kena et al., 2014). A practical impetus for this trend is the growing number of single-parent and dual-earner households. While full-day kindergarten has been associated with small to moderate increases in reading and math skills when compared to a half-day schedule (Votruba-Drzal, Li-Grining & Maldonado-Carreno, 2008), by the end of third grade these differences disappear (Cooper, Allen, Patall & Dent, 2010; Rathbun, West & Germino-Hausken, 2004).

Findings highlight the importance of the preparation a child receives *before* kindergarten. The resources with which children come to kindergarten—preliteracy skills and the richness of a home literacy environment—predict reading achievement in first grade, and these individual differences tend to persist or increase through the first four years of school (Rathbun et al., 2004). Emotional and social adjustment also affect readiness for kindergarten and strongly predict school success. It is important that children have the ability to sit still, follow directions, wait one's turn, and regulate one's own learning (Raver, 2003). Broadly, kindergarten readiness is associated with positive academic and social outcomes for children (Goldstein, McCoach & Yu, 2017; Jones, Greenberg & Crowley, 2015).

There are individual differences in children's ability to self-regulate, but the environment can either promote or impede regulatory activity, suggesting the importance of classroom management in academic achievement (Rimm-Kaufman, Curby, Grimm, Nathanson & Brock, 2009). Adjustment to kindergarten can be eased by enabling preschoolers and parents to visit before the start of kindergarten, shortening school days early in the school year, having teachers make home visits, holding parent orientation sessions, and keeping parents informed about what is going on in school (Schulting, Malone & Dodge, 2005).

Some children are asked to repeat kindergarten, generally out of the belief that a 2nd year of kindergarten will help children gain the skills they need to keep up. Low-SES children, boys, children who are low in school readiness or did not attend preschool, non-native English speakers, and those with developmental delays are most likely to repeat kindergarten (Winsler et al., 2012; Malone, West, Flanagan & Park, 2006). However, it is unclear if there are academic benefits to retention. Some research shows that children who repeat kindergarten still tend to have lower reading and mathematics skills at the end of first grade than those who spent only one year in kindergarten (Malone et al., 2006), while other research suggests there may be some benefits (Dong, 2010).

A variety of strategies—including a pre-class visit and a parent orientation—can help children and parents know what to expect and ease children's adjustment to kindergarten.
©Ariel Skelley/Blend Images/Corbis

mastering the CHAPTER

©Mint Images Limited/Alamy

Piagetian Approach: The Preoperational Child

> Children in the preoperational stage show several important advances, as well as some immature aspects of thought.

> The symbolic function enables children to reflect on people, objects, and events that are not physically present. It is shown in deferred imitation, pretend play, and language.

> Symbolic development helps preoperational children make more accurate judgments of spatial relationships. They can link cause and effect with regard to familiar situations, understand the concept of identity, categorize, compare quantities, and understand principles of counting.

> Preoperational children appear to be less egocentric than Piaget thought.

> Centration keeps preoperational children from understanding principles of conservation. Their logic also is limited by irreversibility and a focus on states rather than transformations.

> Theory of mind, which develops markedly between ages 3 and 5, includes awareness of a child's own thought processes, understanding that people can hold false beliefs, ability to deceive, ability to distinguish appearance from reality, and ability to distinguish fantasy from reality.

> Maturational and environmental influences affect individual differences in theory-of-mind development.

KEY TERMS

Preoperational stage	Animism	Conservation
Symbolic function	Centration	Irreversibility
Pretend play	Decenter	Theory of mind
Transduction	Egocentrism	

Information-Processing Approach: Memory Development

> Information-processing models describe three steps in memory: encoding, storage, and retrieval.

> Although sensory memory shows little change with age, the capacity of working memory increases. The central executive controls the flow of information to and from long-term memory. At all ages, recognition is better than recall, but both increase during early childhood.

> Early episodic memory is only temporary; it fades or is transferred to generic memory. Autobiographical

memory typically begins at about age 3 or 4; it may be related to self-recognition and language development.

> According to the social interaction model, children and adults co-construct autobiographical memories by talking about shared experiences.

> Children are more likely to remember unusual activities that they actively participate in. The way adults talk with children about events influences memory formation.

KEY TERMS

Encoding	Central executive	Generic memory
Storage	Long-term memory	Script
Retrieval	Executive function	Episodic memory
Sensory memory	Recognition	Autobiographic memory
Working memory	Recall	Social interaction model

Psychometric and Vygotskian Approaches: Intelligence

> The two most commonly used psychometric intelligence tests for young children are the Stanford-Binet Intelligence Scales and the Wechsler Preschool and Primary Scale of Intelligence, Revised (WPPSI-IV).

> Intelligence test scores have risen in industrialized countries. Intelligence test scores may be influenced by a number of factors, including the home environment and SES.

> Newer tests based on Vygotsky's concept of the zone of proximal development (ZPD) focus on potential rather than achievement. Such tests, combined with scaffolding, can help parents and teachers guide children's progress.

> KEY TERMS

Stanford-Binet Intelligence Scale

Wechsler Preschool and Primary Scale of Intelligence, Revised (WPPSI-III)

Zone of proximal development (ZPD)

Scaffolding

Language Development

> During early childhood, vocabulary increases greatly, and grammar, syntax, and pragmatics become more sophisticated.

> Private speech is normal and common, and it may aid in self-regulation.

> Causes of delayed language development are multiple. If untreated, language delays may have serious cognitive, social, and emotional consequences.

> Interaction with adults can promote emergent literacy. Reading to children is an effective path to literacy.

> KEY TERMS

Fast mapping

Pragmatics

Private speech

Emergent literacy

Early Childhood Education

> Goals of preschool education vary across cultures. Montessori and Reggio Emilia are two popular child-centered approaches. The academic content of early childhood education programs in the United States has increased.

> Compensatory preschool programs have had positive outcomes, although some gains fade over time. Compensatory programs that start early and extend into the primary grades may have better long-term results.

> Interest in universal preschool has grown as results of pilot programs have shown positive outcomes in terms of children's school readiness and academic success.

> Many children today attend full-day kindergarten. Success in kindergarten depends largely on emotional and social adjustment and kindergarten readiness.

Practice Quiz

1. What are three immature aspects of cognition in early childhood?

_____
_____
_____

2. One reason children typically fail to conserve is:
   a. they have difficulty focusing on one aspect (e.g., height or width) of a substance at a time
   b. they have difficulty understanding that if they were to go backward in time, the original shape or size of the substance would be the same as it was originally
   c. they focus on transformations rather than end-states
   d. children's ability to hold material in short-term memory for extended periods of time is poor

3. Which of the following behaviors requires theory of mind?
   a. smiling at someone after they have smiled at you
   b. hitting another child for taking your toy
   c. getting scared when you see your sister's skinned knee
   d. lying to your mom about eating cookies before dinner

4. Filing papers away in the proper folder in a filing cabinet is most like the _____ aspect of memory.
   a. encoding   **c.** retrieval
   b. storage   **d.** sensory

5. Being able to tell an adult your parent's phone number is an example of _____ memory.

6. Which memory system does not change much with age?
   a. recognition memory
   b. autobiographical memory
   c. sensory memory
   d. working memory

7. Two commonly used intelligence tests for children are:

_____
_____

8. What is the best definition of an IQ score?
   a. it describes a fixed quantity of inborn intelligence
   b. a relatively direct measure of exposure to educational programming, preschools, and formative experiences
   c. a measure of how well a child can do certain tasks at a certain time in comparison to others of the same age
   d. a measure of genetic potential

9. The influence of the family environment:
   a. increases in influence with age
   b. decreases in influence with age
   c. exerts a steady influence across age
   d. has no effect at any age

10. Which is an example of working in a child's zone of proximal development?
   a. doing a child's homework for him or her
   b. giving hints to a child so he or she can complete his or her homework with assistance
   c. encouraging a child to expend more effort to finish his or her homework
   d. hiring a tutor to help a child struggling with homework

11. When young children say things such as, "Daddy goed to the store," this should be viewed as:
   a. a normal developmental occurrence
   b. a sign that a speech problem or delay is likely
   c. a sign that a cognitive development problem or delay is likely
   d. a sign of a specific language impairment

12. What are three things that can contribute to speech delays? _____
_____
_____

13. One of the most effective preliteracy activities for children is:
   a. letter/sound flashcards
   b. reading to them
   c. exposure to television and other media sources
   d. exposure to music

14. With respect to early education programs, "child centered" refers to:
   a. children being allowed to make up most rules for their classrooms
   b. classrooms in which children are allowed to direct their own learning experiences
   c. classrooms in which children of different ages are schooled together
   d. avoiding the use of traditional preschools and teaching children at home

15. What are three characteristics of effective compensatory preschool programs?

_____
_____
_____

16. In addition to academic preparation, another variable that appears to predict success in kindergarten is:
   a. gender
   b. whether children are "younger" or "older" kindergarteners
   c. emotional and social adjustment
   d. whether children have older siblings at home

Answers: 1–Three immature aspects of cognition in early childhood include egocentrism, centration, and irreversibility; 2–b; 3–d; 4–b; 5–recall; 6–d; 7–Two commonly used intelligence tests for children are the Stanford-Binet Intelligence Scales and the Wechsler Preschool and Primary Scale of Intelligence, Revised (WPSSI-III); 8–c; 9–b; 10–b; 11–a; 12–Among the factors that can contribute to speech delays are hearing problems, head and facial abnormalities, premature birth, family history, socioeconomic factors, and developmental delays; 13–b; 14–b; 15–Among the variables associated with effective compensatory preschool programs are early and long-lasting intervention, high parental participation, well-trained teachers, low staff-to-child ratios, longer school days and weeks, and extensive services; 16–c

Five-year-old twins Derek and Sophie have been raised in the same family with the same parents and attend the same day care. Sophie is both more outgoing and more aggressive than Derek, and she frequently gets into arguments with her playmates. Derek is quieter but plays much more actively than Sophie—tumbling around with the other boys and spending much of his free time running and jumping. Derek and Sophie's parents have noted that while Sophie needs a relatively firm hand, Derek responds more quickly to appeals to empathy and to discussions about the ways his actions affect others. Why are these two children so different? Are their differences due to gender? To the different ways in which their parents handle them? To innate differences in their temperament and personality? What influences who they are?

The years from ages 3 to 6 are pivotal in children's psychosocial development. A child's emotional development and sense of self are rooted in the experiences of those years. In this chapter we discuss the developing self, and how sense of male or female identity arises and how it affects behavior. We explore play and why it is so vitally important for children. Finally, we consider the influence of what parents do and why children engage in both prosocial and aggressive behavior.

● ● ● ●

The Developing Self

"Who in the world am I? Ah, that's the great puzzle," said Alice in Wonderland, after her size had abruptly changed—again. Solving Alice's "puzzle" is a lifelong process of getting to know one's self. Our comprehension of the self is informed by self-concept, self-esteem, and our ability to understand and regulate emotions.

THE SELF-CONCEPT AND SELF-DEFINITION

The **self-concept** is our total picture of our abilities and traits that determines how we feel about ourselves—who we think we are. It is a cognitive construction (Harter, 1996) that includes representations of the self. It also has a social aspect that incorporates children's growing understanding of how others see them. For example, a child who other children chronically reject might form a self-concept of herself as unlikable. During the early childhood years, the self-concept develops through changes in self-definition and is impacted by culture.

Changes in Self-Definition

Children develop a sense of self-awareness in toddlerhood that develops along with gains in cognitive abilities. Children's **self-definition**—the way they describe themselves—typically changes between about ages 5 and 7, reflecting this development. At age 4, Jason says:

My name is Jason and I live in a big house with my mother and father and sister, Lisa. I have a kitty that's orange and a television set in my own room. . . . I like pizza and I have a nice teacher. I can count up to 100–want to hear me? I love my dog, Skipper. I can climb to the top of the jungle gym, I'm not scared! Just happy. You can't be happy and scared, no way! I have brown hair, and I go to preschool. I'm really strong. I can lift this chair, watch me (Harter, 1996, p. 208)!

The way Jason describes himself is typical of American children his age. He talks mostly about concrete, observable behaviors; external characteristics, such as physical features; preferences; possessions; and members of his household. He mentions a particular skill (climbing) rather than general abilities (being athletic). His self-descriptions are unrealistically positive. He has difficulty understanding how conflicting emotions can exist simultaneously. Not until around age 7 will he describe himself in terms of generalized traits, such as popular, smart, or dumb; recognize he can have conflicting emotions; and be self-critical while holding a positive overall self-concept. It will take until later in middle childhood for Jason's self-descriptions to become more balanced and realistic ("I'm good at hockey but bad at arithmetic").

Cultural Differences in Self-Definition

Culture helps shape the understanding of the self. For example, one major cultural dimension—individualism versus collectivism—impacts the understanding of the self in relation to others. In highly individualistic cultures like the United States, individuals are seen as separate from one another, and independence and self-reliance are highly valued. In collectivistic cultures, such as India and China, individuals are seen as fundamentally interrelated, and group harmony and cohesiveness take precedence over individual concerns (Oyserman, Coon & Kemmelmeir, 2002).

Parents transmit, often through everyday conversations, cultural ideas and beliefs about how to define the self. For example, Chinese parents tend to encourage interdependent aspects of the self such as compliance with authority, appropriate conduct, humility, and a sense of belonging to the community. European American parents tend to encourage independent aspects of the self: individuality, self-expression, and self-esteem. Children absorb such differing cultural styles of self-definition as early as age 3 or 4, and these differences increase with age (Wang, 2004). For example, when reminiscing about past events with their children, European American mothers are more likely to highlight the child's internal states, a cultural message that highlights the personal meaning of the event and is concordant with the individualistic cultural perspective. By contrast, Chinese parents are more likely to reference the child's relationships with others, emphasizing key cultural values of connectedness and community (Wang, Doan & Song, 2010).

self-concept Sense of self; descriptive and evaluative mental picture of one's abilities and traits.

self-definition Cluster of characteristics used to describe oneself.

SELF-ESTEEM

Self-esteem is the evaluative part of the self-concept, the judgment children make about their overall self-worth. Self-esteem is based on children's growing cognitive ability to describe and define themselves.

Developmental Changes in Self-Esteem

Before about ages 5 to 7, young children's self-esteem is not firmly based on reality, and most young children wildly overestimate their abilities. For example, despite coming in last in a race, 4-year-old Mateo might still believe himself to be the best and the fastest runner. One reason for this positive bias is that self-esteem is, in part, the result of feedback received from others, and adults tend to give positive feedback (Harter, 1998, 2006). For example, a kindergartener's crude lettering is not generally critiqued as being messy; rather, parents are more likely to praise the child's efforts.

self-esteem Judgment a person makes about his or her self-worth.

Children's self-esteem also tends to be unidimensional. In other words, children believe they are either all good or all bad (Harter, 1998). You may notice that this is similar to what is found in the self-concept, and presumably the same cognitive constraints underlie both processes. Not until middle childhood does it become more realistic, as personal evaluations of competence based on internalization of parental and societal standards begin to shape and maintain self-worth (Harter, 1998).

A child whose self-esteem is contingent on success may attribute failures to unchangeable personal deficiencies; this can result in a pattern of learned helplessness.

©OJO Images/AP Images

Contingent Self-Esteem

Consider the praise parents give children for succeeding. If a child is generally praised for working hard, and she fails at a task, the logical implication is that she did not try hard enough. That child might then be motivated to work harder next time. If the same child is praised for being smart, and she fails at a task, the implication is far different. Now, the implication is that the child is no longer smart. The motivation for working hard has been stripped away.

Not surprisingly then, children whose self-esteem is contingent on success tend to become demoralized when they fail. Often, these children attribute failure to their personal deficiencies, which they believe they are unable to change. About one-third to one-half of preschoolers, kindergarteners, and first graders show a "learned helplessness" pattern (Dweck & Grant, 2008). For example, when given a difficult puzzle, "helpless" children are likely to give up. They assume they will fail, and so do not bother to try. Preschoolers who fail may interpret this as a sign of being "bad," whereas older children who fail may conclude that they are "dumb,"

Children with noncontingent self-esteem, in contrast, tend to attribute failure or disappointment to factors outside themselves or to the need to try harder. For example, when faced with the same puzzle, such a child might assume the puzzle was for older children or might continue to try to put it together despite having initial difficult. If initially unsuccessful or rejected, they persevere, trying new strategies until they find one that works (Harter, 1998; Pomerantz & Saxon, 2001). Children who believe that they can succeed if they try, who enjoy challenges, and who have faith in their ability to meet those challenges tend to have parents who praise their efforts, not their inherent abilities, and who focus on specific, focused feedback rather than generic praise (Gunderson et al., 2013).

Did you know?

Giving children generic praise—"great job!"—in response to being shown a drawing is associated with children giving up after failure. This is because if they fail, they assume it's because they lack the critical ability to draw well. However, when praise is targeted—"great job drawing!"—children tend to persevere in the face of failure. This is because this implies their earlier success was due to their efforts related to drawing specifically. When praise is mixed, like in real life, even small amounts of nongeneric praise preserve mastery in children (Zentall & Morris, 2010).

©Comstock/PictureQuest

REGULATING EMOTIONS

At 5-year-old Kayla's birthday party, Kayla opens a present from her grandmother and finds not the doll she was hoping to receive, but a board game. Her face drops as her mother whispers in her ear, "Smile and tell Grandma thank you. You

don't want to hurt her feelings." Kayla tries, but her smile is unconvincing.

The ability to regulate, or control, one's feelings is one of the key advances of early childhood (Dennis, 2006). Emotional self-regulation helps children guide their behavior (Eisenberg, Fabes & Spinrad, 2006) and adjust their responses to meet societal expectations. Children develop the ability to regulate their emotions slowly, via a shift from early reliance on orienting processes supported by the pari-etal and frontal areas of the brain to control of affect using frontal brain networks in the anterior cingulate gyrus (Rothbart, Sheese, Rueda & Posner, 2011).

UNDERSTANDING EMOTIONS

"I hate you!" Maya, age 5, shouts to her mother. "You're a mean mommy!" Angry because her mother sent her to her room for pinching her baby brother, Maya cannot imagine ever loving her mother again. "Aren't you ashamed of your-self for making the baby cry?" her father asks Maya a little later. Maya nods, but only because she knows what response he wants. In truth, she feels a jumble of emotions—not the least of which is feeling sorry for herself.

Emotional understanding appears to proceed in an ordered and hierarchical manner. First, by around 5 years of age, children understand the public aspects of emotions. In other words, they understand the things that cause other people to feel happy or sad, how those emotions look on other people, and that reminding someone of something that happened can elicit that emotion again (Pons, Harris & de Rosnay, 2004). Preschoolers can talk about their feelings and often those of others, and they understand that emotions are connected with experiences and desires (Saarni, Campos, Camras & Witherington, 2006). They also understand that someone who gets what he wants will be happy, and someone who does not get what she wants will be sad (Lagattuta, 2005). By about 4 to 5 years, most children can recognize the facial expressions of joy, sadness, fear, anger, surprise and disgust (Widen & Russsell, 2008), although girls tend to out-perform boys slightly (Denhan, Bassett, Brown, Way & Steed, 2015). They are also able to recognize emotions as reflected in vocal cues (Sauter, Panattoni & Happe, 2013) and body posture, such as found in a sad person's slumped shoulders or an angry person's aggressive stance (Parker, Mathis & Kupersmidt, 2013).

By about 7 years of age, children start to understand that mental states can drive emotions. For example, they under-stand that someone can feel one way and look another. They also understand that what someone believes, even if it is not true, can affect emotional state, and what someone wants, even if they themselves do not want it, can also affect emotional state (Pons, Harris & de Rosnay, 2004). This process is involved in the development of moral behavior. In one study, 4- through 8-year-olds were asked to describe how a young boy would feel if his ball rolled into the street and he either retrieved it—and thus broke the rule of not going into the street—or refrained from retrieving it. The 4- and 5-year-olds tended to believe that the boy would be happy if he got the ball—even though he would be breaking a rule—and unhappy if he didn't. The older children, like adults, were more inclined to believe that obedience to a rule would make the boy feel good and disobedience would make him feel bad—even if they themselves would have preferred to get the ball (Lagattuta, 2005).

Last, by about 9 years of age, children start to under-stand more complex aspects of emotion. For example, they understand that situations can be viewed from multiple per-spectives, that people might have conflicting emotions like feeling angry at someone while loving them, and that they can use cognitive strategies to regulate their emotional state (Pons, Harris & de Rosnay). This process will be discussed more fully in Chapter 14.

Understanding the Social Emotions

Social emotions involve a comparison of one's self or one's actions to social standards. These emotions are directed toward the self and include guilt, shame, and pride. They typically develop by the end of the 3rd year after children gain self-awareness and accept the standards of behavior their parents have set. However, even children a few years older often lack the cognitive sophistication to recognize these emotions and what brings them on (Pons, Harris & de Rosnay, 2004).

social emotions Emotions directed at the self that involve a comparison of one-self or one's actions to social standards.

In one study (Harter, 1993), 4- to 8-year-olds were told two stories. In the first story, a child takes a few coins from a jar after being told not to do so; in the second story, a child performs a difficult gymnastic feat—a flip on the bars. Each story was presented in two versions: one in which a parent sees the child doing the act and another in which no one sees the child. The children were asked how they and the parent would feel in each circumstance.

Again, the answers revealed a gradual progression in understanding of feelings about the self, reflecting the 5 to 7 shift (Harter, 1996). At age 4 to 5, children did not say that either they or their parents would feel pride or shame. Instead they used such terms as *worried* or *scared* (for the money jar incident) and *excited* or *happy* (about the gymnastic accomplishment). At 5 to 6, children said their parents would be ashamed or proud of them but did not acknowledge feeling these emotions themselves. At 6 to 7, children said they would feel ashamed or proud, but only if they were observed. Not until age 7 or 8 did children say they would feel ashamed or proud of themselves even if no one saw them.

Culture seems to influence this process to some degree. Generally, in more collectivistic cultures, where interpersonal interactions and group dynamics are seen as more important, guilt is more common. In individualistic cultures where autonomy and independence are highly valued, pride is more relevant (Eid & Diener, 2001). For example, one study comparing children from three cultural groups found that while patterns of correlations were more similar than different, there were cultural variations. Children from the United States scored higher than other cultures on pride, children from Japan scored higher on shame, and children from Korea scored higher on guilt (Furukawa, Tangney & Higashibara, 2012).

Gender

Five-year-old twins Derek and Sophie argued about what game to play. "I want to play Batman," Derek insisted, "And you can be the Joker, and I will come get you." "No," Sophie replied, "I will be the fairy princess, and you will be my brave knight." "I don't play princess games," Derek replied, "because I am a boy."

Gender identity, awareness of one's femaleness or maleness and all it implies, is an important aspect of the developing self-concept. How different are young boys and girls? What causes those differences? How do children develop gender identity, and how does it affect their attitudes and behavior?

gender identity Awareness, developed in early childhood, that one is male or female.

GENDER DIFFERENCES

Gender differences are psychological or behavioral differences between males and females. As we discussed in Chapter 8, measurable differences between baby boys and girls are few. Although some gender differences become more pronounced after age 3, boys and girls on average remain more alike than different. Extensive evidence from

many studies supports this gender similarities hypothesis. Fully 78 percent of gender differences are small to negligible, and some differences, such as in self-esteem, change with age (Hyde, 2005).

Did you know?

Biologically based gender differences are a controversial area of research precisely because the differences are small. If they were large, there would be no reason to argue their existence.

©Alexander Lysenko/Shutterstock

Physically, among the larger gender differences are boys' higher activity level, superior motor performance, especially after puberty, and their greater propensity for physical aggression (Hyde, 2005; Archer, 2004; Baillargeon et al., 2007; Pellegrini & Archer, 2005; Nielsen, Pfister & Bo Andersen, 2011). These physical differences impact the nature of play. Boys engage in more rough-and-tumble, physically active play than girls do (LaFreniere, 2011; DiPietro, 1981). There are also sex-typed toy preferences; girls prefer to play with dolls and doll accessories, and boys prefer to play with construction and transportation toys (Pasterski et al., 2011). Sex-typed play preferences increase between toddlerhood and middle childhood, and the degree of sex-typed behavior exhibited early in life is a strong indicator of later gender-based behavior (Golombok et al., 2008).

Cognitive gender differences are few and small and are affected by task characteristics (Miller & Halpern, 2014; Ardila, Rosselli, Matute & Inozemtseva, 2011). While there are fine-grain differences in particular areas, there do not appear to be gender differences in overall intelligence (Nisbett et al., 2012).

Boys and girls do equally well on tasks involving basic mathematical skills and are equally capable of learning math, but show variations in specific abilities. Most of these differences emerge in elementary school or later

Gender roles affect the costumes that girls and boys choose to wear, as can be seen here in Mariah Carey's twins, Monroe and Moroccan.
©FilmMagic/Getty Images

(Spelke, 2005). Girls tend to perform better on tests on mathematical computation and memory for lists of numbers and objects. Girls also tend to outperform boys on problems requiring algebraic solutions or short answer responses. Boys generally show an advantage in mental rotations, especially when the task involves 3-D objects and when it is timed (Miller & Halpern, 2014). Boys also tend to do better in mathematical word problems and memory for spatial configurations (Spelke, 2005). Boys' mathematical abilities vary more than girls', with more boys at both the highest and lowest ends of the ability range (Halpern et al., 2007). However, in most studies, mathematics test performance tends to be about the same (Miller & Halpern, 2014).

Girls generally show a verbal advantage (Bornstein, Hahn & Haynes, 2004). Across different languages, they tend to start using language earlier, say more, and combine words earlier (Eriksson et al, 2012). Boys are more likely to stutter or to have a reading disability than girls (Wallentin, 2009; Rutter et al., 2004). In early childhood and again during preadolescence and adolescence, girls tend to use more responsive language, such as praise, agreement, acknowledgment, and elaboration on what someone else has said (Leaper & Smith, 2004). Girls tend to show an advantage in school, and as a group tend to earn higher grades, especially in language classes (Voyer & Voyer, 2014). Some researchers have argued that this early language advantage seems to disappear by adulthood and is no longer detectable (Wallentin, 2009).

We need to remember, of course, that gender differences are valid for large groups of boys and girls but not necessarily for individuals. By knowing a child's sex, we cannot predict whether that *particular* boy or girl will be faster, stronger, smarter, more talkative, or more assertive than another child.

PERSPECTIVES ON GENDER DEVELOPMENT

What accounts for gender differences, and why do some of them emerge as children grow older? Some explanations center on the differing experiences and social expectations boys and girls meet almost from birth. These experiences and expectations concern three related aspects of gender identity: gender roles, gender-typing, and gender stereotypes.

Gender roles are the behaviors, interests, attitudes, skills, and personality traits that a culture considers appropriate for males or females. Historically, in most cultures, women have been expected to devote most of their time to caring for the household and children, and men have been providers and protectors. Women have been expected to be compliant and nurturant; men, to be active, aggressive, and competitive. Today, gender roles in Western cultures have become more diverse and flexible.

Gender-typing, the acquisition of a gender role, takes place early in childhood but children vary greatly in the degree to which they become gender-typed (Iervolino, Hines, Golombok, Rust & Plomin, 2005). **Gender stereotypes**

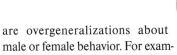

Did you know?

Girls start to love pink, and boys to avoid it, at about the age of 2 to 3 years, just as they're beginning to talk about gender (LoBue & DeLoache, 2011).

©Andrew Paterson/Alamy

are overgeneralizations about male or female behavior. For example, "All females are passive and dependent; all males are aggressive and independent" are gender stereotypes. They appear to some degree in children as young as 2 or 3, increase during the preschool years, and reach a peak at age 5 (Campbell, Shirley & Candy, 2004).

How do children acquire gender roles, and why do they adopt gender stereotypes? Five theoretical perspectives—biological, evolutionary developmental, psychoanalytic, cognitive, and social learning (Table 10.1)—contribute to our understanding of gender development; none fully explains why boys and girls differ in some respects but not in others.

Biological Approach

The existence of similar gender roles in many cultures suggests that some gender differences are biologically based. If gender differences were purely cultural inventions, as has sometimes been argued, we would expect to see more variability in male and female roles and characteristics across cultures. In support of this view, investigators are uncovering evidence of neurological, hormonal, and evolutionary explanations for some gender differences.

In this view, some of the differences we see between boys and girls are influenced by biologically wired brain anatomy. These differences arise from, among other factors, genes coding for differences in anatomy and function between the sexes, prenatal hormonal exposure, differing environmental experiences, or the activating effects of puberty in adolescence.

Across the life span, and starting early in development, men, on average, have larger brain volume than women (Ruigrok et al, 2014). By age 5, when the brain reaches approximate adult size, boys' brains are about 10 percent larger than girls' brains (Reiss, Abrams, Singer, Ross & Denckla, 1996). However, when controlling for total cerebral volume, girls' brains have a higher proportion of gray matter (neurons) and show greater cerebral blood flow, while boys' brains contain more white matter (axons for communication between neurons) (Cosgrove, Mazure & Staley, 2007; Luders, Gaser, Narr & Toga, 2009). What may be even more important is what occurs in the womb when the brain is forming. Hormones in the prenatal environment affect the

gender roles Behaviors, interests, attitudes, skills, and traits that a culture considers appropriate for each sex; differs for males and females.

gender-typing Socialization process whereby children, at an early age, learn appropriate gender roles.

gender stereotypes Preconceived generalizations about male or female role behavior.

TABLE 10.1 Five Perspectives on Gender Development

Theories	Major Theorists	Key Processes	Basic Beliefs
Biological Approach		Genetic, neurological, and hormonal activity	Many or most behavioral differences between the sexes can be traced to biological differences.
Evolutionary Developmental Approach	Charles Darwin	Natural sexual selection	Children develop gender roles in preparation for adult mating and reproductive behavior.
Psychoanalytic Approach Psychosexual theory	Sigmund Freud	Resolution of unconscious emotional conflict	Gender identity occurs when child identifies with same-sex parent.
Cognitive Approach Cognitive-developmental theory	Lawrence Kohlberg	Self-categorization	Once a child learns she is a girl or he is a boy, child sorts information about behavior by gender and acts accordingly.
Gender-schema theory	Sandra Bem, Carol Lynn Martin & Charles F. Halverson	Self-categorization based on processing of cultural information	Child organizes information about what is considered appropriate for a boy or a girl on the basis of what a particular culture dictates and behaves accordingly. Child sorts by gender because the culture dictates that gender is an important schema.
Social Learning Approach Social cognitive theory	Albert Bandura	Observation of models, reinforcement	Child mentally combines observations of multiple models and creates own behavioral variations.

©FatCamera/E+/Getty Images

developing brain. Although levels of the male hormone testosterone do not appear to be directly related to aggressiveness in children (Constantino et al., 1993), an analysis of fetal testosterone levels and the development of gender-typical play has shown a link between higher testosterone levels in utero and male-typical play in boys (Auyeng et al., 2009). Additionally, testosterone has been linked to dominance and status striving behavior in humans (Eisenegger, Haushofer & Fehr, 2011).

Some research focuses on girls with a disorder called *congenital adrenal hyperplasia (CAH)*. These girls have high prenatal levels of *androgens* (male sex hormones). They tend to show preferences for boys' toys, rough play, and male playmates, as well as strong spatial skills. This implies prenatal exposure in utero plays a role in the establishment of these early physical differences between boys and girls. *Estrogens* (female sex hormones), on the other hand, seem to have less influence on boys' gender-typed behavior (Pasterski et al., 2005).

Perhaps the most dramatic examples of biologically based research have to do with infants born with ambiguous sexual organs that are not clearly male or female. John Money and his colleagues (Money, Hampson & Hampson, 1955) recommended that these children be assigned as early as possible to the gender that holds the potential for the most nearly normal functioning. They based this recommendation on the appearance of the genitals.

However, newer studies demonstrate the profound difficulty of predicting the outcome of sex assignment at birth, particularly on the basis of what the genitals looks like. In one study, 14 genetically male children born without normal penises but with testes were legally and surgically assigned female sex during the 1st month of life and were raised as girls. Ultimately, eight declared themselves male, five declared unwavering female identity but expressed difficulty fitting in with other girls, and one refused to discuss the subject with anyone. Meanwhile, the two boys whose parents had refused the initial sexual assignment remained male (Reiner & Gearhart, 2004). This and other similar cases strongly suggest that gender identity is rooted in biological factors and is not easily changed (Meyer-Bahlburg, 2005; Reiner, 2005; Diamond & Sigmundson, 1997). Merely telling a boy or a girl what he or she is is not enough to alter gender identity.

Recently, the issue of transgender children has garnered attention, driven in part by legal challenges regarding which bathroom is appropriate for those individuals who identify with the opposite gender. Transgender people are individuals whose gender identity is different from their biological sex. There are indications that the disparity between gender and sex may be biologically influenced. For example, biological women who later identify as male have markers that suggest high androgen exposure in the womb (Leinung & Wu, 2017;

Wu & Leinung, 2015). Additionally, research on twins suggests there may be genetic influences at play as well (Diamond, 2013). While many young children play with their identity—for example, dressing up in different clothes or pretending to be something they are not—children, especially girls, who will later identify as transgender are far more likely to show strong and persistent gender dysphoria early in childhood (Steensma, McGuire, Kreukels, Beekman & Cohen-Kettenis, 2013). Moreover, the volume of the stria terminalis (an area of the brain involved in sexual behavior) in biological men who later identify as women is more similar to that of other women than to that of other men (Zhou, Hofman, Gooren & Swaab, 1995). The density, but not the volume, of their neurons is more similar to that of biological women as well (Luders et al., 2009). In short, there is emerging evidence that gender identity—a psychological construct housed in the brain—is influenced by biology and is not merely the consequence of biological sex or child-rearing practices. Note that this does not mean the environment does not matter. Gender is complicated and is the result of multiple intersecting lines of influence. An examination of the conditions under which biological sex and gender are not the same, as occurs in transgender people, may offer clues about how these processes interact with each other for people in which development proceeds as expected. Any good theory of gender should be able to account for variation. More research is needed in this controversial area.

Evolutionary Developmental Approach

The evolutionary developmental approach sees gendered behavior as biologically influenced. From this controversial perspective, children's gender roles are a consequence of the evolved mating and child-rearing strategies of adult males and females.

According to Darwin's (1871) **theory of sexual selection**, the selection of sexual partners is a response to the differing reproductive pressures early men and women confronted in the struggle for survival (Wood & Eagly, 2002). In humans, females must contribute far more to raising children because of the constraints placed on them by pregnancy and nursing. Males, however, may contribute as little as a few teaspoonfuls of semen. While survival may be more certain if a man invests resources in a child, that investment is not obligatory. This puts into play different reproductive dynamics for each sex. The more widely a man can engage in sexual activity, the greater his chances to pass on his genetic inheritance. Thus, men tend to prefer more sexual partners than women do. They value physical prowess because it enables them to compete for mates and for control of resources and social status, which women value. Because a woman invests more time and energy in pregnancy and can bear only a limited number of children, each child's survival is of utmost importance to her, so she looks for a mate who will remain with her and support their offspring. More sexual activity after a pregnancy has already been achieved does not result in more children for a woman until after that child has been born and

the woman is ready to carry another pregnancy. The need to raise each child to reproductive maturity and the high degree of care required by human children also explains why women tend to be more caring and nurturing than men (Bjorklund & Pellegrini, 2000; Wood & Eagly, 2002).

According to evolutionary theory, male competitiveness and aggressiveness and female nurturance develop during childhood as preparation for these adult roles. Boys play at fighting; girls play at parenting. Males value physical prowess because it enables them to compete for mates and for control of resources and social status, which women value. Women, by contrast, are the primary caregivers. Thus young girls tend to be more nurturant and better able than young boys to control and inhibit their emotions and to refrain from impulsive behavior (Bjorklund & Pellegrini, 2000).

Critics of evolutionary theory argue that society and culture are more important than biology in determining gender roles. But evolutionary theorists have never argued that culture is insignificant. Rather, they have argued that men and women have cognitive adaptations designed to be sensitive to environmental input. Moreover, they point out that culture does not exist by itself—it is a product of our evolved minds. As such, it reflects our proclivities and who we are. We made it. Thus, to say that culture makes us who we are is a tautological argument (Tooby & Cosmides, 1992).

Moreover, evolutionary psychology is not deterministic, as some critics have argued. Research suggests that men's primary ancestral role was to provide for subsistence while women's was to tend to the children, but this does not mean that we are bound to these roles. Evolution has given us an evolved architecture of the mind that pushes us in certain directions, but it has also given us the ability to reflect upon our choices and make reasoned decisions. Thus, our behavior is flexible and adaptive. For example, in some nonindustrial societies, women are the main or equal providers, and men and women's mate preferences seem to be less pronounced in egalitarian societies where women have more reproductive freedom and educational opportunities (Wood & Eagly, 2012).

theory of sexual selection Darwinian theory, which holds that selection of sexual partners is influenced by the differing reproductive pressures that early men and women confronted in the evolutionary past.

Did you know?

Natural selection depends on reproduction and differential success of descendants. However, the adaptations that evolution works on need not be conscious. For example, most people do not have sex to spread their genes. They have sex because it feels good, and in the ancestral world, the consequence of that was reproduction.

©Jeffrey Blackler/Alamy

Psychoanalytic Approach

"Dad, where will you live when I grow up and marry Mommy?" asks Juan, age 4. From the psychoanalytic perspective, Juan's question is part of his acquisition of gender identity. That process, according to Freud, is one of **identification**, the adoption of characteristics, beliefs, attitudes, values, and behaviors of the same-sex parent. Freud considered identification an important personality development of early childhood.

> **identification** In Freudian theory, process by which a young child adopts characteristics, beliefs, attitudes, values, and behaviors of the parent of the same sex.
>
> **gender constancy** Awareness that one will always be male or female. Also called sex-category constancy.

According to Freud, identification will occur for Juan when he represses or gives up the wish to possess the parent of the other sex (his mother) and identifies with the parent of the same sex (his father). Although this explanation for gender development has been influential, it has been difficult to test and has little research support (Maccoby, 2000). The majority of developmental psychologists today favor other explanations.

Cognitive Approaches

Sarah figures out she is a girl because people call her a girl. As she continues to observe and think about her world, she concludes she will always be a girl. She comes to understand gender by actively thinking about and constructing her own gender-typing. This is the heart of cognitive-developmental theories of gender development. Included in the cognitive approach to understanding gender are Kohlberg's cognitive-developmental theory and gender-schema theory.

Kohlberg's Cognitive-Developmental Theory

In Kohlberg's (1966) theory, gender knowledge ("I am a boy") precedes gendered behavior ("I like to do boy things"). Children actively search for cues about gender in their social world. As children come to realize which gender they belong to, they adopt behaviors they perceive as consistent with being male or female (Martin & Ruble, 2004).

The acquisition of gender roles, said Kohlberg, hinges on **gender constancy**, more recently called sex-category constancy—a child's realization that his or her sex will always be the same. Once children realize this, they are motivated to adopt behaviors appropriate to their sex. Gender constancy seems to develop in three stages: gender identity, gender stability, and gender consistency (Martin, Ruble, & Szkrybalo, 2002).

Cognitive approaches to gender development do not fully explain why some children become more strongly gender-typed than others.
©Inti St Clair/Blend Images

- *Gender identity:* awareness of one's own gender and that of others; typically occurs between ages 2 and 3.
- *Gender stability:* awareness that gender does not change; however, judgments about gender are based on superficial appearances (clothing or hairstyle) and stereotyped behaviors.
- *Gender consistency:* the realization that outward appearances do not affect gender; for example that a girl remains a girl even if she plays with trucks, and a boy remains a boy even if he has long hair; typically occurs between ages 3 and 7, generally corresponds with a decline in rigidity of adherence to gender norms.

What is the support for Kohlberg's theory? Children do start using gendered language, showing their awareness of gender identity, by about 2 years of age, although they are better at doing this for their own gender than for the other gender (Stennes, Burch, Sen & Bauer, 2005; Gelman, Taylor, Nguyen, Leaper & Bigler, 2004). The use of gender labels "girl" and "boy" while playing predict the later use of gender-typed toys in young children (Zosuls et al., 2009). Additionally, gender stability does seem to be related to greater attention toward same-sex models, the adoption of more gender-stereotypical clothing, more positive feelings for one's own gender group, and a more rigid adherence to gender stereotypes (Slaby & Frey, 1975; Halim et al., 2014). These findings are in line with Kohlberg's approach. However, Kohlberg's theory does not fare as well with respect to prediction based on gender constancy. One of the implications of such predictions is that gender constancy should precede gender typing. But, long before children attain the final stage of gender constancy, they show strong gender-typed preferences (Martin & Ruble, 2004). For example, gender preferences in toys and playmates appear as early as 12 months (Jadva, Hines & Golombok, 2010), and by 24 months, toddlers seem to recognize which gender group they belong to (Stennes, Burch, Sen & Bauer, 2005).

However, these findings do not challenge Kohlberg's basic insight: that gender concepts influence behavior (Martin et al., 2002). Today, cognitive-developmental theorists no longer claim that gender constancy must precede gender-typing. Rather, gender-typing is heightened by the more sophisticated understanding that gender constancy brings. Each stage of gender constancy increases children's attention toward and memory for gender-relevant information. The achievement of gender identity may motivate children to learn more about gender; whereas gender stability and gender consistency may motivate them to be sure they are acting "like a boy" or "like a girl."

Gender-Schema Theory

Four-year-old Brandon has watched from his window as a new boy his age moves in next door. When he finally is allowed to visit the new family, he eagerly brings two of his favorite toy trucks, assuming the new boy will like the same toys he likes. How does he reach this conclusion?

One explanation can be found in **gender-schema theory**. Like cognitive-developmental theory, it views children as actively extracting knowledge about gender from their environment *before* engaging in gender-typed behavior. However, gender-schema theory places more emphasis on the influence of culture. Once children know what sex they are, they develop a concept of what it means to be male or female *in their culture*. Children then match their behavior to their culture's view of what boys and girls are "supposed" to be and do (Bem, 1993; Martin et al., 2002). According to this theory, gender schemas promote gender stereotypes by influencing judgments about behavior.

Bem suggests that children who show stereotypical behavior may do so as a result of pressure for gender conformity. However, there is little evidence that gender schemas are at the root of stereotyped behavior or that children who are highly gender-typed necessarily feel pressure to conform (Yunger, Carver & Perry, 2004). Indeed, as many parents will attest, it can be difficult to encourage a young child to behave in ways that are not stereotypically masculine or feminine.

Another problem with both gender-schema theory and Kohlberg's theory is that gender-stereotyping does not always become stronger with increased gender knowledge (Bandura & Bussey, 2004; Banse, Gawronski, Rebetez, Gutt & Morton, 2010). In fact, gender-stereotyping rises and then falls in a developmental pattern (Ruble & Martin, 1998; Welch-Ross & Schmidt, 1996). Around ages 4 to 6, when, according to gender-schema theory, children are constructing and consolidating their gender schemas, they tend to notice and remember only information consistent with these schemas. Indeed, they tend to *mis*remember information that challenges gender stereotypes, such as photos of a girl sawing wood or a boy cooking. They are also quick to accept gender labels; when told that an unfamiliar toy is for the other sex, they will quickly discard it (Martin & Ruble, 2004). By ages 5 and 6, children develop rigid stereotypes about gender that they apply to themselves and others. A boy will pay more attention to what he considers boys' toys and a girl to girls' toys, and both will look to others when they encounter novel toys to determine if the toy is one that is intended for their gender group (Weisgram, Fulcher & Dinella, 2014; Shutts, Banaji & Spelke, 2010). Around age 7 or 8, schemas become more complex as children take in and integrate contradictory information, such as the fact that many girls have short hair. At this point, children develop more complex beliefs about gender and become more flexible in their views about gender roles (Martin & Ruble, 2004; Trautner et al., 2005).

Cognitive approaches to gender development have been an important contribution. However, these approaches may not fully explain the link between knowledge and conduct. There is disagreement about precisely what mechanism prompts children to act out gender roles and why some children become more strongly gender-typed than others (Bussey & Bandura, 1992; 1999; Martin & Ruble, 2004). Some investigators point to socialization.

Social Learning Approach

Five-year-old Sophie loves Disney movies and is particularly enamored with the character of Cinderella. Her parents walk into the kitchen one day to find her on her hands and knees, scrubbing the floor as she sings about a nightingale at the top of her lungs— just as Cinderella does in the film. They smile and laugh at Sophie, and she basks in their approval. What do social interactions such as these do to children's understanding of gender?

gender-schema theory
Theory that children socialize themselves in their gender roles by developing a mentally organized network of information about what it means to be male or female in a particular culture.

Ava Phillipe with her mother Reese Witherspoon. According to social learning theorists, parents are an important influence on children's acquisition of gender roles.
©Jaguar PS/Shutterstock

According to Walter Mischel (1966), a traditional social learning theorist, children acquire gender roles by imitating models and being rewarded for gender-appropriate behavior—in other words, by responding to environmental stimuli. Typically, one model is a parent, often of the same sex, but children also pattern their behavior after other adults, peers, or even characters in books or other media. Behavioral feedback, together with direct teaching by parents and other adults, reinforces gender-typing. A boy who models his behavior after his father is commended for acting "like a boy." A girl gets compliments on a pretty dress or hairstyle. In this model, gendered behavior precedes gender knowledge ("I am rewarded for doing boy things, so I must be a boy").

Since the 1970s, however, studies have cast doubt on the power of same-sex modeling alone to account for gender differences. As cognitive explanations have come to the fore, traditional social learning theory has required updates. Albert Bandura's (1986; Bussey & Bandura, 1999) **social cognitive theory**, an expansion of social learning theory, incorporates some cognitive elements in an attempt to address these issues.

social cognitive theory Albert Bandura's expansion of social learning theory holds that children learn gender roles through socialization.

According to social cognitive theory, observation enables children to learn much about gender-typed behaviors before performing them. Children are active participants, and they mentally combine observations of multiple models and generate their own behavioral variations. In addition, children create their environments through their choice of playmates and activities. However, critics say that social cognitive theory does not explain how children differentiate between boys and girls before they have a concept of gender, or what initially motivates children to acquire gender knowledge, or how gender norms become internalized—questions other cognitive theories attempt to answer (Martin et al., 2002).

Socialization plays a central role and begins in infancy long before a child has a conscious understanding of gender. Gradually, as children begin to regulate their activities, standards of behavior become internalized. A child no longer needs praise, rebukes, or a model's presence to act in socially appropriate ways. Children feel good about themselves when they live up to their internal standards and feel bad when they do not. A substantial part of the shift from socially guided control to self-regulation of gender-related behavior

Boys tend to be more strongly gender-socialized concerning play preferences than girls. Boys are more likely to engage in rough-and-tumble play.
©Sunny studio/Shutterstock

may take place between ages 3 and 4 (Bussey & Bandura, 1992; Bussey, 2011). How do families, peers, and the media influence this development?

Family Influences When former Louisiana Governor Kathleen Blanco's 4-year-old grandson David was asked what he wanted to be when he grew up, he was not sure. He shrugged off all his mother's suggestions—firefighter, soldier, policeman, airplane pilot. Finally, she asked whether he would like to be governor. "Mom," he replied, "I'm a boy!" (Associated Press, 2004a). David's response illustrates how strong family influences may be.

Parents who adhere to traditional gender schemas are more likely to have strongly gender-typed children.
©Tom Grill/Corbis

Usually, experiences in the family seem to reinforce gender-typical preferences and attitudes. We say *seems* because it is difficult to separate parents' genetic influence from the influence of the environment they create. Also, parents may be responding to rather than encouraging children's gender-typed behavior (Iervolino et al., 2005).

Boys tend to be more strongly gender-socialized concerning play preferences than girls. Parents, especially fathers, generally show more discomfort if a boy plays with a doll than if a girl plays with a truck (Ruble, Martin & Berenbaum, 2006; Sandnabba & Ahlberg, 1999). Girls have more freedom than boys in their clothes, games, and choice of playmates (Fagot, Rogers & Leinbach, 2000).

The division of labor in a household matters too. Parents who adhere to traditional gender schemas are more likely to have strongly gender-typed children (Tenenbaum & Leaper, 2002), and the converse is also true. Children from families with lesbian and gay parents tend to show less gender-typed play behavior (Goldberg, Kashy & Smith, 2012); this is especially true for girls and for children raised in families with lesbian parents (Goldberg & Garcia, 2016). There are indications that the father's role in gender socialization is especially important, and that viewing fathers engaged in household and child care work is associated with decreased gender-typing (Deutsch, Servis & Payne, 2001; Turner & Gervai, 1995).

Siblings also influence gender development. Second-borns tend to become more like their older siblings in attitudes, personality, and leisure activities, whereas firstborns are more influenced by their parents and less by their younger siblings (McHale, Updegraff, Helms-Erikson & Crouter, 2001). Young children with an older sibling of the same sex tend to be more gender-typed than those whose older sibling is of the other sex (Iervolino et al., 2005; Rust et al., 2000).

Peer Influences Even in early childhood, the peer group is a major influence on gender-typing. Preschoolers generally play in sex-segregated groups that reinforce gender-typed behavior (Martin et al., 2013), and the influence of the peer group increases with age (Martin et al., 2002). Children who play in same-sex groups (Maccoby, 2002; Martin & Fabes, 2001) or by themselves (Goble, Martin, Hanish & Fabes, 2012) tend to be more gender-typed than children who do not. Additionally, the more children choose to play with particular friends, the more they mutually influence each other (Martin et al., 2012).

Peers can exert negative pressure on each other to behave in normative ways. Being gender atypical is associated with peer victimization (Zosuls, Andrews, Martin, England & Field, 2016) although the relationship is not always simple. For example, in one study, peer harassment is associated with a decrease in gender atypicality for children with many male friends. However, it was also associated with an increase in gender typicality for children with many female friends (Lee & Troop-Gordon, 2011). This illustrates the interactive influence of peer processes and self-socialization. While peers can be a negative influence, friends can also serve as a protective buffer against victimization (Zosuls et al., 2016).

Cultural Influences When a young girl in Nepal touched the plow that her brother was using, she was scolded. In this way she learned that as a girl she must refrain from acts her brother was expected to perform (Skinner, 1989). Social learning theory predicts that the cultural influences around us will influence the degree to which we become gender-typed.

Children's books have long been a source of gender stereotypes. Analyses of top-selling and award-winning children's books have uncovered nearly twice as many male as female main characters, greater representation of males in book titles, and strong gender-stereotyping (McCabe, Fairchild, Grauerholz, Pescosolido & Tope, 2011). Female main characters nurtured more, were portrayed in indoor settings, and appeared to have no paid occupations (Hamilton, Anderson, Broaddus & Young, 2006). Fathers were largely absent, and when they appeared, they were shown as withdrawn and ineffectual (Anderson & Hamilton, 2005). Similar results have been found in coloring books, where females are more typically portrayed as children and boys as superheroes, animals, or adults (Fitzpatrick & McPherson, 2010).

In the United States, television is a major format for the transmission of cultural attitudes toward gender (Collins, 2011). This includes the influences within the content of programming as well as in commercials (Eisend, 2010) and music videos (Wallis, 2011). Theory would predict that those children who watch more television should be more strongly gender-typed. Dramatic supporting evidence emerged from a natural experiment in several Canadian towns. Children who had had relatively unstereotyped attitudes showed marked increases in traditional views 2 years after cable television was introduced to the area (Kimball, 1986). Although television is still an important media influence in young children's lives, new technologies and media sources are becoming increasingly popular as well.

Movies also have an impact on the understanding of gender. Research has shown that males in G-rated movies are more likely to be main characters, and females are more likely to be portrayed as young and as possessing traits such as intelligence and beauty (Smith, Pieper, Granados & Choueiti, 2010). Disney movies, in part because of their popularity, have been frequent targets of criticism because of their stereotypical portrayal of male and female roles. While Disney has made attempts, some more successful than others, at introducing more egalitarian ideals in its line of princess movies (England, Descartes & Collier-Meek, 2011), more work remains. One recent study showed that preschool children, especially girls, who were highly engaged with Disney princess movies showed higher gender-stereotypical behavior a year later than did children less engaged with princess movies (Coyne, Linder, Rasmussen, Nelson & Birkbeck, 2016).

Major strengths of the socialization approach include the breadth and multiplicity of processes it examines and the scope for individual differences it reveals. But this very complexity makes it difficult to establish clear causal connections between the way children are raised and the way they think and act. Just what aspects of the home environment and the peer culture promote gender-typing? Does differential treatment *produce* or *reflect* gender differences? Or, as social cognitive theory suggests, is there a bidirectional relationship? Further research may help us see how socializing agents mesh with children's biological tendencies and cognitive understandings with regard to gender-related attitudes and behavior.

Play

Carmen, age 3, pretends the pieces of cereal floating in her bowl are "fishies" swimming in the milk, and she "fishes," spoonful by spoonful. After breakfast, she puts on her mother's hat, picks up a briefcase, and is a "mommy" going to work. She rides her tricycle through the puddles, comes in for an imaginary telephone conversation, turns a wooden block into a truck, and says, "Vroom, vroom!" Carmen's day is one round of play after another.

It would be a mistake to dismiss Carmen's activities as "just fun." Play has important current and long-term functions (Smith, 2005b; Whitebread, Basilio, Kuvalja & Verma, 2012). It contributes to all domains of development. Through play, children stimulate the senses, exercise their muscles, coordinate sight with movement, gain mastery over their bodies, make decisions, and acquire new skills. As they sort blocks of different shapes, count how many they can pile on each other, or announce "my tower is bigger than yours," they lay the foundation for mathematical concepts. As they cooperate to build sandcastles or tunnels on the beach, they learn negotiation and conflict resolution skills.

Researchers categorize children's play in varying ways. One common classification system is by cognitive complexity. Another classification is based on the social dimension of play. Research has also uncovered gender and cultural influences on play.

functional play Lowest cognitive level of play, involving repetitive muscular movements; also called locomotor play.

constructive play Second cognitive level of play, involving use of objects or materials to make something; also called object play.

dramatic play Play involving imaginary people or situations; also called fantasy play, pretend play, or imaginative play.

formal games with rules Organized games with known procedures and penalties.

©Flavio Coelho/Getty Images

Smilansky (1968) identified four levels of play: functional play, constructive play, dramatic play and, formal games with rules. Although there is a general developmental progression to the types of play, this is not a stage theory.

The simplest level, which begins during infancy, is **functional play**, sometimes called locomotor play. It consists of repeated practice of large muscular movements, such as rolling a ball (Bjorklund & Pellegrini, 2002).

The second level, **constructive play**, also called object play, is the use of objects or materials to make something, such as a house of blocks or a crayon drawing (Bjorklund & Pellegrini, 2002).

The third level, which Smilansky called **dramatic play**—also called pretend play, fantasy play, or imaginative play—involves make-believe objects, actions, or roles; it rests on the symbolic function, which emerges during the last part of the 2nd year (Piaget, 1962). It involves a combination of cognition, emotion, language, and sensorimotor behavior. More advanced cognitive development affords more sophisticated play, but play also helps strengthen the development of dense connections in the brain and promotes later capacity for abstract thought. Play is not just the response to a developing intellect; it is the driver of it as well. For example, studies have found the quality of dramatic play to be associated with social and linguistic competence (Bergen, 2002; Christie, 1998). Pretend play also may further the development of theory-of-mind skills (Smith, 2005). Pretending that a banana is a telephone, for example, and understanding that you and I both agree on that pretense, can help children begin to understand others' thoughts. Although functional play and constructive play precede dramatic play in Smilansky's hierarchy, these three types of play often occur at the same ages (Smith, 2005). Although functional play and constructive play precede dramatic play in Smilanksy's hierarchy, these three types of play often occur at the same ages (Smith, 2005a).

Dramatic play peaks during the preschool years, increasing in frequency and complexity (Bjorklund & Pellegrini, 2002; Smith, 2005a), and then declines as school-age children become more involved in **formal games with rules**—that is, organized games with known procedures and penalties, such as hopscotch and marbles. While most researchers agree on the importance of dramatic play, some theorists have argued that more evidence is needed to establish its causal influence. For example, they argue that dramatic play might be one of many ways to promote positive development, or that, rather than being the driver of development, dramatic play might instead be a secondary consequence of development in other areas (Lillard et al., 2013).

COGNITIVE LEVELS OF PLAY

Jane, at 1, happily banged a spoon on a pot while sitting on the kitchen floor. Courtney, at 3, talked for a doll, using a deeper voice than her own. Miguel, at 4, wore a kitchen towel as a cape and "flew" around as Batman. These children were engaged in various types of play and, as is typical, showed increasing cognitive complexity with age.

THE SOCIAL DIMENSION OF PLAY

In a classic study done in the 1920s, Mildred B. Parten (1932) identified six types of play ranging from the least to the most social (Table 10.2). She found that as children get older, their play tends to become more social—that is, more interactive and more cooperative. At first, children play alone, then alongside other children, and finally together. Today, however, many researchers view Parten's characterization of children's play development as too simplistic, as children of all ages engage in all of Parten's categories of play (Rubin, Bukowski & Parker, 1998).

Parten incorrectly regarded nonsocial play as less mature than social play. She suggested that young children who continue to play alone could develop social, psychological, or educational problems. It is true that solitary play is often a sign of shyness, anxiety, fearfulness, or social rejection (Coplan, Ooi, Rose-Krasnor & Nocita, 2014; Coplan,

©Pixtal/agefotostock

WHAT DO YOU **DO?**

Licensed Clinical Professional Counselor (LCPC)

Licensed clinical professional counselors (LCPCs) provide counseling support to patients. An LCPC can provide psychological and neuropsychological evaluations for young children, help assess concerns about potential disabilities, and provide general counseling. LCPCs work in a variety of health care settings, school settings, and in private practice. After graduating from an accredited college counseling program, a test and clinically supervised hours are required. To learn more about becoming a licensed clinical professional counselor, visit www. counseling.org.

Prakash, O'Neil & Armer, 2004; Henderson, Marshall, Fox & Rubin, 2004; Spinrad et al., 2004). However, researchers now consider not only *whether* a child plays alone but *why*. Some children may just prefer to play alone (Coplan, Ooi & Nocita, 2015). A preference for solitude is not necessarily associated with negative outcomes in adulthood, so it is reasonable to think the same might be true for children (Ooi, Baldwin, Coplan & Rose-Krasnor, 2018). In support of this, among 567 kindergarteners, the teachers, observers, and classmates rated almost 2 out of 3 children who played alone as socially and cognitively competent (Harrist, Zain, Bates, Dodge & Pettit, 1997).

Reticent play, a combination of Parten's unoccupied and onlooker categories, is often a manifestation of shyness (Coplan et al., 2004). Such behaviors as playing near other children, watching what they do, or wandering aimlessly may be a prelude to joining in others' play

Did you know?

Recent research has identified sex differences in play in chimpanzees that mirror those we find in children. Wild female chimpanzees play with sticks as if they were dolls—holding and cuddling them, and even putting them to bed in a "nest." Male chimpanzees, by contrast, are less likely to do so (Kahlenberg & Wrangham, 2010).

©Life on white/Alamy

TABLE 10.2 Parten's Categories of Social and Nonsocial Play

Category	Description
Unoccupied behavior	The child does not seem to be playing but watches anything of momentary interest.
Onlooker behavior	The child spends most of the time watching other children play. The onlooker talks to them, asking questions or making suggestions, but does not enter into the play. The onlooker is definitely observing particular groups of children rather than anything that happens to be exciting.
Solitary independent play	The child plays alone with toys that are different from those used by nearby children and makes no effort to get close to them.
Parallel play	The child plays independently but among the other children, playing with toys like those used by the other children but not necessarily playing with them in the same way. Playing *beside* rather than *with* the others, the parallel player does not try to influence the other children's play.
Associative play	The child plays with other children. They talk about their play, borrow and lend toys, follow one another, and try to control who may play in the group. All the children play similarly if not identically; there is no division of labor and no organization around any goal. Each child acts as she or he wishes and is interested more in being with the other children than in the activity itself.
Cooperative or organized supplementary play	The child plays in a group organized for some goal—to make something, play a formal game, or dramatize a situation. One or two children control who belongs to the group and direct activities. By a division of labor, children take on different roles and supplement each other's efforts.

Source: Adapted from M. B. Parten, "Social Participation Among Preschool Children," *Journal of Abnormal and Social Psychology,* 1932, Vol. 27, Issue 3 (October), pp. 243–269

gender segregation
The tendency of children to select same-sex playmates.

(Spinrad et al., 2004). In a short-term longitudinal study, reticent children were well-liked and showed few problem behaviors (Spinrad et al., 2004). Nonsocial play, then, seems to be far more complex than Parten imagined.

One kind of play that does become more social during the preschool years is dramatic play (Rubin, Bukowski & Parker, 1998). Children typically engage in more dramatic play when playing with someone else than when playing alone (Bjorklund & Pellegrini, 2002). As dramatic play becomes more collaborative, story lines become more complex and innovative, offering rich opportunities to practice interpersonal and language skills and to explore social conventions and roles. In pretending together, children develop joint problem-solving, planning, and goal-seeking skills; gain understanding of other people's perspectives; and construct an image of the social world (Bergen, 2002; Bjorklund & Pellegrini, 2002; Smith, 2005).

A common type of dramatic play involves imaginary companions. This normal phenomenon of childhood is seen most often in firstborn and only children, who lack the close company of siblings. Girls are more likely than boys to have imaginary friends, or at least to acknowledge them (Carlson & Taylor, 2005). Children who have imaginary companions are perfectly capable of distinguishing fantasy from reality (Taylor, Cartwright & Carlson, 1993). They play more imaginatively and cooperatively than other children (Singer & Singer, 1990), they do not lack for friends (Gleason, Sebanc & Hartrup, 2000), and they perform better on theory-of-mind tasks (such as differentiating appearance and reality and recognizing false beliefs) and tasks of emotional understanding (Gimenez-Dasi, Pons & Bender, 2016). The positive associations with imaginary companions continue through preschool. Teachers rate children with imaginary companions as higher in social competence (Gleason & Kalpidou, 2014), and although 5½-year-olds with imaginary companions do not have a bigger vocabulary than children without imaginary companions, they tell more elaborate stories about both personal experiences and a storybook (Trionfi & Reese, 2009). These types of results, as a whole, point to the role of play and imagination in the development of essential cognitive and socio-emotional skills.

HOW GENDER INFLUENCES PLAY

As we have mentioned, sex segregation is common among preschoolers and becomes more prevalent in middle childhood. This tendency seems to be universal across cultures

(Smith, 2005a). By 3, girls are much more likely to play with dolls and tea sets, whereas boys prefer toy guns and trucks (Dunn & Hughes, 2001). Girls tend to select other girls as playmates, and boys prefer other boys (Martin & Fabes, 2001), a phenomenon known as **gender segregation**. Boys' tendency to be more active and physically aggressive compared to girls' more nurturing play styles are likely contributors to gender segregation.

Girls engage in more dramatic play than boys. Boys' pretend play often involves danger or discord and competitive, dominant roles, as in mock battles. Girls' pretend stories generally focus on social relationships and nurturing, domestic roles, as in playing house (Pellegrini & Archer, 2005; Smith, 2005a). However, boys' play is more strongly gender-stereotyped than girls' (Bjorklund & Pellegrini, 2002). Thus, in mixed-sex groups, play tends to revolve around traditionally masculine activities (Fabes, Martin, & Hanish, 2003). See Table 10.3 for a summary of gender differences in play styles.

HOW CULTURE INFLUENCES PLAY

As we have mentioned, sex segregation is common among preschoolers and becomes more prevalent in middle childhood. This tendency seems to be universal across cultures (Smith, 2005b). By 3 years of age girls are much more likely to play with dolls and tea sets whereas boys prefer toy guns and trucks (Dunn & Hughes, 2001). Children will sometimes reprimand each other for playing with the "wrong" toys for their gender (Mayeza, 2017). Girls and boys also prefer to dress in stereotypically gender-typed ways—girls in pink dresses, boys in cowboy hats—and this tendency occurs regardless of the parents' own desires about how their children dress (Halim, Ruble, Tamis-LeMonda, Zosuls, Lurye & Greulich, 2014).

TABLE 10.3 Early Childhood Play Styles

	Boys	Girls
Toys	Toy guns	Dolls
	Trucks and cars	Tea sets
	Trains	Domestic toys
Playmates	Large groups of other boys	Small groups of other girls
	Friendships founded on shared activities and interests	Friendships founded on emotional and physical closeness
Activities	Rough-and-tumble	Conversational
	Physically aggressive	Nurturing
Conflict Resolution	Physical force	Compromise
Communication Style	Talk to give information and commands	Talk to strengthen relationships

Source: S. Golombok, J. Rust, K. Zervoulis, T. Croudace, J. Golding & M. Hines, "Developmental trajectories of sex-typed behaviors in boys and girls: A longitudinal general population study of children aged 2.5–8 years," Child Development, 79 (2008), 1583–1593.
©Dave King/Getty Images; ©McGraw-Hill Education/Ken Karp

Girls tend to select other girls as playmates, and boys prefer other boys (Maccoby & Jacklin, 1987; Martin & Fabes, 2001), a phenomenon known as **gender segregation**. Boys' tendency to be more active and physically aggressive in their play as compared to girls' more nurturing play styles are major contributors (Martin, Fabes, Hanish, Leonard & Dinella, 2011). Boys engage in higher levels of rough-and-tumble play; girls tend to choose more structured, adult-supervised activities (Fabes, Martin & Hanish, 2003; Smith, 2005). Moreover, this does not seem to be driven by social influences. Regardless of the cultural group they come from, boys tend to engage in more exploratory play, and girls enjoy more symbolic and pretend play (Cote & Bornstein, 2009; Smith, 2005b). However, the more salient gender is made (for example, with the use of different clothing for men and women, or when children are separated into groups by gender), the more children believe in gender stereotypes and the less they play with other-sex peers (Hilliard & Liben, 2010).

Girls' pretend stories generally focus on social relationships and nurturing, and they highlight domestic roles as in playing house (Pellegrini & Archer, 2005; Smith, 2005b). Boys' pretend play often involves danger or discord and competitive, dominant roles, as in mock battles. Additionally, boys' play is more strongly gender-stereotyped than girls' (Bjorklund & Pellegrini, 2002). Thus, in mixed-sex groups, play tends to revolve around traditionally masculine activities (Fabes et al., 2003). See Table 10.3 for a summary of gender differences in play styles.

There are cultural differences regarding beliefs about the importance of play. Some cultures actively encourage play, whereas others view play as keeping children busy until they are old enough to assist with work or caregiving (Gaskins, Haight & Lancy, 2007). In Western cultures such as the United States, some argue that adequate amounts of child-directed free play are necessary for optimal development. In other cultures, play may be viewed differently. For example, in one study, parents from China, Korea, Pakistan, Nepal, and India were asked about their beliefs and reported they saw little developmental value in play, preferring to encourage their preschool children in academics. The European parents in the same study, by contrast, believed that play was important for development (Parmar, Harkness & Super, 2004). Cultural values also affect the play environments adults set up for children, and these environments in turn affect the frequency of specific forms of play across cultures (Bodrova & Leong, 2005). Culture also influences the nature of play via peer interactions. Children who behave in ways that are contrary to cultural values may be met with rejection from peers, while those who embody those values are likely to be accepted (Chen, 2012).

As one example, Western-style cultures are more likely to value independence and initiative; collectivistic cultures place a higher value on traits such as self-control and group harmony (Chen, 2012; Rogoff, 2003). One observational study compared 48 middle-class Korean American and 48 middle-class Anglo American children in separate preschools (Farver, Kim & Lee, 1995). The Korean American children played more cooperatively, often offering toys to other children—very likely a reflection of their culture's emphasis on group harmony. Anglo American children were more aggressive and often responded negatively to other children's suggestions, reflecting the competitiveness of American culture.

THE ADAPTIVE NATURE OF PLAY

Why do children play? Play is ubiquitous, not just in young humans—who take almost any opportunity they can to play—but also in the young of many species, especially intelligent ones (Bjorklund & Pellegrini, 2000; Graham & Burghardt, 2010). Why is this pattern of behavior so common across different species? Why is playing so fun?

Evolutionary psychology can help us answer this question. From an evolutionary standpoint, play serves a purpose. During play, physical attributes plus cognitive and social skills necessary for adult life are practiced. Kittens pounce and stalk, puppies wrestle, horses run and kick. Play is a means of experimenting with new behavioral routines that will be needed in adulthood in a relatively risk-free fashion (Pellegrini, Dupuis & Smith, 2007).

In humans, early locomotor play is believed to support gross motor skill and neuromuscular development (Burdette & Whitaker, 2005). Exercise play increases from early childhood to the early primary school years, and vigorous activity may help develop muscle strength, endurance, efficiency of movement, and athletic coordination (Graham & Burghardt, 2010; Smith & Pellegrini, 2013). Active physical play in outdoor settings offers unique problem-solving and creative thinking opportunities as children interact with varied, unstructured features of the environment (Burdette & Whitaker, 2005).

Object play may serve an evolutionary purpose in the development of tools by enabling children to learn the properties of objects and what can be done with them (Bjorklund & Pellegrini, 2000). In non-Western societies, where children as young as 2 or 3 years old spend time observing adults at work, they begin to emulate their activities through object manipulation and sociodramatic play (Morelli, Rogoff & Angellilo, 2003). As children use objects in pretend play, they practice creativity, substituting the purpose or function of one object with another (Russ & Wallace, 2013).

The most complex and difficult thing we will ever have to learn how to navigate is our social world, and social play helps us practice how to do this. Social play is abundant in childhood. Children develop and sustain friendships, practice cooperation, negotiate conflict, and build complex social skills in coordination with peers (Jarvis, Newman & Swiniarski, 2014). Across cultures, social play provides an opportunity to learn and practice societal norms of cooperation, competition, power, and social strategies (Kamp, 2001). Pretend play has been linked to cognitive functions, such as creativity, flexible thinking, perspective taking, and exploring bounds of fantasy and reality (Russ & Wallace, 2013). Play fighting, which is often discouraged by adults, has adaptive functions as children innovate story lines, practice controlled physical movements, and experiment with themes of competition and aggression (Hart & Tannock, 2013).

Evolutionary psychologists argue that for play to be an adaptation, its benefits must outweigh its costs. Potential costs include excess energy expenditure, injury, aggression, and decreased vigilance from predators or other dangers (Graham & Burghardt, 2010). Comparatively, numerous adaptive developmental functions are learned, practiced, and refined through play. Immediate benefits in psychological well-being occur, and there is the potential for a lifelong impact on social and emotional health (Hewes, 2014).

Parenting

As children increasingly become their own persons, their upbringing can be a complex challenge. Parents must deal with small people who have minds and wills of their own but still have a lot to learn about what kinds of behavior work well in society. Two areas that impact child development are forms of discipline and parenting styles.

FORMS OF DISCIPLINE

The word *discipline* means "instruction" or "training." In the field of child development, **discipline** refers to methods of molding character and teaching self-control and acceptable behavior. It can be a powerful tool for socialization with the goal of developing self-discipline. What forms of discipline work best? Researchers have looked at a wide range of techniques, including reinforcement and punishment, inductive reasoning, power assertion, and withdrawal of love.

Reinforcement and Punishment

"You're such a wonderful helper, Derek! Thank you so much for putting away your toys." Derek's mother smiles warmly at her son as he plops his dump truck into the toy box. Her words and actions provide gentle discipline for her son and teach him that putting away his toys is a positive behavior that should be repeated.

Parents sometimes punish children to stop undesirable behavior, but children usually learn more from being reinforced for good behavior. External reinforcements may be tangible (treats, more playtime) or intangible (a smile, a word of praise, a hug). Whatever the reinforcement, the child must see it as rewarding and must receive it consistently and immediately after showing the desired

discipline Methods of molding children's character and of teaching them to exercise self-control and engage in acceptable behavior.

behavior. Eventually, the behavior should provide an internal reinforcement: a sense of pleasure or accomplishment.

Still, punishment, such as isolation or denial of privileges, is necessary at times. Children cannot be permitted to run out into traffic or hit another child. Sometimes a child is willfully defiant. In such situations, punishment, if consistent, immediate, and clearly tied to the offense, may be effective. It is most effective when accompanied by a short, simple explanation of the wrongdoing and an alternative behavior that should have been performed instead (American Academy of Pediatrics [AAP] Committee on Psychosocial Aspects of Child and Family Health, 1998).

Punishment that is too harsh can be harmful. Children who are punished harshly and frequently may have trouble interpreting other people's actions and words, and they may attribute hostile intentions where none exist (Weiss, Dodge, Bates & Pettit, 1992). Young children who have been punished harshly also show more externalizing behaviors such as physical aggression and impulsivity (Erath, El-Sheikh & Cummings, 2009). The link between harsh parenting and aggression is cross-cultural and has been found in research investigating mother-child dyads from China, India, Italy, Kenya, the Philippines and Thailand (Gershoff et al., 2010). Harsh parenting has also been linked to relational aggression, in which attempts are made to damage another's social status or reputation (Kawabata, Alink, Tseng, Van IJzendoorn & Crick, 2011).

The influence of harsh parenting is bidirectional; difficult children elicit more coercive parenting on the part of their parents (Pettit & Arsiwalla, 2008). It is also the case that different children respond differently to harsh parenting. For example, children with attentional issues are particularly likely to respond to coercive parenting with behavior problems (Scott, Doolan, Beckett, Harry & Cartwright, 2012), exacerbating the original problem, and potentially initiating a cascade of increasingly negative interactions between parent and child. By contrast, shyer children may become frightened if parents lose control and may eventually try to avoid a punitive parent, undermining the parent's ability to influence behavior (Grusec & Goodnow, 1994). Essentially, the effectiveness and influence of parenting tactics varies with child temperament, especially with respect to whether or not the child feels guilt or anxiety, a likely

Punishment such as a time-out may be effective if it is immediate and clearly tied to the problem behavior.
©Blend Images/AP Images

Perspectives on Diversity

©Digital Vision/Getty Images

CROSS-CULTURAL DIFFERENCES IN CORPORAL PUNISHMENT

"Spare the rod and spoil the child" may sound old-fashioned, but corporal punishment still exists in the United States. Some form of corporal punishment is widely used on U.S. infants and is nearly universal among parents of toddlers. In a phone survey study, researchers found that parents reported spanking and yelling at infants younger than 9 months, and about a third of parents reported spanking their child under 18 months (Regalado, Sareen, Inkelas, Wissow & Halfon, 2004). While the rates of corporal punishment for preschoolers have trended down by 18 percent in the past three decades, the majority of parents of preschool children—almost 80 percent—still report spanking or slapping their children (Zolotor, Theodore, Runyan, Change & Laskey, 2011). All states except Minnesota allow parents to administer corporal punishment, though some insist that it be reasonable, appropriate, moderate, or necessary, and some recognize that excessive corporal punishment can be abusive (Gershoff, 2002). Corporal punishment is currently allowed in schools in seven states.

This is not the case everywhere, however. Corporal punishment is banned in many countries, including Austria, Bulgaria, Croatia, Cyprus, Denmark, Finland, Germany, Hungary, Iceland, Israel, Latvia, Norway, Romania, Sweden, and Ukraine. One hundred and twelve countries have banned corporal punishment in schools (Center for Effective Discipline, 2009). The United Nations Convention on the Rights of Children opposes all forms of physical violence against children; the United States and Somalia remain the only nations yet to ratify the convention (Zolotar et al., 2011). Many people still believe spanking instills respect for authority, motivates good behavior, and is a necessary part of parenting (Kazdin & Benjet, 2003). However, some professionals view any corporal punishment as verging on child abuse (Straus, 1994b). Other professionals find no harm in corporal punishment in moderation when prudently administered by loving parents (Baumrind, Larzelere & Cowan, 2002). Still others argue the effect depends on cultural norms for behavior (McLoyd & Smith, 2002; Lansford et al., 2005).

prerequisite for the internalization of parental dictates (Kochanska, 1993).

Corporal punishment has been defined as "the use of physical force with the intention of causing a child to experience pain, but not injury, for the purpose of correction or control of the child's behavior" (Straus, 1994a, p. 4). It can include spanking, hitting, slapping, pinching, shaking, and other physical acts. Corporal punishment is common across many cultures and found at all income levels (Runyan et al., 2010). It is popularly believed to be more effective than other methods, to instill respect for parental authority, and to be harmless if done in moderation by loving parents (Kazdin & Benjet, 2003; McLoyd & Smith, 2002). Some researchers have argued that corporal punishment can be one of a number of disciplinary tactics that can be effective under certain circumscribed conditions (Larzelere & Kuhn, 2005).

However, a growing body of evidence suggests that it is often counterproductive and should be avoided (Straus & Stewart, 1999; Gershoff, 2010). Apart from the risk of injury, children who experience corporal punishment may fail to internalize moral messages, develop poor parent-child relationships, and show increased physical aggressiveness or antisocial behavior. As adults they are more likely to suffer from

mental health issues, engage in criminal behavior, and abuse their own children (Gershoff, 2013). A link between spanking and externalizing behaviors has been found in children from different cultural and ethnic groups, both internationally, as well as within white, African American, Latino, and Asian American families in the United States (Gershoff et al., 2010; Gershoff, Lansford, Sexton, Davis-Keen & Sameroff, 2012; Berlin et al., 2009). In addition, spanking has been negatively associated with cognitive development (MacKenzie, Nicklas, Waldfogel & Brooks-Gunn, 2013; Berlin et al., 2009) and there is no clear line between mild and harsh spanking—mild spanking often leads to the other (Kazdiz & Benjet, 2003).

An ongoing debate about the appropriateness of the use of corporal punishment in schools rages in the United States. Fifteen states specifically allow the use of corporal punishment in schools, 7 states do not prohibit it, and 28 states specifically prohibit it (U.S. Department of Education, 2017). Some educators believe it is an effective deterrent to harmful misbehaviors, like fighting, but others assert that corporal punishment degrades the educational environment.

> **corporal punishment** Use of physical force with the intention of causing pain but not injury so as to correct or control behavior.

Moreover, critics point to the fact that ethnic minority children and children with disabilities are subject to corporal punishment more frequently (Human Rights Watch, 2010). The American Academy of Pediatrics Committee on Psychosocial Aspects of Child and Family Health (1998) recommends positive reinforcement to encourage desired behaviors and verbal reprimands, time-outs (brief isolation to give the child a chance to cool down), or removal of privileges to discourage undesired behaviors.

Inductive Reasoning, Power Assertion, and Withdrawal of Love

When Sara took candy from a store, her father did not lecture her on honesty, spank her, or tell her she was bad. Instead, he explained how the owner of the store would be harmed by her failure to pay for the candy, asked her how she thought the store owner might feel, and then took her back to the store to return the candy. Sara, even though she was not asked to do so, told the store owner she was sorry she had made him sad.

Inductive techniques include setting limits, demonstrating logical consequences of an action, explaining, discussing, negotiating, and getting ideas from the child about what is fair. Inductive reasoning tends to arouse empathy for the victim of wrongdoing as well as guilt on the part of the wrongdoer (Kochanska, Gross, Lin & Nichols, 2002). Inductive techniques are usually the most effective method of getting children to accept parental standards (Kerr, Lopez, Olson & Sameroff, 2004). Parents who use inductive techniques are more likely to have children who see the moral wrongness of behavior that hurts other people (Grusec, 2006; Volling, Mahoney & Rauer, 2009).

Two other broad categories of discipline are power assertion and temporary withdrawal of love. **Power assertion** is intended to stop or discourage undesirable behavior through physical or verbal enforcement of parental control; it includes demands, threats, withdrawal of privileges, spanking, and other types of punishment. **Withdrawal of love** may include ignoring, isolating, or showing dislike for a child. Neither of these is as effective as inductive reasoning in most circumstances, and both may be harmful (Baumrind, Larzelere & Owens, 2010).

The effectiveness of parental discipline may hinge on how well the child cognitively and emotionally understands and accepts the parents' message. For the child to accept the message, the parents need to be fair, clear, and consistent about their expectations. They need to fit the discipline to the child's temperament and cognitive and emotional level. A child may be more motivated to accept the message if the parents are normally warm and responsive and if they arouse the child's empathy for someone the child has harmed (Kerr et al., 2004). How well children accept a disciplinary method also may depend on whether the type of discipline used is accepted in the family's culture (Lansford et al., 2005).

One point on which many experts agree is that a child interprets and responds to discipline in the context of an ongoing relationship with the parents. Some researchers, therefore, look beyond specific parental practices to overall styles, or patterns, of parenting.

PARENTING STYLES

Parents differ in their approach to parenting. Children interpret and respond to parenting within the context of an ongoing relationship with their parents. Thus the different styles of parenting may affect children's competence in dealing with their world.

Baumrind's Model of Parenting Styles

In pioneering research, Diana Baumrind (1971; 1996; Baumrind & Black, 1967) studied 103 preschool children from 95 families. Through interviews, testing, and home studies, she measured how the children were functioning, identified three parenting styles, and described typical behavior patterns of children raised according to each. Baumrind's work and the large body of research it inspired established associations between each parenting style and some child behaviors (Baumrind, 1989; Darling & Steinberg, 1993; Pettit, Bates & Dodge, 1997).

Authoritarian parenting emphasizes control and unquestioning obedience. Authoritarian parents try to make children conform rigidly to a set standard of conduct and punish them for violating it, often using power-assertive techniques. They are more detached and less warm than other parents. Their children tend to be more discontented, withdrawn, and distrustful.

Permissive parents make few demands and allow children to monitor their own activities as much as possible. They are warm, noncontrolling, and undemanding or even indulgent. Their preschool children tend to be immature—the least self-controlled and the least exploratory.

Authoritative parents respect children's independent decisions, interests, opinions, and personalities. They are loving and accepting but also demand good behavior and are firm in maintaining standards. They impose limited, judicious punishment when necessary, within the context of a warm, supportive relationship. They favor inductive discipline, explaining the reasoning behind their stand and encouraging verbal negotiation and give-and-take. Their children apparently feel secure in knowing they are loved and what is expected of them. These preschoolers tend to be the most self-reliant, self-controlled, self-assertive, exploratory, and content.

Eleanor Maccoby and John Martin (1983) added a fourth parenting style—**neglectful**, or **uninvolved**—to describe

inductive techniques Disciplinary techniques designed to induce desirable behavior by appealing to a child's sense of reason and fairness.

power assertion Disciplinary strategy designed to discourage undesirable behavior through physical or verbal enforcement of parental control.

withdrawal of love Disciplinary strategy that involves ignoring, isolating, or showing dislike for a child.

authoritarian parenting Parenting style emphasizing control and obedience.

permissive parenting Parenting style emphasizing self-expression and self-regulation.

authoritative parenting Parenting style blending warmth and respect for a child's individuality with an effort to instill social values.

neglectful/uninvolved parenting Parenting style in which parents focus on their own needs rather than those of children.

Preschoolers of parents with an authoritative parenting style tend to be self-reliant, exploratory, and content.

©Stockbyte/PunchStock

parenting practices is crucial to preventing early-onset problem behavior (Dishion & Stormshak, 2007). Families at high-risk for problem behavior in children who participated in parenting support services were able to improve childhood outcomes by an early focus on positive and proactive parenting practices (Dishion et al., 2008).

Also, Baumrind's findings are correlational. Thus, they merely establish associations between each parenting style and a particular set of child behaviors. They do not show that different styles of child rearing cause children to be more or less competent. As with all correlations, the direction of effects is not certain. Baumrind did not consider innate factors, such as temperament, that might have affected children's competence and influenced the parents. Children may elicit parenting styles based on their own behavior. An easy child might, for example, elicit authoritative parenting, and a difficult child, more power assertive techniques as parents search for a way to manage her defiance.

Cultural Differences in Parenting Styles

Another concern is that Baumrind's categories reflect the dominant North American view of child development. In countries such as the United States, the traits of independence and initiative are highly valued. Moreover, constraints on behavior are often viewed as being negative by children. Among Asian Americans, obedience and strictness are not necessarily associated with harshness and domination but instead with caring, concern, and involvement. Traditional Chinese culture, with its emphasis on respect for elders, stresses the responsibility to maintain the social order. This obligation is modeled through firm and just control and governance of the child and even by physical punishment if necessary (Zhao, 2002). Although Asian American parenting is frequently described as authoritarian, the warmth and supportiveness that characterize Asian family relationships may more closely resemble Baumrind's authoritative parenting but without the emphasis on the European American values of individuality, choice, and freedom (Chao, 1994) and with stricter parental control (Chao, 2001).

Parenting strategies reflect cultural values. For example, Mexican American families tend to use more authoritarian parenting than European American families, perhaps in line with the respect for authority characteristic of Mexican culture (Varela et al., 2004). As another example, in African American families, who tend to use more physical punishment, authoritarian parenting is not related to negative behavioral outcomes, although this relationship does exist for white families (Baumrind, 1987; McLeod, Kruttschnitt & Dornfeld, 1994).

parents who focus on their own needs rather than on those of the child. Neglectful parenting has been linked with a variety of behavioral disorders in childhood and adolescence (Steinberg, Eisengart & Cauffman, 2006).

Why does authoritative parenting tend to enhance children's social competence? It may be because by making clear, consistent rules, authoritative parents let children know what is expected of them and give them a standard of behavior by which to judge themselves. In authoritarian homes, children are so strictly controlled they often cannot make independent choices about their behavior; in permissive homes, children receive so little guidance they may be uncertain and anxious about whether they are doing the right thing.

Support and Criticisms of Baumrind's Model

In research based on Baumrind's work, the benefits of authoritative parenting have repeatedly been supported. This is important because identifying and promoting positive

Special Behavioral Concerns

Derek, at 3½, responded to two preschool classmates' complaints that they did not have enough modeling clay, his favorite plaything, by giving them half of his. However, a few days later when his twin sister had a toy he wanted, he hit her on the head in order to take the toy from her. Derek, like most children, is displaying both prosocial—voluntary behavior to help others—and aggressive behaviors. How do such behaviors emerge?

PROSOCIAL BEHAVIOR

Altruism is helping another person with no expectation of reward. It is at the heart of **prosocial behavior**, any voluntary behavior intended to help others. Even before the 2nd birthday, children often help others, share belongings and food, and offer comfort. Research has revealed three preferences: a preference to share with close relations, reciprocity (a preference to share with people who have shared with you), and indirect reciprocity (a preference to share with people who share with others). These preferences are present and functional in children as young as 3½ (Olson & Spelke, 2008).

altruism Motivation to help others without expectation of reward; may involve self-denial or self-sacrifice.

prosocial behavior Any voluntary behavior intended to help others.

instrumental aggression Aggressive behavior used as a means of achieving a goal.

Is there a prosocial personality or disposition? A longitudinal study that followed 32 4- and 5-year-olds suggests there is and that it emerges early and remains somewhat consistent throughout life. Preschoolers who were sympathetic and spontaneously shared with classmates tended to show prosocial understanding and empathic behavior as much as 17 years later (Coplan et al., 2004).

Early appearing and stable individual differences such as these suggest genetic influences. However, while genes matter, so does the environment. Cultures vary in the degree to which they foster prosocial behavior. Traditional cultures in which people live in extended family groups and share work seem to instill prosocial values more than cultures that stress individual achievement (Eisenberg & Fabes, 1998). The more immediate environment matters as well. Parents who show affection and use positive (inductive) disciplinary strategies encourage their children's natural tendency to prosocial behavior (Knafo & Plomin, 2006). Additionally, parents of prosocial children are typically prosocial themselves. They point out models of prosocial behavior and steer children toward stories, films, and television programs that depict cooperation, sharing, and empathy and encourage sympathy, generosity, and helpfulness (Singer & Singer, 1998), which have been shown to increase children's altruism, cooperation, and even tolerance for others (Wilson, 2008). Relationships with siblings, peers, and teachers also can model and reinforce prosocial behavior (Eisenberg, 1992).

AGGRESSIVE BEHAVIOR

When Noah roughly snatches a ball away from Jake, he is interested only in getting the ball, not in hurting or dominating Jake. This is **instrumental aggression**, or aggression used

Cross-cultural studies have found that boys engage in higher levels of overt and physical aggression.
©Image Source/PunchStock

Did you know?

The match between a child and parents' traits can be viewed as a passive genotype–environment correlation. It can either be beneficial or harmful. For example, prosocial parents provide their children with (presumably) prosocial genes as well as an environment that cultivates prosocial behavior. Similarly, antisocial parents may provide their children with both antisocial genes and environments.

©BlackJack3D/Getty Images

as an instrument to reach a goal—the most common type in early childhood. Between ages 2½ and 5, children commonly struggle over toys and control of space. Instrumental aggression surfaces mostly during social play; children who fight the most also tend to be the most sociable and competent. In fact, the ability to show some instrumental aggression may be a necessary step in social development.

As children develop more self-control and become better able to express themselves verbally, they typically shift from showing aggression with blows to doing it with words (Tremblay et. al., 2004). However, individual differences remain. In a longitudinal study of 383 preschoolers, 11 percent of the girls and 9 percent of the boys showed high levels of aggression between ages 2 and 5. Boys and girls who were inattentive at age 2, and girls who showed poor emotion regulation at that age, tended to have conduct problems at age 5 (Hill, Degan, Calkins & Keane, 2006). Children who often engage in violent fantasy play as preschoolers may, at age 6, be prone to violent displays of anger (Dunn & Hughes, 2001).

Gender Differences in Aggression

Aggression is an exception to the generalization that boys and girls are more similar than different (Hyde, 2005). In all cultures studied, as among most mammals, boys are more physically aggressive than girls. This gender difference is apparent by age 2 (Baillargeon et al., 2007).

However, when aggression is looked at more closely, it becomes apparent that, at least in the United States, boys and girls also tend to use different kinds of aggression. Boys engage in more **overt (direct) aggression** and tend to openly direct aggressive acts at a target. Girls, by contrast, tend to engage in a form of indirect social aggression known as **relational aggression** (Putallaz & Bierman, 2004). This more subtle kind of aggression consists of damaging or interfering with relationships, reputation, or psychological well-being, often through teasing, manipulation, ostracism, or bids for control. It may include spreading rumors, name-calling, put-downs, or excluding someone from a group. It can be either overt or covert (indirect)—for example, making mean faces or ignoring someone. Among preschoolers, it tends to be direct and face-to-face ("You can't come to my party if you don't give me that toy") (Archer, 2004; Brendgen et al., 2005).

Cross-cultural research has supported the clear propensity for boys to engage in higher levels of physical aggression. However, the data on relational aggression are less clear. Some studies have found that girls engage in higher levels of relational aggression, and other studies have not found a difference between the genders (Lansford et al., 2012; Hyde, 2014; Archer, 2004). It is safe to say that if a difference does exist, it is quite small.

From an evolutionary perspective, boys' greater overt aggressiveness, like their greater size and strength, may prepare them to compete for a mate (Archer, 2004). Males produce many sperm; females generally produce only one ovum at a time. Males can increase their reproductive output by gaining access to females. Thus males are predicted to be more competitive and more likely to take the risks of physical aggression. Females' reproductive output is limited by their own bodies; thus the need for physical aggression as a means by which to compete is diminished (Pellegrini & Archer, 2005).

Influences on Aggression

Why are some children more aggressive than others? Temperament may play a part. Children who are intensely emotional and low in self-control, or who have a difficult temperament, tend to express anger aggressively (Eisenberg, Fabes, Nyman, Bernzweig & Pinuelas, 1994; Rubin, Burgess, Dwyer & Hastings, 2003; Yaman, Mesman, van IJzendoorn & Bakersmans-Kranenburg, 2010).

Both physical and social aggression have genetic and environmental sources, but their relative influence differs. Among 234 6-year-old twins, physical aggression was 50 to 60 percent heritable; the remainder of the variance was attributable to nonshared environmental influences (unique experiences). Social aggression was much more influenced by the environment; the variance was only 20 percent explained by genetics, 20 percent by shared environmental influences, and 60 percent by nonshared experiences (Brendgen et al., 2005).

Parental behaviors strongly influence aggressiveness. In several longitudinal studies, insecure attachment and lack of maternal warmth and affection in infancy predicted aggressiveness in early childhood (Coie & Dodge, 1998; MacKinnon-Lewis, Starnes, Volling & Johnson, 1997; Rubin, Burgess & Hastings, 2002). Manipulative behaviors such as withdrawal of love and making a child feel guilty or ashamed may foster social aggression (Brendgen et al., 2005).

> **overt (direct) aggression** Aggression that is openly directed at its target.
>
> **relational (indirect or social) aggression** Aggression aimed at damaging or interfering with another person's relationships, reputation, or psychological well-being; can be overt or covert.

Aggressiveness may result from a combination of a stressful and unstimulating home atmosphere, harsh discipline, lack of maternal warmth and social support, family dysfunction, exposure to aggressive adults and neighborhood violence, poverty, and transient peer groups, which prevent stable friendships (Dodge, Pettit & Bates, 1994; Grusec & Goodnow, 1994; Romano, Tremblay, Boulerice & Swisher, 2005). For example, children who witness gang activity, drug trafficking, police pursuits and arrests, or people carrying weapons tend to later show symptoms of distress at home and aggressive behavior at school (Farver, Xu, Eppe, Fernandez & Schwartz, 2005). This violence need not even be real. Cross-culturally, children who are exposed to violent video games show increases in violent behavior, cognition, and affect (Anderson et al., 2010). We discuss the influence of media violence in greater detail in Chapter 14.

Culture can influence how much aggressive behavior a child shows. For example, in countries such as Japan and China, there is a cultural emphasis on harmony, self-control, and group cohesiveness. Anger and aggression contradict these cultural values. Thus, Chinese and Japanese mothers are more likely than U.S. mothers to use inductive discipline, pointing out how aggressive behavior hurts others. They also show strong disappointment when children fail to meet behavioral standards. Moreover, teachers and peers are more likely to reject or exclude such children, and they are more likely than less aggressive children to have low social status (Zahn-Waxler, Friedman, Cole, Mizuta & Hiruma, 1996; Chen, 2010).

FEARFULNESS

Passing fears are common in early childhood. Many 2- to 4-year-olds are afraid of animals, especially dogs. By age 6, children are more likely to be afraid of the dark. Other common fears are of thunderstorms, doctors, and imaginary creatures (DuPont, 1983; Stevenson-Hinde & Shouldice, 1996).

Young children's fears stem largely from their intense fantasy life and their tendency to confuse appearance with reality. Sometimes their imaginations get carried away, making them worry about being attacked by a lion or being abandoned. Young children are more likely to be frightened by something that looks scary, such as a cartoon monster, than by something capable of doing great harm, such as a nuclear explosion (Cantor, 1994). For the most part, older children's fears are more realistic (being kidnapped) and self-evaluative (failing a test) (Stevenson-Hinde & Shouldice, 1996).

Fears may come from hearing about other people's experiences (Muris, Merckelbach & Collaris, 1997). Additionally, fears are also tied to negative events experienced directly by children. Although they come in contact with knives more frequently than needles, most children pay more attention to and fear needles more, presumably as a result of vaccinations (LoBue, Rakison & DeLoache, 2010). Often fears come from appraisals of danger, such as the likelihood of being bitten by a dog. Children who have lived through an earthquake, kidnapping, war, or some other frightening event may fear that it will happen again (Kolbert, 1994).

It is both normal and appropriate for young children to have fears. It is also normal for these fears to fade as children age. Part of the reason many fears are outgrown is because young children get better at distinguishing the real and the imaginary. Additionally, as children master new skills, they develop an emerging sense of autonomy. When that sense of autonomy is coupled with their increased ability to understand and predict events in their environment, children feel more in control, and thus less frightened (National Scientific Council on the Developing Child, 2010).

Parents can help prevent children's fears by instilling a sense of trust and normal caution without being too protective, and also by overcoming their own unrealistic fears. They can help a fearful child by reassurance and by encouraging open expression of feelings: "I know it is scary, but the thunder can't hurt you." Ridicule ("Don't be such a baby!"), coercion ("Pat the nice doggie—it won't hurt you"), and logical persuasion ("The closest bear is 20 miles away, locked in a zoo!") are not helpful (Cantor, 1994).

mastering the CHAPTER

Summary and Key Terms

The Developing Self

> The self-concept undergoes major change in early childhood. Young children do not see the difference between the real self and the ideal self, but over time their self-descriptions become more balanced and realistic.

> Self-esteem in early childhood tends to be global and unrealistic, reflecting adult approval. Targeted praise of efforts rather than global praise or praise of inherent abilities is associated with children who persevere and belief they can succeed if they try.

> Understanding of emotions directed toward the self and of simultaneous emotions develops gradually.

KEY TERMS

Self-concept   Self-esteem   Social emotions

Self-definition

Gender

> Gender identity is an aspect of the developing self-concept.

> The main gender difference in early childhood is boys' greater aggressiveness. Girls tend to be more empathic and prosocial and less prone to problem behavior.

> Children learn gender roles at an early age through gender-typing. Gender stereotypes peak during the preschool years.

> Five major perspectives on gender development are biological, evolutionary, psychoanalytic, cognitive, and social learning.

> Evidence suggests that some gender differences may be biologically based, due to factors such as genes that code for differences in anatomy and function and prenatal hormonal exposure.

> Evolutionary theory sees children's gender roles as preparation for adult mating behavior.

> In Freudian theory, a child identifies with the same-sex parent after giving up the wish to possess the other parent.

> Cognitive-developmental theory maintains that gender identity develops from thinking about one's gender. According to Kohlberg, gender constancy leads to acquisition of gender roles. Gender-schema theory holds that children categorize gender-related information by observing what males and females do in their culture.

> According to social cognitive theory, children learn gender roles through socialization. Parents, peers, and culture influence gender-typing.

KEY TERMS

Gender identity   Gender stereotypes   Gender constancy

Gender roles   Theory of sexual selection   Gender-schema theory

Gender-typing   Identification   Social cognitive theory

Play

> Play has physical, cognitive, and psychosocial benefits. Changes in the types of play children engage in reflect cognitive and social development.

> According to Smilansky, children progress cognitively from functional play to constructive play, dramatic play, and then formal games with rules. Dramatic play and rough-and-tumble play begin during early childhood.

> According to Parten, play becomes more social during early childhood. However, later research has found that nonsocial play is not necessarily immature.

> Children prefer to play with others of their sex.

> Cognitive and social aspects of play are influenced by the culturally approved environments adults create for children.

> **KEY TERMS**

Functional play	**Dramatic play**	**Gender segregation**
Constructive play	**Formal games with rules**	

Parenting

> Discipline can be a powerful tool for socialization.

> Both positive reinforcement and prudently administered punishment can be appropriate tools of discipline within the context of a positive parent-child relationship.

> Inductive techniques, power assertion, and withdrawal of love are three categories of discipline. Reasoning is generally the most effective and power assertion the least effective. Spanking and other forms of corporal punishment can have negative consequences.

> Baumrind identified three parenting styles: authoritarian, permissive, and authoritative. A fourth style, neglectful or uninvolved, was identified later. Authoritative parents tend to raise more competent children. However, Baumrind's findings may be misleading when applied to some cultures.

> **KEY TERMS**

Discipline	**Power assertion**	**Permissive parenting**
Corporal punishment	**Withdrawal of love**	**Authoritative parenting**
Inductive techniques	**Authoritarian parenting**	**Neglectful/uninvolved parenting**

Special Behavioral Concerns

> The roots of altruism and prosocial behavior appear early. This may be an inborn disposition, which can be cultivated by parental modeling and encouragement.

> Instrumental aggression—first physical, then verbal—is most common in early childhood.

> Boys tend to practice overt aggression, whereas girls may more often engage in relational aggression.

> Both genetic and environmental factors influence levels of physical and social aggressiveness. Culture also influences how much aggression children show.

> Preschool children show temporary fears of real and imaginary objects and events; older children's fears tend to be more realistic.

> **KEY TERMS**

Altruism	**Instrumental aggression**	**Relational (indirect or social) aggression**
Prosocial behavior	**Overt (direct) aggression**	

Practice Quiz

1. At age 5, Emma is most likely to describe herself as:
   a. a really nice person
   b. good at school but not good at gym class
   c. a really good runner with brown hair
   d. usually quiet but sometimes loud

2. Children with a "helpless" pattern of self-esteem tend to attribute failure to _____ and are _____ likely to persevere at difficult tasks.
   a. personal characteristics; more
   b. personal characteristics; less
   c. effort; more
   d. effort; less

3. What are three changes in emotions in early childhood? _____
   _____
   _____

4. Cognitive gender differences between girls and boys:
   a. are large
   b. are small
   c. are large in mathematics and small in language
   d. do not exist

5. Dr. Smith believes that hormones are the most important variable in explaining gender differences, while Dr. Frank believes exposure to violent models is more important. Dr. Smith is likely to believe the _____ approach to gender development, while Dr. Frank is more likely to be a proponent of the _____ approach.
   a. cognitive; psychoanalytic
   b. evolutionary; cognitive
   c. social learning; evolutionary
   d. biological; social learning

6. What are three skills that children can learn via play?
   _____
   _____
   _____

7. Which of the following illustrates the most cognitively complex form of play?
   a. two children acting out a family scene with dolls
   b. a child building a tall tower out of blocks
   c. a child feeding a baby doll with a plastic bottle
   d. a child pressing a button to make a toy light up

8. Which of the following types of play is generally considered the most complex?
   a. solitary play   c. functional play
   b. dramatic play   b. rough-and-tumble play

9. What is the primary difference between girls' and boys' play styles?
   a. girls play in a more cognitively complex fashion
   b. boys are more cooperative in their play
   c. boys' play is more active and physically aggressive
   d. there are no established gender differences between girls' and boys' play styles

10. Discuss why children's play styles show cultural differences. _____
    _____
    _____

11. Which of the following is a form of discipline, as defined by developmental psychologists?
    a. reinforcement of desired behaviors
    b. punishment of undesirable behaviors
    c. withdrawal of love
    d. power assertive parenting techniques
    e. all of the above

12. John strongly believes children should be seen and not heard, and he is very strict with his young children. His parenting style sounds most like
    a. authoritarian
    b. permissive
    c. authoritative
    d. neglectful/uninvolved

13. What is a prosocial behavior? _____
    _____
    _____

14. Overall, boys engage in _____ levels of aggression than girls, although girls tend to engage in more _____ aggression.
    a. higher; relational
    b. lower; relational
    c. higher; instrumental
    d. lower; instrumental

Answers: 1–c; 2–b; 3–In early childhood, children get better at regulating emotions, understanding emotions, and at understanding emotions directed at the self; 4–b; 5–d; 6–Through play children stimulate the senses, exercise their muscles, coordinate sight with movement, gain mastery over their bodies, make decisions, acquire new skills, learn to cooperate, and learn about conflict resolution; 7–a; 8–b; 9–c; 10–Children's play styles across different cultures look slightly different because play is influenced both by the play environments that are provided to children as well as cultural values (e.g. cooperation or competition); 11–e; 12–a; 13–Prosocial behavior is defined as voluntary activity intended to benefit another; 14–a

Chapter 11

Physical Development and Health in Middle Childhood

©BananaStock/Getty Images

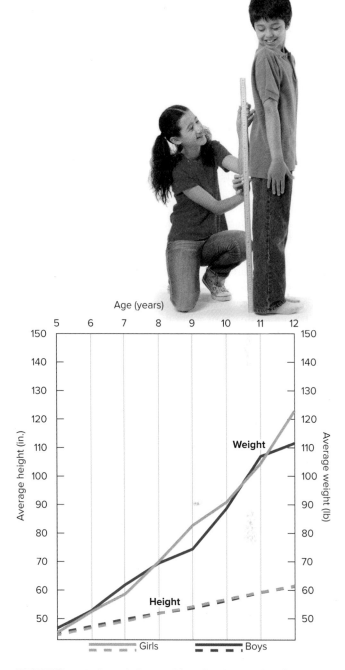

A lex ran as fast as he could through the playground, laughing as his friends tried and failed to catch him. His wide gap-toothed grin flashed at them as he looked back at them in glee. Alex's legs were sturdy and sure as he jumped from the playground onto the soccer field, although his skinned knees and a purple bruise on his arm showed he was not always so lucky when he landed. Alex was doing what children love most—playing. By dinner, Alex would be famished; by night, his physical exertions would sink him into a heavy sleep.

In this chapter, we focus on physical development and health in middle childhood. We explore normal growth and brain development and the factors that promote both, including proper nutrition, adequate sleep, and good health. In addition, we focus on when health is not ideal, and on some of the factors that can put children at risk for obesity, accidental injury, or emotional disturbances.

• • • •

Physical Development

If you walk by a typical elementary school during recess, you would see a virtual explosion of children of all shapes and sizes. Tall ones, short ones, husky ones, and skinny ones would be bursting out of the school doors into the open air, running and jumping, tumbling and scrambling in the grass. We would see them throwing and catching balls, twisting and hanging on the monkey bars, and scrambling over colorful play structures. We would see that school-age children look very different from children a few years younger.

Did you know?

Although most children grow normally, some do not. The little people that played the Munchkins in *The Wizard of Oz*, for example, had growth hormone deficiencies. Today we see few people
©MGM/Kobal/Shutterstock
with conditions such as these because synthetic growth hormone is given to them as children, and they attain a more typical height.

HEIGHT AND WEIGHT

Growth during middle childhood slows considerably. Although the changes may not be obvious day-by-day, they add up to a startling difference between 6-year-olds, who are still small children, and 11-year-olds, many of whom are now beginning to resemble adults.

Children grow about 2 to 3 inches each year between ages 6 and 11 and approximately double their weight during that period (Figure 11.1). Girls retain somewhat more fatty tissue than boys, a characteristic that will persist

FIGURE 11.1 Growth Curves Chart for Boys and Girls Ages 5–12

During middle childhood growth slows, and boys and girls gain height and weight at approximately equivalent rates.

Source: Data from C. D. Fryar, Q. Gu, C. L. Ogden, K. M. Flegal, (2016). "Anthropometric reference data for children and adults: United States, 2011–2014. National Center for Health Statistics," *Vital Health Stat, 3*(39).
©McGraw-Hill Education/Richard Hutchings

through adulthood. The average 10-year-old weighs about 18 pounds more than 40 years ago—just under 91 pounds for a boy and almost 89 pounds for a girl (Fryar, Gu, Ogden & Flegal, 2016). African American boys and girls tend to grow faster than Caucasian (white) children. By about age 6, African American girls have more muscle and bone mass than European American or Mexican American girls;

and Mexican American girls have a higher percentage of body fat than white girls the same size (Ellis, Abrams & Wong, 1997).

TOOTH DEVELOPMENT AND DENTAL CARE

Middle childhood ushers in the excitement of the Tooth Fairy, who sneaks into your room at night to put money under your pillow as a reward for a lost tooth. Primary teeth begin to fall out at about age 6 and are replaced by permanent teeth at a rate of about four teeth per year for the next 5 years.

In the past 20 years, the number of U.S. children ages 6 to 18 with untreated cavities dropped nearly 80 percent (Centers for Disease Control and Prevention, 2014). Nonetheless, tooth decay remains one of the most common chronic untreated conditions in childhood in the United States. Approximately 21 percent of 6- to 11-year-old children have had a cavity, and approximately 5.6 percent of them have not treated their tooth decay. Moreover, there are disparities by racial and ethnic group. While 4 percent of non-Hispanic white children have untreated cavities, 5.7 percent of Asian children, 7.1 percent of African American children, and 8.8 percent of Hispanic children have untreated cavities (Dye, Thornton-Evans, Li & Iafolla, 2015).

The improvements that have been seen can be attributed to a variety of factors, including parental education, access to dental care, fluoridated water supplies or the use of fluoride supplements (discussed in Chapter 8), as well as the use of adhesive sealants on rough chewing surfaces (Centers for Disease Control, 2014). The use of dental sealants in children's teeth has increased. Currently, slightly over one-third of children aged 6 to 8 have a dental sealant on at least one tooth, and nearly half of children aged 9 to 11 have a sealant (Dye et al., 2015). Sealants reduce tooth decay for four years after they are applied (Forss et al., 2013). Because of their efficacy, and because their use is more limited in lower income families, the U.S. Centers for Disease Control has funded programs to offer dental sealants through school programs. In these programs, mobile dental equipment is brought to schools serving low-income families and treatment

WHERE DO YOU STAND?

In many counties in the United States, drinking water is fluoridated as a matter of public health. Many argue that small doses of fluoride help to strengthen tooth enamel and thus promote dental health. However, others argue that levels of fluoride in water supplies are too variable, that the correct dosage depends on weight and nutritional status, and that high doses of fluoride could potentially have adverse effects on health. What's your view?

©Wayhome studio/Shutterstock

is offered to children there during the school day. Such programs have been shown to be effective and cost effective (U.S. Department of Health and Human Services, 2016).

Access to proper dental care is important for young children. Untreated dental caries can result in pain, difficulties chewing food, missed school, problems with concentration, and discomfort with appearance—along with consequent declines in quality of life and ability to succeed (U. S. Department of Health and Human Services, 2016).

BRAIN DEVELOPMENT

Changes in the brain's structure and functioning support the cognitive advances of middle childhood. In general, these changes can be characterized as resulting in faster, more efficient information processing and an increased ability to ignore distracting information (Amso & Casey, 2006; Wendelken, Baym, Gazzaley & Bunge, 2011). For example, it becomes easier for children to concentrate on the teacher—even if it's a boring lesson—while filtering out the antics of the class clown.

The study of the brain's structure is complex and depends on the interaction between genetic, epigenetic, and environment factors. The use of new technologies has allowed us a window into this process. For example, one technology, *magnetic resonance imaging* (MRI), enables researchers to observe how the brain changes over time and how these changes vary from one child to another (Giedd & Rapoport, 2010).

MRI technology shows us that the brain consists of both gray matter and white matter. Gray matter is composed of closely packed neurons in the cerebral cortex. White matter is made of glial cells, which provide support for neurons, and of myelinated axons, which transmit information across neurons. Both types of matter are necessary for effective cognition.

The amount of gray matter in the frontal cortex, which is strongly influenced by genetics, is likely linked with differences in IQ (Toga & Thompson, 2005; Deary, Penke & Johnson, 2010). Gray matter volume shows a U-shaped trajectory. The overall volume increases prepuberty and then declines by postpuberty (Gogtay & Thompson, 2010; Taki et al., 2013). The decline in overall volume is driven primarily by a loss in the density of gray matter. Although "less" gray matter may sound negative, the result is actually the opposite. We are born with more connections than we need. The "loss" reflects pruning of unused dendrites. In other words, those connections that are used remain active; the unused connections eventually disappear. The result is that the brain becomes "tuned" to the experiences of the child. In this way, we can calibrate our growing brains to local conditions.

Changes in the volume of gray matter peak at different times in the different lobes (Figure 11.2). Beneath the cortex, gray matter volume in the caudate—a part of the basal ganglia involved in control of movement and muscle tone and in mediating higher cognitive functions, attention, and emotional states—peaks at age 7 in girls and age 10 in boys (Lenroot & Giedd, 2006). Gray matter volume in the parietal

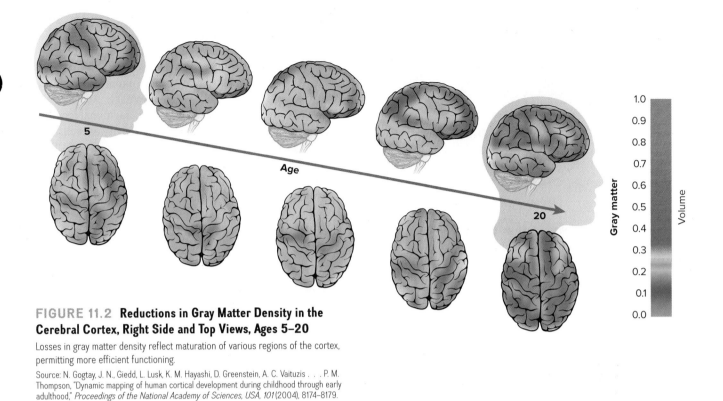

FIGURE 11.2 Reductions in Gray Matter Density in the Cerebral Cortex, Right Side and Top Views, Ages 5–20

Losses in gray matter density reflect maturation of various regions of the cortex, permitting more efficient functioning.

Source: N. Gogtay, J. N., Giedd, L. Lusk, K. M. Hayashi, D. Greenstein, A. C. Vaituzis . . . P. M. Thompson, "Dynamic mapping of human cortical development during childhood through early adulthood," *Proceedings of the National Academy of Sciences, USA, 101* (2004), 8174–8179.

lobes, which deal with spatial understanding, and in the frontal lobes, which handle higher-order functions, peaks at age 11. Gray matter in the temporal lobes, which deal with language, peaks at age 14, while the cerebellum, which regulates motor movements, takes longer. Generally, gray matter volume peaks 1 to 2 years earlier in girls than in boys (Gogtay & Thompson, 2010).

The loss in density of gray matter with age is balanced by another change—a steady increase in white matter. The connections between neurons thicken and myelinate, beginning with the frontal lobes and moving toward the rear of the brain. Between ages 6 and 13, striking growth occurs in connections between the temporal and parietal lobes. In fact, white matter growth may not begin to drop off until well into adulthood (Giedd & Rapoport, 2010; Kuhn, 2006; Lenroot & Giedd, 2006). In addition, changes in the density of the white matter in the corpus callosum may also underlie the advances seen in fine motor control in late childhood (Muetzel et al., 2008), such as the ability to write legibly, tie shoelaces, or play musical instruments.

Children's brains also show changes in the thickness of the cortex. Overall, the volume of the cortex peaks in late childhood to early adolescence (Raznahan et al., 2011). However, this is not a linear process, and different areas show different rates of change. For example, researchers observed cortical thickening between ages 5 and 11 in regions of the temporal and frontal lobes. At the same time, thinning occurred in the rear portion of the frontal and parietal cortex in the brain's left hemisphere. This change correlated with improved performance on the vocabulary portion of an intelligence test (Toga et al., 2006).

Nutrition and Sleep

Emily refuses to eat any vegetables and subsists mostly on pasta and fruit. Nathan learned to read; since then he has stayed up late every night with a flashlight under the covers, reading until he falls asleep. Sarah loves fruits and vegetables and falls asleep promptly at eight. How do different patterns of eating and sleeping affect these children?

NUTRITIONAL NEEDS

The recommended calories per day for schoolchildren 9 to 13 years of age range from 1,600 to 2,600 calories a day, depending on activity level. Nutritionists recommend a varied diet, including plenty of grains, fruits, and vegetables, and high levels of complex carbohydrates such as whole grains. To avoid overweight and prevent cardiac problems, children, like adults, should get only about 25 to 30 percent of their total calories from fat and less than 10 percent of the total from saturated fat. They should consume less than 10 percent of their calories from added sugars (DeSalvo, Olson & Casavale, 2016). Studies have found no negative effects on height, weight, body mass, or neurological development from a moderately low-fat diet at this age (Rask-Nissilä et al., 2000).

As children grow older, pressures and opportunities for unhealthy eating increase. Approximately 20 percent of children skip breakfast, a habit associated with a greater risk of obesity (Deshmukh-Taskar et al., 2010). Most children get almost a third of their daily calories through snacks (Shriver et al., 2018) and are eating almost three snacks a day in

Source: US Department of Agriculture

addition to the typical breakfast, lunch, and dinner (Piernas & Popkin, 2010). In schools in which vending machines are available, 18 percent of children report buying snacks or drinks from vending machines 2 or more days a week rather than lunch. The most frequent items purchased are chips, pretzels, crackers, candy bars, soda, and sports drinks (Park, Sappenfield, Huang, Sherry & Bensyl, 2010).

Approximately one-third of children eat at fast-food restaurants on any given day (Vikraman, Fryar & Ogden, 2015). While socioeconomic status can be a factor in unhealthy eating because healthy, fresh food is often more expensive than highly processed, high-calorie food with low nutrient content, it does not seem to impact fast-food consumption. However, race and ethnicity do. African American (9.8 percent) and white (9.1 percent) children are more likely than Hispanic (8.4 percent) and Asian (5.0 percent) children to eat fast food (Vikraman et al., 2015). The media strongly influence children's food choices, and not for the better. For example, commercials that focus on fast-food restaurants and the enticing toys they often offer are common during children's programming hours. Exposure to fast-food and soft drink advertising is associated with increased consumption of both types of products, especially in overweight or

Did you know?

In September 2011, in response to consumer and government complaints regarding the health value of Happy Meals, McDonald's reduced the volume of French fries, added apple slices, and included a drink option of fat-free chocolate or 1 percent milk. If all healthy options are chosen, this reduces the calories of a four-piece Chicken McNuggets Happy Meal from 520 calories and 26 grams of fat to a more reasonable—but still substantial—410 calories and 19 grams of fat.

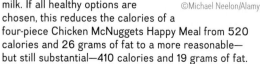

©Michael Neelon/Alamy

obese children (Cairns, Angus, Hastings & Caraher, 2013; Andreyeva, Kelly & Harris, 2011).

Nutrition education in schools can be helpful when combined with parental education and changes in school lunch menus, although they have been more successful in improving fruit intake than vegetable intake. Additionally, efforts to combat obesity benefit from an additional focus on energy expenditure through increased activity as well. Proposed legislative recommendations include changes in food labeling, taxes on unhealthy foods, restrictions on foods in government-supported school lunch programs, regulation of food advertising directed toward children, and requiring restaurants to list nutrition information on their menus (AHA et al., 2006; Evans, Christian, Cleghorn, Greenwood & Cade, 2012; De Bourdeauhuij et al., 2011).

SLEEP PATTERNS AND PROBLEMS

Sleep needs decline from 12.5 hours a day for 3- to 5-year-olds to 10 hours a day for ages 6 to 13 (National Sleep Foundation, 2016). Sleep problems, such as resistance to going to bed, insomnia, and daytime sleepiness, are common in the United States during these years, in part because many children, as they grow older, are allowed to set their own bedtimes (Hoban, 2004).

Did you know?

One study on sleep problems in children reported that girls sleep longer and more soundly than boys (Sadeh, Raviv & Gruber, 2000).

©Morrowind/Shutterstock

Childhood sleep problems are on the rise. In 2011–2012, 41.9 percent of children age 6 to 17 years reported at least one day per week of sleep problems, and 13.6 percent reported at least 2 days of disrupted sleep a week, a significant rise from 2003. A variety of factors seem to be at play, including exposure to media screens, physical inactivity, and secondhand smoke. Additionally, the authors highlighted neighborhood characteristics that were related to sleep problems, such as safety concerns, poor housing, vandalism, and a lack of parks and playgrounds (Singh & Kenney, 2013). The presence of a television in the bedroom can also be highly disruptive. At the age of 7, 23 percent of children have a television in their bedroom, and increased television viewing is associated with fewer hours of sleep (Cespedes et al., 2014).

Estimates of how many children habitually snore vary widely and range from 7 to 21 percent. Whether or not a child snores can be affected by a variety of factors, including age, gender, race, family susceptibility, chronic health problems, and overweight (Goldstein et al., 2011; Bonuck et al., 2011; Li et al., 2010). While children who snore sleep as long as do children who don't snore, their sleep is more fragmented, and fragmented sleep is associated with deficits in language and cognitive skills, fine motor skills and activities of daily living skills, and lower scores on developmental test scores (Yorbik, Mutlu, Koc & Mutluer, 2014).

Persistent snoring, at least 3 times a week, may indicate a child has sleep-disordered breathing (SDB), a condition that has been linked to behavioral and learning difficulties. Obstructive sleep apnea (OSA), a severe form of SDB, affects 1 in 20 children and is associated with significant declines in IQ, memory, and verbal fluency (Halbower et al., 2006). Many children with SDB may have their adenoids and tonsils surgically removed—a treatment that has been found to improve neurobehavioral deficits and improve quality of life (Chervin et al., 2006). Children who are not candidates for surgery may benefit from continuous positive airway pressure (CPAP) therapy, in which an electronic device keeps airways open via air pressure delivered through a nasal mask (Lamberg, 2007).

Failure to get adequate sleep is associated with a variety of adjustment problems, and this effect is particularly marked when children are African American or come from homes of low socioeconomic status (El-Sheikh, Kelly, Buckhalt & Hinnant, 2010; Beebe, 2011). Poor sleep can also negatively impact academic performance. In one study, teachers noted that at least 10 percent of kindergarten through fourth grade students struggled to stay awake in class (Owens, Spirito, McGuinn & Nobile, 2000). Sleep quality, sleep duration, and daytime sleepiness have all been found to affect academic performance and seem to affect younger children, particularly boys, to a greater degree (Dewald, Meijer, Oort, Kerkhof & Bogels, 2010). Moreover, short sleep duration in children is associated with later risk of obesity and overweight (Fatima & Mamun, 2015). Sleep, quite plainly, is necessary for optimal outcomes.

Motor Development and Physical Play

Motor skills continue to improve in middle childhood. By this age, most children in developing countries go to work, and this leaves them little time and freedom for physical play (Larson & Verma, 1999). However, play is an important context for physical and psychological health. In the United States, school-age children now spend less time on sports and other outdoor activities than in the early 1980s and more hours on schooling and homework, in addition to time spent on television and on computer activities, which barely existed 20 years ago (Juster, Ono & Stafford, 2004; Basterfield et al., 2011). In 2016, only 21.6 percent of children ages 6 to 19 reached the recommendations for physical activity on 5 out of 7 days in a week (Centers for Disease Control, 2017a). At the same time, many children participate in organized sports. How do these physical activities—or lack of them—shape development?

©Andrey_Popov/ Shutterstock

RECESS

The games children play at recess tend to be informal and spontaneously organized. Most of recess activity involves socializing with peers (Holmes, 2012). Boys play more physically active games (Rose & Rudolf, 2006), whereas girls favor games that include verbal expression or counting aloud, such as hopscotch and jump rope (Pellegrini, Kato, Blatchford & Baines, 2002). When given the choice, most children opt to play in natural or green areas rather than cement or concrete (Lucas & Dyment, 2010). However, when provided with more playground equipment, children tend to be more active during recess. Not surprisingly, more space to play in also leads to higher levels of activity, and children tend to decrease their activity levels as the temperature rises (Ridgers, Fairclough & Stratton, 2010).

Games at recess tend to be informal and promote both agility and social competence. More space and more playground equipment are both associated with higher levels of activity at recess.
©Stockbyte/PunchStock

Younger children spend more time running and chasing each other (Holmes, 2012). About 10 percent of schoolchildren's free play in the early grades consists of **rough-and-tumble play**—wrestling, kicking, tumbling, grappling, and chasing, often accompanied by laughing and screaming (Bjorklund & Pellegrini, 2002). This kind of play may look like fighting but is done playfully among friends (Jarvis, 2010).

Rough-and-tumble play peaks in middle childhood (Bjorklund & Pellegrini, 2002). It seems to be universal, and boys engage in higher levels of it than girls (Pellegrini et al., 2002; Smith, 2005). These different play styles help explain sex segregation during play (Maccoby, 2000). From an evolutionary standpoint, rough-and-tumble play has important adaptive benefits: It hones skeletal and muscle development, offers safe practice for hunting and fighting skills, and channels aggression and competition (Pellegrini, 2012). By age 11, it often becomes a way to establish dominance within the peer group (Bjorklund & Pellegrini, 2002; Smith, 2005).

Recess-time activities promote growth in agility and social competence and foster adjustment to school. Despite the perception that recess takes time out of the school day that could be better spent learning, recess is also associated with improvements in academic performance (Murray et al., 2013). The improvements may stem from the changes in behavior that occur after children are allowed free time. A recent meta-analysis showed that after recess, children were better able to focus on class material; they were less fidgety, less listless, more focused and on task, and this was true whether or not recess involved physical interaction or social activity (Rasberry et al., 2011).

ORGANIZED SPORTS

When children begin playing games with rules, some join organized, adult-led sports. Estimates are that approximately

Ideally, organized athletic programs should strive to include as many children as possible and focus on building skills rather than winning games.
©isitsharp/Getty Images

37 percent of 6- to 12-year-old children played team sports on a regular basis in 2016, a slow but steady decline from 44.5 percent in 2008. Household income is a major factor impacting the ability of children to participate. In 2016, slightly under 35 percent of children from families that made less than $25,000 a year participated in organized sports on at least one day that year, while over 68 percent of children from families that made more than $100,000 did (The Aspen Institute, 2018). Participation in unorganized physical activity, such as bicycling and shooting baskets, is higher at 77.4 percent (Duke, Huhman, & Heitzler, 2003).

Developmental changes determine what types of organized sports are most effective. Six- to 9-year-olds need more flexible rules, shorter instruction time, and more free time for practice than older children. At this age girls and boys are about equal in weight, height, endurance, and motor skill development. Older children are better able to process instruction and learn team strategies.

Besides improving motor skills, regular physical activity has immediate and long-term health benefits: weight control, lower blood pressure, improved cardiorespiratory functioning, and enhanced self-esteem and well-being. Active children tend to become active adults. Thus, organized athletic programs should include as many children as possible and should focus on building skills rather than winning games (Council on Sports Medicine and Fitness & Council on School Health, 2006).

Health and Safety

Middle childhood is a relatively safe period in the life span, and in the modern world most children enjoy good health. However, while the death rate in the middle childhood years is the lowest in the life span, the increasingly sedentary nature of modern life combined with the easy availability of high-calorie food has resulted in an epidemic of overweight and obesity in the United States. Moreover, some children suffer from chronic medical conditions, accidental injuries, lack of access to health care, or emotional disturbances.

OVERWEIGHT

Overweight, a body mass index between the 85th and 95th percentile, and obesity, a body mass index over the 95th percentile, has become a major health issue for children worldwide. The prevalence rate has risen sharply—in 1975, 4 percent of children and teens ages 5 to 19 were overweight or obese. In 2016, just over 18 percent—or more than 340 million children and adolescents—were overweight or obese. Worldwide, the obesity rate has tripled since 1975. While overweight and obesity were once considered to be problems of high-income and urban countries, it is now found in low- and middle-income countries as well. In fact, many of these countries now carry a "double burden" and must manage the twin issues of undernutrition and obesity and overweight at the same time (World Health Organization, 2018).

In the United States, about 17.2 percent of children between the ages of 2 and 19 are obese and another

16.2 percent are overweight. Boys are slightly more likely to be overweight than girls (Fryar, Carroll & Ogden, 2016). Although overweight has increased in all ethnic groups, it is most prevalent among Mexican American boys (28.9 percent) and non-Hispanic black girls (24.8 percent) (Fryar et al., 2012). While Asians show lower rates of overweight and obesity, there are indications that they may have more body fat than Caucasian (white) children, and thus health risks may begin at a lower weight compared to other ethnic groups (Fryar et al., 2016).

Causes of Overweight

What are the causes of overweight in children? It can be the result of an inherited tendency aggravated by too little exercise and too much or the wrong kinds of food (Sahoo et al., 2015).

Children are more likely to be overweight if they have overweight parents or other relatives. Poor nutrition, encouraged by media advertising and wide availability of snack foods and beverages, also contributes (Council on Sports Medicine and Fitness & Council on School Health, 2006). Eating out is another culprit; children who eat outside the home consume an estimated 200 more calories a day than when they eat at home (French, Story & Jeffery, 2001). Eating fast food has been associated with overweight and obesity (Braithwaite et al., 2014), and on a typical day, approximately one-third of children and adolescents report eating fast foods high in fat, carbohydrates, and sugar additives (Vikraman, Fryar & Ogden, 2015). Children (like adults) should get about 10 percent of their total calories from saturated fat (U.S. Department of Agriculture, 2010). Sugar, especially in the form of sweetened beverages, should be consumed in limited quantities, as sugar consumption has been linked to weight gain (Malik, Pan, Willet & Hu, 2013; Davis, Bennett, Befort & Nollen, 2011).

Inactivity is a major factor in the sharp rise in overweight children. As children get older, activity levels decrease significantly from an average of 180 minutes per day for 9-year-olds to 40 minutes per day for 15-year-olds (Nader, Bradley, Houts, McRitchie & O'Brien, 2008). Television viewing appears to be an important variable. Children who watch TV 5 hours a day are 4.6 times as likely to be overweight as those who watch no more than 2 hours daily (Koplan, Liverman, Kraak & the Committee on Prevention of Obesity in Children and Youth, 2005), and even those who watch TV or play video games for "only" 2 hours daily are still 2 times more likely to be overweight (Sisson, Broyles, Baker & Katzmarzyk, 2010). Preadolescent girls, children with disabilities, children who live in public housing, and children in unsafe neighborhoods with no facilities for outdoor exercise are most likely to be sedentary (Council on Sports Medicine and Fitness & Council on School Health, 2006). Physical inactivity and sedentary behaviors differ among children in various ethnic groups. In a recent study, more than 22 percent of immigrant Hispanic children were physically inactive, compared to 9.5 percent of white, 10.8 percent of Asian, and 14.3 percent of African American U.S. born

children. Overall, immigrant children were significantly more likely to be physically inactive and less likely to participate in sports than native children (Singh, Yu, Siahpush & Kogan, 2008). Where children live also matters. Children who live in rural areas have a 26 percent higher risk of obesity than children who live in urban areas, although the reasons for this are unclear (Johnson & Johnson, 2015).

Impact of Overweight

The adverse health effects of obesity for children are similar to those faced by adults. These children commonly have medical problems, including high blood pressure, high cholesterol, and high insulin levels (National Center for Health Statistics, 2004; Sorof et al., 2004), or they may develop such diseases at a younger age (Sahoo et al., 2015). There is some data that show obese boys have higher levels of cardiometabolic risk factors than obese girls, suggesting they may be at even greater risk for developing disease (Skinner, Perrin, Moss & Skelton, 2015). Childhood diabetes is one of the prime results of rising obesity rates (Malik, Popkin, Bray, Despres & Hu, 2010; Perrin, Finkle & Benjamin, 2007).

Overweight children are also at risk for behavior problems, depression, low self-esteem, and falling behind in physical and social functioning (Datar & Sturm, 2004; Williams, Wake, Hesketh, Maher & Waters, 2005; Sahoo et al., 2015). "Comfort" foods can activate pleasure circuits in the brain similar to those experienced by drug addicts (Kenny, 2011). Thus, overweight children may compensate for their suffering by indulging themselves with treats, making their physical and social problems even worse.

Overweight children tend to become obese adults; they are 5 times more likely to be obese in adulthood than children who are not obese (Simmonds, Llewellyn, Owen & Woolacott, 2016). Obese children are at risk for problems in adulthood with hypertension (high blood pressure), heart disease, orthopedic problems, diabetes, and other problems (Sahoo et al., 2015). Indeed, childhood obesity may be a stronger predictor of some diseases than adult obesity (AAP, 2004; Baker, Olsen & Sorenson, 2007) and may put children at risk of premature death (Franks et al., 2010). By midcentury, obesity that starts in childhood may shorten life expectancy by 2 to 5 years (Ludwig, 2007).

Prevention and Treatment of Overweight

Childhood obesity rates are a significant public health issue. While a temporary plateau in young children (Ogden, Carroll, Kit & Flegal, 2014; Ogden et al., 2016; Wen et al., 2012) gave researchers hope that efforts to combat obesity were finally paying off, more recent data suggest the decline was illusory. Childhood obesity rates continue to rise at alarming rates (Skinner, Ravanbakht, Skelton, Perrin & Armstrong, 2018; Ludwig, 2018).

Healthy attitudes about food and appropriate activity levels are the best way to prevent and treat childhood obesity. Prevention of weight gain is easier, less costly, and more effective than treating overweight (Council on Sports

Prevention of obesity is easier than treatment. Effective prevention programs include more time spent in physical activity and less time in front of computers and television.

©FS Stock/Shutterstock

Medicine and Fitness & Council on School Health, 2006). The U.S. Preventive Services Task Force (USPSTF, 2010) recommends screening children for overweight and obesity starting at the age of 6 years.

Childhood obesity is a risk factor for adult obesity; 55 percent of obese children will become obese adults. However, a typical weight in childhood does not guarantee a healthy weight in adulthood. Seventy percent of obese adults were not obese in childhood (Simmonds, Llewellyn, Owen & Woolacott, 2016). Thus, prevention and intervention programs should target health in all children, not just overweight children.

Generally, research supports efforts focused on overall lifestyle changes rather than narrowly defined diets or exercise programs. Effective programs should include the efforts of parents, schools, physicians, communities, and the larger culture (Krishnamoorthy, Hart & Jelalian, 2006). Treatment should begin early and promote permanent changes in lifestyle, not weight loss alone (Kitzmann & Beech, 2006). Recommendations include less time in front of television and computers, changes in food labeling and advertising, healthier school meals, education to help children make better food choices, more time spent in physical education and informal exercise with family and friends, such as walking and unorganized sports (AAP, 2004).

Schools that serve healthy foods and offer nutrition education have reduced the number of overweight children in their classrooms by 50 percent (Foster et al., 2008). Physical

activity is also an important factor. The Centers for Disease Control (2017a) recommends that children and adolescents should get an hour of physical exercise per day. However, almost 80 percent of children and adolescents fail to achieve the goal on 5 out of 7 days a week. Unfortunately school-based activities do not fill this gap, as the average school offers only 85 to 98 minutes each week (National Center for Education Statistics, 2006). An additional 60 minutes of physical education per week in kindergarten and first grade could reduce by half the number of overweight girls at that age (Datar & Sturm, 2004).

Parental involvement is a crucial factor in successful interventions. The most effective interventions are those in which parents are helped to change their own behaviors as well as those of their children (Kitzmann et al., 2010). Parents can encourage healthy habits by making exercise a family activity and by limiting television. Parents should watch children's eating and activity patterns and address excessive weight gain before a child becomes severely overweight (AAP Committee on Nutrition, 2003). Less time in front of television and computers and changes in food labeling and advertising would also help (American Psychological Association, 2018).

CHRONIC MEDICAL CONDITIONS

Illness in middle childhood tends to be brief. **Acute medical conditions**—occasional, short-term conditions, such as infections and warts—are common. Six or seven bouts a year with colds, flu, or viruses are typical as germs pass among children at school or at play (Behrman, 1992).

Did you know?

The best way to avoid a cold is to wash your hands, and wash them often! And note that hand sanitizers are not effective when hands are visibly dirty (CDC, 2012).

©Ingram Publishing

According to a nationally representative survey of more than 200,000 households, an estimated 12.8 percent of U.S. children have or are at risk for **chronic medical conditions**: long-lasting or recurrent physical, developmental, behavioral, or emotional conditions requiring special health services (Kogan, Newacheck, Honberg & Strickland, 2005). These rates have been rising, as have the rates of hospital admissions for children with more than one medically complex condition (Burns et al., 2010). Still, most will recover, although children who are males, black, Hispanic, or have overweight mothers are at higher risk (Van Cleave, Gortmaker & Perrin, 2010). The most prevalent chronic medical conditions for this age group include asthma, diabetes, hypertension, and stuttering.

Asthma

Asthma is a chronic, allergy-based respiratory disease characterized by sudden attacks of coughing, wheezing, and difficulty breathing. Its prevalence in the United States more than doubled between 1980 and 1995 and has remained high (Akinbami, 2006). More than 9.5 percent of U.S. children and adolescents up to age 17 have been diagnosed with asthma at some time (Akinbami et al., 2012). It is 20 percent more likely to be diagnosed in black children than in white children (McDaniel, Paxson & Waldfogel, 2006). Its prevalence has leveled off in developed countries but is still increasing in developing countries (Asher, 2010).

The causes of the asthma increases are uncertain, but a genetic predisposition is likely to be involved (Eder, Ede & von Mutius, 2006). For example, researchers have identified a gene variant that increases the risk of developing asthma, an effect that is exacerbated in homes where children are exposed to smoke (Caliskan et al., 2013). Smoke exposure is a major environmental risk factor by itself, as is pollution from car emissions (Burke et al., 2012; Gasana, Dillikar, Mendy, Forno & Vieira, 2012). Allergens such as household pets, molds, and cockroach droppings have also been proposed (Bollinger, 2003; Etzel, 2003). Increasing evidence points to an association between obesity and asthma (Weinmayr et al., 2014). Some researchers have focused on genes that might confer a shared genetic risk for asthma and obesity together (Melen et al., 2010) while others have argued that the association exists because of an underlying lifestyle factor related to both conditions (Eder et al., 2006). There is also an association between low levels of vitamin D and increased incidence of asthma in children (Bener, Ehlayel, Tulic & Hamid, 2012). Moreover, vitamin D enhances the anti-inflammatory effects of the inhaled steroids often used to treat asthma attacks in children (Searing et al., 2010).

Diabetes

Diabetes is one of the most common diseases in school-age children. In 2015, more than 132,000 children in the United States had diabetes (Centers for Disease Control and Prevention, 2017b). It is characterized by high levels of glucose in the blood as a result of defective insulin production, ineffective insulin action, or both. Type 1 diabetes is the result of an insulin deficiency that occurs when insulin-producing cells in the pancreas are destroyed. Type 1 diabetes accounts for 5 to 10 percent of all diabetes cases and for almost all diabetes in children under age 10. Symptoms include thirst and urination, hunger, weight loss, blurred vision, and fatigue. Treatment includes insulin administration, nutrition management,

Nick Jonas was diagnosed with Type I diabetes at age 13.
©Dfree/Shutterstock

and physical activity (National Diabetes Education Program, 2008).

Type 2 diabetes is characterized by insulin resistance and used to be found mainly in overweight and older adults. As childhood obesity has increased, so has type 2 diabetes. Increases have been noted in white, Hispanic and African American children (Dabelea et al., 2014), and, if current trends continue, estimates are that by 2050, over 84,000 American children will be diagnosed with type 2 diabetes (Imperatore et al., 2012). Symptoms are similar to type 1 diabetes (Zylke & DeAngelis, 2007). Treatment with nutrition management and increased physical activity can be effective, although glucose-lowering medication or insulin may be needed for resistant cases.

> **diabetes** One of the most common diseases of childhood. It is characterized by high levels of glucose in the blood as a result of defective insulin production, ineffective insulin action, or both.
>
> **hypertension** High blood pressure.

Childhood Hypertension

Hypertension, or high blood pressure, once was relatively rare in childhood, but it has been termed an "evolving epidemic" of cardiovascular risk, especially among ethnic minorities (Sorof, Lai, Turner, Poffenbarger & Portman, 2004, p. 481). Estimates are that 19.2 percent of boys and 12.6 percent of girls have blood pressure at or above the 90th percentile (Rosner, Cook, Daniels & Falkner, 2013). Risk factors include obesity or overweight, salt intake, sedentary lifestyle, poor sleep quality, and race (Bucher et al., 2013; Rosner et al., 2013).

Although high blood pressure in childhood is not generally associated with mortality as it is in adulthood, it does put children at risk for later disease and is associated with damage to organs. For example, it can lead to left ventricular hypertrophy (thickening and hardening of the left wall of the heart), damage to the retina of the eyes, or damage to arteries (Falkner, 2010). Additionally, there are indications that high blood pressure may negatively affect the developing brain. Children with hypertension are more likely to have learning disabilities and may have problems with executive functioning, although some of these issues may be reversible with treatment (Sharma et al., 2010).

Weight reduction through dietary modification and regular physical activity is the primary treatment for overweight-related hypertension. If blood pressure does not come down, drug treatment can be considered. However, care must be taken in prescribing such drugs, as their long-term effects on children are unknown—as are the long-term consequences of untreated hypertension in children (National High Blood Pressure Education Program Working Group on High Blood Pressure in Children and Adolescents, 2004).

Perspectives on Diversity

©Digital Vision/Getty Images

HOW CULTURAL ATTITUDES AFFECT HEALTH CARE

One morning Buddi Kumar Rai, a university-educated resident of Badel, a remote hill village in Nepal, carried his 2½-year-old daughter, Kusum, to the shaman, the local medicine man. Kusum's little face was sober, her golden complexion pale, and her almond-shaped eyes droopy from the upper-respiratory infection she had been suffering with the past week. Two days before, Kusum had been in her father's arms when he had slipped and fallen backward. Neither was hurt, but Kusum had screamed in fright. Now the shaman told Buddi that Kusum's illness was due to that fright. He prescribed incantations and put a mark on the child's forehead to drive away the evil spirit that had entered her body when she had her scare (Olds, 2002).

Adherence to ancient beliefs about illness is common in many parts of the nonindustrialized world, but it is not limited to them. Many cultures see illness and disability as punishment inflicted on someone who has done wrong in this or a previous life or is paying for an ancestor's sin. Another belief, common in Latin America and Southeast Asia, is that an imbalance of elements in the body causes illness, and the patient has to reestablish equilibrium (Groce & Zola, 1993). Arab Americans tend to attribute disease to such causes as the evil eye, grief and loss, exposure to drafts, and eating the wrong combinations of foods (Al-Oballi Kridli, 2002).

How do we address these diverse perspectives? Medical professionals need to explain clearly, in the family's language, what course of treatment they recommend, why they favor it, and what they expect to happen. Such concern can help prevent incidents like one that occurred when an Asian mother became hysterical as an American nurse took her baby to get a urine sample. Three children had been taken from this mother in Cambodia. None had returned (Groce & Zola, 1993).

Stuttering

Stuttering is involuntary audible or silent repetition or prolongation of sounds or syllables. The more common type, persistent developmental stuttering (PDS), is especially noticeable at the beginning of a word or phrase or in long, complex sentences. It usually begins early in life, and by the age of 4, 95 percent of the risk for stuttering is over (Yairi & Ambrose, 2013). By fifth grade, it is 4 times more common in boys than in girls. Five percent of children stutter for a period of 6 months or more, but three quarters of these recover by late childhood, leaving about 1 percent with a long-term problem (Stuttering Foundation, 2006). Previous year prevalence rates, reported by parents of children age 3 to 17 years, are 1.27 percent for non-Hispanic white children, 1.96 percent for Hispanic children, and notably higher at 2.63 percent for non-Hispanic black children (Boyle et al., 2011).

stuttering Involuntary, frequent repetition or prolongation of sounds or syllables.

Stuttering is now widely regarded as a neurological condition. The basic cause may be a structural or functional disorder of the central nervous system. Specifically, functional magnetic resonance imaging has shown that children who stutter show weakened connectivity between the putamen, supplementary motor area, and primary motor cortex. Boys show additional weakened connectivity to ventral premotor areas and the posterior superior temporal gyrus as well, and both boys and girls show decreased white matter connectivity to motor and auditory areas in the left hemisphere. These areas of the brain are believed to support speech planning and execution, and are required for fluid speech (Chang & Zhu, 2013).

A growing body of research has also pointed to genetic influences on stuttering. Behavioral genetics research has found high heritability estimates for stuttering, and molecular genetics studies are beginning to identify particular genes (Frigerio-Domingues & Drayna, 2017; Kang et al., 2010). While there are not temperament differences in shyness or social anxiety for preschool children who stutter compared to those who do not, over time some children develop social anxiety as a result of their difficulty with speaking (Alm, 2014). For example, parental reactions may make the child nervous or anxious about speaking (Büchel & Sommer, 2004).

Did you know?

The actor Bruce Willis treated his stuttering by joining a drama club, which forced him to speak before an audience (Büchel & Sommer, 2004).

©ZUMA Press, Inc./Alamy

There is no known cure for stuttering, but speech therapy can help a child talk more easily and fluently (Stuttering Foundation, 2006).

FACTORS IN CHILDREN'S HEALTH

Social disadvantage plays an important part in children's health. Poor children—who are disproportionately minority children—and those living with a single parent or parents with low educational status are more likely than other children to be in fair or poor health, to have chronic conditions or health-related limitations on activities, to miss school due to illness or injury, to be hospitalized, to have unmet medical and dental needs, and to experience delayed medical care (Bloom, Cohen & Freeman, 2012).

Why does economic disadvantage result in these findings? Parents with higher socioeconomic and educational status tend to know more about good health habits and have better access to insurance and health care. Families that tend to have higher incomes typically have more wholesome diets than families of a lower socioeconomic status (Kirkpatrick, Dodd, Reedy & Krebs-Smith, 2012), and their children are more likely to have health insurance (Bloom et al., 2012). Children in low-income and minority families are more likely than other children to be uninsured, to have no regular health care facility, or to go to clinics or hospital emergency rooms rather than doctors' offices (Bloom et al., 2012). Poor access to health care is a particularly severe problem among Latino children (Scott & Ni, 2004).

ACCIDENTAL INJURIES

As in early childhood, accidental injuries are the leading cause of death among school-age U.S. children (Centers for Disease Control and Prevention, 2017c; Figure 11.3). In 2015, 1,518 U.S. children between the ages of 5 and 14 years died in accidents, the majority—almost 900—in car accidents (Murphy, Xu, Kochanek, Curtin & Arias, 2017).

An estimated 70 percent of children in the United States ride bicycles, making this one of the most popular forms of outdoor recreation and exercise (Mattei et al., 2012). Unfortunately, despite the existence of laws requiring wearing of bicycle helmets in 21 states and the District of Columbia,

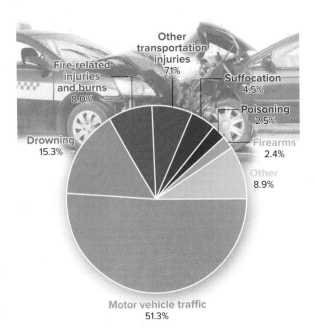

FIGURE 11.3 **Accidental Deaths Ages 5–14, United States**

Traffic accidents, drowning, and burns are the most common causes of unintentional (accidental) deaths among U.S. children ages 5–14 years.

Source: Centers for Disease Control and Prevention, National Center for Injury Prevention and Control, "Web-based Injury Statistics Query and Reporting System (WISQARS)," *Unintentional Injury Deaths, United States, 2016, Ages 5–14* (2018). Accessed at www.cdc.gov/injury/wisqars.

©Vadim Ratnikov/123RF

their use is still low (Kaushik, Krisch, Schroeder, Flick & Nemergut, 2015). An estimated 23,000 children each year suffer serious brain injuries from bicycle accidents, and as many as 88 percent of these injuries could be prevented by using helmets (American Academy of Pediatrics Committee on Injury and Poison Prevention, 2001). Protective headgear also is vital for baseball and softball, football, roller skating, in-line skating, skateboarding, scooter riding, horseback riding, hockey, speed sledding, snowmobiling, skiing, snowboarding, and tobogganing. For soccer, "heading" the ball should be minimized because of the danger of brain injury (AAP Committee on Sports Medicine and Fitness & Committee on School Health, 2001). Also, because of the need for stringent safety precautions and constant supervision for trampoline use, the AAP Council on Injury, Violence and Poison Prevention and the Council on Sports Medicine and Fitness (Briskin et al., 2012) recommend that parents not buy trampolines and that children only be allowed to use trampolines as part of structured training programs.

MENTAL HEALTH

After her parents divorced, 8-year-old Emma started acting differently. She refused to go to her gymnastics class, which she had previously loved; her grades dropped; and she complained of stomachaches and headaches regularly. She was also irritable and had

WHAT DO YOU DO?

Nurse Practitioner (NP)

Nurse practitioners provide routine health care to patients. Those specializing in pediatrics see children for routine and sick child appointments and are able to write prescriptions. Nurse practitioners have a master's degree in nursing—either an MS (master of science) or an MSN (master of science in nursing)—as well as board certification, and they typically work out of hospitals or group practices. To learn more about becoming a nurse practitioner, visit www.aanp.org and www.napnap.org.

©Sheer Photo, Inc/Getty Images

difficulty staying asleep at night. Her concerned mother took her to a therapist, and Emma was diagnosed with depression.

While many people believe young children do not experience mental health issues, in reality, they can suffer from a variety of disruptive conduct disorders, anxiety disorders, and depression.

Did you know?

Children with ADHD or attentional issues are more accident prone (Barkley, 2002).

©Brand X Pictures/PunchStock

Disruptive Conduct Disorders

Children typically outgrow temper tantrums and defiant, argumentative, hostile, or deliberately annoying behaviors by middle childhood. When such a pattern of behavior persists after age 8, children, usually boys, may be diagnosed with oppositional defiant disorder (ODD), a pattern of excessive defiance, disobedience, and hostility toward adult authority figures lasting at least 6 months.

conduct disorder (CD) Repetitive, persistent pattern of aggressive, antisocial behavior violating societal norms or the rights of others.

school phobia Unrealistic fear of going to school.

separation anxiety disorder Condition involving excessive, prolonged anxiety concerning separation from home or from people to whom a person is attached.

social phobia Extreme fear and/or avoidance of social situations.

generalized anxiety disorder Anxiety not focused on any single target.

Children with ODD constantly fight, argue, lose their temper, snatch things, blame others, are angry and resentful, have few friends, are in constant trouble in school, and test the limits of adults' patience (American Psychiatric Association, 2000; American Academy of Child and Adolescent Psychiatry, 2013a).

Some children with ODD also develop **conduct disorder (CD)**, a persistent, repetitive pattern of aggressive, antisocial acts, such as truancy, setting fires, habitual lying, fighting, bullying, theft, vandalism, assaults, and drug and alcohol use (American Academy of Child and Adolescent Psychiatry, 2013b). Between 6 and 16 percent of boys and between 2 and 9 percent of girls under age 18 in the United States have been diagnosed with clinical levels of externalizing behavior or conduct problems (Roosa et al., 2005). Some 11- to 13-year-olds progress from conduct disorder to criminal violence—mugging, rape, and break-ins—and by age 17 may be frequent, serious offenders (Broidy et al., 2003). Between 25 and 50 percent of these highly antisocial children become antisocial adults (USDHHS, 1999b).

In some children, repetitive bullying and fighting is a sign of conduct disorder.
©Digital Vision/Getty Images

What determines whether a particular child with antisocial tendencies will become severely and chronically antisocial? Neurobiological deficits may be important. Children who are at elevated risk of becoming antisocial adults tend to be impulsive, and have low IQ and poor academic achievement. They also tend to experience substandard parenting. Their parents may not supervise them well, or they may be overly punitive or erratic in their care. They may be cold or antisocial, abusive, use hostile parenting strategies, or have high levels of family conflict. Their families are more likely to be large or poor. Additionally, children who later become antisocial are also more likely to have antisocial peers, to go to schools with high delinquency rates, and to live in high crime neighborhoods. These risk factors are additive—the more of them present, the higher the risk (Murray & Farrington, 2010).

School Phobia and Other Anxiety Disorders

Children with **school phobia** have an unrealistic fear of going to school. Some children have realistic reasons to fear going to school: a sarcastic teacher, overly demanding work, or a bully in the schoolyard. In such cases, the environment may need changing, not the child. However, true school phobia may be more closely related to either separation anxiety disorder or social phobia.

Although separation anxiety is normal in infancy, it is cause for concern when it persists in older children. **Separation anxiety disorder** involves excessive anxiety for at least 4 weeks concerning separation from home or from attachment figures. It affects some 4 percent of children and young adolescents. These children often come from close-knit, caring families. They may develop the disorder spontaneously or after a stressful event, such as the death of a pet, an illness, or a move to a new school (American Psychiatric Association, 2000; Harvard Medical School, 2004).

Sometimes school phobia may be a form of **social phobia**, or social anxiety: extreme fear and/or avoidance of social situations, such as speaking in class or meeting an acquaintance on the street. Social phobia affects about 5 percent of children. It runs in families, so there is likely a genetic component. Traumatic experiences, such as a child's mind going blank after being called on in class or writing on the chalkboard, often trigger these phobias (Rao, et al., 2007). Social anxiety tends to increase with age, whereas separation anxiety decreases (Costello, Compton, Keeler & Angold, 2003).

Some children have **generalized anxiety disorder**, which is not focused on any specific aspect of their lives. These children worry about everything: school grades, storms, earthquakes, hurting themselves on the playground, or the amount of gas in the tank. They

Childhood depression affects about 2 percent of children ages 6 to 17; it is more common among girls.
©Royalty-Free/Corbis

tend to be self-conscious, self-doubting, and excessively concerned with meeting others' expectations. They seek approval and need constant reassurance, but their worry seems independent of performance or of how others regard them (Harvard Medical School, 2004).

Far less common is **obsessive-compulsive disorder (OCD)**. Those with OCD may be obsessed by repetitive, intrusive thoughts, images, or impulses that often involve irrational fears, or they may show compulsive behaviors, such as constant hand-washing, or both (Harvard Medical School, 2004).

Anxiety disorders tend to run in families (Harvard Medical School, 2004) and are twice as common among girls as among boys. Anxiety may be neurological or may stem from early experiences. For example, parents who reward an anxious child with attention to the anxiety may unwittingly perpetuate it through operant conditioning (Harvard Medical School, 2004).

Childhood Depression

Childhood depression is a disorder of mood that goes beyond normal, temporary sadness. A recent meta-analysis including 41 studies across 27 cultures estimated the prevalence of childhood and adolescent depressive disorders at 2.6 percent (Polanczyk, Salum, Sugaya, Caye & Rohde, 2015). In the United States, the prevalence rate of depression in 6- to

17-year-old children is estimated to be 2.1 percent, and it becomes proportionately more common in girls with age (Perou et al., 2013). Symptoms include inability to have fun or concentrate, fatigue, extreme activity or apathy, crying, sleep problems, weight change, physical complaints, feelings of worthlessness, a prolonged sense of friendlessness, or frequent thoughts about death or suicide. Childhood depression may signal the beginning of a recurrent problem likely to persist into adulthood (Katz, Conway, Hammen, Brennan & Najman, 2011).

The exact causes of childhood depression are unknown, but depressed children tend to come from families with high levels of parental depression, anxiety, substance abuse, or antisocial behavior. The atmosphere in such families may increase children's risk of depression (Franic, Middeldorp, Dolan, Ligthart & Boomsma, 2010). Genetics are also important, given the existence of gene variants that increase the risk of depression (Dunn et al., 2015; Caspi et al., 2003; Young et al., 2007).

Children as young as 5 or 6 can report depressed moods and feelings that forecast later trouble, from academic problems to major depression and ideas of suicide (Ialongo, Edelsohn & Kellam, 2001). Depression often emerges during the transition to middle school and may be related to the stress of adjusting to adolescence and higher expectations (Stroud et al., 2009), weak self-efficacy beliefs, and lack of personal investment in academic success (Rudolph, Lambert, Clark & Kurlakowsky, 2001). Depression becomes more prevalent during adolescence (Perou et al., 2013; Costello et al., 2003), as discussed in Chapter 15.

Treatment Techniques

Psychological treatment for emotional disturbances can take several forms, and must be adjusted to the child's developmental level. When children have limited verbal and conceptual skills or have suffered emotional trauma, **art therapy** can help them describe what is troubling them without putting their feelings into words (Hanney & Kozlowska, 2002). Likewise, in **play therapy**, a child plays freely while a therapist occasionally comments, asks questions, or makes suggestions. Play therapy has proven effective with a variety of emotional, cognitive, and social problems, especially when consultation with parents or other close family members is part of the process (Bratton & Ray, 2002).

For older children, alternative treatments may be more effective. In **individual psychotherapy**, a therapist sees a child one-on-one to help the child gain insights into his or

obsessive-compulsive disorder (OCD) Anxiety aroused by repetitive, intrusive thoughts, images, or impulses, often leading to compulsive ritual behaviors.

childhood depression Mood disorder characterized by such symptoms as a prolonged sense of friendlessness, inability to have fun or concentrate, fatigue, extreme activity or apathy, feelings of worthlessness, weight change, physical complaints, and thoughts of death or suicide.

art therapy Therapeutic approach that allows a person to express troubled feelings without words, using a variety of art materials and media.

play therapy Therapeutic approach that uses play to help a child cope with emotional distress.

individual psychotherapy Psychological treatment in which a therapist sees a troubled person one-on-one.

family therapy Psychological treatment in which a therapist sees the whole family together to analyze patterns of family functioning.

behavior therapy Therapy that uses principles of learning theory to eliminate undesirable behaviors.

drug therapy Administration of drugs to treat emotional disorders.

her personality and relationships and to interpret feelings and behavior. Such treatment may be helpful at stressful times, such as the death of a parent or parental divorce. In **family therapy**, the therapist sees the family together, observes how members interact, and points out both growth-producing and growth-inhibiting, or destructive, patterns of family functioning. **Behavior therapy**, or behavior modification, is a form of therapy that uses principles of learning theory to eliminate undesirable behaviors or to develop desirable ones. Cognitive behavioral therapy, which seeks to change negative thoughts through gradual exposure, modeling, rewards, or positive self-talk, has proven the most effective treatment for anxiety disorders and depression in children and adolescents (Harvard Medical School, 2004; Zhou et al., 2015).

The use of **drug therapy**—antidepressants, stimulants, tranquilizers, and antipsychotic medications—to treat childhood emotional disorders is controversial. In 2002, antipsychotic medications were prescribed for 1,438 in every 100,000 children and adolescents, as compared with only 275 per 100,000 during the mid-1990s (Olfson, Blanco, Liu, Moreno & Laje, 2006). Sufficient research on the effectiveness and safety of many of these drugs, especially for children, is lacking (Murray, deVries & Wong, 2004). Despite this lack of data, use of such drugs in children has been rising sharply. Much of the increase has involved off-label use. In other words, most children using these drugs are receiving them for nonapproved psychiatric conditions (Pathak, West, Martin, Helm & Henderson, 2010). The reasons for this are varied. Sometimes, a shortage of trained providers, reimbursement for behavioral treatment, or a lack of treatment options leaves parents with few remaining options for managing difficult children. Additionally,

Art therapy can help children who have difficulty expressing their feelings in words describe what is troubling them.
©Phanie/Alamy

Drug therapy for psychological disorders in children is controversial, but rates of use have risen significantly in recent years.
©Comstock/Alamy

increased knowledge and awareness of drugs offerings, as well as increased acceptance of their use, is also a factor (Alexander, Gallagher, Mascola, Moloney & Stafford, 2011).

The use of selective serotonin reuptake inhibitors (SSRIs) to treat obsessive-compulsive, depressive, and anxiety disorders increased rapidly in the 1990s (Leslie, Newman, Chesney & Perrin, 2005) but has since slipped by about 20 percent (Daly, 2005). Some studies show moderate risks of suicidal thought and behavior for children and adolescents taking antidepressants, whereas others show no significant added risk (Hammad, Laughren & Racoosin, 2006; Simon, Savarino, Operskalski & Wang, 2006) or lessened risk (Simon, 2006). An analysis of 27 randomized, placebo-controlled studies found that the benefits of antidepressant use for children and adolescents outweigh the risks (Bridge et al., 2007).

mastering the CHAPTER

©BananaStock/Getty Images

Summary and Key Terms

Physical Development

> Physical development is less rapid in middle childhood than in earlier years. Wide differences in height and weight exist.

> The permanent teeth arrive in middle childhood. Dental health has improved, in part because of the use of sealants on chewing surfaces and the widespread use of fluoride.

> Brain growth continues during childhood with a gradual increase in white matter and decrease in gray matter. The connections between neurons become progressively more myelinated. These changes support cognitive advances and improvements in fine motor control during middle childhood.

Nutrition and Sleep

> A varied and healthy diet can help prevent overweight and chronic disease. As children grow older, they have more opportunities and pressures for unhealthy eating, including fast food and vending machines.

> Proper sleep is essential for growth and health. Most children do not get enough sleep, and many have sleep problems.

Motor Development and Physical Play

> Because of improved motor skills, boys and girls in middle childhood can engage in a wide range of motor activities.

> Informal recess-time activities help develop physical and social skills. Recess time is also associated with improvement in academic performance.

> Boys' games tend to be more physical and girls' games more verbal. About 10 percent of

schoolchildren's play, especially among boys, is rough-and-tumble play.

> Many children engage in organized, competitive sports. Older children are better able to learn team strategies and process more complicated instruction.

> A sound physical education program should aim for skill development and fitness rather than winning games.

> **KEY TERM**
>
> **Rough-and-tumble play**

Health and Safety

> Middle childhood is a relatively healthy period; most children are immunized and the death rate is low.

> Overweight entails multiple risks—physical, emotional, and social. It is influenced by genetic and environmental factors and is more easily prevented than treated. Many children do not get enough physical activity. Healthy attitudes and habits related to diet and physical activity are the best ways to prevent and treat childhood obesity.

> Respiratory infections and other acute medical conditions are common at this age.

> Chronic conditions such as asthma are most prevalent among poor and minority children, as well as those with a genetic predisposition.

> Diabetes is one of the most common childhood chronic conditions, and rates of type 2 diabetes have risen with increased prevalence of obesity.

> Hypertension is becoming more common along with the rise in overweight.

> Stuttering is fairly common but not permanent for most affected children; it is considered a neurological problem influenced by genetics.

> Accidents are the leading cause of death in middle childhood. Use of helmets and other protective devices and avoidance of trampolines and other risky sports can greatly reduce injuries.

> Common emotional and behavior disorders among school-age children include disruptive behavioral disorders, anxiety disorders, and childhood depression.

> Treatment techniques include individual psychotherapy, family therapy, behavior therapy, art therapy, play therapy, and drug therapy.

KEY TERMS

Acute medical conditions

Chronic medical conditions

Asthma

Diabetes

Hypertension

Stuttering

Conduct disorder (CD)

School phobia

Separation anxiety disorder

Social phobia

Generalized anxiety disorder

Obsessive-compulsive disorder (OCD)

Childhood depression

Art therapy

Play therapy

Individual psychotherapy

Family therapy

Behavior therapy

Drug therapy

Practice Quiz

1. Between the ages of 6 and 11, the typical child will grow:
   a. ½ to 1 inch a year
   b. 2 to 3 inches a year
   c. 5 to 6 inches a year
   d. 5 to 6 inches a year, but only if given synthetic growth hormone

2. What are two ways in which children's dental health has been promoted?
   _____
   _____

3. With respect to brain development, the gray matter _____ and the white matter _____ in volume over childhood.

4. Which of the following is the best description of a healthy diet in middle childhood?
   a. a high-protein, high-fat diet
   b. a low-protein diet rich in complex carbohydrates
   c. a varied diet including plenty of grains, fruits, vegetables, and complex carbohydrates
   d. none of the above; what a healthy diet is depends upon the individual child's nutritional needs

5. With respect to sleep, most children:
   a. get adequate sleep
   b. get less sleep than they need
   c. get more sleep than they need
   d. get less sleep than they need on weekdays, and adequate amounts on weekends

6. What are two benefits of recess-time play?
   _____
   _____

7. In general, boys spend _____ time playing sports than girls.

8. Which of the following is most likely to be overweight?
   a. a white girl
   b. an Asian boy
   c. a Hispanic boy
   d. a non-Hispanic black girl

9. Which of the following medical conditions has increased in middle childhood over the past few decades?
   a. asthma
   b. diabetes
   c. hypertension
   d. all of the above

10. What are two ways to explain the relationship between being poor and not having adequate health care?
    _____
    _____

11. What is the leading cause of death in school-age children?
    a. diabetes
    b. cancer
    c. accidents
    d. asthma

12. What are three variables that contribute to childhood depression?
    _____
    _____
    _____

Answers: 1–b; 2–Improvement in children's dental health is also attributed to use of adhesive sealants on the rough, chewing surfaces and better access to preventive dental care; 3–decreases; increases; 4–c; 5–b; 6–Benefits of recess-time play include growth in agility and social competence, better adjustment to school, and improved cognitive performance; 7–more; 8–d; 9–d; 10–Among the reasons for the disparity in health care access for children from lower socioeconomic groups are less knowledgable about good health habits, limited access to health insurance and health care, poor diet, not being able to afford participation in organized sports teams, and the use of clinics or emergency rooms rather than doctor's offices; 11–c; 12–Among the possible variables that put children at risk for depression are parental depression, anxiety, substance abuse or antisocial behavior, and genetic contributions.

What's to Come

©andresr/Getty Images

hat will my new teacher be like? Six-year-old Amira wonders as she walks up the steps to her school, shrugging her small shoulders into her new flowered backpack and pushing her short bob behind her ears. "Will the work be hard? Will the other kids like me? What games will we play at recess?" Amira stops at the front entrance, takes a deep breath, and steps inside. "I hope I like real school," she says softly.

Just like Amira, most children approach first grade with a mixture of eagerness and anxiety. The first day of regular school is a milestone—a sign of the developmental advances that make this new status possible. In this chapter we examine cognitive advances during the first 5 or 6 years of formal schooling, from about ages 6 to 11. Entry into Piaget's stage of concrete operations enables children to think logically and to make more mature moral judgments. As children improve in memory and problem solving, intelligence tests become more accurate in predicting school performance. The abilities to read and write open the door to a wider world. We discuss all these changes, and we look at controversies over IQ testing, bilingual education, homework, and mathematics instruction. Finally, we examine influences on school achievement and how schools try to meet special educational needs.

• • • •

Piagetian Approach: The Concrete Operational Child

At about age 7, according to Piaget, children enter the stage of concrete operations and begin to use mental operations to solve concrete (actual) problems. Children now can think logically because they can take multiple aspects of a situation into account. However, their thinking is still limited to real situations in the here and now.

Children in the stage of concrete operations can perform many tasks at a much higher level than they could in the preoperational stage (Table 12.1). They have a better understanding of spatial concepts, causality, categorization, inductive and deductive reasoning, conservation, and number. In the follow section, we address the cognitive advances typical of this age.

SPATIAL RELATIONSHIPS

Eight-year-old Ella stares intently at the map. "The star means we are here," she points, "so that must mean the store is there!" Ella turns to her mother with a smile and they both begin walking.

Ella is now in the stage of concrete operations. She is better able to understand spatial relationships. This allows her to interpret a map, find her way to and from school,

estimate the time to get from one place to another, and remember routes and landmarks. Children are more easily able to navigate a physical environment with which they have experience, and training can help improve spatial skills as well (Uttal et al., 2015).

CAUSE AND EFFECT

Another key development during middle childhood involves the ability to make judgments about cause and effect. These specific abilities improve as children age. For example, when 5- to 12-year-old children were asked to predict how balance scales worked, the older children gave more correct answers. In addition, earlier in middle childhood they understood that the number of objects on each side of a scale mattered, but it was not until later that they understood that the distance of objects from the center of a scale was also important (Amsel, Goodman, Savoie & Clark, 1996).

Additionally, as children learn more about the world, their growing knowledge about how things work begins to inform the quality of their reasoning. For example, in one study, children age 3 to 11 years were given information about oral health that was either consistent (e.g., going to the dentist is good for teeth) or inconsistent (e.g., drinking cola is good for teeth) with reality, and scenarios in which the outcome was either good or bad oral health. Children were then asked how the causal association provided in the scenarios might be tested. When the information was consistent with reality and had a good outcome, or the information was inconsistent with belief and had a bad outcome, children were more likely to use appropriate hypothesis testing (i.e., manipulate only one variable at a time). In other conditions, they used scientifically invalid procedures (e.g., changing all variables at a time) (Croker & Buchanan, 2011). Thus, the quality of their reasoning was better when they were able to use their understanding of the world to inform their thinking.

CATEGORIZATION

John sits at the table, working on his class project. He is making a timeline of his life. His mother has given him six photographs of himself from infancy to the current time, and John carefully lays them in order from earliest to latest.

Part of the reason John is now able to complete tasks such as this class project is because he is better able to categorize objects. This emerging skill involves a series of relatively sophisticated abilities. One such ability is **seriation**, arranging objects in a series according to one or more dimensions. Children become increasingly better at seriation for dimensions such as time (earliest to latest), length (shortest to longest), or color (lightest to darkest) (Piaget, 1952). Children's later mathematical achievement is dependent on early numeracy, including seriation (Aunio & Niemivirta, 2010), and difficulties in seriation predict later learning disabilities in mathematics (Desoete, 2015; Stock, Desoete & Roeyers, 2010).

seriation Ability to order items along a dimension.

TABLE 12.1 Advances in Selected Cognitive Abilities during Middle Childhood

Ability	Example
Spatial thinking	Danielle can use a map or model to help her search for a hidden object and can give someone else directions for finding the object. She can find her way to and from school, can estimate distances, and can judge how long it will take her to go from one place to another.
Cause and effect	Douglas knows which physical attributes of objects on a balance scale matter (i.e., number of objects matters but color does not). He does not yet know which spatial factors (e.g., position, placement of the objects) matter.
Categorization	Elena can sort objects into categories, such as shape, color, or both. She knows that a subclass (roses) has fewer members than the class of which it is a part (flowers).
Seriation and transitive inference	Catherine can arrange a group of sticks in order, from the shortest to the longest, and can insert an intermediate-size stick into the proper place. She knows that if one stick is longer than a second stick, and the second stick is longer than a third, then the first stick is longer than the third.
Inductive and deductive reasoning	Dominic can solve both inductive and deductive problems and knows that inductive conclusions (based on particular premises) are less certain than deductive ones (based on general premises).
Conservation	Felipe, at age 7, knows that if a clay ball is rolled into a sausage, it still contains the same amount of clay (conservation of substance). At age 9, he knows that the ball and the sausage weigh the same. Not until early adolescence will he understand that they displace the same amount of liquid if dropped in a glass of water.
Number and mathematics	Kevin can count in his head, can add by counting up from the smaller number, and can do simple story problems.

Class inclusion also becomes easier. **Class inclusion** is the ability to see the relationship between a whole and its parts, and to understand the categories within a whole. For example, Piaget (1964) showed preoperational children 10 flowers—seven roses and three carnations—and asked them whether there were more roses or more flowers. Children in the preoperational stage of development tended to say there were more roses because they were comparing the roses with the carnations rather than the whole bunch of flowers. Not until age 7 or 8, and sometimes not even then, do children consistently report that roses are a subclass of flowers and thus there cannot be more roses than flowers (Flavell, Miller & Miller, 2002). More recent research indicates that children actually do have the ability to understand the logic of class inclusion, but usually fail to inhibit the incorrect response in favor of the misleading perceptual comparison. As they get older, and more skilled at inhibitory control, their answers are more likely to be correct (Borst, Poirel, Pineau, Cassotti & Houde, 2013).

transitive inference Understanding the relationship between two objects by knowing the relationship of each to a third object.

class inclusion Understanding the relationship between a whole and its parts.

inductive reasoning Type of logical reasoning that moves from particular observations about members of a class to a general conclusion about that class.

deductive reasoning Type of logical reasoning that moves from a general premise about a class to a conclusion about a particular member or members of the class.

Another characteristic of this age is that of **transitive inferences** (if a < b and b < c, then a < c). For example, Mateo is shown three sticks: a short yellow stick, a medium-length green stick, and a long blue stick. He is shown that the yellow stick is shorter than the green stick, and is then shown that the green stick is shorter than the blue stick. However, he is not shown all three sticks in order of their length. If Mateo is able to understand transitive inferences, he should be able to quickly and easily infer that the yellow stick is shorter than the blue stick without physically comparing them (Piaget & Inhelder, 1967). While Piaget believed that children did not develop this ability until middle childhood, more recent research on visual preferences has shown that children as young as 15 months have some limited ability to reason in this fashion, at least for social stimuli (Gazes, Hampton & Lourenco, 2017; Mascaro & Csibra, 2014; Mou, Province & Luo, 2014).

INDUCTIVE AND DEDUCTIVE REASONING

According to Piaget, children in the stage of concrete operations use only **inductive reasoning**. Starting with observations about particular members of a class of people, animals, objects, or events, they are able to draw general conclusions about the class as a whole. "My dog barks. So does Terry's dog and Melissa's dog. So it looks as if all dogs bark."

During a visit to the zoo, Asher, who loves dinosaurs, asks his mom, "Is that rhinoceros a kind of dinosaur?" "No," his mother responds, "rhinoceroses have warm blood, and dinosaurs have cold blood." Later, in the reptile house, Asher's mother points out that snakes also have cold blood. "Oh," says Asher, "so they are dinosaurs too, right?" Asher has just engaged in deductive reasoning. **Deductive reasoning** starts with a general statement or premise about a class and applies it to particular members of the class. If the premise is true of the whole class and the reasoning is sound, then the conclusion must be true.

Piaget believed that children in the concrete operations stage of cognitive development used only inductive reasoning, and deductive reasoning did not develop until adolescence. However, research suggests Piaget underestimated the abilities of children. In one study, researchers gave reasoning problems to kindergarteners, second graders, fourth graders, and sixth graders. Because they did not want the children to use real-world knowledge, they used imaginary terms and words to create both inductive and deductive reasoning problems. For example, one of the inductive problems was "Tombor is a popgop. Tombor wears blue boots. Do all popgops wear blue boots?" The corresponding deductive reasoning problem was "All popgops wear blue boots. Tombor is a popgop. Does Tombor wear blue boots?" Contrary to Piagetian theory, second graders (but not kindergarteners) were able to answer both kinds of problems correctly (Pillow, 2002). Given age-appropriate testing methods, evidence of inductive and deductive reasoning is present considerably earlier than Piaget predicted. Moreover, children can be encouraged to reason at higher levels via training or intervention programs (Molnar, 2011; Barkl, Porter & Ginns, 2012).

CONSERVATION

In the preoperational stage of development, children are focused on appearances and have difficulty with abstract concepts. For example, Camilla, who is at the preoperational stage of development, is likely to think that if one of two identical clay balls is rolled into a long thin snake, it will now contain more clay because it is longer. She is deceived by appearances and thus fails this conservation task. However, Michael, who is in the stage of concrete operations, will say that the ball and the snake still contain the same amount of clay. What accounts for his ability to understand that the amount of clay remains unchanged regardless of the form it takes?

In solving various types of conservation problems, three primary achievements allow children at this stage

By age 6–7, most children can count on; for example, by starting with 4 blocks and then adding on to reach 5, 6 and finally 7 blocks.
©Marty Heitner/The Image Works

to do this. First, they understand the principle of *identity*. For instance, Michael understands that the clay is still the same clay even though it has a different shape because nothing was added or taken away from it. Second, they understand the principle of *reversibility*. Michael can picture what would happen if he went backward in time and rolled the snake back into a ball, thus the snake must still be the same amount of clay. Third, children at this stage can *decenter*. When Camilla looked at the snake, she focused only on its length, ignoring that it was thinner than the ball. She centered on one dimension (length) while excluding the other (thickness). Michael, however, is able to decenter and look at more than one aspect of the two objects at once. Thus, although the ball is shorter than the snake, it is also thicker.

Typically, children can solve problems involving conservation of substance, such as with the clay, by about age 7 or 8. However, in tasks involving conservation of weight—in which they are asked, for example, whether the ball and the snake weigh the same—children typically do not give correct answers until about age 9 or 10. In tasks involving conservation of volume—in which children must judge whether the snake and the ball displace an equal amount of liquid when placed in a glass of water—correct answers are rare before age 12. Piaget's term for this inconsistency in the development of different types of conservation is **horizontal décalage**. Piaget believed that children's thinking at this stage is so concrete, so closely tied to a particular situation, that they cannot readily transfer what they have learned about one type of conservation to another type, even though the underlying principles are the same.

> **horizontal décalage**
> Piaget's term for an inability to transfer learning about one type of conservation to other types, which causes a child to master different types of conservation tasks at different ages.

Did you know?

The existence of décalage is a major problem for the integrity of Piaget's theory. For example, if identity, reversibility, and decentration really underlie the ability to conserve, then shouldn't children be able to conserve in all areas (e.g., clay, weight, and volume) once they achieve those skills?

©AFP/Getty Images

NUMBER AND MATHEMATICS

By age 6 or 7, many children can count in their heads. They also learn to count on: To add 5 and 3, they start counting at 5 and then go on to 6, 7, and 8. It may take 2 or 3 more years for them to count down for subtraction, but by age 9 most children can count up and down. Children also become more adept at solving simple story problems, such as "Pedro went to the store with $5 and spent $2 on candy. How much did he have left?" When the original amount is unknown—"Pedro went to the store, spent $2 and had $3 left. How much did he start out with?"—the problem is harder because the operation needed to solve it (addition) is not as clearly indicated. Few children can solve this kind of problem before age 8 or 9 (Resnick, 1989).

Some intuitive understanding of fractions seems to exist by age 4 to 5, as children show when they deal a deck of cards or distribute portions of pizza or chips (Bialystock & Codd, 2000; Singer-Freeman & Goswami, 2001; McCrink, Bloom & Santos, 2010). However, children have more difficulty when dealing with numbers, which are more abstract. They tend not to think about the quantity a fraction represents; instead, they focus on the numerals that make it up. Thus they may say that ½ plus ⅓ equals ⅖. It is also difficult for children to grasp that ½ is bigger than ¼—that the smaller fraction (¼) has the larger denominator (Geary, 2006; Sophian & Wood, 1997).

The ability to estimate progresses with age. When asked to place 24 numbers along a line from 0 to 100, kindergartners exaggerate the distances between low numbers and minimize the distances between high numbers. Most second graders produce number lines that are more evenly spaced (Siegler & Booth, 2004). Second, fourth, and sixth graders show a similar progression in producing number lines from 0 to 1,000 (Siegler & Opfer, 2003), most likely reflecting the experience older children gain in dealing with larger numbers (Berteletti, Lucangeli, Piazza, Dehaene & Zorzi, 2010). In support of this, children who play board games that include linear sequences show an advantage in their number line estimation, number estimation and counting-on skills (Whyte & Bull, 2008; Laski & Siegler, 2014). In addition to improving in *number line estimation* with age, school-age children also improve in *computational estimation*, such as estimating the sum in an addition problem; *numerosity estimation*, such as estimating the number of candies in a jar; and *measurement estimation*, such as estimating the length of a line (Booth & Siegler, 2006).

Learning about math does not only happen within the context of school. Research with minimally schooled people in developing countries suggests that the ability to use mathematics can develop through concrete experience in a cultural context (Guberman, 1999; Resnick, 1989). For example, in a study of Brazilian street vendors ages 9 to 15, a researcher said, "I'll take two coconuts." Each coconut cost 40 cruzeiros; she paid with a 500-cruzeiros bill and asked, "What do I get back?" The child counted up from 80: "Eighty, 90, 100. . ." and gave the customer 420 cruzeiros. However, when this same child was given a similar problem in the classroom ("What is 500 minus 80?"), he arrived at the wrong answer by incorrectly using a series of steps learned in school (Carraher, Schliemann & Carraher, 1988). This finding suggests that there are different routes for cultural learning. In cultural contexts in which schooling is not as important or is not as easily available, children do not generally use abstract counting strategies. In these situations, children may develop mathematical abilities in their everyday lives that are not captured by their performance in academic settings, but that are nonetheless complex and arrive at the correct answers (Guberman, 2004; Taylor, 2009; Guberman, 1999).

INFLUENCES OF NEUROLOGICAL, DEVELOPMENT, CULTURE AND SCHOOLING

Piaget maintained that the shift from the rigid, illogical thinking of younger children to the flexible, logical thinking of older children depends on both neurological development and experience. Interestingly, Piaget's careful observations regarding the developing abilities of children have been bolstered by research in brain imaging. This research shows that the ability to pass conservation tasks is related to the development of frontal brain areas believed to be involved in executive functioning, inhibitory control, and attentional shifting (Bolton & Hattie, 2017; Houde et al., 2011). For example, changes in the ability to conserve numbers have been related to the involvement of a parieto-frontal network (Houde et al., 2011), perhaps as a result of an increasing ability to inhibit incorrect assumptions about the pairing of length and quantity (Poirel et al., 2012).

Other data also suggest neurological change is associated with the attainment of cognitive skills. Children who had achieved conservation of volume had different brain wave patterns from those who had not yet achieved it, suggesting that they may have been using different brain regions for the task (Stauder, Molenaar & Van der Molen, 1993). In another study, the time needed to categorize plants and animals decreased with age, and the brain wave data suggested this was due to a progressive decrease in the number of neurons needed to make the assessment (Batty & Taylor, 2002).

But neurological change is not the only influence. While Piaget believed his theories described universal aspects of child development, it may be that some abilities depend in part on familiarity. Children can think more logically about things they know something about. Thus understanding may stem from culturally defined experiences. Children are more likely to learn about skills that are valued and required in their culture. For example, West African children, who produce, store, and exchange food in markets, attain proficiency at conservation of liquid tasks at an earlier age than Inuit children, who traditionally lived a hunter-gatherer lifestyle (Dasen, 1984). Similarly, experiences in school may affect the pace of cognitive development. When 10,000 British 11- and 12-year-olds were tested on conservation of volume and weight, their performance was 2 to 3 years behind that of their counterparts 30 years earlier, presumably because teachers were focusing on the three Rs rather than hands-on experience with the way materials behaved (Shayer, Ginsburg & Coe, 2007).

Information-Processing Approach: Attention, Memory, and Planning

As children move through the school years, they make steady progress in their abilities to regulate and sustain attention, process and retain information, and plan and monitor their own behavior. All of these interrelated developments are central to executive function, the conscious control of thoughts, emotions, and actions to accomplish goals or solve problems. School-age children also understand more about how memory works, and this knowledge enables them to plan and use strategies, or deliberate techniques, to help them remember.

INFLUENCES ON THE DEVELOPMENT OF EXECUTIVE FUNCTION

The gradual development of **executive function** from infancy through adolescence is the result of developmental changes in brain structure. The prefrontal cortex, the region that enables planning, judgment, and decision making, shows significant development during this period (Lamm, Zelazo & Lewis, 2006; Figure 12.1). As unneeded synapses are pruned away and pathways become myelinated, processing speed—usually measured by reaction time—improves dramatically (Camarata & Woodcock, 2006). Faster, more efficient processing increases the amount of information children can keep in working memory (McAuley & White, 2011). As children develop the ability to mentally juggle more concepts at the same time, they are also able to develop more complex thinking and goal-directed planning (Luna et al., 2004).

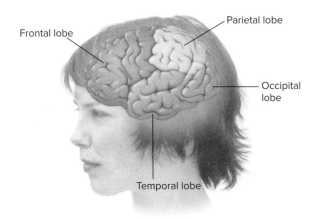

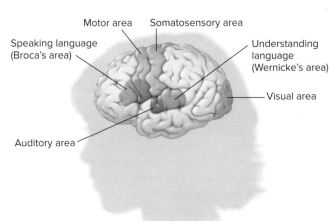

FIGURE 12.1 Major Structures of the Brain
Primary divisions of the brain and major motor, sensory, and associated cortices.

Another aspect of executive function involves the development of self-regulatory capacity, including the ability to regulate attention, inhibit responses and monitor errors. Advances in these areas, as well as in working memory, occur in concert with increases in activity of frontoparietal and frontostraital circuits (Hughes, 2011; Tau & Peterson, 2010).

In addition to the physical development of the brain, environmental influences also matter. Given the slow rate of development of the frontal cortex, environmental influences exert a relatively large effect. For example, parenting quality and family environment—including such factors as cognitive stimulation, parental scaffolding, maternal sensitivity, and attachment—have been found to predict later executive control (Bernier, Carlson & Whipple, 2010; Bernier, Carlson, Deschenes & Matte-Gagne, 2012; Hammond, Muller, Carpendale, Bibok & Liebermann-Finestone, 2012). Moreover, just as high-quality family environments can promote the development of executive functioning, less ideal circumstances can undermine its development. For example, children from disorganized and chaotic families tend to show less advanced executive functioning abilities (Hughes & Ensor, 2009). Environmental circumstances may interact with individual characteristics as well. In one series of studies, poverty did not impact the executive functioning abilities of children who were low in temperamental reactivity, but negatively affected temperamentally reactive children (Raver, Blair & Willoughby, 2013).

> **executive function** Conscious control of thoughts, emotions, and actions to accomplish goals or solve problems.

Children, particularly those with poor executive control, benefit from training. A wide variety of techniques have been successfully used, including computerized training, physical activity such as martial arts or yoga, and mindfulness (meditation) training (Diamond & Lee, 2011). School impacts this developing ability as well. In a 3-year longitudinal study, the responsibility for planning children's informal activities gradually shifted between second and fourth grades from parent to child, and this change was reflected in children's improved ability to plan classroom work (Gauvain & Perez, 2005).

SELECTIVE ATTENTION

School-age children can concentrate longer than younger children and can focus on the information they need and want while screening out irrelevant information (Harnishfeger & Pope, 1996). For example, in school, it may be necessary for a child to focus on a teacher's less-than-exciting lesson while simultaneously ignoring the antics of the class clown. This growth in selective attention—the ability to deliberately direct one's attention and shut out distractions—may hinge on the executive skill of inhibitory control, the voluntary suppression of unwanted responses (Luna et al., 2004).

The increasing capacity for selective attention is believed to be due to neurological maturation and is one of the reasons memory improves during middle childhood (Sanders, Stevens, Coch & Neville, 2006). Older children make fewer mistakes in recall than younger children because they are better able to expect and predict what might be important to remember, to then select and attend to the appropriate stimulus when presented with it, and, when asked, to recall the relevant information from memory while ignoring irrelevant information (Gazzaley & Nobre, 2012).

WORKING MEMORY

Working memory involves the short-term storage of information that is being actively processed, like a mental workspace. For example, if you are asked to compute what 42×60 is, you would use your working memory to solve the answer.

The efficiency of working memory increases greatly in middle childhood, laying the foundation for a wide range of cognitive skills. For example, between the ages of 6 and 10 there are improvements in processing speed (how quickly information is processed) and storage capacity (how many things can be simultaneously held in working memory) (Bayliss, Jarrold, Baddeley, Gunn & Leigh, 2005).

metamemory Understanding of processes of memory.

mnemonic device Strategy to aid memory.

Because working memory is necessary for storing information while other material is being mentally manipulated, the capacity of a child's working memory can directly affect academic success (Alloway & Alloway, 2010). For example, children with low working memory struggle with structured learning activities, especially when there are lengthy instructions (Gathercole & Alloway, 2008). Individual differences in working memory capacity are also linked to a child's ability to acquire knowledge and new skills (Alloway, 2006).

Research has indicated that as many as 10 percent of school-age children suffer from poor working memory (Alloway, Gathercole, Kirkwood & Elliot, 2009). However, working memory is not a fixed entity. Training programs can improve working memory capacity, and indeed training programs have been shown to be associated with changes in brain activity in frontal and parietal cortex, basal ganglia,

and dopamine receptor density (Klingberg, 2010). This is especially true for visuospatial working memory, such as that needed to play concentration games in which pairs of cards must be matched. Thus far, such training effects tend to be absent or short-lived or do not transfer to areas other than the specific form of working memory addressed (Melby-Lervag & Hulme, 2013; Rapport, Orban, Kofler & Friedman, 2013). However, more research is needed in this area, and there are suggestions that the adoption of tools that assess working memory in the classroom could still influence achievement for these children.

METAMEMORY

Between ages 5 and 7, the brain's frontal lobes undergo significant development and reorganization. These changes may make possible improved **metamemory** (Chua, Schacter, Rand-Giovanetti & Sperling, 2006). Metamemory can be described as the knowledge of and reflection about memory processes.

From kindergarten through the elementary school years, children advance steadily in understanding memory (Schneider, 2008). Kindergartners and first graders know that people remember better if they study longer, that people forget things with time, and that relearning something is easier than learning it for the first time (Flavell et al., 2002). However, younger children tend not to use organizational memory strategies such as grouping things by categories to make them easier to remember, and they tend to overestimate their memory capacity (Karably & Zabrucky, 2017). By third grade, children know that some people remember better than others and that some things are easier to remember than others (Flavell et al., 2002), and they become more proficient in their use of memory strategies (Karably & Zabrucky, 2017).

MNEMONICS

Were you ever taught the saying "please excuse my dear Aunt Sally" as a technique to help you remember the order of operations in solving an equation? This is an example of a **mnemonic device**, a strategy to aid memory. The most common mnemonic device among both children and adults is use of *external memory aids*. Other common mnemonic devices are *rehearsal, organization*, and *elaboration*.

Writing down a telephone number, making a list, setting a timer, and putting a library book by the front door are examples of external memory aids: prompts by something outside the person. Saying a telephone number over and over after looking it up, so as not to forget it before dialing, is a form of rehearsal, or conscious repetition. Organization is mentally placing information into categories (such as animals, furniture, vehicles, and clothing) to make it easier to recall. In elaboration, children associate items with something else, such as an imagined scene or story. To remember to buy lemons, ketchup, and napkins, for example, a child might visualize a ketchup bottle balanced on a lemon, with a pile of napkins handy to wipe up any spills.

Did you know?

The reason preoperational children do poorly on Piagetian tasks can be related to their information-processing skills. For example, perhaps these children fail the conservation task because their poor working memory leads them to forget that two differently shaped pieces of clay were originally the same size.

©McGraw-Hill Education/Janette Beckman

There are developmental changes in children's ability to use these memory strategies. For example, when young children are taught to use a memory strategy, they tend to use it only in the particular context in which they were taught. Older children, however, are more likely to apply it to other situations (Flavell et al., 2002). This process occurs for spontaneous learning as well. As children grow older, they develop better strategies, use them more effectively (Bjorklund, 1997; Karably & Zabrucky, 2017), and are better at assessing if they are reaching their memory goals (Schneider, 2008). Older children also often use more than one strategy for a task and choose different kinds of strategies for different problems (Bjorklund, Miller, Coyle & Slawinski, 1997).

Many children say words out loud when they are trying to remember them, and this simple rehearsal strategy does appear to help them remember material more effectively (Icht & Mama, 2015). However, they do not often spontaneously use other mnemonic aids. Although it is difficult to teach young children to use mnemonic strategies, teaching older children about them if they are developmentally ready to learn such skills can result in memory gains. For example, memory can be improved by discussing and modeling the use of different mnemonic strategies and drawing attention to their relative effectiveness. This technique works best if it is integrated into the curricula rather than being taught separately (Schneider, 2008). In one instance, first- and second-grade teachers in a study were asked to use memory relevant language within the context of a science lesson. For example, they might ask the children in their classrooms, "All of these modes of transportation have wheels. What is another vehicle you have seen around town that has wheels?" Later, when the performance of the children in these groups was compared with the performance of children in groups where memory prompts were not used, those children exposed to memory relevant language showed greater strategic knowledge and sophisticated strategy use (Grammer, Coffman & Ornstein, 2013).

Psychometric Approach: Assessment of Intelligence

The colloquial phrase "I know it when I see it" can describe a large variety of somewhat subjective concepts, but it is particularly apt in describing intelligence. Most of us feel we intuitively know what intelligence is, but, as psychologists have found, the process of objectively defining what it is proves to be a challenge. In the following section, we discuss how intelligence has been measured, its relationship to IQ, and whether or not intelligence should be viewed more broadly. Last, we focus on some of the important influences on intelligence.

MEASURING INTELLIGENCE

While there are a variety of ways to assess intelligence, the most widely used individual test is the **Wechsler Intelligence Scale for Children (WISC-III)**. This test for ages 6 through 16

measures verbal and performance abilities; it yields separate scores for each as well as a total score. The separate subtest scores pinpoint a child's strengths and help diagnose specific problems. For example, if a child does well on verbal tests, such as general information and basic arithmetic operations, but poorly on performance tests, such as doing a puzzle or drawing the missing part of a picture, the child may be slow in perceptual or motor development. A child who does well on performance tests but poorly on verbal tests may have a language problem. A popular group test, the **Otis-Lennon School Ability Test (OLSAT8)**, has levels for kindergarten through 12th grade. Children are asked to classify items, show an understanding of verbal and numerical concepts, display general information, and follow directions. Separate scores for verbal comprehension, verbal reasoning, pictorial reasoning, figural reasoning, and quantitative reasoning can identify specific strengths and weaknesses (Otis, 1993).

Some other diagnostic and predictive tools are based on neurological research and information-processing theory. The second edition of the **Kaufman Assessment Battery for Children (K-ABC-II)** (Kaufman & Kaufman, 1983; 2003), an individual test for ages 3 to 18, is designed to evaluate cognitive abilities in children with diverse needs (such as autism, hearing impairments, and language disorders) and from varying cultural and linguistic backgrounds.

Dynamic tests based on Vygotsky's theories emphasize potential rather than present achievement. The focus in these tests is the child's zone of proximal development (ZPD): the difference between the items a child can answer alone and the items the child can answer with help. Thus, dynamic tests contain items up to 2 years above a child's current level of competence. Examiners help the child when necessary by asking leading questions, giving examples or demonstrations, and offering feedback; thus the test itself is a learning situation (Resing, 2013). By pointing to what a child is ready to learn, dynamic testing may give teachers more useful information than does a psychometric test.

THE IQ CONTROVERSY

The use of psychometric intelligence tests such as the Wechsler is controversial. On the positive side, because IQ tests have been standardized and widely used, there is extensive information about their norms, validity, and reliability. Scores on IQ tests can be used as predictors. For example, IQ tests taken during middle childhood are fairly good predictors of school achievement, and IQ at age 11 has even been found to predict length of life, functional independence late in life, and the presence or absence of dementia

Wechsler Intelligence Scale for Children (WISC-III) Individual intelligence test for schoolchildren that yields verbal and performance scores as well as a combined score.

Otis-Lennon School Ability Test (OLSAT8) Group intelligence test for kindergarten through 12th grade.

Kaufman Assessment Battery for Children (K-ABC-II) Nontraditional individual intelligence test designed to provide fair assessments of minority children and children with disabilities.

dynamic tests Tests based on Vygotsky's theory that emphasize potential rather than past learning.

theory of multiple intelligences Gardner's theory that there are eight distinct forms of intelligence.

componential element Sternberg's term for the analytic aspect of intelligence.

(Starr, Deary, Lemmon, & Whalley, 2000; Whalley & Deary, 2001).

On the other hand, critics claim that the tests underestimate the intelligence of children who are in ill health or who do not perform well on tests (Sternberg, 2004). Because the tests are timed, they equate intelligence with speed and penalize a child who works slowly and deliberately. Their appropriateness for diagnosing learning disabilities also has been questioned (Benson, 2003). Moreover, such variables as working memory (Alloway & Alloway, 2010) and self-control (Duckworth, Quinn & Tsukayama, 2012) have also been found to be important in predicting academic achievement.

A more fundamental criticism is that IQ tests do not directly measure native ability; instead, they measure what children already know. Further, the tests are validated against measures of achievement, such as school performance, affected by such factors as schooling and culture. There is also controversy over whether intelligence is a single, general ability or whether there are types of intelligence not captured by IQ tests. For these and other reasons, strong disagreement exists over how accurately these tests assess children's intelligence.

IS THERE MORE THAN ONE INTELLIGENCE?

Another serious criticism of IQ tests is that they focus almost entirely on abilities used in school. They do not cover other important aspects of intelligent behavior, such as common sense, social skills, creative insight, and self-knowledge. Yet these abilities, in which some children with modest academic skills excel, may become equally or more important in later life and may even be considered separate forms of intelligence. Two chief advocates of this position are Howard Gardner and Robert Sternberg.

Gardner's Theory of Multiple Intelligences

Is a child who is good at analyzing paragraphs and making analogies more intelligent than one who can play a challenging violin solo or organize a closet or pitch a curve ball at the right time? The answer is no, according to Gardner's (1993) **theory of multiple intelligences**.

Gardner identified independent types of intelligence. According to Gardner, conventional intelligence tests tap only three "intelligences": verbal-linguistic, logic-mathematical, and, to some extent, visual-spatial. The other five, which are not reflected in IQ scores, are musical, body-kinesthetic, interpersonal, intrapersonal, and naturalistic. In addition, while its inclusion has elicited some criticism, Gardner later proposed a ninth intelligence—that of existential intelligence, akin to spiritual or religious intelligence (Gardner, 1999).

Gardner argued that high intelligence in one area does not necessarily accompany high intelligence in any of the others. A person may be extremely gifted in art (a spatial ability), precision of movement (bodily-kinesthetic), social relations (interpersonal), or self-understanding (intrapersonal), but not have a traditionally high IQ. Thus an athlete, an artist, and a musician could be equally intelligent, each in a different area.

Gardner (1995) assessed each intelligence directly by observing its products—how well a child can tell a story, remember a melody, or get around in a strange area—and not with typical standardized tests. The type of intelligence being assessed would determine the type of test required.

Critics of Gardner argue that his multiple intelligences are actually more accurately labeled as talents or abilities and assert that intelligence is more closely associated with skills that lead to academic achievement. They further question his criteria for defining separate intelligences that largely overlap, such as mathematical and spatial intelligence (Willingham, 2004).

Sternberg's Triarchic Theory of Intelligence

Sternberg's (1985, 2004) triarchic theory of intelligence identifies three elements, or aspects, of intelligence: componential, experiential, and contextual (Figure 12.2).

- The **componential element** is the analytic aspect of intelligence; it encompasses information-processing skills. It tells people how to solve problems, how to monitor solutions, and how to evaluate the results. Conventional IQ tests commonly test this aspect of intelligence.

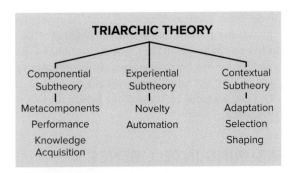

FIGURE 12.2 Sternberg's Triarchic Theory

Sternberg argued that to truly assess intelligence, componential, experiential, and contextual elements all needed to be considered.

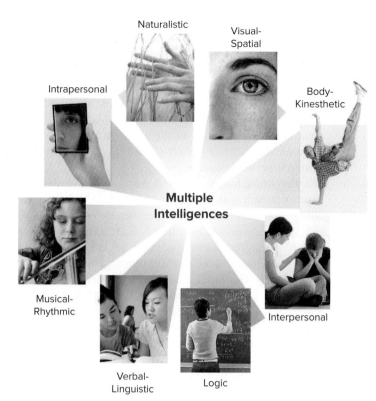

Naturalistic

Visual-Spatial

Intrapersonal

Body-Kinesthetic

Multiple Intelligences

Musical-Rhythmic

Interpersonal

Verbal-Linguistic

Logic

Gardner's Theory of Multiple Intelligences

©Laurence Mouton/Getty Images; ©Barbara Penoyar/Getty Images; ©Mark Andersen/Getty Images; ©Thinkstock/Getty Images; ©Fuse/Getty Images; ©Corbis; ©Mel Curtis/Getty Images; ©Halfdark/Getty Images

- The **experiential element** is insightful or creative; it determines how people approach novel or familiar tasks. It allows people to compare new information with what they already know and to come up with new ways of putting facts together—in other words, to think originally. A creative-verbal test might ask children to solve deductive reasoning problems that start with factually false premises (such as, "Money falls off trees").

- The **contextual element** is practical; it determines how people deal with their environment. It is the ability to size up a situation and decide what to do: adapt to it, change it, or get out of it. A test of practical-quantitative intelligence might be to solve an everyday math problem about buying tickets to a ball game or following a recipe for making cookies.

According to Sternberg, everyone has these three abilities to a greater or lesser extent. The **Sternberg Triarchic Abilities Test** (STAT) (Sternberg, 1993) seeks to measure each of the three aspects of intelligence through multiple-choice and essay questions. Because the ways in which we process information should be applicable across all domains of intelligence, *verbal*, *quantitative*, and *figural* (or spatial) processes are assessed within each domain. For example, an item to test practical quantitative intelligence might be to solve an everyday math problem having to do with buying tickets to a ball game. A creative verbal item might ask children to solve deductive reasoning problems that start with factually false premises (such

as, "Money falls off trees"). An analytical figural item might ask children to identify the missing piece of a figure. Validation studies have found positive correlations between the STAT and several other tests of critical thinking, creativity, and practical problem solving. Additionally, total STAT scores predict academic achievement (Sternberg, Castejon, Prieto, Hautamaki & Grigorenko, 2001; Ekinci, 2014).

Sternberg argued that conventional IQ tests, by focusing only on the componential element and ignoring experiential and contextual elements, have less utility predicting outcomes in the real world. In the real world, book knowledge may not always be helpful. For example, children in many cultures have to learn practical skills, known as *tacit knowledge*, in order to succeed. In studies in Usenge, Kenya, and among Yup'ik children in southwestern Alaska, children's tacit knowledge of medicinal herbs, hunting, fishing, and preserving plants showed no correlation with conventional measures of intelligence but were necessary for survival (Grigorenko et al., 2004; Sternberg, 2004).

INFLUENCES ON INTELLIGENCE

Both heredity and environment influence intelligence. Keeping in mind the controversy over whether IQ tests actually measure intelligence and whether intelligence is one or many things, let's look more closely at these influences.

Genes and Brain Development

Intelligence is highly heritable, and one mechanism of genetic action may be via brain development and structure. Brain imaging research shows a moderate correlation between brain size or amount of gray matter and general intelligence (Rushton & Ankney, 2009), especially for reasoning, problem-solving abilities, and nonverbal performance measures (Gray & Thompson, 2004; Lange, Froimowitz, Bigler, Lainhart & Brain Development Cooperative Group, 2010). One study found that the amount of gray matter in the frontal cortex is largely inherited, varies widely among individuals, and is linked with differences in IQ (Thompson et al., 2001). Moreover, connectivity between frontal and parietal brain regions, especially in girls, has also been associated with nonverbal intelligence (Langeslag et al., 2013).

The developmental changes found in cortical thickness are also strongly influenced by genes (Fjell et al., 2015). Some research has found that in children of average IQ, the prefrontal cortex peaks in thickness by age 8, and then gradually thins as unneeded connections are pruned. In the most intelligent 7-year-olds, however, the cortex does not peak in thickness until age 11 or 12 (Shaw et al., 2006). More recent research has found that intelligence is highest in those children whose cortex thins most quickly

experiential element Sternberg's term for the insightful aspect of intelligence.

contextual element Sternberg's term for the practical aspect of intelligence.

Research suggests that Will Smith and Jada Pinkett-Smith's children will score similarly on intelligence tests to their parents.

©Kathy Hutchins/Shutterstock

(Schnack et al., 2014). While the details remain unclear, it does appear that the *pattern* of development is as important as the *amount* of gray matter. Moreover, while IQ is generally a stable trait, there are sometimes fluctuations. Research has shown that children and adolescents who show declines in IQ over time also show reductions in cortical thickness, suggesting a neural substrate for their declines in intellectual performance (Burgaleta, Johnson, Waber, Colom & Karama, 2014).

Although reasoning, problem solving, and executive function are linked to the prefrontal cortex, other brain regions under strong genetic influence also contribute to intelligent behavior. So does the speed and reliability of transmission of messages in the brain. Environmental factors, such as the family, schooling, and culture, play a strong role early in life, but heritability of intelligence (an estimate of the degree to which individual differences in intelligence are genetically caused) dramatically increases with age as children select or create environments that fit their genetic tendencies (Haworth et al., 2010).

Influences of Race/Ethnicity on IQ

Average test scores vary among racial/ethnic groups. Historically, black children scored about 15 points lower than white children and showed a comparable lag on school achievement tests (Neisser et al., 1996). However, these gaps have narrowed by as much as 4 to 7 points in recent years (Dickens & Flynn, 2006). Average IQ scores of Hispanic American children fall between those of black and white children (Ang, Rodgers & Wangstrom, 2010). Projections for both African Americans and Hispanics are that the IQ gaps will fall even further in the coming decades (Rindermann & Pichelmann, 2015).

What accounts for racial/ethnic differences in IQ? Some researchers have argued for a substantial genetic factor (Herrnstein & Murray, 1994; Jensen, 1969; Rushton & Jensen, 2005). Although there is strong evidence of a genetic influence on *individual* differences in intelligence, there is no

direct evidence that IQ differences among ethnic, cultural, or racial *groups* are hereditary (Gray & Thompson, 2004; Neisser et al., 1996; Sternberg et al., 2005). Instead, many studies attribute ethnic differences in IQ to inequalities in environment (Nisbett, 2005; Nisbett et al., 2012)—in income, nutrition, living conditions, health, parenting practices, early child care, intellectual stimulation, schooling, culture, or other circumstances such as the effects of oppression and discrimination that can affect self-esteem, motivation, and academic performance.

The strength of genetic and environmental influences appears to vary with socioeconomic status (Nisbett et al., 2012). For example, one longitudinal study of over 300 twin pairs showed that children from affluent families showed stronger genetic influences on intelligence than those from poorer families (Turkheimer, Haley, Waldron, D'Onofrio & Gottesman, 2003). In another longitudinal study of 8,716 British twin pairs, researchers found that the genetic influences on intelligence were high but relatively similar for twins of low and high SES. However, a different story emerged for environmental influences. Nonshared environmental experiences—those events and influences experienced differently by each twin—had a greater impact on IQ for children of lower SES (Hanscombe et al., 2012). Results such as these have policy implications, as they suggest that the environment may matter more for children of lower SES.

What about Asian Americans, whose scholastic achievements consistently top those of other ethnic groups? Asian American children's strong scholastic achievement seems to be best explained by their culture's emphasis on obedience and respect for elders, the importance Asian American parents place on education as a route to upward mobility, and the devotion of Asian American students to homework and study (Nisbett et al., 2012).

Influence of Schooling on IQ

Schooling seems to increase tested intelligence (Adey, Csapo, Demetriou, Hautamaki & Shayer, 2007). IQ scores drop during summer vacation and rise again during the academic year (Ceci & Williams, 1997; Huttenlocher, Levine & Vevea, 1998). Additionally, scores attained on various educational assessment tests—which test knowledge, like math and science, unlikely to be learned outside of an educational environment—are strongly correlated with IQ, and this relationship exists in all countries for which data are available (Lynn & Meisenberg, 2010).

However, the cognitive gains associated with schooling do not appear to be general in nature, and instead consist of direct gains in specific cognitive skills that are then tapped by IQ tests (Ritchie, Bates & Deary, 2015). Not surprisingly, the type of schooling also matters. Children who are enrolled in schools with an academic focus tend to show greater gains in intellectual performance than children in schools with a vocational focus (Becker, Ludtke, Trautwein, Koller & Baumert, 2012).

©Digital Vision/Getty Images

Perspectives on Diversity

CULTURE AND IQ

Some critics of IQ tests attribute ethnic differences in IQ to cultural bias: a tendency to include questions that use vocabulary or tasks more familiar to some cultural groups than others (Sternberg, 1985, 1987). These critics argue that intelligence tests are built around the dominant thinking style and language of white people of European ancestry, putting minority children at a disadvantage (Matsumoto & Juang, 2008). Thus, test developers have tried to design **culture-free tests**—tests with no culture-linked content—by posing tasks that do not require language, such as tracing mazes, putting the right shapes in the right holes, and completing pictures; nevertheless, they have been unable to eliminate all cultural influences.

Robert Sternberg (2004) maintains that intelligence and culture are inextricably linked. Behavior seen as intelligent in one culture may be viewed as foolish in another. For example, when given a sorting task, North Americans would be likely to place a robin under the category of birds, whereas the Kpelle people in North Africa would consider it more intelligent to place the robin in the functional category of flying things (Cole, 1998). Thus a test of intelligence developed in one culture may not be equally valid in another. Furthermore, the schooling offered in a culture may prepare a child to do well in certain tasks and not in others, and the competencies taught and tested in school are not necessarily the same as the practical skills needed to succeed in everyday life (Sternberg, 2004, 2005).

Sternberg (2004) defines successful intelligence as the skills and knowledge needed for success within a particular social and cultural context. The mental processes that underlie intelligence may be the same across cultures, says Sternberg, but their products may be different—and so should the means of assessing performance. Sternberg proposes **culture-relevant tests** that take into account the adaptive tasks that confront children in particular cultures.

Language and Literacy

Language abilities continue to grow during middle childhood. School-age children become better at understanding and interpreting oral and written communication and making themselves understood. These tasks are challenging for children who are not native-language speakers. Areas of particular importance during this age stage are vocabulary, grammar, syntax, pragmatics, and literacy.

VOCABULARY, GRAMMAR, AND SYNTAX

As vocabulary grows during the school years, children use increasingly precise verbs. They learn that a word like *run* can have more than one meaning and can tell from the context which meaning is intended. Similes and metaphors become increasingly common (Owens, 1996). Although grammar is quite complex by age 6, children during the early school years rarely use the passive voice ("The sidewalk is being shoveled"). Older children use more subordinate clauses ("The boy who delivers the newspapers rang the doorbell"). Still, some constructions, such as clauses beginning with *however*

and *although*, do not become common until early adolescence (Owens, 1996). Children's understanding of the rules of syntax (how words are organized into phrases and sentences) becomes more sophisticated with age (C. S. Chomsky, 1969). Sentence structure continues to become more elaborate.

PRAGMATICS

The major area of linguistic growth during the school years is in **pragmatics**: the social context of language. For example, there is a pragmatic difference between a child asking, "Can I have the last cookie?" and "You don't want that last cookie do you?" Pragmatics has to do with the speaker's and listener's characteristics, the context of the utterance, the speaker's inferred intent, and the understanding of the "rules" that govern conversation.

Good conversationalists probe by asking questions before introducing a topic with which the other person may not be familiar. They quickly recognize a breakdown in

> **culture-free test** An intelligence test that, if it were possible to design, would have no culturally linked content.
>
> **culture-relevant test** An intelligence test that takes into account the adaptive tasks children face in their culture.
>
> **pragmatics** Practical knowledge needed to use language for communicative purposes.

communication and do something to repair it. There are wide individual differences in such skills; some 7-year-olds are better conversationalists than some adults (Anderson, Clark & Mullin, 1994). There are also gender differences; boys tend to use more controlling statements and utter more negative interactions, while girls phrase their remarks in a more tentative, conciliatory manner (Leman, Ahmed & Ozarow, 2005).

SECOND LANGUAGE LEARNING

In 2013, 22 percent of U.S. children ages 5 to 17 spoke a language other than English at home. The primary language most of these children spoke was Spanish, and 5 percent had difficulty speaking English (Federal Interagency Forum on Child and Family Statistics, 2015). About 9.4 percent of the public school population are defined as **English-language learners** (ELLs) (NCES, 2017).

Some schools use an **English-immersion approach** (sometimes called ESL, or English as a second language), in which language-minority children are immersed in English from the beginning, in special classes. Other schools have adopted programs of **bilingual education**, in which children are taught in two languages, first learning in their native language and then switching to regular classes in English when they become more proficient. These programs can encourage children to become *bilingual* (fluent in two languages) and to feel pride in their cultural identity.

Advocates of early English immersion claim that the sooner children are exposed to English and the more time they spend speaking it, the better they learn it. Proponents of bilingual programs claim that children progress faster academically in their native language and later make a smoother transition to all-English classrooms (Padilla et al., 1991).

Statistical analyses of multiple studies conclude that children in bilingual programs typically outperform those in all-English programs on tests of English proficiency (Crawford, 2007; Krashen & McField, 2005).

Another, less common approach is **two-way (dual-language) learning**, in which English-speaking and foreign-speaking children learn together in their own and each other's languages. By valuing both languages equally, it reinforces self-esteem and improves school performance. However, less than 2 percent of English-language learners nationwide are enrolled in two-way programs (Crawford, 2007).

LITERACY

Literacy—the ability to read and write—is vital to success in the modern world. Moreover, literacy allows children access to the ideas and imagination of people in faraway lands and long-ago times. Once children can translate the marks on a page into patterns of sound and meaning, they can develop increasingly sophisticated strategies to understand what they read. They also learn they can use written words to express ideas, thoughts, and feelings.

Reading and Writing

Think of what must happen in order for a child to learn to read. First, a child must remember the distinctive features of letters—for example, a "c" consists of a curved half-circle and an "o" is a closed circle. Then a child must be able to recognize the different phonemes by breaking down words into their constituent parts. For example, a child must be able to understand that the word *dog* is composed of three different sounds, the "d," the "o," and the "g." Finally, the child must be able to match the visual features of letters and the phonemes and remember which ones go together. This process is known as **decoding**.

Because of the difficulties involved in learning how to read, educators have developed a variety of ways to instruct children. In the traditional approach, called the **phonetic (code-emphasis) approach**, the child sounds out the word, translating it from print to speech before retrieving it from long-term memory. To do this, the child must master the phonetic code that matches the printed alphabet to spoken sounds (as described above). Instruction generally involves rigorous, teacher-directed tasks focused on memorizing sound-letter correspondences.

The **whole-language approach** emphasizes visual retrieval and the use of contextual cues. This approach is based on the belief that children can learn to read and write naturally, much as they learn to understand and use speech. By using **visually based retrieval**, the child simply looks at the word and without analyzing the constituent pieces, pulls it out of memory. Whole-language proponents assert that children learn to read with better comprehension and more enjoyment if they experience written language

Learning to read requires the application of multiple skills. Research supports carefully designed and scaffolded use of e-books for literacy development, especially for children at risk for learning disabilities.
©McGraw-Hill Education

from the outset as a way to gain information and express ideas and feelings, not as a system of isolated sounds and syllables to be learned by memorization and drill. Whole-language programs tend to feature real literature and open-ended, student-initiated activities.

Despite the popularity of the whole-language approach, research has found little support for its claims. Although humans have brains wired for spoken language, there is no theoretical reason to assume that written language, a relatively new invention in human history, has similar evolutionary roots and thus should be learned as naturally as spoken language. A long line of research supports the view that phonemic awareness and early phonetics training are keys to reading proficiency for most children (Jeynes & Littell, 2000; National Reading Panel, 2000).

Many experts recommend a blend of the best features of both approaches (National Reading Panel, 2000). Children can learn phonetic skills along with strategies to help them understand what they read. For example, they might be drilled in sound-letter correspondences, but also be asked to memorize certain common words like *the* and *one* that are more difficult to decode. Children who can summon both visually based and phonetic strategies become better, more versatile, readers (Siegler, 1998; 2000).

Metacognition involves thinking about thinking. It can help children monitor their understanding of what they read and develop strategies to address challenges. Children with good metacognitive skills use strategies such as reading more slowly, rereading difficult passages, trying to visualize information, or thinking of additional examples when trying to learn information in a challenging written passage. Metacognitive abilities can be encouraged by having students recall, summarize, and ask questions about what they read (National Reading Panel, 2000).

The acquisition of writing skills goes hand in hand with the development of reading. Older preschoolers begin using letters, numbers, and letterlike shapes as symbols to represent words or parts of words (syllables or phonemes). Often their spelling is quite inventive—so much so that they may not be able to read it themselves (Oullette & Senechal, 2008).

Writing is difficult for young children. Unlike conversation, which offers constant feedback, writing requires the child to judge independently whether the communicative goal has been met. The child also must keep in mind a variety of other constraints: spelling, punctuation, grammar, and capitalization, as well as the basic physical task of forming letters (Siegler, 1998).

Today's children are growing up in a world saturated with technology, and many of their literary experiences will take place on digital screens rather than on printed books. While some researchers have argued that e-books undermine children's understanding of the thematic content of a story and encourage a passive approach to reading (Labbo & Kuhn, 2000), other researchers have suggested that e-books can be used effectively to help children, especially reluctant readers, develop literacy skills (Maynard, 2010). Research has supported this assertion; a number of

Did you know?

In many classrooms, children are discouraged from discussing their work with other children, but research based on Vygotsky's theory suggests such policies are misguided. In one study, fourth graders working in pairs wrote stories with more solutions to problems, more explanations and goals, and fewer errors in syntax and word use than did children working alone (Daiute, Hartup, Sholl & Zajac, 1993).

©Steve Debenport/Getty Images

school-based interventions have found that e-books supported literacy development to a greater degree than printed books, especially for children at risk for learning disabilities (Ihmeideh, 2014; Shamir, Korat & Fellah, 2012; Shamir & Shlafer, 2011). However, for technology to be useful, it must consist of carefully designed applications that encourage collaborative activity, and be carefully scaffolded by parents or teachers (Moody, 2010; Flewitt, Messer & Kucirkova, 2015).

metacognition Thinking about thinking, or awareness of one's own mental processes.

The Child in School

The earliest school experiences are critical in setting the stage for future success or failure. Even today, when most U.S. children go to kindergarten, children often approach the start of first grade with a mixture of eagerness and anxiety.

SOCIAL AND HOME INFLUENCES ON ACADEMIC ACHIEVEMENT

As Bronfenbrenner's bioecological theory would predict, in addition to children's own characteristics, each level of the context of their lives influences how well they do in school—from the immediate family, to what goes on in the classroom, to the messages children receive from peers and from the larger culture (such as "It's not cool to be smart"). In the following sections we address the social and home influences on school achievement, including self-efficacy beliefs, gender, parenting practices, socioeconomic status, and peer acceptance.

Self-Efficacy Beliefs

Think of how you felt the last time you studied for a big exam. Did you feel you could do well as long as you studied, and were you confident in your ability to master the material? Or did you feel that nothing you could do would matter, and that the material was just too hard? Your attitude can be described as involving a construct called *self-efficacy*. Those students high in self-efficacy believe they can master schoolwork and regulate their own learning (Komarraju & Nadler, 2013). They are more likely to succeed than students who do not believe in their abilities (Caprara et al. 2008). Self-regulated learners try hard, persist despite difficulties, and seek help when necessary. Moreover, doing well in school then results in increases in self-efficacy. Students who do not believe in their ability to succeed tend to become frustrated and depressed—feelings that make success more elusive.

Gender

Girls tend to do better in school than boys. They receive higher marks, on average, in every subject (Voyer & Voyer, 2014; Halpern et al., 2007), are less likely to repeat grades, have fewer school problems, outperform boys in national reading and writing assessments (Freeman, 2004), and tend to do better than boys on timed tests (Camarata & Woodcock, 2006). While some research has suggested that boys outperform girls on science and math tests (Levine, Vasilyeva, Lourenco, Newcombe & Huttenlocher, 2005), other research has not found a gender gap (Lindberg, Hyde, Petersen & Linn, 2010), or has found it varies by culture (Else-Quest, Hyde & Linn, 2010). Research with adults has shown a consistent male advantage for mental rotations. In second grade, boys' and girls' performance on mental rotation tasks does not differ, however, by fourth grade, boys begin to outperform girls (Neuburger, Jansen, Heil & Quaiser-Pohl, 2011).

Gender differences tend to become more prominent in high school. A combination of several factors, including early experience, biological differences, and cultural expectations, may help explain these differences (Nisbett et al., 2012; Halpern et al., 2007).

Parenting Practices

Parents of high-achieving children create an environment for learning. They provide a place to study and to keep books and supplies; they set times for meals, sleep, and homework; they monitor their children's activities; and they talk with their children about school and are involved in school activities (Hill & Taylor, 2004; Hill & Tyson, 2009).

Generally, regardless of how it is defined, parental involvement has a positive effect on academic achievement (Wilder, 2014; LaRocque, Kleiman & Darling, 2011). However, some forms of involvement appear to be more effective than others. For example, homework assistance has not been consistently related to academic achievement (Hill & Tyson, 2009; McNeal, 2012). School involvement, including parental participation in school events and activities and good communication with teachers, is more strongly associated with strong academic performance (Overstreet, Devine, Bevans & Efreom, 2005; Topor, Keane, Shelton & Calkins, 2010). The strongest effects for parent involvement, however, center on parental expectations. Those parents who expect that their children will do well in school have children who live up to those beliefs (Wilder, 2014; Davis-Keane, 2005), perhaps because children also adopt the same attitude about their abilities (Topor et al., 2010).

Socioeconomic Status

Socioeconomic status (SES) can be a powerful factor in educational achievement—not in and of itself, but through its influence on family atmosphere, choice of neighborhood, parenting practices (Evans, 2004; Rouse et al., 2005), and on parents' expectations for children (Davis-Kean, 2005). Generally, achievement gaps between advantaged and disadvantaged students widen from kindergarten to third grade (Rathbun et al., 2004). Summer vacation contributes to these gaps because of differences in the typical home environment and in the summer learning experiences the children have, particularly with respect to reading (Johnston, Riley, Ryan & Kelly-Vance, 2015). This can help account for later differences in high school achievement and completion and college attendance (Alexander, Entwisle & Olson, 2007). Moreover, as the income gap between wealthy and poor families has gotten larger, the achievement gap between wealthy and poor children has also grown (Reardon, 2011).

In addition to these factors, it is likely that socioeconomic status may influence brain development itself. For example, children who live in poverty are more likely to be exposed to environmental toxins such as lead, which can negatively impact brain development. Poor children are also less likely to have access to healthy foods and more likely to suffer from nutrient deficiencies. Moreover, poverty is associated with higher stress, and high levels of chronic stress can have a direct negative effect on development as well as indirect effects on development via its impact on relational processes (Hackman, Farah & Meaney, 2010).

Peer Acceptance

Children who are disliked by their peers tend to do poorly in school, and this association exists for both boys and girls

(Nakamoto & Schwartz, 2010; Van Lier et al., 2012). Among 248 fourth graders, those whose teachers reported that they were not liked by peers had poorer academic self-concepts, more symptoms of anxiety or depression in fifth grade, and lower reading and math grades in sixth grade (Flook, Repetti & Ullman, 2005). It may be that the characteristics of some children, including aggression and oppositional behavior, lead to doing poorly in school *and* not being liked by peers. Then their academic underachievement and peer victimization lead to anxiety, depression, and further declines in academic performance (Van Lier et al., 2012). Early teacher identification of children who exhibit social problems could lead to interventions that would improve such children's academic as well as emotional and social outcomes (Flook et al., 2005). Additionally, teachers can serve as buffers against some of the effects of negative peer interactions, either by establishing a warm relationship with a rejected child, or by promoting a classroom climate in which victimization of disliked children is discouraged and positive social identities are encouraged (Elledge, Elledge, Newgent & Cavell, 2016; Serdiouk, Rodkin, Madill, Logis & Gest, 2015).

©LWA/Dann Tardif/
Blend Images/Corbis

WHAT DO YOU **DO**?

Elementary Teacher

Elementary teachers are responsible for the education of students in their classrooms. They teach children with a range of abilities and needs. While each state has its own curriculum, it is up to the classroom teacher to determine how to implement it in his or her classroom to meet state standards. The typical educational path for a classroom teacher is to receive a bachelor's degree from a teacher education program and then obtain a state license. Some states require teachers to have or be working toward a master's degree as well. To learn more about becoming an elementary teacher, visit www.nea.org and www.aft.org.

Did you know?

Not all low-SES homes involve low levels of intellectual stimulation. Low-income children whose home environment was cognitively stimulating at age 8 showed higher intrinsic motivation for academic learning at ages 9, 10, and 13 than children who had similar economic circumstances but lived in less stimulating homes (Gottfried, Fleming & Gottfried, 1998).

©Jorg Greuel/Getty Images

CLASSROOM AND SCHOOL SYSTEM INFLUENCES ON ACADEMIC ACHIEVEMENT

While certain variables unique to each child impact how well he or she does in school, wider systems variables also impact academic achievement. In the following section we address some of these variables. First, we discuss the impact of educational reforms in the United States. Then, we address the impact of class size, alternative educational models, and the use of computers in the classroom.

Educational Reform

The No Child Left Behind (NCLB) Act of 2001 was a sweeping educational reform emphasizing accountability, expanded parental options, local control, and flexibility. The intent was to funnel federal funding to research-based programs and practices. Students in grades three through eight were tested annually to determine if they were meeting statewide progress objectives. Facing increasing criticism from national education, civil rights, children's and citizens' group that the NCLB emphasized punishment rather than assistance for failing schools; was composed of rigid, unfunded mandates rather than support for proven practices; and had an overly strong focus on standardized testing, NCLB was replaced in 2015 by the Every Student Succeeds Act (ESSA) with bipartisan support. ESSA retained the standardized testing requirements of NCLB but shifted the responsibility and accountability of oversight to the state governments.

What has been the influence of these regulatory systems? The pattern of improvements in achievement scores have been highly variable across states, grades, and subjects

Being liked and accepted by peers is associated with better school performance.
©RubberBall/SuperStock

(Lee & Reeves, 2012). However, test scores do show improvement. In 2007, for example, math scores for fourth and eighth graders on the National Assessment of Educational Progress (NAEP) rose to their highest levels since the test began in 1990. Black, white, and Hispanic students all improved (NCES, 2007c), but ethnic group gaps remain (Hernandez & Macartney, 2008). Efforts to improve the teaching of reading seem to be paying off more slowly (Dee & Jacob, 2011). In the NAEP in 2007, fourth graders' reading scores rose only modestly compared with those in 1990, and eighth graders' scores declined slightly but were better than in 2005 (NCES, 2007d).

Many educators say the only real solution to a high failure rate is to identify at-risk students early and intervene *before* they fail. One way is to provide alternative schools or programs for at-risk students, offering smaller classes, remedial instruction, counseling, and crisis intervention (NCES, 2003). The National Education Policy Center recommends five key factors that represent key educational investments. First, there should be an emphasis on high-quality early education and experiential learning. Second, the school year and day should be expanded and focus on comprehensive learning rather than test prep. Third, children should not be stratified by ability, as this frequently results in the segregation of marginalized students. Fourth, class size should be reduced. Last, school-community partnerships, especially for children who live in areas where stable housing, employment, and other resources are uncertain, should be encouraged and promoted (Mathis & Trujillo, 2016).

Class Size

The evidence on the importance of class size in educational achievement is mixed (Schneider, 2002). Some researchers have not found evidence that reducing class

size benefits academic performance (Chingos, 2012; Hoxby, 2000). Other research has shown that reducing class size has a beneficial effect on academic performance, but that the effects are small and not likely to lead to sizable increases in student learning (Cho, Glewwe & Whitler, 2012).

However, many educators argue that smaller classes do benefit students. In smaller classes, students spend more time interacting with the teacher, are more likely to be the focus of a teacher's attention, and spend more time on task and less time off task (Blatchford, Bassett & Brown, 2011; Folmer-Annevelink, Doolaard, Macareno & Bosker, 2010). There are data to support this view (Shin & Raudenbush, 2011). In classroom observations of 890 first graders, classes with 25 students or less tended to be more social and interactive and to enable higher-quality instruction and emotional support. Students in these classes tended to score higher on standardized achievement tests and beginning reading skills (NICHD Early Childhood Research Network, 2004b). Moreover, data suggest that the students most at risk benefit the most from small classrooms (Blatchford et al., 2011). A longitudinal study found lasting academic benefits for students randomly assigned to classes of about 15 students in kindergarten through third grade and a greater likelihood of finishing high school—and this was especially true for the low-SES students (Finn, Gerber & Boyd-Zaharias, 2005).

Alternative Educational Models

In 2003, the United States ranked 15 out of 29 countries in reading literacy (U.S. Department of Education, National Center for Education Statistics, 2004), 21 out of 30 in scientific literacy, and 25 out of 30 in mathematic literacy (Organisation for Economic Co-operation and Development [OECD], 2007). How to properly educate children is a contentious issue with no easy answers, and some parents and educators have turned to alternative educational models in

Participation in music programs has been associated with a range of positive academic outcomes (Child Trends Databank, 2015).
©Sean Justice/Corbis

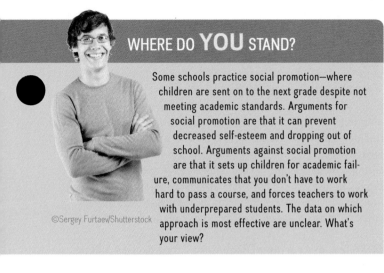
an attempt to remedy low test scores such as these. A variety of different models are currently in use, including alternative programs for at-risk students, charter schooling, and homeschooling.

Many educators say the only real solution to a high failure rate is to identify at-risk students early and intervene before they fail (Bronner, 1999). In 2000–2001, 39 percent of U.S. public school districts provided alternative schools or programs for at-risk students, offering smaller classes, remedial instruction, counseling, and crisis intervention (National Center for Education Statistics [NCES], 2003). Summer school may be effective as an early intervention. In one study, kindergarteners and first graders who attended summer instruction in reading and writing over three summers at an average attendance rate outscored their nonparticipating peers in achievement tests (Borman & Dowling, 2006).

Some parents, unhappy with their public schools or seeking a particular style of education, are choosing charter schools or homeschooling. In 2016–2017, an estimated 3.1 million children attended charter schools, some privately operated and others under charter from public school boards (National Alliance for Public Charter Schools, 2018). Charter schools tend to be smaller than regular public schools and tend to have a unique philosophy, curriculum, structure, or organizational style. Although parents are generally satisfied with their charter schools, studies of their effects on student outcomes have had mixed results. Some studies have found achievement gains, especially in mathematics, for students enrolled in charter schools (Betts & Tang, 2016), some studies have found mixed results (Berends, 2015), and some studies have found negative results (Clark, Gleason, Tuttle & Silverberg, 2015). Currently, not enough data on the factors that make some charter schools successful are available for general recommendations to be made.

Homeschooling is legal in all 50 states. In 2012 1.8 million U.S. students, representing 3.4 percent of the school-age population, were homeschooled (Snyder, de Brey & Dillow, 2016). The main reasons parents give for choosing to homeschool their children is a poor or unsafe learning environment in the schools and the desire to provide religious or moral

instruction (NCES, 2008). Most homeschooled students are white (89 percent), and most (about 90 percent) live above the poverty level (Redford, Battle & Bielick, 2016).

While advocates of homeschooling argue that homeschooling is associated with good academic outcomes (Christian Home Educators Association of California, 2013; Ray, 2010) the studies that have been conducted have serious methodological flaws and tend to come from a limited pool of researchers and organizations with potential biases (Kunzman & Gaither, 2012; Lubienski, Puckett & Brewer, 2013). Thus the efficacy of homeschooling remains in question. Given the variety of methods and materials used (Redford et al., 2016), it is likely the quality of instruction varies widely across different households.

Computer and Internet Use

Access to the Internet in public schools has skyrocketed. In 1995 only 4 percent of classrooms had Internet access, compared with 98 percent in 2008 (National Center for Education Statistics, 2016). However, fewer black, Hispanic, and American Indian children than white and Asian children, and fewer poor children than nonpoor children use these technologies. Girls and boys spend about the same amount of time on computer and Internet use (Day, Janus & Davis, 2005; DeBell & Chapman, 2006).

Media influences from home also play a role in children's development. The predominant influence is television. In 2003, 6- to 12-year-old children spent approximately 14 hours per week watching television. Computers also are an influence, although much less time (1 hour and 20 minutes per week) is spent on computers. Of that, the bulk of time is spent on video games, with e-mail, Internet usage, and studying comprising the remainder. This exposure to media has varying influences depending on what type of media is examined as well as the gender of the child. For example, television is associated with the displacement of other more beneficial experiences such as playing or sleeping for all children. Computer usage is associated with increases in achievement and problem-solving abilities for girls. However, for boys, who are more likely to play violent video games, computer usage is associated with increased aggressive behavior problems (Hofferth, 2010).

Computer literacy is an important skill in today's world. However, this tool poses dangers. Foremost is the risk of exposure to harmful or inappropriate material. Also, students need to learn to critically evaluate information they find in cyberspace and to separate facts from opinion and advertising.

EDUCATING CHILDREN WITH SPECIAL NEEDS

Public schools have a tremendous job educating children of varying abilities from all sorts of families and cultural backgrounds. They must educate children who speak little to no English. They must also educate children with special needs: for example, those who have learning problems and those who are gifted, talented, or creative.

Computer literacy is a critical skill in today's world. Computer usage can improve achievement and problem-solving skills, but students also need to learn to critically evaluate information found online.

©wavebreakmedia/Shutterstock

Educating Children with Disabilities

In 2014–2015, about 13 percent of public school students in the United States were receiving special educational services under the Individuals with Disabilities Education Act, which ensures a free, appropriate public education for all children with disabilities (U.S. Department of Education, 2016). Most of these children had learning disabilities or speech or language impairments. An individualized program (IEP) must be designed for each child, with parental involvement. Children must be educated in the "least restrictive environment" appropriate to their needs—which means, whenever possible, the regular classroom.

Programs in which children with special needs are included in the regular classroom are known as inclusion programs. Children with disabilities are integrated with nondisabled children for all or part of the day, sometimes with assistance. In 2014, 62 percent of students with disabilities spent at least 80 percent of their time in regular classrooms (NCES, 2017).

intellectual disability Significantly subnormal cognitive functioning. Also referred to as cognitive disability or (formerly) mental retardation.

learning disabilities (LDs) Disorders that interfere with specific aspects of learning and school achievement.

Intellectual Disability **Intellectual disability** is significantly subnormal cognitive functioning. It is indicated by an IQ of about 70 or less, coupled with a deficiency in age-appropriate adaptive behavior (such as communication, social skills, and self-care), appearing before age 18 (American Psychiatric Association, 2013). Intellectual disability is sometimes referred to as cognitive disability; the term *mental retardation* was also formerly used to describe this condition. Less than 1 percent of U.S. children are intellectually disabled (NCHS, 2004). Worldwide, about 1 of every 10 people are intellectually disabled (Maulik, Mascrenhas, Mathers, Dua & Saxena, 2011).

In 30 to 50 percent of cases, the cause of intellectual disability is unknown. Known causes include genetic disorders, traumatic accidents, prenatal exposure to infection or alcohol, and environmental exposure to lead or high levels of mercury (Woodruff et al., 2004). Many cases may be preventable through genetic counseling, prenatal care, amniocentesis, routine screening and health care for newborns, and nutritional services for pregnant women and infants.

Most children with an intellectual disability can benefit from schooling. Intervention programs have helped many with mild or moderate disabilities and those considered borderline (with IQs ranging from 70 up to about 85) to hold jobs, live in the community, and function in society. Those with profound disabilities need constant care and supervision, usually in institutions. For some, day care centers, hostels for intellectually disabled adults, and homemaking services for caregivers can be less costly and more humane alternatives.

Overview of Learning Disabilities **Learning disabilities (LDs)** interfere with specific aspects of school achievement, such as listening, speaking, reading, writing, or mathematics, resulting in performance substantially lower than would be expected given a child's age, intelligence, and amount of schooling (American Psychiatric Association, 1994). Children with LDs tend to be less task oriented and more easily distracted than other children; they are less well organized as learners and less likely to use memory strategies. They often have near-average to higher-than-average intelligence and normal vision and hearing, but they seem to have trouble processing sensory information. A growing number of children—almost 4.6 million, or 5 percent of the U.S. school population—have been diagnosed with LDs (Pastor & Reuben, 2008).

The two most commonly diagnosed conditions causing behavioral and learning problems in school-age children are learning disability (LD) and attention-deficit/hyperactivity disorder (ADHD). A recent study of more than 23,000 children in the United States revealed that about 5 percent of children have learning disabilities, 5 percent of children have ADHD, and 4 percent of children have both conditions (Pastor & Reuben, 2008).

Dyslexia The late Nelson Rockefeller, former vice president of the United States, had so much trouble reading that he ad-libbed speeches instead of using a script. Rockefeller is

Dyslexia is the most common learning disability, but with systematic phonological training, most children can learn to read.
©Robin Bartholick/Getty Images

one example of the many people who struggle with **dyslexia**, a language-processing disorder in which reading is substantially below the level predicted by IQ or age. Other famous people reportedly having dyslexia include actors Tom Cruise, Whoopi Goldberg, and Cher; baseball Hall-of-Famer Nolan Ryan; television host Jay Leno; and filmmaker Steven Spielberg. Dyslexia is the most commonly diagnosed of a large number of LDs.

About 4 out of 5 children with LDs have been identified as having dyslexia. Dyslexia is generally considered to be a chronic, persistent medical condition that tends to run in families (Shaywitz, 1998, 2003). It hinders the development of oral as well as written language skills and may cause problems with reading, writing, spelling, grammar, and understanding speech (National Center for Learning Disabilities, 2004a). Reading disability is more frequent in boys than in girls (Rutter, O'Connor & the English and Romanian Adoptees [ERA] Study Team, 2004). Although reading and intelligence are related to each other in children without dyslexia, they are not coupled in children with dyslexia. In other words, dyslexia is not an issue of intelligence (Ferrer et al., 2010).

Brain imaging studies have found that dyslexia is due to a neurological defect that disrupts recognition of speech sounds (Shaywitz, Mody & Shaywitz, 2006). Several identified genes contribute to this disruption (Meng et al., 2005; Kere et al., 2005). Many children—and even adults—with dyslexia can be taught to read through systematic phonological training, but the process does not become automatic, as it does with most readers (Eden et al., 2004; Shaywitz, 1998, 2003).

Did you know?

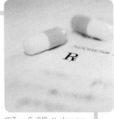

People are sometimes puzzled by why a stimulant such as Ritalin can lead to improved attentional processes. The reason? Children with ADHD can be thought of as having sluggish frontal lobes. The Ritalin "wakes up" those areas and helps them function more effectively.

©Tom Grill/Getty Images

Attention Deficit/Hyperactivity Disorder **Attention-deficit/hyperactivity disorder (ADHD)** is a chronic condition usually marked by persistent inattention, distractibility, impulsivity, low tolerance for frustration, and a great deal of activity at the wrong time and in the wrong place, such as the classroom (Woodruff et al., 2004). Some children with ADHD are inattentive but not hyperactive; others show the reverse pattern (U.S. Department of Health and Human Services [USDHHS], 1999b). Among well-known people reportedly with ADHD are the singer/composer John Lennon, Senator Robert Kennedy, and the actors Robin Williams and Jim Carey.

ADHD may affect an estimated 7.2 percent of school-age children worldwide (Thomas, Sanders, Doust, Beller & Glasziou, 2015). In 2016 about 5.4 million children in the United States had a current diagnosis of ADHD, a rate of about 8.4 percent (Danielson et al., 2018). Previous research indicated the rate of ADHD had increased over previous decades (Pastor & Reuben, 2008), however, more recent research suggests the apparent rise is an artifact of methodological confounds in studies and differences in diagnostic criteria (Polancyzk, Willcut, Salum, Kieling, & Rohde, 2014; Thomas, Sanders, Doust, Beller & Glasziou, 2015; Figure 12.3)

dyslexia Developmental disorder in which reading achievement is substantially lower than predicted by IQ or age.

attention-deficit/hyperactivity disorder (ADHD) Syndrome characterized by persistent inattention and distractibility, impulsivity, low tolerance for frustration, and inappropriate overactivity.

Because hyperactivity and inattention appear to some degree in all children, some practitioners question whether ADHD is actually a distinct neurological or psychological disorder (Bjorklund & Pellegrini, 2002; Furman, 2005). Some research suggests it may be underdiagnosed (Rowland et al., 2002), but physicians warn it may be overdiagnosed, resulting in unnecessary overmedication of children whose parents or teachers do not know how to control them (Elliot, 2000).

Similar to LD, ADHD diagnosis rates vary greatly by gender, ethnicity, geographic area, and other contextual factors. Boys are more likely than girls to have each of the diagnoses and are twice as likely to have ADHD (Pastor & Reuben, 2008). Prevalence rates are higher in non-Hispanic white children (12.5 percent) than black (9.6 percent) and Hispanic (6.4 percent) children (Pastor, Duran & Reuben, 2015). Some of the diagnoses may be environmentally driven and related to the demands or characteristics of the school involved.

Imaging studies reveal that certain regions in the brains of children with ADHD—most notably areas in the frontal cortex—show delays in development. The motor cortex is the only area that matures faster than normal, and this mismatch may account for the restlessness and fidgeting characteristic of the disorder (Shaw, Krause, Liang & Bennett, 2007).

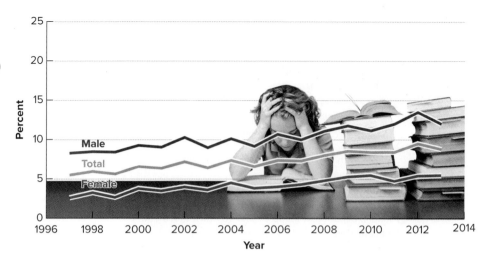

FIGURE 12.3 Prevalence of ADHD by Year and Gender

Diagnosis of learning disabilities has remained constant, but diagnosis of ADHD has risen over the past 20 years. Rates are higher among males than females.

Source: Child Trends DataBank, www.childtrends.org/wp-content/uploads/2014/08/76_ADHD.pdf

©Randy Faris/Getty Images

During tasks that require the deployment of attentional processes, children with ADHD show reduced activation in frontoparietal and ventral attention networks areas (Cortese et al., 2012). These frontal regions enable a person to set goals, focus attention, monitor progress, and inhibit negative impulses—all functions disturbed in children with ADHD.

ADHD is often managed with drugs, sometimes combined with behavioral therapy, counseling, training in social skills, and special classroom placement. Ritalin is a commonly prescribed drug and is generally very effective. However, it is related to slower growth in height and weight (Powell, Frydenberg & Thomsen, 2015); other long-term effects of Ritalin are unclear (Wolraich et al., 2005).

Gifted Children

Giftedness is hard to define and identify. Educators disagree on who qualifies as gifted, on what basis, and on what educational programs these children need. Another source of confusion is that creativity and artistic talent are sometimes viewed as aspects or types of giftedness and sometimes as independent of it.

Identifying Gifted Children The traditional criterion of giftedness is high general intelligence as shown by an IQ score of 130 or higher. This definition tends to exclude highly creative children (whose unusual answers often lower their test scores), children from minority groups (whose abilities may not be well developed, though the potential is there), and children with specific aptitudes (who may be only average or even show learning problems in other areas). Thus, all 50 states have moved beyond a single-score definition of giftedness (McClain & Pfeiffer, 2012).

Most states and school districts have adopted a broader definition of creativity that encompasses children who show high intellectual, creative, artistic, or leadership capacity or ability in specific academic fields and who need special educational services and activities to fully develop those capabilities. Generally, multiple criteria are used for admission to programs for the gifted, including achievement test scores, grades, classroom performance, creative production, parent and teacher nominations, and student interviews. An estimated 6 percent of the student population is considered gifted (National Association for Gifted Children, n.d.). In the 2013–2014 academic year, approximately 3.32 million children were enrolled in gifted and talented programs in the United States (U.S. Department of Education, 2017).

Causes of Giftedness High levels of performance require strong motivation and years of rigorous training (Gardner, 1993; Gottfried, Cook, Gottfried & Morris, 2005; Clinkenbeard, 2012; Al-Dhamit & Kreishan, 2016). However, motivation and training will not produce giftedness unless a child is endowed with unusual ability (Winner, 2000). Conversely, children with innate gifts are unlikely to show exceptional achievement without motivation and hard work (Achter & Lubinski, 2003).

Gifted children tend to grow up in enriched family environments with intellectual or artistic stimulation. Their parents recognize and often devote themselves to nurturing the children's gifts and curiosity and also tend to give their children an unusual degree of independence and expose them to new experiences. Parents of gifted children typically have high expectations and are hard workers and high achievers themselves (Winner, 2000; Al-Dhamit & Kreishan, 2016; Garn, Matthews & Jolly, 2010; Gottfried et al., 2016).

Educating Gifted Children Programs for gifted children generally stress either enrichment or acceleration. **Enrichment** deepens knowledge and skills through extra classroom activities, research projects, field trips, or expert coaching. **Acceleration**, sometimes recommended for highly gifted children, speeds up their education through early school entrance, grade skipping, placement in fast-paced classes, or advanced courses. Other options include ability grouping within the classroom, which has been found to help children academically and not harm them socially (Vogl & Preckel, 2014); dual enrollment, for example, an

enrichment Approach to educating the gifted that broadens and deepens knowledge and skills through extra activities, projects, field trips, or mentoring.

acceleration Approach to educating the gifted that moves them through the curriculum at an unusually rapid pace.

eighth grader taking algebra at a nearby high school; and enrollment in magnet schools and specialized schools for the gifted.

Defining and Measuring Creativity   One definition of *creativity* is the ability to see things in a new light—to produce something never seen before or to discern problems others fail to recognize and find new and unusual solutions to those problems. High creativity and high academic intelligence (IQ) do not necessarily go hand in hand (Anastasi & Schaefer, 1971; Getzels & Jackson, 1963). However, it does appear that a threshold level of intelligence, which varies with the complexity of the creative activity, is necessary. Once the intelligence threshold is met, personality factors become more important (Jauk, Benedek, Dunst & Neubauer, 2013).

The reason creativity is not highly correlated with traditional IQ tests is because traditional tests are measuring a different kind of thinking than is characteristic of creativity. J. P. Guilford (1986) distinguished two kinds of thinking: convergent and divergent. **Convergent thinking**—the kind IQ tests measure—seeks a single correct answer. For example, when solving an arithmetic problem, there is one correct answer upon which everyone is expected to converge. **Divergent thinking**, by contrast, involves coming up with a wide array of fresh possibilities, such as when children are asked to list how many different uses there might be for a paper clip or to write down what a sound brings to mind. There is no one right answer. Tests of creativity call for divergent thinking. This ability can be assessed via the Torrance Tests of Creative Thinking (TTCT) (Torrance & Ball, 1984), one of the most widely known tests of creativity. While there has been controversy about the measurement qualities of the test, a 50-year follow-up showed that scores on the TTCT were related to personal achievement, and when IQ was also taken into account, scores were related to public achievement as well (Runco, Millar, Acar & Cramond, 2010).

convergent thinking Thinking aimed at finding the one right answer to a problem.

divergent thinking Thinking that produces a variety of fresh, diverse possibilities.

Giftedness in children can take different forms, including intellectual or leadership capacity and artistic ability. The key to helping gifted children lies in recognizing and nurturing their natural gifts.
©ERproductions Ltd/Blend Images/Corbis

mastering the CHAPTER

©andresr/Getty Images

Summary and Key Terms

Piagetian Approach: The Concrete Operational Child

> A child from about age 7 to 12 is in the stage of concrete operations. Children are less egocentric than before and are more proficient at tasks requiring logical reasoning, such as spatial thinking, understanding of causality, categorization, inductive and deductive

reasoning, conservation, and number. However, their reasoning is largely limited to the here and now.

> Neurological development, culture, and schooling seem to contribute to the rate of development of Piagetian skills.

KEY TERMS

Seriation	Class inclusion	Deductive reasoning
Transitive inference	Inductive reasoning	Horizontal décalage

Information-Processing Approach: Attention, Memory, and Planning

> Executive function improves during middle childhood as a result of pruning of neurons in the prefrontal cortex. Environmental influences also affect the development of executive function.

> Selective attention, working memory, metamemory, and the use of mnemonic devices improve during the school years.

KEY TERMS

Executive function	Metamemory	Mnemonic device

Psychometric Approach: Assessment of Intelligence

> IQ tests are fairly good predictors of school success but may underestimate the intelligence of some children and depend on prior knowledge.

> IQ tests tap only three of the eight intelligences in Howard Gardner's theory of multiple intelligences.

> According to Robert Sternberg's triarchic theory, IQ tests measure mainly the componential element of intelligence, not the experiential and contextual elements, which may be important in predicting real-world outcomes.

> Other directions in intelligence testing include the Kaufman Assessment Battery for Children (K-ABC-II), and dynamic tests based on Vygotsky's theory.

> Intelligence is highly heritable and may be linked through genetically influenced brain development.

> Differences in IQ among ethnic groups appear to result to a considerable degree from socioeconomic and other environmental differences.

> Schooling increases measured intelligence.

> Attempts to devise culture-free or culture-fair tests have been unsuccessful.

Language and Literacy

> Use of vocabulary, grammar, and syntax become increasingly sophisticated, but the major area of linguistic growth is in pragmatics.

> Methods of second-language education are controversial.

> Despite the popularity of whole-language programs, early phonetics training is a key to reading proficiency. Mixed approaches may be most effective.

> Some research supports carefully designed use of e-books for literacy development, especially for children at risk for learning disabilities.

The Child in School

> Entry into first grade is an important milestone. Children's self-efficacy beliefs affect school achievement.

> Girls tend to do better in school than boys.

> Parents influence children's learning by becoming involved in their schooling and transmitting attitudes about academics. Socioeconomic status can influence parental beliefs and practices that, in turn, influence achievement.

> Peer acceptance and class size affect learning.

> Current educational issues and innovations include social promotion, charter schools, homeschooling, and computer literacy.

> Three frequent sources of learning problems are intellectual disability, learning disabilities (LDs), and attention-deficit/hyperactivity disorder (ADHD). Dyslexia is the most common learning disability.

> In the United States, all children with disabilities are entitled to a free, appropriate education in the least restrictive environment possible, often in the regular classroom.

> An IQ of 130 or higher is a common standard for identifying gifted children.

> Creativity and IQ are *not* closely linked. Tests of creativity seek to measure divergent thinking, but their validity has been questioned.

Practice Quiz

1. What are two factors related to children's increasing skill in understanding spatial relationships?

   _____

   _____

2. When shown a jar of jellybeans containing 30 red jellybeans and 10 blues ones and asked, "Are there more red jellybeans, or are there more blue jellybeans?" Maria correctly answers, "There are more red ones." This illustrates Maria's understanding of:

   a. seriation
   b. transitive inference
   c. class inclusion
   d. conservation

3. Children in the concrete operations stage of development can use _____ but not _____.

   a. inductive reasoning; deductive reasoning
   b. deductive reasoning; inductive reasoning
   c. identity; reversibility
   d. reversibility; identity

4. You are 9 years old and have just gotten back from trick-or-treating. Your mom told you to divide the 20 pieces of candy between yourself and your 5-year-old brother. If you want to get more candy than your brother, what might Piaget suggest you do when you are dividing out the candy?

   a. count backward from 10 instead of forward from 1
   b. use aggression to persuade your brother you should get more candy than him
   c. spread out your brother's smaller pile of candy to make it look bigger and scrunch your pieces of candy closely together to make your pile look smaller
   d. offer your brother a future favor in order to get more candy for yourself now

5. Children generally learn to _____ before they learn to _____.

   a. add; subtract
   b. subtract; add
   c. understand fractions; do word problems
   d. do word problems; understand fractions

6. What are two influences on the development of executive functioning in middle childhood?

   _____

   _____

   _____

7. Selective attention relies on both the ability to _____ as well as _____.

   a. select which stimuli you are interested in; change your selection rapidly if your needs change
   b. deliberately direct attention to target stimuli; inhibit attention to distractions
   c. be able to use inductive reasoning; to be able to use deductive reasoning
   d. all of the above

8. What two abilities underlie the improvements in working memory in middle childhood?

   _____

   _____

9. If you are able to realize that you are better at recognizing the right answer on a multiple-choice exam than you are at writing down the answer without cues, you are engaging in:

   a. selective attention
   b. deductive reasoning
   c. inference activities
   d. metamemory

10. If you are most interested in what children could know with help rather than what they actually know at any point in time, then you are probably most interested in:

    a. the WISC-III
    b. the K-ABC-II
    c. dynamic testing
    d. the influence of schooling on IQ

11. What are two positive aspects and two negative aspects of IQ tests?

    _____

    _____

    _____

    _____

12. List Gardner's eight kinds of intelligence.

    _____

    _____

    _____

13. The reason that race and ethnicity are related to performance on IQ tests is because

    a. there is a genetic factor for intelligence that varies between people of different races
    b. minority children have traditionally scored lower on IQ tests than white children
    c. race and ethnicity are related to socioeconomic status, which in turn affects IQ test scores
    d. this is untrue; the gap in scores has disappeared in recent years

14. Which of the following aspects of language become more common in middle childhood?

    a. metaphors and similes
    b. language errors
    c. active voice
    d. verbs

15. Which of the following sentences illustrates pragmatic knowledge?

    a. I like to eat cookies.
    b. Go away.
    c. I'll wait until she's off the phone before asking for a cookie because she's more likely to say yes that way.
    d. I think butterflies and flowers look kind of the same.

16. Briefly summarize recommendations for promoting literacy in young children.

____

____

____

____

17. Which of the following is NOT positively associated with academic achievement?

a. being high in self-efficacy
b. being a boy rather than a girl
c. being of high socioeconomic status
d. being liked by peers

18. If Bob has difficulty focusing in class, frequently interrupts his teacher, and has problems completing his schoolwork, he is likely to be diagnosed as

a. having intellectual disability
b. having ADHD
c. being gifted
d. uneducable

Answers: 1–increasingly sophisticated symbolic representation; experience; 2–c; 3–a; 4–c; 5–a; 6–Brain development (development of the frontal cortex, pruning, and myelination of axons) and the home environment (available resources, cognitive stimulation, and maternal sensitivity); 7–b; 8–improvements in processing speed; greater storage capacity; 9–d; 10–c; 11–Positive: standardized, extensive information on norms, validity and reliability, good predictors of school achievement. Negative: underestimate the intelligence of children who are ill or do not do well on tests, equate intelligence with speed because they are timed, are not always appropriate for children with learning disabilities, do not measure innate ability; 12–Verbal-linguistic, logic-mathematical, visual-spatial, musical-rhythmic, body-kinesthetic, interpersonal, intrapersonal, and naturalistic; 13–c; 14–a; 15–c; 16–Experts recommend a blend of the phonetic and whole-language approaches. Children can thus use visual retrieval for familiar words and phonetic decoding for unfamiliar words, and become better, more versatile readers; 17–b; 18–b

Chapter 13

Psychosocial Development in Middle Childhood

What's to Come

> The Developing Self

> The Child in the Family

> The Child in the Peer Group

©Sergey Novikov/Shutterstock

m in third grade," Emily says. "I live with my mom and brother, and my dad lives in another house. I like to play with my friends. I'm good at swimming, and I like cats, and I am funny and silly. I think I am helpful, but my mom says that is a lie."

Eight-year-old Emily is typical of girls her age. In this chapter, we trace the rich and varied emotional and social lives of school-age children such as Emily. We see how children develop a more realistic concept of themselves and achieve more competence, self-reliance, and emotional control. Through being with peers, they make discoveries about their own attitudes, values, and skills. Still, the family remains a vital influence. Children's lives are affected, not only by the way parents approach child rearing, but also by whether and how they are employed, by the family's economic circumstances, and by its structure or composition.

• • • •

By age 7 or 8, children have a more balanced and realistic self-concept.
©Dmitri Ma/Shutterstock

The Developing Self

The cognitive growth that takes place during middle childhood enables children to develop more complex concepts of themselves and to grow in emotional understanding and control. In the following section, we address the development of the self-concept and self-esteem, and then we focus on emotional growth and prosocial behavior.

SELF-CONCEPT DEVELOPMENT: REPRESENTATIONAL SYSTEMS

"At school I'm really good at some things. I really like math and science, and I get the best scores on tests of all the other kids," says 8-year-old Emily. "I got A's in them on my last report card and was really proud of myself. But I'm not so good at social studies and English, and sometimes I feel bad when I see how good the other kids are doing. I still like myself as a person though, because I don't really care that much about social studies and English."

Around age 7 or 8, children reach the third stage of self-concept development introduced in Chapter 10. At this time judgments about the self become more conscious, realistic, balanced, and comprehensive as children form **representational systems:** broad, inclusive self-concepts that integrate various aspects of the self (Harter, 1998).

We see these changes in Emily's self-description. She has outgrown her earlier all-or-nothing, black-or-white self-definition. Now she recognizes that she can be "smart" in certain subjects and "dumb" in others. She can verbalize her self-concept better, and she can weigh different aspects of it. She can compare her *real self* (who she is) with her *ideal self* (who she wants to be) and can judge how well she measures

Did you know?

Research suggests that regardless of how good you are, participation in team sports, but not individual sports, is related to higher self-esteem (Slutzky & Simpkins, 2007).

©D. Hurst/Alamy

up to social standards in comparison with others. All of these changes contribute to the development of self-esteem, her assessment of her *global self-worth* ("I still like myself as a person").

SELF-ESTEEM

Middle childhood is the time when children must learn skills valued in their society. Arapesh boys in New Guinea learn to make bows and arrows and to lay traps for rats; Arapesh girls learn to plant, weed, and harvest. Inuit children of Alaska learn to hunt and fish. Children in industrialized countries learn to read, write, do math, and use computers.

representational systems
Broad, inclusive self-concepts that integrate various aspects of the self.

According to Erikson (1982), a major determinant of self-esteem is children's view of their capacity for productive work. Erikson's fourth stage of psychosocial development focuses on **industry versus inferiority**. The virtue that follows successful resolution of this stage is competence, a view of the self as able to master skills and complete tasks. If children feel inadequate compared with their peers, they may retreat to the protective embrace of the family. If, on the other hand, they become too industrious, they may neglect social relationships and turn into workaholics in adulthood.

Parents strongly influence a child's beliefs about competence, and consequently, the amount of effort put into working in an area. In a longitudinal study of 987 European children, parent's beliefs about their children's competence in sports, music, and math were associated with their children's beliefs about their abilities and with their self-reports about motivation. Six years later, children's beliefs were then predictive of the amount of time children spent taking classes or participating in those activities (Yamamoto & Holloway, 2010).

EMOTIONAL GROWTH

As children grow older, they are more aware of their own and other people's feelings. They can better regulate or control their emotions and can respond to others' emotional distress (Saarni, Campos, Camras & Witherington, 2006). Children learn what makes them angry, fearful, or sad and how other people react to displays of these emotions. They know that remembering things that happened in the past and thinking about things that are going to happen in the future can affect your mental state (Lagattuta, 2014). Children also start to understand that they and others can have conflicting emotions (Zajdel, Bloom, Fireman & Larsen, 2013). As Emily says, "I think boys are pretty yucky, and I don't like most of them. My brother is OK, but he can be annoying sometimes. I love him, but he does things that make me mad. But I don't yell at him because if I do, he cries and then I feel guilty."

By age 7 or 8, children typically are aware of feeling shame and pride, and they have a clearer idea of the difference between guilt and shame (Olthof, Shouten, Kuiper, Stegge & Jennekens-Schinkel, 2000). Additionally, cultural values affect the expression of these emotions. For example, one study found that children in the United States expressed the most pride, while Japanese children the most shame, and Korean children the most guilt (Furukawa, Tangney & Higashibara, 2012). These emotions then affect their opinion of themselves (Harter, 1993; 1996). The differential emotional responses are influenced by socialization. For example, another study found that when asked about how they would feel about a difficult interpersonal situation, Brahman children from India reported they would feel anger while Tamang children from Tibet reported shame as their most likely emotion (Cole, Bruschi & Tamang, 2002). Brahman adults generally ignore shame and respond to angry children with reasoning and yield to their demands, presumably as a means by which to socialize them to their future as a high-caste adult. Tamang adults expect children to be socially compliant and are intolerant of anger, but they will reason with and yield to children who are ashamed. Thus, children learn to shape their emotional responses to what is expected and tolerated of them (Cole, Tamang & Shrestha, 2006).

When parents are skilled at the recognition of emotions in others, label emotions, and allow children the latitude to express the emotions they desire, this is associated with greater understanding and recognition of emotions in their children (Castro, Halberstadt, Lozada & Craig, 2015). Parents who acknowledge children's feelings of distress and help them focus on solving the root problem foster empathy, prosocial development, and social skills (Bryant, 1987; Eisenberg et al., 1996). By contrast, when parents respond with excessive disapproval or punishment to the expression of emotions, emotions such as anger and fear may become more intense and may impair children's social adjustment (Fabes, Leonard, Kupanoff & Martin, 2001), or children may become secretive and anxious about negative feelings (Almas, Grusec & Tackett, 2011). As children approach early adolescence, parental intolerance of negative emotion may heighten parent-child conflict (Fabes et al., 2001).

Have you ever received a gift you didn't like or had to hold in your anger to avoid getting in trouble? The ability to fake liking a gift or to smile when you are mad involves emotional self-regulation. Emotional self-regulation is effortful (voluntary) control of emotions, attention, and behavior (Eisenberg et al., 2004), and children get better at this with age. However, some children are better at this than others. For example, children, especially girls, who are securely attached are better at recognizing emotions and producing emotion regulation strategies for handling hypothetical situations than insecurely attached children (Colle & Del Giudice, 2011). How good children are at emotion regulation has behavioral and academic consequences. Children who, at 3 to 4 years of age, had difficulty in delay-of-gratification tasks were more likely to have behavior problems at 5 to 8 years. Similarly, children who were poor at deliberately slowing down, inhibiting their movements in a game, or paying close attention when young were more likely to have academic difficulties when older (Kim, Nordling, Yoon, Boldt & Kochanska, 2013).

Did you know?

Empathy is reflected in the brain. A recent study in 7- to 12-year-olds found parts of their brains were activated when shown pictures of people in pain (Decety, Michalaska, Akitsuki, & Lahey, 2009).

©Creatas/PunchStock

Emotion regulation may also be involved in the development of anxiety disorders, not in the formation of initial fears, but in their maintenance and reinforcement (Cisler, Olatunji, Feldner & Forsyth, 2010).

Children tend to become more empathic and more inclined to prosocial behavior in middle childhood. Children with high self-esteem tend to be more willing to volunteer to help those who are less fortunate than they are, and volunteering, in turn, helps build self-esteem (Karafantis & Levy, 2004). Prosocial children tend to act appropriately in social situations, to be relatively free from negative emotion, and to cope with problems constructively (Eisenberg, Fabes & Murphy, 1996). Empathy—the capacity to understand and feel the emotions of another person—is likely one of the key motivators for prosocial behavior (Eisenberg, Eggum & Di Giunta, 2010). Empathy appears to be hardwired into the brains of typical children. As with adults, empathy has been associated with prefrontal activation in children as young as 4 years of age and continuing throughout childhood (Brink et al., 2011; Light et al., 2009; Decety, Michalaska, Akitsuki & Lahey, 2009).

While children become better at identifying and understanding emotions with age, some children lag behind and this can cause social and behavioral issues. Fortunately, children can be trained to more accurately understand emotions—both their own and those of others—and such interventions show promise for preventive interventions (Sprung, Munch, Harris, Ebesutani & Hofmann, 2015). For example, class interventions have been shown to help children develop empathy for others, increase spontaneous prosocial behavior, and decrease aggressive acts (Schonert-Reichl, Smith, Zaidman-Zait & Hertzman, 2012).

The Child in the Family

School-age children spend more of their free time away from home than when they were younger, visiting and socializing with peers. They also spend more time at school and on their studies and less time at family meals than 20 or so years ago (Juster, Ono & Stafford, 2004). Still, home and the people who live there remain an important part of most children's lives. To understand the child in the family, we need to look at the family environment—its atmosphere and structure—and examine it within the context of the modern world.

FAMILY ATMOSPHERE

The family atmosphere contributes to the family environment. The family atmosphere can be described as the ways in which members interact with each other and the outside world, including the interpersonal dynamics as well as such factors as socioeconomic level and work status. Key influences on the family atmosphere are parenting during this age stage, specifically how parents respond to emerging control of behavior; whether or not they work in or outside the home; and the family's economic status.

Parenting: Emerging Control of Behavior

Babies don't have a lot of say in what happens to them; they experience what their parents decide they should experience. However, as children grow and become more autonomous, control gradually shifts from parents to child.

Family dynamics are a key influence on a school-age child's development.
©Ale Ventura/agefotostock

coregulation Transitional stage in the control of behavior in which parents exercise general supervision and children exercise moment-to-moment self-regulation.

internalizing behaviors Behaviors by which emotional problems are turned inward; for example, anxiety or depression.

externalizing behaviors Behaviors by which a child acts out emotional difficulties; for example, aggression or hostility.

Children begin to request certain types of experiences, demand particular foods, negotiate for desired objects, and communicate their shifting needs to parents. One of the major influences in the family atmosphere is how parents and children navigate this changing balance of power.

Middle childhood brings a transitional stage of **coregulation** in which parent and child share power. While parents still exercise oversight, children enjoy moment-to-moment self-regulation (Maccoby, 1984; 1992). For example, with regard to problems among peers, parents might now rely less on direct intervention and more on discussion with their child (Parke & Buriel, 1998).

The amount of autonomy parents provide affects how their children feel about them. For example, in one study, when parents were overbearing and overly directive when children were toddlers, they tended to also show low support for their child's autonomy at 10 years of age, and this in turn was associated with children's lowered expression of positive feelings for parents (Ispa et al., 2015). But this is a two-way street. How children respond to parents' attempts to regulate their behavior is affected by the overall relationship between parent and child. Children are more apt to follow their parents' wishes when they believe the parents are fair and concerned about the child's welfare and that they may "know better" because of experience. This is particularly true when parents take pains to acknowledge children's maturing judgment and take strong stands only on important issues (Maccoby, 1984; 1992).

The shift to coregulation affects the way parents handle discipline (Kochanska, Aksan, Prisco & Adams, 2008). Parents of school-age children are more likely to use inductive techniques. For example, they might explain how their actions affect others, highlight moral values, or let their children experience the natural consequences of their behaviors. For example, 8-year-old Emily's father might point out: "Hitting John hurts him and makes him feel bad." In other situations, Emily's parents may appeal to her self-esteem ("What happened to the helpful girl who was here yesterday?") or moral values ("A big girl like you shouldn't sit on the train and let an old person stand"). Above all, Emily's parents let her know that she must bear the consequences of her behavior ("No wonder you missed the school bus today—you stayed up too late last night! Now you'll have to walk to school").

However, families vary in what type of discipline they use. Some families are more likely to use coercive parenting practices such as physical punishment, although its use tends to decrease as children get older. Generally, the use of physical punishment is associated with negative outcomes for children. Those parents who continue to spank their children past the age of 10 years tend to have worse relationships with their children in adolescence and to have teens with more severe behavioral problems (Lansford et al., 2009). Exposure to any form of violence and conflict tends to be harmful to children,

both in terms of direct exposure via parental discord (Kaczynski, Lindahl, Malik & Laurenceau, 2006) and via indirect influences on variables like low family cohesion and ineffective anger regulation strategies (Houltberg, Henry & Morris, 2012).

Children exposed to family conflict show a variety of responses that can include externalizing or internalizing behaviors. **Internalizing behaviors** include anxiety, fearfulness, and depression—anger turned inward. **Externalizing behaviors** include aggression, fighting, disobedience, and hostility—anger turned outward. Both internalizing behaviors and externalizing behaviors are more likely in children who come from families with high levels of discord (Kaczynski et al., 2006; Fear et al., 2009; Houltberg et al., 2012).

Family conflict need not always be harmful. How family conflict is resolved is also important. If family conflict is constructive, it can help children see the need for rules and standards, and learn what issues are worth arguing about and what strategies can be effective (Eisenberg, 1996). For example, when family conflict in one longitudinal study was solved in constructive ways, children reported being more emotionally secure one year later, and, one year after that, reported more prosocial behavior (McCoy, Cummings & Davies, 2009). Unfortunately, as children become preadolescents and their striving for autonomy becomes more insistent, the quality of family problem solving often deteriorates (Vuchinich, Angelelli & Gatherum, 1996).

Cultural differences are also important, and tend to exert complex effects. Generally, researchers find that in cultures that stress family interdependence (such as in Turkey, India, and Latin America) authoritarian parenting, with its high degree of control, is not associated with negative maternal feelings or low self-esteem in children as it is in more individualistic cultures (Rudy & Grusec, 2006). Latino parents, for example, have well-adjusted children as often as other groups although they tend to exert more control over their school-age children than European American parents do (Halgunseth, Ispa & Rudy, 2006) and expectations for girls are even more strict (Domenech, Rodriguez, Donovick & Crowley, 2009). However, children in China, also a collectivistic culture, tend to be negatively affected by high control just as are children from the individualistic United States (Pomerantz & Wang, 2009). With respect to low control, children of Iranian (Kazemi, Ardabili & Solokian, 2010), Spanish (Garcia & Gracia, 2009), and some European parents (Calafat, Garcia, Juan, Becona & Fernandez-Hermida, 2014) with a permissive parenting style have good outcomes, contrary to what has been found in American samples (Pinquart, 2017). Thus, the influence of parental control strategies is shaped by the cultural context in which it occurs.

Did you know?

Asking kids to promise to tell the truth makes them more likely to do so (Evans & Lee, 2010).

©Stephen Rees/Shutterstock

Employed Mothers

Most studies of the impact of parents' work on children's well-being have focused on employed mothers. In 1975, the labor force participation rate of mothers with children was 47 percent (U.S. Bureau of Labor Statistics, 2008). By 2015, almost 70 percent of U.S. mothers worked either full- or part-time (U.S. Department of Labor, 2016). Thus, many children have never known a time when their mothers were not working for pay.

In general, the more satisfied a mother is with her employment status, the more effective she is likely to be as a parent. However, the impact of a mother's work depends on many other factors, including the child's age, sex, temperament, and personality; whether the mother works full-time or part-time; why she is working; whether she has a supportive or unsupportive partner, or none; the family's socioeconomic status; and the type of care the child receives before and/or after school (Parke, 2004; Gottfried & Gottfried, 2013). Often a single mother must work to stave off economic disaster. How her working affects her children may hinge on how much time and energy she has left to spend with them. How well parents keep track of their children and monitor their activities may be more important than whether the mother works for pay (Fosco, Stormshak, Dishion & Winter, 2012).

Mothers are far more likely to take on part-time work than fathers (Weeden, Cha & Bucca, 2016), and if possible this arrangement may be preferable. Children tend to do slightly better in school if one parent is able to work part-time (Goldberg, Prause, Lucas-Thompson & Himsel, 2008). While it is difficult to pin down the multiplicity of influences, longitudinal research indicates that overall, children from dual-earner families do well, and there may even be advantages associated with having working parents (Gottfried & Gottfried, 2008).

When both parents work outside the home, child care arrangements are common. Half of grade school children are in some form of child care outside of school, often with relatives (Laughlin, 2013), while others attend organized programs. These programs vary widely in quality. Two important markers of quality are structural features (such as physical facilities and

The impact on their children of parents working outside the home depends on many factors. A working mother who is satisfied with her employment status and who has time and energy to spend with her children is likely to be an effective parent.

WHAT DO YOU **DO**?

After-School Activity Director

An after-school activity director manages after-school programs for children. During after-school programs, children may participate in formal or informal activities and do homework. After-school activity directors are typically responsible for managing all aspects of the program, including hiring and managing staff. Requirements vary by position, but typically directors have a degree in child development or education as well as experience working directly with children. After-school programs are in schools, in organizations like the YMCA, and in private organizations and institutions. To learn more about becoming an after-school activity director, visit www.naaweb.org.

Did you know?

While the numbers have risen, out of the roughly 72.2 million fathers in the United States, approximately 209,000 are stay-at-home-dads (U.S. Census Bureau, 2017b).

staff characteristics) and process features (such as the activities available for children and the overall culture of the program).

self-care Unsupervised situations in which children care for themselves at home.

When children are enrolled in high-quality programs, they show positive changes in academic outcomes, their attachment to their school, peer relationships, and self-confidence, and show declines in problem behaviors and drug use (Durlak, Mahoney, Bohnert & Parente, 2010).

Approximately 11 percent of school-age children and early adolescents are reported to be in **self-care**, regularly caring for themselves at home without adult supervision (Laughlin, 2013). This arrangement is advisable only for older children who are mature, responsible, and resourceful and know how to get help in an emergency—and, even then, only if a parent can stay in touch by telephone.

Poverty and Economic Stress

In 1999, about 14 percent of U.S children lived in poverty, and this number stayed relatively stable until about 2006. In 2007, however, the economic recession drove up the proportion of children living in poverty, a trend that has continued along with the economic challenges the United States has faced (Child Trends, 2011). Recent data suggest that about 20 percent of U.S. children up to age 17 lived in poverty in 2015 (Proctor, Semega & Kollar, 2016). The poverty rate for white children was 12 percent. Rates were much higher for black (37 percent) and Hispanic (32 percent) children. Children under 18 living with single mothers were about 5 times more likely to be poor than children living with married couples—36 percent as compared with 7 percent (U.S. Census Bureau, 2017c; Figure 13.1).

Poor children are more likely than other children to have emotional or behavioral problems (Wadsworth et al., 2008). In addition, their cognitive potential and school performance suffer greatly (Najman et al., 2009).

Poverty can harm children's development through a multitude of pathways. Parents who live in poverty are likely to become anxious, depressed, and irritable and thus may become less affectionate with and responsive to their children. There may be increased levels of parent-child conflict and harsh discipline. Moreover, poverty also affects where children go to school and the neighborhood they live in, features that can exacerbate child stressors. These features in turn also affect parents and their perceived stress. In short, there are cascades of negative interactions that can have a deleterious effect on child outcomes. These outcomes include physical health, behaviors, mental health, and cognitive and intellectual development (Chaudry & Wimer, 2016; Morris et al., 2017; Yoshikawa, Aber & Beardslee, 2012).

Fortunately, this pattern is not inevitable. Effective parenting can buffer children from the effects of poverty. Effective family interventions promote positive parent-child interactions (for example, by encouraging parents to praise their children while also helping them develop reasonable rules and limits) and provide social support for parents (Morris et al., 2017). Parents who can turn to relatives or to other resources for emotional support, help with child care, and child-rearing information often can parent their children more effectively (Brody, Kim, Murry & Brown, 2004). Community organizations, schools, and pediatricians can also be utilized to effectively provide services and advocacy for children affected by poverty (Ellis & Dietz, 2017; Dreyer, Chung, Szilagyi & Wong, 2016; Durlak, Weissberg, Dymnicki, Taylor & Schellinger, 2011).

FAMILY STRUCTURE

Family structure in the United States has changed dramatically. In earlier generations, the vast majority of children grew up in families with two married parents. Today, although about 2 out of 3 children under 18 live with two married biological, adoptive, or stepparents, that proportion represents a dramatic decline—from 85 percent in 1960 to 65 percent in 2015 (Child Trends Databank, 2015). About 10 percent of two-parent families are stepfamilies resulting from divorce and remarriage, and nearly 4 percent are cohabiting families (Kreider & Fields, 2005). Other increasingly common family types are gay and lesbian families and grandparent-headed families.

Other things being equal, children tend to do better in families with two continuously married parents than in cohabiting, divorced, single-parent, or stepfamilies (Brown, 2010). The distinction is even stronger for children growing up with two *happily* married parents. This suggests that the parents' relationship, the quality of their parenting, and their ability to create a favorable family atmosphere may affect children's adjustment more than their marital status does (Amato, 2005).

With respect to variations in two-parent family structures, there are relatively few differences in child well-being regardless of whether children live with biological cohabiting families, married/cohabiting stepfamilies, or blended families

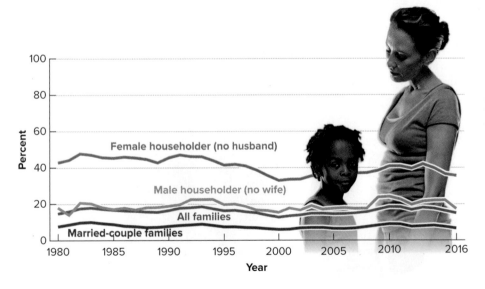

FIGURE 13.1 Percentage of Related Children under 18 Living in Poverty by Family Structure, 1980–2016

Source: U.S. Census Bureau. Current Population Survey, Annual Social and Economic Supplements. "Historical Poverty Tables: People and Families–1959 to 2016." 2017.

©Image Source/Veer

2017a). More than 1.5 million children are involved in divorces each year (National Institute of Mental Health, 2002).

Adjusting to Divorce   When Emily was 6, her parents divorced. In the year following the divorce, Emily was sometimes anxious and upset, and she missed her father as she was no longer able to see him on a daily basis. She wondered if her parents got divorced because of something she did. She was also sad that she and her mother and brother had to move away from their old neighborhood, although she was able to keep attending the same school. However, in about a year, Emily adjusted to her new reality and seemed to return to her previous sunny self. What factors might account for Emily's adjustment? What might be the long-term effects of divorce?

Divorce is stressful for children. First, there is the stress of marital conflict and then of parental separation and the departure of one parent, usually the father. Children may not fully understand what is happening. Of course, divorce is stressful for the parents as well and may negatively affect their parenting. The family's standard of living is likely to drop, and, if a parent moves away, a child's relationship with the noncustodial parent may suffer (Kelly & Emery, 2003; Amato, 2014). A divorced parent's remarriage can increase the stress on children, renewing feelings of loss (Ahrons & Tanner, 2003; Amato, 2003).

Family conflict is a consistently identified risk factor for children (Stallman & Ohan, 2016). Thus, when children exhibit emotional or behavioral problems after a divorce this may actually reflect the influence of parental conflict *before* the divorce. Children whose parents later divorce show more anxiety, depression, or antisocial behavior prior to the divorce than those whose parents stay married (Strohschein, 2012). In fact, if predivorce parental discord is chronic, overt, or destructive, children may be as well or better off after a divorce (Amato, 2003; 2005). Additionally, the quality of parenting prior to divorce matters as well, with maternal sensitivity and support acting as a protective factor for some children whose families divorced (Weaver & Schofield, 2015).

There is wide variability in children's adjustment to divorce. A child's adjustment to divorce depends in part on the child's age, maturity, gender, temperament, and psychosocial adjustment before the divorce. Children who are younger when their parents divorce tend to suffer from more behavioral problems. By contrast, older children are at higher risk with respect to academic and social outcomes (Lansford, 2009). Although previous research suggested boys were at higher risk than girls (Amato, 2005), current data suggest the relationship between gender and negative outcomes is less clear, with no clear disadvantage identified for boys. What is

Divorce is stressful for children but most eventually show good adjustment. Protective factors include parental sensitivity and support and cordial co-parenting relationships.

©S. Olsson/PhotoAlto

(Artis, 2007). Family instability, however, may be harmful. Children who experience more family transitions, such as a divorce or a remarriage, were more likely to have behavior problems and to engage in delinquent behavior than children in stable families (Fomby & Cherlin, 2007; Magnuson & Berger, 2009). The negative effect of family transitions appears to be stronger if they occur earlier in development and for boys (Cavanagh & Huston, 2008).

A father's frequent and positive involvement with his child is directly related to the child's well-being and physical, cognitive, and social development (McLanahan, Tach & Schneider, 2013; Cabrera et al., 2000). Unfortunately, in 2014, more than 23.6 percent of children lived in homes without a biological father present (National Fatherhood Initiative, 2016).

Divorced Parents

Family structure in the United States has changed dramatically. In earlier generations, the vast majority of children grew up in families with two married parents. The United States has one of the highest divorce rates in the world. The divorce rate rose from 1960 (2.2 per 1,000 people) to its peak level in 1980 (3.5 per 1,000 people) (Amato, 2014; Cherlin, 2010). Since then the divorce rate has slowly dropped, and it currently stands at 3.2 per 1,000 people (Centers for Disease Control,

clear, however, is that children who showed poor adjustment prior to their parents' divorce generally fare worse in the long run (Lansford, 2009). Although children whose parents divorce are at slightly higher risk for negative outcomes, most do eventually show good adjustment (Amato & Anthony, 2014).

Custody, Visitation, and Co-parenting

Emily was lucky—her parents established a cordial co-parenting relationship and were able to successfully negotiate conflict, making her adjustment to divorce less painful than it might have been. She spent most of her time at her mother's house, although every other weekend was spent at her father's house, and the holidays were evenly divided between them. Her parents got along well enough that they were both able to attend important events for Emily—like her birthday parties and school plays—without any overt tension, and while Emily still wished sometimes they all lived together in the same house, most of the time she accepted this arrangement without much thought.

There are various types of custody arrangements. In most divorce cases, the mother gets custody, though paternal custody is a growing trend. Joint custody, shared by both parents, is another arrangement. When parents have joint legal custody, they share the right and responsibility to make decisions regarding the child's welfare. When they have joint physical custody (which is less common), the child lives part-time with each parent.

All else being equal, the research suggests children do better with joint custody (Warshak, 2014; Baude, Pearson & Drapeau, 2016), perhaps because fathers are more likely to remain involved. Many children of divorce say that losing contact with a father is one of the most painful results of divorce (Fabricius, 2003). Children living with divorced mothers adjust better when the father pays child support, which may indicate a strong tie between father and child and cooperation between the ex-spouses (Kelly & Emery, 2003).

When one parent has custody, children do better after divorce if the custodial parent is warm, supportive, and authoritative; monitors the child's activities; and holds age-appropriate expectations. In addition, conflict between the divorced parents needs to be minimal, and the nonresident parent should remain closely involved (Stallman & Ohan, 2016; Ahrons & Tanner, 2003). Conflict, as before divorce, is damaging and can result in lower life satisfaction, negative affect, externalizing symptoms, and adolescent delinquency (Lamela, Figueiredo, Bastos & Feinberg, 2016; Teubert & Pinquart, 2010; Esmaeili & Yaacob, 2011). High conflict between parents, especially if a child is drawn into the conflict and forced to choose sides, can be extremely damaging (Fosco & Grych, 2010).

Co-parenting is a parenting relationship in which two people, who may or may not be romantically involved, work together in a cooperative fashion to raise a child. With respect to divorced couples, it involves shared responsibility and active consultation between both partners on parenting decisions. Co-parenting has been consistently linked to positive child outcomes (Teubert & Pinquart, 2010), in part because it is strongly associated with more frequent contact between father and child (Sobolewski & King, 2005). For instance, children whose parents are able to parent cooperatively following a divorce tend to have closer ties to their fathers—and fewer behavioral problems—than children whose parents have more conflict following divorce (Amato, Kane & James, 2011). Unfortunately, cooperative parenting is not the norm (Amato, 2005). Parent education programs that teach separated or divorced couples how to prevent or deal with conflict, keep lines of communication open, and help children adjust to divorce have been introduced in many states with measurable success (Ferraro, Malespin, Oehme, Bruker & Opel, 2016).

Long-Term Effects of Divorce Most children of divorce adjust well (Amato & Anthony, 2014). However, there are nonetheless negative consequences. Children who experience their parent's divorce are more likely to develop internalizing or externalizing problems (Lansford et al., 2006), to have emotional issues, to initiate sexual activity early, to be at risk for depression and suicidal thoughts (D'Onofrio et al., 2006), and, in adolescence, to be at risk for antisocial behavior and difficulties with authority figures (Amato, 2005; Kelly & Emery, 2003). As adults, they are more likely to have poorer psychological well-being and a higher risk of depression (Amato, 2005; Uphold-Carrier & Utz, 2012).

Children of divorced parents also tend to have lower academic achievement (Lansford, 2009). In one study across 14 countries, children from divorced families were less likely to graduate from college, and this difference was most pronounced for children who came from highly educated families (Bernardi & Radl, 2014). This may account for the finding that children of divorce are more likely to have lower SES as adults (Amato, 2005; Gruber, 2004). Moreover, there are indications that these effects may persist across generations. Parental divorce can result in lower educational achievement in adult children of divorce; and the challenges created by this decline in achievement can then affect the subsequent generation in a similar fashion (Amato & Cheadle, 2005).

The anxiety connected with parental divorce may surface as children enter adulthood and form intimate relationships of their own. For example, children whose parents divorced have

WHAT DO YOU DO?

Forensic Psychologist

A forensic psychologist works in the field of criminal justice. In relation to cases involving children, forensic psychologists may be involved in custody disputes, investigating suspected child abuse, and assessing parental visitation risk. Forensic psychologists typically have doctoral degrees and then must receive certification from the American Board of Forensic Psychology. Forensic psychologists typically work within the court system, in prisons, and in private practice. To learn more about becoming a forensic psychologist, go to www.abfp.com.

higher separation and divorce rates (Mustonen, Huurre, Kiviruusu, Huakkala & Aro, 2011). Having experienced their parents' divorce, some young adults are afraid of making commitments that might end in disappointment (Glenn & Marquardt, 2001). Although these differences are small, as adults, the children of divorce tend to have a greater chance of having a birth outside marriage. Their marriages tend to be less satisfying and are more likely to end in divorce (Amato, 2005). Additionally, adults whose parents divorced when they were children and who endured multiple or prolonged separation from a parent later show compromised parenting themselves, including lower sensitivity and warmth, and more parent-child conflict and physical punishment (Friesen, Horwood, Fergusson & Woodward, 2017).

However, much depends on how young people resolve and interpret the experience of parental divorce. Some who saw a high degree of conflict between their parents are able to learn from that negative example and to form highly intimate relationships themselves (Shulman, Scharf, Lumer & Maurer, 2001). Interventions can help. One counseling intervention designed to improve children's post-divorce adjustment focused on increasing effective child coping strategies, reducing negative thoughts about divorce-related stressors, and improving mother-child relationships showed positive effects at both 6 months and 6 years after the counseling sessions had concluded (Velez, Wolchik, Tein & Sandler, 2011). Thus, negative effects are not inevitable.

One-Parent Families

One-parent families can result from divorce or separation, unwed parenthood, or death. With rising rates of divorce and of parenthood outside of marriage, the number of single-parent families in the United States has increased by approximately 3.5 times since 1960 (U.S. Census Bureau, 2017a). Currently, about 27 percent of children live in a single-parent household. More than half of all black children live with a single parent, as compared with 21 percent of non-Hispanic white children and 31 percent of Hispanic children (Vespa, Lewis & Kreider, 2013). The issue is even more pressing when low-income families are examined, with 66 percent of African American families and 35 percent of both non-Hispanic and Hispanic white children living in single-parent homes (Mather, 2010). Although children are far more likely to live with a single mother than with a single father, the number of father-only families has more than quadrupled since 1960, due largely to the increase in paternal custody after divorce (U.S. Census Bureau, 2017a; Fields, 2004; Figure 13.2).

Children in single-parent families do fairly well overall but tend to lag socially and educationally behind peers in two-parent families (Waldfogel, Craigie & Brooks-Gunn, 2010; Brown, 2010). Children living with married parents tend to have more daily interaction with their parents, are read to more often, progress more steadily in school, and participate more in extracurricular activities than children living with a single parent (Lugaila, 2003).

However, negative outcomes for children in one-parent families are not inevitable. The child's age and level of development, the family's financial circumstances and educational level, whether there are frequent moves, and a nonresident father's involvement make a difference (Amato, 2005; Seltzer, 2000; Ricciuti, 2004). One important variable appears to be family stability, or whether or not children grow up with the same parent(s) that were present at birth (Heiland & Liu, 2006). In general, single-parent families are more unstable than married families (Craigie, 2008). However, when single-parent or cohabiting families are stable, children fare as well on cognitive and health outcomes as children from two-parent families (Waldfogel, Craigie & Brooks-Gunn, 2010). Income is a key factor; many of the negative effects of single-parenthood appear to be driven by lower socioeconomic status. Because single parents often lack resources, potential risks to children in these families can be reduced through increased access to economic, social, educational, and parenting support. Indeed, in countries with a more robust welfare support system for single mothers, children in such families report higher levels of well-being than children in countries who do not provide as much aid to single mothers (Bjarnason et al., 2012).

Cohabiting Families

Approximately 20 percent of births in the United States are to cohabitating couples—in other words, unmarried partners living together (Smock & Greenland, 2010), and about

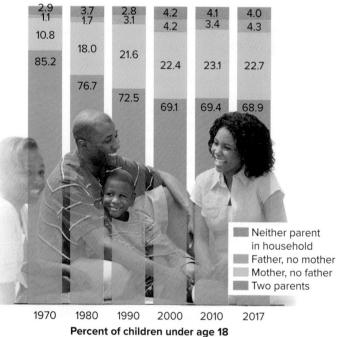

			Neither parent in household
			Father, no mother
			Mother, no father
			Two parents

1970 1980 1990 2000 2010 2017
Percent of children under age 18

FIGURE 13.2 **Living Arrangements of Children Younger than 18, 1970–2017**

Source: U.S. Census Bureau. "Historical Living Arrangements of Children Under 18 Years Old: 1960 to Present." 2017.
©Fancy/Alamy

40 percent of children will spend at least part of their life in a cohabitating household (Manning, 2017). Cohabiting families are similar in many ways to married families, but the parents tend to be more disadvantaged (Mather, 2010). They traditionally have less income and education, report poorer relationships, and have more mental health problems. Research shows worse emotional, behavioral, and academic outcomes for children living with cohabiting biological parents than for those living with married biological parents (Waldfogel et al., 2010; Brown, 2004). However, this difference in outcomes is primarily the result of differences in economic resources and family instability (Manning, 2017). Parenting differences, by contrast, explain only a small amount of the variation in child outcomes for cohabiting versus married couples (Thomson & McLanahan, 2012).

Cohabiting families are more likely to break up than married families. Although about 40 percent of unwed mothers are living with the child's father at the time of birth, 25 percent of cohabiting parents are no longer together 1 year later, and 31 percent break up after 5 years (Amato, 2005). The average cohabiting relationship lasts 18 months (Kennedy & Bumpass, 2008). However, there are social class differences. When cohabiting couples are from higher social classes, cohabitation is more likely to be seen as a step to marriage, and eventually lead to marriage. By contrast, couples from lower socioeconomic classes are more likely to see their cohabiting relationship end, or to enter into a number of cohabiting unions over the course of a lifetime (Kroeger & Smock, 2014).

Stepfamilies

Most divorced parents eventually remarry, and many unwed mothers marry men who were not the father of their children, forming step-, or blended, families. Sixteen percent of U.S. children live in blended families (Kreider & Ellis, 2011).

Adjusting to a new stepparent may be stressful. A child's loyalties to an absent or dead parent may interfere with forming ties to a stepparent (Amato, 2005). For example, when children are emotionally closer to a nonresident biological parent, this is associated with increased levels of stress during stepfamily formation in comparison to children who are not close to their nonresident parent (Jensen, Shafer & Holmes, 2017). Both children and parents have to navigate shifting relationships, adapt to a new power structure in the family, and adjust to household changes. Studies have found small to moderate, but consistent, negative effects for children living in stepparent families when compared to married families (Sweeney, 2010; Barrett & Turner, 2005; Hofferth, 2006). Adjustment to the stepparents and the potential negative influence of that on development appear to be influenced by family relationships prior to the formation of the stepfamily.

The popular ABC sitcom Modern Family includes a characteristically modern family—gay couple Cameron and Mitchell and their adopted daughter, Lily, a Vietnamese girl.
©AF archive/Alamy

When there is a good relationship with the biological parent (usually the mother) before the introduction of a stepparent, children show more positive relationships with their stepparent and better adjustment (King, Amato & Lindstrom, 2015; Jensen & Shafer, 2013).

Gay or Lesbian Parents

An estimated 6 million U.S. children and adolescents have at least one gay or lesbian parent (Gates, 2013). About 25 percent of lesbian couples and 7 percent of gay couples have children living with them (Carpenter & Gates, 2008). Some gays and lesbians are raising children born of previous heterosexual relationships. Others conceive by artificial means, use surrogate mothers, or adopt children.

Did you know?

An estimated 220,000 children under age 18 live in same-sex couple households (Gates, 2013). Same sex parents are 4 times more likely to be raising adopted children than different sex parents (Gates, 2013).

©Billy Farrell/BFA/Shutterstock

A considerable body of research has examined the development of children of gays and lesbians and has found no special concerns (APA, 2004, July). There are *no* consistent differences between homosexual and heterosexual parents in emotional health or parenting skills and attitudes; and where there are differences, they tend to favor gay and lesbian parents (Golombok et al., 2013; Meezan & Rauch, 2005; Pawelski et al., 2006; Wainright, Russell & Patterson, 2004; Biblarz & Stacey, 2010). Gay or lesbian parents usually have positive relationships with their children, and the children are no more likely than children raised by heterosexual parents to have emotional, social, academic, or psychological problems (APA, 2004, July; Perrin, Siegel & Committee on Psychosocial Aspects of Child and Family Health, 2013; Fedewa, Black & Ahn, 2015; Manning, Fettro & Lamidi, 2014). Furthermore, children of gays and lesbians are no more likely to be homosexual or to be confused about their gender than are children of heterosexuals (Fedewa et al., 2015; Meezan & Rauch, 2005; Pawelski et al., 2006; Wainright et al., 2004).

Such findings have social policy implications for legal decisions on custody and visitation disputes, foster care, and adoptions (Manning et al., 2014). In the face of controversy, several states have considered or adopted legislation sanctioning second-parent adoption by

same-sex partners. The American Academy of Pediatrics supports legislative and legal efforts to permit a partner in a same-sex couple to adopt the other partner's child (AAP Committee on Psychosocial Aspects of Child and Family Health, 2002).

Adoptive Families

Adoption is found in all cultures throughout history. It is not only for infertile people; single people, older people, gay and lesbian couples, and people who already have biological children have become adoptive parents. In 2010, 1.5 million U.S. children under 18 (about 2 percent) lived with at least one adoptive parent (Kreider & Lofquist, 2010) and about 120,000 children are adopted annually (Child Welfare Information Gateway, 2016). An estimated 60 percent of legal adoptions are by stepparents or relatives, usually grandparents (Kreider, 2003).

Adoptions usually take place through public or private agencies. Traditionally, agency adoptions were intended to be confidential, with no contact between the birth mother and the adoptive parents. However, independent adoptions, made by direct agreement between birth parents and adoptive parents, have become more common. Often these are *open adoptions*, in which both parties share information or have direct contact with the child (Grotevant, 2012).

Studies suggest that the presumed risks of open adoption, such as fear that a birth mother who knows her child's whereabouts will try to reclaim the child, are overstated (Grotevant, McRoy, Eide & Fravel, 1994). In fact, birth mothers who participate in open adoptions have less unresolved grief than those that participate in closed adoptions, and many tend to show less interest in contact as the child gets older and they become more certain the child is being well cared for (Grotevant, McRoy, Wrobel & Ayers-Lopez, 2013). Whether an adoption is open or closed bears no relation to the children's adjustment or to the parents' satisfaction with the adoption, both of which are generally high (Berry, Dylla, Barth & Needell, 1998). Likewise, adoptive parents of adolescents report no significant difference in their children's adjustment whether the adoption is open or confidential (VonKorff, Grotevant & McRoy, 2006).

While adopted children do tend to have more psychological and academic difficulties than non-adopted children, these differences are small, and most adopted children fall within the normal range of development (Palacios & Brodzinsky, 2010; Haugaard, 1998). Age at adoption matters, however. For example, one large meta-analysis of more than 60 studies including 17,767 children showed that

Pop singer Madonna and her adopted children David and Mercy.
©AFP/Getty Images

adopted children were not at risk of lower intelligence. However, those children adopted after the age of 1, especially if they experienced significant pre-adoption adversity, were more likely to show lower school achievement (Juffer et al., 2011). Children adopted after the age of 1 are also more likely to show disturbances in their attachment patterns than children adopted before their first birthday (van IJzendoorn & Bakermans-Kranenburg, 2009). Similar findings have emerged for adjustment problems. Children adopted in infancy are least likely to have adjustment problems, as are younger children (Julian, 2013; Sharma, McGue & Benson, 1996b). Any problems that do occur may surface during middle childhood, when children become more aware of differences in the way families are formed (Freeark et al., 2005), or in adolescence (Goodman, Emery & Haugaard, 1998; Sharma, McGue & Benson, 1996a), particularly among boys (Freeark et al., 2005) and international adoptees (Juffer et al., 2011).

The demographics of adopted children have changed dramatically in the past 50 years. Prior to the 1960s, most adopted children in the United States were healthy, white infants, adopted as newborns and surrendered by unmarried teen mothers. Adoption rates for children born to women of color were extremely low. In the 1960s a variety of social and economic changes, including the growing acceptance of single motherhood and the rise of social support programs, led to an increase in the number of women who opted to keep their babies. Additionally, the growing availability of birth control and the legalization of abortion led to a decrease in unintentional pregnancies. These changes resulted in fewer white babies available for adoption (Brodzinsky & Pinderhughes, 2014), and thus prospective parents began to look elsewhere for adoption. Currently, only about 37 percent of adopted children are non-Hispanic white. The remainder are black (23 percent), Hispanic (15 percent), Asian (15 percent), and other (9 percent). Transracial adoptions, where at least one parent is of a different race than the child, are common and comprise about 40 percent of adoptions (Vandivere, Malm & Radel, 2009). Most transracial adoptions involve white parents adopting an Asian or Latin American child (Kreider, 2003). Rules governing interracial adoption vary from state to state; some states give priority to same-race adoption, whereas others require that race not be a factor in approval of an adoption.

As the number of babies available for adoption in the United States declined, adoptions of foreign-born children rose from the 1970s to a peak of nearly 23,000 children in 2004; rates have since declined significantly due to changing international adoption protocols (Bosch et al., 2003; Crary, 2007; U.S. Department of State, 2017). Does foreign adoption entail special problems? Aside from the possibility of malnourishment or medical conditions in children from developing countries (Bosch et al., 2003), a number of studies find no significant problems with the children's psychological adjustment, school adjustment, and performance (Palacios & Brodzinsky, 2010). However, when foreign adoptees reach adolescence, they may experience feelings of loss of their native culture and growing awareness of racism and discrimination in their adopted culture. Parents who expose their adopted children to experiences that help them identify with their native culture and speak with their children about racism and discrimination may help buffer adopted children from negative effects (Lee, Grotevant, Hellerstedt, Gunnar & The Minnesota International Adoption Project Team, 2006).

SIBLING RELATIONSHIPS

"Give it back!" Emily screamed at her brother John, "It's mine." "No fair," whined 6-year-old John back, "it was supposed to be for sharing, so you have to share." Their mother stepped into the room and sighed. "Patch it up guys, or we won't go to the park later," she warned. "Emily, you're older. You should know better." While Emily and John scowled at each other for a few minutes, within a short while they were once again playing together happily.

Sibling relations have both positive and negative aspects to them. Having a warm and supportive sibling relationship is associated with better adjustment (Noller, 2005), social competence (Kim, McHale, Crouter & Osgood, 2007), and better emotion regulation (Kennedy & Kramer, 2008). Sibling relationships are also marked by conflict. While generally perceived as negative, conflict can nonetheless be a laboratory for conflict resolution. Siblings are motivated to make up after quarrels because they know they will see each other every day. They learn that expressing anger does not end a relationship. Through these conflicts, siblings learn about others' points of view, negotiation, and problem solving (McHale, Updegraff & Whiteman, 2012).

However, sibling conflict is not always beneficial. High sibling conflict has been associated with internalizing (e.g., depression and anxiety) and externalizing (e.g., delinquency and aggression) problems as well as risky behaviors (Buist, Dekovic & Prinzie, 2013; Solmeyer, McHale & Crouter, 2014). Siblings can exert a negative effect via modeling antisocial actions, introducing undesirable behaviors to younger siblings, or encouraging antisocial acts or collusion against parents (McHale et al., 2012). For example, when older siblings use drugs or alcohol, or engage in early sexual activity, their younger siblings are more likely to do so as well (Low, Shortt & Snyder, 2012; McHale, Bissell & Kim, 2009). Interestingly, there is also another side to the positive effects of sibling warmth. In the presence of antisocial behaviors, sibling warmth can actually be a risk factor (McHale, Bissell & Kim, 2009). For example, an older teen who is abusing substances might be more likely to introduce those substances to a sibling he is close to than to one he is not.

Gender, too, appears to be an influence on sibling relationships. Sisters are higher in sibling intimacy than brothers or mixed-sex dyads (Kim, McHale, Osgood & Crouter, 2006). Children are more likely to squabble with same-sex siblings. However, two brothers quarrel (Cicirelli, 1976; 1995) and show less caring and intimacy than any other combination (Cole & Kerns, 2001). Additionally, the negative influence of an older antisocial sibling on a younger sibling, in some research, has been limited to same-sex siblings (Buist, 2010).

Sibling conflict and warmth are direct influences. However, siblings also influence each other indirectly, through their impact on each other's relationship with their parents. Parents' experience with an older sibling influences their expectations and treatment of a younger one (Brody, 2004). And behavior patterns a child establishes with parents tend to spill over into the child's behavior with siblings. When a parent-child relationship is warm and affectionate, siblings tend to have positive relationships as well. When the parent-child relationship is conflictual, sibling conflict is more likely (Pike, Coldwell & Dunn, 2005).

The Child in the Peer Group

Emily was glad her parents' divorce did not mean she had to change schools. Although she had a number of friends and was well liked by most of her peers, she was by nature a bit shy, and the thought of navigating a new social world filled her with dread. Luckily, she and her best friend were able to continue to play together and even ended up in the same classroom that year.

Perspectives on Diversity

©Digital Vision/Getty Images

BULLYING ACROSS THE WORLD

Bullying is the use of power and aggression to control, cause distress to, or harm someone or destroy property, and can include nonphysical acts such as name-calling, spreading rumors, and taunting.

In a global status report, UNESCO (2017) examined bullying prevalence rates across a number of countries. In France, 32 percent of students reported being the victim of verbal bullying, and 35 percent were the victims of physical bullying. In Australia, 27 percent of students reported experiencing frequent bullying and 9 percent admitted to bullying others. In Kenya, between 63 and 82 percent of students reported being subjected to various types of bullying, and in South Africa, more than half of respondents had experienced bullying. Reports vary widely—in Sweden, 15 percent reported bullying, while in Lithuania 67 percent of students reported being bullied. Though the statistics vary from country to country, bullying is a global problem and it is having a negative impact on the world's children.

Bullying occurs regardless of whether a country is wealthy or poor. In 2014 UNICEF released a report including information collected from approximately 100,000 young people in 18 countries (UNICEF, 2014). Bullying occurred in every country measured, ranging from 7 percent in Tajikistan to a high of 74 percent in Samoa. Wealthy countries likewise showed a similar range, with prevalence rates ranging from a low of 14 percent in the Czech Republic and a high of 69 percent in Latvia and Romania.

Just as in the United States, research shows that children may suffer negative social, behavioral, and psychological outcomes as a result of bullying. Moreover, cross-cultural research conducted with adults in 30 European countries indicated that those adults who had been bullied as children showed lower life satisfaction (29 percent) than those who had not been bullied (40 percent) (UNESCO, 2017). Thus, both the immediate negative consequences and the long-term effects of bullying make it an issue worthy of attention. Health promotion and prevention strategies need to address bullying problems to make the world safer for all.

In middle childhood the peer group comes into its own. Groups form naturally among children who live near one another or go to school together and often consist of children of the same racial or ethnic origin and similar socioeconomic status. Children who play together are usually close in age and of the same sex (Hartup, 1992; Pellegrini, Kato, Blatchford & Baines, 2002).

How does the peer group influence children? What determines their acceptance by peers and their ability to make friends?

POSITIVE AND NEGATIVE EFFECTS OF PEER RELATIONS

As children begin to move away from parental influence, the peer group opens new perspectives. The peer group helps children learn how to adjust their needs and desires to those of others, when to yield, and when to stand firm. Within the context of peer groups, children develop skills needed for sociability and intimacy, and they gain a sense of belonging. They are motivated to achieve, and they attain a sense of identity.

The peer group can sometimes foster antisocial tendencies. While, some degree of conformity to group standards is healthy, it is unhealthy when it becomes destructive or prompts young people to act against their better judgment. It is usually in the company of peers that some children shoplift and begin to use drugs (Dishion & Tipsord, 2011; Hartup, 1992).

> **prejudice** Unfavorable attitude toward members of certain groups outside one's own, especially racial or ethnic groups.

Unfortunately, peer groups may also reinforce **prejudice**: unfavorable attitudes toward outsiders, especially members of certain racial or ethnic groups. Children tend to be biased toward children like themselves. These biases peak at about 5 to 7 years of age and then decrease through late childhood. As children move into adolescence, social context and what children learn from others seem to matter more (Raabe & Beelman, 2011).

Children can be negatively affected by discrimination. The perception of being discriminated against has been linked to reductions in well-being, self-esteem, and life satisfaction, and increases in anxiety, depression, and conduct problems (Schmitt, Branscombe, Postmes & Garcia, 2014;

Brody et al., 2006). However, prejudice is not inevitable. In one study, children who were prejudiced against refugees showed reductions in that bias when they were read stories about close friendships between English children and refugee children, followed by group discussions (Cameron, Rutland, Brown & Douch, 2006). In another study, the degree of bias toward immigrants was related to whether the adolescents in the study had immigrant friends. Those who did were more tolerant of differences and showed less bias toward immigrants (van Zalk & Kerr, 2014). Group norms also matter. Children whose social groups or schools have a norm of inclusion are less likely to show prejudiced behavior (Nesdale, 2011; Tropp, O'Brien & Migacheva, 2014; Tezanos-Pinto, Bratt & Brown, 2010). Intervention programs, including direct or extended contact, imagined contact, the promotion of empathy, and perspective-taking, have been moderately successful at reducing prejudice (Beelmann & Hienemann, 2014; Jones & Rutland, 2018).

GENDER AND PEER GROUPS

Boys' and girls' peer groups engage in different types of activities. Groups of boys more consistently pursue strongly gender-typed activities (Rose & Rudolf, 2006), while girls are more likely to engage in cross-gender activities, such as academic clubs (McHale, Kim, Whiteman & Crouter, 2004). Boys play in large groups with well-defined leadership hierarchies and engage in more competitive and rough-and-tumble play. Girls have more intimate conversations characterized by prosocial interactions and shared confidences (Rose & Rudolph, 2006). Boys and girls prefer different characteristics in their friends. Boys report liking friends high in positive affect and low in anxiety, and they are not overly concerned with how empathic their friends are. Girls, by contrast, prefer friends high in empathy and optimism, but low in positive affect (Oberle, Schonert-Reichl & Thomson, 2010).

Why do children segregate themselves by sex and engage in such different activities? One of the most clearly identified reasons is because of boys' higher activity levels and more vigorous play (Pellegrini & Archer, 2005; Trost, Rozencranz & Dzewatowski, 2011). However, it also appears that socialization influences are at play. Even very active girls often end up in same-sex groups (Pellegrini, Long, Roseth, Bohm & Van Ryzin, 2007). One reason may be that same-sex peer groups may help children learn gender-appropriate behaviors and incorporate gender roles into their self-concept. A sense of being typical of one's gender and being content with that gender increases self-esteem and well-being, whereas feeling pressure—from parents, oneself, or peers—to conform to gender stereotypes lessens well-being (Yunger et al., 2004). Indeed, such pressure may result in children adopting more gender-typical behaviors as a result. In one study, peer harassment predicted decreases in gender-atypical behavior for boys. For girls, at least those with many female friends, peer harassment was not associated with a decrease in gender atypicality (Lee & Troop-Gordon, 2011), perhaps because girls are generally subject to less pressure to conform to gender norms at this age (Katz & Walsh, 1991).

POPULARITY

As children age, peer relationships become increasingly important. Because children most often interact with each other within the context of school and in groups, researchers have developed means by which to assess their standing in the social group.

Much of research in child development depends on asking children the right questions in the right way. If a researcher asked schoolchildren to tell her the social ranking of all the children in a classroom, she would most likely be met with a blank stare. However, children can easily say who they like to play with, who they like the most, or who they think other kids like the most. This is known as a *positive nomination.*

Children can also easily describe which children they don't like to play with, like the least, or think other kids don't like—this is a *negative nomination.* By asking these types of questions of every child in a classroom, a researcher can use the aggregated responses to get an overall score, or tally, for each child. The tally may be composed of positive nominations, negative nominations, or no nominations. This measure is known as *sociometric popularity* (Figure 13.3).

Sociometrically *popular* children receive many positive nominations and few negative nominations. They generally

FIGURE 13.3 Measured Popularity: Five Peer Status Groups

(rejected): ©MBI/Alamy; (neglected): ©AP Images; (average): ©Image Source/AP Images; (controversial): ©Andi Berger/Shutterstock; (popular): ©Blend Images/Image Source

have good cognitive abilities, are high achievers, are good at solving social problems, are kind and help other children, and are assertive without being disruptive or aggressive. Their superior social skills make others enjoy being with them (Cillessen & Mayeux, 2004; LaFontana & Cillessen, 2002).

Children can be unpopular in one of two ways. Some children are *rejected*, and they receive a large number of negative nominations. Other children are *neglected* and receive few nominations of any kind. Some unpopular children are aggressive; others are hyperactive, inattentive, or withdrawn (Dodge, Coie, Pettit & Price, 1990; LaFontana & Cillessen, 2002). Still others act silly and immature or anxious and uncertain. Unpopular children are often insensitive to other children's feelings and do not adapt well to new situations (Bierman, Smoot & Aumiller, 1993).

Other children can be *average* in their ratings and do not receive an unusual number of either positive or negative nominations. Finally, some children are *controversial* and receive many positive and negative nominations, indicating that some children like them a great deal and some dislike them a great deal. Less is known about outcomes related to average and controversial sociometric categories.

Popularity is important in middle childhood. Schoolchildren whose peers like them are likely to be well adjusted as adolescents. Those who have trouble getting along with peers are more likely to develop psychological problems, drop out of school, or become delinquent (Dishion & Tipsort, 2011; Mrug et al., 2012; Hartup, 1992). Peer rejection has also been linked to lower levels of classroom participation and poor academic achievement (Ladd, Herald-Brown & Reiser, 2008; Wentzel & Muenks, 2016).

Children's sociometric popularity is influenced by family context. It is often in the family that children acquire behaviors that affect popularity. In one study, fourth-grade children were more socially competent when they were from families in which the parent-child relationships were warm and nurturing, parents provided direct advice about how to manage conflictual social interactions, and parents provided children with appropriate high-quality peer experiences (McDowell & Parke, 2009). By contrast, parents who are very controlling or negative in their interactions with their children are more likely to have children who are aggressive, low in social competence, and rejected by peers (Li, Putallaz & Su, 2011; Attili, Vermigli & Roazzi, 2011; Attili, Vermigli & Roazzi, 2010).

Did you know?

Culture also can affect criteria for popularity. In the late 1990s, China shifted from a collectivist system in which the government owned all means of production and distribution to a more individualistic and competitive market economy with private ownership. In 1990, shy children were accepted by peers and were high in academic achievement, leadership, and teacher-rated competence. However, by 2002, the results were the reverse. Shy children were more likely to be rejected, depressed, and rated by teachers as low in competence (Chen, Cen, Li & He, 2005). Similar findings were obtained in more recent research on urban and rural children. Shy urban children were more likely to be depressed or have social and school problems. However, shy rural children, in the more traditional environment of the countryside, had more positive outcomes (Chen, Wang & Wang, 2009). In the quasi-capitalist society that China has become, social assertiveness and initiative may be more highly appreciated and encouraged than in the past, and shyness and sensitivity may lead to social and psychological difficulties for children.

FRIENDSHIP

Friends are an important developmental influence. Children look for friends who are like them in age, sex, activity level, and interests (McDonald et al., 2013; Mehta & Strough, 2009; Macdonald-Wallis, Jago, Page, Brockman & Thompson, 2011). Though children tend to choose friends with similar ethnic backgrounds, cross-racial/ethnic friendships are associated with positive developmental outcomes (Kawabata & Crick, 2008). Friends agree they are friends, derive pleasure from each other's company, and the relationship, unlike that of siblings, is voluntary (Bagwell & Schmidt, 2011).

With their friends, children learn to communicate and cooperate. They help each other weather stressful situations, such as starting at a new school or adjusting to parents' divorce. The inevitable quarrels help children learn to resolve conflicts. In short, friendships are a means by which children practice and hone social interaction skills (Glick & Rose, 2011; Newcomb & Bagwell, 1995). Friendship seems to help children feel good about themselves, although it's also likely that children who feel good about themselves have an easier time making friends.

Children's concepts of friendship and the ways they act with their friends change with age, reflecting cognitive and emotional growth. Preschool friends play together and have preferred playmates, but they are not friends in the same sense that older children are. Children cannot be or have true friends until they achieve the cognitive maturity to consider other people's views and needs as well as their own (Dodge, Coie & Lynam, 2006; Hartup & Stevens, 1999). Friendship among school-age children is thus deeper, more reciprocal, and more stable.

School-age children distinguish among "best friends," "good friends," and "casual friends" on the basis of intimacy and time spent together. Children this age typically have three to five best friends but usually

Through interactions with friends, children learn to communicate, cooperate, resolve conflicts, and deal with stressful situations.

©John Lund/Sam Diephuis/Blend Images

AGGRESSION AND BULLYING

Aggression declines and changes in form during the early school years. After age 6 or 7, most children become less physically aggressive as they grow less egocentric, more empathic, more cooperative, and better able to communicate. They can now put themselves in someone else's place, understand another person's motives, and find positive ways of asserting themselves. **Instrumental aggression**, aggression aimed at achieving an objective, the hallmark of the preschool period, becomes much less common. However, as aggression declines overall, **hostile aggression**—action intended to hurt another person—proportionately increases (Dodge et al., 2006), often taking verbal rather than physical form (Pellegrini & Archer, 2005). Past research indicated that boys were more likely to engage in more direct aggression and girls were increasingly more likely to engage in social or relational aggression (Archer, 2004). More recent research suggests that the differences have been overstated, calling into question the common portrayal of indirect aggression as a predominantly female form of aggression (Card, Stucky, Sawalani & Little, 2008).

A small minority of children do not learn to control physical aggression (Coie & Dodge, 1998). These children tend to have social and psychological problems, but it is not clear whether aggression causes these problems or is a response to them, or both (Crick & Grotpeter, 1995). Not surprisingly, school-age boys who are physically aggressive may become juvenile delinquents in adolescence (Broidy et al., 2003; Hay, Meldrum, Widdowson & Piquero, 2017). Being a boy, having a reactive temperament, parental separation, early onset of motherhood, and controlling parenting have all been shown to contribute to physical aggression in 6- to 12-year olds (Joussemet et al., 2008). Generally, those children who are high in physical aggression are disliked, although there are indications that how much these children are disliked is moderated by age. Physically aggressive children sometimes can attain higher social status as they get older (Garandeau, Ahn & Rodkin, 2011; Cillessen & Mayeux, 2004).

Relational aggression does not appear to show the same dynamic and has been associated with increased social influence and popularity (Vaillancourt & Hymel, 2006). Girls—those who, for example, talk behind another girl's back or exclude her socially—are sometimes perceived as being among the most popular in the classroom (Cillessen & Mayeux, 2004; Rodkin, Farmer, Pearl & Van Acker, 2000). There is evidence that relationally aggressive children seek out other relationally aggressive children as friends, and that both interaction members then mutually influence each other (Sijtsema et al., 2010; Dijkstra, Berger & Lindenberg, 2011). Children who are high in relational aggression tend to have parents low in positive parenting and high in harsh parenting, mothers who are uninvolved, and fathers who are psychologically controlling (Kawabata, Alink, Tseng, Van IJzendoorn & Crick, 2011).

instrumental aggression Aggressive behavior used as a means of achieving a goal.

hostile aggression Aggressive behavior intended to hurt another person.

play with only one or two at a time (Hartup & Stevens, 1999). School-age girls seem to care less about having many friends than about having a few close friends they can rely on. Boys have more friendships, but they tend to be less intimate and affectionate (Furman & Buhrmester, 1985; Hartup & Stevens, 1999). The prevalence of friends is similar across cultures (French, Purwono & Rodkin, 2012).

Unpopular children can make friends, but they tend to have fewer friends than popular children, and they demonstrate a preference for younger friends, other unpopular children, or children in a different class or a different school (Hartup, 1996; Deptula & Cohen, 2004). This can put children on a negative trajectory, as having few friends or low friendship quality in grade school has been associated longitudinally with loneliness in middle school (Kingery, Erdley & Marshall, 2011).

Adults can help children curb aggression by teaching them how to recognize when they are getting angry and how to control their anger. In a New York City school study, children exposed to a conflict resolution curriculum that involved discussions and group role-playing showed less aggression, fewer behavior problems, and more effective responses to social situations than children who did not participate in the program (Aber, Brown & Jones, 2003).

Aggression and Social Information Processing

What makes some children act aggressively? One answer may lie in the way they process social information.

Instrumental, or *proactive*, aggressors view force and coercion as effective ways to get what they want. They act deliberately, not out of anger. In social learning terms, they are aggressive because they expect to be rewarded for it (Crick & Dodge, 1996). For example, such a child might learn that he can force another child to trade lunch items with him by threatening to hit the other child. If that strategy works, the child has been reinforced for his aggressive acts, and his belief in aggression is confirmed.

Other children are more likely to engage in hostile, or *reactive*, aggression. Such a child might, after being accidentally pushed by someone in the lunch line, assume that the bump was on purpose and push back angrily. All children might sometimes assume the worst of others, but children who habitually assume the worst of others in situations such as these are said to have a **hostile attribution bias**. They quickly conclude, in ambiguous situations, that others were acting with ill intent and are likely to strike out in retaliation or self-defense. In part, this is because they are poor at processing social information. They

tend to be hypervigilant to hostile cues, and, once they attribute hostile intent, generate fewer possible responses for social situations, are more likely to use aggressive responses, and tend to believe that aggression will lead to a successful resolution. Generally, other children then respond to this hostility with aggression, thereby confirming the original hostile attributional bias and strengthening it (Crick & Dodge, 1996; de Castro, Veerman, Koops, Bosch & Monshouwer, 2002). This pattern of behavior has been documented in a variety of different cultures suggesting a universal psychological mechanism underlying at least one aspect of interpersonal conflict (Dodge et al., 2015).

> **hostile attribution bias**
> Tendency for individuals to perceive others as trying to hurt them and to strike out in retaliation or self-defense.

Rejected children and those exposed to harsh parenting also tend to have a hostile attribution bias, as do children who seek dominance and control (Coie & Dodge, 1998; de Castro, Veerman, Koops, Bosch & Monshouwer, 2002; Masten & Coatsworth, 1998; Goraya & Shamama-tus-Sabah, 2013). Because people often *do* become hostile toward someone who acts aggressively toward them, a hostile bias may become a self-fulfilling prophecy, setting in motion a cycle of aggression (Lansford, Malone, Dodge, Pettit & Bates, 2010; de Castro et al., 2002).

Influence of Media on Aggression

"Please, please, please Mom," Emily begged, "I really want to see it! It's only PG-13, and all my friends saw it!"

As television, movies, video games, cell phones, and computers take on larger roles in children's daily lives, it is critical to understand the impact mass media has on children's behavior. Children spend more time on entertainment media than on any other activities except school and sleeping. On average, children spend more than 7 hours a day in front of a television or computer screen (Anderson, Bushman, Donnerstein, Hummer & Warburton, 2015; Rideout, Foehr & Roberts, 2010).

Violence is prevalent in U.S. media. About 6 out of 10 television programs portray violence, usually glamorized, glorified, or trivialized (Yokota & Thompson, 2000). Music videos disproportionately feature violence against women and blacks. The motion picture, music, and video game industries aggressively market violent, adult-rated products to children (AAP Committee on Public Education, 2001). In a study of U.S. children, 40 movies that were rated R for violence were seen by a median of 12.5 percent of an estimated 22 million children aged 10 to 14 (Worth et al., 2008).

Because of the significant amount of time that children spend interacting with media, the images they see can become primary role models and sources of information about how people behave. Evidence from research conducted over the past 50 years on exposure to violence on TV, movies, and video games supports a causal relationship between media violence and violent behavior on the viewer's part (Anderson et al., 2015; Huesmann, 2007). Although the strongest single correlate of violent behavior is previous exposure to violence (AAP Committee on Public Education, 2001;

The vast majority of children learn to control direct and physical aggression after age 6 or 7.

©BananaStock/agefotostock

In 2012's The Hunger Games, teenagers are pitted against each other in publicly televised fights to the death.
©Pictorial Press Ltd/Alamy

bullying Aggression deliberately and persistently directed against a particular target, or victim, typically one who is weak, vulnerable, and defenseless.

Anderson et al., 2003; Huesmann, Moise-Titus, Podolski & Eron, 2003), the effect of exposure to violence via mass media is significant. Moreover, cross-cultural research has shown that the positive relationship between violent media exposure and increases in aggressive behavior holds across different cultures (Anderson, Suzuki et al., 2017; Anderson et al., 2010).

How does media violence lead to long-term aggressiveness? Longitudinal studies have demonstrated that children's exposure to violent media increases their risk for long-term effects based on observational learning, desensitization, and enactive learning that occurs automatically in human children (Huesmann, 2007). Children who see characters use violence to achieve their goals are likely to conclude that force is an effective way to resolve conflicts. Media provides visceral thrills without showing the human cost, leads children to view aggression as acceptable, and desensitizes them to violence. Negative reactions to violent scenes have been shown to decline in intensity with repeated exposure (Huesmann & Kirwil, 2007). The more realistically violence is portrayed, the more likely it is to be accepted (AAP Committee on Public Education, 2001; Anderson et al., 2003).

Children are more vulnerable than adults to the influence of televised violence (AAP Committee on Public Education, 2001; Coie & Dodge, 1998). The influence is stronger if the child believes the violence on the screen is real, identifies with the violent character, finds that character attractive, and watches without parental supervision or intervention (Anderson et al., 2003; Coie & Dodge, 1998). Children who are aggressive to start with fare worse. Highly aggressive children are more strongly affected by media violence than are less aggressive children (Anderson et al., 2003).

More than 90 percent of children play video games (Gentile, 2009). Research on effects of video games and

the Internet suggest that long-term increases in violent behavior could be even greater for video games than for TV and movies. Players of violent games are active participants who receive positive reinforcement for violent actions (Huesmann, 2007). Violent video game players show less prosocial behavior and empathy, more aggressive behaviors and thoughts, more angry feelings, physiological arousal, hostile appraisals, desensitization to violence, and they are more likely to respond violently to provocation (Anderson, Bushman et al., 2017; Ferguson, 2015; Gentile, Bender & Anderson, 2017).

Although the majority of researchers endorse the link between viewing violence and aggression (Bushman, Gollwitzer & Cruz, 2015), some believe the link between media violence and aggression may have been overstated (Ferguson, 2013). For example, some researchers argue that methodological flaws such as a failure to consider confounding variables, difficulty generalizing from laboratory studies of aggression to real-world aggressive acts, and inappropriate statistical modeling call into question some of the claims (Ferguson & Savage, 2012). Moreover, researchers have also pointed out that media violence is just one of many factors, and perhaps not even the most important one (Bushman, Anderson, Donnerstein, Hummer & Warburton, 2016). In support of these assertions are data indicating that youth violence has declined even though exposure to violent media has remained stable (Ferguson, 2013) and video game consumption is inversely related to youth violence (Ferguson, 2015).

Media-induced aggressiveness can be minimized by cutting down on television use and by parental monitoring and guidance of the shows children watch (Anderson et al., 2003). Additionally, just as viewing violent media promotes aggression, viewing media that promotes messages of empathy and helping promotes prosocial behavior in children (Anderson et al., 2015).

Bullies and Victims

Aggression becomes bullying when it is deliberately, persistently directed against a particular target: a victim. **Bullying** can be physical (hitting, punching, kicking, or damaging or taking of personal belongings), verbal (name-calling or threatening), or relational or emotional (isolating and gossiping, often behind the victim's back) (Berger, 2007; Veenstra et al., 2005). Bullying can be proactive—done to

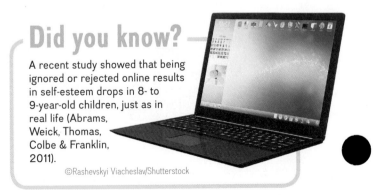

Did you know?

A recent study showed that being ignored or rejected online results in self-esteem drops in 8- to 9-year-old children, just as in real life (Abrams, Weick, Thomas, Colbe & Franklin, 2011).

©Rashevskyi Viacheslav/Shutterstock

show dominance, bolster power, or win admiration—or reactive, responding to a real or imagined attack. Cyberbullying—posting negative comments or derogatory photos of the victim on a website—has become increasingly common (Berger, 2007). The increase in use of cell phones, text messaging, e-mail, and chat rooms has opened new venues for bullies that provide access to victims without the protection of family and community (Huesmann, 2007).

Bullying may reflect a genetic tendency toward aggressiveness combined with environmental influences, such as coercive parents and antisocial friends (Berger, 2007). Bullies also tend to be low in empathy, especially with respect to the ability to experience the emotions that other people are feeling, or the affective component of empathy (Fink, Deighton, Humphrey & Wolpert, 2015). Most bullies are boys who tend to victimize other boys; female bullies tend to target other girls (Berger, 2007; Pellegrini & Long, 2002; Veenstra et al., 2005). Patterns of bullying and victimization may become established as early as kindergarten; as tentative peer groups form, aggressors soon get to know which children make the easiest targets. The frequency of bullying increases from elementary school to middle school before declining again in high school (Hong & Espelage, 2012). Some 24 percent of U.S. primary schools, 42 percent of middle schools, and 21 percent of high schools report student bullying at school at least once a week (Guerino, Hurwitz, Noonan & Kaffenberger, 2006). Whereas younger children reject an aggressive child, by early adolescence bullies are sometimes dominant, respected, feared, and even liked (Berger, 2007). Both bullies and victims tend to be deficient in social problem-solving skills, and those who also have academic problems are more likely to be bullies than victims (Cook, Williams, Guerra, Kim & Sadek, 2010).

Risk factors for victimization seem to be similar across cultures (Schwartz, Chang & Farver, 2001). Victims do not fit in. They tend to be anxious, depressed, cautious, quiet, and submissive and to cry easily, or to be argumentative and provocative (Hodges, Boivin, Vitaro & Bukowski, 1999; Veenstra et al., 2005). They have few friends and may live in harsh, punitive family environments (Nansel et al., 2001; Schwartz, Dodge, Pettit, Bates & Conduct Problems Prevention Research Group, 2000). Victims are apt to have low self-esteem, though it is not clear whether low self-esteem leads to or follows from victimization (Boulton & Smith, 1994; Olweus, 1995). Some victims are small, passive,

Bullying increases from elementary to middle school before declining in high school.
©Lopolo/Shutterstock

weak, and submissive and may blame themselves for being bullied. Other victims are provocative; they goad their attackers, and they may even attack other children themselves (Berger, 2007; Veenstra et al., 2005). Children who are overweight are more likely to become either victims or bullies (Janssen, Craig, Boyce & Pickett, 2004; Bacchini et al., 2015; Van Geel, Vedder & Tanilon, 2014).

Bullying, especially emotional bullying, is harmful to both bullies and victims (Berger, 2007). Both bullies and victims tend to have conduct problems and lower academic achievement (Golmaryami et al., 2016; Shetgiri, Espelage & Carroll, 2015). Bullies are at increased risk of delinquency, crime, or alcohol abuse. They are also more likely to be diagnosed with anxiety or depression. Victims of chronic bullying tend to develop behavior problems. They may become more aggressive themselves or may become depressed (Schwartz, McFadyen-Ketchum, Dodge, Pettit & Bates, 1998; Veenstra et al., 2005; Turcotte Benedict, Vivier & Gjelsvik, 2015). Furthermore, frequent bullying affects the school atmosphere, leading to widespread underachievement, alienation from school, stomachaches and headaches, reluctance to go to school, and frequent absences (Berger, 2007).

As more and more children gain access to electronic devices and participate in social media at younger and younger ages, there has been a rise in incidents of cyberbullying. Estimates for prevalence rates vary widely, and range from 10 percent to 40 percent (Kowalski, Giumetti, Schroeder & Lattanner, 2014), with higher rates reported for the United States (Selkie, Fales & Moreno, 2016) than Europe (Brochado, Soares & Fraga, 2017). Research suggests that cyberbullying is often an extension of face-to-face bullying, as cyberbullies also tend to engage in aggressive acts in person as well as online (Modecki, Minchin, Harbaugh, Guerra & Runions, 2014; Kowalski et al., 2014). Cyberbullies tend to

Did you know?

Children seem to treat obesity as if it is contagious, perhaps leading to easier stigmatization of overweight kids (Klaczynski, 2008).

©Stockbyte/Getty Images

believe that aggression is normative and show low empathy for others (Kowalski et al., 2014). While overall, boys cyberbully at higher levels than do girls, girls engage in more cyberbullying in early to midadolescence, while boys' cyberbullying peaks somewhat later (Barlett & Coyne, 2014). Being a victim of cyberbullying is associated with a wealth of mental health and academic issues, and, for some children, an elevated risk of suicidal ideation and suicide (Van Geel, Vedder & Tanilon, 2014).

The U.S. Department of Health and Human Services has promoted Steps to Respect, a program for third through sixth grades that aims to (1) increase staff awareness and responsiveness to bullying, (2) teach students social and emotional skills, and (3) foster socially responsible beliefs. Some research has found a reduction in playground bullying and argumentative behavior and an increase in harmonious interactions among children who participated in the program (Frey et al., 2005). However, other data have indicated the impact on actual bullying behavior is minimal although the programs may enhance students' social competence and self-esteem (Merrell, Gueldner, Ross & Isava, 2008).

mastering the CHAPTER

©Sergey Novikov/Shutterstock

Summary and Key Terms

The Developing Self

> The self-concept becomes more realistic during middle childhood, when children form representational systems.

> According to Erikson, the source of self-esteem is children's competence. This virtue develops through resolution of the fourth psychosocial conflict, industry versus inferiority.

> School-age children have internalized shame and pride and can better understand and regulate negative emotions. Empathy and prosocial behavior increase.

> Emotional growth is affected by parents' reactions to displays of negative emotions and involves effortful control.

> **KEY TERMS**

> **Representational systems**   **Industry versus inferiority**

The Child in the Family

> School-age children spend less time with parents and are less close to them than before, but relationships with parents continue to be important. Culture influences family relationships and roles.

> The family environment has two major components: family structure and family atmosphere.

> The emotional tone of the home, the way parents handle disciplinary issues and conflict, the effects of parents' work, and the adequacy of financial resources all contribute to family atmosphere.

> Development of coregulation may affect the way a family handles conflicts and discipline.

> The impact of mothers' employment depends on many factors.

> Poverty can harm children's development indirectly through its effects on parents' well-being and parenting practices.

> Many children today grow up in nontraditional family structures. Other things being equal, children tend to do better in two-parent families than in cohabiting, divorced, single-parent, or stepfamilies.

> Children's adjustment to divorce depends on factors concerning the child, the parents' handling of the situation, custody and visitation arrangements, financial circumstances, contact with the

noncustodial parent (usually the father), and a parent's remarriage.

> The amount of conflict in a marriage and after divorce may influence whether children are better off if the parents stay together.

> In most divorces the mother gets custody, though paternal custody is a growing trend. Joint custody can be beneficial to children when the parents can cooperate. Joint legal custody is more common than joint physical custody.

> Although parental divorce increases the risk of long-term problems for children, most adjust reasonably well.

> Children living with only one parent are at heightened risk of behavioral and academic problems, largely related to socioeconomic status.

> Studies have found positive developmental outcomes in children living with gay or lesbian parents.

> Adopted children are generally well adjusted, though they face special challenges.

> The roles and responsibilities of siblings in nonindustrialized societies are more structured than in industrialized societies.

> Siblings learn about conflict resolution from their relationships with each other. Relationships with parents affect sibling relationships.

The Child in the Peer Group

> The peer group becomes more important in middle childhood. Peer groups generally consist of children who are similar in age, sex, ethnicity, and socioeconomic status and who live near one another or go to school together.

> The peer group helps children develop social skills, allows them to test and adopt values independent of parents, gives them a sense of belonging, and helps develop their self-concept and gender identity. It also may encourage conformity and prejudice.

> Popularity in middle childhood tends to influence future adjustment. Popular children tend to have good cognitive abilities and social skills. Behaviors that affect popularity may be influenced by family relationships and cultural values.

> Intimacy and stability of friendships increase during middle childhood. Boys tend to have more friends, whereas girls tend to have closer friends.

> During middle childhood, aggression typically declines. Instrumental aggression generally gives way to hostile aggression, often with a hostile bias. Highly physically aggressive children tend to be unpopular.

> Aggressiveness is promoted by exposure to media violence and can extend into adult life.

> Middle childhood is a prime time for bullying. Victims tend to be weak and submissive or argumentative and provocative and to have low self-esteem.

1. What are two changes that occur in children's self-concept in middle childhood?

_____
_____
_____

2. Which of Erikson's stages is relevant to the development of self-esteem in middle childhood?
   a. trust vs. mistrust
   b. industry vs. inferiority
   c. identity vs. identity confusion
   d. generativity vs. stagnation

3. Which of the following traits is related to the ability to effectively regulate emotions?
   a. anxiety
   b. empathy
   c. effortful control
   d. aggression

4. Which of the following variables affects the impact of maternal employment on children's well-being?
   a. how satisfied the mother is
   b. the child's temperament
   c. how well the child is monitored and kept track of
   d. all of the above

5. When all other factors are held equal, what type of family structure seems to be the best for children?

_____
_____
_____

6. Which of the following is an indirect sibling influence?
   a. A child's parents are warm and loving toward her, so she tends to treat her sister the same way.
   b. A child's parents are happy that he is a boy.
   c. Two siblings are punished for fighting with each other.
   d. Siblings from large families receive less one-on-one time with parents.

7. What are two positive and two negative effects of peer relations?

_____
_____

8. What is the most clearly identified gender difference between boys' and girls' play groups?
   a. loyalty
   b. activity level
   c. tendency to cooperate
   d. inclusion of all group members in joint activities

9. When a sociometric study is conducted at his school, Mark gets a large number of negative nominations and almost no positive nominations. This suggests that Mark is a/an _____ child.

10. Children generally look for friends that:
    a. are like them in age, sex, and interests
    b. can help them climb socially
    c. their parents approve of
    d. are unique from them

11. Children who have a hostile attributional bias:
    a. tend to have a low IQ
    b. are usually girls
    c. chronically misinterpret social cues
    d. are usually bullied

Answers: 1–Changes that occur in children's self-concepts include their becoming more comprehensive, realistic, balanced. 2–b; 3–c; 4–d; 5–When all other factors are held equal, children tend to do best in families with two continuously married parents, regardless of whether they are adoptive or gay parents. 6–a; 7–Positive influences include the development of skills needed for sociability and intimacy, a sense of belonging, a sense of identity, learning to get along with others, and emotional security. Negative influences include the reinforcement of prejudice and the fostering of antisocial tendencies. 8–b; 9–rejected; 10–a; 11–c

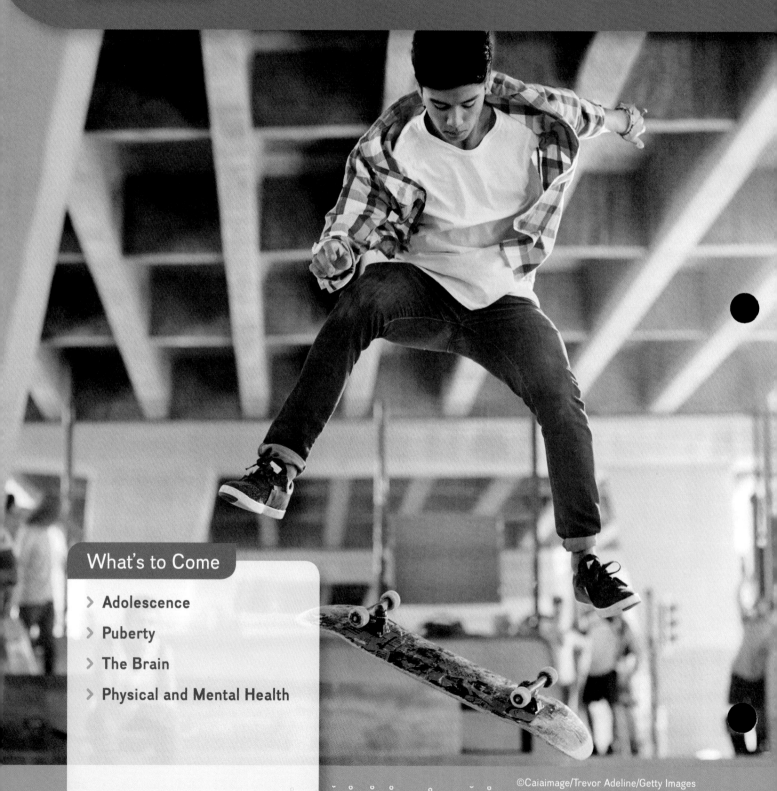

Chapter 14

Physical Development and Health in Adolescence

What's to Come

©Caiaimage/Trevor Adeline/Getty Images

"It was *so* embarrassing," Sara wrote in her diary. "I went shopping with Mom today for my first bra, and she kept picking up bras and just basically *shouting*, "Do you like this one? What about this one?" and she just would *not* stop. She drives me nuts. It's like she goes out of her way to embarrass me. We finally found one and brought it home, and I put it on and it just feels weird." Sara, stopped, chewing thoughtfully on the tip of her pen. "It's just *all* so weird," she finally wrote. Sara, like all typical girls, had hit puberty and embarked upon life's next chapter: adolescence.

In this chapter, we address the physical transformations of adolescence and how they affect young people's feelings. We consider the impact of early or late maturation. We discuss health issues associated with this time of life, and we address a variety of risks, including eating disorders, depression, and mortality.

● ● ● ●

Adolescence

In most modern societies, the passage from childhood to adulthood is marked, not by a single event, but by a long period known as **adolescence**—a developmental transition that involves physical, cognitive, emotional, and social changes and takes varying forms in different social, cultural, and economic settings (Larson & Wilson, 2004). In *Child*, we define adolescence as encompassing the years between 11 and 20.

ADOLESCENCE AS A SOCIAL CONSTRUCTION

Adolescence is a social construction. In preindustrial societies, children entered the adult world when they matured physically or when they began a vocational apprenticeship.

> **adolescence** Developmental transition between childhood and adulthood entailing major physical, cognitive, and psychosocial changes.

Perspectives on Diversity

©Digital Vision/Getty Images

THE GLOBALIZATION OF ADOLESCENCE

Young people today live in a global neighborhood, a web of interconnections and interdependencies. Goods, information, electronic images, songs, entertainment, and fads sweep almost instantaneously around the planet. Western youth dance to Latin rhythms, and Arabic girls draw their images of romance from Indian cinema. Maori youth in New Zealand listen to African American rap music to symbolize their separation from adult society. Adolescence is no longer solely a Western phenomenon. Globalization and modernization have set in motion societal changes the world over.

Globalization of adolescence does not mean adolescence is the same the world over. The strong hand of culture shapes its meaning differently in different societies. In the United States, adolescents are spending less time with their parents and confiding in them less. In India, adolescents may wear Western clothing and use computers, but they maintain strong family ties, and their life decisions often are influenced by traditional Hindu values. In Western countries, teenage girls strive to be as thin as possible. In Niger and other African countries, obesity is considered beautiful.

In many non-Western countries, adolescent boys and girls seem to live in two separate worlds. In parts of the Middle East, Latin America, Africa, and Asia, puberty brings more restrictions on girls, whose honor must be protected to uphold family status and ensure girls' marriageability. Boys, on the other hand, gain more freedom and mobility, and their sexual exploits are tolerated by parents and admired by peers.

In addition, puberty heightens preparation for gender roles, which, for girls in most parts of the world, means preparation for domesticity. In Laos, a girl may spend 2½ hours a day husking, washing, and steaming rice. In Istanbul, a girl must learn the proper way to serve tea when a suitor comes to call. In some cultures, girls are expected to spend most of their time helping at home.

This traditional pattern is changing in some parts of the developing world as women's employment and self-reliance become financial necessities. During the past quarter-century, the advent of public education has enabled more girls to go to school, breaking down some of the taboos and restrictions on feminine activities. Better-educated girls tend to marry later and have fewer children, enabling them to seek skilled employment in the new technological society.

Cultural change is complex; it can be both liberating and challenging. Today's adolescents are charting a new course, not always certain where it will lead.

puberty Process by which a person attains sexual maturity and the ability to reproduce.

Adolescence was not defined as a separate stage of life in the Western world until the twentieth century. Today, adolescence is a global concept, though it may take different forms in different cultures. In most parts of the world, entry into adulthood takes longer and is less clear-cut than in the past. Puberty begins earlier than it used to, and entrance into a vocation occurs later, often requiring longer periods of education or vocational training to prepare for adult responsibilities. Marriage with its attendant responsibilities typically comes later as well (Larson & Wilson, 2004).

A TIME OF OPPORTUNITIES AND RISKS

Adolescence offers opportunities for growth, not only in physical dimensions but also in cognitive and social competence, autonomy, self-esteem, and intimacy. Young people who have supportive connections with parents, school, and community tend to develop in a positive, healthful way (Youngblade et al., 2007). However, U.S. adolescents today face hazards to their physical and mental well-being, including high death rates from accidents, homicide, and suicide (Eaton et al., 2008; Murphy et al, 2017).

Risky behaviors may reflect immaturity of the adolescent brain, but a national survey of some 14,000 high school students reveals encouraging trends. Since the 1990s, students have become less likely to use alcohol, tobacco, or marijuana; to ride in a car without wearing a seat belt or to ride with a driver who has been drinking; to carry weapons; to have sexual intercourse or to have it without condoms; or to attempt suicide (Centers for Disease Control and Prevention [CDC], 2012; Eaton et al., 2008). Avoidance of such risky behaviors increases the chances that young people will come through the adolescent years in good physical and mental health.

Puberty

An important physical change in adolescence is the onset of puberty, the process that leads to sexual maturity, or fertility—the ability to reproduce. **Puberty** involves dramatic biological changes. In the following section, we discuss the hormonal changes that mark the beginning of puberty, and then we focus on the changes that occur during that period. Last, we discuss the psychological effects of early and late maturation.

HOW PUBERTY BEGINS: HORMONAL CHANGES

Sara got her first bra when outward signs of puberty—breast development in her case—became apparent. However, these changes were part of a long, complex process of maturation that begins even before birth.

Puberty results from the production of various hormones. An increase in gonadatropin releasing hormone (GnRH) in the hypothalamus leads to a rise in two key reproductive hormones: follicle-stimulating hormone (FSH) and luteinizing hormone (LH). In girls, increased levels of FSH lead to the onset of menstruation. In boys, LH initiates the secretion of testosterone and androstenedione (Buck Louis et al., 2008). Puberty is marked by two stages: (1) the activation of the adrenal glands and (2) the maturing of the sex organs a few years later.

The first stage of puberty occurs between ages 6 and 8. During this stage, the adrenal glands located above the kidneys secrete gradually increasing levels of androgens, principally dehydroepiandrosterone (DHEA) (Susman & Rogol, 2004). By age 10, levels of DHEA are 10 times what they were between ages 1 and 4. DHEA influences the growth of pubic, axillary (underarm), and facial hair. It also contributes to faster body growth, oilier skin, and the development of body odor.

The maturing of the sex organs triggers a second burst of DHEA production, which then rises to adult levels (Herdt & McClintock, 2000). In this second stage, a girl's ovaries increase their output of estrogen, which stimulates growth of female genitals and development of breasts and pubic and underarm hair. In boys, the testes increase the manufacture of androgens, particularly testosterone, which stimulate growth of male genitals, muscle mass, and body hair. Boys and girls have both types of hormones, but girls have higher levels of estrogen, and boys have higher levels of androgens. In girls, testosterone influences growth of the clitoris as well as of the bones and of pubic and axillary hair (Figure 14.1).

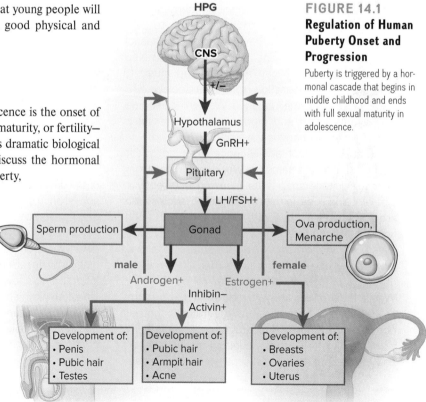

FIGURE 14.1

Regulation of Human Puberty Onset and Progression

Puberty is triggered by a hormonal cascade that begins in middle childhood and ends with full sexual maturity in adolescence.

TIMING, CHARACTERISTICS OF, AND INFLUENCES ON PUBERTY

Changes that herald puberty typically begin at age 8 in girls and age 9 in boys (Susman & Rogol, 2004), but a wide range of ages exists for various changes (Figure 14.2). The pubertal process typically takes about 3 to 4 years for both sexes.

Race and ethnicity also impact pubertal development. African American and Mexican American girls generally enter puberty earlier than white and Asian girls (Wu, Mendola & Buck, 2002; Biro et al., 2013), although recent data suggest the proportion of white girls who enter puberty early may be increasing (Biro et al., 2010). Recent data in boys suggest a similar pattern, with African American boys developing at a more rapid pace than white or Hispanic boys (Papadimitriou, 2016; Herman-Giddens et al., 2012).

Primary and Secondary Sex Characteristics

The **primary sex characteristics** are the organs necessary for reproduction. In the female, the sex organs include the ovaries, fallopian tubes, uterus, clitoris, and vagina. In the male, they include the testes, penis, scrotum, seminal vesicles, and prostate gland. During puberty, these organs enlarge and mature.

The **secondary sex characteristics** (Table 14.1) are physiological signs of sexual maturation that do not directly involve the sex organs, for example, the breasts of females and the broad shoulders of males. Other secondary sex characteristics are changes in the voice and skin texture; muscular development; and the growth of pubic, facial, axillary, and body hair. These changes unfold in a sequence that is much more consistent than their timing. One girl may develop breasts and body hair at about the same rate; in another girl, body hair may reach adultlike growth a year or so before breasts develop. Similar variations in pubertal status (degree of pubertal development) and timing occur among boys. Let's look more closely at these changes.

Signs of Puberty

The first external signs of puberty typically are breast tissue and pubic hair in girls and enlargement of the testes in boys (Susman & Rogol, 2004). A girl's nipples enlarge and protrude; the areolae, the pigmented areas surrounding the nipples, enlarge; and the breasts assume first a conical and then a rounded shape. Some adolescent boys experience temporary breast enlargement, much to their distress. This development is normal and generally does not last longer than 18 months.

Pubic hair, at first straight and silky, eventually becomes coarse, dark, and curly. It appears in different patterns in males and females. Adolescent boys are usually happy to see hair on the face and chest, but girls are usually dismayed at the appearance of even a slight amount of hair on the face or around the nipples, though this is normal.

primary sex characteristics Organs directly related to reproduction, which enlarge and mature during adolescence.

secondary sex characteristics Physiological signs of sexual maturation (such as breast development and growth of body hair) that do not involve the sex organs.

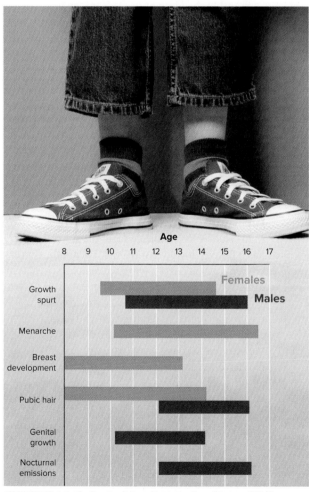

FIGURE 14.2 Typical Age Ranges for Signs of Puberty
Note that while one can talk about an average age at which pubertal events take place, the range of ages is actually quite variable.
©Leonard McLane/Getty Images

TABLE 14.1 Secondary Sex Characteristics

Girls	Boys
Breasts	Pubic hair
Pubic hair	Axillary (underarm) hair
Axillary (underarm) hair	Muscular development
Changes in voice	Facial hair
Changes in skin	Changes in voice
Increased width and depth of pelvis	Changes in skin
Muscular development	Broadening of shoulders

The voice deepens, especially in boys, partly in response to the growth of the larynx and partly in response to the production of male hormones. The skin becomes coarser and oilier. Increased activity of the sebaceous glands may cause pimples and blackheads. Acne is more common in boys and seems related to increased amounts of testosterone.

The Adolescent Growth Spurt

The **adolescent growth spurt** generally begins in girls between ages 9½ and 14½, on average at about 10, and in boys, between 10½ and 16, on average at 12 or 13 (Figure 14.3). It typically lasts about 2 years; soon after it ends, the young person reaches sexual maturity, generally defined as the age at which an organism can reproduce. Both growth hormone and the sex hormones, androgens and estrogen, contribute to this normal pubertal growth (Susman & Rogol, 2004).

Because girls' growth spurt usually occurs 2 years earlier than that of boys, girls between ages 11 and 13 tend to be taller, heavier, and stronger than boys the same age. After their growth spurt, boys are again larger, as before. Girls usually reach full height by age 15 and boys by age 17. Boys and girls grow differently, not only in rate of growth but also in form and shape. A boy becomes larger overall: his shoulders wider, his legs longer relative to his trunk, and his forearms longer relative to his upper arms and his height. A girl's pelvis widens to make childbearing easier, and layers of fat accumulate under her skin, giving her a more rounded appearance. Fat accumulates twice as rapidly in girls as in boys (Susman & Rogol, 2004).

Because each of these changes follows its own timetable, parts of the body may be out of proportion for a while. The result is the familiar teenage gawkiness that accompanies unbalanced, accelerated growth.

The striking physical changes of puberty have psychological ramifications. Most young teenagers are more concerned about their appearance than about any other aspect of themselves, and some do not like what they see in the mirror. As we discuss in a subsequent section, these attitudes can lead to eating problems.

Signs of Sexual Maturity

The maturation of the reproductive organs brings the beginning of menstruation in girls and the production of sperm in boys. The principal sign of sexual maturity in boys is sperm production. The first ejaculation, or **spermarche**, occurs at an average age of 13. A boy may wake up to find a wet spot or a dried, hardened spot on the sheets—the result of a nocturnal emission, an involuntary ejaculation of semen (commonly referred to as a wet dream).

The principal sign of sexual maturity in girls is *menstruation*, a monthly shedding of tissue from the lining of the womb. The first menstruation, called **menarche**, occurs fairly late in the sequence of female development; its normal timing can vary from age 10 to 16½ (see Figure 14.2). The average age of menarche in U.S. girls fell from greater than 14 years before 1900 to the current 12.8 years. On average, black girls experience menarche 6 months earlier than white girls (Cabrera, Bright, Frane, Blethen & Lee, 2014; Anderson, Dallal & Must, 2003). While menarche is a significant event, the reproductive system may not yet be functionally mature, as menstrual cycles may occur without ova, especially in very young girls (Eveleth, 2017).

Influences on Pubertal Timing

Many studies have indicated that the start of puberty has shifted downward in the twentieth century (Papadimitriou, 2016). Developmental scientists call a pattern such as this a **secular trend**—a trend that spans several generations. The trend, which also involves increases in adult height and weight, began about 100 years ago. It has occurred in such places as the United States, Western Europe, and Japan (Anderson et al., 2003), with better evidence existing for girls than for boys (Papadimitriou, 2016; Euling, Selevan, Pescovitz & Skakkebaek, 2008). This may not be the only change in pubertal processes; recent research indicates there may be a compensatory delay in pubertal maturation that is associated with earlier puberty. In other words, children may be starting puberty earlier, but spending more time to reach full sexual maturity (Papadimitriou, 2016; Mendle, 2014).

One set of proposed explanations for the secular trend focuses on environmental factors that influence the pace of pubertal development. One such

adolescent growth spurt Sharp increase in height and weight that precedes sexual maturity.

spermarche A boy's first ejaculation.

menarche A girl's first menstruation.

secular trend Trend that can be seen only by observing several generations, such as the trend toward earlier attainment of adult height and sexual maturity, which began a century ago.

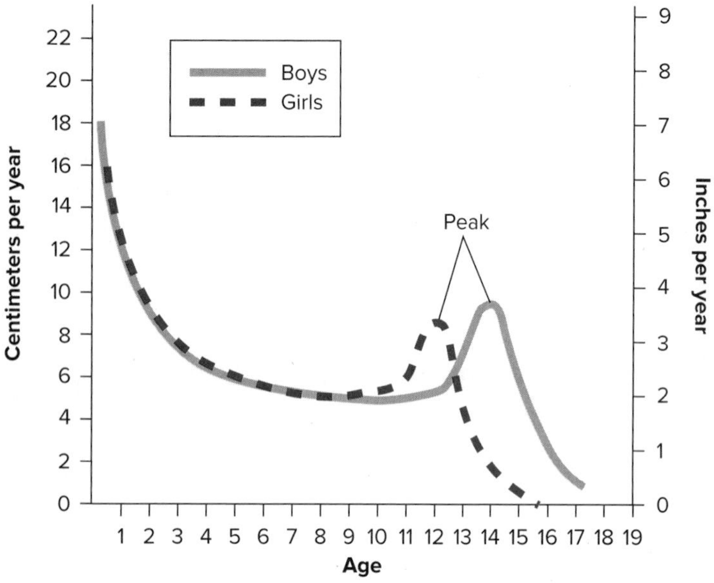

FIGURE 14.3 Adolescent Growth Chart

The adolescent growth spurt begins slightly earlier in girls than in boys and typically lasts about two years.

Source: Thompson, Peter J. L. "Rate of Height Increase." *Introduction to Coaching Theory.* Lincolnshire, UK: International Amateur Athletic Federation, 1991.

factor is a higher standard of living. Undernutrition, whether because of insufficient food supply or because of disease, has been associated with delayed onset of puberty and a reduced puberty growth spurt (Soliman, De Sanctis & Elalaily, 2014). Children who are healthier, better nourished, and better cared for might be expected to mature earlier and grow bigger (Slyper, 2006). Thus, the average age of sexual maturity is earlier in developed countries than in developing countries.

The timing of hormonal activity signaling the start of puberty seems to depend in part on reaching a critical amount of body fat necessary for successful reproduction. Because of the role of body fat in triggering puberty, a contributing factor in the United States during the last part of the twentieth century may have been the increase in obesity among young girls (Anderson et al., 2003; Lee et al., 2007). Girls with a higher percentage of body fat in early childhood and those who experience unusual weight gain between ages 5 and 9 tend to show earlier pubertal development (Davison, Susman, & Birch, 2003; Lee et al., 2007).

Studies suggest that an accumulation of leptin, a hormone associated with obesity, may be the link between body fat and earlier puberty in girls (Kaplowitz, 2008). Increased levels of leptin may signal the pituitary and sex glands to increase their secretion of hormones (Susman & Rogol, 2004). This suggests that leptin may play a permissive role for puberty to start. In other words, leptin may need to be present in sufficient amounts for puberty to occur, but leptin alone does not initiate puberty (Kaplowitz, 2008).

Weight and leptin appear to influence pubertal timing differently in boys. While leptin still plays a permissive role (Clayton et al., 1997), having a high body mass index in childhood or being obese appears to delay puberty rather than accelerate it (Lee et al., 2010; Wang, 2002). Interestingly, recent research has found that being overweight, rather than either thin or obese, results in an earlier start to puberty in boys (Lee et al., 2016). More research is needed in this area.

Another environmental explanation focuses on exposure to endocrine-disrupting chemicals, such as those found in some plastics, flame retardants, and pesticides. Research has indicated that exposure to such substances appears to be related to earlier pubertal timing (Lee & Styne, 2013;

Ozen & Darcan, 2011). Some of this exposure may be during childhood and adolescence, most commonly through foods and liquids or the inhalation of dust or sprays, and some of it is likely via prenatal exposure in utero (Frye et al., 2012). Other toxins may also have an effect. With respect to prenatal influences, studies have also shown that earlier menarche is associated with maternal smoking during pregnancy (Maisonet et al., 2010).

Genetic factors are also important. One genetic influence seems to be the age at which parents themselves began puberty. Both maternal and paternal pubertal timing are associated with an individual's pubertal timing, although this is less true for girls' breast and pubic hair development (Wohlfahrt-Veje et al., 2016). Additionally, twin studies have documented the heritability of age of menarche (Mendle et al., 2006), and further support for genetic influences is illustrated by the finding that the age of a girl's first menstruation tends to be similar to that of her mother's (Maisonet et al., 2010) if nutrition and standards of living remain stable from one generation to the next (Susman & Rogol, 2004).

A variety of social factors also influence when puberty begins. With respect to mothers, studies have shown that earlier menarche is associated with being the firstborn child (Maisonet et al., 2010) as well as single motherhood (Belsky et al., 2007; Ellis, McFadyen-Ketchum, Dodge, Pettit & Bates, 1999) and harsh maternal parenting practices (Belsky, Steinberg, Houts & Halpren-Felsher, 2010). Fathers also play a role. Girls with absent, distant, or conflictual relationships with their fathers tend to reach menarche earlier than girls with close supportive paternal relationships (Belsky et al., 2007; Mendle et al., 2006; Ellis et al., 1999; Tither & Ellis, 2008). The unifying theme in these influences is stress, which has been proposed to mediate the above associations. In other words, it is not being firstborn, or being born to a single mother, or having a conflictual relationship per se that influences puberty; rather, it is the presence or absence of high levels of stress. Those children who are exposed to high stress when young tend to reach pubertal milestones earlier than those who are not (Belsky, Ruttle, Boyce, Armstrong & Essex, 2015; Ellis & Del Giudice, 2014; Bleil et al., 2013).

IMPLICATIONS OF EARLY AND LATE MATURATION

The onset of puberty can vary by as many as 5 years among typical boys and girls. Early maturation increases the likelihood of accelerated skeletal maturation and psychosocial difficulties and has been linked to adult health issues, including reproductive-tract cancers, type 2 diabetes, and cardiovascular disease (Golub et al., 2008). Early puberty is also predictive of adult obesity, and this effect is partially independent of childhood body mass index. In other words, the finding that early puberty predicts adult obesity is not entirely a consequence of the accelerant influence childhood obesity has on puberty, and the association between childhood and adult obesity (Prentice & Viner, 2013). As adults, women who had early puberty are somewhat more likely to have polycystic ovarian syndrome, a hormonal disorder causing acne, irregular periods, excess hair growth, and the growth of cysts on the ovaries (Fuqua, 2013; Franceschi et al., 2010). Other effects of early and late maturation vary in boys and girls, and the timing of maturation tends to influence adolescent mental health and health-related behaviors in adulthood (Susman & Rogol, 2004).

Research on early maturing boys has had mixed results. The most consistent trends to emerge from the literature are that early maturing boys are at significant risk for a wide variety of negative outcomes (Mendle & Ferrero, 2012). Earlier studies found that early maturing boys reported being better adjusted than later maturing boys (Graber, Brooks-Gunn & Warren, 2006). However, more recent research suggested greater risk for early maturing boys, particularly for substance use and delinquent behavior (Hummel, Shelton, Heron, Moore & Bree, 2013; Westling, Andrews, Hampson & Peterson, 2008). Early maturing boys also demonstrate a higher incidence of conduct and behavioral disorders during adolescence (Golub et al., 2008). The data for late maturing boys are less consistent and more characteristic of internalizing symptoms (Mendle & Ferrero, 2012). Late maturing boys have been found to feel more inadequate, self-conscious, rejected, and dominated; to be more dependent, aggressive, insecure, or depressed; to have more conflict with parents and more trouble in school; and to have poorer social and coping skills and higher risk for aggression problems (Graber, Lewinsohn, Seeley & Brooks-Gunn, 1997; Sontag, Graber & Clemans, 2011).

Early maturing girls are at increased risk of anxiety and depression, disruptive behavior, eating disorders, early smoking, drinking, substance abuse, antisocial behavior, precocious sexual activity, early pregnancy, and attempted suicide (Copeland et al., 2010; Galvao et al., 2014; Blumenthal et al., 2011; Belsky et al., 2010; Deardorff, Gonzalez, Christopher, Roosa, & Millsap, 2005; Susman & Rogol, 2004, Golub et al., 2008). Early maturers tend to be particularly vulnerable to risky behavior and the influence of deviant peers (Mrug et al., 2014; Orr & Ingersoll, 1995; Susman & Rogol, 2004). There is much less data on late maturing girls. Generally, they are not at risk for poor psychological outcomes when compared to "on-time" girls (Ge, Conger & Elder, 2001a); however, there are some indications that they may be more reactive to interpersonal stress (Smith & Powers, 2009).

It is hard to generalize about the psychological effects of pubertal timing because they depend on how the adolescent and other people in his or her world interpret the accompanying changes. Effects of early or late maturation are most likely to be negative when adolescents are much more or less developed than their peers; when they do not see the changes as advantageous; and when several stressful events, such as the advent of puberty and the transition to junior high school, occur about the same time (Petersen, 1993; Simmons, Blyth & McKinney, 1983). Contextual factors such as ethnicity, school, and neighborhood can make a difference. For example, African American and Hispanic late maturers report less satisfaction with their bodies, but timing of puberty for Asian American and European American youth does not seem to affect body image to the same degree (Susman & Rogol, 2004). Additionally, early maturing girls are more likely to show problem behavior in mixed-gender schools than in all-girl schools, and in disadvantaged urban communities than in rural or middle-class urban communities (Dick, Rose, Kaprio & Viken, 2000; Ge, Brody, Conger, Simons & Murry, 2002).

The Brain

"I got in *huge* trouble today," Sara wrote, "I'm grounded for pretty much forever. Siobhan asked me to cut class with her, and even though I knew I would get in trouble, I did it anyway. I don't know what I was thinking."

Adolescents tend to engage in certain types of behaviors. They become more interested in and influenced by their peers and social relationships. Additionally, they show an increased tendency for impulsivity and risk-taking, are more likely to experiment with drugs and alcohol, have a propensity for reckless behavior, seek out fun and exciting experiences, and find it hard to focus on long-term goals. Nonetheless they are able to think in more complex and sophisticated ways, and can imagine possible futures and alternative realities. While there are certainly individual differences among teens, the adolescent brain contributes to some of these characteristic teen behaviors. Adolescents process information differently than adults do. To understand the immaturity of the adolescent brain, we need to look at changes in the structure and composition of the brain.

On the positive side, a steady increase in white matter, nerve fibers that connect distant portions of the brain, permits

Did you know?

Because of the still-developing brain, the Supreme Court ruled the death penalty unconstitutional for murderers 17 years of age or younger when the crime was committed (Mears, 2005).

©OJO Images/AP Images

faster transmission of information and better communication across hemispheres (Casey, Jones & Somerville, 2011). In adolescence, this process continues in the frontal lobes (Bava et al., 2010; Blakemore & Choudhury, 2006), occurring earlier in women than men (Asato, Terwilliger, Woo & Luna, 2010). In addition, there is a major spurt in production of gray matter in the frontal lobes (Blakemore & Choudhury, 2006; Kuhn, 2006). The pruning of unused dendritic connections during childhood results in a reduction in density of gray matter, or nerve cells, thus increasing the brain's efficiency. This process begins in the rear portions of the brain and moves forward (Konrad, Firk & Uhlhaas, 2013; Casey et al., 2011). Thus, by mid- to late adolescence young people have fewer but stronger, smoother, and more effective neuronal connections, making cognitive processing more efficient (Kuhn, 2006).

Unfortunately, this process takes time, and in large part it has not yet reached the frontal lobes by adolescence. There are consequences to this timeline. The frontal lobes are generally associated with problem solving, impulse control, goal setting, planning, and other similar behaviors generally associated with monitoring social behavior. Given the relatively slow development of the prefrontal cortex, we might expect to see a similar slow improvement in social behavior and decision making as children age into the teen years. However, we are more likely to see a rapid shift in trajectory (Casey et al., 2011; Windle et al., 2008). Why do adolescents so suddenly shift into a pattern of impulsivity and risk-taking?

One possible explanation lies with the pattern these changes take. Because development starts in the back of the brain and moves forward (Konrad et al., 2013; Casey et al., 2011), subcortical brain areas, including the limbic and reward systems, mature earlier (Konrad et al., 2013; Albert, Chein & Steinberg, 2013). The underdevelopment of frontal cortical systems by comparison to these areas may help explain why adolescents tend to seek thrills and novelty and why many of them find it hard to focus on long-term goals (Bjork et al., 2004; Chambers, Taylor & Potenza, 2003). While teens are *capable* of thinking in a sophisticated fashion, the more advanced development in reward areas biases them toward thinking with their subcortical "gas pedal" rather than with the "brakes" that might be provided by their prefrontal cortex (Casey et al., 2011).

Other behavioral changes are related to brain structure. Adolescence is a time of social change. Compared with children, adolescents tend

Exercise provides a variety of physical benefits, but it is also associated with enhanced well-being, lower anxiety, higher self-esteem and academic performance, and decreases in risky behavior.
©Ron Levine/Digital Vision/Getty Images

to form more complex relationships and are more concerned with social hierarchies (Steinberg & Morris, 2001). Adolescents grapple with changes in identity and feelings of self-consciousness, and they become more sensitive to acceptance and rejection from their peers. (Blakemore, 2012). These social changes have a neural substrate. Peers tend to exert a stronger influence in adolescence in part because of a heightened neurobehavioral susceptibility to social reward cues and concurrent immaturity in the cognitive control system (Albert et al., 2013). There are also changes in the brain that specifically affect the processing of social information. The changes have been demonstrated most clearly in the temporoparietal junction and the posterior superior temporal sulcus, areas believed to be involved in the processing of social information. Generally, these areas decrease in volume (suggesting dendritic pruning) from adolescence into the early twenties (Mills, Lalonde, Clasen, Giedd & Blakemore, 2012). Moreover, there is also a decline in medial pre-frontal cortex activity and grey matter volume at the same time (Blakemore, 2012).

We live lives of great complexity, and our slowly developing brains give us the time and flexibility to learn about the wide variety of environments in which we find ourselves. However, because the brain develops so slowly and extensively during the teen years, this makes it particularly susceptible to both beneficial and harmful environmental influences (Konrad et al., 2013). Thus, cognitive stimulation in adolescence makes a critical difference in the brain's development. Likewise, adolescent drug use can have particularly devastating effects, depending on how drugs interact with the growing brain.

Physical and Mental Health

"I really like playing soccer," Sara wrote in her diary, "but I don't know if I want to play it anymore. But I'm afraid that if I stop I might get fat. But I *hate* getting up early on Saturday—I'm always *so* sleepy in the morning now. I don't know. I guess I'll see if any of my friends are doing it too."

Like Sara, about 1.2 billion people in the world—1 in 6—are adolescents (World Health Organization, 2017a). Nine out of ten 11- to 15-year-olds in Western industrialized countries consider themselves healthy (Scheidt, Overpeck, Wyatt & Aszmann, 2000). Still, many adolescents, especially girls, report frequent health problems, such as headache, backache, stomachache, nervousness, and feeling tired, lonely, or low.

Some of the lifestyle patterns Sara sets down now will have effects many years later. Many health problems are preventable and stem from lifestyle choices (World Health Organization, 2017a). Because adolescents are generally healthy, they may not feel the effects of their choices for decades. Lifestyle patterns tend to solidify in adolescence, which may result in poor lifelong health habits and early death in adults.

Across many countries, adolescents from less affluent families tend to report poorer health and more frequent symptoms. Adolescents from more affluent families tend to have healthier diets and to be more physically active (Elgar et al., 2015; Mullan & Currie, 2000; Scheidt et al., 2000). Health concerns related to adolescence include physical fitness, sleep needs, eating disorders, drug abuse, depression, and causes of death in adolescence.

PHYSICAL ACTIVITY

Exercise, or lack of it, affects both physical and mental health. The benefits of regular exercise include improved strength and endurance, healthier bones and muscles, weight control, and reduced anxiety and stress, as well as increased self-esteem, school grades, and well-being. Exercise also decreases the likelihood an adolescent will participate in risky behavior. Even moderate physical activity has health benefits if done regularly for at least 30 minutes almost every day. A sedentary lifestyle may result in increased risk of poor mental health, obesity, type 2 diabetes, and an increased likelihood of heart disease and cancer in adulthood (Janssen & LeBlanc, 2010; National Center for Health Statistics, 2004; Nelson & Gordon-Larsen, 2006; Biddle & Asare, 2011).

The Centers for Disease Control (2016a) recommends that adolescents do one hour of or more of physical activity a day. Unfortunately, only 27.1 percent of U.S. high school students engage in the recommended amounts of physical activity. Males are almost twice as likely to meet the guidelines as females (CDC, 2016b). Age also matters. Adolescents show a steep drop in physical activity upon entering puberty, shifting from an average of 3 hours per day of physical activity at age 9 to an average of only 49 minutes of activity per day at age 15 (Nader et al., 2008), and the proportion of young people who are inactive increases even more throughout the high school years (CDC, 2016a; Eaton et al., 2008). Additionally, adolescents from less affluent families and ethnic minorities tend to be less physically active (Foltz et al., 2011). U.S. adolescents exercise less frequently than in past years and less than adolescents in most other industrialized countries (Centers for Disease Control, 2000a; Hickman et al., 2000).

SLEEP NEEDS AND PROBLEMS

Sleep deprivation among adolescents has been called an epidemic (Hansen, Janssen, Schiff, Zee & Dubocovich, 2005). The American Academy of Sleep Medicine (2016) recommends that adolescents age 13 to 18 should regularly sleep a minimum of 8 to 10 hours per 24-hour period. However, most do not. A national poll found the prevalence of short sleep duration in middle school students was 57.8 percent, but rose to 72.7 percent by the high school years. Girls (75.6 percent) were slightly more likely to be sleep deprived than boys (69.9 percent). There were some relatively small differences between ethnic groups as well. Asian (79.3 percent), African American (76.5 percent), and Native American (75 percent) students were the most likely to be sleep deprived, while white (72 percent) and Hispanic (70.2 percent) students fared slightly better. (Wheaton, Jones, Cooper & Croft, 2018).

Children generally go to sleep later and sleep less on school days the older they get. While 61.3 percent of U.S. sixth graders report sleeping less than 8 hours a night, by 12th grade, almost 78 percent do not sleep a full 8 hours (Wheaton et al., 2018), a pattern that is true internationally (Owens & Adolescent Sleep Working Group, 2014). This is particularly distressing as both children and adolescents need sleep, and adolescents need even more sleep than when they were younger (Hoban, 2004; Iglowstein et al., 2003). Although many teens attempt to catch up with the sleep

Sleep deprivation among adolescents is extremely common and can lead to declines in school performance.
©S. Olsson/PhotoAlto

deficit on weekends (Owens & Adolescent Sleep Working Group, 2014), sleeping in on weekends does not make up for the loss of sleep on school nights (Hoban, 2004).

Sleep deprivation can sap motivation and cause irritability, and concentration and school performance can suffer. Sleepiness has also been associated with impaired driving and automobile accidents (Garner et al., 2015; Owens & Adolescent Sleep Working Group, 2014). Studies have found that young people ages 16 to 29 are most likely to be involved in crashes caused by the driver falling asleep (Millman et al., 2005). Moreover, insufficient sleep is associated with increased risk for obesity, diabetes, injuries, poor mental health, attention and behavioral problems, and poor academic performance (Wheaton et al., 2018).

Why do adolescents stay up late? They may need to do homework, listen to music, play video games, or talk to or text friends and surf the Web. Such behavior has been clearly linked to the chronic sleep deprivation of modern teenagers (Bartel, Gradisar & Williamson, 2015; Owens & Adolescent Sleep Working Group, 2014). However, sleep experts now recognize that biological changes are also behind adolescents' sleep problems. The timing of secretion of the hormone *melatonin* is a gauge of when the brain is ready for sleep. After puberty, this secretion takes place later at night (Carskadon, Vieira & Acebo, 1993) But adolescents still need just as much sleep as before, so when they go to bed later than younger children, they need to get up later as well. Yet most secondary schools start *earlier* than elementary schools. Their schedules are out of sync with students' biological rhythms (Carskadon, 2011). Teenagers tend to be least alert and most stressed early in the morning and more alert in the afternoon (Hansen et al., 2005). Starting school later, or at least offering difficult courses later in the day, would positively influence key outcomes such as student attendance, fatigue, and academic achievement (Adolescent Sleep Working Group, 2014; Boergers, Gable & Owens, 2014; Carrell, Maghakian & West, 2011).

NUTRITION AND EATING DISORDERS

Good nutrition is important to support the rapid growth of adolescence and to establish healthy eating habits that will last through adulthood. Unfortunately, many adolescents eat fewer fruits and vegetables and consume more foods high in cholesterol, fat, and calories and low in nutrients than they should.

Prevalence of Overweight and Obesity

Worldwide, overweight and obesity in children and adolescents has increased substantially. The prevalence rates have increased by nearly 50 percent over the past 30 years. In the developing world, nearly 13 percent of boys and more than 13 percent of girls were overweight or obese in 2013. In developed countries, more than 22 percent of girls and nearly 24 percent of boys were overweight or obese (Murray & Ng, 2017).

Within high-income countries, such as the United States, Canada, Greece, and Italy, approximately a third of teens are overweight, with boys more likely to be overweight than girls (Patton et al., 2012). In middle- and especially lower-income countries, undernutrition often co-occurs with overweight. For example, between a fifth to a third of boys in China, the eastern Mediterranean, Latin American countries, Mauritania, Thailand, and the region of Oceania are overweight (Patton et al., 2012).

In the United States, 13- to 15-year-olds are about twice as likely to be overweight as their age-mates in 14 other industrialized countries (Lissau et al., 2004). About 34 percent of U.S. teens have a body mass index (BMI) at or above the 85th percentile for age and sex. The percentage of U.S. adolescents with BMIs at this level rose from 5 percent in 1980 (Ogden et al., 2010) to over 20 percent in 2014 (National Center for Health Statistics, 2017). Among older adolescents, obesity is 50 percent more prevalent in those from poor families (Miech et al., 2006). Mexican American girls and boys and non-Hispanic black girls, who tend to be poorer than their peers, are more likely to be overweight than non-Hispanic white adolescents (Hernandez & Macartney, 2008; Ogden et al., 2010).

Causes and Consequences of Overweight and Obesity

There are clear genetic contributions to obesity. Being born to overweight or obese parents is a risk factor for childhood and adolescent obesity, and overweight and BMI appear to be strongly influenced genetically (Wardle, Carnell, Haworth & Plomin, 2008; Silventoinen, Rokholm, Kaprio & Sorenson, 2010). It is important to remember, however, that in addition to genes, parents also provide a nutritional environment to their children.

Moreover, the rise in obesity rates has happened too quickly for it to be due purely to genetic influences. An obesogenic environment in conjunction with genetic influences is to blame. This trend is being driven by increased consumption of animal fat and protein, refined grains, and added

Did you know?

In one study, teens who were obese were significantly less likely to get as much sleep as teens of normal weight (Liou, Liou & Chang, 2010).

©National Geographic/AP Images

sugar, and concurrent decreases in physical activity. These diet and lifestyle changes are brought about by global trade liberalization, economic growth, and urbanization (Malik, Willett & Hu, 2013).

body image Descriptive and evaluative beliefs about one's appearance.

Overweight teenagers tend to be in poorer health than their peers and are more likely to have difficulty attending school or engaging in strenuous activity or personal care (Swallen, Reither, Haas & Meier, 2005). They are at heightened risk of hypertension, diabetes, and cardiac disease (Sahoo et al., 2015; Flynn, 2013; Pulgaron, 2013). One in 5 have abnormal lipid levels, including either too much bad cholesterol, too little good cholesterol, or high blood triglycerides (Centers for Disease Control, 2010). They tend to become obese adults, subject to a variety of physical, social, and psychological risks (Singh, Mulder, Twisk, Van Mechelen & Chinapaw, 2008). Given how many adolescents are overweight today, one research team projects that by 2035 more than 100,000 additional cases of cardiovascular disease will be attributable to an increased prevalence of overweight in young and middle-aged men and women (Bibbins-Domingo, Coxson, Pletcher, Lightwood & Goldman, 2007).

Dieting for adolescents may be counterproductive as interventions in which dieting is encouraged can sometimes result in weight gain for participants (Field et al., 2003). Programs that use behavioral modification techniques to help adolescents make lifestyle changes have had better success. For example, interventions that have encouraged increases in physical activity, reductions in television viewing, and encouragement of healthier eating habits, either home- or school-based, have been shown to reduce body mass index and other weight-related outcome measures (Wang et al., 2013; Doak, Visscher, Renders & Seidell, 2006). Still, despite many interventions, a recent study showed that the number of 15-year-olds who are overweight or obese has steadily

Repeated exposure to photographs of thin women like the Duchess of Cambridge lead some young women to feel dissatisfied with their bodies.
©Mirrorpix/Splash News/Newscom

increased since 2000 in most countries that have implemented such programs (World Health Organization, 2017a).

Body Image and Eating Disorders

Sometimes a determination not to become overweight can result in problems more serious than overweight itself. Concern with body image may lead to obsessive efforts at weight control. This pattern is more common among girls than boys.

Boys and girls respond differently to the body changes that result from puberty. **Body image**—or one's perceptions, thoughts, and feelings about his or her body—can be affected by puberty. Overall, boys tend to be more satisfied with their bodies than girls (Makinen, Puukko-Viertomies, Lindberg, Siimes & Aalberg, 2012; Lawler & Nixon, 2011). Because of the normal increase in girls' body fat during puberty, many become unhappy with their appearance, reflecting the cultural emphasis on women's physical attributes (Susman & Rogol, 2004). Girls tend to express the highest levels of body satisfaction when underweight, some dissatisfaction when average weight, and the most dissatisfaction when overweight. Boys express the most dissatisfaction when overweight and underweight, but are more satisfied with an average weight body (Makinen et al., 2012; Lawler & Nixon, 2011). Body satisfaction is important because it has been related to self-esteem (Wichstrom & von Soest, 2016), dieting, and disordered eating (Bucchianeri et al., 2016). In fact, body satisfaction actually may be protective for overweight girls. In one study, overweight girls with low body satisfaction gained significantly more weight over a decade—an almost 3 unit increase in body mass index—than overweight girls with high body satisfaction. This suggests that the common belief held by many people that being dissatisfied with one's body motivates weight loss, at least in girls, is not correct (Loth, Watts, Van Den Berg & Newmark-Sztainer, 2015).

There are also ethnic differences in body satisfaction. Asian American boys and girls have the highest levels of body dissatisfaction, followed by Hispanics, whites, and African Americans (Buccianeri et al., 2016). African American girls are generally more satisfied with their bodies and less concerned about weight and dieting than are white girls (Gillen & Lefkowitz, 2012; Wardle et al., 2004).

By age 15, more than half the girls sampled in 16 countries were dieting or thought they should be. The United States was at the top of the list, with 47 percent of 11-year-old girls and 62 percent of 15-year-old girls concerned about their weight (Vereecken & Maes, 2000). Part of this may be driven by the ways in which parents discuss weight concerns with their children. When fathers talk to their sons, they are more likely to focus on healthy eating and exercise. By contrast, when mothers talk to their daughters, they are more likely to talk about weight management (Berge et al., 2015).

There are clearly other influences at play as well. Friends are one important influence. For example, friends' dieting, teasing about weight, and pressure to conform to weight ideals predict weight-control behaviors and negative body image (Balantekin, Birch & Savage, 2018; Kenny, O'Malley-Keighran, Molchro & Kelly, 2017; Eisenberg & Neumark-Sztainer, 2010). Media also exert a powerful influence. When adolescents, especially young women, are exposed to images of a thin ideal in mass media content such as magazines, television, and videos, they show more dissatisfaction with their bodies, more concern with their appearance and greater endorsement of disordered eating behaviors (Grabe, Ward & Hyde, 2008). Similar findings have emerged with respect to social media. Research indicates that the use of social media such as Facebook and Instagram is associated with body image concerns in adolescents, and that these concerns become more pronounced over time (Fardouly & Vartanian, 2016).

Excessive concern with weight control and body image may be signs of anorexia nervosa or bulimia nervosa, both of which involve abnormal patterns of food intake. These chronic disorders occur worldwide, mostly in adolescent girls and young women.

Katharine McPhee, a 2006 American idol runner-up who is currently working as an actress and singer, struggled with bulimia.
©Paul Morigi/Stringer/Getty Images

Anorexia Nervosa An estimated 0.3 to 0.5 percent of adolescent girls and young women and a smaller but growing percentage of boys and men in Western countries have **anorexia nervosa**. People with anorexia have a distorted body image and, though typically severely underweight, think they are too fat. They are often good students but may be withdrawn or depressed and may engage in repetitive, perfectionist behavior. They are extremely afraid of losing self-control and becoming overweight (American Academy of Pediatrics [AAP] Committee on Adolescence, 2003; Martínez-González et al., 2003; Wilson, Grilo, & Vitousek, 2007). Early warning signs include determined, secret dieting; dissatisfaction after losing weight; setting new, lower weight goals after reaching an initial desired weight; excessive exercising; and interruption of regular menstruation.

Anorexia is, paradoxically, both deliberate and involuntary: an affected person deliberately refuses food needed for sustenance yet cannot stop doing so even when rewarded or punished. These behavior patterns have been traced back to medieval times and seem to have existed in all parts of the world. Thus, anorexia may be in part a reaction to societal pressure to be slender, but this does not seem to be the only factor or even a necessary one (Keel & Klump, 2003; Striegel-Moore & Bulik, 2007).

Bulimia Nervosa **Bulimia nervosa** is an eating disorder that affects about 1 to 2 percent of international populations (Wilson et al., 2007). A person with bulimia regularly goes on huge, short-lived eating binges (2 hours or less) and then may try to purge the high caloric intake through self-induced vomiting; strict dieting or fasting; excessively vigorous exercise; or laxatives, enemas, or diuretics. These episodes occur at least once a week for at least 3 months (American Psychiatric Association, 2013). People with bulimia are usually within normal weight ranges, but they are obsessed with their weight and shape. They tend to have low self-esteem

and may become overwhelmed with shame, self-contempt, and depression (Wilson et al., 2007).

There is some overlap between anorexia and bulimia; some people with anorexia have bulimic episodes, and some people with bulimia lose large amounts of weight (Eddy et al., 2008).

A related *binge eating disorder* (BED) involves frequent binging but without subsequent fasting, exercise, or vomiting (American Psychiatric Association, 2013). Not surprisingly, people who binge frequently tend to be overweight and to experience emotional distress and other medical and psychological disorders. BED is the most common eating disorder in the United States, affecting approximately 1.6 percent of adolescents and becoming more common in adulthood. Approximately 2 percent of adult men and 3.5 percent of adult women meet the criteria for diagnosis (Swanson, Crow, Le Grange, Swendsen & Merikangas, 2011).

Treatment and Outcomes of Eating Disorders The immediate goal of treatment for anorexia is to get patients to eat and gain weight—goals that are often difficult to achieve given the strength of patients' beliefs about their bodies. Patients who show signs of severe malnutrition, are resistant to treatment, or do not make progress on an outpatient basis may be admitted to a hospital, where they can be given 24-hour care. Once their weight is stabilized, patients may enter less intensive daytime care (McCallum & Bruton, 2003).

One widely used treatment is a type of family therapy in which parents take control of their child's eating patterns. When the child begins to comply

anorexia nervosa Eating disorder characterized by self-starvation and extreme weight loss.

bulimia nervosa Eating disorder in which a person regularly eats huge quantities of food and then purges the body by laxatives, induced vomiting, fasting, or excessive exercise.

with parental directives, she (or he) may be given more age-appropriate autonomy. Cognitive behavioral therapy, which seeks to change a distorted body image and rewards eating with such privileges as being allowed to get out of bed and leave the room, appears to be the most effective treatment (Hay, 2013). Patients may keep daily diaries of their eating patterns and are taught ways to avoid the temptation to binge. Bulimia, too, is best treated with cognitive behavioral therapy (Wilson et al., 2007).

Individual, group, or family psychotherapy can help both anorexia and bulimia patients, usually after initial behavior therapy has brought symptoms under control. Initially, both family and individual therapy show similar outcomes. However, at 6 to 12 months posttreatment, teens who participated in family therapy show more lasting gains than those who participated in individual therapy (Couturier, Kimber & Szatmari, 2013).

Because these patients are at risk for depression and suicide, antidepressant drugs are often combined with psychotherapy (Chesney, Goodwin & Fazel, 2014; McCallum & Bruton, 2003), but evidence of their long-term effectiveness on either anorexia or bulimia is lacking (Wilson et al., 2007).

Mortality rates among those affected with anorexia nervosa have been estimated at about 10 percent of cases. Among the surviving anorexia patients, less than one-half make a full recovery and only one-third actually improve; 20 percent remain chronically ill (Steinhausen, 2002). Up to one-third of patients drop out of treatment before achieving an appropriate weight (McCallum & Bruton, 2003). Those who drop out are most likely to have had low motivation and engaged in more binge and purge behaviors (Vall & Wade, 2015). Recovery rates from bulimia are a bit better and average 30 to 50 percent after cognitive behavioral therapy (Wilson et al., 2007).

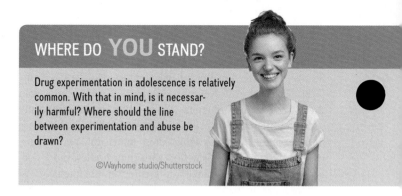

DRUG USE

Although the great majority of adolescents do not abuse drugs, a significant minority do. **Substance abuse** is harmful use of alcohol or other drugs. It can lead to substance dependence, or addiction, which may be physiological, psychological, or both and is likely to continue into adulthood. Addictive drugs are especially dangerous because they stimulate parts of the brain that are still developing in adolescence (Crews, He & Hodge, 2007). About 12 percent of teens ages 13 to 17 will at some point receive treatment for alcohol use and more than 18 percent for illicit drug use (Substance Abuse and Mental Health Services Administration [SAMHSA], 2013).

Trends in Drug Use

Nearly half (47 percent) of U.S. adolescents have tried illicit drugs by the time they leave high school (Johnston, O'Malley, Bachman & Schulenberg, 2013). There was an upsurge in drug use during the mid- to late 1990s, then drug use started to go down in the late '90s until 2008, where it once again started to rise (Figure 4.4). This pattern once

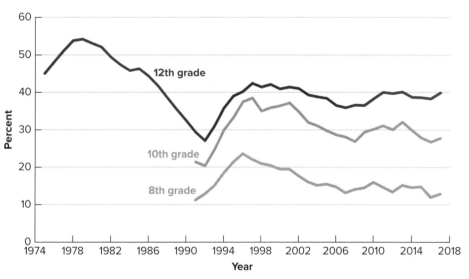

FIGURE 4.4 Trends in High School Students' Use of Illicit Drugs over the Previous 12 Months

Source: R. A. Miech, L. D. Johnston, P. M. O'Malley, J. G. Bachman, J. E. Schulenberg & M. E. Patrick, *Monitoring the Future national survey results on drug use, 1975–2017: Volume I, Secondary school students*. Ann Arbor: Institute for Social Research, The University of Michigan, 2018.

©PhotoAlto/Getty Images

again reversed in 2011, and illicit drug use started to decline again, although less so for marijuana (Johnston, O'Malley, Bachman, Schulenberg & Miech, 2016).

These findings come from the latest in a series of annual government surveys of a nationally representative sample of 8th, 10th, and 12th graders from more than 400 schools across the United States. These surveys probably underestimate adolescent drug use because they are based on self-reports and do not reach high school dropouts, who are more likely to use drugs. Continued progress in eliminating drug abuse is slow because new drugs are continually introduced or rediscovered by a new generation, and young people do not necessarily generalize the adverse consequences of one drug to another (Johnston et al., 2016).

A recent trend is the abuse of nonprescription cough and cold medications; 3 percent of 8th graders, 4.7 percent of 10th graders, and 5.6 percent of 12th graders report taking medicines containing dextromethorphan (DXM), a cough suppressant, to get high within the past year (Johnston et al., 2013).

In the past two decades, there has also been a general increase in opioid abuse. This involves both prescription and street drugs (Dart et al., 2015; Substance Abuse and Mental Health Services Administration, 2013). With respect to adolescents, use of legal narcotics nearly tripled from 1992 to 2009, and then declined slightly. Use of heroin by children in 8th through 12th grade peaked in the mid to late '90s, and then showed a downward path since that time (Johnston, O'Malley, Miech, Bachman & Schulenberg, 2016). The sharp rise in heroin usage reported in the United States has primarily been limited to older teens and emerging adults, where peak levels of usage were reached in the mid 2000s (Schulenberg et al., 2017).

Alcohol

Alcohol is a potent, mind-altering drug with major effects on physical, emotional, and social well-being. Worldwide, approximately 34.1 percent of adolescents age 15 to 19 years reported themselves to be current drinkers, and another 12 percent reported having consumed alcohol previously. Drinking alcohol was more common in European and American regions,

and least common in Southeast Asian and Eastern Mediterranean regions. Adolescents also reported heavy episodic drinking in the previous month at relatively high rates—11.7 percent, compared to a rate of 7.5 percent in adults. Adolescent women reported drinking less on average, less often, and were less likely to report heavy episodic drinking than adolescent men (World Health Organization & WHO Management of Substance Abuse Unit, 2014).

Alcohol use in U.S. teenagers showed a dramatic rise in the 1990s, followed by a smaller, gradual decline (Johnston et al., 2013; Miech, Johnston, O'Malley, Bachman & Schulenberg 2016). In 2016, 26 percent of U.S. 8th graders, 47 percent of 10th graders, and 64 percent of 12th graders said they had tried alcohol, and current use (in the past 30 days) is likewise high. (Miech et al., 2016). **Binge drinking**—consuming five or more drinks on one occasion—puts teens at particularly high risk. While 17 percent of 12th graders report binge drinking during the previous 2 weeks, (Miech et al., 2016), this does represent a decline from levels found in the early 2000s, when 25 percent of high school seniors admitted to binge drinking (McQueeny et al., 2009).

> **binge drinking** Consuming five or more drinks on one occasion.

From a theoretical perspective, it would be expected that adolescence, when the brain is undergoing significant structural and functional change, might be a period of the life span during which teens should be particularly sensitive to environmental influences (Gogtay et al., 2004). Additionally, alcohol interacts with inhibitory (e.g., GABA) and excitatory (e.g., N-methyl-d-aspartate) receptor systems that are developing in adolescence, making adolescents more sensitive to the rewarding effects of alcohol and less sensitive to its negative features (Spear, 2014).

Brain imaging studies have documented structural brain changes in adolescents as a result of alcohol consumption. Generally, those changes can be characterized as consisting of dose-dependent smaller gray matter volume and lower white matter integrity as a result of alcohol use. When compared to teens who do not drink alcohol, a recent meta-analysis showed that those who do drink show changes in key prefrontal areas, including the middle frontal gyrus, superior frontal gyrus, left frontal cortex, frontal pole, and left frontal gyrus—all areas involved in executive control. Structural differences have also been found in areas of the brain involved in reward mechanisms, including the dorsal striatum, thalamus, anterior cingulate, and inferior frontal gyrus (Ewing, Sakhardande & Blakemore, 2014).

MRI-based studies have revealed that binge drinking in teenagers may affect thinking and memory by damaging sensitive "white matter" in the brain (McQueeny et al., 2009). In one study, 15- and 16-year-old alcohol abusers who stopped drinking showed cognitive impairments weeks later in comparison with nonabusing peers (Brown, Tapert, Granholm & Delis, 2000). Moreover, teenage binge drinkers are more likely than other students to report poor school performance and to engage in other risky behaviors (Miller, Naimi, Brewer & Jones, 2007). The effects of alcohol on brain development may be more severe for young women than men (Ewing et al., 2014).

Marijuana

Despite the decline in marijuana use since 1996–1997, it is still by far the most widely used illicit drug in the United States. In 2012, about 11 percent of 8th graders, 28 percent of 10th graders, and 36 percent of 12th graders admitted to having used it in the past year (Johnston et al., 2013). Approximately 1 in every 17 high school seniors uses marijuana daily (Johnston et al., 2016). The impact of recent movements to legalize marijuana for recreational use, such as has happened in nine states as of 2018, remains to be seen. There are some indications that the legalization of marijuana may lead to increased usage (Johnston et al., 2016) as well as an increase in the number of people who develop problems with its abuse (Chou, Zhang, Jung, Pickering & Ruan, 2015). However, such research has focused on adults, and other data suggest that marijuana usage by teens has not shown a rise in response to its legalization (Anderson, Hansen & Rees, 2015).

Marijuana potency quadrupled from 1980 to 2014 (ElSohly et al, 2016). Heavy use has been associated with damage to the brain, heart, and lungs. It has been correlated with declines in school performance, memory problems, and increased risk for anxiety and depression. Like any drug, if used while driving, it can contribute to traffic accidents. Given the higher potency of modern marijuana, older studies may not fully capture potential for harm at current levels. Additionally, it is difficult to disentangle the direct effects of marijuana with indirect effects, such as concurrent use of other drugs. The debate about marijuana use is also complicated by the fact that marijuana does have legitimate medical applications and has been used to manage such conditions as nausea, chronic pain, and epilepsy (Volkow, Baler, Compton & Weiss, 2014).

Did you know?

Urea, a chemical compound found in urine, is used to add flavor to cigarettes.

©Matti/Alamy

Tobacco

The use of cigarettes and other tobacco products is a global health issue. Adolescent use is particularly concerning because the vast majority of smokers begin smoking prior to adulthood, and became addicted in adolescence. Cigarettes will kill approximately half of all lifetime users and increase the risk of multiple cancers, especially lung cancer, as well as

heart disease, stroke, emphysema, and multiple other diseases (Eriksen, Mackay & Ross, 2013).

Adolescent tobacco use is a less widespread problem in the United States than in most other industrialized countries (Gabhainn & Francois, 2000). Still, in the United States, approximately 5 percent of 8th graders, 11 percent of 10th graders, and 17 percent of 12th graders are current (past-month) tobacco smokers (Johnston et al., 2013). Black youth tend to smoke less but metabolize nicotine more slowly than white youth, so their bodies take longer to get rid of it and they are quicker to become dependent (Moolchan, Franken & Jaszyna-Gasior, 2006).

Although this number is high and cause for concern, there is some good news. In the late 1990s, about 28 percent of 9th to 12th graders reported being current smokers. Current data now put this number at 7 percent (Johnston, O'Malley, Miech, Bachman & Schulenberg, 2016). In 2015, e-cigarettes were the most commonly used form of tobacco among middle and high school students (Singh et al., 2016). This is troubling, as there is reason to suspect that e-cigarette users may eventually graduate to cigarettes.

A randomized, controlled trial found nicotine replacement therapy plus behavioral skills training effective in helping adolescents stop smoking (Killen et al., 2004). Additionally, parents can provide a positive influence by discouraging friendships with peers who smoke (Simons-Morton & Farhat, 2010).

The Initiation of Nicotine and Alcohol Use

Generally, alcohol, along with tobacco, is one of the first substances that is tried. The peak period for trying alcohol is between 7th and 11th grade, although some children start earlier (Miech, Johnston, O'Malley, Bachman & Schulenberg, 2016). The earlier young people start to use a drug, the more frequently they are likely to use it and the greater their tendency to abuse it (Wong et al., 2006).

The average age for starting to drink is 13 to 14 (Faden, 2006), and those who start drinking before age 15 are more than 5 times more likely to become alcohol dependent or alcohol abusers than those who do not start drinking until age 21 or later (SAMHSA, 2004). Young people who begin drinking early tend to have behavior problems, siblings who are alcohol dependent, or an alcoholic parent (Kuperman et al., 2005; Wong et al., 2006). Adolescents exposed to alcohol before age 15 demonstrate an increased risk for substance disorders (Hingson, Heeren & Winter, 2006), risky sexual behavior (Stueve & O'Donnell, 2005), low educational attainment, and crime (King, Meehan, Trim & Chassin, 2006).

Smoking often begins in the early teenage years as a sign of toughness, rebelliousness, and passage from childhood to adulthood. This desired image enables a young initiate to tolerate initial distaste for the first few puffs, after which the effects of nicotine begin to take over to sustain the habit. Within a year or two after starting to smoke, these young people inhale the same amount of nicotine as adults and experience the same cravings and withdrawal effects if they try to quit. Young adolescents attracted to smoking often come from homes, schools, and neighborhoods where smoking is common. They also tend to be overweight, have low self-esteem, and are unsuccessful at school (Jarvis, 2004). The omnipresence of substance use in the media is another important influence. Movies that depict smoking increase early initiation of smoking (Charlesworth & Glantz, 2005).

Peer influences on both smoking and drinking have been documented extensively (Cleveland & Wiebe, 2003). As with hard drugs, older siblings and friends can increase the likelihood of tobacco and alcohol use (Rende, Slomkowski, Lloyd-Richardson & Niaura, 2005), and closer friends have a stronger influence on each other than more distant friends (Fujimoto & Valente, 2012). Recent research indicates that peer and sibling influences can also act via media such as online social media postings and messaging content (Huang et al., 2014). However, it is important to remember that there are also selection issues at play. For example, adolescents who smoke are likely to seek out friends who share their habit (Simons-Morton & Farhat, 2010).

Parents, too, can influence the likelihood of smoking and drinking in their children. Parents who smoke significantly increase the risk that their adolescent will smoke (Leonardi-Bee, Jere & Britton, 2011). Similarly, parents who have more alcohol-related problems or more lenient attitudes about alcohol are more likely to have teen children who drink excessively or have alcohol-related problems. Overall, parents who monitor their adolescent's activities and exert some control, while also maintaining a warm and positive relationship are less likely to have teens who smoke and drink (Piko & Balazs, 2012).

DEPRESSION

The prevalence of depression increases during adolescence, as shown in Figure 14.5. In 2016, 12.8 percent of young people ages 12 to 17 experienced at least one episode of major depression, and only 40.9 percent of them had been treated

(SAHMSA, 2017). Rates generally increase with increasing age. Depression in young people does not necessarily appear as sadness but as irritability, boredom, or inability to experience pleasure. At least 1 in 5 persons who experience bouts of depression in childhood or adolescence are at risk for bipolar disorder, in which depressive episodes ("low" periods) alternate with manic episodes ("high" periods) characterized by increased energy, euphoria, grandiosity, and risk-taking (Brent & Birmaher, 2002).

Being female is a risk factor for depression. Adolescent girls, especially early maturing girls, are more likely to be depressed than adolescent boys (Galvao et al., 2014; NSDUH, 2012). This gender difference may be related to biological changes associated with puberty; studies show a correlation between advancing puberty status and depressive symptoms (Susman & Rogol, 2004). Other possible factors are the way girls are socialized (Birmaher et al., 1996) and their greater vulnerability to stress in social relationships (Hankin, Mermelstein & Roesch, 2007).

In addition to female gender, risk factors for depression include anxiety, fear of social contact, stressful life events, chronic illnesses such as diabetes or epilepsy, parent-child conflict, abuse or neglect, alcohol and drug use, sexual activity, and having a parent with a history of depression. Alcohol and drug use and sexual activity are more likely to lead to depression in girls than in boys (Hallfors, Waller, Bauer, Ford & Halpern, 2005; NSDUH, 2012; Waller et al., 2006).

Depressed adolescents who do not respond to outpatient treatment or who have substance dependence or psychosis or seem suicidal may need to be hospitalized. Another treatment option for depression is psychotherapy. Studies have found that although psychotherapy can be effective in the short term, its effects last no more than a year (Weisz, McCarty & Valeri, 2006). More commonly, medications are used. Selective serotonin reuptake inhibitors (SSRIs) are currently approved for use in children and adolescents and commonly prescribed. Although there are concerns about

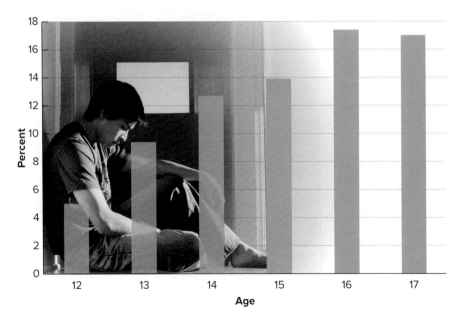

FIGURE 14.5 Depression Rates for 12- to 17-Year-Olds

Rates of depression typically go up with increasing age during adolescence.

Source: National Institute of Mental Health, National Institutes of Health. *Statistics: Major depression* (2017). Retrieved from www.nimh.nih.gov/health/statistics/major-depression.shtml.

©Nathan Lau/Design Pics

their safety, research suggests that the benefits outweigh the risks (Bridge et al., 2007). The most effective treatment for depressed adolescents, at least in the short term, seems to be a combination of medications and cognitive behavioral therapy (Dubicka et al., 2010; March & the TADS Team, 2007).

DEATH

Death this early in life is always tragic and usually but not always accidental. Worldwide in 2012, a 50-year downward trend for lower adolescent mortality continued, although that number still comprised some 1.3 million teens. The top five causes of death were automobile accidents, HIV, suicide, lower respiratory infection, and violence (World Health Organization, 2016).

In the United States, 75 percent of all deaths among adolescents resulted from motor vehicle crashes, other unintentional injuries, homicide, and suicide, with the remainder of deaths stemming from medical causes such as cancer, heart disease, and congenital malformations. Violent death is a relatively frequent occurrence for adolescents. For instance, in people ages 15 to 24, homicide is the second leading cause of death. For people age 25 to 44, homicide drops to the fifth leading cause, and after the age of 45 years, it does not appear in the top 10 (NCHS, 2011). The mortality rate of 15- to 19-year-old American males is more than twice that of female adolescents (Child Health USA, 2012). The frequency of violent deaths in this age group reflects a violent culture as well as adolescents' inexperience and immaturity, which often lead to risk-taking and carelessness.

Deaths from Motor Accidents

Motor vehicle collisions are the leading cause of death among U.S. teenagers, accounting for approximately one-third of all deaths in adolescence (Miniño, 2010). The risk of collision is greater among 16- to 19-year-olds than for any other age group, and especially so for males (Miniño, Anderson, Fingerhut, Boureault & Warner, 2006; National Center for Injury Prevention and Control, 2004). Collisions are more likely to be fatal when teenage passengers are in the vehicle, probably because adolescents tend to drive more recklessly in the presence of peers (Chen, Baker, Braver & Li, 2000). In the United States, about 1 in 5 teens involved in fatal traffic crashes had been drinking, suggesting that alcohol is a major factor in accident-related fatalities (National Highway Traffic Safety Administration, 2017).

Another important risk factor is distracted driving, which includes texting, talking on a cell phone, or eating. While all drivers risk a crash if distracted, novice drivers are at the highest risk (Miniño et al., 2006). For example, they are 8 times more likely to crash or have a near miss when dialing a phone in comparison to experienced drivers who are 2 times more likely to do so (Klauer et al., 2014).

Despite efforts aimed at increasing seat belt use among teens, observed use among teens and young adults was 61 percent in 2015—the lowest of any age group (Centers for Disease Control, 2017b). In fact, in 2015, 58 percent of young people 16 to 20 years old involved in fatal motor vehicle crashes were unbuckled (National Highway Traffic Safety Administration, 2017).

Firearm-Related Deaths

Homicides are the second leading cause of death for adolescents in the United States (Child Trends DataBank, 2015). Firearm-related deaths are far more common in the United States than in other industrialized countries (Grinshteyn & Hemenway, 2016). The United States has a higher firearm mortality rate than the next highest 25 industrialized nations combined (Blum & Qureshi, 2011).

Adolescent boys are eight times more likely to be fatally shot than girls (Price & Khubchandani, 2017). Race and ethnicity matter as well; the homicide rate for African American male teens is more than 20 times higher that that of white male teens (Child Trends DataBank, 2015; Price & Khubchandani, 2017). Gun fatalities make up about one-third of all injury deaths and more than 85 percent of homicides in that age group. The chief reason for these grim statistics seems to be

Dan Savage, pictured here with his long-term partner, created the *It Gets Better Project*, which has the goal of preventing suicide among LGBT youth.
©ZUMA Wire Service/Alamy

the ease of obtaining a gun in the United States (AAP Committee on Injury and Poison Prevention, 2000). Indeed, having a firearm in the home is correlated with being the victim of a homicide (Anglemyer, Horvath & Rutherford, 2014).

Suicide

"We found out Dan—the guy in my fourth period homeroom—shot and killed himself last weekend," wrote Sara. "It's so sad. It's terrible really. I knew he was weird and quiet and everything, but to kill yourself? That's so awful. I can't imagine what he was going through. I feel sad now that I never really paid him any attention."

Suicide is the third leading cause of death among U.S. 15- to 19-year-olds (Miniño, 2010). The teenage suicide rate fell by 34 percent between 1990 and 2006, perhaps in part due to restrictions on children's access to firearms (CDC, 2008b; Lubell, Kegler, Crosby & Karch, 2007). Indeed, having a firearm in the home is strongly associated with an increased risk of completed suicide (Anglemyer, Hovarth & Rutherford, 2014). In 2004, however, the suicide rate increased by 8 percent, with the largest increases among teenage girls (Lubell et al., 2007). Rates continued to rise through 2015, with firearms remaining the most common method used (Kegler, 2017).

Adolescent girls are more likely to attempt suicide, but tend to use less lethal methods, such as suffocation or poisoning, and thus are more likely to survive. Although adolescent boys are less likely to attempt suicide, their greater propensity to use firearms results in a greater chance of a successful attempt (Price & Khubchandani, 2017; Child Trends DataBank, 2015).

Although suicide occurs in all ethnic groups, white adolescents have the highest rates, followed by Hispanics and African Americans (Price & Khubchandani, 2017). Gay, lesbian, and bisexual youths, who have high rates of depression, also have unusually high rates of suicide and attempted suicide (AAP Committee on Adolescence, 2000). The highest rates of suicide are found in transgender and gender nonconforming individuals. A recent study found that 41 percent of such adults reported attempting suicide at some point in their life (Herman, Haas & Rogers, 2014).

Young people who consider or attempt suicide tend to have histories of emotional illness. They are likely to be either perpetrators or victims of violence and to have school problems, academic or behavioral. Many have suffered from maltreatment in childhood and have severe problems with relationships. They tend to think poorly of themselves, to feel hopeless, and to have poor impulse control and a low tolerance for frustration and stress. These young people are often alienated from their parents and have no one outside the family to turn to. They also tend to have attempted suicide before, to have friends or family members who did so, or to report suicidal ideation (Borowsky, Ireland & Resnick, 2001; Brent & Mann, 2006; Nock et al., 2013). Substance abuse, especially heroin, is also a risk factor, and that risk increases with the number of illicit substances being used (Wong, Zhou, Goebert & Hishinuma, 2013). Protective factors that reduce the risk of suicide include a sense of connectedness to family and school, emotional well-being, and academic achievement (Taliaferro & Muehlenkamp, 2014; Borowsky et al., 2001).

Whenever a person expresses suicidal feelings, it is essential to address the statements. For instance, one might ask direct questions such as "Have you thought about how you would do it?" or "Are you thinking of hurting yourself?" If the person answers affirmatively, emergency help is needed. Do not leave the person alone, and seek help from trained professionals (such as in an emergency room) immediately (Mayo Clinic, 2012).

mastering the CHAPTER

©Caiaimage/Trevor Adeline/Getty Images

Summary and Key Terms

Adolescence

> Adolescence, in modern industrial societies, is the transition from childhood to adulthood. It lasts from about age 11 to about 20.

> Early adolescence involves physical, cognitive, and psychosocial growth, but risks. Risky behavior

patterns, such as drinking alcohol, drug abuse, sexual activity, and use of firearms, tend to increase throughout the teenage years, but most young people experience no major problems.

> **KEY TERM**
>
> **Adolescence**

Puberty

> Puberty is triggered by hormonal changes. Puberty takes about 4 years, typically begins earlier in girls than in boys, and ends when a person can reproduce.

> Puberty is marked by two stages: (1) the activation of the adrenal glands and (2) the maturing of the sex organs a few years later.

> During puberty, both boys and girls undergo an adolescent growth spurt. The reproductive organs enlarge and mature, and secondary sex characteristics appear.

> A secular trend toward earlier attainment of adult height and sexual maturity began about 100 years ago, probably because of improvements in living standards.

> The principal signs of sexual maturity are production of sperm (for males) and menstruation (for females).

> Teenagers can be sensitive about their physical appearance. The timing of maturation can affect mental health and health-related behaviors in adulthood.

> **KEY TERMS**
>
> **Puberty** **Adolescent growth spurt** **Menarche**
>
> **Primary sex characteristics** **Spermarche** **Secular trend**
>
> **Secondary sex characteristics**

The Brain

> The adolescent brain is not yet fully mature, and adolescents process information differently than adults do. The brain undergoes a second wave of overproduction of gray matter, especially in the frontal lobes, followed by pruning of excess nerve cells. Continuing myelination of the frontal lobes facilitates the maturation of cognitive processing.

> Underdevelopment of frontal cortical systems connected with motivation, impulsivity, and addiction relative to the development of the frontal cortex may help explain adolescents' tendency toward risk-taking.

Physical and Mental Health

> Many adolescents do not engage in regular vigorous physical activity.

> Many adolescents do not get enough sleep because of electronics use and because the high school schedule is out of sync with their natural body rhythms.

> Three common eating disorders in adolescence are obesity, anorexia nervosa, and bulimia nervosa. All can have serious long-term effects. Concern with body image, especially among girls, may lead to eating disorders. Anorexia and bulimia affect mostly girls and young women. Outcomes for bulimia tend to be better than for anorexia.

> Adolescent substance use has lessened in recent years; still, drug use often begins as children move into middle school.

> Marijuana, alcohol, and tobacco are the most popular drugs with adolescents. All involve serious risks. Nonmedical use of prescription and over-the-counter drugs is an increasing problem.

> The prevalence of depression increases in adolescence, especially among girls.

> Leading causes of death among adolescents include motor vehicle accidents, firearm use, and suicide.

KEY TERMS

| Body image | Bulimia nervosa | Binge drinking |
| Anorexia nervosa | Substance abuse | |

Practice Quiz

1. Adolescence is best thought of as:
   a. a biological stage
   b. a social construction
   c. the first stage of adulthood
   d. a universal stage of development

2. Name two possible opportunities for growth in adolescence and two risks.

   _____

   _____

   _____

   _____

3. What are the two stages of puberty?

   _____

   _____

4. What are secondary sexual characteristics?
   a. male sexual characteristics
   b. female sexual characteristics
   c. sexual organs necessary for reproduction
   d. physiological signs of sexual maturation that do not directly involve the sex organs

5. Overall, early maturation:
   a. is strongly associated with positive outcomes for both girls and boys
   b. is strongly associated with positive outcomes for girls, and risks for boys
   c. is strongly associated with positive outcomes for boys, and risks for girls
   d. is associated with risks for both boys and girls

6. In adolescence, there is continued development of:
   a. the frontal lobes
   b. the temporal lobes
   c. the gray matter of the brain
   d. white matter of the brain, but only in girls

7. Adolescent drug use can have such devastating effects on the brain because:
   a. the majority of fibers in the corpus callosum are being laid down during adolescence
   b. a young person's activities and experiences determine which neuronal connections will be retained and strengthened
   c. drug use can stop the development of the frontal cortex
   d. this is a myth; drug use is equally damaging to the brain across the lifespan

8. What are three benefits associated with exercise?

   _____

   _____

   _____

9. Why have some psychologists suggested that classes for adolescents should start later in the morning?

   _____

   _____

   _____

10. Which of the following is a key difference between anorexia and bulimia?
    a. In anorexia there is an unhealthy preoccupation with food, in bulimia there is not.
    b. Anorexia is more common in girls, while bulimia is more common in boys.
    c. Anorexia is associated with a low weight, while girls with bulimia are more likely to be of typical weight.
    d. Anorexia is common in industrialized countries, while bulimia is common in nonindustrialized countries.

11. Adolescents who use drugs or alcohol are at higher risk if they:
    a. are girls
    b. are boys
    c. start using at an early age
    d. are honest with their parents about their usage

12. What are three factors associated with elevated risk for depression?

    _____

    _____

    _____

13. What is the leading cause of death in adolescence?
    a. motor fatalities
    b. firearm-related deaths
    c. suicide
    d. drug overdose

Answers: 1–b; 2–Among the opportunities for growth in adolescence are physical growth, cognitive and social competence, autonomy, self-esteem, and intimacy. Risks include accidents, homicide, suicide, drug or alcohol use, vehicle accidents, and risky sexual behavior. 3–The stages of puberty include (1) the activation of the adrenal glands and (2) the maturing of the sex organs; 4–d; 5–d; 6–a; 7–b; 8–The benefits of regular exercise include improved strength and endurance, healthier bones and muscles, weight control, reduced anxiety and stress, increased self-esteem, higher school grades, higher well-being, and a decrease in risky behaviors. 9–Psychologists have suggested schooling for adolescents start later because teens secrete melanin (a hormone associated with sleep) later than children, making it likely they will stay up later than do children. But, they still need as much sleep as children and are often groggy and sleepy in the early morning. Starting school later would be in sync with their biological rhythm and help improve their concentration. 10–c; 11–c; 12–Among the risk factors for depression are being female, having high anxiety or fear of social contact, stressful life events, chronic illnesses, parent-child conflict, abuse or neglect, alcohol and drug use, sexual activity, and having a parent with a history of depression. 13–a

What's to Come

> **Cognitive Development**

> **Moral Development**

> **Educational and Vocational Issues**

Adam is 15 years old. Sometimes he feels his parents just don't understand the world today—that their view of life is old fashioned. They think Adam is obsessed with his phone, and they worry about video games and cable television. Adam is beginning to question some of his parents' moral beliefs that he accepted as a child, and struggles to reconcile his views with theirs. "I'm not sure what I think or feel really, or even what I want to do when I get older," he says, "I'm still figuring it out. I don't even know if I really want to go to college." Like most 15-year-olds, Adam is on the cusp of adulthood. How he navigates these next few years will have profound consequences for his life's trajectory.

In this chapter, we examine the Piagetian stage of formal operations that allows Adam to think about different systems of knowledge. We look at adolescents' growth in information processing, including memory, knowledge, and reasoning, and in vocabulary and other linguistic skills. We note some immature aspects of adolescents' thought, and we examine adolescents' moral development. Finally, we explore practical aspects of cognitive growth—issues of school and vocational choice.

● ● ● ●

Cognitive Development

Adolescents not only look different from younger children, they also think and talk differently. Their speed of information processing and language abilities continue to increase, though not as dramatically as in middle childhood. However, at the same time they show increases in abilities, they nonetheless retain immature aspects of thought that are characteristically adolescent. These changes are reflected in the physical structure of the brain. In this section, we address these changes and discuss their impact.

PIAGET'S STAGE OF FORMAL OPERATIONS

Adolescents enter what Piaget called the highest level of cognitive development—**formal operations**—when they develop the capacity for abstract thought. This development, usually around age 11, gives them a new, more flexible way to manipulate information. No longer limited to the here and now, they can understand historical time and extraterrestrial space. They can use symbols for symbols, for example, letting the letter *x* stand for an unknown numeral, and thus can learn algebra and calculus. They can better appreciate metaphor and allegory and thus can find richer meanings in literature. They can think in terms of what might be, not just what is. They can imagine possibilities and can form and test hypotheses. People in the stage of formal operations

formal operations In Piaget's theory, final stage of cognitive development, characterized by the ability to think abstractly.

can integrate what they have learned in the past with the challenges of the present and make plans for the future.

Hypothetical-Deductive Reasoning

Hypothetical-deductive reasoning involves a methodical, scientific approach to problem solving. It involves the ability to develop, consider, and systematically test hypotheses. To appreciate the difference formal reasoning makes, let us follow the progress of a typical child in dealing with a classic Piagetian problem, the pendulum problem (adapted from Ginsburg & Opper, 1979).

Adam is shown the pendulum, an object hanging from a string. He is then shown how he can change any of four factors: the length of the string, the weight of the object, the height from which the object is released, and the amount of force he uses to push the object. He is asked to figure out which factor or combination of factors determines how fast the pendulum swings. (Figure 15.1 depicts this and other Piagetian tasks for assessing the achievement of formal operations.)

When Adam first sees the pendulum, he is not yet 7 years old and is in the preoperational stage. Unable to formulate a plan for attacking the problem, he tries one thing after another in a hit-or-miss manner. First he puts a light weight on a long string and pushes it; then he tries swinging a heavy weight on a short string; then he removes the weight entirely. Not only is his method random, but he also cannot understand or report what has happened.

Adam next encounters the pendulum at age 10, when he is in the stage of concrete operations. This time, he discovers that varying the length of the string and the weight of the object affects the speed of the swing. However, because he varies both factors at the same time, he cannot tell which is critical or whether both are.

Adam is confronted with the pendulum for a third time at age 15; this time he goes at the problem systematically. He designs an experiment to test all the possible hypotheses, varying one factor at a time—first, the length of the string; next, the weight of the object; then, the height from which it is released; and finally, the amount of force used—each time

In Piaget's stage of formal operations adolescents develop the ability to reason abstractly, for example by using letters as symbols for unknown numbers.
©Darren Greenwood/Design Pics

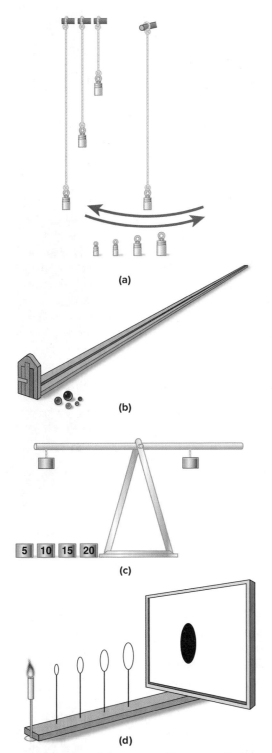

FIGURE 15.1 Formal Operations Reasoning Tasks

(a) Pendulum. The pendulum's string can be shortened or lengthened, and weights of varying sizes can be attached to it. The student must determine what variables affect the speed of the pendulum's swing. (b) Motion in a horizontal plane. A spring device launches balls of varying sizes that roll in a horizontal plane. The student must predict their stopping points. (c) Balance beam. A balance scale comes with weights of varying sizes that can be hung at different points along the crossbar. The student must determine what factors affect whether the scale will balance. (d) Shadows. A board containing a row of peg holes is attached perpendicular to the base of a screen. A light source and rings of varying diameters can be placed in the holes, at varying distances from the screen. The student must produce two shadows of the same size, using different-sized rings.

Source: Adapted from M. Y. Small, *Cognitive development.* New York: Harcourt Brace, 1990. Fig 8-12.

holding the other three factors constant. In this way, he is able to determine that only one factor—the length of the string—determines how fast the pendulum swings.

hypothetical-deductive reasoning Ability, believed by Piaget to accompany the stage of formal operations, to develop, consider, and test hypotheses.

Adam's solution of the pendulum problem shows he has arrived at the stage of formal operations. He is now capable of **hypothetical-deductive reasoning**: He can develop a hypothesis and design an experiment to test it. He considers all the relationships he can imagine and tests them systematically, one by one, to eliminate the false and arrive at the true.

What brings about the shift to formal reasoning? Piaget attributed it chiefly to a combination of brain maturation and expanding environmental opportunities. Both are essential: Even if young people's neurological development has advanced enough to permit formal reasoning, they can attain it only with appropriate environmental stimulation.

Evaluating Piaget's Theory

Although adolescents tend to think more abstractly than younger children, there is debate about the precise age at which this advance occurs (Eccles, Wigfield & Byrnes, 2003). Piaget's writings provide many examples of children displaying aspects of scientific thinking well before adolescence. At the same time, Piaget seems to have overestimated some older children's abilities. Many late adolescents and adults—perhaps one-third to one-half—seem incapable of abstract thought as Piaget defined it (Gardiner & Kozmitzki, 2005), and even those who are capable of abstract thinking do not always use it.

Piaget, in most of his early writings, paid little attention to individual differences, to variations in the same child's performance on different kinds of tasks, or to social and cultural influences. However, neo-Piagetian research suggests children's cognitive processes are closely tied to specific content, what a child is thinking about, as well as to the context of a problem and the kinds of information and thought a culture considers important (Kuhn, 2006). So, for example, when children and adolescents are asked to reason within the context of familiar situations or objects, they perform at higher levels, suggesting that prior knowledge affects their ability to reason formally.

Furthermore, Piaget's theory does not adequately consider such cognitive advances as gains in information-processing capacity, accumulation of knowledge and expertise in specific fields, and the role of metacognition, which is the awareness and monitoring of one's own mental processes and strategies (Flavell, Miller & Miller, 2002). This ability to "think about what one is thinking about" and, thus, to manage one's mental processes—in other words, enhanced executive function—may be the chief advance of adolescent thought, the result of changes occurring in the adolescent brain (Kuhn, 2006).

IMMATURE CHARACTERISTICS OF ADOLESCENT THOUGHT

Adam believes parents who test positive for drug use should have their children removed permanently from their homes.

Perspectives on Diversity

©Digital Vision/Getty Images

CULTURE AND COGNITION

When Piaget first developed his theories, it was assumed his stages of cognitive development represented universal aspects of human development, and that all people in all cultures went through the same processes as those in Western countries. However, as research in different cultures began to be carried out, it became clear this original conception was simplistic and that culture profoundly affects the path development takes.

For example, when adolescents in New Guinea were tested on the pendulum task, none were able to solve it. In Rwanda (Gardiner & Kozmitzki, 2005) and Nigeria (Hollos & Richards, 1993), only a handful of teens were able to adequately solve the puzzle. On the other hand, Chinese children in Hong Kong, who had been to British schools, did at least as well if not better than U.S. and European children. Apparently, formal reasoning is a learned ability that is not equally necessary or equally valued in all cultures, and the experiences children have shape their developing abilities.

Does this mean, then, that adults in cultures other than Western ones function at lower levels of cognitive complexity? Even Piaget (1972) eventually realized this was not the case. Rather, adults learn to reason in the ways their culture demands and while doing culturally relevant activities. For example, when African men from the Côte d'Ivoire play Baoule, a board game in which opponents capture seeds from each other, they use a mix of sophisticated cognitive strategies, including complex rules, offensive and defensive moves, and abstract calculations (Retschitzki, 1989).

That Piaget had to change his theories does not make them bad theories; rather, this is how science works. Piaget was instrumental in developing the field of cognitive and developmental psychology we know today and stimulated a wide variety of important research. However, his original theories require modification in light of what we know today.

---

imaginary audience
Elkind's term for observer who exists only in an adolescent's mind and is as concerned with the adolescent's thoughts and actions as the adolescent is.

"But where would those kids go?" asks his friend Maria. "I mean, yeah, their parents are bad, but are there better places for them to go? What if their parents agree to go into treatment?" Adam stops—he had not considered these issues. As we will see, Adam's focus on the big picture while neglecting the details of how it would play out in reality is typical of adolescents his age. We have seen how children develop from egocentric beings to persons capable of solving abstract problems and imagining ideal societies. Yet in some ways adolescents' thinking seems strangely immature. According to the psychologist David Elkind (2001), such behavior stems from adolescents' inexperienced ventures into formal operational thought. This new way of thinking, which fundamentally transforms the way they look at themselves and their world, is as unfamiliar to them as their reshaped bodies, and they sometimes feel just as awkward in its use. As they try their new powers, they may sometimes stumble, like an infant learning to walk.

So, for example, in addition to their idealism, they are often rude to adults, they have trouble making up their minds what to wear each day, and they tend to act as if the whole world revolves around them.

Their immaturity of thinking, Elkind suggests, manifests itself in at least six characteristic ways:

1. *Idealism and criticalness*: As adolescents envision an ideal world, they realize how far the real world, for which they hold adults responsible, falls short. They become ultra-conscious of hypocrisy. Convinced they know better than adults how to run the world, they frequently find fault with their parents and other authority figures.

2. *Argumentativeness*: Adolescents are constantly looking for opportunities to try out their reasoning abilities. They often become argumentative as they build a case for, say, staying out past their curfew.

3. *Indecisiveness*: Adolescents can keep many alternatives in mind at the same time yet may lack effective strategies for choosing among them. They may struggle with simple decisions like whether they should go to the mall with a friend or work on a school assignment.

4. *Apparent hypocrisy*: Young adolescents often do not recognize the difference between expressing an ideal, such as conserving energy, and making the sacrifices necessary to live up to it, such as driving less often.

5. *Self-consciousness*: Adolescents can think about thinking—their own and other people's. However, in their preoccupation with their own mental state, adolescents often assume everyone else is thinking about the same thing they are thinking about: themselves. Elkind refers to this as the **imaginary audience**, a

According to Elkind, one of the common expressions of immature teen thinking is a tendency toward argumentativeness.
©Rubberball/Getty Images

conceptualized "observer" who is as concerned with a young person's thoughts and behavior as he or she is. The certainty, for example, that everyone is staring at a small pimple all day long is one example of this. The imaginary audience fantasy is especially strong in the early teens but persists to a lesser degree into adult life.

6. *Specialness and invulnerability*: Elkind uses the term **personal fable** to describe a belief by adolescents that they are special, their experience is unique, and they are not subject to the rules that govern the rest of the world. This belief might encourage adolescents to believe they can drive fast and recklessly and not get into an accident. According to Elkind, this form of egocentrism underlies much risky, self-destructive behavior. Like the imaginary audience, the personal fable continues into adulthood.

How has Elkind's model stood up to research? In general, research support has been spotty. For example, research has generally shown that, rather than being indecisive, adolescents are more likely to make impulsive or risky decisions (Albert & Steinberg, 2011). This tendency to make risky decisions does not come from an inability to reason effectively about the consequences nor does it stem from an adolescent belief about being special or unique. Rather, brain immaturity, as described in Chapter 14, biases adolescents toward risky decision making. Data on the decline of egocentrism, another key feature, have also been equivocal. While some studies have found that levels of egocentrism are similar in teens and adults (Rai, Mitchell, Kadar & Mackenzie, 2016), others have found that egocentrism, especially in girls, declines over adolescence (Van der Graaf et al., 2014). Others have found no influence of egocentrism on the imaginary audience, but have found support for the role of

self-consciousness (Galanaki, 2012). Moreover, the characteristic thinking patterns described by Elkind do not seem to be confined to adolescence. For example, research has shown that smokers and ex-smokers develop a personal fable about the risk of health problems as a result of their smoking. Smokers are overly optimistic about their health risks, while ex-smokers believe that quitting and the adoption of a healthy lifestyle has afforded them with greater risk reduction than it actually has. This is not limited to teens—the age range in this particular study was from 19 to 74 years of age (Masiero, Lucchiari & Pravettoni, 2015).

> **personal fable** Elkind's term for conviction that one is special, unique, and not subject to the rules that govern the rest of the world.

CHANGES IN INFORMATION PROCESSING IN ADOLESCENCE

Changes in the way adolescents process information reflect the maturation of the brain's frontal lobes and may help explain the cognitive advances Piaget described. Which neural connections wither and which become strengthened are highly responsive to experience. Thus progress in cognitive processing varies greatly among individual adolescents (Kuhn, 2006).

Researchers have identified two broad categories of measurable change in information processing: structural change and functional change (Eccles et al., 2003). Let's look at each.

Structural Change

Structural changes in adolescence may include growth of information-processing capacity and an increase in the amount of knowledge stored in long-term memory. The capacity of working memory, which enlarges rapidly in middle childhood, may continue to increase during adolescence.

The amount of knowledge stored in long term memory increases during adolescence.
©C Squared Studios/Getty Images

The expansion of working memory enables older adolescents to deal with complex problems or decisions involving multiple pieces of information.

Information stored in long-term memory can be declarative, procedural, or conceptual.

- **Declarative knowledge** ("knowing that . . .") consists of all the factual knowledge a person has acquired (for example, knowing 2 + 2 = 4 and George Washington was the first U.S. president).

- **Procedural knowledge** ("knowing how to . . .") consists of all the skills a person has acquired, such as being able to use a computer and tie a bow.

- **Conceptual knowledge** ("knowing why") is an understanding of, for example, why an algebraic equation remains true if the same amount is added or subtracted from both sides.

Did you know?

We remember the things we learned and what happened to us in our teenage years more clearly than during any other point in the life span—a memory quirk known as the reminiscence bump (Janssen, Murre & Meeter, 2007).

©Design Pics Inc/Alamy

Functional Change

Processes for obtaining, handling, and retaining information are functional aspects of cognition. Among these are learning, remembering, and reasoning, all of which improve during adolescence.

Among the most important functional changes are a continued increase in processing speed (Kuhn, 2006) and further development of executive function, which includes such skills as selective attention, decision making, inhibitory control of impulsive responses, and management of working memory. These skills seem to develop at varying rates (Blakemore & Choudbury, 2006; Kuhn, 2006). Although each process appears to mature independently, each seems to aid in the development of the others (Luna, Garver, Urban, Lazar & Sweeney, 2004). These skills seem to develop at varying rates (Blakemore & Choudhury, 2006; Kuhn, 2006) and they seem to be related. Adolescents reach adult-level performance in response inhibition at age 14, processing speed at 15, and working memory at 19 (Luna, Garver, Urban, Lazar & Sweeney, 2004). These advances are important as increases in processing speed are associated with improvements in reasoning (Kail, Lervag & Hulme, 2016).

However, improvements in information-processing skills do not necessarily carry over to real life, where behavior depends in part on motivation and emotion regulation. Many older adolescents make poorer real-world decisions than younger adolescents do. As we discussed in Chapter 14, adolescents' rash judgments may be related to immature brain development, which may permit feelings to override reason.

LANGUAGE DEVELOPMENT

Children's use of language generally reflects their level of cognitive development. School-age children are quite proficient in use of language, but adolescence brings further refinements. Vocabulary continues to grow as reading matter becomes more adult. By ages 16 to 18 the average young person knows approximately 80,000 words (Owens, 1996). This is important for academic success—vocabulary knowledge is crucial for reading comprehension (Lesaux, Crosson, Kieffer & Pierce, 2010).

With the advent of abstract thought, adolescents can define and discuss such abstractions as love, justice, and freedom. They more frequently use such terms as *however, otherwise, anyway, therefore, really,* and *probably* to express logical relationships. They become more conscious of words as symbols that can have multiple meanings, and they take pleasure in using irony, puns, and metaphors (Duthie, Nippold, Billow & Mansfield, 2008; Katz, Blasko & Kazmerski, 2004).

Adolescents also become more skilled in social perspective-taking, the ability to tailor their speech to another person's point of view. So, for example, a teen might use simpler words when talking to a child, or swear among friends and show deference when speaking to an adult. This ability is essential for skilled conversation.

Language is not static; it is fluid and the words and phrases used by people change over time. These changes are striking in the speech of adolescents, who often develop their own unique terms. Vocabulary may differ by gender, ethnicity, age, geographical region, neighborhood, and type of school (Eckert, 2003) and varies from one clique to another. Teenage slang is part of the process of developing an independent identity separate from parents and the adult world. This specialized vocabulary even extends to electronic communication, with its own rules for spelling, abbreviations, and the use of emoticons and emojis to convey emotional content (Haas, Takayoshi, Carr, Hudson & Pollock, 2011).

Moral Development

Adam's parents talked him into working at a homeless shelter on Thanksgiving one year; although he complained about it at the time, the experience was pivotal for him. Over the holiday season he thought about how fortunate he was. He thought a great deal about what his life might have been like had he been born into a different family, and about whether or not it was fair that some had so much and some so little. Eventually, as his New Year's resolution, he decided to volunteer at a homeless shelter once a week. Adam, as many people his age, was showing gains in his moral development.

As children grow older and attain higher cognitive levels, they become capable of more complex reasoning about moral issues. Their tendencies toward altruism and empathy increase as well. Adolescents are better able than younger children to take another person's perspective, solve social problems, deal with interpersonal relationships, and see themselves as social beings. All of these tendencies foster moral development.

Lawrence Kohlberg's theory of moral reasoning, Carol Gilligan's work on moral development in women and girls, and research on prosocial behavior in adolescence all provide insight into adolescents' moral development.

KOHLBERG'S THEORY OF MORAL REASONING

A woman is near death from cancer. A druggist has discovered a drug that doctors believe might save her. The druggist is charging $2,000 for a small dose—10 times what the drug costs him to make. The sick woman's husband, Heinz, borrows from everyone he knows but can scrape together only $1,000. He begs the druggist to sell him the drug for $1,000 or let him pay the rest later. The druggist refuses, saying, "I discovered the drug, and I'm going to make money from it." Heinz, desperate, breaks into the man's store and steals the drug. Should Heinz have done that? Why or why not? (Kohlberg, 1969).

Heinz's problem is the most famous example of Lawrence Kohlberg's approach to studying moral development. Starting in the 1950s, Kohlberg and his colleagues posed hypothetical dilemmas like this one to 75 boys ages 10, 13, and 16 and continued to question them periodically for more than 30 years. By asking respondents how they arrived at their answers, Kohlberg, like Piaget, concluded that the way people look at moral issues reflects cognitive development. Moreover, he believed that at the heart of every dilemma was the concept of justice—a universal principle.

Kohlberg's Levels and Stages

On the basis of thought processes shown by responses to his dilemmas, Kohlberg (1969) described three levels of moral reasoning and their substages (Table 15.1):

- Level I: **Preconventional morality**. People act under external controls. They obey rules to avoid punishment or reap rewards, or they act out of self-interest. This level is typical of children ages 4 to 10.

- Level II: **Conventional morality** (or morality of conventional role conformity). People have internalized the standards of authority figures. They are concerned about being "good," pleasing others, and maintaining the social order. This level is typically reached after age 10; many people never move beyond it, even in adulthood.

- Level III: **Postconventional morality** (or morality of autonomous moral principles). People recognize conflicts between moral standards and make judgments on the basis of principles of right, fairness, and justice.

People generally do not reach this level of moral reasoning until at least early adolescence, or more commonly in young adulthood, if ever.

In Kohlberg's theory, it is the reasoning underlying a person's response to a moral dilemma, not the answer itself, that indicates the stage of moral development. Two people who give opposite answers may be at the same stage if their reasoning is based on similar factors. For example, a young person at the conventional stage of morality might argue Heinz should steal the drug because it is the husband's responsibility to try to save his wife's life. Alternatively, another person might argue that although Heinz might be tempted to steal the drug, he should not because it's always wrong to steal. Despite arriving at different answers, both young people would be classified as being at the conventional stage of moral development because their reasoning focuses on social concern and conscience.

Some adolescents and even some adults remain at Kohlberg's level I. Like young children, they seek to avoid punishment or satisfy their needs. Most adolescents and most adults seem to be at level II, usually in stage 3 as in Table 15.1. They conform to social conventions, support the status quo, and do the "right" thing to please others or to obey the law. Stage 4 reasoning, upholding social norms, is less common but increases from early adolescence into adulthood. Often adolescents show periods of apparent disequilibrium when advancing from one level to another (Eisenberg & Morris, 2004).

Kohlberg added a transitional level between levels II and III, when people no longer feel bound by society's moral standards but have not yet reasoned out their own principles of justice. Instead, they base their moral decisions on personal feelings. Before people can develop a fully principled (level III) morality, he said, they must recognize the relativity of moral standards. Many young people question their earlier moral views when they enter high school or college or the world of work and encounter people whose values, culture, and ethnic background are different from their own. Still, few people

preconventional morality First level of Kohlberg's theory of moral reasoning in which control is external and rules are obeyed in order to gain rewards or avoid punishment or out of self-interest.

conventional morality (or morality of conventional role conformity) Second level in Kohlberg's theory of moral reasoning in which standards of authority figures are internalized.

postconventional morality (or morality of autonomous moral principles) Third level in Kohlberg's theory of moral reasoning in which people follow internally held moral principles and can decide among conflicting moral standards.

WHERE DO YOU STAND?

Five percent of Internet users have paid for "cheats or codes" to help them win video games (Janson, 2010). Is this moral?

©Wayhome studio/Shutterstock

TABLE 15.1 Kohlberg's Six Stages of Moral Reasoning

Levels	Stages of Reasoning	Typical Answers to Heinz's Dilemma
Level I: Preconventional morality (ages 4 to 10)	*Stage 1: Orientation toward punishment and obedience.* "What will happen to me?" Children obey rules to avoid punishment. They ignore the motives of an act and focus on its physical form (such as the size of a lie) or its consequences (such as the amount of physical damage). "He did a lot of damage and stole a very expensive drug."	*Pro:* "He should steal the drug. It isn't really bad to take it. It isn't as if he hadn't asked to pay for it first. The drug he'd take is worth only $200; he's not really taking a $2,000 drug." *Con:* "He shouldn't steal the drug. It's a big crime. He didn't get permission; he used force and broke and entered."
	Stage 2: Instrumental purpose and exchange. "You scratch my back, I'll scratch yours." Children conform to rules out of self-interest and consideration for what others can do for them. They look at an act in terms of the human needs it meets and differentiate this value from the act's physical form and consequences.	*Pro:* "It's all right to steal the drug, because his wife needs it and he wants her to live. It isn't that he wants to steal, but that's what he has to do to save her." *Con:* "He shouldn't steal it. The druggist isn't wrong or bad; he just wants to make a profit. That's what you're in business for—to make money."
Level II: Conventional morality (ages 10 to 13 or beyond)	*Stage 3: Maintaining mutual relations, approval of others, the golden rule.* "Am I a good boy or girl?" Children want to please and help others, can judge the intentions of others, and develop ideas of what a good person performing it, and they take circumstances into account.	*Pro:* "He should steal the drug. He is only doing something that is natural for a good husband to do. You can't blame him for doing something out of love for his wife." *Con:* "He shouldn't steal. If his wife dies, he can't be blamed. It isn't because he's heartless or that he doesn't love her enough. The druggist is the selfish or heartless one."
	Stage 4: Social concern and conscience. "What if everybody did it?" People are concerned with doing their duty, showing respect for higher authority, and maintaining the social order. They consider an act always wrong, regardless of motive or circumstances, if it violates a rule and harms others.	*Pro:* "He should steal it. If he did nothing, he'd be letting his wife die. It's his responsibility if she dies. He has to take it with the idea of paying the druggist." *Con:* "It is a natural thing for Heinz to want to save his wife, but it's still always wrong to steal."
Level III: Postconventional morality (early adolescence, or not until young adulthood, or never)	*Stage 5: Morality of contract, of individual rights, and of democratically accepted law.* People think in rational terms, valuing the will of the majority and the welfare of society. They generally see these values as best supported by adherence to the law. While they recognize that there are times when human need and the law conflict, they believe it is better for society in the long run if they obey the law.	*Pro:* "The law wasn't set up for these circumstances. Taking the drug in this situation isn't really right, but it's justified." *Con:* "You can't completely blame someone for stealing, but extreme circumstances don't really justify taking the law into your own hands. You can't have people stealing whenever they are desperate. The end may be good, but the ends don't justify the means."
	Stage 6: Morality of universal ethical principles. People do what they as individuals think is right, regardless of legal restrictions or the opinions of others. They act in accordance with internalized standards, knowing that they would condemn themselves if they did not.	*Pro:* "This is a situation that forces him to choose between stealing and letting his wife die. In a situation where the choice must be made, it is morally right to steal. He has to act in terms of the principle of preserving and respecting life." *Con:* "Heinz is faced with the decision of whether to consider the other people who need the drug just as badly as his wife. Heinz ought to act not according to his feelings for his wife, but considering the value of all the lives involved."

Source: L. Kohlberg, "Stage and Sequence: The cognitive-development approach to socialization," in *Handbook of Socialiation Theory and Research* by David A. Goslin. Skokie, IL: Rand McNally, 1969.

reach a level where they can choose among differing moral standards. In fact, at one point Kohlberg questioned the validity of stage 6, morality based on universal ethical principles, because so few people seem to attain it. Later, he proposed a seventh "cosmic" stage in which people consider the effect of their actions not only on other people but on the universe as a whole (Kohlberg, 1981; Kohlberg & Ryncarz, 1990).

Evaluating Kohlberg's Theory

Kohlberg inaugurated a profound shift in the way we look at moral development. Instead of viewing morality solely as the attainment of control over self-gratifying instincts, investigators became interested in how children and adults based moral judgments on their growing understanding of the social world.

Initial research supported Kohlberg's theory. The American boys whom Kohlberg and his colleagues followed through adulthood progressed through Kohlberg's stages in sequence, and none skipped a stage. Their moral judgments correlated positively with age, education, IQ, and socioeconomic status (Colby, Kohlberg, Gibbs & Lieberman, 1983). It is true that generally, adolescents who are more advanced in moral reasoning do tend to be more moral in their behavior, whereas antisocial adolescents tend to use less mature moral reasoning (Eisenberg & Morris, 2004). More recent research, however, has cast doubt on the delineation of some of Kohlberg's stages. For example, some children can reason flexibly about moral issues as early as 6 years of age (Helwig & Jasiobedzka, 2001). It also has been argued that Kohlberg's stages 5 and 6 cannot fairly be called the most mature stages of moral development because they restrict maturity to a select group of people given to philosophical reflection and to people who hold a particular view about the value of moral relativism.

One of the problems with Kohlberg's approach is that people who have achieved a high level of cognitive development do not necessarily reach a comparably high level of moral development. A certain level of cognitive development is *necessary* but not *sufficient* for an equivalent level of moral development. For example, most people would characterize the actions of Pol Pot, the despotic Cambodian leader of the Khmer Rouge, as amoral. From 1974 to 1979, the Khmer Rouge killed 1 million to 3 million Cambodian people. Most people would consider this mass murder to be profoundly evil. But Pol Pot was driven by his belief in an idyllic Communist agrarian society. He believed that the actions he took were in the service of a higher ideal, and the justifications for the actions he took were cognitively complex and well formed. Although this is an extreme example, it is clear that people at postconventional levels of reasoning do not necessarily act more morally than those at lower levels.

Moreover, there are influences on moral behavior other than cognitive complexity. Some investigators suggest that moral activity is motivated not only by abstract considerations of justice, but also by such emotions as empathy, guilt, distress, and the internalization of prosocial norms (Eisenberg & Morris, 2004; Gibbs, 1995). In addition, while Kohlberg paid little attention to these influences, both parents and peers also influence moral development. Having supportive, authoritarian parents or close friends to talk to, or being perceived as a leader, are both associated with higher moral reasoning (Eisenberg & Morris, 2004).

Last, Kohlberg's system does not seem to represent moral reasoning in non-Western cultures as accurately as in the Western culture in which it was originally developed (Eisenberg & Morris, 2004). Older people in countries other than the United States do tend to score at higher stages than younger people. However, people in non-Western cultures rarely score above stage 4 (Shweder et al., 2006), suggesting that some aspects of Kohlberg's model may not fit these societies' cultural values. The context in which reasoning occurs affects the type of reasoning that people tend to exhibit. For example, an analysis of the moral content in annual letters to stakeholders from chief executive officers (CEOs) of large automobile companies showed the level of moral reasoning to overwhelmingly be conventional in nature at stage 2 despite an average age of 58 years, although CEOs of companies based in Asia were slightly more likely to reason at stage 3 (Weber, 2010).

GILLIGAN'S THEORY: AN ETHIC OF CARE

On the basis of research on women, Carol Gilligan (1982) asserted Kohlberg's theory is oriented toward values more important to men than to women. Gilligan claimed women see morality not so much in terms of justice and fairness as in responsibility to show caring and avoid harm. They focus on not turning away from others rather than on not treating others unfairly (Eisenberg & Morris, 2004).

Research has not found much support for Gilligan's claim of a male bias in Kohlberg's stages (Brabeck & Shore, 2003; Jaffee & Hyde, 2000), and she has since modified her position. However, research has found small gender differences in moral reasoning among adolescents (Jaffee & Hyde, 2000; Eisenberg & Morris, 2004). For example, early adolescent girls in the United States tend to emphasize care-related concerns more than boys do, or self-chosen moral dilemmas related to their own experience (Garmon, Basinger, Gregg & Gibbs, 1996; Jaffee & Hyde, 2000). This may be because girls generally mature earlier and have more intimate social relationships (Skoe & Diessner, 1994).

PROSOCIAL BEHAVIOR AND VOLUNTEER ACTIVITY

Some researchers have studied prosocial moral reasoning, similar to care-oriented moral reasoning, as an alternative to Kohlberg's justice-based system. Prosocial moral reasoning is reasoning about moral dilemmas in which one person's needs conflict with those of others in situations in which social rules or norms are unclear or nonexistent. For example, a child faced with the dilemma of deciding whether or not to intervene when a friend is being teased might run the risk of becoming a target of the bullies too. Such a child

Selena Gomez at a charity event.
©Michael Buckner/Getty Images

might engage in prosocial moral reasoning when deciding on a course of action. Research has shown that, from childhood to early adulthood, prosocial reasoning based on personal reflection about consequences and on internalized values and norms increases with age, whereas reasoning based on stereotypes such as "it's nice to help" decreases with age (Eisenberg & Morris, 2004).

Prosocial behavior typically increases from childhood through adolescence (Eisenberg & Morris, 2004). Parents play a role in this; parents who are warm, are sympathetic, and use prosocial reasoning themselves are more likely to have teens who behave in prosocial ways (Carlo, Mestre, Samper, Tur & Armenta, 2011; Padilla-Walker, Nielson & Day, 2016). Girls tend to show more prosocial behavior and empathic concern than boys (Eisenberg & Morris, 2004; Van der Graaff et al., 2014), and this difference becomes more pronounced in adolescence (Eisenberg, Fabes & Spinrad, 2006). This may be in part because cross-culturally, parents of girls emphasize social responsibility more than parents of boys do. This has been validated in Australia, the United States, Sweden, Hungary, Czech Republic, Bulgaria, and Russia (Flannagan, Bowes, Jonsson, Csapo & Sheblanova, 1998).

Peers also matter. Although generally most people conceptualize peer pressure as negative, peers may reinforce positive prosocial development in each other (Farrell, Thompson & Mehari, 2017; Lee, Padilla-Walker & Memmott-Elison, 2017). Experiments show that peer feedback about the value of prosocial behavior can, depending on whether the peer group is perceived as supporting or disliking such behavior, increase or decrease the occurrence of prosocial behavior (Hoorn, Dijk, Meuwese, Rieffe & Crone, 2016), and this is particularly true when peers are considered to be high-status (Choukas-Bradley, Giletta, Cohen & Prinstein, 2015).

Volunteering is a common form of prosocial behavior. About half of adolescents engage in some sort of community service or volunteer activity, although adolescents with high SES volunteer more than those with lower SES (Schmidt, Shumow & Kackar, 2007). Students who do volunteer work tend to be more engaged in their communities than those who do not as adults. In addition, adolescent volunteers tend to have a higher degree of self-understanding and commitment to others (Eccles, 2004) and better academic and civic outcomes (Schmidt et al., 2007). The effects of community service also apply to inner city, racial minority youth (Chan, Ou & Reynolds, 2014), suggesting that intervention programs promoting community service might be an important means by which to promote characteristics associated with positive development.

Educational and Vocational Issues

School is a central organizing experience in most adolescents' lives. It offers opportunities to learn information, master new skills, and sharpen old skills; to participate in sports, the arts, and other activities; to explore vocational choices; and to be with friends. It widens intellectual and social horizons. Some adolescents, however, experience school not as an opportunity but as one more hindrance on the road to adulthood. What factors might impact adolescents' trajectory?

In the following section, we focus on the influences on school achievement and then take a look at young people who drop out of school. Then, we'll consider planning for higher education and vocations.

WHAT DO YOU **DO**?

Youth Minister

Youth ministers work within a range of religious denominations to support the youth of their religious institution, organizing and coordinating activities to engage the institution's youth. For example, the youth minister might orchestrate the weekly youth group meeting, schedule guest speakers relevant to the adolescents in the community, or plan special mission trips. Educational requirements vary by denomination and community. A degree in an area such as pastoral ministry may be needed for some positions, while experience working with youth in the denomination may be acceptable for other positions. To learn more about becoming a youth minister, search for youth ministry by denomination.

©Don Hammond/Design Pics

INFLUENCES ON SCHOOL ACHIEVEMENT

In the United States, as in all other industrialized countries and in some developing countries as well, more students finish high school than ever before, and many enroll in higher education (OECD, 2004). In the 2015–2016 academic year, the 4-year graduation rate for U.S. public high school students hit a high of 84 percent (McFarland et al., 2017).

Among the 35 member countries of the Organisation for Economic Cooperation and Development (OECD, 2008), graduation rates vary—for example, 15 percent in Turkey and 62 percent in Iceland. The United States, with an average of 12.7 years of schooling, is on the high end of this international comparison. However, despite our wealth and technological sophistication, U.S. adolescents remain solidly in the middle with respect to academics. Compared to other countries, U.S. students score average in scientific literacy and reading, and below average in math (OECD, 2016). As in the elementary grades, such factors as parenting practices, socioeconomic status, and the quality of the home environment influence the course of school achievement in adolescence. Other factors include gender, ethnicity, peer influence, quality of schooling, and students' belief in themselves.

Student Motivation and Self-Efficacy

In Western countries, particularly the Unites States, educational practices are based on the assumption that students are, or can be, motivated to learn. Educators emphasize the value of intrinsic motivation—the student's desire to learn for the sake of learning—because research has shown this orientation is associated with academic achievement (Cerasoli, Nicklin & Ford, 2014). Unfortunately, many U.S. students are *not* self-motivated, and motivation often declines as they enter high school (Eccles, 2004; Larson & Wilson, 2004).

Students high in **self-efficacy**—who believe that they can successfully achieve academic goals—are likely to do well in school (Komarraju & Nadler, 2013). So, for example, after failing a test, a student with high self-efficacy might conclude that he didn't study enough and that to do well in future tests he should study more. A student with low self-efficacy, by contrast, might conclude that the material was too hard or the test was unfair, a belief system that undermines work ethic and motivation. Similarly, students' beliefs about their ability to self-regulate their learning (Zuffiano et al., 2013) as well as their actual levels of self-discipline (Duckworth & Seligman, 2005) impact academic achievement.

In the United States, where opportunities exist for many children, personal motivation can have a strong effect on how much children learn. Future-oriented cognitions—hopes and dreams about future jobs—are related to greater achievement as well as participation in extracurricular activities. It may be that future-oriented cognitions are helpful in part because they motivate participation in activities that relate to later success (Beal & Crockett, 2010).

But in many cultures, education is based on such factors as duty (India), submission to authority (Islamic countries), and participation in the family and community (sub-Saharan Africa). In the countries of east Asia, students are expected to learn to meet family and societal expectations. Learning is expected to require intense effort, and students who fail or fall behind feel obligated to try again. This expectation may help explain why, in international comparisons in science and math, east Asian students substantially surpass U.S. students. In developing countries, issues of motivation pale in the light of social and economic barriers to education: inadequate or absent schools, the need for child labor to support the family, barriers to schooling for girls, and early marriage (Larson & Wilson, 2004). Thus, as we discuss factors in educational success, which are drawn largely from studies in the United States and other Western countries, we need to remember that they do not apply to all cultures.

self-efficacy Sense of one's capability to master challenges and achieve goals

Self-efficacy, self-regulation of learning, and self-discipline are all associated with academic achievement.
©Monkey Business Images/Shutterstock

Did you know?

Middle schoolers prefer to do their homework with their friends, high schoolers prefer to do it alone (Kackar, Shumow, Schmidt & Grzetich, 2011).

Gender

Reading tests conducted on 15-year-olds in 72 countries show an advantage for girls, although the difference in scores for girls and boys narrowed between 2009 and 2015. Although gender differences in science are small, boys are more likely to be top performers in all countries with the exception of Finland (OECD, 2016). However, despite having a greater proportion of high performers, boys are more likely to fail to achieve a baseline of proficiency in reading, mathematics, and science (OECD, 2015). Overall, beginning in adolescence, girls do better on verbal tasks that involve writing and language usage; boys do better in activities that involve visual and spatial functions helpful in math and science. An evaluation of SAT results and math scores from 7 million students found few gender differences in math performance (Hyde, Lindberg, Linn, Ellis & Williams, 2008).

Why might we expect gender differences? As with all aspects of development, research points to interacting biological and environmental contribution. Male and female brains show some differences in structure and organization, and these differences tend to become more pronounced with age. Girls have more gray matter and the growth of gray matter peaks earlier. Their neurons also have more connections (Halpern et al., 2007). The brain structure of girls appears to better integrate verbal and analytic tasks (which occur in the left brain) with spatial and holistic tasks (which occur in the right brain) (Ingalhalikar et al., 2014).

On average, boys have bigger brains (Ruigrok et al., 2014). Boys also have more connective white matter (Ingalhalikar et al., 2014). They also have more cerebrospinal fluid, which cushions the longer paths of nerve impulses. Boys' brains seem to be optimized for activity within each hemisphere—their brains are more modular

and seem to show an advantage for visual and spatial performance (Halpern et al., 2007; Ingalhalikar et al., 2014). Earlier reports about sex differences in the size of the corpus callosum (a band of nerve fibers connecting both hemispheres of the brain) appear to be an artifact of overall brain size (Luders, Toga & Thompson, 2014).

Social and cultural forces that influence gender differences include (Halpern et al., 2007):

- Home influences: Across cultures, parents' educational level correlates with their children's math achievement. Except for highly gifted sons and daughters, the amount of parental involvement in children's education affects math performance. Parents' gender attitudes and expectations also have an effect.

- School influences: Subtle differences in the way teachers treat boys and girls, especially in math and science classes, have been documented.

- Neighborhood influences: Boys benefit more from enriched neighborhoods and are hurt more by deprived neighborhoods. In other words, they are generally more sensitive to this environmental influence.

- Women's and men's roles in society help shape girls' and boys' choices of courses and occupations.

- Cultural influences: Cross-cultural studies show that the size of gender differences in math performance varies among nations and becomes greater by the end of secondary school. These differences correlate with the degree of gender equality in the society. Countries with greater gender equality demonstrate less variance in math scores between boys and girls (Hyde & Mertz, 2009).

Science continues to search for the ways in which boys' and girls' academic abilities differ and the reasons those differences exist. As changes in attitudes and perceptions open opportunities, these differences seem to be shrinking. The rate of U.S. doctoral degrees in the sciences and math awarded to women is strong evidence: In 1970 only 14 percent of PhDs in biology and 8 percent of PhDs in mathematics and statistics were granted to women. By 2006, the rates rose to 46 and 32 percent, respectively (Hyde & Mertz, 2009). By 2016, 54.1 percent of PhDs in biology and 37.8 percent of PhDs in mathematics and computer science were women. Overall, 52.1 percent of doctoral degrees across all fields of study were awarded to women (Okahana & Zhou, 2017).

Technology

In 2013, approximately 78 percent of teens had a cell phone, 23 percent had a tablet computer, and 93 percent had access to a computer at home (Madden, Lenhart, Duggan, Cortesi & Gassar, 2013). The expansion of technology and the major role it plays in children's lives has affected learning. Teachers often ask students to conduct research online, as well

While the expansion of technology has had a positive impact on visual skills, critical-thinking and analysis skills have declined, and students spend less time reading for pleasure.

as to access (79 percent) and submit (76 percent) homework and assignments online (Purcell, Heaps, Buchanan & Fried, 2013). Unfortunately, research indicates that while visual skills have improved as a result of the increased use of computers and video games, critical-thinking and analysis skills have declined. Also, students are spending more time with visual media and less time reading for pleasure (Greenfield, 2009). Reading develops vocabulary, imagination, and induction, skills that are critical to solving more complex problems.

Another primary concern involves the tendency to multitask while using electronic devices. Adolescents, who have grown up with portable electronic media at their fingertips, are particularly prone to multitasking (Voorveld & van der Goot, 2013). Studies show that more than 25 percent of adolescents' media consumption occurs using two media types simultaneously (Rideout et al., 2010). Adolescents may believe that they are producing high-quality work while texting with friends or listening to music, but evidence suggests the opposite. Students given access to the Internet during class do not process what was presented as well and perform more poorly than students without access (Greenfield, 2009).

Moreover, there are indications that repeated multitasking may affect later performance, and these potential deficits in executive function may have far-reaching implications in school. Research has demonstrated that adolescents who frequently media multitask report more problems in staying focused, inhibiting inappropriate behavior, and switching effectively between tasks (Baumgartner, Weeda, van der Hejiden & Huizinga, 2014). Moreover, multitasking in adolescents is associated with poorer academic performance on standardized English and math tests and decreased working memory capacity (Cain, Leonard, Gabrieli & Finn, 2016).

Parenting Practices, Ethnicity, and Peer Influence

Family and school experiences are subject to a phenomenon referred to as spillover, wherein experiences in different contexts influence each other (Grzywacz, Almeida & McDonald, 2002). Stress at home has been shown to predict problems with attendance and learning; conversely, problems with attendance and learning contribute to family stress (Flook & Fuligni, 2008).

Does parenting style influence academic performance? *Authoritative parents,* who strike a balance between making demands and being responsive, tend to have teens who do better academically. Both *authoritarian parents,* who tend to use more punishment and harsh control, and *permissive parents,* who seem indifferent to grades, have children who show slightly lower achievement. However, while statistically significant, all of these differences are small to very small (Pinquart, 2016). In other words, they have little predictive value in the real world.

Parental involvement in academic activities is a far better predictor of which teens will do well academically (Castro et al., 2015). Parents who emphasize the value of education, connect academic performance to future goals, and discuss learning strategies have a significant impact on student academic achievement (Hill & Tyson, 2009). Parents' educational level and family income also indirectly affect educational attainment based on how they influence parenting style, sibling relationships, and adolescent academic engagement (Melby, Conger, Fang, Wickrama & Conger, 2008).

Children of minority status, while sharing many common developmental influences with their majority status peers, are exposed to additional potentially negative influences such as discrimination and racism (Coll et al., 1996). Also, in the United States, minority status is generally correlated with poverty, and socioeconomic status in turn is strongly associated with school achievement. Thus, we might expect ethnicity to be an important factor. This is indeed the case. High school graduation rates in 2014–2015 were highest for Asian Americans (90 percent), followed by whites (88 percent), Hispanics (78 percent), blacks (75 percent), and Native Americans (72 percent) (NCES, 2017).

Peer influences on motivation are also important. In one study, Latino and African American adolescents did less well in school than European American students, apparently because of lack of peer support for academic achievement (Steinberg, Dornbusch & Brown, 1992). On the other hand, Asian American students get high grades and score better than European American students on math achievement tests, apparently because both parents and peers prize achievement (Chen & Stevenson, 1995). Peer influence may also help explain the downward trend in academic motivation and achievement that begins for many students in early adolescence. In one study, students whose peer group included high achievers showed less of a decline in achievement and enjoyment of school, whereas those who associated with low achievers showed greater declines (Ryan, 2001).

The School

The quality of schooling strongly influences student achievement. A good middle school or high school has an orderly, safe environment; adequate material resources; a stable teaching staff; and a positive sense of community. The school culture places a strong emphasis on academics and fosters the belief that all students can learn. It also offers opportunities for extracurricular activities, which keep students engaged and prevent them from getting into trouble after school. Teachers trust, respect, and care about students and have high expectations for them as well as confidence in their own ability to help students succeed (Eccles, 2004).

Adolescents are more satisfied with school if allowed to participate in making rules, if they feel support from teachers and other students (Samdal & Dür, 2000), and if the curriculum and instruction are meaningful and appropriately challenging and fit their interests, skill level, and needs (Eccles, 2004). In part, the positive effects of a school are a function of the unique peer culture—including both how students relate to each other and what they perceive the academic culture of the school to be (Lynch, Lerner & Leventhal, 2013). High teacher expectations are the most consistent positive predictor of students' goals and interests,

and negative feedback is the most consistent negative predictor of academic performance and classroom behavior (Wentzel, 2002).

A decline in academic motivation and achievement often begins with the transition from the intimacy and familiarity of elementary school to the larger, more pressured, and less supportive environment of middle school or junior high school (Eccles, 2004). For this reason, some cities have tried eliminating the middle school transition by extending elementary school to eighth grade or have consolidated some middle schools with small high schools (Gootman, 2007). Some big-city school systems, such as in New York City, Philadelphia, and Chicago, are experimenting with small schools in which students, teachers, and parents form a learning community united by a common vision of good education and often a special curricular focus, such as music or ethnic studies (Meier, 1995; Rossi, 1996). In one evaluation of a small-school initiative in Chicago, researchers found that students who attended the schools were more likely to stay in school and graduate (Barrow, Claessens & Schanzenbach, 2010)

Characteristics of good schools include fostering a positive sense of community and placing an emphasis on academic success.

©Hill Street Studios/Blend Images

DROPPING OUT OF HIGH SCHOOL

As noted, more U.S. youths are completing high school than ever before. The percentage of those who drop out, known as the status dropout rate, includes all people in the 16- to 24-year-old age group who are not enrolled in school and who have not completed a high school program, regardless of when they left school (Figure 15.2). In 2015, the status dropout rate for this group was 5.9 percent, and it was higher for boys (6.3 percent) than girls (5.4 percent). Average dropout rates are lower for non-Hispanic white students (4.5 percent) than for both blacks (7.2 percent) and Hispanics (9.9 percent). Asian students at 2.4 percent are the least likely to drop out (NCES, 2017).

Why are poor and minority adolescents more likely to drop out? Reasons include low teacher expectations, differential treatment of these students, less teacher support than at the elementary level, and the perceived irrelevance of the curriculum to culturally underrepresented groups. The transition to high school for African American and Latino students seems to be most risky for those students transitioning from smaller, more supportive junior high schools with significant numbers of minority peers to larger, more impersonal high schools with fewer minority peers (Benner & Graham, 2009).

There are consequences both for society and for individuals to dropping out. Society suffers when young people do not finish school. Dropouts are more likely to be unemployed or to have low incomes, to end up on welfare, to become involved with drugs, crime, and delinquency. They also tend to be in poorer health (Laird et al., 2006; NCES, 2004).

There are also personal consequences. As young adults, those who successfully complete high school are most likely to obtain postsecondary education, to have jobs, and to be employed (Finn, 2006; U.S. Department of Labor, 2013). For example, in 2017, the unemployment rate for young adults without a high school degree was 43 percent, while those with at least a high school degree had an unemployment rate of 30 percent, and those with a bachelor's degree had a 14 percent unemployment rate (NCES, 2018). High school completers are also likely to earn more money. In 2012, the median income of people who did not complete high school was approximately $25,000. However, those with at least a high school degree earned a median income of approximately $46,000. Over a lifetime of work this results in a difference of $670,000 (Stark & Noel, 2015).

PREPARING FOR HIGHER EDUCATION OR VOCATIONS

Adam was graduating high school. After his work volunteering at a homeless shelter, he had realized he wanted to work in a way that would help out the less fortunate. However, he also wanted to have a career in which he made decent money. Was college the best path toward this? Should he try working first, and then going to college later?

In the following section, we address the development of career goals. We also look at how young people decide

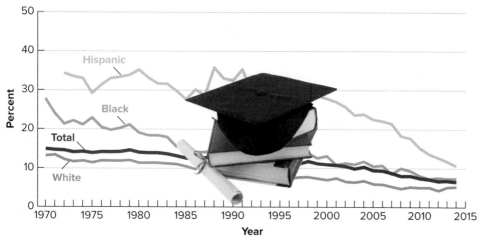

Figure 15.2 Percentage of High School Dropouts among 16-to-24-Year-Olds, 1970–2014

While rates have fallen, the dropout rate remains higher than average for blacks and Hispanics.

Source: J. McFarland, J. Cui & P. Stark, *Trends in high school dropout and completion rates in the United States: 2014* (NCES 2018-117). U.S. Department of Education. Washington, DC: National Center for Education Statistics, 2018. Retrieved from http://nces.ed.gov/pubsearch.

©Ingram Publishing/agefotostock

whether to go to college and, if not, how they enter the world of work. Many factors enter in, including individual ability and personality, education, socioeconomic and ethnic background, the advice of school counselors, life experiences, and societal values.

Influences on Students' Aspirations

Self-efficacy beliefs help shape the occupational options students consider and the way they prepare for careers (Bandura, Barbaranelli, Caprara & Pastorelli, 2001). In addition, parents' values with regard to academic achievement influence adolescents' values and occupational goals (Jodl, Michael, Malanchuk, Eccles & Sameroff, 2001).

Despite the greater flexibility in career goals today, there are still gender differences in career choices. Women receive more than half of all undergraduate degrees in biology, chemistry, and math. However, they are underrepresented—earning only 20 percent of degrees—in computer science, engineering, and physics (Cheryan, Ziegler, Montoya & Jiang, 2017). While the reasons for this are varied, one factor is gender-stereotyping, which still influences vocational choice. Young men and women in the United States are now equally likely to plan careers in math and science. However, women are still more likely to go into fields such as nursing, social welfare professions, and teaching (Eccles, 2004). Much the same is true in other industrialized countries (OECD, 2004). Another factor may be that those individuals who are high in both mathematical and verbal abilities—of whom more are female—have a wider variety of career options available to them. These individuals are less likely to pursue careers in science, technology, engineering, or mathematical career areas (Wang, Eccles & Kenny, 2013).

The educational system itself may act as a brake on vocational aspirations. Students who can memorize and analyze tend to do well academically. Students whose strength is in creative or practical thinking—areas critical to success in certain fields—rarely get a chance to show what they can do (Sternberg, 1997). Recognition of a broader range of intelligences and more flexible teaching and career counseling could allow more students to meet their educational goals.

Guiding Students Not Bound for College

Adolescents decide to forgo college for a variety of reasons. Some young adults, who tend to come from low-income families and have low academic achievement, have financial constraints that prevent them from attending college despite their desire to do so. A second smaller group is composed of young people who have the financial means to go to college as well as the academic ability, but prefer to begin working and earning money. The remainder of non-college-bound young adults give a wide variety of reasons for their decision not to attend college (Bozick & DeLuca, 2011).

Most industrialized countries offer guidance to non-college-bound students. Germany, for example, has an apprenticeship system in which high school students go to school part-time and spend the rest of the week in paid on-the-job training supervised by an employer-mentor.

The United States lacks coordinated policies to help non-college-bound youth make a successful transition from high school to the labor market (Eccles, 2004). Vocational counseling is generally oriented toward college-bound youth. Whatever vocational training programs do exist tend to be less comprehensive than the German system and less closely

©Pixtal/agefotostock

WHAT DO YOU DO?

College Counselor

Private college counselors help students and their families select and apply to college. They help students determine the best programs based on their goals as well as their strengths and weaknesses, and they can work at schools or own private practices. A master's degree and state-specific licensure are typically required to become a college counselor. To learn more about becoming a college counselor, visit www.nacacnet.org.

tied to the needs of businesses and industries. Most of these young people must get training on the job or in community college courses. Many, ignorant about the job market, do not obtain the skills they need. Others take jobs beneath their abilities. Some do not find work at all (NCES, 2002).

In some communities, demonstration programs help in the school-to-work transition. The most successful ones offer instruction in basic skills, counseling, peer support, mentoring, apprenticeship, and job placement (Kash, 2008). In 1994, Congress allocated $1.1 billion to help states and local governments establish school-to-work programs in partnership with employers. Participating students improved their school performance and graduation rates and, when they entered the labor market, were more likely to find jobs and earned higher wages than students who did not participate (Hughes, Bailey & Mechur, 2001).

Adolescents in the Workplace

In the United States, about 18 percent of students are employed during a given school year (Child Trends DataBank, 2016), and the vast majority of adolescents are employed at some time during high school, mostly in service and retail jobs. Researchers disagree over whether part-time work is beneficial to high school students (by helping them develop real-world skills and a work ethic) or detrimental (by distracting them from long-term educational and occupational goals). How

much students work matters—those that work more than 20 hours a week generally suffer academically and are more likely to drop out of school (Warren & Lee, 2003). However, there is research that suggests this association is not causal and is a consequence of the fact that those students who are poor achievers may prefer to work more hours (Staff, Schulenberg & Bachman, 2010). Some data, however, suggest that while working may not affect the academic performance in high school, it may nonetheless lower the probability of going to college (Lee & Orazem, 2010).

Some research suggests that working students fall into two groups: those who are on an accelerated path to adulthood, and those who make a more leisurely transition, balancing schoolwork, paid jobs, and extracurricular activities. The "accelerators" work more than 20 hours a week during high school and spend little time on school-related leisure activities. Exposure to an adult world may lead them into alcohol and drug use, sexual activity, and delinquent behavior. Many of these adolescents have relatively low SES; they tend to look for full-time work right after high school and not to obtain college degrees. The "balancers," in contrast, often come from more privileged backgrounds. For them, part-time work helps them to gain a sense of responsibility, independence, and self-confidence and to appreciate the value of work, but it does not deter them from their educational paths (Staff et al., 2004).

Although research on the association between academic performance and part-time employment for high school students working less than 20 hours a week is conflicting, those students who work more than 20 hours a week generally suffer academically and are more likely to drop out of school.
©Andersen Ross/Getty Images

mastering the CHAPTER

©Ian Lishman/Juice Images/Getty Images

Summary and Key Terms

Cognitive Development

> Adolescents who reach Piaget's stage of formal operations can engage in hypothetical-deductive reasoning. They can think in terms of possibilities, deal flexibly with problems, and test hypotheses.

> Because environmental stimulation plays an important part in attaining this stage, not all people become capable of formal operations.

> Piaget's proposed stage of formal operations does not take into account such developments as accumulation of knowledge and expertise, gains in information processing, and the growth of metacognition. Piaget also paid little attention to individual differences, between-task variations, and the role of the situation.

> According to Elkind, immature thought patterns can result from adolescents' inexperience with formal thinking. These thought patterns include idealism and criticalness, argumentativeness, indecisiveness, apparent hypocrisy, self-consciousness, and specialness and invulnerability. Research has cast doubt on whether all the patterns are confined to adolescence.

> Research has found both structural and functional changes in adolescents' information processing. Structural changes include increases in declarative, procedural, and conceptual knowledge and expansion of the capacity of working memory. Functional changes include progress in reasoning.

> Vocabulary and other aspects of language development, such as social perspective-taking, improve in adolescence. Adolescents enjoy wordplay and may create their own dialect.

KEY TERMS

Formal operations
Hypothetical-deductive reasoning
Imaginary audience

Personal fable
Declarative knowledge

Procedural knowledge
Conceptual knowledge

Moral Development

> According to Kohlberg, moral reasoning is based on a developing sense of justice and growing cognitive abilities. Kohlberg proposed that moral development progresses from external control to internalized societal standards to personal, principled moral codes.

> Kohlberg's theory has been criticized on several grounds, including failure to credit the roles of emotion, socialization, and parental and peer guidance, and being biased toward Western cultures.

> Gilligan proposed an alternative theory of moral development based on an ethic of caring, rather than on justice.

> Prosocial behavior continues to increase during adolescence, especially among girls. Many adolescents engage in volunteer community service.

KEY TERMS

Preconventional morality
Conventional morality (or morality of conventional role conformity)

Postconventional morality (or morality of autonomous moral principles)

Educational and Vocational Issues

> Self-efficacy beliefs, parental practices, cultural and peer influences, gender, and quality of schooling affect adolescents' educational achievement.

> Use of technology can have both positive and negative impacts on skill development—with improvements seen for visual skills but declines in critical thinking and analysis skills. Multitasking has negative effects on academic performance and memory capacity.

> Although most Americans graduate from high school, the dropout rate is higher among poor, Hispanic, and African American students. However, this racial/ethnic gap is narrowing. Active engagement in studies is an important factor in keeping adolescents in school.

> Educational and vocational aspirations are influenced by several factors, including self-efficacy, parental values, and gender stereotypes.

> High school graduates who do not immediately go on to college can benefit from vocational training.

> Part-time work can have both positive and negative effects on educational, social, and occupational development. The long-term effects tend to be best when working hours are limited.

KEY TERM

Self-efficacy

1. A research participant is given a balance beam with weight of various sizes that can be hung at different points on the crossbar and asked to figure out what factors affect whether the scale will balance. A person in the formal operations stage of development would be most likely to:
   a. attack the problem in a hit-or miss fashion, randomly varying the size of the weight and the hanging position
   b. understand that both the size of the weight and the hanging position matter, but not vary them in a systematic way
   c. start with one size weight, and then go through the hanging positions, and then take one hanging position and vary all the weights
   d. it is impossible to answer this question without knowing the age of the participant

2. What are the six immature aspects of adolescent thought? _____
   _____
   _____

3. What are two of the changes in adolescent language?
   _____
   _____
   _____

4. John is better able to concentrate on his teacher while ignoring the class clown. This is due to _____ in information processing.
   a. structural change
   b. declarative memory
   c. procedural knowledge
   d. functional change

5. Kohlberg believed moral development depended upon:
   a. complexity of reasoning
   b. whether or not an individual was a morally good or morally bad person

c. cultural influences
d. whether or not a person was male or female

6. Gilligan believed that rather than being focused on justice and fairness, women were focused on _____.

7. Which two factors are positively related to prosocial behavior?
   a. being male, getting older
   b. being female, getting older
   c. volunteering, being male
   d. being forced to volunteer, being younger

8. "I don't know why I even bother studying. These tests are just too hard!" says Craig. Craig is showing:
   a. high self-efficacy
   b. low self-efficacy
   c. authoritarian parenting
   d. transitory motivation

9. What are two reasons poor and minority adolescents are more likely to drop out of school?
   _____
   _____

10. Which of the following adolescents could be best described as an "accelerator"?
    a. Jenny, who did not work at all while attending high school
    b. Enzo, who worked five hours during the week and was on the track team
    c. Sara, who worked every night after school as a hostess at a local restaurant
    d. Jake, who was failing all his classes and did not have a job

Answers: 1–c; 2–The immature aspects of adolescent thought include (1) idealism and criticalness, (2) argumentativeness, (3) indecisiveness, (4) apparent hypocrisy, (5) self-consciousness, and (6) specialness and invulnerability; 3–The development of abstract thought allows for adolescents to define and discuss abstract concepts; to express logical relationships; to become conscious of words as symbols; to use irony, puns and metaphors more effectively; and to better take the perspective of others; 4–d; 5–a; 6–showing caring and avoiding harm; 7–a; 8–b; 9–Among the reasons poor or minority adolescents may drop out of school are low teacher expectations, differential treatment, less teacher support, perceived irrelevance of the curriculum, tracking to low ability or noncollege tracks, being placed with alienated peers, feeling incompetent, and having negative attitudes about school; 10–c

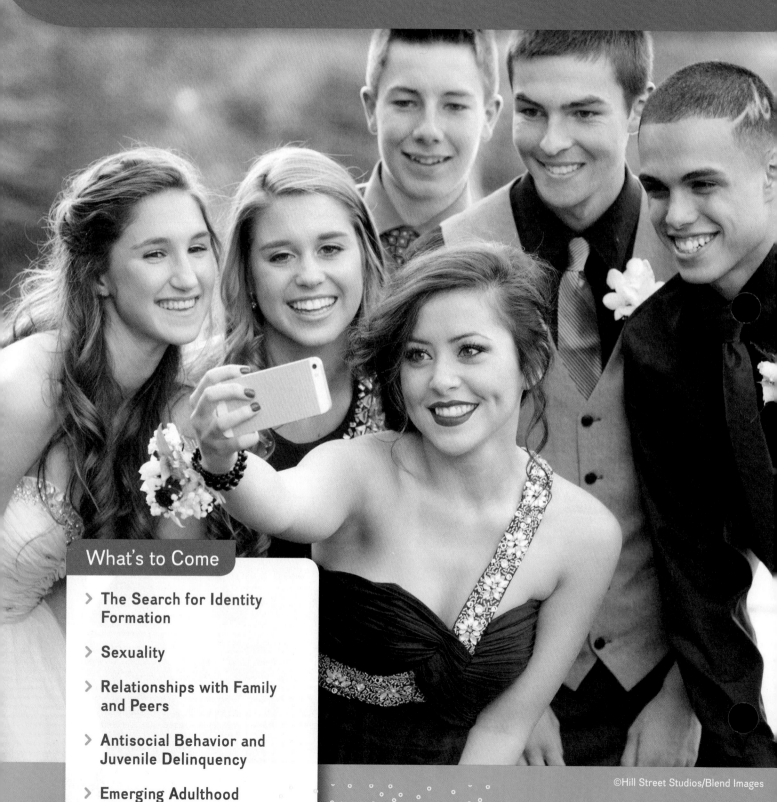

Chapter 16

Psychosocial Development in Adolescence

What's to Come

> **The Search for Identity Formation**

> **Sexuality**

> **Relationships with Family and Peers**

> **Antisocial Behavior and Juvenile Delinquency**

> **Emerging Adulthood**

©Hill Street Studios/Blend Images

John's parents were horrified when he dyed his hair green and started wearing black clothing, but they held back from making it an issue, assuming this was just a teenage phase. John's parents knew that, as many teens do, John was likely experimenting with identity and who he wanted to be. In the next few years, his search for identity would lead beyond mere clothes and focus on the multitude of paths his future held.

In this chapter, we consider John's path through focusing on the quest for identity in adolescence. We discuss how adolescents come to terms with their sexuality and how teenagers' burgeoning individuality expresses itself in relationships with parents, siblings, and peers. We examine sources of antisocial behavior and ways of reducing the risks of adolescence in order to make it a time of positive growth and expanding possibilities. Finally, we look at late adolescence and the emerging adult.

● ● ● ●

The Search for Identity

The search for **identity**—according to Erikson, a coherent conception of the self made up of goals, values, and beliefs to which the person is solidly committed—comes into focus during the teenage years. As Erikson (1950) emphasized, the effort to make sense of the self is part of a healthy process that builds on the achievements of earlier stages—on trust, autonomy, initiative, and industry—and lays the groundwork for coping with the challenges of adult life. Both Erikson and Marcia provide insight into identity development in adolescence, which is also influenced by gender and ethnicity.

ERIKSON: IDENTITY VERSUS IDENTITY CONFUSION

The chief task of adolescence, said Erikson (1968), is to confront the crisis of **identity versus identity confusion** in order to become a unique adult with a coherent sense of self and a valued role in society. Identity forms as young people resolve three major issues: the choice of an occupation, the adoption of values to live by, and the development of a satisfying sexual identity.

According to Erikson (1982), the **psychosocial moratorium**, the time-out period that adolescence provides, allows young people to search for commitments to which they can be faithful. For example, going to college allows adolescents the time and opportunity to think about different career paths before taking on all the responsibilities of adulthood. Adolescents who resolve the identity crisis satisfactorily develop the virtue of fidelity: sustained loyalty, faith, or a sense of belonging to a loved one or to friends and companions. Fidelity also can mean identification with a set of values, an ideology, a religion, a political movement, a creative pursuit, or an ethnic group.

Erikson saw the prime danger of this stage as identity confusion, which can greatly delay reaching psychological adulthood. According to Erikson, the identity confusion typical during this time accounts for the seemingly chaotic nature of much adolescent behavior and for teenagers' painful self-consciousness. Cliquishness and intolerance of differences, both hallmarks of adolescence, are defenses against identity confusion.

Erikson's theory describes male identity development as the norm. According to Erikson, a man is not capable of real intimacy until after he has achieved a stable identity, whereas women define themselves through marriage and motherhood, something that was likely truer when Erikson developed his theory than it is today. Thus, said Erikson, women develop identity through intimacy, not before it. As we will see, this male orientation of Erikson's theory has prompted criticism. Still, Erikson's concept of the identity crisis has inspired much valuable research.

MARCIA: IDENTITY STATUS—CRISIS AND COMMITMENT

What does the process of forming an identity look like? Are there individual differences? Erikson's perspective was extended by work in identity statuses. Marcia (1966, 2002) distinguished between four types of identity statuses that differ according to the presence or absence of crisis and commitment: identity achievement, foreclosure, moratorium, and identity diffusion. Crisis, within the context of Erikson's theories, does not refer to a stressful event such as losing your job or not being able to pay your bills. Rather, it refers to the process of actively grappling with what to believe and who to be. Commitment, the other aspect

identity In Erikson's terminology, a coherent conception of the self made up of goals, values, and beliefs to which a person is solidly committed.

identity versus identity confusion Erikson's fifth stage of psychosocial development in which an adolescent seeks to develop a coherent sense of self, including the role she or he is to play in society. Also called *identity versus role confusion.*

psychosocial moratorium A period of time that allows young people to search for commitments to which they can be faithful.

During the teen years, identity comes into focus.
©JGI/Jamie Grill/Blend Images/ AP Images

Earlier research on identity formation suggested that, for women, relationships and intimacy figured more prominently than for men. More recent work has failed to find gender differences in this area.
©Halfdark/Getty Images

of identity formation, involves a personal investment in an occupation or ideology (system of beliefs). Commitments can be held after they have been deeply considered, after crisis, or they can be adopted without much thought put into them. Following are sketches of the typical young person in each identity status.

identity diffusion Identity status characterized by absence of commitment and lack of serious consideration of alternatives.

foreclosure Identity status in which a person who has not spent time considering alternatives (that is, has not been in crisis) is committed to other people's plans for his or her life.

moratorium Identity status in which a person is considering alternatives (in crisis) and seems headed for commitment.

identity achievement Identity status, described by Marcia, characterized by commitment to choices made following a crisis; a period spent in exploring alternatives.

- **Identity diffusion** (no commitment, no crisis). Mark has not seriously considered options and has avoided commitments. He is unsure of himself and tends to be uncooperative. His parents do not discuss his future with him; they say it is up to him. People in this category tend to be unhappy and often lonely.

- **Foreclosure** (commitment without crisis). Andrea has made commitments, not as a result of exploring possible choices, but by accepting someone else's plans for her life. She is happy and self-assured, perhaps even smug and self-satisfied, and she becomes dogmatic when her opinions are questioned. She has close family ties, is obedient, and tends to follow a powerful leader like her mother, who accepts no disagreement.

- **Moratorium** (crisis with no commitment yet). Nick is in crisis, struggling with decisions. He is lively, talkative, self-confident, and scrupulous but also anxious and fearful. He is close to his mother but resists her authority. He will probably come out of his crisis eventually with the ability to make commitments and achieve identity.

- **Identity achievement** (crisis and commitment). Caterina has resolved her identity crisis. During the crisis period, she devoted much thought and some emotional struggle to major issues in her life. She has come to her own conclusions about what she believes, and she expresses strong commitment about her beliefs. Her parents have encouraged her to make her own decisions; they have listened to her ideas and given their opinions without pressuring her to adopt them. Research in a number of cultures has found people in this category to be more mature and more socially competent than people in the other three (Marcia, 1993).

From late adolescence on, as Marcia proposed, more and more people are in moratorium or achievement: seeking or finding their identity. About half of late adolescents remain in foreclosure or diffusion, but when development does occur, it is typically in the direction Marcia described (Kroger, 2003). When middle-aged people look back on their lives, they most commonly trace a path from foreclosure to moratorium to identity achievement (Kroger & Haslett, 1991). However, these categories are not stages. Rather, they represent the status of identity development at a particular time, and they are likely to change in any direction as young people continue to develop. Also, because our identity is multidimensional, our identity development is as well. For example, a young person may have decided upon a career path but not yet considered political or religious affiliation.

GENDER DIFFERENCES IN IDENTITY FORMATION

Some earlier research supports Erikson's view that, for women, identity and intimacy develop together. However, according to Carol Gilligan (1982, 1987a, 1987b; Brown & Gilligan, 1990), the female sense of self develops not so much through achieving a separate identity as through establishing relationships. Girls and women, says Gilligan, judge themselves on their handling of their responsibilities and on their ability to care for others as well as for themselves.

However, given changes in social structure and the increased role of women in the workplace, it may be that these gender differences are less important than they were previously, and individual differences play more of a role now (Archer, 1993; Marcia, 1993). Some data suggest this may be the case. Earlier studies described young women as more competent at intimacy than men (Fischer, 1981). Such research also suggested that intimacy was more closely related to identity formation for women than men, and that self-esteem and the understanding of the self was interpersonally based for women and intrapersonally based for men (Hodgson & Fischer, 1979). Moreover, a meta-analysis using data from studies conducted in the 1970s and 1980s showed that identity status and intimacy were associated with each other in both men and women, but that the relationship was more robust for men (Arseth, Kroger, Martinussen & Marcia, 2009). However, a few decades later, a longitudinal study on German young adults found no gender differences. While ego identity at age 15 strongly predicted intimacy in romantic relationships at age 25, this was true for both men and women (Beyers & Seiffge-Krenke, 2010). Similarly, other research has failed to find gender differences in the link between adolescent romantic attachment and identity exploration (Kerpelman et al., 2012).

ETHNIC FACTORS IN IDENTITY FORMATION

If you are part of the majority culture, ethnic identity formation tends not to be a primary concern. For many young people in minority groups, however, race or ethnicity is central to identity formation. Following Marcia's model, some research has identified four ethnic identity statuses (Phinney, 1998; 2008):

- *Diffused:* Juanita hasn't really thought about her identity. She has done little or no exploration of what her heritage means or what she thinks about it.

- *Foreclosed:* Caleb has strong feelings about his identity, but those feelings are not really based on any serious exploration of his identity. Rather, he has absorbed the attitudes of other important people in his life. These feelings may be positive or negative.

- *Moratorium:* Cho-san has begun to think about what her ethnicity means to her but is still confused about it. She asks questions of others, talks about it with her parents, and thinks a great deal about it.

- *Achieved:* Diego has spent a good deal of time thinking about who he is and what his ethnicity means within that context. He now understands and accepts his ethnicity.

Research shows evidence of the existence of these categories, with the highest proportion of adolescents falling into the moratorium status. In addition, the proportion of people in achieved rises throughout adolescence and into adulthood, and those people who attain identity achievement are more likely to view race as central to their identity (Yip, Seaton & Sellers, 2006). More recent research, rather than focusing on the categorization of adolescents and young adults into identity statuses, has shifted toward examining longitudinal change in and the consequences of exploration and commitment/belongingness to one's ethnic group (Phinney & Ong, 2007).

Exploration of the meaning of ethnicity, which increases in middle adolescence and may reflect the transition to a more ethnically diverse high school, is an important variable (French, Seidman, Allen & Aber, 2006). Friends are likely to

report similar levels of identity exploration and commitment, especially if they are both ethnic minority members, and if they frequently discuss issues of race or ethnicity (Syed & Juan, 2012). Girls may undergo the process of identity formation earlier than boys (Portes, Dunham & Del Castillo, 2000). For example, one study showed that, over a 4-year period, Latina girls went through exploration, resolution, and affirmation of positive feelings about their ethnic identities, whereas boys showed increases only in affirmation (Umana-Taylor, Gonzales-Backen & Guimond, 2009).

cultural socialization Parental practices that teach children about their racial/ethnic heritage and promote cultural practices and cultural pride.

Generally, research has found that developing a sense of ethnic identity is beneficial. Several reviews have found that ethnic identity development has been related to higher self-esteem and better well-being, mental and physical health, and academic outcomes, especially for African American adolescents (Smith & Silvia, 2011; Rivas-Drake et al., 2014).

Perceived discrimination during the transition to adolescence can interfere with positive identity formation and lead to conduct problems or depression. As an example, perceptions of discrimination are associated with depressive symptoms, alienation, and a drop in academic performance in Chinese American adolescents (Benner & Kim, 2009) and decreases in self-esteem and increases in depression in Asian American, black and Latino teens (Greene, Way & Pahl, 2006). Although the effect is stronger for males than for females, increases in racial identity over 1 year have been related to a decreased risk of depressive symptoms (Mandara, Gaylord-Harden, Richards & Ragsdale, 2009). Other protective factors are nurturant, involved parenting; secure attachment with parents; prosocial friends; and strong academic performance (Myrick & Martorell, 2011; Brody et al., 2006).

Cultural socialization includes practices that teach children about their racial or ethnic heritage, promote cultural customs and traditions, and foster racial/ethnic and cultural pride. For example, think about the holidays you celebrate. Participating in those traditions and rituals was part of your cultural socialization, and it impacts identity formation. Adolescents who have experienced cultural socialization tend to have stronger and more positive ethnic identities than those who have not (Juang & Syed, 2010; Hughes et al., 2006). Note that in some cases, cultural socialization is not positive in nature. For example, in some African American families, some ethnic socialization practices involve preparing children to experience oppression and racism, or emphasizing the need to exercise caution in interracial interactions with majority group members (Else-Quest & Morse, 2015).

Sexuality

When John was young, he used to wonder if he was like the other kids. "I always felt different," he later said, "I just didn't know what part of me was different." Not until adolescence,

sexual orientation Focus of consistent sexual, romantic, and affectionate interest, either heterosexual, homosexual, or bisexual.

when he developed a full-blown, and secret, crush on a schoolmate, did John realize he might be gay. Afraid of being laughed at or ridiculed, he kept it to himself until his senior year of high school.

Seeing oneself as a sexual being, recognizing one's sexual orientation, coming to terms with sexual stirrings, and forming romantic or sexual attachments are all parts of achieving sexual identity. Awareness of sexuality is an important aspect of identity formation, profoundly affecting self-image and relationships.

During the twentieth century, a major change in sexual attitudes and behavior in the United States and other industrialized countries brought more widespread acceptance of premarital sex, homosexuality, and other previously disapproved forms of sexual activity. The Internet, cell phones, e-mail, and instant messaging make it easy for adolescents to arrange casual sex and engage in sexual risk-taking. On the other hand, the AIDS epidemic and better sexual education programs have led many young people to abstain from sexual activity outside of committed relationships or to engage in safer sexual practices. In the following section, we discuss important factors in sexual identity formation and sexual behavior, and focus on some of the risks today's adolescents face.

SEXUAL ORIENTATION AND IDENTITY

Although present in younger children, **sexual orientation** generally becomes a pressing issue in adolescence: whether that person will consistently be sexually attracted to persons of the other sex (heterosexual), of the same sex (homosexual), or of both sexes (bisexual). Heterosexuality predominates in nearly every known culture throughout the world. The prevalence of homosexual orientation varies widely, depending on how it is defined and measured. Depending on whether it is measured by sexual, or romantic, attraction or arousal, by sexual behavior, or by sexual identity, the rate of homosexuality in the U.S. population ranges from 1 to 15 percent (Savin-Williams & Ream, 2007). Many young people have one or more homosexual experiences, but isolated experiences or even occasional attractions or fantasies do not determine sexual orientation. In a national survey, 3 percent of 18- to 19-year-old boys and 8 percent of girls in that age group reported being gay, lesbian, or bisexual, but 4 percent of the boys and 12 percent of the girls reported same-sex sexual behaviors (Guttmacher Institute, 2016). Social stigma may bias such self-reports, underestimating the prevalence of homosexuality and bisexuality.

Origins of Sexual Orientation

Sexual orientation seems to be at least partly genetic (Diamond & Savin-Williams, 2003). For example, research has found stretches of DNA on chromosomes 7, 8, 10, and 28 that appear to be involved (Mustanski et al., 2005; Sanders et al., 2015). Twin studies have led to similar conclusions about genetic influences. Researchers have found the concordance rates of monozygotic (identical) twins is always higher than

Chris Colter, formerly of the hit television show *Glee*, is an openly gay singer and actor. He is also the author of a popular middle-school reading series, The Land of Stories, which has recently been optioned for a film adaptation.
©AF archive/Alamy

that of dizygotic (fraternal) twins. However, despite having the exact same copy of genes, identical twins are not perfectly concordant for sexual orientation (Ngun & Vilain, 2014). This implies that nongenetic factors must also play a part. One large twin study found that genes explained about 34 percent of the variation in men and 18 percent in women (Langstrom, Rahman, Carlstrom & Lichtenstein, 2008). But what of the remaining influence? What are the environmental experiences that might impact sexual orientation?

It is important to note that when discussing environmental influences, researchers are not referring to older, discredited theories about domineering mothers, absent fathers, or sexual abuse as causal factors in the development of

Did you know?

Same-sex activity is widespread in the animal kingdom and found in animals as disparate as zebra finches, dolphins, and bonobos (Bailey & Zuk, 2009).

©Kuttelvaserova Stuchelova/Shutterstock

homosexual orientation (Ngun & Vilain, 2014). Rather, environmental experiences refer, most commonly, to the 9 months of prenatal influences in the womb. Those experiences have shaped the brain in significant ways that may impact later sexual orientation.

One environmental influence on development involves biological correlates of family structure. The more older biological brothers a man has, the more likely he is to be gay (Blanchard, 2017). Each older biological brother increases the chances of homosexuality in a younger brother by 33 percent (Bogaert, 2006). Furthermore, there are indications that male babies that will later identify as gay are more likely to weigh less at birth and are more likely to have mothers who experience miscarriages (VanderLaan, Blanchard, Wood, Garzon & Zucker, 2015; Skorska, Blanchard, VanderLaan, Zucker & Bogaert, 2017). These phenomena may be a cumulative immune-like response to the presence of successive male fetuses in the womb.

Another variable that has been implicated in sexual orientation is the 2D:4D ratio. This ratio—that of the pointer finger to the ring finger—is, through a quirk of development, affected by hormone exposure in utero. A lower 2D:4D ratio indicates high prenatal androgen exposure and is more typical of men than women. Interestingly, one meta-analysis showed that lesbian women had a significantly more masculinized 2D:4D ratio when compared to heterosexual women, suggesting androgen exposure in utero affected their sexual orientation. Gay men, by contrast, did not appear to have a different 2D:4D ratio than heterosexual men (Grimbos, Dawood, Burriss, Zucker & Puts, 2010). Other research with girls who have a condition called congenital adrenal hyperplasia (CAH) also speaks to the influence of prenatal hormone exposure. Girls with CAH, who are exposed to higher than average levels of androgens in utero, are more likely to later identify as lesbian or bisexual (Bao & Swaab, 2010).

Imaging studies have found similarities of brain structure and function between homosexuals and heterosexuals of the other sex. While correlational, they are intriguing. Brains of gay men and straight women are more symmetrical, whereas in lesbians and straight men the right hemisphere is slightly larger. Also, in gays and lesbians, connections in the amygdala, which is involved in emotion, are more typical of the other sex (Savic & Lindstrom, 2008). One researcher reported a difference in the size of the hypothalamus, a brain structure that governs sexual activity, in heterosexual and gay men (LeVay, 1991). In brain imaging studies on pheromones, odors that attract mates, the odor of male sweat activated the hypothalamus in gay men much as it did in heterosexual women. Similarly, lesbian women and straight men reacted more positively to female pheromones than to male ones (Savic, Berglund & Lindstrom, 2005; 2006).

Homosexual and Bisexual Identity Development

Despite the increased acceptance of homosexuality in the United States, many adolescents who openly identify as gay, lesbian, or bisexual sometimes fear disclosing their sexual

orientation, even to their parents (Hillier, 2002). They may also find it difficult to meet potential same-sex partners. Most gay, lesbian, and bisexual youth begin to identify as such between the ages of 12 and 17 years (Calzo, Masyn, Austin, Jun & Corliss, 2017). However, because of the lack of socially sanctioned ways to explore their sexuality, many gay and lesbian adolescents experience identity confusion (Sieving, Oliphant & Blum, 2002). Gay, lesbian, and bisexual youth who are unable to establish peer groups that share their sexual orientation may struggle with the recognition of same-sex attractions (Bouchey & Furman, 2003), although the Internet has increasingly provided an anonymous and accessible means for young adults to explore their sexuality (Harper, Serrano, Bruce & Bauermeister, 2016).

Gay and lesbian youth who experience rejection and low support for their sexual orientation from their parents after coming out are more likely to adopt a negative view of their sexuality (Bregman, Malik, Page, Makynen & Lindahl, 2013). Additionally, those gay, lesbian, and bisexual youth who do not successfully integrate their sexual identity in their self-concept are at risk for issues with anxiety, depression, or conduct problems (Rosario, Schrimshaw & Hunter, 2011).

SEXUAL BEHAVIOR

According to national surveys, slightly over 41 percent of high school students have had sexual intercourse (Kann, 2016) and 77 percent of young people in the United States have had sex by age 20 (Finer, 2007). Teenage boys historically have been more likely to be sexually experienced than teenage girls; however, trends are shifting. In 2011, 44 percent of 12th grade boys and 51 percent of girls in that age group reported being sexually active (USDHHS, 2012; Figure 16.1). The median age for girls to first have sex is 17.8 years, and boys follow shortly thereafter with a median age of 18.1 years (Finer & Philbin, 2014).

African Americans tend to begin sexual activity earlier than white youth (Kaiser Family Foundation, Hoff, Greene & Davis, 2003). While Latino boys are also likely to have sex at an earlier age, Latino girls tend to have sex slightly later than their non-Latino white counterparts (Finer & Philbin, 2014).

Early Sexual Activity and Risk-Taking

Two major concerns about adolescent sexual activity are the risks of contracting sexually transmitted infections (STIs) and, for heterosexual activity, of pregnancy. Most at risk are

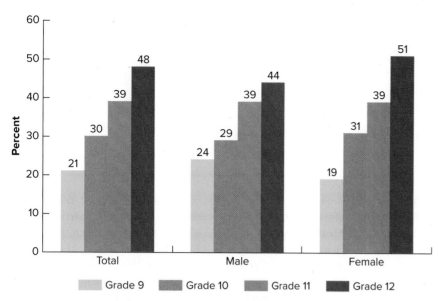

FIGURE 16.1 Percentage of Students in Grades 9 through 12 Who Report They Are Sexually Active

Source: U.S. Department of Health and Human Services (USDHHS). "Youth risk behavior surveillance: United States 2011." MMWR Surveillance Summaries, 61(4), 2012, Table 65.

young people who start sexual activity early, have multiple partners, do not use contraceptives regularly, and have inadequate information—or misinformation—about sex (Abma, Chandra, Mosher, Peterson & Piccinino, 1997; Meade & Ickovics, 2005). Other risk factors are living in a socioeconomically disadvantaged community, substance use, antisocial behavior, and association with deviant peers. Parental monitoring can help reduce these risks (Centers for Disease Control, 2017c; Baumer & South, 2001; Capaldi, Stoolmiller, Clark & Owen, 2002).

Why do some adolescents become sexually active at an early age? Various factors, including early entrance into puberty, poverty, poor school performance, lack of academic and career goals, a history of sexual abuse or parental neglect, and cultural or family patterns of early sexual experience, may play a part (Klein & AAP Committee on Adolescence, 2005).

One of the most powerful influences is perception of peer group norms. Young people often feel under pressure to engage in activities they do not feel ready for. In a nationally representative survey, nearly one-third of 15- to 17-year-olds, especially boys, said they had experienced pressure to have sex (Kaiser Family Foundation et al., 2003). Teens are more likely to have sex and to take risks while having sex if they believe their peers are also having and approve of sex, or are pressuring them to have sex (Van de Bongardt, Reitz, Sandfort & Dekovic, 2015). As a teen's number of close friends who initiate sex grows, the likelihood they themselves will initiate sex also rises (Ali & Dwyer, 2011).

Generally, an involved and engaged relationship between teens and parents is associated with a decreased risk of early sexual activity. Participating in regular family activities predicts declines in teenage sexual activity (Coley, Votruba-Drzal & Schindler, 2009), and more parent-child communication is

sexting The sharing or sending of sexually explicit or suggestive photos or videos to others.

associated with delayed sexual intercourse (Parkes, Henderson, Wight & Nixon, 2011). Teens who have supportive relationships with their parents are more likely to delay intercourse and to use safe sex practices when they finally do so (Deptula, Henry & Schoeny, 2010). Teenagers who have close, warm relationships with their mothers are also likely to delay sexual activity, especially if they perceive that their mothers would disapprove (Jaccard & Dittus, 2000; Sieving, McNeely & Blum, 2000). Warm and accepting parenting may be particularly important for girls (Kincaid, Jones, Sterrett & McKee, 2012). For those teens in two-parent families, having fathers who know more about their friends and activities is associated with delays in sexual activity (Coley, Votruba-Drzal & Schindler, 2009), whereas the absence of a father, especially early in life, is a predictor of early sexual activity (Ellis et al., 2003).

One proposed protective factor is a sense of meaning in life, which is theorized to provide protection against health risk behaviors. Meaning in life has been associated with a decreased risk of unsafe sexual activity, but only in adolescent women (Brassai, Piko & Steger, 2011). However, religiosity, which for many people provides a sense of meaning and community, has repeatedly been associated with decreased risk (Haglund & Fehring, 2010). For instance, a common reason teenagers give for not yet having had sex include that it is against their religion or morals (Abma, Martinez & Copen, 2010). The relationship between religiosity and decreased risk of sexual activity may in part be driven by peers. Religious teens are less likely to be friends with peers who have positive views of sexual activity (Landor, Simons, Simons, Brody & Gibbons, 2011).

Non-Intercourse Sexual Behavior

The percentage of U.S. adolescents who have had intercourse has declined over the past few decades (Kann et al., 2014). However, noncoital forms of genital sexual activity, such as oral and anal sex and mutual masturbation, are common. Many heterosexual teens do not regard these activities as "sex" but as substitutes for, or precursors of, sex, or even as abstinence (Remez, 2000). In one national survey, just under half of teenage boys and girls reported having given or received oral sex (Copen, Chandra & Martinez, 2012).

As with many areas of modern life, social media and electronics have also impacted sexual behavior. In particular, **sexting**, the sharing or sending of sexually explicit or suggestive photos or videos to others, has been a rising concern. Estimates of how many teens either send or receive sexts vary widely. One study found that 7 percent of ages 10 through 17 years had sent or shown sexts, with older teens and girls reporting higher levels (Mitchell, Finkelhor, Jones & Wolak, 2012). This percentage rises to 17 percent if the teen pays for the cell service (Lenhart, 2009). Girls are more likely to send sexually explicit photographs, and sending photographs

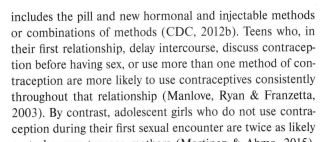
is in turn associated with a great likelihood of engaging in sexual activity (Houck et al., 2014). As with other sexual behaviors, adolescents' perception that their friends approve of their risky online sexual behaviors increases their participation in those behaviors (Sasson & Mesch, 2014).

While this represents a minority of teens, it is nonetheless concerning. Sexting has been associated with an increased likelihood of teens having oral, anal, or vaginal sex; more frequent sexual partners; substance abuse; low self-esteem; depression; and anxiety (Ybarra & Mitchell, 2014; Mitchell et al., 2012). Moreover, the electronic transmission of photographs of nude teens is subject to prosecution under child pornography laws. For example, in 2008–2009, law enforcement agencies handled an estimated 3,477 cases of youth-produced sexual images. Although some of the cases involved either the participation of an adult or were related to malicious intent or bullying, 18 percent of the "non-aggravated" youth-only cases that consisted of experimental and romantic sexual and attention seeking resulted in arrest (Wolak, Finkelhor & Mitchell, 2012). Last, arrest is not the only issue. Once released to the Internet, such photos may be available to future employers, schools, or romantic partners and may follow a young person over time and to their detriment.

Sexting by teens is associated with increased likelihood of sexual activity, substance abuse, low self-esteem, depression, and anxiety.

©Grzegorz Czapski/Shutterstock

Use of Contraceptives

The use of contraceptives among sexually active teenage girls has increased since the 1990s (Abma et al., 2004), and

includes the pill and new hormonal and injectable methods or combinations of methods (CDC, 2012b). Teens who, in their first relationship, delay intercourse, discuss contraception before having sex, or use more than one method of contraception are more likely to use contraceptives consistently throughout that relationship (Manlove, Ryan & Franzetta, 2003). By contrast, adolescent girls who do not use contraception during their first sexual encounter are twice as likely to become teenage mothers (Martinez & Abma, 2015). One nationwide study found that 13 percent of currently sexually active teens did not use any form of birth control during their last sexual encounter (Kann et al., 2014).

The best safeguard for sexually active teens is regular use of condoms, which give some protection against STIs as well as against pregnancy. Slightly over 80 percent of teenage girls and almost 80 percent of teenage boys who are having sex for the first time use a condom (Abma & Martinez, 2017). This does not necessarily ensure continued use, however. While condoms are still the most common form of contraception used, almost half of adolescent females and about a third of adolescent males report not using a condom during their last sexual encounter (Martinez & Abma, 2015). Approximately 5.8 percent of adolescent women use a long-term reversible method such as an intrauterine implant (Abma & Martinez, 2017). Adolescents who start using prescription contraceptives often stop using condoms, in some cases not realizing that they leave themselves unprotected against STIs (Klein & AAP Committee on Adolescence, 2005).

Sex Education

Adolescents get their information about sex primarily from friends, parents, sex education in school, and the media (Kaiser Family Foundation et al., 2003). Adolescents who can talk about sex with older siblings as well as with parents are more likely to have positive attitudes toward safer sexual practices (Kowal & Pike, 2004). However, approximately 22 percent of teen girls and 30 percent of teen boys report that their parents do not talk to them about any sexual or reproductive health topics (Lindberg, Maddow-Zimet & Boonstra, 2016).

Many teenagers get much of their "sex education" from the media, which present a distorted view of sexual activity, associating it with fun, excitement, competition, or violence and rarely showing the risks of unprotected sex. Surprisingly, teens report more exposure to sexual media from television, movies, and music than they do from the Internet (Ybarra, Strasburger & Mitchell, 2014). Teens who watch highly sexual television content are twice as likely to experience a pregnancy compared to those with lower level or no exposure (Chandra et al., 2008). Additionally, teens exposed to sexually explicit content—including pornography and erotica—are more likely to have oral sex and sexual intercourse at earlier ages (Brown & L'Engle, 2009).

From 2011 to 2013, approximately 80 percent of teens received formal sexual education—generally at a school, church, or community center—on preventing STIs or how to say no to sex. However, only 55 percent of males and 60 percent of females received information on the use of birth control methods (Lindberg, Maddow-Zimet & Boonstra, 2016). This is in part driven by policies promoting abstinence research over more comprehensive programs. Programs that encourage abstinence but also discuss STI prevention and safer sexual practices—known as comprehensive sexual education—have been found to delay sexual initiation and increase contraceptive use (Breuner, Mattson & Committee on Psychosocial Aspects of Child and Family Health, 2016). However, since 1998, federal- and state-funded sex education programs stressing abstinence until marriage as the best option have become common.

sexually transmitted infections (STIs) Diseases spread by sexual contact.

Some school programs promote abstinence as the *only* option, even though most abstinence-only courses have not been found to delay sexual activity (Breuner et al., 2016; Satcher, 2001; Trenholm et al., 2007). Abstinence-based courses, even when they have been found to reduce some sexual activity, do not reduce pregnancy rates or sexually transmitted infections. This may be because abstinence-only programs do not impact whether or not teens use safe sex practices such as condoms (Chin et al., 2012). Thus, if teens do have sex, they are less likely to be protected. Likewise, pledges to maintain virginity have shown little impact on sexual behavior other than a *decrease* in the likelihood to take precautions during sex (Rosenbaum, 2009).

Unfortunately, policies promoting abstinence programs have not only undermined the quality of the information taught in the United States, but also in foreign aid programs. These policies have harmed both family planning and HIV prevention programs in other countries (Santelli et al., 2017). Comprehensive sexual education programs, by contrast, have been shown to be effective in preventing pregnancy and disease across a number of countries (Fonner, Armstrong, Kennedy, O'Reilly & Sweat, 2014). Under the Trump administration, federal funding for abstinence education programming is again on the rise, and comprehensive sexual education programs previously demonstrated to be effective are in danger of being defunded (Guttmacher Institute, 2017).

SEXUALLY TRANSMITTED INFECTIONS (STIs)

When John told his parents he was gay, after their initial surprise and adjustment, his parents accepted his sexuality without issue. However, they were worried about sexually risky behavior and talked to John, to his great embarrassment, about the necessity of always using condoms during sexual activity. "Just because pregnancy might not be an issue," his mother said, "doesn't mean sex carries no risk."

Sexually transmitted infections (STIs) are diseases spread by sexual contact. Globally, more than 1 million STIs are acquired each day (World Health Organization, 2016). The highest rates of infection occur among 20- to 24-year-olds, followed by 15- to 19-year-olds (Dehne, Reidner, Berer & World Health Organization, 2005). Rates in the United States are higher than in other developed nations, although the majority of cases are found in developing countries (Advocates for Youth, 2010).

In the United States, an estimated 19.7 million new STIs are diagnosed each year, over half in young men and women (CDC, 2013a). Approximately 65 million Americans have an uncurable STI (Wildsmith, Schelar, Peterson & Manlove, 2010). An estimated 3.2 million adolescent girls in the United States—about 1 in 4 of those ages 14 to 19—has at least one STI (Forhan et al., 2008). The chief reasons for the prevalence of STIs among teenagers include early sexual activity; multiple partners; failure to use condoms or to use them regularly and correctly; and, for women, a tendency to have sex with older partners (CDC, 2000b; Forhan et al., 2008). Additionally, there are often barriers to sexual health services such as lack of transportation to clinics, inability to pay, conflict between school and clinic hours, and concerns about confidentiality (CDC, 2016c). Despite the fact that teens are at higher risk for contracting STIs, they perceive their own personal risk as low (Wildsmith et al., 2010).

STIs in adolescent girls are most likely to develop undetected. In a *single* unprotected sexual encounter with an infected partner, a girl runs a 1 percent risk of acquiring HIV, a 30 percent risk of acquiring genital herpes, and a 50 percent risk of acquiring gonorrhea (Alan Guttmacher Institute, 1999). Although teenagers tend to view oral sex as less risky than intercourse, a number of STIs, especially pharyngeal gonorrhea, can be transmitted in that way (Remez, 2000).

Did you know?

Teens exposed to highly sexual television content are twice as likely to experience a pregnancy compared with lower level or no exposure (Chandra et al., 2008).

©Tony Cardoza/Getty Images

Human Papillomavirus (HPV)

The most common STI, accounting for about half of all STI infections diagnosed in 15- to 24-year-olds each year, is human papillomavirus (HPV), or genital warts, the leading cause of cervical cancer in women (Weinstock, Berman & Cates, 2004). Among girls with three or more partners, the risk jumps to 50 percent (Forhan et al., 2008). There are approximately 40 types of HPV, a number of which have been identified as the leading cause of cervical cancer in women.

In 2006, a vaccine that targets the types of HPV that cause most cases of cervical cancer and genital warts became available. The Centers for Disease Control (2016c) recommends routine vaccination for all female adolescents and young adults starting at age 11 or 12. Vaccination rates are low but growing. In 2010, about half of girls age 14 to 17 had received at least one dose and only 32 percent had received the recommended three doses (Markowitz et al., 2013). Rates are even lower in adolescent boys; in 2013, only 32.6 percent of teen boys had received at least one dose, and 13.9 percent received the entire series (Lu et al., 2015). Despite low vaccination rates, HPV incidence since the introduction of the vaccine has dropped from 11.5 percent to 5.1 percent, indicating a high level of protection is conferred by the vaccine (Markowitz et al., 2013).

Some parents avoid vaccinating their children out of a fear it might lead to increased sexual activity. However, research has shown that vaccination for HPV does not lead to more or riskier sexual behavior in adolescents (Mayhew et al., 2014). Additionally, parental concerns about the safety of the vaccine are also unfounded, as multiple, large-scale studies have shown little to no evidence of adverse side effects or safety risks (Chao et al., 2012; Lu, Kumar, Castellsague & Guiliano, 2011; Gee et al., 2011).

Chlamydia, Gonorrhea, Genital Herpes, and Trichomoniasis

The most common *curable* STIs are chlamydia and gonorrhea. These diseases, if undetected and untreated, can lead to severe health problems, including, in women, pelvic inflammatory disease (PID), a serious abdominal infection. The rates of all three STIs have recently increased. In 2015-2016, the reported rate of chlamydia rose by 4 percent in 15- to 19-year-olds, especially in young women. After a period of decline, rates of syphilis (11.3 percent) and gonorrhea (13.0 percent) both rose during the same time period (CDC, 2016c). Both gonorrhea and chlamydia are currently treated with antibiotics. There are growing concerns that antibiotic resistance will eventually result in an inability to successfully treat gonorrhea (Kirkcaldy, 2016; CDC, 2013a).

Genital herpes simplex is a chronic, recurring, often painful, and highly contagious disease. It can be fatal to a person with a deficiency of the immune system or to the newborn infant of a mother who has an outbreak at the time of delivery. There are two variants: herpes simplex virus type 1 (HSV-1), which causes cold sores; and herpes simplex virus type 2 (HSV-2), which causes genital sores. Teens today are less likely to have been infected with HSV-1 because of public health education efforts such as the discouraging of shared cosmetics. However, their lack of exposure to this virus means they have not had the opportunity to form HSV-1 antibodies, which may result in a higher risk of HSV-2 if they are exposed when they become sexually active. (Bradley, Markowitz, Gibson & McQuillan, 2013).

Hepatitis B is a virus that affects the liver, causing both acute and chronic issues that can lead to cirrhosis, liver cancer, and death. Hepatitis B has been affecting humans for at least 4,500 years, as evidence of its presence has been found in the bones of ancient humans (Muhlemann et al., 2018). Currently, it affects an estimated 257 million people globally (World Health Organization, 2018c), and in 2012 there were approximately 847,000 infected people in the United States (Roberts et al., 2016). Rates have dropped sharply as a result of the availability, for more than 20 years, of a preventive vaccine.

Also common among young people is trichomoniasis, a parasitic infection that is most commonly transmitted during sexual activity, but may be passed along by moist towels and swimsuits (Weinstock et al., 2004). An estimated 3.7 million U.S. citizens are infected, although the majority of people show no symptoms. Trichomoniasis can be easily treated with medication such as metronidazole or tinidazole (CDC, 2017d).

Human Immunodeficiency Virus (HIV)

The human immunodeficiency virus (HIV), which causes acquired immune deficiency syndrome, AIDS, is transmitted through bodily fluids, usually by sharing intravenous drug needles or by sexual contact with an infected partner. The virus attacks the body's immune system, leaving a person vulnerable to a variety of fatal diseases. Symptoms of AIDS include extreme fatigue, fever, swollen lymph nodes, weight loss, diarrhea, and night sweats. There were 1.8 million new HIV infections worldwide in 2016, representing an 11 percent decline from 2010 (UNAIDS, 2018). As of now, AIDS is incurable, but increasingly the related infections that kill people are being stopped with antiviral therapy (UNAIDS, 2013).

Globally, estimates are that there were 36.7 million people living with HIV/AIDS worldwide in 2016. Of those, approximately 2.1 million were young people between the ages of 10 and 19 years. Moreover, 260,000 teens age 15 to 19 years were newly infected with HIV that same year (World Health Organization, 2018b).

In the United States at the end of 2015, slightly over 60,000 young adults were living with HIV. In 2016, 8,451 young adults, most between the ages of 20 and 24, received a new HIV diagnosis, and most contracted the virus through sexual contact. This represents a 24 percent decline from 2010, a promising trend. However, approximately half of these young adults were diagnosed, only 41 percent received HIV medical care, and only 27 percent had a suppressed viral load (a sign of successful management of the disease) (CDC, 2018b).

Comprehensive sex and STI/HIV education is critical to promoting responsible decision making and controlling the spread of STIs. Evidence for the positive impact of such programs is strong: More than 60 percent of programs that emphasized abstinence and condom use delayed and/or reduced sexually activity and increased the use of condoms or contraceptives. Further, the programs did not increase sexual activity. In contrast, programs that emphasize abstinence-only have shown little evidence of affecting sexual behavior (Kirby & Laris, 2009). Unfortunately, fewer than half of schools teach all 19 sexual health topics recommended by the Centers for Disease Control and the percentage of schools that are required to provide HIV prevention information is declining (CDC, 2018b).

TEENAGE PREGNANCY AND CHILDBEARING

Estimates are that 21 million girls between the ages of 15 and 19 years in developing regions of the world become pregnant each year, as do an additional 2 million girls under the age of 15 years. Moreover, approximately 3.9 million girls age 15 to 19 years receive an unsafe abortion (World Health Organization, 2018a).

Pregnancy rates vary widely across countries for which data are available. With respect to the developed world, the United States has higher rates of teen pregnancy than other similar countries despite comparable rates of teenage sexual activity. For example, the rate of teenage birth and pregnancy is six times higher than that of Switzerland and more than twice as high as France (Lindberg et al., 2016). Other areas with high pregnancy rates include Mexico, sub-Saharan Africa, Azerbaijan, Georgia, and Romania. The lowest pregnancy rates are found in Switzerland, the Netherlands, Singapore, and Slovenia. Abortion rates also vary, with a low of 17 percent of teen pregnancies ending in abortion in Slovakia to a high of 69 percent in Sweden (Sedgh, Finer, Bankole, Eilers & Singh, 2015).

Birthrates for U.S. teenagers peaked in 1957 at 96.3 births per 1,000 women and have fallen dramatically since then to 22.2 births per 1,000 women in 2013 (Ventura, Hamilton & Mathews, 2014; Martin, Hamilton, Osterman, Driscoll & Mathews, 2017). The declines reflect a variety of factors, including, most importantly, increased use of contraception (Lindberg, Santelli & Desai, 2016). The declines also have accompanied steady decreases in early intercourse and in sex with multiple partners (Martin et al., 2017). The declines do not reflect increased use of abortion (Kost, Maddow-Zimmet & Arpaia, 2017).

About 7 in 100 girls in the United States have been pregnant at least once before age 20 (Kost, Henshaw & Carlin, 2013). More than half (51 percent) of pregnant teenagers in the United States have their babies (Klein & AAP Committee on Adolescence, 2005). Sixty-seven percent of teens who carry the pregnancies to term are between the

MTV's Teen Mom franchise, originally criticized for glamorizing teen pregnancy, may instead be partially responsible for the recent declines in teenage motherhood. Internet searches for birth control and abortion spiked after episodes of the reality drama aired. (Kearney & Levine, 2015).
©MediaPunch/Shutterstock

ages of 18 and 19 years, and 31 percent are 15 to 17 years of age, with 2 percent of live births accounted for by teens under the age of 15 (National Center for Health Statistics, 2009). Overall, 29 percent of adolescents choose to abort (Kost et al., 2017), the lowest percentage recorded since the legalization of abortion in 1973 (Santelli & Melnikas, 2010). Fourteen percent of teen pregnancies end in miscarriage or stillbirth (Klein & AAP Committee on Adolescence, 2004).

Although declines in teenage pregnancy and childbearing have occurred among all population groups, birthrates have fallen most sharply among non-Hispanic black teenagers. Still, non-Hispanic black and Hispanic girls are more likely to have babies than non-Hispanic white or Asian American girls (Martin et al., 2017).

More than 90 percent of pregnant teenagers describe their pregnancies as unintended, and 50 percent of teen pregnancies occur within 6 months of sexual initiation (Klein & AAP Committee on Adolescence, 2005). Research suggests contributing factors include having been physically or sexually abused and/or exposed to parental divorce

More than 90 percent of pregnant teenagers describe their pregnancies as unintended.
©Comstock Images/Alamy

or separation, domestic violence, substance abuse, or a household member who was mentally ill or engaged in criminal behavior, and growing up fatherless (Madigan, Wade, Tarabulsy, Jenkins & Shouldice, 2014; Hillis et al., 2004; Ellis et al., 2003). Teenage fathers tend to have limited financial resources, poor academic performance, and high dropout rates. Many teenage parents are themselves products of adolescent pregnancy (Campa & Eckenrode, 2006).

Outcomes of Teen Pregnancy

Teenage pregnancies often have poor outcomes. Many of the mothers are impoverished and poorly educated, and some are drug users. Many do not eat properly, do not gain enough weight, and get inadequate prenatal care or none at all. Their babies are likely to be premature or dangerously small and are at heightened risk of other birth complications (Jeha, Usta, Ghulmiyya & Nassar, 2015; Wen et al., 2007). They are also at heightened risk for health and academic problems, abuse and neglect, and developmental disabilities that may continue into adolescence (Children's Defense Fund, 2004; Menacker, Martin, MacDorman & Ventura, 2004).

Teenage unwed mothers and their families are likely to suffer financially. Child support laws are spottily enforced, court-ordered payments are often inadequate, and many young fathers cannot afford the payments (AAP Committee on Adolescence, 1999). In addition, teenage mothers are likely to drop out of school and to have repeated pregnancies, and they are less likely to go to college. They and their partners may lack the maturity, skills, and social support to be good parents. Their children, in turn, tend to have developmental and academic problems, to be depressed, to engage in substance abuse and early sexual activity, to engage in gang activity, to be unemployed, and to become adolescent parents themselves (Basch, 2011; Klein & AAP Committee on Adolescence, 2005; Pogarsky, Thornberry & Lizotte, 2006).

Poor outcomes of teenage parenting are far from inevitable, however. Several long-term studies find that, two decades after giving birth, most former adolescent mothers are not on welfare; many have finished high school and secured steady jobs; and they do not have large families. Comprehensive adolescent pregnancy and home visitation programs seem to contribute to good outcomes (Basch, 2011; Klein & AAP Committee on Adolescence, 2005), as do contact with the father (Howard, Lefever, Borkowski & Whitman, 2006) and involvement in a religious community (Carothers, Borkowski, Lefever & Whitman, 2005).

Preventing Teen Pregnancy

Europe's industrialized countries have provided universal, comprehensive sex education for a much longer time than the United States. Comprehensive programs encourage young teenagers to delay intercourse and improve contraceptive use. They include education about sexuality, birth control, and responsible sexual decisions, and information about risks and consequences of teenage pregnancy (AAP Committee on Psychosocial Aspects of Child and Family Health & Committee

on Adolescence, 2001). Contraceptives are provided free to adolescents in many countries. Sweden showed a fivefold reduction in the teenage birthrate following introduction of birth control education, free access to contraceptives, and free abortion on demand (Bracher & Santow, 1999).

In the United States, programs that focus on teen outreach have had success. Such programs generally combine comprehensive sex education and access to family planning services. With the use of such a program, California—the only state that refused abstinence-only federal dollars—went from having the highest teen pregnancy rate to showing the steepest decline, effectively halving rates (Boonstra, 2010). Similar results have been found with teen outreach programs that also focus on raising self-esteem, handling emotions, and dealing effectively with peers and adults (Allen & Philliber, 2001).

Unfortunately, the provision and content of American sex education programs are political issues. Some critics claim that community- and school-based sex education leads to more or earlier sexual activity, even though evidence shows otherwise (Boonstra, 2010; Kirby & Laris, 2009).

The problem of teenage pregnancy requires a multifaceted solution. It must include programs and policies to encourage postponing or refraining from sexual activity, but it also must recognize that many young people do become sexually active and need education and information to prevent pregnancy and STIs. It requires attention to underlying factors that put teenagers and families at risk—reducing poverty, school failure, behavioral and family problems, and expanding employment, skills training, and family life education (CDC, 2013c)—and it should target those young people at highest risk.

Relationships with Family and Peers

Age becomes a powerful bonding agent in adolescence. Adolescents spend more time with peers and less with family. However, most teenagers' fundamental values remain closer to their parents' than is generally realized (Steinberg, 2008). Even as adolescents turn to peers for role models, companionship, and intimacy, they still look to parents for a secure base from which they can try their wings.

IS ADOLESCENT REBELLION A MYTH?

The teenage years have been called a time of **adolescent rebellion**, involving emotional turmoil, conflict within the family, alienation from adult society, reckless behavior, and rejection of adult values. But is this characterization of teens true?

Most young people feel close to and positive about their parents, share similar opinions on major issues, and value their parents' approval (Blum & Reinhart, 2000; Offer, Ostrov & Howard, 1989). The vast majority of teens adapt

adolescent rebellion Pattern of emotional turmoil, characteristic of a minority of adolescents that may involve conflict with family, alienation from adult society, reckless behavior, and rejection of adult values.

Perspectives on Diversity

©Digital Vision/Getty Images

CULTURE AND DISCRETIONARY TIME

One way to assess changes in adolescents' relationships with the important people in their lives is to see how they spend their discretionary time. Cultural variations in time use reflect varying cultural needs, values, and practices (Verma & Larson, 2003).

Young people in tribal or peasant societies spend most of their time producing bare necessities of life and have much less time for socializing than adolescents in technologically advanced societies (Larson & Verma, 1999). In some postindustrial societies such as Korea and Japan, where the pressures of schoolwork and family obligations are strong, adolescents have relatively little free time. To relieve stress, they spend their time in passive pursuits, such as watching television and "doing nothing" (Verma & Larson, 2003). In India's family-centered culture, on the other hand, middle-class urban eighth graders spend 39 percent of their waking hours with family, compared with 23 percent for U.S. eighth graders, and report being happier when with their families than U.S. eighth graders do. For these young people, the task of adolescence is not to separate from the family but to become more integrated with it. Similar findings have been reported in Indonesia, Bangladesh, Morocco, and Argentina (Larson & Wilson, 2004).

In comparison, U.S. adolescents have a good deal of discretionary time. Approximately half of teens' waking hours outside of school are spent in discretionary activities (Larson & Verma, 1999).

Americans spend a great deal of this time on electronic media or interacting with friends, increasingly of the other sex, and less of this time, in comparison to other countries, on homework, (Larson, 2001; Rideout, Foehr& Roberts, 2010). Some students participate in extracurricular activities such as organized sports, community work, or school clubs. In general, participation in these activities is associated with positive academic outcomes, a decrease in risk for internalizing and externalizing behavior, less alcohol and drug use, and increases in civic engagement following graduation from high school (Fredricks & Eccles, 2010).

Ethnicity may affect family connectedness. In some research, African American teenagers, who may look on their families as havens in a hostile world, tended to maintain more intimate family relationships and less intense peer relations than white teenagers (Giordano, Cernkovich & DeMaris, 1993). On the other hand, those from Mexican and Chinese families, particularly immigrant families, reported a stronger sense of family obligation and assistance and spent more time on activities that carried out those obligations (Hardway & Fuligni, 2006). Asian, Latino, and European American teens all tend to show higher levels of happiness when they participate in activities that help the family (Telzer & Fulingi, 2009). For some ethnic and cultural groups, providing assistance to the family is associated with connectedness and is thus beneficial.

---

well to their life experiences. The relatively few deeply troubled adolescents tend to come from disrupted families and, as adults, continue to have unstable family lives and reject cultural norms (Offer, Offer & Ostrov, 2004; Offer, Kaiz, Ostrov & Albert, 2002).

Still, adolescence can be a tough time for young people and their parents. Family conflict, depression, and risky behavior are more common than during other parts of the life span (Arnett, 1999). Negative emotionality and mood swings are most intense during early adolescence, perhaps due to the stress connected with puberty. It may also

©Don Hammond/ Design Pics

WHAT DO YOU DO?

Art Therapist

Art therapists use art as a part of the therapeutic process for individuals with emotional problems, disabilities, or acute or chronic health problems. Through the process of creating art, art therapists help their clients better understand their thoughts and emotions. Art therapists typically work within health and non-profit organizations, as well as in private practice. A master's degree in art therapy or a degree with an art therapy concentration is required to become an art therapist. In addition, each state has its own licensure requirements. To learn more about becoming an art therapist, visit www.atcb.org and www.arttherapy.org.

be that some level of rebellious behavior in the teenage years is developmentally normal (Moffitt, 1993; Steinberg, 2001). By late adolescence, emotionality tends to become more stable (Larson, Moneta, Richards & Wilson, 2002).

ADOLESCENTS AND PARENTS

Adolescence brings special challenges. Just as adolescents feel tension between dependency on their parents and the need to break away, parents want their children to be independent yet find it hard to let go. These tensions can lead to family conflict, and parenting styles and monitoring can influence outcomes and teens' willingness to self-disclose. Also, adolescents' relationships with parents are affected by the parents' life situation—their work and marital and socio-economic status (SES).

Individuation and Family Conflict

If you were like most teens, you probably listened to different music from your parents, dressed in a different style of clothing, and felt it was reasonable to keep certain things private from them. This process, called **individuation** by psychologists, begins in infancy and continues throughout adolescence. It involves the struggle for autonomy and differentiation, or personal identity. An important aspect of individuation is carving out boundaries of control between self and parents (Nucci, Hasabe & Lins-Dyer, 2005), and this process may entail family conflict. Somewhat paradoxically, a warm, interconnected relationship with parents can help teens individuate successfully (Ponappa, Bartle-Haring & Day, 2014).

Both family conflict and positive identification with parents are highest at age 13 and then diminish through age 17, when they stabilize or increase somewhat. This shift reflects increased opportunities for independent adolescent decision making (Gutman & Eccles, 2007). Parents of young adolescents must strike a delicate balance between too much freedom and too much intrusiveness during this process. For instance, seventh and eighth graders are at elevated risk for problem behaviors because of decreased parental monitoring and involvement, which allows the behavior of antisocial peers to exert increased influence (Van Ryzin, Stormshak & Dishion, 2012). By 11th grade, those young people who see themselves as having a great deal of autonomy tend to spend more time in unsupervised socializing with peers, again increasing risk. But too little autonomy can also have negative effects. Those students who perceive their parents as highly intrusive in their personal lives are also more likely to be influenced by negative peer interactions (Goldstein, Davis-Kean & Eccles, 2005).

Despite common beliefs about adolescence being a time of great rebellion and chaos, family arguments most often concern control over everyday personal matters—chores, schoolwork, dress, money, curfews, dating, and friends—rather than issues of health and safety or right and wrong (Steinberg, 2005). The emotional intensity of these conflicts—out of all proportion with the subject matter—may reflect the underlying individuation process.

There are also cultural differences. One primary distinction is that drawn between collectivistic and individualistic societies. Research in this area shows that connectedness between teens and parents is higher in collectivistic countries such as India, Saudi Arabia, and Algeria than in individualistic Western countries such as France, Poland, and Argentina. In collectivistic cultures, emphasis is placed more on family than on individual desires (Dwairy & Achoui, 2010).

> **individuation** Adolescent's struggle for autonomy and differentiation, or personal identity.

Especially for girls, family relations can affect mental health. Negative family interactions are related to adolescent depression (Gutman & Eccles, 2007). Family conflict predicts multiple adjustment problems in addition to depression, including anxiety, conduct problems, and problems with peers (Cummings, Koss & Davies, 2015), and it tends to increase over time in harsh, coercive, or hostile families (Rueter & Conger, 1995). Additionally, adolescent maltreatment has been linked to criminal offenses and violent crime, alcohol and drug use, risky sexual behavior and suicidal thoughts (Thornberry, Henry, Ireland & Smith, 2010).

Alternatively, healthy family interactions have a positive effect. Family conflict tends to go down over time in warm, supportive families (Rueter & Conger, 1995). In addition, autonomy support on the part of parents is associated with more adaptive self-regulation of negative emotions and academic engagement (Roth, Assor, Niemiec, Ryan & Deci, 2009) and positive family identification is related to less depression (Gutman & Eccles, 2007). Adolescents who are given more decision-making opportunities report higher self-esteem than those who are given fewer such opportunities (Gutman & Eccles, 2007. Last, both individuation and family connectedness during adolescence predict well-being in middle age (Bell & Bell, 2005).

Parenting Styles

Authoritative parenting continues to foster healthy psychosocial development (Baumrind, 2005; Hoskins, 2014). Authoritative parents insist on important rules, norms, and values but are willing to listen, explain, and negotiate. They exercise appropriate control over a child's conduct (*behavioral control*) but not over the child's feelings, beliefs, and sense of self (*psychological control*) (Steinberg & Darling, 1994). So, for example, they might ground their teenage son for breaking a rule, but they would not insist that the teen agree with them about the wisdom of the broken rule. Generally, behavioral control is preferable. Psychological control and harsh control can harm adolescents' psychosocial development and mental health (Steinberg, 2005), and are associated with externalizing problems (Pinquart, 2017). For example, withdrawal of love as a control strategy is associated with an increase in resentment toward parents and a decrease in teens' ability to self-regulate negative emotions (Roth et al., 2009). Parents who are psychologically controlling tend to be unresponsive to their children's growing need for *psychological autonomy*, the right to their own thoughts and feelings (Steinberg, 2005). By contrast, parents who are open to new experiences themselves are more likely to allow their teens greater freedom (Denissen, van Aken & Dubas, 2009).

Teens whose parents firmly enforce behavioral rules have more self-discipline and fewer behavior problems than those with more permissive parents. Those whose parents grant them psychological autonomy tend to be self-confident and competent academically and socially (Gray & Steinberg, 1999).

Problems arise when parents overstep what adolescents perceive as appropriate bounds of legitimate parental authority. The existence of a mutually agreed personal domain in which authority belongs to the adolescent has been found in various cultures and social classes from Japan to Brazil. This domain expands as parents and adolescents continually renegotiate its boundaries (Nucci et al., 2005).

The literature on parenting styles has been critiqued on the grounds it is primarily unidirectional. In other words, the original model considered the effect of parenting on adolescents, but minimized the effect that teens' behaviors had on parenting. For example, a rebellious and confrontational adolescent is likely to elicit a far different set of parenting behaviors than will a compliant and cooperative teen. There is evidence that this is indeed the case. For example, meta-analyses indicate that many effects of parenting on teen behavior are bidirectional (Pinquart, 2017). Additionally, some research suggests that adolescents may actually exert a stronger effect on their parents' behavior than parenting exerts on their behavior (Kerr, Stattin & Ozdemir, 2012), perhaps via their own genetically influenced personality traits (Klahr & Burt, 2014).

Parental Monitoring and Adolescents' Self-Disclosure

A large body of research shows that parental monitoring is one of the most consistently identified protective factors for teens (Barnes, Hoffman & Welte, 2006; Racz & McMahon, 2011). Parental monitoring broadly involves keeping track of the young person's activities, for example, by signing the teen up for after-school activities, checking in with parents of their teen's friends, and keeping track of a teen's where-abouts (Barnes et al., 2006).

Part of monitoring involves knowing what a teen is up to. Young people's growing autonomy and the shrinking areas of perceived parental authority redefine the types of behavior adolescents are expected to disclose to parents (Smetana, Crean & Campione-Barr, 2005). Both adolescents and parents see *prudential* issues, behavior related to health and safety (such as smoking, drinking, and drug use), as most subject to disclosure; followed by *moral* issues (such as lying); *conventional* issues (such as bad manners or swearing); and *multifaceted*, or borderline, issues (such as seeing an R-rated movie), which lie at the boundary between personal matters and one of the other categories. Both adolescents and parents see *personal* issues (such as how teens spend their time and money) as least subject to disclosure. However, for each type of behavior parents tend to want more disclosure than adolescents are willing to provide, although this discrepancy diminishes with age (Smetana,

Metzger, Gettman & Campione-Barr, 2006). Importantly, adolescent disclosure to parents is predictive of delinquency; those teens who disclose more are less likely to engage in problem behaviors (Keijsers, Branje, VanderValk & Meeus, 2010).

In a study of 690 Belgian adolescents, teens disclosed more information when parents maintained a warm, responsive family climate and provided clear expectations without being overly controlling (Soenens, Vansteenkiste, Luyckx & Goossens, 2006)—in other words, when parenting was authoritative. This link between warmth and disclosure also has been found in various ethnic groups in the United States, including Chinese, Mexican American, and European American youth (Yau, Tasopoulos-Chan & Smetana, 2009). Adolescents, especially girls, tend to have closer, more supportive relationships with their mothers than with their fathers (Smetana et al., 2006), and girls confide more in their mothers (Yau et al, 2009). Moreover, relationship quality seems to matter more in girls' willingness to confide in their parents. In other words, boys' secret keeping depends less on relationship warmth than does that of girls' (Keijsers et al., 2010).

Family Structure and Family Atmosphere

Conflict in the home can affect the process of individuation. Changes in marital distress or conflict predict corresponding changes in adolescents' adjustment (Cui, Conger & Lorenz, 2005). Divorce can affect this process as well. Adolescents whose parents later divorced showed more academic, psychological, and behavioral problems before the breakup than peers whose parents did not later divorce (Sun, 2001).

Adolescents living with their continuously married parents tend to have significantly fewer behavioral problems than those in other family structures

Authoritative parenting—characterized by listening, explaining, and negotiating as well as by insistence on important rules, values, and norms—fosters healthy psychosocial development.
©PhotoAlto/PunchStock

(single-parent, cohabiting, or stepfamilies). Divorce negatively impacts outcomes in part via its influence on the paternal relationship. Teens whose parents were still married reported a close relationship with their father 48 percent of the time, whereas those whose parents were divorced reported being close to their father only 25 percent of the time (Scott, Booth, King & Johnson, 2007). High-quality involvement by a nonresident father helps a great deal, but not as much as the involvement of a father living in the home (Carlson, 2006).

Adolescents, especially boys, from single-parent families are at higher risk for problem behaviors such as substance abuse or aggression. However, this risk can be mitigated by other family structures. For example, parental monitoring (Griffin, Botvin, Scheier, Diaz & Miller, 2000) and mother's educational level, family income, and quality of the home environment (Ricciuti, 2004) have been associated with a reduction in risk.

Adolescents in cohabiting families, like younger children, tend to have greater behavioral and emotional problems than adolescents in married families (Brown, 2004). However, a better comparison group may be that of adolescents in stepparent families. Some of the data on cohabitation is driven by family instability—a documented negative influence on development—rather than cohabitation per se. Adolescents in stepparent families have also experienced family instability and thus may be considered a more appropriate comparison group. When compared to teens in married stepparent families, a recent review suggested that adolescents in cohabitating families are similar in outcomes. They have similar rates of delinquency, substance abuse, risky sexual activity, academic outcomes, physical health, and emotional well-being (Manning, 2017).

Adolescents from families headed by gay or lesbian parents do not appear to show differences in a wide variety of outcomes, including cognitive development, gender identity, and adjustment problems (Fedewa, Black & Ahn, 2015). Rather, as with traditional two-parent families, the quality of the relationship—not the sexual orientation of the parents—is the key variable influencing outcomes (Wainright & Patterson, 2006).

Mothers' Employment and Economic Stress

The impact of a mother's work outside the home may depend on how many parents are present in the household. Single mothers may find that work affects how much time and energy is left to spend with children or monitor their activities. For example, in one study, mothers who worked at night spent less time with their teen children, had lower quality home environments, and were less close to their children. These variables, in turn, were related to an increase in risky adolescent behaviors (Han, Miller & Waldfogel, 2010). Additionally, maternal employment has repeatedly been associated with a less healthy nutritional environment in the home (Bauer, Hearst, Escoto, Berge & Neumark-Sztainer, 2012) and an increased risk of overweight (Miller, 2011).

The type of after-school care and supervision is particularly important. Those teens who are on their own, away from home, tend to become involved in alcohol and drug use and in misconduct in school, especially if they have an early history of problem behavior (Coley, Morris & Hernandez, 2004). Participation in organized after school activities can serve as a protective factor (Mahatmya & Lohman, 2011).

As discussed earlier, a major problem in many single-parent families is lack of money. For example, teens are more likely to drop out of school and show declines in self-esteem and mastery if their mothers have unstable employment or are out of work for 2 years (Kalil & Ziol-Guest, 2005). Job displacement—where employees lose their jobs due to organizational changes such as restructuring, downsizing, or relocating—has also been associated with declines in educational attainment and well-being in adolescents from single-parent families (Brand & Thomas, 2014). Family economic hardship during adolescence affects adult well-being in part because it is stressful, and that stress interferes with family relationships and affects children's educational and occupational attainments (Sobelewski & Amato, 2005).

ADOLESCENTS AND SIBLINGS

There are several trends in sibling relationships across adolescence. In general, siblings spend less time together, their relationships become more equal, and they become more similar in their levels of competence.

Many mothers, such as designer Vera Wang, seen here with her daughter, must juggle the demands of both a career and family life.
©Theo Wargo/WireImage/Getty Images

Changes in sibling relationships in many ways mirror the changes we see in the relationships of adolescents and their parents. As adolescents spend more time with peers, they spend less time with siblings. Generally, and perhaps as a result of this, adolescents tend to be less close to siblings than to friends and are less influenced by them. This distance grows across adolescence (Laursen, 1996). Moreover, as children move through adolescence, their relationships with their siblings become progressively more equal (Campione-Barr, 2017).

Sibling conflict declines across middle adolescence. Research has shown that sisters report more intimacy than brothers or mixed pairs. Mixed-sex siblings become less intimate between middle childhood and early adolescence, but more so in middle adolescence, a time when most young people become more interested in the other sex (Kim, McHale, Osgood & Courter, 2006). Teens who have opposite-sex siblings report increases in their perceived romantic competence from early adolescence into adulthood (Doughty, Lam, Stanik & McHale, 2015).

Sibling relationships also interact with parent-child relations and the parents' marital relationship. For example, in one study siblings were more intimate if their mother was warm and accepting. Parent-child conflict was associated with sibling conflict. However, when fathers became less happy in their marriage, siblings became closer and quarreled less (Kim et al., 2006). Additionally, research has shown that differential treatment, where teens perceive a parent as favoring their sibling, is associated with both externalizing and internalizing behavior problems (Buist, Dekovic & Prinzie, 2013).

Siblings can exert positive or negative effects on each other. Older siblings may influence a younger one to smoke, drink, or use drugs (Pomery et al., 2005; Rende, Slomkowski, Lloyd-Richardson & Niaura, 2005). Younger siblings hanging out with an antisocial older brother are at serious risk for adolescent antisocial behavior, drug use, sexual behavior, and violence (Snyder, Bank & Burraston, 2005; Solmeyer, McHale & Crouter, 2014). However, siblings can also be protective. In single-mother homes, a warm and nurturing relationship with an older sister tended to prevent a younger sister from engaging in substance use and risky sexual behavior (East & Khoo, 2005). A recent meta-analysis supports the strong connection between warm relationships with little conflict and healthier psychological adjustment in siblings (Buist et al., 2013).

PEERS AND FRIENDS

"I came out to my parents first," John said, "I mean, I knew they would always love me. But my friends were harder. I didn't know what they would do. I was lucky. While I had one friend that dumped me after learning I was gay, for the most part, everyone was really supportive."

An important source of emotional support during the complex transition of adolescence is the peer group. The peer group is a source of affection, sympathy, understanding, and moral guidance; a place for experimentation; and a setting for achieving autonomy and independence from parents. It is a place to form intimate relationships that serve as rehearsals for adult intimacy.

In childhood, most peer interactions are one-to-one, though somewhat larger groupings begin to form in middle childhood. As children move into adolescence, cliques—structured groups of friends who do things together—become more important. In adolescence, crowds emerge. Crowd membership is a social construction, a set of labels such as the jocks, the nerds, the skaters, the stoners. All three levels of peer groupings may exist simultaneously, and some may overlap in membership, which may change over time. Both clique and crowd affiliations become looser as adolescence progresses (Brown & Klute, 2003).

The influence of peers normally peaks at ages 12 to 13 and declines during middle and late adolescence. Risk-taking, especially in early adolescence, is higher in the company of peers than when alone (Gardner & Steinberg, 2005), even when potential negative consequences are made clear (Smith, Chein & Steinberg, 2014). For example, at age 13 or 14, popular adolescents may engage in mildly antisocial behaviors, such as trying drugs or sneaking into a movie without paying, to demonstrate to their peers their independence from parental rules (Allen, Porter, McFarland, March & McElhaney, 2005). However, attachment to peers in early adolescence is not likely to forecast real trouble unless the attachment is so strong that the young person is willing to give up obeying household rules, doing schoolwork, and developing his or her own talents in order to win peer approval and popularity (Fuligni, Eccles, Barber & Clements, 2001).

Friendships

The intensity and importance of friendships and the amount of time spent with friends are probably greater in adolescence than at any other time in the life span. Friendships tend to become more reciprocal, more equal, and more stable, although many friendships are still fleeting. High-quality friendships are more stable (Hiatt, Laursen, Mooney & Rubin, 2015). Those that are less satisfying become less important or are abandoned. Often, differences in such areas as peer acceptance, physical aggression, school competence, and especially sex predict friendship dissolution (Hartl, Laursen & Cillessen, 2015).

Greater intimacy, loyalty, and sharing with friends mark a transition toward adultlike friendships. Adolescents begin to rely more on friends than on parents for intimacy and support, and they share confidences more than younger friends do (Buhrmester & Chong, 2009). Girls' friendships tend to be more intimate than boys', with frequent sharing of confidences (Brown & Klute, 2003). Intimacy with same-sex friends increases during early to midadolescence, after which it typically declines as intimacy with the other sex grows (Laursen, 1996).

The increased intimacy of adolescent friendship reflects cognitive as well as emotional development. Adolescents are now better able to express their private thoughts and feelings and consider another person's point of view. Confiding in a friend helps young people explore their own feelings, define

Friendships during adolescence become more equal and stable, and adolescents typically spend more time with friends than at any other time of life.
©PeopleImages.com/Getty Images

their identity, and validate their self-worth. The capacity for intimacy is related to psychological adjustment and social competence. Adolescents who are more intimate with their friends feel closer to and have less conflict with them (Chow, Ruhl & Buhrmester, 2013).

Adolescents with high-quality friendships have a high opinion of themselves, do well in school, are sociable, and are less likely to be hostile, anxious, or depressed (Berndt & Perry, 1990; Hartup & Stevens, 1999; Hiatt et al., 2015). They also tend to have established strong bonds with parents (Brown & Klute, 2003). This may be part of a more general process. When adolescents have high-quality friendships, those friendships tend to be deeply embedded within their other supportive social relationships, including other friends, romantic partners, and family members (Flynn, Felmlee & Conger, 2017). A bidirectional process seems to be at work: Good relationships foster adjustment, which in turn fosters good relationships.

Social Consequences of Online Communication

The explosion of online communication technologies such as e-mail, social networking sites, and text messaging has changed the way many adolescents communicate. As a group, adolescents are the primary users of these technologies. They spend more time online than adults (Pew Research Center, 2012), and they spend a majority of their online time using the Internet to communicate. More than 99 percent of teens use the Internet (van den Eijnden, Meerkerk, Vermulst, Spijkerman & Engels, 2008) and 88 percent of teens use the Internet daily for interaction and communication with their peers (Pew Research Center, 2012). Moreover, 88 percent of adolescents report using at least one social media site, with Facebook, Instagram, and

Did you know?

Facebook may be a good social outlet, but can harm academic performance. Students who are on Facebook while they study earn 20 percent lower grades than their friends who avoid it while working (Kirschner & Karpinski, 2010).

©Tomislav Pinter/Shutterstock

Twitter reported as the most commonly used sites (Pew Research Center, 2018). Adolescents who are active users of social media sites, especially if they are not guarded about their personal privacy, are more vulnerable to online harassment and cyberbullying (Ang, 2015).

In general, screen-based media usage is related to poorer physical health, quality of life, and quality of family relationships (Iannotti, Kogan, Janssen & Boyce, 2009). However, what type of media is used appears to be important. For example, studies indicate that instant messaging (van den Eijnden et al., 2008) and video game usage (Mathers et al., 2009) are associated with depression, while television is associated with obesity, socio-emotional problems, and lower self-esteem (Russ, Larson, Franke & Halfon, 2009). Additionally, some people can develop problematic Internet usage, a condition akin to addiction, in which continued Internet and electronic use can impact everyday functioning, relationships, and overall well-being (Akin, 2012). Men, perhaps because of their generally greater interest in video games and online gaming, are at higher risk of developing addiction-related behaviors, although there are some indications that when women do develop similar difficulties they may be more profoundly affected (Anderson, Steen & Stavropoulos, 2017).

However, not all access to the Internet is harmful. As access to the Internet increased and technology became more sophisticated and easy to use, studies began to show that at times online communication can stimulate rather than reduce social connectedness (Kraut et al., 2002). For example, studies have found instant messaging can have a positive effect on relationship quality in adolescence (Valkenburg & Peter, 2009b), and social competence in lonely adolescents can be strengthened using the Internet to communicate with others and experiment with their identities (Valkenburg & Peter, 2008). This has been particularly true for LGBTQ adolescents, possibly because they often have difficulty finding partners or safe supportive places in which to be themselves in real life (Korchmaros, Ybarra & Mitchell, 2015).

Individuals often become unusually intimate in an online environment and feel free to express themselves (Valkenburg & Peter, 2009). Because adolescents connect self-disclosure with quality friendships, the elevated level of self-disclosure in online environments is linked to friendship quality and formation (Valkenburg & Peter, 2007), which in turn elevates social connectedness and well-being. However, there is a dark side to this. One aspect of online communication that enhances intimacy—anonymity—has made it appealing for electronic bullies. This, in conjunction with limited contextual cues, and especially for teens whose parents do not monitor their child's online activities, increases the risk of cyberbullying (Ang, 2015). Estimates for prevalence rates across middle and high school vary widely, with cyberbullying perpetration reported from 1 to 41 percent, victimization from 3 to 72 percent, and cyberbully/victim rates from 2.3 percent to 16.7 percent (Selkie, Fales & Moreno, 2016). Most studies on cyberbullying have been conducted in North America, but cross-cultural work also shows variable estimates across different countries, with countries such as

Did you know?

Of teens who blog, 57.1 percent claim they "never lie" on their blogs (Blinka & Smahal, 2009).

©AP Images

Canada (23.8 percent) and China (23 percent) showing higher median prevalence rates and countries such as Australia (5 percent), Sweden (5.2 percent), and Germany (6.3 percent) lower levels (Brochado, Soares & Fraga, 2017).

Romantic Relationships

Romantic relationships are a central part of most adolescents' social worlds. With the onset of puberty, most heterosexual boys and girls begin to think about and interact more with members of the other sex. Romantic relationships tend to become more intense and intimate across adolescence. By age 16, adolescents interact with and think about romantic partners more than parents, friends, or siblings (Bouchey & Furman, 2003).

Typically, romantic relationships move from mixed groups or group dates to one-on-one romantic relationships that, unlike other-sex friendships, are described as involving passion and a sense of commitment (Lantagne & Furman, 2017). While teens practice interacting with the opposite sex within the context of friendships, opposite-sex friends are unlikely to become romantic partners. Rather, romantic partners tend to come from different friendship networks (Kreager, Molloy, Moody & Feinberg, 2016). Boys appear to be less confident than girls about these early romantic relationships (Giordano, Longmore & Manning, 2006).

Early adolescents think primarily about how a relationship might affect their status in the peer group and pay little attention to attachment or support needs (Bouchey & Furman, 2003). By midadolescence, most young people have had at least one exclusive partner lasting for several months to about a year, and the effect of the choice of partner on peer status tends to become less important. Not until late adolescence or early adulthood, though, do romantic relationships begin to serve the full gamut of emotional needs that such relationships can serve and then only in relatively long-term relationships (Furman & Wehner, 1997).

Relationships with parents may affect the quality of romantic relationships. For example, those teens who have a good relationship with their parents as teens have higher self-esteem and better relationship quality as young adults (Johnson & Galambos, 2014). Additionally, parental divorce and marital conflict is associated with poorer relationship quality in teens, expressed as low commitment and high conflict (Cui & Fincham, 2010; Cui, Fincham & Durtschi, 2011).

As with other social relationships, technology is playing an increasingly large role in adolescent romantic relationships (Vaterlaus, Tulane, Porter & Beckert, 2017). For example, while most teens meet their romantic partners at school, some relationships do develop online (Korchmaros et al., 2015). Moreover, information available online via social media sites is often used to "check out" new romantic interests, gauge and signal interest in potential partners, and initiate communication (Subrahmanyam & Greenfield, 2008; Van Ouystel, Van Gool, Walrave, Ponnet & Peeters, 2016). Once a relationship is established, social media may also be used to communicate daily, to convey affection, to argue, to publicly broadcast relationship status, and to break and make up (Vaterlaus et al., 2017; Van Oustel et al., 2016).

More problematically, electronic communication can also be used for the exchange of sexually charged conversation or explicit photographs, often referred to as "sexting." Large, nationally representative studies suggest that only 4 percent of teenagers send nude or nearly nude photos of themselves via text, instant messaging, or online (Lenhart, 2009). Adolescents who do so tend to be sexually active and intend to share photos privately with a romantic partner (Kletke, Hallford & Mellor, 2014). Sexting has been linked with other risky behaviors, such as higher substance use, having concurrent sexual partners, and more current sexual partners (Ybarra & Mitchell, 2014).

Dating Violence

Dating violence is a significant problem in the United States. The three common forms of dating violence are:

Physical—when a partner is hit, pinched, shoved, or kicked.

Emotional—when a partner is threatened or verbally abused.

Sexual—when a partner is forced to engage in a non-consensual sex act

Statistics indicate that about 10 percent of students have been victims of teen dating violence, including both physical and sexual abuse, but the rate is almost certainly underreported. When analyses are limited to only those students who were dating in the previous year, almost 21 percent of girls and 10.4 percent of boys reported experiencing some form of teen dating violence (Vagi, Olsen, Basile & Vivole-Kantor, 2015). The rates for emotional abuse are even higher: As many as 3 in 10 adolescents report being verbally or psychologically abused (Halpern, Young, Waller, Martin & Kupper, 2003). White students generally report lower levels of teen dating violence than African American or Hispanic students (Vagi et al., 2015).

In addition to the physical harm caused by this type of abuse, teens who are victims of dating violence are more likely to do poorly in school and to engage in risky behaviors such as drug and alcohol use. These students are also subject to eating disorders, depression, and suicide (Mulford & Giordano, 2008).

Risk factors that may predict violence include substance abuse, conflict and/or abuse in the home, and living in neighborhoods with high rates of crime and drug use (Child Trends, 2010a; 2010b). Additionally, attitudes about the acceptability of violence within relationships, poor family relationship quality, mental health problems, and the use of aggressive media also predict violence (Vagi et al., 2013). Peers are a particularly important influence. A recent meta-analysis found that a variety of peer behaviors, but especially peer dating violence, peers' aggressive and/or antisocial behavior, and being victimized by peers, were all significantly related to both dating violence perpetration and victimization (Garthe, Sullivan & McDaniel, 2017).

Unhealthy relationships can last a lifetime as victims carry patterns of violence into future relationships. Adolescent dating violence is a predictor of adult partner violence (Exner-Cortens, Eckenrode, Bunge & Rothman, 2017).

Antisocial Behavior and Juvenile Delinquency

John had always been a "good kid," but one night, his parents got a phone call from the police department.

John, now a high school senior, had been booked for shoplifting at a local mall. John's parents were furious, and John was embarrassed and ashamed. "We didn't raise you to be like this," they sternly told him, and took away his car, television, and cell phone privileges.

John's behavior, while upsetting to his parents, was not out of the norm for teenagers. Many teens engage in some degree of antisocial or delinquent behavior.

Antisocial behavior and juvenile delinquency is influenced, as Bronfenbrenner's theory would suggest, by interacting factors ranging from microsystem influences, such as genetic and biological factors, parent-child hostility, poor parenting practices, and peer deviance, to macrosystem influences, such as community structure and neighborhood social support. In the following section, we outline some factors that influence these behaviors.

BIOLOGICAL INFLUENCES

Antisocial behavior tends to run in families. Analyses of many studies have concluded that genes influence 40 to 56 percent of the variation in antisocial behavior within a population, and 60 to 65 percent of the variation in aggressive antisociality (Ferguson, 2010; Rhee & Waldman, 2002; Tackett, Krueger, Iacono & McGue, 2005). Genes alone, however, are not predictive of antisocial behavior. Research suggests that although genetics influences delinquency, environmental influences including family, friends, and school affect gene expression (Guo, Roettger & Cai, 2008; Silberg, Maes & Eaves, 2012).

Neurobiological deficits, particularly in the portions of the brain that regulate reactions to stress, may help explain why some children become antisocial adolescents. As a result of these neurological deficits, children may not receive or heed normal warning signals to restrain impulsive or reckless behavior (van Goozen, Fairchild, Snoek & Harold, 2007). For example, they tend to have abnormal or blunted responses to events that generally evoke fear in others (Marsh et al., 2011).

Part of this abnormal physiological profile may involve arousal processes. Specifically, individuals who have low arousal levels may be prone to antisocial behaviors as a form of sensation seeking to achieve arousal levels that a typical person experiences. In support of this, high frontal EEG power (FAP, which is associated with low brain arousal) is associated with adolescent aggressive antisocial behavior in male twins (Niv et al., 2015). Low heart rate has also been found to be repeatedly associated with antisocial behavior in

both men and women (Portnoy & Farrington, 2015; Hammerton et al., 2018).

Attentional processes may also be involved. Children with attention-deficit/hyperactivity disorder (ADHD) are at higher risk for the development of comorbid conduct disorder (CD) and depression that contribute to antisocial behavior (Drabick, Gadow & Sprafkin, 2006). There is some dispute about whether or not ADHD by itself is a direct risk factor for the development of antisocial behavior, although more recent research does seem to indicate this is the case (Storebo & Simonsen, 2016).

Also, findings of an MRI investigation of empathetic response have indicated youth with aggressive conduct disorders have atypical responses to seeing others in pain (Decety, Michalaska, Akitsuki & Lahey, 2009). Moreover, those that have traits associated with psychopathy seem to have reduced gray matter volume in the anterior rostral prefrontal cortex and temporal poles, areas involved in the processing of empathy, moral reasoning, and emotions such as shame and guilt (Gregory et al., 2012).

A crucial variable that must be taken into account is the age at which antisocial behavior begins. Researchers have identified two types of antisocial behavior: an early-onset type, beginning by age 11, which tends to lead to chronic juvenile delinquency in adolescence, and a milder, late-onset type, beginning after puberty, which tends to arise temporarily in adolescence. Late-onset adolescents tend to commit relatively minor offenses (Schulenberg & Zarrett, 2006) and tend to come from families with standard family backgrounds (Collins, Maccoby, Steinberg, Hetherington & Bornstein, 2000). Evidence suggests that early-onset offenders are likely different from very early on, explaining both the early onset of their behaviors as well as their persistence into adulthood. For example, such adolescents show poor impulse control, are aggressive, and tend not to think about their future (Barker, Oliver & Maughan, 2010; Monahan, Steinberg & Cauffman, 2009).

FAMILY INFLUENCES

Parents of children who become chronically antisocial may have failed to reinforce good behavior in early childhood and may have been harsh or inconsistent in their discipline (Coie & Dodge, 1998; Snyder, Cramer, Frank & Patterson, 2005; Neppl, Dhalewadikar & Lohman, 2016). The children may get payoffs for antisocial behavior: When they act up, they may gain attention or get their own way. These early negative patterns pave the way for negative peer influences that promote and reinforce antisocial behavior (Brown, Mounts, Lamborn & Steinberg, 1993; Collins et al., 2000). When constant criticism, angry coercion, or rude, uncooperative behavior characterizes parent-child interactions, the child tends to show aggressive behavior problems, which worsen the parent-child relationship (Buehler, 2006).

Many teens experiment with behaviors considered antisocial or deliquent, but the vast majority do not develop long-term problems or become adult criminals.
©Image Source

However, when parents show high warmth and low hostility, even delinquent teens tend to reduce their problematic behavior and behave more positively (Williams & Steinberg, 2011). Parents can also inoculate their teens from delinquency by discouraging association with deviant peers (Simons et al., 2001). Adolescents whose parents know where they are and what they are doing are less likely to engage in delinquent acts (Laird, Pettit, Bates & Dodge, 2003) or to associate with deviant peers (Lloyd & Anthony, 2003). Teens who are open with their parents and disclose information are less likely to engage in antisocial acts (Criss et al., 2015), although it may very well be the case that teens who are engaging in acts their parents would not approve of are less likely to disclose.

ENVIRONMENTAL INFLUENCES

The choice of antisocial peers is affected mainly by environmental factors (Iervolino et al., 2002). Young people gravitate to others brought up like themselves who are similar in school achievement, adjustment, and antisocial tendencies (Collins et al., 2000). Antisocial adolescents tend to have antisocial friends, and their antisocial behavior increases when they associate with each other (Monahan, Steinberg & Cauffman, 2009). The way antisocial teenagers talk, laugh, or smirk about rule-breaking and nod knowingly among themselves seems to constitute a sort of "deviancy training" (Dishion & Tipsord, 2011). Not all children respond in the same way, however. Teens who are genetically predisposed to antisocial behavior respond more strongly to maladaptive peer group norms than other children (Vitaro et al., 2015). These adolescents then continue to elicit ineffective parenting, which then predicts delinquent behavior and association with deviant peer groups (Simons, Chao, Conger & Elder, 2001; Tolan, Gorman-Smith & Henry, 2003). Notably, peer influences can also be positive. For example, exposure to altruistic peers can buffer adolescents against the negative effects of violent or dangerous neighborhoods (Criss, Smith, Morris, Liu & Hubbard, 2017; Rious & Cunningham, 2018).

Family economic circumstances may influence the development of antisocial behavior. Poor children are more likely than other children to commit antisocial acts, and those whose families are continuously poor tend to become more antisocial with time (Macmillan, McMorris & Kruttschnitt, 2004). Even within individual children, those whose families rose in and out of poverty showed more delinquent behavior when their families had less money than when they were financially well off (Rekker et al., 2015). When families rise from poverty while a child is still young, the child is no more likely to develop behavior problems than a child whose family was never poor (Macmillan et al., 2004). Boys, but not girls, who live in poor neighborhoods that border wealthier areas are at greater risk of antisocial behaviors than boys who live in areas of concentrated poverty, perhaps as a result of the feelings of unfairness the obvious social disparities may bring about (Odgers, Donley, Caspi, Bates & Moffit, 2015).

Weak neighborhood social organization in a disadvantaged community can influence delinquency through its effects on parenting behavior and peer deviance (Chung & Steinberg, 2006) as well as on norms about antisocial or violent acts (Stewart & Simons, 2010). For example, exposure to community violence and living in a dangerous community are strong predictors of future antisocial behavior (Slatterly & Meyers, 2014; Criss et al., 2017). By contrast, collective efficacy—the strength of social connections within a neighborhood and the extent to which residents monitor or supervise each other's children—can positively influence outcomes (Odgers et al., 2009).

LONG-TERM PROSPECTS

The vast majority of young people who engage in juvenile delinquency do not become adult criminals (Kosterman, Graham, Hawkins, Catalano & Herrenkohl, 2001). Delinquency peaks about age 15 and then declines. However, teenagers who do not see positive alternatives or who come from dysfunctional families are more likely to adopt a permanently antisocial lifestyle (Schulenberg & Zarrett, 2006).

Those most likely to persist in violence are those who had early antisocial influences. For example, teens who show antisocial behavior prior to the age of 15 are at higher risk of death, substance abuse, self-inflicted harm, crime, and poverty (Molero, Samuelson, Hodgins, Larsson, Larm & Tengstrom, 2010). In one study, 75 percent of individuals who were delinquent at age 14 remained so at high or moderate levels through age 29 (Brook, Lee, Finch, Brown & Brook, 2013). Least likely to persist are boys and girls who were early school achievers and girls who showed early prosocial development (Kosterman et al., 2001).

PREVENTING AND TREATING DELINQUENCY

Because juvenile delinquency has roots early in childhood, so should preventive efforts that attack the multiple factors that can lead to delinquency. Adolescents who have taken part in certain early childhood intervention programs are less likely to get in trouble than their equally underprivileged peers (Reynolds, Temple, Ou, Arteaga & White, 2011). Effective programs target high-risk urban children and last at least 2 years during the child's first 5 years. They influence children directly, through high-quality day care or education, and at the same time indirectly, by offering families assistance and support geared to their needs (Yoshikawa, 1994; Loeber, Farrington & Petechuck, 2003).

These programs operate on Bronfenbrenner's mesosystem by affecting interactions between the home and the school or child care center. The programs also go one step further, to the exosystem, by creating supportive parent networks and linking parents with such community services as prenatal and postnatal care and educational and vocational counseling (Yoshikawa, 1994; Zigler, Taussig & Black, 1992; Reynolds et al., 2011). Through their multipronged approach, these interventions have an impact on several early risk factors for delinquency.

Once children reach adolescence, especially in poor, crime-ridden neighborhoods, interventions need to focus on spotting troubled adolescents and preventing gang recruitment (Tolan et al., 2003). Successful programs boost parenting skills through better monitoring, behavioral management, and neighborhood social support. For example, recent research has shown that in early adolescence, maintaining appropriate levels of control and nurturing a close and positive relationship has protective effects against teenage antisocial behaviors later in adolescence, especially for mothers (Vieno, Nation, Pastore & Santinello, 2009).

Programs such as teen hangouts and summer camps for behaviorally disturbed youth can be counterproductive because they bring together groups of deviant youth who tend to reinforce each other's deviancy. Similarly, programs such as Scared Straight, in which at-risk teens visit prisons and speak with inmates, tend to result in higher levels of delinquency and thus have fallen out of favor (Petrosino, Turpin-Petrosino, Hollis-Peel & Lavenberg, 2013). Moving juveniles through the juvenile court system rather than diversion programs (such as counseling referrals) also tends to increase future offending (Petitclerc, Gatti, Vitaro & Tremblay, 2013; Petrosino, Guckenburg & Turpin-Petrosino, 2013). More effective programs—Scouts, sports, and church activities—integrate deviant youth into the nondeviant mainstream. Structured, adult-monitored or school-based activities after school, on weekend evenings, and in summer, when adolescents are most likely to be idle and to get in trouble, can reduce their exposure to settings that encourage antisocial behavior (Dodge, Dishion & Lansford, 2006).

emerging adulthood Proposed transitional period between adolescence and adulthood, usually extending from the late teens through the midtwenties.

Did you know?

Programs such as teen hangouts and summer camps for behaviorally disturbed youth can be counterproductive because they bring together groups of deviant youth who tend to reinforce each other's deviancy. More effective programs integrate deviant youth into the nondeviant mainstream. (Dodge, Dishion & Lansford, 2006).

©Oleksiy Maksymenko/ Getty Images

Fortunately, the great majority of adolescents do not get into serious trouble. Those who show disturbed behavior can—and should—be helped. With love, guidance, and support, adolescents can avoid risks, build on their strengths, and explore their possibilities as they approach adult life.

Emerging Adulthood

When does a person become an adult? For most people, three criteria define adulthood: (1) accepting responsibility for oneself, (2) making independent decisions, and (3) becoming financially independent (Arnett, 2006).

In industrialized countries, entrance into adulthood takes longer and follows far more varied routes than in the past. Before the mid-twentieth century, a young man just out of high school typically would seek a stable job, marry, and start a family. For a young woman, the usual route to adulthood was marriage, which occurred as soon as she found a suitable mate.

Since the 1950s, the technological revolution made specialized training increasingly essential. The gender revolution has brought more women into the workforce and broadened female roles. The ages at first marriage and childbirth have shifted sharply upward as both women and men pursued higher education or vocational opportunities and as cohabitation became more acceptable (Furstenberg, Rumbaut & Setterstein, 2005; Lundberg & Pollack, 2014). Today the road to adulthood may be marked by multiple milestones—entering college, working, moving away from home, getting married, and having children—and the order and timing of these transitions vary (Schulenberg, O'Malley, Bachman & Johnston, 2005).

Thus some developmental scientists suggest that, for the many young people in industrialized societies, the late teens through the mid- to late twenties has become a distinct period of the life span now known as **emerging adulthood**. It is a time during which young people are no longer adolescents but have not yet settled into adult roles (Arnett, 2007). In the minds of many people today, the onset of adulthood is marked not so much by external criteria but rather by a sense of autonomy, self-control, and personal responsibility (Shanahan, Porfeli & Morimer, 2005). Although the uncertainty and turmoil that can mark this process can be distressing, overall most young people have a positive view of their future and look forward to their adult lives (Arnett, 2007). It is important to note that this exploratory process is not shared by all young adults in the world. It is largely tied to development in Western countries, especially among relatively affluent young people.

Earlier theorists critiqued the view of emerging adulthood as being relevant only to upper-class European Americans and suggested that ethnic minorities and people from lower socioeconomic classes, even when confined to analyses of developed countries, might not share the same processes. For example, some work suggested that African Americans and Latinos who came from lower-SES families tended to believe they had reached adulthood at an earlier age than European Americans and Asian Americans, probably because of greater and earlier family responsibilities (Arnett, 2003).

Did you know?

The top three criteria for adulthood cited by emerging adult Americans are "accepting responsibility for oneself, making independent decisions, and becoming financially independent"— criteria that reflect the U.S. cultural values of individualism and self-sufficiency (Arnett & Galambos, 2003, p. 92).

©AP Images

However, more recent work suggests that there are more commonalities in the experience of emerging adulthood than differences, at least within different social classes within the United States (Arnett, 2016). We are, at our core, more alike than different.

The normal developmental changes in the early years of life are obvious and dramatic signs of growth. The infant lying in the crib becomes an active, exploring toddler. The young child enters and embraces the worlds of school and society. The adolescent, with a new body and new awareness, prepares to step into adulthood.

Growth and development do not screech to a stop even then. People change in important ways throughout adulthood. They continue to shape their development, as they have been doing since birth. What occurs in a child's world is significant, but it is not the whole story. We each continue to write the story of human development for ourselves and our society for as long as we live.

Emerging adulthood, extending from the late teens through the mid-twenties, is a transitional period during which individuals establish adult roles.
©skynesher/Getty Images

mastering the CHAPTER

©Hill Street Studios/Blend Images

Summary and Key Terms

The Search for Identity Formation

> A central concern during adolescence is the search for identity. Erik Erikson described this psychosocial conflict as *identity versus identity confusion*. The virtue that should arise from this conflict is *fidelity*.

> James Marcia described four identity statuses: identity diffusion, foreclosure, moratorium, and identity achievement.

> Researchers differ on whether girls and boys take different paths to identity formation.

> Ethnicity is an important part of identity. Minority adolescents seem to go through stages of ethnic identity development much like Marcia's identity statuses.

KEY TERMS

Identity

Identity versus identity confusion

Psychosocial moratorium

Identity diffusion

Foreclosure

Moratorium

Identity achievement

Cultural socialization

Sexuality

> Sexual orientation appears to be influenced by an interaction of biological and environmental factors.

> Because of lack of social acceptance, the course of homosexual identity and relationship development may vary.

> Teenage sexual activity involves risks of pregnancy and sexually transmitted infections. Adolescents at greatest risk are those who begin sexual activity early, have multiple partners, do not use contraceptives, and are ill-informed about sex.

> Regular condom use is the best safeguard for sexually active teens.

> Comprehensive sex education programs delay sexual initiation and encourage contraceptive use. Abstinence-only programs are not as effective.

> Teenage pregnancy and birthrates in the United States have declined.

> Teenage childbearing often has negative outcomes, including ill health and financial hardship, and risk of ineffective parenting.

KEY TERMS

Sexual orientation

Sexting

Sexually transmitted infections (STIs)

Relationships with Family and Peers

> Full-scale adolescent rebellion is unusual. For the majority of teens, adolescence is a fairly smooth transition. For the few deeply troubled teens, it can predict a difficult adulthood.

> Adolescents spend an increasing amount of time with peers, but relationships with parents continue to be influential.

> Conflict with parents tends to be greatest during early adolescence. Authoritative parenting is associated with the most positive outcomes.

> Effects of family structure and maternal employment on adolescents' development may depend on such factors as economic resources, the quality of the home environment, and how closely parents monitor adolescents.

> Relationships with siblings tend to become more distant during adolescence, and the balance of power between older and younger siblings becomes more equal.

> The influence of the peer group is strongest in early adolescence. The structure of the peer group

becomes more elaborate, involving cliques and crowds as well as friendships.

> Friendships, especially among girls, become more intimate, stable, and supportive in adolescence.

> Digital communication can have both positive and negative impacts on social connectedness and emotional well-being.

> Romantic relationships meet a variety of needs and develop with age and experience.

KEY TERMS

Adolescent rebellion   **Individuation**

Antisocial Behavior and Juvenile Delinquency

> Chronic delinquency generally stems from early-onset antisociality. It is associated with multiple, interacting risk factors, including ineffective parenting, school failure, peer and neighborhood influence, and low socioeconomic status.

> Programs that attack risk factors from an early age have had success.

Emerging Adulthood

> For many people, three criteria define adulthood: Accepting responsibility for oneself, making independent decisions, and becoming financially independent.

> As the age at first marriage and childbirth have shifted to later in life, other milestones may mark adulthood.

> In industrialized societies, a period known as emerging adulthood is characterized as a transitional period between adolescence and adulthood.

KEY TERM

Emerging adulthood

Practice Quiz

1. What are the three issues in identity formation that Erikson believed needed to be resolved?

   _____
   _____
   _____

2. Nick is agonizing over his future and is trying to decide if he should attend a community college or join the army. He is probably best described as being in Marcia's _____ stage of identity status.

   a. identity diffusion
   b. moratorium
   c. foreclosure
   d. identity achievement

3. According to Gilligan, identity is developed through intimate relationships to a greater degree in:

   a. women
   b. men
   c. adolescents who came from difficult family circumstances
   d. neither gender; it is equally important

4. Ethnic identity formation is more important for adolescents:

   a. as they reach adulthood
   b. when they start working full time
   c. from the majority group in a culture
   d. from minority groups in a culture

5. What are two factors that impact sexual orientation?

   _____
   _____
   _____

6. What are four risk factors for contracting STIs and/or becoming pregnant in adolescence?

   _____
   _____
   _____
   _____

7. What is the most common STI?

   a. HIV   c. syphilis
   b. genital herpes   d. HPV

8. Overall, teen pregnancy has a _____ effect on outcomes.

   a. neutral
   b. negative
   c. positive
   d. variable, depending on race/ethnicity

9. Is the characterization of adolescence as a time of rebellion and alienation true?

   a. Yes, it is true for the vast majority of teens, although most outgrow it.
   b. Yes, and adolescent rebellion and alienation have increased in the last 20 years.
   c. No, only a small minority of teens rebel and become alienated.
   d. No, because in the modern world there is little to rebel against.

10. What is individuation? _____
    _____
    _____

11. Generally, _____ report greater levels of intimacy in adolescence.

    a. same-sex siblings
    b. cross-sex siblings
    c. siblings with more than a 4-year gap in age
    d. siblings with less than a 2-year gap in age

12. "I guess I would describe myself as a jock," says John. What type of peer group is he referring to?

    a. friend   c. crowd
    b. clique   d. individualistic

13. If Colin began shoplifting at age 9 and was committing armed robberies and abusing drugs by age 17, we would likely characterize Colin as being:

    a. an early-onset delinquent
    b. a temperamentally delayed delinquent
    c. a late-onset delinquent
    d. an imitative adopter

14. What are four characteristics of effective early intervention programs for delinquency?

    _____
    _____
    _____
    _____

15. What is the onset of adulthood marked by for most young people today?

    a. getting a stable job
    b. getting married
    c. a sense of autonomy, self-control, and personal responsibility
    d. being able to vote

Answers: 1–choice of an occupation; the adoption of values to live by; the development of a satisfying sexual identity; 2–b; 3–a; 4–d; 5–Among the factors that impact sexual orientation are genes, having older biological brothers (for gay men), and brain structure; 6–Among the risk factors are starting sexual activity early, having multiple partners, not using contraceptives regularly, having inadequate or incorrect information about sex, living in a socioeconomically disadvantaged community, substance use, antisocial behavior, association with deviant peers, and low parental monitoring; 7–d; 8–b; 9–c; 10–Individuation is an adolescent's struggle for autonomy and differentiation, or personal identity; 11–a; 12–c; 13–a; 14–Effective programs are those that target high-risk urban children, last at least 2 years during the child's first 5 years of life, provide high-quality day care or education, and provide family support; 15–c

The words in this glossary are found throughout the book and will help the student better understand the concepts.

A

acceleration Approach to educating the gifted that moves them through the curriculum at an unusually rapid pace. *274*

accommodation Piaget's term for changes in a cognitive structure to include new information. *19*

acquired immune deficiency syndrome (AIDS) Viral disease that undermines effective functioning of the immune system. *64*

acute medical conditions Occasional illnesses that last a short time. *244*

adaptation Piaget's term for adjustment to new information about the environment. *19*

adolescence Developmental transition between childhood and adulthood entailing major physical, cognitive, and psychosocial changes. *305*

adolescent growth spurt Sharp increase in height and weight that precedes sexual maturity. *308*

adolescent rebellion Pattern of emotional turmoil, characteristic of a minority of adolescents that may involve conflict with family, alienation from adult society, reckless behavior, and rejection of adult values. *355*

alleles Two or more alternative forms of a gene that can occupy the same position on paired chromosomes and affect the same trait. *40*

altruism Motivation to help others without expectation of reward; may involve self-denial or self-sacrifice. *230*

altruistic behavior Activity intended to help another person with no expectation of reward. *150*

animism Tendency to attribute life to objects that are not alive. *190*

anorexia nervosa Eating disorder characterized by self-starvation and extreme weight loss. *315*

anoxia Lack of oxygen, which may cause brain damage. *83*

anticipatory smiling Infant smiles at an object and then gazes at an adult while still smiling. *150*

Apgar scale Standard measurement of a newborn's condition; it assesses appearance, pulse, grimace, activity, and respiration. *83*

art therapy Therapeutic approach that allows a person to express troubled feelings without words, using a variety of art materials and media. *249*

assimilation Piaget's term for incorporation of new information into an existing cognitive structure. *19*

assisted reproductive technology (ART) Methods used to achieve conception through artificial means. *35*

asthma A chronic respiratory disease characterized by sudden attacks of coughing, wheezing, and difficulty in breathing. *244*

attachment Reciprocal, enduring tie between two people—especially between infant and caregiver—each of whom contributes to the quality of the relationship. *155*

attention-deficit/hyperactivity disorder (ADHD) Syndrome characterized by persistent inattention and distractibility, impulsivity, low tolerance for frustration, and inappropriate overactivity. *273*

authoritarian parenting Parenting style emphasizing control and obedience. *228*

authoritative parenting Parenting style blending warmth and respect for a child's individuality with an effort to instill social values. *228*

autobiographical memory A type of episodic memory of distinctive experiences that form a person's life history. *198*

autonomy versus shame and doubt Erikson's second stage in psychosocial development, in which children achieve a balance between self-determination and control by others. *160*

autosomes In humans, the 22 pairs of chromosomes not related to sexual expression. *39*

avoidant attachment Pattern in which an infant rarely cries when separated from the primary caregiver and avoids contact on his or her return. *155*

B

basic trust versus basic mistrust Erikson's first stage in psychosocial development, in which infants develop a sense of the reliability of people and objects. *154*

Bayley Scales of Infant and Toddler Development Standardized test of infants' and toddlers' mental and motor development. *122*

behaviorist approach Approach to the study of cognitive development that is concerned with the basic mechanics of learning. *121*

behavior therapy Therapy that uses principles of learning theory to eliminate undesirable behaviors. *250*

bilingual education System of teaching non-English-speaking children in their native language while they learn English and later switching to all-English instruction. *266*

binge drinking Consuming five or more drinks on one occasion. *317*

bioecological theory Bronfenbrenner's approach to understanding processes and contexts of child development that identifies five levels of environmental influence. *21*

body image Descriptive and evaluative beliefs about one's appearance. *314*

Brazelton Neonatal Behavioral Assessment Scale (NBAS) Neurological and behavioral test to measure a neonate's responses to the environment. *84*

bulimia nervosa Eating disorder in which a person regularly eats huge quantities of food and then purges the body by laxatives, induced vomiting, fasting, or excessive exercise. *315*

bullying Aggression deliberately and persistently directed against a particular target, or victim, typically one who is weak, vulnerable, and defenseless. *298*

C

canalization Limitation on variance of expression of certain inherited characteristics. *48*

case study A study of a single subject, such as an individual or family. *25*

cell death In brain development, normal elimination of excess cells to achieve more efficient functioning. *103*

central executive In Baddeley's model, element of working memory that controls the processing of information. *197*

centration In Piaget's theory, tendency of preoperational children to focus on one aspect of a situation and neglect others. *191*

cephalocaudal principle Principle that development proceeds in a head-to-tail direction; that is, that upper parts of the body develop before lower parts of the trunk. *57*

cesarean delivery Delivery of a baby by surgical removal from the uterus. *79*

child development The scientific study of processes of change and stability in human children. *2*

child-directed speech (CDS) Form of speech often used in talking to babies or toddlers; includes slow, simplified speech, a high-pitched tone, exaggerated vowel sounds, short words and sentences, and much repetition; also called *parentese*. *141*

childhood depression Mood disorder characterized by such symptoms as a prolonged sense of friendlessness, inability to have fun or concentrate, fatigue, extreme activity or apathy, feelings of worthlessness, weight change, physical complaints, and thoughts of death or suicide. *249*

chromosomes Coils of DNA that consist of genes. *38*

chronic medical conditions Long-lasting or recurrent physical, developmental, behavioral, and/or emotional conditions that require special health services. *244*

circular reactions Piaget's term for behaviors performed by an infant that stimulate their own repetition. *124*

class inclusion Understanding the relationship between a whole and its parts. *256*

classical conditioning Learning based on association of a stimulus that does not ordinarily elicit a particular response with another stimulus that does elicit the response. *16, 121*

cognitive development Pattern of change in mental abilities, such as learning, attention, memory, language, thinking, reasoning, and creativity. *3*

cognitive neuroscience approach Approach to the study of cognitive development that links brain processes with cognitive ones. *133*

cognitive perspective Perspective that looks at the development of mental processes such as thinking. *18*

cohort A group of people born at about the same time. *9*

committed compliance Kochanska's term for wholehearted obedience of a parent's orders without reminders or lapses. *162*

componential element Sternberg's term for the analytic aspect of intelligence. *262*

conceptual knowledge Acquired interpretive understandings stored in long-term memory. *330*

conduct disorder (CD) Repetitive, persistent pattern of aggressive, antisocial behavior violating societal norms or the rights of others. *248*

conscience Internal standards of behavior, which usually control one's conduct and produce emotional discomfort when violated. *162*

conservation Piaget's term for awareness that two objects that are equal according to a certain measure remain equal in the face of perceptual alteration so long as nothing has been added to or taken away from either object. *192*

constructive play Second cognitive level of play, involving use of objects or materials to make something; also called object play. *222*

contextual element Sternberg's term for the practical aspect of intelligence. *263*

contextual perspective View of child development that sees the individual as inseparable from the social context. *21*

control group In an experiment, a comparison group of people similar to those in the experimental group who do not receive the treatment under study. *26*

conventional morality (or morality of conventional role conformity) Second level in Kohlberg's theory of moral reasoning in which standards of authority figures are internalized. *331*

convergent thinking Thinking aimed at finding the one right answer to a problem. *275*

coregulation Transitional stage in the control of behavior in which parents exercise general supervision and children exercise moment-to-moment self-regulation. *284*

corporal punishment Use of physical force with the intention of causing pain but not injury so as to correct or control behavior. *227*

correlational study Research design intended to discover whether a statistical relationship between variables exists. *25*

critical period Specific time when a given event or its absence has a profound and specific impact on development. *9*

cross-sectional study Study designed to assess age-related differences, in which people of different ages are assessed on one occasion. *27*

cultural socialization Parental practices that teach children about their racial/ethnic heritage and promote cultural practices and cultural pride. *347*

culture A society's or group's total way of life, including customs, traditions, beliefs, values, language, and physical products—all learned behavior passed on from adults to children. *5*

culture-free test An intelligence test that, if it were possible to design, would have no culturally linked content. *265*

culture-relevant test An intelligence test that takes into account the adaptive tasks children face in their culture. *265*

D

decenter In Piaget's terminology, to think simultaneously about several aspects of a situation. *191*

declarative knowledge Acquired factual knowledge stored in long-term memory. *330*

decoding Process of phonetic analysis by which a printed word is converted to spoken form before retrieval from long-term memory. *266*

deductive reasoning Type of logical reasoning that moves from a general premise about a class to a conclusion about a particular member or members of the class. *256*

deferred imitation Piaget's term for reproduction of an observed behavior after the passage of time by calling up a stored symbol of it. *126*

dental caries Tooth decay, a cavity. *180*

Denver Developmental Screening Test Screening test given to children age 1 month to 6 years to determine whether they are developing normally. *106*

deoxyribonucleic acid (DNA) Chemical that carries inherited instructions for the development of all cellular forms of life. *38*

dependent variable In an experiment, the condition that may or may not change as a result of changes in the independent variable. *26*

depth perception Ability to perceive objects and surfaces in three dimensions. *108*

diabetes One of the most common diseases of childhood. It is characterized by high levels of glucose in the blood as a result of defective insulin production, ineffective insulin action, or both. *245*

differentiation Process by which cells acquire specialized structures and functions. *101*

difficult children Children with irritable temperament, irregular biological rhythms, and intense emotional responses. *152*

discipline Methods of molding children's character and of teaching them to exercise self-control and engage in acceptable behavior. *226*

dishabituation Increase in responsiveness after presentation of a new stimulus. *128*

disorganized-disoriented attachment Pattern in which an infant, after separation from the primary caregiver, shows contradictory behaviors on his or her return. *156*

divergent thinking Thinking that produces a variety of fresh, diverse possibilities. *275*

dominant inheritance Pattern of inheritance in which, when a child receives different alleles, only the dominant one is expressed. *40*

Down syndrome Chromosomal disorder characterized by moderate-to-severe intellectual disability and by such physical signs as a downward-sloping skin fold at the inner corners of the eyes. *45*

dramatic play Play involving imaginary people or situations; also called fantasy play, pretend play, or imaginative play. *222*

drug therapy Administration of drugs to treat emotional disorders. *250*

dual representation hypothesis Proposal that children under age 3 have difficulty grasping spatial relationships because of the need to keep more than one mental representation in mind at the same time. *128*

dynamic systems theory (DST) Thelen's theory that holds that motor development is a dynamic process of active coordination of multiple systems within the infant in relation to the environment. *109*

dynamic tests Tests based on Vygotsky's theory that emphasize potential rather than past learning. *261*

dyslexia Developmental disorder in which reading achievement is substantially lower than predicted by IQ or age. *273*

E

early intervention Systematic process of providing services to help families meet young children's developmental needs. *123*

easy children Children with a generally happy temperament, regular biological rhythms, and a readiness to accept new experiences. *152*

ecological theory of perception Theory developed by Eleanor and James Gibson that describes developing motor and perceptual abilities as interdependent parts of a functional system that guides behavior in varying contexts. *108*

egocentrism Piaget's term for an inability to consider another person's point of view; a characteristic of young children's thought. *191*

electronic fetal monitoring Mechanical monitoring of fetal heartbeat during labor and delivery. *79*

embryonic stage Second stage of prenatal development (2 to 8 weeks), characterized by rapid growth and development of major body systems and organs. *59*

emergent literacy Preschoolers' development of skills, knowledge, and attitudes that underlie reading and writing. *203*

emerging adulthood Proposed transitional period between adolescence and adulthood, usually extending from the late teens through the midtwenties. *366*

emotions Subjective reactions to experience that are associated with physiological and behavioral changes. *148*

empathy Ability to put oneself in another person's place and feel what the other person feels. *151*

encoding Process by which information is prepared for long-term storage and later retrieval. *196*

English-immersion approach Approach to teaching English as a second language in which instruction is presented only in English. *266*

enrichment Approach to educating the gifted that broadens and deepens knowledge and skills through extra activities, projects, field trips, or mentoring. *274*

enuresis Repeated urination in clothing or in bed. *174*

environment Totality of nonhereditary, or experiential, influences on development. *10*

epigenesis Mechanism that turns genes on or off and determines functions of body cells. *41*

episodic memory Long-term memory of specific experiences or events, linked to time and place. *198*

equilibration Piaget's term for the tendency to seek a stable balance among cognitive elements; achieved through a balance between assimilation and accommodation. *19*

ethnic group A group united by ancestry, race, religion, language, or national origin that contributes to a sense of shared identity. *5*

ethnographic study In-depth study of a culture, which uses a variety of methods including participant observation. *25*

ethology Study of distinctive adaptive behaviors of species of animals that have evolved to increase survival of the species. *22*

evolutionary psychology Application of Darwinian principles of natural selection and survival of the fittest to human psychology. *22*

evolutionary/sociobiological perspective View of human development that focuses on evolutionary and biological bases of social behavior. *22*

executive function Conscious control of thoughts, emotions, and actions to accomplish goals or solve problems. *197, 259*

experiential element Sternberg's term for the insightful aspect of intelligence. *263*

experimental group In an experiment, the group receiving the treatment under study. *26*

explicit memory Intentional and conscious memory, generally of facts, names, and events; sometimes called *declarative memory.* *133*

extended family Multigenerational kinship network of parents, children, and other relatives, sometimes living together in an extended-family household. *5*

externalizing behaviors Behaviors by which a child acts out emotional difficulties; for example, aggression or hostility. *284*

F

family therapy Psychological treatment in which a therapist sees the whole family together to analyze patterns of family functioning. *250*

fast mapping Process by which a child absorbs the meaning of a new word after hearing it once or twice in conversation. *202*

fertilization Union of sperm and ovum to produce a zygote; also called *conception.* *34*

fetal alcohol syndrome (FAS) Combination of mental, motor, and developmental abnormalities affecting the offspring of some women who drink heavily during pregnancy. *68*

fetal stage Final stage of prenatal development (from 8 weeks to birth), characterized by increased differentiation of body parts and greatly enlarged body size. *60*

fine motor skills Physical skills that involve the small muscles and eye-hand coordination. *106, 175*

foreclosure Identity status in which a person who has not spent time considering alternatives (that is, has not been in crisis) is committed to other people's plans for his or her life. *346*

formal games with rules Organized games with known procedures and penalties. *222*

formal operations In Piaget's theory, final stage of cognitive development, characterized by the ability to think abstractly. *326*

functional play Lowest cognitive level of play, involving repetitive muscular movements; also called locomotor play. *222*

G

gender constancy Awareness that one will always be male or female. Also called sex-category constancy. *218*

gender identity Awareness, developed in early childhood, that one is male or female. *214*

gender roles Behaviors, interests, attitudes, skills, and traits that a culture considers appropriate for each sex; differs for males and females. *215*

gender segregation The tendency of children to select same-sex playmates. *224*

gender stereotypes Preconceived generalizations about male or female role behavior. *215*

gender-schema theory Theory that children socialize themselves in their gender roles by developing a mentally organized network of information about what it means to be male or female in a particular culture. *219*

gender-typing Socialization process by which children, at an early age, learn appropriate gender roles. *164, 215*

generalized anxiety disorder Anxiety not focused on any single target. *248*

generic memory Memory that produces scripts of familiar routines to guide behavior. *198*

genes Small segments of DNA located in definite positions on particular chromosomes; functional units of heredity. *38*

genetic counseling Clinical service that advises prospective parents of their probable risk of having children with hereditary defects. *45*

genotype Genetic makeup of a person, containing both expressed and unexpressed characteristics. *41*

genotype–environment correlation Tendency of certain genetic and environmental influences to reinforce each other; may be passive, reactive (evocative), or active. *48*

genotype–environment interaction Effect of the interaction between genes and the environment on phenotypic variation. *48*

germinal stage First 2 weeks of prenatal development, characterized by rapid cell division, increasing complexity and differentiation, and implantation in the wall of the uterus. *57*

gestation The prenatal period of development, between conception and birth. *57*

goodness of fit Appropriateness of environmental demands and constraints to a child's temperament. *153*

gross motor skills Physical skills that involve the large muscles. *106, 175*

guided participation Participation of an adult in a child's activity in a manner that helps to structure the activity and to bring the child's understanding of it closer to that of the adult. *133*

H

habituation Type of learning in which familiarity with a stimulus reduces, slows, or stops a response. *128*

handedness Preference for using a particular hand. *176*

haptic perception Ability to acquire information about properties of objects, such as size, weight, and texture, by handling them. *108*

heredity Inborn characteristics inherited from the biological parents. *10*

heritability Statistical estimate of contribution of heredity to individual differences in a specific trait within a given population at a particular time. *46*

heterozygous Possessing differing alleles for a trait. *40*

historical generation A group of people strongly influenced by a major historical event during their formative period. *9*

holophrase Single word that conveys a complete thought. *137*

Home Observation for Measurement of the Environment (HOME) Instrument designed to measure the influence of the home environment on children's cognitive growth. *122*

homozygous Possessing two identical alleles for a trait. *40*

horizontal décalage Piaget's term for an inability to transfer learning about one type of conservation to other types, which causes a child to master different types of conservation tasks at different ages. *257*

hostile aggression Aggressive behavior intended to hurt another person. *296*

hostile attribution bias Tendency for individuals to perceive others as trying to hurt them and to strike out in retaliation or self-defense. *297*

human genome The complete sequence of genes in the human body. *38*

hypertension High blood pressure. *245*

hypotheses Possible explanations for phenomena, used to predict the outcome of research. *23*

hypothetical-deductive reasoning Ability, believed by Piaget to accompany the stage of formal operations, to develop, consider, and test hypotheses. *327*

I

identification In Freudian theory, process by which a young child adopts characteristics, beliefs, attitudes, values, and behaviors of the parent of the same sex. *218*

identity In Erikson's terminology, a coherent conception of the self made up of goals, values, and beliefs to which a person is solidly committed. *345*

identity achievement Identity status, described by Marcia, characterized by commitment to choices made following a crisis; a period spent in exploring alternatives. *346*

identity diffusion Identity status characterized by absence of commitment and lack of serious consideration of alternatives. *346*

identity versus identity confusion Erikson's fifth stage of psychosocial development in which an adolescent seeks to develop a coherent sense of self, including the role she or he is to play in society. Also called *identity versus role confusion*. *345*

imaginary audience Elkind's term for observer who exists only in an adolescent's mind and is as concerned with the adolescent's thoughts and actions as the adolescent is. *328*

implicit memory Unconscious recall, generally of habits and skills; sometimes called *procedural memory*. *133*

imprinting Instinctive form of learning in which, during a critical period in early development, a young animal forms an attachment to the first moving object it sees, usually the mother. *9*

incomplete dominance Pattern of inheritance in which a child receives two different alleles, resulting in partial expression of a trait. *44*

independent variable In an experiment, the variable or condition the researcher directly manipulates to see if it has an effect on another variable. *26*

individual differences Differences among children in characteristics, influences, or developmental outcomes. *3*

individual psychotherapy Psychological treatment in which a therapist sees a troubled person one-on-one. *249*

individuation Adolescent's struggle for autonomy and differentiation, or personal identity. *357*

inductive reasoning Type of logical reasoning that moves from particular observations about members of a class to a general conclusion about that class. *256*

inductive techniques Disciplinary techniques designed to induce desirable behavior by appealing to a child's sense of reason and fairness. *228*

industry versus inferiority Erikson's fourth crisis of psychosocial development, in which children must learn the productive skills their culture requires or else face feelings of inferiority. *282*

infant mortality rate Proportion of babies born alive who die within the 1st year. *110*

information-processing approach Approach to the study of cognitive development by observing and analyzing the mental processes involved in perceiving and handling information. *20, 128*

instrumental aggression Aggressive behavior used as a means of achieving a goal. *230, 296*

integration Process by which neurons coordinate the activities of muscle groups. *101*

intellectual disability Significantly subnormal cognitive functioning. Also referred to as cognitive disability or (formerly) mental retardation. *272*

intelligent behavior Behavior that is goal oriented and adaptive to circumstances and conditions of life. *122*

interactional synchrony The synchronized coordination of behavior and affect between a caregiver and infant. *158*

internalization During socialization, process by which children accept societal standards of conduct as their own. *161*

internalizing behaviors Behaviors by which emotional problems are turned inward; for example, anxiety or depression. *284*

invisible imitation Imitation with parts of one's body that one cannot see. *126*

IQ (intelligence quotient) tests Psychometric tests that seek to measure intelligence by comparing a test-taker's performance with standardized norms. *122*

irreversibility Piaget's term for a preoperational child's failure to understand that an operation can go in two or more directions. *192*

J

joint attention Involves understanding that you and I have a shared focus of attention. *129*

K

Kaufman Assessment Battery for Children (K-ABC-II) Nontraditional individual intelligence test designed to provide fair assessments of minority children and children with disabilities. *261*

L

laboratory observation Research method in which all participants are observed under the same controlled conditions. *24*

learning disabilities (LDs) Disorders that interfere with specific aspects of learning and school achievement. *272*

learning perspective View of human development that holds that changes in behavior result from experience. *16*

linguistic speech Verbal expression designed to convey meaning. *137*

longitudinal study Study designed to assess changes in a sample over time. *27*

long-term memory Storage of virtually unlimited capacity that holds information for long periods. *197*

low-birth-weight babies Infants who weigh less than 5½ pounds (2,500 grams) at birth because of prematurity or being small-for-date. *86*

M

maturation Unfolding of a universal natural sequence of physical and behavioral changes. *3*

menarche A girl's first menstruation. *308*

metacognition Thinking about thinking, or awareness of one's own mental processes. *267*

metamemory Understanding of processes of memory. *260*

mirror neurons Neurons that fire when a person does something or observes someone else doing the same thing. *151*

mnemonic device Strategy to aid memory. *260*

moratorium Identity status in which a person is considering alternatives (in crisis) and seems headed for commitment. *346*

multifactorial transmission Combination of genetic and environmental factors to produce certain complex traits. *40*

mutations Permanent alterations in genes or chromosomes that usually produce harmful characteristics but provide the raw material of evolution. *40*

mutual regulation Process by which infant and caregiver communicate emotional states to each other and respond appropriately. *158*

myelination Process of coating neural pathways with a fatty substance called myelin, which enables faster communication between cells. *102*

N

nativism Theory that human beings have an inborn capacity for language acquisition. *135*

natural, or prepared, childbirth Method of childbirth that seeks to reduce or eliminate the use of drugs, enable both parents to participate fully, and control perceptions of pain. *80*

naturalistic observation Research method in which behavior is studied in natural settings without intervention or manipulation. *24*

neglectful/uninvolved parenting Parenting style in which parents focus on their own needs rather than those of children. *228*

neonatal jaundice Condition in many newborn babies caused by immaturity of the liver and evidenced by a yellowish appearance; can cause brain damage if not treated promptly. *83*

neonatal period First 4 weeks of life, a time of transition from intrauterine dependency to independent existence. *81*

neonate Newborn baby, up to 4 weeks old. *81*

neurons Nerve cells. *61, 101*

night terrors Abrupt awakening from a deep sleep in a state of agitation. *173*

nightmares A bad dream, sometimes brought on by staying up too late, eating a heavy meal close to bedtime, or overexcitement. *174*

nonnormative Characteristic of an unusual event that happens to a particular person or a typical event that happens at an unusual time of life. *8*

nonorganic failure to thrive In infancy, lack of appropriate growth for no known medical cause, accompanied by poor developmental and emotional functioning. *114*

nonshared environmental effects The unique environment in which each child grows up, consisting of distinctive influences or influences that affect one child differently than another. *49*

normative Characteristic of an event that occurs in a similar way for most people in a group. *8*

nuclear family Two-generational household unit consisting of one or two parents and their biological children, adopted children, or stepchildren. *5*

O

obesity Extreme overweight in relation to age, sex, height, and body type. *50*

observational learning Learning through watching the behavior of others. *18*

obsessive-compulsive disorder (OCD) Anxiety aroused by repetitive, intrusive thoughts, images, or impulses, often leading to compulsive ritual behaviors. *249*

operant conditioning Learning based on association of behavior with its consequences. *17, 121*

organization Piaget's term for the creation of categories or systems of knowledge. *18*

Otis-Lennon School Ability Test (OLSAT8) Group intelligence test for kindergarten through 12th grade. *261*

overt (direct) aggression Aggression that is openly directed at its target. *231*

P

participant observation Research method in which the observer lives with the people or participates in the activity being observed. *25*

permissive parenting Parenting style emphasizing self-expression and self-regulation. *228*

personal fable Elkind's term for conviction that one is special, unique, and not subject to the rules that govern the rest of the world. *329*

phenotype Observable characteristics of a person. *41*

phonetic (code-emphasis) approach Approach to teaching reading that emphasizes decoding unfamiliar words. *266*

physical development Growth of body and brain, including biological and physiological patterns of change in sensory capacities, motor skills, and health. *3*

Piagetian approach Approach to the study of cognitive development that describes qualitative stages in cognitive functioning. *124*

plasticity Modifiability of the brain through experience. *9, 103*

play therapy Therapeutic approach that uses play to help a child cope with emotional distress. *249*

postconventional morality (or morality of autonomous moral principles) Third level in Kohlberg's theory of moral reasoning in which people follow internally held moral principles and can decide among conflicting moral standards. *331*

postmature A fetus not yet born as of 42 weeks' gestation. *89*

power assertion Disciplinary strategy designed to discourage undesirable behavior through physical or verbal enforcement of parental control. *228*

pragmatics Practical knowledge needed to use language for communicative purposes. *203, 265*

preconventional morality First level of Kohlberg's theory of moral reasoning in which control is external and rules are obeyed in order to gain rewards or avoid punishment or out of self-interest. *331*

prejudice Unfavorable attitude toward members of certain groups outside one's own, especially racial or ethnic groups. *293*

prelinguistic speech Forerunner of linguistic speech; utterance of sounds that are not words. Includes crying, cooing, babbling, and accidental and deliberate imitation of sounds without understanding their meaning. *136*

preoperational stage In Piaget's theory, the second major stage of cognitive development in which children become more sophisticated in their use of symbolic thought but are not yet able to use logic. *189*

pretend play Play involving imaginary people or situations; also called fantasy play, dramatic play, or imaginary play. *189*

preterm (premature) infants Infants born before completing the 37th week of gestation. *86*

primary sex characteristics Organs directly related to reproduction, which enlarge and mature during adolescence. *307*

private speech Talking aloud to oneself with no intent to communicate with others. *203*

procedural knowledge Acquired skills stored in long-term memory. *330*

prosocial behavior Any voluntary behavior intended to help others. *230*

proximodistal principle Principle that development proceeds from within to without; that is, that parts of the body near the center develop before the extremities. *57*

psychoanalytic perspective View of human development as being shaped by unconscious forces. *13*

psychometric approach Approach that seeks to quantitatively measure the different factors that make up intelligence and predict future performance. *122*

psychosexual development In Freudian theory, an unvarying sequence of stages of personality development during infancy, childhood, and adolescence in which gratification shifts from the mouth to the anus and then to the genitals. *14*

psychosocial development (1) In Erikson's eight-stage theory, the socially and culturally influenced process of development of the ego, or self. (2) Pattern of change in emotions, personality, and social relationships. *3, 14*

psychosocial moratorium A period of time that allows young people to search for commitments to which they can be faithful. *345*

puberty Process by which a person attains sexual maturity and the ability to reproduce. *306*

punishment In operant conditioning, a process that decreases the likelihood that a behavior will be repeated. *17*

Q

qualitative change Change in kind, structure, or organization, such as the change from nonverbal to verbal communication. *11*

quantitative change Change in number or amount, such as in height, weight, or size of vocabulary. *10*

R

reaction range Potential variability, depending on environmental conditions, in the expression of a hereditary trait. *47*

recall Ability to reproduce material from memory. *197*

receptive cooperation Kochanska's term for eager willingness to cooperate harmoniously with a parent in daily interactions, including routines, chores, hygiene, and play. *162*

recessive inheritance Pattern of inheritance in which a child receives identical recessive alleles, resulting in expression of a nondominant trait. *40*

reciprocal determinism Bandura's term for bidirectional forces that affect development. *18*

recognition Ability to identify a previously encountered stimulus. *197*

reflex behaviors Automatic, involuntary, innate responses to stimulation. *102*

reinforcement In operant conditioning, a process that increases the likelihood that a behavior will be repeated. *17*

relational (indirect or social) aggression Aggression aimed at damaging or interfering with another person's relationships, reputation, or psychological well-being; can be overt or covert. *231*

representational systems Broad, inclusive self-concepts that integrate various aspects of the self. *281*

resistant (ambivalent) attachment Pattern in which an infant becomes anxious before the primary caregiver leaves, is extremely upset during his or her absence, and both seeks and resists contact on his or her return. *155*

retrieval Process by which information is accessed or recalled from memory storage. *196*

risk factors Conditions that increase the likelihood of a negative developmental outcome. *8*

rough-and-tumble play Vigorous play involving wrestling, hitting, and chasing, often accompanied by laughing and screaming. *242*

S

scaffolding Temporary support to help a child master a task. *200*

schemes Piaget's term for organized patterns of thought and behavior used in particular situations. *19*

school phobia Unrealistic fear of going to school. *248*

script General remembered outline of a familiar, repeated event, used to guide behavior. *198*

secondary sex characteristics Physiological signs of sexual maturation (such as breast development and growth of body hair) that do not involve the sex organs. *307*

secular trend Trend that can be seen only by observing several generations, such as the trend toward earlier attainment of adult height and sexual maturity, which began a century ago. *308*

secure attachment Pattern in which an infant is quickly and effectively able to find comfort from a caregiver when faced with a stressful situation. *155*

self-awareness Realization that one's existence and functioning are separate from those of other people and things. *150*

self-care Unsupervised situations in which children care for themselves at home. *285*

self-concept Sense of self; descriptive and evaluative mental picture of one's abilities and traits. *159, 211*

self-conscious emotions Emotions, such as embarrassment, shame, and pride, that depend on self-awareness. *150*

self-definition Cluster of characteristics used to describe oneself. *211*

self-efficacy Sense of one's capability to master challenges and achieve goals. *18, 335*

self-esteem Judgment a person makes about his or her self-worth. *212*

self-regulation A person's independent control of behavior to conform to understood social expectations. *162*

sensitive periods Times in development when a given event or its absence usually has a strong effect on development. *9*

sensory memory Initial, brief, temporary storage of sensory information. *196*

separation anxiety Distress shown by someone, typically an infant, when a familiar caregiver leaves. *157*

separation anxiety disorder Condition involving excessive, prolonged anxiety concerning separation from home or from people to whom a person is attached. *248*

sequential study Study design that combines cross-sectional and longitudinal designs. *28*

seriation Ability to order items along a dimension. *255*

sex chromosomes Pair of chromosomes that determines sex; XY in the normal human male, XX in the normal human female. *39*

sex-linked inheritance Pattern of inheritance in which certain characteristics carried on the X chromosome inherited from the mother are transmitted differently to her male and female offspring. *44*

sexting The sharing or sending of sexually explicit or suggestive photos or videos to others. *350*

sexual orientation Focus of consistent sexual, romantic, and affectionate interest, either heterosexual, homosexual, or bisexual. *348*

sexually transmitted infections (STIs) Diseases spread by sexual contact. *352*

shaken baby syndrome Form of maltreatment in which shaking an infant or toddler can cause brain damage, paralysis, or death. *114*

situational compliance Kochanska's term for obedience of a parent's orders only in the presence of signs of ongoing parental control. *162*

sleeptalking Talking while asleep. *174*

sleepwalking Walking around and sometimes performing other functions while asleep. *174*

slow-to-warm-up children Children whose temperament is generally mild but who are hesitant about accepting new experiences. *152*

small-for-date (small-for-gestational-age) infants Infants whose birth weight is less than that of 90 percent of babies of the same gestational age as a result of slow fetal growth. *86*

social cognitive theory Albert Bandura's expansion of social learning theory holds that children learn gender roles through socialization. *220*

social construction Concept about the nature of reality based on societally shared perceptions or assumptions. *2*

social emotions Emotions directed at the self that involve a comparison of oneself or one's actions to social standards. *213*

social interaction model Model, based on Vygotsky's sociocultural theory, that proposes children construct autobiographical memories through conversation with adults about shared events. *198*

social phobia Extreme fear and/or avoidance of social situations. *248*

social promotion Policy of automatically promoting children even if they do not meet academic standards. *271*

social referencing Understanding an ambiguous situation by seeking out another person's perception of it. *159*

social-contextual approach Approach to the study of cognitive development that focuses on environmental influences, particularly parents and other caregivers. *133*

socialization Development of habits, skills, values, and motives shared by responsible, productive members of a society. *161*

socioeconomic status (SES) Combination of economic and social factors, that describe an individual or family, including income, education, and occupation. *6*

spermarche A boy's first ejaculation. *308*

spontaneous abortion Natural expulsion from the uterus of an embryo that cannot survive outside the womb; also called *miscarriage*. *59*

Stanford-Binet Intelligence Scale Individual intelligence test for ages 2 and up, used to measure knowledge, quantitative reasoning, visual-spatial processing, and working memory. *199*

state of arousal Infant's physiological and behavioral status at a given moment in the periodic daily cycle of wakefulness, sleep, and activity. *85*

still-face paradigm Research procedure used to measure mutual regulation in infants 2 to 9 months old. *159*

stillbirth Death of a fetus at or after the 20th week of gestation. *89*

storage Retention of information in memory for future use. *196*

Strange Situation Laboratory technique used to study infant attachment. *155*

stranger anxiety Wariness of strange people and places, shown by some infants from age 6 to 12 months. *157*

stuttering Involuntary, frequent repetition or prolongation of sounds or syllables. *246*

substance abuse Repeated, harmful use of a substance, usually alcohol or other drugs. *316*

sudden infant death syndrome (SIDS) Sudden and unexplained death of an apparently healthy infant. *111*

symbolic function Piaget's term for ability to use mental representations (words, numbers, or images) to which a child has attached meaning. *189*

T

telegraphic speech Early form of sentence use consisting of only a few essential words. *138*

temperament Characteristic disposition or style of approaching and reacting to situations. *51, 151*

teratogen Environmental agent, such as a virus, a drug, or radiation, that can interfere with normal prenatal development and cause developmental abnormalities. *62*

theory Coherent set of logically related concepts that seeks to organize, explain, and predict data. *12*

theory of mind Awareness and understanding of mental processes of others. *192*

theory of multiple intelligences Gardner's theory that there are eight distinct forms of intelligence. *262*

theory of sexual selection Darwinian theory, which holds that selection of sexual partners is influenced by the differing reproductive pressures that early men and women confronted in the evolutionary past. *217*

transduction In Piaget's terminology, preoperational child's tendency to mentally link particular experiences, whether or not there is logically a causal relationship. *190*

transitive inference Understanding the relationship between two objects by knowing the relationship of each to a third object. *256*

two-way (dual-language) learning Approach to second-language education in which English speakers and non-English-speakers learn together in their own and each other's languages. *266*

U

ultrasound Prenatal medical procedure using high-frequency sound waves to detect the outline of a fetus and its movements; used to determine whether a pregnancy is progressing normally. *61*

universal preschool A national system for early care and education that makes access to preschool similar to kindergarten by using the public schools. *205*

V

violation-of-expectations research Research method in which dishabituation to a stimulus that conflicts with experience is taken as evidence that an infant recognizes the new stimulus as surprising. *131*

visible imitation Imitation with parts of one's body that one can see. *126*

visual cliff Apparatus designed to give an illusion of depth and used to assess depth perception in infants. *108*

visual preference Tendency of infants to spend more time looking at one sight than another. *129*

visual recognition memory Ability to distinguish a familiar visual stimulus from an unfamiliar stimulus when shown both at the same time. *129*

visually based retrieval Process of retrieving the sound of a printed word when seeing the word as a whole. *266*

W

Wechsler Intelligence Scale for Children (WISC-III) Individual intelligence test for schoolchildren that yields verbal and performance scores as well as a combined score. *261*

Wechsler Preschool and Primary Scale of Intelligence, Revised (WPPSI-III) Individual intelligence test for children ages 2½ to 7 that yields verbal and performance scores as well as a combined score. *199*

whole-language approach Approach to teaching reading that emphasizes visual retrieval and use of contextual clues. *266*

withdrawal of love Disciplinary strategy that involves ignoring, isolating, or showing dislike for a child. *228*

working memory Short-term storage of information being actively processed. *197*

Z

zone of proximal development (ZPD) Vygotsky's term for the difference between what a child can do alone and what the child can do with help. *20, 200*

zygote One-celled organism resulting from fertilization. *34*

Abma, J. C., & Martinez, G. M. (2017). Sexual activity and contraceptive use among teenagers in the United States, 2011–2015. *National Health Statistics Reports,104*, 1–23.

Abma, J. C., Martinez, G. M., & Copen, C. E. (2010). Teenagers in the United States: Sexual activity, contraceptive use, and childbearing, National Survey of Family Growth 2006–2008. *Vital Health Statistics, 23*(30). Washington, DC: National Center for Health Statistics.

Abramovitch, R., Corter, C., Pepler, D., & Stanhope, L. (1986). Sibling and peer interactions: A final follow-up and comparison. *Child Development, 57*, 217–229.

Abu-Akel, A., & Shamay-Tsoory, S. (2011). Neuroanatomical and neurochemical bases of theory of mind. *Neuropsychologia, 49*(11), 2971–2984.

Adamson, G. D., Tabangin, M., Macaluso, M., & de Mouzon, J. (2013). The number of babies born globally after treatment with the assisted reproductive technologies (ART). *Fertility and Sterility, 100*(3), S42.

Adey, P., Csapó, B., Demetriou, A., Hautamäki, J., & Shayer, M. (2007). Can we be intelligent about intelligence? Why education needs the concept of plastic general ability. *Educational Research Review, 2*(2), 75–97.

Adolescent Sleep Working Group. (2014). School start times for adolescents. *Pediatrics, 134*(3), 642–649.

Advocates for Youth. (2010). Adolescents and sexually transmitted infections: A costly and dangerous global phenomenon. Retrieved from www.advocatesforyouth.org/storage/advfy/documents/thefacts_adolescents_sti.pdf

Ahern, E. C., Lyon, T. D., & Quas, J. A. (2011). Young children's emerging ability to make false statements. *Developmental Psychology, 47*(1), 61.

Akin, A. (2012). The relationships between Internet addiction, subjective vitality, and subjective happiness. *CyberPsychology, Behavior, and Social Networking, 15*, 404–410. doi:10.1089/cyber.2011.0609

Akinbami, O. J., Moorman, J. E., Bailey, C., Zahran, H. S., King, M., Johnson, C. A., & Liu, X. (2012). Trends in asthma prevalence, health care use, and mortality in the United States, 2001–2010. *NCHS Data Brief, 94*.

Alan Guttmacher Institute (AGI). (1999). *Facts in brief: Teen sex and pregnancy.* Retrieved from www.agi_usa.org/pubs/fb_teen_sex.html#sfd

Albert, D., Chein, J., & Steinberg, L. (2013). The teenage brain: Peer influences on adolescent decision making. *Current Directions in Psychological Science, 22*(2), 114–120.

Albert, D., & Steinberg, L. (2011). Judgment and decision making in adolescence. *Journal of Research on Adolescence, 21*(1), 211–224.

Al-Dhamit, Y., & Kreishan, L. (2016). Gifted students' intrinsic and extrinsic motivations and parental influence on their motivation: From the self-determination theory perspective. *Journal of Research in Special Educational Needs, 16*(1), 13–23.

Alexander, G. C., Gallagher, S. A., Mascola, A., Moloney, R. M., & Stafford, R. S. (2011). Increasing off-label use of antipsychotic medications in the United States, 1995–2008. *Pharmacoepidemiology and Drug Safety, 20*(2), 177–184.

Alexander, G. M., & Hines, M. (2002). Sex differences in response to children's toys in nonhuman primates (Cercopithecus aethiopssabaeus). *Evolution and Human Behavior, 23*(6), 467–479.

Alexander, G. M., & Wilcox, T. (2012). Sex differences in early infancy. *Child Development Perspectives, 6*(4), 400–406.

Alexander, G. M., Wilcox, T., & Woods, R. (2009). Sex differences in infants' visual interest in toys. *Archives of Sexual Behavior, 38*(3), 427–433.

Allen, J. P., & Philliber, S. (2001). Who benefits most from a broadly targeted prevention program? Differential efficacy across populations in the Teen Outreach Program. *Journal of Community Psychology, 29*(6), 637–655.

Allen, J. P., Porter, M. R., McFarland, F. C., Marsh, P., & McElhaney, K. B. (2005). The two faces of adolescents' success with peers: Adolescent popularity, social adaptation, and deviant behavior. *Child Development, 76*(3), 747–760.

Alloway, T. P., & Alloway, R. G. (2010). Investigating the predictive roles of working memory and IQ in academic attainment. *Journal of Experimental Child Psychology, 106*(1), 20–29.

Alloway, T. P., Gathercole, S. E., & Elliott, J. (2010). Examining the link between working memory behaviour and academic attainment in children with ADHD. *Developmental Medicine & Child Neurology, 52*(7), 632–636.

Alm, P. A. (2014). Stuttering in relation to anxiety, temperament, and personality: Review and analysis with focus on causality. *Journal of Fluency Disorders, 40*, 5–21.

Almas, A. N., Grusec, J. E., & Tackett, J. L. (2011). Children's disclosure and secrecy: Links to maternal parenting characteristics and children's coping skills. *Social Development, 20*(3), 624–643.

Al-Namlah, A. S., Meins, E., & Fernyhough, C. (2012). Self-regulatory private speech relates to children's recall and organization of autobiographical memories. *Early Childhood Research Quarterly, 27*(3), 441–446.

Altschul, I., Oyserman, D., & Bybee, D. (2006). Racial-ethnic identity in mid-adolescence: Content and change as predictors of academic achievement. *Child Development, 77*, 1155–1169.

Amato, P. R. (2014). The consequences of divorce for adults and children: An update. *Drustvena Istrazivanja, 23*(1), 5.

Amato, P. R., & Anthony, C. J. (2014). Estimating the effects of parental divorce and death with fixed effects models. *Journal of Marriage and Family, 76*(2).

Amato, P. R., & Cheadle, J. (2005). The long reach of divorce: Divorce and child well-being across three generations. *Journal of Marriage and Family, 67*(1), 191–206.

Amato, P. R., Kane, J. B., & James, S. (2011). Reconsidering the "good divorce." *Family Relations, 60*(5), 511–524.

America's youngest outcasts 2014. (2014). Needham, MA: National Center on Family Homelessness. Retrieved from www.homelesschildrenamerica.org

American Academy of Child and Adolescent Psychiatry. (2013a). Children with oppositional defiant disorder. [Fact sheet]. Retrieved from www.aacap.org/aaCaP/Families_and_Youth/Facts_for_Families/Facts_for_Families_Pages/Children_With_Oppositional_Defiant_Disorder_72.aspx

American Academy of Child and Adolescent Psychiatry. (2013b). Children with conduct disorder. [Fact sheet]. Retrieved from www.aacap.org/aacap/families_and_youth/facts_for_families/FFF-Guide/Conduct-Disorder-033.aspx

American Academy of Pediatrics (AAP) Committee on Psychosocial Aspects of Child and Family Health. (1998). Guidance for effective discipline. *Pediatrics, 101*, 723–728.

American Academy of Pediatrics Committee on Injury and Poison Prevention. (2001). Bicycle helmets. *Pediatrics, 108*(4), 1030–1032.

American Academy of Pediatrics. (2009). *A pediatric guide to children's oral health.* Elk Grove Village, IL: American Academy of Pediatrics.

American Academy of Pediatrics. (2016). American Academy of Pediatrics announces new guidelines for children's media use. Retrieved from www.aap.org/en-us/about-the-aap/aap-press-room/pages/american-academy-of-pediatrics-announces-new-recommendations-for-childrens-media-use.aspx

American Academy of Sleep Medicine. (2016). Recharge with sleep: Pediatric sleep recommendations promoting optimal health [Consensus statement]. Retrieved from https://aasm.org/recharge-with-sleep-pediatric-sleep-recommendations-promoting-optimal-health/

American College of Nurse-Midwives. (2016). *Position statement: Planned home births.* Silver Spring, MD: Author.

American College of Obstetricians and Gynecologists. (2013). Weight gain during pregnancy. Committee Opinion No. 548. Obstet Gynecol, 121, 210-212.

American College of Obstetricians and Gynecologists. (2015a). Cell-free DNA screening for fetal aneuploidy. Committee Opinion No. 640. *Obstet Gynecol, 126*(3), e31-e37.

American College of Obstetricians and Gynecologists. (2015b). *Committee opinion: Cell-free fetal screening for fetal aneuploidy.* Retrieved from www.acog.org/Clinical-Guidance-and-Publications/Committee-Opinions/Committee-on-Genetics/Cell-free-DNA-Screening-for-Fetal-Aneuploidy

American College of Obstetricians and Gynecologists. (2015c). Committee Opinion: The Apgar Score. Retrived from www.acog.org/Clinical-Guidance-and-Publications/Committee-Opinions/Committee-on-Obstetric-Practice/The-Apgar-Score

American College of Obstetricians and Gynecologists. (2015d, May). Early pregnancy loss. Practice Bulletin No. 150. *Obstet Gynecol, 125*(5), 1258-67.

American College of Obstetricians and Gynecologists. (2016). Exercise during pregnancy. Retrieved from www.acog.org/Patients/FAQs/Exercise-During-Pregnancy#precautions

American College of Obstetricians and Gynecologists. (2017). Planned home birth. Committee Opinion No. 697. *Obstet Gynecol, 129,* e117-e122.

American Medical Association House of Delegates. (2008, June). Resolution 205: Home deliveries. Proceedings of the American Medical Association House of Delegates, Fifteenth Annual Meeting, Chicago, IL. Retrieved from www.ama-assn.org/ama1/pub/upload/mm/471/205.doc

American Optometric Association. (2018). Recommended eye examination frequency for pediatric patients and adults. Retrieved from www.aoa.org/patients-and-public/caring-for-your-vision/comprehensive-eye-and-vision-examination/recommended-examination-frequency-for-pediatric-patients-and-adults

American Psychiatric Association (2013). *Diagnostic and statistical manual of mental disorders* (5th ed.). Arlington, VA: American Psychiatric Publishing.

American Psychological Association. (2018). Obesity. [Fact sheet]. Retrieved from www.apa.org/topics/obesity/index.aspx

Amsel, E., Goodman, G., Savoie, D., & Clark, M. (1996). The development of reasoning about causal and noncausal influences on levers. *Child Development, 67*(4), 1624-1646.

Anastasiou, A., Karras, S. N., Bais, A., Grant, W. B., Kotsa, K., & Goulis, D. G. (2017). Ultraviolet radiation and effects on humans: The paradigm of maternal vitamin D production during pregnancy. *European Journal of Clinical Nutrition, 71*(11), 1268.

Anderson, C. A., Bushman, B. J., Bartholow, B. D., Cantor, J., Christakis, D., Coyne, S. M., . . . & Huesmann, R. (2017). Screen violence and youth behavior. *Pediatrics, 140* (Supplement 2), S142-S147.

Anderson, C. A., Bushman, B. J., Donnerstein, E., Hummer, T. A., & Warburton, W. (2015). SPSSI research summary on media violence. *Analyses of Social Issues and Public Policy, 15*(1), 4-19.

Anderson, C. A., Shibuya, A., Ihori, N., Swing, E. L., Bushman, B. J., Sakamoto, A., . . . & Saleem, M. (2010). Violent video game effects on aggression, empathy, and prosocial behavior in Eastern and Western countries: A meta-analytic review. *Psychological Bulletin, 136*(2), 151.

Anderson, C. A., Suzuki, K., Swing, E. L., Groves, C. L., Gentile, D. A., Prot, S., . . . & Jelic, M. (2017). Media violence and other aggression risk factors in seven nations. *Personality and social psychology bulletin, 43*(7), 986-998.

Anderson, D. M., Hansen, B., & Rees, D. I. (2015). Medical marijuana laws and teen marijuana use. *American Law and Economics Review, 17*(2), 495-528.

Anderson, E. L., Steen, E., & Stavropoulos, V. (2017). Internet use and problematic Internet use: A systematic review of longitudinal research trends in adolescence and emergent adulthood. *International Journal of Adolescence and Youth, 22*(4), 430-454.

Anderson, S. E., & Whitaker, R. C. (2010). Household routines and obesity in US preschool-aged children. *Pediatrics, 125*(3), 420-428. doi: 10.1542/peds.2009-0417

Andreyeva, T., Kelly, I. R., & Harris, J. L. (2011). Exposure to food advertising on television: Associations with children's fast food and soft drink consumption and obesity. *Economics & Human Biology, 9*(3), 221-233.

Ang, R. P. (2015). Adolescent cyberbullying: A review of characteristics, prevention and intervention strategies. *Aggression and Violent Behavior, 25,* 35-42.

Ang, S., Rodgers, J. L., & Wanstrom, L. (2010). The Flynn Effect within subgroups in the U.S.: Gender, race, income, education, and urbanization differences in the NLSY-Children data. *Intelligence, 38*(4), 367-384.

Anglemyer, A., Horvath, T., & Rutherford, G. (2014). The accessibility of firearms and risk for suicide and homicide victimization among household members: A systematic review and meta-analysis. *Annals of Internal Medicine, 160*(2), 101-110.

Angulo-Barroso, R. M., Schapiro, L., Liang, W., Rodrigues, O., Shafir, T., Kaciroti, N., . . . & Lozoff, B. (2011). Motor development in 9-month-old infants in relation to cultural differences and iron status. *Developmental Psychobiology, 53*(2), 196-210.

Aram, D., Abiri, S., & Elad, L. (2014). Predicting early spelling: The contribution of children's early literacy, private speech during spelling, behavioral regulation, and parental spelling support. *Reading and Writing, 27*(4), 685-707.

Archer, J. (2004). Sex differences in aggression in real-world settings: A meta-analytic review. *Review of General Psychology, 8,* 291-322.

Archer, S. L. (1993). Identity in relational contexts: A methodological proposal. In J. Kroger (Ed.), *Discussions on ego identity* (pp. 75-99). Hillsdale, NJ: Erlbaum.

Ardila, A., Rosselli, M., Matute, E., & Inozemtseva, O. (2011). Gender differences in cognitive development. *Developmental Psychology, 47*(4), 984.

Armour, J. A., Davison, A., & McManus, I. C. (2014). Genome-wide association study of handedness excludes simple genetic models. *Heredity, 112*(3), 221.

Arnestad, M., Crotti, L., Rognum, T. O., Insolia, R., Pedrazzini, M., Ferrandi, C., . . . Schwartz, P. J. (2007). Prevalence of long-qt syndrome gene variants in sudden infant death syndrome. *Circulation, 115,* 361-367.

Arnett, J. J. (2006). Emerging adulthood: Understanding the new way of coming of age. In J. J. Arnett & J. L. Tanner (Eds.), *Emerging adults in America: Coming of age in the 21st century* (pp. 3-19). Washington, DC: American Psychological Association.

Arnett, J. J. (2016). Does emerging adulthood theory apply across social classes? National data on a persistent question. *Emerging Adulthood, 4*(4), 227-235.

Årseth, A. K., Kroger, J., Martinussen, M., & Marcia, J. E. (2009). Meta-analytic studies of identity status and the relational issues of attachment and intimacy. *Identity: An International Journal of Theory and Research, 9*(1), 1-32.

Artis, J. E. (2007). Maternal cohabitation and child well-being among kindergarten children. *Journal of Marriage and Family, 69*(1), 222-236.

Asato, M. R., Terwilliger, R., Woo, J., & Luna, B. S. (2010). White matter development in adolescence: A DTI study. *Cerebral Cortex, 20*(9), 2122-2131.

Aschersleben, G., Hofer, T., & Jovanovic, B. (2008). The link between infant attention to goal-directed action and later theory of mind abilities. *Developmental Science, 11*(6), 862-868.

Asher, M. I. (2010). Recent perspectives on global epidemiology of asthma in childhood. *Allergologia et Immunopathologia, 38*(2), 83-87.

Attili, G., Vermigli, P., & Roazzi, A. (2010). Children's social competence, peer status, and the quality of mother-child and father-child relationships. *European Psychologist, 15*, 23-33.

Attili, G., Vermigli, P., & Roazzi, A. (2011). Rearing styles, parents' attachment mental state, and children's social abilities: The link to peer acceptance. *Child Development Research, 2*, 1-12.

Audet, K., & Le Mare, L. (2011). Mitigating effects of the adoptive caregiving environment on inattention/overactivity in children adopted from Romanian orphanages. *International Journal of Behavioral Development, 35*(2), 107-115.

Aunio, P., & Niemivirta, M. (2010). Predicting children's mathematical performance in grade one by early numeracy. *Learning and Individual Differences, 20*(5), 427-435.

Auyeung, B., Baron-Cohen, S., Ashwin, E., Kinckmeyer, R., Taylor, K., Hackett, G., & Hines, M. (2009). Fetal testosterone predicts sexually differentiated childhood behavior in girls and in boys. *Psychological Science, 20*, 144-148.

B

Bacchini, D., Licenziati, M. R., Garrasi, A., Corciulo, N., Driul, D., Tanas, R., . . . & Maltoni, G. (2015). Bullying and victimization in overweight and obese outpatient children and adolescents: An Italian multicentric study. *PLoS One, 10*(11), e0142715.

Baddeley, A. (1998). Recent developments in working memory. *Current Opinion in Neurobiology, 8*, 234-238.

Bagwell, C., & Schmidt, M. E. (2011). *Friendships in childhood and adolescence.* New York: Guilford Press.

Baidal, J. A. W., Locks, L. M., Cheng, E. R., Blake-Lamb, T. L., Perkins, M. E., & Taveras, E. M. (2016). Risk factors for childhood obesity in the first 1,000 days: A systematic review. *American Journal of Preventive Medicine, 50*(6), 761-779.

Baillargeon, R. (2004). Infants' reasoning about hidden objects: Evidence for event-general and event-specific expectations. *Developmental Science, 7*(4), 391-414.

Baillargeon, R., & Carey, S. (2012). Core cognition and beyond: The acquisition of physical and numerical knowledge. In S. Pauen (Ed.), *Early childhood development and later outcome* (pp. 33-65). New York: Cambridge University Press.

Baillargeon, R., Li, J., Gertner, Y., & Wu, D. (2011). How do infants reason about physical events. *The Wiley-Blackwell Handbook of Childhood Cognitive Development* (pp. 11-48). Hoboken, NJ: Wiley.

Baillargeon, R., Scott, R. M., & He, Z. (2010). False-belief understanding in infants. *Trends in Cognitive Sciences, 14*(3), 110-118.

Baillargeon, R. H., Zoccolillo, M., Keenan, K., Côté, S., Pérusse, D., Wu, H.-X., . . . Tremblay, R. E. (2007). Gender differences in physical aggression: A prospective population-based survey of children before and after 2 years of age. *Developmental Psychology, 43*, 13-26.

Baker, C. E. (2013). Fathers' and mothers' home literacy involvement and children's cognitive and social emotional development: Implications for family literacy programs. *Applied Developmental Science, 17*(4), 184-197.

Baker, J. L., Olsen, L. W., & Sørensen, T. I. (2007). Childhood body-mass index and the risk of coronary heart disease in adulthood. *New England Journal of Medicine, 357*(23), 2329-2337.

Balantekin, K. N., Birch, L. L., & Savage, J. S. (2018). Family, friend, and media factors are associated with patterns of weight-control behavior among adolescent girls. *Eating and Weight Disorders-Studies on Anorexia, Bulimia and Obesity, 23*(2), 215-223.

Bale, T. L., & Epperson, C. N. (2015). Sex differences and stress across the lifespan. *Nature Neuroscience, 18*(10), 1413.

Banse, R., Gawronski, B., Rebetez, C., Gutt, H., & Bruce Morton, J. (2010). The development of spontaneous gender stereotyping in childhood: Relations to stereotype knowledge and stereotype flexibility. *Developmental Science, 13*(2), 298-306.

Bao, A. M., & Swaab, D. F. (2010). Sex differences in the brain, behavior, and neuropsychiatric disorders. *The Neuroscientist, 16*(5), 550-565.

Barclay, N. L., & Gregory, A. M. (2013). Quantitative genetic research on sleep: A review of normal sleep, sleep disturbances and associated emotional, behavioural, and health-related difficulties. *Sleep Medicine Reviews, 17*(1), 29-40.

Barker, E. D., Oliver, B. R., & Maughan, B. (2010). Co-occurring problems of early onset persistent, childhood limited, and adolescent onset conduct problem youth. *Journal of Child Psychology and Psychiatry, 51*(11), 1217-1226.

Barkl, S., Porter, A., & Ginns, P. (2012). Cognitive training for children: Effects on inductive reasoning, deductive reasoning, and mathematics achievement in an Australian school setting. *Psychology in the Schools, 49*(9), 828-842.

Barlett, C., & Coyne, S. M. (2014). A meta-analysis of sex differences in cyber-bullying behavior: The moderating role of age. *Aggressive Behavior, 40*(5), 474-488.

Barnes, G. M., Hoffman, J. H., & Welte, J. W. (2006). Effects of parental monitoring and peer deviance in substance abuse and delinquency. *Journal of Marriage and Family, 68*, 1084-1104.

Barnett, L. M., Van Beurden, E., Morgan, P. J., Brooks, L. O., & Beard, J. R. (2009). Childhood motor skill proficiency as a predictor of adolescent physical activity. *Journal of Adolescent Health, 44*(3), 252-259.

Barnett, W. S., Jung, K., Yarosc, D. J., Thomas, J., Hornbeck, A., Stechuk, R. A., & Burns, M. S. (2008). Educational effects of the tools of the mind curriculum: A randomized trial. *Early Childhood Research Quarterly, 23*(3), 299-313.

Baron-Cohen, S., Leslie, A. M., & Frith, U. (1985). Does the autistic child have a "theory of mind"? *Cognition, 21*(1), 37-46.

Barr, R. (2010). Transfer of learning between 2D and 3D sources during infancy: Informing theory and practice. *Developmental Review, 30*(2), 128-154.

Barr, R., Lauricella, A., Zack, E., & Calvert, S. L. (2010). Infant and early childhood exposure to adult-directed and child-directed television programming: Relations with cognitive skills at age four. *Merrill-Palmer Quarterly, 56*(1), 21-48.

Barr, R., Muentener, P., & Garcia, A. (2007). Age-related changes in deferred imitation from television by 6- to 18-month-olds. *Developmental Science, 10*(6), 910-921.

Barrett, A. E., & Turner, R. J. (2005). Family structure and mental health: The mediating effects of socioeconomic status, family process, and social stress. *Journal of Health and Social Behavior, 46*(2), 156-169.

Bartel, K. A., Gradisar, M., & Williamson, P. (2015). Protective and risk factors for adolescent sleep: A meta-analytic review. *Sleep Medicine Reviews, 21*, 72-85.

Bartzokis, G., Lu, P. H., Tingus, K., Mendez, M. F., Richard, A., Peters, D. G., . . . & Thompson, P. M. (2010). Lifespan trajectory of myelin integrity and maximum motor speed. *Neurobiology of Aging, 31*(9), 1554-1562.

Basch, C. E. (2011). Teen pregnancy and the achievement gap among urban minority youth. *Journal of School Health, 81*(10), 614–618.

Bassuk, E. L., Murphy, C., Coupe, N. T., Kenney, R. R., Beach, C. A. (2011). America's youngest outcasts 2010: State report card on child homelessness. *The National Center on Family Homelessness.* Retrieved from www.homelesschildrenamerica.org/media/NCFH_AmericaOutcast2010_web.pdf

Bassuk, E. L., Richard, M. K., & Tsertsvadze, A. (2015). The prevalence of mental illness in homeless children: A systematic review and meta-analysis. *Journal of the American Academy of Child & Adolescent Psychiatry, 54*(2), 86–96.

Baste, V., Moen, B. E., Oftedal, G., Strand, L. Å., Bjørge, L., & Mild, K. H. (2012). Pregnancy outcomes after paternal radiofrequency field exposure aboard fast patrol boats. *Journal of Occupational and Environmental Medicine, 54*(4), 431–438.

Basterfield, L., Adamson, A. J., Frary, J. K., Parkinson, K. N., Pearce, M. S., Reilly, J. J., & Gateshead Millennium Study Core Team. (2011). Longitudinal study of physical activity and sedentary behavior in children. *Pediatrics, 127*(1), e24–e30.

Batty, M., & Taylor, M. J. (2002). Visual categorization during childhood: An ERP study. *Psychophysiology, 39*(4), 482–490.

Baude, A., Pearson, J., & Drapeau, S. (2016). Child adjustment in joint physical custody versus sole custody: A meta-analytic review. *Journal of Divorce & Remarriage, 57*(5), 338–360.

Bauer, K. W., Hearst, M. O., Escoto, K., Berge, J. M., & Neumark-Sztainer, D. (2012). Parental employment and work-family stress: Associations with family food environments. *Social Science & Medicine, 75*(3), 496–504.

Bauer, P. J. (2002). Long-term recall memory: Behavioral and neurodevelopmental changes in the first 2 years of life. *Current Directions in Psychological Science, 11*, 137–141.

Bauer, P. J., DeBoer, T., & Lukowski, A. F. (2007). In the language of multiple memory systems, defining and describing developments in long-term explicit memory. In L. M. Oakes & P. J. Bauer (Eds.), *Short- and long-term memory in infancy and early childhood* (pp. 240–270). New York: Oxford University Press.

Bauer, P. J., Wenner, J. A., Dropik, P. L., Wewerka, S. S., & Howe, M. L. (2000). Parameters of remembering and forgetting in the transition from infancy to early childhood. *Monographs of the Society for Research in Child Development*, i–213.

Bauer, P. J., Wiebe, S. A., Carver, L. J., Waters, J. M., & Nelson, C. A. (2003). Developments in long-term explicit memory late in the first year of life: Behavioral and electrophysiological indices. *Psychological Science, 14*, 629–635.

Baumgartner, S. E., Weeda, W. D., van der Heijden, L. L., & Huizinga, M. (2014). The relationship between media multitasking and executive function in early adolescents. *Journal of Early Adolescence, 34*, 1120–1144.

Baumrind, D. (1971). Harmonious parents and their preschool children. *Developmental Psychology, 41*, 92–102.

Baumrind, D. (1972). An exploratory study of socialization effects on black children: Some black-white comparisons. *Child Development*, 261–267.

Baumrind, D. (1996). The discipline controversy revisited. *Family Relations, 45*, 405–414.

Bava, S., Thayer, R., Jacobus, J., Ward, M., Jernigan, T. L., & Tapert, S. F. (2010). Longitudinal characterization of white matter maturation during adolescence. *Brain Research, 1327*, 38–46.

Beal, S. J., & Crockett, L. J. (2010). Adolescents' occupational and educational aspirations and expectations: Links to high school activities and adult educational achievement. *Developmental Psychology, 46*(1), 258–265.

Beauchamp, G. K., & Mennella, J. A. (2011). Flavor perception in human infants: Development and functional significance. *Digestion, 83* (Suppl. 1), 1–6.

Becker, M., Lüdtke, O., Trautwein, U., Köller, O., & Baumert, J. (2012). The differential effects of school tracking on psychometric intelligence: Do academic-track schools make students smarter? *Journal of Educational Psychology, 104*(3), 682.

Beebe, D. W. (2011). Cognitive, behavioral, and functional consequences of inadequate sleep in children and adolescents. *Pediatric Clinics, 58*(3), 649–665.

Beelmann, A., & Heinemann, K. S. (2014). Preventing prejudice and improving intergroup attitudes: A meta-analysis of child and adolescent training programs. *Journal of Applied Developmental Psychology, 35*(1), 10–24.

Behne, R., Carpenter, M., Call, J., & Tomasello, M. (2005). Unwilling versus unable: Infants' understanding of intentional action. *Developmental Psychology, 41*, 328–337.

Behne, T., Liszkowski, U., Carpenter, M., & Tomasello, M. (2012). Twelve-month-olds' comprehension and production of pointing. *British Journal of Developmental Psychology, 30*(3), 359–375.

Behnke, M., Smith, V. C., & Committee on Substance Abuse. (2013). Prenatal substance abuse: Short-and long-term effects on the exposed fetus. *Pediatrics, 131*(3), e1009–e1024.

Bell, M. A. (2012). A psychobiological perspective on working memory performance at 8 months of age. *Child Development, 83*(1), 251–265.

Bell, M. A., & Fox, N. A. (1992). The relations between frontal brain electrical activity and cognitive development during infancy. *Child Development, 63*, 1142–1163.

Bellieni, C. V., & Buonocore, G. (2012). Is fetal pain a real evidence? *The Journal of Maternal-Fetal & Neonatal Medicine, 25*(8), 1203–1208.

Belsky, J., Fish, M., & Isabella, R. (1991). Continuity and discontinuity in infant negative and positive emotionality: Family antecedents and attachment consequences. *Developmental Psychology, 27*, 421–431.

Belsky, J., Ruttle, P. L., Boyce, W. T., Armstrong, J. M., & Essex, M. J. (2015). Early adversity, elevated stress physiology, accelerated sexual maturation, and poor health in females. *Developmental Psychology, 51*(6), 816.

Belsky, J., Steinberg, L. D., Houts, R. M., Friedman, S. L., DeHart, G., Cauffman, E., . . . NICHD Early Child Care Research Network. (2007). Family rearing antecedents of pubertal timing. *Child Development, 78*(4), 1302–1321.

Belsky, J., Steinberg, L., Houts, R. M., & Halpern-Felsher, B. L. (2010). The development of reproductive strategy in females: Early maternal harshness—earlier menarch—increased sexual risk taking. *Developmental Psychology, 46*(1), 120–128.

Bem, S. L. (1993). *The lenses of gender: Transforming the debate on sexual inequality.* New Haven, CT: Yale University Press.

Benavides-Varela, S., Gómez, D. M., Macagno, F., Bion, R. A., Peretz, I., & Mehler, J. (2011). Memory in the neonate brain. *PLoS One, 6*(11), e27497.

Benenson, J. F., Philippoussis, M., & Leeb, R. (1999). Sex differences in neonates' cuddliness. *The Journal of Genetic Psychology, 160*(3), 332–342.

Bener, A., Ehlayel, M. S., Tulic, M. K., & Hamid, Q. (2012). Vitamin D deficiency as a strong predictor of asthma in children. *International Archives of Allergy and Immunology, 157*(2), 168–175.

Benes, F. M., Turtle, M., Khan, Y., & Farol, P. (1994). Myelination of a key relay zone in the hippocampal formation occurs in the human brain during childhood, adolescence, and adulthood. *Archives of General Psychiatry, 51*, 447–484.

Benner, A. D., & Graham, S. (2009). The transition to high schools as a developmental process among multiethnic urban youth. *Child Development, 80*(2), 356–376.

Benner, A. D., & Kim, S. Y. (2009). Experiences of discrimination among Chinese American adolescents and the consequences for socioemotional and academic development. *Developmental Psychology, 45*(6), 1682-1694.

Benson, E. (2003). Intelligent intelligence testing. *Monitor on Psychology, 43*(2), 48-51.

Beran, T. N., Ramirez-Serrano, A., Kuzyk, R., Fior, M., & Nugent, S. (2011). Understanding how children understand robots: Perceived animism in child-robot interaction. *International Journal of Human-Computer Studies, 69*(7-8), 539-550.

Berends, M. (2015). Sociology and school choice: What we know after two decades of charter schools. *Annual Review of Sociology, 41*, 159-180.

Berge, J. M., MacLehose, R. F., Loth, K. A., Eisenberg, M. E., Fulkerson, J. A., & Neumark-Sztainer, D. (2015). Parent-adolescent conversations about eating, physical activity and weight: Prevalence across sociodemographic characteristics and associations with adolescent weight and weight-related behaviors. *Journal of Behavioral Medicine, 38*(1), 122-135.

Bergen, D. (2002). The role of pretend play in children's cognitive development. *Early Childhood Research & Practice, 4*(1). Retrieved from http://ecrp.uiuc.edu/v4n1/bergen.html

Berk, L. E. (1992). Children's private speech: An overview of theory and the status of research. In R. M. Diaz & L. E. Berk (Eds.), *Private speech: From social interaction to self-regulation* (pp. 17-53). Hillsdale, NJ: Erlbaum.

Berlin, L. J., Ispa, J. M., Fine, M. A., Malone, P. S., Brooks-Gunn, J., Brady-Smith, C., . . . & Bai, Y. (2009). Correlates and consequences of spanking and verbal punishment for low-income white, African American, and Mexican American toddlers. *Child Development, 80*(5), 1403-1420.

Bernardi, F., & Radl, J. (2014). The long-term consequences of parental divorce for children's educational attainment. *Demographic Research, 30*, 1653-1680.

Bernier, A., Carlson, S. M., & Whipple, N. (2010). From external regulation to self-regulation: Early parenting precursors of young children's executive functioning. *Child Development, 81*(1), 326-339.

Bernier, A., Carlson, S. M., Deschênes, M., & Matte-Gagné, C. (2012). Social factors in the development of early executive functioning: A closer look at the caregiving environment. *Developmental Science, 15*(1), 12-24.

Berrick, J. D. (1998). When children cannot remain home: Foster family care and kinship care. *Future of Children, 8*, 72-87.

Berry, M., Dylla, D. J., Barth, R. P., & Needell, B. (1998). The role of open adoption in the adjustment of adopted children and their families. *Children and Youth Services Review, 20*, 151-171.

Berteletti, I., Lucangeli, D., Piazza, M., Dehaene, S., & Zorzi, M. (2010). Numerical estimation in preschoolers. *Developmental psychology, 46*(2), 545.

Berthiaume, V. G., Shultz, T. R., & Onishi, K. H. (2013). A constructivist connectionist model of transitions on false-belief tasks. *Cognition, 126*(3), 441-458.

Berthier, N. E. (2011). The syntax of human infant reaching. In *8th International Conference on Complex Systems* (pp. 1477-1487). Cambridge, MA: New England Complex Systems Institute.

Berthier, N. E., & Carrico, R. L. (2010). Visual information and object size in infant reaching. *Infant Behavior and Development, 33*(4), 555-566.

Betancourt, J. R., Green, A. R., Carrillo, J. E., & Ananeh-Firempong, O. (2016). Defining cultural competence: A practical framework for addressing racial/ethnic disparities in health and health care. *Public Health Reports, 118*(4), 293-302.

Betts, J. R., & Tang, Y. E. (2016). A meta-analysis of the literature on the effect of charter schools on student achievement. *Society for Research on Educational Effectiveness.*

Bevan, S., Traylor, M., Adib-Samii, P., Malik, R., Paul, N. L., Jackson, C., . . . & Markus, H. S. (2012). Genetic heritability of ischemic stroke and the contribution of previously reported candidate gene and genomewide associations. *Stroke, 43*(12), 3161-3167.

Beyers, W., & Seiffge-Krenke, I. (2010). Does identity precede intimacy? Testing Erikson's theory on romantic development in emerging adults of the 21st century. *Journal of Adolescent Research, 25*(3), 387-415.

Bhutta, Z. A., Yakoob, M. Y., Lawn, J. E., Rizvi, A., Friberg, I. K., Weissman, E., . . . & Lancet's Stillbirths Series steering committee. (2011). Stillbirths: What difference can we make and at what cost? *The Lancet, 377*(9776), 1523-1538.

Bialik, K. (2017). Key facts about race and marriage, 50 years after Loving v. Virginia. Pew Research Center. Retrieved from http://www.pewresearch.org/fact-tank/2017/06/12/key-facts-about-race-and-marriage-50-years-after-loving-v-virginia/

Bialystok, E., & Codd, J. (2000). Representing quantity beyond whole numbers: Some, none, and part. *Canadian Journal of Experimental Psychology/Revue canadienne de psychologie expérimentale, 54*(2), 117.

Bianchi, S., Robinson, J., & Milkie, M. (2006). *The changing rhythms of American family life.* New York: Russell Sage Foundation.

Bibbins-Domingo, K., Coxson, P., Pletcher, M. J., Lightwood, J., & Goldman, L. (2007). Adolescent overweight and future adult coronary heart disease. *New England Journal of Medicine, 357*, 2371-2379.

Biblarz, T. J., & Stacey, J. (2010). How does the gender of parents matter? *Journal of Marriage and Family, 72*(1), 3-22.

Biddle, S. J., & Asare, M. (2011). Physical activity and mental health in children and adolescents: A review of reviews. *British Journal of Sports Medicine*, bjsports90185.

Bigelow, A. E., & Dugas, K. (2009). Relations among preschool children's understanding of visual perspective taking, false belief, and lying. *Journal of Cognition and Development, 9*(4), 411-433.

Biro, F. M., & Wien, M. (2010). Childhood obesity and adult morbidities. *The American Journal of Clinical Nutrition, 91*(5), 1499S-1505S.

Biro, F. M., Galvez, M. P., Greenspan, L. C., Succop, P. A., Vangeepuram, N., Pinney, S. N., . . . Wolff, M. S. (2010). Pubertal assessment method and baseline characteristics in a mixed longitudinal study of girls. *Pediatrics, 126*(3), e583-e590.

Biro, F. M., Greenspan, L. C., Galvez, M. P., Pinney, S. M., Teitelbaum, S., Windham, G. C., . . . & Kushi, L. H. (2013). Onset of breast development in a longitudinal cohort. *Pediatrics, 132*(6), 1019-1027.

Bitler, M. P., Hoynes, H. W., & Domina, T. (2014). *Experimental evidence on distributional effects of Head Start* (No. w20434). Cambridge, MA: National Bureau of Economic Research.

Bixler, E. O., Vgontzas, A. N., Lin, H. M., Liao, D., Calhoun, S., Vela-Bueno, A., . . . & Graff, G. (2009). Sleep disordered breathing in children in a general population sample: Prevalence and risk factors. *Sleep, 32*(6), 731-736.

Bjarnason, T., Bendtsen, P., Arnarsson, A. M., Borup, I., Iannotti, R. J., Löfstedt, P., . . . & Niclasen, B. (2012). Life satisfaction among children in different family structures: A comparative study of 36 western societies. *Children & Society, 26*(1), 51-62.

Bjorklund, D. F. (1997). The role of immaturity in human development. *Psychological Bulletin, 122*, 153-169.

Bjorklund, D. F., & Causey, K. B. (2017). *Children's thinking: Cognitive development and individual differences* (p. 572). Thousand Oaks, CA: Sage.

Bjorklund, D. F., & Pellegrini, A. D. (2000). Child development and evolutionary psychology. *Child Development, 71*, 1687-1708.

Bjorklund, D. F., & Pellegrini, A. D. (2002). *The origins of human nature: Evolutionary developmental psychology.* Washington, DC: American Psychological Association.

Bjorklund, D. F., Miller, P. H., Coyle, T. R., & Slawinski, J. L. (1997). Instructing children to use memory strategies: Evidence of utilization deficiencies in memory training studies. *Developmental Review, 17*(4), 411-441.

Black, R. E., Allen, L. H., Bhutta, Z. A., Caulfield, L. E., De Onis, M., Ezzati, M., . . . & Maternal and Child Undernutrition Study Group. (2008). Maternal and child undernutrition: Global and regional exposures and health consequences. *The Lancet, 371*(9608), 243-260.

Black, R. E., Victora, C. G., Walker, S. P., Bhutta, Z. A., Christian, P., De Onis, M., . . . & Uauy, R. (2013). Maternal and child undernutrition and overweight in low-income and middle-income countries. *The Lancet, 382*(9890), 427-451.

Blakemore, S. J. (2012). Development of the social brain in adolescence. *Journal of the Royal Society of Medicine, 105*(3), 111-116.

Blanchard, R. (2017). Fraternal birth order, family size, and male homosexuality: Meta-analysis of studies spanning 25 years. *Archives of Sexual Behavior*, 1-15.

Blatchford, P., Bassett, P., & Brown, P. (2011). Examining the effect of class size on classroom engagement and teacher-pupil interaction: Differences in relation to pupil prior attainment and primary vs. secondary schools. *Learning and Instruction, 21*(6), 715-730.

Bleil, M. E., Adler, N. E., Appelhans, B. M., Gregorich, S. E., Sternfeld, B., & Cedars, M. I. (2013). Childhood adversity and pubertal timing: Understanding the origins of adulthood cardiovascular risk. *Biological Psychology, 93*(1), 213-219.

Bloom, B., Cohen, R. A., & Freeman, G. (2012). Summary health statistics for U.S. children. *National Health Interview Survey, 2011.*

Bloom, B., Jones, L. I., & Freeman, G. (2013). Summary health statistics for U.S. children: National Health Interview Survey, 2012. *National Center for Health Statistics, 10*, 258.

Blum, R. W., & Qureshi, F. (2011). *Morbidity and mortality among adolescents and young adults in the United States.* Baltimore, MD: Johns Hopkins Bloomberg School of Public Health.

Blum, R., & Reinhart, P. (2000). *Reducing the risk: Connections that make a difference in the lives of youth.* Minneapolis: University of Minnesota, Division of General Pediatrics and Adolescent Health.

Blumenthal, H., Leen-Feldner, E. W., Babson, K. A., Gahr, J. L., Trainor, C. D., & Frala, J. L. (2011). Elevated social anxiety among early maturing girls. *Developmental Psychology, 47*(4), 1133.

Bochukova, E. G., Huang, N., Keogh, J., Henning, E., Plurmann, C., Blaszczyk, K., . . . Faroqui, I. S. (2009). Large, rare chromosomal deletions associated with severe early-onset obesity. *Nature, 463*, 666-670.

Bodrova, E. (2008). Make-believe play versus academic skills: A Vygotskian approach to today's dilemma of early childhood education. *European Early Childhood Education Research Journal, 16*(3), 357-369.

Boergers, J., Gable, C. J., & Owens, J. A. (2014). Later school start time is associated with improved sleep and daytime functioning in adolescents. *Journal of Developmental & Behavioral Pediatrics, 35*(1), 11-17.

Bogard, K., & Takanishi, R. (2005). Pre-K through 3: An aligned and coordinated approach to education for children 3-8 years old. *Social Policy Report, 19*(3).

Bolton, S., & Hattie, J. (2017). Cognitive and brain development: Executive function, Piaget, and the prefrontal cortex. *Archives of Psychology, 1*(3).

Bonny, J. W., & Lourenco, S. F. (2013). The approximate number system and its relation to early math achievement: Evidence from the preschool years. *Journal of Experimental Child Psychology, 114*(3), 375-388.

Bönsch, D., Wunschel, M., Lenz, B., Janssen, G., Weisbrod, M., & Sauer, H. (2012). Methylation matters? Decreased methylation status of genomic DNA in the blood of schizophrenic twins. *Psychiatry Research, 198*(3), 533-537.

Bonuck, K. A., Chervin, R. D., Cole, T. J., Emond, A., Henderson, J., Xu, L., & Freeman, K. (2011). Prevalence and persistence of sleep disordered breathing symptoms in young children: a 6-year population-based cohort study. *Sleep, 34*(7), 875-884.

Boonstra, H. D. (2010). Winning campaign: California's concerted effort to reduce its teen pregnancy rate. *Gottmacher Policy Review, 13*(2), 18-24.

Bornstein, M. H., Hahn, C. S., & Haynes, O. M. (2004). Specific and general language performance across early childhood: Stability and gender considerations. *First Language, 24*(3), 267-304.

Bornstein, M. H., Putnick, D. L., Gartstein, M. A., Hahn, C. S., Auestad, N., & O'Connor, D. L. (2015). Infant temperament: Stability by age, gender, birth order, term status, and socioeconomic status. *Child Development, 86*(3), 844-863.

Borst, G., Poirel, N., Pineau, A., Cassotti, M., & Houdé, O. (2013). Inhibitory control efficiency in a Piaget-like class-inclusion task in school-age children and adults: A developmental negative priming study. *Developmental Psychology, 49*(7), 1366.

Bouchard, T. J. (2013). The Wilson effect: The increase in heritability of IQ with age. *Twin Research and Human Genetics, 16*(5), 923-930.

Boulton, M. J. (1995). Playground behaviour and peer interaction patterns of primary school boys classified as bullies, victims and not involved. *British Journal of Educational Psychology, 65*, 165-177.

Boulton, M. J., & Smith, P. K. (1994). Bully/victim problems in middle school children: Stability, self-perceived competence, peer perception, and peer acceptance. *British Journal of Developmental Psychology, 12*, 315-329.

Bowlby, J. (1960). *Attachment and loss: Vol. I. Attachment.* London, UK: Hogarth Press & the Institute of Psychoanalysis.

Bowman, S. A., Gortmaker, S. L., Ebbeling, C. B., Pereira, M. A., & Ludwig, D. S. (2004). Effects of fast food consumption on energy intake and diet quality among children in a national household survey. *Pediatrics, 113*, 112-118.

Boyce, J. A., Assa'ad, A., Burks A. W., et al. (2010). Guidelines for the diagnosis and management of food allergy in the United States: Report of the NIAID-sponsored expert panel. *Journal of Allergy and Clinical Immunology, 126* (suppl 6), S1-S58.

Boyle, C. A., Boulet, S., Schieve, L. A., Cohen, R. A., Blumberg, S. J., Yeargin-Allsopp, M., . . . & Kogan, M. D. (2011). Trends in the prevalence of developmental disabilities in U.S. children, 1997-2008. *Pediatrics, 127*(6), 1034-1042.

Boyles, S. (2002, January 27). Toxic landfills may boost birth defects. *WebMD Medical News.* Retrieved from www.webmd.com/content/article/25/3606_1181.htm

Bozick, R., & DeLuca, S. (2011). Not making the transition to college: School, work, and opportunities in the lives of American youth. *Social Science Research, 40*(4), 1249-1262.

Bracher, G., & Santow, M. (1999). Explaining trends in teenage childbearing in Sweden. *Studies in Family Planning, 30*, 169-182.

Bradbury, J. (2011). Docosahexaenoic acid (DHA): An ancient nutrient for the modern human brain. *Nutrients, 3*(5), 529-554.

Braddick, O., & Atkinson, J. (2011). Development of human visual function. *Vision Research, 51*(13), 1588-1609.

Bradley, H., Markowitz, L. E., Gibson, T., & McQuillan, G. M. (2013). Seroprevalence of herpes simplex virus types 1 and 2—United States, 1999-2010. *The Journal of Infectious Diseases, 209*(3), 325-333.

Braithwaite, I., Stewart, A. W., Hancox, R. J., Beasley, R., Murphy, R., Mitchell, E. A., & ISAAC Phase Three Study Group. (2014). Fast-food consumption and body mass index in children and adolescents: An international cross-sectional study. *BMJ Open, 4*(12), e005813.

Brand, J. E., & Simon Thomas, J. (2014). Job displacement among single mothers: Effects on children's outcomes in young adulthood. *American Journal of Sociology, 119*(4), 955–1001.

Brandone, A. C. (2015). Infants' social and motor experience and the emerging understanding of intentional actions. *Developmental Psychology, 51*(4), 512.

Branum, A., & Lukacs, S. L. (2008). *Food allergy among U.S. children: Trends in prevalence and hospitalizations* (Data Brief No. 10). Hyattsville, MD: National Center for Health Statistics.

Brassai, L., Piko, B. F., & Steger, M. F. (2011). Meaning in life: Is it a protective factor for adolescents' psychological health? *International Journal of Behavioral Medicine, 18*(1), 44–51.

Braungart, J. M., Plomin, R., DeFries, J. C., & Fulker, D. W. (1992). Genetic influence on tester-rated infant temperament as assessed by Bayley's Infant Behavior Record: Nonadoptive and adoptive siblings and twins. *Developmental Psychology, 28,* 40–47.

Braveman, P. A., Cubbin, C., Egerter, S., Williams, D. R., & Pamuk, E. (2010). Socioeconomic disparities in health in the United States: What the patterns tell us. *American Journal of Public Health, 100*(S1), S186–S196.

Bregman, H. R., Malik, N. M., Page, M. J., Makynen, E., & Lindahl, K. M. (2013). Identity profiles in lesbian, gay, and bisexual youth: The role of family influences. *Journal of Youth and Adolescence, 42*(3), 417–430.

Brenneman, K., Massey, C., Machado, S. F., & Gelman, R. (1996). Young children's plans differ for writing and drawing. *Cognitive Development, 11,* 397–419.

Breuner, C. C., Mattson, G., & Committee on Psychosocial Aspects of Child and Family Health. (2016). Sexuality education for children and adolescents. *Pediatrics, 138*(2), e20161348.

Brezina, P. R., & Zhao, Y. (2012). The ethical, legal, and social issues impacted by modern assisted reproductive technologies. *Obstetrics and Gynecology International,* 2012.

Bridgett, D. J., Laake, L. M., Gartstein, M. A., & Dorn, D. (2013). Development of infant positive emotionality: The contribution of maternal characteristics and effects on subsequent parenting. *Infant and Child Development, 22*(4), 362–382.

Briggs, G. G., Freeman, R. K., & Yaffe, S. J. (2012). *Drugs in pregnancy and lactation: A reference guide to fetal and neonatal risk.* Baltimore, MD: Lippincott Williams & Wilkins.

Briley, D. A., & Tucker-Drob, E. M. (2014). Genetic and environmental continuity in personality development: A meta-analysis. *Psychological Bulletin, 140*(5), 1303.

Brink, T. T., Urton, K., Held, D., Kirilina, E., Hofmann, M., Klann-Delius, G., . . . & Kuchinke, L. (2011). The role of orbitofrontal cortex in processing empathy stories in 4- to 8-year-old children. *Frontiers in Psychology, 2,* 80.

Briskin, S., LaBotz, M., Brenner, J. S., Benjamin, H. J., Cappetta, C. T., Demorest, R. A., . . . & Martin, S. S. (2012). Trampoline safety in childhood and adolescence. *Pediatrics, 130*(4), 774–779.

Broadbent, J. M., Thomson, W. M., Ramrakha, S., Moffitt, T. E., Zeng, J., Foster Page, L. A., & Poulton, R. (2015). Community water fluoridation and intelligence: Prospective study in New Zealand. *American Journal of Public Health, 105*(1), 72–76.

Brochado, S., Soares, S., & Fraga, S. (2017). A scoping review on studies of cyberbullying prevalence among adolescents. *Trauma, Violence, & Abuse, 18*(5), 523–531.

Brody, E. M. (2004). *Women in the middle: Their parent care years* (2nd ed.). New York: Springer.

Brody, G. H., Chen, Y.-F., Murry, V. M., Ge, X., Simons, R. L., Gibbons, F. X., . . . Cutrona, C. E. (2006). Perceived discrimination and the adjustment of African American youths: A five-year longitudinal analysis with contextual moderation effects. *Child Development, 77*(5), 1170–1189.

Brodzinsky, D. M., & Pinderhughes, E. (2013). Parenting and child development in adoptive families. *Handbook of Parenting, 1,* 279–312.

Brook, J. S., Lee, J. Y., Finch, S. J., Brown, E. N., & Brook, D. W. (2013). Long-term consequences of membership in trajectory groups of delinquent behavior in an urban sample: Violence, drug use, interpersonal, and neighborhood attributes. *Aggressive Behavior, 39*(6), 440–452.

Brooks, R., & Meltzoff, A. N. (2005). The development of gaze following and its relation to language. *Developmental Science, 8,* 535–543.

Brooks, R., & Meltzoff, A. N. (2008). Infant gaze following and pointing predict accelerated vocabulary growth through two years of age: A longitudinal, growth curve modeling study. *Journal of Child Language, 35*(1), 207–220.

Brooks, R., & Meltzoff, A. N. (2015). Connecting the dots from infancy to childhood: A longitudinal study connecting gaze following, language, and explicit theory of mind. *Journal of Experimental Child Psychology, 130,* 67–78.

Brown, A. S. (2012). Epidemiologic studies of exposure to prenatal infection and risk of schizophrenia and autism. *Developmental Neurobiology, 72*(10), 1272–1276.

Brown, B. B., & Larson, J. (2009). Peer relationships in adolescence. In R. M. Lerner & L. Steinberg(Eds.), *Handbook of adolescent psychology: Vol. 2. Contextual influences on adolescent development* (3rd ed., pp. 74–103). Hoboken, NJ: Wiley.

Brown, B. B., Mounts, N., Lamborn, S. D., & Steinberg, L. (1993). *Parenting practices and peer group affiliation in adolescence* (pp. 245–270). Cambridge, England: Cambridge University Press.

Brown, J. D., & L'Engle, K. L. (2009). X-rated: Sexual attitudes and behaviors associated with U.S. early adolescents' exposure to sexually explicit media. *Communication Research, 36*(1), 129–151.

Brown, S. L. (2010). Marriage and child well-being: Research and policy perspectives. *Journal of Marriage and Family, 72*(5), 1059–1077.

Brownell, C. A., Svetlova, M., Anderson, R., Nichols, S. R., & Drummond, J. (2013). Socialization of early prosocial behavior: Parents' talk about emotions is associated with sharing and helping in toddlers. *Infancy, 18*(1), 91–119.

Brubacher, S. P., Glisic, U., Roberts, K. P., & Powell, M. (2011). Children's ability to recall unique aspects of one occurrence of a repeated event. *Applied Cognitive Psychology, 25*(3), 351–358.

Bruni, O., & Novelli, L. (2010). Sleep disorders in children. *BMJ Clinical Evidence,* 2010.

Brunson, K. L., Kramar, E., Lin, B., Chen, Y., Colgin, L. L., Yanagihara, T., . . . & Baram, T. Z. (2005). Mechanisms of late-onset cognitive decline after early-life stress. *Journal of Neuroscience, 25*(41), 9328–9338.

Bryant, A. S., Worjoloh, A., Caughey, A. B., & Washington, A. E. (2010). Racial/ethnic disparities in obstetric outcomes and care: Prevalence and determinants. *American Journal of Obstetrics & Gynecology, 202*(4), 335–343.

Bucchianeri, M. M., Fernandes, N., Loth, K., Hannan, P. J., Eisenberg, M. E., & Neumark-Sztainer, D. (2016). Body dissatisfaction: Do associations with disordered eating and psychological well-being differ across race/ethnicity in adolescent girls and boys? *Cultural Diversity and Ethnic Minority Psychology, 22*(1), 137.

Buchanan, D. W., & Sobel, D. M. (2011). Mechanism-based causal reasoning in young children. *Child Development, 82*(6), 2053–2066.

Buchanan, T. W. (2007). Retrieval of emotional memories. *Psychological Bulletin, 133*(5), 761.

Bucher, B. S., Ferrarini, A., Weber, N., Bullo, M., Bianchetti, M. G., & Simonetti, G. D. (2013). Primary hypertension in childhood. *Current Hypertension Reports, 15*(5), 444-452.

Bugental, D. B., Ellerson, P. C., Lin, E. K., Rainey, B., Kokotovic, A., & O'Hara, N. (2010). A cognitive approach to child abuse prevention. *Journal of Family Psychology, 16*(3), 243-258.

Buist, K. L. (2010). Sibling relationship quality and adolescent delinquency: A latent growth curve approach. *Journal of Family Psychology, 24*(4), 400.

Buist, K. L., Deković, M., & Prinzie, P. (2013). Sibling relationship quality and psychopathology of children and adolescents: A meta-analysis. *Clinical Psychology Review, 33*(1), 97-106.

Burdette, H. L., & Whitaker, R. C. (2005). Resurrecting free play in young children. *Archives of Pediatrics and Adolescent Medicine, 159,* 46-50.

Burgaleta, M., Johnson, W., Waber, D. P., Colom, R., & Karama, S. (2014). Cognitive ability changes and dynamics of cortical thickness development in healthy children and adolescents. *NeuroImage, 84,* 810-819.

Burke, H., Leonardi-Bee, J., Hashim, A., Pine-Abata, H., Chen, Y., Cook, D. G., . . . & McKeever, T. M. (2012). Prenatal and passive smoke exposure and incidence of asthma and wheeze: Systematic review and meta-analysis. *Pediatrics, 129*(4), 735-744.

Burns, K. H., Casey, P. H., Lyle, R. E., Mac Bird, T., Fussell, J. J., & Robbins, J. M. (2010). Increasing prevalence of medically complex children in US hospitals. *Pediatrics, 126*(4), 638-646.

Bushman, B. J., Anderson, C. A., Donnerstein, E., Hummer, T. A., & Warburton, W. A. (2016). Reply to comments on SPSSI Research Summary on Media Violence by Cupit (2016), Gentile (2016), Glackin and Gray (2016), Gollwitzer (2016), and Krahé (2016). *Analyses of Social Issues and Public Policy, 16*(1), 443-450.

Bushman, B. J., Gollwitzer, M., & Cruz, C. (2015). There is broad consensus: Media researchers agree that violent media increase aggression in children, and pediatricians and parents concur. *Psychology of Popular Media Culture, 4*(3), 200.

Bushnell, E. W. (1985). The decline of visually guided reaching during infancy. *Infant Behavior and Development, 8*(2), 139-155.

Bussey, K., & Bandura, A. (1992). Self-regulatory mechanisms governing gender development. *Child Development, 63,* 1236-1250.

Buttelmann, D., Zmyj, N., Daum, M., & Carpenter, M. (2013). Selective imitation of in-group over out-group members in 14-month-old infants. *Child Development, 84*(2), 422-428.

Buzalaf, M. A. R., & Levy, S. M. (2011). Fluoride intake of children: considerations for dental caries and dental fluorosis. In M. A. R. Buzalaf (Ed.), *Fluoride and the oral environment* (Vol. 22, pp. 1-19). Basel, Switzerland: Karger Publishers.

Byers-Heinlein, K., Burns, T. C., & Werker, J. F. (2010). The roots of bilingualism in newborns. *Psychological Science, 21*(3), 343-348. doi:10.1177/0956797609360758

Bystron, I., Rakic, P., Molnar, Z., & Blakemore, C. (2006). The first neurons of the human cerebral cortex. *Nature Neuroscience, 9*(7), 880-886.

C

Cabrera, N. J., Tamis-LeMonda, C. S., Bradley, R. H., Hofferth, S., & Lamb, M. E. (2000). Fatherhood in the twenty-first century. *Child Development, 71,* 127-136.

Cabrera, S. M., Bright, G. M., Frane, J. W., Blethen, S. L., & Lee, P. A. (2014). Age of thelarche and menarche in contemporary U.S. females: A cross-sectional analysis. *Journal of Pediatric Endocrinology and Metabolism, 27*(1-2), 47-51.

Cain, M. S., Leonard, J. A., Gabrieli, J. D. E., & Finn, A. S. (2016). Media multitasking in adolescence. *Psychonomic Bulletin & Review.* 23, 1932-1941.

Cairns, G., Angus, K., Hastings, G., & Caraher, M. (2013). Systematic reviews of the evidence on the nature, extent and effects of food marketing to children. A retrospective summary. *Appetite, 62,* 209-215.

Calafat, A., García, F., Juan, M., Becoña, E., & Fernández-Hermida, J. R. (2014). Which parenting style is more protective against adolescent substance use? Evidence within the European context. *Drug and Alcohol Dependence, 138,* 185-192.

Çalışkan, M., Bochkov, Y. A., Kreiner-Møller, E., Bønnelykke, K., Stein, M. M., Du, G., . . . & Nicolae, D. L. (2013). Rhinovirus wheezing illness and genetic risk of childhood-onset asthma. *New England Journal of Medicine, 368*(15), 1398-1407.

Callaghan, T., Rochat, P., Lillard, A., Claux, M. L., Odden, H., Itakura, S., . . . & Singh, S. (2005). Synchrony in the onset of mental-state reasoning: Evidence from five cultures. *Psychological Science, 16*(5), 378-384.

Calzo, J. P., Masyn, K. E., Austin, S. B., Jun, H. J., & Corliss, H. L. (2017). Developmental latent patterns of identification as mostly heterosexual versus lesbian, gay, or bisexual. *Journal of Research on Adolescence, 27*(1), 246-253.

Cameron, L., Rutland, A., Brown, R., & Douch, R. (2006). Changing children's intergroup attitudes towards refugees: Testing different models of extended contact. *Child Development, 77,* 1208-1219.

Camilli, G., Vargas, S., Ryan, S., & Barnett, W. S. (2010). Meta-analysis of the effects of early education interventions on cognitive and social development. *Teachers College Record, 112*(3), 579-620.

Campa, M. J., & Eckenrode, J. J. (2006). Pathways to intergenerational adolescent childbearing in a high-risk sample. *Journal of Marriage and Family, 68,* 558-572.

Campione-Barr, N. (2017). The changing nature of power, control, and influence in sibling relationships. *New Directions for Child and Adolescent Development, 2017*(156), 7-14.

Campos, J. J., Sorce, J. F., Emde, R. N., & Svejda, M. (2013). Emotions as behavior regulators: Social referencing in infancy. *Emotions in Early Development, 5*

Canfield, M. A., Mai, C. T., Wang, Y., O'Halloran, A., Marengo, L. K., Olney, R. S., . . . & Copeland, G. (2014). The association between race/ethnicity and major birth defects in the United States, 1999-2007. *American Journal of Public Health, 104*(9), e14-e23.

Cantor, J. (1994). Confronting children's fright responses to mass media. In D. Zillman, J. Bryant, & A. C. Huston (Eds.), *Media, children, and the family: Social scientific, psychoanalytic, and clinical perspectives* (pp. 139-150). Hillsdale, NJ: Erlbaum.

Capps, R., Fix, M., & Zong, J. (2016). A profile of US children with unauthorized immigrant parents. Migration Policy Institute.

Carlo, G., Mestre, M. V., Samper, P., Tur, A., & Armenta, B. E. (2011). The longitudinal relations among dimensions of parenting styles, sympathy, prosocial moral reasoning, and prosocial behaviors. *International Journal of Behavioral Development, 35*(2), 116-124.

Carlson, S. E., Colombo, J., Gajewski, B. J., Gustafson, K. M., Mundy, D., Yeast, J., . . . & Shaddy, D. J. (2013). DHA supplementation and pregnancy outcomes. *The American Journal of Clinical Nutrition, 97*(4), 808-815.

Carlson, S. M., & Taylor, M. (2005). Imaginary companions and impersonated characters: Sex differences in children's fantasy play. *Merrill-Palmer Quarterly, 51*(1), 93-118.

Carpenter, C., & Gates, G. J. (2008). Gay and lesbian partnership: Evidence from California. *Demography, 45,* 573-590.

Carraher, T. N., Schliemann, A. D., & Carraher, D. W. (1988). Mathematical concepts in everyday life. *New Directions for Child and Adolescent Development, 1988*(41), 71-87.

Carrell, S. E., Maghakian, T., & West, J. E. (2011). A's from Zzzz's? The causal effect of school start time on the academic achievement of adolescents. *American Economic Journal: Economic Policy, 3*(3), 62-81.

Carskadon, M. A. (2011). Sleep in adolescents: The perfect storm. *Pediatric Clinics, 58*(3), 637-647.

Carskadon, M. A., Vieira, C., & Acebo, C. (1993). Association between puberty and delayed phase preference. *Sleep, 16*(3), 258-262.

Casey, B. J., Jones, R. M., & Somerville, L. H. (2011). Braking and accelerating of the adolescent brain. *Journal of Research on Adolescence, 21*(1), 21-33.

Caspi, A. (2000). The child is father of the man: Personality continuities from childhood to adulthood. *Journal of Personality and Social Psychology, 78*(1), 158

Caspi, A., McClay, J., Moffitt, T. E., Mill, J., Martin, J., Craig, I. W., . . . Poulton, R. (2002). Role of genotype in the cycle of violence in maltreated children. *Science, 297,* 851-854.

Castro, M., Expósito-Casas, E., López-Martín, E., Lizasoain, L., Navarro-Asencio, E., & Gaviria, J. L. (2015). Parental involvement on student academic achievement: A meta-analysis. *Educational Research Review, 14,* 33-46.

Castro, V. L., Halberstadt, A. G., Lozada, F. T., & Craig, A. B. (2015). Parents' emotion-related beliefs, behaviours, and skills predict children's recognition of emotion. *Infant and Child Development, 24*(1), 1-22.

Cavanagh, S. E., & Huston, A. C. (2008). The timing of family instability and children's social development. *Journal of Marriage and Family, 70*(5), 1258-1270.

Caylak, E. (2009). The genetics of sleep disorders in humans: Narcolepsy, restless legs syndrome, and obstructive sleep apnea syndrome. *American Journal of Medical Genetics Part A, 149*(11), 2612-2626.

Ceci, S. J., & Williams, W. M. (1997). Schooling, intelligence, and income. *American Psychologist, 52*(10), 1051-1058.

Center for Effective Discipline. 2009. *Discipline and the law.* Retrieved from www. stophitting.com/index.php?page=laws-main.

Center for Substance Abuse Treatment. (2008). *Medication-assisted treatment for opioid addiction during pregnancy. SAHMSA/CSAT treatment improvement protocols.* Rockville,MD: Substance Abuse and Mental Health Services Administration. Available at: www.ncbi.nlm. nih.gov/books/NBK26113.

Centers for Disease Control and Prevention (2017). 2015 Assisted Reproductive Technology National Summary Report. Retrieved from https://www.cdc.gov/art/pdf/2015-report/ART-2015-National-Summary-Report.pdf

Centers for Disease Control and Prevention (CDC). (2010). *Mortality among teenagers aged 12-19 years: United States, 1999-2006.* NCHS Data Brief. Retrieved from www.cdc.gov/nchs/data/databriefs/db37.htm

Centers for Disease Control and Prevention (CDC). (2012a). Death rates for suicide, by sex, race, Hispanic origin, and age: United States, selected years 1950-2010. Retrieved from www.cdc.gov/nchs/data/hus/2012/035.pdf

Centers for Disease Control and Prevention (CDC). (2012b). Sexual experience and contraceptive use among female teens—United States, 1995, 2002, and 2006-2010. *Morbidity and Mortality Weekly Report, 61*(17), 297-301.

Centers for Disease Control and Prevention. (2013a). Incidence, prevalence and cost of sexually transmitted infections in the United States. Retrieved from www.cdc.gov/std/stats/STI-Estimates-Fact-Sheet-Feb-2013.pdf

Centers for Disease Control and Prevention (CDC). (2013c). Reducing teen pregnancy: Engaging communities. Retrieved from http://www.cdc.gov/Features/TeenPregnancy/

Centers for Disease Control and Prevention. (2014a). Children's oral health. [Data sheet]. Retrieved from www.cdc.gov/oralhealth/children_adults/child.htm

Centers for Disease Control and Prevention. (2014b). U.S. infant vaccinations rates still high: Unvaccinated still vulnerable. Retrieved from www.cdc.gov/media/releases/2014/p0828-infant-vaccination.html

Centers for Disease Control and Prevention. (2015). *Severe maternal morbidity in the United States.* Atlanta, GA: Author.

Centers for Disease Control and Prevention. (2016a). Current physical activity guidelines. Retrieved from www.cdc.gov/cancer/dcpc/prevention/policies_practices/physical_activity/guidelines.htm

Centers for Disease Control and Prevention. (2016b). Physical activity among youth. Retrieved from www.cdc.gov/cancer/dcpc/prevention/policies_practices/physical_activity/youth.htm

Centers for Disease Control and Prevention. (2016c). STDs in adolescents and young adults. Retrieved from https://www.cdc.gov/std/stats16/adolescents.htm

Centers for Disease Control and Prevention. (2016d). CDC recommends only two HPV shots for younger adolescents. Retrieved from https://www.cdc.gov/media/releases/2016/p1020-hpv-shots.html

Centers for Disease Control and Prevention. (2017). National Immunization Survey (NIS): Results. Retrieved from www.cdc.gov/breastfeeding/data/nis_data/results.html

Centers for Disease Control and Prevention. (2017a). National marriage and divorce rate trends: 2000-2015. [Data file]. Retrieved from www.cdc.gov/nchs/data/dvs/national_marriage_divorce_rates_00-15.pdf

Centers for Disease Control and Prevention. (2017b). National diabetes statistics report: Estimates of diabetes and its burden in the United States, 2017. Atlanta, GA: US Department of Health and Human Services.

Centers for Disease Control and Prevention. (2017c). 10 leading causes of death by age group: United States - 2015. Retrieved from https://www.cdc.gov/injury/wisqars/pdf/leading_causes_of_death_by_age_group_2015-a.pdf

Centers for Disease Control and Prevention. (2017d). Trichomoniasis—CDC fact sheet. Retrieved from www.cdc.gov/std/trichomonas/stdfact-trichomoniasis.htm

Centers for Disease Control and Prevention. (2018). Birth defects [fact sheet]. Accessed from https://www.cdc.gov/ncbddd/birthdefects/data.html

Centers for Disease Control and Prevention. (2018a). Antibiotic resistance threats in the United States, 2013. (2013). [Report]. Retrieved from https://www.cdc.gov/drugresistance/threat-report-2013/pdf/ar-threats-2013-508.pdf#page=6

Centers for Disease Control and Prevention. (2018b). HIV among youth. [Fact sheet]. Retrieved from https://www.cdc.gov/hiv/group/age/youth/index.html

Centers for Disease Control and Prevention. (2017a). Microcephaly [fact sheet]. Retrieved from https://www.cdc.gov/ncbddd/birthdefects/microcephaly.html

Centers for Disease Control and Prevention. (2017b). Zika virus [fact sheet]. Retrieved from www.cdc.gov/zika/about/overview.html

Centers for Disease Control and Prevention. (2017c). Physical activity facts. Retrieved from https://www.cdc.gov/healthyschools/physicalactivity/facts.htm

Centers for Disease Control and Prevention. (2017d). Teen drivers: Get the facts. Retrieved from www.cdc.gov/motorvehiclesafety/teen_drivers/teendrivers_factsheet.html

Centers for Disease Control and Prevention. (2017e). Social determinants and eliminating disparities in teen pregnancy. Retrieved from www.cdc.gov/teenpregnancy/about/social-determinants-disparities-teen-pregnancy.htm

Centers for Disease Control and Prevention. (2017f). Infertility FAQs [Fact sheet]. Retrieved from www.cdc.gov/reproductivehealth/infertility/index.htm

Cerasoli, C. P., Nicklin, J. M., & Ford, M. T. (2014). Intrinsic motivation and extrinsic incentives jointly predict performance: A 40-year meta-analysis. *Psychological Bulletin, 140*(4), 980.

Cespedes, E. M., Gillman, M. W., Kleinman, K., Rifas-Shiman, S. L., Redline, S., & Taveras, E. M. (2014). Television viewing, bedroom television, and sleep duration from infancy to mid-childhood. *Pediatrics, 133*(5), e1163-e1171.

Chan, W. Y., Ou, S. R., & Reynolds, A. J. (2014). Adolescent civic engagement and adult outcomes: An examination among urban racial minorities. *Journal of Youth and Adolescence, 43*(11), 1829-1843.

Chandra, A., Martin, S., Collins, R., Elliott, M., Berry, S., Kanouse, D., & Miu, A. (2008). Does watching sex on television predict teen pregnancy? Findings from a National Longitudinal Survey of Youth. *Pediatrics, 122*(5), 1047-1054.

Chang, S. E., & Zhu, D. C. (2013). Neural network connectivity differences in children who stutter. *Brain, 136*(12), 3709-3726.

Chao, C., Klein, N. P., Velicer, C. M., Sy, L. S., Slezak, J. M., Takhar, H., . . . & Emery, M. (2012). Surveillance of autoimmune conditions following routine use of quadrivalent human papillomavirus vaccine. *Journal of Internal Medicine, 271*(2), 193-203.

Chao, R. K. (1994). Beyond parental control and authoritarian parenting style: Understanding Chinese parenting through the cultural notion of training. *Child Development, 65*, 1111-1119.

Chaplin, T. M., & Aldao, A. (2013). Gender differences in emotion expression in children: A meta-analytic review. *Psychological Bulletin, 139*(4), 735.

Chaudry, A., & Wimer, C. (2016). Poverty is not just an indicator: the relationship between income, poverty, and child well-being. *Academic Pediatrics, 16*(3), S23-S29.

Chen, H., Chauhan, S. P., Ananth, C. V., Vintzileos, A. M., & Abuhamad, A. Z. (2013). Electronic fetal heart rate monitoring and its relationship to neonatal and infant mortality in the United States. *American Journal of Obstetrics and Gynecology, 204*(6), 491-501.

Chen, L. W., Wu, Y., Neelakantan, N., Chong, M. F. F., Pan, A., & van Dam, R. M. (2014). Maternal caffeine intake during pregnancy is associated with risk of low birth weight: A systematic review and dose-response meta-analysis. *BMC Medicine, 12*(1), 174.

Chen, X. (2010). Socioemotional development in Chinese children. *Handbook of Chinese Psychology*, 37-52.

Chen, X. (2012). Culture, peer interaction, and socioemotional development. *Child Development Perspectives, 6*(1), 27-34.

Chen, X., Cen, G., Li, D., & He, Y. (2005). Social functioning and adjustment in Chinese children: The imprint of historical time. *Child Development, 76*, 182-195.

Chen, X., Wang, L., & Wang, Z. (2009). Shyness-sensitivity and social, school, and psychological adjustment in rural migrant and urban children in China. *Child Development, 80*(5), 1499-1513.

Cherlin, A. J. (2010). Demographic trends in the United States: A review of research in the 2000s. *Journal of Marriage and Family, 72*(3), 403-419.

Cheryan, S., Ziegler, S. A., Montoya, A. K., & Jiang, L. (2017). Why are some STEM fields more gender balanced than others? *Psychological Bulletin, 143*(1), 1.

Chesney, E., Goodwin, G. M., & Fazel, S. (2014). Risks of all-cause and suicide mortality in mental disorders: A meta-review. *World Psychiatry, 13*(2), 153-160.

Chian, R., Uzelac, P.S., & Nargund, G. (2013). In vitro maturation of human immature oocytes for fertility preservation. *Fertility and Sterility, 99*, 1173-1181.

Child Health USA. (2012). Adolescent mortality. Retrieved from https://mchb.hrsa.gov/chusa12/hs/hsa/pages/am.html

Child Trends DataBank. (2012). Number and percentage distribution of all children and adopted children, ages 0-17, by selected characteristics, United States, 2007. [Data file]. Retrieved from https://www.childtrends.org/wp-content/uploads/2012/08/113_appendix1.pdf

Child Trends DataBank. (2015). Family structure: Indicators of child and youth well-being. Retrieved from www.childtrends.org/wp-content/uploads/2015/12/59_Family_Structure.pdf

Child Trends Databank. (2015). Late or no prenatal care [report]. Retrieved from https://www.childtrends.org/?late-or-no-prenatal-care

Child Trends DataBank. (2015). Teen homicide, suicide and firearm deaths. Retrieved from www.childtrends.org/wp-content/uploads/2015/12/70_Homicide_Suicide_Firearms.pdf

Child Trends DataBank. (2016). Youth employment. Retrieved from www.childtrends.org/?indicators=youth-employment

Child Trends. (2010a). Children in poverty. Retrieved from www.childtrendsdatabank.org/?q=node/221

Child Trends. (2010b). Physical fighting by youth. Retrieved from www.childtrendsdatabank.org/?q=node/136

Child Welfare Information Gateway. (2013). *Long-term consequences of child abuse and neglect.* Washington, DC: U.S. Department of Health and Human Services, Children's Bureau.

Child Welfare Information Gateway. (2016a). Who may adopt, be adopted, or place a child for adoption. Washington, DC: U.S. Department of Health and Human Services, Children's Bureau.

Child Welfare Information Gateway. (2016b). *Trends in U.S. Adoptions: 2008-2012.* Washington, DC: U.S. Department of Health and Human Services, Children's Bureau.

Child Welfare Information Gateway. (2017). *Child abuse and neglect fatalities 2015: Statistics and interventions.* Washington, DC: U.S. Department of Health and Human Services, Children's Bureau.

Children's Defense Fund. (2017). Ending child poverty now. Retrieved from http://www.childrensdefense.org/library/PovertyReport/EndingChildPovertyNow.html

Children's Legal Defense Fund. (2014). The state of America's children 2014. Retrieved from www.childrensdefense.org/library/state-of-americas-children/2014-soac.pdf?utm_source=2014-SOAC-PDF & utm_medium=link & utm_campaign=2014-SOAC

Chin, H. B., Sipe, T. A., Elder, R., Mercer, S. L., Chattopadhyay, S. K., Jacob, V., . . . & Chuke, S. O. (2012). The effectiveness of group-based comprehensive risk-reduction and abstinence education interventions to prevent or reduce the risk of adolescent pregnancy, human immunodeficiency virus, and sexually transmitted infections: Two systematic reviews for the Guide to Community Preventive Services. *American Journal of Preventive Medicine, 42*(3), 272-294.

Chingos, M. M. (2012). The impact of a universal class-size reduction policy: Evidence from Florida's statewide mandate. *Economics of Education Review, 31*(5), 543-562.

Chiriboga, C. A., Brust, J. C. M., Bateman, D., & Hauser, W. A. (1999). Dose-response effect of fetal cocaine exposure on newborn neurologic function. *Pediatrics, 103*, 79-85.

Cho, H., Glewwe, P., & Whitler, M. (2012). Do reductions in class size raise students' test scores? Evidence from population variation in Minnesota's elementary schools. *Economics of Education Review, 31*(3), 77-95.

Choi, A. L., Sun, G., Zhang, Y., & Grandjean, P. (2012). Developmental fluoride neurotoxicity: A systematic review and meta-analysis. *Environmental Health Perspectives, 120*(10), 1362.

Chou, S. P., Zhang, H., Jung, J., Pickering, R. P., & Ruan, W. J. (2015). Prevalence of marijuana use disorders in the United States. *JAMA, 72*(12).

Choukas-Bradley, S., Giletta, M., Cohen, G. L., & Prinstein, M. J. (2015). Peer influence, peer status, and prosocial behavior: An experimental investigation of peer socialization of adolescents' intentions to volunteer. *Journal of Youth and Adolescence, 44*(12), 2197-2210.

Chow, C. M., Ruhl, H., & Buhrmester, D. (2013). The mediating role of interpersonal competence between adolescents' empathy and friendship quality: A dyadic approach. *Journal of Adolescence, 36*(1), 191-200.

Christakis, D. A., Zimmerman, F. J., DiGiuseppe, D. L., & McCarty, C. A. (2004). Early television exposure and subsequent attentional problems in children. *Pediatrics, 113,* 708-713.

Christian Home Educators Association of California. (2013). *Considering homeschooling?* Norwalk, CA: Christian Home Educators Association of California. Retrieved from www.cheaofca.org/index.cfm?fuseaction=Page.viewPage & pageId=1033

Christie, J. F. (1998). Play as a medium for literacy development. In D. P. Fromberg & D. Bergen (Eds.), *Play from birth to 12 and beyond: Contexts, perspectives, and meanings* (pp. 50-55). New York: Garland.

Cicchino, J. B., & Rakison, D. H. (2008). Producing and processing self-propelled motion in infancy. *Developmental Psychology, 44,* 1232-1241.

Cisler, J. M., Olatunji, B. O., Feldner, M. T., & Forsyth, J. P. (2010). Emotion regulation and the anxiety disorders: An integrative review. *Journal of Psychopathology and Behavioral Assessment, 32*(1), 68-82.

Clark, M. A., Gleason, P. M., Tuttle, C. C., & Silverberg, M. K. (2015). Do charter schools improve student achievement? *Educational Evaluation and Policy Analysis, 37*(4), 419-436.

Clauss, J. A., & Blackford, J. U. (2012). Behavioral inhibition and risk for developing social anxiety disorder: A meta-analytic study. *Journal of the American Academy of Child & Adolescent Psychiatry, 51*(10), 1066-1075.

Clayton, P. E., Gill, M. S., Hall, C. M., Tillmann, V., Whatmore, A. J., & Price, D. A. (1997). Serum leptin through childhood and adolescence. *Clinical Endocrinology, 46*(6), 727-733.

Clemmons, N. S., Gastanaduy, P. A., Fiebelkorn, A. P., Redd, S. B., Wallace, G. S., & Centers for Disease Control and Prevention (CDC). (2015). Measles—United States, January 4-April 2, 2015. *Morbidity and Mortality Weekly Report, 64*(14), 373-376.

Clinkenbeard, P. R. (2012). Motivation and gifted students: Implications of theory and research. *Psychology in the Schools, 49*(7), 622-630.

Cloak, C. C., Ernst, T., Fujii, L., Hedemark, B., & Chang, L. (2009). Lower diffusion in white matter of children with prenatal methamphetamine exposure. *Neurology, 72*(24), 2068-2975. doi: 10.1212/01.wnl.0000346516.49126.20 Ch. 3

Coan, J. A., & Allen, J. J. (2004). Frontal EEG asymmetry as a moderator and mediator of emotion. *Biological Psychology, 67*(1-2), 7-50.

Coffman, J. L., Ornstein, P. A., McCall, L. W., & Curran, P. J. (2008). Linking teachers' memory-relevant language and the development of children's memory skills. *Developmental Psychology, 44,* 1640-1654.

Cohen, L. B., & Amsel, L. B. (1998). Precursors to infants' perception of the causality of a simple event. *Infant Behavior and Development, 21,* 713-732.

Cohen, L. B., Chaput, H. H., & Cashon, C. H. (2002). A constructivist model of infant cognition. *Cognitive Development, 17,* 1323-1343.

Cohen, L. B., & Marks, K. S. (2002). How infants process addition and subtraction events. *Developmental Science, 5,* 186-201.

Cohn, D., & Passel, J. S. (2016). A record 60.6 million Americans live in multigenerational households. Pew Research Center. Retrieved from www.pewresearch.org/fact-tank/2016/08/11/a-record-60-6-million-americans-live-in-multigenerational-households/

Colby, S. L., & Ortman, J. M. (2015). *Projections of the size and composition of the U.S. population: 2014 to 2060.* P25-1143. Washington, DC: U.S. Census Bureau, 9.

Cole, A., & Kerns, K. A. (2001). Perceptions of sibling qualities and activities of early adolescents. *The Journal of Early Adolescence, 21*(2), 204-227.

Cole, P. M., Barrett, K. C., & Zahn-Waxler, C. (1992). Emotion displays in two-year-olds during mishaps. *Child Development, 63,* 314-324.

Cole, P. M., Bruschi, C. J., & Tamang, B. L. (2002). Cultural differences in children's emotional reactions to difficult situations. *Child Development, 73*(3), 983-996.

Cole, P. M., Tamang, B. L., & Shrestha, S. (2006). Cultural variations in the socialization of young children's anger and shame. *Child Development, 77*(5), 1237-1251.

Cole, S. W. (2009). Social regulation of human gene expression. *Current Directions in Psychological Science, 18*(3), 132-137.

Cole, T. J. (2003). The secular trend in human physical growth: A biological view. *Economics & Human Biology, 1*(2), 161-168.

Coleman-Jensen, A., Nord, M., Andrews, M., Carlson, S., 2011. Household food security in the United States in 2010. Economic Research Service (ERS), US Department of Agriculture.

Coll, C. G., Crnic, K., Lamberty, G., Wasik, B. H., Jenkins, R., Garcia, H. V., & McAdoo, H. P. (1996). An integrative model for the study of developmental competencies in minority children. *Child Development, 67*(5), 1891-1914.

Colle, L., & Del Giudice, M. (2011). Patterns of attachment and emotional competence in middle childhood. *Social Development, 20*(1), 51-72.

Collins, R. L. (2011). Content analysis of gender roles in media: Where are we now and where should we go? *Sex Roles, 64*(3-4), 290-298.

Colombo, J. (2002). Infant attention grows up: The emergence of a developmental cognitive neuroscience perspective. *Current Directions in Psychological Science, 11,* 196-200.

Colombo, J., Kannass, K. N., Shaddy, J., Kundurthi, S., Maikranz, J. M., Anderson, C. J., . . . Carlson, S. E. (2004). Maternal DHA and the development of attention in infancy and toddlerhood. *Child Development, 75,* 1254-1267.

Colombo, J., Kapa, L., & Curtindale, L. (2010). Varieties of attention in infancy. In L. Oakes, C. Cashon, M. Casasola & D. Rakison (Eds.), *Infant perception and cognition: Recent advances, emerging theories, and future directions* (pp. 3-26). Oxford, England: Oxford University Press.

Colombo, J., Shaddy, D. J., Anderson, C. J., Gibson, L. J., Blaga, O. M., & Kannass, K. N. (2010). What habituates in infant visual habituation? A psychophysiological analysis. *Infancy, 15*(2), 107-124.

Colonnesi, C., Stams, G. J. J., Koster, I., & Noom, M. J. (2010). The relation between pointing and language development: A meta-analysis. *Developmental Review, 30*(4), 352-366.

Congressional Budget Office (2017). *Repealing the individual health insurance mandate: An updated estimate* [report]. Retrieved from www.cbo.gov/publication/53300

Connellan, J., Baron-Cohen, S., Wheelwright, S., Batki, A., & Ahluwalia, J. (2000). Sex differences in human neonatal social perception. *Infant Behavior and Development, 23*(1), 113-118.

Constantino, J. N., Grosz, D., Saenger, P., Chandler, D. W., Nandi, R., & Earls, F. J. (1993). Testosterone and aggression in children. *Journal of the Academy of Child and Adolescent Psychiatry, 32,* 1217-1222.

Cook, C. R., Williams, K. R., Guerra, N. G., Kim, T. E., & Sadek, S. (2010). Predictors of bullying and victimization in childhood and adolescence: A meta-analytic investigation. *Social Psychology Quarterly, 25*(2), 65-83.

Cooke, L., & Fildes, A. (2011). The impact of flavour exposure in utero and during milk feeding on food acceptance at weaning and beyond. *Appetite, 57*(3), 808-811.

Cooper, H., Allen, A. B., Patall, E. A., & Dent, A. L. (2010). Effects of full-day kindergarten on academic achievement and social development. *Review of Educational Research, 80*(1), 34-70.

Cooper, R. P., & Aslin, R. N. (1990). Preference for infant-directed speech in the first month after birth. *Child Development, 61*(5), 1584-1595.

Copeland, W., Shanahan, L., Miller, S., Costello, E. J., Angold, A., & Maughan, B. (2010). Outcomes of early pubertal timing in young women: A prospective population-based study. *American Journal of Psychiatry, 167*(10), 1218-1225.

Copen, C. E., Chandra, A., & Martinez, G. (2012). *Prevalence and timing of oral sex with opposite-sex partners among females and males aged 15-24 years: United States, 2007-2010*. Washington, DC: U.S. Department of Health and Human Services, Centers for Disease Control and Prevention, National Center for Health Statistics.

Coplan, R. J., Ooi, L. L., & Nocita, G. (2015). When one is company and two is a crowd: Why some children prefer solitude. *Child Development Perspectives, 9*(3), 133-137.

Coplan, R. J., Ooi, L. L., Rose-Krasnor, L., & Nocita, G. (2014). 'I want to play alone': Assessment and correlates of self-reported preference for solitary play in young children. *Infant and Child Development, 23*(3), 229-238.

Corbetta, D., Thurman, S. L., Wiener, R. F., Guan, Y., & Williams, J. L. (2014). Mapping the feel of the arm with the sight of the object: On the embodied origins of infant reaching. *Frontiers in Psychology, 5*, 576.

Coren, S. (2012). *The left-hander syndrome: The causes and consequences of left-handedness*. New York: Simon and Schuster.

Correa, A., Botto, L., Liu, V., Mulinare, J., & Erickson, J. D. (2003). Do multivitamin supplements attenuate the risk for diabetes-associated birth defects? *Pediatrics, 111*, 1146-1151.

Corriveau, K. H., Chen, E. E., & Harris, P. L. (2015). Judgments about fact and fiction by children from religious and nonreligious backgrounds. *Cognitive Science, 39*(2), 353-382.

Corriveau, K. H., Harris, P. L., Meins, E., Fernyhough, C., Arnott, B., Elliott, L., . . . deRosnay, M. (2009). Young children's trust in their mother's claims: Longitudinal links with attachment security in infancy. *Child Development, 80*(3), 750-761.

Cortese, S., Kelly, C., Chabernaud, C., Proal, E., Di Martino, A., Milham, M. P., & Castellanos, F. X. (2012). Toward systems neuroscience of ADHD: A meta-analysis of 55 fMRI studies. *American Journal of Psychiatry, 169*(10), 1038-1055.

Cosgrove, K. P., Mazure, C. M., & Staley, J. K. (2007). Evolving knowledge of sex differences in brain structure, function, and chemistry. *Biological Psychiatry, 62*(8), 847-855.

Cote, L. R., & Bornstein, M. H. (2009). Child and mother play in three U.S. cultural groups: Comparisons and associations. *Journal of Family Psychology, 23*(3), 355-363.

Council on Sports Medicine and Fitness & Council on School Health. (2006). Active healthy living: Prevention of childhood obesity through increased physical activity. *Pediatrics, 117*, 1834-1842.

Courage, M. L., & Howe, M. L. (2002). From infant to child: The dynamics of cognitive change in the second year of life. *Psychological Bulletin, 128*, 250-277.

Couturier, J., Kimber, M., & Szatmari, P. (2013). Efficacy of family-based treatment for adolescents with eating disorders: A systematic review and meta-analysis. *International Journal of Eating Disorders, 46*(1), 3-11.

Cox, M. J., & Paley, B. (2003). Understanding families as systems. *Current Directions in Psychological Science, 12*(5), 193-196.

Coyne, S. M., Linder, J. R., Rasmussen, E. E., Nelson, D. A., & Birkbeck, V. (2016). Pretty as a princess: Longitudinal effects of engagement with Disney princesses on gender stereotypes, body esteem, and prosocial behavior in children. *Child Development, 87*(6), 1909-1925.

Cozzi, P., Putnam, S. P., Menesini, E., Gartstein, M. A., Aureli, T., Calussi, P., & Montirosso, R. (2013). Studying cross-cultural differences in temperament in toddlerhood: United States of America (US) and Italy. *Infant Behavior and Development, 36*(3), 480-483.

Craigie, T. A. (2008). Effects of paternal presence and family instability on child cognitive performance. *Center for Research on Child Wellbeing Working Paper*.

Crawford, J. (2007). The decline of bilingual education: How to reverse a troubling trend? *International Multilingual Research Journal, 1*(1), 33-38.

Crews, F., He, J., & Hodge, C. (2007). Adolescent cortical development: A critical period of vulnerability for addiction. *Pharmacology Biochemistry and Behavior, 86*(2), 189-199.

Crick, N. R., & Dodge, K. A. (1996). Social information-processing mechanisms in reactive and proactive aggression. *Child Development, 67*, 993-1002.

Crino, M., Sacks, G., Vandevijvere, S., Swinburn, B., & Neal, B. (2015). The influence on population weight gain and obesity of the macronutrient composition and energy density of the food supply. *Current Obesity Reports, 4*(1), 1-10.

Criss, M. M., Lee, T. K., Morris, A. S., Cui, L., Bosler, C. D., Shreffler, K. M., & Silk, J. S. (2015). Link between monitoring behavior and adolescent adjustment: An analysis of direct and indirect effects. *Journal of Child and Family Studies, 24*(3), 668-678.

Criss, M. M., Smith, A. M., Morris, A. S., Liu, C., & Hubbard, R. L. (2017). Parents and peers as protective factors among adolescents exposed to neighborhood risk. *Journal of Applied Developmental Psychology, 53*, 127-138.

Croker, S., & Buchanan, H. (2011). Scientific reasoning in a real-world context: The effect of prior belief and outcome on children's hypothesis-testing strategies. *British Journal of Developmental Psychology, 29*(3), 409-424.

Crosnoe, R., Cavanagh, S., & Elder Jr, G. H. (2003). Adolescent friendships as academic resources: The intersection of friendship, race, and school disadvantage. *Sociological Perspectives, 46*(3), 331-352.

Cuevas, K., & Bell, M. A. (2010). Developmental progression of looking and reaching performance on the A-not-B task. *Developmental Psychology, 46*(5), 1363.

Cui, M., & Fincham, F. D. (2010). The differential effects of parental divorce and marital conflict on young adult romantic relationships. *Personal Relationships, 17*(3), 331-343.

Cui, M., Fincham, F. D., & Durtschi, J. A. (2011). The effect of parental divorce on young adults' romantic relationship dissolution: What makes a difference? *Personal Relationships, 18*(3), 410-426.

Cummings, A. J., Knibb, R. C., King, R. M., & Lucas, J. S. (2010). The psychosocial impact of food allergy and food hypersensitivity in children, adolescents and their families: A review. *Allergy, 65*(8), 933-945.

Cummings, E. M., Koss, K. J., & Davies, P. T. (2015). Prospective relations between family conflict and adolescent maladjustment: Security in the family system as a mediating process. *Journal of Abnormal Child Psychology, 43*(3), 503-515.

Currie, J., & SpatzWidom, C. (2010). Long-term consequences of child abuse and neglect on adult economic well-being. *Child Maltreatment, 15*(2), 111-120.

Curtin, S. C., & Mathews, T. J. (2016). Smoking prevalence and cessation before and during pregnancy: Data from the birth certificate, 2014. *National Vital Statistics Reports 65*(1). Hyattsville, MD: National Center for Health Statistics.

D

D'Hondt, E., Deforche, B., Gentier, I., De Bourdeaudhuij, I., Vaeyens, R., Philippaerts, R., & Lenoir, M. (2013). A longitudinal analysis of gross motor coordination in overweight and obese children versus normal-weight peers. *International Journal of Obesity, 37*(1), 61.

D'Hondt, E., Deforche, B., Gentier, I., Verstuyf, J., Vaeyens, R., Bourdeaudhuij, I., . . . & Lenoir, M. (2014). A longitudinal study of gross motor coordination and weight status in children. *Obesity, 22*(6), 1505-1511.

Dabelea, D., Mayer-Davis, E. J., Saydah, S., Imperatore, G., Linder, B., Divers, J., . . . & Liese, A. D. (2014). Prevalence of type 1 and type

2 diabetes among children and adolescents from 2001 to 2009. *JAMA, 311*(17), 1778–1786.

Dahlin, K. I. (2011). Effects of working memory training on reading in children with special needs. *Reading and Writing, 24*(4), 479–491.

Danielson, M. L., Bitsko, R. H., Ghandour, R. M., Holbrook, J. R., Kogan, M. D., & Blumberg, S. J. (2018). Prevalence of parent-reported ADHD diagnosis and associated treatment among U.S. children and adolescents, 2016. *Journal of Clinical Child & Adolescent Psychology*, 1–14.

Dart, R. C., Surratt, H. L., Cicero, T. J., Parrino, M. W., Severtson, S. G., Bucher-Bartelson, B., & Green, J. L. (2015). Trends in opioid analgesic abuse and mortality in the United States. *New England Journal of Medicine, 372*(3), 241–248.

Darwin, C. (1877). A biographical sketch of an infant. *Mind, 2*, 285–294.

Dasen, P. R. (1984). The cross-cultural study of intelligence: Piaget and the Baoule. *International Journal of Psychology, 19*(1–4), 407–434.

Daugherty, M., & White, C. S. (2008). Relationships among private speech and creativity in Head Start and low-socioeconomic status preschool children. *Gifted Child Quarterly, 52*(1), 30–39.

David and Lucile Packard Foundation. (2004). Children, families, and foster care: Executive summary. *Future of Children, 14*(1). Retrieved from www.futureofchildren.org

Davis, A. M., Bennett, K. J., Befort, C., & Nollen, N. (2011). Obesity and related health behaviors among urban and rural children in the United States: Data from the National Health and Nutrition Examination Survey 2003–2004 and 2005–2006. *Journal of Pediatric Psychology, 36*(6), 669–676.

Davis, E. L., Levine, L. J., Lench, H. C., & Quas, J. A. (2010). Metacognitive emotion regulation: Children's awareness that changing thoughts and goals can alleviate negative emotions. *Emotion, 10*(4), 498.

Davis, O. S. P., Haworth, C. M. A., & Plomin, R. (2009). Dramatic increases in heritability of cognitive development from early to middle childhood: An 8-year longitudinal study of 8,700 pairs of twins. *Psychological Science, 20*(10), 1301–1308.

Davis-Kean, P. E. (2005). The influence of parent education and family income on child achievement: The indirect role of parental expectations and the home environment. *Journal of Family Psychology, 19*(2), 294.

Dawson, M. A., & Kouzarides, T. (2012). Cancer epigenetics: From mechanism to therapy. *Cell, 150*(1), 12–27.

Day, K. L., & Smith, C. L. (2013). Understanding the role of private speech in children's emotion regulation. *Early Childhood Research Quarterly, 28*(2), 405–414.

De Bourdeaudhuij, I., Van Cauwenberghe, E., Spittaels, H., Oppert, J. M., Rostami, C., Brug, J., . . . & Maes, L. (2011). School-based interventions promoting both physical activity and healthy eating in Europe: A systematic review within the HOPE project. *Obesity Reviews, 12*(3), 205–216.

De Kieviet, J. F., Piek, J. P., Aarnoudse-Moens, C. S., & Oosterlaan, J. (2009). Motor development in very preterm and very low-birth-weight children from birth to adolescence: A meta-analysis. *JAMA, 302*(20), 2235–2242.

De Onis, M., Blössner, M., & Borghi, E. (2010). Global prevalence and trends of overweight and obesity among preschool children. *The American Journal of Clinical Nutrition, 92*(5), 1257–1264.

Deary, I. J., Penke, L., & Johnson, W. (2010). The neuroscience of human intelligence differences. *Nature Reviews. Neuroscience, 11*(3), 201.

Deave, T., Heron, J., Evans, J., & Emond, A. (2008). The impact of maternal depression in pregnancy on early child development. *BJOG: An International Journal of Obstetrics & Gynaecology, 115*(8), 1043–1051.

Debnath, M., Venkatasubramanian, G., & Berk, M. (2015). Fetal programming of schizophrenia: Select mechanisms. *Neuroscience & Biobehavioral Reviews, 49*, 90–104.

DeCasper, A. J., Lecanuet, J. P., Busnel, M. C., Granier-Deferre, C., & Maugeais, R. (1994). Fetal reactions to recurrent maternal speech. *Infant Behavior and Development, 17*, 159–164.

Decety, J., Michalaska, K., Akitsuki, Y., & Lahey, B. (2009). Atypical empathetic responses in adolescents with aggressive conduct disorder: A functional MRI investigation. *Biological Psychology, 80*, 203–211.

Dee, T. S., & Jacob, B. (2011). The impact of No Child Left Behind on student achievement. *Journal of Policy Analysis and management, 30*(3), 418–446.

Dehaene-Lambertz, G., Hertz-Pannier, L., Dubois, J., Mériaux, S., Roche, A., Sigman, M., & Dehaene, S. (2006). Functional organization of perisylvian activation during presentation of sentences in preverbal infants. *Proceedings of the National Academy of Sciences, 103*(38), 14240–14245.

Dehne, K. L., Riedner, G., Berer, M., & World Health Organization. (2005). Sexually transmitted infections among adolescents: The need for adequate health services. [Report]. Retrieved from http://apps. who.int/iris/bitstream/handle/10665/43221/9241562889. pdf?sequence=1 & isAllowed=y

Deli, E., Bakle, I., & Zachopoulou, E. (2006). Implementing intervention movement programs for kindergarten children. *Journal of Early Childhood Research, 4*(1), 5–18.

DeLoache, J. S. (2011). Early development of the understanding and use of symbolic artifacts. In U. Goswami (Ed.), *The Wiley-Blackwell handbook of childhood cognitive development* (2nd ed., pp. 312–336). Hoboken, NJ: Wiley.

DeLoache, J. S., Chiong, C., Sherman, K., Islam, N., Vanderborght, M., Troseth, G. L., . . . & O'Doherty, K. (2010). Do babies learn from baby media? *Psychological Science, 21*(11), 1570–1574.

DeLoache, J. S., LoBue, V., Vanderborght, M., & Chiong, C. (2013). On the validity and robustness of the scale error phenomenon in early childhood. *Infant Behavior and Development, 36*(1), 63–70.

DeLoache, J. S., Pierroutsakos, S. L., & Uttal, D. H. (2003). The origins of pictorial competence. *Current Directions in Psychological Science, 12*, 114–118.

DeLoache, J. S., Uttal, D. H., & Rosengren, K. S. (2004). Scale errors offer evidence for a perception-action dissociation early in life. *Science, 304*(5673), 1027–1029.

Deng, K., Liu, Z., Lin, Y., Mu, D., Chen, X., Li, J., . . . & Li, S. (2013). Periconceptional paternal smoking and the risk of congenital heart defects: A case-control study. *Birth Defects Research Part A: Clinical and Molecular Teratology, 97*(4), 210–216.

Deng, W., Aimone, J. B., & Gage, F. H. (2010). New neurons and new memories: How does adult hippocampal neurogenesis affect learning and memory? *Nature Reviews. Neuroscience, 11*(5), 339.

Denham, S. A., Bassett, H. H., Brown, C., Way, E., & Steed, J. (2015). "I Know How You Feel": Preschoolers' emotion knowledge contributes to early school success. *Journal of Early Childhood Research, 13*(3), 252–262.

Denissen, J. J. A., van Aken, M. A. G., & Dubas, J. S. (2009). It takes two to tango: How parents' and adolescents' personalities link to the quality of their mutual relationship. *Developmental Psychology, 45*(4), 928–941.

Dennis, T. (2006). Emotional self-regulation in preschoolers: The interplay of child approach reactivity, parenting, and control capacities. *Developmental Psychology, 42*, 84–97.

Dennis, W. (1936). A bibliography of baby biographies. *Child Development*, 71–73.

Deoni, S. C., Dean III, D. C., O'muircheartaigh, J., Dirks, H., & Jerskey, B. A. (2012). Investigating white matter development in infancy and early childhood using myelin water faction and relaxation time mapping. *Neuroimage, 63*(3), 1038–1053.

Deoni, S. C., Mercure, E., Blasi, A., Gasston, D., Thomson, A., Johnson, M., . . . & Murphy, D. G. (2011). Mapping infant brain myelination with magnetic resonance imaging. *Journal of Neuroscience, 31*(2), 784–791.

Department of Immunization, Vaccines, and Biologicals, World Health Organization; United Nations Children's Fund; Global Immunization Division, National Center for Immunization and Respiratory Diseases (proposed); & McMorrow, M. (2006). Vaccine preventable deaths and the global immunization vision and strategy, 2006–2015. *Morbidity and Mortality Weekly Report, 55*, 511–515.

Deptula, D. P., Henry, D. B., & Schoeny, M. E. (2010). How can parents make a difference? Longitudinal associations with adolescent sexual behavior. *Journal of Family Psychology, 24*(6), 731.

DeSalvo, K. B., Olson, R., & Casavale, K. O. (2016). Dietary guidelines for Americans. *JAMA, 315*(5), 457–458.

Deshmukh-Taskar, P. R., Nicklas, T. A., O'Neil, C. E., Keast, D. R., Radcliffe, J. D., & Cho, S. (2010). The relationship of breakfast skipping and type of breakfast consumption with nutrient intake and weight status in children and adolescents: The National Health and Nutrition Examination Survey 1999–2006. *Journal of the American Dietetic Association, 110*(6), 869–878.

Desoete, A. (2015). Predictive indicators for mathematical learning disabilities/dyscalculia in kindergarten children. In S. Chinn (Ed.), *The Routledge international handbook of dyscalculia and mathematical learning difficulties.* (New York: Routledge), 90–100.

Deutsch, F. M., Servis, L. J., & Payne, J. D. (2001). Paternal participation in child care and its effects on children's self-esteem and attitudes toward gendered roles. *Journal of Family Issues, 22*(8), 1000–1024.

Devine, R. T., & Hughes, C. (2014). Relations between false belief understanding and executive function in early childhood: A meta-analysis. *Child Development, 85*(5), 1777–1794.

Devoe, J. E., Ray, M., Krois, L., & Carlson, M. J. (2010). Uncertain health insurance coverage and unmet children's health care needs. *Family Medicine, 42*(2), 121–132.

Dew, J., & Wilcox, W. B. (2011). If Momma ain't happy: Explaining declines in marital satisfaction among new mothers. *Journal of Marriage and Family, 73*(1), 1–12.

Dewald, J. F., Meijer, A. M., Oort, F. J., Kerkhof, G. A., & Bögels, S. M. (2010). The influence of sleep quality, sleep duration and sleepiness on school performance in children and adolescents: A meta-analytic review. *Sleep Medicine Reviews, 14*(3), 179–189.

Diamond, A. (1991). Neuropsychological insights into the meaning of object concept development. In S. Carey & R. Gelman (Eds.), *Epigensis of mind* (pp. 67–110). Hillsdale, NJ: Erlbaum.

Diamond, A. (2002). Normal development of prefrontal cortex from birth to young adulthood: Cognitive functions, anatomy, and biochemistry. In D. T. Strauss & R. T. Knight (Eds.), *Principles of frontal lobe function* (pp. 466–503). New York: Oxford University Press.

Diamond, A., & Lee, K. (2011). Interventions shown to aid executive function development in children 4 to 12 years old. *Science, 333*(6045), 959–964.

Diamond, M. (2013). Transsexuality among twins: Identity concordance, transition, rearing, and orientation. *International Journal of Transgenderism, 14*(1), 24–38.

Diamond, M., & Sigmundson, H. K. (1997). Sex reassignment at birth: Long-term review and clinical implications. *Archives of Pediatrics & Adolescent Medicine, 151*(3), 298–304.

Dickens, W. T., & Flynn, J. R. (2006). Black Americans reduce the racial IQ gap: Evidence from standardization samples. *Psychological Science, 17*(10), 913–920.

Dickinson, D. K., & Porche, M. V. (2011). Relation between language experiences in preschool classrooms and children's kindergarten and fourth-grade language and reading abilities. *Child Development, 82*(3), 870–886.

Dietert, R. R. (2005). Developmental immunotoxicology (DIT): Is DIT testing necessary to ensure safety? *Proceedings of the 14th Immunotoxicology Summer School, Lyon, France, October 2005*, 246–257.

DiFranza, J. R., Aligne, C. A., & Weitzman, M. (2004). Prenatal and postnatal environmental tobacco smoke exposure and children's health. *Pediatrics, 113*, 1007–1015.

Dijkstra, J. K., Berger, C., & Lindenberg, S. (2011). Do physical and relational aggression explain adolescents' friendship selection? The competing roles of network characteristics, gender, and social status. *Aggressive Behavior, 37*(5), 417–429.

DiPietro, J. A. (1981). Rough and tumble play: A function of gender. *Developmental Psychology, 17*(1), 50.

DiPietro, J. A. (2004). The role of prenatal maternal stress in child development. *Current Directions in Psychological Science, 13*(2), 71–74.

DiPietro, J. A., Kivlighan, K. T., Costigan, K. A., Rubin, S. E., Shiffler, D. E., Henderson, J. L., & Pillion, J. P. (2010). Prenatal antecedents of newborn neurological maturation. *Child Development, 81*(1), 115–130. doi: 10.1111/j.1467-8624.2009.01384.x

Dirix, C. E. H., Nijhuis, J. G., Jongsma, H. W., & Hornstra, G. (2009). Aspects of fetal learning and memory. *Child Development, 80*(4), 1251–1258.

Dishion, T. J., & Stormshak, E. (2007). *Intervening in children's lives: An ecological, family-centered approach to mental healthcare.* Washington, DC: APA Books.

Dishion, T. J., Shaw, D., Connell, A., Gardner, F., Weaver, C., & Wilson, M. (2008). The family check-up with high-risk indigent families: Preventing problem behavior by increasing parents' positive behavior support in early childhood. *Child Development, 79,* 1395–1414.

Doak, C. M., Visscher, T. L. S., Renders, C. M., & Seidell, J. C. (2006). The prevention of overweight and obesity in children and adolescents: A review of interventions and programmes. *Obesity Reviews, 7*(1), 111–136.

Dodge, K. A., Coie, J. D., & Lynam, D. (2006). Aggression and antisocial behavior in youth. In N. Eisenberg, W. Damon, & R. Lerner (Eds.), *Handbook of child psychology: Vol. 3, Social, emotional and personality development* (6th ed., pp. 719–788). Hoboken, NJ: Wiley.

Dodge, K. A., Malone, P. S., Lansford, J. E., Sorbring, E., Skinner, A. T., Tapanya, S., . . . & Bacchini, D. (2015). Hostile attributional bias and aggressive behavior in global context. *Proceedings of the National Academy of Sciences, 112*(30), 9310–9315.

Domellöf, E., Johansson, A. M., & Rönnqvist, L. (2011). Handedness in preterm born children: A systematic review and a meta-analysis. *Neuropsychologia, 49*(9), 2299–2310.

Domènech Rodríguez, M. M., Donovick, M. R., & Crowley, S. L. (2009). Parenting styles in a cultural context: Observations of "protective parenting" in first-generation Latinos. *Family Process, 48*(2), 195–210.

Dong, Y. (2010). Kept back to get ahead? Kindergarten retention and academic performance. *European Economic Review, 54*(2), 219–236.

dos Santos, A. P. P., Nadanovsky, P., & de Oliveira, B. H. (2013). A systematic review and meta-analysis of the effects of fluoride toothpastes on the prevention of dental caries in the primary dentition of preschool children. *Community Dentistry and Oral Epidemiology, 41*(1), 1–12.

Doughty, S. E., Lam, C. B., Stanik, C. E., & McHale, S. M. (2015). Links between sibling experiences and romantic competence from adolescence through young adulthood. *Journal of Youth and Adolescence, 44*(11), 2054–2066.

Doyle, L. W., & Anderson, P. J. (2010). Adult outcome of extremely preterm infants. *Pediatrics, 126*(2), 342–351.

Dreyer, B., Chung, P. J., Szilagyi, P., & Wong, S. (2016). Child poverty in the United States today: Introduction and executive summary. *Academic Pediatrics, 16*(3), S1-S5.

Dube, S. R., Felitti, V. J., Dong, M., Chapman, D. P., Giles, W. H., & Anda, R. F. (2003, March). Childhood abuse, neglect, and household dysfunction and the risk of illicit drug use: The Adverse Childhood Experiences Study. *Pediatrics, 111*(3), 564-572.

Dubicka, B., Elvins, R., Roberts, C., Chick, G., Wilkinson, P., & Goodyer, I. M. (2010). Combined treatment with cognitive–behavioural therapy in adolescent depression: Meta-analysis. *The British Journal of Psychiatry, 197*(6), 433-440.

Dubois, J., Dehaene-Lambertz, G., Kulikova, S., Poupon, C., Hüppi, P. S., & Hertz-Pannier, L. (2014). The early development of brain white matter: A review of imaging studies in fetuses, newborns and infants. *Neuroscience, 276*, 48-71.

Dubowitz, H., Kim, J., Black, M. M., Weisbart, C., Semiatin, J., & Magder, L. S. (2011). Identifying children at high risk for a child maltreatment report. *Child Abuse & Neglect, 35*(2), 96-104.

Duckworth, A. L., Quinn, P. D., & Tsukayama, E. (2012). What No Child Left Behind leaves behind: The roles of IQ and self-control in predicting standardized achievement test scores and report card grades. *Journal of Educational Psychology, 104*(2), 439.

Duncan, J. R., Paterson, D. S., Hoffman, J. M., Mokler, D. J., Borenstein, N. S., Belliveau, R. A., . . . Kinney, H. C. (2010). Brainstem serotonergic deficiency in sudden infant death syndrome. *Journal of the American Medical Association, 303*(5), 430-437. doi: 10.1001/jama.2010.45

Dunfield, K. A., & Kuhlmeier, V. A. (2013). Classifying prosocial behavior: Children's responses to instrumental need, emotional distress, and material desire. *Child Development, 84*(5), 1766-1776.

Dunfield, K., Kuhlmeier, V. A., O'Connell, L., & Kelley, E. (2011). Examining the diversity of prosocial behavior: Helping, sharing, and comforting in infancy. *Infancy, 16*(3), 227-247.

Dunn, E. C., Brown, R. C., Dai, Y., Rosand, J., Nugent, N. R., Amstadter, A. B., & Smoller, J. W. (2015). Genetic determinants of depression: Recent findings and future directions. *Harvard Review of Psychiatry, 23*(1), 1.

Dunning, D. L., Holmes, J., & Gathercole, S. E. (2013). Does working memory training lead to generalized improvements in children with low working memory? A randomized controlled trial. *Developmental Science, 16*(6), 915-925.

Dunson, D. B., Colombo, B., & Baird, D. D. (2002). Changes with age in the level and duration of fertility in the menstrual cycle. *Human Reproduction, 17*, 1399-1403.

Dunst, C., Gorman, E., & Hamby, D. (2012). Preference for infant-directed speech in preverbal young children. *Center for Early Literacy Learning, 5*(1), 1-13.

Dupierrix, E., de Boisferon, A. H., Méary, D., Lee, K., Quinn, P. C., Di Giorgio, E., . . . & Pascalis, O. (2014). Preference for human eyes in human infants. *Journal of Experimental Child Psychology, 123*, 138-146.

DuPont, R. L. (1983). Phobias in children. *Journal of Pediatrics, 102*, 999-1002.

Durbin, D. R. (2011). Child passenger safety. *Pediatrics, 127*(4), e1050-e1066.

Durlak, J. A., Mahoney, J. L., Bohnert, A. M., & Parente, M. E. (2010). Developing and improving after-school programs to enhance youth's personal growth and adjustment. *American Journal of Community Psychology, 45*(3-4), 285-293.

Durlak, J. A., Weissberg, R. P., Dymnicki, A. B., Taylor, R. D., & Schellinger, K. B. (2011). Enhancing students' social and emotional development promotes success in school: Results of a meta-analysis. *Child Development, 82*(1), 405-432.

Dwairy, M., & Achoui, M. (2010). Adolescents-family connectedness: A first cross-cultural research on parenting and psychological adjustment of children. *Journal of Child and Family Studies, 19*(1), 8-15.

Dwyer, T., Ponsonby, A. L., Blizzard, L., Newman, N. M., & Cochrane, J. A. (1995). The contribution of changes in the prevalence of prone sleeping position to the decline in sudden infant death syndrome in Tasmania. *Journal of the American Medical Association, 273*, 783-789.

Dye, B. A., Thornton-Evans, G., Li, X., & Iafolla, T. J. (2015). *Dental caries and sealant prevalence in children and adolescents in the United States, 2011-2012.* Hyattsville, MD: U.S. Department of Health and Human Services, Centers for Disease Control and Prevention, National Center for Health Statistics.

Dye, J. L., & Johnson, T. D. (2009). A child's day: 2006 (selected indicators of child well-being). *Current Population Reports,* P70-118. Washington, DC: U.S. Census Bureau

Dykas, M. J., & Cassidy, J. (2011). Attachment and the processing of social information across the life span: theory and evidence. *Psychological Bulletin, 137*(1), 19.

E

Eckenrode, J., Smith, E. G., McCarthy, M. E., & Dineen, M. (2014). Income inequality and child maltreatment in the United States. *Pediatrics, 133*(3), 454-461.

Eddy, K. T., Dorer, D. J., Franko, D. L., Tahilani, K., Thompson-Brenner, H., & Herzog, D. B. (2008). Diagnostic crossover in anorexia nervosa and bulimia nervosa: Implications for DSM-V. *American Journal of Psychiatry, 165*(2), 245-250.

Eid, M., & Diener, E. (2001). Norms for experiencing emotions in different cultures: Inter- and intranational differences. *Journal of Personality and Social Psychology, 81*(5), 869.

Eidelman, A. I., Schanler, R. J., Johnston, M., Landers, S., Noble, L., Szucs, K., & Viehmann, L. (2012). Breastfeeding and the use of human milk. *Pediatrics, 129*(3), e827-e841.

Einarson, A., & Boskovic, R. (2009). Use and safety of antipsychotic drugs during pregnancy. *Journal of Psychiatric Practice, 15*(3), 183-192.

Eisenberg, M. E., & Neumark-Sztainer, D. (2010). Friends' dieting and disordered eating behaviors among adolescents five years later: Findings from Project EAT. *Journal of Adolescent Health, 47*(1), 67-73.

Eisenberg, N., Eggum, N. D., & Di Giunta, L. (2010). Empathy-related responding: Associations with prosocial behavior, aggression, and intergroup relations. *Social Issues and Policy Review, 4*(1), 143-180.

Eisenberg, N., Fabes, R. A., Nyman, M., Bernzweig, J., & Pinuelas, A. (1994). The relations of emotionality and regulation to children's anger-related reactions. *Child Development, 65*, 109-128.

Eisend, M. (2010). A meta-analysis of gender roles in advertising. *Journal of the Academy of Marketing Science, 38*(4), 418-440.

Eisenegger, C., Haushofer, J., & Fehr, E. (2011). The role of testosterone in social interaction. *Trends in Cognitive Sciences, 15*(6), 263-271.

Ekinci, B. (2014). The relationships among Sternberg's Triarchic Abilities, Gardner's multiple intelligences, and academic achievement. *Social Behavior and Personality: An International Journal, 42*(4), 625-633.

Elgar, F. J., Pförtner, T. K., Moor, I., De Clercq, B., Stevens, G. W., & Currie, C. (2015). Socioeconomic inequalities in adolescent health 2002-2010: A time-series analysis of 34 countries participating in the Health Behaviour in School-aged Children study. *The Lancet, 385*(9982), 2088-2095.

Elledge, L. C., Elledge, A. R., Newgent, R. A., & Cavell, T. A. (2016). Social risk and peer victimization in elementary school children: The protective role of teacher-student relationships. *Journal of Abnormal Child Psychology, 44*(4), 691-703.

Elliot, V. S. (2000). Doctors caught in the middle of ADHD treatment controversy: Critics charge that medications are being both underprescribed and overprescribed. *AMNews*. Retrieved from www.ama.assn.org/ amednews/2000/11/20/hlsb1120.htm

Ellis, A., & Oakes, L. M. (2006). Infants flexibly use different dimensions to categorize objects. *Developmental Psychology, 42*, 1000–1011.

Ellis, B. J., & Del Giudice, M. (2014). Beyond allostatic load: Rethinking the role of stress in regulating human development. *Development and Psychopathology, 26*(1), 1–20.

Ellis, B. J., McFadyen-Ketchum, S., Dodge, K. A., Pettit, G. S., & Bates, J. E. (1999). Quality of early family relationships and individual differences in the timing of pubertal maturation in girls: A longitudinal test of an evolutionary model. *Journal of Personality and Social Psychology, 77*, 387–401.

Ellis, K. J., Abrams, S. A., & Wong, W. W. (1997). Body composition of a young, multiethnic female population. *American Journal of Clinical Nutrition, 65*, 724–731.

Ellis, W. R., & Dietz, W. H. (2017). A new framework for addressing adverse childhood and community experiences: The Building Community Resilience Model. *Academic Pediatrics, 17*(7), S86–S93.

Else-Quest, N. M., Hyde, J. S., & Linn, M. C. (2010). Cross-national patterns of gender differences in mathematics: a meta-analysis. *Psychological Bulletin, 136*(1), 103.

Else-Quest, N. M., & Morse, E. (2015). Ethnic variations in parental ethnic socialization and adolescent ethnic identity: A longitudinal study. *Cultural Diversity and Ethnic Minority Psychology, 21*(1), 54.

El-Sheikh, M., Kelly, R. J., Buckhalt, J. A., & Hinnant, J. B. (2010). Children's sleep and adjustment over time: The role of socioeconomic context. *Child Development, 81*, 870–883. doi: 10.1111/j.1467-8624.2010.01439.x

ElSohly, M. A., Mehmedic, Z., Foster, S., Gon, C., Chandra, S., & Church, J. C. (2016). Changes in cannabis potency over the last 2 decades (1995-2014): Analysis of current data in the United States. *Biological Psychiatry, 79*(7), 613–619.

England, D. E., Descartes, L., & Collier-Meek, M. A. (2011). Gender role portrayal and the Disney princesses. *Sex Roles, 64*(7–8), 555–567.

Erath, S. A., El-Sheikh, M., & Mark Cummings, E. (2009). Harsh parenting and child externalizing behavior: Skin conductance level reactivity as a moderator. *Child Development, 80*(2), 578–592.

Eriksen, M., Mackay, J., & Ross, H. (2013). *The tobacco atlas* (No. Ed. 4). Atlanta: American Cancer Society.

Eriksson, M., Marschik, P. B., Tulviste, T., Almgren, M., Pérez Pereira, M., Wehberg, S., . . . & Gallego, C. (2012). Differences between girls and boys in emerging language skills: Evidence from 10 language communities. *British Journal of Developmental Psychology, 30*(2), 326–343.

Esmaeili, N. S., & Yaacob, S. N. (2011). Post-divorce parental conflict and adolescents' delinquency in divorced families. *Asian Culture and History, 3*(2), 34.

Euling, S. Y., Selevan, S. G., Pescovitz, O. H., & Skakkebaek, N. E. (2008). Role of environmental factors in the timing of puberty. *Pediatrics, 121* (Supplement 3), S167–S171.

Evans, A. D., & Lee, K. (2013). Emergence of lying in very young children. *Developmental Psychology, 49*(10), 1958.

Evans, C. E., Christian, M. S., Cleghorn, C. L., Greenwood, D. C., & Cade, J. E. (2012). Systematic review and meta-analysis of school-based interventions to improve daily fruit and vegetable intake in children aged 5 to 12 years. *The American Journal of Clinical Nutrition, 96*(4), 889–901.

Evans, M. A., & Shaw, D. (2008). Home grown for reading: Parental contributions to young children's emergent literacy and word recognition. *Canadian Psychology/Psychologiecanadienne, 49*(2), 89.

Eveleth, P. B. (2017). Timing of menarche: Secular trend and population differences. In J. B. Lancaster & B. A. Hamburg (Eds.), *School-age pregnancy and parenthood* (pp. 39–52). New York: Routledge.

Ewing, S. W. F., Sakhardande, A., & Blakemore, S. J. (2014). The effect of alcohol consumption on the adolescent brain: A systematic review of MRI and fMRI studies of alcohol-using youth. *NeuroImage: Clinical, 5*, 420–437.

Exner-Cortens, D., Eckenrode, J., Bunge, J., & Rothman, E. (2017). Revictimization after adolescent dating violence in a matched, national sample of youth. *Journal of Adolescent Health, 60*(2), 176–183.

F

Fabes, R. A., Carlo, G., Kupanoff, K., & Laible, D. (1999). Early adolescence and prosocial/moral behavior: I. The role of individual processes. *Journal of Early Adolescence, 19*, 5–16.

Fabes, R. A., Martin, C. L., & Hanish, L. D. (2003). Young children's play qualities in same-, other-, and mixed-gender peer groups. *Child Development, 74*(3), 921–932.

Falkner, B. (2010). Hypertension in children and adolescents: Epidemiology and natural history. *Pediatric Nephrology, 25*(7), 1219–1224.

Fardouly, J., & Vartanian, L. R. (2016). Social media and body image concerns: Current research and future directions. *Current Opinion in Psychology, 9*, 1–5.

Farrell, A. D., Thompson, E. L., & Mehari, K. R. (2017). Dimensions of peer influences and their relationship to adolescents' aggression, other problem behaviors and prosocial behavior. *Journal of Youth and Adolescence, 46*(6), 1351–1369.

Fatima, Y., & Mamun, A. A. (2015). Longitudinal impact of sleep on overweight and obesity in children and adolescents: A systematic review and bias-adjusted meta-analysis. *Obesity Reviews, 16*(2), 137–149.

Fear, J. M., Champion, J. E., Reeslund, K. L., Forehand, R., Colletti, C., Roberts, L., & Compas, B. E. (2009). Parental depression and interparental conflict: Children and adolescents' self-blame and coping responses. *Journal of Family Psychology, 23*(5), 762.

Fearon, R. P., Bakermans-Kranenburg, M. J., Van IJzendoorn, M. H., Lapsley, A. M., & Roisman, G. I. (2010). The significance of insecure attachment and disorganization in the development of children's externalizing behavior: A meta-analytic study. *Child Development, 81*(2), 435–456.

Federal Interagency Forum on Child and Family Statistics. (2015). America's children: Key national indicators of well-being, 2015. Retrieved from www.childstats.gov/pdf/ac2015/ac_15.pdf

Federal Interagency Forum on Child and Family Statistics. (2017). *America's children: Key national indicators of well-being, 2017.* Washington, DC: U.S. Government Printing Office.

Federal Interagency Forum on Child and Family Statistics. *America's Children in Brief: Key National Indicators of Well-Being, 2016.* Washington, DC: U.S. Government Printing Office.

Fedewa, A. L., Black, W. W., & Ahn, S. (2015). Children and adolescents with same-gender parents: A meta-analytic approach in assessing outcomes. *Journal of GLBT Family Studies, 11*(1), 1–34.

Feigenson, L., Dehaene, S., & Spelke, E. (2004). Core systems of number. *Trends in Cognitive Sciences, 8*(7), 307–314.

Feldman, R. (2007). Parent-infant synchrony: Biological foundations and developmental outcomes. *Current Directions in Psychological Science, 16*(6), 340–345.

Feldman, R., Magori-Cohen, R., Galili, G., Singer, M., & Louzoun, Y. (2011). Mother and infant coordinate heart rhythms through episodes of interaction synchrony. *Infant Behavior and Development, 34*(4), 569–577.

Ferguson, C. A. (1964). Baby talk in six languages. *American Anthropologist, 66*(6_PART2), 103–114.

Ferguson, C. J. (2010). Genetic contributions to antisocial personality and behavior: A meta-analytic review from an evolutionary perspective. *The Journal of Social Psychology, 150*(2), 160-180.

Ferguson, C. J. (2013). Violent video games and the Supreme Court: Lessons for the scientific community in the wake of Brown vs. Entertainment Merchant's Association. *American Psychologist, 68*(2), 57-74.

Ferguson, C. J. (2015a). Do angry birds make for angry children? A meta-analysis of video game influences on children's and adolescents' aggression, mental health, prosocial behavior, and academic performance. *Perspectives on Psychological Science, 10*(5), 646-666.

Ferguson, C. J. (2015b). Does media violence predict societal violence? It depends on what you look at and when. *Journal of Communication, 65*(1).

Ferguson, C. J., & Savage, J. (2012). Have recent studies addressed methodological issues raised by five decades of televised violence research? A critical review. *Aggression and Violent Behavior, 17,* 129-139.

Fergusson, D. M., McLeod, G. F., & Horwood, L. J. (2013). Childhood sexual abuse and adult developmental outcomes: Findings from a 30-year longitudinal study in New Zealand. *Child Abuse & Neglect, 37*(9), 664-674.

Fernald, A., Perfors, A., & Marchman, V. A. (2006). Picking up speed in understanding: Speech processing efficiency and vocabulary growth across the second year. *Developmental Psychology, 42,* 98-116.

Fernald, A., Swingley, D., & Pinto, J. P. (2001). When half a word is enough: Infants can recognize spoken words using partial phonetic information. *Child Development, 72,* 1003-1015.

Fernbach, P. M., Macris, D. M., & Sobel, D. M. (2012). Which one made it go? The emergence of diagnostic reasoning in preschoolers. *Cognitive Development, 27*(1), 39-53.

Ferraro, A. J., Malespin, T., Oehme, K., Bruker, M., & Opel, A. (2016). Advancing co-parenting education: Toward a foundation for supporting positive post-divorce adjustment. *Child and Adolescent Social Work Journal, 33*(5), 407-415.

Ferrer, E., Shaywitz, B. A., Holahan, J. M., Marchione, K., & Shaywitz, S. E. (2010). Uncoupling of reading and IQ over time: Empirical evidence for a definition of dyslexia. *Psychological Science, 21*(1), 93-101.

Ferry, A. L., Hespos, S. J., & Waxman, S. R. (2010). Categorization in 3- and 4-month-old infants: An advantage of words over tones. *Child Development, 81*(2), 472-479.

Finer, L. B., & Philbin, J. M. (2014). Trends in ages at key reproductive transitions in the United States, 1951-2010. *Women's Health Issues, 24*(3), e271-e279.

Fink, E., Deighton, J., Humphrey, N., & Wolpert, M. (2015). Assessing the bullying and victimisation experiences of children with special educational needs in mainstream schools: Development and validation of the Bullying Behaviour and Experience Scale. *Research in Developmental Disabilities, 36,* 611-619.

Finn, J. D. (2006). *The adult lives of at-risk students: The roles of attainment and engagement in high school* (NCES 2006-328). Washington, DC: U.S. Department of Education, National Center for Education Statistics.

Fischer, J. L. (1981). Transitions in relationship style from adolescence to young adulthood. *Journal of Youth and Adolescence, 10*(1), 11-23.

Fishbein, H. D., & Imai, S. (1993). Preschoolers select playmates on the basis of gender and race. *Journal of Applied Developmental Psychology, 14*(3), 303-316.

Fisher, K. R., Hirsh-Pasek, K., Newcombe, N., & Golinkoff, R. M. (2013). Taking shape: Supporting preschoolers' acquisition of geometric knowledge through guided play. *Child Development, 84*(6), 1872-1878.

Fitzpatrick, E. M., Thibert, J., Grandpierre, V., & Johnston, J. C. (2014). How HANDy are baby signs? A systematic review of the impact of gestural communication on typically developing, hearing infants under the age of 36 months. *First Language, 34*(6), 486-509.

Fitzpatrick, M. J., & McPherson, B. J. (2010). Coloring within the lines: Gender stereotypes in contemporary coloring books. *Sex Roles, 62*(1-2), 127-137.

Fivush, R. (2011). The development of autobiographical memory. *Annual Review of Psychology, 62,* 559-582.

Fivush, R., Habermas, T., Waters, T. E., & Zaman, W. (2011). The making of autobiographical memory: Intersections of culture, narratives and identity. *International Journal of Psychology, 46*(5), 321-345.

Fivush, R., & Haden, C. A. (2006). Elaborating on elaborations: Role of maternal reminiscing style in cognitive and socioemotional development. *Child Development, 77,* 1568-1588.

Fjell, A. M., Grydeland, H., Krogsrud, S. K., Amlien, I., Rohani, D. A., Ferschmann, L., . . . & Bjørnerud, A. (2015). Development and aging of cortical thickness correspond to genetic organization patterns. *Proceedings of the National Academy of Sciences, 112*(50), 15462-15467.

Flammarion, S., Santos, C., Guimber, D., Jouannic, L., Thumerelle, C., Gottrand, F., & Deschildre, A. (2011). Diet and nutritional status of children with food allergies. *Pediatric Allergy and Immunology, 22*(2), 161-165.

Flannagan, C. A., Bowes, J. M., Jonsson, B., Csapo, B., & Sheblanova, E. (1998). Ties that bind: Correlates of adolescents' civic commitment in seven countries. *Journal of Social Issues, 54,* 457-475.

Flavell, J. H., Flavell, E. R., & Green, F. L. (1983). Development of the appearance-reality distinction. *Cognitive Psychology, 15*(1), 95-120.

Flavell, J. H., Green, F. L., & Flavell, E. R. (1986). Development of knowledge about the appearance-reality distinction. *Monographs of the Society for Research in Child Development, 51*(1, Serial No. 212).

Flavell, J. H., Green, F. L., Flavell, E. R., & Grossman, J. B. (1997). The development of children's knowledge about inner speech. *Child Development, 68,* 39-47.

Flavell, J. H., Miller, P. H., & Miller, S. A. (2002). *Cognitive development.* Englewood Cliffs, NJ: Prentice Hall.

Flewitt, R., Messer, D., & Kucirkova, N. (2015). New directions for early literacy in a digital age: The iPad. *Journal of Early Childhood Literacy, 15*(3), 289-310.

Flores, G. (2010). Technical report—racial and ethnic disparities in the health and health care of children. *Pediatrics,* peds-2010.

Flynn, H. K., Felmlee, D. H., & Conger, R. D. (2017). The social context of adolescent friendships: Parents, peers, and romantic partners. *Youth & Society, 49*(5), 679-705.

Flynn, J. (2013). The changing face of pediatric hypertension in the era of the childhood obesity epidemic. *Pediatric Nephrology, 28*(7), 1059-1066.

Folmer-Annevelink, E., Doolaard, S., Mascareño, M., & Bosker, R. J. (2010). Class size effects on the number and types of student-teacher interactions in primary classrooms. *The Journal of Classroom Interaction,* 30-38.

Foltz, J. L., Cook, S. R., Szilagyi, P. G., Auinger, P., Stewart, P. A., Bucher, S., & Baldwin, C. D. (2011). U.S. adolescent nutrition, exercise, and screen time baseline levels prior to national recommendations. *Clinical Pediatrics, 50*(5), 424-433.

Fong, A., King, E., Duffy, J., Wu, E., Pan, D., & Ogunyemi, D. (2016). Declining VBAC rates despite improved delivery outcomes compared to repeat cesarean delivery [20Q]. *Obstetrics & Gynecology, 127,* 144S.

Fonner, V. A., Armstrong, K. S., Kennedy, C. E., O'Reilly, K. R., & Sweat, M. D. (2014). School based sex education and HIV prevention in low-and middle-income countries: A systematic review and meta-analysis. *PloS One, 9*(3), e89692.

Forget-Dubois, N., Dionne, G., Lemelin, J.-P., Pérusse, D., Tremblay, R. E., & Boivin, M. (2009). Early child language mediates the relation between home environment and school readiness. *Child Development, 80,* 736-749. doi: 10.1111/j.1467-8624.2009.01294.x

Forss, H., Walsh, T., Hiiri, A., Nordblad, A., Mäkelä, M., & Hv, W. (2013). Sealants for preventing dental decay in the permanent teeth. *Cochrane Database Syst Rev, 3*, CD001830.

Fortinguerra, F., Clavenna, A., & Bonati, M. (2009). Psychotropic drug use during breastfeeding: A review of the evidence. *Pediatrics, 124*(4), e547–e556.

Fosco, G. M., & Grych, J. H. (2010). Adolescent triangulation into parental conflicts: Longitudinal implications for appraisals and adolescent-parent relations. *Journal of Marriage and Family, 72*(2), 254–266.

Fosco, G. M., Stormshak, E. A., Dishion, T. J., & Winter, C. E. (2012). Family relationships and parental monitoring during middle school as predictors of early adolescent problem behavior. *Journal of Clinical Child & Adolescent Psychology, 41*(2), 202–213.

Foster, E. M., & Watkins, S. (2010). The value of reanalysis: TV viewing and attention problems. *Child Development, 81*(1), 368–375. doi: 10.1111/j.1467-8624.2009.01400.x

Foundation for Child Development. (2015). Children's experience with parental employment insecurity and income inequality. Retrieved from https://www.fcd-us.org/childrens-experience-parental-employment-insecurity-family-income-inequality/

Fox, N. A., Hane, A. A., & Pine, D. S. (2007). Plasticity for affective neurocircuitry: How the environment affects gene expression. *Current Directions in Psychological Science, 16*(1), 1–5.

Fox, N. A., Henderson, H. A., Rubin, K. H., Calkins, S. D., & Schmidt, L. A. (2001). Continuity and discontinuity of behavioral inhibition and exuberance: Psychophysiological and behavioral influences across the first four years of life. *Child Development, 72*(1), 1–21.

Franceschi, R., Gaudino, R., Marcolongo, A., Gallo, M. C., Rossi, L., Antoniazzi, F., & Tatò, L. (2010). Prevalence of polycystic ovary syndrome in young women who had idiopathic central precocious puberty. *Fertility and Sterility, 93*(4), 1185–1191.

Frank, D. A., Augustyn, M., Knight, W. G., Pell, T., & Zuckerman, B. (2001). Growth, development, and behavior in early childhood following prenatal cocaine exposure. *Journal of the American Medical Association, 285*, 1613–1625.

Franks, P. W., Hanson, R. L., Knowler, W. C., Sievers, M. L., Bennett, P. H., & Looker, H. C. (2010). Childhood obesity, other cardiovascular risk factors, and premature death. *New England Journal of Medicine, 362*(6), 485–493.

Franks, S. (2009). Polycystic ovary syndrome. *Medicine, 37*(9), 441–444.

Fredricks, J. A., & Eccles, J. S. (2010). Breadth of extracurricular participation and adolescent adjustment among African-American and European-American youth. *Journal of Research on Adolescence, 20*(2), 307–333.

Freeark, K., Rosenberg, E. B., Bornstein, J., Jozefowicz-Simbeni, D., Linkevich, M., & Lohnes, K. (2005). Gender differences and dynamics shaping the adoption life cycle: Review of the literature and recommendations. *American Journal of Orthopsychiatry, 75*, 86–101.

Freeman, C. E. (2004). Trends in educational equity of girls & women: 2004. NCES 2005–016. *National Center for Education Statistics*.

French, D. C., Purwono, U., & Rodkin, P. C. (2012). Religiosity of adolescents and their friends and network associates: Homophily and associations with antisocial behavior. *Journal of Research on Adolescence, 22*, 326–333. doi:10.1111/j.1532-7795.2012.00778.x

French, S. E., Seidman, E., Allen, L., & Aber, J. L. (2006). The development of ethnic identity during adolescence. *Developmental Psychology, 42*, 1–10.

Fried, P. A. (2002). Adolescents prenatally exposed to marijuana: Examination of facets of complex behaviors and comparisons with the influence of in utero cigarettes. *The Journal of Clinical Pharmacology, 42*(S1).

Friederici, A. D. (2011). The brain basis of language processing: From structure to function. *Physiological Reviews, 91*(4), 1357–1392.

Fries, A. B. W., Ziegler, T. E., Kurian, J. R., Jacoris, S., & Pollak, S. D. (2005). Early experiences in humans is associated with changes in neuropeptides critical for regulating social behavior. *Proceedings of the National Academy of Sciences, USA, 102*, 17237–17240.

Friesen, M. D., Horwood, L. J., Fergusson, D. M., & Woodward, L. J. (2017). Exposure to parental separation in childhood and later parenting quality as an adult: Evidence from a 30-year longitudinal study. *Journal of Child Psychology and Psychiatry, 58*(1), 30–37.

Frigerio-Domingues, C., & Drayna, D. (2017). Genetic contributions to stuttering: The current evidence. *Molecular Genetics & Genomic Medicine, 5*(2), 95–102.

Froehlich, T. E., Lanphear, B. P., Auinger, P., Hornung, R., Epstein, J. N., Braun, J., & Kahn, R. S. (2009). Association of tobacco and lead exposures with attention-deficit/hyperactivity disorder. *Pediatrics, 124*(6), e1054–e1063. doi: 10.1542/peds.2009-0738

Fromkin, V., Krashen, S., Curtiss, S., Rigler, D., & Rigler, M. (1974). The development of language in Genie: A case of language acquisition beyond the "critical period." *Brain and Language, 1*(1), 81–107.

Fryar, C. D., Carroll, M. D., & Ogden, C. L. (2012). Prevalence of obesity among children and adolescents: United States, trends 1963–1965 through 2009–2010. National Center for Health Statistics. *Health E-Stats, 1*–6.

Fryar, C. D., Carroll, M. D., & Ogden, C. (2016). Prevalence of overweight and obesity among children and adolescents aged 2–19 years: United States, 1963–1965 through 2013–2014. *Health E-Stats, 1*–5.

Fryar, C. D., Gu, Q., Ogden, C. L., & Flegal, K. M. (2016). Anthropometric reference data for children and adults; United States, 2011–2014. *Vital and Health Statistics, 3*(39). Hyattsville, MD: National Center for Health Statistics.

Frye, C., Bo, E., Calamandrei, G., Calza, L., Dessi-Fulgheri, F., Fernández, M., . . . & Patisaul, H. B. (2012). Endocrine disrupters: A review of some sources, effects, and mechanisms of actions on behaviour and neuroendocrine systems. *Journal of Neuroendocrinology, 24*(1), 144–159.

Frye, D. (2014). *Children's theories of mind: Mental states and social understanding*. London: Psychology Press.

Fujimoto, K., & Valente, T. W. (2012). Decomposing the components of friendship and friends' influence on adolescent drinking and smoking. *Journal of Adolescent Health, 51*(2), 136–143.

Fuqua, J. S. (2013). Treatment and outcomes of precocious puberty: An update. *The Journal of Clinical Endocrinology & Metabolism, 98*(6), 2198–2207.

Furman, W., & Bierman, K. L. (1983). Developmental changes in young children's conception of friendship. *Child Development, 54*, 549–556.

Furukawa, E., Tangney, J., & Higashibara, F. (2012). Cross-cultural continuities and discontinuities in shame, guilt, and pride: A study of children residing in Japan, Korea and the USA. *Self and Identity, 11*(1), 90–113.

G

Gagne, J. R., & Saudino, K. J. (2010). Wait for it! A twin study of inhibitory control in early childhood. *Behavioral Genetics, 40*(3), 327–337.

Galal, M., Symonds, I., Murray, H., Petraglia, F., & Smith, R. (2012). Postterm pregnancy. *Facts, Views & Vision in ObGyn, 4*(3), 175.

Galanaki, E. P. (2012). The imaginary audience and the personal fable: A test of Elkind's theory of adolescent egocentrism. *Psychology, 3*(6), 457.

Galland, B. C., Taylor, B. J., Elder, D. E., & Herbison, P. (2012). Normal sleep patterns in infants and children: A systematic review of observational studies. *Sleep Medicine Reviews, 16*(3), 213–222.

Galvao, T. F., Silva, M. T., Zimmermann, I. R., Souza, K. M., Martins, S. S., & Pereira, M. G. (2014). Pubertal timing in girls and depression: A systematic review. *Journal of Affective Disorders, 155*, 13–19.

Gameiro, S., & Finnigan, A. (2017). Long-term adjustment to unmet parenthood goals following ART: A systematic review and meta-analysis. *Human Reproduction Update, 23*(3), 322–337.

Ganger, J., & Brent, M. R. (2004). Reexamining the vocabulary spurt. *Developmental Psychology, 40*, 621–632.

Garandeau, C. F., Ahn, H. J., & Rodkin, P. C. (2011). The social status of aggressive students across contexts: The role of classroom status hierarchy, academic achievement, and grade. *Developmental Psychology, 47*(6), 1699.

Garcia, F., & Gracia, E. (2009). Is always authoritative the optimum parenting style? Evidence from Spanish families. *Adolescence, 44*(173), 101.

Gardner, H. (1993). *Frames of mind: The theory of multiple intelligences.* New York: Basic Books. (Original work published 1983)

Gardner, H. (1998). Are there additional intelligences? In J. Kane (Ed.), *Education, information, and transformation: Essays on learning and thinking.* Englewood Cliffs, NJ: Prentice Hall.

Garn, A. C., Matthews, M. S., & Jolly, J. L. (2010). Parental influences on the academic motivation of gifted students: A self-determination theory perspective. *Gifted Child Quarterly, 54*(4), 263–272.

Garner, A. A., Miller, M. M., Field, J., Noe, O., Smith, Z., & Beebe, D. W. (2015). Impact of experimentally manipulated sleep on adolescent simulated driving. *Sleep Medicine, 16*(6), 796–799.

Garthe, R. C., Sullivan, T. N., & McDaniel, M. A. (2017). A meta-analytic review of peer risk factors and adolescent dating violence. *Psychology of Violence, 7*(1), 45.

Gartstein, M. A., Slobodskaya, H. R., Olaf Zylicz, P., Gosztyla, D., & Nakagawa, A. (2010). A cross-cultural evaluation of temperament: Japan, USA, Poland and Russia. *International Journal of Psychology and Psychological Therapy, 10*(1).

Gasana, J., Dillikar, D., Mendy, A., Forno, E., & Vieira, E. R. (2012). Motor vehicle air pollution and asthma in children: A meta-analysis. *Environmental Research, 117*, 36–45.

Gaskins, S., Haight, W., & Lancy, D. F. (2007). The cultural construction of play. In A. Göncü & S. Gaskins (Eds.), *Play and development: Evolutionary, sociocultural, and functional perspectives* (pp. 179–202), New York: Lawrence Erlbaum Associates.

Gates, G. J. (2013). LBGT parenting in the United States. Retrieved from http://williamsinstitute.law.ucla.edu/wp-content/uploads/LGBT-Parenting.pdf

Gatewood, J. D., Wills, A., Shetty, S., Xu, J., Arnold, A. P., Burgoyne, P. S., & Rissman, E. F. (2006). Sex chromosome complement and gonadal sex influence aggressive and parental behaviors in mice. *Journal of Neuroscience, 26*, 2335–2342.

Gathercole, S. E., & Alloway, T. P. (2008). Working memory and classroom learning. In S. K. Thurman & C. A. Fiorello (Eds.), *Applied cognitive research in K-3 classrooms* (pp. 17–40), New York: Routledge.

Gathercole, S. E., Pickering, S. J., Ambridge, B., & Wearing, H. (2004). The structure of working memory from 4 to 15 years of age. *Developmental Psychology, 40*(2), 177.

Gauvain, M., & Perez, S. M. (2005). Parent-child participation in planning children's activities outside of school in European American and Latino families. *Child Development, 76*, 371–383.

Gazes, R. P., Hampton, R. R., & Lourenco, S. F. (2017). Transitive inference of social dominance by human infants. *Developmental Science, 20*(2).

Gazzaley, A., & Nobre, A. C. (2012). Top-down modulation: Bridging selective attention and working memory. *Trends in Cognitive Sciences, 16*(2), 129–135.

Geangu, E., Benga, O., Stahl, D., & Striano, T. (2010). Contagious crying beyond the first days of life. *Infant Behavior and Development, 33*(3), 279–288.

Gee, J., Naleway, A., Shui, I., Baggs, J., Yin, R., Li R., . . . & Klein, N. P. (2011). Monitoring the safety of quadrivalent human papillomavirus vaccine: Findings from the Vaccine Safety Datalink. *Vaccine, 29*(46), 8279–8284.

Geen, R. (2004). The evolution of kinship care: Policy and practice. *Future of Children 14 (1).* (David and Lucile Packard Foundation). Retrieved from wwww.futureofchildren.org

Gelman, R., Spelke, E. S., & Meck, E. (1983). What preschoolers know about animate and inanimate objects. In D. R. Rogers & J. S. Sloboda (Eds.), *The acquisition of symbolic skills* (pp. 297–326). New York: Plenum Press.

Gelman, S. A., Taylor, M. G., Nguyen, S. P., Leaper, C., & Bigler, R. S. (2004). Mother-child conversations about gender: Understanding the acquisition of essentialist beliefs. *Monographs of the Society for Research in Child Development*, i-142.

Genesee, F., Nicoladis, E., & Paradis, J. (1995). Language differentiation in early bilingual development. *Journal of Child Language, 22*, 611–631.

Gentile, D. (2009). Pathological video-game use among youth ages 8 to 18: A national study. *Psychological Science, 20*(5), 594–602.

Gentile, D. A., Bender, P. K., & Anderson, C. A. (2017). Violent video game effects on salivary cortisol, arousal, and aggressive thoughts in children. *Computers in Human Behavior, 70*, 39–43.

Gershoff, E. T. (2002). Corporal punishment by parents and associated child behaviors and experiences: A meta-analytic and theoretical review. *Psychological Bulletin, 128*(4), 539.

Gershoff, E. T. (2010). More harm than good: A summary of scientific research on the intended and unintended effects of corporal punishment on children. *Law and Contemporary Problems, 73*(2), 31–56.

Gershoff, E. T. (2013). Spanking and child development: We know enough now to stop hitting our children. *Child Development Perspectives, 7*(3), 133–137.

Gershoff, E. T., Grogan-Kaylor, A., Lansford, J. E., Chang, L., Zelli, A., Deater-Deckard, K., & Dodge, K. A. (2010). Parent discipline practices in an international sample: Associations with child behaviors and moderation by perceived normativeness. *Child Development, 81*(2), 487–502.

Gershoff, E. T., Lansford, J. E., Sexton, H. R., Davis-Kean, P., & Sameroff, A. J. (2012). Longitudinal links between spanking and children's externalizing behaviors in a national sample of white, black, Hispanic, and Asian American families. *Child Development, 83*(3), 838–843.

Gervain, J., & Mehler, J. (2010). Speech perception and language acquisition in the first year of life. *Annual Review of Psychology, 61*, 191–218.

Gest, S. D. (1997). Behavioral inhibition: Stability and associations with adaptation from childhood to early adulthood. *Journal of Personality and Social Psychology, 72*(2), 467.

Gibson, E. J., & Walker, A. S. (1984). Development of knowledge of visual-tactual affordances of substance. *Child Development*, 453–460.

Giedd, J. N., & Rapoport, J. L. (2010). Structural MRI of pediatric brain development: What have we learned and where are we going? *Neuron, 67*(5), 728–734.

Giedd, J. N., Lalonde, F. M., Celano, M. J., White, S. L., Wallace, G. L., Lee, N. R., & Lenroot, R. K. (2009). Anatomical brain magnetic resonance imaging of typically developing children and adolescents. *Journal of the American Academy of Child and Adolescent Psychiatry, 48*(5), 465.

Gilboa, S., Correa, A., Botto, L., Rasmussen, S., Waller, D., Hobbs, C., . . . Riehle-Colarusso, T. J. (2009). Association between prepregnancy body mass index and congenital heart defects. *American Journal of Obstetrics and Gynecology, 202*(1), 51–61.

Gillen, M. M., & Lefkowitz, E. S. (2012). Gender and racial/ethnic differences in body image development among college students. *Body Image, 9*(1), 126–130.

Giménez-Dasí, M., Pons, F., & Bender, P. K. (2016). Imaginary companions, theory of mind and emotion understanding in young children. *European Early Childhood Education Research Journal, 24*(2), 186–197.

Giri, B. (2016). Fluoride fact on human health and health problems: A review. *Medical & Clinical Reviews, 2*(1).

Glaser, D. (2000). Child abuse and neglect and the brain: A review. *Journal of Child Psychiatry, 41*, 97-116.

Glass, H. C., Costarino, A. T., Stayer, S. A., Brett, C., Cladis, F., & Davis, P. J. (2015). Outcomes for extremely premature infants. *Anesthesia and Analgesia, 120*(6), 1337.

Gleason, T. R., & Kalpidou, M. (2014). Imaginary companions and young children's coping and competence. *Social Development, 23*(4), 820-839.

Gleason, T. R., Sebanc, A. M., & Hartup, W. W. (2000). Imaginary companions of preschool children. *Developmental Psychology, 36*, 419-428.

Glick, G. C., & Rose, A. J. (2011). Prospective associations between friendship adjustment and social strategies: Friendship as a context for building social skills. *Developmental Psychology, 47*(4), 1117.

Goble, P., Martin, C. L., Hanish, L. D., & Fabes, R. A. (2012). Children's gender-typed activity choices across preschool social contexts. *Sex Roles, 67*(7-8), 435-451.

Goertz, C., Lamm, B., Graf, F., Kolling, T., Knopf, M., & Keller, H. (2011). Deferred imitation in 6-month-old German and Cameroonian Nso infants. *Journal of Cognitive Education and Psychology, 10*(1), 44.

Gogtay, N., & Thompson, P. M. (2010). Mapping gray matter development: Implications for typical development and vulnerability to psychopathology. *Brain and Cognition, 72*(1), 6-15.

Gogtay, N., Giedd, J. N., Lusk, L., Hayashi, K. M., Greenstein, D., Vaituzis, A. C., . . . & Rapoport, J. L. (2004). Dynamic mapping of human cortical development during childhood through early adulthood. *Proceedings of the National academy of Sciences of the United States of America, 101*(21), 8174-8179.

Goldberg, A. E., & Garcia, R. L. (2016). Gender-typed behavior over time in children with lesbian, gay, and heterosexual parents. *Journal of Family Psychology, 30*(7), 854.

Goldberg, A. E., Kashy, D. A., & Smith, J. Z. (2012). Gender-typed play behavior in early childhood: Adopted children with lesbian, gay, and heterosexual parents. *Sex Roles, 67*(9-10), 503-515.

Goldberg, W. A., Prause, J. A., Lucas-Thompson, R., & Himsel, A. (2008). Maternal employment and children's achievement in context: A meta-analysis of four decades of research. *Psychological Bulletin, 134*, 77-108.

Goldin-Meadow, S. (2007). Pointing sets the stage for learning language—And creating language. *Child Development, 78*(3), 741-745.

Goldschmidt, L., Richardson, G. A., Cornelius, M. D., & Day, N. L. (2004). Prenatal marijuana and alcohol exposure and academic achievement at age 10. *Neurotoxicology and Teratology, 26*(4), 521-532.

Goldstein, J., McCoach, D. B., & Yu, H. (2017). The predictive validity of kindergarten readiness judgments: Lessons from one state. *The Journal of Educational Research, 110*(1), 50-60.

Goldstein, M. H., Schwade, J. A., & Bornstein, M. H. (2009). The value of vocalizing: Five-month-old infants associate their own noncry vocalizations with responses from caregivers. *Child Development, 80*(3), 636-644.

Goldstein, N. A., Abramowitz, T., Weedon, J., Koliskor, B., Turner, S., & Taioli, E. (2011). Racial/ethnic differences in the prevalence of snoring and sleep disordered breathing in young children. *Journal of Clinical Sleep Medicine: JCSM: Official Publication of the American Academy of Sleep Medicine, 7*(2), 163.

Goldstein, S. E., Davis-Kean, P. E., & Eccles, J. E. (2005). Parents, peers, and problem behavior: A longitudinal investigation of the impact of relationship perceptions and characteristics on the development of adolescent problem behavior. *Developmental Psychology, 2*, 401-413.

Golinkoff, R. M., Can, D. D., Soderstrom, M., & Hirsh-Pasek, K. (2015). (Baby) talk to me: The social context of infant-directed speech and its effects on early language acquisition. *Current Directions in Psychological Science, 24*(5), 339-344.

Golinkoff, R. M., & Hirsch-Pasek, K. (2006). Baby wordsmith. *Current Directions in Psychological Science, 15*, 30-33.

Golmaryami, F. N., Frick, P. J., Hemphill, S. A., Kahn, R. E., Crapanzano, A. M., & Terranova, A. M. (2016). The social, behavioral, and emotional correlates of bullying and victimization in a school-based sample. *Journal of Abnormal Child Psychology, 44*(2), 381-391.

Golombok, S., Mellish, L., Jennings, S., Casey, P., Tasker, F., & Lamb, M. E. (2013). Adoptive gay father families: Parent-child relationships and children's psychological adjustment. *Child Development.* doi: 10.1111/cdev.12155

Gómez-Robles, A., Hopkins, W. D., & Sherwood, C. C. (2013, June). Increased morphological asymmetry, evolvability and plasticity in human brain evolution. In *Proc. R. Soc. B* (Vol. 280, No. 1761, p. 20130575). London: The Royal Society.

Goodman, G. S., Emery, R. E., & Haugaard, J. J. (1998). Developmental psychology and law: Divorce, child maltreatment, foster care, and adoption. In W. Damon (Series Ed.), I. E. Sigel & K. A. Renninger (Vol. Eds.), *Handbook of child psychology* (Vol. 4, pp. 775-874). New York: Wiley.

Goraya, F., & Shamama-tus-Sabah, S. (2013). Parenting, children's behavioral problems, and the social information processing among children. *Pakistan Journal of Psychological Research, 28*(1), 107.

Gordon, I., Zagoory-Sharon, O., Leckman, J. F., & Feldman, R. (2010). Oxytocin and the development of parenting in humans. *Biological Psychiatry, 68*(4), 377-382.

Gottfried, A. E., & Gottfried, A. W. (Eds.). (2013). *Maternal employment and children's development: Longitudinal research.* Berlin: Springer Science & Business Media.

Gottfried, A. E., Preston, K. S. J., Gottfried, A. W., Oliver, P. H., Delany, D. E., & Ibrahim, S. M. (2016). Pathways from parental stimulation of children's curiosity to high school science course accomplishments and science career interest and skill. *International Journal of Science Education, 38*(12), 1972-1995.

Gould, E., Reeves, A. J., Graziano, M. S. A., & Gross, C. G. (1999). Neurogenesis in the neocortex of adult primates. *Science, 286*, 548-552.

Grabe, S., Ward, L. M., & Hyde, J. S. (2008). The role of the media in body image concerns among women: A meta-analysis of experimental and correlational studies. *Psychological Bulletin, 134*(3), 460.

Grace, D. M., David, B. J., & Ryan, M. K. (2008). Investigating preschoolers' categorical thinking about gender through imitation, attention, and the use of self-categories. *Child Development, 79*(6), 1928-1941.

Graham, K. L., & Burghardt, G. M. (2010). Current perspectives on the biological study of play: Signs of progress. *The Quarterly Review of Biology, 85*, 393-418.

Grammer, J., Coffman, J. L., & Ornstein, P. (2013). The effect of teachers' memory-relevant language on children's strategy use and knowledge. *Child Development, 84*(6), 1989-2002.

Granier-Deferre, C., Ribeiro, A., Jacquet, A. Y., & Bassereau, S. (2011). Near-term fetuses process temporal features of speech. *Developmental Science, 14*(2), 336-352.

Greene, M. L., Way, N., & Pahl, K. (2006). Trajectories of perceived adult and peer discrimination among black, Latino, and Asian American adolescents: Patterns and psychological correlates. *Developmental Psychology, 42*(2), 218.

Greenwood, D. C., Thatcher, N. J., Ye, J., Garrard, L., Keogh, G., King, L. G., & Cade, J. E. (2014). Caffeine intake during pregnancy and adverse birth outcomes: A systematic review and dose-response meta-analysis. *European Journal of Epidemiology, 29*(10), 725.

Gregory, S., Simmons, A., Kumari, V., Howard, M., Hodgins, S., & Blackwood, N. (2012). The antisocial brain: Psychopathy matters: A structural MRI investigation of antisocial male violent offenders. *Archives of General Psychiatry, 69*(9), 962-972.

Griffin, K. W., Botvin, G. J., Scheier, L. M., Diaz, T., & Miller, N. L. (2000). Parenting practices as predictors of substance use, delinquency, and aggression among urban minority youth: Moderating effects of family structure and gender. *Psychology of Addictive Behaviors: Journal of the Society of Psychologists in Addictive Behaviors, 14*(2), 174.

Grigorenko, E. L., Meier, E., Lipka, J., Mohatt, G., Yanez, E., & Sternberg, R. J. (2004). Academic and practical intelligence: A case study of the Yup'ik in Alaska. *Learning and Individual Differences, 14*(4), 183-207.

Grigoriadis, S., VonderPorten, E. H., Mamisashvili, L., Tomlinson, G., Dennis, C. L., Koren, G., . . . & Martinovic, J. (2013). The impact of maternal depression during pregnancy on perinatal outcomes: A systematic review and meta-analysis. *Journal of Clinical Psychiatry, 74*(4), e321-e341.

Grimbos, T., Dawood, K., Burriss, R. P., Zucker, K. J., & Puts, D. A. (2010). Sexual orientation and the second to fourth finger length ratio: A meta-analysis in men and women. *Behavioral Neuroscience, 124*(2), 278-287.

Grinshteyn, E., & Hemenway, D. (2016). Violent death rates: The US compared with other high-income OECD countries, 2010. *The American Journal of Medicine, 129*(3), 266-273.

Groen, R. S., Bae, J. Y., & Lim, K. J. (2012). Fear of the unknown: Ionizing radiation exposure during pregnancy. *American Journal of Obstetrics & Gynecology, 206*(6), 456-462.

Groh, A. M., Fearon, R. P., Bakermans-Kranenburg, M. J., Van IJzendoorn, M. H., Steele, R. D., & Roisman, G. I. (2014). The significance of attachment security for children's social competence with peers: A meta-analytic study. *Attachment & Human Development, 16*(2), 103-136.

Grotevant, H. D. (2012). What works in open adoption. In P. A. Curtis & G. Alexander (Eds). *What works in child welfare.* Washington, DC: Child Welfare League of America.

Grotevant, H. D., McRoy, R. G., Eide, C. L., & Fravel, D. L. (1994). Adoptive family system dynamics: Variations by level of openness in the adoption. *Family Process, 33*(2), 125-146.

Grotevant, H. D., McRoy, R. G., Wrobel, G. M., & Ayers-Lopez, S. (2013). Contact between adoptive and birth families: Perspectives from the Minnesota/Texas Adoption Research Project. *Child Development Perspectives, 7*(3), 193-198.

Gruber, J. (2004). Is making divorce easier bad for children? The long-run implications of unilateral divorce. *Journal of Labor Economics, 22*(4), 799-833.

Gruber, K. J., Cupito, S. H., & Dobson, C. F. (2013). Impact of doulas on healthy birth outcomes. *The Journal of Perinatal Education, 22*(1), 49.

Grusec, J. E. (2006). The development of moral behavior and conscience from a socialization perspective. *Handbook of Moral Development,* 243-265.

Grusec, J. E., & Goodnow, J. J. (1994). Impact of parental discipline methods on the child's internalization of values: A reconceptualization of current points of view. *Developmental Psychology, 30,* 4-19.

Guberman, S. R. (1999). Cultural aspects of young children's mathematics knowledge.

Guberman, S. R. (2004). A comparative study of children's out-of-school activities and arithmetic achievements. *Journal for Research in Mathematics Education,* 117-150.

Guedes, A., & Mikton, C. (2013). Examining the intersections between child maltreatment and intimate partner violence. *Western Journal of Emergency Medicine, 14*(4), 377.

Guendelman, S., Kosa, J. L., Pearl, M., Graham, S., Goodman, J., & Kharrazi, M. (2009). Juggling work and breastfeeding: Effects of maternity leave and occupational characteristics. *Pediatrics, 123,* e38-e46.

Guillery, R. W. (2005). Is postnatal neocortical maturation hierarchical? *Trends in Neurosciences, 28*(10), 512-517.

Gunderson, E. A., Gripshover, S. J., Romero, C., Dweck, C. S., Goldin-Meadow, S., & Levine, S. C. (2013). Parent praise to 1- to 3-year-olds predicts children's motivational frameworks 5 years later. *Child Development, 84*(5), 1526-1541.

Gurteen, P. M., Horne, P. J., & Erjavec, M. (2011). Rapid word learning in 13- and 17-month-olds in a naturalistic two-word procedure: Looking versus reaching measures. *Journal of Experimental Child Psychology, 109*(2), 201-217.

Guttmacher Institute. (2013). Facts on American teens' sexual and reproductive health. Retrieved from http://www.guttmacher.org/pubs/FB-ATSRH.html#6

Guttmacher Institute. (2016). American teens' sexual and reproductive health [fact sheet]. Retrieved from www.guttmacher.org/fact-sheet/american-teens-sexual-and-reproductive-health-old

Guttmacher Institute. (2017). The looming threat to sex education: A resurgence of federal funding for abstinence-on programs? [News release]. Retrieved from www.guttmacher.org/gpr/2017/03/looming-threat-sex-education-resurgence-federal-funding-abstinence-only-programs

Guzzetta, A., D'Acunto, M. G., Carotenuto, M., Berardi, N., Bancale, A., Biagioni, E., . . . & Cioni, G. (2011). The effects of preterm infant massage on brain electrical activity. *Developmental Medicine & Child Neurology, 53*(s4), 46-51.

H

Haas, C., Takayoshi, P., Carr, B., Hudson, K., & Pollock, R. (2011). Young people's everyday literacies: The language features of instant messaging. *Research in the Teaching of English,* 378-404.

Haastrup, M. B., Pottegård, A., & Damkier, P. (2014). Alcohol and breastfeeding. *Basic & Clinical Pharmacology & Toxicology, 114*(2), 168-173.

Hackman, D. A., Farah, M. J., & Meaney, M. J. (2010). Socioeconomic status and the brain: Mechanistic insights from human and animal research. *Nature Reviews Neuroscience, 11*(9), 651.

Haglund, K. A., & Fehring, R. J. (2010). The association of religiosity, sexual education, and parental factors with risky sexual behaviors among adolescents and young adults. *Journal of Religion and Health, 49*(4), 460-472.

Haider, B. A., & Bhutta, Z. A. (2012). Multiple-micronutrient supplementation for women during pregnancy. *Cochrane Database Syst Rev, 11.*

Hair, N. L., Hanson, J. L., Wolfe, B. L., & Pollak, S. D. (2015). Association of child poverty, brain development, and academic achievement. *JAMA Pediatrics, 169*(9), 822-829.

Haith, M. M. (1998). Who put the cog in infant cognition? Is rich interpretation too costly? *Infant Behavior and Development, 21*(2), 167-179.

Hales, C. M., Carroll, M. D., Fryar, C. D., & Ogden, C. L. (2017). *Prevalence of obesity among adults and youth: United States, 2015-2016.* Washington, DC: U.S. Department of Health and Human Services, Centers for Disease Control and Prevention, National Center for Health Statistics.

Haley, D. W., & Stansbury, K. (2003). Infant stress and parent responsiveness: Regulation of physiology and behavior during still-face and reunion. *Child Development, 74*(5), 1534-1546.

Halgunseth, L. C., Ispa, J. M., & Rudy, D. (2006). Parental control in Latino families: An integrated review of the literature. *Child Development, 77,* 1282-1297.

Halim, M. L., Ruble, D. N., Tamis-LeMonda, C. S., Zosuls, K. M., Lurye, L. E., & Greulich, F. K. (2014). Pink frilly dresses and the avoidance of all things "girly": Children's appearance rigidity and cognitive theories of gender development. *Developmental Psychology, 50*(4), 1091.

Hamby, S., Finkelhor, D., Turner, H., & Ormrod, R. (2010). The overlap of witnessing partner violence with child maltreatment and other victimizations in a nationally representative survey of youth. *Child Abuse & Neglect, 34*(10), 734-741.

Hamilton, B. E., & Ventura, S. J. (2012). *Birthrates for US teenagers reach historic lows for all age and ethnic groups (Vol. 89).* Atlanta, GA: US Department of Health and Human Services, Centers for Disease Control and Prevention, National Center for Health Statistics.

Hamilton, S. F., & Hamilton, M. A. (2006). School, work, and emerging adulthood. In J. J. Arnett & J. J. Tanner (Eds.). *Emerging adults in America: Coming of age in the 21st century* (pp. 257-277). Washington, DC: American Psychological Association.

Hamlin, J. K., & Wynn, K. (2011). Young infants prefer prosocial to antisocial others. *Cognitive Development, 26*(1), 30-39.

Hammerton, G., Heron, J., Mahedy, L., Maughan, B., Hickman, M., & Murray, J. (2018). Low resting heart rate, sensation seeking and the course of antisocial behaviour across adolescence and young adulthood. *Psychological Medicine*, 1-8.

Hammond, S. I., Müller, U., Carpendale, J. I., Bibok, M. B., & Liebermann-Finestone, D. P. (2012). The effects of parental scaffolding on preschoolers' executive function. *Developmental Psychology, 48*(1), 271.

Han, W. J., Miller, D. P., & Waldfogel, J. (2010). Parental work schedules and adolescent risky behaviors. *Developmental Psychology, 46*(5), 1245.

Hankin, B. L., Mermelstein, R., & Roesch, L. (2007). Sex differences in adolescent depression: Exposure and reactivity models. *Child Development, 78*, 279-295.

Hanscombe, K. B., Trzaskowski, M., Haworth, C. M., Davis, O. S., Dale, P. S., & Plomin, R. (2012). Socioeconomic status (SES) and children's intelligence (IQ): In a UK-representative sample SES moderates the environmental, not genetic, effect on IQ. *PLoS One, 7*(2), e30320.

Harper, G. W., Serrano, P. A., Bruce, D., & Bauermeister, J. A. (2016). The Internet's multiple roles in facilitating the sexual orientation identity development of gay and bisexual male adolescents. *American Journal of Men's Health, 10*(5), 359-376.

Harrist, A. W., Zain, A. F., Bates, J. E., Dodge, K. A., & Pettit, G. S. (1997). Subtypes of social withdrawal in early childhood: Sociometric status and social-cognitive differences across four years. *Child Development, 68*, 278-294.

Hart, C. H., DeWolf, M., Wozniak, P., & Burts, D. C. (1992). Maternal and paternal disciplinary styles: Relations with preschoolers' playground behavioral orientation and peer status. *Child Development, 63*, 879-892.

Hart, J. L., & Tannock, M. T. (2013). Young children's play fighting and use of war toys. In R. E. Tremblay, M. Boivin, & R. Peters (Eds.), *Encyclopedia on early childhood development* [online]. www.child-encyclopedia.com/play/according-experts/learning-through-play

Harter, S. (1998). The development of self-representations. In W. Damon (Series Ed.) & N. Eisenberg (Vol. Ed.), *Handbook of child psychology: Vol. 3. Social, emotional, and personality development* (5th ed., pp. 553-617). New York: Wiley.

Hartl, A. C., Laursen, B., & Cillessen, A. H. (2015). A survival analysis of adolescent friendships: The downside of dissimilarity. *Psychological Science, 26*(8), 1304-1315.

Hartup, W. W. (1992). Peer relations in early and middle childhood. In V. B. Van Hasselt & M. Hersen (Eds.), *Handbook of social development: A lifespan perspective* (pp. 257-281). New York: Plenum Press.

Hartup, W. W., & Stevens, N. (1999). Friendships and adaptation across the life span. *Current Directions in Psychological Science, 8*, 76-79.

Hassett, J. M., Siebert, E. R., & Wallen, K. (2008). Sex differences in rhesus monkey toy preferences parallel those of children. *Hormones and Behavior, 54*(3), 359-364.

Haugaard, J. J. (1998). Is adoption a risk factor for the development of adjustment problems? *Clinical Psychology Review, 18*, 47-69.

Haun, D., & Tomasello, M. (2011). Conformity to peer pressure in preschool children. *Child Development, 82*(6), 1759-1767.

Haworth, C. M., Wright, M. J., Luciano, M., Martin, N. G., De Geus, E. J. C., Van Beijsterveldt, C. E. M., . . . & Kovas, Y. (2010). The heritability of general cognitive ability increases linearly from childhood to young adulthood. *Molecular Psychiatry, 15*(11), 1112.

Hay, C., Meldrum, R. C., Widdowson, A. O., & Piquero, A. R. (2017). Early aggression and later delinquency: Considering the redirecting role of good parenting. *Youth Violence and Juvenile Justice, 15*(4), 374-395.

Hay, D. F., Pawlby, S., Waters, C. S., Perra, O., & Sharp, D. (2010). Mothers' antenatal depression and their children's antisocial outcomes. *Child Development, 81*(1), 149-165.

Hay, P. (2013). A systematic review of evidence for psychological treatments in eating disorders: 2005-2012. *International Journal of Eating Disorders, 46*(5), 462-469.

Heckman, J. J., Moon, S. H., Pinto, R., Savelyev, P. A., & Yavitz, A. (2010). The rate of return to the High/Scope Perry Preschool Program. *Journal of Public Economics, 94*(1), 114-128.

Heiland, F., & Liu, S. H. (2006). Family structure and wellbeing of out-of-wedlock children: The significance of the biological parents' relationship. *Demographic Research, 15*, 61-104.

Helwig, C. C., & Jasiobedzka, U. (2001). The relation between law and morality: Children's reasoning about socially beneficial and unjust laws. *Child Development, 72*, 1382-1393.

Henry, M., Cortes, A., & Morris, S. (2013). *The 2013 Annual Homeless Assessment Report (AHAR) to Congress.* Washington, DC: U.S. Department of Housing and Urban Development.

Hepach, R., Vaish, A., & Tomasello, M. (2012). Young children are intrinsically motivated to see others helped. *Psychological Science, 23*(9), 967-972.

Herbers, J. E., Cutuli, J. J., Supkoff, L. M., Heistad, D., Chan, C. K., Hinz, E., & Masten, A. S. (2012). Early reading skills and academic achievement trajectories of students facing poverty, homelessness, and high residential mobility. *Educational Researcher, 41*(9), 366-374.

Herman, J. L., Haas, A. P., & Rodgers, P. L. (2014). *Suicide attempts among transgender and gender non-conforming adults.* Los Angeles: UCLA, The Williams Institute.

Herman-Giddens, M. E., Steffes, J., Harris, D., Slora, E., Hussey, M., Dowshen, S. A., . . . & Reiter, E. O. (2012). Secondary sexual characteristics in boys: Data from the Pediatric Research in Office Settings Network. *Pediatrics, 130*(5), e1058-e1068.

Hernandez, D. J., & Macartney, S. E. (2008, January). *Racial-ethnic inequality in child well- being from 1985-2004: Gaps narrowing, but persist* (No. 9). New York: Foundation for Child Development.

Herrnstein, R. J., & Murray, C. (1994). *The bell curve: Intelligence and class structure in American life.* New York: Free Press.

Hertenstein, M. J., & Campos, J. J. (2004). The retention effects of an adult's emotional displays on infant behavior. *Child Development, 75*, 595-613.

Hetherington, E. M., Reiss, D., & Plomin, R. (Eds.). (2013). *Separate social worlds of siblings: The impact of nonshared environment on development.* New York: Routledge.

Hewes, J. (2014). Seeking balance in motion: The role of spontaneous free play in promoting social and emotional health in early childhood care and education. *Children, 1*, 280-301.

Hiatt, C., Laursen, B., Mooney, K. S., & Rubin, K. H. (2015). Forms of friendship: A person-centered assessment of the quality, stability, and outcomes of different types of adolescent friends. *Personality and Individual Differences, 77*, 149-155.

Hill, N. E., & Tyson, D. F. (2009). Parental involvement in middle school: A meta-analytic assessment of the strategies that promote achievement. *Developmental Psychology, 45*(3), 740.

Hilliard, L. J., & Liben, L. S. (2010). Differing levels of gender salience in preschool classrooms: Effects on children's gender attitudes and intergroup bias. *Child Development, 81*(6), 1787-1798.

Hillis, S. D., Anda, R. F., Dubé, S. R., Felitti, V. J., Marchbanks, P. A., & Marks, J. S. (2004). The association between adverse childhood experiences and adolescent pregnancy, long-term psychosocial consequences, and fetal death. *Pediatrics, 113,* 320-327.

Hirsh-Pasek, K. (1991). Pressure or challenge in preschool? How academic environments affect children. *New Directions for Child and Adolescent Development, 1991*(53), 39-46.

Hitzert, M. M., Van Braeckel, K. N., Bos, A. F., Hunnius, S., & Geuze, R. H. (2014). Early visual attention in preterm and fullterm infants in relation to cognitive and motor outcomes at school age: An exploratory study. *Frontiers in Pediatrics, 2.*

Hobson, J. A., & Silvestri, L. (1999, February). Parasomnias. *Harvard Mental Health Letter,* 3-5.

Hodges, E. V. E., Boivin, M., Vitaro, F., & Bukowski, W. M. (1999). The power of friendship: Protection against an escalating cycle of peer victimization. *Developmental Psychology, 35,* 94-101.

Hodgson, J. W., & Fischer, J. L. (1979). Sex differences in identity and intimacy development in college youth. *Journal of Youth and Adolescence, 8*(1), 37-50.

Hoff, E. (2006). How social contexts support and shape language development. *Developmental Review, 26,* 55-88.

Hofferth, S. L. (2006). Residential father family type and child well-being: Investment versus selection. *Demography, 43*(1), 53-77.

Hofferth, S. L. (2010). Home media and children's achievement and behavior, *Child Development, 81,* 1598-1619. doi: 10.1111/j.1467-8624.2010.01494.x

Hogge, W. A. (2003). The clinical use of karyotyping spontaneous abortions. *American Journal of Obstetrics and Gynecology, 189,* 397-402.

Holland, G., & Tiggemann, M. (2016). A systematic review of the impact of the use of social networking sites on body image and disordered eating outcomes. *Body Image, 17,* 100-110.

Holmes, J., & Gathercole, S. E. (2014). Taking working memory training from the laboratory into schools. *Educational Psychology, 34*(4), 440-450.

Holmes, R. M. (2012). The outdoor recess activities of children at an urban school: Longitudinal and intraperiod patterns. *American Journal of Play, 4*(3), 327.

Homan, G. F., Davies, M., & Norman, R. (2007). The impact of lifestyle factors on reproductive performance in the general population and those undergoing infertility treatment: A review. *Human Reproduction Update, 13*(3), 209-223.

Honein, M. A., Dawson, A. L., Petersen, E. E., Jones, A. M., Lee, E. H., Yazdy, M. M., . . . & Ellington, S. R. (2017). Birth defects among fetuses and infants of US women with evidence of possible Zika virus infection during pregnancy. *JAMA, 317*(1), 59-68.

Hong, J. S., & Espelage, D. L. (2012). A review of research on bullying and peer victimization in school: An ecological system analysis. *Aggression and Violent Behavior, 17*(4), 311-322.

Hoorn, J., Dijk, E., Meuwese, R., Rieffe, C., & Crone, E. A. (2016). Peer influence on prosocial behavior in adolescence. *Journal of Research on Adolescence, 26*(1), 90-100.

Hopkins, B., & Westra, T. (1988). Maternal handling and motor development: An intracultural study. *Genetic, Social and General Psychology Monographs, 14,* 377-420.

Hopkins, B., & Westra, T. (1990). Motor development, maternal expectations and the role of handling. *Infant Behavior and Development, 13,* 117-122.

Hoskins, D. H. (2014). Consequences of parenting on adolescent outcomes. *Societies, 4*(3), 506-531.

Houck, C. D., Barker, D., Rizzo, C., Hancock, E., Norton, A., & Brown, L. K. (2014). Sexting and sexual behavior in at-risk adolescents. *Pediatrics, 133*(2), e276-e282.

Houdé, O., Pineau, A., Leroux, G., Poirel, N., Perchey, G., Lanoë, C., . . . & Delcroix, N. (2011). Functional magnetic resonance imaging study of Piaget's conservation-of-number task in preschool and school-age children: A neo-Piagetian approach. *Journal of Experimental Child Psychology, 110*(3), 332-346.

Houltberg, B. J., Henry, C. S., & Morris, A. S. (2012). Family interactions, exposure to violence, and emotion regulation: Perceptions of children and early adolescents at risk. *Family Relations, 61,* 283-296. doi: 10.1111/j.1741-3729.2011.00699.x

Howe, N., Petrakos, H., Rinaldi, C. M., & LeFebvre, R. (2005). "This is a bad dog, you know . . . ": Constructing shared meanings during sibling pretend play. *Child Development, 76,* 783-794.

Howe, N., Rinaldi, C. M., Jennings, M., & Petrakos, H. (2002). "No! The lambs can stay out because they got cozies": Constructive and destructive sibling conflict, pretend play, and social understanding. *Child Development, 73*(5), 1460-1473.

Hoxby, C. M. (2000). The effects of class size on student achievement: New evidence from population variation. *The Quarterly Journal of Economics, 115*(4), 1239-1285. http://dx.doi.org/10.1037/bul0000116

Huang, G. C., Unger, J. B., Soto, D., Fujimoto, K., Pentz, M. A., Jordan-Marsh, M., & Valente, T. W. (2014). Peer influences: The impact of online and offline friendship networks on adolescent smoking and alcohol use. *Journal of Adolescent Health, 54*(5), 508-514.

Hudak, M. L., & Tan, R. C. (2012). Neonatal drug withdrawal. *Pediatrics, 129*(2), e540-e560.

Huesmann, L. R., Moise-Titus, J., Podolski, C. L., & Eron, L. D. (2003). Longitudinal relations between children's exposure to TV violence and their aggressive and violent behavior in young adulthood: 1977-1992. *Developmental Psychology, 39*(2), 201.

Hughes, C. (2011). Changes and challenges in 20 years of research into the development of executive functions. *Infant and Child Development, 20*(3), 251-271.

Hughes, C., Devine, R. T., Ensor, R., Koyasu, M., Mizokawa, A., & Lecce, S. (2014). Lost in translation? Comparing British, Japanese, and Italian children's theory-of-mind performance. *Child Development Research,* 893492. doi:10.1155/2014/893492

Hughes, C. H., & Ensor, R. A. (2009). How do families help or hinder the emergence of early executive function? *New Directions for Child and Adolescent Development, 2009*(123), 35-50.

Hughes, D., Rodriguez, J., Smith, E. P., Johnson, D. J., Stevenson, H. C., & Spicer, P. (2006). Parents' ethnic-racial socialization practices: A review of research and directions for future study. *Developmental Psychology, 42,* 747-770.

Hughes, I. A. (2004). Female development—All by default? *New England Journal of Medicine, 351,* 748-750.

Huizink, A., Robles de Medina, P., Mulder, E., Visser, G., & Buitelaar, J. (2002). Psychological measures of prenatal stress as predictors of infant temperament. *Journal of the American Academy of Child and Adolescent Psychiatry, 41,* 1078-1085.

Hujoel, P. P., Bollen, A.-M., Noonan, C. J., & del Aguila, M. A. (2004). Antepartum dental radiography and infant low birth weight. *Journal of the American Medical Association, 291,* 1987-1993.

Human Rights Watch. (2010). Corporal punishment and its effect on students' academic performance. Retrieved from www.hrw.org/news/2010/04/15/corporal-punishment-schools-and-its-effect-academic-success-joint-hrw/aclu-statement

Hummel, A., Shelton, K. H., Heron, J., Moore, L., & Bree, M. (2013). A systematic review of the relationships between family functioning, pubertal timing and adolescent substance use. *Addiction, 108*(3), 487–496.

Hunt, C. E. (1996). Prone sleeping in healthy infants and victims of sudden infant death syndrome. *Journal of Pediatrics, 128*, 594–596.

Hutchinson, E. A., De Luca, C. R., Doyle, L. W., Roberts, G., Anderson, P. J., & Victorian Infant Collaborative Study Group. (2013). School-age outcomes of extremely preterm or extremely low birth weight children. *Pediatrics*, peds-2012.

Huttenlocher, J., Levine, S., & Vevea, J. (1998). Environmental input and cognitive growth: A study using time period comparisons. *Child Development, 69*, 1012–1029.

Hwang, S. W., Ueng, J. J., Chiu, S., Kiss, A., Tolomiczenko, G., Cowan, L., . . . & Redelmeier, D. A. (2010). Universal health insurance and health care access for homeless persons. *American Journal of Public Health, 100*(8), 1454–1461.

Hyde, D. C., & Spelke, E. S. (2011). Neural signatures of number processing in human infants: Evidence for two core systems underlying numerical cognition. *Developmental Science, 14*(2), 360–371.

Hyde, J., Lindberg, S., Linn, M., Ellis, A., & Williams, C. (2008). Gender similarities characterize math performance. *Science, 321*, 494–495.

I

Iacoboni, M. (2008). *Mirroring people: The new science of how we connect with others.* New York: Farrar, Straus, & Giroux.

Iacoboni, M., & Mazziotta, J. C. (2007). Mirror neuron system: Basic findings and clinical applications. *Annals of Neurology, 62*, 213–218.

Icht, M., & Mama, Y. (2015). The production effect in memory: A prominent mnemonic in children. *Journal of Child Language, 42*(5), 1102–1124.

Iervolino, A. C., Hines, M., Golombok, S. E., Rust, J., & Plomin, R. (2005). Genetic and environmental influences on sex-types behavior during the preschool years. *Child Development, 76*, 826–840.

Ihmeideh, F. M. (2014). The effect of electronic books on enhancing emergent literacy skills of pre-school children. *Computers & Education, 79*, 40–48.

Imai, M., Li, L., Haryu, E., Okada, H., Hirsh-Pasek, K., Golinkoff, R. M., & Shigematsu, J. (2008). Novel noun and verb learning in Chinese-, English-, and Japanese-speaking children. *Child Development, 79*(4), 979–1000.

Imdad, A., & Bhutta, Z. A. (2011). Effect of balanced protein energy supplementation during pregnancy on birth outcomes. *BMC Public Health, 11*(3), S17.

Imperatore, G., Boyle, J. P., Thompson, T. J., Case, D., Dabelea, D., Hamman, R. F., . . . & Rodriguez, B. L. (2012). Projections of type 1 and type 2 diabetes burden in the US population aged <20 years through 2050: Dynamic modeling of incidence, mortality, and population growth. *Diabetes Care, 35*(12), 2515–2520.

Ingalhalikar, M., Smith, A., Parker, D., Satterthwaite, T. D., Elliott, M. A., Ruparel, K., . . . & Verma, R. (2014). Sex differences in the structural connectome of the human brain. *Proceedings of the National Academy of Sciences, 111*(2), 823–828.

Innocenti, G. M., & Price, D. J. (2005). Exuberance in the development of cortical networks. *Nature Reviews Neuroscience, 6*(12), 955.

International Food Policy Research Institute. 2016. *Global nutrition report 2016: From promise to impact: Ending malnutrition by 2030.* Washington, DC: Author.

Ispa, J. M., Carlo, G., Palermo, F., Su-Russell, C., Harmeyer, E., & Streit, C. (2015). Middle childhood feelings toward mothers: Predictions from maternal directiveness at the age of two and respect for autonomy currently. *Social Development, 24*(3), 541–560.

Izard, V., Sann, C., Spelke, E. S., & Streri, A. (2009). Newborn infants perceive abstract numbers. *Proceedings of the National Academy of Sciences, 106*(25), 10382–10385.

J

Jaccard, J., & Dittus, P. J. (2000). Adolescent perceptions of maternal approval of birth control and sexual risk behavior. *American Journal of Public Health, 90*, 1426–1430.

Jackson, K. D., Howie, L. D., & Akinbami, L. J. (2013). *Trends in allergic conditions among children: United States, 1997–2011.* NCHS Data Brief No 121. Hyattsville, MD: National Center for Health Statistics.

Jackson, K. D., Howie, L. D., & Akinbami, O. J. (2013). *Trends in allergic conditions among children: United States, 1997–2011.* NCHS Data Brief, No. 121. Hyattsville, MD: National Center for Health Statistics; 201.

Jadallah, M., Anderson, R. C., Nguyen-Jahiel, K., Miller, B. W., Kim, I. H., Kuo, L. J., . . . & Wu, X. (2011). Influence of a teacher's scaffolding moves during child-led small-group discussions. *American Educational Research Journal, 48*(1), 194–230.

Jadva, V., Hines, M., & Golombok, S. (2010). Infants' preferences for toys, colors, and shapes: Sex differences and similarities. *Archives of Sexual Behavior, 39*(6), 1261–1273.

Jaffari-Bimmel, N., Juffer, F., van IJzendoorn, M. H., Bakermans-Kranenburg, M. J., & Mooijaart, A. (2006). Social development from infancy to adolescence: Longitudinal and concurrent factors in an adoption sample. *Developmental Psychology, 42*, 1143–1153.

Jaffe, A. C. (2011). Failure to thrive: current clinical concepts. *Pediatrics in Review-Elk Grove, 32*(3), 100.

Jaffe, S. R., Caspi, A., Moffitt, T. E., Dodge, K. A., Rutter, M., Taylor, A., & Tully, L. A. (2005). Nature x nature: Genetic vulnerabilities interact with physical maltreatment to promote conduct problems. *Developmental Psychopathology, 17*, 67–84.

Janssen, I., & LeBlanc, A. G. (2010). Systematic review of the health benefits of physical activity and fitness in school-aged children and youth. *International Journal of Behavioral Nutrition and Physical Activity, 7*(1), 40.

Jansson, L. M., & Velez, M. (2012). Neonatal abstinence syndrome. *Current Opinion in Pediatrics, 24*(2), 252–258.

Jardri, R., Houfflin-Debarge, V., Delion, P., Pruvo, J. P., Thomas, P., & Pins, D. (2012). Assessing fetal response to maternal speech using a noninvasive functional brain imaging technique. *International Journal of Developmental Neuroscience, 30*(2), 159–161.

Jarlenski, M., Baller, J., Borrero, S., & Bennett, W. L. (2016). Trends in disparities in low-income children's health insurance coverage and access to care by family immigration status. *Academic Pediatrics, 16*(2), 208–215.

Jarvis, P. (2010). Born to play: The biocultural roots of rough and tumble play, and its impact upon young children's learning and development. *Play and Learning in the Early Years*, 61–77.

Jarvis, P., Newman, S., & Swiniarski, L. (2014). On becoming social: The importance of collaborative free play in childhood. *International Journal of Play, 3*, 53–68.

Jauk, E., Benedek, M., Dunst, B., & Neubauer, A. C. (2013). The relationship between intelligence and creativity: New support for the threshold hypothesis by means of empirical breakpoint detection. *Intelligence, 41*(4), 212-221.

Jeha, D., Usta, I., Ghulmiyyah, L., & Nassar, A. (2015). A review of the risks and consequences of adolescent pregnancy. *Journal of Neonatal-Perinatal Medicine, 8*(1), 1-8.

Jenkins, J. V. M., Woolley, D. P., Hooper, S. R., & De Bellis, M. D. (2014). Direct and indirect effects of brain volume, socioeconomic status and family stress on child IQ. *Journal of Child and Adolescent Behavior, 1*(2).

Jensen, A. R. (1969). How much can we boost IQ and scholastic achievement? *Harvard Educational Review, 39,* 1-123.

Jensen, T. M., & Shafer, K. (2013). Stepfamily functioning and closeness: Children's views on second marriages and stepfather relationships. *Social Work, 58*(2), 127-136.

Jensen, T. M., Shafer, K., & Holmes, E. K. (2017). Transitioning to stepfamily life: The influence of closeness with biological parents and stepparents on children's stress. *Child & Family Social Work, 22*(1), 275-286.

Ji, B. T., Shu, X. O., Zheng, W., Ying, D. M., Linet, M. S., Wacholder, S., . . . & Jin, F. (1997). Paternal cigarette smoking and the risk of childhood cancer among offspring of nonsmoking mothers. *Journal of the National Cancer Institute, 89*(3), 238-243.

Jia, Y., Way, N., Ling, G., Yoshikawa, H., Chen, X., Hughes, D., . . . Lu, Z. (2009). The influence of student perceptions of school climate on socioemotional and academic adjustment: A comparison of Chinese and American adolescents. *Child Development, 80*(5), 1514-1530.

Jiang, Y., Ekono, M., & Skinner, C. (2015). *Basic facts about low-income children: Children aged 12 through 17 years, 2013.* National Center for Children in Poverty; Columbia University. Accessed atwww.nccp.org/publications/pub_1099.html.

Johnson III, J. A., & Johnson, A. M. (2015). Urban-rural differences in childhood and adolescent obesity in the United States: A systematic review and meta-analysis. *Childhood Obesity, 11*(3), 233-241.

Johnson, M. D., & Galambos, N. L. (2014). Paths to intimate relationship quality from parent–adolescent relations and mental health. *Journal of Marriage and Family, 76*(1), 145-160.

Johnston, C. C., Fernandes, A. M., & Campbell-Yeo, M. (2011). Pain in neonates is different. *Pain, 152*(3), S65-S73.

Johnston, C., Campbell-Yeo, M., Fernandes, A., Inglis, D., Streiner, D., & Zee, R. (2014). Skin-to-skin care for procedural pain in neonates. *Cochrane Database Syst Rev, 1*(1).

Johnston, J., Riley, J., Ryan, C., & Kelly-Vance, L. (2015). Evaluation of a summer reading program to reduce summer setback. *Reading & Writing Quarterly, 31*(4), 334-350.

Johnston, L. D., O'Malley, P. M., Bachman, J. G., & Schulenberg, J. E. (2013). *Monitoring the Future: National results on drug use: 2012 Overview, key findings on adolescent drug use.* Ann Arbor: Institute for Social Research, The University of Michigan.

Johnston, L. D., O'Malley, P. M., Miech, R. A., Bachman, J. G., & Schulenberg, J. E. (2016). *Monitoring the Future national survey results on drug use, 1975-2015: Overview, key findings on adolescent drug use.* Ann Arbor, MI: Institute for Social Research, The University of Michigan. Retrieved from www.monitoringthefuture.org/pubs/monographs/mtf-overview2015.pdf - PDF.

Jones, D. E., Greenberg, M., & Crowley, M. (2015). Early social-emotional functioning and public health: The relationship between kindergarten social competence and future wellness. *Journal Information, 105*(11).

Jones, S., & Rutland, A. (2018). Attitudes toward immigrants among the youth. *European Psychologist, 23*(1), 83-92.

Jordan, N. C., Glutting, J., & Ramineni, C. (2010). The importance of number sense to mathematics achievement in first and third grades. *Learning and individual differences, 20*(2), 82-88.

Juang, L., & Syed, M. (2010). Family cultural socialization practices and ethnic identity in college-going emerging adults. *Journal of Adolescence, 33*(3), 347-354.

Juffer, F., Palacios, J., Le Mare, L., Sonuga-Barke, E. J., Tieman, W., Bakermans-Kranenburg, M. J., . . . & Verhulst, F. C. (2011). II. Development of adopted children with histories of early adversity. *Monographs of the Society for Research in Child Development, 76*(4), 31-61.

Julian, M. M. (2013). Age at adoption from institutional care as a window into the lasting effects of early experiences. *Clinical Child and Family Psychology Review, 16*(2), 101-145.

Jurewicz, J., & Hanke, W. (2008). Prenatal and childhood exposure to pesticides and neurobehavioral development: Review of epidemiological studies. *International Journal of Occupational Medicine and Environmental Health, 21*(2), 121-132.

Juvonen, J., & Gross, E. F. (2008). Extending the school grounds?—Bullying experiences in cyberspace. *Journal of School health, 78*(9), 496-505.

K

Kaczynski, K. J., Lindahl, K. M., Malik, N. M., & Laurenceau, J. (2006). Marital conflict, maternal and paternal parenting, and child adjustment: A test of mediation and moderation. *Journal of Family Psychology, 20*, 199-208.

Kagan, J. (1997). Temperament and the reactions to unfamiliarity. *Child Development, 68*, 139-143.

Kagan, J. (2008). In defense of qualitative changes in development. *Child Development, 79*, 1606-1624.

Kagan, J. (2012). The biography of behavioral inhibition. In M. Zentner & R. L. Shiner (Eds.), *Handbook of temperament* (pp. 69-82). New York: Guilford Press.

Kagan, J., Reznick, J. S., Clarke, C., Snidman, N., & Garcia-Coll, C. (1984). Behavioral inhibition to the unfamiliar. *Child Development*, 2212-2225.

Kagan, J., Reznick, J. S., Snidman, N., Gibbons, J., & Johnson, M. O. (1988). Childhood derivatives of inhibition and lack of inhibition to the unfamiliar. *Child Development*, 1580-1589.

Kagan, J., & Snidman, N. (2004). *The long shadow of temperament.* Cambridge, MA: Belknap Press.

Kail, R. V., Lervåg, A., & Hulme, C. (2016). Longitudinal evidence linking processing speed to the development of reasoning. *Developmental Science, 19*(6), 1067-1074.

Kaiser Family Foundation. (2017). OECD Health Data: Health status: Health status indicators. *OECD Health Statistics database.*

Kaiser Family Foundation, Hoff, T., Greene, L., & Davis, J. (2003). *National survey of adolescents and young adults: Sexual health knowledge, attitudes and experiences.* Menlo Park, CA: Henry J. Kaiser Foundation.

Kalmuss, D., Davidson, A., & Cushman, L. (1992). Parenting expectations, experiences, and adjustment to parenthood: A test of the violated expectations framework. *Journal of Marriage and Family, 54*(3), 516-526.

Kamp, K. A. (2001). Where have all the children gone?: The archaeology of childhood. *Journal of Archaeological Method and Theory, 8*(1), 1-34.

Kandler, C., & Zapko-Willmes, A. (2017). Theoretical perspectives on the interplay of nature and nurture in personality development. In *Personality development across the lifespan* (pp. 101-115). Elsevier Academic Press. https://doi.org/ 10.1016/B978-0-12-804674-6.00008-9.

Kann, L. (2016). Youth risk behavior surveillance—United States, 2015. *MMWR. Surveillance Summaries, 65.*

Kann, L., Kinchen, S., Shanklin, S. L., Flint, K. H., Hawkins, J., Harris, W. A., . . . & Whittle, L. (2014). Youth risk behavior surveillance–United States, 2013. *Morbidity and Mortality Weekly Report, 63*(SS04), 1–168.

Kaplan, H., & Dove, H. (1987). Infant development among the Ache of East Paraguay. *Developmental Psychology, 23*, 190–198.

Karably, K., & Zabrucky, K. M. (2017). Children's metamemory: A review of the literature and implications for the classroom. *International Electronic Journal of Elementary Education, 2*(1), 32–52.

Karafantis, D. M., & Levy, S. R. (2004). The role of children's lay theories about the malleability of human attributes in beliefs about and volunteering for disadvantaged groups. *Child Development, 75*, 236–250.

Kärtner, J., Keller, H., Chaudhary, N., & Yovsi, R. D. (2012). The development of mirror self-recognition in different sociocultural contexts. *Monographs of the Society for Research in Child Development, 77*(4), i-101.

Kashimada, K., & Koopman, P. (2010). Sry: The master switch in mammalian sex determination. *Development, 137*(23), 3921–3930.

Katz, P. A., & Walsh, V. (1991). Modification of children's gender-stereotyped behavior. *Child Development, 62*, 338–351.

Kaufman, A. S., & Kaufman, N. L. (1983). *Kaufman Assessment Battery for Children: Administration and scoring manual.* Circle Pines, MN: American Guidance Service.

Kaufman, A. S., & Kaufman, N. L. (2003). *Kaufman Assessment Battery for Children* (2nd ed.). Circle Pines, MN: American Guidance Service.

Kaushik, R., Krisch, I. M., Schroeder, D. R., Flick, R., & Nemergut, M. E. (2015). Pediatric bicycle-related head injuries: A population-based study in a county without a helmet law. *Injury Epidemiology, 2*(1), 16.

Kawabata, Y., Alink, L. R., Tseng, W. L., Van Ijzendoorn, M. H., & Crick, N. R. (2011). Maternal and paternal parenting styles associated with relational aggression in children and adolescents: A conceptual analysis and meta-analytic review. *Developmental Review, 31*(4), 240–278.

Kazdin, A. E., & Benjet, C. (2003). Spanking children: Evidence and issues. *Current Directions in Psychological Science, 12*, 99–103.

Kazemi, A., Ardabili, H. E., & Solokian, S. (2010). The association between social competence in adolescents and mothers' parenting style: A cross sectional study on Iranian girls. *Child and Adolescent Social Work Journal, 27*(6), 395–403.

Kegler, S. R. (2017). Trends in suicide by level of urbanization–United States, 1999–2015. *Morbidity and Mortality Weekly Report, 66.*

Keijsers, L., Branje, S. J. T., Frijns, T., Finkenauer, C., & Meeus, W. (2010). Gender differences in keeping secrets from parents in adolescence. *Developmental Psychology, 46*(1), 293–298.

Keijsers, L., Branje, S. J., VanderValk, I. E., & Meeus, W. (2010). Reciprocal effects between parental solicitation, parental control, adolescent disclosure, and adolescent delinquency. *Journal of Research on Adolescence, 20*(1), 88–113.

Kellogg, N., & Committee on Child Abuse and Neglect (2005). The evaluation of sexual abuse in children. *Pediatrics, 116* (2), 506–512.

Kena, G., Aud, S., Johnson, F., Wang, X., Zhang, J., Rathbun, A., Wilkinson-Flicker, S., and Kristapovich, P. (2014). *The condition of education 2014 (NCES 2014-083).* Washington, DC: U.S. Department of Education, National Center for Education Statistics. Retrieved from http://nces.ed.gov/pubsearch

Kennedy, D. E., & Kramer, L. (2008). Improving emotion regulation and sibling relationship quality: The more fun with sisters and brothers program. *Family Relations, 57*(5), 567–578.

Kennedy, S., & Bumpass, L. (2008). Cohabitation and children's living arrangements: New estimates from the United States. *Demographic Research, 19*, 1663.

Kenny, P. J. (2011). Reward mechanisms in obesity: New insights and future directions. *Neuron, 69*(4), 664–679.

Kenny, U., O'Malley-Keighran, M. P., Molcho, M., & Kelly, C. (2017). Peer influences on adolescent body image: Friends or foes? *Journal of Adolescent Research, 32*(6), 768–799.

Kerpelman, J. L., Pittman, J. F., Cadely, H. S. E., Tuggle, F. J., Harrell-Levy, M. K., & Adler-Baeder, F. M. (2012). Identity and intimacy during adolescence: Connections among identity styles, romantic attachment and identity commitment. *Journal of Adolescence, 35*(6), 1427–1439.

Kerr, M., Stattin, H., & Özdemir, M. (2012). Perceived parenting style and adolescent adjustment: Revisiting directions of effects and the role of parental knowledge. *Developmental Psychology, 48*(6), 1540.

Kids Count Data Center. (2017). Children in poverty by race and ethnicity [interactive data sheet]. Retrieved from http://datacenter.kidscount. org/data/tables/44-children-in-poverty-by-race-and-ethnicity#detailed/1/ any/false/870,573,869,36,868/10,11,9,12,1,185,13/324,323

Kier, C., & Lewis, C. (1998). Preschool sibling interaction in separated and married families: Are same-sex pairs or older sisters more sociable? *Journal of Child Psychology and Psychiatry, 39*, 191–201.

Kim, G., & Kwak, K. (2011). Uncertainty matters: Impact of stimulus ambiguity on infant social referencing. *Infant and Child Development, 20*(5), 449–463.

Kim, J., & Cicchetti, D. (2010). Longitudinal pathways linking child maltreatment, emotion regulation, peer relations, and psychopathology. *Journal of Child Psychology and Psychiatry, 51*(6), 706–716.

Kim, J. Y., McHale, S. M., Crouter, A. C., & Osgood, D. W. (2007). Longitudinal linkages between sibling relationships and adjustment from middle childhood through adolescence. *Developmental Psychology, 43*(4), 960.

Kim, J. Y., McHale, S. M., Osgood, D. W., & Crouter, A. C. (2006). Longitudinal course and family correlates of sibling relationships from childhood through adolescence. *Child Development, 77*(6), 1746–1761.

Kim, P., Feldman, R., Mayes, L. C., Eicher, V., Thompson, N., Leckman, J. F., & Swain, J. E. (2011). Breastfeeding, brain activation to own infant cry, and maternal sensitivity. *Journal of Child Psychology and Psychiatry, 52*(8), 907–915.

Kim, P., Strathearn, L., & Swain, J. E. (2016). The maternal brain and its plasticity in humans. *Hormones and Behavior, 77*, 113–123.

Kim, S., Nordling, J. K., Yoon, J. E., Boldt, L. J., & Kochanska, G. (2013). Effortful control in "hot" and "cool" tasks differentially predicts children's behavior problems and academic performance. *Journal of Abnormal Child Psychology, 41*(1), 43–56.

Kimball, M. M. (1986). Television and sex-role attitudes. In T. M. Williams (Ed.), *The impact of television: A natural experiment in three communities* (pp. 265–301). Orlando, FL: Academic Press.

Kim-Cohen, J., Moffitt, T. E., Caspi, A., & Taylor, A. (2004). Genetic and environmental processes in young children's resilience and vulnerability to socioeconomic deprivation. *Child Development, 75*, 651–668.

Kincaid, C., Jones, D. J., Sterrett, E., & McKee, L. (2012). A review of parenting and adolescent sexual behavior: The moderating role of gender. *Clinical Psychology Review, 32*(3), 177–188.

King, B. M. (1996). *Human sexuality today.* Englewood Cliffs, NJ: Prentice Hall.

King, V., Amato, P. R., & Lindstrom, R. (2015). Stepfather–adolescent relationship quality during the first year of transitioning to a stepfamily. *Journal of Marriage and Family, 77*(5), 1179–1189.

Kingery, J. N., Erdley, C. A., & Marshall, K. C. (2011). Peer acceptance and friendship as predictors of early adolescents' adjustment across the middle school transition. *Merrill-Palmer Quarterly, 57*(3), 215–243.

Kirby, D., & Laris, B. (2009). Effective curriculum-based sex and STD/HIV education programs for adolescents. *Child Development Perspectives, 3,* 21-29.

Kirk, E., Howlett, N., Pine, K. J., & Fletcher, B. C. (2013). To sign or not to sign? The impact of encouraging infants to gesture on infant language and maternal mind-mindedness. *Child Development, 84*(2), 574-590.

Kirkcaldy, R. D. (2016). Neisseria gonorrhoeae antimicrobial susceptibility surveillance—the gonococcal isolate surveillance project, 27 sites, United States, 2014. *MMWR. Surveillance Summaries, 65.*

Kirkorian, H. L., Wartella, E. A., & Anderson, D. R. (2008). Media and young children's learning. *Future of Children, 18,* 39-61.

Kirkpatrick, S. I., Dodd, K. W., Reedy, J., & Krebs-Smith, S. M. (2012). Income and race/ethnicity are associated with adherence to food-based dietary guidance among U.S. adults and children. *Journal of the Academy of Nutrition and Dietetics, 112*(5), 624-635.

Kisilevsky, B. S., & Haines, S. M. J. (2010). Exploring the relationship between fetal heart rate and cognition. *Infant and Child Development, 19,* 60-75.

Kisilevsky, B. S., Hains, S. M., Brown, C. A., Lee, C. T., Cowperthwaite, B., Stutzman, S. S., . . . & Ye, H. H. (2009). Fetal sensitivity to properties of maternal speech and language. *Infant Behavior and Development, 32*(1), 59-71.

Kisilevsky, B. S., Hains, S. M. J., Jacquet, A. Y., Granier-Deferre, C., & Lecanuet, J. P. (2004). Maturation of fetal responses to music. *Developmental Science, 7*(5), 550-559.

Kisilevsky, B. S., Muir, D. W., & Low, J. A. (1992). Maturation of human fetal responses to vibroacoustic stimulation. *Child Development, 63,* 1497-1508.

Kissin, D. M., Kulkarni, A. D., Mneimneh, A., Warner, L., Boulet, S. L., Crawford, S., & Jamieson, D. J. (2015). Embryo transfer practices and multiple births resulting from assisted reproductive technology: an opportunity for prevention. *Fertility and Sterility, 103*(4), 954-961.

Kitamura, C., Thanavishuth, C., Burnham, D., & Luksaneeyanawin, S. (2001). Universality and specificity in infant-directed speech: Pitch modifications as a function of infant age and sex in a tonal and non-tonal language. *Infant Behavior and Development, 24*(4), 372-392.

Kitzmann, K. M., & Beech, B. (2006). Family-based interventions for pediatric obesity: Methodological and conceptual challenges from family psychology. *Journal of Family Psychology, 20,* 175-189.

Kitzmann, K. M., Dalton, W. T., III, Stanley, C. M., Beech, B. M., Reeves, T. P., Bescemi, J., . . . Midgett, E. L. (2010). Lifestyle interventions for youth who are overweight: A meta-analytic review. *Health Psychology, 29*(1), 91-101.

Klahr, A. M., & Burt, S. A. (2014). Elucidating the etiology of individual differences in parenting: A meta-analysis of behavioral genetic research. *Psychological Bulletin, 140*(2), 544.

Klauer, S. G., Guo, F., Simons-Morton, B. G., Ouimet, M. C., Lee, S. E., & Dingus, T. A. (2014). Distracted driving and risk of road crashes among novice and experienced drivers. *New England Journal of Medicine, 370*(1), 54-59.

Klein, N. P., Hansen, J., Chao, C., Velicer, C., Emery, M., Slezak, J., . . . & Cheetham, T. C. (2012). Safety of quadrivalent human papillomavirus vaccine administered routinely to females. *Archives of Pediatrics & Adolescent Medicine, 166*(12), 1140-1148.

Kletke, B., Hallford, D.J., & Mellor, D.J. (2014). Sexting prevalence and correlates: A systematic literature review. *Clinical Psychology Review, 34,* 44-53.

Klingberg, T. (2010). Training and plasticity of working memory. *Trends in Cognitive Sciences, 14*(7), 317-324.

Ko, T. J., Tsai, L. Y., Chu, L. C., Yeh, S. J., Leung, C., Chen, C. Y., . . . & Hsieh, W. S. (2014). Parental smoking during pregnancy and its association with low birth weight, small for gestational age, and preterm birth offspring: A birth cohort study. *Pediatrics & Neonatology, 55*(1), 20-27.

Kochanek, K. D., Murphy, S. L., Xu, J. Q. & Tejada-Vera, B. (2016). Deaths: Final data for 2014. *National Vital Statistics Reports, 65*(4). Hyattsville, MD: National Center for Health Statistics.

Kochanska, G. (1993). Toward a synthesis of parental socialization and child temperament in early development of conscience. *Child Development, 64*(2), 325-347.

Kochanska, G., Aksan, N., & Carlson, J. J. (2005). Temperament, relationships, and young children's receptive cooperation with their parents. *Developmental Psychology, 41,* 648-660.

Kochanska, G., Friesenborg, A. E., Lange, L. A., & Martel, M. M. (2004). Parents' personality and infants' temperament as contributors to their emerging relationship. *Journal of Personality and Social Psychology, 86,* 744-759.

Kochanska, G., Tjebkes, T. L., & Forman, D. R. (1998). Children's emerging regulation of conduct: Restraint, compliance, and internalization from infancy to the second year. *Child Development, 69*(5), 1378-1389.

Kochanska, G., Woodard, J., Kim, S., Koenig, J. L., Yoon, J. E., & Barry, R. A. (2010). Positive socialization mechanisms in secure and insecure parent-child dyads: Two longitudinal studies. *Journal of Child Psychology and Psychiatry, 51*(9), 998-1009.

Kocherlakota, P. (2014). Neonatal abstinence syndrome. *Pediatrics, 134*(2), e547-e561.

Kohn, J. L., Rholes, S. W., Simpson, J. A., Martin III, A. M., Tran, S., & Wilson, C. L. (2012). Changes in marital satisfaction across the transition to parenthood: The role of adult attachment orientations. *Personality and Social Psychology Bulletin, 38*(11), 1506-1522.

Kolb, B., Mychasiuk, R., Muhammad, A., Li, Y., Frost, D. O., & Gibb, R. (2012). Experience and the developing prefrontal cortex. *Proceedings of the National Academy of Sciences, 109*(Supplement 2), 17186-17193.

Kolbert, E. (1994, January 11). Canadians curbing TV violence. *The New York Times,* pp. C15, C19.

Komarraju, M., & Nadler, D. (2013). Self-efficacy and academic achievement: Why do implicit beliefs, goals, and effort regulation matter? *Learning and Individual Differences, 25,* 67-72.

Konrad, K., Firk, C., & Uhlhaas, P. J. (2013). Brain development during adolescence: Neuroscientific insights into this developmental period. *Deutsches Ärzteblatt International, 110*(25), 425.

Korat, O., & Or, T. (2010). How new technology influences parent—child interaction: The case of e-book reading. *First Language, 30*(2), 139-154.

Korchmaros, J. D., Ybarra, M. L., & Mitchell, K. J. (2015). Adolescent online romantic relationship initiation: Differences by sexual and gender identification. *Journal of Adolescence, 40,* 54-64.

Kost, K., & Henshaw, S. (2013). U.S. teenage pregnancies, births and abortions, 2008: State trends by age, race and ethnicity.

Kost, K., Henshaw, S., & Carlin, L. (2013). U.S. teenage pregnancies, births and abortions: National and state trends and trends by race and ethnicity, 2010. Retrieved from www.guttmacher.org/pubs/USTPtrends.pdf

Kost, K., Maddow-Zimet, I., and Arpaia, A. (2017). *Pregnancies, births and abortions among adolescents and young women in the United States, 2013: National and state trends by age, race and ethnicity.* New York: Guttmacher Institute. Retrieved from www.guttmacher.org/report/us-adolescent-pregnancy-trends-2013

Kosterman, R., Graham, J. W., Hawkins, J. D., Catalano, R. F., & Herrenkohl, T. I. (2001). Childhood risk factors for persistence of violence in the transition to adulthood: A social development perspective. *Violence & Victims. Special Issue: Developmental Perspectives on Violence and Victimization, 16*(4), 355-369.

Kostović, I., & Judaš, M. (2010). The development of the subplate and thalamocortical connections in the human foetal brain. *Acta Paediatrica, 99*(8), 1119-1127.

Kovachy, B., O'Hara, R., Hawkins, N., Gershon, A., Primeau, M. M., Madej, J., & Carrion, V. (2013). Sleep disturbance in pediatric PTSD: Current findings and future directions. *Journal of Clinical Sleep Medicine: JCSM: Official Publication of the American Academy of Sleep Medicine, 9*(5), 501.

Kovack-Lesh, K. A., Horst, J. S., & Oakes, L. M. (2008). The cat is out of the bag: The joint influence of previous experience and looking behavior on infant categorization. *Infancy, 13*(4), 285-307.

Kovács, Á. M. (2009). Early bilingualism enhances mechanisms of false-belief reasoning. *Developmental Science, 12*(1), 48-54.

Kowal, A. K., & Pike, L. B. (2004). Sibling influences on adolescents' attitudes toward safe sex practices. *Family Relations, 53*, 377-384.

Kowalski, R. M., Giumetti, G. W., Schroeder, A. N., & Lattanner, M. R. (2014). Bullying in the digital age: A critical review and meta-analysis of cyberbullying research among youth. *Psychological Bulletin, 140*(4), 1137.

Kozhimannil, K. B., Hardeman, R. R., Alarid-Escudero, F., Vogelsang, C. A., Blauer-Peterson, C., & Howell, E. A. (2016). Modeling the cost-effectiveness of doula care associated with reductions in preterm birth and cesarean delivery. *Birth, 43*(1), 20-27.

Kozhimannil, K. B., Hardeman, R. R., Attanasio, L. B., Blauer-Peterson, C., & O'Brien, M. (2013). Doula care, birth outcomes, and costs among Medicaid beneficiaries. *American Journal of Public Health, 103*(4), e113-e121.

Kramer, L., & Kowal, A. K. (2005). Sibling relationship quality from birth to adolescence: The enduring contributions of friends. *Journal of Family Psychology, 19*, 503-511.

Krashen, S., & McField, G. (2005). What works? Reviewing the latest evidence on bilingual education. *Language Learner 1*(2), 7-10, 34.

Kraut, R., Kiesler, S., Boneva, B., Cummings, J., Helgeson, V., & Crawford, A. (2002). Internet paradox revisited. *Journal of Social Issues, 58*(1), 49-74.

Krcmar, M. (2011). Word learning in very young children from infant-directed DVDs. *Journal of Communication, 61*(4), 780-794.

Kreager, D. A., Molloy, L. E., Moody, J., & Feinberg, M. E. (2016). Friends first? The peer network origins of adolescent dating. *Journal of Research on Adolescence, 26*(2), 257-269.

Kreider, R. M. (2003). Adopted children and stepchildren: 2000. *Census 2000 Special Reports.* Washington, DC: U.S. Bureau of the Census.

Kreider, R. M., & Ellis, R. (2011). Living arrangements of children: 2009. *Current Population Reports,* P70-126. Washington, DC: U.S. Census Bureau.

Kreider, R. M., & Fields, J. (2005). Living arrangements of children: 2001. *Current Population Reports* (P70-104). Washington, DC: U.S. Census Bureau.

Kreider, R. M., & Lofquist, D. A. (2010). Adopted children and stepchildren: 2010. *Adoption Quarterly, 13*, 268-291.

Kreider, R. M., & Lofquist, D. A. (2014). Adopted children and stepchildren: 2010. US Census Bureau.

Kringelbach, M. L., Stark, E. A., Alexander, C., Bornstein, M. H., & Stein, A. (2016). On cuteness: Unlocking the parental brain and beyond. *Trends in Cognitive Sciences, 20*(7), 545-558.

Kroeger, R. A., & Smock, P. J. (2014). Cohabitation: Recent research and implications. In J. Treas, J. Scott & M. Richards (Eds.), *The Wiley-Blackwell companion to the sociology of families* (pp. 217-235) New York: Wiley.

Kroger, J. (2003). Identity development during adolescence. In G. R. Adams & M. D. Berzonsky (Eds.), *Blackwell handbook of adolescence* (pp. 205-226). Malden, MA: Blackwell.

Krogstad, P. (2014). 5 facts about the modern American family. Pew Research Center. Retrieved from http://www.pewresearch.org/fact-tank/2014/04/30/5-facts-about-the-modern-american-family/

Kuczmarski, R. J., Ogden, C. L., Grummer-Strawn, L. M., Flegal, K. M., Guo, S. S., Wei, R., . . . Johnson, C. L. (2000). *CDC growth charts: United States* (Advance Data, No. 314). Washington, DC: Centers for Disease Control and Prevention, U.S. Department of Health and Human Services.

Kuhl, P., & Rivera-Gaxiola, M. (2008). Neural substrates of language acquisition. *Annual Review of Neuroscience, 31*, 511-534.

Kuhl, P. K. (2004). Early language acquisition: Cracking the speech code. *Nature Reviews Neuroscience, 5*, 831-843.

Kuhl, P. K. (2010). Brain mechanisms in early language acquisition. *Neuron, 67*(5), 713-727.

Kuhl, P. K. (2010). Brain mechanisms in early language acquisition. *Neuron, 67*(5), 713-727.

Kuhl, P. K., Conboy, B. T., Padden, D., Nelson, T., & Pruitt, J. (2005). Early speech perception and later language development: Implications for the "critical period." *Language Learning and Development, 1*, 237-264.

Kuhl, P. K., Williams, K. A., Lacerda, F., Stevens, K. N., & Lindblom, B. (1992). Linguistic experience alters phonetic perception in infants by 6 months of age. *Science, 255*, 606-608.

Kuipersmidt, J. B., & Coie, J. D. (1990). Preadolescent peer status, aggression, and school adjustment as predictors of externalizing problems in adolescence. *Child Development, 61*, 1350-1362.

Kunzman, R., & Gaither, M. (2013). Homeschooling: A comprehensive survey of the research. *Other Education, 2*(1), 4-59.

Kuperman, S., Chan, G., Kramer, J. R., Bierut, L., Buckholz, K. K., Fox, L., . . . Schuckit, M. A. (2005). Relationship of age of first drink to child behavioral problems and family psychopathology. *Alcoholism: Clinical and Experimental Research, 29*(10), 1869-1876.

L

Labbo, L. D., & Kuhn, M. R. (2000). Weaving chains of affect and cognition: A young child's understanding of CD-ROM talking books. *Journal of Literacy Research, 32*(2), 187-210.

LaFreniere, P. (2011). Evolutionary functions of social play: Life histories, sex differences, and emotion regulation. *American Journal of Play, 3*(4), 464-488.

Lagattuta, K. H. (2014). Linking past, present, and future: Children's ability to connect mental states and emotions across time. *Child Development Perspectives, 8*(2), 90-95.

Laird, J., Lew, S., DeBell, M., & Chapman, C. (2006). *Dropout rates in the United States: 2002 and 2003* (NCES 2006-062). Washington, DC: U.S. Department of Education, National Center for Education Statistics.

Lake, A. (2015, November). *For every child, a fair chance: The promise of equity.* Retrieved from UNICEF: www.unicef.org/publications/files/For_every_child_a_fair_chance.pdf

Lamela, D., Figueiredo, B., Bastos, A., & Feinberg, M. (2016). Typologies of post-divorce coparenting and parental well-being, parenting quality and children's psychological adjustment. *Child Psychiatry & Human Development, 47*(5), 716-728.

Lamm, C., & Majdandžić, J. (2015). The role of shared neural activations, mirror neurons, and morality in empathy-a critical comment. *Neuroscience Research, 90*, 15-24.

Lamminmäki, A., Hines, M., Kuiri-Hänninen, T., Kilpeläinen, L., Dunkel, L., & Sankilampi, U. (2012). Testosterone measured in infancy predicts subsequent sex-typed behavior in boys and in girls. *Hormones and Behavior, 61*(4), 611–616.

Landor, A., Simons, L. G., Simons, R. L., Brody, G. H., & Gibbons, F. X. (2011). The role of religiosity in the relationship between parents, peers, and adolescent risky sexual behavior. *Journal of Youth and Adolescence, 40*(3), 296–309.

Landry, S. H., Smith, K. E., Swank, P. R., & Miller-Loncar, C. L. (2000). Early maternal and child influences on children's later independent cognitive and social functioning. *Child Development, 71,* 358–375.

Lange, N., Froimowitz, M. P., Bigler, E. D., Lainhart, J. E., & Brain Development Cooperative Group. (2010). Associations between IQ, total and regional brain volumes, and demography in a large normative sample of healthy children and adolescents. *Developmental Neuropsychology, 35*(3), 296–317.

Langeslag, S. J., Schmidt, M., Ghassabian, A., Jaddoe, V. W., Hofman, A., Lugt, A., . . . & White, T. J. (2013). Functional connectivity between parietal and frontal brain regions and intelligence in young children: The Generation R study. *Human Brain Mapping, 34*(12), 3299–3307.

Langley, K., Heron, J., Smith, G. D., & Thapar, A. (2012). Maternal and paternal smoking during pregnancy and risk of ADHD symptoms in offspring: Testing for intrauterine effects. *American Journal of Epidemiology, 176*(3), 261–268.

Lansford, J. E. (2009). Parental divorce and children's adjustment. *Perspectives on Psychological Science, 4*(2), 140–152.

Lansford, J. E., Dodge, K. A., Pettit, G. S., Bates, J. E., Crozier, J., & Kaplow, J. (2002). A 12-year prospective study of the long-term effects of early child physical maltreatment on psychological, behavioral, and academic problems in adolescence. *Archives of Pediatric and Adolescent Medicine, 156*(8), 824–830.

Lansford, J. E., Malone, P. S., Dodge, K. A., Pettit, G. S., & Bates, J. E. (2010). Developmental cascades of peer rejection, social information processing biases, and aggression during middle childhood. *Development and Psychopathology, 22*(3), 593–602.

Lansford, J. E., Skinner, A. T., Sorbring, E., Giunta, L. D., Deater-Deckard, K., Dodge, K. A., . . . & Uribe Tirado, L. M. (2012). Boys' and girls' relational and physical aggression in nine countries. *Aggressive Behavior, 38*(4), 298–308.

Lantagne, A., & Furman, W. (2017). Romantic relationship development: The interplay between age and relationship length. *Developmental Psychology, 53*(9), 1738.

LaRocque, M., Kleiman, I., & Darling, S. M. (2011). Parental involvement: The missing link in school achievement. *Preventing School Failure, 55*(3), 115–122.

Larson, R. W. (2001). How U.S. children and adolescents spend time: What it does (and doesn't) tell us about their development. *Current Directions in Psychological Science, 10*(5), 160–164.

Larson, R. W., & Verma, S. (1999). How children and adolescents spend time across the world: Work, play, and developmental opportunities. *Psychological Bulletin, 125*(6), 701.

Larzelere, R. E., & Kuhn, B. R. (2005). Comparing child outcomes of physical punishment and alternative disciplinary tactics: A meta-analysis. *Clinical Child and Family Psychology Review, 8*(1), 1–37.

Laski, E. V., & Siegler, R. S. (2014). Learning from number board games: You learn what you encode. *Developmental Psychology, 50*(3), 853.

Laughlin, L. (2013). Who's minding the kids? Child care arrangements: Spring 2011. *Current Population Reports,* 70–135.

Lavenex, P., & Lavenex, P. B. (2013). Building hippocampal circuits to learn and remember: Insights into the development of human memory. *Behavioural Brain Research, 254,* 8–21.

Lawler, M., & Nixon, E. (2011). Body dissatisfaction among adolescent boys and girls: The effects of body mass, peer appearance culture and internalization of appearance ideals. *Journal of Youth and Adolescence, 40*(1), 59–71.

Lawn, J. E., Mwansa-Kambafwile, J., Horta, B. L., Barros, F. C., & Cousens, S. (2010). 'Kangaroo mother care' to prevent neonatal deaths due to preterm birth complications. *International Journal of Epidemiology, 39*(suppl_1), i144–i154.

Lawrence, E., Rothman, A. D., Cobb, R., Rothman, M. T., & Bradbury, T. (2008). Marital satisfaction across the transition to parenthood. *Journal of Family Psychology, 22*(1), 41–50.

Leaper, C., & Smith, T. E. (2004). A meta-analytic review of gender variations in children's language use: Talkativeness, affiliative speech, and assertive speech. *Developmental Psychology, 40,* 993–1027.

Lederberg, A. R., Schick, B., & Spencer, P. E. (2013). Language and literacy development of deaf and hard-of-hearing children: Successes and challenges. *Developmental Psychology, 49*(1), 15.

Lee, C., & Orazem, P. F. (2010). High school employment, school performance, and college entry. *Economics of Education Review, 29*(1), 29–39.

Lee, C. T., Padilla-Walker, L. M., & Memmott-Elison, M. K. (2017). The role of parents and peers on adolescents' prosocial behavior and substance use. *Journal of Social and Personal Relationships, 34*(7), 1053–1069.

Lee, E. A. E., & Troop-Gordon, W. (2011). Peer processes and gender role development: Changes in gender atypicality related to negative peer treatment and children's friendships. *Sex Roles, 64*(1–2), 90–102.

Lee, G. Y., & Kisilevsky, B. S. (2014). Fetuses respond to father's voice but prefer mother's voice after birth. *Developmental Psychobiology, 56*(1), 1–11.

Lee, J., & Reeves, T. (2012). Revisiting the impact of NCLB high-stakes school accountability, capacity, and resources: State NAEP 1990–2009 reading and math achievement gaps and trends. *Educational Evaluation and Policy Analysis, 34*(2), 209–231.

Lee, J. M., Appugliese, D., Kaciroti, N., Corwyn, R. F., Bradley, R., & Lumeng, J. C. (2007). Weight status in young girls and the onset of puberty. *Pediatrics, 119,* e624–e630.

Lee, J. M., Kaciroti, N., Appugliese, D., Corwyn, R. F., Bradley, R. H., & Lumeng, J. C. (2010). Body mass index and timing of pubertal initiation in boys. *Archives of Pediatrics & Adolescent Medicine, 164*(2), 139–144.

Lee, J. M., Wasserman, R., Kaciroti, N., Gebremariam, A., Steffes, J., Dowshen, S., . . . & Reiter, E. (2016). Timing of puberty in overweight versus obese boys. *Pediatrics,* peds-2015.

Lee, K. (2013). Little liars: Development of verbal deception in children. *Child Development Perspectives, 7*(2), 91–96.

Lee, R., Zhai, F., Brooks-Gunn, J., Han, W. J., & Waldfogel, J. (2014). Head Start participation and school readiness: Evidence from the early childhood longitudinal study–birth cohort. *Developmental Psychology, 50*(1), 202.

Lee, R. M., Grotevant, H. D., Hellerstedt, W. L., Gunnar, M. R., & The Minnesota International Adoption Project Team. (2006). Cultural socialization in families with internationally adopted children. *Journal of Family Psychology, 20*(4), 571–580.

Lee, Y., & Styne, D. (2013). Influences on the onset and tempo of puberty in human beings and implications for adolescent psychological development. *Hormones and Behavior, 64*(2), 250–261.

Leerkes, E. M., Blankson, A. N., & O'Brien, M. (2009). Differential effects of maternal sensitivity to infant distress and nondistress on social-emotional functioning. *Child Development, 80*(3), 762–775.

Leinung, M., & Wu, C. (2017). The biologic basis of transgender identity: 2D:4D finger length ratios implicate a role for prenatal androgen activity. *Endocrine Practice, 23*(6), 669–671.

Lenhart, A. (2009). Teens and sexting. Retrieved from Pew Research Center: www.pewinternet.org/2009/12/15/teens-and-sexting/

Leonardi-Bee, J., Jere, M. L., & Britton, J. (2011). Exposure to parental and sibling smoking and the risk of smoking uptake in childhood and adolescence: A systematic review and meta-analysis. *Thorax*, thx-2010.

Leonardi-Bee, J., Nderi, M., & Britton, J. (2016). Smoking in movies and smoking initiation in adolescents: Systematic review and meta-analysis. *Addiction*, *111*(10), 1750-1763.

Lesaux, N. K., Crosson, A. C., Kieffer, M. J., & Pierce, M. (2010). Uneven profiles: Language minority learners' word reading, vocabulary, and reading comprehension skills. *Journal of Applied Developmental Psychology*, *31*(6), 475-483.

Leslie, A. M. (1995). A theory of agency. In D. Sperber, D. Premack, & A. J. Premack (Eds.), *Causal cognition* (pp. 121-149). Oxford, England: Clarendon Press.

Leslie, A. M., Friedman, O., & German, T. P. (2004). Core mechanisms in 'theory of mind.' *Trends in Cognitive Sciences*, *8*(12), 528-533.

Levine, L. J., & Edelstein, R. S. (2009). Emotion and memory narrowing: A review and goal-relevance approach. *Cognition and Emotion, 23*(5), 833-875.

Levitt, P. (2003). Structural and functional maturation of the developing primate brain. *The Journal of Pediatrics*, *143*(4), 35-45.

Lewis, C., & Lamb, M. E. (2003). Fathers' influences on children's development: The evidence from two-parent families. *European Journal of Psychology of Education*, *18*(2), 211-228.

Lewis-Morrarty, E., Degnan, K. A., Chronis-Tuscano, A., Rubin, K. H., Cheah, C. S., Pine, D. S., . . . & Fox, N. A. (2012). Maternal over-control moderates the association between early childhood behavioral inhibition and adolescent social anxiety symptoms. *Journal of Abnormal Child Psychology*, *40*(8), 1363-1373.

Lewkowicz, D. J., & Hansen-Tift, A. M. (2012). Infants deploy selective attention to the mouth of a talking face when learning speech. *Proceedings of the National Academy of Sciences*, *109*(5), 1431-1436.

Li, A. M., Au, C. T., So, H. K., Lau, J., Ng, P. C., & Wing, Y. K. (2010). Prevalence and risk factors of habitual snoring in primary school children. *Chest*, *138*(3), 519-527.

Li, S. X., Yu, M. W. M., Lam, S. P., Zhang, J., Li, A. M., Lai, K. Y. C., & Wing, Y. K. (2011). Frequent nightmares in children: Familial aggregation and associations with parent-reported behavioral and mood problems. *Sleep*, *34*(4), 487-493.

Li, Y., Putallaz, M., & Su, Y. (2011). Interparental conflict styles and parenting behaviors: Associations with overt and relational aggression among Chinese children. *Merrill-Palmer Quarterly*, *57*(4), 402-428.

Libertus, M. E., & Brannon, E. M. (2010). Stable individual differences in number discrimination in infancy. *Developmental Science*, *13*(6), 900-906.

Lidstone, J., Meins, E., & Fernyhough, C. (2011). Individual differences in children's private speech: Consistency across tasks, timepoints, and contexts. *Cognitive Development*, *26*(3), 203-213.

Lien, Y. J., Chen, W. J., Hsiao, P. C., & Tsuang, H. C. (2015). Estimation of heritability for varied indexes of handedness. *Laterality: Asymmetries of Body, Brain and Cognition*, *20*(4), 469-482.

Light, S. N., Coan, J. A., Zahn-Waxler, C., Frye, C., Goldsmith, H. H., & Davidson, R. J. (2009). Empathy is associated with dynamic change in prefrontal brain electrical activity during positive emotion in children. *Child Development, 80*, 1210-1231. doi: 10.1111/j.1467-8624.2009.01326.x

Lillard, A., & Curenton, S. (1999). Do young children understand what others feel, want, and know? *Young Children, 54*(5), 52-57.

Lillard, A. S., Lerner, M. D., Hopkins, E. J., Dore, R. A., Smith, E. D., & Palmquist, C. M. (2013). The impact of pretend play on children's development: A review of the evidence. *Psychological Bulletin*, *139*(1), 1.

Lillard, A. S., & Peterson, J. (2011). The immediate impact of different types of television on young children's executive function. *Pediatrics*, *128*(4), 644-649.

Lin, S., Hwang, S. A., Marshall, E. G., & Marion, D. (1998). Does paternal occupational lead exposure increase the risks of low birth weight or prematurity? *American Journal of Epidemiology, 148*, 173-181.

Lindberg, L., Santelli, J., & Desai, S. (2016). Understanding the decline in adolescent fertility in the United States, 2007-2012. *Journal of Adolescent Health*, *59*(5), 577-583.

Lindberg, L. D., Maddow-Zimet, I., & Boonstra, H. (2016). Changes in adolescents' receipt of sex education, 2006-2013. *Journal of Adolescent Health*, *58*(6), 621-627.

Lindberg, S. M., Hyde, J. S., Petersen, J. L., & Linn, M. C. (2010). New trends in gender and mathematics performance: A meta-analysis. *Psychological Bulletin*, *136*(6), 1123.

Linnet, K. M., Wisborg, K., Obel, C., Secher, N. J., Thomsen, P. H., Agerbo, E., & Henriksen, T. B. (2005). Smoking during pregnancy and the risk of hyperkinetic disorder in offspring. *Pediatrics, 116*, 462-467.

Litt, J. S., Gerry Taylor, H., Margevicius, S., Schluchter, M., Andreias, L., & Hack, M. (2012). Academic achievement of adolescents born with extremely low birth weight. *Acta Paediatrica*, *101*(12), 1240-1245.

Liu, D., Sabbagh, M. A., Gehring, W. J., & Wellman, H. M. (2009). Neural correlates of children's theory of mind development. *Child Development*, *80*(2), 318-326.

Liu, S., Xiao, W. S., Xiao, N. G., Quinn, P. C., Zhang, Y., Chen, H., . . . & Lee, K. (2015). Development of visual preference for own- versus other-race faces in infancy. *Developmental Psychology*, *51*(4), 500.

LoBue, V., Rakison, D. H., & DeLoache, J. S. (2010). Threat perception across the life span: Evidence for multiple converging pathways. *Current Directions in Psychological Science*, *19*(6), 375-379.

Lopes, V. P., Rodrigues, L. P., Maia, J. A., & Malina, R. M. (2011). Motor coordination as predictor of physical activity in childhood. *Scandinavian Journal of Medicine & Science in Sports*, *21*(5), 663-669.

Loth, K. A., Watts, A. W., Van Den Berg, P., & Neumark-Sztainer, D. (2015). Does body satisfaction help or harm overweight teens? A 10-year longitudinal study of the relationship between body satisfaction and body mass index. *Journal of Adolescent Health*, *57*(5), 559-561.

Low, J. (2010). Preschoolers' implicit and explicit false-belief understanding: Relations with complex syntactical mastery. *Child Development*, *81*(2), 597-615.

Low, S., Shortt, J. W., & Snyder, J. (2012). Sibling influences on adolescent substance use: The role of modeling, collusion, and conflict. *Development and Psychopathology*, *24*(1), 287-300.

Lowe, J. R., MacLean, P. C., Duncan, A. F., Aragón, C., Schrader, R. M., Caprihan, A., & Phillips, J. P. (2012). Association of maternal interaction with emotional regulation in 4- and 9-month infants during the Still Face Paradigm. *Infant Behavior and Development*, *35*(2), 295-302.

Lu, B., Kumar, A., Castellsagué, X., & Giuliano, A. R. (2011). Efficacy and safety of prophylactic vaccines against cervical HPV infection and diseases among women: A systematic review & meta-analysis. *BMC Infectious Diseases*, *11*(1), 13.

Lu, P. J., Yankey, D., Jeyarajah, J., O'Halloran, A., Elam-Evans, L. D., Smith, P. J., . . . & Dunne, E. F. (2015). HPV vaccination coverage of male adolescents in the United States. *Pediatrics*, peds-2015.

Lubienski, C., Puckett, T., & Brewer, T. J. (2013). Does homeschooling "work"? A critique of the empirical claims and agenda of advocacy organizations. *Peabody Journal of Education*, *88*(3), 378-392.

Lucas, A. J., & Dyment, J. E. (2010). Where do children choose to play on the school ground? The influence of green design. *Education 3-13*, *38*(2), 177-189.

Luders, E., Gaser, C., Narr, K. L., & Toga, A. W. (2009). Why sex matters: Brain size independent differences in gray matter distributions between men and women. *Journal of Neuroscience, 29*(45), 14265–14270.

Luders, E., Sánchez, F. J., Gaser, C., Toga, A. W., Narr, K. L., Hamilton, L. S., & Vilain, E. (2009). Regional gray matter variation in male-to-female transsexualism. *Neuroimage, 46*(4), 904–907.

Luders, E., Thompson, P. M., & Toga, A. W. (2010). The development of the corpus callosum in the healthy human brain. *Journal of Neuroscience, 30*(33), 10985–10990.

Luders, E., Toga, A. W., & Thompson, P. M. (2014). Why size matters: Differences in brain volume account for apparent sex differences in callosal anatomy: The sexual dimorphism of the corpus callosum. *Neuroimage, 84*, 820–824.

Ludwig, D. S. (2007). Childhood obesity—the shape of things to come. *New England Journal of Medicine, 357*(23), 2325–2327.

Ludwig, D. S. (2018). Epidemic childhood obesity: Not yet the end of the beginning. *Pediatrics*, e20174078.

Lundberg, S., & Pollak, R. A. (2014). Cohabitation and the uneven retreat from marriage in the United States, 1950-2010. In L. P. Boustan, C. Frydman & R. A. Margo (Eds.), *Human capital in history: The American record* (pp. 241–272). Chicago: University of Chicago Press.

Lynch, A. D., Lerner, R. M., & Leventhal, T. (2013). Adolescent academic achievement and school engagement: An examination of the role of school-wide peer culture. *Journal of Youth and Adolescence, 42*(1), 6–19.

Lynn, R., & Meisenberg, G. (2010). National IQs calculated and validated for 108 nations. *Intelligence, 38*(4), 353–360.

M

Ma, W., Golinkoff, R. M., Houston, D. M., & Hirsh-Pasek, K. (2011). Word learning in infant- and adult-directed speech. *Language Learning and Development, 7*(3), 185–201.

Maccoby, E. E. (1990). Gender and relationships: A developmental account. *American Psychologist, 45*(4), 513.

Maccoby, E. E. (1992). The role of parents in the socialization of children: An historical overview. *Developmental Psychology, 28*(6), 1006.

Maccoby, E. E., & Jacklin, C. N. (1987). Gender segregation in childhood. *Advances in Child Development and Behavior, 20,* 239–287.

Macdonald-Wallis, K., Jago, R., Page, A. S., Brockman, R., & Thompson, J. L. (2011). School-based friendship networks and children's physical activity: A spatial analytical approach. *Social Science & Medicine, 73*(1), 6–12.

MacDorman, M. F., & Gregory, E. C. (2015). Fetal and perinatal mortality: United States, 2013. *National Vital Statistics Reports 64*(8), 1–24. Hyattsville, MD: National Center for Health Statistics.

MacDorman, M. F., & Mathews, T. J. (2009). *Behind international rankings of infant mortality: How the United States compares with Europe* (No. 23). Washington, DC: Department of Health and Human Services, Centers for Disease Control and Prevention, National Center for Health Statistics.

MacDorman, M. F., Menacker, F., & Declercq, E. (2010). Trends and characteristics of home and other out-of-hospital births in the United States, 1990-2006. *National Vital Statistics Reports, 58*(11), 1–14, 16. Hyattsville, MD: National Center for Health Statistics.

Machaalani, R., & Waters, K. A. (2014). Neurochemical abnormalities in the brainstem of the sudden infant death syndrome (SIDS). *Paediatric Respiratory Reviews, 15*(4), 293–300.

MacKenzie, M. J., Nicklas, E., Waldfogel, J., & Brooks-Gunn, J. (2013). Spanking and child development across the first decade of life. *Pediatrics, 132*(5), e1118–e1125.

MacKinnon-Lewis, C., Starnes, R., Volling, B., & Johnson, S. (1997). Perceptions of parenting as predictors of boys' sibling and peer relations. *Developmental Psychology, 33,* 1024–1031.

Madden, M., Lenhart, A., Duggan, M., Cortesi, S., & Gasser, U. (2013). *Teens and technology 2013* (pp. 1–19). Washington, DC: Pew Internet & American Life Project.

Madigan, S., Wade, M., Tarabulsy, G., Jenkins, J. M., & Shouldice, M. (2014). Association between abuse history and adolescent pregnancy: A meta-analysis. *Journal of Adolescent Health, 55*(2), 151–159.

Magnuson, K., & Berger, L. M. (2009). Family structure states and transitions: Associations with children's well-being during middle childhood. *Journal of Marriage and Family, 71*(3), 575–591.

Mahatmya, D., & Lohman, B. (2011). Predictors of late adolescent delinquency: The protective role of after-school activities in low-income families. *Children and Youth Services Review, 33*(7), 1309–1317.

Maheshwari, A. (2010). Overweight and obesity in infertility: Cost and consequences. *Human Reproductive Updates, 16*(3), 229–230.

Maheshwari, A., Griffiths, S., & Bhattacharya, S. (2010). Global variations in the uptake of single embryo transfer. *Human Reproduction Update, 17*(1), 107–120.

Maisonet, M., Christensen, K. Y., & Rubin, C., Holmes, A., Flanders, A. H., Heron, J., . . . Ong, K. K. (2010). Role of prenatal characteristics and early growth on pubertal attainment of British girls. *Pediatrics, 126*(3), 591–600.

Mäkinen, M., Puukko-Viertomies, L. R., Lindberg, N., Siimes, M. A., & Aalberg, V. (2012). Body dissatisfaction and body mass in girls and boys transitioning from early to mid-adolescence: Additional role of self-esteem and eating habits. *BMC Psychiatry, 12*(1), 35.

Malabarey, O. T., Balayla, J., Klam, S. L., Shrim, A., & Abenhaim, H. A. (2012). Pregnancies in young adolescent mothers: A population-based study on 37 million births. *Journal of Pediatric and Adolescent Gynecology, 25*(2), 98–102.

Malik, V. S., Pan, A., Willett, W. C., & Hu, F. B. (2013). Sugar-sweetened beverages and weight gain in children and adults: A systematic review and meta-analysis. *The American Journal of Clinical Nutrition, 98*(4), 1084–1102.

Malik, V. S., Popkin, B. M., Bray, G. A., Després, J. P., & Hu, F. B. (2010). Sugar-sweetened beverages, obesity, type 2 diabetes mellitus, and cardiovascular disease risk. *Circulation, 121*(11), 1356–1364.

Malik, V. S., Willett, W. C., & Hu, F. B. (2013). Global obesity: Trends, risk factors and policy implications. *Nature Reviews Endocrinology, 9*(1), 13–27.

Mampe, B., Friederici, A. D., Christophe, A., & Wermke, K. (2009). Newborns' cry melody is shaped by their native language. *Current Biology, 19*(23), 1994–1997. doi: 10.1016/j.cub.2009.09.064

Mandara, J., Gaylord-Harden, N. K., Richards, M. H., & Ragsdale, B. L. (2009). The effects of change in racial identity and self-esteem on changes in African American adolescents' mental health. *Child Development, 80*(6), 1660–1675.

Mandler, J. M. (1998). Representation. In D. Kuhn & R. S. Siegler (Eds.), *Handbook of child psychology: Vol. 2. Cognition, perception, and language* (5th ed., pp. 255–308). New York: Wiley.

Manning, W. D. (2017). Cohabitation and child well-being. In D. J. Besharov (Ed.), *Family and child well-being after welfare reform* (pp. 127–142). New York: Routledge.

Manning, W. D., Fettro, M. N., & Lamidi, E. (2014). Child well-being in same-sex parent families: Review of research prepared for American Sociological Association Amicus Brief. *Population Research and Policy Review, 33*(4), 485–502.

Mar, R. A., Tackett, J. L., & Moore, C. (2010). Exposure to media and theory-of-mind development in preschoolers. *Cognitive Development, 25*(1), 69–78.

March of Dimes Foundation. (2012). Toxoplasmosis [Fact sheet]. Wilkes-Barre, PA: Author.

March, J., & the TADS Team. (2007). The Treatment for Adolescents with Depression Study (TADS): Long-term effectiveness and safety outcomes. *Archives of General Psychiatry, 64,* 1132–1143.

Marcon, R. A. (2002). Moving up the grades: Relationship between preschool model and later school success. *Early Childhood Research & Practice, 4*(1), n1.

Marcus, L., Lejeune, F., Berne-Audéoud, F., Gentaz, E., & Debillon, T. (2012). Tactile sensory capacity of the preterm infant: Manual perception of shape from 28 gestational weeks. *Pediatrics, 130*(1), e88–e94.

Mares, M. L., & Pan, Z. (2013). Effects of Sesame Street: A meta-analysis of children's learning in 15 countries. *Journal of Applied Developmental Psychology, 34*(3), 140–151.

Mark, K., Desai, A., & Terplan, M. (2016). Marijuana use and pregnancy: Prevalence, associated characteristics, and birth outcomes. *Archives of Women's Mental Health, 19*(1), 105.

Markant, J., & Amso, D. (2014). Leveling the playing field: Attention mitigates the effects of intelligence on memory. *Cognition, 131*(2), 195–204.

Markowitz, L. E., Hariri, S., Lin, C., Dunne, E. F., Steinau, M., McQuillan, G., & Unger, E. R. (2013). Reduction in human papillomavirus (HPV) prevalence among young women following HPV vaccine introduction in the United States, National Health and Nutrition Examination Surveys, 2003–2010. *The Journal of Infectious Diseases, 208*(3), 385–393.

Marks, H. M. (2000). Student engagement in instructional activity: Patterns in the elementary, middle, and high school years. *American educational research journal, 37*(1), 153–184.

Marsh, A. A., Finger, E. C., Schechter, J. C., Jurkowitz, I. T., Reid, M. E., & Blair, R. J. R. (2011). Adolescents with psychopathic traits report reductions in physiological responses to fear. *Journal of Child Psychology and Psychiatry, 52*(8), 834–841.

Martin, C. E., Longinaker, N., Mark, K., Chisolm, M. S., & Terplan, M. (2015). Recent trends in treatment admissions for marijuana use during pregnancy. *Journal of Addiction Medicine, 9*(2), 99–104.

Martin, C. E., Longinaker, N., & Terplan, M. (2015). Recent trends in treatment admissions for prescription opioid abuse during pregnancy. *Journal of Substance Abuse Treatment, 48*(1), 37–42.

Martin, C. L., Fabes, R. A., Hanish, L., Leonard, S., & Dinella, L. M. (2011). Experienced and expected similarity to same-gender peers: Moving toward a comprehensive model of gender segregation. *Sex Roles, 65*(5-6), 421–434.

Martin, C. L., Kornienko, O., Schaefer, D. R., Hanish, L. D., Fabes, R. A., & Goble, P. (2013). The role of sex of peers and gender-typed activities in young children's peer affiliative networks: A longitudinal analysis of selection and influence. *Child Development, 84*(3), 921–937.

Martin, C. L., Ruble, D. N., & Szkrybalo, J. (2002). Cognitive theories of early gender development. *Psychological Bulletin, 128,* 903–933.

Martin, J. A., Hamilton, B. E., & Osterman, M. J. K. (2012). *Three decades of twin births in the United States, 1980–2009.* NCHS Data Brief No 80. Hyattsville, MD: National Center for Health Statistics.

Martin, J. A., Hamilton, B. E., Osterman, M. J., Driscoll, A. K., & Drake, P. (2018). Births: Final data for 2016. *National Vital Statistics Reports, 67*(1). Hyattsville, MD: National Center for Health Statistics.

Martin, J. A., Hamilton, B. E., Osterman, M. J., Driscoll, A. K., & Mathews, T. J. (2017). Births: Final data for 2015. *National Vital Statistics Report, 66*(1), 1. Hyattsville, MD: National Center for Health Statistics.

Martin, J. A., Hamilton, B. E., Sutton, P. D., Ventura, S. J., Mathews, T. J., Kirmeyer, S., & Osterman, M. J. (2010). Births: Final data for 2007.

National Vital Statistics Reports, 59(1), 1–72. Hyattsville, MD: National Center for Health Statistics.

Martin, J. A., Hamilton, B. E., Sutton, P. D., Ventura, S. J., Mathews, T. J., & Osterman, M. J. K. (2010). Births: Final data for 2008. *National Vital Statistics Reports, 59*(1). Hyattsville, MD: National Center for Health Statistics.

Martin, J. A., Hamilton, B. E., Sutton, P. D., Ventura, S. J., Menacker, F., Kirmeyer, S., & Mathews, T. J. (2009). Births: Final data for 2006. *National Vital Statistics Reports, 57*(7). Hyattsville, MD: National Center for Health Statistics.

Martin, J. A., Hamilton, B. E., Ventura, S. J., Osterman, M. J. K., & Mathews, M. S. (2013). Births: Final data for 2011. *National Vital Statistics Reports, 62*(1). Hyattsville, MD: National Center for Health Statistics.

Martin, J. A., Hamilton, B. E., Osterman, M. J. K., Driscoll, A. K., & Drake, P. (2018). Births: Final data for 2016. *National Vital Statistics Reports 67*(1), Hyattsville, MD: National Center for Health Statistics.

Martin, R., Noyes, J., Wisenbaker, J., & Huttunen, M. (2000). Prediction of early childhood negative emotionality and inhibition from maternal distress during pregnancy. *Merrill-Palmer Quarterly, 45,* 370–391.

Martin, S. P., & Parashar, S. (2006). Women's changing attitudes toward divorce, 1974–2002: Evidence for an educational crossover. *Journal of Marriage and Family, 68,* 29–40.

Martinez, G., & Abma, J. C. (2015). *Sexual activity, contraceptive use, and childbearing of teenagers aged 15–19 in the United States.* Washington, DC: National Center for Health Statistics. Retrieved from www.cdc.gov/mmwr/pdf/ss/ss6304.pdf - PDF.

Martinez, G., Copen, C. E., & Abma, J. C. (2011). Teenagers in the United States: Sexual activity, contraceptive use, and childbearing, 2006–2010. National Survey of Family Growth. National Center for Health Statistics. *Vital Health Statistics 23*(31).

Martínez-Ortega, J. M., Carretero, M. D., Gutiérrez-Rojas, L., Díaz-Atienza, F., Jurado, D., & Gurpegui, M. (2011). Winter birth excess in schizophrenia and in non-schizophrenic psychosis: Sex and birth-cohort differences. *Progress in Neuro-Psychopharmacology and Biological Psychiatry, 35*(7), 1780–1784.

Martorell, R. (2010). Physical growth and development of the malnourished child: Contributions from 50 years of research at INCAP. *Food and Nutrition Bulletin, 31*(1), 68–82.

Martorell, R., Melgar, P., Maluccio, J. A., Stein, A. D., & Rivera, J. A. (2010). The nutrition intervention improved adult human capital and economic productivity. *The Journal of Nutrition, 140*(2), 411–414.

Martorell, R., & Zongrone, A. (2012). Intergenerational influences on child growth and undernutrition. *Paediatric and Perinatal Epidemiology, 26*(s1), 302–314.

Mascarenhas, M. N., Flaxman, S. R., Boerma, T., Vanderpoel, S., & Stevens, G. A. (2012). National, regional, and global trends in infertility prevalence since 1990: A systematic analysis of 277 health surveys. *PLoS medicine, 9*(12), e1001356.

Mascaro, O., & Csibra, G. (2014). Human infants' learning of social structures: The case of dominance hierarchy. *Psychological Science, 25*(1), 250–255.

Mashburn, A. J., Justice, L. M., Downer, J. T., & Pianta, R. C. (2009). Peer effects on children's language achievement during prekindergarten. *Child Development, 80*(3), 686–702.

Masiero, M., Lucchiari, C., & Pravettoni, G. (2015). Personal fable: Optimistic bias in cigarette smokers. *International Journal of High Risk Behaviors & Addiction, 4*(1).

Mason, T. B., & Pack, A. I. (2007). Pediatric parasomnias. *Sleep, 30*(2), 141–151.

Masten, A. S., & Coatsworth, J. D. (1998). The development of competence in favorable and unfavorable environments: Lessons from research on successful children. *American Psychologist, 53*(2), 205.

Mather, M. (2010). *U.S. children in single-mother families.* Washington, DC: Population Reference Bureau.

Mathews, T. J., & Hamilton, B. E. (2016). Mean age of mothers is on the rise: United States, 2000–2014. *NCHS Data Brief, 232,* 1–8.

Mathews, T. J., MacDorman, M. F., & Thoma, M. E. (2015). Infant mortality statistics from the 2013 period linked birth/infant death data set. *National Vital Statistics Reports, 64*(9). Hyattsville, MD: National Center for Health Statistics.

Mathis, W.J. & Trujillo, T.M. (2016). *Lessons from NCLB for the Every Student Succeeds Act.* Boulder, CO: National Education Policy Center. Retrieved from http://nepc.colorado.edu/ publication/lessons-from-NCLB

Mattei, T. A., Bond, B. J., Goulart, C. R., Sloffer, C. A., Morris, M. J., & Lin, J. J. (2012). Performance analysis of the protective effects of bicycle helmets during impact and crush tests in pediatric skull models. *Journal of Neurosurgery: Pediatrics, 10*(6), 490–497.

Maulik, P. K., Mascarenhas, M. N., Mathers, C. D., Dua, T., & Saxena, S. (2011). Prevalence of intellectual disability: A meta-analysis of population-based studies. *Research in Developmental Disabilities, 32*(2), 419–436.

Mayeza, E. (2017). 'It's not right for boys to play with dolls': Young children constructing and policing gender during 'free play' in a South African classroom. *Discourse: Studies in the Cultural Politics of Education,* 1–13.

Mayhew, A., Mullins, T. L. K., Ding, L., Rosenthal, S. L., Zimet, G. D., Morrow, C., & Kahn, J. A. (2014). Risk perceptions and subsequent sexual behaviors after HPV vaccination in adolescents. *Pediatrics,* peds-2013.

Maynard, S. (2010). The impact of e-books on young children's reading habits. *Publishing Research Quarterly, 26*(4), 236–248.

Mayo Foundation for Medical Education and Research. (2009, January). Beyond the human genome: Meet the epigenome. *Mayo Clinic Health Letter, 27*(1), pp. 4–5.

Mazloom, A. R., Džakula, Ž., Oeth, P., Wang, H., Jensen, T., Tynan, J., . . . & Bombard, A. T. (2013). Noninvasive prenatal detection of sex chromosomal aneuploidies by sequencing circulating cell-free DNA from maternal plasma. *Prenatal diagnosis, 33*(6), 591–597.

Mazzocco, M. M., Feigenson, L., & Halberda, J. (2011). Impaired acuity of the approximate number system underlies mathematical learning disability (dyscalculia). *Child Development, 82*(4), 1224–1237.

McAlister, A. R., & Peterson, C. C. (2013). Siblings, theory of mind, and executive functioning in children aged 3–6 years: New longitudinal evidence. *Child Development, 84*(4), 1442–1458.

McAuley, T., & White, D. A. (2011). A latent variables examination of processing speed, response inhibition, and working memory during typical development. *Journal of Experimental Child Psychology, 108*(3), 453–468.

McCabe, D. P., Roediger III, H. L., McDaniel, M. A., Balota, D. A., & Hambrick, D. Z. (2010). The relationship between working memory capacity and executive functioning: Evidence for a common executive attention construct. *Neuropsychology, 24*(2), 222.

McCabe, J., Fairchild, E., Grauerholz, L., Pescosolido, B. A., & Tope, D. (2011). Gender in twentieth-century children's books: Patterns of disparity in titles and central characters. *Gender & Society, 25*(2), 197–226.

McClain, M. C., & Pfeiffer, S. (2012). Identification of gifted students in the United States today: A look at state definitions, policies, and practices. *Journal of Applied School Psychology, 28*(1), 59–88.

McClure, E. B. (2000). A meta-analytic review of sex differences in facial expression processing and their development in infants, children, and adolescents. *Psychological Bulletin, 126*(3), 424.

McCoy, K., Cummings, E. M., & Davies, P. T. (2009). Constructive and destructive marital conflict, emotional security and children's prosocial behavior. *Journal of Child Psychology and Psychiatry, 50*(3), 270–279.

McCrink, K., & Wynn, K. (2004). Large-number addition and subtraction by 9-month-old infants. *Psychological Science, 15,* 776–781.

McCrink, K., Bloom, P., & Santos, L. R. (2010). Children's and adults' judgments of equitable resource distributions. *Developmental Science, 13*(1), 37–45.

McDonald, K. L., Dashiell-Aje, E., Menzer, M. M., Rubin, K. H., Oh, W., & Bowker, J. C. (2013). Contributions of racial and sociobehavioral homophily to friendship stability and quality among same-race and cross-race friends. *Journal of Early Adolescence.* doi:10.1177/0272431612472259

McDonnell, P. M. (1975). The development of visually guided reaching. *Perception & Psychophysics, 18*(3), 181–185.

McDonough, C., Song, L., Hirsh-Pasek, K., Golinkoff, R. M., & Lannon, R. (2011). An image is worth a thousand words: Why nouns tend to dominate verbs in early word learning. *Developmental Science, 14*(2), 181–189.

McDowell, D. J., & Parke, R. (2009). Parental correlates of children's peer relations: An empirical test of a tripartite model. *Developmental Psychology, 45*(1), 224–235.

McElwain, N. L., & Volling, B. L. (2005). Preschool children's interactions with friends and older siblings: Relationship specificity and joint contributions to problem behavior. *Journal of Family Psychology, 19,* 486–496.

McFarland, J., Hussar, B., de Brey, C., Snyder, T., Wang, X., Wilkinson-Flicker, S., . . . & Hinz, S. (2017). *The condition of education 2017* (NCES 2017- 144). U.S. Department of Education. Washington, DC: National Center for Education Statistics. Retrieved from https://nces.ed.gov/pubsearch/pubsinfo.asp?pubid=2017144.

McHale, S. M., & Huston, T. L. (1985). The effect of the transition to parenthood on the marriage relationship. *Journal of Family Issues, 6*(4), 409–433.

McHale, S. M., Bissell, J., & Kim, J. Y. (2009). Sibling relationship, family, and genetic factors in sibling similarity in sexual risk. *Journal of Family Psychology, 23*(4), 562.

McHale, S. M., Updegraff, K. A., & Whiteman, S. D. (2012). Sibling relationships and influences in childhood and adolescence. *Journal of Marriage and Family, 74*(5), 913–930.

McLanahan, S., Tach, L., & Schneider, D. (2013). The causal effects of father absence. *Annual Review of Sociology, 39,* 399–427.

McLaughlin, M. R. (2011). Speech and language delay in children. *American Family Physician, 83*(10).

McLeod, J. D., Kruttschnitt, C., & Dornfeld, M. (1994). Does parenting explain the effects of structural conditions on children's antisocial behavior? A comparison of blacks and whites. *Social Forces, 73*(2), 575–604.

McManus, I. C., Davison, A., & Armour, J. A. (2013). Multilocus genetic models of handedness closely resemble single-locus models in explaining family data and are compatible with genome-wide association studies. *Annals of the New York Academy of Sciences, 1288*(1), 48–58.

McNeal Jr, R. B. (2012). Checking in or checking out? Investigating the parent involvement reactive hypothesis. *The Journal of Educational Research, 105*(2), 79–89.

McQuaid, N., Bigelow, A. E., McLaughlin, J., & MacLean, K. (2008). Maternal mental state language and preschool children's attachment security: Relation to children's mental state language and expressions of emotional understanding. *Social Development, 17*(1), 61–83.

Meador, K. J., Baker, G. A., Browning, N., Clayton-Smith, J., Combs-Cantrell, D. T., Cohen, M., . . . & Privitera, M. (2009). Cognitive function at 3 years of age after fetal exposure to antiepileptic drugs. *New England Journal of Medicine, 360*(16), 1597–1605.

Meador, K. J., Baker, G. A., Browning, N., Cohen, M. J., Bromley, R. L., Clayton-Smith, J., . . . & Privitera, M. (2014). Breastfeeding in children of women taking antiepileptic drugs: Cognitive outcomes at age 6 years. *JAMA Pediatrics, 168*(8), 729–736.

Mehta, C. M., & Strough, J. (2009). Sex segregation in friendships and normative contexts across the life span. *Developmental Review, 29,* 201–220. doi:10.1016/j.dr.2009.06.001

Meier, R. (1991, January–February). Language acquisition by deaf children. *American Scientist, 79,* 60–70.

Meinhardt, J., Sodian, B., Thoermer, C., Döhnel, K., & Sommer, M. (2011). True- and false-belief reasoning in children and adults: An event-related potential study of theory of mind. *Developmental Cognitive Neuroscience, 1*(1), 67–76.

Meins, E. (1998). The effects of security of attachment and maternal attribution of meaning on children's linguistic acquisitional style. *Infant Behavior and Development, 21,* 237–252.

Melby, J., Conger, R., Fang, S., Wickrama, K., & Conger, K. (2008). Adolescent family experiences and educational attainment during early adulthood. *Developmental Psychology, 44*(6), 1519–1536.

Melby-Lervåg, M., & Hulme, C. (2013). Is working memory training effective? A meta-analytic review. *Developmental Psychology, 49*(2), 270.

Melén, E., Himes, B. E., Brehm, J. M., Boutaoui, N., Klanderman, B. J., Sylvia, J. S., & Lasky-Su, J. (2010). Analyses of shared genetic factors between asthma and obesity in children. *Journal of Allergy and Clinical Immunology, 126*(3), 631–637.

Meltzoff, A. N. (2007). "Like me": A foundation for social cognition. *Developmental Science, 10,* 126–134.

Meltzoff, A. N., & Moore, M. K. (1989). Imitation in newborn infants: Exploring the range of gestures imitated and the underlying mechanisms. *Developmental Psychology, 25,* 954–962.

Meltzoff, A. N., Murray, L., Simpson, E., Heimann, M., Nagy, E., Nadel, J., . . . & Subiaul, F. (2017). Re-examination of Oostenbroek et al.(2016): Evidence for neonatal imitation of tongue protrusion. *Developmental Science.*

Mendle, J. (2014). Beyond pubertal timing: New directions for studying individual differences in development. *Current Directions in Psychological Science, 23*(3), 215–219.

Mendle, J., & Ferrero, J. (2012). Detrimental psychological outcomes associated with pubertal timing in adolescent boys. *Developmental Review, 32*(1), 49–66.

Menegaux, F., Baruchel, A., Bertrand, Y., Lescoeur, B., Leverger, G., Nelken, B., . . . & Clavel, J. (2006). Household exposure to pesticides and risk of childhood acute leukaemia. *Occupational and Environmental Medicine, 63*(2), 131–134.

Mennella, J. A. (2014). Ontogeny of taste preferences: Basic biology and implications for health. *The American Journal of Clinical Nutrition, 99*(3), 704S–711S.

Mennella, J. A., & Bobowski, N. K. (2015). The sweetness and bitterness of childhood: Insights from basic research on taste preferences. *Physiology & Behavior, 152,* 502–507.

Mesman, J., van IJzendoorn, M. H., & Bakermans-Kranenburg, M. J. (2009). The many faces of the Still-Face Paradigm: A review and meta-analysis. *Developmental Review, 29*(2), 120–162.

Metz, T. D., & Stickrath, E. H. (2015). Marijuana use in pregnancy and lactation: A review of the evidence. *American Journal of Obstetrics and Gynecology, 213*(6), 761–778.

Meyer-Bahlburg, H. F. (2005). Gender identity outcome in female-raised 46, XY persons with penile agenesis, cloacal exstrophy of the bladder, or penile ablation. *Archives of Sexual Behavior, 34*(4), 423–438.

Miech, R. A., Johnston, L. D., O'Malley, P. M., Bachman, J. G., & Schulenberg, J. E. (2016). *Monitoring the Future national survey results on drug use, 1975-2015: Volume I, Secondary school students.* Ann Arbor: Institute for Social Research, The University of Michigan.

Milkie, M. A., Mattingly, M. J., Nomaguchi, S. M., Bianchi, S. M., & Robinson, J. P. (2004). The time squeeze: Parental statuses and feelings about time with children. *Journal of Marriage and Family, 66,* 739–761.

Miller, B., Messias, E., Miettunen, J., Alaräisänen, A., Järvelin, M. R., Koponen, H., . . . & Kirkpatrick, B. (2010). Meta-analysis of paternal age and schizophrenia risk in male versus female offspring. *Schizophrenia Bulletin, 37*(5), 1039–1047.

Miller, D. I., & Halpern, D. F. (2014). The new science of cognitive sex differences. *Trends in Cognitive Sciences, 18*(1), 37–45.

Miller, D. P. (2011). Maternal work and child overweight and obesity: The importance of timing. *Journal of Family and Economic Issues, 32*(2), 204–218.

Miller, S. A. (2009). Children's understanding of second-order mental states. *Psychological Bulletin, 135*(5), 749.

Mills, K. L., Lalonde, F., Clasen, L. S., Giedd, J. N., & Blakemore, S. J. (2012). Developmental changes in the structure of the social brain in late childhood and adolescence. *Social Cognitive and Affective Neuroscience, 9*(1), 123–131.

Min, J., Chiu, D. T., & Wang, Y. (2013). Variation in the heritability of body mass index based on diverse twin studies: A systematic review. *Obesity Reviews, 14*(11), 871–882.

Minagawa-Kawai, Y., Van Der Lely, H., Ramus, F., Sato, Y., Mazuka, R., & Dupoux, E. (2010). Optical brain imaging reveals general auditory and language-specific processing in early infant development. *Cerebral Cortex, 21*(2), 254–261.

Mindell, J. A., & Owens, J. A. (2015). *A clinical guide to pediatric sleep: Diagnosis and management of sleep problems.* Philadelphia, PA: Lippincott Williams & Wilkins.

Mindell, J. A., Sadeh, A., Kwon, R., & Goh, D. Y. (2013). Cross-cultural differences in the sleep of preschool children. *Sleep Medicine, 14*(12), 1283–1289.

Miniño, A. M. (2010). Mortality among teenagers aged 12–19 years: United States, 1999-2006. *NCHS Data Brief, 37.* Hyattsville, MD: National Center for Health Statistics.

Mintz, T. H. (2005). Linguistic and conceptual influences on adjective acquisition in 24- to 36-month-olds. *Developmental Psychology, 41,* 17–29.

Mireault, G., Poutre, M., Sargent-Hier, M., Dias, C., Perdue, B., & Myrick, A. (2012). Humour perception and creation between parents and 3- to 6-month-old infants. *Infant and Child Development, 21*(4), 338–347.

Mireault, G., Sparrow, J., Poutre, M., Perdue, B., & Macke, L. (2012). Infant humor perception from 3 to 6 months and attachment at one year. *Infant Behavior and Development, 35*(4), 797–802.

Mitchell, J. P., Banaji, M. R., & MacRae, C. N. (2005). The link between social cognition and self-referential thought in the medial prefrontal cortex. *Journal of Cognitive Neuroscience, 17*(8), 1306–1315.

Mitchell, K. J., Finkelhor, D., Jones, L. M., & Wolak, J. (2012). Prevalence and characteristics of youth sexting: A national study. *Pediatrics, 129*(1), 13–20.

Mitnick, D. M., Heyman, R. E., & Slep, A. M. S. (2009). Changes in relationship satisfaction across the transition to parenthood: A meta-analysis. *Journal of Family Psychology, 23*(6), 848-852.

Mix, K. S., Huttenlocher, J., & Levine, S. C. (2002). Multiple cues for quantification in infancy: Is number one of them? *Psychological Bulletin, 128*, 278-294.

Modecki, K. L., Minchin, J., Harbaugh, A. G., Guerra, N. G., & Runions, K. C. (2014). Bullying prevalence across contexts: A meta-analysis measuring cyber and traditional bullying. *Journal of Adolescent Health, 55*(5), 602-611.

Molero Samuelson, Y., Hodgins, S., Larsson, A., Larm, P., & Tengström, A. (2010). Adolescent antisocial behavior as predictor of adverse outcomes to age 50: A follow-up study of 1,947 individuals. *Criminal Justice and Behavior, 37*(2), 158-174.

Moll, H., & Meltzoff, A. N. (2011). How does it look? Level 2 perspective-taking at 36 months of age. *Child Development, 82*(2), 661-673.

Moll, H., & Tomasello, M. (2012). Three-year-olds understand appearance and reality—just not about the same object at the same time. *Developmental Psychology, 48*(4), 1124.

Moller, L. C., & Serbin, L. A. (1996). Antecedents of toddler gender segregation: Cognitive consonance, gender-typed toy preferences and behavioral compatibility. *Sex Roles, 35*(7-8), 445-460.

Molnár, G. (2011). Playful fostering of 6- to 8-year-old students' inductive reasoning. *Thinking Skills and Creativity, 6*(2), 91-99.

Moody, A. K. (2010). Using electronic books in the classroom to enhance emergent literacy skills in young children. *Journal of Literacy and Technology, 11*(4), 22-52.

Mook-Kanamori, D. O., Steegers, E. A., Eilers, P. H., Raat, H., Hofman, A., & Jaddoe, V. W. (2010). Risk factors and outcomes associated with first-trimester fetal growth restriction. *Journal of the American Medical Association, 303*(6), 527-534. doi: 10.1001/jama.2010.78

Moon, R. Y., & Fu, L. (2012). Sudden infant death syndrome: An update. *Pediatrics in Review-Elk Grove, 33*(7), 314.

Moore, M. (2012). Behavioral sleep problems in children and adolescents. *Journal of Clinical Psychology in Medical Settings, 19*(1), 77-83.

Morelli, G. A., Rogoff, B., & Angellilo, C. (2003). Cultural involvement in young children's access to work or involvement in specialized child-focused activities. *International Journal of Behavioral Development, 27*, 264-274.

Moreno, M. A. (2015). Sleep terrors and sleepwalking: Common parasomnias of childhood. *JAMA Pediatrics, 169*(7), 704-704.

Morris, A. S., Robinson, L. R., Hays-Grudo, J., Claussen, A. H., Hartwig, S. A., & Treat, A. E. (2017). Targeting parenting in early childhood: A public health approach to improve outcomes for children living in poverty. *Child Development, 88*(2), 388-397.

Mou, Y., Province, J. M., & Luo, Y. (2014). Can infants make transitive inferences? *Cognitive Psychology, 68*, 98-112.

Mrug, S., Elliott, M. N., Davies, S., Tortolero, S. R., Cuccaro, P., & Schuster, M. A. (2014). Early puberty, negative peer influence, and problem behaviors in adolescent girls. *Pediatrics, 133*(1), 7-14.

Mrug, S., Molina, B. S., Hoza, B., Gerdes, A. C., Hinshaw, S. P., Hechtman, L., & Arnold, L. E. (2012). Peer rejection and friendships in children with attention-deficit/hyperactivity disorder: Contributions to long-term outcomes. *Journal of Abnormal Child Psychology, 40*(6), 1013-1026.

Muentener, P., & Carey, S. (2010). Infants' causal representations of state change events. *Cognitive Psychology, 61*(2), 63-86.

Mühlemann, B., Jones, T. C., de Barros Damgaard, P., Allentoft, M. E., Shevnina, I., Logvin, A., . . . & Tashbaeva, K. (2018). Ancient hepatitis B viruses from the Bronze Age to the Medieval period. *Nature*, 1.

Mulder, H., Pitchford, N. J., & Marlow, N. (2010). Processing speed and working memory underlie academic attainment in very preterm children. *Archives of Disease in Childhood-Fetal and Neonatal Edition, 95*(4), F267-F272.

Mullan, D., & Currie, C. (2000). Socioeconomic equalities in adolescent health. In C. Currie, K. Hurrelmann, W. Settertobulte, R. Smith, & J. Todd (Eds.), *Health and health behaviour among young people: A WHO cross-national study (HBSC) international report* (pp. 65-72). (WHO Policy Series: Healthy Policy for Children and Adolescents, Series No. 1.) Copenhagen, Denmark: World Health Organization Regional Office for Europe.

Murachver, T., Pipe, M., Gordon, R., Owens, J. L., & Fivush, R. (1996). Do, show, and tell: Children's event memories acquired through direct experience, observation, and stories. *Child Development, 67*, 3029-3044.

Muris, P., Merckelbach, H., & Collaris, R. (1997). Common childhood fears and their origins. *Behaviour Research and Therapy, 35*, 929-937.

Murphy S. L., Xu, J.Q., Kochanek, K. D., Curtin, S.C., & Arias, E. (2017). Deaths: Final data for 2015. *National Vital Statistics Reports, 66*(6). Hyattsville, MD: National Center for Health Statistics.

Murray, C. J., & Ng, M. (2017). Nearly one-third of the world's population is obese or overweight, new data show. Retrieved from Institute for Health Metrics and Evaluation: www.healthdata.org/news-release/nearly-one-third-world%E2%80%99s-population-obese-or-overweight-new-data-show

Murray, J., & Farrington, D. P. (2010). Risk factors for conduct disorder and delinquency: Key findings from longitudinal studies. *The Canadian Journal of Psychiatry, 55*(10), 633-642.

Murray, R., Ramstetter, C., Devore, C., Allison, M., Ancona, R., Barnett, S., . . . & Okamoto, J. (2013). The crucial role of recess in school. *Pediatrics, 131*(1), 183-188.

Mustonen, U., Huurre, T., Kiviruusu, O., Haukkala, A., & Aro, H. (2011). Long-term impact of parental divorce on intimate relationship quality in adulthood and the mediating role of psychosocial resources. *Journal of Family Psychology, 25*(4), 615.

Myrick, S. E., & Martorell, G. A. (2011). Sticks and stones may break my bones: Protective factors for the effects of perceived discrimination on social competence in adolescence. *Personal Relationships, 18*(3), 487-501.

N

Nader, P. R., Bradley, R. H., Houts, R. M., McRitchie, S. L., & O'Brien, M. (2008). Moderate-to-vigorous physical activity from ages 9 to 15 years. *Journal of the American Medical Association, 300*, 295-305.

Nakamoto, J., & Schwartz, D. (2010). Is peer victimization associated with academic achievement? A meta-analytic review. *Social Development, 19*(2), 221-242.

Nansel, T. R., Overpeck, M., Pilla, R. S., Ruan, W. J., Simons-Morton, B., & Scheidt, P. (2001). Bullying behaviors among U.S. youth: Prevalence and association with psychosocial adjustment. *Journal of the American Medical Association, 285*, 2094-2100.

National Alliance for Public Charter Schools. (2018). Estimated charter public school enrollment, 2016-17. [Report]. Retrieved from www.publiccharters.org/sites/default/files/migrated/wp-content/uploads/2017/01/EER_Report_V5.pdf.

National Center for Education Statistics (NCES). (2003). *The condition of education, 2003* (NCES 2003-067). Washington, DC: Author.

National Center for Education Statistics (NCES). (2004). *The condition of education 2004* (NCES 2004-077). Washington, DC: U.S. Government Printing Office.

National Center for Education Statistics (NCES). (2007c). *The Nation's Report Card: Mathematics 2007* (NCES 2007-494). Washington, DC: Author.

National Center for Education Statistics (NCES). (2007d). *The Nation's Report Card: Reading 2007* (NCES 2007-496). Washington, DC: Author.

National Center for Education Statistics. (2016). Number and Internet access of instructional computers and rooms in public schools, by selected school characteristics: Selected years, 1995 through 2008. [Data sheet]. Retrieved from https://nces.ed.gov/programs/digest/d16/tables/dt16_218.10.asp?current=yes

National Center for Education Statistics. (2017a). Status dropout rates. [Fact sheet]. Retrieved from https://nces.ed.gov/programs/coe/indicator_coj.asp

National Center for Education Statistics. (2017b). The condition of education: Children and youth with disabilities. Retrieved from https://nces.ed.gov/programs/coe/indicator_cgg.asp

National Center for Education Statistics. (2018). Employment and unemployment rates by educational attainment. [Fact sheet]. Retrieved from https://nces.ed.gov/programs/coe/indicator_cbc.asp

National Center for Health Statistics (2017). Health, United States, 2016: Chartbook on long-term trends in health. Retrieved from www.cdc.gov/nchs/data/hus/hus16.pdf

National Center for Health Statistics (U.S.). (2016). Health, United States, 2015: With special feature on racial and ethnic health disparities. Retrieved from www.ncbi.nlm.nih.gov/pubmed/27308685

National Center for Health Statistics. (2004). Health, United States, 2004 with chartbook on trends in the health of Americans (DHHS Publication No. 2004-1232). Hyattsville, MD: Author.

National Center for Health Statistics. (2015). The public use natality file. Retrieved from ftp://ftp.cdc.gov/pub/Health_Statistics/NCHS/Dataset_Documentation/DVS/natality/UserGuide2015.pdf

National Clearinghouse on Child Abuse and Neglect Information (NCCANI). (2004). Long-term consequences of child abuse and neglect. Retrieved from http://nccanch.acf.hhs.gov/pubs/factsheets/longtermconsequences.cfm

National Coalition for the Homeless. (2017). Homelessness in America. Retrieved from http://nationalhomeless.org/about-homelessness/

National Coalition for the Homeless. (2018). Homelessness in America. [Fact sheet]. Retrieved from http://nationalhomeless.org/about-homelessness/

National Fatherhood Initiative. (2016). Father facts 7. Retrieved from www.fatherhood.org/father-absence-statistics-2016?

National Forum on Early Childhood Policy and Programs. (2010). Understanding the Head Start Impact Study. Retrieved from www.developingchild.harvard.edu/

National Highway Traffic Safety Administration. (2017). Teen driving. Retrieved from https://www.nhtsa.gov/road-safety/teen-driving

National Institute for Early Education Research (2017). The state of preschool, 2016. [Report]. Retrieved from http://nieer.org/wp-content/uploads/2017/09/Full_State_of_Preschool_2016_9.15.17_compressed.pdf

National Institute of Child Health and Development. (2008). Facts about Down syndrome. Retrieved from www.nichd.nihgov/publications/pubs/downsyndrome.cfm

National Institute of Child Health and Human Development (NICHD). (2017). Phenylketonuria (PKU). Retrieved from www.nichd.nih.gov/health/topics/pku/Pages/default.aspx

National Institutes of Health (NIH). (2010a, February 4). NIH scientists identify maternal and fetal genes that increase preterm birth risk [Press release]. Retrieved from http://www.nih.gov/news/health/feb2010/nichd-04.htm

National Scientific Council on the Developing Child. (2010). Persistent fear and anxiety can affect young children's learning and development: Working paper #9. Retrieved from www.developingchild.net

National Sleep Foundation. (2016). National Sleep Foundation recommends new sleep times. Retrieved from https://sleepfoundation.org/press-release/national-sleep-foundation-recommends-new-sleep-times/page/0/1

National Survey on Drug Use and Health (NSDUH). (2012). *Results from the 2011 national survey on drug use and health: Mental health findings.* NSDUH Series H-45. HHS Publication No. (SMA) 12-4725. Rockville, MD: Substance Abuse and Mental Health Services Administration. Retrieved from www.samhsa.gov/data/NSDUH/2k11MH_FindingsandDetTables/2K11MHFR/NSDUHmhfr2011.htm

Neisser, U., Boodoo, G., Bouchard, T. J., Jr., Boykin, A. W., Brody, N., Ceci, S. J., . . . Urbina, S. (1996). Intelligence: Knowns and unknowns. *American Psychologist, 51*(2), 77-101.

Nelson, C. A. (1995). The ontogeny of human memory: A cognitive neuroscience perspective. *Developmental Psychology, 31*, 723-738.

Nelson, K. (2005). Evolution and development of human memory systems. In B. J. Ellis and D. F. Bjorklund (Eds.), *Origins of the social mind: Evolutionary psychology and child development* (pp. 354-382). New York: Guilford Press.

Nelson, S. K., Kushlev, K., English, T., Dunn, E. W., & Lyubomirsky, S. (2013). In defense of parenthood: Children are associated with more joy than misery. *Psychological Science, 24*(1), 3-10.

Neppl, T. K., Dhalewadikar, J., & Lohman, B. J. (2016). Harsh parenting, deviant peers, adolescent risky behavior: Understanding the meditational effect of attitudes and intentions. *Journal of Research on Adolescence, 26*(3), 538-551.

Neppl, T. K., Donnellan, M. B., Scaramella, L. V., Widaman, K. F., Spilman, S. K., Ontai, L. L., & Conger, R. D. (2010). Differential stability of temperament and personality from toddlerhood to middle childhood. *Journal of Research in Personality, 44*(3), 386-396.

Nesdale, D. (2011). Social groups and children's intergroup prejudice: Just how influential are social group norms? *Anales de Psicología/Annals of Psychology, 27*(3), 600-610.

Neuburger, S., Jansen, P., Heil, M., & Quaiser-Pohl, C. (2011). Gender differences in pre-adolescents' mental-rotation performance: Do they depend on grade and stimulus type? *Personality and Individual Differences, 50*(8), 1238-1242.

Newbury, D. F., & Monaco, A. P. (2010). Genetic advances in the study of speech and language disorders. *Neuron, 68*(2), 309-320.

Ng, M., Fleming, T., Robinson, M., Thomson, B., Graetz, N., Margono, C., . . . & Abraham, J. P. (2014). Global, regional, and national prevalence of overweight and obesity in children and adults during 1980-2013: A systematic analysis for the Global Burden of Disease Study 2013. *The Lancet, 384*(9945), 766-781.

Ngun, T. C., & Vilain, E. (2014). The biological basis of human sexual orientation: Is there a role for epigenetics. *Adv Genet, 86*, 167-184.

Nguyen, B. H., Pérusse, D., Paquet, J., Petit, D., Boivin, M., Tremblay, R. E., & Montplaisir, J. (2008). Sleep terrors in children: A prospective study of twins. *Pediatrics, 122*(6), e1164-e1167.

Nielsen, G., Pfister, G., & Bo Andersen, L. (2011). Gender differences in the daily physical activities of Danish school children. *European Physical Education Review, 17*(1), 69-90.

Nieuwenhuijsen, M. J., Dadvand, P., Grellier, J., Martinez, D., & Vrijheid, M. (2013). Environmental risk factors of pregnancy outcomes: A summary of recent meta-analyses of epidemiological studies. *Environmental Health, 12*(1), 6.

Nisbett, R. E., Aronson, J., Blair, C., Dickens, W., Flynn, J., Halpern, D. F., & Turkheimer, E. (2012). Intelligence: New findings and theoretical developments. *American Psychologist, 67*(2), 130.

Niv, S., Ashrafulla, S., Tuvblad, C., Joshi, A., Raine, A., Leahy, R., & Baker, L. A. (2015). Childhood EEG frontal alpha power as a predictor of adolescent antisocial behavior: A twin heritability study. *Biological Psychology, 105*, 72-76.

Nobes, G., Panagiotaki, G., & Pawson, C. (2009). The influence of negligence, intentions and outcome on children's moral judgments. *Journal of Experimental Child Psychology, 104*(4), 382-397.

Noble, Y., & Boyd, R. (2012). Neonatal assessments for the preterm infant up to 4 months corrected age: A systematic review. *Developmental Medicine & Child Neurology, 54*(2), 129-139.

Nock, M. K., Green, J. G., Hwang, I., McLaughlin, K. A., Sampson, N. A., Zaslavsky, A. M., & Kessler, R. C. (2013). Prevalence, correlates, and treatment of lifetime suicidal behavior among adolescents: Results from the National Comorbidity Survey Replication Adolescent Supplement. *JAMA Psychiatry, 70*(3), 300-310.

Noller, P. (2005). Sibling relationships in adolescence: Learning and growing together. *Personal Relationships, 12*(1), 1-22.

Norman, R. E., Byambaa, M., De, R., Butchart, A., Scott, J., & Vos, T. (2012). The long-term health consequences of child physical abuse, emotional abuse, and neglect: A systematic review and meta-analysis. *PLoS medicine, 9*(11), e1001349.

O

O'Connor, T., Heron, J., Golding, J., Beveridge, M., & Glover, V. (2002). Maternal antenatal anxiety and children's behavioural/emotional problems at 4 years. *British Journal of Psychiatry, 180*, 502-508.

O'Flynn O'Brien, K. L. F., Varghese, A. C., & Agarwal, A. (2010). The genetic causes of male factor infertility: A review. *Fertility and Sterility, 93*, 1-12.

Oberle, E., Schonert-Reichl, K. A., & Thomson, K. C. (2010). Understanding the link between social and emotional well-being and peer relations in early adolescence: Gender-specific predictors of peer acceptance. *Journal of Youth and Adolescence, 39*(11), 1330-1342.

Oberman, L. M., & Ramachandran, V. S. (2007). The simulating social mind: The role of the mirror neuron system and simulation in the social and communicative deficits of autism spectrum disorders. *Psychological Bulletin, 133*, 310-327.

Odgers, C. L., Donley, S., Caspi, A., Bates, C. J., & Moffitt, T. E. (2015). Living alongside more affluent neighbors predicts greater involvement in antisocial behavior among low-income boys. *Journal of Child Psychology and Psychiatry, 56*(10), 1055-1064.

Offer, D., Offer, M. K., & Ostrov, E. (2004). *Regular guys: 34 years beyond adolescence.* Dordrecht, The Netherlands: Kluwer-Academic.

Ogden, C. L., Carroll, M. D., Curtin, L. R., Lamb, M. M., & Flegal, K. M. (2010). Prevalence of high body mass index in U.S. children and adolescents, 2007-2008. *Journal of the American Medical Association, 303*(3), 242-249.

Ogden, C. L., Carroll, M. D., Fryar, C. D., & Flegal, K. M. (2015). *Prevalence of obesity among adults and youth: United States, 2011-2014* (pp. 1-8). Washington, DC: U.S. Department of Health and Human Services, Centers for Disease Control and Prevention, National Center for Health Statistics.

Ogden, C. L., Carroll, M. D., Kit, B. K., & Flegal, K. M. (2014). Prevalence of childhood and adult obesity in the United States, 2011-2012. *JAMA, 311*(8), 806-814.

Ogden, C. L., Carroll, M. D., Lawman, H. G., Fryar, C. D., Kruszon-Moran, D., Kit, B. K., & Flegal, K. M. (2016). Trends in obesity prevalence among children and adolescents in the United States, 1988-1994 through 2013-2014. *JAMA, 315*(21), 2292-2299.

Ogden, C. L., Lamb, M. M., Carroll, M. D., & Flegal, K. M. (2010). Obesity and socioeconomic status in children and adolescents: United

States, 2005-2008. NCHS Data Brief. Number 51. *National Center for Health Statistics.*

Okahana, H., & Zhou, E. (2017). *Graduate enrollment and degrees: 2006 to 2016.* Washington, DC: Council of Graduate Schools.

Olson, M. E., Diekema, D., Elliott, B. A., & Renier, C. M. (2010). Impact of income and income inequality on infant health outcomes in the United States. *Pediatrics, 126*(6), 1165-1173.

Olweus, D. (1995). Bullying or peer abuse at school: Facts and intervention. *Current Directions in Psychological Science, 4*, 196-200.

O'Neill, W. (2005). Word-imagery effects on recollection and familiarity in recognition memory. *Perceptual and Motor Skills, 100*(3), 716-722.

Ono, M., & Harley, V. R. (2013). Disorders of sex development: New genes, new concepts. *Nature Reviews Endocrinology, 9*(2), 79-91.

Ooi, L. L., Baldwin, D., Coplan, R. J., & Rose-Krasnor, L. (2018). Young children's preference for solitary play: Implications for socio-emotional and school adjustment. *British Journal of Developmental Psychology, 22.*

Oostenbroek, J., Suddendorf, T., Nielsen, M., Redshaw, J., Kennedy-Costantini, S., Davis, J., . . . & Slaughter, V. (2016). Comprehensive longitudinal study challenges the existence of neonatal imitation in humans. *Current Biology, 26*(10), 1334-1338.

Opfer, J. E., & Gelman, S. A. (2011). Development of the animate-inanimate distinction. In U. Goswami (Ed.), *The Wiley-Blackwell handbook of childhood cognitive development* (2nd ed., pp. 213-238). Hoboken, NJ: Wiley.

Organisation for Economic Cooperation and Development (OECD). (2008). *Education at a glance.* Paris: Author.

Organisation for Economic Cooperation and Development. (2015). The ABC of gender equity in education: Aptitude, behavior, confidence. Retrieved from www.oecd.org/pisa/keyfindings/pisa-2012-results-gender-eng.pdf

Organisation for Economic Cooperation and Development. (2016). PISA 2015 results in focus. Retrieved from www.oecd.org/pisa/pisa-2015-results-in-focus.pdf

Ostfeld, B. M., Esposity, L., Perl, H., & Hegyl, T. (2010). Concurrent risks in sudden infant death syndrome. *Pediatrics, 125*(3), 447-453.

Otis, A. S. (1993). *Otis-Lennon School Ability Test: OLSAT.* New York: The Psychological Corp.

Out, D., Pieper, S., Bakermans-Kranenburg, M. J., Zeskind, P. S., & van IJzendoorn, M. H. (2010). Intended sensitive and harsh caregiving responses to infant crying: The role of cry pitch and perceived urgency in an adult twin sample. *Child Abuse & Neglect, 34*(11), 863-873.

Overstreet, S., Devine, J., Bevans, K., & Efreom, Y. (2005). Predicting parental involvement in children's schooling within an economically disadvantaged African American sample. *Psychology in the Schools, 42*(1), 101-111.

Owens, J., & Adolescent Sleep Working Group. (2014). Insufficient sleep in adolescents and young adults: An update on causes and consequences. *Pediatrics, 134*(3), e921-e932.

Özçalışkan, Ş., & Goldin-Meadow, S. (2010). Sex differences in language first appear in gesture. *Developmental Science, 13*(5), 752-760.

Özen, S., & Darcan, Ş. (2011). Effects of environmental endocrine disruptors on pubertal development. *Journal of Clinical Research in Pediatric Endocrinology, 3*(1), 1.

P

Padilla, A. M., Lindholm, K. J., Chen, A., Duran, R., Hakuta, K., Lambert, W., & Tucker, G. R. (1991). The English-only movement: Myths, reality, and implications for psychology. *American Psychologist, 46*(2), 120-130.

Padilla-Walker, L. M., Nielson, M. G., & Day, R. D. (2016). The role of parental warmth and hostility on adolescents' prosocial behavior toward multiple targets. *Journal of Family Psychology, 30*(3), 331.

Pagani, L. S., Fitzpatrick, C., Barnett, T. A., & Dubow, E. (2010). Prospective associations between early childhood television exposure and academic, psychosocial, and physical well-being by middle childhood. *Archives of Pediatrics & Adolescent Medicine, 164*(5), 425-431.

Palacios, J., & Brodzinsky, D. (2010). Adoption research: Trends, topics, outcomes. *International Journal of Behavioral Development, 34*(3), 270-284.

Pan, B. A., Rowe, M. L., Singer, J. D., & Snow, C. E. (2005). Maternal correlates of growth in toddler vocabulary production in low-income families. *Child Development, 76*, 763-782.

Panigrahy, A., Filiano, J., Sleeper, L. A., Mandell, F., Valdes-Dapena, M., Krous, H. F., . . . Kinney, H. C. (2000). Decreased serotonergic receptor binding in rhombic lip-derived regions of the medulla oblongata in the sudden infant death syndrome. *Journal of Neuropathology and Experimental Neurology, 59*, 377-384.

Papadimitriou, A. (2016). Timing of puberty and secular trend in human maturation. In P. Kumanov & A. Agarwal (Eds.), *Puberty* (pp. 121-136). Geneva: Springer.

Parish-Morris, J., Mahajan, N., Hirsh-Pasek, K., Golinkoff, R. M., & Collins, M. F. (2013). Once upon a time: Parent–child dialogue and storybook reading in the electronic era. *Mind, Brain, and Education, 7*(3), 200-211.

Park, S., Belsky, J., Putnam, S., & Crnic, K. (1997). Infant emotionality, parenting, and 3-year inhibition: Exploring stability and lawful discontinuity in a male sample. *Developmental Psychology, 33*, 218-227.

Park, S., Sappenfield, W. M., Huang, Y., Sherry, B., & Bensyl, D. M. (2010). The impact of the availability of school vending machines on eating behavior during lunch: The Youth Physical Activity and Nutrition Survey. *Journal of the American Dietetic Association, 110*(10), 1532-1536.

Parker, A. E., Mathis, E. T., & Kupersmidt, J. B. (2013). How is this child feeling? Preschool-aged children's ability to recognize emotion in faces and body poses. *Early Education & Development, 24*(2), 188-211.

Parker, S. E., Mai, C. T., Canfield, M. A., Rickard, R., Wang, Y., Meyer, R. E., . . . & Correa, A. (2010). Updated national birth prevalence estimates for selected birth defects in the United States, 2004-2006. *Birth Defects Research Part A: Clinical and Molecular Teratology, 88*(12), 1008-1016.

Parkes, A., Henderson, M., Wight, D., & Nixon, C. (2011). Is parenting associated with teenagers' early sexual risk-taking, autonomy and relationship with sexual partners? *Perspectives on Sexual and Reproductive Health, 43*(1), 30-40.

Parkinson, J. R., Hyde, M. J., Gale, C., Santhakumaran, S., & Modi, N. (2013). Preterm birth and the metabolic syndrome in adult life: A systematic review and meta-analysis. *Pediatrics*, peds-2012.

Parmar, P., Harkness, S., & Super, C. (2004). Asian and Euro-American parents' ethnotheories of play and learning: Effects on preschool children's home routines and school behaviour. *International Journal of Behavioral Development, 28*(2), 97-104.

Partanen, E., Kujala, T., Näätänen, R., Liitola, A., Sambeth, A., & Huotilainen, M. (2013). Learning-induced neural plasticity of speech processing before birth. *Proceedings of the National Academy of Sciences, 110*(37), 15145-15150.

Partridge, S., Balayla, J., Holcroft, C. A., & Abenhaim, H. A. (2012). Inadequate prenatal care utilization and risks of infant mortality and poor birth outcome: A retrospective analysis of 28,729,765 US deliveries over 8 years. *American Journal of Perinatology, 29*(10), 787-794.

Pascalis, O., & Kelly, D. J. (2009). The origins of face processing in humans: Phylogeny and ontogeny. *Perspectives on Psychological Science, 4*(2), 200-209.

Pasterski, V. L., Geffner, M. E., Brain, C., Hindmarsh, P., Brook, C., & Hines, M. (2005). Prenatal hormones and postnatal socialization by parents as determinants of male-typical toy play in girls with congenital adrenal hyperplasia. *Child Development, 76*(1), 264-278.

Pasterski, V., Geffner, M. E., Brain, C., Hindmarsh, P., Brook, C., & Hines, M. (2011). Prenatal hormones and childhood sex segregation: Playmate and play style preferences in girls with congenital adrenal hyperplasia. *Hormones and Behavior, 59*(4), 549-555.

Pastor, P. N., & Reuben, C. A. (2008). Diagnosed attention deficit hyperactivity disorder and learning disability: United States, 2004-2006. *Vital and Health Statistics. Series 10, Data from the National Health Survey, 237*, 1-14.

Pastor, P. N., Duran, C., & Reuben, C. (2015). Quickstats: Percentage of children and adolescents aged 5-17 years with diagnosed attention-deficit/hyperactivity disorder (ADHD), by race and hispanic ethnicity—National health interview survey, United States, 1997-2014. *Morbidity and Mortality Weekly Report (MMWR), 64*(33), 925-925.

Pathak, P., West, D., Martin, B. C., Helm, M. E., & Henderson, C. (2010). Evidence-based use of second-generation antipsychotics in a state Medicaid pediatric population, 2001-2005. *Psychiatric Services, 61*(2), 123-129.

Patrick, S. W., & Schiff, D. M. (2017). A public health response to opioid use in pregnancy. *Pediatrics*, e20164070.

Patterson, T. (2017, June 15). Why does America have so many hungry kids? Retrieved from CNN: www.cnn.com/2017/06/09/health/champions-for-change-child-hunger-in-america/index.html

Patton, G. C., Coffey, C., Cappa, C., Currie, D., Riley, L., Gore, F., . . . & Mokdad, A. (2012). Health of the world's adolescents: A synthesis of internationally comparable data. *The Lancet, 379*(9826), 1665-1675.

Pauen, S. (2002). Evidence for knowledge-based category discrimination in infancy. *Child Development, 73*, 1016-1033.

Pedersen, M., Giorgis-Allemand, L., Bernard, C., Aguilera, I., Andersen, A. M. N., Ballester, F., . . . & Dedele, A. (2013). Ambient air pollution and low birthweight: A European cohort study (ESCAPE). *The Lancet Respiratory Medicine, 1*(9), 695-704.

Pellegrini, A. D. (2012). The development and function of rough-and-tumble play in childhood and adolescence: A sexual selection theory perspective. In *Play and development* (pp. 85-106). London: Psychology Press.

Pellegrini, A. D., & Archer, J. (2005). Sex differences in competitive and aggressive behavior: A view from sexual selection theory. In B. J. Ellis & D. F. Bjorklund (Eds.), *Origins of the social mind: Evolutionary psychology and child development* (pp. 219-244). New York: Guilford Press.

Pellegrini, A. D., Dupuis, D., & Smith, P.K. (2007). Play in evolution and development. *Developmental Review, 27*, 261-276.

Pelphrey, K. A., Reznick, J. S., Davis Goldman, B., Sasson, N., Morrow, J., Donahoe, A., & Hodgson, K. (2004). Development of visuospatial short-term memory in the second half of the 1st year. *Developmental Psychology, 40*(5), 836.

Perera, F., Tang, W-Y., Herbstman, J., Tang, D., Levin, L., Miller, R., & Ho, S.-M. (2009). Relation of DNA methylation of 5'-CpG island of ACSL3 to transplacental exposure to airborne polycyclic aromatic hydrocarbons and childhood asthma. *PloS ONE, 4*, e44-e48.

Perera, F. P., Rauh, V., Whyatt, R. M., Tsai, W. Y., Bernert, J. T., Tu, Y. H., . . . & Tang, D. (2004). Molecular evidence of an interaction between prenatal environmental exposures and birth outcomes in a multiethnic population. *Environmental Health Perspectives, 112*(5), 626.

Pérez-Edgar, K., Bar-Haim, Y., McDermott, J. M., Chronis-Tuscano, A., Pine, D. S., & Fox, N. A. (2010). Attention biases to threat and behavioral inhibition in early childhood shape adolescent social withdrawal. *Emotion, 10*(3), 349.

Pérez-Edgar, K., Reeb-Sutherland, B. C., McDermott, J. M., White, L. K., Henderson, H. A., Degnan, K. A., . . . & Fox, N. A. (2011). Attention biases to threat link behavioral inhibition to social withdrawal over time in very young children. *Journal of Abnormal Child Psychology, 39*(6), 885-895.

Perkins, K. M., Boulet, S. L., Jamieson, D. J., & Kissin, D. M. (2016). Trends and outcomes of gestational surrogacy in the United States. *Fertility and Sterility, 106*(2), 435-442.

Perkins, K. M., Boulet, S. L., Levine, A. D., Jamieson, D. J., & Kissin, D. M. (2018). Differences in the utilization of gestational surrogacy between states in the U.S. *Reproductive Biomedicine & Society Online, 5*, 1-4.

Perou, R., Bitsko, R. H., Blumberg, S. J., Pastor, P., Ghandour, R. M., Gfroerer, J. C., . . . & Parks, S. E. (2013). Mental health surveillance among children—United States, 2005-2011. *MMWR Surveill Summ, 62*(Suppl 2), 1-35.

Perrin, E. C., Siegel, B. S., & Committee on Psychosocial Aspects of Child and Family Health. (2013). Promoting the well-being of children whose parents are gay or lesbian. *Pediatrics, 131*(4), e1374-e1383.

Pesonen, A. K., Räikkönen, K., Keltikangas-Järvinen, L., Strandberg, T., & Järvenpää, A. L. (2003). Parental perception of infant temperament: Does parents' joint attachment matter? *Infant Behavior and Development, 26*(2), 167-182.

Petersen, A. C. (1993). Presidential address: Creating adolescents: The role of context and process in developmental transitions. *Journal of Research on Adolescents, 3*(1), 1-18.

Peterson, C. (2011). Children's memory reports over time: Getting both better and worse. *Journal of Experimental Child Psychology, 109*(3), 275-293.

Petit, D., Pennestri, M. H., Paquet, J., Desautels, A., Zadra, A., Vitaro, F., . . . & Montplaisir, J. (2015). Childhood sleepwalking and sleep terrors: A longitudinal study of prevalence and familial aggregation. *JAMA Pediatrics, 169*(7), 653-658.

Petit, D., Touchette, E., Tremblay, R. E., Boivin, M., & Montplaisir, J. (2007). Dyssomnias and parasomnias in early childhoold. *Pediatrics, 119*(5), e1016-e1025.

Petitclerc, A., Gatti, U., Vitaro, F., & Tremblay, R. E. (2013). Effects of juvenile court exposure on crime in young adulthood. *Journal of Child Psychology and Psychiatry, 54*(3), 291-297.

Petitto, L. A., Holowka, S., Sergio, L., & Ostry, D. (2001). Language rhythms in babies' hand movements. *Nature, 413*, 35-36.

Petitto, L. A., & Kovelman, I. (2003). The bilingual paradox: How signing-speaking bilingual children help us to resolve it and teach us about the brain's mechanisms underlying all language acquisition. *Learning Languages, 8*, 5-18.

Petitto, L. A., & Marentette, P. F. (1991). Babbling in the manual mode: Evidence for the ontogeny of language. *Science, 251*, 1493-1495.

Petrosino, A. J., Guckenburg, S., & Turpin-Petrosino, C. (2013). *Formal system processing of juveniles: Effects on delinquency* (Vol. 9). Washington, DC: U.S. Department of Justice, Office of Community Oriented Policing Services.

Petrosino, A., Turpin-Petrosino, C., Hollis-Peel, M. E., & Lavenberg, J. G. (2013). 'Scared Straight' and other juvenile awareness programs for preventing juvenile delinquency. *The Cochrane Library*.

Pettit, G. S., & Arsiwalla, D. D. (2008). Commentary on special section on "bidirectional parent–child relationships": The continuing evolution of dynamic, transactional models of parenting and youth behavior problems. *Journal of Abnormal Child Psychology, 36*(5), 711.

Pew Research Center. (2012). Parents, teens and online privacy: Main report. Retrieved from www.pewinternet.org/2012/11/20/main-report-10/

Pew Research Center. (2018). Social media fact sheet. [Data report]. Retrieved from www.pewinternet.org/fact-sheet/social-media/

Phinney, J. S. (1992). The multigroup ethnic identity measure: A new scale for use with diverse groups. *Journal of adolescent research, 7*(2), 156-176.

Phinney, J. S., & Ong, A. D. (2007). Conceptualization and measurement of ethnic identity: Current status and future directions. *Journal of Counseling Psychology, 54*(3), 271.

Piaget, J. (1929). *The child's conception of the world*. New York: Harcourt Brace.

Piaget, J. (1932). *The moral judgment of the child*. New York: Harcourt Brace.

Piaget, J. (1954). *The construction of reality in the child*. Basic Books, New York.

Piaget, J. (1962). *The language and thought of the child* (M. Gabain, Trans.). Cleveland, OH: Meridian. (Original work published 1923)

Piaget, J., & Inhelder, B. (1969). *The psychology of the child*. New York: Basic Books.

Piernas, C., & Popkin, B. M. (2010). Trends in snacking among U.S. children. *Health Affairs, 29*(3), 398-404.

Pike, A., Coldwell, J., & Dunn, J. F. (2005). Sibling relationships in early/middle childhood: Links with individual adjustment. *Journal of Family Psychology, 19*, 523-532.

Piko, B. F., & Balázs, M. Á. (2012). Authoritative parenting style and adolescent smoking and drinking. *Addictive Behaviors, 37*(3), 353-356.

Pino, O. (2016). Fetal memory: The effects of prenatal auditory experience on human development. *BAOJ Med Nursing, 2*, 20.

Pinquart, M. (2016). Associations of parenting styles and dimensions with academic achievement in children and adolescents: A meta-analysis. *Educational Psychology Review, 28*(3), 475-493.

Pinquart, M. (2017). Associations of parenting dimensions and styles with externalizing problems of children and adolescents: An updated meta-analysis. *Developmental Psychology, 53*(5), 873-932.

Plomin, R. (1996). Nature and nurture. In M. R. Merrens & G. G. Brannigan (Eds.), *The developmental psychologist: Research adventures across the life span* (pp. 3-19). New York: McGraw-Hill.

Plomin, R. (2011). Commentary: Why are children in the same family so different? Non-shared environment three decades later. *International Journal of Epidemiology, 40*(3), 582-592.

Poehlmann-Tynan, J., Gerstein, E. D., Burnson, C., Weymouth, L., Bolt, D. M., Maleck, S., & Schwichtenberg, A. J. (2015). Risk and resilience in preterm children at age 6. *Development and Psychopathology, 27*(3), 843-858.

Poirel, N., Borst, G., Simon, G., Rossi, S., Cassotti, M., Pineau, A., & Houdé, O. (2012). Number conservation is related to children's prefrontal inhibitory control: An fMRI study of a Piagetian task. *PloS One, 7*(7), e40802.

Polanczyk, G. V., Salum, G. A., Sugaya, L. S., Caye, A., & Rohde, L. A. (2015). Annual research review: A meta-analysis of the worldwide prevalence of mental disorders in children and adolescents. *Journal of Child Psychology and Psychiatry, 56*(3), 345-365.

Polanczyk, G. V., Willcutt, E. G., Salum, G. A., Kieling, C., & Rohde, L. A. (2014). ADHD prevalence estimates across three decades: An updated systematic review and meta-regression analysis. *International Journal of Epidemiology, 43*(2), 434-442.

Pomerantz, E. M., & Wang, Q. (2009). The role of parental control in children's development in Western and Asian countries. *Current Directions in Psychological Science, 18*(5), 285-289.

Ponappa, S., Bartle-Haring, S., & Day, R. (2014). Connection to parents and healthy separation during adolescence: A longitudinal perspective. *Journal of Adolescence, 37*(5), 555–566.

Pons, F., Harris, P. L., & de Rosnay, M. (2004). Emotion comprehension between 3 and 11 years: Developmental periods and hierarchical organization. *European Journal of Developmental Psychology, 1*(2), 127–152.

Portes, P. R., Dunham, R., & Del Castillo, K. (2000). Identity formation and status across cultures: Exploring the cultural validity of Eriksonian Theory. In A. L. Communian & U. Geilen (Eds.), *International perspectives on human development* (pp. 449–460). Berlin: abst Science.

Portnoy, J., & Farrington, D. P. (2015). Resting heart rate and antisocial behavior: An updated systematic review and meta-analysis. *Aggression and Violent Behavior, 22*, 33–45.

Povinelli, D. J., & Giambrone, S. (2001). Reasoning about beliefs: A human specialization? *Child Development, 72*, 691–695.

Powell, S. G., Frydenberg, M., & Thomsen, P. H. (2015). The effects of long-term medication on growth in children and adolescents with ADHD: An observational study of a large cohort of real-life patients. *Child and Adolescent Psychiatry and Mental Health, 9*(1), 50.

Preissler, M., & Bloom, P. (2007). Two-year-olds appreciate the dual nature of pictures. *Psychological Science, 18*(1), 1–2.

Prentice, P., & Viner, R. M. (2013). Pubertal timing and adult obesity and cardiometabolic risk in women and men: A systematic review and meta-analysis. *International Journal of Obesity, 37*(8), 1036.

Pressley, J. C., Barlow, B., Kendig, T., & Paneth-Pollak, R. (2007). Twenty-year trends in fatal injuries to very young children: The persistence of racial disparities. *Pediatrics, 119*, 875–884.

Price, J. H., & Khubchandani, J. (2017). Adolescent homicides, suicides, and the role of firearms: A narrative review. *American Journal of Health Education, 48*(2), 67–79.

Price, T. S., Grosser, T., Plomin, R., & Jaffee, S. R. (2010). Fetal genotype for the xenobiotic metabolizing enzyme NQO1 influences intrauterine growth among infants whose mothers smoked during pregnancy. *Child Development, 81*(1), 101–114.

Procianoy, R. S., Mendes, E. W., & Silveira, R. C. (2010). Massage therapy improves neurodevelopment outcome at two years corrected age for very low birth weight infants. *Early Human Development, 86*(1), 7–11.

Proctor, B. D., Semega, J. L., & Kollar, M. A. (2016). *U.S. Census Bureau, current population reports, P60-256 (RV): Income and poverty in the United States: 2015.* Washington, DC: U.S. Government Printing Office.

Pruden, S. M., Hirsch-Pasek, K., Golinkoff, R. M., & Hennon, E. A. (2006). The birth of words: Ten-month-olds learn words through perceptual salience. *Child Development, 77*, 266–280.

Pulgarón, E. R. (2013). Childhood obesity: A review of increased risk for physical and psychological comorbidities. *Clinical Therapeutics, 35*(1), A18–A32.

Puma, M., Bell, S., Cook, R., Heid, C., Broene, P., Jenkins, F., . . . Downer, J. (2012). *Third grade follow-up to the Head Start impact study: Final report.* OPRE Report 2012-45. Washington, DC: Administration for Children & Families.

Purcell, K., Heaps, A., Buchanan, J. & Fried, L. (2013). *How teachers are using technology in the classroom.* Washington, DC: Pew Internet & American Life Project.

Q

Qin, J., Wang, H., Sheng, X., Liang, D., Tan, H., & Xia, J. (2015). Pregnancy-related complications and adverse pregnancy outcomes in multiple pregnancies resulting from assisted reproductive technology: A meta-analysis of cohort studies. *Fertility and Sterility, 103*(6), 1492–1508.

Qiu, A., Mori, S., & Miller, M. I. (2015). Diffusion tensor imaging for understanding brain development in early life. *Annual Review of Psychology, 66*, 853–876.

Quattrin, T., Liu, E., Shaw, N., Shine, B., & Chiang, E. (2005). Obese children who are referred to the pediatric oncologist: Characteristics and outcome. *Pediatrics, 115*, 348–351.

Quinn, P. C., Westerlund, A., & Nelson, C. A. (2006). Neural markers of categorization in 6-month-old infants. *Psychological Science, 17*, 59–66.

R

Raabe, T., & Beelmann, A. (2011). Development of ethnic, racial, and national prejudice in childhood and adolescence: A multinational meta-analysis of age differences. *Child Development, 82*(6), 1715–1737.

Racz, S. J., & McMahon, R. J. (2011). The relationship between parental knowledge and monitoring and child and adolescent conduct: A 10-year update. *Clinical Child and Family Psychology Review, 14*(4), 377–398.

Rai, R., Mitchell, P., Kadar, T., & Mackenzie, L. (2016). Adolescent egocentrism and the illusion of transparency: Are adolescents as egocentric as we might think? *Current Psychology, 35*(3), 285–294.

Rakison, D. H. (2005). Infant perception and cognition. In B. J. Ellis & D. F. Bjorklund (Eds.), *Origins of the social mind* (pp. 317–353). New York: Guilford Press.

Rakison, D. H., & Krogh, L. (2012). Does causal action facilitate causal perception in infants younger than 6 months of age? *Developmental Science, 15*(1), 43–53.

Rakyan, V., & Beck., S. (2006). Epigenetic inheritance and variation in mammals. *Current Opinion in Genetics and Development, 16*(6), 573–577.

Ramsey, P. G., & Lasquade, C. (1996). Preschool children's entry attempts. *Journal of Applied Developmental Psychology, 17*, 135–150.

Rapoport, J. L., Giedd, J. N., & Gogtay, N. (2012). Neurodevelopmental model of schizophrenia: Update 2012. *Molecular Psychiatry, 17*(12), 1228–1238.

Rapport, M. D., Orban, S. A., Kofler, M. J., & Friedman, L. M. (2013). Do programs designed to train working memory, other executive functions, and attention benefit children with ADHD? A meta-analytic review of cognitive, academic, and behavioral outcomes. *Clinical Psychology Review, 33*(8), 1237–1252.

Rasberry, C. N., Lee, S. M., Robin, L., Laris, B. A., Russell, L. A., Coyle, K. K., & Nihiser, A. J. (2011). The association between school-based physical activity, including physical education, and academic performance: A systematic review of the literature. *Preventive Medicine, 52*, S10–S20.

Rauh, V. A., Whyatt, R. M., Garfinkel, R., Andrews, H., Hoepner, L., Reyes, A., . . . Perera, F. P. (2004). Developmental effects of exposure to environmental tobacco smoke and material hardship among inner-city children. *Neurotoxicology and Teratology, 26*, 373–385.

Raver, C. (2003). Young children's emotional development and school readiness. *Social Policy Report, 16*(3), 3–19.

Raver, C. C., Blair, C., & Willoughby, M. (2013). Poverty as a predictor of 4-year-olds' executive function: New perspectives on models of differential susceptibility. *Developmental Psychology, 49*(2), 292.

Ray, B. D. (2010). Academic achievement and demographic traits of homeschool students: A nationwide study. *Academic Leadership, 8*(1).

Raznahan, A., Shaw, P., Lalonde, F., Stockman, M., Wallace, G. L., Greenstein, D., . . . & Giedd, J. N. (2011). How does your cortex grow? *Journal of Neuroscience, 31*(19), 7174–7177.

Reardon, S. F. (2011). The widening academic achievement gap between the rich and the poor: New evidence and possible explanations. In

R. Murnane & G. Duncan (Eds.), *Whither opportunity* (pp. 91–116). New York: Russell Sage.

Recchia, H. E., & Howe, N. (2009). Associations between social understanding, sibling relationship quality, and siblings' conflict strategies and outcomes. *Child Development, 80*(5), 1564–1578.

Redford, J., Battle, D., & Bielick, S. (2016). *Homeschooling in the United States: 2012 (NCES 2016–096).* Washington, DC: National Center for Education Statistics, Institute of Education Sciences, U.S. Department of Education.

Reese, E., & Newcombe, R. (2007). Training mothers in elaborative reminiscing enhances children's autobiographical memory and narrative. *Child Development, 78*(4), 1153–1170.

Reese, E., Sparks, A., & Leyva, D. (2010). A review of parent interventions for preschool children's language and emergent literacy. *Journal of Early Childhood Literacy, 10*(1), 97–117.

Reiner, W. G. (2005). Gender identity and sex-of-rearing in children with disorders of sexual differentiation. *Journal of Pediatric Endocrinology and Metabolism, 18*(6), 549–554.

Reiss, A. L., Abrams, M. T., Singer, H. S., Ross, J. L., & Denckla, M. B. (1996). Brain development, gender and IQ in children: A volumetric imaging study. *Brain, 119*, 1763–1774.

Reissland, N., Francis, B., & Mason, J. (2013). Can healthy fetuses show facial expressions of "pain" or "distress"? *PLoS One, 8*(6), e65530.

Rekker, R., Pardini, D., Keijsers, L., Branje, S., Loeber, R., & Meeus, W. (2015). Moving in and out of poverty: The within-individual association between socioeconomic status and juvenile delinquency. *PLoS One, 10*(11), e0136461.

Resing, W. C. (2013). Dynamic testing and individualized instruction: Helpful in cognitive education? *Journal of Cognitive Education and Psychology, 12*(1), 81.

Reynolds, A. J., Temple, J. A., Ou, S. R., Arteaga, I. A., & White, B. A. (2011). School-based early childhood education and age-28 well-being: Effects by timing, dosage, and subgroups. *Science, 333*(6040), 360–364.

Reynolds, G. D., Guy, M. W., & Zhang, D. (2011). Neural correlates of individual differences in infant visual attention and recognition memory. *Infancy, 16*(4), 368–391.

Rice, M. L., Smolik, F., Perpich, D., Thompson, T., Rytting, N., & Blossom, M. (2010). Mean length of utterance levels in 6-month intervals for children 3 to 9 years with and without language impairments. *Journal of Speech, Language, and Hearing Research, 53*(2), 333–349.

Richards, R., Merrill, R. M., & Baksh, L. (2011). Health behaviors and infant health outcomes in homeless pregnant women in the United States. *Pediatrics, 128*(3), 438–446.

Richardson, G. A., Ryan, C., Willford, J., Day, N. L., & Goldschmidt, L. (2002). Prenatal alcohol and marijuana exposure: Effects on neuropsychological outcomes at 10 years. *Neurotoxicology and Teratology, 24*(3), 309–320.

Richert, R. A., Robb, M. B., Fender, J. G., & Wartella, E. (2010). Word learning from baby videos. *Archives of Pediatrics & Adolescent Medicine, 164*(5), 432–437.

Rideout, V., Foehr, U., & Roberts, D. (2010). *Generation M2: Media in the lives of 8 to 18-year-olds.* Kaiser Family Foundation Study. Retrieved from www.kff.org/entmedia/8010.cfm

Ridgers, N. D., Fairclough, S. J., & Stratton, G. (2010). Variables associated with children's physical activity levels during recess: The A-CLASS project. *International Journal of Behavioral Nutrition and Physical Activity, 7*(1), 74.

Riegle-Crumb, C., Farkas, G., & Muller, C. (2006). The role of gender and friendship in advanced course taking. *Sociology of Education, 79*(3), 206–228.

Riem, M. M., Bakermans-Kranenburg, M. J., van IJzendoorn, M. H., Out, D., & Rombouts, S. A. (2012). Attachment in the brain: Adult attachment representations predict amygdala and behavioral responses to infant crying. *Attachment & Human Development, 14*(6), 533–551.

Riethmuller, A. M., Jones, R. A., & Okely, A. D. (2009). Efficacy of interventions to improve motor development in young children: A systematic review. *Pediatrics, 124*(4), e782–e792.

Rimm-Kaufman, S. E., Curby, T. W., Grimm, K. J., Nathanson, L., & Brock, L. L. (2009). The contribution of children's self-regulation and classroom quality to children's adaptive behaviors in the kindergarten classroom. *Developmental Psychology, 45*(4), 958–972.

Rindermann, H., & Pichelmann, S. (2015). Future cognitive ability: U.S. IQ prediction until 2060 based on NAEP. *PLoS One, 10*(10), e0138412.

Rious, J. B., & Cunningham, M. (2018). Altruism as a buffer for antisocial behavior for African American adolescents exposed to community violence. *Journal of Community Psychology, 46*(2), 224–237.

Ritchie, S. J., Bates, T. C., & Deary, I. J. (2015). Is education associated with improvements in general cognitive ability, or in specific skills? *Developmental Psychology, 51*(5), 573.

Rivas-Drake, D., Seaton, E. K., Markstrom, C., Quintana, S., Syed, M., Lee, R. M., . . . & Ethnic and Racial Identity in the 21st Century Study Group. (2014). Ethnic and racial identity in adolescence: Implications for psychosocial, academic, and health outcomes. *Child Development, 85*(1), 40–57.

Roberts, G., Quach, J., Spencer-Smith, M., Anderson, P. J., Gathercole, S., Gold, L., . . . & Wake, M. (2016). Academic outcomes 2 years after working memory training for children with low working memory: A randomized clinical trial. *JAMA Pediatrics, 170*(5), e154568–e154568.

Roberts, H., Kruszon-Moran, D., Ly, K. N., Hughes, E., Iqbal, K., Jiles, R. B., & Holmberg, S. D. (2016). Prevalence of chronic hepatitis B virus (HBV) infection in U.S. households: National Health and Nutrition Examination Survey (NHANES), 1988–2012. *Hepatology, 63*(2), 388–397.

Rodgers, B., Gray, P., Davidson, T., & Butterworth, P. (2011). Parental divorce and adult family, social and psychological outcomes: The contribution of childhood family adversity. (Social Policy Research Paper No. 42). Canberra: Department of Families, Housing, Community Services & Indigenous Affairs.

Rodgers, E., D'Agostino, J. V., Harmey, S. J., Kelly, R. H., & Brownfield, K. (2016). Examining the nature of scaffolding in an early literacy intervention. *Reading Research Quarterly, 51*(3), 345–360.

Rogoff, B. (2003). *The cultural nature of human development.* Oxford, England: Oxford University Press.

Roopnarine, J., & Honig, A. S. (1985, September). The unpopular child. *Young Children,* 59–64.

Root, A. K., & Stifter, C. (2010). Temperament and maternal emotion socialization beliefs as predictors of early childhood social behavior in the laboratory and classroom. *Parenting: Science and Practice, 10*(4), 241–257.

Rosario, M., Schrimshaw, E. W., & Hunter, J. (2011). Different patterns of sexual identity development over time: Implications for the psychological adjustment of lesbian, gay, and bisexual youths. *Journal of Sex Research, 48*(1), 3–15.

Rose, A. J., & Rudolph, K. D. (2006). A review of sex differences in peer relationship processes: Potential trade-offs for the emotional and behavioral development of girls and boys. *Psychological Bulletin, 132*(1), 98.

Rose, S. A., Feldman, J. F., & Jankowski, J. J. (2002). Processing speed in the 1st year of life: A longitudinal study of preterm and full-term infants. *Developmental Psychology, 38*, 895–902.

Rose, S. A., Feldman, J. F., Jankowski, J. J., & Van Rossem, R. (2012). Information processing from infancy to 11 years: Continuities and prediction of IQ. *Intelligence, 40*(5), 445–457.

Roseberry, S., Hirsh-Pasek, K., & Golinkoff, R. M. (2014). Skype me! Socially contingent interactions help toddlers learn language. *Child Development, 85*(3), 956-970.

Rosner, B., Cook, N. R., Daniels, S., & Falkner, B. (2013). Childhood blood pressure trends and risk factors for high blood pressure novelty and significance: The NHANES experience 1988-2008. *Hypertension, 62*(2), 247-254.

Roth, G., Assor, A., Niemiec, C. P., Ryan, R. M., & Deci, E. L. (2009). The emotional and academic consequences of parental conditional regard: Comparing conditional positive regard, conditional negative regard, and autonomy supports as parenting practices. *Developmental Psychology, 45*(4), 1119-1142.

Rothbart, M. K., Ahadi, S. A., & Evans, D. E. (2000). Temperament and personality: Origins and outcomes. *Journal of Personality and Social Psychology, 78*, 122-135.

Rothbart, M. K., Sheese, B. E., Rueda, M. R., & Posner, M. I. (2011). Developing mechanisms of self-regulation in early life. *Emotion Review, 3*(2), 207-213.

Roussotte, F. F., Bramen, J. E., Nunez, C., Quandt, L. C., Smith, L., O'Connor, M. J., . . . Sowell, E. R. (2011). Abnormal brain activation during working memory in children with prenatal exposure to drugs of abuse: The effects of methamphetamine, alcohol, and polydrug exposure. *NeuroImage, 54*(4), 3067-3075.

Rovee-Collier, C. (1999). The development of infant memory. *Current Directions in Psychological Science, 8*, 80-85.

Rowe, M. L. (2012). A longitudinal investigation of the role of quantity and quality of child-directed speech in vocabulary development. *Child Development, 83*(5), 1762-1774.

Rubin, D., Leventhal, J., Krasilnikoff, P., Weile, B., & Berget, A. (1986). Effect of passive smoking on birth-weight. *The Lancet, 328*(8504), 415-417.

Rubin, K. H., Bukowski, W., & Parker, J. G. (1998). Peer interactions, relationships, and groups. In W. Damon (Series Ed.) & N. Eisenberg (Vol. Ed.), *Handbook of child psychology: Vol. 3. Social, emotional, and personality development* (5th ed., pp. 619-700). New York: Wiley.

Rubio-Fernández, P., & Geurts, B. (2013). How to pass the false-belief task before your fourth birthday. *Psychological Science, 24*(1), 27-33.

Ruble, D. N., & Martin, C. L. (1998). Gender development. In W. Damon (Series Ed.) & N. Eisenberg (Vol. Ed.), *Handbook of child psychology: Vol. 3. Social, emotional, and personality development* (5th ed., pp. 933-1016). New York: Wiley.

Rudy, D., & Grusec, J. E. (2006). Authoritarian parenting in individualistic and collectivistic groups: Associations with maternal emotion and cognition and children's self-esteem. *Journal of Family Psychology, 20*, 68-78.

Rueter, M. A., & Conger, R. D. (1995). Antecedents of parent-adolescent disagreements. *Journal of Marriage and Family, 57*, 435-448.

Ruigrok, A. N., Salimi-Khorshidi, G., Lai, M. C., Baron-Cohen, S., Lombardo, M. V., Tait, R. J., & Suckling, J. (2014). A meta-analysis of sex differences in human brain structure. *Neuroscience & Biobehavioral Reviews, 39*, 34-50.

Runco, M. A., Millar, G., Acar, S., & Cramond, B. (2010). Torrance tests of creative thinking as predictors of personal and public achievement: A fifty-year follow-up. *Creativity Research Journal, 22*(4), 361-368.

Runyan, D. K., Shankar, V., Hassan, F., Hunter, W. M., Jain, D., Paula, C. S., . . . & Bordin, I. A. (2010). International variations in harsh child discipline. *Pediatrics*, peds-2008.

Rushton, J. P., & Ankney, C. D. (2009). Whole brain size and general mental ability: A review. *International Journal of Neuroscience, 119*(5), 692-732.

Rushton, J. P., & Jensen, A. R. (2005). Thirty years of research on race differences in cognitive ability. *Psychology, Public Policy, and Law, 11*, 235-294.

Russ, S. W., & Wallace, C. E. (2013). Pretend play and creative processes. *American Journal of Play, 6*, 136-148.

Rust, J., Golombok, S., Hines, M., Johnston, K., Golding, J., & ALSPAC Study Team. (2000). The role of brothers and sisters in the gender development of preschool children. *Journal of Experimental Child Psychology, 77*(4), 292-303.

Rutter, M., Caspi, A., Fergusson, D., Horwood, L. J., Goodman, R., Maughan, B., . . . & Carroll, J. (2004). Sex differences in developmental reading disability: New findings from 4 epidemiological studies. *JAMA, 291*(16), 2007-2012.

Ryan, A. S., Wenjun, Z., & Acosta, A. (2002). Breastfeeding continues to increase into the new millennium. *Pediatrics, 110*, 1103-1109.

S

Sachs, H. C. (2013). The transfer of drugs and therapeutics into human breast milk: An update on selected topics. *Pediatrics, 132*(3), e796-e809.

Sacks, J. J., Gonzales, K. R., Bouchery, E. E., Tomedi, L. E., & Brewer, R. D. (2015). 2010 national and state costs of excessive alcohol consumption. *American Journal of Preventive Medicine, 49*(5), e73-e79.

Sadeh, A., De Marcas, G., Guri, Y., Berger, A., Tikotzky, L., & Bar-Haim, Y. (2015). Infant sleep predicts attention regulation and behavior problems at 3-4 years of age. *Developmental Neuropsychology, 40*(3), 122-137.

Sadeh, A., Tikotzky, L., & Scher, A. (2010). Parenting and infant sleep. *Sleep Medicine Reviews, 14*(2), 89-96.

Saffran, J. R., Pollak, S. D., Seibel, R. L., & Shkolnik, A. (2007). Dog is a dog is a dog: Infant rule learning is not specific to language. *Cognition, 105*(3), 669-680.

Sahoo, K., Sahoo, B., Choudhury, A. K., Sofi, N. Y., Kumar, R., & Bhadoria, A. S. (2015). Childhood obesity: Causes and consequences. *Journal of Family Medicine and Primary Care, 4*(2), 187.

Sallmen, M., Sandler, D. P., Hoppin, J. A., Blair, A., & Day, D. (2006). Reduced fertility among overweight and obese men. *Epidemiology, 17*(5), 520-523.

Salvig, J. D., & Lamont, R. F. (2011). Evidence regarding an effect of marine n-3 fatty acids on preterm birth: A systematic review and meta-analysis. *Acta Obstetricia et Gynecologica Scandinavica, 90*(8), 825-838.

Sanders, A. R., Martin, E. R., Beecham, G. W., Guo, S., Dawood, K., Rieger, G., . . . & Duan, J. (2015). Genome-wide scan demonstrates significant linkage for male sexual orientation. *Psychological Medicine, 45*(7), 1379-1388.

Sanders, L. D., Stevens, C., Coch, D., & Neville, H. J. (2006). Selective auditory attention in 3- to 5-year-old children: An event-related potential study. *Neuropsychologia, 44*(11), 2126-2138.

Sandnabba, N. K., & Ahlberg, C. (1999). Parents' attitudes and expectations about children's cross-gender behavior. *Sex Roles, 40*(3-4), 249-263.

Santelli, J. S., Kantor, L. M., Grilo, S. A., Speizer, I. S., Lindberg, L. D., Heitel, J., . . . & Heck, C. J. (2017). Abstinence-only-until-marriage: An updated review of U.S. policies and programs and their impact. *Journal of Adolescent Health, 61*(3), 273-280.

Santelli, J. S., & Melnikas, A. J. (2010). Teen fertility in transition: Recent and historic trends in the United States. *Annual Review of Public Health, 31*, 371-383.

Sapp, F., Lee, K., & Muir, D. (2000). Three-year-olds' difficulty with the appearance–reality distinction: Is it real or is it apparent? *Developmental Psychology, 36*(5), 547.

Sasson, H., & Mesch, G. (2014). Parental mediation, peer norms and risky online behavior among adolescents. *Computers in Human Behavior, 33*, 32-38.

Satcher, D. (2001). The Surgeon General's call to action to promote sexual health and responsible sexual behavior. *American Journal of Health Education, 32*(6), 356–368.

Saudino, K. J., & Micalizzi, L. (2015). Emerging trends in behavioral genetic studies of child temperament. *Child Development Perspectives, 9*(3), 144–148.

Sauter, D. A., Panattoni, C., & Happé, F. (2013). Children's recognition of emotions from vocal cues. *British Journal of Developmental Psychology, 31*(1), 97–113.

Savic, I., Berglund, H., & Lindström, P. (2005). Brain response to putative pheromones in homosexual men. *Proceedings of the National Academy of Sciences, 102*, 7356–7361.

Saxe, R., Tenenbaum, J. B., & Carey, S. (2005). Secret agents: Inferences about hidden causes by 10- and 12-month old infants. *Psychological Science, 16*, 995–1001.

Sazonova, A., Kallen, K., Thurin-Kjellberg, A., Wennerholm, U., & Bergh, C. (2013). Neonatal and maternal outcomes comparing women undergoing two in vitro fertilization (IVF) singleton pregnancies and women undergoing one IVF twin pregnancy. *Fertility and Sterility, 99*, 731–737.

Scarr, S. (1992). Developmental theories for the 1990s: Development and individual differences. *Child Development, 63*, 1–19.

Schanzenbach, D.W. (2014). Does class size matter? Boulder, CO: National Education Policy Center. Retrieved [date] from http://nepc.colorado.edu/publication/does-class-size-matter.

Scharf, R. J., Stroustrup, A., Conaway, M. R., & DeBoer, M. D. (2016). Growth and development in children born very low birthweight. *Archives of Disease in Childhood-Fetal and Neonatal Edition, 101*(5), F433–F438.

Scheidt, P., Overpeck, M. D., Whatt, W., & Aszmann, A. (2000). Adolescents' general health and wellbeing. In C. Currie, K. Hurrelmann, W. Settertobulte, R. Smith, & J. Todd (Eds.), *Health and health behaviour among young people: A WHO cross-national study (HBSC) international report* (pp. 24–38). (WHO Policy Series: Healthy Policy for Children and Adolescents, Series No. 1.) Copenhagen, Denmark: World Health Organization Regional Office for Europe.

Schetter, C. D. (2009). Stress processes in pregnancy and preterm birth. *Current Directions in Psychological Science, 18*(4), 205–209.

Schickedanz, A., Dreyer, B. P., & Halfon, N. (2015). Childhood poverty: Understanding and preventing the adverse impacts of a most-prevalent risk to pediatric health and well-being. *Pediatric Clinics, 62*(5), 1111–1135.

Schlotz, W., Jones, A., Phillips, D. I. W., Gale, C. R., Robinson, S. M., & Godrey, K. M. (2009). Lower maternal folate status in early pregnancy is associated with childhood hyperactivity and peer problems in offspring. *Journal of Child Psychology and Psychiatry, 51*(5), 594–602. doi: 10.1111/j.1469-7610.2009.02182.x

Schmidt, J. A., Shumow, L., & Kackar, H. (2007). Adolescents' participation in service activities and its impact on academic, behavioral, and civic outcomes. *Journal of Youth and Adolescence, 36*(2), 127–140.

Schmitt, M. T., Branscombe, N. R., Postmes, T., & Garcia, A. (2014). The consequences of perceived discrimination for psychological well-being: A meta-analytic review. *Psychological Bulletin, 140*(4), 921.

Schmitz, S., Saudino, K. J., Plomin, R., Fulker, D. W., & DeFries, J. C. (1996). Genetic and environmental influences on temperament in middle childhood: Analyses of teacher and tester ratings. *Child Development, 67*, 409–422.

Schnaas, L., Rothenberg, S. J., Flores, M., Martinez, S., Hernandez, C., Osorio, E., . . . Perroni, E. (2006). Reduced intellectual development in children with prenatal lead exposure. *Environmental Health Perspectives, 114*(5), 791–797.

Schnack, H. G., Van Haren, N. E., Brouwer, R. M., Evans, A., Durston, S., Boomsma, D. I., . . . & Hulshoff Pol, H. E. (2014). Changes in thickness and surface area of the human cortex and their relationship with intelligence. *Cerebral Cortex, 25*(6), 1608–1617.

Schneider, B. H., Atkinson, L., & Tardif, C. (2001). Child-parent attachment and children's peer relations: A quantitative review. *Developmental Psychology, 37*, 86–100.

Schneider, W. (2008). The development of metacognitive knowledge in children and adolescents: Major trends and implications for education. *Mind, Brain, and Education, 2*(3), 114–121.

Schonert-Reichl, K. A., Smith, V., Zaidman-Zait, A., & Hertzman, C. (2012). Promoting children's prosocial behaviors in school: Impact of the "Roots of Empathy" program on the social and emotional competence of school-aged children. *School Mental Health, 4*(1), 1–21.

Schredl, M., Anders, A., Hellriegel, S., & Rehm, A. (2008). TV viewing, computer game playing and nightmares in school children. *Dreaming, 18*(2), 69–76. http://dx.doi.org.vwu.idm.oclc.org/10.1037/1053-0797.18.2.69

Schredl, M., Fricke-Oerkermann, L., Mitschke, A., Wiater, A., & Lehmkuhl, G. (2009). Longitudinal study of nightmares in children: Stability and effect of emotional symptoms. *Child Psychiatry and Human Development, 40*(3), 439–449.

Schulenberg, J. E., Johnston, L. D., O'Malley, P. M., Bachman, J. G., Miech, R. A. & Patrick, M. E. (2017). Monitoring the Future national survey results on drug use, 1975–2016: Volume II, College students and adults ages 19–55. Ann Arbor: Institute for Social Research, The University of Michigan. Available at http://monitoringthefuture.org/pubs.html#monographs

Schulenberg, J. E., & Zarrett, N. R. (2006). Mental health during emerging adulthood: Continuity and discontinuity in courses, causes, and functions. In J. J. Arnett & J. L. Tanner (Eds.), *Emerging adults in America: Coming of age in the 21st century* (pp. 135–172). Washington, DC: American Psychological Association

Schulting, A. B., Malone, P. S., & Dodge, K. A. (2005). The effect of school-based kindergarten transition policies and practices on child academic outcomes. *Developmental Psychology, 41*, 860–871.

Schurz, M., Aichhorn, M., Martin, A., & Perner, J. (2013). Common brain areas engaged in false belief reasoning and visual perspective taking: A meta-analysis of functional brain imaging studies. *Frontiers in Human Neuroscience, 7*.

Schwab, S. G., & Wildenauer, D. B. (2013). Genetics of psychiatric disorders in the GWAS era: An update on schizophrenia. *European Archives of Psychiatry and Clinical Neuroscience, 263,* 147.

Schwartz, D., McFadyen-Ketchum, S. A., Dodge, K. A., Pettit, G. S., & Bates, J. E. (1998). Peer group victimization as a predictor of children's behavior problems at home and in school. *Development and Psychopathology, 10*, 87–99.

Scott, M. E., Booth, A., King, V., & Johnson, D. R. (2007). Postdivorce father-adolescent closeness. *Journal of Marriage and Family, 69*(5), 1194–1209.

Scott, R. M., & Baillargeon, R. (2009). Which penguin is this? Attributing false beliefs about object identity at 18 months. *Child Development, 80*(4), 1172–1196.

Scott, S., Doolan, M., Beckett, C., Harry, S., & Cartwright, S. (2012). How is parenting style related to child antisocial behaviour? Preliminary findings from the Helping Children Achieve study [research report]. Retrieved from http://dera.ioe.ac.uk/13827/1/DFE-RR185a.pdf

Searing, D. A., Zhang, Y., Murphy, J. R., Hauk, P. J., Goleva, E., & Leung, D. Y. (2010). Decreased serum vitamin D levels in children with asthma are associated with increased corticosteroid use. *Journal of Allergy and Clinical Immunology, 125*(5), 995–1000.

Sebanc, A. M. (2003). The friendship features of preschool children: Links with prosocial behavior and aggression. *Social Development, 12*(2), 249-268.

Sedgh, G., Finer, L. B., Bankole, A., Eilers, M. A., & Singh, S. (2015). Adolescent pregnancy, birth, and abortion rates across countries: Levels and recent trends. *Journal of Adolescent Health, 56*(2), 223-230.

Seehagen, S., & Herbert, J. S. (2011). Infant imitation from televised peer and adult models. *Infancy, 16*(2), 113-136.

Selkie, E. M., Fales, J. L., & Moreno, M. A. (2016). Cyberbullying prevalence among U.S. middle and high school-aged adolescents: A systematic review and quality assessment. *Journal of Adolescent Health, 58*(2), 125-133.

Semega, J. L., Fontenot, K. R., & Kollar, M. A. (2017). *U.S. Census Bureau, current population reports, p60-259, income and poverty in the United States: 2016.* Washington, DC: U.S. Government Printing Office.

Serdiouk, M., Rodkin, P., Madill, R., Logis, H., & Gest, S. (2015). Rejection and victimization among elementary school children: The buffering role of classroom-level predictors. *Journal of Abnormal Child Psychology, 43*(1), 5-17.

Shah, T., Sullivan, K., & Carter, J. (2006). Sudden infant death syndrome and reported maternal smoking during pregnancy. *American Journal of Public Health, 96*(10), 1757-1759.

Shahaeian, A., Nielsen, M., Peterson, C. C., & Slaughter, V. (2014). Cultural and family influences on children's theory of mind development: A comparison of Australian and Iranian school-age children. *Journal of Cross-Cultural Psychology, 45*(4), 555-568.

Shamir, A., Korat, O., & Fellah, R. (2012). Promoting vocabulary, phonological awareness and concept about print among children at risk for learning disability: Can e-books help? *Reading and Writing, 25*(1), 45-69.

Shamir, A., & Shlafer, I. (2011). E-books effectiveness in promoting phonological awareness and concept about print: A comparison between children at risk for learning disabilities and typically developing kindergarteners. *Computers & Education, 57*(3), 1989-1997.

Shapiro-Mendoza, C. K., Rice, M. E., Galang, R. R., Fulton, A. C., VanMaldeghem, K., Prado, M. V., . . . & Ellington, S. R. (2017). Pregnancy outcomes after maternal Zika virus infection during pregnancy-US territories, January 1, 2016-April 25, 2017. *Morbidity and Mortality Weekly Report, 66*(23), 615-621.

Sharma, A. R., McGue, M. K., & Benson, P. L. (1996b). The emotional and behavioral adjustment of United States adopted adolescents, Part II: Age at adoption. *Children and Youth Services Review, 18*, 101-114.

Sharma, M., Kupferman, J. C., Brosgol, Y., Paterno, K., Goodman, S., Prohovnik, I., . . . & Pavlakis, S. G. (2010). The effects of hypertension on the paediatric brain: A justifiable concern. *The Lancet Neurology, 9*(9), 933-940.

Shayer, M., Ginsburg, D., & Coe, R. (2007). Thirty years on—A large anti-Flynn effect? The Piagetian Test Volume & Heaviness norms 1975-2003. *British Journal of Educational Psychology, 77*(1), 25-41.

Shea, K. M., Little, R. E., & the ALSPAC Study Team. (1997). Is there an association between preconceptual paternal X-ray exposure and birth outcome? *American Journal of Epidemiology, 145,* 546-551.

Shetgiri, R., Espelage, D. L., & Carroll, L. (2015). Bullying trends, correlates, consequences, and characteristics. In *Practical strategies for clinical management of bullying* (pp. 3-11). New York: Springer International Publishing.

Shields, B., Wacogne, I., & Wright, C. M. (2012). Weight faltering and failure to thrive in infancy and early childhood. *BMJ, 345,* e5931.

Shin, Y., & Raudenbush, S. W. (2011). The causal effect of class size on academic achievement: Multivariate instrumental variable estimators with data missing at random. *Journal of Educational and Behavioral Statistics, 36*(2), 154-185.

Shiner, R. L., Buss, K. A., McClowry, S. G., Putnam, S. P., Saudino, K. J., & Zentner, M. (2012). What is temperament now? Assessing progress in temperament research on the twenty-fifth anniversary of Goldsmith et al. *Child Development Perspectives, 6*(4), 436-444.

Shinya, Y., Kawai, M., Niwa, F., & Myowa-Yamakoshi, M. (2016). Associations between respiratory arrhythmia and fundamental frequency of spontaneous crying in preterm and term infants at term-equivalent age. *Developmental Psychobiology, 58*(6), 724-733.

Shriver, L. H., Marriage, B. J., Bloch, T. D., Spees, C. K., Ramsay, S. A., Watowicz, R. P., & Taylor, C. A. (2018). Contribution of snacks to dietary intakes of young children in the United States. *Maternal & Child Nutrition, 14*(1).

Shutts, K., Banaji, M. R., & Spelke, E. S. (2010). Social categories guide young children's preferences for novel objects. *Developmental Science, 13*(4), 599-610.

Siegler, R. S. (1998). *Children's thinking* (3rd ed.). Upper Saddle River, NJ: Prentice Hall.

Siegler, R. S. (2009). Improving the numerical understanding of children from low-income families. *Child Development Perspectives, 3*(2), 118-124.

Siegler, R. S., & Booth, J. L. (2004). Development of numerical estimation in young children. *Child Development, 75,* 428-444.

Sieving, R. E., McNeely, C. S., & Blum, R. W. (2000). Maternal expectations, mother-child connectedness, and adolescent sexual debut. *Archives of Pediatric & Adolescent Medicine, 154,* 809-816.

Sijtsema, J. J., Ojanen, T., Veenstra, R., Lindenberg, S., Hawley, P. H., & Little, T. D. (2010). Forms and functions of aggression in adolescent friendship selection and influence: A longitudinal social network analysis. *Social Development, 19*(3), 515-534.

Silberg, J. L., Maes, H., & Eaves, L. J. (2012). Unraveling the effect of genes and environment in the transmission of parental antisocial behavior to children's conduct disturbance, depression and hyperactivity. *Journal of Child Psychology and Psychiatry, 53*(6), 668-677.

Silventoinen, K., Rokholm, B., Kaprio, J., & Sørensen, T. I. A. (2010). The genetic and environmental influences on childhood obesity: A systematic review of twin and adoption studies. *International Journal of Obesity, 34*(1), 29.

Simmonds, M., Llewellyn, A., Owen, C. G., & Woolacott, N. (2016). Predicting adult obesity from childhood obesity: A systematic review and meta-analysis. *Obesity Reviews, 17*(2), 95-107.

Simmons, R. G., Blyth, D. A., & McKinney, K. L. (1983). The social and psychological effect of puberty on white females. In J. Brooks-Gunn & A. C. Petersen (Eds.), *Girls at puberty: Biological and psychological perspectives.* New York: Plenum Press.

Simons, E., To, T., Moineddin, R., Stieb, D., & Dell, S. D. (2014). Maternal second-hand smoke exposure in pregnancy is associated with childhood asthma development. *The Journal of Allergy and Clinical Immunology: In Practice, 2*(2), 201-207.

Simons-Morton, B. G., & Farhat, T. (2010). Recent findings on peer group influences on adolescent smoking. *The Journal of Primary Prevention, 31*(4), 191-208.

Simpson, J. A., Collins, A., Tran, S., & Haydon, K. C. (2007). Attachment and the experience and expression of emotions in romantic relationships: A developmental perspective. *Journal of Personality and Social Psychology, 92,* 355-367.

Sines, E., Syed, U., Wall, S., & Worley, H. (2007). Postnatal care: A critical opportunity to save mothers and newborns. *Policy Perspectives on Newborn Health.* Washington, DC: Save the Children and Population Reference Bureau.

Singer, D. G., & Singer, J. L. (1990). *The house of make-believe: Play and the developing imagination.* Cambridge, MA: Harvard University Press.

Singer, T. (2006). The neuronal basis and ontogeny of empathy and mind reading: Review of literature and implications for future research. *Neuroscience & Biobehavioral Reviews, 30*(6), 855–863.

Singh, A. S., Mulder, C., Twisk, J. W., Van Mechelen, W., & Chinapaw, M. J. (2008). Tracking of childhood overweight into adulthood: A systematic review of the literature. *Obesity Reviews, 9*(5), 474–488.

Singh, G. K., & Kenney, M. K. (2013). Rising prevalence and neighborhood, social, and behavioral determinants of sleep problems in U.S. children and adolescents, 2003–2012. *Sleep Disorders.*

Singh, T., Arrazola, R. A., Corey, C. G., Husten, C. G., Neff, L. J., Homa, D. M., & King, B. A. (2016) Tobacco use among middle and high school students–United States, 2011–2015. *Morbidity and Mortality Weekly Report, 65*(14), 361–367. Retrieved from www.cdc.gov/mmwr/volumes/65/wr/mm6514a1.htm.

Skadberg, B. T., Morild, I., & Markestad, T. (1998). Abandoning prone sleeping: Effects on the risk of sudden infant death syndrome. *Journal of Pediatrics, 132,* 234–239.

Skinner, A. C., Perrin, E. M., Moss, L. A., & Skelton, J. A. (2015). Cardiometabolic risks and severity of obesity in children and young adults. *New England Journal of Medicine, 373*(14), 1307–1317.

Skinner, A. C., Ravanbakht, S. N., Skelton, J. A., Perrin, E. M., & Armstrong, S. C. (2018). Prevalence of obesity and severe obesity in U.S. children, 1999–2016. *Pediatrics,* e20173459.

Skinner, D. (1989). The socialization of gender identity: Observations from Nepal. In J. Valsiner (Ed.), *Child development in cultural context* (pp. 181–192). Toronto, Canada: Hogrefe & Huber.

Skorska, M. N., Blanchard, R., VanderLaan, D. P., Zucker, K. J., & Bogaert, A. F. (2017). Gay male only-children: Evidence for low birth weight and high maternal miscarriage rates. *Archives of Sexual Behavior, 46*(1), 205–215.

Slaby, R. G., & Frey, K. S. (1975). Development of gender constancy and selective attention to same-sex models. *Child Development, 46*(4), 849–856.

Slattery, T. L., & Meyers, S. A. (2014). Contextual predictors of adolescent antisocial behavior: The developmental influence of family, peer, and neighborhood factors. *Child and Adolescent Social Work Journal, 31*(1), 39–59.

Slaughter, V., Imuta, K., Peterson, C. C., & Henry, J. D. (2015). Meta-analysis of theory of mind and peer popularity in the preschool and early school years. *Child Development, 86*(4), 1159–1174.

Slomko, H., Heo, H. J., & Einstein, F. H. (2012). Minireview: Epigenetics of obesity and diabetes in humans. *Endocrinology, 153*(3), 1025–1030.

Smith, A. R., Chein, J., & Steinberg, L. (2014). Peers increase adolescent risk taking even when the probabilities of negative outcomes are known. *Developmental Psychology, 50*(5), 1564.

Smith, C. L., & Bell, M. A. (2010). Stability in infant frontal asymmetry as a predictor of toddlerhood internalizing and externalizing behaviors. *Developmental Psychobiology, 52*(2), 158–167.

Smith, L. M., LaGasse, L. L., Derauf, C., Grant, P., Shah, R., Arria, A., . . . Lester, B. M. (2006). The infant development, environment, and lifestyle study: Effects of prenatal methamphetamine exposure, polydrug exposure, and poverty on intrauterine growth. *Pediatrics, 118,* 1149–1156.

Smith, P. K. (2005). Social and pretend play in children. In A. D. Pellegrini & P. K. Smith (Eds.), *The nature of play* (pp. 173–209). New York: Guilford Press.

Smith, P. K., & Pellegrini, A. D. (2013). Learning through play. In R. E. Tremblay, M. Boivin, & R. Peters, R. (Eds.), *Encyclopedia on early childhood development* [online]. www.child-encyclopedia.com/play/according-experts/learning-through-play

Smith, S. L., Pieper, K. M., Granados, A., & Choueiti, M. (2010). Assessing gender-related portrayals in top-grossing G-rated films. *Sex Roles, 62,* 774–786. doi: 10-1007/s11199-009-9736z

Smith, T. B., & Silva, L. (2011). Ethnic identity and personal well-being of people of color: A meta-analysis. *Journal of Counseling Psychology, 58*(1), 42.

Smock, P. J., & Greenland, F. R. (2010). Diversity in pathways to parenthood: Patterns, implications, and emerging research directions. *Journal of Marriage and Family, 72*(3), 576–593.

Snyder, J., Bank, L., & Burraston, B. (2005). The consequences of antisocial behavior in older male siblings for younger brothers and sisters. *Journal of Family Psychology, 19,* 643–653.

Snyder, T.D., de Brey, C., and Dillow, S.A. (2016). *Digest of education statistics 2015 (NCES 2016-014).* Washington, DC: National Center for Education Statistics, Institute of Education Sciences, U.S. Department of Education.

Society for Neuroscience. (2008). Neural disorders: Advances and challenges. In *Brain facts: A primer on the brain and nervous system* (pp. 36–54). Washington, DC: Author.

Soley, G., & Hannon, E. E. (2010). Infants prefer the musical meter of their own culture: A cross-cultural comparison. *Developmental Psychology, 46*(1), 286.

Soliman, A., De Sanctis, V., & Elalaily, R. (2014). Nutrition and pubertal development. *Indian Journal of Endocrinology and Metabolism, 18*(Suppl 1), S39.

Solmeyer, A. R., McHale, S. M., & Crouter, A. C. (2014). Longitudinal associations between sibling relationship qualities and risky behavior across adolescence. *Developmental Psychology, 50*(2), 600.

Sommerville, J. A., Schmidt, M. F., Yun, J. E., & Burns, M. (2013). The development of fairness expectations and prosocial behavior in the second year of life. *Infancy, 18*(1), 40–66.

Sophian, C., & Wood, A. (1997). Proportional reasoning in young children: The parts and the whole of it. *Journal of Educational Psychology, 89,* 309–317.

Sophian, C., Wood, A. M., & Vong, K. I. (1995). Making numbers count: The early development of numerical inferences. *Developmental Psychology, 31*(2), 263.

Sordillo, J. E., Kelly, R., Bunyavanich, S., McGeachie, M., Qiu, W., Croteau-Chonka, D. C., . . . & Weiss, S. T. (2015). Genome-wide expression profiles identify potential targets for gene-environment interactions in asthma severity. *Journal of Allergy and Clinical Immunology, 136*(4), 885–892.

Sova, C., Feuling, M. B., Baumler, M., Gleason, L., Tam, J. S., Zafra, H., & Goday, P. S. (2013). Systematic review of nutrient intake and growth in children with multiple IgE-mediated food allergies. *Nutrition in Clinical Practice, 28*(6), 669–675.

Sparks, A. B., Struble, C. A., Wang, E. T., Song, K., & Oliphant, A. (2012). Noninvasive prenatal detection and selective analysis of cell-free DNA obtained from maternal blood: evaluation for trisomy 21 and trisomy 18. *American Journal of Obstetrics & Gynecology, 206*(4), 319-e1.

Spear, L. P. (2014). Adolescents and alcohol: Acute sensitivities, enhanced intake, and later consequences. *Neurotoxicology and Teratology, 41,* 51–59.

Spelke, E. S. (2017). Core knowledge, language, and number. *Language Learning and Development, 13*(2), 147–170.

Spiegel, C., & Halberda, J. (2011). Rapid fast-mapping abilities in 2-year-olds. *Journal of Experimental Child Psychology, 109*(1), 132–140.

Spinelli, M., Fasolo, M., & Mesman, J. (2017). Does prosody make the difference? A meta-analysis on relations between prosodic aspects of infant-directed speech and infant outcomes. *Developmental Review, 44,* 1–18.

Sprung, M., Münch, H. M., Harris, P. L., Ebesutani, C., & Hofmann, S. G. (2015). Children's emotion understanding: A meta-analysis of training studies. *Developmental Review, 37*, 41–65.

Staff, J., Schulenberg, J. E., & Bachman, J. G. (2010). Adolescent work intensity, school performance, and academic engagement. *Sociology of Education, 83*(3), 183–200.

Stallman, H. M., & Kohler, M. (2016). Prevalence of sleepwalking: A systematic review and meta-analysis. *PloSOne, 11*(11), e0164769.

Stallman, H. M., & Ohan, J. L. (2016). Parenting style, parental adjustment, and co-parental conflict: Differential predictors of child psychosocial adjustment following divorce. *Behaviour Change, 33*(2), 112–126.

Stark, P., & Noel, A. M. (2015). Trends in high school dropout and completion rates in the United States: 1972–2012. Compendium report. NCES 2015-015. *National Center for Education Statistics.*

Stauder, J. E. A., Molenaar, P. C. M., & Van der Molen, M. W. (1993). Event-related brain potential analysis of the conservation of liquid quantity. *Child Development, 64*, 769–788.

Steensma, T. D., McGuire, J. K., Kreukels, B. P., Beekman, A. J., & Cohen-Kettenis, P. T. (2013). Factors associated with desistence and persistence of childhood gender dysphoria: A quantitative follow-up study. *Journal of the American Academy of Child & Adolescent Psychiatry, 52*(6), 582–590.

Steinberg, L., & Darling, N. (1994). The broader context of social influence in adolescence. In R. Silberstein & E. Todt (Eds.), *Adolescence in context.* New York: Springer.

Steinberg, L., & Morris, A. S. (2001). Adolescent development. *Annual Review of Psychology, 52*(1), 83–110.

Steinberg, L., & Scott, E. S. (2003). Less guilty by reason of adolescence: Developmental immaturity, diminished responsibility, and the juvenile death penalty. *American Psychologist, 58*, 1009–1018.

Stennes, L. M., Burch, M. M., Sen, M. G., & Bauer, P. J. (2005). A longitudinal study of gendered vocabulary and communicative action in young children. *Developmental Psychology, 41*(1), 75.

Sternberg, R. J. (1993). *Sternberg Triarchic Abilities Test.* Unpublished manuscript.

Sternberg, R. J. (1997). The concept of intelligence and its role in lifelong learning and success. *American Psychologist, 52*, 1030–1037.

Sternberg, R. J., Castejón, J. L., Prieto, M. D., Hautamäki, J., & Grigorenko, E. L. (2001). Confirmatory factor analysis of the Sternberg Triarchic Abilities Test in three international samples: An empirical test of the triarchic theory of intelligence. *European Journal of Psychological Assessment, 17*(1), 1.

Stevenson-Hinde, J., & Shouldice, A. (1996). Fearfulness: Developmental consistency. In A. J. Sameroff & M. M. Haith (Eds.), *The five- to seven-year shift: The age of reason and responsibility* (pp. 237–252). Chicago: University of Chicago Press.

Stevenson-Hinde, J., Shouldice, A., & Chicot, R. (2011). Maternal anxiety, behavioral inhibition, and attachment. *Attachment & Human Development, 13*(3), 199–215.

Stewart, A. M., Lewis, G. F., Heilman, K. J., Davila, M. I., Coleman, D. D., Aylward, S. A., & Porges, S. W. (2013). The covariation of acoustic features of infant cries and autonomic state. *Physiology & Behavior, 120*, 203–210.

Stewart, E. A., & Simons, R. L. (2010). Race, code of the street, and violent delinquency: A multilevel investigation of neighborhood street culture and individual norms of violence. *Criminology, 48*(2), 569–605.

Stiles, J., & Jernigan, T. L. (2010). The basics of brain development. *Neuropsychology Review, 20*(4), 327–348.

Stipek, D., Feiler, R., Daniels, D., & Milburn, S. (1995). Effects of different instructional approaches on young children's achievement and motivation. *Child Development, 66*(1), 209–223.

Stock, P., Desoete, A., & Roeyers, H. (2010). Detecting children with arithmetic disabilities from kindergarten: Evidence from a 3-year longitudinal study on the role of preparatory arithmetic abilities. *Journal of Learning Disabilities, 43*(3), 250–268.

Storebø, O. J., & Simonsen, E. (2016). The association between ADHD and antisocial personality disorder (ASPD) a review. *Journal of Attention Disorders, 20*(10), 815–824.

Strathearn, L., Fonagy, P., Amico, J., & Montague, P. R. (2009). Adult attachment predicts maternal brain and oxytocin response to infant cues. *Neuropsychopharmacology, 34*(13), 2655.

Straus, M. A. (1994a). *Beating the devil out of them: Corporal punishment in American families.* San Francisco: Jossey-Bass.

Straus, M. A. (1999). The benefits of avoiding corporal punishment: New and more definitive evidence. Submitted for publication in K. C. Blaine (Ed.), *Raising America's children.*

Strauss, N., Giessler, K., & McAllister, E. (2015). How doula care can advance the goals of the Affordable Care Act: A snapshot from New York City. *The Journal of Perinatal Education, 24*(1), 8.

Strohschein, L. (2012). Parental divorce and child mental health: Accounting for predisruption differences. *Journal of Divorce & Remarriage, 53*, 489–502. doi:10.1080/10502556.2012.682903

Stroop, J. R. (1935). Studies of interference in serial verbal reactions. *Journal of Experimental Psychology, 18*(6), 643.

Strouse, G. A., & Ganea, P. A. (2017). Toddlers' word learning and transfer from electronic and print books. *Journal of Experimental Child Psychology, 156*, 129–142.

Suanda, S. H., Tompson, W., & Brannon, E. M. (2008). Changes in the ability to detect ordinal numerical relationships between 9 and 11 months of age. *Infancy, 13*(4), 308–337.

Subbotsky, E., Hysted, C., & Jones, N. (2010). Watching films with magical content facilitates creativity in children. *Perceptual and Motor Skills, 111*(1), 261–277.

Subrahmanyam, K., & Greenfield, P. (2008). Online communication and adolescent relationships. *The Future of Children 18*, 119–146.

Substance Abuse and Mental Health Services Administration (SAMHSA). (2004a, October 22). Alcohol dependence or abuse and age at first use. *The NSDUH Report.* Retrieved from http://oas.samhsa.gov/2k4/ageDependence/ageDependence.htm

Substance Abuse and Mental Health Services Administration [SAMHSA]. (2013). *Results from the 2012 national survey on drug use and health: Mental health findings.* NSDUH Series H-47, HHS Publication No. (SMA) 13-4805. Rockville, MD. Author. Retrieved from www.samhsa.gov/data/NSDUH/2k12MH_FindingsandDetTables/2K12MHF/NSDUHmhfr2012.htm#fig3-2

Substance Abuse and Mental Health Services Administration. (2017). *Key substance use and mental health indicators in the United States: Results from the 2016 National Survey on Drug Use and Health* (HHS Publication No. SMA 17-5044, NSDUH Series H-52). Rockville, MD: Center for Behavioral Health Statistics and Quality, Substance Abuse and Mental Health Services Administration. Retrieved from www.samhsa.gov/data/

Sugden, N. A., & Marquis, A. R. (2017). Meta-analytic review of the development of face discrimination in infancy: Face race, face gender, infant age, and methodology moderate face discrimination. *Psychological Bulletin, 143*(11), 1201–1244.

Sundet, J., Barlaug, D., & Torjussen, T. (2004). The end of the Flynn Effect? A study of secular trends in mean intelligence test scores of Norwegian conscripts during half a century. *Intelligence, 32*, 349–362.

Sung, J., Beijers, R., Gartstein, M. A., de Weerth, C., & Putnam, S. P. (2015). Exploring temperamental differences in infants from the USA and the Netherlands. *European Journal of Developmental Psychology, 12*(1), 15–28.

Suss, C., Gaylord, S., & Fagen, J. (2012). Odor as a contextual cue in memory reactivation in young infants. *Infant Behavior and Development, 35*(3), 580-583.

Swain, I., Zelano, P., & Clifton, R. (1993). Newborn infants' memory for speech sounds retained over 24 hours. *Developmental Psychology, 29,* 312-323.

Swain, J. E., Lorberbaum, J. P., Kose, S., & Strathearn, L. (2007). Brain basis of early parent–infant interactions: Psychology, physiology, and in vivo functional neuroimaging studies. *Journal of Child Psychology and Psychiatry, 48*(3-4), 262-287.

Swain, J. E., Tasgin, E., Mayes, L. C., Feldman, R., Constable, R. T., & Leckman, J. F. (2008). Maternal brain response to own baby cry is affected by cesarean section delivery. *Journal of Child Psychology and Psychiatry, 49,* 1042-1052.

Swanson, S. A., Crow, S. J., Le Grange, D., Swendsen, J., & Merikangas, K. R. (2011). Prevalence and correlates of eating disorders in adolescents: Results from the national comorbidity survey replication adolescent supplement. *Archives of General Psychiatry, 68*(7), 714-723.

Swanston, H. Y., Tebbutt, J. S., O'Toole, B. I., & Oates, R. K. (1997). Sexually abused children 5 years after presentation: A case-control study. *Pediatrics, 100,* 600-608.

Sweeney, M. M. (2010). Remarriage and stepfamilies: Strategic sites for family scholarship in the 21st century. *Journal of Marriage and Family, 72*(3), 667-684.

Swingley, D. (2008). The roots of the early vocabulary in infants' learning from speech. *Current Directions in Psychological Science, 17,* 308-312.

Swingley, D., & Fernald, A. (2002). Recognition of words referring to present and absent objects by 24-month-olds. *Journal of Memory and Language, 46,* 39-56.

Syed, M., & Juan, M. J. D. (2012). Birds of an ethnic feather? Ethnic identity homophily among college-age friends. *Journal of Adolescence, 35*(6), 1505-1514.

T

Taki, Y., Hashizume, H., Thyreau, B., Sassa, Y., Takeuchi, H., Wu, K., . . . & Fukuda, H. (2013). Linear and curvilinear correlations of brain gray matter volume and density with age using voxel-based morphometry with the Akaike information criterion in 291 healthy children. *Human Brain Mapping, 34*(8), 1857-1871.

Taliaferro, L. A., & Muehlenkamp, J. J. (2014). Risk and protective factors that distinguish adolescents who attempt suicide from those who only consider suicide in the past year. *Suicide and Life-Threatening Behavior, 44*(1), 6-22.

Talwar, V., & Lee, K. (2008). Social and cognitive correlates of children's lying behavior. *Child Development, 79*(4), 866-881.

Tau, G. Z., & Peterson, B. S. (2010). Normal development of brain circuits. *Neuropsychopharmacology, 35*(1), 147.

Taumoepeau, M., & Reese, E. (2014). Understanding the self through siblings: Self-awareness mediates the sibling effect on social understanding. *Social Development, 23*(1), 1-18.

Taveras, E. M., Capra, A. M., Braveman, P. A., Jensvold, N. G., Escobar, G. J., & Lieu, T. A. (2003). Clinician support and psychosocial risk factors associated with breastfeeding discontinuation. *Pediatrics, 112,* 108-115.

Taylor, E. V. (2009). The purchasing practice of low-income students: The relationship to mathematical development. *The Journal of the Learning Sciences, 18*(3), 370-415.

Taylor, L. E., Swerdfeger, A. L., & Eslick, G. D. (2014). Vaccines are not associated with autism: An evidence-based meta-analysis of case-control and cohort studies. *Vaccine, 32*(29), 3623-3629.

Taylor, M., & Carlson, S. M. (1997). The relation between individual differences in fantasy and theory of mind. *Child Development, 68,* 436-455.

Taylor, M., Cartwright, B. S., & Carlson, S. M. (1993). A developmental investigation of children's imaginary companions. *Developmental Psychology, 28,* 276-285.

Teasdale, T. W., & Owen, D. R. (2008). Secular declines in cognitive test scores: A reversal of the Flynn effect. *Intelligence, 36,* 121-126.

Teffer, K., & Semendeferi, K. (2012). Human prefrontal cortex: evolution, development, and pathology. In *Progress in brain research* (Vol. 195, pp. 191-218). Amsterdam: Elsevier.

Telzer, E. H., & Fuligni, A. J. (2009). Daily family assistance and the psychological well-being of adolescents from Latin American, Asian and European backgrounds. *Developmental Psychology, 45*(4), 1177-1189.

Teubert, D., & Pinquart, M. (2010). The association between coparenting and child adjustment: A meta-analysis. *Parenting: Science and Practice, 10*(4), 286-307.

Tezanos-Pinto, P., Bratt, C., & Brown, R. (2010). What will the others think? In-group norms as a mediator of the effects of intergroup contact. *British Journal of Social Psychology, 49*(3), 507-523.

The Aspen Institute. (2018). Sport participation and physical activity rates. [Data sheet]. Retrieved from www.aspenprojectplay.org/kids-sports-participation-rates

Thomas, A., Chess, S., & Birch, H. G. (1968). *Temperament and behavior disorders in children.* New York: New York University Press.

Thomas, R., Sanders, S., Doust, J., Beller, E., & Glasziou, P. (2015). Prevalence of attention-deficit/hyperactivity disorder: A systematic review and meta-analysis. *Pediatrics, 135*(4), e994-e1001.

Thomson, E., & McLanahan, S. S. (2012). Reflections on "Family structure and child well-being: Economic resources vs. parental socialization." *Social Forces, 91*(1), 45-53.

Tiedemann, D. (1787/1972). Observations on the mental development of a child. (1927). In W. Dennis (Ed.), *Historical readings in developmental psychology* (pp. 11-31). New York: Appleton-Century-Crofts.

Tippett, N., & Wolke, D. (2015). Aggression between siblings: Associations with the home environment and peer bullying. *Aggressive Behavior, 41*(1), 14-24.

Tither, J., & Ellis, B. (2008). Impact of fathers on daughter's age at menarche: A genetically and environmentally controlled sibling study. *Developmental Psychology, 44*(5), 1409-1420.

Titz, C., & Karbach, J. (2014). Working memory and executive functions: Effects of training on academic achievement. *Psychological Research, 78*(6), 852-868.

Toga, A. W., Thompson, P. M., & Sowell, E. R. (2006). Mapping brain maturation. *Trends in Neurosciences, 29*(3), 148-159.

Tokariev, A., Videman, M., Palva, J. M., & Vanhatalo, S. (2016). Functional brain connectivity develops rapidly around term age and changes between vigilance states in the human newborn. *Cerebral Cortex, 26*(12), 4540-4550.

Tomasello, M., & Moll, H. (2010). The gap is social: Human shared intentionality and culture. In *Mind the gap* (pp. 331-349). Berlin: Springer.

Tomashek, K. M., Hsia, J., & Iyasu, S. (2003). Trends in postneonatal mortality attributable to injury, United States, 1988-1998. *Pediatrics, 111,* 1215-1218.

Tooby, J., & Cosmides, L. (1992). The psychological foundations of culture. In J. Barkow, L. Cosmides & J. Tooby (Eds.), *The adapted mind: Evolutionary psychology and the generation of culture* (p. 19), New York: Oxford University Press.

Topor, D. R., Keane, S. P., Shelton, T. L., & Calkins, S. D. (2010). Parent involvement and student academic performance: A multiple mediational analysis. *Journal of Prevention & Intervention in the Community, 38*(3), 183–197.

Torrance, E. P., & Ball, O. E. (1984). *The Torrance tests of creative thinking streamlined (revised) manual, figural A and B.* Bensenville, IL: Scholastic Testing Service.

Trabulsi, J. C., & Mennella, J. A. (2012). Diet, sensitive periods in flavour learning, and growth. *International Review of Psychiatry, 24.* https://doi.org/10.3109/09540261.2012.675573

Trahan, L. H., Stuebing, K. K., Fletcher, J. M., & Hiscock, M. (2014). The Flynn effect: A meta-analysis. *Psychological Bulletin, 140*(5), 1332.

Trenholm, C., Devaney, B., Fortson, K., Quay, L., Wheeler, J., & Clark, M. (2007). *Impacts of four Title V, Section 510 abstinence education programs: Final report.* Princeton, NJ: Mathematica Policy Research.

Trentacosta, C. J., & Fine, S. E. (2010). Emotion knowledge, social competence, and behavior problems in childhood and adolescence: A meta-analytic review. *Social Development, 19*(1), 1–29.

Trionfi, G., & Reese, E. (2009). A good story: Children with imaginary companions create richer narratives. *Child Development, 80*(4), 1301–1313.

Tropp, L. R., O'Brien, T. C., & Migacheva, K. (2014). How peer norms of inclusion and exclusion predict children's interest in cross-ethnic friendships. *Journal of Social Issues, 70*(1), 151–166.

Troseth, G. L., & DeLoache, J. S. (1998). The medium can obscure the message: Young children's understanding of video. *Child Development, 69*, 950–965.

Troseth, G. L., Saylor, M. M., & Archer, A. H. (2006). Young children's use of video as a source of socially relevant information. *Child Development, 77*, 786–799.

Tsao, F. M., Liu, H. M., & Kuhl, P. K. (2004). Speech perception in infancy predicts language development in the second year of life: A longitudinal study. *Child Development, 75*, 1067–1084.

Tubert-Jeannin, S., Auclair, C., Amsallem, E., Tramini, P., Gerbaud, L., Ruffieux, C., . . . & Ismail, A. (2011). Fluoride supplements (tablets, drops, lozenges or chewing gums) for preventing dental caries in children. *Cochrane Database Syst Rev, 12.*

Turcotte Benedict, F., Vivier, P. M., & Gjelsvik, A. (2015). Mental health and bullying in the United States among children aged 6 to 17 years. *Journal of Interpersonal Violence, 30*(5), 782–795.

Turkheimer, E., Haley, A., Waldron, M., d'Onofrio, B., & Gottesman, I. I. (2003). Socioeconomic status modifies heritability of IQ in young children. *Psychological Science, 14*(6), 623–628.

U

U.S. Census Bureau. (2016). Historical living arrangements of children under 18 years old: 1960 to present. [Data file]. Retrieved from https://www.census.gov/data/tables/time-series/demo/families/children.html

U.S. Census Bureau. (2017a). Historical living arrangements of children under 18 years old: 1960 to present. [Data file]. Retrieved from www.census.gov/data/tables/time-series/demo/families/children.html

U.S. Census Bureau. (2017b). Facts for features: Father's Day. Release CB17-FF.12 (June 18, 2017). Retrieved from www.census.gov/newsroom/facts-for-features/2017/cb17-ff12-fathers-day.html

U.S. Census Bureau. (2017c). Historical poverty tables: People and families—1959 to 2016. Current population survey, annual social and economic supplements. Retrieved from www.census.gov/data/tables/time-series/demo/income-poverty/historical-poverty-people.html

U.S. Census Bureau. (2018). Annual estimates of the resident population by single year of age and sex for the United States: April 1, 2010 to July 1, 2017 [Data file]. Retrieved from www.census.gov/data/datasets/2017/demo/popest/nation-detail.html

U.S. Department of Agriculture. (2010). *Dietary guidelines.* Retrieved from www.cnpp.usda.gov/Publications/DietaryGuidelines/2010/PolicyDoc/ExecSumm.pdf

U.S. Department of Education, Office of Special Education Programs, Individuals with Disabilities Education Act (IDEA) database, retrieved July 26, 2016, from www2.ed.gov/programs/osepidea/618-data/state-level-data-files/index.html#bcc.

U.S. Department of Education. (2017a). School discipline laws and regulation by category. [interactive database]. Retrieved from https://safesupportivelearning.ed.gov/node/3510

U.S. Department of Education. (2017b). Number and percentage of public school students enrolled in gifted/talented programs, by race/ethnicity, disability status, and English proficiency, by state, School Year, 2013–14 [data file]. Retrieved from https://ocrdata.ed.gov/StateNationalEstimations/Estimations_2013_14

U.S. Department of Health & Human Services, Administration for Children and Families, Administration on Children, Youth and Families, Children's Bureau. (2017). *Child maltreatment 2015.* Available from www.acf.hhs.gov/programs/cb/research-data-technology/statistics-research/child-maltreatment

U.S. Department of Health and Human Services (USDHHS). (2012). Youth risk behavior surveillance: United States 2011. *MMWR Surveillance Summaries, 61*(4): Table 65. Retrieved from www.cdc.gov/mmwr/pdf/ss/ss6104.pdf

U.S. Department of Health and Human Services, Centers for Disease Control and Prevention (CDC). (2016). Oral health: Working to improve oral health for all Americans: At a glance 2016. Retrieved from www.cdc.gov/chronicdisease/pdf/aag-oral-health.pdf

U.S. Department of Labor, Bureau of Labor Statistics. (2013). Tabulations retrieved November 22, 2013, from www.bls.gov/cps/cpsaat07.htm.

U.S. Department of Labor. (2016). Working brief: Working mothers. Retrieved from www.dol.gov/wb/resources/WB_WorkingMothers_508_FinalJune13.pdf

U.S. Department of State, Bureau of Consular Affairs. (2017). Intercountry adoption: Adoption statistics. Retrieved from https://travel.state.gov/content/travel/en/Intercountry-Adoption/adopt_ref/adoption-statistics.html

U.S. Preventive Services Task Force. (2010). Screening for obesity in children and adolescents: Recommendation statement. *Pediatrics, 125*(2), 361–367. doi: 10.1542/peds.2009-2037

Uematsu, A., Matsui, M., Tanaka, C., Takahashi, T., Noguchi, K., Suzuki, M., & Nishijo, H. (2012). Developmental trajectories of amygdala and hippocampus from infancy to early adulthood in healthy individuals. *PloS one, 7*(10), e46970.

Umana-Taylor, A. J., Gonzalez-Backen, M. A., & Guimond, A. B. (2009). Latino adolescents' ethnic identity: Is there a developmental progression and does growth in ethnic identity predict growth in self-esteem? *Child Development, 80*(2), 391–405.

UNAIDS. (2013). UNAIDS report on the global AIDS epidemic. Retrieved from www.unaids.org/en/media/unaids/contentassets/documents/epidemiology/2013/gr2013/UNAIDS_Global_Report_2013_en.pdf

UNAIDS. (2018). Fact sheet: Latest statistics on the status of the AIDS epidemic. Retrieved from www.unaids.org/en/resources/fact-sheet

UNESCO. (2017). School violence and bullying: Global status report. Retrieved from http://unesdoc.unesco.org/images/0024/002469/246970e.pdf

UNICEF. (2013). Undernourishment in the womb can lead to diminished potential and predispose infants to early death. *UNICEF Data: Monitoring the Situation of Children and Women.* http://data.unicef.org/nutrition/low-birthweight# sthash. BG4IvrwC. Dpuf

UNICEF. (2013b). Improving child nutrition: The achievable imperative for global progress. Retrieved from http://www.unicef.org/media/files/nutrition_report_2013.pdf

UNICEF. (2014). The state of the world's children 2014 in numbers. Every child counts. Revealing disparities, advancing children's rights. https://www.unicef.org/sowc2014/numbers/

UNICEF. (2014, September). Hidden in plain sight: A statistical analysis of violence against children. Retrieved from www.unicef.org/publications/index_74865.html

UNICEF. (2015). Goal: Reduce child mortality. Retrieved from UNICEF Millennium Development Goals: www.un.org/sustainabledevelopment

UNICEF. (2015a). UNICEF data: Monitoring the situation for children and women: Neonatal mortality. Retrieved from https://data.unicef.org/topic/child-survival/neonatal-mortality/#

UNICEF. (2015b). UNICEF data: Monitoring the situation for children and women: Maternal mortality. Retrieved from https://data.unicef.org/topic/maternal-health/maternal-mortality/#

UNICEF. (2015c). Undernutrition contributes to nearly half of all deaths in children under 5 and is widespread in Asia and Africa. Retrieved from https://data.unicef.org/topic/nutrition/malnutrition/

UNICEF. (2016, October). Under-five and infant mortality rates and number of deaths. Retrieved from UNICEF: https://data.unicef.org/topic/child-survival/under-five-mortality

UNICEF. (2017). UNICEF data: Monitoring the situation for children and women: Immunizations. Retrieved from https://data.unicef.org/topic/child-health/immunization/#

UNICEF. (2017, May 16). Joint child malnutrition estimates—2017 edition. Retrieved from UNICEF: https://data.unicef.org/topic/nutrition/malnutrition

United Nations. (2009). Rethinking poverty: Report on the world social situation (No. E.09.IV.10). Retrieved from http://www.un.org/esa/socdev/rwss/docs/2010/fullreport.pdf

United States Census Bureau. (2016). Quick facts: United States [data sheet]. Retrieved from https://www.census.gov/quickfacts/fact/table/US#viewtop

United States Department of Health and Human Services. (2017). Recommended Uniform Screening Panel. Retrieved from www.hrsa.gov/advisorycommittees/mchbadvisory/heritabledisorders/recommendedpanel/index.html

Uphold-Carrier, H., & Utz, R. (2012). Parental divorce among young and adult children: A long-term quantitative analysis of mental health and family solidarity. Journal of Divorce & Remarriage, 53(4), 247-266.

Uttal, D. H., Meadow, N. G., Tipton, E., Hand, L. L., Alden, A. R., Warren, C., & Newcombe, N. S. (2013). The malleability of spatial skills: A meta-analysis of training studies. Psychological Bulletin, 139, 352-402. doi:10.1037/a0028446

V

Vagi, K. J., Olsen, E. O. M., Basile, K. C., & Vivolo-Kantor, A. M. (2015). Teen dating violence (physical and sexual) among U.S. high school students: Findings from the 2013 National Youth Risk Behavior Survey. JAMA Pediatrics, 169(5), 474-482.

Vagi, K. J., Rothman, E. F., Latzman, N. E., Tharp, A. T., Hall, D. M., & Breiding, M. J. (2013). Beyond correlates: A review of risk and protective factors for adolescent dating violence perpetration. Journal of Youth and Adolescence, 42(4), 633-649.

Vaillancourt, T., & Hymel, S. (2006). Aggression and social status: The moderating roles of sex and peer-valued characteristics. Aggressive Behavior, 32(4), 396-408.

Vall, E., & Wade, T. D. (2015). Predictors of treatment outcome in individuals with eating disorders: A systematic review and meta-analysis. International Journal of Eating Disorders, 48(7), 946-971.

Valladares, S., & Moore, K. A. (2009). The strengths of poor families. Research brief. Publication# 2009-26. Child Trends.

Van Cleave, J., Gortmaker, S. L., & Perrin, J. M. (2010). Dynamics of obesity and chronic health conditions among children and youth. Journal of the American Medical Association, 303(7), 623-630.

Van de Bongardt, D., Reitz, E., Sandfort, T., & Deković, M. (2015). A meta-analysis of the relations between three types of peer norms and adolescent sexual behavior. Personality and Social Psychology Review, 19(3), 203-234.

Van der Graaff, J., Branje, S., De Wied, M., Hawk, S., Van Lier, P., & Meeus, W. (2014). Perspective taking and empathic concern in adolescence: Gender differences in developmental changes. Developmental Psychology, 50(3), 881.

Van Geel, M., Vedder, P., & Tanilon, J. (2014a). Are overweight and obese youths more often bullied by their peers? A meta-analysis on the relation between weight status and bullying. International Journal of Obesity, 38(10), 1263.

Van Geel, M., Vedder, P., & Tanilon, J. (2014b). Relationship between peer victimization, cyberbullying, and suicide in children and adolescents: A meta-analysis. JAMA Pediatrics, 168(5), 435-442.

van Lier, P. A., Vitaro, F., Barker, E. D., Brendgen, M., Tremblay, R. E., & Boivin, M. (2012). Peer victimization, poor academic achievement, and the link between childhood externalizing and internalizing problems. Child Development, 83(5), 1775-1788.

Van Ouystel, J., Van Gool, E., Walrave, M., Ponnet, K., & Peeters, E. (2016). Exploring the role of social networking sites within adolescent romantic relationships and dating experiences. Computers in Human Behavior, 55, 76-86.

Van Ryzin, M. J., Stormshak, E. A., & Dishion, T. J. (2012). Engaging parents in the family check-up in middle school: Longitudinal effects on family conflict and problem behavior through the high school transition. Journal of Adolescent Health, 50(6), 627-633.

van Steenbergen, E. F., Kluwer, E. S., & Karney, B. R. (2011). Workload and the trajectory of marital satisfaction in newlyweds: job satisfaction, gender, and parental status as moderators. Journal of Family Psychology, 25(3), 345.

van Zalk, M. H. W., & Kerr, M. (2014). Developmental trajectories of prejudice and tolerance toward immigrants from early to late adolescence. Journal of Youth and Adolescence, 43(10), 1658-1671.

VanderLaan, D. P., Blanchard, R., Wood, H., Garzon, L. C., & Zucker, K. J. (2015). Birth weight and two possible types of maternal effects on male sexual orientation: A clinical study of children and adolescents referred to a Gender Identity Service. Developmental Psychobiology, 57(1), 25-34.

Vandivere, S., Malm, K., & Radel, L. (2009). Adoption USA: A chartbook based on the 2007 National Survey of Adoptive Parents. Washington, DC: U.S. Department of Health and Human Services, Office of the Assistant Secretary for Planning and Evaluation.

Vandorpe, B., Vandendriessche, J., Vaeyens, R., Pion, J., Matthys, S., Lefevre, J., . . . & Lenoir, M. (2012). Relationship between sports participation and the level of motor coordination in childhood: A longitudinal approach. Journal of Science and Medicine in Sport, 15(3), 220-225.

Varela, R. E., Vernberg, E. M., Sanchez-Sosa, J. J., Riveros, A., Mitchell, M., & Mashunkashey, J. (2004). Parenting style of Mexican, Mexican American, and Caucasian-non-Hispanic families: Social context and cultural influences. Journal of Family Psychology, 18(4), 651.

Vaterlaus, J. M., Tulane, S., Porter, B. D., & Beckert, T. E. (2017). The perceived influence of media and technology on adolescent romantic relationships. Journal of Adolescent Research. doi: 10.1177/0743558417712611

Vélez, C. E., Wolchik, S. A., Tein, J. Y., & Sandler, I. (2011). Protecting children from the consequences of divorce: A longitudinal study of the effects of parenting on children's coping processes. Child Development, 82(1), 244-257.

Venetsanou, F., & Kambas, A. (2010). Environmental factors affecting preschoolers' motor development. *Early Childhood Education Journal, 37*(4), 319-327.

Ventola, C. L. (2016). Immunization in the United States: Recommendations, barriers, and measures to improve compliance: Part 1: Childhood vaccinations. *Pharmacy and Therapeutics, 41*(7), 426.

Ventura, A. K., & Worobey, J. (2013). Early influences on the development of food preferences. *Current Biology, 23*(9), R401-R408.

Ventura, S. J., Hamilton, B. E., & Mathews, T. J. (2014). National and state patterns of teen births in the United States, 1940-2013. *National Vital Statistics Reports, 63*(4), 1-34. Hyattsville, MD: National Center for Health Statistics.

Véronneau, M. H., & Dishion, T. J. (2011). Middle school friendships and academic achievement in early adolescence: A longitudinal analysis. *The Journal of Early Adolescence, 31*(1), 99-124.

Véronneau, M. H., Vitaro, F., Brendgen, M., Dishion, T. J., & Tremblay, R. E. (2010). Transactional analysis of the reciprocal links between peer experiences and academic achievement from middle childhood to early adolescence. *Developmental Psychology, 46*(4), 773.

Vespa, J., Lewis, J. M., & Kreider, R. M. (2013). America's families and living arrangements: 2012. *Current Population Reports,* P20-570. Washington, DC: U.S. Census Bureau.

Victora, C. G., Adair, L., Fall, C., Hallal, P. C., Martorell, R., Richter, L., . . . & Maternal and Child Undernutrition Study Group. (2008). Maternal and child undernutrition: Consequences for adult health and human capital. *The Lancet, 371*(9609), 340-357.

Victora, M., Victora, C., & Barros, F. (1990). Cross-cultural differences in developmental rates: A comparison between British and Brazilian children. *Child: Care, Health and Development, 16,* 151-164.

Vieno, A., Nation, M., Pastore, M., & Santinello, M. (2009). *Developmental Psychology, 45*(6), 1509-1519.

Vikraman, S., Fryar, C. D., & Ogden, C. L. (2015). Caloric intake from fast food among children and adolescents in the United States, 2011-2012. *NCHS Data Brief, 213.*

Viner, R. M., & Cole, T. J. (2005). Television viewing in early childhood predicts adult body mass index. *Journal of Pediatrics, 147,* 429-435

Vinkhuyzen, A. A., Pedersen, N. L., Yang, J., Lee, S. H., Magnusson, P. K., Iacono, W. G., . . . & Payton, A. (2012). Common SNPs explain some of the variation in the personality dimensions of neuroticism and extraversion. *Translational Psychiatry, 2*(4), e102.

Virtala, P., Huotilainen, M., Partanen, E., Fellman, V., & Tervaniemi, M. (2013). Newborn infants' auditory system is sensitive to Western music chord categories. *Frontiers in Psychology, 4.*

Vitaro, F., Brendgen, M., Girard, A., Boivin, M., Dionne, G., & Tremblay, R. E. (2015). The expression of genetic risk for aggressive and non-aggressive antisocial behavior is moderated by peer group norms. *Journal of Youth and Adolescence, 44*(7), 1379-1395.

Voegtline, K. M., Costigan, K. A., Pater, H. A., & DiPietro, J. A. (2013). Near-term fetal response to maternal spoken voice. *Infant Behavior and Development, 36*(4), 526-533.

Vogl, K., & Preckel, F. (2014). Full-time ability grouping of gifted students: Impacts on social self-concept and school-related attitudes. *Gifted Child Quarterly, 58*(1), 51-68.

Volkow, N. D., Baler, R. D., Compton, W. M., & Weiss, S. R. (2014). Adverse health effects of marijuana use. *New England Journal of Medicine, 370*(23), 2219-2227.

Volling, B. L., Mahoney, A., & Rauer, A. J. (2009). Sanctification of parenting, moral socialization, and young children's conscience development. *Psychology of Religion and Spirituality, 1*(1), 53.

Von Korff, L., Grotevant, H. D., & McRoy, R. G. (2006). Openness arrangements and psychological adjustment in adolescent adoptees. *Journal of Family Psychology, 20*(3), 531.

Voorveld, H.A.M., & van der Goot, M. (2013). Age differences in media multitasking: A diary study. *Journal of Broadcasting & Electronic Media, 57,* 392-408.

Voss, W., Jungmann, T., Wachtendorf, M., & Neubauer, A. P. (2012). Long-term cognitive outcomes of extremely low-birth-weight infants: The influence of the maternal educational background. *Acta Paediatrica, 101*(6), 569-573.

Voyer, D., & Voyer, S. D. (2014). Gender differences in scholastic achievement: A meta-analysis. *Psychological Bulletin, 140*(4), 1174.

Vrijenhoek, T., Buizer-Voskamp, J. E., van der Stelt, I., Strengman, E., Sabatti, C., van Kessel, A. G., . . . Veltman, J. A. (2008). Recurrent CNVs disrupt three candidate genes in schizophrenia patients. *American Journal of Human Genetics, 83,* 504-510.

Vuchinich, S., Angelelli, J., & Gatherum, A. (1996). Context and development in family problem solving with preadolescent children. *Child Development, 67,* 1276-1288.

Vukasović, T., & Bratko, D. (2015). Heritability of personality: A meta-analysis of behavior genetic studies. *Psychological bulletin, 141*(4), 769.

Vuoksimaa, E., Eriksson, C. P., Pulkkinen, L., Rose, R. J., & Kaprio, J. (2010). Decreased prevalence of left-handedness among females with male co-twins: Evidence suggesting prenatal testosterone transfer in humans? *Psychoneuroendocrinology, 35*(10), 1462-1472.

Vygotsky, L. S. (1962). *Thought and language.* Cambridge, MA: MIT Press. (Original work published 1934)

Vygotsky, L. S. (1980). *Mind in society: The development of higher psychological processes.* Harvard University Press.

W

Wainright, J. L., & Patterson, C. J. (2006). Delinquency, victimization, and substance use among adolescents with female same-sex parents. *Journal of Family Psychology, 20*(3), 526.

Wald, N. J. (2004). Folic acid and the prevention of neural-tube defects. *New England Journal of Medicine, 350,* 101-103.

Waldfogel, J., Craigie, T. A., & Brooks-Gunn, J. (2010). Fragile families and child wellbeing. *The Future of Children/Center for the Future of Children, the David and Lucile Packard Foundation, 20*(2), 87.

Walker, C. M., Walker, L. B., & Ganea, P. A. (2013). The role of symbol-based experience in early learning and transfer from pictures: Evidence from Tanzania. *Developmental Psychology, 49*(7), 1315.

Walle, J. V., Rittig, S., Bauer, S., Eggert, P., Marschall-Kehrel, D., & Tekgul, S. (2012). Practical consensus guidelines for the management of enuresis. *European Journal of Pediatrics, 171*(6), 971-983.

Wallentin, M. (2009). Putative sex differences in verbal abilities and language cortex: A critical review. *Brain and Language, 108*(3), 175-183.

Wallis, C. (2011). Performing gender: A content analysis of gender display in music videos. *Sex Roles, 64*(3-4), 160-172.

Walsh, T., McClellan, J. M., McCarthy, S. E., Addington, A. M., Pierce, S. B., Cooper, G. M., . . . Sebat, J. (2008). Rare structural variants disrupt multiple genes in neurodevelopmental pathways in schizophrenia. *Science, 320,* 539-543.

Wang, D. W., Desai, R. R., Crotti, L., Arnestad, M., Insolia, R., Pedrazzini, M., . . . George, A. L. (2007). Cardiac sodium channel dysfunction in sudden infant death syndrome. *Circulation, 115,* 368-376

Wang, M. T., Eccles, J. S., & Kenny, S. (2013). Not lack of ability but more choice: Individual and gender differences in choice of careers in science, technology, engineering, and mathematics. *Psychological Science, 24*(5), 770-775.

Wang, Q., Doan, S. N., & Song, Q. (2010). Talking about internal states in mother-child reminiscing influences children's self-representations: A cross-cultural study. *Cognitive Development, 25*(4), 380-393.

Wang, Y. (2002). Is obesity associated with early sexual maturation? A comparison of the association in American boys versus girls. *Pediatrics, 110*(5), 903–910.

Wang, Y., Liu, G., Canfield, M. A., Mai, C. T., Gilboa, S. M., Meyer, R. E., . . . & Kirby, R. S. (2015). Racial/ethnic differences in survival of United States children with birth defects: A population-based study. *The Journal of Pediatrics, 166*(4), 819–826.

Wang, Y., Wu, Y., Wilson, R. F., Bleich, S., Cheskin, L., Weston, C., . . . & Segal, J. (2013). *Childhood obesity prevention programs: Comparative effectiveness review and meta-analysis.* Rockville, MD: Agency for Healthcare Research and Quality.

Wardle, J., Carnell, S., Haworth, C. M., & Plomin, R. (2008). Evidence for a strong genetic influence on childhood adiposity despite the force of the obesogenic environment. *The American Journal of Clinical Nutrition, 87*(2), 398–404.

Wardle, J., Robb, K. A., Johnson, F., Griffith, J., Brunner, E., Power, C., & Tovée, M. (2004). Socioeconomic variation in attitudes to eating and weight in female adolescents. *Health Psychology, 23*, 275–282.

Warneken, F., & Tomasello, M. (2009). The roots of human altruism. *British Journal of Psychology, 100*(3), 455–471.

Warren, J. R., & Lee, J. C. (2003). The impact of adolescent employment on high school dropout: Differences by individual and labor-market characteristics. *Social Science Research, 32*(1), 98–128.

Warshak, R. A. (2014). Social science and parenting plans for young children: A consensus report. *Psychology, Public Policy, and Law, 20*(1), 46.

Watson, A. C., Nixon, C. L., Wilson, A., & Capage, L. (1999). Social interaction skills and theory of mind in young children. *Developmental Psychology, 35*(2), 386–391.

Waxman, S., Fu, X., Arunachalam, S., Leddon, E., Geraghty, K., & Song, H. J. (2013). Are nouns learned before verbs? Infants provide insight into a long-standing debate. *Child Development Perspectives, 7*(3), 155–159.

Weaver, J. M., & Schofield, T. J. (2015). Mediation and moderation of divorce effects on children's behavior problems. *Journal of Family Psychology, 29*(1), 39.

Weber, J. (2010). Assessing the "Tone at the Top": The moral reasoning of CEOs in the automobile industry. *Journal of Business Ethics, 92*(2), 167–182.

Webster, A. L., Yan, M. S. C., & Marsden, P. A. (2013). Epigenetics and cardiovascular disease. *Canadian Journal of Cardiology, 29*(1), 46–57.

Weeden, K. A., Cha, Y., & Bucca, M. (2016). Long work hours, part-time work, and trends in the gender gap in pay, the motherhood wage penalty, and the fatherhood wage premium. *RSF: The Russell Sage Foundation Journal of the Social Sciences, 2*(4), 71–102.

Weinberg, M. K., Tronick, E. Z., Cohn, J. F., & Olson, K. L. (1999). Gender differences in emotional expressivity and self-regulation during early infancy. *Developmental Psychology, 35*(1), 175.

Weinmayr, G., Forastiere, F., Büchele, G., Jaensch, A., Strachan, D. P., Nagel, G., & ISAAC Phase Two Study Group. (2014). Overweight/obesity and respiratory and allergic disease in children: International study of asthma and allergies in childhood (ISAAC) phase two. *PloS One, 9*(12), e113996.

Weisberg, D. S., Sobel, D. M., Goodstein, J., & Bloom, P. (2013). Young children are reality-prone when thinking about stories. *Journal of Cognition and Culture, 13*(3–4), 383–407.

Weisgram, E. S., Fulcher, M., & Dinella, L. M. (2014). Pink gives girls permission: Exploring the roles of explicit gender labels and gender-typed colors on preschool children's toy preferences. *Journal of Applied Developmental Psychology, 35*(5), 401–409.

Weisleder, A., & Fernald, A. (2013). Talking to children matters: Early language experience strengthens processing and builds vocabulary. *Psychological Science, 24*(11), 2143–2152.

Weisman, O., Magori-Cohen, R., Louzoun, Y., Eidelman, A. I., & Feldman, R. (2011). Sleep-wake transitions in premature neonates predict early development. *Pediatrics, 128*(4), 706–714.

Weiss, B., Dodge, K. A., Bates, J. E., & Pettit, G. S. (1992). Some consequences of early harsh discipline: Child aggression and a maladaptive social information processing style. *Child Development, 63*, 1321–1335.

Welch-Ross, M. K., & Schmidt, C. R. (1996). Gender-schema development and children's story memory: Evidence for a developmental model. *Child Development, 67*, 820–835.

Wellman, H. M. (2014). *Making minds: How theory of mind develops.* Oxford: Oxford University Press.

Welsh, J. A., Nix, R. L., Blair, C., Bierman, K. L., & Nelson, K. E. (2010). The development of cognitive skills and gains in academic school readiness for children from low-income families. *Journal of Educational Psychology, 102*(1), 43.

Welt, C. K. (2008). Primary ovarian insufficiency: A more accurate term for premature ovarian failure. *Clinical Endocrinology, 68*(4), 499–509.

Wen, X., Wen, S. W., Fleming, N., Demissie, K., Rhoads, G. G., & Walker, M. (2007). Teenage pregnancy and adverse birth outcomes: A large population based retrospective cohort study. *International Journal of Epidemiology, 36*(2), 368–373.

Wendelken, C., Baym, C. L., Gazzaley, A., & Bunge, S. A. (2011). Neural indices of improved attentional modulation over middle childhood. *Developmental Cognitive Neuroscience, 1*(2), 175–186.

Wentzel, K. R., & Muenks, K. (2016). Peer influence on students' motivation, academic achievement, and social behavior. In K. R. Wentel & G. B. Ramani (Eds.), *Handbook of social influences in school contexts: Social-emotional, motivation, and cognitive outcomes* (pp. 13–30). New York: Routledge.

Werker, J. F., Yeung, H. H., & Yoshida, K. A. (2012). How do infants become experts at native-speech perception? *Current Directions in Psychological Science, 21*(4), 221–226.

Wheaton, A. G., Jones, S. E., Cooper, A. C., & Croft, J. B. (2018). Short sleep duration among middle school and high school students—United States, 2015. *Morbidity and Mortality Weekly Report, 67*(3), 85.

White, B. L., Castle, P., & Held, R. (1964). Observations on the development of visually directed reaching. *Child Development*, 349–364.

White, L. K., McDermott, J. M., Degnan, K. A., Henderson, H. A., & Fox, N. A. (2011). Behavioral inhibition and anxiety: The moderating roles of inhibitory control and attention shifting. *Journal of Abnormal Child Psychology, 39*(5), 735–747.

Whitebread, D., Basilio, M., Kuvalja, M., & Verma, M. (2012). *The importance of play.* Brussels, Belgium: Toy Industries of Europe (TIE).

Whitebread, D., Coltman, P., Pasternak, D. P., Sangster, C., Grau, V., Bingham, S., . . . & Demetriou, D. (2009). The development of two observational tools for assessing metacognition and self-regulated learning in young children. *Metacognition and Learning, 4*(1), 63–85.

Whitehurst, G. J., & Lonigan, C. J. (1998). Child development and emergent literacy. *Child Development, 69*(3), 848–872.

Whyatt, R. M., Rauh, V., Barr, D. B., Camann, D. E., Andrews, H. F., Garfinkel, R., . . . Perera, F. P. (2004). Prenatal insecticide exposures and birth weight and length among an urban minority cohort. *Environmental Health Perspectives, 112*(110), 1125–1132.

Whyte, J. C., & Bull, R. (2008). Number games, magnitude representation, and basic number skills in preschoolers. *Developmental Psychology, 44*(2), 588.

Wichstrøm, L., & von Soest, T. (2016). Reciprocal relations between body satisfaction and self-esteem: A large 13-year prospective study of adolescents. *Journal of Adolescence, 47*, 16–27.

Widen, S. C., & Russell, J. A. (2008). Children acquire emotion categories gradually. *Cognitive Development, 23*(2), 291–312.

Wilder, S. (2014). Effects of parental involvement on academic achievement: a meta-synthesis. *Educational Review, 66*(3), 377–397.

Wildsmith, E., Schelar, E., Peterson, K., & Manlove, J. (2010). *Sexually transmitted diseases among young adults: Prevalence, perceived risk and risk-taking behaviors* (2010–21). Retrieved from www.childtrends.org/Files/Child_Trends-2010_ 05_01_RB_STD.pdf

Williams, J., Mai, C. T., Mulinare, J., Isenburg, J., Flood, T. J., Ethen, M., . . . & Kirby, R. S. (2015). Updated estimates of neural tube defects prevented by mandatory folic acid fortification-United States, 1995–2011. MMWR. *Morbidity and Mortality Weekly Report, 64*(1), 1–5.

Williams, J., Wake, M., Hesketh, K., Maher, E., & Waters, E. (2005). Health-related quality of life of overweight and obese children. *JAMA, 293*(1), 70–76.

Williams, L. R., & Steinberg, L. (2011). Reciprocal relations between parenting and adjustment in a sample of juvenile offenders. *Child Development, 82*(2), 633–645.

Willinger, M., Hoffman, H. T., & Hartford, R. B. (1994). Infant sleep position and risk for sudden infant death syndrome: Report of meeting held January 13 and 14, 1994. *Pediatrics, 93*, 814–819.

Willingham, D. T. (2004). Reframing the mind. *Education Next, 4*, 19–24.

Willyard, C. (2014). Heritability: The family roots of obesity. *Nature, 508* (7496), 558–560.

Wilson, D. R. (2010). Health consequences of childhood sexual abuse. *Perspectives in Psychiatric Care, 46*(1), 56–64.

Windle, M., Spear, L. P., Fuligni, A. J., Angold, A., Brown, J. D., Pine, D., . . . & Dahl, R. E. (2008). Transitions into underage and problem drinking: Developmental processes and mechanisms between 10 and 15 years of age. *Pediatrics, 121*(Supplement 4), S273–S289.

Winsler, A., Hutchison, L. A., De Feyter, J. J., Manfra, L., Bleiker, C., Hartman, S. C., & Levitt, J. (2012). Child, family, and childcare predictors of delayed school entry and kindergarten retention among linguistically and ethnically diverse children. *Developmental Psychology, 48*(5), 1299.

Wohlfahrt-Veje, C., Mouritsen, A., Hagen, C. P., Tinggaard, J., Mieritz, M. G., Boas, M., . . . & Main, K. M. (2016). Pubertal onset in boys and girls is influenced by pubertal timing of both parents. *The Journal of Clinical Endocrinology & Metabolism, 101*(7), 2667–2674.

Wolf, S., Magnuson, K. A., & Kimbro, R. T. (2017). Family poverty and neighborhood poverty: Links with children's school readiness before and after the Great Recession. *Children and Youth Services Review, 79*, 368–384.

Wong, C. C. Y., Meaburn, E. L., Ronald, A., Price, T. S., Jeffries, A. R., Schalkwyk, L. C., . . . & Mill, J. (2014). Methylomic analysis of monozygotic twins discordant for autism spectrum disorder and related behavioural traits. *Molecular Psychiatry, 19*(4), 495–503.

Wong, K.M., Masternbroek, S., & Repping, S. (2014). Cryopreservation of human embryos and its contribution to in vitro success rates. *Fertility and Sterility, 102*, 19–26.

Wong, M. M., Nigg, J. T., Zucker, R. A., Puttler, L. I., Fitzgerald, H. E., Jester, J. M., . . . Adams, K. (2006). Behavioral control and resiliency in the onset of alcohol and illicit drug use: A prospective study from preschool to adolescence. *Child Development, 77*, 1016–1033.

Wong, S. S., Zhou, B., Goebert, D., & Hishinuma, E. S. (2013). The risk of adolescent suicide across patterns of drug use: A nationally representative study of high school students in the United States from 1999 to 2009. *Social Psychiatry and Psychiatric Epidemiology, 48*(10), 1611–1620.

Wood, R. M., & Gustafson, G. E. (2001). Infant crying and adults' anticipated caregiving responses: Acoustic and contextual influences. *Child Development, 72*(5), 1287–1300.

Wood, W., & Eagly, A. H. (2012). Biosocial construction of sex differences and similarities in behavior. *Advances in Experimental Social Psychology, 46*(1), 55–123.

Woodruff, T. J., Axelrad, D. A., Kyle, A. D., Nweke, O., Miller, G. G., & Hurley, B. J. (2004). Trends in environmentally related childhood illnesses. *Pediatrics, 113*, 1133–1140.

Woodward, A. L., Markman, E. M., & Fitzsimmons, C. M. (1994). Rapid word learning in 13- and 18-month-olds. *Developmental Psychology, 30*(4), 553.

Woolley, J. D., & Cox, V. (2007). Development of beliefs about storybook reality. *Developmental Science, 10*(5), 681–693.

World Bank. (2016). Poverty and shared prosperity 2016: Taking on inequality. Washington, DC: World Bank. doi:10.1596/978-1-4648-0958-3.

World Health Organization & UNICEF. (2014). Trends in maternal mortality: 1990 to 2013: Estimates by WHO, UNICEF, UNFPA, The World Bank and the United Nations Population Division.

World Health Organization (WHO). (2013). Levels and trends in child mortality. Retrieved from www.who.int/maternal_child_adolescent/documents/levels_trends_child_mortality_2013/en/

World Health Organization & WHO Management of Substance Abuse Unit. (2014). *Global status report on alcohol and health, 2014*. Geneva: World Health Organization.

World Health Organization. (2013). *Essential nutrition actions: improving maternal, newborn, infant and young child health and nutrition*. Geneva: Author.

World Health Organization. (2015). Global Health Observatory (GHO) data: Under five mortality. Retrieved from www.who.int/gho/child_health/mortality/mortality_under_five_text/en/

World Health Organization. (2015, May). *MDG 4: Reduce child mortality*. Retrieved from WHO: www.who.int/topics/millennium_development_goals/child_mortality/en

World Health Organization. (2016a). Adolescent health epidemiology. Retrieved from www.who.int/maternal_child_adolescent/epidemiology/adolescence/en/

World Health Organization. (2016b). Sexually transmitted infections (STIs). [Fact sheet]. Retrieved from www.who.int/en/news-room/fact-sheets/detail/sexually-transmitted-infections-(stis)

World Health Organization. (2017a). Malnutrition [fact sheet]. Retrieved from http://www.who.int/mediacentre/factsheets/malnutrition/en/

World Health Organization. (2017b). Commission on ending childhood obesity. Retrieved from www.who.int/end-childhood-obesity/en/

World Health Organization. (2017c). Adolescence: Health risks and solutions. [Fact sheet]. Retrieved from www.who.int/mediacentre/factsheets/fs345/en/

World Health Organization. (2017d). Global Health Observatory (GHO) data: Skilled attendants at birth. Retrieved from www.who.int/gho/maternal_health/skilled_care/skilled_birth_attendance/en/

World Health Organization. (2017e). Newborns: Reducing mortality [data sheet]. Retrieved from www.who.int/mediacentre/factsheets/fs333/en/

World Health Organization. (2017f). Growing up unequal. HBSC 2016 study (2013/2014 survey). Retrieved from World Health Organization: http://www.euro.who.int/en/publications/abstracts/growing-up-unequal.-hbsc-2016-study-20132014-survey

World Health Organization. (2018). Obesity and overweight. [Fact sheet]. Retrieved from www.who.int/mediacentre/factsheets/fs311/en/

World Health Organization. (2018a). Adolescent pregnancy. [Fact sheet]. Retrieved from http://www.who.int/en/news-room/fact-sheets/detail/adolescent-pregnancy

World Health Organization. (2018b). The AIDS epidemic continues to take a staggering toll but progress is possible. [Data tables]. Retrieved from https://data.unicef.org/topic/hivaids/global-regional-trends/

World Health Organization. (2018c). What is Hepatitis B? [Fact sheet]. Retrieved from www.wpro.who.int/hepatitis/hepatitis_b/en/

Wörmann, V., Holodynski, M., Kärtner, J., & Keller, H. (2012). A cross-cultural comparison of the development of the social smile: A longitudinal study of maternal and infant imitation in 6- and 12-week-old infants. *Infant Behavior and Development, 35*(3), 335-347.

Wu, C., & Leinung, M. C. (2015). The biologic basis of transgender Identity: Finger length ratios in transgender individuals implicates a role for prenatal androgen activity. *Basic and Clinical Aspects of Sexual Development*, SAT-081.

Wu, Z., Hou, F., & Schimmele, C. M. (2008). Family structure and children's psychosocial outcomes. *Journal of Family Issues, 29,* 1600-1624.

Wulczyn, F. (2004). Family reunification. In David and Lucile Packard Foundation, Children, families, and foster care. *Future of Children, 14*(1). Retrieved from www.futureofchildren.org

X

Xiao, W. S., Xiao, N. G., Quinn, P. C., Anzures, G., & Lee, K. (2013). Development of face scanning for own- and other-race faces in infancy. *International Journal of Behavioral Development, 37*(2), 100-105.

Xie, X., Ding, G., Cui, C., Chen, L., Gao, Y., Zhou, Y., . . . & Tian, Y. (2013). The effects of low-level prenatal lead exposure on birth outcomes. *Environmental Pollution, 175,* 30-34.

Xu, F., Bao, X., Fu, G., Talwar, V., & Lee, K. (2010). Lying and truth-telling in children: From concept to action. *Child Development, 81*(2), 581-596.

Y

Yairi, E., & Ambrose, N. (2013). Epidemiology of stuttering: 21st century advances. *Journal of Fluency Disorders, 38*(2), 66-87.

Yamamoto, Y., & Holloway, S. D. (2010). Parental expectations and children's academic performance in sociocultural context. *Educational Psychology Review, 22*(3), 189-214.

Yaman, A., Mesman, J., van IJzendoorn, M. H., & Bakermans-Kranenburg, M. J. (2010). Parenting and toddler aggression in second-generation immigrant families: The moderating role of child temperament. *Journal of Family Psychology, 24*(2), 208.

Yang, L., Neale, B. M., Liu, L., Lee, S. H., Wray, N. R., Ji, N., . . . & Faraone, S. V. (2013). Polygenic transmission and complex neuro developmental network for attention deficit hyperactivity disorder: Genome-wide association study of both common and rare variants. *American Journal of Medical Genetics Part B: Neuropsychiatric Genetics, 162*(5), 419-430.

Yau, J. P., Tausopoulos-Chan, M., & Smetana, J. G. (2009). Disclosure to parents about everyday activities among American adolescents from Mexican, Chinese and European backgrounds. *Child Development, 80*(5), 1481-1498.

Ybarra, M. L., & Mitchell, K. J. (2014). "Sexting" and its relation to sexual activity and sexual risk behavior in a national survey of adolescents. *Journal of Adolescent Health, 55*(6), 757-764.

Ybarra, M. L., Strasburger, V. C., & Mitchell, K. J. (2014). Sexual media exposure, sexual behavior, and sexual violence victimization in adolescence. *Clinical Pediatrics, 53*(13), 1239-1247.

Yeung, W. J., Sandberg, J. F., Davis-Kean, P. E., & Hofferth, S. L. (2001). Children's time with fathers in intact families. *Journal of Marriage and Family, 63,* 136-154.

Yorbik, O., Mutlu, C., Koc, D., & Mutluer, T. (2014). Possible negative effects of snoring and increased sleep fragmentation on developmental status of preschool children. *Sleep and Biological Rhythms, 12*(1), 30-36.

Yoshikawa, H., Aber, J. L., & Beardslee, W. R. (2012). The effects of poverty on the mental, emotional, and behavioral health of children and youth: implications for prevention. *American Psychologist, 67*(4), 272.

You, D., Hug, L., Ejdemyr, S., & Beise, J. (2015). *Levels and trends in child mortality. Report 2015. Estimates developed by the UN Inter-agency Group for Child Mortality Estimation.* New York: UNICEF.

Young, K. S., Parsons, C. E., Jegindoe Elmholdt, E. M., Woolrich, M. W., van Hartevelt, T. J., Stevner, A. B., . . . & Kringelbach, M. L. (2015). Evidence for a caregiving instinct: Rapid differentiation of infant from adult vocalizations using magnetoencephalography. *Cerebral Cortex, 26*(3), 1309-1321.

Yunger, J. L., Carver, P. R., & Perry, D. G. (2004). Does gender identity influence children's psychological well-being? *Developmental Psychology, 40,* 572-582.

Z

Zahn-Waxler, C., Friedman, R. J., Cole, P. M., Mizuta, I., & Hiruma, N. (1996). Japanese and U.S. preschool children's responses to conflict and distress. *Child Development, 67,* 2462-2477.

Zajdel, R. T., Bloom, J. M., Fireman, G., & Larsen, J. T. (2013). Children's understanding and experience of mixed emotions: The roles of age, gender, and empathy. *The Journal of Genetic Psychology, 174*(5), 582-603.

Zelazo, P. D., & Carlson, S. M. (2012). Hot and cool executive function in childhood and adolescence: Development and plasticity. *Child Development Perspectives, 6*(4), 354-360.

Zelazo, P. R., Kearsley, R. B., & Stack, D. M. (1995). Mental representations for visual sequences: Increased speed of central processing from 22 to 32 months. *Intelligence, 20,* 41-63.

Zelkowitz, P., Na, S., Wang, T., Bardin, C., & Papageorgiou, A. (2011). Early maternal anxiety predicts cognitive and behavioural outcomes of VLBW children at 24 months corrected age. *Acta Paediatrica, 100*(5), 700-704.

Zentall, S. R., & Morris, B. J. (2010). "Good job, you're so smart": The effects of inconsistency of praise type on young children's motivation. *Journal of Experimental Child Psychology, 107*(2), 155-163.

Zhai, F., Raver, C. C., & Jones, S. M. (2012). Academic performance of subsequent schools and impacts of early interventions: Evidence from a randomized controlled trial in Head Start settings. *Children and Youth Services Review, 34*(5), 946-954.

Zhou, J. N., Hofman, M. A., Gooren, L. J., & Swaab, D. F. (1995). A sex difference in the human brain and its relation to transsexuality. *Nature, 378*(6552), 68.

Zhou, X., Hetrick, S. E., Cuijpers, P., Qin, B., Barth, J., Whittington, C. J., . . . & Zhang, Y. (2015). Comparative efficacy and acceptability of psychotherapies for depression in children and adolescents: A systematic review and network meta-analysis. *World Psychiatry, 14*(2), 207-222.

Zlotnick, C., Tam, T. W., & Soman, L. A. (2012). Life course outcomes on mental and physical health: The impact of foster care on adulthood. *American Journal of Public Health, 102*(3), 534-540.

Zlotnick, C., Tam, T., & Zerger, S. (2012). Common needs but divergent interventions for U.S. homeless and foster care children: Results from a systematic review. *Health & Social Care in the Community, 20*(5), 449–476.

Zmyj, N., & Seehagen, S. (2013). The role of a model's age for young children's imitation: A research review. *Infant and Child Development, 22*(6), 622–641.

Zolotor, A. J., Theodore, A. D., Runyan, D. K., Chang, J. J., & Laskey, A. L. (2011). Corporal punishment and physical abuse: Population-based trends for three- to-11-year-old children in the United States. *Child Abuse Review, 20*(1), 57–66.

Zosuls, K. M., Andrews, N. C., Martin, C. L., England, D. E., & Field, R. D. (2016). Developmental changes in the link between gender typicality and peer victimization and exclusion. *Sex Roles, 75*(5–6), 243–256.

Zosuls, K. M., Ruble, D. N., Tamis-LeMonda, C. S., Shrout, P. E., Bornstein, M. H., & Greulich, F. K. (2009). The acquisition of gender labels in infancy: Implications for gender-typed play. *Developmental Psychology, 45*(3), 688.

Zuffianò, A., Alessandri, G., Gerbino, M., Kanacri, B. P. L., Di Giunta, L., Milioni, M., & Caprara, G. V. (2013). Academic achievement: The unique contribution of self-efficacy beliefs in self-regulated learning beyond intelligence, personality traits, and self-esteem. *Learning and Individual Differences, 23*, 158–162.

Page numbers followed by *f* indicate figures, and page numbers followed by *t* indicate tables.

Kennedy-Costantini, S., 126
Kennedy-Stephenson, J., 98
Kenney, M. K., 240
Kenney, R. R., 183
Kenny, L. C., 51
Kenny, P. J., 243
Kenny, S., 314, 339
Kenny, U., 315
Keogh, G., 69
Keogh, J., 50
Kere, J., 273
Kerkhof, G. A., 241
Kerns, K. A., 68, 292
Kerpelman, J. L., 347
Kerr, D. C. R., 228
Kerr, M., 294, 358
Kessler, R. C., 321
Kharrazi, M., 69, 98, 99
Khashan, A. S., 51
Khoo, S. T., 360
Khubchandani, J., 320, 321
Kidd, K. K., 6, 264
Kids Count Data Center, 8
Kieffer, M. J., 330
Kieling, C., 273
Kier, C., 165
Kiesler, S., 362
Killen, J. D., 318
Kilpeläinen, L., 164
Kim, E., 70
Kim, G., 159
Kim, I. H., 201
Kim, J., 114, 115, 292, 294, 360
Kim, J. Y., 165, 292
Kim, P., 149
Kim, S., 162, 163, 282, 286
Kim, S. Y., 347
Kim, T. E., 299
Kim, Y. K., 225
Kimball, M. M., 221
Kimber, M., 316
Kimbro, R. T., 8
Kim-Cohen, J., 8, 200
Kimmel, C., 310
Kimmerly, N. L., 155
Kincaid, C., 350
Kinchen, S., 306, 312, 350, 351
Kinckmeyer, R., 216
King, A., 141
King, B. A., 318
King, B. M., 35
King, E., 79
King, K. M., 318
King, L. G., 69
King, M., 245
King, R. M., 179
King, V., 288, 290, 359
Kingdon, C. K., 91
Kingery, J. N., 296
Kinney, H. C., 111
Kinsella, K., 5
Kirby, D., 354, 355
Kirby, R., 89
Kirby, R. S., 42, 63
Kirilina, E., 283
Kirk, E., 137
Kirkaldy, R. D., 353
Kirkorian, H. L., 200
Kirkpatrick, B., 51
Kirkpatrick, S. I., 247
Kirkwood, H., 260
Kirmeyer, S., 57, 63, 66, 68, 71, 72, 79, 84, 86, 87, 89
Kirschner, P. A., 25, 361
Kirsten, B., 219
Kirwil, L., 298
Kisilevsky, B. S., 61, 62, 129

Kiss, A., 183
Kissin, D. M., 35, 37
Kit, B. K., 99, 178, 243
Kita, S., 139
Kitzmann, K. M., 244
Kiviruusu, O., 289
Kivlighan, K. T., 65, 66, 249
Klaczynski, P., 299
Klahr, A. M., 358
Klam, S. L., 66–67
Klanderman, B. J., 245
Klann-Delius, G., 283
Klauer, S. G., 320
Kleiman, I., 268
Klein, J. D., 178, 350, 351, 354, 355
Klein, N., 89
Klein, N. P., 353
Kleinman, K., 240, 243
Klein-Velderman, M., 158
Kletke, B., 363
Klibanoff, R. S., 191
Klingberg, T., 197, 260
Klockau, L., 292
Klump, K. L., 315
Klute, C., 360, 361
Kluwer, E. S., 92
Knafo, A., 230
Knecht, S., 140
Knibb, R. C., 179
Knight, D. B., 88
Knight, J. R., 274
Knight, W. G., 69
Knopf, M., 126
Knowler, W. C., 178, 243
Knutson, B., 311
Ko, T. J., 69
Koc, D., 241
Kochanek, K. D., 77, 87, 110, 111, 112, 177, 181, 247, 306
Kochanska, G., 157, 161, 162, 163, 227, 228, 282, 284
Koenig, J. L., 162, 163
Kofler, M. J., 260
Kogan, M. D., 179, 243, 244, 246, 273, 362
Kohlberg, L., 11, 216t, 218, 331–333
Kohler, M., 174
Kohn, J. L., 92
Kokotovic, A., 114
Kolata, G., 46
Kolb, B., 133
Kolbert, E., 232
Koliskor, B., 240
Kolko, D. J., 115
Kollar, M. A., 7f, 8, 286
Köller, O., 264
Kolling, T., 126
Kollman, T. R., 113
Komarraju, M., 268, 335
Konrad, D., 39
Konrad, K., 311
Koopman, P., 39
Koops, W., 297
Koplan, J. P., 243
Koponen, H., 51
Korat, O., 204, 267
Korchmaros, J. D., 362, 363
Koren, G., 66, 68
Kornienko, O., 221
Kosa, J. L., 98, 99
Kose, S., 149
Koskenvuo, M., 50
Koss, K. J., 357
Kost, K., 354
Koster, I., 130, 137

Kosterman, R., 365
Kostović, I., 104
Kotsa, K., 64
Kouzarides, T., 41
Kovachy, B., 174
Kovack-Lesh, K. A., 130
Kovács, Á. M., 195
Kovas, Y., 200, 264
Kovelman, I., 141
Kowal, A. K., 166, 351
Kowalski, R. M., 299, 300
Koyasu, M., 195
Kozhevnikova, E. V., 142
Kozhimannil, K. B., 80, 81
Kozlowska, K., 249
Kozmitzki, C., 76, 106, 327, 328
Kraak, V. I., 243
Kraft, P., 70
Kramer, J. R., 318
Kramer, L., 166, 292
Kramer, M. S., 99t
Krashen, S., 140, 266
Krasilnikoff, P., 71
Krasnewich, D., 246
Krause, N., 273
Krausz, C., 35
Kraut, R., 362
Krcmar, M., 140
Kreager, D. A., 362
Krebs, N. F., 114
Krebs-Smith, S. M., 247
Kreider, R. M., 37, 38, 286, 289, 290, 291, 292
Kreiner-Møller, E., 245
Kreishan, L., 274
Kreukels, B. P., 217
Kringelbach, M. L., 90
Krisch, I. M., 247
Krishnamoorthy, J. S., 244
Kristapovich, P., 206
Kroeger, R. A., 290
Kroger, J., 346, 347
Krogh, L., 131
Krogsrud, S. K., 263
Krogstad, P., 5
Krois, L., 183
Krous, H. F., 111
Krueger, R. F., 363
Kruszon-Moran, D., 243, 353
Kruttschnitt, C., 229, 365
Kuchinke, L., 283
Kucirkova, N., 267
Kuczmarski, R. J., 98
Kuh, D., 89
Kuhl, P. K., 9, 135t, 136, 137, 138, 139, 140, 141, 142
Kuhlmeier, V. A., 151
Kuhn, B. R., 227
Kuhn, D., 239, 311, 327, 329, 330
Kuhn, M. R., 267
Kuiper, H., 282
Kuiri-Hänninen, T., 164
Kujala, T., 104
Kulikova, S., 102
Kulkarni, A., 35
Kumanyika, S. K., 313
Kumar, A., 353
Kumar, R., 178, 243, 314
Kumari, V., 364
Kumwenda, N. I., 99
Kundurthi, S., 63, 129
Kunz, A., 295
Kunzman, R., 271
Kuo, L. J., 201
Kupanoff, K., 223, 224, 282
Kuperman, S., 318
Kupersmidt, J. B., 213

Kupferman, J. C., 245
Kupper, L., 363
Kurachi, M., 309
Kurinczuk, J., 87
Kurlakowsky, K. D., 249
Kurowski, C. O., 135
Kurukulaaratchy, R. J., 99t
Kushlev, K., 92
Kuvalja, M., 222
Kuzawa, C. W., 91
Kuzyk, R., 190
Kwak, K., 159
Kwon, R., 86
Kyle, A. D., 184, 272, 273

L

Laake, L. M., 150
Labbo, L. D., 267
Laberge, L., 174
LaBotz, M., 247
LaBounty, J., 195
Lacerda, F., 136
Lack, G., 179
Ladd, G., 295
Ladewig, P., 58t
LaFontana, K. M., 295
LaFreniere, P., 214
Lagasse, L. L., 69
Lagattuta, K. H., 193, 213, 282
Lagercrantz, H., 79
Lahey, B., 282, 283, 364
Lahortiga, F., 315
Lai, D., 243, 245
Lai, K. Y. C., 174
Lai, M. C., 163, 215, 336
Laible, D. J., 163
Lainhart, J. E., 263
Laird, J., 338
Laird, R., 248, 296
Laird, R. D., 365
Laje, G., 250
Lake, A., 100
Lalonde, C. E., 135t
Lalonde, F., 239, 311
Lam, C. B., 360
Lam, S. P., 174
Lamaze, F., 80
Lamb, M. E., 90, 91, 92, 141, 157, 164, 165, 287, 290
Lamb, M. M., 50, 178, 313
Lamberg, A., 241
Lambert, S. F., 249
Lambert, W., 266
Lamberty, G., 337
Lamborn, S. D., 364
Lamela, D., 288
Lamidi, E., 290
Lamm, B., 126
Lamm, C., 151, 259
Lamminmäki, A., 164
Lamont, R. F., 63
Lancy, D. F., 225
Landers, S., 99
Landon, M. B., 79
Landor, A., 350
Landry, S. H., 201
Landsverk, J., 115
Lange, L. A., 162
Lange, N., 263
Langenberg, C., 89
Langer, J. C., 69
Langeslag, S. J., 263
Langley, K., 70–71
Långström, N., 71, 348
Lannon, R., 138
Lanoë, C., 258

Romero, C., 212
Romney, D. M., 164
Ronald, A., 41
Ronnemaa, T., 239
Rönnqvist, L., 176
Roopnarine, J. L., 165, 166
Roosa, M. W., 248, 310
Root, A. K., 162
Ropero, S., 41
Rosand, J., 249
Rosario, M., 349
Rosatelli, M. C., 46
Rose, A. J., 241, 294, 295
Rose, R. J., 176, 310
Rose, S. A., 89, 129, 130
Roseberry, S., 141
Rose-Krasnor, L., 223
Rosenbaum, J., 352
Rosenberg, E. B., 291
Rosengren, K. S., 127
Rosenkranz, R. R., 294
Rosenthal, S. L., 353
Rosicky, J. G., 159
Rosner, B., 245, 314
Ross, H., 318
Ross, J., 306, 312
Ross, J. L., 215
Ross, S., 300
Rosselli, M., 214
Rossi, L., 310
Rossi, R., 338
Rossi, S., 258
Rostami, C., 240
Roth, G., 357
Rothbart, M. K., 151, 152, 157, 213
Rothenberg, S. J., 67
Rothman, A. D., 92
Rothman, E. F., 363
Rothman, M. T., 92
Rourke, M., 195
Rouse, C., 268
Rousseau, J. J., 10
Roussotte, F. F., 70
Rowe, M. L., 137, 141
Rowland, A. S., 273
Roy, K., 91
Ruan, J., 313
Ruan, W. J., 299, 318
Rubens, C. E., 89
Rubin, C., 309
Rubin, D., 71
Rubin, K. H., 154, 223, 224, 231, 295, 360, 361
Rubin, S. E., 65, 66
Rubio-Fernández, P., 193
Ruble, D. N., 218, 219, 220, 221, 224
Rudd, R. A., 112
Rudolph, K. D., 241, 249, 294
Rudy, D., 284
Rueda, M. R., 151, 213
Rueter, M. A., 357
Ruffieux, C., 180
Ruhl, H., 361
Ruigrok, A. N., 163, 215, 336
Rumbaut, R. G., 366
Runco, M. A., 275
Runions, K. C., 299
Runyan, D. K., 115, 227
Ruparel, K., 336
Rushton, J. P., 263, 264
Russ, S. A., 362
Russ, S. W., 225
Russell, J. A., 213
Russell, L. A., 242
Russell, S. T., 290
Rust, J., 214, 215, 221, 224*t*
Rutherford, G., 321

Rutland, A., 294
Rutter, M., 47, 103, 116, 215, 273
Ruttle, P. L., 309
Ruzicka, D. L., 241
Ryan, A., 337
Ryan, A. S., 98
Ryan, C., 69, 268
Ryan, M. K., 127
Ryan, N. D., 319
Ryan, R. M., 357
Ryan, S., 123, 205, 351
Ryncarz, R. A., 333
Ryskina, V. L., 142
Rytting, N., 138
Ryu, E., 248

S

Saarni, C., 213, 282
Sabatti, C., 51
Sabbagh, M. A., 195
Sachs, H. C., 70
Sacks, G., 178
Sacks, J. J., 68
Sadeh, A., 86, 173, 240
Sadek, S., 299
Saenger, P., 216
Saffran, J. R., 137
Sagi-Schwartz, A., 156
Sahoo, B., 178, 243, 314
Sahoo, K., 178, 243, 314
Saigal, S., 89
Sakamoto, A., 231, 298
Sakhardande, A., 317, 318
Salary, C. B., 250, 320
Saleem, M., 231, 298
Salgueiro, M., 183
Salimi-Khorshidi, G., 163, 215, 336
Salkind, N. J., 150
Sallee, F. R., 248
Sallmen, M., 35
Salum, G. A., 249, 273
Salvig, J. D., 63
Samara, M., 88
Samara, R., 351
Sambeth, A., 104
Samdal, O., 115, 337
Sameroff, A., 227, 228, 339
Sampaio, I., 183
Samper, P., 334
Sampson, N. A., 321
Sampson, P. D., 68
Sánchez, F. J., 217
Sanchez-Sosa, J. J., 229
Sandberg, J. F., 91
Sanders, A. R., 348
Sanders, L. D., 259
Sanders, P., 164
Sanders, S., 273
Sanders, S. A., 99*t*
Sandfort, T., 350
Sandin, S., 71
Sandler, D. P., 35, 273
Sandler, I., 289
Sandnabba, N. K., 221
Sangster, C., 197
Sankilampi, U., 164
Sann, C., 132
Santelli, J. S., 352, 354
Santhakumaran, S., 88
Santiago, C. D., 286
Santinello, M., 366
Santos, C., 179
Santos, L. R., 258
Santow, M., 355
Sapp, F., 194
Sappenfield, W. M., 240

Sareen, H., 227
Sargent, J., 297
Sargent-Hier, M., 150
Sarnecka, B. W., 190
Sassa, Y., 238
Sasson, H., 351
Sasson, N., 133
Saswati, S., 35
Satcher, D., 352
Sato, Y., 104
Satterthwaite, T. D., 336
Saudino, K. J., 51, 152
Sauer, H., 51
Saunders, N., 76
Sauter, D. A., 213
Savage, J., 298
Savage, J. S., 61, 315
Savarino, J., 250
Savelyev, P. A., 205
Savic, I., 349
Savin-Williams, R. C., 348
Savoie, D., 255
Sawalani, G., 296
Sawhill, I., 205
Saxe, R., 131
Saxena, S., 272
Saxon, J. L., 212
Saydah, S., 245
Saylor, M. M., 127
Sazonova, A., 35
Scaramella, L. V., 152
Scarr, S., 49
Schaafsma, S. M., 176
Schacter, D. L., 260
Schaefer, C. E., 275
Schaefer, D. R., 221
Schafer, W. D., 155
Schalkwyk, L. C., 41
Schanler, R. J., 99
Schanzenbach, D. W., 338
Schapiro, L., 109
Scharf, M., 289
Scharf, R. J., 87
Schatzberg, A. F., 318
Schechter, J. C., 364
Scheidt, P., 299, 311, 312
Scheier, L. M., 359
Schelar, E., 352
Schellinger, K. B., 286
Scher, A., 85, 173
Scher, M., 88
Schetter, C. D., 66
Schick, B., 139
Schickedanz, A., 8
Schiefenhovel, W., 176
Schieve, L. A., 35, 179, 246
Schiff, A., 312, 313
Schiff, D. M., 68
Schindler, H. S., 350, 351
Schissel, A., 239
Schliemann, A. D., 258
Schlotz, W., 63
Schluchter, M., 88, 89
Schmelzer, D., 174
Schmidt, C. R., 219
Schmidt, J., 334, 336
Schmidt, L. A., 154
Schmidt, M., 263
Schmidt, M. E., 295
Schmidt, M. F., 150–151
Schmidt, M. M., 63
Schmitt, M. T., 293
Schmitt, S. A., 141
Schmitz, S., 152
Schnaas, L., 67
Schnack, H. G., 264
Schneider, B. H., 157

Schneider, D., 287
Schneider, M., 270
Schneider, W., 197, 198, 260, 261
Schoefs, V., 157
Schoendorf, K. C., 67
Schoenle, E. J., 39
Schoeny, M. E., 350
Schofield, T. J., 287
Schölmerich, A., 90
Scholten, C. M., 76
Schonert-Reichl, K. A., 283, 294
Schoppe-Sullivan, S. J., 155
Schork, N. J., 348
Schouten, A., 282
Schrader, R. M., 158
Schredl, M., 174
Schrimshaw, E. W., 349
Schroeder, A. N., 299, 300
Schroeder, D. R., 247
Schuckit, M. A., 318
Schulenberg, J. E., 306, 316, 316*f*, 317, 318, 340, 364, 365, 366
Schulting, A. B., 206
Schulz, M. S., 92
Schurz, M., 193
Schuster, M. A., 310
Schwab, S. G., 51
Schwade, J. A., 149
Schwartz, D., 231, 269, 299
Schwartz, L. L., 37
Schwartz, P. J., 111
Schwartz, T., 88
Schweinhart, L J., 205
Schweinsburg, A. D., 317
Schweinsburg, B. C., 317
Schwenck, C., 197
Schwichtenberg, A. J., 89
Scott, G., 247
Scott, J., 115
Scott, M. E., 359
Scott, R. M., 193
Scott, S., 226
Searing, D. A., 245
Seaton, E. K., 347
Sebanc, A. M., 166, 224
Sebat, J., 51
Sedgh, G., 354
Seehagen, S., 127
Seeley, J. R., 310
Séguin, J. R., 230
Seibel, R. L., 137
Seidell, J. C., 314
Seidman, E., 347
Seifen, S., 174
Seifer, R., 69
Seiffge-Krenke, I., 347
Selevan, S. G., 308
Seligman, M. E. P., 335
Selkie, E. M., 299, 362
Sellers, R. M., 347
Seltzer, J. A., 289
Semega, J. L., 7*f*, 8, 286
Semendeferi, K., 133
Semiatin, J., 114
Sen, M. G., 218
Sénéchal, M., 142, 267
Senghas, A., 139
Senman, L., 193, 195
Sentelle, G., 35
Serbin, L. A., 164
Serdiouk, M., 269
Sergio, L., 139
Serrano, P. A., 349
Service, V., 137
Servis, L. J., 221
Sethi, A., 162
Setien, F., 41